New Perspectives on

Microsoft® Office 2007

Second Course

**Microsoft®
CERTIFIED**

Approved Courseware

*Application
Specialist*

The application-specific tutorials in this book are included as part of the New Perspectives Series texts shown below, each of which meets the certification requirements for the corresponding Microsoft Certified Application Specialist exam, "Using Microsoft® Office Word 2007," "Using Microsoft® Office Excel 2007,"Using Microsoft® Office Access 2007," and "Using Microsoft® Office PowerPoint 2007."

1-4239-0582-2

1-4239-0585-7

1-4239-0589-X

1-4239-0593-8

New Perspectives on

Microsoft® Office 2007

Second Course

Ann Shaffer
Patrick Carey
Roy Ageloff

June Jamrich Parsons
Dan Oja

S. Scott Zimmerman
Brigham Young University

Joseph J. Adamski
Grand Valley State University

Beverly B. Zimmerman
Brigham Young University

COURSE TECHNOLOGY
CENGAGE Learning™

Australia • Brazil • Japan • Korea • Mexico • Singapore • Spain • United Kingdom • United States

COURSE TECHNOLOGY
CENGAGE Learning

New Perspectives on Microsoft® Office 2007—Second Course

Executive Editor: Marie L. Lee

Senior Product Manager: Kathy Finnegan

Product Manager: Erik Herman

Associate Acquisitions Editor: Brandi Henson

Associate Product Manager: Leigh Robbins

Editorial Assistant: Patrick Frank

Director of Marketing: Cheryl Costantini

Marketing Manager: Ryan DeGrote

Marketing Specialist: Jennifer Hankin

Developmental Editors: Jessica Evans, Mary Kemper, Katherine T. Pinard, Robin M. Romer

Senior Content Project Managers: Catherine G. DiMassa, Jennifer Goguen McGrail

Content Project Manager: Daphne Barbas

Composition: GEX Publishing Services

Text Designer: Steve Deschene

Art Director: Marissa Falco

Cover Designer: Elizabeth Paquin

Cover Art: Bill Brown

Indexer: Alexandra Nickerson

Some of the product names and company names used in this book have been used for identification purposes only and may be trademarks or registered trademarks of their respective manufacturers and sellers.

Microsoft and the Office logo are either registered trademarks or trademarks of Microsoft Corporation in the United States and/or other countries. Course Technology, Cengage Learning is an independent entity from the Microsoft Corporation, and not affiliated with Microsoft in any manner.

Disclaimer: Any fictional data related to persons or companies or URLs used throughout this book is intended for instructional purposes only. At the time this book was printed, any such data was fictional and not belonging to any real persons or companies.

ISBN-13: 978-0-324-59841-4

ISBN-10: 0-324-59841-6

Course Technology
25 Thomson Place
Boston, Massachusetts 02210
USA

Cengage Learning is a leading provider of customized learning solutions with office locations around the globe, including Singapore, the United Kingdom, Australia, Mexico, Brazil, and Japan. Locate your local office at: **international.cengage.com/region**

Cengage Learning products are represented in Canada by Nelson Education, Ltd.

For your lifelong learning solutions, visit **course.cengage.com**

Purchase any of our products at your local college store or at our preferred online store **www.ichapters.com**

Printed in the United States of America
1 2 3 4 5 6 7 12 11 10 09 08

Preface

The New Perspectives Series' critical-thinking, problem-solving approach is the ideal way to prepare students to transcend point-and-click skills and take advantage of all that Microsoft Office 2007 has to offer.

In developing the New Perspectives Series for Microsoft Office 2007, our goal was to create books that give students the software concepts and practical skills they need to succeed beyond the classroom. We've updated our proven case-based pedagogy with more practical content to make learning skills more meaningful to students.

With the New Perspectives Series, students understand *why* they are learning *what* they are learning, and are fully prepared to apply their skills to real-life situations.

"I really love the Margin Tips, which add 'tricks of the trade' to students' skills package. In addition, the Reality Check exercises provide for practical application of students' knowledge. I can't wait to use them in the classroom."
—Terry Morse Colucci
Institute of Technology, Inc.

About This Book

This book provides complete coverage of introductory-to-advanced concepts and skills for the new Microsoft Office 2007 suite, and includes the following:

- Three Word 2007 tutorials on working with templates and outlines, performing a mail merge, collaborating with others, and creating Web pages
- Four Excel 2007 tutorials plus two Appendices that cover working with Excel tables, PivotTables, and PivotCharts; managing multiple worksheets and workbooks; using advanced functions, conditional formatting, and filtering; developing an Excel application; working with Text functions and creating custom formats; and integrating Excel with other Windows programs
- Four Access 2007 tutorials plus one Appendix that cover creating advanced queries and enhancing table design; using form tools and creating custom forms; creating custom reports; sharing, integrating, and analyzing data; and understanding relational databases and database design
- Two PowerPoint 2007 tutorials on presenting a slide show with special effects, integrating PowerPoint with other programs, and collaborating with workgroups
- New business case scenarios throughout, which provide a rich and realistic context for students to apply the concepts and skills presented

System Requirements

This book assumes a typical installation of Microsoft Office 2007 and a typical installation of Microsoft Windows Vista Ultimate (with the Aero feature turned off), Windows Vista Home Premium, or Windows Vista Business. Note that you can also complete the tutorials in this book using Windows XP; you will notice only minor differences in the appearance of some screen elements and dialog boxes, but no major functional differences, if you are using Windows XP. The browser used for any steps that require a browser is Internet Explorer 7.

The New Perspectives Approach

"I appreciate the real-world approach that the New Perspectives Series takes. It enables the transference of knowledge from step-by-step instructions to a far broader application of the software tools."

—Monique Sluymers
Kaplan University

Context
Each tutorial begins with a problem presented in a "real-world" case that is meaningful to students. The case sets the scene to help students understand what they will do in the tutorial.

Hands-on Approach
Each tutorial is divided into manageable sessions that combine reading and hands-on, step-by-step work. Colorful screenshots help guide students through the steps. **Trouble?** tips anticipate common mistakes or problems to help students stay on track and continue with the tutorial.

InSight

InSight Boxes
New for Office 2007! InSight boxes offer expert advice and best practices to help students better understand how to work with the software. With the information provided in the InSight boxes, students achieve a deeper understanding of the concepts behind the software features and skills.

Tip

Margin Tips
New for Office 2007! Margin Tips provide helpful hints and shortcuts for more efficient use of the software. The Tips appear in the margin at key points throughout each tutorial, giving students extra information when and where they need it.

Reality Check

Reality Checks
New for Office 2007! Comprehensive, open-ended Reality Check exercises give students the opportunity to practice skills by creating practical, real-world documents, such as resumes and budgets, which they are likely to use in their everyday lives at school, home, or work.

Review

In New Perspectives, retention is a key component to learning. At the end of each session, a series of Quick Check questions helps students test their understanding of the concepts before moving on. Each tutorial also contains an end-of-tutorial summary and a list of key terms for further reinforcement.

Apply

Assessment
Engaging and challenging Review Assignments and Case Problems have always been a hallmark feature of the New Perspectives Series. Colorful icons and brief descriptions accompany the exercises, making it easy to understand, at a glance, both the goal and level of challenge a particular assignment holds.

Reference Window

Task Reference

Reference
While contextual learning is excellent for retention, there are times when students will want a high-level understanding of how to accomplish a task. Within each tutorial, Reference Windows appear before a set of steps to provide a succinct summary and preview of how to perform a task. In addition, a complete Task Reference at the back of the book provides quick access to information on how to carry out common tasks. Finally, each book includes a combination Glossary/Index to promote easy reference of material.

Our Complete System of Instruction

Coverage To Meet Your Needs

Whether you're looking for just a small amount of coverage or enough to fill a semester-long class, we can provide you with a textbook that meets your needs.

- Brief books typically cover the essential skills in just 2 to 4 tutorials.
- Introductory books build and expand on those skills and contain an average of 5 to 8 tutorials.
- Comprehensive books are great for a full-semester class, and contain 9 to 12+ tutorials.

So if the book you're holding does not provide the right amount of coverage for you, there's probably another offering available. Visit our Web site or contact your Course Technology sales representative to find out what else we offer.

Student Online Companion

This book has an accompanying online companion Web site designed to enhance learning. This Web site, www.course.com/np/office2007, includes the following:

- Internet Assignments for selected tutorials
- Student Data Files
- PowerPoint presentations

CourseCasts – Learning on the Go. Always available...always relevant.

Want to keep up with the latest technology trends relevant to you? Visit our site to find a library of podcasts, CourseCasts, featuring a "CourseCast of the Week," and download them to your mp3 player at http://coursecasts.course.com.

Our fast-paced world is driven by technology. You know because you're an active participant— always on the go, always keeping up with technological trends, and always learning new ways to embrace technology to power your life.

Ken Baldauf, host of CourseCasts, is a faculty member of the Florida State University Computer Science Department where he is responsible for teaching technology classes to thousands of FSU students each year. Ken is an expert in the latest technology trends; he gathers and sorts through the most pertinent news and information for CourseCasts so your students can spend their time enjoying technology, rather than trying to figure it out. Open or close your lecture with a discussion based on the latest CourseCast.

Visit us at http://coursecasts.course.com to learn on the go!

Instructor Resources

We offer more than just a book. We have all the tools you need to enhance your lectures, check students' work, and generate exams in a new, easier-to-use and completely revised package. This book's Instructor's Manual, ExamView testbank, PowerPoint presentations, data files, solution files, figure files, and a sample syllabus are all available on a single CD-ROM or for downloading at www.course.com.

Skills Assessment and Training

SAM 2007 helps bridge the gap between the classroom and the real world by allowing students to train and test on important computer skills in an active, hands-on environment.

SAM 2007's easy-to-use system includes powerful interactive exams, training or projects on critical applications such as Word, Excel, Access, PowerPoint, Outlook, Windows, the Internet, and much more. SAM simulates the application environment, allowing students to demonstrate their knowledge and think through the skills by performing real-world tasks.

Designed to be used with the New Perspectives Series, SAM 2007 includes built-in page references so students can print helpful study guides that match the New Perspectives textbooks used in class. Powerful administrative options allow instructors to schedule exams and assignments, secure tests, and run reports with almost limitless flexibility.

Blackboard

Online Content

Blackboard is the leading distance learning solution provider and class-management platform today. Course Technology has partnered with Blackboard to bring you premium online content. Content for use with *New Perspectives on Microsoft Office 2007, Second Course* is available in a Blackboard Course Cartridge and may include topic reviews, case projects, review questions, test banks, practice tests, custom syllabi, and more.

Course Technology also has solutions for several other learning management systems. Please visit http://www.course.com today to see what's available for this title.

Acknowledgments

The entire New Perspectives team would like to extend its sincere thanks to the New Perspectives Office 2007 advisory board members and textbook reviewers listed below. We are extremely grateful to all of them for their contributions in the development of this text. Their valuable insights and excellent feedback helped us to shape this text, ensuring that it will meet the needs of instructors and students both in the classroom and beyond. Thank you all!

Advisory Board Members

Earl Belcher, Sinclair Community College
Steve Belville, Bryant & Stratton College
Alan Fisher, Walters State Community College
Patti J. Impink, Macon State College
Diane M. Larson, Indiana University Northwest
Gayle E. Larson, Dakota County Technical College
Cindy J. Miller, Ivy Tech Community College, Lafayette
Terry Morse Colucci, Institute of Technology, Inc., Clovis, CA
Ryan Murphy, Sinclair Community College
Lucy Parakhovnik, California State University, Northridge
Debi Revelle, Sanford-Brown College
Monique Sluymers, Kaplan University
Kenneth J. Sousa, Bryant University
Cathy Van Landuyt, Missouri State University

Textbook Reviewers

Bashar Elkhatib, Grantham University
Ranida B. Harris, Indiana University Southeast
Carla K. Jones, Middle Tennessee State University
Brian Kovar, Kansas State University
Karleen Nordquist, Rasmussen College
Diane Perreault, California State University, Sacramento
Janet Reckmeyer, Glendale Community College
Pamela Silvers, Asheville-Buncombe Technical Community College
Candice Spangler, Columbus State Community College
Lynne Stuhr, Trident Technical College
Martha Taylor, Sinclair Community College
Barbara Tollinger, Sinclair Community College
Robert Van Cleave, Laramie County Community College

Brief Contents

Table of Contents

Word Level II Tutorials

Tutorial 5 Working with Templates and Outlines

Creating a Site Selection Report . . . . *WD 201*

Tutorial 6 Using Mail Merge

Creating a Form Letter, Mailing Labels, and a List . . . *WD 261*

Tutorial 7 Collaborating with Others and Creating Web Pages

Writing a Program Description

Excel Level II Tutorials

Tutorial 5 Working with Excel Tables, PivotTables, and PivotCharts
Tracking Museum Art Objects ....EX 217

Tutorial 6 Managing Multiple Worksheets and Workbooks
Summarizing Ticket Sales ....EX 281

Tutorial 7 Using Advanced Functions, Conditional Formatting, and Filtering
Reviewing Employee Data ....EX 337

Appendix A Working with Text Functions and Creating Custom Formats
Cleaning Data in a Spreadsheet . . . .*EX A1*

Appendix B Integrating Excel with Other Windows Programs
Creating Integrated Documents . . . .*EX B1*

Access Level II Tutorials

Tutorial 5 Creating Advanced Queries and Enhancing Table Design
Making the Panorama Database Easier to Use . . . . .*AC 201*

Tutorial 6 Using Form Tools and Creating Custom Forms

Tutorial 7 Creating Custom Reports

Tutorial 8 Sharing, Integrating, and Analyzing Data

Working with Templates and Outlines

Creating a Site Selection Report

Case | Department of City Planning

Clarenbach, Tennessee is a rapidly growing suburb of Nashville. Clarenbach's Department of City Planning prepares reports on many public projects that contribute to this growing community. Sam Hooper, a senior member of the department, has asked you to help prepare a report on possible sites for a new public swimming pool. He'd like you to use one of Word's templates as the basis for the new report. He'd also like you to create a template that can be used for all the reports the department creates.

Starting Data Files

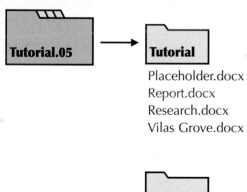

Tutorial.05 →	Tutorial	Review	Case1	Case2
	Placeholder.docx	Body.docx	Characteristics.docx	Star.docx
	Report.docx	Future.docx	Crabapple.jpg	Video.docx
	Research.docx	Placeholder.docx	Height.docx	
	Vilas Grove.docx	Research.docx	Plant Headings.docx	
			Requirements.docx	

Case3	Case4
Text.docx	(none)

Session 5.1

Creating a New Document from an Installed Template

A **template** is a file that you use as a starting point to create other files so that you don't have to re-create formatting and text for each new file. You can think of a template as a pattern for a series of similar documents. A template can contain customized Quick Styles (often referred to simply as styles), text, graphics, or any other element that you want to repeat from one document to another. Word provides numerous types of templates that you can use to create reports, fax cover sheets, letters, and other types of documents. For an even wider selection of templates, you can look online, where you'll find templates for certificates, contracts, brochures, and greeting cards, just to name a few. As you'll learn in this tutorial, you can also create your own templates to suit your specific needs.

Although you might not realize it, you already have experience working with templates. Every new, blank document that you open in Word is a copy of the Normal template. Unlike all other templates, the **Normal template** does not have any text, formatting, or graphics, but it does include all the default settings that you are accustomed to in Word. For example, the default theme in the Normal template is the Office theme. The Office theme, in turn, supplies the default body font (Calibri) and the default heading font (Cambria). The default 1.5 line spacing and the extra space after paragraphs are also specified in the Normal template.

InSight	**Changing the Normal Template**

If the settings in the Normal template don't suit your needs or tastes, you can change them. For example, you could change the default theme for the Normal template from Office to Oriel; or, instead of changing the entire theme, you could change just the default body font from Calibri to Verdana or another font. You could also change the default line spacing or the space that is supplied after each paragraph by default. It's important to remember, though, that when you change the default settings for the Normal template, the new settings will be apparent in all the new documents that you open in Word.

Tip

Templates have the file extension .dotx to differentiate them from regular Word documents, which have the extension .docx.

Sam would like to base his report on the Equity Report template, which is one of the templates installed along with Word. You open a template from the New Document dialog box. By default, when you open a new template, Word actually opens a document that is an exact copy of the template. The template itself remains untouched, so that you can continue to use it as the basis of future documents.

To open a new document based on the Equity Report template:

▶ 1. Start Word, click the **Office Button** 🗐, and then click **New**. The New Document dialog box opens. You've used the Blank document option in this dialog box before to open a new, blank document. The Templates panel on the left side of this dialog box gives you access to templates that are stored on your computer and to templates available online. In this case, you want to open a template that was installed with Word.

2. Click **Installed Templates**. The middle pane of the New Documents dialog box displays thumbnail images of the templates that were installed with Word. Scroll down, if necessary, and then click **Equity Report**. See Figure 5-1. In the lower-right corner of the New Document dialog box, the Document option button is selected by default. This indicates that Word will open a new document that is a copy of the template, not the template itself.

Selecting the Equity Report template | **Figure 5-1**

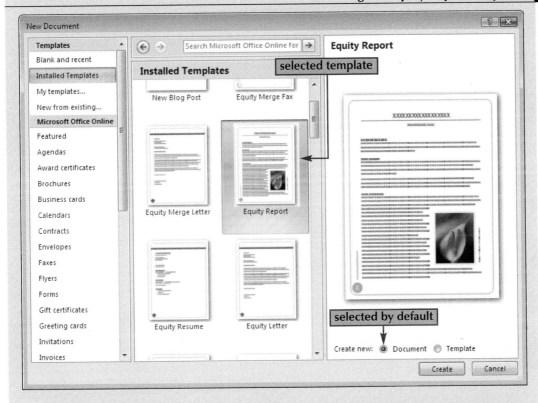

3. Click **Create**. The New Document dialog box closes, and a new document, named Document2, opens.

4. Switch to Print Layout if necessary, change the Zoom setting to Page width, display nonprinting characters if necessary, and then scroll down and review the parts of the document. The first page is a cover page with five controls: the document title, the subtitle, the company name, the date, and the author. The second page contains controls for the title and subtitle. It also contains heading and body text and a sample photograph. To the right of the photograph is a vertically formatted figure caption, which also contains a control. The lower-left corner of the second page contains a page number in an orange circle and a footer that is formatted vertically so that it runs up the left side of the page. The footer consists of two controls—one for the document title and one for the date. Each page is surrounded by a border with rounded corners. Figure 5-2 shows all the elements of the Equity Report template. The colors, the fonts, and the other elements you see in the document are specified by the Equity theme, which is the default theme for the Equity Report template.

Figure 5-2 ▶ **Equity Report template**

Tip

The sample text in the Equity Report is actually a helpful summary of techniques for working with templates, rather than text one might use in a report.

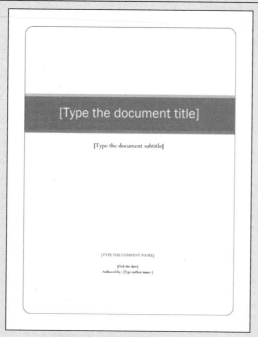

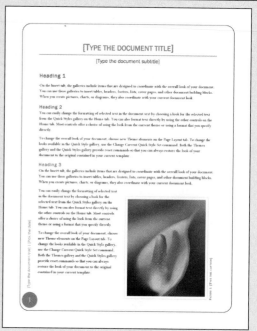

▶ **5.** Save the document as **Pool Sites** in the Tutorial.05\Tutorial folder included with your Data Files.

InSight | **Using Template Elements**

When you create a document from a template, you don't have to use all the elements the template provides. For example, you could replace the default cover page with a different one by using the Cover Page button on the Insert tab, or you could delete the cover page entirely. Likewise, the sample photograph in the Equity Report template is just a suggestion; it shows how to format a photograph so that it blends harmoniously with the other elements of the Equity Report template. The same is true of the page number inside the orange circle. If you don't like it, you can switch to Header and Footer view, click the orange circle, and delete it. The secret to getting the most out of templates is to use only the elements that suit your needs.

After you open a new document based on a template, you can type the appropriate text in the controls and then replace the sample body text with text that is specific to your document. As you learned in Tutorial 3, a document control (also known as a **content control**, or just a control) serves as a repository of information; Word reuses the information from a document control in various places within the same document. For example, if you enter the title in a title document control, it will appear in all the title document controls in that document. You'll gain more practice with document controls in the following steps as you begin work on the pools report.

To enter text into the document controls:

▶ **1.** In the orange bar on the cover page, click the **[Type the document title]** place-holder text. The text is selected within the document control, ready for you to replace it. Sam wants to use the department name as the document title.

▶ **2.** Type **Department of City Planning**. The new title replaces the placeholder text. The document control is still visible around the new title, because it contains the insertion point. Next, you need to enter the subtitle.

▶ **3.** Click the **[Type the document subtitle]** placeholder text and type **Sites for New Swimming Pool**. The new subtitle appears in the control.

▶ **4.** Scroll down, if necessary, and click the **[TYPE THE COMPANY NAME]** placeholder text. The placeholder text is selected inside the company name control. A blue dot-ted rectangle with selection handles appears, enclosing the bottom of the cover page, including the company name, date, and author controls. This rectangle is part of the formatting that governs the placement of the controls on the page. You can ignore it. Sam does not want to include anything in the company name control, so you will delete it.

▶ **5.** Right-click the selected text. A shortcut menu appears. The Mini toolbar also appears, but you can ignore it. See Figure 5-3. Note that the Zoom in Figure 5-3 is set to 80% so you can see all the parts of the cover page in one figure. On your computer, the Zoom should be set to Page width.

Shortcut menu for the company name control ◀ Figure 5-3

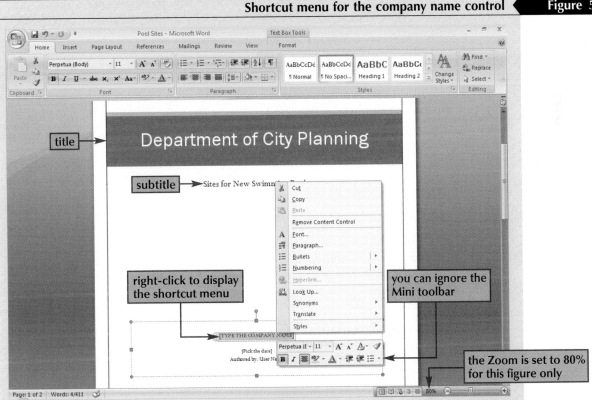

▶ **6.** Click **Remove Content Control**. The company name control is deleted.

Next, you turn your attention to inserting the date and your name as the author.

To insert the date and your name:

▶ **1.** Click the **[Pick the date]** placeholder text. A document control with an arrow button appears, surrounding the placeholder text.

▶ **2.** Click the arrow button next to the date control. A calendar appears, with a rectangle around the current date. See Figure 5-4.

Figure 5-4 ▶ **Cover page with calendar displayed**

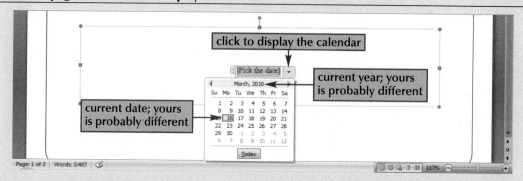

▶ **3.** Click the current date. The calendar closes and the current date is displayed in the Date control.

▶ **4.** Click to the right of the text "Authored by" to display a control where you can insert the name of the author of the report. Depending on how your computer is set up, you might see a name displayed in this control, you might see the placeholder text "[Type the author name]," or the control might be empty. See Figure 5-5.

Figure 5-5 ▶ **Author control**

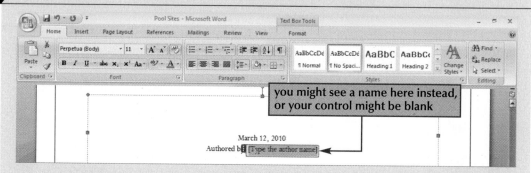

▶ **5.** If the Author control is empty, click it and type your first and last name. If the control contains a name, delete it, and then type your first and last name. Press the **Escape** key to deselect the control. Your name is now displayed in the control.

The cover page for Sam's report is finished. Now you can work on the second page. Sam wants the report to begin with the heading "Contents" followed by a table of contents. You'll insert the heading now; you'll work on inserting a table of contents in Session 3 of this tutorial.

To enter the "Contents" heading on page 2:

▶ **1.** Scroll down to display page 2. Notice that the title and subtitle controls at the top of page 2 now display the title and subtitles you typed on the cover page. Likewise, the controls in the vertical footer (in the lower-left corner of the page) display the document title and the current date.

2. Move the mouse pointer over the text in the body of the report, which begins "Heading 1." The text area is highlighted in blue.

3. Click anywhere in the body of the report. The blue highlight darkens and now covers only the text itself. A blue tag above the highlighted text indicates that the body of the report is actually a content control. See Figure 5-6. This control is included in the document only so you can see a sample of the heading and body fonts and a suggestion for how to format a photograph, should you decide to include one in the report. Before you can create the body of the report, you need to delete this control.

Document with sample text highlighted | **Figure 5-6**

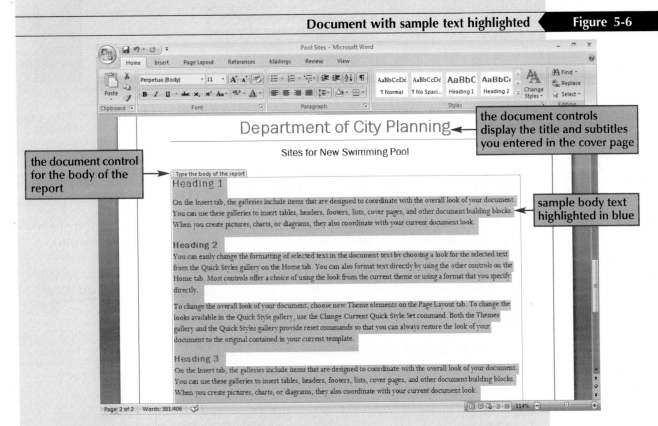

the document controls display the title and subtitles you entered in the cover page

the document control for the body of the report

sample body text highlighted in blue

4. Right-click the **body control** to display a shortcut menu, and then click **Remove Content Control**. The control is deleted. You are ready to start typing the body of the report.

5. Verify that the insertion point is located in the blank paragraph on the left margin below the subtitle, and then type **Contents**. The text is formatted in the Perpetua font, which is the default body font for the Equity Report template. In the next step, you'll format the text using a heading style.

6. In the Styles group, click the **Heading 1** Quick Style. The Contents heading is formatted in 14-point Franklin Gothic Book font with a dark orange color.

7. Press the **Enter** key to start a new paragraph, type **[Insert a table of contents.]**, and then press the **Enter** key. This placeholder text will remind Sam to insert a table of contents later. Notice that the new text is formatted in the Normal style, not in the Heading 1 style. A new paragraph after a heading is formatted in the Normal style by default. See Figure 5-7.

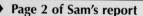

Figure 5-7 ▶ **Page 2 of Sam's report**

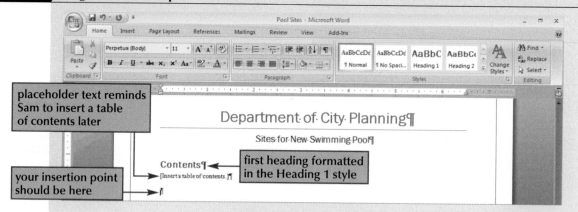

Sam has already typed the remainder of his report and saved it in a separate Word document. In the next section, you'll learn how to insert this Word file into the Pool Sites document.

Inserting a File into a Word Document

To insert a file into a document, you start by clicking the Object button in the Text group on the Insert tab. When you insert a Word file into an open Word document, the text of the inserted file is inserted at the location of the insertion point, so you need to make sure the insertion point is at the correct location. Word always inserts a blank paragraph at the end of text inserted from another file. If you don't want to include this extra paragraph, you can delete it.

To insert a file into the Pool Sites document:

▶ 1. Verify that the insertion point is located in the blank paragraph below the placeholder text, as shown earlier in Figure 5-7.

▶ 2. Click the **Insert** tab, and then, in the Text group, click the **Object** button arrow. (Take care to click the Object button arrow, and not the Object button itself.) A menu appears with two options.

   Trouble? If the Object dialog box opens, you clicked the Object button instead of the Object button arrow. Close the dialog box, and then click the Object button arrow instead.

▶ 3. In the Object menu, click **Text from File**. The Insert File dialog box opens. This looks like the Open dialog box, which you've used many times before.

▶ 4. If necessary, navigate to the Tutorial.05\Tutorial folder included with your Data Files, click the **Report** document, and then click the **Insert** button. The text of the Report document is inserted in the Pool Sites document. Sam formatted the headings of the Report document with Quick Styles when he first typed the document, so you don't need to format the headings now. Note that Word inserted a blank paragraph after the report text. You can leave that extra paragraph there for now. See Figure 5-8.

Trouble? If a menu appears below the Insert button in the Insert File dialog box, you clicked the Insert button arrow, rather than the Insert button itself. Press the Escape key to close the menu, and then click the Insert button.

Report document inserted into the Pool Sites document ◀ **Figure 5-8**

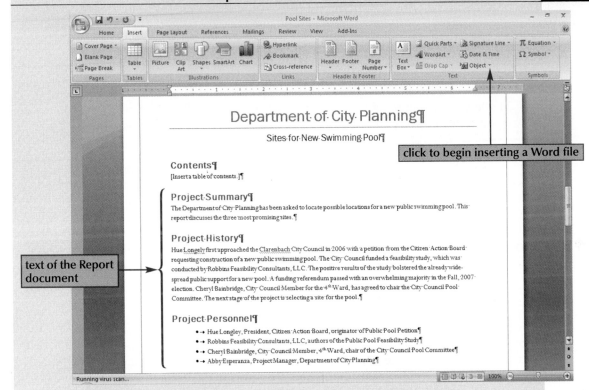

Review the document and notice that it now includes five main headings formatted with the Heading 1 style: Contents (which you typed earlier), Project Summary, Project History, Project Personnel, and Project Description. Below the Project Description heading are three subheadings: Breese Terrace Park, Langbrook Farm, and Flora Park. The subheadings Breese Terrace Park and Flora Park are formatted with the Heading 2 style. Sam mistakenly formatted the Langbrook Farm heading in the Heading 3 style. Later in this tutorial, when you learn about outlines, you will fix this problem.

▶ **5.** Save your work.

Now that the document contains the report text, you can turn your attention to customizing its formatting. You'll start with the document theme.

Customizing the Document Theme

A document theme consists of three main components: colors, fonts, and effects. The **theme colors** control the colors used for every element in a document, including text, shading, hyperlinks, and so on. The **theme fonts** control the document's heading and body fonts. Remember that each theme specifies one font to be used for headings and one font to be used for body text. These two fonts appear at the top of the Font list on the Home tab. The **theme effects** control the look of a document's graphics. A specific set of colors, fonts, and effects is associated with each theme, but you can mix and match them to create a customized theme for your document. You change the theme colors, fonts, and effects for a document using the options in the Themes group on the Page Layout tab. When you change the theme colors, fonts, and effects for a document, the new elements affect only that document.

Reference Window | **Customizing the Document Theme**

- To select a different set of theme colors, click the Theme Colors button in the Themes group on the Page Layout tab, and then click the color palette you want.
- To select a different combination of heading and body fonts, click the Theme Fonts button in the Themes group on the Page Layout tab, and then click the font combination you want.
- To select a different set of theme effects, click the Theme Effects button in the Themes group on the Page Layout tab, and then click the icon for the effects you want.

The Pool Sites document, which was based on the Equity Report template, is formatted with the Equity theme. That means it draws its colors, fonts, and effects from the default settings of the Equity theme. Although Sam likes the overall layout of the document, which was provided by the Equity Report template, he doesn't like the colors or the fonts supplied by the Equity theme. He decides to select different theme colors and theme fonts for the Pool Sites document. He doesn't plan to include any graphics, so he will not take the time to customize the theme effects. He'll start with the theme colors.

Changing the Theme Colors

To get a better understanding of what happens when you change a document's theme colors, suppose you are working on a new document with the Office theme selected. The colors associated with the Office theme format headings in blue. If you prefer headings formatted in pink instead, you could select the colors of the Verve theme, which formats headings in pink.

Sam doesn't like the orange and red colors used in the Equity theme and asks you to change it to something more neutral. Before you begin customizing the theme, you will take a moment to verify that the Equity theme is in fact the current theme.

To change the theme colors in the Pool Sites document:

1. Verify that the second page of the document is displayed, so that you can see the document headings.

2. Click the **Page Layout** tab, and then position the mouse pointer over the **Themes** button. A ScreenTip appears indicating that the current theme is Equity. Next, you begin customizing the Equity theme's colors.

3. In the Themes group, click the **Theme Colors** button. A gallery of color sets appears, with one color set for each theme. A pale orange outline indicates that the Equity color set is the current color set. You see eight colors in each color set. The third color from the left in each set is the color used for headings. For example, the third color from the left in the Equity color set is dark orange, which is the color currently applied to the headings in the document. The remaining colors are used for other types of elements, such as hyperlinks, shading on cover pages, and so on. See Figure 5-9.

Tip

To see a ScreenTip that tells you the current theme colors, move the mouse pointer over the Theme Colors button in the Themes group on the Page Layout tab.

Theme Colors gallery **Figure 5-9**

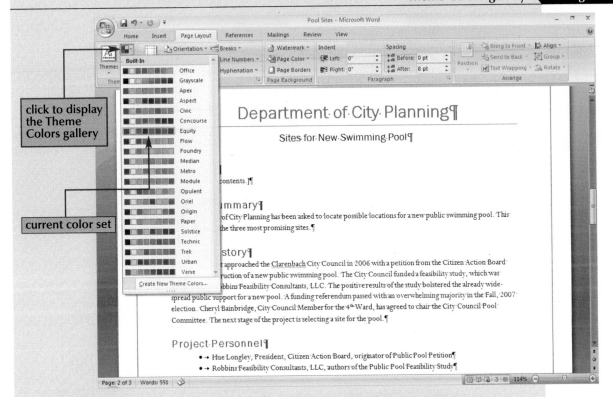

Trouble? If you see additional color sets at the top of the menu under the heading Custom, someone else created custom color sets on your computer. You can ignore them.

4. Move the mouse pointer over the options in the gallery and observe the live pre-view of the colors in the document.

5. Scroll down if necessary, and then click the **Urban** color set, which is the second from the bottom. The document headings are now formatted in dark blue. The page number circle in the document footing changes from orange to blue.

6. Scroll up and review the new colors applied to the cover page. The colored bar is dark blue with a brown bottom border, instead of dark orange with a light orange bottom border.

7. Save your work.

Keep in mind that the new colors you just selected affect only the Pool Sites document. Your changes do not affect the Equity theme that was installed with Word and that is available to all new documents. In the next section, you will finish customizing the document's theme by changing the theme fonts.

Customizing the Theme Fonts

Before you get to work changing the theme fonts for the Pool Sites document, you need to take a moment to learn some general principles that are useful when deciding which fonts to use in your documents:

- Fonts are divided into two types: serif and sans serif fonts. A **serif** is a small embellishment at the tips of the lines of a character, as shown in Figure 5-10. "Sans" is French for "without," thus, a **sans serif font** is a font without embellishments.

Figure 5-10   **Elements of fonts**

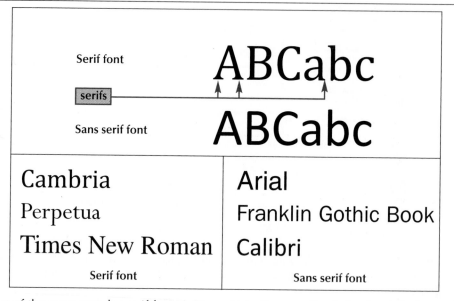

- One of the most popular serif fonts is Times New Roman. Cambria, the default Headings font in the Office theme, is a new serif font created specifically by Microsoft for Office 2007. Perpetua, the default Body font for the Equity theme, is also a serif font.
- Arial is a popular sans serif font. Calibri, the default body font in the Office theme, is a new sans serif font created specifically by Microsoft for Office 2007. Franklin Gothic Book, the default Headings font for the Equity theme, is also a sans serif font.
- As a rule, you should avoid unusual fonts, or fonts that look like handwriting, except in certificates, invitations, advertisements, and other specialty documents.
- You can add special effects to most fonts by adjusting the settings in the Font dialog box, which you open by clicking the Dialog Box Launcher in the Font group on the Home tab. For example, you can format a font as small caps (a reduced version of regular capital letters), superscript (slightly above the main line), subscript (slightly below the main line), outline (only the outline of the letters), or with shadows (light shading in the shape of the letter).

With these guidelines in mind, you are ready to select a new set of fonts for the Pool Sites document. As with theme colors, when changing the theme fonts, you can select from all the font combinations available in any of the themes installed with Word.

To select a different set of theme fonts for the Pool Sites document:

▶ **1.** Scroll down so you can see page 2 of the document.

▶ **2.** In the Themes group, move the mouse pointer over the **Theme Fonts** button ⒶⓋ. A ScreenTip appears, indicating that the current fonts are Franklin Gothic book for headings and Perpetua for body text.

▶ **3.** Click ⒶⓋ. The Theme Fonts gallery opens, displaying the heading and body font combinations for each theme.

▶ **4.** Scroll down until you see the heading and body fonts for the Equity theme. The orange highlighting indicates that these are the current fonts for the Pool Sites document. Sam prefers the Lucida Sans Unicode font, which has a bolder, more modern look than the default fonts for the Equity theme. The Concourse theme uses the Lucida Sans Unicode font for both headings and body text, so you will select the Concourse font set in the next step. (Although the Concourse font set consists of the same font for headings and body text, it's still called a "set.") See Figure 5-11.

Theme Fonts gallery ◀ **Figure 5-11**

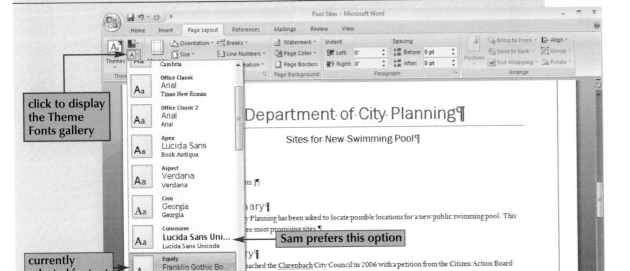

▶ **5.** Click the **Concourse** font set. The Theme Fonts gallery closes, and the Lucida Sans Unicode Font is applied to the headings and body text in the Pool Sites document. See Figure 5-12.

Figure 5-12 | **Pool Sites document with new theme fonts and colors**

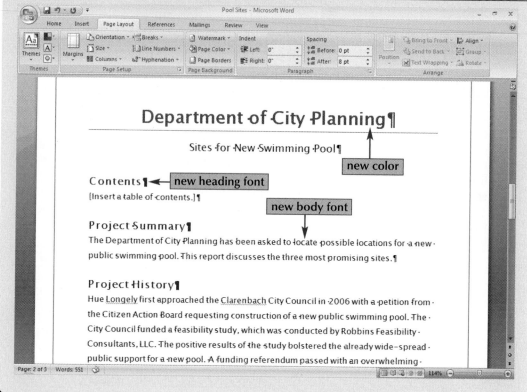

6. Save your work.

Remember that the new font set you just selected affects only the Pool Sites document. The new fonts do not affect the original Equity theme that was installed with Word and that is available to all new documents.

Creating Custom Theme Colors and Theme Fonts

It is possible to create customized sets of theme fonts and theme colors. Customized sets of theme colors and theme fonts include combinations that are not included in any of the themes installed with Word. (It is not possible to create customized theme effects in Word.) When you create a customized set of theme fonts or theme colors, they are saved as part of Word, so that you can use them in other documents.

Creating Custom Theme Colors and Theme Fonts | Reference Window

- To create a custom set of theme colors, click the Theme Colors button in the Themes group on the Page Layout tab, click Create New Theme Colors to open the Create New Theme Colors dialog box, click the arrow for the color you want to change, click a color, repeat for additional colors as necessary, type a descriptive name for the new color scheme in the Name text box, and then click the Save button. The custom set of theme colors appears as an option in the Themes Color menu.
- To delete a custom set of theme colors, click the Theme Colors button in the Themes group on the Page Layout tab, right-click the custom set of colors you want to delete, click Delete, and then click Yes.
- To create a custom set of heading and body fonts, click the Theme Fonts button in the Themes group on the Page Layout tab, click Create New Theme Fonts to open the Create New Theme Fonts dialog box, use the list boxes to select the Heading and Body fonts you want, type a descriptive name for the new set of fonts in the Name text box, and then click the Save button. The custom set of theme fonts appears as an option in the Theme Fonts menu.
- To delete a new set of theme colors or fonts, click the Theme Colors or Theme Fonts button in the Themes group on the Page Layout tab, right-click the custom set of colors or fonts you want to delete, click Delete, and then click Yes.

The sets of theme colors and theme fonts installed with Word were created by Microsoft designers who are experts in creating harmonious-looking documents. As a rule, it's best to stick with these predesigned options, rather than trying to create your own.

Creating a Custom Theme

Keep in mind that the new theme colors and theme fonts you selected for the Pool Sites document affect only that document. To make your new choices available to other documents, you would need to create a custom theme. When you create a custom theme, it is saved as part of Word and appears as an option in the Themes gallery so that you can apply it to any document.

Creating a Custom Theme | Reference Window

- Modify the document theme as much as you want by selecting new theme colors, theme fonts, and theme effects.
- In the Themes group on the Page Layout tab, click the Themes button.
- Click Save Current Theme to open the Save Current Theme dialog box, type a name for the theme in the File name text box, and then click the Save button. The new theme appears at the top of the Themes menu, under the "Custom" heading.
- To delete a custom theme, click the Themes button in the Themes group on the Page Layout tab, right-click the theme you want to delete, click Delete, and then click Yes.

Sam is happy with the new look of the Pool Sites document. He doesn't need to save his changes to the fonts and colors as a custom theme, though. In the next session, you will focus on modifying the Quick Styles used in Sam's report.

1. Which template includes all the default settings that you are accustomed to in Word?
2. How do you delete a content control?
3. What tab should you click if you want to insert a Word file into a document?
4. What are the three main components of a document theme?
5. List the two types of fonts.
6. True or False. It is not possible to create a new theme.

Session 5.2

Understanding Themes, Styles, and Style Sets

Before you begin working more extensively with styles, you need to make sure you understand the relationship between styles and themes. The elements of a theme (colors, fonts, and effects) are like the building materials for a house. Styles, on the other hand, are like blueprints for the many types of houses that you can create with those building materials.

For example, by default, the Heading 1 style applies the heading font specified in the document theme. However, it doesn't just apply to the heading font. That would be like a blueprint that said only that a house should be made out of brick, but failed to specify the number of rooms, the style of windows, and so on. The Heading 1 style, for example, includes numerous additional details that, taken together, format text with a particular look—its style. Among other things, the Heading 1 style applies a particular font size and adds boldface. It also adds color—whatever color specified by the current Accent 1 color for the current theme.

As you know, you select a style from the Quick Styles gallery on the Home tab. By default, the Quick Styles gallery displays 20 different styles. Additional sets of styles are also available via the Change Styles button in the Styles group on the Home tab.

You can modify an existing style, or you can create a new style by modifying an existing one and saving it with a new name. By default, a new or modified style is saved only in the current document. If you prefer, you can save a new or modified style as part of the current template, so that it is available in all new documents based on that template.

InSight | **Saving Styles to the Current Document**

Keep in mind that all new, blank documents are based on the Normal template. So if you open a blank document, modify or create a style, and then save the style to the current template (rather than to the current document), the style will be available in all new blank documents that you open in Word in the future. Continually modifying or creating styles in the Normal template can result in a Quick Styles gallery that is disorganized, making it hard to find the styles you want. To avoid this problem, consider saving specialized styles to the current document (rather than to the current template), and then saving the current document as a template. All future documents based on that new template will contain your new styles. Meanwhile, the Normal template will remain unaffected by the new styles.

Sam wants to select a different style set for the Pool Sites document. Then he would like to modify the Heading 1 style, and finally, create a new style for the Project Summary heading.

Selecting a Style Set

Every built-in theme comes with 11 sets of styles, with names such as Elegant, Modern, and Manuscript. Each style set is, in turn, made up of 31 styles. So far, you've worked with only the sixteen styles, such as Heading 1 and Heading 2, that are available from the Quick Styles gallery on the Home tab. You can access additional styles via the Styles window, by clicking the More button in the Styles group on the Home tab.

The **style sets** have the same names in each theme, but they look different from one theme to the next. Likewise, the styles that make up the style sets have the same name in each style set, but they look different from one style set to the next. The default style set for built-in themes is the Office 2007 style set. This is the style set you are used to seeing in the Quick Styles gallery whenever you open a new, blank document.

Each set of styles includes a Normal style for formatting body text, several heading styles, and styles for titles, captions, and other special types of text. To select a different style set, you use the Change Styles button in the Styles group on the Home tab. The Style Sets menu allows you to preview the various style sets in your document before actually selecting one.

In the following steps, you select a new style set for the Pool Sites document.

To select a new style set for the Pool Sites document:

▶ **1.** Verify that the Pool Sites document is open, in Print Layout view, the Zoom set at Page width, and nonprinting characters displayed. If necessary, scroll down so the second page of the document is visible. This will allow you to see how changing the style set affects the document headings. Recall that some headings are formatted with various heading styles. The body text below each of the headings is formatted in the Normal style.

▶ **2.** Click the **Home** tab if necessary, and then in the Styles group, click the **Change Styles** button. The Change Styles menu opens. To select a new style set, you use the Style Set option.

▶ **3.** Point to **Style Set**. The Style Set menu opens, displaying a list of style sets.

▶ **4.** Drag the mouse pointer down and point to **Modern**. In the document, you see a preview of some of the styles that make up the Modern style set. In the Modern style set, the Heading 1 style applies a blue box that spans the left and right margins, with the heading text in white. The font for the document is still Lucida Sans Unicode for both headings and the body text, as you specified in Session 1 when you changed the theme fonts. The colors are still the colors you picked when you changed the theme colors in Session 1. See Figure 5-13.

Tip

To restore the default style set specified by the document's template, click Reset to Quick Styles from *Name* Template (where *Name* stands for the template's name) at the bottom of the Style Set menu.

Figure 5-13 **Live Preview of the Modern style set**

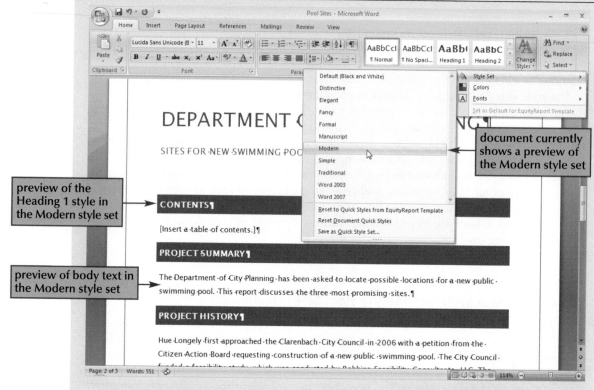

5. Move the mouse pointer over other options in the Style Set menu and observe the live preview in the document.

6. Click **Modern** in the Style Set menu. The styles in the document change to reflect the styles in the Modern style set, and the Quick Styles gallery in the Styles group displays the first four styles in the Modern Style set.

7. In the Styles group, click the **More** button ☰ to review the set of styles available in the Quick Styles gallery, and then click anywhere in the document to close the Quick Styles gallery.

Tip

If you forget which style set is currently applied to a document, you can always check the Style Set menu to see which style has a check mark next to it.

Now that you've selected the Modern style set for Sam's document, you can customize the styles in the Modern style set. You'll start by modifying the Heading 1 style.

Modifying Styles

To modify a style, you select text formatted with the style you want to modify, apply new formatting, and then save your changes to the style. You'll start modifying the Heading 1 style by selecting some text formatted in that style and then applying the new formatting. Specifically, you will expand its character spacing, paragraph spacing, and apply italics. After you finish applying this new formatting, you will modify the Heading 1 style to match the newly formatted heading. To apply this formatting, you need to turn your attention briefly away from styles to focus on character spacing and paragraph spacing.

Changing Character Spacing

Word offers a number of ways to adjust the spacing between characters—that is, to adjust **character spacing**. In some situations, you might want to use **kerning**, the process of adjusting the spacing between characters to make them look like they are spaced evenly. Kerning is helpful because in text formatted in large font sizes, characters sometimes look unevenly spaced, even though they are in fact spaced evenly. Turning on Word's automatic kerning feature ensures that the spacing is adjusted automatically so that letters appear evenly spaced. In most documents, however, it's easiest to select a group of characters and then uniformly expand or condense the spacing between them. Notice that space between characters is measured in points, with one point equal to 1/72 of an inch.

Adjusting Character Spacing | Reference Window

- Select the text whose character spacing you want to adjust.
- In the Font group on the Home tab, click the Dialog Box Launcher to open the Font dialog box, and then click the Character Spacing tab.
- Click the Spacing arrow, and then click Expanded or Condensed. If you like, you can specify the amount of spacing to apply to each character by adjusting the setting in the By text box.
- To switch from Expanded or Condensed spacing back to regular spacing, click the Spacing arrow, and then click Normal.
- To turn on automatic kerning, click the Kerning for fonts check box to insert a check, and then select a point size in the Points and above check box.

You are ready to modify the character spacing of the Contents heading. While you have the Font dialog box open, you will also add italics.

To modify the character spacing of the Contents heading:

▶ 1. Click in the left margin to select the heading **Contents**. Note that the blue selection highlighting might be hard to see in the blue box surrounding the "Contents" heading.

▶ 2. In the Font group on the Home tab, click the Dialog Box Launcher. The Font dialog box opens.

▶ 3. Click the **Character Spacing** tab. This tab includes several options for changing the space between characters. Currently, the setting in the Spacing list box is Expanded. The setting you see here depends on the style applied to the text that is selected in the document. If you wanted to move the selected character closer together, you could click the Spacing arrow and then click Condensed. In this case, you will keep the Expanded setting but increase the space between the characters by changing the setting in the By box next to the Spacing list box.

▶ 4. Next to the Spacing list box, delete the contents of the By text box, type **2** (you don't have to type "pt"), and then press the **Tab** key. The Preview section shows a sample of the expanded character spacing. See Figure 5-14.

Figure 5-14 | **Changing character spacing in the Font dialog box**

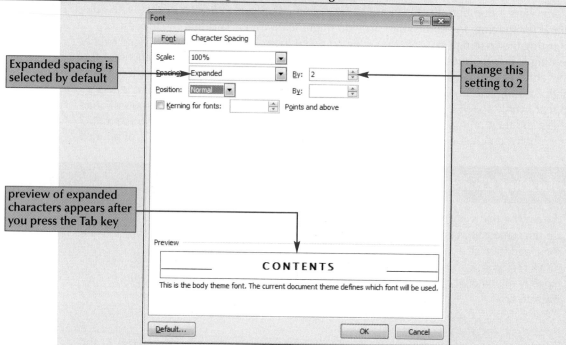

Expanded spacing is selected by default

change this setting to 2

preview of expanded characters appears after you press the Tab key

Next, you need to apply italics. It's normally easiest to use the buttons on the Home tab to perform this task. However, since the Font dialog box is open, it makes sense to make these changes there.

5. In the Font dialog box, click the **Font** tab. Here you can make numerous changes affecting the appearance of the selected text, including adding special effects such as shadows or outlines. The "Contents" heading is already formatted in all capital letters, so the All caps check box is selected. This setting was specified by the Heading 1 style. In the Font style list box, Bold is also selected, indicating that the Heading 1 style also applied bold formatting to the "Contents" heading. (In the case of the white font color applied to the "Contents" heading, bold makes the white characters thicker rather than darker.) You want to keep the bold formatting and also add italics.

6. In the Font style list box, click **Bold Italic**. The Preview section of the Font tab shows a preview of the new formatting. See Figure 5-15.

Applying italics in the Font dialog box ◀ **Figure 5-15**

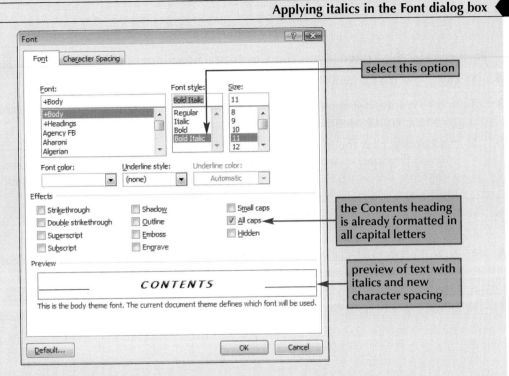

7. Click the **OK** button to close the Font dialog box. The selected heading is now italicized, with the individual characters spread slightly farther apart.

8. Save your work.

Next, you need to change the Heading 1 style so there is some extra spacing below each heading formatted with this style. Increasing the paragraph spacing is the last change Sam wants for the headings. After you're done formatting the Contents heading, you will tell Word that you want to modify the Heading 1 style to match the formatting of the Contents heading. This will affect all the headings that are currently formatted with the Heading 1 style.

Changing Paragraph Spacing

You already know how to add or delete a default amount of space before or after a paragraph using the Line spacing button in the Paragraph group on the Home tab. To specify an exact amount of space, you use the Paragraph dialog box.

Adjusting Spacing Between Paragraphs | Reference Window

- Select the paragraph whose spacing you want to adjust.
- To add or delete Word's default amount of space, click the Line spacing button in the Paragraph group on the Home tab, and then click Add Space Before Paragraph or Remove Space After Paragraph.
- To add or delete a specific amount of space, in the Paragraph group on the Home tab, click the Dialog Box Launcher to open the Paragraph dialog box, click the Indents and Spacing tab, and then use the Before box to specify the amount of space you want to insert above the selected paragraph. Use the After box to specify the amount of space you want to insert below the selected paragraph.

Sam wants 6 points of space after the Contents heading. The extra space will help draw attention to the heading.

To increase the space after the Contents heading:

▶ **1.** Verify that the Contents heading is still selected.

▶ **2.** In the Paragraph group on the Home tab, click the Dialog Box Launcher. The Paragraph dialog box opens.

▶ **3.** If necessary, click the **Indents and Spacing** tab. You use the Before and After boxes in the Spacing section of this tab to add space before or after the selected paragraph. Currently, there are 10 points of space before the selected paragraph and no points after it. Sam wants to change the After setting to 15.

▶ **4.** In the Spacing section, select the contents of the After box, and then type **15**. (You don't have to type "pt.")

▶ **5.** Press the **Tab** key to enter the new setting. The Preview section of the dialog box shows a sample of the increased paragraph spacing. See Figure 5-16.

Figure 5-16 ▶ **Changing paragraph spacing**

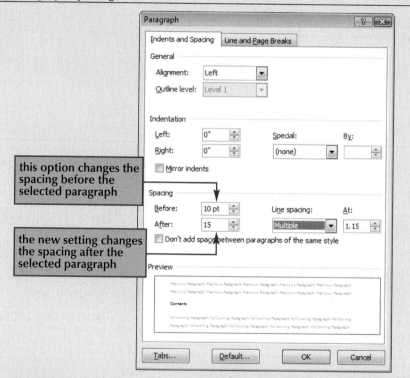

▶ **6.** Click the **OK** button. The Paragraph dialog box closes. Notice that there is now a little extra space below the Contents heading and above the paragraph of body text that says "[Insert a table of contents.]."

You might be tempted to increase the space before or after a paragraph by pressing the Enter key to insert a blank paragraph. However, inserting blank paragraphs in a document is rarely a good idea. For one thing, inserting a blank paragraph after a heading prevents Word from keeping a heading and its body text together when they span page or column breaks. Also, if you insert a blank paragraph, and then later increase the paragraph spacing in the entire document, you may end up with more blank space in the document than you really want. As a rule, using the Line spacing button in the Paragraph group on the Home tab or using the Paragraph dialog box gives you much more control over spacing before and after paragraphs. Make it a habit to use these options rather than inserting blank paragraphs.

Updating a Style to Match Selected Text

Now that the selected text is formatted the way you want, you can modify the Heading 1 style to match the selected text. As mentioned earlier, to modify a style, you select text formatted with the style you want to modify, apply new formatting, and then save your changes to the style. When saving the style, you need to decide whether you want to save the style to the current document or to the current template. If Sam modified the Heading 1 style and saved it to the current template, the modified version of the Heading 1 style would appear in all new documents based on the Equity Report template (the template his document is based on). However, Sam doesn't want to alter the Equity Report template. So in this case, it makes sense to save the modified version of the Heading 1 style just to the current document. You'll start by opening the Styles window.

- In the Styles group on the Home tab, click the Dialog Box Launcher to open the Styles window.
- In the document, select text formatted with the style you want to modify.
- Format the selected text with the font, paragraph, and other formatting you want.
- With the text still selected in the document, move the mouse pointer over the style you want to modify in the Styles window. A down arrow appears next to the style's name in the Styles window.
- Click the down arrow next to the style's name.
- To save the modified style to the current document, click Update *Style Name* to Match Selection (where *Style Name* is the name of the style you want to modify).
- To save the modified style to the current template, click Modify to open the Modify Style dialog box, click the New documents based on this template option button, and then click the OK button.

The **Styles window** displays a complete list of all the document's styles and provides easy access to the relevant commands. If you're doing a lot of work with styles in a document, it's often easier to use the Styles window rather than the Quick Styles gallery. You open the Styles window with the Dialog Box Launcher in the Styles group on the Home tab. You can click a style in the Styles window to apply it to selected text, just as you would click a style in the Quick Styles gallery.

To open the Styles window and modify the Heading 1 style:

▶ **1.** In the Styles group on the Home tab, click the Dialog Box Launcher. The Styles window opens. It might be located on the right or left side of the document window, floating over the document text, or it might be locked on the right side, in which case the document window has been resized to accommodate it. In the following step, you will lock the Styles window on the right side of the document window, if it isn't there already.

▶ **2.** Click the title bar of the Styles window, and then drag the Styles window to the right as far as you can, almost as if you are going to drag it off the screen. The Styles window snaps in place on the right side of the screen, and the document window resizes accordingly. The blue outline around the Heading 1 style in the Styles window tells you that the text currently selected in your document, the Contents heading, is formatted with the Heading 1 style—even though you've made several changes to that heading. See Figure 5-17.

Tip

To remove formatting from selected text and return it to the Normal style, click the Clear Formatting button in the Font group on the Home tab.

Figure 5-17 **Styles window**

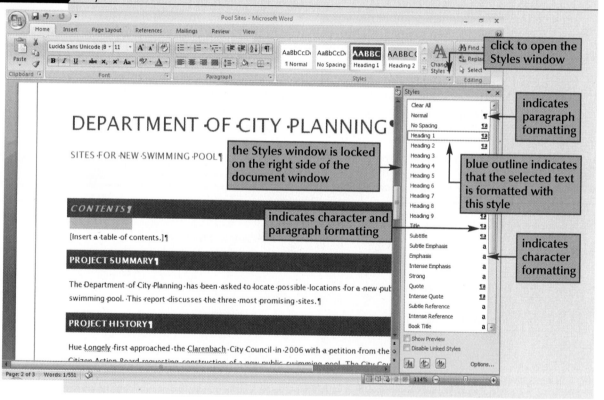

The Styles window contains a complete list of all the styles available in the document, along with some helpful commands and buttons. You can apply styles from the Styles window, just as you would from the Quick Styles gallery; just select the text you want to format and click a style in the Styles window.

Using the Styles Window | InSight

There are a lot of advantages to using the Styles window instead of the Quick Styles gallery. First, the Styles window includes styles that are not displayed in the Quick Styles gallery. Also, in the Styles window, styles are listed alphabetically, making it easier to locate a specific style in a document that contains lots of styles. So if you are looking for a style and can't find it in the Quick Styles gallery, check the Styles window. Another advantage of the Styles window is that it remains open until you close it. This makes the Styles window easier to use than the Quick Styles gallery when you need to apply a lot of styles. Finally, the symbols next to each style in the Styles window allow you to see quickly if a style is considered a paragraph style, a character style, or both.

Note that a paragraph symbol to the right of a style name in the Styles window indicates that the style applies paragraph formatting—such as line spacing, indentation, a border, and so on. A lowercase letter "a" to the right of a style name indicates the style applies character formatting—such as bold, italics, or a particular font size. Styles with both symbols next to their names apply both character and paragraph formatting. As you'll see in the following steps, you can display even more information about a style by moving the mouse pointer over the style's name in the Styles window.

To use the Styles Window to modify the Heading 1 style:

▶ **1.** In the Styles window, move the mouse pointer over **Heading 1**. A blue box with detailed information about the Heading 1 style appears, and a down arrow appears next to the style. Note that this information makes no mention of italics because, although you added italics to the "Contents" heading, you haven't yet altered the Heading 1 style itself. The information in this box relates only to the Heading 1 style.

▶ **2.** Click the **Heading 1** down arrow. A menu opens with options related to working with the Heading 1 style. The first option on the menu modifies the Heading 1 style to match the selected text and saves the newly modified style to the current document. To open a dialog box where you can save the modified style to the current template instead, you click the Modify option. Sam wants to save the newly modified Heading 1 style to the current document, so you'll use the first option. See Figure 5-18.

Figure 5-18 | **Modifying the Heading 1 style**

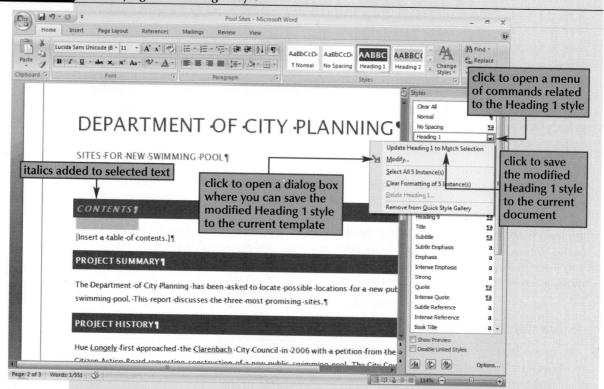

3. Click **Update Heading 1 to Match Selection**. The Heading 1 style changes to include expanded character spacing, italics, and additional paragraph spacing— all the changes Sam asked you to make to the Contents heading. All the headings in the document formatted in the Heading 1 style are now formatted this way as well, and any other text you format with the Heading 1 style in this document will also have the italics, expanded character spacing, and additional paragraph spacing.

4. Save your work. The modified version of the Heading 1 style is saved along with the document. No other documents are affected by this change to the Heading 1 style.

You've successfully modified the Heading 1 style by adding italics and by expanding its character and paragraph spacing. Next, you will create a new style to be used for the Project Summary heading, because it's helpful to set off a summary and its heading from the rest of a report.

Creating a New Style

When creating a new style, you have two important choices. First, as when modifying styles, you need to decide whether to save the style to the current document or to the current template. Second, you need to decide whether you want to base your new style on an existing style or create a new style from scratch.

When you base a new style on an existing style, you modify a style, as explained in the preceding section, and then, instead of updating the style to match your changes, you save the style with a new name. For example, suppose you modify the Heading 1 style by removing the bold formatting, and then save the modified style with the name "Budget," so that you can use it exclusively for formatting a "Budget" heading. A new style created in this way is called a **linked style**, because it remains linked to the style on which it is based; changes to the original style also affect the new style. This means that if you change the font for the Heading 1 style to Algerian, the font for the new Budget style would also change to Algerian. Note that the opposite is not true: changes to the new style do *not* affect the style on which it is based.

If you instead choose to create a new style from scratch—that is, if you create a style that is not based on any existing styles—the new style has no connection to any other styles. This usually isn't a good idea, because it prevents Word from enforcing the kind of formatting consistency that is possible with linked styles. As you'll see later in this tutorial, creating a style from scratch is especially troublesome in long documents, where you might want to work in Outline view.

Creating a New Style | Reference Window

- In the Styles group on the Home tab, click the Dialog Box Launcher to open the Styles window.
- Select text formatted with the style that most closely resembles the new style you want to create.
- Format the selected text with the font and paragraph formatting you want.
- In the lower-left corner of the Styles window, click the New Style button to open the Create New Style from Formatting dialog box.
- Type a name for the new style in the Name text box.
- The Style based on list box tells you which existing style the new style will be based on. If you don't want to base the new style on an existing style, click the Style based on arrow, and then click (no style).
- To save the new style to the current document, verify that the Only in this document option button is selected, and then click the OK button.
- To save the style to the current template, click the New documents based on this template option button, and then click the OK button.
- To delete a style you have created, point to the style's name in the Styles window, click the down arrow next to the style's name, click Revert to *Style Name*, (where *Style Name* is the style it was based on), and then click Yes.

Sam is ready to create a new style for the Project Summary heading. The new style will be based on the Heading 1 style. It will look just like the Heading 1 style, except that it will be not be in all uppercase (capital) letters, and it will include an underline. You'll start by selecting the text you want to format.

To format the Project Summary heading in uppercase and lowercase, with an underline:

▶ **1.** Select the **Project Summary** heading. A quick way to change uppercase letters to lowercase, or vice versa, is to use the Change Case button in the Font group on the Home tab. However, in the next step you'll use the Font dialog box instead, because there you can apply a shadow effect at the same time.

▶ **2.** In the Font group on the Home tab, click the Dialog Box Launcher, and then, in the Font dialog box, click the **Font** tab if necessary.

▶ **3.** In the Effects section, click the **All caps** check box to remove the checkmark, click the **Underline style** arrow, scroll to the bottom of the list, and select the double-wavy underline style. The Preview section of the Font dialog box displays a preview of the new formatting. See Figure 5-19.

Figure 5-19

Formatting the Project Summary heading

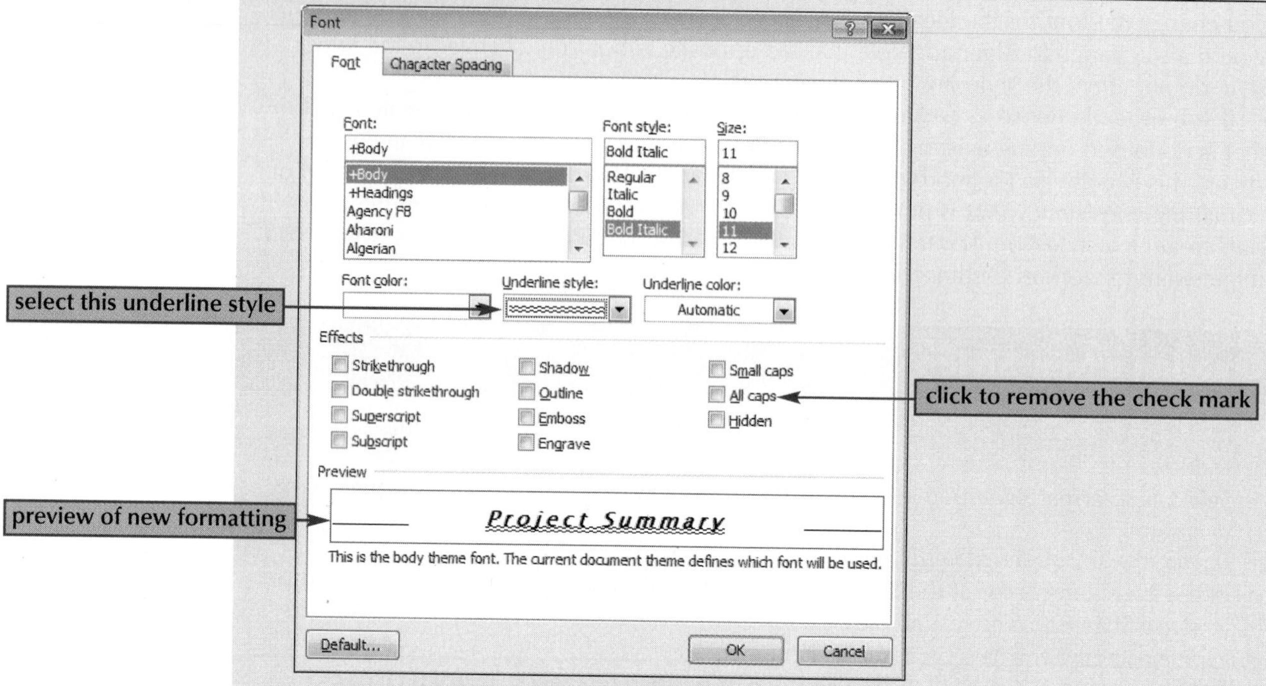

select this underline style

click to remove the check mark

preview of new formatting

► **4.** Click the **OK** button. The Font dialog box closes.

► **5.** Click anywhere in the document to deselect the "Project Summary" heading so you can clearly see its new formatting.

Now that the text is formatted the way you want, you can create the new style.

To create a new style for the Project Summary heading:

► **1.** Select the **Project Summary** heading, and then verify that the Styles window is still open.

► **2.** In the lower-left corner of the Styles window, click the **New Style** button [44]. The Create New Style from Formatting dialog box opens. A default name for the new style, "Style1," appears in the Name text box. In the next step, you will change the default name to something more meaningful.

► **3.** In the **Name** text box, select the default name, if necessary, and then type **Summary**. The default style name is replaced with the new one. The Style based on list box tells you that the new Summary style is based on the Heading 1 style, which is what you want. See Figure 5-20.

Naming a new style | Figure 5-20

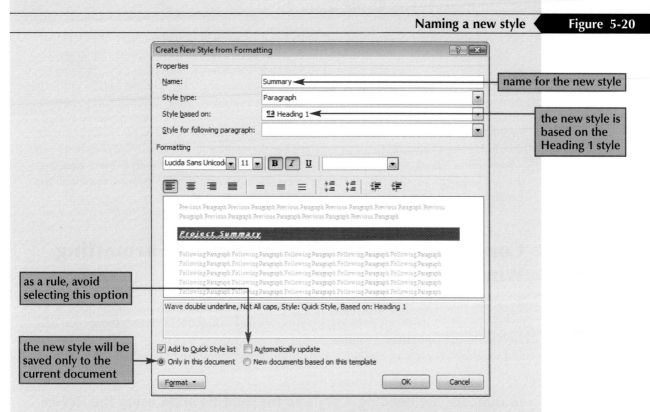

If you wanted to make the new style available to all future documents based on the current template, you would click the New documents based on this template option button. However, you want to save the new Summary style only to the current document, so you will accept the default setting, with the Only in this document option button selected. Note that, by default, the Automatically update check box is *not* selected. As a general rule, you should never select this check box. If you do select it, subsequent changes to the Summary style in future documents will be automatically updated in all documents based on the same template. This can produce unpredictable results and introduce problems that you might have difficulty resolving.

▶ 4. Click the **OK** button. The Create New Style from Formatting dialog box closes. The new Summary style is added to the Quick Styles gallery and to the Styles window. If Sam needs to format additional headings with this new style, he can access it in either location. See Figure 5-21.

Summary style added to Quick Styles gallery and Styles window | Figure 5-21

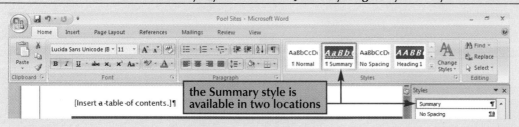

▶ 5. Save the document.

Although it's possible create a new style that is not based on any other style, it's rarely a good idea. The link between a new style and the style it is based on ensures that changes affecting the overall look of a document are made consistently throughout the document. For example, suppose that, after creating his new Summary style, Sam decides to add extra paragraph spacing above and below the headings in the Pool Sites document. He can do that by modifying the Heading 1 style. Because his new Summary style is based on the Heading 1 style, the new paragraph spacing will automatically apply to the Summary style, thus enforcing a consistent appearance among all headings in the document. Another advantage to basing a new style on an existing style has to do with using Outline view. As you will see later in this tutorial, basing a new style on an existing style ensures that all the headings appear in the proper level in the document's outline.

Comparing Styles with the Reveal Formatting Window

If you create a document with many new or modified styles, it's easy to lose track of the formatting associated with each style. To see a quick comparison of two styles, you can use the **Reveal Formatting window**. In the following steps, you'll use the Reveal Formatting window to compare the Normal style to the Subtitle style in the document.

To compare the Heading 1 style to the Subtitle style using the Reveal Formatting window:

▶ **1.** Click in the left margin to select the **[Insert a table of contents.]** paragraph.

▶ **2.** At the bottom of the Styles window, click the **Style Inspector** button ⊞. The Style Inspector window opens, displaying options that allow you to quickly inspect the formatting associated with a particular style. In most situations, you'll find the Reveal Formatting window more useful, so you'll open that next.

▶ **3.** At the bottom of the Style Inspector window, click the **Reveal Formatting** button ⊞. The Reveal Formatting window opens, displaying information about the style applied to the text that is currently selected in the document. Your Reveal Formatting window and Style Inspector windows might be positioned as in Figure 5-22, or they might be located elsewhere in the document window. Their position is unimportant.

Reveal Formatting window   Figure 5-22

4. In the Reveal Formatting window, click the **Compare to another selection** check box to select it. The options in the Reveal Formatting window change to allow you to compare one style to another. Under Selected text, both text boxes display copies of the text that is currently selected in the document, "[Insert a table of contents.]" This tells you that, currently the Normal style, the style applied to the text "[Insert a table of contents.]," is being compared to itself. In the next step, you'll compare the Normal style to the Subtitle style.

5. In the document, click in the left margin to select the text **SITES FOR NEW SWIMMING POOL**, which is formatted with the Subtitle style. The text "SITES FOR NEW SWIMMING POOL" appears in the Reveal Formatting window, in the text box below "[Insert a table of contents.]" The Formatting differences section displays information about the styles to the two different text samples. This information is divided into two sections, Font and Paragraph. The information in the Reveal Formatting can sometimes be hard to interpret. But generally, if you see two settings separated by a hyphen and a greater than sign (->),the setting on the left relates to the top text box, and the item on the right relates to the bottom text box. For example, in the Font section, you see "10pt -> 12 pt." This tells you that the item in the top text box, "[Insert a table of contents.]," is formatted in a 10-point font, whereas the item in the bottom text box, "SAMPLE TEXT," is formatted in a 12-point font. See Figure 5-23.

Tip

Text formatted in a white font, such as the Contents heading, is not visible in the text boxes at the top of the Reveal Formatting window. To use the Reveal Formatting window with white text, temporarily format it in black.

Figure 5-23 ▶ Comparing two styles

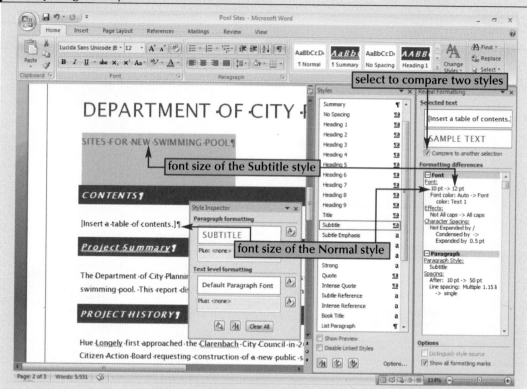

6. Click the **Close** button ☒ in the title bars of the Style Inspector window, the Reveal Formatting window, and the Styles window to close them. The document window readjusts, displaying the document at Page width zoom.

You are finished formatting the Pool Sites document. Sam likes its appearance so much that he would like to be able to reuse its formatting in the future reports issued by his department. To do that, you need to save the Pool Sites document as a template.

Saving a Document as a Template

If you know you'll often need to create a particular type of document, it's a good idea to create your own template for that type of document. In this case, Sam wants to create a template that will be used for all reports issued by the Department of City Planning. When creating a template, you can save it to any folder on the computer. However, if you save it to the Templates folder that is installed with Word, you can easily open the template later by clicking My templates in the New Document dialog box.

Saving a Document as a Template

- Click the Office Button, point to Save As, and then click Word Template.
- Navigate to the folder in which you want to save the template. To save the template to the Templates folder that is installed as part of Word, click the Templates folder under "Favorite Links."
- In the File name text box, type a name for the template.
- Click the Save button.

In the following steps, you will save the new template in the Tutorial folder for Tutorial 5, so that you can easily submit the completed tutorial files to your instructor. You'll start by saving the Pool Sites document again, just in case you didn't earlier.

To save the Pool Sites document as a new template:

1. Save the Pool Sites document.

2. Click the **Office Button** , point to **Save As**, and then click **Word Template**. The Save As dialog box opens, with Word Template selected in the Save as type list box.

3. If necessary, navigate to the Tutorial.05\Tutorial included with your Data Files. You'll type the new filename next using "DCP," the acronym for "Department of City Planning," in the filename.

4. Delete the default filename in the File name text box, and then type **DCP Report**. See Figure 5-24.

Saving a document as a template | Figure 5-24

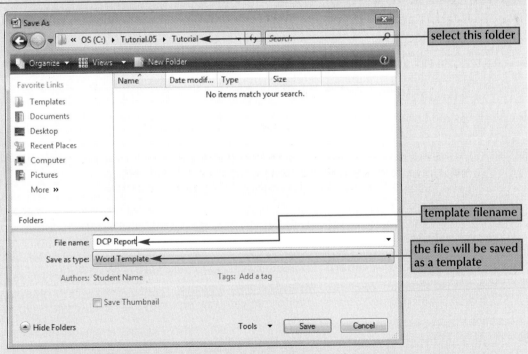

5. Click the **Save** button. The Save As dialog box closes, and the document, which is now a template with the .dotx file extension, remains open.

To make the new DCP Report template really useful, you need to delete the specific information related to the Pool Sites report and replace it with placeholder text explaining what type of information is required in each section. You'll start by editing the document controls on page 1. Then you will delete the body of the report and replace it with some placeholder text that Sam has already typed and saved as a separate Word document.

To replace the Pool Sites report information with placeholder text:

▶ 1. Scroll up to page 1. Sam wants to use the current title, "Department of City Planning," as the title in all department reports, so there's no need to change it. However, the subtitle will vary from one report to the next, so you need to replace it with a suitable placeholder.

▶ 2. Delete the subtitle "Sites for New Swimming Pool," and then type **[Insert subtitle here.]** as a replacement. Be sure to include the brackets, so Sam's co-workers will quickly see that this is placeholder text.

▶ 3. Scroll down, if necessary, so you can see the date, select the date in the date control, delete it, and then type **[Select current date.]** as a replacement. You'll leave your name in the Author control, so you can find the template later when you print it.

▶ 4. Scroll down to page 2 and notice that the new subtitle placeholder has been inserted in the subtitle control at the top of page 2. Also, the placeholder for the date has been inserted in the vertical footer on the lower-left side of the page.

▶ 5. Click in the left margin to select the **Project Summary** heading, drag down to select the remainder of the document, and press the **Delete** key. Deleting the text deleted some of the formatting codes that are included as hidden text in a Word document. (You can't see these codes, but they control the way the document is formatted.) As a result, the text "[Insert a table of contents.]" is now formatted in the Heading 1 style. You need to change it back to the Normal style.

▶ 6. Verify that the insertion point is located within the paragraph containing the text "[Insert a table of contents.]," and then in the Quick Styles gallery in the Styles group, click the **Normal** style. The text returns to its original formatting.

▶ 7. Press the **Enter** key to start a new paragraph. Now you are ready to insert a file containing placeholder text for the body of the report template.

▶ 8. Click the **Insert** tab, in the Text group click the **Object** arrow, click **Text from File**, use the options in the Insert File dialog box to select the file **Placeholder** from the Tutorial.05\Tutorial folder included with your Data Files, and then click the **Insert** button. The placeholder text is inserted in the document. Scroll down to review the document and notice that the headings are all correctly formatted with the Heading 1 style. When Sam created the Placeholder document, he formatted the text in the default Heading 1 style provided by the Office theme. But when you inserted the file into the Pool Sites document, Word automatically reformatted the headings with your modified Heading 1 style. The only remaining issue is the "Project Summary" heading, which you need to format with the Summary style you created earlier.

▶ 9. Click in the left margin to select the **Project Summary** heading, click the **Home** tab, and then in the Quick Styles gallery, click the **Summary** style. The heading is formatted with the wavy underline.

▶ 10. Save your work and close the template.

The template you just created will simplify the process of creating new reports in Sam's department. In the next section, you'll have a chance to use the template as the basis of a new document.

| **Working Around Hidden Formatting Codes** | | InSight |

When you are working with a highly formatted document, you may sometimes encounter unexpected issues, such as in Step 5 in the preceding set of steps, when the Heading 1 style was applied to the text "[Insert a table of contents.]." Such problems are related to formatting codes that are included in a Word document, but which you can't normally see. Sometimes when you delete or insert a large amount of text, these hidden formatting codes are disrupted, causing unexpected results. Keep in mind that many hidden formatting codes are attached to the last paragraph symbol in a Word document. You can avoid formatting problems in a document by inserting a blank paragraph at the end of the document, and then taking care never to delete that last paragraph. Alternatively, if you encounter a formatting problem that you can't resolve, insert a blank paragraph at the end of the document, copy everything in the document except the last paragraph to a new document, and work with that new document instead.

Opening a New Document Based on Your Template

At this point, the new template is ready to be used by the Department of City Planning for all new reports. In fact, Sam would like to use it now to begin a report on possible sites for a new public library.

To begin a new document based on the DCP Report template:

▶ 1. Start Word, if necessary, click the **Office Button** 🔘 , and then click **New**. The New Document dialog box opens.

▶ 2. In the Templates section on the left, click **My templates**. The New dialog box opens. If you had saved the DCP Report template to Word's Template folder, you would see an icon for it here. To open a new document based on the template, you could click the template's icon and then click the OK button. However, because you saved the DCP Reports template with your Data Files, you need to open it using a different method. See Figure 5-25.

Figure 5-25 ▶ New dialog box

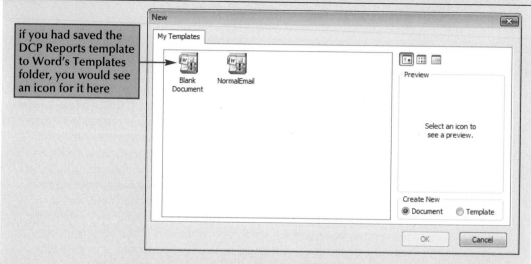

if you had saved the DCP Reports template to Word's Templates folder, you would see an icon for it here

3. Click the **Cancel** button. The New dialog box closes, and you return to the New Document dialog box.

4. On the left side of the New Document dialog box, under Templates, click **New from existing**. The New from Existing Document dialog box opens. This dialog box looks like the Open dialog box, which you have used many times before.

5. If necessary, select the Tutorial.05\Tutorial folder included with your Data Files, click **DCP Report**, and then click the **Create New** button. A new document opens containing the text and formatting from the DCP Report template. The document is named "Document2" (or possibly "Document3" or "Document4," depending on whether Word was closed earlier in this tutorial). Changes you make to this new document will not affect the DCP Report template file, which remains untouched in the Tutorial.05\Tutorial folder.

6. Delete the placeholder **[Insert subtitle here.]** on the cover page and type **Possible Sites for New Public Library**, and then click anywhere outside the Subtitle control to deselect it. That's all the work you need to do on the library report for now. Sam will finish it later. You can save the document with a new name and close it.

7. Save the document as **Library Sites** in the Tutorial.05\Tutorial folder included with your Data Files.

Trouble? If the Subtitle control displays the placeholder text "[Insert subtitle here.]" after you save the document, you didn't deselect the control before saving the document. Retype the subtitle, deselect the control, and save your changes to the document.

8. Preview the document, print it, and then close it.

1. True or False. By default, a new or modified style is saved only in the current document.
2. Explain the relationship between the themes installed with Word, style sets, and styles.
3. If you can't see the style you want in the Quick Styles gallery, where should you look?
4. Explain how to open a dialog box tab where you can adjust the character spacing for selected text.
5. Explain how to open a dialog box tab where you can add a specific amount of space below a selected paragraph.
6. Where can you see a quick comparison of two styles?
7. True or False. If you save a template to the Templates folder that is installed with Word, you can easily open the template later by clicking My templates in the New Document dialog box.

Session 5.3

Using Outline View

An **outline** is a list of the basic points of a document, usually organized into main topics and subtopics. Once you have formatted a document with heading styles, you can use these headings and Word's **Outline view** to display the various levels of headings as an outline. For instance, you can display only the Heading 1 headings, or the Heading 1 and Heading 2 headings, or all the text in the document, including text formatted with the Normal style. In fact, you can display and work with as many as nine levels of headings in Outline view. The top level heading (the Heading 1 style) is Level 1, with subheadings (Heading 2, Heading 3, etc.) labeled as Level 2, Level 3, and so on.

If your document contains a heading style that you created, that heading style is assigned to the same outline level as the style on which your heading style is based. For example, the "Project Summary" heading in the Pool Sites document is formatted in the Summary style you created, which is based on the Heading 1 style. That means the "Project Summary" heading appears as Level 1 in the outline, just like the other main headings in the document. A new heading style that is not based on any other heading style is assigned an outline level that is one level lower than the lowest heading style in the document. This is why it's much wiser to base a new heading style on an existing style, rather than creating new styles from scratch.

The purpose of Outline view is to simplify the process of reorganizing a document. Imagine a long document with many Level 1 headings, several Level 2 headings for each Level 1 heading, and body text below each heading. With Outline view, you can click a heading and move it below or above other headings; the subheadings and body text associated with the heading you are moving get moved along with the heading. This is a powerful tool when you are reorganizing a large document.

Outline view has several symbols and buttons that you use in viewing and reorganizing your document. An **outline symbol** is displayed to the left of each paragraph. An outline symbol in the shape of a plus sign indicates a heading with subordinate text below it, a minus sign indicates a heading without subordinate text, and an empty gray circle indicates body text (that is, text that is not formatted with a heading style). To select an entire section, you click the outline symbol next to that section's heading. To move a section after you select it, you click the Move Up or Move Down button on the Outlining tab, which is visible only in Outline view. You can also use buttons on the Outlining tab to change the precedence of headings. For instance, you might want to change a Level 1 heading to a Level 2 heading, or to change a Level 3 heading to a Level 1 heading.

Reference Window | **Creating and Editing Outlines**

- Format a document with heading styles, such as Heading 1, Heading 2, and so on.
- Click the Outline view button in the lower-right corner of the Word window.
- If necessary, select the Show Text Formatting check box in the Outline Tools group on the Outlining tab. This ensures that you can see the document formatting.
- Use the Show Level arrow in the Outline Tools group to display the desired number of headings. For example, to see only text formatted with heading styles 1 through 3, click Level 3. To see all the document text, including the body text, click All Levels.
- To select a section, click the Outline symbol next to the section's heading.
- To move a section, select the section, and then in the Outline Tools group, click the Move Up button or the Move Down button until the section is at the desired location.
- Use the Promote button or the Demote button in the Outline Tools group to increase or decrease the levels of headings.
- Click the Page Layout button to return to Page Layout view.

Sam wants to do some more work on the Pool Sites document. Specifically, he wants to reorganize some of the sections. Outline view is the perfect tool for this task. You'll start by reopening the Pool Sites document and reviewing its organization.

To open the Pool Sites document and review its organization:

▶ 1. Open the **Pool Sites** document from the Tutorial.05\Tutorial folder included with your Data Files.

▶ 2. If necessary, switch to Print Layout view, set the Zoom to Page width, and display nonprinting characters.

▶ 3. Review pages 2 and 3 so you are familiar with the report's structure. Notice that the headings "Breese Terrace Park," "Langbrook Farm," and "Flora Park," are formatted as subheadings below the "Project Description" heading.

Sam decides that the Flora Park section should appear before the Breese Terrace Park section. First you need to switch to Outline view and display the appropriate heading levels.

To switch to Outline view and view the outline levels:

▶ 1. Scroll up, if necessary, to display the first page of the document.

▶ 2. Click the **Outline** button 📄 in the lower-right corner of the Word window. The document is displayed in Outline view, and the Outlining tab appears on the Ribbon. At this point, you may see all of the document, just some of the headings, or all of the document except for some of the headings. In the next two steps, you will check to make sure you can see the entire document.

3. If necessary, in the Outline Tools group on the Outlining tab, click the **Show Text Formatting** check box to remove the checkmark. When this check box is selected, Word displays the document headings in the same font, font color, and font size that you see in Page Layout view. Because the major headings in the Pool Sites document are formatted in a white font, you don't want to show the document formatting in Outline view, because you wouldn't be able to see the white text on the white background. With the Show Text Formatting check box deselected, all the text in Outline view is displayed in the body text font.

4. If necessary, in the Outlining tools group on the Outlining tab, click the **Show Level** arrow, and then click **All Levels**. This tells Word to display the entire document, including the headings and the body text. At this point, your document should look like the one in Figure 5-26.

Pool Sites document in Outline view ◄ Figure 5-26

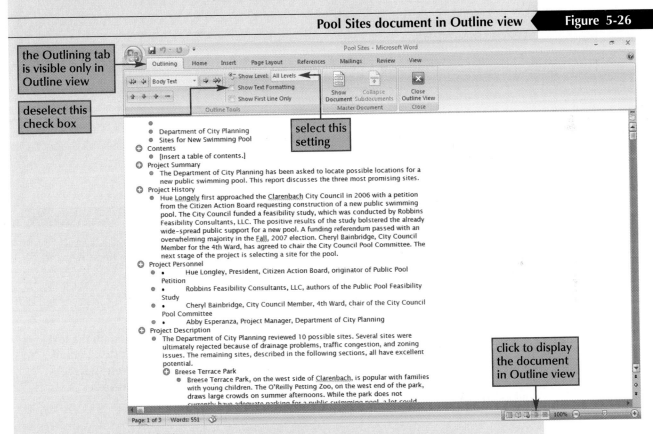

You can use the Show Level list box to display only the document headings. This is especially useful in long documents, because it allows you to see all the document headings at a glance, without having to scroll through several pages of body text. In the next step, you will display only the document headings.

5. In the Outline Tools group, click the **Show Level** arrow, and then click **Level 3**. You see only Level 1, Level 2, and Level 3 headings. In other words, you see only the text formatted with the Heading 1, Heading 2, and Heading 3 styles. Sam was concerned that he might have mistakenly applied the Heading 3 style to a heading that actually required the Heading 2 style. As you can see in Figure 5-27, he did make this mistake. You'll fix this problem later. Notice the plus sign next to each heading, indicating that the text is a heading with subordinate text. The gray lines represent text that is not currently visible.

Figure 5-27 **Levels 1 through 3 displayed in Outline view**

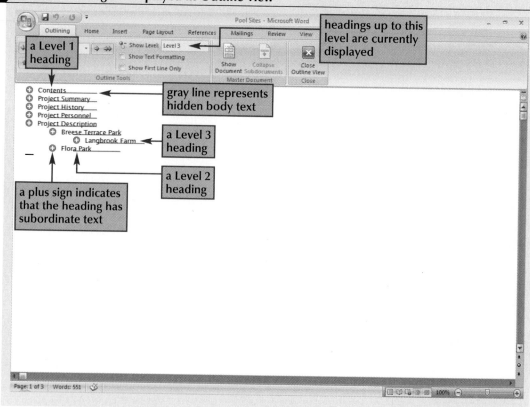

Now that you see only the document headings, you can reorder some headings and change the level of another.

Working with Headings in Outline View

When you move a heading in Outline view, any subordinate headings and all the text associated with those headings moves with the heading. In the following steps, you'll move the heading "Flora Park" so that it appears before the heading "Breese Terrace Park." As you work in Outline view, keep in mind that the Undo button reverses any mistakes, just as in Print Layout view.

To move the "Flora Park" heading and its subordinate text:

1. Double-click the **plus sign** ⊕ next to the heading "Flora Park." The subordinate text below the heading is now visible.

2. Double-click the **plus sign** ⊕ next to the heading "Flora Park" again. The subordinate text is again hidden.

3. Verify that the "Flora Park" heading and the paragraph mark following it are selected, and then click the **Move Up** button ⬆ in the Outline Tools group. The heading moves up above the heading "Langbrook Farm." Its subordinate text moved along with the heading, even though you can't see it.

4. Click the **Move Up** button ⬆ again. The "Flora Park" heading (and its subordinate text) move up above the heading "Breese Terrace Park." See Figure 5-28.

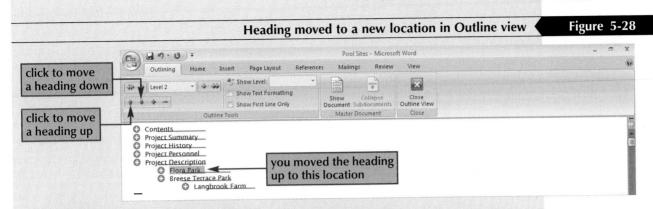

Figure 5-28

Heading moved to a new location in Outline view

5. Double-click the **plus symbol** ⊕ next to the heading "Flora Park," verify that the subordinate text did indeed move along with the heading, and then double-click ⊕ next to the heading "Flora Park" again to hide the subordinate text. Note that each time you click the Move Up button, the selected section moves up above the preceding section. To move a section down, you would use the Move Down button. Note that to select a section before moving it, you need to click the Outline symbol only once. You double-clicked it in these steps to display and then hide the subtext.

Now that the topics of the outline are in the desired order, you need to change the level of the Langbrook Farm heading, so it matches the level of the other two headings under "Project Description."

Promoting and Demoting Headings in an Outline

To **promote** a heading means to increase the level of a heading—for example, to change a Level 3 heading to a Level 2 heading. To **demote** a heading means to decrease the level—for example, to change a Level 1 heading to a Level 2 heading. When you promote or demote a heading in Outline view, the heading style applied to the heading changes accordingly. For example, if you promote a Level 3 heading to a Level 2 heading, the style applied to the heading changes from Heading 3 to Heading 2.

Sam wants to correct the error he made earlier by promoting the "Langbrook Farm" heading to a Level 2 heading.

To promote the Langbrook Farm heading:

1. Click anywhere in the heading **Langbrook Farm**, and then in the Outline Tools group on the Outlining tab, click the **Promote** button. (Take care not to click the Promote to Heading 1 button by mistake.) The heading moves left and becomes a Level 2 heading, formatted with the Heading 2 style. Note that demoting a heading in Outline view is similar to promoting a heading. You place the insertion point in the heading and click the Demote button. See Figure 5-29.

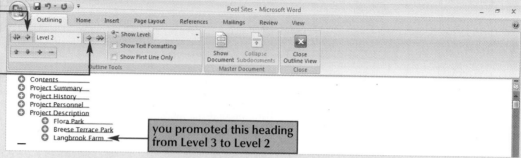

Figure 5-29 ▶ **Heading promoted in Outline view**

click to promote selected headings

click to demote selected headings

you promoted this heading from Level 3 to Level 2

Trouble? If the "Langbrook Farm" heading moved all the way to the left margin, you clicked the Promote to Heading 1 button by mistake. Undo the change, and then repeat Step 1.

2. Print the outline as you would print any other Word document.

3. Return to Print Layout view, and then review the Project Description section and its subheadings. Note that the "Langbrook Farm" heading is formatted in the Heading 2 style, and that the Flora Park section now appears before the Breese Terrace Park section. However, the blank paragraph that was originally at the end of the document, after the Flora Park section, moved up along with the Flora Park section. You need to delete it.

4. Click at the end of the Flora Park Section, press the **Delete** key to delete the blank paragraph, and then save your work.

Tip

It's important to review a document in Page Layout view after you make changes in Outline view, to make sure the document looks the way you expect.

Next, Sam would like to create a table of contents for his report.

Creating a Table of Contents

You can use Word to create a **table of contents** with page numbers for any paragraphs to which you have applied heading styles. The page numbers and headings in a table of contents in Word are actually hyperlinks that you can click to jump to a particular part of the document. If you add or delete text in the document later, and one or more headings move to a new page, you can quickly update the table of contents by clicking the Update Table button in the Table of Contents group on the References tab. After you create a table of contents, you can select additional text in the document and add it to the table of contents.

When inserting a table of contents, you can insert one of the predesigned formats available via the Table of Contents button in the Table of Contents group on the References tab. If you prefer to select from more options, you can open the Table of Contents dialog box.

Working with a Table of Contents | Reference Window

- Make sure you have applied heading styles such as Heading 1, Heading 2, and Heading 3 to the appropriate headings in your document.
- Move the insertion point to the location in the document where you want to insert the table of contents.
- Click the References tab, and then in the Table of Contents group, click the Table of Contents button. This opens the Table of contents menu.
- To insert a predesigned table of contents, click one of the Automatic table of contents styles in the Table of Contents menu.
- To open a dialog box where you can choose from an array of table of contents settings, click Insert Table of Contents in the Table of Contents menu, and then in the Table of Contents dialog box, click the Table of Contents tab if necessary. Click the Formats arrow and select a style, change the Show levels setting to the number of heading levels you want to include in the table of contents, verify that the Show page numbers check box is selected, and then click the OK button.
- To update a table of contents, click the Update Table button in the Table of Contents group on the References tab.
- To add text to a table of contents, select the text in the document, then in the Table of Contents group on the References tab, click the Add Text button. In the Add Text menu, click the level at which you want to insert the selected text, and then update the table of contents.
- To delete a table of contents, click the Table of Contents button, and then click Remove Table of Contents.

The current draft of Sam's report is fairly short, but the final document will be much longer. He asks you to create a table of contents for the report now, just after the "Contents" heading. Then, as Sam adds sections to the report, he can update the table of contents.

To insert the table of contents into the Pool Sites document:

▶ 1. Below the heading "Contents," select and delete the placeholder text [**Insert a table of contents.**]. Do not delete the paragraph mark after the placeholder text. When you are finished, your insertion point should be in the blank paragraph between the "Contents" heading and the "Project Summary" heading.

▶ 2. Click the **References** tab, and then in the Table of Contents group, click the **Table of Contents** button. The Table of Contents menu opens, displaying two Automatic table of contents formats, one Manual Table option, and two commands to insert and delete a table of contents. The Automatic options insert a table of contents made up of the first three levels of document headings, in a predefined format. Each of the Automatic options also includes a heading for the Table of Contents. Because Sam's document already contains the heading "Contents," you do not want to use either of the Automatic options. The Manual option is useful only if you need to type the table of contents yourself. In this case, you want to take advantage of the document headings and allow Word to build the table of contents for you, so you will use the Insert Table of Contents command at the bottom of the menu. See Figure 5-30.

Figure 5-30 | **Table of Contents menu**

click either one to insert a table of contents made up of the document headings with the default settings

click to insert a table of contents with placeholder text that you can replace

click to open a dialog box where you can select from numerous table of contents settings

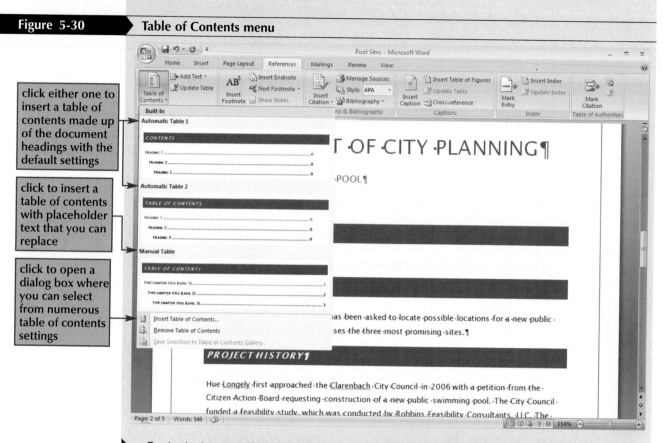

3. At the bottom of the Table of Contents menu, click **Insert Table of Contents**. The Table of Contents dialog box opens, with the Table of Contents tab displayed. The Formats list box allows you to select a format for your table of contents. The default option, From template, uses the styles provided by the document's template. In this case, you'll accept that default setting. Note that the Show page numbers check box is selected by default, so the table of contents will include a page number for each heading. Also by default, the "Use hyperlinks instead of page numbers" check box is selected. This setting means that Word will make each entry in the table of contents a hyperlink that links to the relevant section in the document. You can accept this default setting. Finally, you need to consider the Show levels headings. The document contains two levels of headings (Heading 1 and Heading 2). However, Sam might add some headings formatted in the Heading 3 style later, so you will leave the Show levels setting at 3. See Figure 5-31.

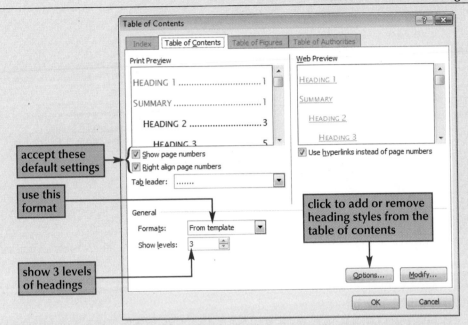

Sam knows that Word will compile the table of contents based on the heading styles in the document. But what about the Summary style, which you created earlier? Remember that the Summary style is based on the Heading 1 style, so Word will treat it as a heading of the same level as the Heading 1 style, just like in Outline view. To verify that this is true, you can check the heading levels by clicking the Options button.

4. Click the **Options** button in the lower-right corner of the Table of Contents dialog box. The Table of Contents Options dialog box opens. The Styles check box is selected, indicating that Word will compile the table of contents based on the styles applied to the document headings.

5. Use the vertical scroll in the TOC level list to see how the various styles in the document are assigned levels in the table of contents. (Note that "TOC" is short for "Table of Contents.") You can see that Heading 1 is assigned to Level 1, and Heading 2 is assigned to Level 2. Like Heading 1, the Summary style is also assigned to Level 1. If you wanted to change the level of a heading style, you could type a different number for it in the style's TOC level text box. To add a style to the table of contents, you could type a level number in the style's TOC level text box. See Figure 5-32.

Figure 5-32 | Checking the styles used in the table of contents

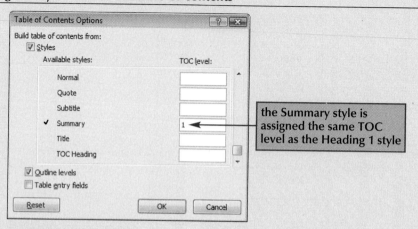

the Summary style is assigned the same TOC level as the Heading 1 style

The settings in the Table of Contents Options dialog box are all correct, so you can close it.

▶ **6.** Click the **Cancel** button to close the Table of Contents Options dialog box without making any changes.

▶ **7.** Click the **OK** button to accept the default settings in the Table of Contents dialog box. Word searches for text formatted with styles Heading 1, Heading 2, and Heading 3, and then places those headings and their corresponding page numbers in a table of contents. The table of contents is inserted below the "Contents" heading, where you placed the insertion point in Step 1. Depending on how your computer is set up, the table of contents might appear on a light gray background. See Figure 5-33.

Figure 5-33 | Table of contents inserted into document

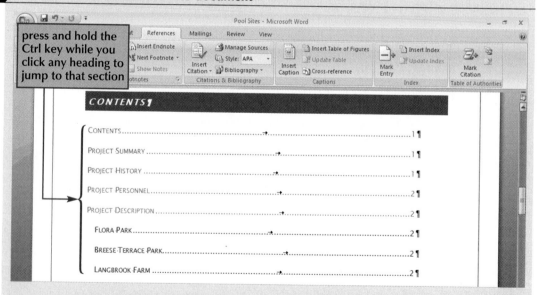

press and hold the Ctrl key while you click any heading to jump to that section

In the following step, you'll check the hyperlink formatting to make sure the headings really do function as links.

8. Press and hold down the **Ctrl** key while you click **LANGBROOK FARM** in the table of contents. The Langbrook Farm section is displayed.

9. Save the report.

Sam remembers that he needs to add a new section to the document describing another potential pool site. He's already typed the new section and saved it as a Word file. He asks you to insert it at the end of the Pool Sites document and then add the new heading to the table of contents. You can do this using the Add Text button in the Table of Contents group in the References tab. You start by selecting the text you want to add to the table of contents. Then you use the Add Text button in the Table of Contents group on the References tab to format the text in the appropriate heading level. Finally, you update the table of contents.

To add a section to the Pool Sites document, add the heading text to the table of contents, and update the table of contents:

1. Press the **Ctrl+End** keys to move the insertion point to the end of the document, insert a new blank paragraph, and then insert the file **Vilas Grove** from the Tutorial.05\Tutorial folder included with your Data Files.

2. Select the heading **Vilas Grove**.

3. Click the **References** tab, and then, in the Table of Contents group on the References tab, click the **Add Text** button. The Add Text menu opens. See Figure 5-34.

Add Text menu | Figure 5-34

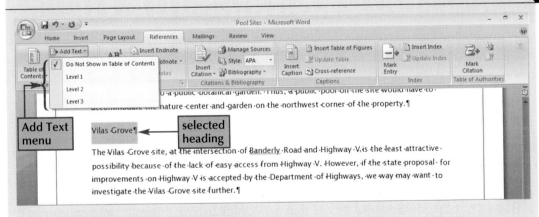

In the Add Text menu, you need to indicate at what level you want to insert the selected text in the table of contents.

4. Click **Level 2**. The text is formatted with the Heading 2 style, to match the headings for the sections about the other possible pool sites. Now that the text is formatted with a heading style, you can update the table of contents.

5. Scroll up so you can see the table of contents, and then in the Table of Contents group in the References tab, click the **Update Table** button. The Update Table of Contents dialog box opens. You can use the Update page numbers only option button if you don't want to update the headings in the table of contents. However, it's usually best to use the Update entire table option because it ensures that the table of contents is completely up to date.

6. Click the **Update entire table** option button to select it, and then click the **OK** button. The table of contents is updated to include the Vilas Grove heading. See Figure 5-35.

Tip

You can also format new text with a heading style in the Quick Styles gallery, and then update the table of contents.

Figure 5-35 ▶ **Updated table of contents**

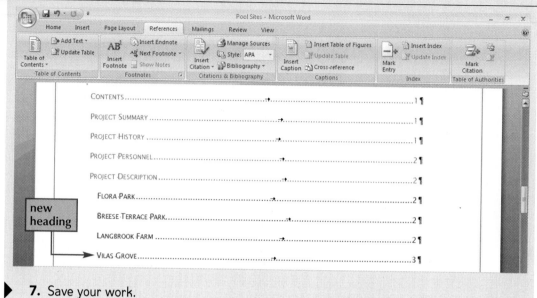

7. Save your work.

Sam is finished with the Pool Sites report for now, so you can print it and close it.

To print the document:

▶ **1.** Preview the document, and then print it. If you see a dialog box asking about updating the table of contents, update the entire table.

▶ **2.** Close the document.

Sam will continue work on the Pool Sites report later. Right now, he needs to do some research for another city project: an open-air theater.

Using the Research Task Pane

You can use the **Research task pane** to look up dictionary definitions and to search for synonyms in Word's thesaurus. In addition, you can search for information in online general interest encyclopedias and in sources devoted to particular topics, such as business and finance. If you prefer, you can use the MSN search engine to search the entire Web from the Research task pane. You can even use the Research task pane to translate a word or phrase into the language of your choice.

The Department of City Planning has been asked to evaluate a proposed open-air theater, which will be funded by a grant from a state arts organization. The proposal includes a number of theater-related terms. Sam wants to make sure he understands the term *proscenium* and decides to use Word's Research task pane to look it up in Encarta, the dictionary installed with Word. He also wants to experiment with looking up synonyms in Word's thesaurus.

To look up a definition in the Research task pane:

1. Open the document named **Research** from the Tutorial.05\Tutorial folder and save it as **Theater Research** in the same folder. This document contains the terms you will look up, along with space to insert the results of your research.

2. If necessary, set the Zoom to Page width and display nonprinting characters. To open the Research task pane, you need to switch to the Review tab.

3. Click the **Review** tab, and then locate the Proofing group on the left side of the Review tab. The Research, Thesaurus, and Translate buttons in the Proofing group all open the Research task pane, although each with different options displayed. Once the Research task pane is open, you can easily switch among the various options, depending on whether you want to research a topic, look up a word in the thesaurus, or translate some text.

4. In the Proofing group, click the **Research** button. The Research task pane opens on the right side of the document window. For starters, Sam wants to look up the word *proscenium*, one of the terms in the theater proposal.

5. Delete any text in the Search for text box, and then type **proscenium**. Next, you need to specify where you want to search for information.

6. In the list box that currently contains the text "All Reference Books," click the arrow to open a drop-down menu, and then click **Encarta Dictionary: English (North America)**. Two definitions of the term *proscenium* are displayed in the Research task pane. See Figure 5-36.

> **Tip**
>
> If you select a new reference source and don't see the information you expect in the Research task pane, click the green Start searching arrow at the top of the task pane to start the search.

Definitions displayed in the Research task pane **Figure 5-36**

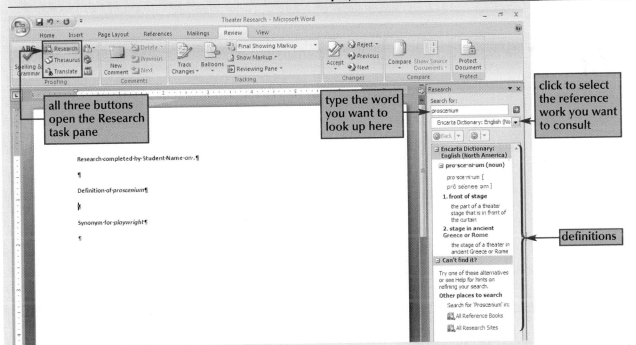

7. Drag the mouse pointer to select the first definition, which reads **the part of a theater stage that is in front of the curtain**, right-click the selected text, click **Copy**, click in the blank paragraph below the text "Definition of *proscenium*" in the document, and press the **Ctrl+V** keys to paste the definition into the document.

Next, Sam wants to look up a synonym for *playwright*. If he didn't have the Research task pane open already, he would begin his search by clicking the Thesaurus button in the Proofing group. But because the Research task pane is already open, he can simply select a new reference work.

To look up a synonym in the thesaurus:

1. In the document, click in the blank paragraph below the text "Synonym for *playwright*."

2. In the Research task pane, delete the word **proscenium** from the Search for text box, and then type **playwright**.

3. Click the arrow button below the Search for text box, and then click **Thesaurus: English (United States)**. Synonyms for *playwright* are displayed in the Research task pane, where the definitions for *proscenium* appeared earlier.

4. Move the mouse pointer over **writer**, the second synonym in the list. A list box appears around the word.

5. Click the down arrow next to the word "writer." A menu of options appears. See Figure 5-37.

Tip

To move back to previous search items, click the Previous Search button in the Research task pane. To return to later search items, click the Next Search button.

Figure 5-37 | **Synonyms displayed in the Research task pane**

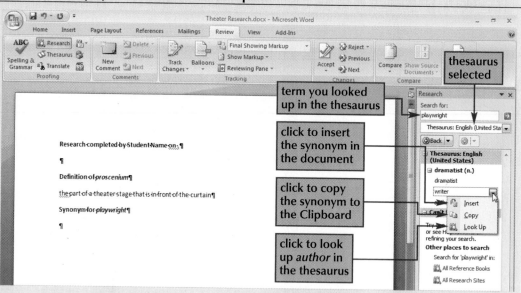

You can click Insert to insert the synonym in the document at the insertion point, or you can click Copy to copy the synonym to the Clipboard, so that you can paste it into other locations in the document or in other documents. To look up synonyms of *writer*, you could click Look Up. Right now, Sam simply wants to insert the word *writer* into the document.

6. Click **Insert**. The term *writer* is inserted into the document, below "Synonym for *playwright*."

7. Save the document, and then click the **Close** button in the title bar of the Research task pane to close it.

If your computer is connected to the Internet, you can type a word or phrase in the Search for box, click the down arrow and select Translation, and then use the options that appear in the Research task pane to retrieve a translation of your word or phrase over the Internet. The translations provided by the Research task pane are performed by computers, and therefore are useful only when you need a quick idea of what a term or phrase refers to.

You are finished with your research. All that remains is to insert your name and the current date at the top of the document.

Inserting the Current Date

You could begin typing the current date and have Word finish it for you using AutoComplete. But by using the Date and Time button in the Text group on the Insert tab, you can take advantage of several formatting options. These formats allow you to include the time or the day of the week. You can also choose to have Word update the date every time you open the document. Sam wants to use one of the date formats available via the Date and Time dialog box.

To insert your name and the current date into the Theater Research document:

▶ **1.** In the first line of the document, replace **Student Name** with your first and last name.

▶ **2.** Click at the end of the first line, just to the left of the period. This is where you want to insert the current date.

▶ **3.** Click the **Insert** tab, and then, in the Text group, click the **Date & Time** button. The Date and Time dialog box opens. The Available formats list shows the different ways you can insert the current date.

▶ **4.** In the Available formats list box, click the format that provides the day of the week and the date—for example, Friday, March 05, 2010. This is probably the second item in the Available formats list. See Figure 5-38.

Date and Time dialog box ◀ **Figure 5-38**

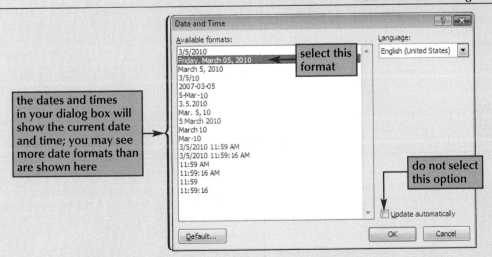

Note that your Date & Time dialog box will show the current date, and not the date shown in Figure 5-38. Notice the Update automatically check box, which you could click if you wanted Word to update the date and time each time you open the document. In this case, you want to insert today's date without Word updating it when you reopen the document.

▶ **5.** Verify that the Update automatically check box is *not* selected.

▶ **6.** Click the **OK** button. Word inserts the date into the document.

▶ **7.** Save the document, print it, and then close it.

Review | **Session 5.3 Quick Check**

1. What type of outline symbol indicates a heading with subordinate text under it?
2. Define *promote* as it relates to Outline view.
3. What do you have to do before you can create a table of contents?
4. What button can you click to revise a table of contents, and where is the button located?
5. True or False. You can use the Research task pane to look up definitions, but not synonyms.
6. What's the advantage of using the Date & Time button in the Text group on the Insert tab to insert a date?

Review | **Tutorial Summary**

In this tutorial, you learned how to create a new document from a template, insert a Word file into a document, and customize the document theme. You also learned how to select a style set, modify a style, create a new style, and compare styles with the Reveal Formatting window. Finally, you learned how to create a new template, use Outline view, create a table of contents, use the Research task pane, and insert the current date into the document.

Key Terms

character spacing	outline symbol	style sets
content control	Outline view	Styles window
demote	promote	table of contents
kerning	Research task pane	template
linked style	Reveal Formatting window	theme colors
Normal template	sans serif font	theme fonts
outline	serif	theme effects

| Practice | **Review Assignments** |

Apply the skills you learned in the tutorial using the same case scenario.

Data Files needed for the Review Assignments: Body.docx, Placeholder.docx, Future.docx, Research.docx

Sam's DCP Report template is now used for all reports created by employees of Clarenbach Department of City Planning. Inspired by Sam's success with the template, the director of the Department of Water Safety (DWS), Heather Sheehan, wants you to help with a report on improving the city's water testing system. After you format the report, she'd like you to save the document as a new template. Finally, she'd like you to look up some terms using the Research task pane. (*Note:* Text you need to type is shown in bold for ease of reference only; do not bold the text unless otherwise instructed.)

Complete the following:

1. Start Word if necessary, open a new document based on the **Oriel Report** template, and then save the document as **Water Testing** in the Tutorial.05\Review folder included with your Data Files.
2. Make sure that nonprinting characters are displayed, and if necessary, switch to Print Layout view.
3. Replace the placeholder text in the Title control with **Department of Water Safety**. Replace the subtitle placeholder text with **Plans for Improving City Water Testing**.
4. Replace the placeholder text in the Abstract control with **This report analyzes possibilities for improving the city's water testing system.** Type your name in the Author control and select the current date in the Date control.
5. Delete the placeholder text in the Body control on page 2, and then insert the file named **Body** from the Tutorial.05\Review folder included with your Data Files. This is just a skeletal draft of the report, but it includes the necessary headings.
6. Format the five headings (Table of Contents, Project History, Improved Bacterial Testing, Protecting the Municipal Reservoir, and Installing New Pumping Stations) with the Heading 1 style.
7. Change the theme colors to Concourse, and then change the theme's fonts to the Apex fonts.
8. Select the Formal style set, and then open the Styles window.
9. Select the Project History heading and modify it by changing its character spacing to condensed, changing the paragraph spacing after the heading to 20 points, and adding italics.
10. Update the Heading 1 style to match the newly formatted Project History heading.
11. Create a new style for the Table of Contents heading that is based on the Heading 1 style. The style should be identical to the Heading 1 style, except that it should format text in 18-point font, in bold. Name the new style **Contents** and save it to the current document.
12. Open the Reveal Formatting window and compare the Contents style with the Heading 1 style.
13. Save your changes to the Water Testing document.
14. Save the Water Testing document as a template named **DWS Template** in the Tutorial.05\Review folder included with your Data Files.
15. On page 1, replace the subtitle with the placeholder **[Insert subtitle here.]**. Replace the abstract with the placeholder **[Insert report abstract here.]**.
16. Delete the body of the report, beginning with the Table of Contents heading to the end of the report (Tip: To maintain the formatting of the subtitle at the top of page 2, do not delete the last paragraph of the document.)

17. In the blank paragraph below the subtitle on page 2, insert the Word file **Placeholder** from the Tutorial.05\Review folder included with your Data Files.

18. Format the Table of Contents heading with the Contents style.

19. Save the template, preview it, print it, and close it.

20. Open a new document based on the DWS Template, enter **Estimate for New Wells** as the document subtitle, save the new document as **New Wells** in the Tutorial.05\Review folder included with your Data Files, preview it, print it, and close it.

21. Open the **Water Testing** document from the Tutorial.05\Review folder included with your Data Files.

22. In Outline view, demote the last three headings in the document to Level 2, and then move the heading Protecting the Municipal Reservoir up so it comes before the heading Improved Bacterial Testing.

23. Save your work and print the outline.

24. Insert a table of contents below the Table of Contents heading. Use the default settings in the Table of Contents dialog box.

25. At the end of the document, insert the Word file **Future** from the Tutorial.05\Review folder included with your Data Files, and then add the heading Future Plans to the table contents as a Level 1 heading.

26. Save, preview, print, and close the Water Testing document.

27. Open the document named **Research** from the Tutorial.05\Review folder included with your Data Files, and then save it as **Water Research** in the same folder.

28. Open the Research task pane, look up the definition of *aquifer*, and then insert the definition into the document in the appropriate place. Look up synonyms for *reservoir*, and insert the third synonym in the list into the appropriate place in the document.

29. At the top of the document, replace STUDENT NAME with your first and last name, replace DATE with the current date and time in the format 3/04/10 10:25 AM, and then save, preview, print, and close the document.

30. Submit the finished documents to your instructor, either in printed or electronic form, as requested.

| Apply | | **Case Problem 1** |

Apply the skills you learned to create a template for a plant information handout.

Data Files needed for this Case Problem: Characteristics.docx, Crabapple.jpg, Height.docx, Plant Headings.docx, Requirements.docx.

Bluestem Landscape Design Carla Niedenthal is the manager of the retail store owned by Bluestem Landscape Design. Customers often ask her for information about particular plants. Over the years, she has created fact sheets for some of the most popular plants, but now Carla would like to create a set of one-page plant descriptions. Her first step is to create a template that will serve as the basis of the handouts. As you'll see in the following steps, you can use templates intended for one purpose, such as a letter, for another purpose, such as a handout. (*Note:* Text you need to type is shown in bold for ease of reference only; do not bold the text unless otherwise instructed.)

Complete the following:

1. Open a new document based on the **Median Letter** template, and then save the document as **Plant** in the Tutorial.05\Case1 folder included with your Data Files.

2. Make sure that nonprinting characters are displayed and that Print Layout view is selected.

3. Replace the placeholder text in the Company Name control with **Bluestem Landscape Design**. Replace the company address placeholder text with **Plant-at-a-Glance**.

4. Delete the date control, and then type **[Insert common plant name]** in the brown box that used to contain the date control. Click the blue bar next to the brown box and type **[Insert Latin plant name.]**.

5. Below the blue bar, delete the sender company address control, the recipient title control, the recipient address control, and the salutation control. Delete the body text control, the closing control, and the name control. If a name remains visible in the document after you delete the name control, delete the name as well.

6. Delete all the blank paragraphs in the document below the brown and blue boxes except one. Make sure the remaining blank paragraph below the brown box is formatted with the Normal style, and that it is positioned at the left margin.

7. With the insertion point located in the blank paragraph below the brown box, insert the file Plant Headings from the Tutorial.05\Case1 folder included with your Data Files.

8. Format the three headings with the Heading 1 style. Remember that if you can't find a style in the Quick Styles gallery, you can look in the Styles window.

9. Change the theme colors to Foundry.

10. Change the theme's fonts to Verve.

11. Modify the Heading 1 style for the current document by changing its character spacing to Expanded, changing the paragraph spacing after the heading to 12 points, and adding italics.

12. At the bottom of the document, replace "STUDENT NAME" with your first and last name. Save and print the Plant document.

13. Save the Plant document as a template named **Plant Template** in the Tutorial.05\Case1 folder included with your Data Files, and then close the template.

14. Open a document based on your template. Save the new document as **Crabapple** in the Tutorial.05\Case1 folder included with your Data Files.

15. For the common plant name, enter **Crabapple**. For the Latin plant name, enter **Malus**.

16. Under the Characteristics heading, delete the placeholder text but not the paragraph mark at the end of the paragraph, verify that the blank paragraph is formatted in the Normal style, and insert the Word file **Characteristics** from the Tutorial.05\Case1 folder included with your Data Files. Delete the extra paragraph mark at the end of the new text. Replace the placeholder text below the Mature Height heading and the Requirements heading with the files **Height** and **Requirements** from the Tutorial.05\Case1 folder included with your Data Files. Delete any extra new paragraphs.

17. At the bottom of the document, read the placeholder text about inserting a photograph. Select the placeholder text (but not the paragraph mark at the end of it), and delete it so you can insert a photo in its place.

⊕ EXPLORE

18. Verify that the insertion point is positioned in the blank paragraph just above the line that begins "Created by..." and then insert the photo named **Crabapple.jpg** from the Tutorial.05\Case1 folder included with your Data Files. (*Hint*: Use the Picture button in the Illustrations group on the Insert tab.) With the photograph selected, click the Drop Shadow Rectangle style in the Picture Styles group on the Picture Tools Format tab.

19. At the bottom of the document, replace DATE with the current date, including the day of the week.

20. Save, print, and close the Crabapple document.

21. Submit the finished documents to your instructor, either in printed or electronic form, as requested.

Apply		**Case Problem 2**

Apply the skills you learned to create a template for a consultant's report.

Data Files needed for this Case Problem: Star.docx, Video.docx

Star Avenue Consulting   Steven Yang is a consultant for Star Avenue Consulting, a firm that helps retail chains evaluate and improve the organization of their retail floor space. Steven and his colleagues often have to produce reports that summarize their recommendations. Your job is to create a template they can use to generate these reports. (*Note:* Text you need to type is shown in bold for ease of reference only; do not bold the text unless otherwise instructed.)

Complete the following:

1. Open the document **Star** from the Tutorial.05\Case2 folder included with your Data Files, and then save it as **Star Report** in the same folder.
2. Make sure that nonprinting characters are displayed. If necessary, switch to Print Layout view. This document is based on the Normal template, and was created using all the default settings.
3. Format the five headings (starting with Recommendation and ending with Advantages of Current Layout) with the Heading 1 style.
4. Select the Opulent theme, and change the theme colors to Flow. Change the style set to Traditional.
5. Format the "Recommendation" heading by changing its character spacing to Expanded, changing the font size to 16 points, and changing the paragraph spacing after the paragraph to 12 points. Update the Heading 1 style for the current document to match the "Recommendation" heading.
6. Create a new style for the company name at the top of the document that is based on the Title style. The style should be identical to the Title style, except that it should format text in 20-point font, with bold and italic formatting, and should include 6 points of space after the paragraph. Name the new style **Company**, and save it to the current document.
7. Open the Reveal Formatting window and compare the Company style to the Title style.
8. In Outline view, move the Recommendation section down so it is the last section in the document. Demote the headings "Variations by Location," "Disadvantages of Current Layout," and "Advantages of Current Layout" to Level 2 headings.
9. In the blank paragraph above the heading "Assessment of Current Store Layout," insert a table of contents using the Automatic Table 2 format. Delete any extra blank paragraphs after the table of contents. The table of contents might seem unnecessary in such a short document, but as consultants create their multipage reports, they will need a table of contents.
10. Save your changes to the Star Report document, and then save the Star Report document as a template named **Star Report Template** in the Tutorial.05\Case2 folder included with your Data Files. Close the template.
11. Open a document based on your new template. You will use this document as the basis of a new report for HomeFlix Video Outlets. You will not complete the entire report; instead you'll leave the placeholder text in the body of the report for another consultant to replace.
12. Save the new document as **HomeFlix** in the Tutorial.05\Case2 folder included with your Data Files.
13. For the client name, insert **HomeFlix Video Outlets**. Replace CONSULTANT NAME with your first and last name.

⊕ EXPLORE

14. Replace DATE with the current date and time in the format 3/4/2010 3:25:25 PM. Select the Update automatically check box. Note the exact time inserted into the document, save the document, close it, pause briefly, and reopen the document. Note the updated time. Click the date, and then click Update. Note the updated time.

15. Save, print, and close the HomeFlix document.

16. Open the document named **Video** from the Tutorial.05\Case2 folder included with your Data Files, and then save it as **Video Research**. Open the Research task pane, look up the definition of *video*, and insert the third definition into the document in the appropriate place. Look up synonyms for *video* and insert the last synonym under "videotape" into the appropriate place in the document.

17. Save, print, and close the document.

18. Submit the finished documents to your instructor, either in printed or electronic form, as requested.

Challenge | **Case Problem 3**

Go beyond what you've learned to edit a business plan for a new Internet company named AllSecure, Incorporated.

Data File needed for this Case Problem: Text.docx

AllSecure, Inc. Camden Lui has written a business plan for his new Internet business, AllSecure, Incorporated. On its Web site, the company will publish security information on data storage and transmission services. Camden has written part of the report and needs help formatting it. (*Note:* Text you need to type is shown in bold for ease of reference only; do not bold the text unless otherwise instructed.)

Complete the following:

1. Open a new document based on the Origin Report template and save it as **AllSecure Plan** in the Tutorial.05\Case3 folder included with your Data Files.

2. Remove the cover page at the beginning of the document. (*Hint:* Use the Cover Page button on the Insert tab.)

3. Use **AllSecure, Inc.** for the document title and **Business Plan** for the subtitle.

4. Delete the body control, and insert the file named **Text** from the Tutorial.05\Case3 folder included with your Data Files.

5. Format the four headings in the left column with the Heading 1 style. In the right column, format the first three headings in the Heading 1 style. Format the last three headings in the right column in the Heading 2 style.

⊕ EXPLORE

6. Create a new character style for the company name where it is used in the body of the report. Base the style on the Intense Reference style. It should be identical to the Intense Reference style, but without underline formatting. In the Create New Style from Formatting dialog box, select Character in the Style type list box. If necessary, select Intense Reference in the Style based on list box and deselect the Underline button. Name the style **Company Name** and save it to the current document.

⊕ EXPLORE

7. Open the Find and Replace dialog box, find all instances of "AllSecure" in the body of the document, and format them with the new Company Name style. After you find the first instance using the Find and Replace dialog box, close the dialog box, and click the button with the double blue down arrows at the bottom of the vertical scroll bar to find additional instances without using the Find and Replace dialog box. Use the button with the double blue up arrows at the bottom of the vertical scroll bar to move back to preceding instances.

⊕ EXPLORE

8. Use Word Help to look up information on Find and Replace. Click the "Find and replace text or other items" topic, and then read about how to find and highlight text on the screen. Use this feature to highlight all instances of "AllSecure" in the document. Turn off the highlighting and close the Find and Replace dialog box.

9. Insert a new paragraph before the Executive Summary heading, format the new paragraph with the Normal style, type **Contents**, and insert a new paragraph. Format the paragraph containing the heading Contents in the Heading 1 style.

10. Use the Table of Contents dialog box to insert a table of contents in the blank paragraph below the Contents heading. Use the Distinctive format. Deselect the Right align page numbers check box so the entire table of contents is aligned in the left column.

11. At the end of the document, change the heading Audience Needs to **Audience Requirements**, and then update the table of contents.

⊕ EXPLORE

12. Click the Select Browse Object button (the circle near the bottom of the vertical scroll bar). Move the pointer over the buttons in the palette and review the name of each option. Click the Go To button in the palette, and then use the Go To tab of the Find and Replace dialog box to move the insertion point to the top of page 2. Close the Find and Replace dialog box. Click the Select Browse Object button again, click the Browse by Heading button, and then click the button with the double blue down arrows (at the bottom of the vertical scroll bar) to move from one heading to the next. Use the double blue up arrow button to browse up through the document by heading.

13. Save, print, and close the document.

14. Submit the finished documents to your instructor, either in printed or electronic form, as requested.

Create	**Case Problem 4**

Create the outline shown in Figure 5-39 by using the Numbering button in the Paragraph group on the Home tab.

There are no Data Files needed for this Case Problem.

Public Health Report Outline   Shakira Ankor is a communications specialist at the Municipal Association for Public Health (MAPH). Each year she begins her work on the association's annual report by creating an outline using Word's multilevel list feature. She has asked you to help. (*Note:* Text you need to type is shown in bold for ease of reference only; do not bold the text unless otherwise instructed.)

1. Open a new Word document, and save it as **MAPH Report** in the Tutorial.05\Case4 folder included with your Data Files.

2. Switch to Print Layout view, if necessary, and make sure nonprinting characters are displayed.

3. To begin creating the report outline, insert a new paragraph, click the Numbering button in the Paragraph group on the Home tab, and type **A Message from the Director**. Press the Enter key, and then type **Report Highlights**. Press the Enter key, and then type **Summaries from Regional Committees**.

⊕ EXPLORE

4. To demote a heading to a lower level, you can press the Tab key or click the Increase Indent button in the Paragraph group on the Home tab. Press the Enter key, press the Tab key, and then type **Northeast Region**. Continue typing the names of the following regions on separate lines: **Southeast Region**, **Midwest Region**, **West Region**. Insert another paragraph, click the Decrease Indent button, and then type **National Health Information Campaigns**.

5. Continue using the techniques described in Step 4 to complete the outline shown in Figure 5-39.

Figure 5-39

1. A Message from the Director
2. Report Highlights
3. Summaries from Regional Committees
   a. Northeast Region
   b. Southeast Region
   c. Midwest Region
   d. West Region
4. National Health Information Campaigns
   a. Vaccinations for Adolescents and Young Adults
      i. Special Needs of High School Students
      ii. Considerations for the College-Bound
   b. Lupus Signs and Symptoms
   c. Childhood Obesity
   d. Geriatric Nutrition Needs
      i. Calcium Intake
      ii. Protein Requirements

⊕ EXPLORE

6. Select the outline, click the Multilevel List button in the Paragraph group on the Home tab, and then select the style that uses Roman numerals and capital letters (in the lower-left corner of the Multilevel List gallery).

7. In Outline view, move the Southeast Region heading up before the Northeast Region heading.

8. Switch to Print Layout view, click at the beginning of the document, and then add **Municipal Association for Public Health** and the subtitle **Annual Report Outline**. Below the subtitle, insert **Created by Student Name**. (Replace "Student Name" with your first and last name.) On a line below your name, insert the current date in the March 7, 2010, format.

9. Format the title in the Title style, and then reduce the title's font size to 18 point. (Do not modify the Title style.) Format the subtitle in the Subtitle style.

10. Save your work, preview the document, and print it.

11. Submit the finished documents to your instructor, either in printed or electronic form, as requested.

Research | Internet Assignments

Go to the Web to find information you can use to create documents.

The purpose of the Internet Assignments is to challenge you to find information on the Internet that you can use to work effectively with this software. The actual assignments are updated and maintained on the Course Technology Web site. Log on to the Internet and use your Web browser to go to the Student Online Companion for New Perspectives Office 2007 at **www.course.com/np/office2007**. Then navigate to the Internet Assignments for this tutorial.

Assess | SAM Assessment and Training

If you have a SAM user profile, you may have access to hands-on instruction, practice, and assessment of the skills covered in this tutorial. Log in to your SAM account (**http://sam2007.course.com**) to launch any assigned training activities or exams that relate to the skills covered in this tutorial.

Review | **Quick Check Answers**

Session 5.1

1. Normal template
2. Right-click the content control, and then click Remove Content Control.
3. Insert tab
4. Colors, fonts, effects
5. Serif and sans serif
6. False

Session 5.2

1. True
2. Every built-in theme comes with 11 sets of styles. Each style set is, in turn, made up of 31 styles.
3. Styles window
4. In the Font group on the Home tab, click the Dialog Box Launcher to open the Font dialog box, and then click the Character Spacing tab.
5. Click the Dialog Box Launcher in the Paragraph group on the Home tab to open the Paragraph dialog box, and then click the Indents and Spacing tab.
6. Reveal Formatting window
7. True

Session 5.3

1. Plus sign
2. To increase the level of a heading
3. Format the document headings with heading styles.
4. Update Table button in the Table of Contents group in the References tab
5. False
6. It allows you to choose from a variety of date and time formats.

Ending Data Files

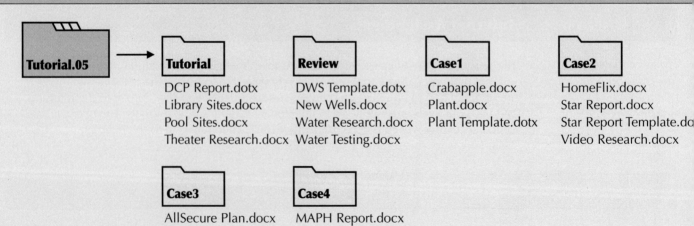

Tutorial.05 →

Tutorial
DCP Report.dotx
Library Sites.docx
Pool Sites.docx
Theater Research.docx

Review
DWS Template.dotx
New Wells.docx
Water Research.docx
Water Testing.docx

Case1
Crabapple.docx
Plant.docx
Plant Template.dotx

Case2
HomeFlix.docx
Star Report.docx
Star Report Template.do
Video Research.docx

Case3
AllSecure Plan.docx

Case4
MAPH Report.docx

Objectives

Session 6.1
- Learn about the mail merge process
- Use the Mail Merge task pane
- Select a main document
- Create a data source
- Insert mail merge fields into a main document
- Edit a main document
- Preview a merged document
- Complete a mail merge

Session 6.2
- Edit an existing data source
- Sort records
- Create mailing labels and a phone directory
- Convert tables to text and text to tables
- Create a multilevel list

Using Mail Merge

Creating a Form Letter, Mailing Labels, and a List

Case | Lily Road Yoga Studio

Nina Ranabhat is the owner and chief instructor at Lily Road Yoga Studio in Boise, Idaho. The studio has just moved to a new, expanded location. Nina wants to invite clients to try out the new facility during free, open-studio days in the month of June. She plans to send a letter to each client announcing the new location and the open-studio days.

Nina doesn't have time to type a personal letter to each of the studio's many clients. Instead, she plans to create a **form letter** that contains the information she wants to send to all clients. The form letter will also contain specific details for individual clients, such as name, address, and each client's favorite class and instructor. Nina has already written the text of the form letter. She plans to use the mail merge process to add the personal information for each client. She asks you to create the form letter using Word's Mail Merge feature. She also needs a set of letters that will go just to the clients who take power yoga classes. After you create the merged letters, she'd like you to create the mailing labels for the envelopes and a telephone directory that lists a phone number for each teacher. Next, you will create an additional document with name and address information by converting text to a table. Finally, you will create and format a list of names by converting a table to text.

Starting Data Files

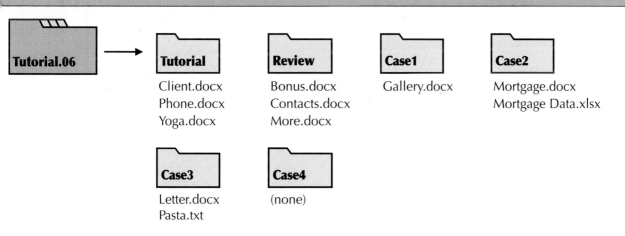

Tutorial.06 →

Tutorial
Client.docx
Phone.docx
Yoga.docx

Review
Bonus.docx
Contacts.docx
More.docx

Case1
Gallery.docx

Case2
Mortgage.docx
Mortgage Data.xlsx

Case3
Letter.docx
Pasta.txt

Case4
(none)

Session 6.1

Understanding the Mail Merge Process

To insert individualized information into a form letter, you combine, or **merge**, a form letter with a separate file containing specific information, whether that information is names and addresses, product information, or another type of data. The form letter is called a **main document**, and the file containing the specific information is called the **data source**.

A main document can be a letter or any other kind of document. It contains codes called **fields** that tell Word where to insert names, addresses, and other variable information. A field can be a data field, such as date and time fields, or **merge fields**, such as First Name and Last Name fields. As you will see in this tutorial, one of the steps you must complete before merging the main document with the data source is inserting the merge fields into the main document. Nina's main document is the letter shown in Figure 6-1. As you complete the steps in this tutorial, you will replace the red text with merge fields.

Figure 6-1	Nina's main document

[Date]

[First Name] [Last Name]
[Street Address]
[City], ID [ZIP Code]

Dear [First Name]:

I am happy to announce that Lily Road Yoga Studio has moved to an expanded location at 4722 Lily Road. This is just two blocks south of our original location, but it feels like a whole new world. Our sunny new studio offers off-street parking, private changing rooms, and a much larger studio space. We also have a separate, smaller space for individual instruction.

To welcome you to our new home, we are hosting open studio hours every Thursday through the month of June. Classes on open studio days are free. Of course, we will continue to offer a full range of yoga instruction, including group classes and private practice.

Please check out our schedule online at *www.lilyroad.course.com*. You'll be glad to know that we now offer two additional [Favorite Type] classes. Also, keep in mind that [Favorite Teacher] is available for individual instruction.

We hope to see you soon at one of our open-studio Thursdays. Come soon, and bring a friend!

Sincerely yours,

Nina Ranabhat

Owner and Certified Ashtanga Instructor

Nina's data source will include the name and address of each client, as well as information about each client's preferred type of class and favorite teacher.

Inserting information from a data source into a main document produces a final document called a **merged document**. Figure 6-2 illustrates how the data source and main document combine to form a merged document.

Merging a main document with a data source to create a merged document | **Figure 6-2**

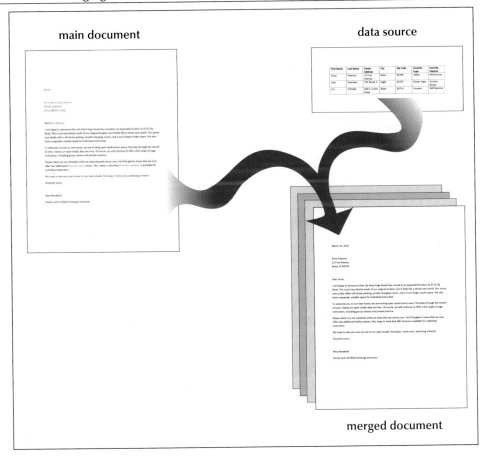

Merge Fields and Records

Merge fields appear in the main document and tell Word which pieces of information to retrieve from the data source. One merge field might retrieve an address from the data source; another merge field might retrieve a telephone number. Merge fields are easy to spot in the main document because each merge field name is enclosed by pairs of angled brackets, which look like this: << >>. You can insert merge fields into a main document only by using the Mail Merge task pane or the tools in the Mailings tab. You cannot simply type merge fields into the main document—even if you type the brackets.

A data source is a table of information similar to the one shown in Figure 6-3. The header row, the first row of the table, contains the name of each merge field. The cells below the header row contain the specific information that replaces the merge fields in the main document. This information is called **data**. Each row of data in the table makes up a complete **record**. You can also think of a record as the information about one individual or object.

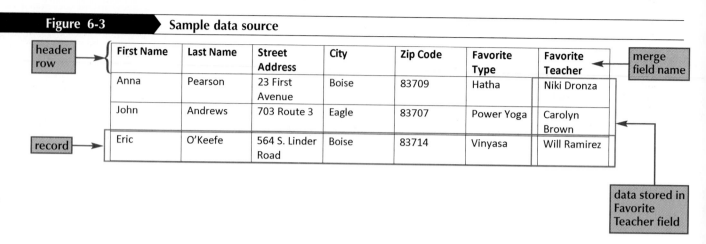

Figure 6-3 ▶ Sample data source

First Name	Last Name	Street Address	City	Zip Code	Favorite Type	Favorite Teacher
Anna	Pearson	23 First Avenue	Boise	83709	Hatha	Niki Dronza
John	Andrews	703 Route 3	Eagle	83707	Power Yoga	Carolyn Brown
Eric	O'Keefe	564 S. Linder Road	Boise	83714	Vinyasa	Will Ramirez

header row

merge field name

record

data stored in Favorite Teacher field

Data sources are commonly used to store names and addresses. However, you can also create data sources with inventory records, records of suppliers, or records of equipment. After you understand how to manage and manipulate the records in a data source, you'll be able to use them for many different types of information.

Using the Mail Merge Task Pane

The **Mail Merge task pane** walks you through the following six steps for merging documents:

1. Select the type of document you want to use as the main document. Possible types of main documents include letters, envelopes, e-mails, labels, and directories.
2. Select the document you want to use as the main document. You can create a new document or edit an existing one.
3. Select the list of recipients (that is, the data source) you want to use for the merge or create a new list of recipients.
4. Complete the main document by adding merge fields.
5. Preview the merged document.
6. Complete the mail merge.

To ensure that you see the same thing in the Mail Merge task pane each time you open it, start with a new, blank document before you open the Mail Merge task pane. Once you are familiar with merging documents, you can also use the options on the Mailings tab to perform the same tasks described in the Mail Merge task pane.

Nina is ready for you to start the mail merge process for her form letter.

To start Word and open the Mail Merge task pane:

▶ **1.** Start Word and make sure a new, blank document is displayed. Note that this new document is named "Document1."

▶ **2.** Switch to Print Layout view, and then display nonprinting characters, if necessary. Use any Zoom setting you want for now. You won't need the rulers in this tutorial, so close them if they are displayed.

▶ **3.** Click the **Mailings** tab, then in the Start Mail Merge group, click the **Start Mail Merge** button, and then click **Step by Step Mail Merge Wizard**. The Mail Merge task pane opens, displaying information and options related to the first step in merging documents. See Figure 6-4.

Starting the mail merge process ◂ Figure 6-4

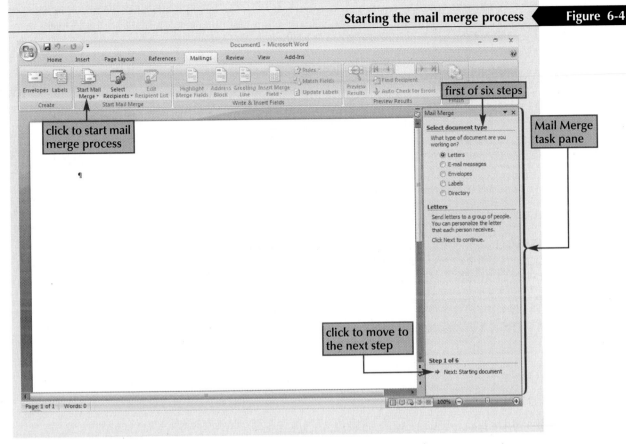

With the Mail Merge task pane open, you are ready to perform the first two steps in merging a document.

Selecting a Main Document

According to the Mail Merge task pane, your first task is to specify the type of main document you want to use for the merge. The Mail Merge task pane provides a number of options, including e-mail messages and labels. In this case, you want to create a letter.

To specify the type of merged document to create:

▶ 1. Verify that the **Letters** option button is selected in the Mail Merge task pane.

▶ 2. At the bottom of the task pane, click **Next: Starting document**. The Mail Merge task pane displays information and options that you can use to select a starting document—that is, to select a main document.

Now that you've selected letters as the type of document you'll use for your main document, you need to specify which document you'll use for Nina's form letter. When selecting a main document, you have three choices: use the document currently displayed in the document window; start a new document from a pre-installed mail merge template; or open an existing document. Nina has already written the letter she wants to send to all of her yoga clients, so you don't need to create a new document. Instead, you'll use her existing document, which she saved in a file named Yoga.

When you open an existing document from the Mail Merge task pane, Word actually opens a *copy* of the document you select so that any changes you make to the file will not affect the original file. You'll see how this works in the following steps.

To select a main document for the form letter:

▶ **1.** In the Mail Merge task pane, click the **Start from existing document** option button (just below the "Select starting document" heading). A list box appears, with an Open button below it. The list box contains names of files that have been used for a mail merge on your computer in the past. (If this is the first time anyone has performed a mail merge on your computer, the list box will be blank except for a More Files link.) If you perform mail merges regularly with the same group of files, you can click the name of the file you want in this list box. For now, however, you will use the Open button below the list box.

▶ **2.** In the Start from existing section of the Mail Merge task pane, click the **Open** button. The Open dialog box is displayed. You'll use this dialog box to select Nina's document.

▶ **3.** Navigate to the **Tutorial.06\Tutorial** folder included with your Data Files.

▶ **4.** Click **Yoga**, and then click the **Open** button. A copy of the file named Yoga is opened and is named Document1. The Use the current document option button is now selected in the task pane because you are now ready to use the current document as the main document. Because Nina had set the top margin of the Yoga document at 2 inches, the top margin of the Document1 document changes to 2 inches as well. This will leave enough room for Nina's letterhead.

▶ **5.** Make sure nonprinting characters are displayed.

▶ **6.** Change the zoom so you can see the entire width of the text, but not the left or right margins. On most monitors, **120%** is a good zoom setting. At the bottom of the task pane, you see the next step in the mail merge process. See Figure 6-5.

Main document Normal view | Figure 6-5

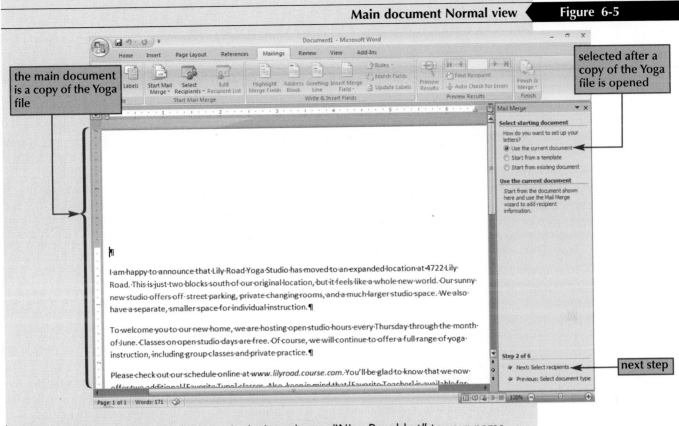

7. Scroll down to display the letter's closing, change "Nina Ranabhat" to your name, and then scroll back up to the beginning of the letter.

8. Save the file as **Yoga Letter with Merge Fields** in the Tutorial.06\Tutorial folder.

Next, you need to specify your data source—the list of recipients for Nina's letter.

Creating a Data Source

As you learned earlier, a data source is a file with information organized into fields and records. Typically, the data source for a mail merge contains a list of names and addresses, but it can also contain e-mail addresses, telephone numbers, and other data. Various kinds of files can be used as the data source, including a simple text file, a Word table, an Excel worksheet, an Access database, or a Microsoft Office Address Lists file, which stores addresses for Microsoft Outlook and other Microsoft Office applications. (In Word Help, this type of file is sometimes called a Microsoft Office Contacts Lists file.) In this tutorial, you will create a Microsoft Office Address Lists file to use as your data source. Word's Mail Merge task pane walks you through the steps required to create the data source.

When performing a mail merge, you can select a data source file that already contains names and addresses, or you can create a new data source and enter names and addresses into it. When you create a new data source, the file is saved by default as a Microsoft Office Address Lists file. In this section, you will create a data source using the tools provided by the Mail Merge task pane. This involves two steps: deciding which fields to include in the data source and entering address information.

You need to create a data source that contains information on Nina's clients, including the name, address, preferred type of class, and favorite teacher. Nina collected all the necessary information by asking clients to fill out a form when they registered for their first yoga class. Figure 6-6 shows one of these forms.

Figure 6-6 **Client information form**

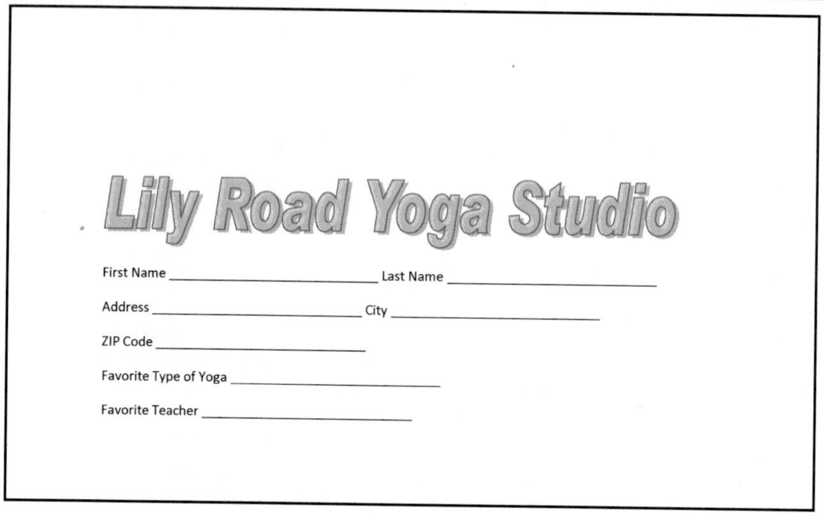

Lily Road Yoga Studio

First Name ____________ Last Name ____________

Address ____________ City ____________

ZIP Code ____________

Favorite Type of Yoga ____________

Favorite Teacher ____________

The information on each form will make up one record in the data source. Your job is to create a data source for three of Nina's clients, which means you'll have just three records. A real yoga studio would of course have tens or hundreds of records, one for each client. When you create your data source, you must include the field names shown in Figure 6-7.

Figure 6-7 **Field names to include in data source**

Field Names	Description
First Name	Client's first name
Last Name	Client's last name
Address	Client's street address
City	City in Idaho
ZIP Code	ZIP code in Idaho
Favorite Type of Yoga	Client's preferred type of yoga
Favorite Teacher	Client's preferred yoga teacher

When you create a new data source from within the Mail Merge task pane, Word provides a number of default fields, such as First Name, Last Name, and Company. You can customize the data source by adding new fields and removing the default fields that you don't plan to use. As you create a data source, keep in mind that each field name must be unique; you can't have two fields with the same name.

Creating a Data Source for a Mail Merge

- In Step 3 of the Mail Merge task pane, select the Type a new list option button, and then click Create; or, in the Start Mail Merge group on the Mailings tab, click the Select Recipients button, and then click Type New List.
- In the New Address List dialog box, click the Customize Columns button.
- To delete unnecessary fields, in the Customize Address List dialog box, click a field you want to delete, click the Delete button, and then click the Yes button. Continue to delete any other unnecessary fields.
- To add a new field, click the Add button, type the name of the field in the Add Field dialog box, and then click the OK button.
- To rearrange the order of the field names, click a field name, and then click the Move Up or Move Down button.
- Click the OK button to close the Customize Address List dialog box.
- In the New Address List dialog box, enter information for the first record, click the New Entry button, and type another record. Continue until you are finished entering information into the data source, and then click the OK button to open the Save Address List dialog box.
- Type a name for the data source in the File name text box, and then click the Save button. The file is saved with the .mdb file extension.

You're ready to begin creating the data source for Nina's form letter.

To begin creating the data source:

▶ 1. In the bottom of the Mail Merge task pane, click **Next: Select recipients**, and then click the **Type a new list** option button.

▶ 2. Below the heading "Type a new list," click **Create**. The New Address List dialog box opens, as shown in Figure 6-8.

Creating a data source ◀ Figure 6-8

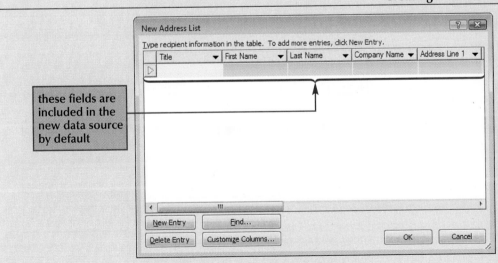

these fields are included in the new data source by default

You will use the New Address List dialog box to enter a complete set of information for one person—that is, you will enter one record into the data source. However, before you begin entering information, you need to customize the list of fields to match the fields shown earlier in Figure 6-7.

To customize the list of fields:

▶ **1.** Click the **Customize Columns** button. The Customize Address List dialog box opens. Here you can delete the fields you don't need, add new ones, and arrange the fields in the order you want. You'll start by deleting fields.

▶ **2.** In the Field Names list box, verify that **Title** is selected, and then click the **Delete** button. A message appears asking you to confirm the deletion.

▶ **3.** Click the **Yes** button. The Title field is deleted from the list of field names.

▶ **4.** Continue using the Delete button to delete the following fields: **Company Name**, **Address Line 2**, **State**, **Country or Region**, **Home Phone**, **Work Phone**, and **E-mail Address**. Next, you need to add some new fields. When you add a new field, it is inserted below the selected field, so you will start by selecting the last field in the list if it is not already selected.

▶ **5.** In the Field Names list box, verify that **ZIP Code** is selected, and then click the **Add** button. The Add Field dialog box opens, instructing you to type a name for your field.

▶ **6.** Type **Favorite Type**, and then click the **OK** button. The field "Favorite Type" is added.

▶ **7.** Use the Add button to add a **Favorite Teacher** field below the Favorite Type field. When you are finished, your Customize Address List dialog box should look like the one shown in Figure 6-9. You could use the Move Up and Move Down buttons to rearrange the field names (for instance, to move the Favorite Teacher field above the Favorite Type field), but in this case the order is fine. You are finished customizing the list of field names.

Figure 6-9 ▶ **Customized list of field names**

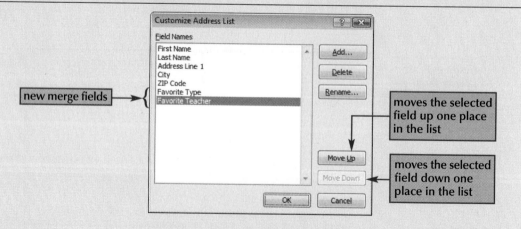

8. Click the **OK** button in the Customize Address List dialog box. The Customize Address List dialog box closes, and you return to the New Address List dialog box. This dialog box reflects the changes you just made. For instance, it no longer includes the Title field. The fields are listed in the same order they appeared in the Customize Address List dialog box. In the next step, you'll scroll right so you can see the fields you just added.

9. Use the horizontal scroll bar near the bottom of the New Address List dialog box to display the Favorite Type and Favorite Teacher fields. Although part of "Favorite Teacher" is cut off in the dialog box, the entire field name is stored as part of the data source. See Figure 6-10.

Changes made to New Address List dialog box ◀ Figure 6-10

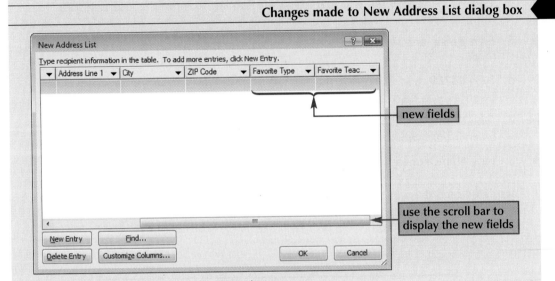

Organizing Field Names | InSight

Although the order of field names in the data source doesn't affect their placement in the main document, it's a good idea to arrange field names logically in the data source so you can enter information quickly and efficiently. For example, you'll probably want the First Name field next to the Last Name field. Also, note that if you include spaces in your field names, Word will replace the spaces with underscores when you insert the fields into the main document. For example, Word transforms the field name First Name into First_Name.

Now that you have specified the fields you want to use, you are ready to enter the client information into the data source.

Entering Data into a Data Source

You are now ready to begin entering information about each client into the data source. Nina gives you three copies of the form shown earlier in Figure 6-6, with information entered in each form. She asks you to transfer the information from the paper forms into the data source. Each paper form will be used to create one new record in the data source. You'll use the New Address List dialog box to enter the information.

To enter data into a record using the New Address List dialog box:

▶ **1.** Scroll left to display the First Name field, click in the **First Name** text box, if necessary, and then type **Anna** to enter the first name of the first client. Make sure you do not press the spacebar after you finish typing an entry in the New Address List dialog box. You should add spaces only in the text of the main document, not in the data source, to prevent too many or too few spaces between words.

▶ **2.** Press the **Tab** key to move the insertion point to the Last Name field.

▶ **3.** Type **Pearson**, and then press the **Tab** key to move the insertion point to the Address Line 1 field.

▶ **4.** Type **23 First Avenue**, and then press the **Tab** key to move the insertion point to the City field.

▶ **5.** Type **Boise**, and then press the **Tab** key to move the insertion point to the ZIP Code field.

▶ **6.** Type **83709**, and then press the **Tab** key to move to the Favorite Type field. The Favorite Type field scrolls into view on the right side of the dialog box.

▶ **7.** Type **Hatha**, and then press the **Tab** key. The insertion point is now in the Favorite Teacher field, which has scrolled into view on the right side of the dialog box.

▶ **8.** Type **Niki Dronza**, but do *not* press the Tab key. See Figure 6-11.

Tip

You can press the Shift+Tab keys to move the insertion point to the previous text box.

Figure 6-11 | Completed record 1

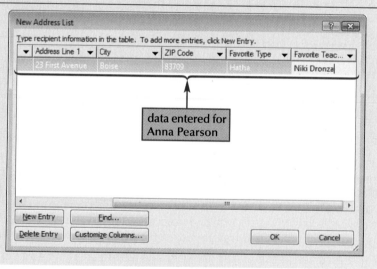

data entered for
Anna Pearson

You have completed the information for the first record of the data source document. Now you're ready to enter the information for the next two records. You can create a new record by clicking the New Entry button. When the insertion point is in the far-right text box in the New Address List dialog box, you can also create a new record by pressing the Tab key. In the steps that follow, you use both methods.

To add additional records to the data source:

▶ **1.** In the New Address List dialog box, click the **New Entry** button. This creates a new, blank record.

▶ **2.** Enter the information shown in Figure 6-12 into the new record.

Information for record 2 ◀ **Figure 6-12**

First Name	Last Name	Street Address	City	Zip Code	Favorite Type	Favorite Teacher
John	Andrews	703 Route 3	Eagle	83707	Power Yoga	Carolyn Brown

> **3.** After entering data into the last field, press the **Tab** key.

> **4.** Enter the information for the third record, as shown in Figure 6-13. After entering the information for the third record, do not create a fourth record.

Information for record 3 ◀ **Figure 6-13**

First Name	Last Name	Street Address	City	Zip Code	Favorite Type	Favorite Teacher
Eric	O'Keefe	564 S. Linder Road	Boise	83714	Vinyasa	Will Ramirez

Trouble? If you create a fourth record by mistake, click the Delete Entry button to remove the blank fourth record.

You have entered the records for three clients. Next, you need to proofread each record to make sure you typed the information correctly.

To proof the records in the data source:

> **1.** Review the information about Anna Pearson in the first record. Compare the record to Figure 6-11, which shows all the data for Anna Pearson except for her name. Make any necessary corrections by selecting the text and retyping it.

> **2.** Proofread record 2 by comparing your information with Figure 6-12. Make any necessary corrections.

> **3.** Proofread record 3 by comparing your information with Figure 6-13. Make any necessary corrections.

Nina's data source eventually will contain hundreds of records for Lily Road Yoga Studio clients. The current data source, however, contains only the records Nina wants to work with now. Next, you need to save the data source.

Saving a Data Source

You have finished entering data, so you are ready to close the New Address List dialog box. When you close this dialog box, a new dialog box opens, where you can save the data source as a Microsoft Office Address Lists file.

To save the data source:

▶ **1.** In the New Address List dialog box, click the **OK** button. The New Address List dialog box closes, and the Save Address List dialog box opens, as shown in Figure 6-14. By default, Word offers to save the file to the My Data Sources folder, which is a subfolder of the Documents folder. In this case, however, you will save the data source in the Tutorial.06\Tutorial folder. Notice that the Save as type box indicates that the data source will be saved as a Microsoft Office Address Lists file.

Figure 6-14 ▶ Saving the data source

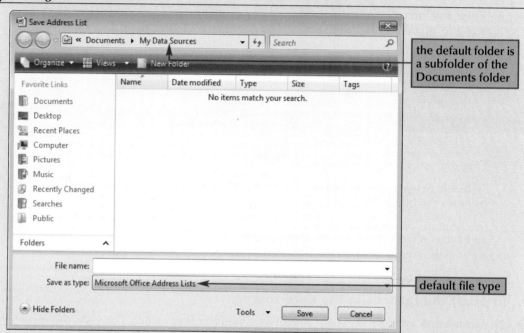

2. Navigate to the **Tutorial.06\Tutorial** folder.

▶ **3.** Click the **File name** text box, type **Yoga Data**, and then click the **Save** button. The Mail Merge Recipients dialog box opens, as shown in Figure 6-15. As in the New Address List dialog box, the header row in this dialog box contains the names of the fields. You need to scroll right to see all the fields. You can use the Mail Merge Recipients dialog box to rearrange the records in the list and to choose which clients you want to include in the mail merge. You'll use this dialog box later in this tutorial.

Mail Merge Recipients dialog box ◄ Figure 6-15

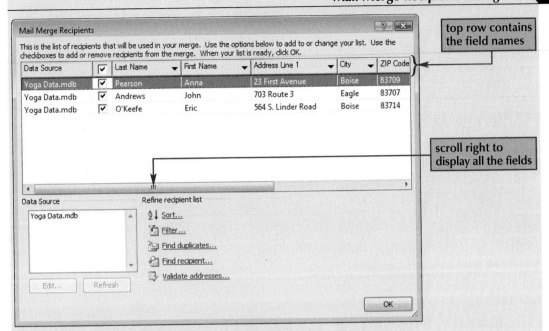

4. Click the **OK** button. The Mail Merge Recipients dialog box closes and you return to the document window. The Mail Merge task pane indicates that you have selected an Office Address List file named "Yoga Data.mdb" as your data source. The task pane also indicates that the next step in the mail merge process is writing (in this case, editing) the main document. See Figure 6-16.

Tip

You can also open the Mail Recipients dialog box by clicking the Edit Recipient List button in the Start Mail Merge group on the Mailings tab.

Selected data source ◄ Figure 6-16

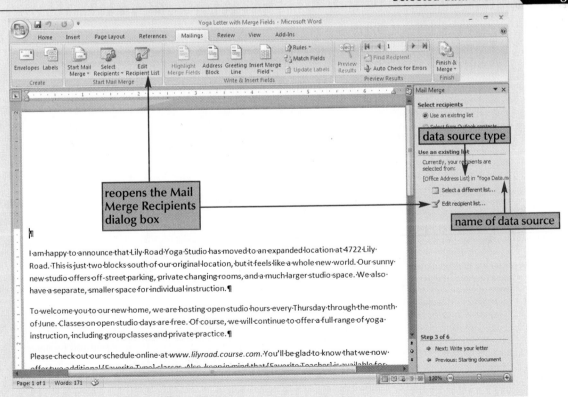

Editing a Main Document

In the first two steps of the mail merge process, you selected Nina's letter as your main document. A copy of this letter is open on your screen, next to the Mail Merge task pane. In the third step, you created and saved the data source. Now you will turn your attention back to the main document. You'll edit Nina's letter to add the current date and the merge fields.

Adding a Date Field

As you've learned, merge fields tell Word where to insert information from the data source. You can also insert other kinds of fields in a document, including a **date field**, which inserts the current date. You can set up a date field up so Word updates the field each time the document is opened.

You insert a date field via the Insert Date and Time dialog box. You already know how to use this dialog box to add the current date as text. To insert a date field that Word updates automatically, you select the Update automatically check box.

Nina wants the date to appear at the top of the document, just below where the yoga studio logo appears on the printed stationery.

To insert the date field:

1. In the Mail Merge task pane, click **Next: Write your letter**. The Mail Merge task pane displays information and options related to working with the main document. If you had originally selected a new, blank document as your main document, you would need to write the text of the form letter now. In this case, you will edit the existing letter.

2. Make sure the insertion point is at the beginning of the form letter on the first blank line. You will insert the date on the first line of the document.

3. Click the **Insert** tab, and then, in the Text group, click the **Date & Time** button. The Date and Time dialog box opens.

4. Click the third format in the Available formats list, which includes the month, the day, and the year, as in March 5, 2010.

5. If it's not selected, click the **Update automatically** check box to select it. See Figure 6-17.

Figure 6-17 ▶ Inserting a date field

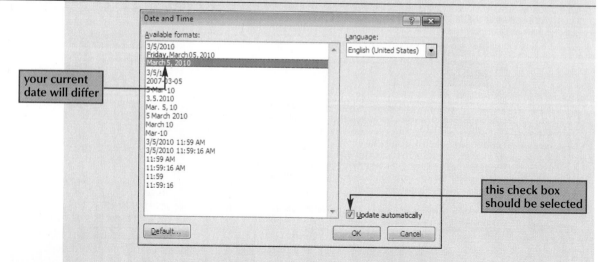

> **6.** Click the **OK** button. The current date appears in the document.
>
> **Trouble?** If you see {DATE \@ "MMMM d, yyyy"} instead of the current date, your system is set to display field codes. To view the date instead of the field code, click the Office Button, click Word Options, click Advanced, scroll down to display the Show document content section, deselect the "Show field codes instead of their values" check box, and then click the OK button.

Now, whenever you print the merged document, the current date will appear in the document. Next, you will insert the merge fields for the letter's inside address.

Inserting Merge Fields

Nina's letter is a standard business letter, so you'll place the client's name and address below the date. You'll use merge fields for the client's first name, last name, address, city, and zip code. You must enter proper spacing and punctuation around the fields so that the information in the merged document will be formatted correctly.

The Mail Merge task pane includes links, such as the Address block link, which you can use to insert a standard set of fields. The More items link offers more flexibility because it allows you to insert fields one at a time, rather than in predefined groups. In the following steps you will use the More link in the Mail Merge task pane to begin inserting merge fields in the main document. But first, you will re-display the Mailings tab, so that you can see the options on the Mailings tab that correspond to the options in the Mail merge task pane.

To insert a merge field:

> **1.** Click the **Mailings** tab.
>
> **2.** Verify that the insertion point is positioned in the first line immediately to the right of the date field, and then press the **Enter** key two times to leave space between the date and the first line of the inside address.
>
> **3.** In the Mail Merge task pane, click **More items**. The Insert Merge Field dialog box opens. As shown in Figure 6-18, the Database Fields option button is selected, indicating that the dialog box displays all the fields in the data source.

Inserting merge fields into the main document Figure 6-18

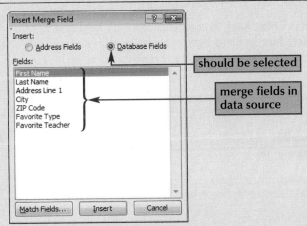

> **Trouble?** If you see a different list than the one shown in Figure 6-18, the Address Fields option button might be selected rather than the Database Fields option button. Click the Database Fields option button to select it, and then continue with Step 4.

▶ **4.** In the Fields list, click **First Name** if necessary to select it, click the **Insert** button, and then click the **Close** button. The Insert Merge Field dialog box closes, and the merge field is inserted into the document. The merge field consists of the field name surrounded by double angled brackets << >>, also called **chevrons**. Note that Word replaces spaces in field names with underscores, so the field name "First Name" is displayed as "First_Name." Also note that the Highlight Merge Fields button is now available, which means you can use it to display the merge field on a gray background.

Trouble? If you make a mistake and insert the wrong merge field, click to the left of the merge field, press the Delete key to select the field, and then press the Delete key again to delete it.

▶ **5.** In the Write & Insert Fields group, click the **Highlight Merge Fields** button. The First Name merge field is displayed on a gray background, making it easier to see in the document.

Later, when you merge the main document with the data source, Word will replace this merge field with information from the First Name field in the data source. Now, you're ready to insert the merge fields for the rest of the inside address. You'll add the necessary spacing and punctuation to the main document as well.

To insert the remaining merge fields for the inside address:

▶ **1.** Press the **spacebar** to insert a space after the First Name field, and then on the Mailings tab, click the **Insert Merge Field** button arrow. A menu appears displaying a list of the fields in the data source.

Trouble? If the Insert Merge Field dialog box opens, you clicked the Insert Merge Field button instead of the Insert Merge Field button arrow. Close the dialog box, and then click the Insert Merge Field button arrow.

▶ **2.** Click **Last_Name**. The Last_Name merge field is inserted in the document. As you continue entering the remaining merge fields in the inside address, you will use manual line breaks to avoid inserting paragraph spacing after each line. Remember that a manual line break moves the insertion point to the next line without actually starting a new paragraph, so no extra space is inserted.

▶ **3.** Press the **Shift+Enter** keys to create a manual line break, click the **Insert Merge Field** button arrow, and then click **Address Line 1**. Word inserts the Address Line 1 merge field into the form letter.

▶ **4.** Press the **Shift+Enter** keys to create another manual line break, and then, using either the Insert Merge Field button arrow on the Mailings tab or the More items link in the task pane, insert the **City** merge field. Word inserts the City merge field into the form letter.

▶ **5.** Type **,** (a comma), press the **spacebar** to insert a space after the comma, and then type **ID** to insert the abbreviation for the state of Idaho.

▶ **6.** Press the **spacebar** to insert a space after ID, and then insert the **ZIP Code** merge field. See Figure 6-19.

Form letter with merge fields | Figure 6-19

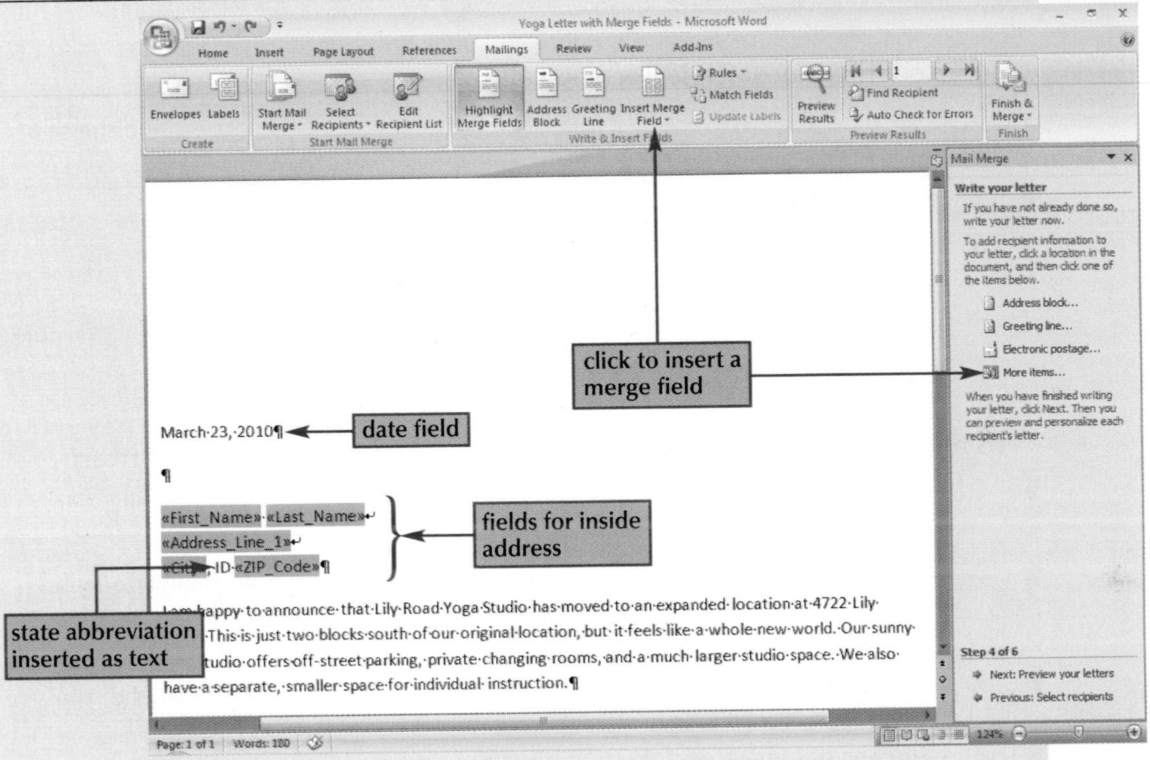

Planning Your Data Source | InSight

It's important to take some time to think about the structure of your data source before you create it. As you plan a data source, try to break information down into as many fields as seems reasonable. For example, it's always better to include a First Name field and a Last Name field, rather than simply a Name field, because including two separate fields makes it possible, later, to alphabetize the information in the data source by last name. If you entered first and last names in a single Name field, you could only alphabetize by first name, because the first name would appear first in the Name field.

If you're working with a very small data source, breaking information down into as many fields as possible is less important. However, it's very common to start with a small data source, and then, as time goes on, find that you need to keep adding information to the data source, until you have a large file. If you failed to plan the data source adequately at the beginning, the expanded data source could be hard to work with.

In this tutorial, you are working with a data source that does not include a State field because all of the yoga studio's clients live in the state of Idaho. This allows you to get some practice building an inside address out of merge fields and text. As a general rule, however, it's smart to include a State field in every address data source you create. That way, if your pool of addresses should expand in the future to include residents of other states, you won't have to make major changes to your data source to accommodate the new records. Also, if your data source includes a State field, you can use the Address Block merge field to insert an entire address at once, as you did in Tutorial 4. Finally, as you'll see later in this tutorial, including a State field in your data source simplifies the process of creating mailing labels.

The inside address is set up to match the form for a standard business letter. You can now add the salutation of the letter, which will contain each client's first name.

To insert the merge field for the salutation:

▶ **1.** Press the **Enter** key twice to insert a line between the inside address and the salutation, type **Dear**, and then press the **spacebar**.

▶ **2.** Insert the **First Name** field into the document.

▶ **3.** Type **:** (a colon), and then save your work. This completes the salutation.

You'll personalize the letter even more by including references to each client's favorite type of class and teacher.

To add each client's favorite type of class and teacher to the letter:

▶ **1.** Scroll down to display the third main paragraph of the letter, which begins "Please check out our schedule...."

▶ **2.** In the third main paragraph of the letter, select the placeholder **[Favorite Type]** (including the brackets). You'll replace this phrase with a merge field. (Don't be concerned if you also select the space following the closing bracket.)

▶ **3.** Insert the **Favorite Type** merge field. Word replaces the selected text with the Favorite Type merge field.

▶ **4.** Verify that the field has a single space before it and after it. Add a space on either side if necessary.

▶ **5.** Replace **[Favorite Teacher]** in the third main paragraph of the form letter with the **Favorite Teacher** field, and adjust the spacing as necessary.

▶ **6.** Carefully check your document to make sure the field names and spacing are correct. Your document should look like Figure 6-20.

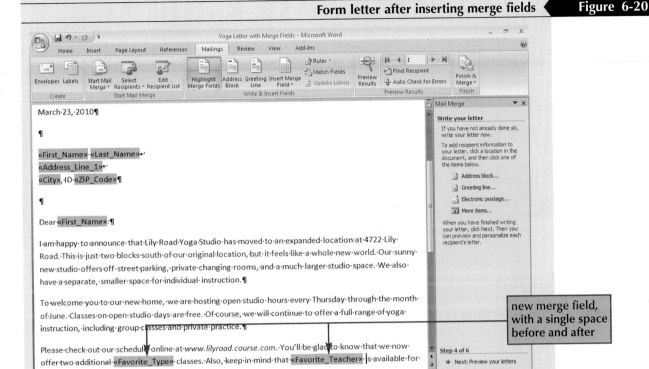

Trouble? If you see an error, edit the document as you would any other Word document. If you inserted an incorrect merge field, drag the mouse pointer to select the entire merge field, press the Delete key, and then insert the correct merge field.

▶ **7.** Save the document.

The main document now contains all the necessary merge fields. The next step is to merge the main document and the data source. Word allows you to preview the merged document before you complete the merge.

Previewing the Merged Document

Referring again to the Mail Merge task pane, your next step is to preview the merged document to see how the letter will look after Word inserts the information for each client. When you preview the merged document, you can check one last time for any missing spaces between the merge fields and the surrounding text. You can also look for any other formatting problems, and, if necessary, make final changes to the data source.

To preview the merged document:

▸ **1.** In the Mail Merge task pane, click **Next: Preview your letters**. The Mail Merge task pane displays information and options related to previewing the merged document. The data for the first record (Anna Pearson) replaces the merge fields in the form letter. See Figure 6-21. Carefully check the letter to make sure the text and formatting are correct. In particular, check to make sure that the spaces before and after the merged data are correct; it is easy to accidentally omit spaces or add extra spaces around merge fields. Finally, notice that both the task pane and the Go to Record box in the Preview Results group show which record is currently displayed in the document.

Figure 6-21 ▸ First letter with merged data

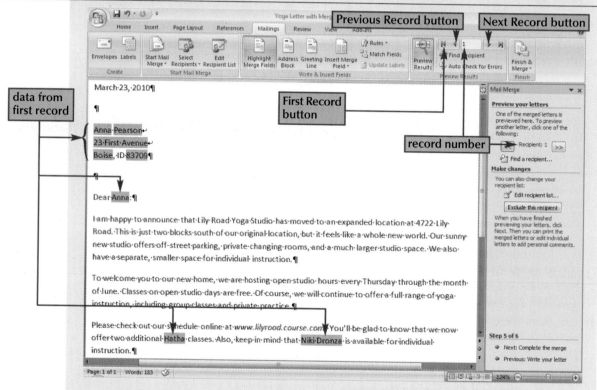

▸ **2.** If you need to make any changes to the form letter, click **Previous: Write your letter** in the Mail Merge task pane, edit the document, save your changes, and then click **Next: Preview your letters** in the task pane. When you are finished, your screen should look like Figure 6-21. Before you complete the merge, you should review the data for the other two records.

▸ **3.** In the Preview Results group on the Mailings tab, click the **Next Record** button ▸. The data for John Andrews is displayed in the letter.

▸ **4.** Click the **Next Record** button ▸ to display the data for Eric O'Keefe in the letter.

▸ **5.** Click the **First Record** button ◂ in the Preview Results group to redisplay the first record in the letter (with data for Anna Pearson).

Tip

You can also use the right-facing double-arrow button in the Mail Merge task pane to display the next record and the left-facing double-arrow button to display the previous record.

The main document of the mail merge is completed. At this stage, you could also use the Mail Merge task pane to make changes to the data source, but Nina says the data source is fine for now. You are ready for the final step, completing the merge.

Merging the Main Document and Data Source

Now that you've created the form letter (main document) and the list of client information (data source), you're ready to merge the two files and create personalized letters to send to Nina's clients. Because the data source consists of three records, your merged document will contain three letters; each will be one page long.

When you complete a merge, you can choose to merge directly to the printer. In other words, you can choose to have Word print the merged document immediately without saving it as a separate file. However, Nina wants to keep a copy of the merged document on disk for her records. So you'll merge the data source and main document to a new document first, and then print it.

> ### Tip
> You can use the Finish & Merge button in the Finish group on the Mailings tab to merge to a new document, merge to the printer, or send out the merged documents as e-mails.

To complete the mail merge:

▶ 1. In the Mail Merge task pane, click **Next: Complete the merge**. As shown in Figure 6-22, the task pane displays options related to merging the main document and the data source. You can use the Print option to merge directly to the printer. Alternatively, you can use the Edit individual letters option to merge to a new document.

Last step in Mail Merge task pane ◀ **Figure 6-22**

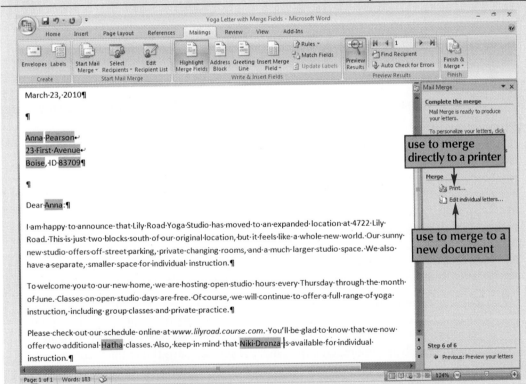

▶ 2. In the Mail Merge task pane, click **Edit individual letters**. The Merge to New Document dialog box opens. Here, you need to specify which records to include in the merge. You want to include all three records from the data source.

▶ 3. Verify that the **All** option button is selected, and then click the **OK** button. Word creates a new document called Letters1, which contains three pages, one for each record in the data source. In this new document, the merge fields have been replaced by the specific names, addresses, and so on, from the data source. See Figure 6-23. The date field, however, has not been replaced. Instead, a date field appears at the top of every page, highlighted in gray. The gray highlighting will not print.

Figure 6-23 ▶ Merged document

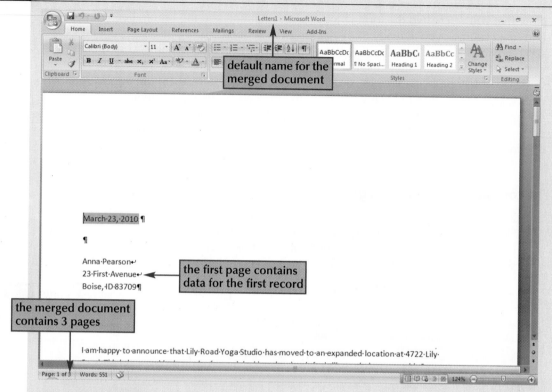

4. Save the merged document in the Tutorial.06\Tutorial folder, using the filename **Yoga Merged Letters 1**.

5. Zoom out so the text is large enough to read. Next, you will use the Select Browse Object button at the bottom of the vertical scroll bar to move from one page to the next.

6. Click the **Select Browse Object** button 🔘 near the bottom of the vertical scroll bar, click the **Browse by Page** button 🔲 on the palette, and then click the **Previous Page** button ⬍ or **Next Page** button ⬎ to move among the letters. Note that each letter is addressed to a different client and that the favorite type and teacher vary from one letter to the next. A page break separates each letter from the one that follows. Nina will print the letters later. For now, you will close the file.

7. Close the **Yoga Merged Letters 1** document. The document named "Yoga Letter with Merge Fields" is now the active document. You see the Mail Merge task pane again, displaying the last step of the mail merge process. Note that if you need to take a break while working on a mail merge, you can save the main document and close it. The data source and field information are saved along with the document. When you're ready to work on the merge again, you can open the main document again and update the connection to the data source. You'll see how this works at the beginning of the next session. For now, you will close the main document.

8. Save and close the **Yoga Letter with Merge Fields** document.

You have completed the six steps of the Mail Merge task pane and generated a merged document. In the next session, you will learn how to use additional Mail Merge features.

Session 6.1 Quick Check | Review

1. Define the following in your own words:
   a. date field
   b. main document
   c. merge field
   d. record
2. A _____ is a file with information organized into fields and records.
3. True or False. In the Mail Merge task pane, you can select a data source file that already contains names and addresses, or you can create a new data source and enter names and addresses into it.
4. True or False. You cannot use an Excel worksheet as a data source.
5. Explain how to insert a merge field into a main document.
6. Explain how to add a date field to a document.

Session 6.2

Editing a Data Source

After you complete a mail merge, you might find that you need to make some changes to the data source and redo the merge. You can edit a data source in two ways—from within the program used to create the data source in the first place, or via the Mail Merge Recipients dialog box in Word. If you are familiar with the program used to create the data source, it's often simplest to edit the file from within that program. For example, if you were using an Excel worksheet as your data source, you could open the file in Excel, edit it (perhaps by adding new records), save it, and then reselect the file as your data source. To edit a Microsoft Office Address Lists file from within Word, you can use the Mail Merge Recipients dialog box.

Editing a Data Source in Word | Reference Window

- Open the main document for the data source you want to edit.
- In the Start Mail Merge group on the Mailings tab, click the Edit Recipient List button.
- In the Data Source list box in the Mail Merge Recipients dialog box, select the data source you want to edit, and then click the Edit button.
- To add a record, click the New Entry button, and then type a new record.
- To delete a record, click any field in the record, and then click the Delete Entry button.
- To add or remove fields from the data source, click the Customize Columns button, make any changes, and then click the OK button. Remember that if you remove a field, you will delete any data entered into that field.

In the following steps, you will reopen the main document, which you closed at the end of the last session.

InSight		**Restoring a Connection to the Data Source**

After you complete a mail merge, a connection exists between the main document file and the data source file, even after you close the main document and exit Word. You can be certain the connection is maintained as long as you keep both files in their original locations. The two files don't have to be in the same folder; each file just has to remain in the folder it was in when you first created the connection between the two files.

What happens if you move one of the files to a different folder? That depends on how your computer is set up and where you move the files. On most Windows Vista computers, you can't move the *data source* file on its own, but if you move the *main document* file to another location on the same computer, the connection is usually maintained. However, if you move the document to another computer on a network, or to a different storage media (say from the hard drive to a memory stick), the connection might be broken. In that case, when you open the main document, you'll see a series of message boxes informing you that the connection to the data source has been broken. Eventually, you will see a Microsoft Word dialog box with a button labeled Find Data Source, which you can click, and then use the Select Data Source dialog box to select your data source.

To avoid difficulties with locating a data source, it's a good idea to either store the data source in the default My Data Sources folder and keep it there, or store the data source and the main document in the same folder (a folder other than the My Data Sources folder) and keep them there. The latter option is best if you think you might need to move the files to a different computer. That way, if you do need to move them, you can move the entire folder.

To add records to Nina's data source:

1. Open the document named **Yoga Letter with Merge Fields** from the Tutorial.06\Tutorial folder. You see a warning message indicating that opening the document will run an SQL command. SQL is the database programming language that controls the connection between the main document and the data source.

2. Click **Yes** to continue, and then click the **Mailings** tab. The main document still displays the data for the last record you displayed in the document when you previewed the merged document (probably Anna Pearson). As you'll see in the next step, you can alternate between displaying the merge fields and the client data by toggling the Preview Results button on the Mailings tab.

   Trouble? If you see data for a client other than Anna Pearson, don't be concerned. Simply proceed to Step 3.

   Trouble? If you see the merge fields instead of the data for one of the yoga clients, read but do not perform Step 3, and then proceed to Step 4.

3. In the Preview Results group, click the **Preview Results** button to deselect it. The merge fields are displayed in the main document.

   Trouble? If you see the data for one of the clients instead of the merge fields, click the Preview Results button again to deselect it.

4. If necessary, highlight the merge fields by clicking the **Highlight Merge Fields** button in the Write & Insert Fields group.

5. In the Start Mail Merge group, click the **Edit Recipient List** button. The Mail Merge Recipients dialog box opens. You saw this dialog box earlier, when you first selected the data source to use for the mail merge. The Data Source list box in the lower-left corner allows you to select a data source to edit. If you had multiple data sources stored in the Tutorial.06\Tutorial folder, you would see them all in this list box.

6. In the Data Source list box, in the lower-left corner of the Mail Merge Recipients dialog box, click **Yoga Data.mdb**. The filename is selected.

7. Click the **Edit** button. The Edit Data Source dialog box opens. Note that this dialog box looks similar to the New Address List dialog box, which you used earlier when you first entered information into the data source.

8. Use the New Entry button to enter the information shown in Figure 6-24 into the data source. When you are finished, you should have added three new records, for a total of six.

New data ◀ **Figure 6-24**

First Name	Last Name	Street Address	City	Zip Code	Favorite Type	Favorite Teacher
Hannah	Blackmore	2054 First Avenue	Boise	83709	Hatha	Niki Dronza
Antonio	Morelos	55 Moraine Road	Eagle	83707	Hatha	Niki Dronza
Clara	Beck	34 Vilas Street	Boise	83710	Power Yoga	Carolyn Brown

After you finish entering the data for Clara Beck, review your work and make any necessary corrections.

9. Click the **OK** button. When you are asked if you want to update the Yoga Data.mdb file, click the **Yes** button. You return to the Mail Merge Recipients dialog box, as shown in Figure 6-25. If your records look different from those in Figure 6-25, select the data source, click the Edit button, edit the data source, and then click the OK button.

New records added to data source ◀ **Figure 6-25**

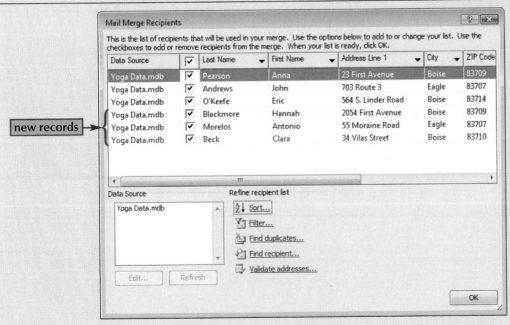

new records

You'll leave the Mail Merge Recipients dialog box open so you can use it to make other changes to the data source.

Sorting Records

As Nina looks through the letters to her clients in the merged document, she notices one problem—the letters are not grouped by zip codes. Currently, the letters are in the order in which clients were added to the data source file. She plans to use bulk mailing rates to send her letters, and the U.S. Postal Service requires bulk mailings to be separated into groups according to zip code. She asks you to sort the data file by zip code and perform another merge, this time merging the main document with the sorted data source.

You can sort information in a data source table just as you sort information in any other table. Recall that to **sort** means to rearrange a list or a document in alphabetical, numerical, or chronological order. You can sort information in ascending order (*A* to *Z*, lowest to highest, or earliest to latest) or in descending order (*Z* to *A*, highest to lowest, or latest to earliest) by clicking a column heading in the Mail Merge Recipients dialog box. The first time you click the heading, the records are sorted in ascending order. If you click it twice, the records are sorted in descending order.

Reference Window | **Sorting a Data Source**

- In the Start Mail Merge group on the Mailings tab, click the Edit Recipient List button to display the Mail Merge Recipients dialog box.
- To sort data in ascending order, click the heading for the column you want to sort. For example, if you want to arrange the records alphabetically according to the contents of the First Name column, click the First Name column heading.
- To sort data in descending order, click the column heading a second time.

Currently, the records in the data source are listed in the order you entered them, with the information for Anna Pearson at the top. You'll sort the records in ascending order, based on the contents of the ZIP Code column.

To sort the data source by zip code:

▶ **1.** Verify that the Mail Merge Recipients dialog box is still open.

▶ **2.** Scroll right, if necessary, to display the entire ZIP code column.

▶ **3.** Click the **ZIP Code** column heading. Word sorts the rows of the data table from lowest zip code number to highest. The information for Antonio Morelos is now at the top of the list. See Figure 6-26. When you merge the data source with the form letter, the letters will appear in the merged document in this order.

Records sorted in ascending order by ZIP code | Figure 6-26

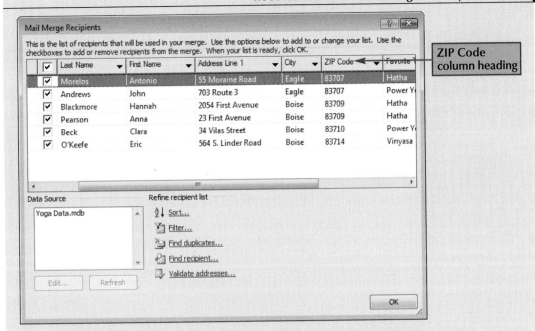

4. Click the **OK** button. The Mail Merge Recipients dialog box closes.

5. In the Finish group, click the **Finish & Merge** button, click **Edit Individual Documents**, verify that the **All** option button is selected in the Merge to New Document dialog box, and then click the **OK** button. Word generates the new merged document with six letters, one letter per page as before—but this time the first letter is to Antonio Morelos, who has the lowest zip code (83707).

6. Use the Select Browse Object button  to browse by page and verify that the letters in the newly merged document are arranged in ascending order by zip code. Nina will print the letters later. For now, you will close the document.

7. Save the new merged document in the Tutorial.06\Tutorial folder, using the filename **Yoga Merged Letters 2**, and then close it. You return to the main document.

As Nina requested, you've created a merged document with the letters to her clients sorted by zip code. Now she would like you to create a set of letters to just those clients who attend power yoga classes.

Selecting Records to Merge

Nina wants to inform students of Carolyn Brown that she is available for individual instruction only on Tuesdays and Thursdays. She asks you to modify the form letter slightly and then merge it with only those records of clients who have indicated that Carolyn is their favorite teacher. To select specific records in a data source, you use the Mail Merge Recipients dialog box.

To select specific records for a merge:

1. Make sure the document named Yoga Letter with Merge Fields is displayed in the document window.

▶ **2.** Click at the end of the third main paragraph, which begins "Please check out our schedule online...."

▶ **3.** Press the ← key to move the insertion point to the left of the period, insert a space, and type **on Tuesdays and Thursdays** and then verify that the sentence reads "...is available for individual instruction on Tuesdays and Thursdays."

▶ **4.** Save the document as **Carolyn Letter with Merge Fields** in the Tutorial.06\Tutorial folder.

▶ **5.** Click the **Edit Recipient List** button in the Start Mail Merge group. The Mail Merge Recipients dialog box opens. To remove an individual record from a merge, you can deselect its check box. You want to include only the records for John Andrews and Clara Beck in this merge, because they are the only clients who listed Carolyn Brown as their favorite teacher.

▶ **6.** Click the **check box** next to the first record (for Antonio Morelos). The check mark is removed.

▶ **7.** Remove the check marks for all the records *except* for the John Andrews and Clara Beck records. See Figure 6-27. Now that you have selected only the records you want, you can complete the merge.

Figure 6-27 ▶ **Specific records selected in data source**

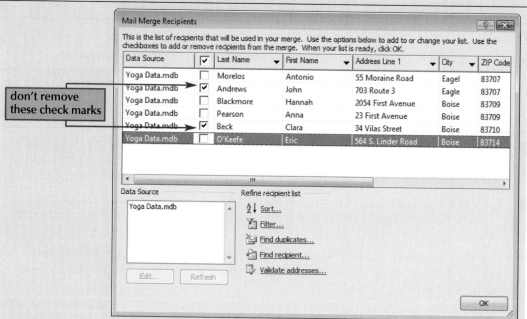

▶ **8.** Click the **OK** button. The Mail Merge Recipients dialog box closes.

▶ **9.** In the Finish group, click the **Finish & Merge** button, click **Edit Individual Documents**, in the Merge to New Document dialog box verify that the **All** option button is selected, and then click the **OK** button. Word generates the new merged document with two letters, one letter per page. This time the first letter is to John Andrews.

▶ **10.** Scroll through the letters in the new merged document to see that they are both addressed to clients who listed Carolyn Brown as their favorite teacher.

11. Save the new merged document in the Tutorial.06\Tutorial folder using the file-name **Yoga Merged Letters 3**, close it, save your changes to the document named **Carolyn Letter with Merge Fields**, and then close it.

Next, you'll create and print mailing labels for the form letter so Nina doesn't have to address the letters by hand.

Creating Mailing Labels

Now that you've created and printed the personalized letters, Nina is ready to prepare envelopes in which to mail the letters. She could print the names and addresses directly on envelopes, or she could create mailing labels to stick on the envelopes. The latter method is easier because she can print 14 labels at once, rather than printing one envelope at a time.

Nina has purchased Avery® Laser Printer labels, which are available in most office-supply stores. Word supports most of the Avery label formats, allowing you to choose the layout that works best for you. The labels Nina has come in 8½ × 11-inch sheets designed to feed through a laser printer. Each label measures 4 × 1.33 inches. There are seven rows of labels per sheet, with two labels in each row, for a total of 14 labels. See Figure 6-28.

Layout of a sheet of Avery® labels ◀ **Figure 6-28**

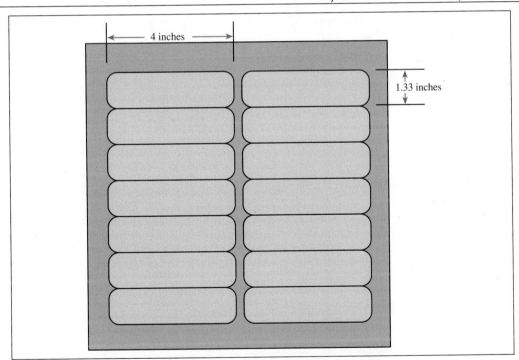

Creating mailing labels is similar to creating form letters, and the Mail Merge task pane walks you through all six steps. You'll begin creating the mailing labels by opening a blank document and the Mail Merge task pane. You can use the same data source file (Yoga Data.mdb) that you used earlier.

To specify the main document for creating mailing labels:

▶ **1.** Open a new, blank document, make sure nonprinting characters are displayed, and zoom out so you can see the whole page.

▶ **2.** Click the **Mailings** tab, and then open the Mail Merge task pane.

▶ **3.** In the Mail Merge task pane, click the **Labels** option button, and then click **Next: Starting document**. The Mail Merge task pane displays information and options for setting up the document layout for labels. (*Note:* If Nina wanted you to print envelopes instead of mailing labels, you would have selected Envelopes as the type of main document.)

▶ **4.** Under "Select starting document," verify that the **Change document layout** option button is selected, and then, under "Change document layout," click **Label options**. The Label Options dialog box opens.

▶ **5.** Click the **Label vendors** arrow, and then click **Avery US Letter**.

▶ **6.** Scroll down the Product number list box, and then click **5162**. This number is found on the packages of most labels that you buy at office supply stores. Your Label Options dialog box should look like Figure 6-29.

Figure 6-29 ▶ **Label Options dialog box**

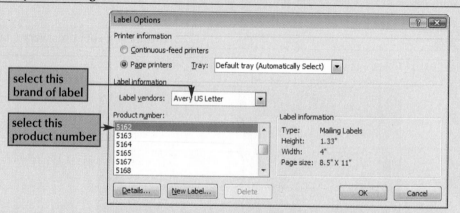

▶ **7.** Click the **OK** button. The Label Options dialog box closes. Word inserts a table structure into the document, with one cell for each of the 14 labels on the page. You might not be able to see the table structure if the table gridlines are not displayed.

▶ **8.** If you don't see the table structure, click the **Table Tools Layout** tab, and then, in the Table group, click the **View Gridlines** button to select it. You can now see that the document is divided into label-sized rectangles, as shown in Figure 6-30. The gridlines are visible only on the screen; they will not be visible on the printed labels.

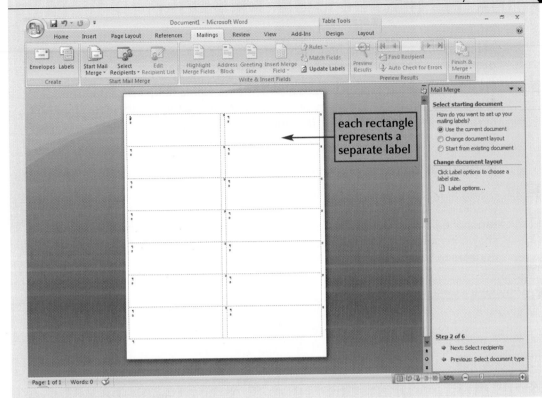

You are finished setting up the document. Next, you need to save the main document and select the data source you created earlier.

To continue the mail merge for the labels:

▶ **1.** Save the main document to the Tutorial.06\Tutorial folder using the filename **Yoga Labels with Merge Fields**.

▶ **2.** Click **Next: Select recipients**. Under "Select recipients," verify that the **Use an existing list** option button is selected, and then, under "Use an existing list," click **Browse**. The Select Data Source dialog box opens.

▶ **3.** Navigate to and select the file named **Yoga Data** in the Tutorial.06\Tutorial folder, and then click the **Open** button. The Mail Merge Recipients dialog box opens.

▶ **4.** Verify that all the records are displayed with all check boxes selected, and then click the **OK** button. The Mail Merge Recipients dialog box closes. A special code (<<Next Record>>) is inserted into all the labels except the one in the upper-left corner. To see the <<Next Record>> code, you need to adjust the Zoom setting.

▶ **5.** Zoom in so you can read the document. The <<Next Record>> code is a special code that tells Word how to insert data into the document. You can ignore it.

▶ **6.** Click **Next: Arrange your labels**. The Mail Merge task pane displays options for inserting merge fields into the document. Note that if the data source included a State field, you could use the Address block option to insert a complete set of fields for a single address. However, because the data source does not include a State field, you need to insert the fields individually, as you did when creating the form letter.

7. Verify that the insertion point is located in the upper-left label, and then, in the Write & Insert Fields group on the Mailings tab, click the **Insert Merge Field** button arrow.

8. Click **First_Name**, and then in the Write & Insert Fields group, click the **Highlight Merge Fields** button. The First_Name merge field is inserted in the document and displayed on a gray background.

9. Press the **spacebar** to add a space after the First Name field, insert the **Last_Name** field, press the **Enter** key, insert the **Address_Line_1** field, press the **Enter** key, insert the **City** field, type **,** (a comma), press the **spacebar** to insert a space, type **ID**, press the **spacebar**, and then insert the **ZIP_Code** field. You are finished inserting the fields for the first label. Now you will update your labels so the merge fields appear on all the labels.

10. Near the bottom of the Mail Merge task pane, click the **Update all labels** button. (You might have to scroll down to see it; use the scroll button at the bottom of the task pane.) The address fields are inserted into all the labels in the document, as shown in Figure 6-31. In all except the upper-left label, the Next Record code appears to the left of the First Name merge field.

Figure 6-31 ▶ **Field codes inserted into document**

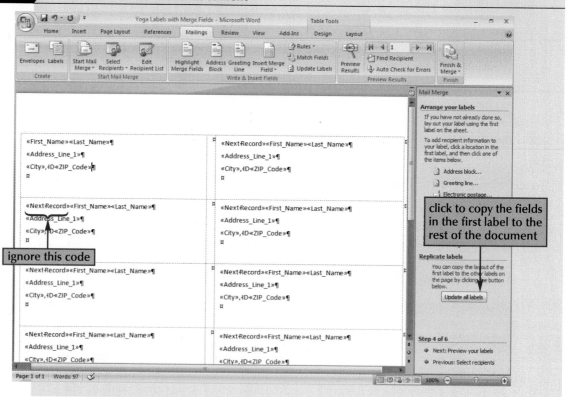

You are ready to preview the labels and complete the merge.

To preview the labels and complete the merge:

1. Click **Next: Preview your labels** in the Mail Merge task pane. (You might have to scroll down to display this option, again using the scroll button at the bottom of the task pane.) The data for the clients is displayed in the labels. For now, ignore the extra ", ID" in labels that would otherwise be blank. You are ready to merge to a new document.

2. Click **Next: Complete the merge** in the task pane, click **Edit individual labels** in the task pane, verify that the **All** option button is selected in the Merge to New Document dialog box, and then click the **OK** button. The finished labels are displayed in a new document.

The labels are almost finished. All you need to do is edit the document to remove the "ID" text from the unused labels, save the document, and print the labels. For now, you'll just print the labels on an 8½ × 11-inch sheet of paper so you can see what they look like. Later, Nina will print them on the sheet of labels.

To edit, save, and print the labels:

1. Scroll through the document. The document contains space for 14 labels, but the data source contained only six records. However, when you clicked the Update Labels button in the task pane earlier, the comma and the state abbreviation (ID) were copied to all the labels, including those that don't contain any address information. See Figure 6-32, where the document is zoomed to show the whole page, so you can see all the labels. You can solve this problem with the extra text by deleting the extra text in the bottom four rows of labels.

Extra text in labels document ◄ **Figure 6-32**

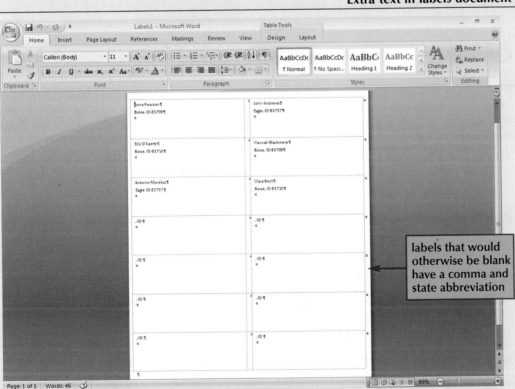

labels that would otherwise be blank have a comma and state abbreviation

2. Change the Zoom setting to **Whole Page**, drag the mouse pointer to select the bottom four rows of labels, and then press the **Delete** key. The extra text is deleted.

3. In the upper-left label, change "Anna Pearson" to your name, and then save the merged document in the Tutorial.06\Tutorial folder using the filename **Yoga Merged Labels**.

▶ **4.** Print the labels on a sheet of paper, just as you would print any other document.

Trouble? If you want to print on a sheet of labels, ask your instructor or technical support person how to feed the label sheet into the printer. If you're using a shared printer, you might need to make special arrangements so other users' documents aren't accidentally printed on your label sheet.

▶ **5.** Close the merged document, and then close the task pane if necessary.

▶ **6.** Save changes to the main document, and then close it.

InSight	**Printing Labels**

Labels are expensive, so it's extra important to take care in completing the merge to avoid wasting label sheets. When you create labels, keep these tips in mind:

- It's a good idea to print one page of a label document on regular paper so you can check your work before printing on the more expensive sheets of adhesive labels.
- Always check the few rows of a labels document for extra text, just as you did with the Yoga studio labels.
- If you include a State field in your data source, you can avoid the problem with extra text in unused labels by inserting an Address Block merge field instead of individual merge fields mixed with regular text.

Creating a Telephone Directory

Next, Nina wants you to create a list of telephone numbers for all the teachers at Lily Road Yoga Studio. Nina has already created a Word document containing the phone numbers; you will use that document as the data source for the merge. You'll set up a mail merge as before, except this time you'll select Directory as the main document type. You'll start by examining the Word document that Nina wants you to use as the data source.

To begin creating the telephone list:

▶ **1.** Open the document named **Phone** from the Tutorial.06\Tutorial folder, and then save it as **Phone Data** in the same folder.

▶ **2.** Review the document. Note that the information is arranged in a table with three column headings: "First Name," "Last Name," and "Phone." The information in the table has already been sorted in alphabetical order by last name.

▶ **3.** In the bottom row, replace "Nina Ranabhat" with your name.

▶ **4.** Save and close the Phone Data document, open a new, blank document, display nonprinting characters, if necessary, and display the rulers.

▶ **5.** Open the Mail Merge task pane, and then zoom out if necessary so you can see the 6-inch mark on the ruler.

▶ **6.** In the Mail Merge task pane under "Select document type," click the **Directory** option button, click **Next: Starting document**, verify that the **Use the current document** option button is selected, click **Next: Select recipients**, verify that the **Use an existing list** option button is selected, and then click **Browse**. The Select Data Source dialog box opens.

> **7.** Navigate to and select the file named **Phone Data** in the Tutorial.06\Tutorial folder as the data source, click the **Open** button, review the records in the Mail Merge Recipients dialog box, and then click the **OK** button.

> **8.** In the task pane, click **Next: Arrange your directory**. The document is still blank; you'll insert the merge fields next.

You're ready to insert the fields in the main document. Nina wants the telephone list to include the names at the left margin of the page and the phone number at the right margin. You'll set up the main document so that the phone number is preceded by a dot leader. A **dot leader** is a dotted line that extends from the last letter of text on the left margin to the beginning of the nearest text aligned at a tab stop.

To create the main document with dot leaders:

> **1.** With the insertion point at the top of the blank document, insert the **First_Name** merge field, insert a space, insert the **Last_Name** merge field, and then in the Write & Insert Fields group, click the **Highlight Merge Fields** button. The First Name and Last Name merge fields are displayed on a gray background. Now you'll set a tab stop at the right margin (at the 6-inch mark on the ruler) with a dot leader.

> **2.** Click the **Page Layout** tab, then in the Paragraph group, click the **Dialog Box Launcher** to open the Paragraph dialog box, and then in the lower-left corner of the Paragraph dialog box, click the **Tabs** button. The Tabs dialog box opens.

> **3.** Type **6** in the Tab stop position text box, then in the Alignment section, click the **Right** option button, and then in the Leader section, click the **2 ....** option button. See Figure 6-33. While the Tabs dialog box is open, notice the Clear All button, which you could click to delete all the current tab stops.

Creating a tab with a dot leader | **Figure 6-33**

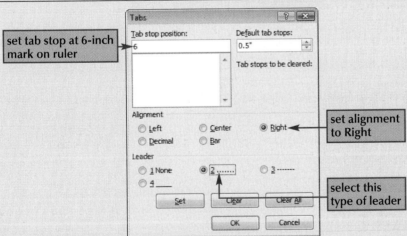

> **4.** Click the **OK** button. Word clears the current tab stops and inserts a right-aligned tab stop at the 6-inch mark on the horizontal ruler.

> **5.** Press the **Tab** key to move the insertion point to the new tab stop. A dotted line stretches across the page, from the Last Name field to the right margin.

> **6.** Switch back to the Mailings tab, and then insert the **Phone** merge field at the location of the insertion point.

7. Press the **Enter** key. You must insert a hard return here so that each name and telephone number will appear on a separate line. Notice that the dot leader shortened to accommodate the inserted field. The completed main document should look like Figure 6-34.

Figure 6-34 ▶ Completed main document for telephone directory

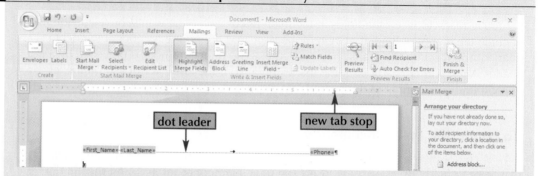

8. Save the main document in the Tutorial.06\Tutorial folder using the filename **Phone Directory with Merge Fields**.

You are now ready to merge this file with Nina's data source.

To merge the files for the phone list:

1. In the Mail Merge task pane, click **Next: Preview your directory**, and then review the data for the first record in the document.

2. Click **Next: Complete the merge** in the task pane, click **To New Document** in the task pane, verify that the **All** option button is selected in the Merge to New Document dialog box, and then click the **OK** button. Word creates a new document that contains the completed telephone list. See Figure 6-35.

Figure 6-35 ▶ Completed telephone directory

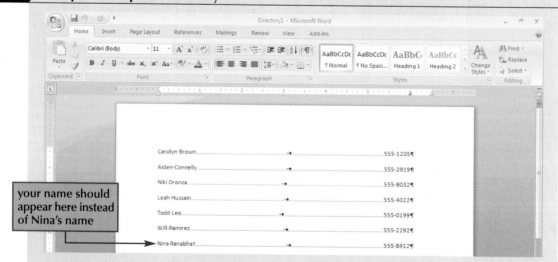

3. Save the document as **Phone Directory** in the Tutorial.06\Tutorial folder, and then close it.

4. Save and close the **Phone Directory with Merge Fields** document.

You have created the telephone list. Nina will print it and distribute it to each of the teachers. Now that you are familiar with the many types of documents you can create using Word's Mail Merge feature, you can use mail merge whenever you need to distribute customized information to a group of people.

Converting Text to Tables and Tables to Text

Nina needs your help with a few other tasks related to managing information about the teachers and clients at Lily Road Yoga Studio. First, she needs to convert names and addresses of new clients, which her assistant typed for her, into a table. She will then use the table later as the data source in a mail merge.

Before you can convert text into a table, you need to verify that the information in the document is set up properly. That is, you need to make sure that **separator characters**—typically commas or tabs—are used consistently to divide the text into individual pieces of data. Upon conversion, each data item is formatted as a separate cell in a column, and each paragraph mark starts a new row.

To convert text into a table:

1. Open the document named **Client** from the Tutorial.06\Tutorial folder, and then save it as **Client Table** in the same folder. Display nonprinting characters, if necessary.

2. Review the document. Notice that it consists of three paragraphs. Each paragraph contains seven separate pieces of information (first name, last name, address, city, zip code, favorite type of yoga, and favorite teacher) separated by commas.

3. Drag the mouse to select the three paragraphs, click the **Insert** tab, click the **Table** button, and then, at the bottom of the Table menu, click **Convert Text to Table**. The Convert Text to Table dialog box opens. See Figure 6-36. Because the information in each paragraph is separated by commas, the Commas option button at the bottom of the dialog box is selected. Note that the Number of columns setting is 7. This corresponds to the seven pieces of information in each paragraph.

Converting text to a table | **Figure 6-36**

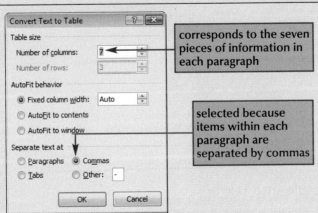

Tip

When converting text to a table, if the result is not what you expect, undo the conversion and then review the text to make sure it is set up consistently, with each paragraph containing the same number of data items, and with the data items broken up by the same separator character.

4. Click the **OK** button. The Convert Text to Table dialog box closes, and the text in the document is converted into a table consisting of seven columns and three rows. Next, you need to add the column headings.

5. Click in the left margin to select the top row of the table, click the **Table Tools Layout** tab, and then in the Rows & Columns group, click the **Insert Above** button. A blank row is added at the top of the table.

6. Enter the following column headings: **First Name**, **Last Name**, **Street Address**, **City**, **ZIP Code**, **Favorite Type**, and **Favorite Teacher**. Format the column headings in bold. When you are finished, your table should look like the one in Figure 6-37.

| Figure 6-37 | Text changed to table |

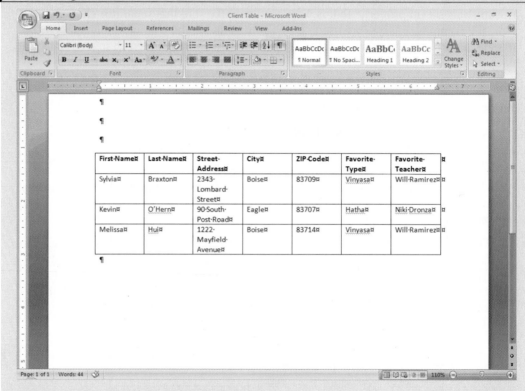

7. Save the document, and then close it. Nina will use the Client Table in another mail merge she has planned for next month, and eventually she'll combine it with her current list of clients.

You have finished converting text into a table. Now, Nina needs your help doing the opposite—that is, converting a table into text. After the conversion, she will use the text to create a list of yoga teachers for the studio.

To convert a table into text:

1. Open the document named **Phone Data** from the Tutorial.06\Tutorial folder, and then save it as **Teacher List** in the same folder. Display nonprinting characters, if necessary. You want to include only the names of Nina's teachers, so you will start by deleting the header row and the Phone column.

▶ **2.** Click in the left margin to select the header row, click the **Table Tools Layout** tab, then in the Rows & Columns group, click the **Delete** button, and then click **Delete Rows**.

▶ **3.** Select the column containing the phone numbers, and then use the Delete button in the Rows & Columns group to delete the column. The table now contains only the first and last name of each yoga teacher. You are ready to convert this table into text.

▶ **4.** Select the entire table, verify that the Table Tools Layout tab is displayed, and then in the Data group, click **Convert to Text**. The Convert to Text dialog box opens.

▶ **5.** Click the **Other** option button. In the text box next to this option button, you can specify how you want to divide the information in each row. In this case, you want to separate the first and last names by a space.

▶ **6.** In the text box next to the Other option button, delete the hyphen, verify that the insertion point is at the far-left edge of the text box, and then press the **spacebar** to insert a space. See Figure 6-38.

Converting a table to text ◀ **Figure 6-38**

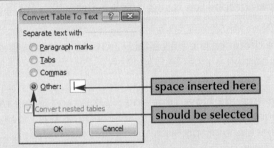

▶ **7.** Click the **OK** button. The Convert Table to Text dialog box closes. The contents of the table are now formatted as seven separate paragraphs, one for each row in the table. Each first name is separated from its corresponding last name by a space.

You now have seven paragraphs, each containing the name of a teacher at Lily Road Yoga studio. In the next section, you will use Word's list features to manipulate these paragraphs, creating a useful list for Nina.

Working with Lists

Nina often has to respond to calls from potential clients asking about teachers at the yoga studio. To make her job easier, Nina wants to create a quick reference list with information about each teacher, such as what they teach and how strenuous their classes are. She wants you to format the names of the yoga teachers as a list, alphabetize it, and then add more information.

To convert the text to a list and sort it:

▶ **1.** If necessary, select the seven paragraphs containing the names of the yoga teachers, and then format the selected text as a bulleted list using the default bullet style.

▶ **2.** Select the bulleted list, and then, in the Paragraph group, click the **Sort** button. The Sort Text dialog box opens. This is similar to the dialog box you've already used several times before to sort tables. You want to sort the paragraphs in the list in ascending alphabetical order.

3. Verify that **Paragraphs** appears in the Sort by text box and that the **Ascending** option button is selected, and then click the **OK** button. The Sort Text dialog box closes, and the bulleted paragraphs are arranged alphabetically. The list begins with Aiden Connelly, unless your name comes alphabetically before "Aiden," in which case your name appears at the top of the list.

4. Save the document.

Now that the list is sorted, you need to add some more information about each teacher. When working with a bulleted or numbered list, you can indent items in the list. When you do, Word automatically applies a different bullet or numbering style to the indented item, to help create a visual distinction between the various levels of the list. Indenting an item in a numbered or bulleted list is known as **demoting** the item. Moving an item in a list back to the left is known as **promoting** the item. You'll see how this works in the following steps.

To add information to the list:

1. Click to the right of Aiden Connelly's name, and then press the **Enter** key to insert a new bulleted paragraph. The round, black bullet looks just like the other bullets in the list.

2. In the Paragraph group on the Home tab, click the **Increase Indent** button ▤. The bulleted paragraph is indented, and the bullet changes to a white bullet with a black outline.

3. Type **Specialties include Flow Yoga and Pilates**, and then press the **Enter** key to insert another bulleted paragraph. The new paragraph is indented at the same level as the previous paragraph, with the same style of bullet.

4. Click the **Increase Indent** button ▤. The bulleted paragraph is indented even more. The bullet changes to a black square.

5. Type **Flow Yoga is not recommended for beginners**, press the **Enter** key, and then type **Pilates requires four hours of individual instruction**.

6. Press the **Enter** key to insert a new bulleted paragraph, click the **Decrease Indent** button ▤ in the Paragraph group to promote the new bulleted paragraph, and then type **His classes are generally considered very challenging**. When you are finished, your bulleted list should look like the list in Figure 6-39. Nina's assistant will finish adding information to the bulleted list later. For now, you can save and close it.

Figure 6-39 | **Bulleted list with multiple levels**

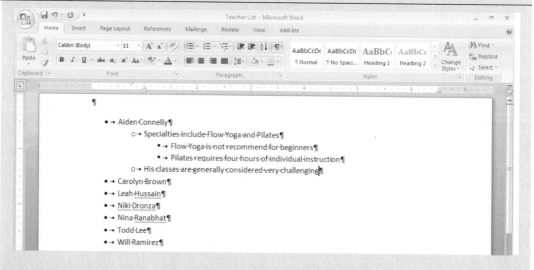

▶ **7.** Save the document and close it.

Session 6.2 Quick Check | Review

1. True or False: After you complete a mail merge and close the main document, the connection between the main document file and the data source file is broken.
2. Explain how to edit a data source for a main document that is already open.
3. Explain how to select records to merge.
4. When you create a directory with a dot leader, what do you have to do after you insert the merge field on the right side of the page?
5. True or False. You can convert data in a document to a table only if the individual pieces of data are separated by tabs.

Tutorial Summary | Review

In this tutorial, you opened the Mail Merge task pane and then completed a mail merge by selecting a main document, creating a data source, inserting merge fields into the main document, and merging the form letter with the data source. You then used the Mail Merge feature to create mailing labels and a telephone directory. In the process, you edited a data source and sorted records in a data source. Finally, you converted text to a table to create a new data source, and you converted a table to text, which you then formatted as a bulleted list with multiple levels.

Key Terms

chevrons	fields	merged document
data	form letter	promote
data source	Mail Merge task pane	record
date field	main document	sort
demote	merge	separator character
dot leader	merge fields	

| Practice | **Review Assignments** |

Apply the skills you learned in the tutorial using the same case scenario.

Data Files needed for the Review Assignments: Bonus.docx, Contacts.docx, More.docx

Nina's clients are happy with the new facility, and the open-studio days she offered in June were a big success. Nina was pleased with how convenient it was to send out form letters with the Word Mail Merge feature. Now she wants to send a letter inviting clients who have purchased an annual membership to sign up for their membership bonus—either a massage or a meditation session, depending on which option they selected when they purchased their membership. (*Note:* As you complete the following steps, print only those documents your instructor asks you to print.)

1. Start Word if necessary with a new, blank document, and then open the Mail Merge task pane.
2. Verify that Letters is selected as the type of main document, then in Step 2 of the Mail Merge Task pane, select the file **Bonus** in the Tutorial.06\Review folder included with your Data Files as the main document, and then save the current document as **Bonus Letter with Merge Fields** in the Tutorial.06\Review folder. In the letter's closing, replace Nina's name with yours.
3. In Step 3 of the Mail Merge task pane, create a new data source with the following fields: First Name, Last Name, Address Line 1, City, State, ZIP Code, and Bonus. Remove any extra fields so that the data source contains only seven fields.
4. Create four records using the following information (don't include the commas in the records; they are inserted here to help you see which text belongs in which fields):
    - Jane Cussler, 299 Hollister Street, Boise, ID, 83710, massage
    - May Simon, 922 Flambeau Road, Cloverdale, ID, 83712, meditation session
    - Carl Hesse, 933 Wildway Avenue, Beatty, ID, 83722, massage
    - William Greely, 52 Eton Way # 3, Boise, ID, 83714, meditation session
5. Save the data source as **Bonus Data** in the Tutorial.06\Review folder.
6. Edit the data source to replace "William Greely" with your first and last name.
7. Sort the data source by zip code from the lowest to the highest.
8. In Step 4 of the Mail Merge task pane, insert a date field in the format "March 7, 2010" at the top of the letter. Create an inside address consisting of the necessary merge fields; don't forget to use the Shift+Enter keys to prevent extra paragraph spacing. Add a salutation that includes the First Name merge field. Insert the Bonus field into the body of the letter where indicated. Add the appropriate number of blank paragraphs so the letter is formatted like a standard business letter. Insert blank paragraphs as necessary to center the letter vertically on the page.
9. Save your changes to the main document, and then preview the merged document. Correct any formatting or spacing problems.

10. In Step 6 of the Mail Merge task pane, merge to a new document and view all the letters. Save the merged document as **Merged Bonus Letters**, scroll to view the letters, and then close the file.

11. Return to Step 5 in the Mail Merge task pane, edit the data source to select only records for clients interested in a meditation session, and then complete a second merge. Save the new merged document as **Merged Meditation Letters**. Close all documents, saving all changes.

12. Open a new, blank document, open the Mail Merge task pane, and create a set of mailing labels using the vendor Avery US Letters and product number 5162. Save the main document as **Labels with Merge Fields** in the Tutorial.06\Review folder.

13. In Step 3 of the Mail Merge task pane, select the Bonus Data file you created earlier as the data source.

14. In Step 4 of the Mail Merge task pane, insert the necessary merge fields.

15. Update all the labels, preview the merged labels, merge all the records to a new document, and then save the new document as **Merged Labels** in the Tutorial.06\Review folder and close it. Save and close all open documents.

16. Create a telephone directory using the same format as the telephone directory you created in the tutorial. Use the file named **Contacts** from the Tutorial.06\Review folder as the data source. Set a right tab at six inches and use a dot leader. Save the main document as **Directory with Merge Fields** in the Tutorial.06\Review folder and the merged document as **Merged Directory** in the same folder. Close the files.

17. Open the document named **More** from the Tutorial.06\Review folder and save it as **More Bonus Data**. Convert the data in the document to a table. Insert a header row with the following column headers: First Name, Last Name, Street Address, City, State, ZIP Code, and Bonus. Replace "Sandy Martinez" with your name. Save and close the document.

18. Open the document named **Contacts** from the Tutorial.06\Review folder and save it as **Contacts Info** in the same folder. Delete the header row and the phone number column, and then convert the table to four paragraphs of text.

19. Format the company names as a bulleted list, and then add the extra information shown in Figure 6-40. Be sure to demote the subordinate bullets, as shown in Figure 6-40.

Figure 6-40

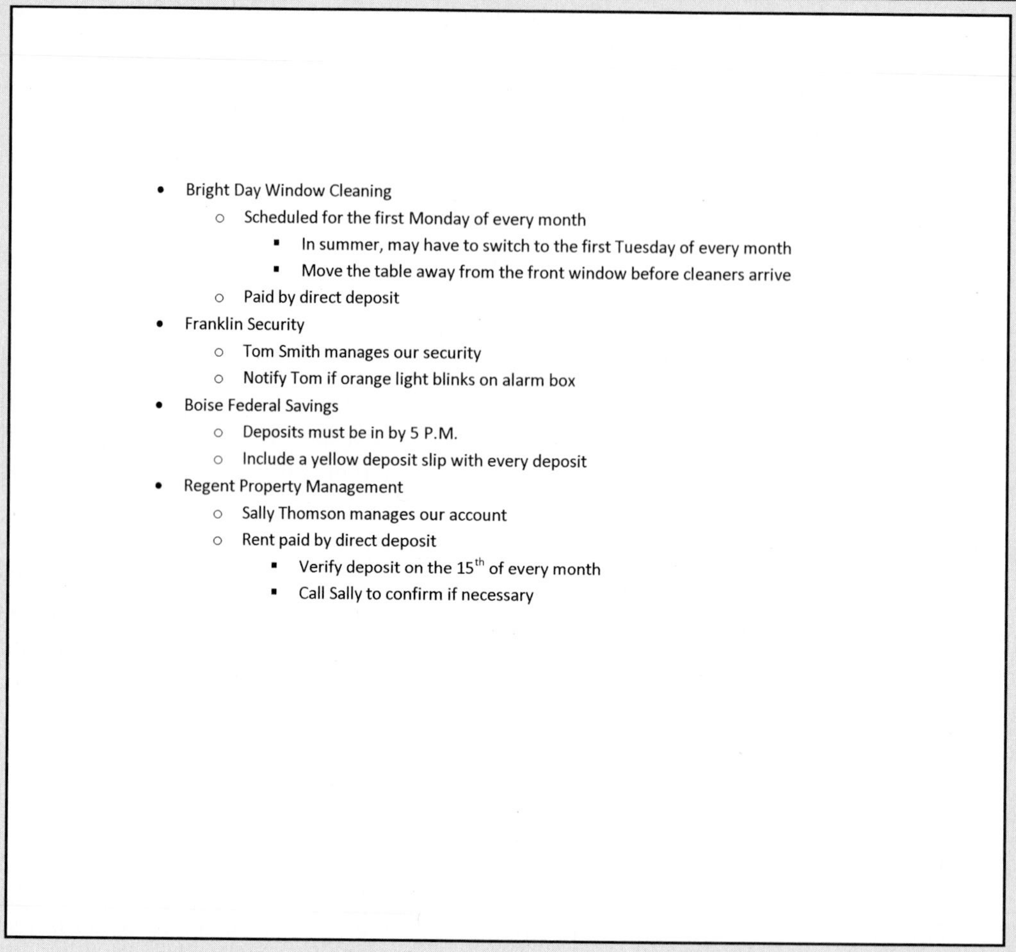

- Bright Day Window Cleaning
  - o Scheduled for the first Monday of every month
    - In summer, may have to switch to the first Tuesday of every month
    - Move the table away from the front window before cleaners arrive
  - o Paid by direct deposit
- Franklin Security
  - o Tom Smith manages our security
  - o Notify Tom if orange light blinks on alarm box
- Boise Federal Savings
  - o Deposits must be in by 5 P.M.
  - o Include a yellow deposit slip with every deposit
- Regent Property Management
  - o Sally Thomson manages our account
  - o Rent paid by direct deposit
    - Verify deposit on the 15th of every month
    - Call Sally to confirm if necessary

20. In the bullet under "Regent Property Management," change "Sally Thomson" to your name. Save and close the document.
21. Submit the documents to your instructor, either in printed or electronic form, as requested.

| Apply | **Case Problem 1** |

Apply the skills you learned to create a letter to customers of an art gallery.

Data File needed for this Case Problem: Gallery.docx

Nightingale Gallery Nell Williams owns Nightingale Gallery, a purveyor of fine art photography in Saginaw, Michigan. She wants to send out a letter to past customers informing them of an upcoming show by a local photographer. (*Note:* As you complete the following, print only those documents your instructor asks you to print.)

1. Open a new, blank document, and then begin a mail merge using Letters as the document type. For the starting document, select the document named **Gallery** from the Tutorial.06\Case1 folder, and then save it in the same folder as **Gallery Letter**. In the closing, replace "Student Name" with your name.
2. Create a data source with the following field names: Title, First Name, Last Name, Address Line1, ZIP Code, and E-mail Address.

3. Enter the following four records into the data source (don't include the commas in the records; they are inserted here to help you see what text belongs in what fields):
   - Mr., David, Joliet, 1577 Cooperville Drive, 48601, joliet@world.net
   - Mr., Paul, Robertson, 633 Wentworth, 48603, d_roberts@pmc.org
   - Ms., Maya, Suyemoto, 4424 Bedford, 48602, m_suyemoto@TaylorCulkins.com
   - Ms., Kira, Gascoyne, 844 Winter Way, 48601, gascoyne@saginaw.school.edu

4. Save the data source as **Gallery Data** in the Tutorial.06\Case1 folder, and then sort the records alphabetically by last name.

5. Edit the data source to replace "Kira Gascoyne" with your name. Change the title to "Mr." if necessary. Replace the e-mail address for that record with your e-mail address.

6. Add an inside address (use the Shift+Enter keys after each line) and a salutation to the document, using merge fields where necessary. Use "Saginaw, MI" as the city and state. Use the Title merge field and the Last Name merge field in the salutation.

7. Save your changes to the main document. Preview the merged document, and then merge to a new document. If you don't see the row of photographs at the top of the first letter, don't be concerned. You may not have a fast enough video card or enough memory to display them properly. After you close the document in the next step, and then re-open it, you will see the photographs on the first page.

8. Save the merged letters document as **Merged Gallery Letters** in the Tutorial.06\Case1 folder and then close it. If you did not see the photographs on the first page of the document in Step 7, re-open the document, verify that the photographs are properly displayed, and then close the document again.

9. Close the **Gallery Letter** document, saving any changes.

10. Open a new blank document, save it as **Gallery Envelopes** in the Tutorial.06\Case1 folder, and then open the Mail Merge task pane.

⊕ EXPLORE   11. Use the Mail Merge task pane to create envelopes, as follows:
   - In Step 1 of the Mail Merge task pane, select Envelopes as the type of main document.
   - In Step 2 of the Mail Merge task pane, verify that the Change document layout option button is selected, and then click Envelope options. In the Envelope Options dialog box, verify that Envelope size 10 ($4\frac{1}{8} \times 9\frac{1}{2}$ in) is selected in the Envelope size box, and then click the OK button.
   - In Step 3 of the Mail Merge task pane, select the **Gallery Data** file you created earlier as the data source.
   - In Step 4 of the Mail Merge task pane, click the recipient address area of the envelope, and then insert the necessary merge fields to print a title, first name, last name, and street address and zip code on each envelope. For the city and state, use "Saginaw, MI."
   - In Step 5, preview the merged envelopes.
   - In Step 6, merge to a new document, and then save the document as **Merged Gallery Envelopes**.

12. Close all open documents, saving changes as necessary.

13. Create a customer e-mail directory that includes first and last names but not titles. Use the file named **Gallery Data** (which you created earlier) as the data source. Do not include the record for David Joliet in the merge. Use a dot leader, with the right tab stop set at the 6-inch mark, to separate the name on the left from the e-mail address on the right.

14. Save the main document for the e-mail directory as **E-mail Directory** in the Tutorial.06\Case1 folder.

15. Save the merged document as **Merged E-mail Directory** in the Tutorial.06\Case1 folder.

16. Save and close all open documents. Submit the documents to your instructor, in either printed or electronic form, as requested.

Apply | **Case Problem 2**

Apply the skills you learned to create a form letter for a mortgage company using an Excel file as a data source.

Data Files needed for this Case Problem: Mortgage.docx, Mortgage Data.xlsx

Lensville Mortgage Corporation   As an account manager at Lensville Mortgage Corporation, you need to send out letters to past customers asking them to consider refinancing with a new loan. Your data source for this case problem is in an Excel file. (*Note:* As you work on this Case Problem, print only those documents your instructor asks you to print.)

1. Open a new, blank document, and begin a mail merge using Letters as the document type. For the starting document, select the document named **Mortgage** from the Tutorial.06\Case2 folder, and then save it in the same folder as **Mortgage Letter**. In the closing, replace "Student Name" with your name.

⊕ **EXPLORE**   2. For the data source, select the Excel file **Mortgage Data** from the Tutorial.06\Case2 folder.

3. Edit the data source to replace "Barb Russ" with your name.

4. At the beginning of the main document, insert a date field.

5. Insert an Address Block merge field for the inside address in the form "Joshua Randall Jr.," and format the Address block merge field using the No Spacing Quick Style. Insert a salutation using the First Name merge field. Use a proper business-letter format throughout.

6. In the body of the letter, replace the placeholders [NUMBER OF YEARS], [CURRENT LOAN TERM], and [NEW LOAN TERM] with the appropriate merge fields.

7. Open the Mail Merge Recipients dialog box, and then sort the records in ascending order by Current Loan Term.

8. Preview the merged document, and then merge to a new document. Save the merged document as **Merged Mortgage Letters** in the Tutorial.06\Case2 folder.

9. Close all open documents, saving all changes.

10. Create a main document for generating mailing labels on sheets of Avery US Letter Address labels, product number 5162, using the **Mortgage Data** file as your data source. Use the same Address Block merge field code that you used for the inside address of the Mortgage Letter file. Save the main document as **Mortgage Labels** in the Tutorial.06\Case2 folder.

11. Preview the merged document, merge to a new document, and then save the merged document as **Merged Mortgage Labels** in the Tutorial.06\Case2 folder. Close all open documents, saving any changes.

⊕ **EXPLORE**   12. Use Word Help to look up the topic "Use mail merge to create and print letters and other documents" and learn how to filter records in a data source. Open your **Mortgage Letter** file from the Tutorial.06\Case2 folder (click Yes if you are asked to run an SQL command), and save it as **Mortgage Letter Filtered**. Start a mail merge, and then select the **Mortgage Data** file as the data source. Use what you learned from Help to filter out all records except records for customers in Fort Myers. You should end up with two records displayed in the Mail Merge Recipients dialog box.

13. Preview the merged document, and then complete the merge to a new document. Save the merged document as **Merged Fort Myers** in the Tutorial.06\Case2 folder.

14. Close all open documents, saving any changes. Submit the documents to your instructor, in either printed or electronic form, as requested.

Challenge | Case Problem 3

Perform a mail merge using the Mailings tab instead of the Mail Merge task pane.

Data Files needed for this Case Problem: Letter.docx, Pasta.txt

Fierenze Pasta   Kayla Souza is manager of Fierenze, a manufacturer of fresh pasta in Racine, Wisconsin. Fierenze has just bought out a competitor, JD Pasta. Now Kayla wants to send a letter to JD Pasta's longtime customers, who she hopes will become Fierenze customers. She wants to use Word's mail merge feature to create a letter that informs each customer of the price of his or her favorite type of pasta. Kayla retrieved the customer data from the JD Pasta's computer system in the form of a text file, with the data fields separated by commas. Kayla needs your help to convert the text file to a Word table, which she can then use as the data source for a mail merge. (*Note:* As you complete the following steps, print only those documents your instructor asks you to print.)

✪ EXPLORE

1. In Word, open the text file named **Pasta.txt** from the Tutorial.06\Case3 folder. To find the text file in the Open dialog box, click the arrow next to the Files of type list box, and then click All Files. Once the file is open, save it as a Word document (in the Save As dialog box, click Word document in the Files of type list box) in the same folder using the filename **Pasta Data**.

2. Format the data in the Normal style, and then convert it to a table. Insert your first and last name where indicated. Insert a header row with the following column headers: First Name, Last Name, Street Address, City, State, ZIP Code, Type, and Price. Save the document and close it.

3. Open the file **Letter** from the Tutorial.06\Case3 folder, and then save it as **Pasta Letter** in the same folder. In the closing, replace "Student Name" with your first and last name.

✪ EXPLORE

4. Begin a mail merge using the buttons on the Mailings tab instead of the Mail Merge task pane. Start by using the Start Mail Merge button to create a letter main document using the current document. As you perform the remaining steps in this case problem, continue to use the options on the Mailings tab rather than the Mail Merge task pane.

5. Use the Select Recipients button to select the **Pasta Data** document as the data source, and then use the Edit Recipient List button to sort the records in ascending alphabetical order by type of pasta.

6. Insert a date field where indicated by the brackets at the top of the document, and then use the Insert Merge Field button to replace the placeholder text that appears in brackets with an inside address.

✪ EXPLORE

7. For the salutation, experiment with the Greeting Line button on the Mailings tab. Use the Greeting Line dialog box to insert a salutation that includes "Dear" and the customer's first name, followed by a colon.

8. Edit the body of the form letter to replace the placeholder text with the corresponding merge field names.

9. Save the document. Use the Preview Results button to view the merged document, and then use the Finish & Merge button to merge all the records to a new document. Save the merged document as **Merged Pasta Letters** in the Tutorial.06\Case3 folder.

10. Close all open documents, saving changes as necessary. Submit the documents to your instructor, in either printed or electronic form, as requested.

Create | **Case Problem 4**

Use the skills you learned in the tutorial to create the list shown in Figure 6-41.

There are no Data Files needed for this Case Problem.

Chronos Steel Corporation As a public relations specialist at Chronos Steel Corporation, you are often asked to explain the process of making steel to a general audience. To save time, you have decided to create a handout that summarizes the process. (*Note:* As you complete the following steps, print only those documents your instructor asks you to print.)

Figure 6-41

Steel Production

➢ Raw materials
  ○ Usually three components
    ▪ Iron ore
    ▪ Limestone
    ▪ Coke
      • Coke is a byproduct of coal
      • Created when coal is baked at a high temperature to purify it
  ○ Raw materials can vary by manufacturer
➢ Raw materials are heated in a blast furnace
➢ Slag floats to top and is drained, leaving molten iron suitable for steel
➢ Molten iron is transformed into steel
  ○ Molten iron is mixed with scrap metals
  ○ The iron and scrap metals are heated in an oxygen furnace
  ○ The resulting liquid steel is formed into slabs
➢ Slabs are milled to desired thickness and treated with acid

1. Open a new, blank document, save it as **Steel Handout** in the Tutorial.06\Case4 folder, and then change the document theme to Verve.

2. Type the multilevel bulleted list shown in Figure 6-41; don't specify the bullet type yet. Format the title, "Steel Production," in the Heading 1 style and center it.

✛ EXPLORE

3. Click in the "Raw Materials" bulleted paragraph, and then select the arrow bullet style to change all the top-level bullets to the arrow style.

EXPLORE

4. In Word Help, look up *bullets* and then read the topic that explains how to add picture bullets or symbols to a list. Use what you learned to change the second-level bullets (the first of which is "Usually three components") from a white circle to an orange square. Then change the third-level bullets (the first of which is "Iron ore") to green squares and the lowest level bullets to brown squares.

5. Save your changes to the document, and then save it as **Numbered Handout** in the same folder so that you can change the bullets to numbering in the next step.

6. Select the bulleted list and use the Numbering button to format it as a numbered list instead. The multiple levels of the new numbered list are numbered in outline form.

7. Delete items 1.a and 1.b, but not the items under 1.a.

 EXPLORE

8. Using the same technique you used to promote items in a bulleted list, promote the three paragraphs containing the three raw materials so they are lettered a, b, and c. Promote the two items about coke so they are numbered i and ii.

9. Save the document and close it. Submit the documents to your instructor, in either printed or electronic form, as requested.

Research | Internet Assignments

Go to the Web to find information you can use to create documents.

The purpose of the Internet Assignments is to challenge you to find information on the Internet that you can use to work effectively with this software. The actual assignments are updated and maintained on the Course Technology Web site. Log on to the Internet and use your Web browser to go to the Student Online Companion for New Perspectives Office 2007 at **www.course.com/np/office2007**. Then navigate to the Internet Assignments for this tutorial.

Assess | SAM Assessment and Training

If you have a SAM user profile, you may have access to hands-on instruction, practice, and assessment of the skills covered in this tutorial. Log in to your SAM account (**http://sam2007.course.com**) to launch any assigned training activities or exams that relate to the skills covered in this tutorial.

Session 6.1

1. a. A date field is an instruction that tells Word to insert the current date.
    b. A main document is a document (such as a letter) that, in addition to text, contains merge fields to mark where variable information (such as a name or an address) from the data source will be inserted.
    c. A merge field is a code in a main document that tells Word where to insert specific information from the data source.
    d. A record is a collection of information about one individual or object in a data source. For example, a record might include the first name, last name, address, and phone number for a client.
2. data source
3. True
4. False
5. Position the insertion point in the main document where you want to insert the merge field. Click More Items in the Mail Merge task pane, click the field you want to insert in the Insert Merge Field dialog box, click Insert, and then click Close. Alternately, in the Write & Insert Fields group on the Mailings tab, click the Insert Merge Field button, and then click the field you want to insert. Adjust the spacing or formatting around the merge field as necessary.
6. Click the Insert tab, and then, in the Text group, click the Date and Time button. In the Date and Time dialog box, click the date format you want, select the Update automatically check box, and then click the OK button.

Session 6.2

1. False
2. In the Start Mail Merge group on the Mailings tab, click the Edit Recipient List button. In the Data Source list box in the Mail Merge Recipients dialog box, select the data source you want to edit, and then click the Edit button. To add a record, click the New Entry button, and then type a new record. To delete a record, click any field in the record, and then click the Delete Entry button. To add or remove fields from the data source, click the Customize Columns button, and make any changes.
3. Click the Edit Recipients button in the Start Mail Merge group on the Mailings tab and then deselect the check boxes for the records you do not want to include in the merge.
4. Press the Enter key to insert a blank paragraph below the directory merge fields.
5. False

Ending Data Files

Tutorial.06 → **Tutorial**

Carolyn Letter with
  Merge Fields.docx
Client Table.docx
Phone Data.docx
Phone Directory.docx
Phone Directory with
  Merge Fields.docx
Teacher List.docx
Yoga Data.mdb
Yoga Labels with
  Merge Fields.docx
Yoga Letter with
  Merge Fields.docx
Yoga Merged Labels.docx
Yoga Merged Letters 1.docx
Yoga Merged Letters 2.docx
Yoga Merged Letters 3.docx

Review

Bonus Data.mdb
Bonus Letter with
  Merge Fields.docx
Contacts.docx
Contacts Info.docx
Directory with
  Merge Fields.docx
Labels with
  Merge Fields.docx
Merged Bonus Letters.docx
Merged Directory.docx
Merged Labels.docx
Merged Meditation
  Letters.docx
More Bonus Data.docx

Case1

E-mail Directory.docx
Gallery Data.mdb
Gallery Envelopes.docx
Gallery Letter.docx
Merged E-mail Directory.docx
Merged Gallery Envelopes.docx
Merged Gallery Letters.docx

Case2

Merged Fort Myers.docx
Merged Mortgage Labels.docx
Merged Mortgage Letters.docx
Mortgage Data.xlsx
Mortgage Labels.docx
Mortgage Letter.docx
Mortgage Letter Filtered.docx

Case3

Merged Pasta Letters.docx
Pasta Data.docx
Pasta Letter.docx

Case4

Numbered Handout.docx
Steel Handout.docx

Objectives

Session 7.1
- Track changes in a document
- Insert and delete comments
- Accept and reject changes
- Compare and combine documents
- Embed and modify an Excel worksheet
- Link an Excel chart
- Modify and update a linked chart

Session 7.2
- Modify a document for online distribution
- Insert and edit hyperlinks
- Use Web Layout view
- Save a Word document as a Web page
- Format a Web document
- View a Web document in a Web browser

Collaborating with Others and Creating Web Pages

Writing a Program Description

Case | Green Fields Fresh Lunch Program

Zoe Rios is the owner and president of Rios Communications in Dubuque, Iowa, a public relations company that specializes in developing publicity documents and Web sites. She is currently working on a program description for Green Fields, an organization that is devoted to improving the quality of meals served in area schools.

As a professional writer, Zoe knows the importance of writing and revising several drafts of a document, and she knows it's vital to ask her clients and colleagues to review her documents and make suggestions. As a first step, she asked Henry Davis, a writer at Rios Communications, to review a draft of the program description. He will read the document in Word, make some corrections, and insert some comments. While Henry is revising the program description, Zoe has asked you to work on it, making additional changes. When you are finished, Zoe wants you to merge Henry's edited version of the document with your most recent draft.

After you create a new version of the document for Zoe, she wants you to add some budget figures compiled by Alison Jorgenson, the Program Director for the Green Fields organization. She also needs you to add a pie chart created by Henry. When you are finished, she wants you to e-mail the program description to Alison. Finally, to make the program description available to the organization's members, she asks for your help to distribute it in printed form and publish it on her company's Web site.

Starting Data Files

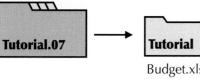

Tutorial.07 →	Tutorial	Review	Case1	Case2	Case3	Case4
	Budget.xlsx	Expenses.xlsx	Cook.docx	Kreelie.docx	Survey.xlsx	FAQ.docx
	Chart.xlsx	Menu.docx	Statement.xlsx	Sun.docx		
	Green.docx	Progress.docx				
	Green Fields HD.docx	Progress HD.docx				
	Resume.docx	Rates.xlsx				

Session 7.1

Tracking Changes and Making Comments in a Document

When you edit a printed copy of a document, it's common to use a brightly colored pen to draw lines through words or phrases you want to delete. You might write new text in the margin and then draw a line to the place in the document where you want to insert the text. You might also write notes to yourself or the writer in the margin, reminding you about facts you need to check or suggesting new sections for the writer to add. The problem with this revision method is that after you finish marking up the printed copy, you or the writer must go back to the computer and enter your changes into the document. In a long document, this can be very time-consuming. Instead of writing marks on a printed copy, it's more efficient to use Microsoft Word's Track Changes feature and the Comments feature.

Tracking Changes

When you turn on **Track Changes**, Word uses a variety of ways to mark the changes you make to the document. Any text that you insert appears in a contrasting color, with an underline. Text that you delete appears with a strikeout line, just as if you'd drawn a line through it on the printed page. If you make formatting changes, they are listed in the margin in oblong boxes known as **balloons**. In addition, a vertical line appears in the left margin next to text that has been changed in any way. Collectively, the colored text, the strikeout lines, the margin balloons, and the vertical margin lines are known as **revision marks**.

You can use the mouse to point to any marked revision in a document; this displays a ScreenTip that indicates who made the change and the date and time the change was made. By default, the name assigned to each change is taken from the User name text box on the Popular tab of the Word Options dialog box. This indication of who made a particular edit is especially useful when you are sharing revisions among a group of reviewers.

When you feel confident about the changes you or someone else has made to your document, you can accept the changes, at which point Word removes the revision marks from your document. You can accept all the changes at once, or you can go through them one by one, accepting or rejecting each one individually. When you reject a change, depending on what change you are rejecting, Word removes the text you inserted, or undoes the formatting you applied, or restores the text you deleted.

The Review tab contains all the options you need for working with track changes. Among other things, you can use the options on the Review tab to move from one change to another, to accept or reject changes, and to hide revision marks. When you hide revision marks, Word continues to track changes, but doesn't display them on the screen.

Reference Window | **Tracking Changes in a Document**

- Verify that the document is displayed in Print Layout view, click the Review tab, and then in the Tracking group, click the Track Changes button.
- Verify that Final Showing Markup is displayed in the Display for Review list box in the Tracking group.
- Edit the document as you ordinarily would. Adjust the document zoom as necessary, so you can easily see tracked changes in the document and in the margin.

Working with Comments

In addition to making changes to a document, you can also insert margin notes known as **comments**. You can attach a comment to a selected word, phrase, or paragraph. Text to which a comment has been attached is highlighted in a contrasting color so that you can easily see what the comment refers to. You type the text of your comment in a balloon that appears in the right margin. In addition to the text of your comment, the comment balloon displays the name of the person who made the comment, as well as the date and time it was made. As with tracked changes, the name assigned to each comment is taken from the User name text box on the Popular tab of the Word Options dialog box.

Although comments are often used in conjunction with the tracked changes, you don't have to turn on Track Changes in order to insert comments in a document. They are separate features. The Review tab contains all the options you need for working with Comments.

Inserting Comments | Reference Window

- Select the text to which you want to attach a comment.
- Click the Review tab, and then in the Comments group, click the New Comment button.
- Type the text of your comment in the balloon that appears in the margin.
- Adjust the document zoom as necessary so you can read the document text as well as the comment balloons in the margin.

Revising a Document with Tracked Changes and Comments

Zoe has already e-mailed a copy of her document to Henry. He will review it for her while she makes some additional changes. She decides to turn on Track Changes before she begins making these additional changes so she will have a record of the changes she makes after sending the file to Henry.

To edit Zoe's document with Track Changes turned on:

▶ 1. Open the document named **Green** from the Tutorial.07\Tutorial folder included with your Data Files, and then save it as **Green Fields** in the same folder.

▶ 2. Switch to Print Layout view if necessary, display nonprinting characters, and change the document zoom to Page width. There's no need to display the ruler.

▶ 3. Review the document, and notice that it includes three headings formatted with the Heading 1 style for the Office theme. The first heading in the document is not formatted in a heading style; instead it is simply formatted in the heading font (Cambria) and in blue. Page 1 includes two placeholders in brackets, which you will eventually replace with an Excel chart and an Excel worksheet. Also notice the photograph on page 2.

▶ 4. Click the **Review** tab, and then in the Tracking group, click the **Track Changes** button. (Do not click the Track Changes button arrow.) The Track Changes button is highlighted in orange, indicating that the Track Changes feature is turned on. You won't see any revision marks until you begin editing the document.

Trouble? If a menu appears below the Track Changes button, you clicked the Track Changes button arrow by mistake. Press the Escape key to close the menu, and then click the Track Changes button.

5. In the Tracking group, verify that Final Showing Markup appears in the Display for Review list box. This is a default setting which tells Word to display the revision marks on the screen. See Figure 7-1.

Figure 7-1 | **Track Changes turned on**

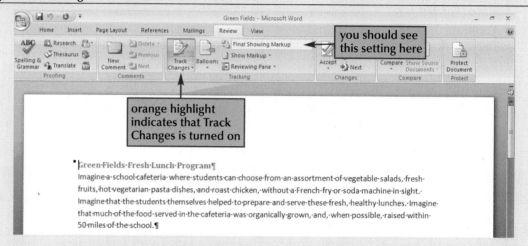

You'll start by making a change in the first main paragraph.

6. In the paragraph below the first heading, select the number **50** in the last sentence, and then type **100**. A strikeout line appears through the number 50, and the new number, 100, appears in color. In Figure 7-2, the number 100 is red, but depending on how your computer is set up, it might be a different color. The new number is also underlined, and a vertical line appears in the left margin, drawing attention to the change.

Figure 7-2 | **Edit with revision marks turned on**

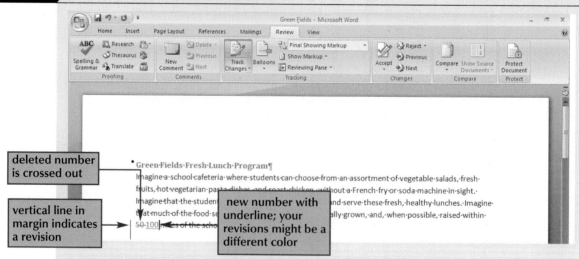

Next, you need to move a sentence. Zoe wants the second to last sentence in this paragraph to be the last sentence in the paragraph.

7. Select the sentence **Imagine that the students themselves helped to prepare and serve these fresh, healthy lunches.** Take care to select the space after the sentence as well.

8. Drag the sentence down to insert it at the end of the paragraph, and then click anywhere in the document to deselect it. The sentence is inserted with a double underline, in color. This time the color is different from the one used for the number "100" earlier, because Word uses a separate color to denote moved text. In Figure 7-3, the sentence appears in green, but it might be a different color on your computer. The sentence is still visible in its original location, but now it is also displayed in color, with a double strikeout line through it. A vertical line appears in the left margin, next to the sentence in its original location, and also next to the sentence in its new location. When you inserted the sentence, Word automatically deleted the space after it and added a space before it, to the left of the "I" in "Imagine."

Tracked changes showing text moved to a new location ◄ **Figure 7-3**

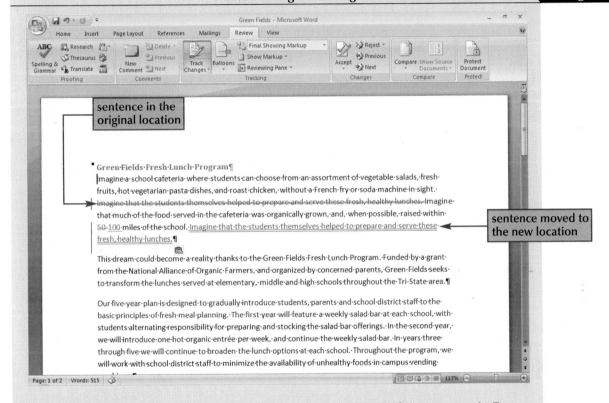

After reviewing the sentence in its new location at the end of the paragraph, Zoe decides she wants to shorten it slightly by deleting the word "healthy."

9. Click to the left of the comma after "fresh," and then press the **Delete** key repeatedly to delete the comma, the space after it, and the word **healthy**. The deleted text ", healthy" appears with a strikeout line through it, so that the sentence reads "...serve these fresh lunches."

Finally, you need to format the first heading in the document with the Heading 1 style.

10. Click in the left margin to select the heading **Green Fields Fresh Lunch Program**, click the **Home** tab, and then click the **Heading 1** style in the Quick Styles gallery. The heading is formatted with the larger font size of the Heading 1 style, a vertical line appears in the left margin next to the heading, and a balloon appears in the right margin containing the text "Formatted: Heading 1," indicating that you formatted the paragraph with the Heading 1 style. Because you selected Page width zoom earlier, the document zoom automatically adjusts to allow you to see the document text as well as the balloon in the right margin. See Figure 7-4.

Figure 7-4 **Tracked changes showing formatted text**

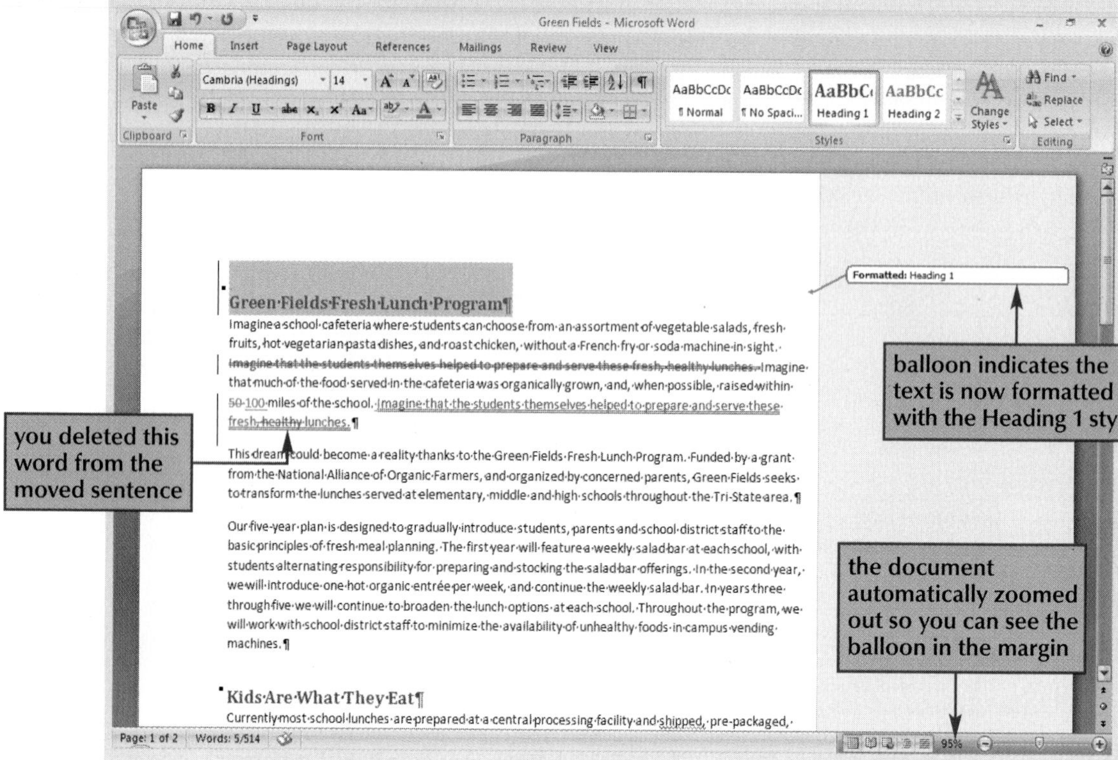

You are finished editing the document for now. For each edit, Word noted the current user name for the copy of Word on your computer, as well as the current date and time. You can display this information by moving the mouse pointer over one of your edits.

To display a ScreenTip that indicates the user name, date, and time for an edit:

1. Move the mouse pointer over the newly inserted number **100**. A ScreenTip appears displaying the type of edit (an insertion), the user name for the copy of Word in which the edit was made, and the date and time the edit was made. In Figure 7-5, the user name is Zoe Rios, but you should see either your name or another name. See Figure 7-5. Later in this tutorial you will learn how to change the user name.

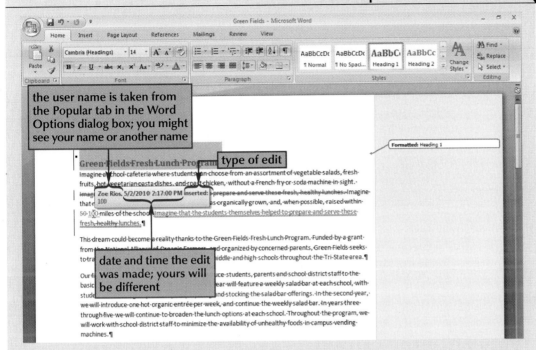

2. Move the mouse pointer over the moved sentence, the deleted sentence, and the newly formatted heading, and review the ScreenTip that appears over each edit.

Zoe would like you to add a comment in the Budget section on page 2.

To add a comment to page 2:

1. Scroll down until you can see the Budget section on the top of page 2. The second sentence says that a complete budget will be available soon. Zoe wants to include a reminder to be more precise, if possible, about exactly when the full budget will be ready. She wants to attach the comment to the word "soon," so you start by selecting that word.

2. At the end of the Budget section, select the word **soon**.

3. Click the **Review** tab, and then in the Comments group click the **New Comment** button. The word "soon" is highlighted in color, a balloon is inserted in the right margin, and the insertion point moves to the balloon, ready for you to begin typing the comment. In Figure 7-6, the highlighting and the balloon are red, but they might be a different color on your computer. Also, in Figure 7-6, you see "Comment [ZR1]." The letters "ZR" are Zoe's initials; the number 1 after the initials tells you that this is the first comment inserted by Zoe Rios. On your computer, you see your initials or some other set of initials, depending on the settings on the Popular tab of the Word Options dialog box.

Figure 7-6   **Inserting a comment**

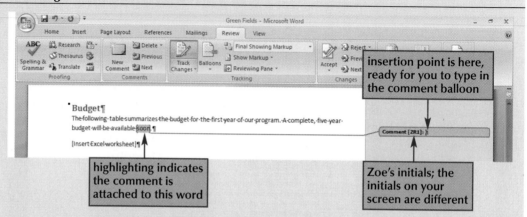

highlighting indicates the comment is attached to this word

insertion point is here, ready for you to type in the comment balloon

Zoe's initials; the initials on your screen are different

▶ **4.** With the insertion point in the comment balloon, as shown in Figure 7-6, type **Can we give a precise date for the new budget?** The comment is displayed in the balloon in the right margin. The insertion point remains in the comment balloon until you click in the document.

▶ **5.** Click anywhere in the document text, and then save your work.

Adjusting Track Changes Options

The default settings for Track Changes worked well as you edited Zoe's document. Note, however, that you can change these settings if you prefer. For instance, you could select a larger balloon for comments or a different color for inserted text. You could also change the user name that appears in the ScreenTip for each edit. You don't need to change any options now, but you will take a moment to learn how to change them, in case you want to later.

To learn how to change the Track Changes options:

▶ **1.** Click the **Track Changes** button arrow. A menu appears below the Track Changes button.

Trouble? If you don't see a menu and if the Track Changes button is now deselected, you clicked the Track Changes button rather than the arrow below it. Click the Track Changes button again to select it, and then click the Track Changes button arrow to open the menu.

Tip

You can also open the Popular tab of the Word Options dialog box by clicking the Office Button and then clicking the Word Options button.

▶ **2.** Click **Change User Name**. The Popular tab of the Word Options dialog box opens. You've seen this tab before, when you used the Word Options dialog box to adjust Word settings. The User name text box on the Popular tab contains the current user name for the copy of Word installed on your computer. This is the name that appears in the ScreenTip associated with each edit when Track Changes is turned on. The letters in the Initials text box are the initials that appear in comment balloons. Do not change the user name or initials now. Simply note their location, and keep in mind that when you are working on your own computer, you should make sure the User name text box contains your full name, and that the Initials text box contains your initials.

▶ **3.** Click the **Cancel** button to close the Word Options dialog box. You return to the Green Fields document.

4. Click the **Track Changes** arrow to display the menu again, and then click **Change Tracking Options**. The Track Changes Options dialog box opens. As shown in Figure 7-7, you can use the options in the Balloons section to control the size and location of the balloons in the margins. Other options in this dialog box allow you to select the colors you want to use for various types of edits. For example, you can use the Color list box next to the Insertions list box to select a color to use for inserted text. Note that the default setting for Insertions, Deletions, Comments, and Formatting is By author. This means that Word assigns one color to each person who edits the document. You'll see the significance of that later in this tutorial, when you merge your copy of the document with Henry's. Finally, note that you can deselect the Track moves check box or the Track formatting check box if you don't want to track those types of changes. Right now there's no need to change any of the settings in the Track Changes Options dialog box, so you can close it.

Examining the Track Changes Options dialog box ◀ **Figure 7-7**

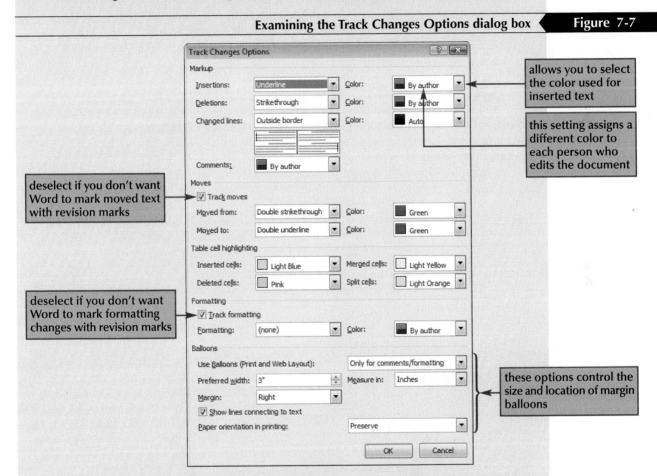

allows you to select the color used for inserted text

this setting assigns a different color to each person who edits the document

deselect if you don't want Word to mark moved text with revision marks

deselect if you don't want Word to mark formatting changes with revision marks

these options control the size and location of margin balloons

5. Click the **Cancel** button to close the Track Changes Options dialog box, and then click the **Balloons** button in the Tracking group. A menu opens, displaying options related to the way tracked changes are displayed in margin balloons. Currently, "Show Only Comments and Formatting in Balloons" is selected. To hide the margin balloons, you could click Show All Revisions Inline. To display a margin balloon for every edit (including insertions, moves, and deletions), you could click Show Revisions in Balloons. Right now, there's no need to change the default setting.

6. Press the **Escape** key to close the Balloons menu.

You are finished making Zoe's additional changes in the document. She has received Henry's edited copy via e-mail, and now she'd like your help in combining her copy of the Green Fields document with Henry's.

Comparing and Combining Documents

When you work in a collaborative environment, where multiple people work on the same document, Word's Compare and Combine features are essential tools. They allow you to compare documents, with revision marks highlighting the differences. The Compare and Combine features are similar, but they have different purposes.

Use the **Compare** feature when you have two different versions of a document that do not contain revision marks and you want to see the differences between the two. Use the **Combine** feature when you have two or more versions of a document that contain revision marks, which you want to combine into a single document. Note that it's also common to use the term **merge** rather than "combine" when talking about combining documents. However, keep in mind that merging, when used in this context, is different from the mail merge operation you learned about earlier.

When you compare two documents, you select one document as the original document and one as the revised document. Word then creates a new, third document, which consists of the original document with revision marks added to show how the revised document differs from the original document. The original document and the revised document are left unchanged.

For example, suppose the original document contains the sentence "The sky is blue." Also, suppose that in the revised document, the sentence reads "The sky is dark blue." When you compare these two documents, you create a third document where the sentence looks like you took the original document, turned on revision marks, and inserted the word "dark." See Figure 7-8.

| Figure 7-8 | Comparing two documents |

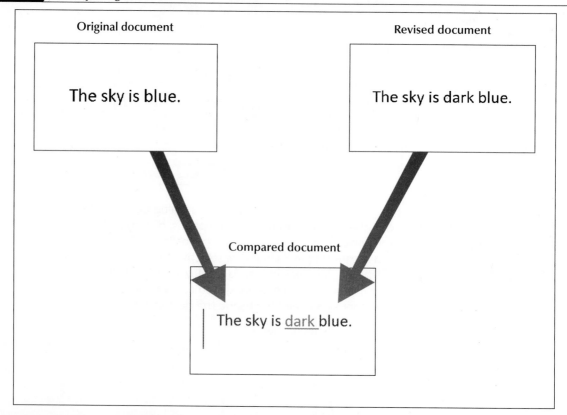

As when comparing documents, when you combine documents, you start by selecting one document as the original document and the other document as the revised document. Word then creates a new document that contains the revision marks from both the original document and the revised document. If you want, you can then take this new document and combine it with a third. In this way, you can continue, incorporating changes from as many authors as you want.

Comparing and Combining Documents | Reference Window

- With any document open in Word, click the Compare button in the Compare group on the Review tab.
- Click either Compare (to open the Compare Documents dialog box) or Combine (to open the Combine Documents dialog box). Except for their names, the two dialog boxes are identical.
- Next to the Original document list box, click the Browse for Original button, navigate to the location of the document, select the document, and then click the Open button.
- Next to the Revised document list box, click the Browse for Revised button, navigate to the location of the document, select the document, and then click the Open button.
- Click the More button, if necessary, to display options that allow you to select which items you want marked with revision marks. If the Less button is visible, these options are already displayed.
- Select or deselect any options as necessary. Verify that the New document option button is selected in the Show changes in list.
- Click the OK button, and then review the revision marks in the new document. Most likely you will want to save the combined or compared document.

You are ready to combine your document with Henry's. When you start combining or comparing documents, it doesn't matter what document is currently open in Word. It's not even necessary to have either the original document or the revised document open. In this case, the Green Fields document, which you will use as the original document, is currently open.

To combine your document with Henry's document:

▶ 1. Verify that you have saved your changes to the **Green Fields** document.

▶ 2. In the Compare group, click the **Compare** button. A menu opens. Here, you could click Compare if you wanted to compare two documents. However, you want to combine two documents, not compare them.

▶ 3. Click **Combine**. The Combine Documents dialog box opens. If you see a Less button, you also see a number of check boxes in the lower part of the document, which you can use to specify which items you want marked with revision marks. If you see a More button, you need to display these options.

▶ 4. If it is visible, click the **More** button. If the Less button is showing, skip this step. If you didn't see the check boxes earlier, you see them now. See Figure 7-9.

Figure 7-9 **Combine Documents dialog box**

Browse for
Original button

options in bottom
half of dialog box
control which items
will be marked by
revision marks

Browse for
Revised button

this default option tells
Word to create a new,
combined document

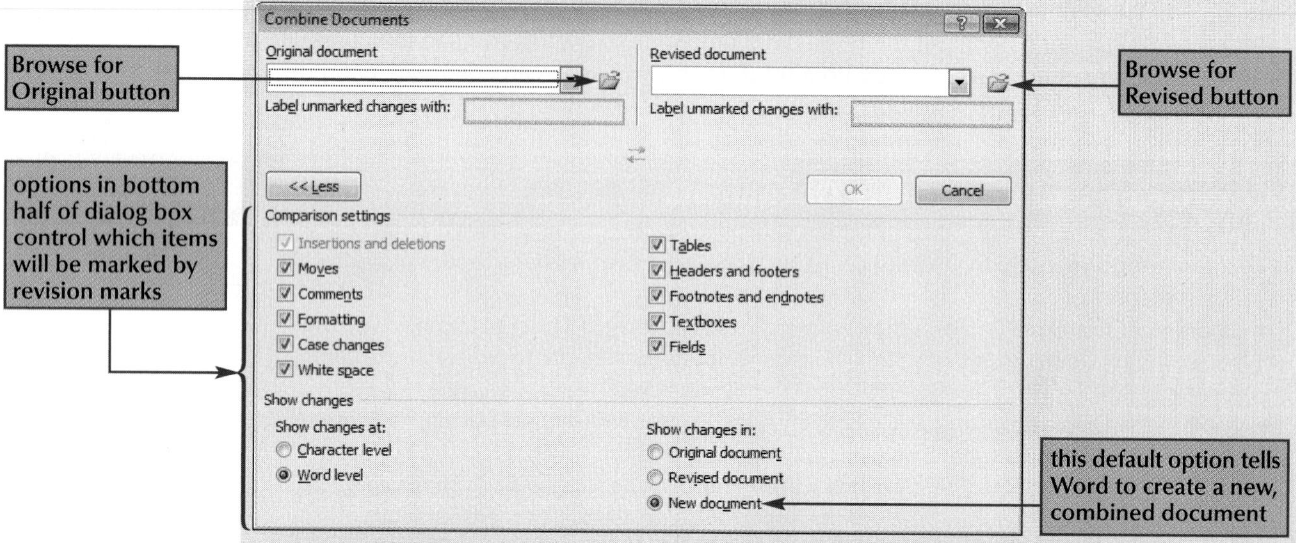

Note especially the New document option button, in the lower-right corner of the dialog box, which is selected by default. This tells Word to create a new, combined document, rather than importing the revision marks from the original document into the revised document, or vice versa. There's no reason to change any of the default options, so you can proceed with selecting the document you want to use as the original document. In this case, you want to use the Green Fields document as the original document. Even though this document is currently displayed on the screen, you need to select it.

▶ **5.** Next to the Original document list box, click the **Browse for Original** button 📷. This opens an Open dialog box that is identical to the Open dialog box you have used many times before.

▶ **6.** Use the options in the Open dialog box to select the **Green Fields** document from the Tutorial.07\Tutorial folder included with your Data Files, and then click the **Open** button. You return to the Combine Documents dialog box, where the filename "Green Fields" now appears in the Original document list box. In the "Label unmarked changes with" text box, you see the user name from the Popular tab of the Word options dialog box. When you combine the documents, the edits you made earlier will be marked with this user name. Next, you need to select the document you want to use as the revised document. Henry took the file named "Green Fields" that Zoe sent to him earlier, and added his initials to the file name, to create the filename "Green Fields HD." This file is included with your Data Files.

▶ **7.** Next to the Revised document list box, click the **Browse for Revised** button 📷, use the options in the Open dialog box to navigate to and select the file named **Green Fields HD** in the Tutorial.07\Tutorial folder included with your Data Files, and then click the **Open** button. The filename "Green Fields HD" appears in the Revised document list box, and Henry's first and last name appear in the "Label unmarked changes with" text box. See Figure 7-10.

Tip

You can also use the Original document list arrow or the Revised document list arrow to select files that you have previously opened on your computer, but using the Browse for Original and Browse for Revised buttons ensures that you select the correct file from the correct folder.

Selecting the original and revised documents | **Figure 7-10**

the user name from
the Popular tab in the
Word Options dialog
box is displayed here;
yours will be different

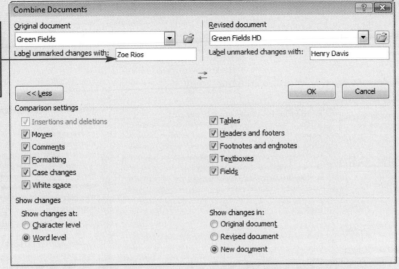

8. Click the **OK** button. A new document opens and is named "Document1," "Document2," "Combine Result 1," or something similar. It contains the revision marks from both the original document and revised document. At this point, you might see only the new, combined document, or you might also see the original and revised documents open in separate windows. You might also see the Reviewing Pane, which lists each change in the new, combined document. In the next two steps, you will make sure your screen is set up to show the original and revised documents and the Reviewing Pane.

9. In the Compare group, click the **Show Source Documents** button, and, if you do not see a check mark next to Show Both, click **Show Both**. If you do see a check mark next to Show Both, press the **Escape** key to close the menu.

10. In the Tracking group, locate the Reviewing Pane button. If it is orange, then the Reviewing Pane is currently displayed. If it is not orange, click the **Reviewing Pane** button to display the Reviewing Pane. At this point, the Reviewing Pane might be displayed in a horizontal window at the bottom of the screen or vertically on the left side of the screen. In Figure 7-11, it is displayed vertically.

Figure 7-11 Combining two documents

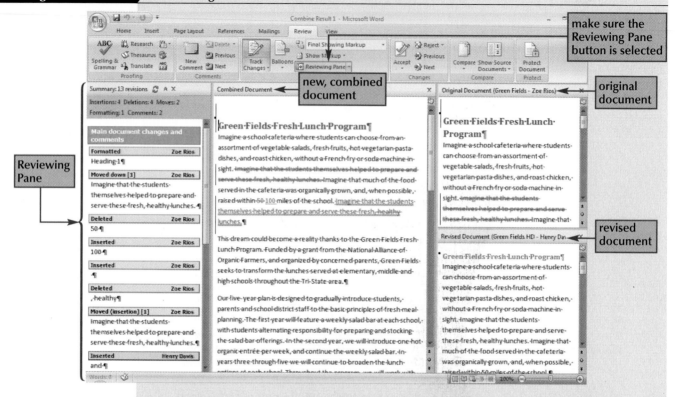

11. If your Reviewing Pane is displayed horizontally, in the Tracking group click the **Reviewing Pane** button arrow, and then click **Reviewing Pane Vertical**.

It's helpful to know how to display the original and revised documents, but if you have a small screen, having them displayed makes it harder to read the new document. You will close them in the next set of steps, and then you will take a moment to explore some options for displaying the edits made by multiple reviewers. Finally, you will save the new document with a new name.

To hide the source documents and change the reviewer options:

1. In the Compare group, click the **Show Source Documents** button, and then click **Hide Source Documents**. The panes displaying the original and revised documents close.

2. Use the vertical scroll bar in the Reviewing Pane to scroll down and review the list of edits. Notice that the document contains the edits you made earlier, as well as edits made by Henry Davis. By default, Word displays all the edits by all reviewers, but you can choose to display only the edits made by a specific reviewer or reviewers. You'll see how this works in the following step.

3. In the Tracking group, click the **Show Markup** button, and then point to **Reviewers**. A menu opens with check marks next to Henry's name and the user name for your computer. Also, you see a check mark next to "All Reviewers." This tells you that currently the document displays all the edits of all the reviewers. To hide Henry's edits, you need to deselect his name.

▶ **4.** Click **Henry Davis**. The menu closes, and the Reviewing Pane and document show only the edits you made earlier.

▶ **5.** Scroll down, if necessary, so you can see that the edits for Henry Davis are no longer displayed.

▶ **6.** Click the **Show Markup** button again, point to **Reviewers**, and then click **Henry Davis**. Henry's edits are again displayed in the Reviewing Pane and in the document. At this point, you are finished with the Reviewing Pane, so you can close it.

▶ **7.** In the Tracking group, click the **Reviewing Pane** button. (Do not click the arrow next to the Reviewing Pane button.) The Reviewing Pane closes, and the document window adjusts to show the new document in Page width zoom.

▶ **8.** Save the document as **Green Fields Rev** in the Tutorial.07\Tutorial folder included with your Data Files.

▶ **9.** Scroll down to review the document. Notice that Henry's changes, at the bottom of page 1, appear in a different color than the changes you made earlier at the top of page 1. On some computers, the word "soon" at the end of the Budget section (where you inserted a comment) might be marked as a deletion, with another instance of the word "soon" also marked as an insertion. Combining documents that contain revision marks can sometimes produce unexpected results like this. You will fix this problem later, when you accept and reject the changes in the document.

As you have seen, the document you just created contains Zoe's edits, your edits, and Henry's edits. In the following section, you will review the edits, accepting most of the changes and rejecting one.

Accepting and Rejecting Changes

When you go through revision marks in a document, it's important to be systematic, so you don't accidentally miss a change. The best approach is to move the insertion point to the beginning of the document, and then go through the document one change at a time using the Next and Previous buttons. When you click the Next button, Word moves to and selects the first change after the insertion point. Likewise, when you click the Previous button, Word moves to and selects the first change before the insertion point.

Accepting and Rejecting Changes and Deleting Comments | Reference Window

- Move the insertion point to the beginning of the document.
- To move the insertion point from one edit or comment to another, in the Changes group on the Review tab click the Next button. To move the insertion point from one comment to another, in the Comments group on the Review tab click the Next button.
- To accept a change that currently contains the insertion point, in the Changes group on the Review tab click the Accept button. To accept all the changes in the document, click the Accept button arrow, and then click Accept All Changes in Document.
- To reject the change that currently contains the insertion point, click the Reject button in the Changes group on the Review tab. To reject all the changes in the document, click the Reject button arrow, and then click Reject All Changes in Document.
- To delete a comment, click in the comment balloon, and then click the Delete button in the Comment group. To delete all the comments in a document, click the Delete button arrow, and then click Delete All Comments in Document.

You are ready to review the changes in the Green Fields Rev document, so Zoe can decide which to accept and which to reject.

To accept and reject changes in the Green Fields Rev document:

▶ 1. Press the **Ctrl+Home** keys to move the insertion point to the beginning of the document.

▶ 2. In the Changes group on the Review tab, click the **Next** button.

▶ 3. The heading "Green Fields Fresh Lunch Program" is highlighted. As you saw earlier, the margin bubble tells you that you formatted this paragraph with the Heading 1 style. This is one of your changes, and you need to accept it.

▶ 4. In the Changes group, click the **Accept** button. The heading remains formatted with the Heading 1 style, and the margin bubble disappears, indicating that the change has been accepted. The highlighting moves to the next change, which is the deleted sentence, currently displayed in green (or another color) and with a strikeout line through it. You also need to accept this change.

   Trouble? If you see a menu below the Accept button, you clicked the Accept button arrow by mistake. Press the Escape key to close the menu, and then click the Accept button.

▶ 5. Click the **Accept** button. The sentence with the strikeout line through it is removed from the document, and the highlighting moves to the deleted number 50.

▶ 6. Accept the deletion of the number 50, the insertion of the number 100, the insertion of the space before the word "Imagine," and the deletion of word "healthy." After you accept the deletion of "healthy," the word "and," near the bottom of page 1, is highlighted. This is one of Henry's changes to the document. In this same paragraph, he also added a comment and deleted the word "coronary." See Figure 7-12.

Figure 7-12 ⟩ **Reviewing Henry's changes**

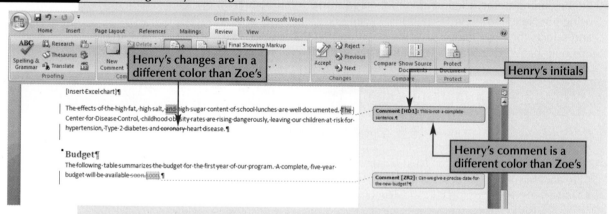

▶ 7. Click the **Accept** button to accept the insertion of the word "and." The insertion point moves to Henry's comment, which reads "This is not a complete sentence."

Henry is correct; something is missing from the sentence to which the comment is attached. You need to edit the sentence to correct it. Before you edit the sentence that Henry was concerned about, you need to turn off Track Changes if it was turned on by default when you created the combined document.

To continue accepting and rejecting changes:

▶ **1.** In the Tracking group, if the Track Changes button is highlighted, click the **Track Changes** button to deselect it.

▶ **2.** Click to the left of the word "The," press the **Delete** key to delete the "T" in "The" and then type **According to t** so that the sentence reads "According to the Center for Disease Control...". Because you turned off tracked changes, the new text looks like ordinary text. It is not displayed in revision marks. The last two letters in "The" are highlighted, indicating that the comment is still attached to them. You will delete the comment later in this set of steps.

▶ **3.** In the Changes group, click the **Next** button. The insertion point moves to the first change or comment after the insertion point, which is Henry's comment.

Trouble? If the insertion point moves to the deleted word "coronary" instead of to Henry's comment, then the insertion point was located somewhere after the comment. In that case, skip the following step.

▶ **4.** In the Changes group, click the **Next** button again. The deleted word "coronary," which appears with a strikeout line through it, is highlighted. Both "coronary" and "heart" are unnecessary; Zoe prefers to keep "coronary" and delete "heart." That means you need to reject Henry's deletion of "coronary." You don't want to move on to the next change in the document, because you need to remain at this location and edit this sentence. So instead of using the Reject button (which would reject the change and move the insertion point to the next change in the document), you will use the Reject arrow button.

▶ **5.** In the Changes group, click the **Reject** button arrow, and then click **Reject Change**. The word "coronary" appears as ordinary text and is selected. It is no longer marked as a deletion. See Figure 7-13. Next, you will delete the word "heart," which is next to the word "coronary" and is unnecessary.

Rejected change ◀ **Figure 7-13**

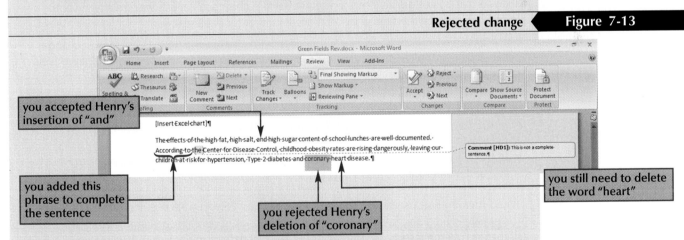

- you accepted Henry's insertion of "and"
- you added this phrase to complete the sentence
- you rejected Henry's deletion of "coronary"
- you still need to delete the word "heart"

▶ **6.** Double-click the word **heart** to select it, and then delete it, so the sentence reads "...and coronary disease." Next, as she reviews the edited sentence, Zoe notices that a comma is missing after the word "diabetes." You'll add the comma in the next step.

▶ **7.** Click to the right of the "s" in "diabetes," and then insert a comma. Finally, Zoe asks you to remove her comment, which she decides is no longer necessary. At the same time, you will delete Henry's comment. First, you need to move the insertion point to one of the comments.

▶ **8.** Click anywhere in the margin bubble for Henry's comment.

▶ **9.** In the Comments group, click the **Delete** button arrow, and then click **Delete All Comments in Document**. The comments are removed from the document.

Trouble? If only Henry's comment is deleted, and you do not see a menu with the command Delete All Comments in Document, you clicked the Delete button rather than the Delete button arrow. Undo the change, and then repeat Step 9.

If the word "soon" is marked as a deletion in your document and also marked as an insertion, then you need to complete Step 10. If the word "soon" appears in ordinary text, skip to Step 11.

▶ **10.** In the Changes group, click the **Next** button to select the deleted word "soon," accept the deletion of the word "soon," accept the insertion of the word "soon," and then click the **OK** button in the dialog box informing you that the document now contains no comments or tracked changes.

▶ **11.** Save your work on the Green Fields Rev document, click the button for the **Green Fields** document in the taskbar to display the document, and then close the **Green Fields** document. If you are asked if you want to save changes, click **Yes**. You return to the Green Fields Rev document.

| InSight | | **Understanding Tracked Changes** |

Tracked changes allow you to see the evolution of a document from draft form to the finished product. They can be extremely useful during the revision process. However, you do not want the final readers of your document to encounter any tracked changes. Inadvertently including tracked changes in a final document can be embarrassing; in other situations, it could result in serious consequences. For example, suppose you sent out a letter offering a job and specifying a salary, but you accidentally left in tracked changes that showed that you originally contemplated offering a higher salary. Such a mistake would greatly complicate the salary negotiations with a potential employee.

The problem is, you can't always tell if a document contains comments or tracked changes, because the comments or changes for some or all of the reviewers might be hidden. Also, the Display for Review list box in the Tracking group on the Review tab might be set to something other than Final Showing Markup. To determine whether or not a document contains any tracked changes or comments:

- In the Tracking group on the Review tab, verify that the Display for Review list box is set to Final Showing Markup.
- In the Tracking group on the Review tab, click the Show Markup button, point to Reviewers, and make sure you see a check mark next to All Reviewers.
- Press the Ctrl+Home keys to move the insertion point to the beginning of the document, and then in the Changes group on the Review tab, click the Next button. This will either display a dialog box informing you that the document contains no comments or tracked changes, or the insertion point will move to the next comment or tracked changes.

Now that you have incorporated Henry's suggestions, you are ready to add Alison's budget and Henry's pie chart to the document.

Embedding and Linking Objects from Other Programs

Every software program is designed to accomplish a set of specific tasks. As you've seen with Word, you can use a word-processing program to create, edit, and format documents such as letters, reports, newsletters, and proposals. A **spreadsheet program**, on the other hand, allows you to organize, calculate, and analyze numerical data. A spreadsheet created in Microsoft Excel is known as a **worksheet**. Alison created the budget for the Green Fields Fresh Lunch Program in an Excel worksheet. Henry also used Excel to create his chart.

Both the worksheet and the chart are objects. An **object** is an item such as a graphic, WordArt, chart, or paragraph of text that you can modify and move from one document to another. Zoe asks you to place the worksheet and chart objects into her document, but she also wants to be able to modify the Excel objects after they are inserted into the document. A technology called **object linking and embedding**, or **OLE**, allows you to integrate information created in one program (such as Excel) into a document created in another program (such as Word), and then modify that information using the tools originally used to create it.

The program used to create the original version of the object is called the **source program** (in this case, Excel). The program into which the object is integrated is called the **destination program** (in this case, Word). Similarly, the original file that contains the object you are inserting is called the **source file**, and the file into which you insert the object is called the **destination file**.

The next two sections describe two options for transferring data between source files and destination files: embedding and linking.

Embedding is a technique that allows you to insert a copy of an existing object into a destination document. In the destination document, you can double-click an embedded object to access the tools of the source program. This allows you to edit the object within the destination document using the tools of the source program. Because the embedded object is a copy, any changes you make to it are not reflected in the original source file, and vice versa. For instance, you could embed a worksheet named Itemized Expenses into a Word document named Travel Report. Later, if you change the Itemized Expenses file, those revisions would not appear in the Travel Report document. The opposite is also true. If you edit the embedded object from within the Travel Report file, those changes will not be reflected in the source file Itemized Expenses. The embedded object retains a connection to the source program, Excel, but not to the source file.

Figure 7-14 illustrates the relationship between an embedded Excel object in Zoe's Word document and the source file.

Figure 7-14 > **Embedding an Excel worksheet in a Word document**

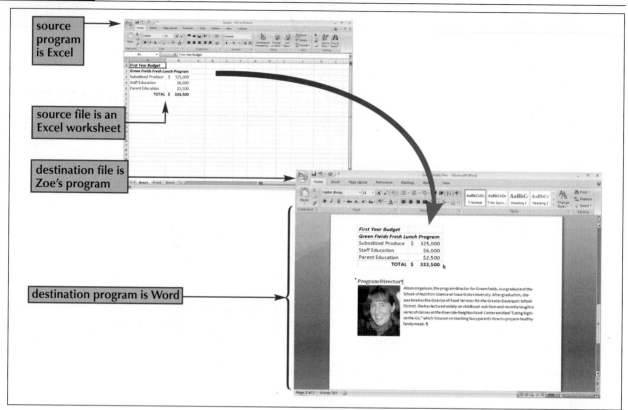

Linking is similar to embedding, except that the object inserted into the destination file maintains a connection to the source file—not just the source program. Just as with an embedded object, you can double-click a linked object to access the tools of the source program. However, unlike with an embedded object, if you edit the source file in the source program, those changes appear in the linked object; likewise, if you change the object from the destination program, the changes will also appear in the file in the source program. The linked object in the destination document is not a copy; it is a shortcut to the original object in the source file. As a result, a document that contains a linked object usually takes up less space on a disk than does a document containing an embedded version of the same object.

Figure 7-15 illustrates the relationship between the data in Henry's Excel chart and the linked object in Zoe's Word document.

Linking an Excel chart to a Word document | Figure 7-15

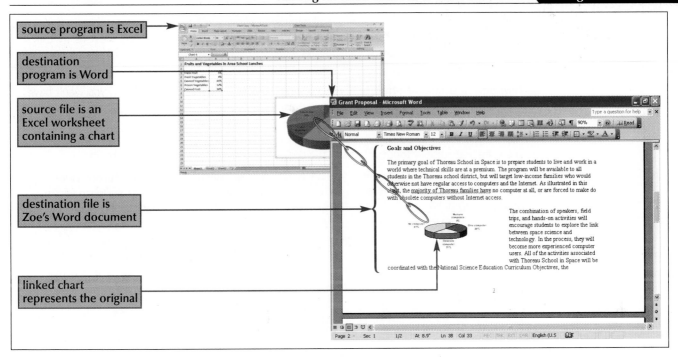

   One drawback to linking is that by moving files or folders, you can accidentally disrupt the connection between the source file and the document containing the linked object. For example, suppose you insert a linked Excel file into a Word document, close the Word document and the Excel file, and then go home. Suppose then that later a colleague moves the source file (the Excel file) to a different folder or even deletes it. The next time you open the Word document containing the linked object, you will get an error message, or you won't be able to update the linked object.

InSight | **Choosing Between Embedding and Linking**

Embedding and linking are both useful when you know you'll want to edit an object after inserting it into Word. Before you can use either embedding or linking, you must verify that you have the source program installed on your computer. Then you can decide if you want to embed or link the object.

How do you decide whether to embed or link? Create an embedded object if you won't have access to the original source file in the future, or if you don't need to maintain the connection between the source file and the document containing the linked object. The source file is unaffected by any editing in the destination document. You could even delete the source file from your disk without affecting the copy embedded in your Word document.

Create a linked object whenever you have data that is likely to change over time and when you want your document to be updated with those changes. For example, suppose you created a Word document called Refinancing Options into which you want to insert an Excel file containing the latest interest rates for home mortgages. Suppose also that your assistant updates the Excel file daily to make sure it reflects current rates. By linking the Excel file to the Refinancing Options Word document, you can be certain that the mortgage rates are updated every time your assistant updates the Excel file. The advantage to linking is that the data in both the source file (the Excel file) and destination file (the Word document) can reflect recent revisions. A disadvantage to linking is that you have to keep track of two files (the Excel file and the Word file) rather than just one.

If you won't need to edit the object, you can also simply paste a copy of the object into a Word document, using the regular Paste button, similar to the way you paste a selection of copied text.

Keep in mind that you must have Excel installed on your computer to perform the steps in the rest of this session. If Excel is not installed on your computer, read the remainder of this session, but you won't be able to perform the steps.

Embedding an Excel Worksheet

Embedding all or part of an Excel worksheet in a Word document is really a special form of pasting. You start by opening the Excel file and selecting the worksheet or part of a worksheet that you want to embed in the Word document. Then you copy the selection to the Office Clipboard. When you return to Word, you click the Paste button arrow in the Clipboard group on the Home tab and select the Paste Special command to open the Paste Special dialog box. In this dialog box, you can choose to paste the copied worksheet data in a number of different forms. To embed the worksheet data, you select Microsoft Office Excel Worksheet Object.

Zoe asks you to embed the budget from Alison's Excel file into the Green Fields Rev document. In OLE terminology, the budget is the object, the Excel file is the source file, and the Green Fields Rev document is the destination file. In the following steps, you will embed the Excel object in the Word document, replacing the "[Insert Excel worksheet]" placeholder at the top of page 2. (It was originally on page 1, but it moved to page 2 after you formatted the first heading with the Heading 1 style.) Then you can use Excel commands to modify the embedded object from within Word.

To embed the Excel worksheet:

▶ **1.** Press the **Ctrl+Home** keys to move the insertion point to the beginning of the document, click the **Home** tab, in the Editing group click the **Find** button, find the placeholder **[Insert Excel worksheet]**, click **Cancel** to close the Find and Replace dialog box, and then press the **Delete** key. Take care to delete only the placeholder text and not the paragraph mark after it. When you are finished, the insertion point should be located in a blank paragraph above the heading Program Director. This is where you will embed the Excel worksheet. Now you are ready to open Alison's Excel file and copy the budget.

▶ **2.** Click the **Start** button, point to **All Programs**, click **Microsoft Office**, and then click **Microsoft Office Excel 2007**. The Excel window opens, displaying a blank worksheet named Book1.

   Trouble? If you don't see Microsoft Office Excel 2007 as an option in the Start menu, or if a message indicates that Word can't find the source program, Excel might not be installed on your computer. Ask your instructor or technical support person for assistance.

▶ **3.** In Excel, click the **Office Button** 🔘, click **Open**, navigate to the Tutorial. 07\Tutorial folder included with your Data Files, click the file named **Budget,** and then click the **Open** button. The Budget worksheet opens, as shown in Figure 7-16.

Budget file open in Excel ◀ Figure 7-16

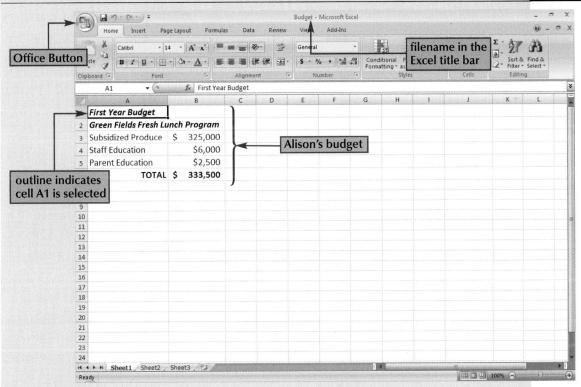

Notice that an Excel worksheet is arranged in rows and columns, just like a Word table. The intersection between a row and column is called a **cell**; an individual cell takes its name from its column letter and row number. For example, the intersection of column B and row 2 is "cell B2." Currently cell A1, in the upper-left corner of the worksheet, is selected, as indicated by its dark outline. To copy the budget data to the Office Clipboard, you need to select the entire block of cells containing the budget.

4. Click cell **A1** (the cell containing the text "First Year Budget"), drag the mouse down to select cells A1 through A6 (that is, down to the cell containing "TOTAL"), and then drag the mouse right to select the data in column B. See Figure 7-17.

Figure 7-17 **Budget data selected in the worksheet**

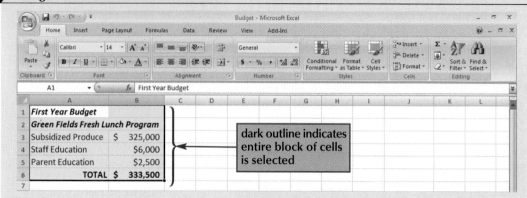

Now that the data is selected, you can copy it to the Office Clipboard and return to Word.

5. Press the **Ctrl+C** keys. The border around the selected cells is animated, indicating that you have copied the data in these cells to the Office Clipboard.

6. Click the **Green Fields Rev** button in the taskbar. You return to the Word window.

7. Verify that the insertion point is located at the top of page 2, in the blank paragraph above the heading "Program Director." You are ready to embed the copied budget into the Word document. As mentioned earlier, you need to use the Paste button arrow to do this, and not the Paste button. If you click the Paste button instead, the budget won't be embedded. Instead, Word will insert the Excel data as a Word table, which would prevent you from editing it using the Excel tabs and tools.

8. Click the **Home** tab if necessary, in the Clipboard group click the **Paste** button arrow, and then click **Paste Special**. The Paste Special dialog box opens.

   Trouble? If the budget is inserted in the document, you clicked the Paste button rather than the Paste button arrow. Undo the change, and then repeat Step 8.

   Here you can choose to embed the Excel object or link it, depending on whether you select the Paste option button or the Paste link option button. The Paste option button, which tells Word you want to embed the object, is selected by default. In the As list box, you can select the format in which you want to paste the Excel data. For example, you could click Picture (Enhanced Metafile) to insert a picture of the data, which you could not edit. In this case, you want to paste the data as a Microsoft Office Excel Worksheet Object, so you can edit it later.

9. In the As list, click **Microsoft Office Excel Worksheet Object**. See Figure 7-18.

Embedding an Excel object | **Figure 7-18**

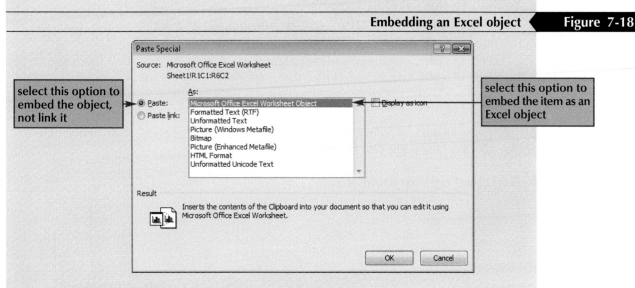

select this option to embed the object, not link it

select this option to embed the item as an Excel object

10. Click the **OK** button. The Excel object is inserted in the Word document, as shown in Figure 7-19.

Excel object embedded in Word document | **Figure 7-19**

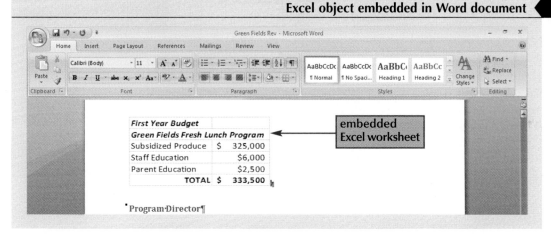

embedded Excel worksheet

Because the object is embedded, you can make changes to the object from within Word, which you'll do in the next section.

Modifying the Embedded Worksheet

After you embed an object in Word, you can modify it two different ways. First, you can click it to select it, and then move it or resize it, just as you would a picture or a piece of clip art. You can think of this as modifying the object's container—the box in which it is displayed. Second, you can double-click the object to display the tools of the source program, and then edit the contents of the object. After you modify the embedded object using the tools of the source program, you can click anywhere else in the Word document to deselect the embedded object and redisplay the usual Word tools.

Zoe would like to center the Excel object on the page. Also, Alison just e-mailed Zoe to tell her that she used an incorrect value for Staff Education, so Zoe needs to revise the worksheet data.

To modify the Excel object:

▶ **1.** Click anywhere inside the borders of the budget data. A dotted blue outline and selection handles appear around the Excel object, indicating that it is selected. With the object selected, you can center it as you would center any other selected item in a Word document. Notice that merely selecting the Excel object does not display the Excel tabs and buttons. That will happen later when you double-click the object.

▶ **2.** In the Paragraph group, click the **Center** button ≡. The Excel object moves to the center of the page. See Figure 7-20.

Figure 7-20	Excel object centered on the page

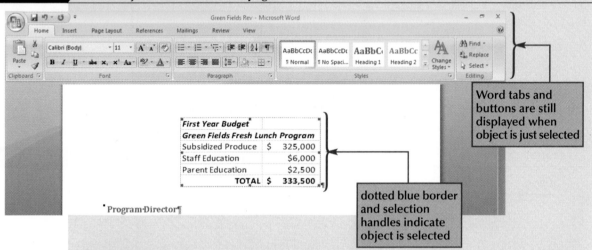

Word tabs and buttons are still displayed when object is just selected

First Year Budget
Green Fields Fresh Lunch Program
Subsidized Produce $ 325,000
Staff Education $6,000
Parent Education $2,500
TOTAL $ 333,500

dotted blue border and selection handles indicate object is selected

Program·Director¶

▶ **3.** Double-click the Excel object. The object's border changes to resemble the borders of an Excel worksheet, with horizontal and vertical scroll bars, row numbers, and column letters. The Word tabs at the top of the screen are replaced with Excel tabs. You need to change the value for Staff Education from $6,000 to $5,000. Decreasing the Staff Education value by $1,000 should also decrease the budget total by $1,000 because of the formula Alison entered in the worksheet.

▶ **4.** Click cell **B4**, which contains the number $6,000, type **5000** (you don't have to type a dollar sign or a comma), and then press the **Enter** key. The new value of "$5,000" replaces the old value of "$6,000." The budget total, in cell B6, decreases from $333,500 to $332,500. See Figure 7-21.

Figure 7-21 Revised data in Excel object

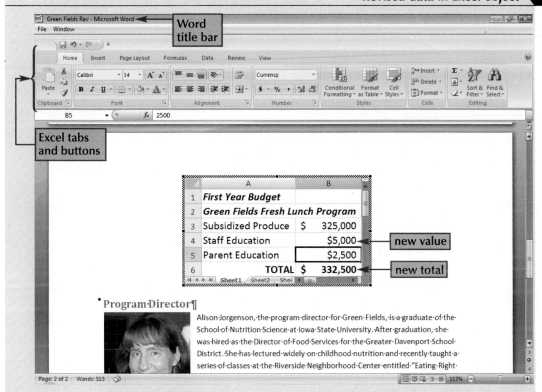

5. Click in the blank area to the left or right of the Excel object (outside its borders) to deselect it.

The source file, Budget.xlsx, remains in its original form in your Data Files, with the $6,000 as the Staff Education value. You have modified only the object in Zoe's document because it is embedded, not linked. You'll see how linking works in the next section.

Linking an Excel Chart

Next, Zoe wants you to incorporate the chart that illustrates the percentage of fresh fruits and vegetables served in school lunches in her area. Because Henry plans to revise the data soon, Zoe decides to link the chart in the Excel file rather than embed it. That way, once Henry updates the chart in the source file, the update will appear in Zoe's program description as well.

You'll use the Chart file Henry created in Excel to create the linked object in the program description document. This file is located in the Tutorial.07\Tutorial folder included with your Data Files. Because you'll make changes to the chart after you link it, you should make a copy of the Chart file before you link it. This leaves the original file in the Tutorial folder unchanged in case you want to repeat the tutorial steps later. Normally you don't need to copy a file before you link it to a Word document.

To link an Excel chart to the program description document:

1. Use the Find dialog box to find and select the placeholder **[Insert Excel chart]**, click **Cancel** to close the Find and Replace dialog box, and then delete the placeholder **[Insert Excel chart]**. Make sure the insertion point is positioned on a blank line between the two paragraphs of text.

2. Click the **Microsoft Excel** button in the taskbar to display the Excel window. Next, you will close the Budget file before you open the Chart file.

3. Click the **Office Button** , and then click **Close**. The Budget worksheet closes.

4. Click the **Office Button** , click **Open**, and then open the file named **Chart** from the Tutorial.07\Tutorial folder included with your Data Files. The worksheet includes some data in the upper-left corner and the pie chart created from the data in the lower-right corner.

5. Click the **Office Button** , click **Save As**, and then save the Excel file with the name **Chart Copy** in the Tutorial.07\Tutorial folder included with your Data Files.

    As with embedding, to link an Excel object, you start by selecting the object and copying it to the Office Clipboard. You want to copy the chart, not the data.

6. Click the chart border. Do not click any part of the chart itself. A selection border appears around the chart. The worksheet data is also outlined in color, indicating that this is the data used to create the chart. Note that the colored outlines do not indicate that the data itself is selected. See Figure 7-22.

Figure 7-22 ▶ **Pie chart selected in worksheet**

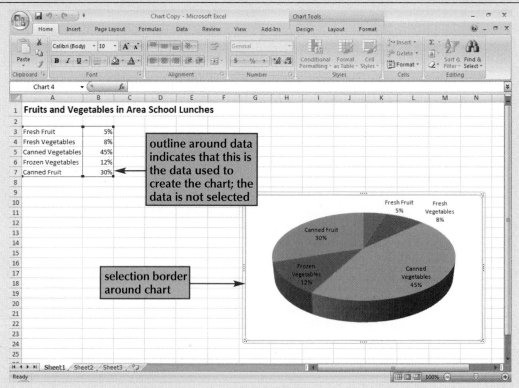

Trouble? If you see borders or handles around parts of the pie chart, click in the worksheet outside the chart border, and then repeat Step 6.

7. Press the **Ctrl+C** keys to copy the pie chart to the Office Clipboard, and then click the **Green Fields Rev** button in the taskbar. The Green Fields Rev document is displayed in the Word window. You'll leave the Excel window open, so you can return to it in a moment.

8. Verify that the insertion point is located in the blank paragraph between the two paragraphs of text, click the **Paste** button arrow, and then click **Paste Special**. The Paste Special dialog box opens. To link the worksheet chart to Zoe's Word document, you need to click the Paste link option button. You also need to specify that the chart is an object.

9. Click the **Paste link** option button to select it, and then click **Microsoft Office Excel Chart Object** in the As list box. See Figure 7-23.

Inserting a linked object ◄ **Figure 7-23**

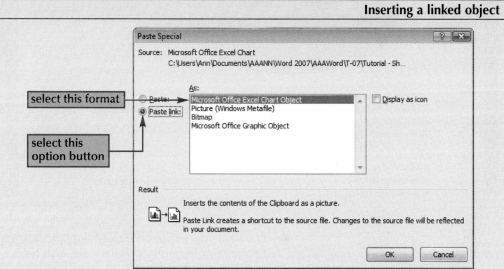

10. Click the **OK** button. The Paste Special dialog box closes, and the Excel chart is inserted in the Word document. See Figure 7-24. It is too large to fit on page 1, so Word moved it to the top of page 2.

Figure 7-24 | **Linked chart inserted in Word document**

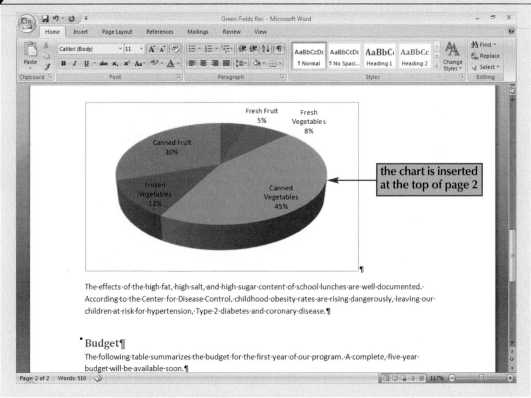

You can resize and move a linked object just as you would an embedded object. Later on, after Zoe incorporates suggestions and comments from other readers, she will resize the chart and wrap text around it. For now, she'll leave it as it is.

Modifying the Linked Chart

The advantage of linking a file over embedding it is that you can update the destination file to reflect modifications to the source file. If the destination file is closed while the source file is being modified, the linked object in the destination file will be updated automatically the next time you open the destination file. If the destination file is open while the source file is being modified, you need to right-click the linked object and then click Update Link.

In the following steps, you'll return to the Chart Copy file in Excel, change some values, and then view the updated information in the Word document.

To modify the chart in the source program:

▶ 1. Click the **Microsoft Excel** button in the taskbar. The Chart Copy workbook is displayed in the Excel window, with the chart still selected.

▶ 2. Click anywhere outside the chart to deselect it. To modify the chart, you need to edit the data in the upper-left corner of the worksheet. Currently the percentage for Fresh Fruit is 5%, and the percentage for Fresh Vegetables is 8%. In the next step, you will edit these values.

3. Click cell **B3**, which contains the percentage for Fresh Fruit, type **9** (you don't have to type the percentage sign), and then press the **Enter** key. The new percentage is entered in cell B3, and the label in the Fresh Fruit section of the pie chart changes from 5% to 9%. Cell B4, which contains the percentage for Fresh Vegetables, is now selected, ready for you to enter a new value.

4. Type **4**, and then press the **Enter** key. The new percentage is entered in cell B4, and the label in the Fresh Vegetables section of the pie chart changes from 8% to 4%. See Figure 7-25.

Modifying the chart in Excel ◄ **Figure 7-25**

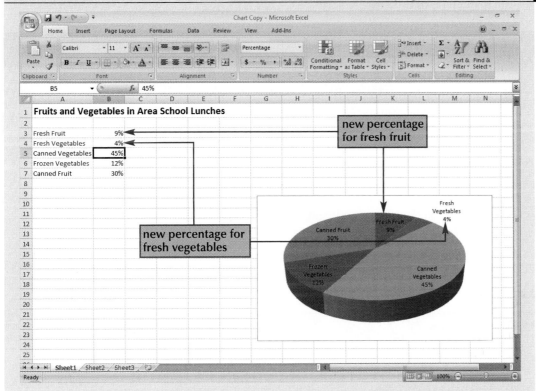

5. On the Quick Access Toolbar, click the **Save** button, and then close the Chart Copy file and Excel. You return to the Word window, with the pie chart displayed. Because the destination file, Green Fields Rev, was open when you edited the source file, you need to update the chart before it will show the new percentages. If the Word file had been closed, the chart would be updated when you reopened the file in Word.

6. Right-click the chart in the Word window, and then in the shortcut menu click **Update Link**. After a pause, the chart is updated and shows a percentage of 9% for Fresh Fruit and 4% for Fresh Vegetables, just like the chart shown in Figure 7-25.

7. Click anywhere outside the chart to deselect it, and then save your work.

Zoe's program description is finished for now. Later, after she receives everyone's comments, she will further revise it. At that time, she will add additional text, adjust the size of the pie chart, and wrap text around it.

You are ready to print the program description for distribution to the parent volunteers at Green Fields who ask for printed copies.

To print and then close the document:

▶ **1.** Preview the document. Don't be concerned if the page breaks seem awkward. Zoe will add additional text to the document after her colleagues review it, so at this point she isn't concerned about adjusting page breaks in the document.

▶ **2.** Print the document, click the **Office Button** ⊚, and then click **Close**. You closed the document so you can see what happens later when you open a document that contains a linked object.

Next, Zoe wants to focus on the task of distributing the document electronically, which you'll do in the next session.

Review | **Session 7.1 Quick Check**

1. Explain how to use Track Changes to edit a document.
2. What button do you use to insert a comment and on what tab is it located?
3. Suppose you want to merge two documents, each containing revision marks. Should you combine them or compare them?
4. Explain the difference between a linked object and an embedded object.
5. What term refers to an item such as a graphic, WordArt, or chart that you can modify and move from one document to another?
6. What button do you use to begin embedding or linking an object that you've copied to the Clipboard? On what tab is the button located?
7. True or False. When you modify a linked object in the destination file, your changes are also made to the source file.

Session 7.2

Distributing Word Documents Online

> **Tip**
>
> You can save a document as a PDF file, which can be opened on any computer running Adobe Acrobat Reader. To learn how, search for "Enable support for other file formats, such as PDF and XPS" in Word Help.

In addition to printing the document for Green Fields members, Zoe wants to make the program description available to the organization's members **online**, which means they can read it on a computer screen rather than on a printed page. You can make a document available online in one of two ways—you can either e-mail the document to specific people, or you can make it available as a Web page.

Whichever online option you choose, keep in mind that reading a document online is different from reading it in printed form. If you are certain a document will be read only online, and therefore don't have to worry about how the document will look when printed on a black and white printer, you can sometimes use more interesting formatting options, such as a fancy background. Because it is difficult to "flip through pages" online, you might also need to organize online information for easy access, or provide hyperlinks for opening related files. (You'll learn more about hyperlinks later in this tutorial.) Finally, remember that when distributing documents online, large document files can be problematic.

E-Mailing Word Documents	InSight

To e-mail a Word document, you need to use an e-mail program such as Microsoft Outlook or a Web mail service such as Yahoo. First, you create an e-mail message, type the recipient's e-mail address, and then type the text of the e-mail. Finally, you need to attach the Word document to the e-mail message. The exact steps for attaching a document to an e-mail message vary from one e-mail program to another, but in all of them, you need to find and then select the file you want to attach.

When you e-mail documents, you should keep in mind a few basic rules:

- Many e-mail programs have difficulty handling large attachments. Consider storing large files in a compressed (or zipped) folder to reduce their size before e-mailing. Alternately, you could convert the Word document to a Web page as described later in this tutorial. A Web page is usually much smaller than a Word document containing the same amount of text.
- Other word-processing programs and early versions of Word are unable to open files created in Word 2007. Before e-mailing a file, ask the recipient what word processor he or she is using. To avoid problems with conflicting versions, save the Word document as a rich text file (using the Rich Text File document, type in the Save As dialog box) before e-mailing it. All versions of Word can open rich text files.
- If you plan to e-mail a document that contains links to other files, remember to e-mail all the linked files.
- Attachments, including Word documents, are sometimes used maliciously to spread computer viruses. Remember to include an explanatory note with any e-mail attachment so that the recipient can be certain the attachment is legitimate. Also, while every computer should have a reliable virus checker program installed, this is even more important if you plan to send and receive e-mail attachments.

E-mailing Word documents is especially useful when you are collaborating with a group. You can exchange documents with colleagues in the office or around the world with just a click of the mouse. To make a document available to a larger audience, however, it's easier to publish it as a Web page, because then you don't have to take time to read and manage numerous e-mail messages. You'll learn more about working with Web pages in the next section.

Publishing Word Documents as Web Pages

Web pages are special documents designed to be viewed in a program called a **browser**. The two most popular browsers are **Microsoft Internet Explorer** and **Mozilla Firefox**. You can create a Web page on just about any kind of computer, but if you want other people to be able to view your Web page, you must store it on a computer called a **Web server**. The Web server communicates with a computer user's browser in order to display the Web page in the browser window. The process of making a Web page available to others via a Web server is called **publishing** the Web page.

Web servers are found on two different types of networks—intranets and the Internet. An **intranet** is a self-contained network belonging to a single organization. For example, the computers at Zoe's company, Rios Communications, are connected via an intranet. Zoe could publish a document as a Web page on her company's intranet Web site, so that her coworkers could view it—but it would not be available to the general public.

At the same time, Zoe's computer is also connected to the largest, most widely used computer network in the world, the **Internet**. The part of the Internet that transfers and displays Web pages is called the **World Wide Web**, or simply, the **Web**. Each Web page has its own **Web address** (or **URL**), such as *www.course.com* or *www.microsoft.com*. A group of related Web pages is called a **Web site**. The main Web page within a Web site (the one that is usually displayed first) is called a **home page**.

You probably have experience using a browser to view Web pages. If so, you know that Web pages usually contain both text and graphics, and also can contain audio and video. Web pages also include **hyperlinks**, which you can click to open or "jump to" other Web pages. A hyperlink can be a word, a phrase, or a graphic. Text hyperlinks are usually underlined and appear in a different color from the rest of the document. Hyperlinks are usually referred to as **links**, but take care not to confuse them with the OLE links you worked with earlier in this tutorial.

While hyperlinks are widely used in Web pages, you can also use them in ordinary Word documents that are intended for online reading. In the next section, you will learn more about using hyperlinks in online Word documents and Web pages.

Using Hyperlinks in Word

Hyperlinks in Word documents can link to a Web page, to a separate Word document, or to another part of the same document as the one containing the link. You can also include e-mail links, which you can click to create an e-mail message from a document. Finally, if you have many Office 2007 documents that are related to each other, you can create a useful hyperlink system that allows users to retrieve and view related material. For example, a business proposal might include links to a budget stored in an Excel file and to product photographs stored in a PowerPoint presentation. In fact, instead of inserting Henry's chart as a linked object, you could have inserted a hyperlink that users could click to open the chart in Excel. You used a linked object instead, because you wanted the chart to appear in the printed version of the program description.

Zoe wants you to add two hyperlinks to the program description—one hyperlink that jumps to a location within the program description and one that will open a different document.

Inserting a Hyperlink to a Bookmark in the Same Document

Creating a hyperlink within a document is actually a two-part process. First, you need to mark the text you want the link to jump to—either by formatting the text with a heading style or by inserting a bookmark. A **bookmark** is an electronic marker that refers to a specific point in a document. Second, you need to select the text that you want users to click, format it as a hyperlink, and specify the bookmark or heading as the target of the hyperlink. The **target** is the place in the document to which the link connects.

In this case, Zoe wants to create a hyperlink that targets Alison's name, near the end of the document. Figure 7-26 illustrates this process.

Hyperlink that targets a bookmark ◀ **Figure 7-26**

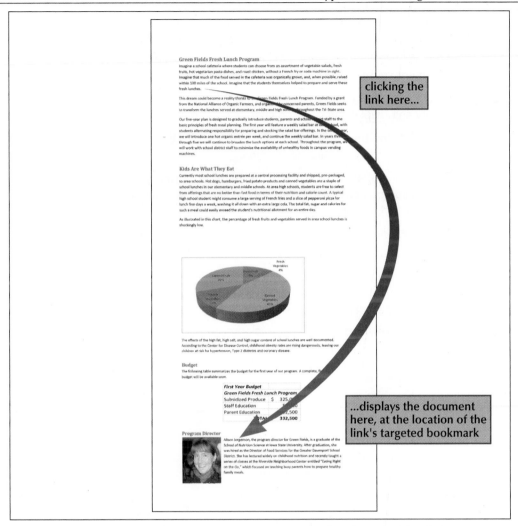

clicking the link here...

...displays the document here, at the location of the link's targeted bookmark

---

Linking to a Location in the Same Document | Reference Window

- Insert a bookmark at the target location or format text at the target location with a heading style. To insert a bookmark, select the text you want to mark as a bookmark, click the Insert tab, in the Links group click Bookmark, type a name for the bookmark, and then click the Add button.
- Select the text or graphic you want to use as the hyperlink.
- On the Insert tab in the Links group, click Hyperlink.
- Under Link to, click the Place in This Document option.
- Click the bookmark you want to link to, and then click the OK button.

To create a hyperlink in the Green Fields Rev document, you'll need to insert a bookmark in the Program Director section. But first, you need to reopen the Green Fields Rev document and update the linked object.

To reopen the document and insert a bookmark:

1. Open the **Green Fields Rev** document from the Tutorial.07\Tutorial folder included with your Data Files. A dialog box opens, explaining that the document contains links (in this case, just one link) and asking if you want to update the data from the linked file. It's usually a good idea to click Yes in this dialog box, so you can be sure your document contains the latest version of all linked objects.

2. Click **Yes** to update the links and close the dialog box, and then switch to Print Layout view and display nonprinting characters, if necessary.

3. Use the Find dialog box to find and select the name **Alison Jorgenson** at the beginning of the Program Director section.

4. Click the **Insert** tab, and then click the **Bookmark** button in the Links group. The Bookmark dialog box opens. You can now type the bookmark name, which must be one word, without spaces.

5. Type **Director**. See Figure 7-27.

| **Figure 7-27** | Creating a bookmark |

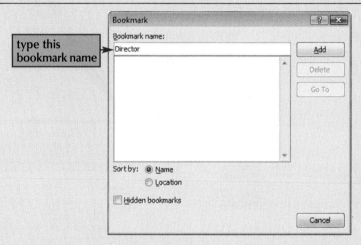

6. Click the **Add** button. The Bookmark dialog box closes. Although you can't see it, a bookmark has been inserted before Alison's name.

This bookmark you just created will be the target of the hyperlink. When you click the hyperlink, which you will create in the next set of steps, the insertion point will jump to this bookmark.

To create a hyperlink to the bookmark:

1. Press the **Ctrl+Home** keys to move the insertion point to the beginning of the document, and then click at the end of the second paragraph under the heading Green Fields Fresh Lunch Program. The insertion point should be positioned immediately following the phrase "...throughout the Tri-State area."

2. Insert a space, and then type **The program director is Alison Jorgenson, an expert in childhood nutrition.** (Include the period.) Next, you'll format part of this sentence as a hyperlink.

3. Select the name **Alison Jorgenson** in the sentence you just typed, and then in the Links group on the Insert tab, click the **Hyperlink** button. The Insert Hyperlink dialog box opens.

4. Under Link to (on the left side of the dialog box), click **Place in This Document**. See Figure 7-28. The right side of the dialog box now lists the headings and bookmarks in the document. Here you can click the bookmark or heading you want the hyperlink to jump to.

Inserting a hyperlink ◄ **Figure 7-28**

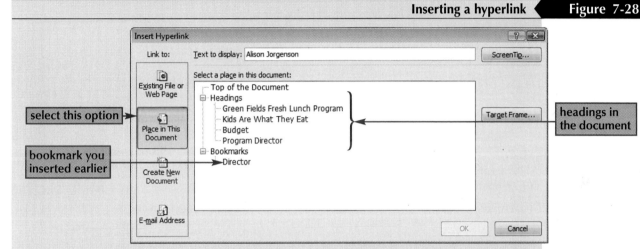

Trouble? If you don't see the document headings or the bookmark in the dialog box, click the plus signs next to Headings and Bookmarks.

5. Under Bookmarks, click **Director**, and then click the **OK** button. The name "Alison Jorgenson" appears in underlined blue text. The hyperlink now targets the Director bookmark that you created in the last set of steps.

Trouble? If you formatted the wrong text as a hyperlink, click the Undo button and begin again with Step 3.

After inserting a hyperlink into a document, you should test it.

To test the hyperlink in your document:

1. Without clicking, move the mouse pointer over the blue underlined hyperlink, **Alison Jorgenson**. After a moment, a ScreenTip appears with the name of the bookmark (Director) and instructions for following the link. See Figure 7-29.

Figure 7-29	Displaying the hyperlink ScreenTip

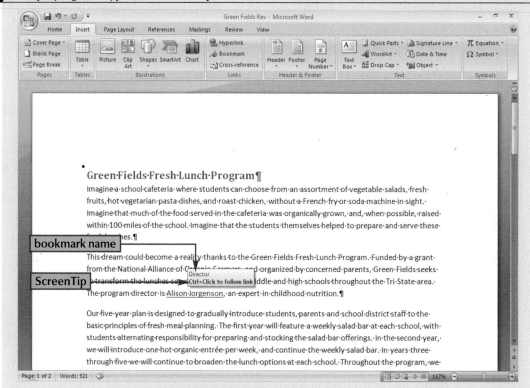

2. Press and hold the **Ctrl** key, and then click the **Alison Jorgenson** hyperlink. The insertion point jumps to the beginning of Alison's name in the Program Director section, where you inserted the bookmark.

3. Press the **Ctrl+Home** keys to move the insertion point back to the beginning of the document. The hyperlink has changed color, indicating that it has been used. If you were to close and then reopen the document, the hyperlink would again be blue until you clicked it.

4. Save your work.

You have finished creating a hyperlink that jumps to a location in the same document. Next, you will create a hyperlink that jumps to a location in a different document.

Creating Hyperlinks to Other Documents

The greatest power of hyperlinks lies not in jumping to another location within the same document, but in jumping to other documents. These documents can be located on the World Wide Web, on your computer's hard drive, or on your company's network server. When you create a hyperlink to another document, you can target the URL of a document stored on the Web or the path and filename of a file on your computer or network. When you click a hyperlink to another document, the document opens on your computer, with the beginning of the document displayed. If you want, you can also specify a particular bookmark within the other document. In that case, when you click the link, the document opens, with the bookmarked location in the document displayed.

Creating a Hyperlink to Another Document | Reference Window

- Select the text you want to format as a hyperlink.
- In the Links group on the Insert tab, click the Hyperlink button.
- Under Link to, click Existing File or Web Page.
- To target a specific file on your computer or network, use the Look in list arrow to open the folder containing the file, and then click the file in the file list.
- To target a Web page, type the URL in the Address text box.

Zoe wants to insert a hyperlink that will open a Word document containing Alison's resume. Because she wants the hyperlink to take users to the beginning of the resume, you don't need to insert a bookmark. Instead, you can use just the name of the target document.

To create a hyperlink to another document:

▶ **1.** Use the hyperlink again to jump to the bookmark in the Program Director section.

▶ **2.** Click at the end of the Program Director section. The insertion point should be located immediately to the right of the period that concludes the phrase "healthy family meals." This is where you'll insert text, some of which will become the hyperlink.

▶ **3.** Press the **spacebar**, and type **(See her resume.)**, making sure to include the parentheses.

▶ **4.** Select the word **resume** in the text you just typed.

▶ **5.** In the Links group on the Insert tab, click the **Hyperlink** button. The Insert Hyperlink dialog box opens.

▶ **6.** Under Link to, click **Existing File or Web Page**. The right side of the dialog box displays options related to selecting a file or a Web page.

▶ **7.** If necessary, use the **Look in** list arrow to open the Tutorial.07\Tutorial folder.

▶ **8.** Click **Resume** in the file list. See Figure 7-30.

Inserting a hyperlink to a different document | Figure 7-30

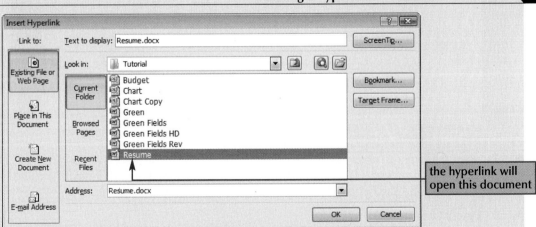

▶ **9.** Click the **OK** button. The word "resume" is now formatted as a hyperlink, in blue with an underline.

InSight	**Keeping Track of Documents Containing Hyperlinks**

When your documents include hyperlinks to other documents, you must keep track of where you store the target documents. If you move a target document to a different location, hyperlinks to it might not function properly. In this case, you created a hyperlink in the Green Fields Rev document that links to the Resume document. Both documents are stored in the Tutorial.07\Tutorial folder, which is most likely located on your computer's hard disk. To ensure that the hyperlink in the program description document will continue to function, you must keep the two documents in the same folder as when you created the link. If you have to move a target document, then be sure to edit the hyperlink to select the target document in its new location. You'll learn how to edit hyperlinks later in this tutorial.

Now you're ready to test the hyperlink you just created.

To test the resume hyperlink:

▶ 1. Press and hold the **Ctrl** key and click the **resume** hyperlink. The Resume document opens. See Figure 7-31.

Figure 7-31	**Resume document**

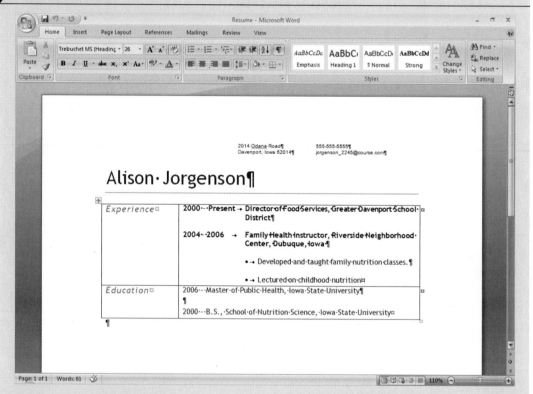

▶ 2. Read through the Resume document, and then close it. You return to the Green Fields Rev document. Notice that the hyperlink color has changed, indicating that you have used the hyperlink.

▶ 3. Save your work.

As you can see, hyperlinks allow you to display information instantaneously. When used thoughtfully, hyperlinks make it possible to navigate a complicated document or a set of files quickly and easily.

Viewing a Document in Web Layout View

Because the version of the program description you are now working on is intended for an online audience, Zoe suggests that you switch to Web Layout view. **Web Layout view** offers several advantages for online viewers:

- Text automatically wraps to suit the size of your screen, not the printed page.
- Documents can be displayed with a variety of background effects.
- Page setup elements, such as footers, headers, and breaks, are not displayed. Because users don't view the document as printed pages, these elements aren't necessary.

Web Layout view is useful when you need to format a document for online viewing. Text wrapping doesn't always survive the conversion from a Word document to a Web page, and graphics often shift position when you save a document as a Web page. Web Layout view prepares you for this by showing you what the graphics look like in their new positions.

Keep in mind that, despite its name, Web Layout view does not show you exactly how a document will look when saved as a Web page. Some features you see in Web Layout view, such as the embedded chart, might look different when you save the document as a Web page. (You will learn more about saving a document as a Web page later in this tutorial.)

If you switch to Web Layout view and then save the document in that view, the next time you open it, it will by default open in Web Layout view. Zoe asks you to display the program description document in Web Layout view, and then save it. Then when she e-mails the file to Alison, it will open for her in Web Layout view.

To display a document in Web Layout view:

▶ 1. Scroll to the beginning of the document, and then click the **Web Layout** button 🔲. This button is located in the status bar in the lower-right corner of the document window. Notice that paragraphs now span the width of the document window. The line widths are no longer constrained by the margin settings for the printed page. See Figure 7-32.

Figure 7-32 ▸ Document displayed in Web Layout view

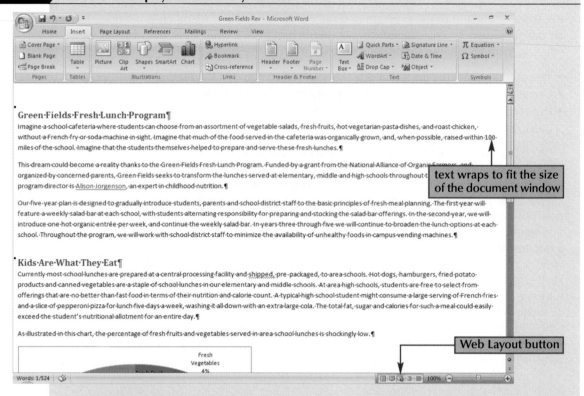

Trouble? Depending on the size of your monitor, the line breaks in your document may differ from those in Figure 7-32. This has to do with the fact that Web Layout view wraps text to fit the size of the screen, and is not a problem.

▸ **2.** Scroll through the document to review its appearance in Web Layout view.

▸ **3.** Save the document.

Next, you'll make some changes to the Green Fields Rev document that will improve its online appearance.

Applying a Background Effect

To make the document more visually interesting for online viewers, Zoe would like to add a background effect. You can apply one of the following background effects:

• Solid color
• Gradient—a single color or combination of colors that varies in intensity
• Texture—a design that mimics the look of various textured materials, including linen and marble
• Pattern—a repetitive design such as checks, polka dots, and stripes, in colors you specify
• Picture—a graphic image

Note that backgrounds do not appear in printed documents; they are visible only on the screen in Web Layout view and in documents saved as Web pages. After you apply a background color or texture, you should make sure your text is still readable. In poorly designed online documents, the background might be so dark or the pattern so obtrusive that the text is illegible. Zoe suggests you use an unobtrusive textured background.

To apply a background effect to a document:

1. Click the **Page Layout** tab, and then in the Page Background group, click the **Page Color** button. The Page Color palette opens, with a menu at the bottom. You could click a color in the palette to select it as a background color for the page. To select any other type of background effect, you need to click Fill Effects.

2. Click **Fill Effects**, and then click the **Texture** tab if necessary. The Texture list box displays a variety of textured backgrounds.

3. Click the gray box in the left column, fourth row down. An outline appears around the gray box, indicating that it is selected, and the name of the texture, "Newsprint," appears below the palette of tiles. See Figure 7-33.

Selecting a texture background   **Figure 7-33**

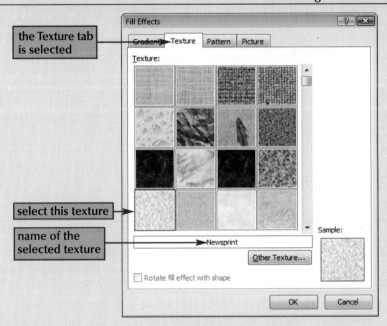

4. Click the **OK** button. The gray texture fills the background of the Green Fields Rev document.

5. Save the document in Web Layout view.

The texture background is attractive and light enough to make the document text easy to read. Note that it's a good idea to make sure linked documents have a similar appearance. Later, Zoe plans to add a similar background to the Resume document. That way both of the linked documents will have a consistent look. She'll take care of that task, though. Instead, you can focus on saving the current document as a Web page.

Saving a Word Document as a Web Page

To create sophisticated Web pages (or a complete Web site), you'll probably want to use a dedicated HTML editor, such as Adobe Dreamweaver. But to create a simple Web page from an existing document, you can convert a document to a Web page from within Word.

So far, Zoe has created printed copies of her program description and an online version to e-mail to Alison. Next, she wants to convert her document to a Web page so she can make it available on the World Wide Web.

Another term for a Web page is **HTML document**. The acronym "HTML" is short for **Hypertext Markup Language**, a language that tells a Web browser how a Web page should look on the screen. When you save a Word document as a Web page, Word inserts HTML codes that tell the browser how to format the text and graphics. Fortunately, you don't have to learn the Hypertext Markup Language to create Web pages with Word. When you save the document as a Web page, Word creates all the necessary HTML codes (called markings, or tags). This process is transparent to you, so you won't actually see the HTML codes in your Web pages.

When you save a document as a Web page, Word saves the document as an HTML file and places the graphics that appear in the document in a separate folder. A group of smaller files travels across the Web faster than one large file, so this division of files makes it easier to share your documents on the Web.

You can choose from three different Web page file types in Word. The main differences among these file types are file size and the way special elements, such as WordArt, or embedded or linked objects, are treated when they are displayed in a browser:

- Single File Web Page—Saves the document as an MHTML file, which is slightly different from an HTML file. All graphics are stored in the file. When the Web page is open in Word, the linked and embedded objects continue to function as usual. When displayed in a browser, the file, including its linked or embedded objects, looks exactly as it did in Word. However, the linked and embedded objects do not function as embedded or linked objects when displayed in a browser. A Single File Web Page can be more than twice the size of the original Word document.

- Web Page—Saves the document as an HTML file, with all graphics stored in a separate folder. When the Web page is open in Word, the linked and embedded objects continue to function as usual. When displayed in a browser, the file, including its linked or embedded objects, looks exactly as it did in Word, but the linked and embedded objects no longer function as embedded or linked objects. A file saved using the Web Page file type might be 30 kilobytes, with 100 KB of accompanying files.

- Web Page, Filtered—Saves the document as an HTML file that contains only HTML codes, without any of the codes that ensure that special elements are displayed as they are in the Word document. Instead, these special elements are formatted by HTML codes. For example, the labels on an embedded Excel chart might look different than they did in the original Word document. Such formatting differences are apparent when you open the filtered Web page in a browser, or the next time you open the file in Word. A filtered Web page is very small, allowing it to travel quickly across the Web. A typical filtered Web page of a few hundred words might be about 4 KB, with 25 KB of accompanying files.

The Single File Web Page file type is a good choice when you plan to share your Web page only over a small network and not over the Internet. Having to manage only one file is more convenient than having to keep track of a group of files. But when you want to share your files over the Internet, it's better to use the Web Page, Filtered option. This will keep your overall file size as small as possible. Note that the folder Word creates to store the accompanying graphics files has the same name as your Web page, plus an underscore and the word "files." For instance, a Web page saved as "Finance Summary" would be accompanied by a folder named "Finance Summary_files."

Although saving a Word document as a Web page is easy, it's not foolproof, particularly when it comes to formatting. When you save your document as a Web page, some document formatting might be lost, or the formatting might look different. This is especially true if you use the Web Page, Filtered file type. Sometimes you might need to reapply formatting after a document has been saved as a Web page. As a general rule, once you save a document as a Web page, you'll want to modify it to make it more attractive for users of the Web. At the very least, you will probably need to reposition graphics.

Saving a Word Document as a Web Page | Reference Window

- Click the Office Button, and then click Save As.
- To save the Web page as a single file, click the Save as type list arrow, and then click Single File Web Page. To ensure that your Web page file is as small as possible, click the Save as type list arrow, and then click Web Page, Filtered.
- If desired, give the file a new filename. For files saved using the Single File Web Page type, Word automatically adds the .mht file extension. For files saved using the Web Page file type, Word automatically adds the .htm file extension. These extensions probably won't be visible in the Save As dialog box.
- Click the Change Title button, type a title for the Web page in the Set Page Title dialog box, and then click the OK button. This title will appear in the browser title bar.
- Click the Save button in the Save As dialog box.
- If you saved the document using the Web Page, Filtered option, click Yes in the warning dialog box.

To save the Green Fields Rev document as a Web page:

▶ **1.** Close any Internet-related programs, such as e-mail editors and browsers.

▶ **2.** Click the **Office Button** 🏢, and then click **Save As**. The Save As dialog box opens.

▶ **3.** Click the **Save as type** list arrow, and then click **Web Page, Filtered**.

▶ **4.** Change the filename to **Green Fields Web Page**.

▶ **5.** Click the **Change Title** button to open the Set Page Title dialog box, and then type **Green Fields Fresh Lunch Program** in the Page title text box. This title will appear in the browser title bar.

▶ **6.** Click the **OK** button in the Set Page Title dialog box.

▶ **7.** Click the **Save** button in the Save As dialog box. A dialog box appears warning you that using the Web Page, Filtered file type will remove special codes, called tags, that control how the document is displayed in Word. That's fine, because you are concerned only with creating a file that is small enough to transmit quickly across the Web and that will be displayed properly in a Web browser.

▶ **8.** Click the **Yes** button. The document is converted into a Web page, although it looks the same as it did before you saved it as a Web page. The revised filename, "Green Fields Web Page," appears in the Word title bar, as usual. The title you specified in Step 5 won't be visible until you open the Web page in a browser, at which point it will be displayed in the browser's title bar.

At this point, the new Green Fields Web page looks identical to the Green Fields Rev Word document when you displayed it in Web Layout view. Because you used the Web Page, Filtered file type, you might have expected the new Web page to look different. In particular, you might have expected the linked chart or the embedded worksheet to have changed appearance. Their appearance hasn't changed yet, because your computer's memory still retains the image of these elements with the proper Word formatting. Later, when you close the Web page file and open it in a browser, you will see some differences.

Although you can't see any visible change in the file, the file size has decreased from about 61 KB to only about 9 KB, plus about 29 KB of related files. Even though you are currently looking at the Web page in Word, the new HTML file is optimized for viewing in a Web browser such as Internet Explorer.

Formatting a Web Page

You can edit and format text and graphics in a Web page the same way you edit and format a normal Word document. After you have saved a Word document as a Web page, you need to format the Web page so that it is attractive when it is displayed in a browser—you need to format it for online viewing.

Inserting Horizontal Lines

Web pages sometimes include horizontal lines that separate sections of a document. These lines make it easy to see at a glance where one section ends and another begins. You can also add horizontal lines to Word documents that you plan to read in Web Layout view. If you don't like a horizontal line after you insert one into a document, you can delete it by clicking the line and then pressing the Delete key.

Zoe wants you to add a horizontal line below the title and at the end of each section except the last one.

To insert horizontal lines into the Web page:

▶ **1.** Click at the beginning of the heading "Kids Are What They Eat."

▶ **2.** Click the **Home** tab, if necessary, click the **Borders** button arrow ▦ ▾, and then, at the bottom of the menu, click **Borders and Shading**. The Borders and Shading dialog box opens.

▶ **3.** Click the **Borders** tab in the Borders and Shading dialog box if it is not already selected, and then click the **Horizontal Line** button. The Horizontal Line dialog box opens, displaying many styles of horizontal lines.

▶ **4.** Click the line in the left column, second box from the top. The line is selected, as shown in Figure 7-34.

Figure 7-34 ▶ **Selecting a horizontal line style**

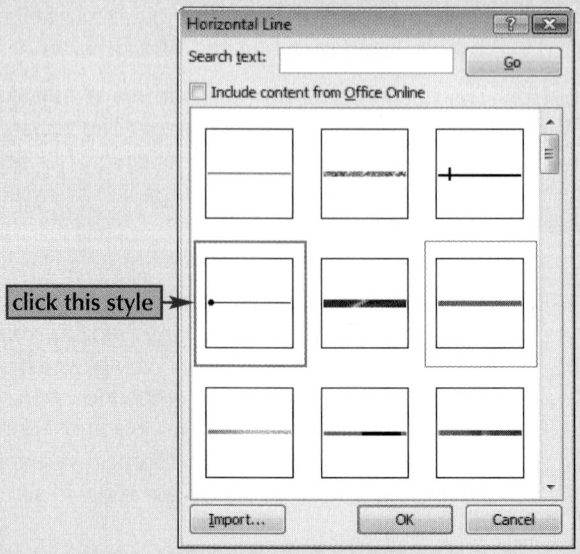

5. Click the **OK** button. A black line with a small, black circle on each end is inserted into the Web page above the "Kids Are What They Eat" heading. Your Web page should look similar to Figure 7-35.

Newly inserted horizontal line ◄ **Figure 7-35**

6. Scroll down, click to the left of the "B" in the Budget heading, and then insert the same style of horizontal line.

7. Insert the same style of horizontal line above the Program Director heading.

8. Scroll back to the top of the document and save your work. If you see the warning dialog box you saw earlier, click the **Yes** button.

Tip

You can use the F4 key to open the Horizontal Line dialog box after you complete Step 5.

Now that you've used horizontal lines to give shape to the document, you decide to improve the appearance of the document's text.

Modifying Text Size and Color

It's often helpful to format headings in a Web page in a larger size than you might use in a document that would be printed. Zoe wants you to increase the font size of the first heading in the document. She also wants you to center it.

To increase the font size for the first heading and center it:

1. Select the heading **Green Fields Fresh Lunch Program** at the beginning of the Web page.

2. In the Font group on the Home tab, click the **Grow Font** button A to increase the font size from 14-point to 16-point.

3. Continue clicking the **Grow Font** button A until the font size of the selected heading is **28-point**. Use the Font Size list box to see the current size of the selected text. If you increase the font size too much, use the Shrink Font button A to reduce the font size.

4. In the Paragraph group, click the **Center** button ≡ to center the heading at the top of the document, and then click anywhere in the document to deselect the heading.

5. Save your work. If you see the warning dialog box, click the **Yes** button.

You've formatted Zoe's document so that it will be visually appealing when displayed in a browser. Next, you'll create additional hypertext links and edit the existing link.

Creating and Editing Hyperlinks in a Web Page

As you looked through the HTML version of the program description, you probably noticed that it still contains two hyperlinks. The Alison Jorgenson link still jumps to the Program Director section at the end of the Web page, and the resume link still jumps to a Word document containing Alison's resume. Zoe wants to save the Resume document as a Web page and then format it to match the Green Fields Rev document. She also wants you to add a hyperlink in the resume that will jump back to the Green Fields Web page. Finally, because you'll save the Resume document with a new name, you have to edit the resume hyperlink (in the Green Fields Web page) to make sure it opens the right file.

In the following steps, you will convert the resume to a Web page, create a new link from the resume back to the Green Fields Web page, and then modify the hyperlink in the Green Fields Web page so that browsers can easily jump between the two documents.

To convert the resume to a Web page:

▶ **1.** Open the file named **Resume** from the Tutorial.07\Tutorial folder included with your Data Files.

▶ **2.** Click the **Office Button** , click **Save As**, navigate to the Tutorial.07\Tutorial folder, select the **Web Page, Filtered** file type, use **Resume Web Page** as the file-name, and use **Alison Jorgenson's Resume** as the Web page title.

▶ **3.** While the Save As dialog box is open, notice that Word has created a new folder, named "Green Fields Web Page_files," in which to store the files related to the Green Fields Web page. You should never save any other documents in this folder.

▶ **4.** Click the **Save** button to save the file and close the Save As dialog box, and then click **Yes** in the warning dialog box. Word automatically switches to Web Layout view.

Next, you'll make some formatting changes to give the Resume Web page the same look as the Green Fields Web page. You'll use the procedures you learned earlier in this tutorial.

To format the resume Web page:

▶ **1.** Click the **Page Layout** tab, click the **Page Color** button, click **Fill Effects**, click the **Texture** tab, and then apply the **Newsprint** style textured background.

▶ **2.** Save your work. Click the **Yes** button in the warning dialog box.

The resume and the program description Web pages now have a similar appearance.

Inserting a Hyperlink to a Web Page

After users read Alison's resume, they most likely will want to return to the program description, so Zoe asks you to insert a hyperlink that jumps to the program description. You insert hyperlinks into Web pages just as you do in Word documents.

To insert a hyperlink in the Resume Web page:

▶ **1.** Press the **Ctrl+End** keys to move the insertion point to the end of the Web page, press the **Enter** key to insert a blank paragraph, and then type **Return to Green Fields Web page.** (Include the period.)

▶ **2.** Select the text **Return to Green Fields Web Page.**, click the **Insert** tab, click the **Hyperlink** button, and then, under Link to, click **Existing File or Web Page** if it is not already selected.

▶ **3.** If necessary, navigate to the Tutorial.07\Tutorial folder included with your Data Files, click **Green Fields Web Page**, and then click the **OK** button. Word inserts the hyperlink to the program description.

▶ **4.** Save the Resume Web page (clicking Yes in the warning dialog box), and then close the Web page. You return to the Green Fields Web Page.

The resume now contains a hyperlink that takes users back to the Green Fields Web page. You will test this hyperlink later in this tutorial, when you view both Web pages in a browser.

Editing a Hyperlink

The Green Fields Web page contains a hyperlink that targets the Resume document. You need to edit the hyperlink so that it targets the Web page version of the resume. Rather than deleting the hyperlink and reinserting a new one, you can edit the existing hyperlink to target the Resume Web Page document.

To edit a hyperlink:

▶ **1.** Scroll to the end of the program description, and then position the pointer over the hyperlink. A ScreenTip appears indicating that the link will jump to a document named Resume.docx.

▶ **2.** Right-click the **resume** hyperlink. A shortcut menu opens.

▶ **3.** Click **Edit Hyperlink** in the shortcut menu. The Edit Hyperlink dialog box opens. This looks just like the Insert Hyperlink dialog box, which you have already used. To edit the hyperlink, you simply select a different target file.

▶ **4.** Under Link to, verify that the **Existing File or Web Page** option is selected.

▶ **5.** If necessary, navigate to the Tutorial.07\Tutorial folder.

▶ **6.** Click **Resume Web Page** in the file list (you might have to scroll to see it), and then click the **OK** button. You return to the Green Fields Web page.

▶ **7.** Place the mouse pointer over the resume hyperlink. A ScreenTip appears, indicating that the link will now jump to a Web page named Resume Web Page.htm.

▶ **8.** Save your work, click the **Yes** button if you see a warning dialog box about the removal of Word tags, and then close Word.

The edited hyperlink in the program description Web page now correctly targets the Resume Web page. Note that if you move your Web page files to another folder or e-mail them to someone, the hyperlinks you created won't work because they refer to a specific location on your computer. Such links that refer to a specific location on a specific computer are known as absolute links. To avoid problems with absolute links, after moving a document, be sure to review all hyperlinks in the document, editing the hyperlinks as necessary to make sure they work correctly.

Breaking a Link Between Objects

When you convert a Word document to a Web page using the Single File Web Page file type or the Web Page file type, any embedded objects or linked objects continue to function as usual as long as the Web page is displayed in Word. That is, you can double-click them to display the tools of the source program. If you use the Web Page, Filtered file type, embedded and linked objects continue to function only as long as you don't close the Web page in Word. If you reopen the filtered Web page in Word, embedded and linked objects will no longer function. No matter what file type you use, when you display a Web page in a browser, the embedded or linked objects do not function. They are displayed in the Web page, but double-clicking them does not display the tools of the source program.

Even though the links to a source program continue to function in some types of Web pages when they are displayed in Word, they can be problematic. After all, the main reason to save a document as a Web page is to make transmitting it over the Web as easy as possible. You probably won't want to increase the total file size by transmitting the source file along with the Web page. Also, your readers will naturally open your Web page in a browser, not in Word, so even if the links were functional, the readers wouldn't notice them.

For these reasons, it's good idea to break any links between a Web page and a source file. When you **break a link**, the linked object becomes an embedded object, and any connection between the source file and the Web page is severed. Note that you can also break a link between a Word document and a source file. The steps are the same, whether you are working with a Word document or a Web page.

Reference Window | **Breaking the Link to a Source File**

- Click the Office Button, point to Prepare, and then click Edit Links to Files.
- Click the link that you want to break, and then click Break Link.
- To break all the links in a document, press the Ctrl+Shift+F9 keys.

Because you used the Web Page, Filtered file type, the link to the worksheet containing Alison's chart was broken automatically. There's no need to break the link now. Instead, you can proceed with viewing the new Web page in a browser.

Viewing the Web Page in a Browser

You're now ready to view the finished Web pages in a Web browser and to test the hyperlinks. In a browser, you don't have to press the Ctrl key to use a hyperlink. Instead, you simply click the link.

To view the Web page in a Web browser and test the links:

▶ 1. Click the **Start** button 🍥 on the taskbar, and then click **Internet Explorer**. If you are asked if you want to connect to the Internet, click No. If your browser automatically attempts to connect to the Internet, wait until the connection is established before proceeding to Step 2.

▶ 2. If you see a menu bar in Internet Explorer, click **File** on the Internet Explorer menu bar, and then click **Open** to display the Open dialog box. If you do not see a menu bar, press the **Ctrl+O** keys to display the Open dialog box.

▶ 3. Click the **Browse** button, navigate to the Tutorial.07\Tutorial folder included with your Data Files, click **Green Fields Web Page**, click the **Open** button, and then click the **OK** button. If you see a warning dialog box indicating that Internet Explorer needs to open a new window, click the **OK** button. The Green Fields Web Page file opens in Internet Explorer. See Figure 7-36.

Internet Explorer title bar

lettering in chart labels is darker and thicker than in Word

4. Scroll down and review the Web page. Notice that the labels in the pie chart are darker and less elegant-looking than they appeared in Word. Likewise, the embedded worksheet is a bit harder to read. This decrease in visual quality is a disadvantage of choosing the Web Page, Filtered file type. Keep in mind, however, that this file type has the all-important advantage of very small files, which makes transmitting the Web page faster and easier. If you preferred a better-looking Web page, you could choose one of the other Web page file types. Zoe is primarily concerned with making sure the Green Fields members can easily retrieve the Web page over the Internet, so she prefers to stick with the small-sized files provided by the Web Page, Filtered file type, at the expense of readability.

5. Near the beginning of the Web page, click the **Alison Jorgenson** hyperlink. The Program Director section is displayed in the browser window.

6. In the last paragraph of the document, click the **resume** hyperlink. The browser opens the Resume Web page.

7. Scroll through the resume. Notice that when you view the resume in the browser, the table format disappears and Alison's address information is left-aligned. In this case, the format is still acceptable, so you don't have to make any additional changes in Word. But in another type of document, such a change might necessitate another round of editing in Word.

8. At the bottom of the resume, click the **Return to Green Fields Web page** hyperlink. The browser displays the Green Fields Web page.

   Trouble? If any of the hyperlinks don't work properly, close the browser, return to Word, and then edit the hyperlinks so they link to the proper document.

▶ **9.** Close the browser window, start Word, open the **Green Fields Web Page** document from the Tutorial.07\Tutorial folder included with your Data Files, click the **Yes** button to update links, press the **Ctrl+End** keys to move the insertion point to the bottom of the Web page, press the **Enter** key twice, and insert the text **Prepared by** followed by your first and last name and a period.

▶ **10.** Save the Web page, print it, and close it. The printed Web page looks similar, but not identical, to the printed Word document.

Review | **Session 7.2 Quick Check**

1. True or False. A Web page is the same thing as an HTML document.
2. True or False. The Web Page file type results in the smallest possible total file size.
3. What's the difference between an intranet and the Internet?
4. What is the first step in creating a hyperlink to a location in the same document?
5. What term refers to the part of the Internet that transfers and displays Web pages?
6. Explain how to edit a hyperlink.
7. When saving a document as a Web page, which file type should you choose if you want to ensure that all OLE links to a source file are severed automatically?

Review | **Tutorial Summary**

In this tutorial, you turned on Track Changes in a document and inserted comments. Then you compared and combined documents, accepted and rejected changes, deleted comments, embedded an Excel file in a Word document, linked an Excel file with a Word document, edited an embedded Excel file, and edited a linked Excel file. You made a document suitable for online reading by adding hyperlinks, previewing the document in Web Layout view, and modifying the document's appearance to make it more interesting. Finally, you converted a Word document into a Web page, added additional hyperlinks, edited a hyperlink, and previewed the Web page in a browser.

Key Terms

bookmark	Internet	source file
balloons	intranet	source program
break a link	link	spreadsheet program
browser	linking	target
cell	merge	URL
combine	Microsoft Internet Explorer	Web
compare	Mozilla Firefox	Web address
destination file	object	Web Layout view
destination program	object linking and embed-	Web page
embedding	ding (OLE)	Web server
HTML document	online	Web site
home page	publish	worksheet
hyperlink	revision marks	World Wide Web
Hypertext Markup Language (HTML)		

| Practice | **Review Assignments** |

Apply the skills you learned in the tutorial using the same case scenario.

Data Files needed for the Review Assignments: Expenses.xlsx, Menu.docx, Progress.docx, Progress HD.docx, Rates.xlsx

The first year of the Green Fields Fresh Lunch program was a success. Now Zoe and the staff of Rios Communication need to create a progress report to summarize the program's effectiveness. Zoe has written a draft of the progress report and e-mailed it to Henry. While Henry reviews it, she plans to turn on Track Changes and continue work on the document. Then she can combine her edited version of the document with Henry's, accepting or rejecting changes. Next, she needs to insert an Excel worksheet as an embedded object and insert an Excel chart as a linked object. She then wants to create an online version of the document with hyperlinks, format the document for online viewing, save it as a Web page, and view it in a browser. (Note: Text you need to type is shown in bold for ease of reference only; do not bold the text unless otherwise instructed.)

1. Open the file named **Progress** from the Tutorial.07\Review folder included with your Data Files. Save the file as **Progress Report** in the same folder.

2. Turn on Track Changes, and then edit the document by formatting the first two headings with the Heading 1 style. Delete "concerned" in the first main paragraph.

3. In the last line of the first main paragraph, insert the word **generous** before the word "grant," so the sentence reads "...by a generous grant...." In the middle line of the third main paragraph, select the word "thirty" and insert a comment that reads **Remember to verify this number**.

4. In the Current Membership section at the end of the document, replace "Marti Sundra" with your name. Save your work.

5. Combine the Progress Report document with Henry's edited version, named **Progress HD**. This file is in the Tutorial.07\Review folder included with your Data Files.

6. Close the Progress Report document (saving changes if necessary) and save the new document as **Progress Report Rev** in the Tutorial.07\Review folder included with your Data Files.

7. Turn off Track Changes, and then accept all the changes in the document except Henry's deletion of "extremely." Review the comments and then delete all comments in the document. Save your work.

8. Replace the placeholder [Insert Excel worksheet] with the budget in the Expenses.xlsx file in the Tutorial.07\Review folder included with your Data Files. Insert the budget as an embedded object, and then close Excel.

9. Center the embedded object, and then edit it to change the Parent Education value from $2,500 to **$3,000**.

10. Delete the placeholder [Insert Excel chart], make sure the insertion point is located in a blank paragraph between the two paragraphs of text, start Excel, open the workbook named **Rates.xlsx** file in the Tutorial.07\Review folder included with your Data Files, and then save it as **Rates Copy.xlsx**. Copy the chart and insert it as a linked object in the **Progress Report Rev** document at the insertion point. Save your work.

11. Return to Excel and change the Last Month participation rate for middle schools from 40% to **90%**. Save and close the **Rates Copy.xlsx** file and close Excel. Update the linked object in Word.

12. Print the **Progress Report Rev** document.

13. In the list of board members at the end of the document, select the word "Chair" and insert a bookmark named **Board**. At the end of the first main paragraph, insert the sentence **The Board of Directors is responsible for overseeing the grant.** Format "Board of Directors" as a hyperlink that targets the Board bookmark. Test the hyperlink to make sure it works.

14. In the paragraph below the heading "Year One: What Went Right?," click after the first sentence and insert the following: **(Click here for a typical salad bar menu.)** Select the word **here** and insert a hyperlink that targets the Word document named **Menu** in the Tutorial.07\Review folder included with your Data Files. Test the hyperlink to make sure it works, and then close the Menu document.

15. Switch to Web Layout view, and then format the report's background with the Newsprint texture.

16. Before every heading except the first, insert a black horizontal line with circles on each end.

17. Increase the font size for the first heading, "Green Fields Progress Report," to 28-point, and then center the heading. Save the document.

18. Save the report as a Web page in the Tutorial.07\Review folder using the Web Page, Filtered file type. Use **Progress Report Web Page** for the filename and **Green Fields First Year Progress** as the page title.

19. Use the hyperlink to open the **Menu** document, and save then save the Menu document in the Tutorial.07\Review folder as a Web Page using the Web Page, Filtered file type. Use **Menu Web Page** as the filename, and **Green Fields Typical Menu** as the page title. Format the menu's background with the Newsprint texture, and then save the close the file.

20. Close Word, open your browser, open the **Progress Report Web Page** from the Tutorial.07\Review folder, review the Web page in the browser, test the hyperlinks, and then close the browser.

21. Use your e-mail program to send the **Progress Report Rev** document to a fellow student. In most e-mail programs, you need to create a new message, and then attach the file to the message. Ask the recipient of the file to open it and test the various links. Can he or she access the source file for the Excel file? Why or why not? Do the other links in the document work? Why or why not?

22. Submit the documents to your instructor, in printed or electronic form, as requested.

Apply | **Case Problem 1**

Apply the skills you learned to create an investment statement.

Data Files needed for this Case Problem: Cook.docx, Statement.xlsx

KingFish Financial Planning   You have just started work as a certified financial planner at KingFish Financial Planning. At the end of every quarter, you need to send a letter to each client containing a statement that summarizes the client's investment portfolio. The letter is a Word document, and the investment data for each client is stored in an Excel file. You need to insert the Excel data in the Word document. Because your assistant updates this data every morning, you plan to insert the data as a linked object. That way, when you print and mail the statement at the end of the quarter, you can be sure that it will contain the most current data. In the following steps, you will create a statement for a client named Isabella Cook. You will also practice pasting copied worksheet data into a document as a Word table. (Note: Text you need to type is shown in bold for ease of reference only; do not bold the text unless otherwise instructed.)

1. Open the file named **Cook** from the Tutorial.07\Case1 folder included with your Data Files. Save the file as **Cook Letter** in the same folder. The letter is based on the Oriel Letter template.

2. Use the Date document control to select the current date. In the signature line, replace "Student Name" with your name.

3. Delete the placeholder "[Insert Excel worksheet.]."

4. Start Excel and open the file named **Statement** from the Tutorial.07\Case1 folder included with your Data Files. Save the file as **Cook Statement** in the same folder.

5. Copy the worksheet data to the Clipboard and insert it into the Word document in the blank paragraph that previously contained the placeholder text. Insert the data as a linked Microsoft Office Excel Worksheet Object.

6. Save and close the Word document.

7. Return to the **Cook Statement** worksheet and change the Year to Date value for the Roth IRA to **$28,000**. Save and close the Excel file.

8. Open the **Cook Letter** document in Word and verify that the Year to Date value for the Roth IRA has been updated to $28,000.

9. Save and print and the **Cook Letter** document.

10. Save the letter again as **Cook Letter** 2 in the same folder. Delete the worksheet object.

⊕ EXPLORE 11. Open the **Cook Statement** file in Excel again, and then copy the worksheet data to the Office Clipboard again. Return to the Word document, and this time simply paste the worksheet data into the document using the Paste button. Adjust column widths in the new table as necessary to make the statement easy to read.

12. Save and print the document.

13. Close Excel.

14. Submit the finished documents to your instructor, either in printed or electronic form, as requested.

Apply | **Case Problem 2**

Apply the skills you learned to create a Web page for an upscale dog kennel.

Data Files needed for this Case Problem: Kreelie.docx, Sun.docx

Kreelie Kennels Web Page Brianna Kreelie is the owner of Kreelie Kennels, an upscale dog boarding facility in Knoxville, Kentucky. She would like your help in creating a Web page for her business. She has created a first draft and saved it as a Word document. In the document, she included some comments explaining the edits she would like you to make. After you edit the document and remove the comments, she would like you to format it for online viewing and save it as a Web page. (Note: Text you need to type is shown in bold for ease of reference only; do not bold the text unless otherwise instructed.)

1. Open the file **Kreelie** from the Tutorial.07\Case2 folder included with your Data Files, and then save it as **Kreelie Edits** in the same folder.

2. Turn on Track Changes, review the comments, and make the changes requested in the comments. When you are finished, delete the comments. At the end of the document, insert a comment that reads **I made all the changes you requested**.

⊕ EXPLORE 3. Save and print the document using the default print settings. Notice that the margin balloons and revision marks are printed by default.

4. Save the document as **Kreelie Final** in the Tutorial.07\Case2 folder.

5. Turn off Track Changes, and then accept all your changes in the document except for the deletion of the word "fleece," which you should reject. Delete your comment at the end of the document, and then save your work.

6. Open the document named **Sun** from the Tutorial.07\Case2 folder, save it as **Sundeck** in the same folder, and then close it.

7. In the **Kreelie Final** document, at the end of the "Fun in the Sun" section, format the word "here" as a hyperlink that opens the **Sundeck** document. For now, don't be concerned if the link is formatted in a color that is hard to see. Test the link, and then return to the **Kreelie Final** document.

8. Open the Theme Colors menu and preview the various color sets, noticing the different color applied to the hyperlink in each theme. Select the Technic theme colors.

◆ EXPLORE　　9. Format the page background for the **Kreelie Final** document and the **Sundeck** document using the yellow tile under Standard Colors in the Page Color menu.

10. Review the Kreelie Final document and the Sundeck document in Web Layout view. Save both documents in Web Layout view. Do not print the documents unless your instructor asks you to, because the yellow background could be problematic on some printers.

11. Save the Kreelie Final document as **Kreelie Web Page** in the Tutorial.07\Case2 folder, using the Web Page, Filtered file type. Use **Kreelie Kennels** as the page title. Save the Sundeck document as **Sundeck Web Page** in the same folder, using the same file type. Use **Kreelie Kennels Sundeck** as the page title.

12. Edit the hyperlink so it targets the correct file, and then save your work.

13. Close Word and open the **Kreelie Web Page** file in a browser. Test the hyperlink. Close the browser.

14. Submit the finished file to your instructor, either in printed or electronic form, as requested.

| Create | | **Case Problem 3** |

Use your Web page skills to create the Web page shown in Figure 7-37.

Data File needed for this Case Problem: Survey.xlsx

Seabird Optical Web Page　　You have been asked to create a Web page for Seabird Optical, a supplier of high-quality eyeglasses in Bellingham, Washington. Perform the following steps to create the Web page shown in Figure 7-37.

Figure 7-37

Seabird Optical

3421 Island Way, Bellingham, Washington 98225

Think you don't need glasses? Think again. Our customer surveys show a surprising number of people don't discover they need glasses until they have an eye exam. The following chart prepared by Student Name summarizes our findings:

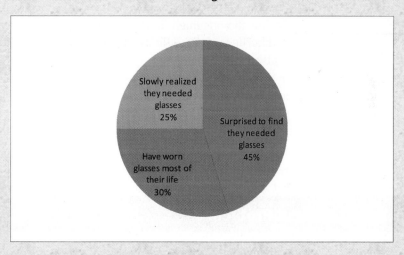

1. Open a new, blank document and save it as a document (not as a Web page) using the name **Sea** in the Tutorial.07\Case3 folder included with your Data Files. Insert two blank paragraphs.

⊕ EXPLORE

2. When creating Web pages and online documents, you might sometimes need to create simple graphics. To learn how, click the Start button on the taskbar, click All Programs, click Accessories, and then click Paint.

   a. Click Image on the menu bar, click Attributes, and then change the Width setting to 500 and the Height setting to 200.

      b. Click the Brush button on the toolbar, click a blue box in the color palette, and draw the waves shown in Figure 7-37. Continue using these tools to draw the yellow sun and the black birds. (If you don't like your first attempt, use the Erase button to erase your work.) Don't expect to produce a perfect work of art; your goal is just to get familiar with using Paint.

      c. Save the logo as a JPEG file named **Birds** in the Tutorial.07\Case3 folder, and then close Paint.

3. On the Insert tab, use the Insert Picture button to insert the **Birds** file into the first blank paragraph of the document. Center the picture at the top of the document.

4. In the second paragraph of the document, insert the company name as WordArt, as shown in Figure 7-37. Center the WordArt object.

5. Below the WordArt title, insert the text shown in Figure 7-37. Replace "Student Name" with your name. Format the text as shown in Figure 7-37.

6. Open the Excel file named **Survey** from the Tutorial.07\Case3 folder included with your Data Files, and then save it as **Survey Copy**.

7. Insert a linked copy of the chart from the Survey Copy file in the Word document. Close Excel.

8. From within Word, revise the linked chart to change the percentage for "Surprised to find they needed glasses" to 45%. Change the percentage for "Have worn glasses most of their life" to 30%. Update the link.

9. Format the page background with the Blue tissue paper texture. Insert a turquoise horizontal line as shown in Figure 7-37.

10. Break the link to the Excel file.

11. Review the document in Web Layout view, and then save it as a Web page using the Single File Web Page file type. Use **Seabird Web Page** as the filename and **Seabird Optical** as the page title.

12. In Web Layout view, resize the Excel chart to make it as wide as the last line of text in the paragraph above it, and then save your changes.

13. Close Word and open the Web page in a browser.

⊕ **EXPLORE**   14. Print the Web page from your browser, and then close your browser.

15. Submit the finished files to your instructor, either in printed or electronic form, as requested.

Challenge | **Case Problem 4**

Go beyond the skills you've learned to create a FAQ Web page.

Data File needed for this Case Problem: FAQ.docx

Great Falls Health Resource   Sebastian Morey is publications director at Great Falls Health Resource, a county agency in Great Falls, Montana, that helps county residents manage health and health insurance-related issues. Sebastian asks you to help create a FAQ (Frequently Asked Questions) page that answers some basic questions related to health insurance. So far, he has created the basic structure of the FAQ and inserted a few questions. He wants you to add the necessary hyperlinks.

1. Open the file named **FAQ** from the Tutorial.07\Case4 folder included with your Data Files, and then save it as a Word document using the name **Insurance FAQ** in the same folder.

2. At the bottom of the document, replace "Student Name" with your name. Replace "Date" with the current date.

EXPLORE

3. Create a system of hyperlinks that makes it possible for a user to click a topic in the Table of Contents and jump immediately to the relevant section in the Web page. Add hyperlinks to the "Back to top" text that jump to the "Table of Contents" heading at the beginning of the document. Use a heading as the target of each hyperlink rather than a bookmark.

4. At the bottom of page 1, delete the placeholder "[Insert chart here.]," and then verify that the insertion point is located in a blank paragraph between two other blank paragraphs.

EXPLORE

5. In the Illustrations group on the Insert tab, use the Chart button to insert the default type of column chart. Drag the mouse to select the bottom row of data and then delete it. In the same way, delete the data in columns C and D. Drag the border between the column headers for Columns A and B to the right to make Column A about four times wider than its default width. Replace the first three rows of data with the following data:
   - No employee contribution: 5%
   - Required for family coverage: 60%
   - Required for employee coverage: 80%

   Replace "Series1" with **Employee Contributions**. Locate the bottom-right corner of the selection box around the data, and drag it up and to the left so that it encloses the data you just typed. Close the Chart in Microsoft Office Word window. There's no need to save the chart in this window because it will be saved with the Word document.

EXPLORE

6. Double-click the chart in the Word document, and then examine the various Chart Tools tabs. Use a button on the Chart Tools Layout tab to turn off the chart legend. Use a button on the Design tab to edit the data, changing the percentage for "Required for family coverage" from 60% to 93%.

EXPLORE

7. Near the end of page 2, in the section on finding health insurance statistics on the Web, format the word "here" as a hyperlink that targets the Web site for the U.S. Census Bureau. In the Address box of the Insert Hyperlink dialog box, enter the following URL: **www.census.gov**. (Do not include the period at the end.) If your computer is connected to the Internet, test the hyperlink, and then close the browser.

8. Save the document and print it.

9. Save the document as a Web page using the file type that results in the lowest total file size. Use **Insurance FAQ Web Page** as the filename and **Insurance FAQ** as the page title.

10. Close Word and open the **Insurance FAQ Web Page** in a browser. Test all the table of contents and "Back to top" hyperlinks. If your computer is connected to the Internet, test the U.S. Census Bureau hyperlink.

11. Submit the finished files to your instructor, either in printed or electronic form, as requested.

Research | Internet Assignments

Go to the Web to find information you can use to create documents.

The purpose of the Internet Assignments is to challenge you to find information on the Internet that you can use to work effectively with this software. The actual assignments are updated and maintained on the Course Technology Web site. Log on to the Internet and use your Web browser to go to the Student Online Companion for New Perspectives Office 2007 at **www.course.com/np/office2007**. Then navigate to the Internet Assignments for this tutorial.

Assess | SAM Assessment and Training

If you have a SAM user profile, you may have access to hands-on instruction, practice, and assessment of the skills covered in this tutorial. Log in to your SAM account (**http://sam2007.course.com**) to launch any assigned training activities or exams that relate to the skills covered in this tutorial.

Review | Quick Check Answers

Session 7.1

1. Verify that the document is displayed in Print Layout view, click the Review tab, and then click the Track Changes button in the Tracking group. Verify that Final Showing Markup is displayed in the Display for Review list box in the Tracking group. Edit the document as you ordinarily would.
2. New Comment button on the Review tab
3. Combine
4. An embedded object is a copy of the original object; edits to an embedded object do not affect the original. A linked object is shortcut to the original object in the source file; edits to a linked object also affect the original object.
5. Object
6. Paste button arrow on the Home tab
7. True

Session 7.2

1. True
2. True
3. An intranet is a self-contained Web-based network that is owned by a single organization. The Internet is a worldwide network incorporating many organizations.
4. Create a bookmark
5. World Wide Web
6. Right-click the hyperlink, click Edit Hyperlink in the shortcut menu, and then select a different target file.
7. Web Page, Filtered

Ending Data Files

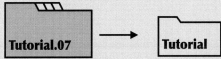

Tutorial

Green Fields Web Page_files (folder)
Resume Web Page_files (folder)
Chart Copy.xlsx
Green Fields.docx
Green Fields Rev.docx
Green Fields Web Page.htm
Resume.docx
Resume Web Page.htm

Review

Menu Web Page_files (folder)
Progress Report Web
    Page_files (folder)
Menu.docx
Menu Web Page.htm
Progress Report.docx
Progress Report Rev.docx
Progress Report Web Page.htm
Rates Copy.xlsx

Case1

Cook Letter.docx
Cook Letter 2.docx
Cook Statement.xlsx

Case2

Kreelie Web Page_files (folder)
Sundeck Web Page_files (folder)
Kreelie Edits.docx
Kreelie Final.docx
Kreelie Web Page.htm
Sundeck.docx
Sundeck Web Page.htm

Case3

Birds.jpg
Sea.docx
Seabird Web Page.mht
Survey Copy.xlsx

Case4

Insurance FAQ Web
    Page_files (folder)
Insurance FAQ.docx
Insurance FAQ
    Web Page.htm

Reality Check

At this point, you should feel confident that you have the word-processing skills to create, revise, and distribute polished, useful documents in the business world. But there's no need to wait to use your new word-processing skills. You can use them to create some practical documents right now. In the following exercise, you'll create documents using the Word skills and features presented in Tutorials 5 through 7.

Note: Please be sure *not* to include any personal information of a sensitive nature in the documents you create to be submitted to your instructor for this exercise. Later on, you can update the documents with such information for your own personal use.

1. Create a new report template to use for school reports or another type of report that you might have to create on a regular basis. Start with one of the templates installed with Word, delete or edit document controls as necessary, insert placeholder text as necessary, and customize the theme. Select an appropriate style set, and create at least one new style that will be useful in your report.

2. Use your template as the basis for a new report. Insert a file containing the text of a report you wrote for one of your classes, or insert appropriate text of your choosing, and then format the text using the template styles. Remember to include a table of contents in the report. At the end of the report, include a hyperlink that jumps to the beginning of the report.

3. If you are familiar with Excel, open a new workbook, enter some data that supports one of the points in your report, and then embed the worksheet data in your report. If you don't know how to enter data in Excel, you can embed the data from the Budget file in the Tutorial.07\Tutorial folder included with your Data Files, and then edit the data as necessary. Note that you can widen a column in Excel by dragging the right border of the column's header (the letter at the top of the column).

4. If possible, e-mail a copy of your report to a fellow student and have him or her edit the document with Track Changes turned on.

5. Turn on Track Changes in your copy of the report, and then edit it carefully for grammar, word choice, and punctuation. If you were able to ask a fellow student to edit another copy of the report, combine the two documents, and then accept or reject changes as necessary. Save the new, combined combined document with a new name.

6. Choose a type of information, such as e-mail addresses or birthdays, that you would like to organize in a single document. Create a Word table, and then enter fictitious versions of the information into the table. You can replace this with real information later for your personal use, after you've handed in your assignments. Sort the information based on one of the columns.

7. Create a main document for a directory that includes a dot leader. Use your Word table from Step 6 as the data source. Insert the necessary merge codes into the main document and complete the merge.

8. Format the merged document with a textured background and add a title. Format the title appropriately. Save the document as a Web page that consists of only one file.

9. Submit your documents to your instructor in electronic or printed form, as requested.

Working with Excel Tables, PivotTables, and PivotCharts

Tracking Museum Art Objects

Case | LaFouch Museum

Henry LaFouch, a rancher in Missoula, Montana, amassed a huge collection of North American art, particularly art of the West. Henry was a well-respected, active member of the community, and he often donated art to the town. Similarly, he loaned the town artwork to place in public locations and community centers. Upon his death, Henry donated his art collection to the town of Missoula and its people. They established an art museum in his name.

Mary Littlefield was recently hired as the curator and director of the LaFouch Museum. She is responsible for assessing the current holdings and using the endowment set aside by Henry to purchase additional art in keeping with his vision for the collection. One of Mary's first tasks was to establish an accurate inventory of the museum's holdings. For each piece of artwork, she identified the title, the artist, the date acquired, the type of art, and other pertinent facts such as its location in the museum, its condition, and its appraised value. Then, she entered all this data in an Excel worksheet.

Mary asks you to help her maintain this data so she can provide current and accurate information to the administration and board of directors about the art objects. You'll work with the data using Excel table features. You will sort the data and add, modify, and delete the data to ensure it is current. You'll also filter the information to display only data that meets certain criteria. Finally, you'll summarize the data using a PivotTable and a PivotChart.

Starting Data Files

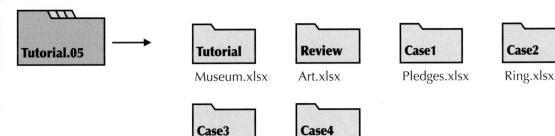

Tutorial.05 →

Tutorial
Museum.xlsx

Review
Art.xlsx

Case1
Pledges.xlsx

Case2
Ring.xlsx

Case3
CustLoans.xlsx

Case4
Bowls.xlsx

Session 5.1

Planning a Structured Range of Data

One of the more common uses of a worksheet is to manage data, such as lists of clients, products, and transactions. Using Excel, you can store and update data, sort data, search for and retrieve subsets of data, summarize data, and create reports. In Excel, a collection of similar data can be structured in a range of rows and columns. Each column in the range represents a **field** that describes some attribute or characteristic of a person, place, or thing, such as a last name, address, city, or state. Each row in the range represents a **record**, or a collection of related fields that are grouped together. The first row of the range contains column headers that describe the data fields in each column. Figure 5-1 shows a portion of the data Mary compiled for the LaFouch Museum's art objects. In this data, the ArtID, Artist, and Title columns are the first three fields. Each row is a record that stores the data for each art object—art ID, artist name, title, date acquired, category, condition, location, and appraised value. All the art object records make up the structured range of data. A structured range of data is commonly referred to as a list or table.

Figure 5-1 | LaFouch Museum art objects data

ArtID	Artist	Title	Date Acquired	Category	Condition	Location	Appraised Value
1	Mogan	Red Rock Mountain	3/19/2005	Painting	Excellent	East Pavilion	$ 18,000
2	Novarre	Offerings	5/16/2005	Painting	Excellent	East Pavilion	$ 10,000
3	Chico	Spring Flowers	3/20/2004	Sculpture	Excellent	East Pavilion	$ 2,400
4	Roman	Seeking Shelter	10/8/2005	Sculpture	Excellent	Courtyard	$ 52,000
5	DiGrigoro	The Hang	7/16/2004	Painting	Excellent	East Pavilion	$ 8,000
6	Ibe	House Remembered	8/16/2004	Sculpture	Good	East Pavilion	$ 700
7	Zischke	Homage to the Ancestors	7/17/2004	Textile	Excellent	East Pavilion	$ 1,200
8	Gilhooly	End of the Path	8/16/2004	Sculpture	Excellent	East Pavilion	$ 1,900
9	Guys	Amen	12/13/2003	Sculpture	Excellent	East Pavilion	$ 3,000
10	Swartz	Untitled (two figures)	9/8/2007	Sculpture	Excellent	East Pavilion	$ 800
11	Dill	Eve	7/16/2004	Sculpture	Excellent	East Pavilion	$ 975
12	Udinotti	Man on horseback	11/10/2007	Painting	Good	East Pavilion	$ 8,000
13	Aserty	Superstitions	1/10/2009	Painting	Excellent	Courtyard	$ 78,000
14	McGraw	Plenty	2/19/2005	Sculpture	Excellent	West Pavilion	$ 500
15	McIver	Punch	3/19/2005	Painting	Excellent	East Pavilion	$ 10,000
16	Schenck	Untitled	1/7/2006	Painting	Excellent	East Pavilion	$ 6,000
17	Bindner	Brittlecone	1/10/2004	Sculpture	Excellent	East Pavilion	$ 1,300
18	Blum	Mountain Scene	1/10/2004	Sculpture	Excellent	East Pavilion	$ 2,500

The Importance of Planning | InSight

Before you create a structured range of data, you should do some planning. Spend time thinking about how you will use the data. Consider what reports you want to create for different audiences (supervisors, customers, directors, and so forth) and the fields needed to produce those reports. Also consider the various questions, or queries, you want answered and the fields needed to create these results. The end results you want to achieve will help you determine the kind of data to include in each record and how to divide that data into fields. Careful and thorough planning will help to prevent having to redesign a structured range of data later on.

Before creating the list of art objects, Mary carefully planned what information she needs and how she wants to use it. Mary plans to use the data to track where each art object is located in the museum, its condition, the date it was acquired, its art category, and its appraised value. She wants to be able to create reports that show specific lists of art objects, such as all the objects by a specific artist or all the objects that are paintings. Based on her needs, Mary developed a **data definition table**, which is documentation that lists the fields to be maintained for each record (in this case, each art object) and a description of the information each field will include. Figure 5-2 shows Mary's completed data definition table.

Data definition table for the art objects | Figure 5-2

Field	Description
ArtID	Unique number
Artist	Name of artist
Title	Title of art object
Date Acquired	Date of purchase or donation of art object
Category	Painting, Sculpture, Installation, Textile
Condition	Excellent, Good, Fair, Poor
Location	Location of art object
Appraised Value	Appraised value of art object

After you determine the fields and records you need, you can enter the data in a blank worksheet or use a range of data that is already entered in a worksheet. You can then work with the data in many ways. The following is a list of common operations you can perform on a structured range of data:

- Add, edit, and delete data in the range
- Sort the data range
- Filter to display only rows that meet specified criteria
- Insert formulas to calculate subtotals
- Create summary tables based on the data in the range (usually with PivotTables)
- Add data validation to ensure the integrity of the data
- Apply conditional formatting

You'll perform many of these operations on the art objects data.

For a range of data to be used effectively, it must have the same structure throughout. Keep in mind the following guidelines:

- Enter field names in the top row of the range. A **field name** (also called a **column header**) is a unique label that describes the contents of the data in that column. The row of field names is called the **header row**. Although the header row often is row 1, it can be any row.
- Use short, descriptive field names. Shorter field names are easier to remember and enable more fields to appear in the workbook window at once.
- Format field names to distinguish the header row from the data. For example, apply bold, color, and a different font size.
- Enter the same kind of data for a field in each record.
- Separate the data from other information in the worksheet by *at least* one blank row and one blank column. The blank row and column enable Excel to accurately determine the range of the data.

You'll open the workbook in which Mary entered the art objects data according to the data definition table.

To open and review the Museum workbook:

▶ **1.** Open the **Museum** workbook located in the **Tutorial.05\Tutorial** folder included with your Data Files, and then save the workbook as **LaFouch Museum** in the same folder.

▶ **2.** In the Documentation worksheet, enter your name in cell B3 and the current date in cell B4.

▶ **3.** Switch to the **Art Collection** worksheet. This worksheet (which is shown in Figure 5-1) contains data about the museum's art objects. Currently, the worksheet lists 115 art objects. Each art object record is a separate row (rows 2 through 116) and contains eight fields (columns A through H). The top row, the header row, contains labels that describe the data in each column. The field names are boldface to make it easier to distinguish them from the data.

▶ **4.** Scroll the worksheet to row 116, the last record. The column headers, in the top row, are no longer visible.

▶ **5.** Press the **Ctrl+Home** keys to return to cell A1.

Freezing Rows and Columns

You want to see the column headers as you scroll the art objects data. Without the column headers visible, it is difficult to know what the data entered in each column represents. You can select rows and columns to remain visible in the workbook window as you scroll around the worksheet. **Freezing** a row or column lets you keep headings visible as you work with the data in a large worksheet. To freeze a row or column, you select the cell immediately below the row(s) and to the right of the column(s) you want to freeze. For example, if you want to keep only the column headers in the top row displayed on the screen, you click cell A2 (first column, second row), and then freeze the panes. As you scroll the data, the first row remains on the screen so the column headers are visible, making it easier to identify the data in each record.

You'll freeze the first row, which contains the column headers, so that they remain on the screen as you scroll the data.

To freeze the top row in the worksheet:

▶ **1.** Click the **View** tab on the Ribbon. The Ribbon changes to display the View options.

▶ **2.** In the Window group, click the **Freeze Panes** button, and then click **Freeze Top Row**. A dark, horizontal line appears below the column headers to indicate which row is frozen.

▶ **3.** Scroll the worksheet to row 116. This time, the column headers remain visible as you scroll. See Figure 5-3.

Freezing the top row of the worksheet ◀ **Figure 5-3**

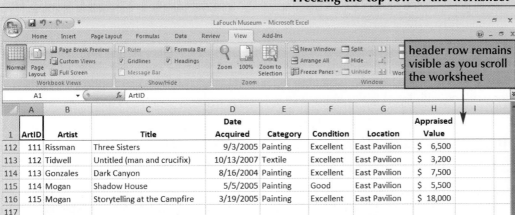

▶ **4.** Press the **Ctrl+Home** keys to return to cell A2, the cell directly below the frozen row.

After you freeze panes, the first option on the Freeze Panes menu changes to Unfreeze Panes. This option unlocks all the rows and columns so you can scroll the entire worksheet. You will use a different method to keep the column headers visible, so you will unfreeze the top row of the worksheet.

To unfreeze the top row of the worksheet:

▶ **1.** In the Window group on the View tab, click the **Freeze Panes** button. The first Freeze Panes option is now Unfreeze Panes.

▶ **2.** Click **Unfreeze Panes**. The dark, horizontal line below the column headers is removed, and you can scroll all the rows and columns in the worksheet.

Creating an Excel Table

You can convert a structured range of data, such as the art objects data in the range A1:H116, to an Excel table. Recall that an Excel table is a range of related data that is managed independently from the data in other rows and columns in the worksheet. An Excel table uses features designed to make it easier to identify, manage, and analyze the groups of related data. You can create more than one Excel table in a worksheet.

InSight	**Saving Time with Excel Table Features**

Excel tables provide many advantages to structured ranges of data. When you create an Excel table, you can perform the same operations as you can for a structured range of data. In addition, you can do the following:

- Format the Excel table quickly using a table style.
- Add new rows and columns to the Excel table that automatically expand the range.
- Add a Total row to calculate the summary function you select, such as SUM, AVERAGE, COUNT, MIN, and MAX.
- Enter a formula in one table cell that is automatically copied to all other cells in that table column.
- Create formulas that reference cells in a table by using table and column names instead of cell addresses.

These Excel table features let you focus on analyzing and understanding the data, letting the program perform the more time-consuming tasks. You will use these Excel table features in this and other tutorials.

Next, you'll create an Excel table from the art objects data in the Art Collection worksheet. By doing so, you'll be able to take advantage of the many features and tools for working with Excel tables to analyze data effectively.

Tip

If your data does not contain column headers, Excel adds headers with the default names Column1, Column2, and so forth to the table.

To create an Excel table from the art objects data:

1. Verify that the active cell is cell **A2**, which is in the range of art objects data.

2. Click the **Insert** tab on the Ribbon, and then, in the Tables group, click the **Table** button. The Create Table dialog box opens. The range of data for the table is entered in the dialog box. See Figure 5-4.

Figure 5-4	Create Table dialog box

range reference for the art objects table data

option checked because the art objects table includes column headers

3. Click the **OK** button. The dialog box closes, and the range of data is converted to an Excel table. Filter arrows appear in the header row, the table is formatted with a predefined table style, and the Table Tools Design contextual tab appears on the Ribbon. See Figure 5-5.

Excel table created for the art objects data ◀ Figure 5-5

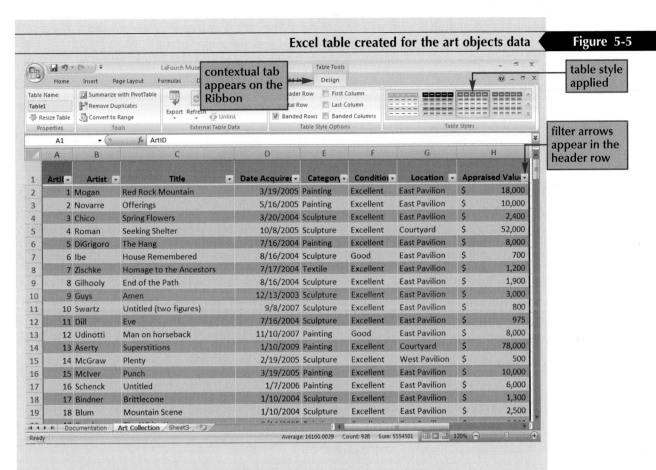

4. Scroll the table down. The text of the header row replaces the standard lettered column headings (A, B, C, and so on) as you scroll so that you don't need to freeze panes to keep the header row visible. See Figure 5-6.

Art objects table scrolled ◀ Figure 5-6

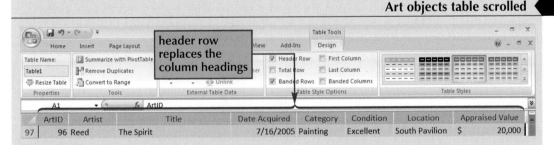

5. Press the **Ctrl+Home** keys to make cell A1 active. The column headings return to the standard display, and the header row scrolls back into view as row 1.

Renaming an Excel Table

Excel assigns the name Table1 to the first Excel table created in a workbook. Any additional Excel tables you create in the workbook are named consecutively, Table2, Table3, and so forth. You can assign a more descriptive name to a table, which makes it easier to identify a particular table by its content. Descriptive names are especially useful when you create more than one Excel table in the same workbook. Table names must start with a letter or an underscore and can use any combination of letters, numbers, and underscores for the rest of the name. Table names cannot include spaces.

Mary asks you to change the name of the Excel table you just created from the art objects data to ArtObjects.

To rename the Table1 table:

▶ **1.** In the Properties group on the Table Tools Design tab, select **Table1** in the Table Name box. See Figure 5-7.

Figure 5-7	Table Name box

enter a descriptive table name

▶ **2.** Type **ArtObjects**, and then press the **Enter** key. The Excel table is renamed ArtObjects.

Formatting an Excel Table

Refer to Figure 5-7 and note the check boxes in the Table Style Options group on the Table Tools Design tab. These check boxes enable you to quickly and easily add or remove table elements or change the format of the table elements. For example, you can choose to remove the header row in a table by deselecting the Header Row check box; you can easily toggle back to display the header row by clicking to select this check box. Similarly, you can change the appearance of a table from banded rows to banded columns by deselecting the Banded Rows check box and then clicking to select the Banded Columns check box. With these options readily available on the Table Tools Design tab, it's easy to achieve the exact content and look for a table.

Mary likes the default table style applied to the Excel table, but asks you to make a few modifications to improve the table's appearance. She wants the ArtID values in the first column of the table highlighted for emphasis. She also wants the width in the Date Acquired and Appraised Value columns reduced to better fit the values.

To format the ArtObjects table:

▶ **1.** In the Table Style Options group on the Table Tools Design tab, click the **First Column** check box to insert a check mark. The text in the ArtID column is bold, and the fill color is the same as the header row.

▶ **2.** Change the width of column D to **12**. The Date Acquired column width better fits the dates.

▶ **3.** Change the width of column H to **12**. The Appraised Value column better fits the monetary values.

▶ **4.** Click cell **A1**, if necessary.

Maintaining an Excel Table

Mary has several changes that need to be reflected in the ArtObjects table. First, the museum acquired a new painting and received a sculpture from an anonymous donor; both art objects need to be added to the table. Second, Mary just learned that the Moonlight painting needs to be repaired as its condition has deteriorated; the condition of this art object needs to be changed from Fair to Poor. Finally, one of the paintings has been sold to raise money for new acquisitions; the record for this art object needs to be deleted from the table. Mary asks you to update the ArtObjects table to reflect these changes.

Adding Records

As you maintain an Excel table, you often need to add new records. You add a record to an Excel table in a blank row. The simplest and most convenient way to add a record to an Excel table is to enter the data in the first blank row below the last record. You can then sort the data to arrange the table in the order you want. You can also insert a row within the table for the new record, if you want the record in a specific location.

Adding a Record to an Excel Table | Reference Window

- Click in the row below the last row of the Excel table.
- Type the values for the new record, pressing the Tab key to move from field to field.
- Press the Tab key to create another new record, or press the Enter key if this is the last record.

Next, you'll add records for the new painting and sculpture to the ArtObjects table.

To add two records to the ArtObjects table:

▶ 1. Press the **End+↓** keys to make cell A116 the active cell. This cell is in the last row of the table.

▶ 2. Press the **↓** key to move the active cell to cell A117. This is the first blank row below the table.

▶ 3. Type **116** in cell A117, and then press the **Tab** key. Cell B117 in the Artist column becomes the active cell. The table expands to include a new row in the table structure with the same formatting as the rest of the table. The AutoCorrect Options button appears so you can undo the table formatting if you hadn't intended the new data to be part of the existing table. The sizing handle in the lower-right corner of the table indicates the last row and column in the table. You can use the sizing handle to add columns or rows to the Excel table to expand it or remove them to make the table smaller. See Figure 5-8.

New row added to the ArtObjects table | Figure 5-8

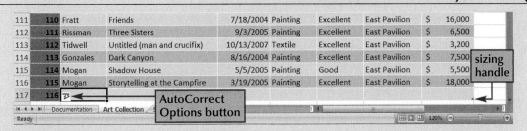

111	110	Fratt	Friends	7/18/2004	Painting	Excellent	East Pavilion	$	16,000	
112	111	Rissman	Three Sisters	9/3/2005	Painting	Excellent	East Pavilion	$	6,500	
113	112	Tidwell	Untitled (man and crucifix)	10/13/2007	Textile	Excellent	East Pavilion	$	3,200	
114	113	Gonzales	Dark Canyon	8/16/2004	Painting	Excellent	East Pavilion	$	7,500	sizing
115	114	Mogan	Shadow House	5/5/2005	Painting	Good	East Pavilion	$	5,500	handle
116	115	Mogan	Storytelling at the Campfire	3/19/2005	Painting	Excellent	East Pavilion	$	18,000	
117	116									

AutoCorrect Options button

Documentation Art Collection

Ready   120%

Tip

As you type in a cell, Auto-Complete displays any existing entry in the column that matches the characters you typed. Press the Tab key to accept the entry or continue typing to replace it.

Trouble? If cell A118 is the active cell, you probably pressed the Enter key instead of the Tab key. Click cell B117 and then continue entering the data in Step 4.

▶ 4. In the range B117:H117, enter **Giama**, **Starry Night**, **4/3/2010**, **Painting**, **Excellent**, **South Pavilion**, and **8500** for the Artist, Title, Date Acquired, Category, Condition, Location, and Appraised Value fields, pressing the **Tab** key to move from cell to cell, and pressing the **Tab** key after you enter all the data for the record. Cell A118 becomes the active cell and the table expands to incorporate row 118.

Next, you'll enter the second record.

▶ 5. In the range A118:H118, enter **117**, **Higgins**, **Apache Warrior**, **4/5/2010**, **Sculpture**, **Excellent**, **Garden**, and **23000**, and then click cell **A119** after the last entry. The record for the sculpture is added to the table. See Figure 5-9.

| Figure 5-9 | Two records added to the ArtObjects table |

115	**114**	Mogan	Shadow House	5/5/2005	Painting	Good	East Pavilion	$ 5,500
116	**115**	Mogan	Storytelling at the Campfire	3/19/2005	Painting	Excellent	East Pavilion	$ 18,000
117	**116**	Giama	Starry Night	4/3/2010	Painting	Excellent	South Pavilion	$ 8,500
118	**117**	Higgins	Apache Warrior	4/5/2010	Sculpture	Excellent	Garden	$ 23,000
119								

Documentation Art Collection Sheet3

Ready   120%

two new records

Trouble? If a new row is added to the table, you probably pressed the Tab key instead of the Enter key after the last entry in the record. On the Quick Access Toolbar, click the Undo button to remove the extra row.

Finding and Editing Records

You need to update the condition for the art object with the title Moonlight. Although you can manually scroll through the table to find a specific record, a quicker and more accurate way to locate a record is to use the Find command. You edit the data in a field the same way as you edit data in a worksheet cell. You'll use the Find command to locate the record for the Moonlight painting, which has deteriorated to poor condition. Then, you'll edit the record in the table to change the condition to "Poor."

To find and edit the record for the Moonlight painting:

▶ 1. Press the **Ctrl+Home** keys to move to the top of the worksheet, and then click cell **C2** to make it the active cell.

▶ 2. In the Editing group on the Home tab, click the **Find & Select** button, and then click **Find**. The Find and Replace dialog box opens.

▶ 3. Type **Moonlight** in the Find what box, and then click the **Find Next** button. Cell C69, which contains the title Moonlight, is selected. This is the record you want. If it weren't, you would click the Find Next button again to display the next record that meets the search criteria.

▶ 4. Click the **Close** button. The Find and Replace dialog box closes.

▶ 5. Press the **Tab** key three times to move the active cell to the Condition column, and then type **P**. AutoComplete displays Poor in the cell, which is the condition text you want to enter.

▶ **6.** Press the **Tab** key to enter the AutoComplete entry. The painting's condition is changed in the table.

▶ **7.** Press the **Ctrl+Home** keys to make cell A1 active.

Deleting a Record

The final update you need to make to the ArtObjects table is to delete the record for the Trappers painting (art ID 90), which is the art object that was sold. You'll use the Find command to locate the painting's record. Then, you'll delete the record from the table.

To find and delete the Trappers painting record:

▶ **1.** In the Editing group on the Home tab, click the **Find & Select** button, and then click **Find**. The Find and Replace dialog box opens.

▶ **2.** Type **90** in the Find what box, and then click the **Find Next** button. Because Excel searches the entire worksheet (not just the current column), and because it finds the search value even if it is part of another value, the appraised value $1,900 is selected. This is not the record you want to delete.

▶ **3.** Click the **Find Next** button to highlight the appraised value $1,900 for a different record, and then click the **Find Next** button again to highlight the value 90 in the ArtID column. This is the record you need to delete.

▶ **4.** Click the **Close** button. The Find and Replace dialog box closes.

Next, you'll delete the record for the Trappers painting.

▶ **5.** In the Cells group on the Home tab, click the **Delete button arrow**, and then click **Delete Table Rows**. The record for the Trappers painting is deleted from the table.

Trouble? If a different record was deleted, the active cell was not in the record for the Trappers painting. On the Quick Access Toolbar, click the Undo button 🔄 to restore the record, and then repeat Steps 1 through 5.

▶ **6.** Press the **Ctrl+Home** keys to make cell A1 active.

Tip

You can find fields whose contents match a value (such as 90) exactly by clicking the Options button in the Find & Replace dialog box, and checking the Match entire cell contents check box.

Tip

Be sure to verify that you select the correct record to delete, because a dialog box does not open for you to confirm the delete operation.

Sorting Data

The records in the ArtObjects table appear in the order that Mary entered them. As you work with tables, however, you'll want to view the same records in a different order, such as by the artist name or by the art object's location in the museum. You can rearrange, or **sort**, the records in a table or range based on the data in one or more fields. The fields you use to order the data are called **sort fields**. For example, to arrange the art objects by artist name, you can sort the data using the Artist column as the sort field.

You can sort data in ascending or descending order. **Ascending order** arranges text alphabetically from A to Z, numbers from smallest to largest, and dates from oldest to newest. **Descending order** arranges text in reverse alphabetical order from Z to A, numbers from largest to smallest, and dates from newest to oldest. In both ascending and descending order, blank fields are placed at the end of the table.

Sorting One Column Using the Sort Buttons

The simplest way to sort data with one sort field is to use the ⬆ or ⬇ button. Mary wants you to sort the art objects in ascending order by the artist. This will rearrange the table data so that the records appear in alphabetical order by the artist name.

Tip

You can also access the Sort buttons in the Editing group on the Home tab by clicking the Sort & Filter button and clicking a sort option.

To sort the art objects table in ascending order by the artist name:

▶ 1. Click any cell in the Artist column. You do not need to select the entire ArtObjects table, which consists of the range A1:H117. Excel determines the table's range when you click any cell in the table.

▶ 2. Click the **Data** tab on the Ribbon, and then, in the Sort & Filter group, click the **Sort A to Z** button ⬆. The data is sorted in ascending order by Artist. The Artist filter arrow indicates the data is sorted by that column. See Figure 5-10.

Figure 5-10 ArtObjects table sorted by Artist

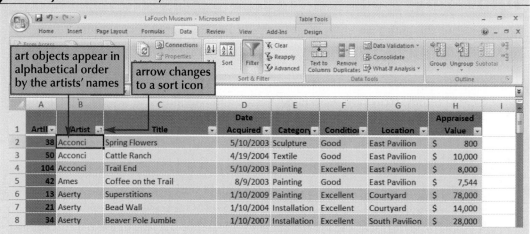

Trouble? If the data is sorted in the wrong order, you might have clicked in a different column than the Artist column. Repeat Steps 1 and 2.

Sorting Multiple Columns Using the Sort Dialog Box

Sometimes, sorting by one sort field is not adequate for your needs. For example, Mary wants you to arrange the ArtObjects table so that all the art objects in each location are together, and then all the objects for each artist within each location are together, and then each artist's work is arranged by the date acquired. You must sort on more than one column to accomplish this. The first sort field is called the **primary sort field**, the second sort field is called the **secondary sort field**, and so forth. You can use up to 64 sort fields in a single sort. In this case, the Location field is the primary sort field, the Artist field is the secondary sort field, and the Date Acquired field is the tertiary sort field. When you have more than one sort field, you should use the Sort dialog box to specify the sort criteria.

Sorting Data Using Multiple Sort Fields | Reference Window

- Click any cell in a table or range.
- In the Sort & Filter group on the Data tab, click the Sort button to open the Sort dialog box.
- If the Sort by row exists, modify the primary sort by selections; otherwise, click the Add Level button to insert the Sort by row.
- Click the Sort by arrow, select the column heading that you want to specify as the primary sort field, click the Sort On arrow to select the type of data, and then click the Order arrow to select the sort order.
- To sort by a second column, click the Add Level button to add the first Then by row. Click the Sort by arrow, select the column heading that you want to specify as the secondary sort field, click the Sort On arrow to select the type of data, and then click the Order arrow to select the sort order.
- To sort by additional columns, click the Add Level button and select appropriate Then by, Sort On, and Order values.
- Click the OK button.

Mary wants you to sort the art objects by location, and then within location by artist, and then within artist by date acquired with the most recently acquired objects for the artist appearing before the older ones. This will make it faster for her to find information about the location and the creator of the art objects in each location.

To sort the art objects table by location, then by artist, and then by date acquired:

▶ **1.** Click cell **A1** in the ArtObjects table. Cell A1 is the active cell, although you can click any cell in the table to sort the table data.

▶ **2.** In the Sort & Filter group on the Data tab, click the **Sort** button. The Sort dialog box opens. Any sort specifications (sort field, type of data sorted on, and sort order) from the last sort appear in the dialog box.

You'll set the primary sort field—Location.

▶ **3.** Click the **Sort by** arrow to display the list of the column headers in the ArtObjects table, and then click **Location**.

▶ **4.** If necessary, click the **Sort On** arrow to display the type of sort, and then click **Values**. Typically, you want to sort by the numbers, text, or dates stored in the cells, which are all values. However, you can also sort by formats, such as cell color, font color, and cell icon (a graphic that appears in a cell as a result of applying a conditional format).

▶ **5.** If necessary, click the **Order** arrow to display sort order options, and then click **A to Z**. The sort order is set to ascending.

The specification for the primary sort field are complete. Next, you will specify the secondary sort field—Artist. First, you need to insert a blank sort level.

▶ **6.** Click the **Add Level** button. A Then by row is added below the primary sort field.

▶ **7.** Click the **Then by** arrow and click **Artist**, and then verify that **Values** appears in the Sort On box and **A to Z** appears in the Order box.

The second sort field is specified. You'll add the third sort field—Date Acquired.

▶ **8.** Click the **Add Level** button to add a second Then by row.

▶ **9.** Click the second **Then by** arrow and click **Date Acquired**, verify that **Values** appears in the Sort On box, click the **Order** arrow, and then click **Newest to Oldest** to specify a descending sort order for the Date Acquired values. See Figure 5-11.

| Figure 5-11 | Sort dialog box with complete sort specifications |

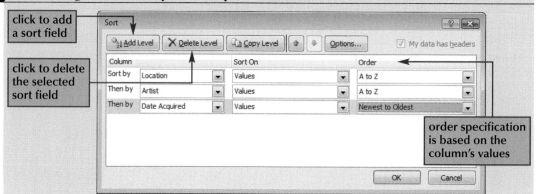

▶ **10.** Click the **OK** button. Excel sorts the table records first in ascending order by Location, then within each location by Artist (again, in ascending order), and then within each artist by Date Acquired. For example, notice the three works by Acconci located in the East Pavilion; the works are arranged in descending order by the value in the Date Acquired column, so that the newer works appear before the older works. See Figure 5-12.

| Figure 5-12 | Art objects sorted by Location, then by Artist, and then by Date Acquired |

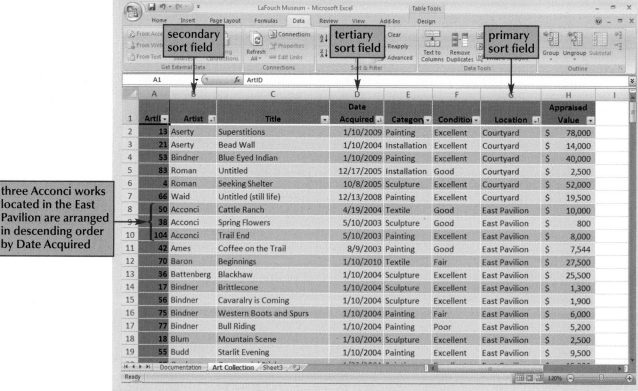

▶ **11.** Scroll the table to view the sorted table data.

Mary wants to review the condition of each art object to determine how many objects need repairs. To do this more easily, she asks you to sort the objects by Condition. Because she wants to sort by only one field, you'll use the Sort A to Z button.

To sort the table by condition:

▶ **1.** Click any cell in the **Condition** column.

▶ **2.** In the Sort & Filter group on the Data tab, click the **Sort A to Z** button 🔼. The previous sort is removed and the art objects are now sorted in ascending order by Condition.

▶ **3.** Scroll the table to see the reordered art objects.

As Mary reviews the sorted table, she realizes that the data is sorted in alphabetical order by the condition of the art objects: Excellent, Fair, Good, and Poor. This default sort order for fields with text values is not appropriate for the condition ratings. Instead, Mary wants you to base the sort on quality ranking rather than alphabetical. You'll use a custom sort list to set up the sort order Mary wants.

Sorting Using a Custom List

Text is sorted in ascending or descending alphabetical order unless you specify a different order using a custom list. A **custom list** indicates the sequence in which you want data ordered. Excel provides four predefined custom sort lists. Two days-of-the-week custom lists (Sun, Mon, Tues, ... and Sunday, Monday, Tuesday, ...) and two months-of-the-year custom lists (Jan, Feb, Mar, Apr, ... and January, February, March, April, ...). If a column consists of day or month labels, you can sort them in their correct chronological order using one of these predefined custom lists. You can also create custom lists to sort records in a sequence you define. In this case, you want to create a custom list to arrange the art objects based on their condition, with the top-quality condition appearing first, as follows: Excellent, Good, Fair, Poor.

Creating a Custom List | Reference Window

- In the Sort & Filter group on the Data tab, click the Sort button.
- Click the Order arrow, and then click Custom List.
- In the List entries box, type each entry for the custom list, pressing the Enter key after each entry.
- Click the Add button.
- Click the OK button.

You'll create a custom list that Mary can use to sort the records by the Condition field.

To create the custom list based on the Condition field:

▶ **1.** Make sure the active cell is in the table, and then, in the Sort & Filter group on the Data tab, click the **Sort** button. The Sort dialog box opens, showing the sort specifications from the previous sort.

▶ **2.** Click the **Sort by** arrow, click **Condition** to select the sort field (if necessary), and then verify that **Values** appears in the Sort On box.

> 3. Click the **Order** arrow to display the sort order options, and then click **Custom List**. The Custom Lists dialog box opens.

> 4. Click **NEW LIST** in the Custom lists box to place the insertion point in the List entries box.
>
>   Next, you'll enter the condition values in the order you want them sorted. You must press the Enter key after each entry.

> 5. Type **Excellent**, press the **Enter** key to move the insertion point to the next line, type **Good**, press the **Enter** key, type **Fair**, press the **Enter** key, type **Poor**, and then press the **Enter** key. The four items appear in the List entries box.

> 6. Click the **Add** button. The custom list entries are added to the Custom lists box. See Figure 5-13.

Figure 5-13 ▶ **Custom Lists dialog box with custom list defined**

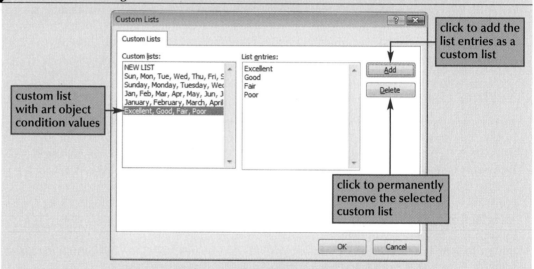

> 7. Click the **OK** button to return to the Sort dialog box. The custom sort list—Excellent, Good, Fair, Poor—appears in the Order box.

> 8. Click the **OK** button. The table is sorted based on the custom list.

> 9. Scroll the sorted table to verify that the art objects are sorted by their condition rankings: Excellent, Good, Fair, and Poor. Note that there are six art objects in poor condition.

In this session, you created an Excel table for the art objects, and then named and formatted the table. Next, you updated the table by adding records, editing a record, and deleting a record. You sorted the records by one field and then by three fields. Finally, you created a custom list to sort the Condition field by its quality ratings. In the next session, you will filter the ArtObjects table to retrieve specific information on some of the art objects.

Review | **Session 5.1 Quick Check**

1. What is the purpose of the Freeze Panes button in the Window group on the View tab? Why is this feature helpful?

2. What three elements indicate an Excel table has been created in the worksheet?

3. What fields do you use to order data?
4. An Excel table of college students tracks each student's first name, last name, major, and year of graduation. How can you order the table so students graduating the same year appear together in alphabetical order by the student's last name?
5. How do you enter a new record in an Excel table?
6. An Excel table of faculty data includes the Rank field with the values Full, Associate, Assistant, and Instructor. How can you sort the data by rank in the following order: Full, Associate, Assistant, and Instructor?
7. If you sort table data from the most recent purchase date to the oldest purchase date, in what order have you sorted the data?

Session 5.2

Filtering Data

Mary is working on her budget for the upcoming year. She needs to determine which art objects the museum can afford to repair this year. She asks you to prepare a list of all paintings in poor condition. Mary will then examine these paintings, estimate the repair costs, and decide which ones to place on the upcoming year's repairs list.

Although you could sort the list of paintings by condition to group those in poor condition, you are still working with the entire table. A better solution is to display only the specific records you want. The process of displaying a subset of rows in the table that meets the criteria you specify is called **filtering**. Filtering, rather than rearranging the data as sorting does, temporarily hides any records that do not meet the specified criteria. After data is filtered, you can sort, copy, format, chart, and print it.

Filtering Using One Column

When you create an Excel table, filter arrows appear in each of the column headers. You can see these filter arrows in the ArtObjects table you created for Mary. You click a filter arrow to open the Filter menu for that field. You can use options on the Filter menu to create three types of filters. You can filter a column of data by its cell colors or font colors; by a specific text, number, or date filter, although the specific choices depend on the type of data in the column; or by selecting one or more of the exact values by which you want to filter in the column. After you filter a column, the Clear Filter command becomes available so you can remove the filter and redisplay all the records.

Mary wants to see only paintings in poor condition. First, you need to filter the ArtObjects table to show only those records with the value "Paintings" in the Category column. Remember, filtering the data only hides some of the records.

> **Tip**
>
> You can display or hide filter arrows for an Excel table or a range of data by using the Filter button in the Sort & Filter group on the Data tab.

To filter the ArtObjects table to show only paintings:

▶ **1.** If you took a break after the previous session, make sure the LaFouch Museum workbook is open, the Art Collection worksheet is active, and the ArtObjects table is active.

▶ **2.** Click the **Category filter arrow**. The Filter menu opens, as shown in Figure 5-14, listing the unique entries in the Category column: Installation, Painting, Sculpture, and Textile. Initially, all the items are selected, but you can select which items you want to use to filter the data. In this case, you want to select the Painting item.

| Figure 5-14 | Filter menu for the Category column |

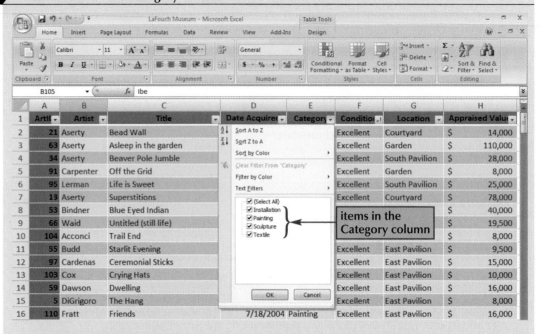

Notice the **Sort by Color** and **Filter by Color** options in the filter menu. These options enable you to filter and sort data using color, one of many cell attributes. Suppose that Mary used specific cell background colors for certain works of art in the ArtObjects table. For example, she might want to highlight those works given to the museum by its two most generous donors, using yellow for one and red for the other. So, the cells in the Title column for the two donors would be formatted with these colors. You could then click the Sort by Color option in the filter menu to display a list of available colors by which to sort, and then click the specific color so that all the records for the first donor (formatted with yellow) would appear together, and all the records for the second donor (formatted with red) would appear together. Similarly, you could click the Filter by Color option to display a submenu with the available colors by which to filter, and then click a color. In this example, if you selected yellow, only the records for the first donor would be displayed in the table, allowing you to focus on just those records.

▶ 3. Click the **(Select All)** check box to remove the check marks from all the Category items, and then click the **Painting** check box to insert a check mark. The filter will show only those records that match the checked item and hide records that contain the unchecked items.

▶ 4. Click the **OK** button. The filter is applied. The status bar lists the number of paintings found in the entire table. Fifty-seven of the 116 records in the table are displayed. See Figure 5-15.

ArtObjects table filtered to show only paintings ◂ **Figure 5-15**

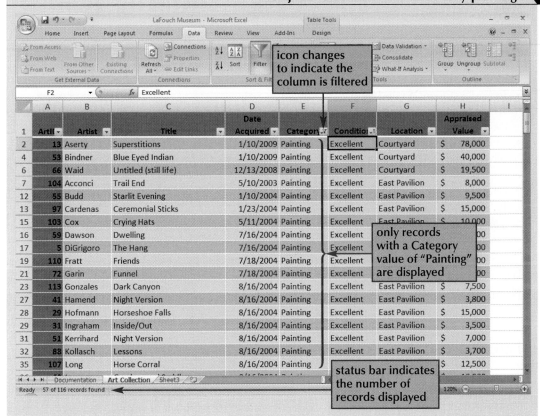

5. Review the records to verify that only records with a value equal to Painting in the Category column are visible. All records that do not have the value Painting in this column are hidden. Notice the gaps in the row numbers in the worksheet. As a reminder that the records are filtered, the row numbers of the filtered records are blue and the Category filter arrow changes to indicate that this column is being used to filter the table.

6. Point to the **Category filter arrow**. A ScreenTip—Category: Equals "Painting"—describes the filter applied to the column.

| InSight | | **Exploring Text Filters** |

You can use different text filters to display the records you want. If you know only part of a text value or want to match a certain pattern, you can use the Begins With, Ends With, and Contains operators to filter a text field to match the pattern you specify.

The following examples are based on a student directory table that includes First Name, Last Name, Address, City, State, and Zip fields:

- To find a student named Smith, Smithe, or Smythe, create a text filter using the Begins With operator. In this example, use Begins With *Sm* to display all records that have *Sm* at the beginning of the text value.
- To Find anyone whose Last Name ends in "son" (such as Robertson, Anderson, Dawson, Gibson, and so forth), create a text filter using the Ends With operator. In this example, use Ends With *son* to display all records that have *son* as the last characters in the text value.
- To find anyone whose street address includes *Central* (such as 101 Central Ave, 1024 Central Road, or 457 Avenue De Central), create a text filter using the Contains operator. In this example, use Contains *Central* to display all records that have *Central* anywhere in the text value.

When you create a text filter, think about the results you want. Then, consider what text filter you can use to best achieve those results.

Filtering Using Multiple Columns

If you need to further restrict the records that appear in a filtered table, you can filter by one or more of the other columns. Each additional filter is applied to the currently filtered data and further reduces the records that are displayed. Mary wants to see only paintings that are in poor condition, rather than all the paintings in the ArtObjects table. To do this, you need to filter the paintings records to display only those with the value "Poor" in the Condition column. You'll use the filter arrow in the Condition column to add this second filter criterion to the filtered data.

To filter the painting records to show only those in poor condition:

▶ **1.** Click the **Condition filter arrow**. The Filter menu opens.

▶ **2.** Click the **Excellent**, **Good**, and **Fair** check boxes to remove the check marks. The Poor check box remains checked, so only paintings in poor condition will be displayed.

▶ **3.** Click the **OK** button. The ArtObjects table is further filtered and shows the three paintings that are in poor condition. See Figure 5-16.

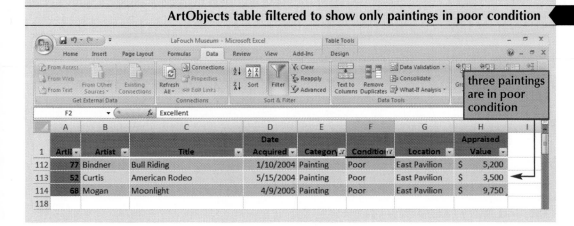

ArtObjects table filtered to show only paintings in poor condition Figure 5-16

Clearing Filters

When you want to see all the data in a filtered table, you can **clear** (or remove) the filters. When you clear a filter from a column, any other filters are still applied. For example, in the ArtObjects table, you would see all the paintings in the table if you cleared the filter from the Condition field, or you would see all the art objects in poor condition if you cleared the filter from the Category field. To redisplay all the art objects in the table, you need to clear both the Condition filter and the Category filter. You will do this now to restore the entire table of art objects.

To clear the filters to show all the records in the ArtObjects table:

▶ 1. Click the **Condition filter arrow**, and then click **Clear Filter From "Condition"**. The Condition filter is removed from the table. The table shows only paintings because the Category filter is still in effect.

▶ 2. Click the **Category filter arrow**, and then click **Clear Filter From "Category"**. The Category condition is removed, and all the records in the ArtObjects table are displayed again.

Selecting Multiple Filter Items

You can often find the information you need by selecting a single filter item from a list of filter items. Sometimes, however, you need to specify a more complex set of criteria to find the records you want. Earlier, you selected one filter item for the Category column and one filter item for the Condition column to display the records whose Category field value equals Painting AND whose Condition field value equals Poor. The records had to have both values to be displayed. The AND condition requires that all of the selected criteria be true for the record to be displayed. Now you want to select two filter items for the Category column to display records whose Category field value equals Installation OR whose Category field value equals Sculpture. The records must have at least one of these values to be displayed. A filter that selects more than one item from the list of items uses the OR condition, which requires that only one of the selected criteria be true for a record to be displayed. For example, if you check the Installation and Sculpture check boxes in the Category filter items, you create the filter condition "Category equal to installation" OR "Category equal to sculpture."

The museum's board of directors wants a list of all installations or sculptures valued above $20,000. Mary asks you to create a list of these holdings.

To select multiple filter items:

► 1. Click the **Category filter arrow**, and then click the **Painting** and **Textile** check boxes to remove the check marks.

► 2. Verify that the **Installation** and **Sculpture** check boxes remain checked. When you select more than one item, you create a multiselect filter.

► 3. Click the **OK** button. The ArtObjects table is filtered, and the status bar indicates that 51 out of 116 records are either an installation or a sculpture.

Creating Criteria Filters to Specify More Complex Criteria

Filter items enable you to filter a range of data or an Excel table based on exact values in a column. However, many times you need broader criteria. **Criteria filters** enable you to specify various conditions in addition to those that are based on an "equals" criterion. For example, you might want to find all art objects with an appraised value greater than $20,000 or acquired after 7/1/2009. You use criteria filters to create these conditions.

The type of criteria filters available change depending on whether the data in a column contains text, numbers, or dates. Figure 5-17 shows some of the options for text, number, and date criteria filters.

Figure 5-17 ▶ **Options for text, number, and date criteria filters**

Filter	Criteria	Records displayed
Text	Equals	Exactly match the specified text string
	Does Not Equal	Do not exactly match the specified text string
	Begins With	Begin with the specified text spring
	Ends With	End with the specified text string
	Contains	Have the specified text string anywhere
	Does Not Contain	Do not have the specified text string anywhere
Number	Equals	Exactly match the specified number
	Greater Than or Equal to	Are greater than or equal to the specified number
	Less Than	Are less than the specified number
	Between	Are greater than or equal to *and* less than or equal to the specified numbers
	Top 10	Are the top or bottom 10 (or the specified number)
	Above Average	Are greater than the average
Date	Today	Have the current date
	Last Week	Are in the prior week
	Next Month	Are in the month following the current month
	Last Quarter	Are in the previous quarter of the year (quarters defined Jan, Feb, Mar; Apr, May, June; and so on)
	Year to Date	Are since January 1 of the current year to the current date
	Last Year	Are in the previous year (based on the current date)

You will modify the filtered ArtObjects table to add a criteria filter that includes only objects valued greater than $20,000.

To create a number criteria filter:

▶ **1.** Click the **Appraised Value filter arrow**, and then point to **Number Filters**. A menu opens displaying the comparison operators available for columns of numbers.

▶ **2.** Click **Greater Than**. The Custom AutoFilter dialog box opens. The upper-left box lists *is greater than*, the comparison operator you want to use to filter the Appraised Value column. You enter the value you want to use for the filter criteria in the upper-right box, which, in this case, is 20,000.

▶ **3.** Type **20000** in the upper-right box. See Figure 5-18. You use the lower set of boxes if you want the filter to meet a second condition. You click the And option button to display rows that meet both criteria. You click the Or option button to display rows that meet either of the two criteria. You only want to set one criteria for this filter, so you'll leave the lower boxes empty.

Custom AutoFilter dialog box ◀ **Figure 5-18**

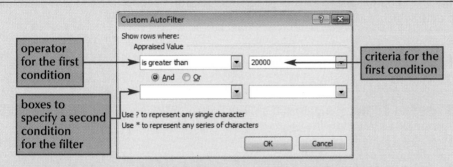

▶ **4.** Click the **OK** button. The status bar indicates that 7 of 116 records were found. The seven records that appear in the ArtObjects table are either installations or sculptures and have an appraised value greater than $20,000.

Before Mary sends this list to the board of directors, you'll sort the filtered data to show the largest appraised value first. Although you can sort the data using Sort buttons, as you did earlier, these sort options are also available on the Filter menu for your convenience. If you want to perform a more complex sort, you still need to use the Sort dialog box.

To sort the filtered table data:

▶ **1.** Click the **Appraised Value filter arrow**. The Filter menu opens. The sort options are at the top of the menu.

▶ **2.** Click **Sort Largest to Smallest**. The filtered table now displays installations and sculptures with an appraised valued above $20,000 sorted in descending order. See Figure 5-19.

| Figure 5-19 | Filtered ArtObjects table |

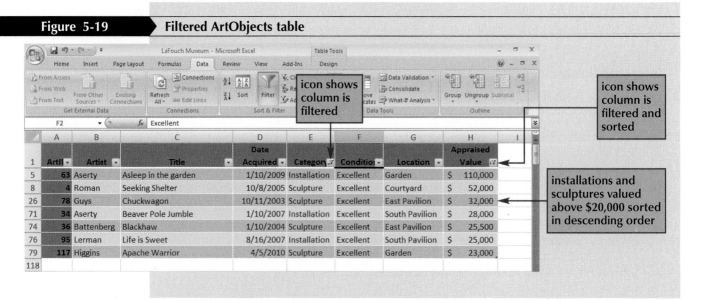

Mary will send this list to the board of directors. You need to restore the entire table of art objects, which you can do by clearing all the filters at one time.

To clear all the filters from the ArtObjects table:

▶ **1.** Click the **Data** tab on the Ribbon, if necessary.

▶ **2.** In the Sort & Filter group, click the **Clear** button. All the records appear in the table.

Using the Total Row to Calculate Summary Statistics

You can calculate summary statistics (including sum, average, count, maximum, and minimum) on all the columns in an Excel table or on a filtered table in a Total row. A **Total row**, which you can display at the end of the table, is used to calculate summary statistics for the columns in an Excel table. When you click in each cell in the Total row, an arrow appears that you can click to open a list of the most commonly used functions.

Mary is creating a brochure for an upcoming fund-raising event, and wants to know the number and value of the items in the current museum collection, excluding art objects in poor condition. She asks you to filter the table to display art objects that are in excellent, good, and fair condition. Then, you will display the Total row for the ArtObjects table to count the number of art objects and add their total appraised value.

To add a Total row and select summary statistics:

▶ **1.** Click the **Condition filter arrow**, click the **Poor** check box to remove the check mark, and then click the **OK** button. The ArtObjects table displays objects that are in excellent, good, or fair condition. The status bar indicates that 110 of 116 records remain in the filtered table.

Next, you will display the Total row.

▶ **2.** Click the **Table Tools Design** tab on the Ribbon, and then, in the Table Style Options group, click the **Total Row** check box to insert a check mark.

3. Scroll to the end of the table. The Total row is the last row of the table, the word "Total" appears in the leftmost cell, and the total appraised value $1,118,723 appears in the rightmost cell. By default, the Total row adds the numbers in the last column of the Excel table or counts the number of records if the data in the last column contains text. See Figure 5-20.

Total row added to the ArtObjects table ◄ Figure 5-20

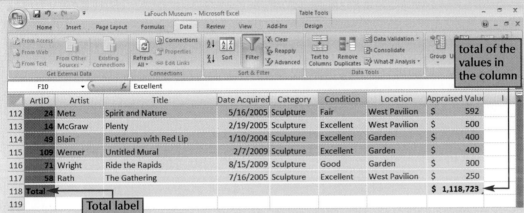

Total label

In the Artist cell of the Total row, you want to count the number of records whose Appraised Values were added in the last column.

4. Click cell **B118** (the Artist cell in the Total row), and then click the **arrow button** to display a list of functions. None is the default function in all columns except the last column. See Figure 5-21.

Total row functions ◄ Figure 5-21

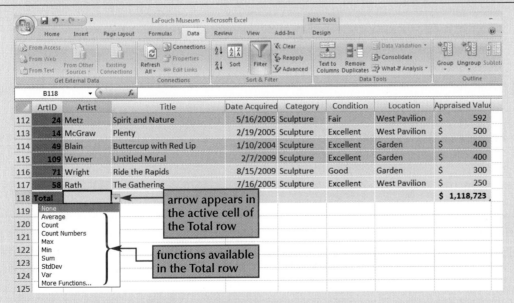

arrow appears in the active cell of the Total row

functions available in the Total row

> **Tip**
>
> You can click the More Functions command to open the Insert Function dialog box and select any available function.

5. Click **Count**. The number 110 appears in the cell, which is the number of records in the filtered ArtObjects table. See Figure 5-22.

| Figure 5-22 | Count of records in the filtered table |

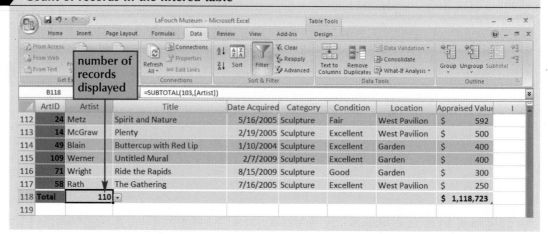

Mary will include this information in her fund-raising brochure. You will remove the Total row and clear the filter.

To remove the Total row and clear the filter from the ArtObjects table:

1. In the Table Style Options group on the Table Tools Design tab, click the **Total Row** check box to remove the check mark. The Total row is no longer visible.

2. Scroll to the top of the table, click the **Condition filter arrow**, and then click **Clear Filter From "Condition"**. The ArtObjects table displays all the art objects.

The board of directors asked Mary to create a report that shows all the museum's art objects sorted by Category with the total appraised value of the art objects in each category. The board also wants to see the total appraised value for each category after the last item of that category. Although you could use the Total row in the Excel table to calculate the results, you would need to filter, total, and print the data for each category separately. A faster way to provide the information Mary needs is to use the Subtotal command.

Inserting Subtotals

You can summarize data in a range of data by inserting subtotals. The Subtotal command offers many kinds of summary information, including counts, sums, averages, minimums, and maximums. The Subtotal command inserts a subtotal row into the range for each group of data and adds a grand total row below the last row of data. Because Excel inserts subtotals whenever the value in a specified field changes, you need to sort the data so that records with the same value in a specified field are grouped together *before* you use the Subtotal command. The Subtotal command cannot be used in an Excel table, so you must first convert the Excel table to a range.

Calculating Subtotals for a Range of Data | Reference Window

- Sort the data by the column for which you want a subtotal.
- If the data is in an Excel table, in the Tools group on the Table Tools Design tab, click the Convert to Range button, and then click the Yes button to convert the Excel table to a range.
- In the Outline group on the Data tab, click the Subtotal button.
- Click the At each change in arrow, and then click the column that contains the group you want to subtotal.
- Click the Use function arrow, and then click the function you want to use to summarize the data.
- In the Add subtotal to box, click the check box for each column that contains the values you want to summarize.
- To calculate another category of subtotals, click the Replace current subtotals check box to remove the check mark, and then repeat the previous three steps.
- Click the OK button.

To produce the results Mary needs, you will sort the art objects by category and calculate subtotals in the Appraised Value column for each category grouping.

To calculate appraised values subtotals for each category of art object:

▶ **1.** Click the **Category filter** arrow, and then click **Sort A to Z** on the Filter menu. The ArtObjects table is sorted in ascending order by the Category field. This ensures one subtotal is created for each category.

▶ **2.** In the Tools group on the Table Tools Design tab, click the **Convert to Range** button. A dialog box opens, asking if you want to convert the table to a normal range.

▶ **3.** Click the **Yes** button. The Excel table is converted to a range. You can tell this because the filter arrows and the Table Tools Design tab disappear, and the Home tab on the Ribbon is selected.

Next, you'll calculate the subtotals. The active cell needs to be in the header row so you can select the correct column.

▶ **4.** Press the **Ctrl+Home** keys to make cell A1 the active cell, click the **Data** tab on the Ribbon, and then, in the Outline group, click the **Subtotal** button. The Subtotal dialog box opens. See Figure 5-23.

Subtotal dialog box | Figure 5-23

▶ **5.** Click the **At each change in** arrow, and then click **Category**. This is the column you want Excel to use to determine where to insert the subtotals; it's the column you sorted. A subtotal will be calculated at every change in the Category value.

▶ **6.** If necessary, click the **Use function** arrow, and then click **Sum**. The Use function list provides several options for subtotaling data, including counts, averages, minimums, maximums, and products.

▶ **7.** In the Add subtotal to list box, make sure only the **Appraised Value** check box is checked. This specifies the Appraised Value field as the field to be subtotaled. If the data already included subtotals, you would check the Replace current subtotals check box to replace the existing subtotals or uncheck the option to display the new subtotals on separate rows above the existing subtotals. Because the data has no subtotals, it makes no difference whether you select this option.

▶ **8.** Make sure the **Summary below data** check box is checked. This option places the subtotals below each group of data, instead of above the first entry in each group, and places the grand total at the end of the data, instead of at the top of the column just below the row of column headings.

▶ **9.** Click the **OK** button to insert subtotals into the data. Excel inserts rows below each category group and displays the subtotals for the appraised value of each art category. A series of Outline buttons appears to the left of the worksheet so you can display or hide the detail rows within each subtotal.

Trouble? If each item has a subtotal following it, you probably forgot to sort the data by Category. Repeat Steps 1 through 9.

▶ **10.** Scroll through the data to see the subtotals below each category and the grand total at the end of the data. See Figure 5-24.

Figure 5-24 | **Subtotals and grand total added to the art objects data**

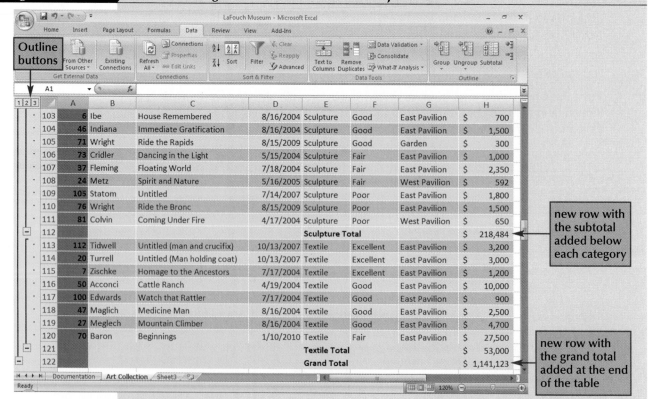

Trouble? If necessary, increase the column width so you can view the subtotal values.

Using the Subtotal Outline View

In addition to displaying subtotals, the Subtotal feature "outlines" your worksheet so you can control the level of detail that is displayed. The three Outline buttons at the top of the outline area, as shown in Figure 5-24, allow you to show or hide different levels of detail in the worksheet. By default, the highest level is active, in this case, Level 3. Level 3 displays the most detail—the individual art object records, the subtotals, and the grand total. Level 2 displays the subtotals and the grand total, but not the individual records. Level 1 displays only the grand total.

The subtotals are useful, but Mary wants you to isolate the different subtotal sections so that she can focus on them individually. You will use the Outline buttons to prepare a report for Mary that includes only subtotals and the grand total.

To use the Outline buttons to hide records:

▶ **1.** Click the **Level 2 Outline** button. The individual art object records are hidden, and you see only the subtotals for each category and the grand total. See Figure 5-25.

Table displaying only subtotals and grand total ◀ **Figure 5-25**

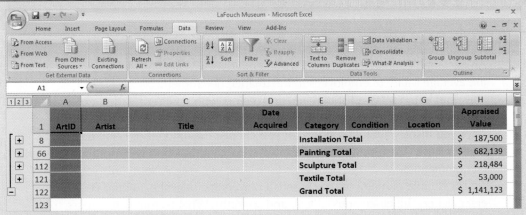

Trouble? If necessary, scroll the worksheet up to see the complete Level 2 list.

▶ **2.** Click the **Level 1 Outline** button. The individual art object records and the subtotals for each category are hidden. Only the grand total remains visible.

▶ **3.** Click the **Level 3 Outline** button. All the records along with the subtotals and the grand total are visible.

Mary has all the information she needs for her meeting with the board to review financial plans for the next fiscal cycle. So you can remove the subtotals from the data.

To remove the subtotals from the art objects data:

▶ **1.** In the Outline group on the Data tab, click the **Subtotal** button. The Subtotal dialog box opens.

▶ **2.** Click the **Remove All** button to remove the subtotals from the data. Only the records appear in the worksheet.

   You'll reset the art objects data as an Excel table.

▶ **3.** Make sure the active cell is a cell within the structured range of data.

▶ **4.** Click the **Insert** tab on the Ribbon, and then, in the Tables group, click the **Table** button. The Create Table dialog box opens.

▶ **5.** Click the **OK** button to create the Excel table, and then click any cell in the table. The table structure is active.

   You need to rename the table as ArtObjects.

▶ **6.** In the Properties group on the Table Tools Design tab, type **ArtObjects** in the Table Name box, and then press the **Enter** key. The Excel table is again named ArtObjects.

Mary needs to generate some information for a meeting with the budget director to review financial plans for the next fiscal cycle. You will work with the art objects data in the next session to gather the information she needs for that meeting.

Review | **Session 5.2 Quick Check**

1. Explain the relationship between the Sort and Subtotal commands.
2. An Excel table includes records for 500 employees. What can you use to calculate the average salary of employees in the finance department?
3. How can you display a list of marketing majors with a GPA of 3.0 or greater from an Excel table with records for 300 students?
4. After you display subtotals, how can you change the amount of detail displayed?
5. True or False: The Count function is a valid subtotal function when using the Subtotal command.
6. An Excel table of major league baseball players includes the column Position (pitchers, catchers, infielders, outfielders, and so forth). What feature can you use to display only pitchers and catchers in the table?
7. If you have a list of employees that includes fields for gender and salary, among others, how can you determine the average salary for females using the Total row feature?

Session 5.3

Analyzing Data with PivotTables

An Excel table can contain a wealth of information, but the large amounts of detailed data often make it difficult to form a clear, overall view of that information. You can use a PivotTable to help organize the data into a meaningful summary. A **PivotTable** is an interactive table that enables you to group and summarize either a range of data or an Excel table into a concise, tabular format for easier reporting and analysis. A PivotTable summarizes data into categories using functions such as COUNT, SUM, AVERAGE, MAX, and MIN. For example, Mary is preparing a presentation for the museum's board of directors that will include a report of the appraised value of the museum's art objects by location, category, and condition. A PivotTable can generate the information she needs.

To create a PivotTable report, you need to specify which fields in your data source you want to summarize. In the ArtObjects table, the Appraised Value field is the most likely field to summarize. In other applications, fields such as salaries, sales, and costs are frequently summarized fields for PivotTables. In PivotTable terminology, the fields that contain summary data are known as **value fields**. **Category fields** group the values in a PivotTable by fields, such as condition, location, and year acquired. Category fields appear in PivotTables as row labels, column labels, and report filters, which allows you to focus on a subset of the PivotTable by displaying one, several, or all items. Figure 5-26 shows the PivotTable you will create.

Sample PivotTable ◀ **Figure 5-26**

	A	B	C	D	E	F
1	Location	(All)				
2						
3	Sum of Appraised Value	Column Labels				
4	Row Labels	Excellent	Good	Fair	Poor	Grand Total
5	Installation	$185,000	$2,500			$187,500
6	Painting	$611,520	$41,669	$10,500	$18,450	$682,139
7	Sculpture	$194,292	$16,300	$3,942	$3,950	$218,484
8	Textile	$7,400	$18,100	$27,500		$53,000
9	Grand Total	$998,212	$78,569	$41,942	$22,400	$1,141,123

You can easily rearrange, hide, and display different category fields in the PivotTable to provide alternative views of the data. This ability to "pivot" the table—for example, change row headings to column positions and vice versa—gives the PivotTable its name and makes it a powerful analytical tool. The PivotTable in Figure 5-26 could be rearranged so that the Condition items appear as row labels and the Category items appear as column labels.

To conceptualize the layout of a PivotTable and convey your ideas to others who might implement them, a useful first step in creating a PivotTable is to sketch its layout. Mary's sketch, shown in Figure 5-27, illustrates the PivotTable you will create to show the appraised value of the art objects organized by location, category, and condition.

PivotTable sketch ◀ **Figure 5-27**

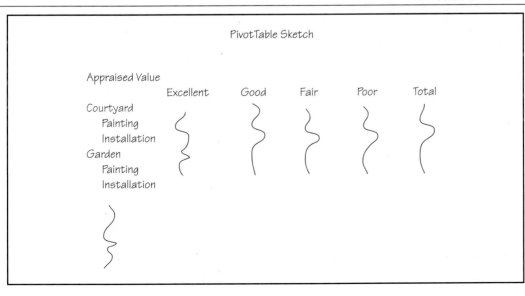

You are ready to create a PivotTable summarizing the total appraised value of art objects by location, category, and condition.

Creating a PivotTable

To create the PivotTable that will provide Mary with the information she needs, you will use the PivotTable dialog box to select the data to analyze and the location of the Pivot-Table report. Often when creating a PivotTable, you begin with data stored in a worksheet, although a PivotTable can also be created using data stored in an external database file, such as one in Access. In this case, you will use the ArtObjects table to create the PivotTable and place the PivotTable in a new worksheet.

To create a PivotTable using the ArtObjects table:

▶ **1.** If you took a break after the previous session, make sure the LaFouch Museum workbook is open, the Art Collection worksheet is active, and the Excel table is active.

▶ **2.** Click the **Insert** tab on the Ribbon, and then, in the Tables group, click the **PivotTable** button. The Create PivotTable dialog box opens. See Figure 5-28.

Create PivotTable dialog box ◀ **Figure 5-28**

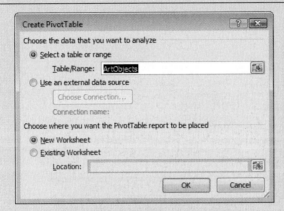

In this dialog box, you specify where to find the data for the PivotTable. The data can be an Excel table or range in the current workbook or an external data source such as an Access database file. You also specify whether to place the PivotTable in a new or existing worksheet. If you place the PivotTable in an existing worksheet, you must also specify the cell in which you want the upper-left corner of the Pivot-Table to appear. For the appraised value PivotTable report, you will use the ArtObjects table and place the PivotTable in a new worksheet.

Tip

You can also create a PivotTable by clicking the Summarize with Pivot-Table button in the Tools group on the Table Tools Design tab.

▶ **3.** Make sure the **Select a table or range** option button is selected and **ArtObjects** appears in the Table/Range box.

▶ **4.** Click the **New Worksheet** option button, if necessary. This sets the PivotTable report to be placed in a new worksheet.

▶ **5.** Click the **OK** button. A new worksheet, Sheet1, is inserted to the left of the Art Collection worksheet and the PivotTable Tools contextual tabs appear on the Ribbon. The left side of Sheet1 shows an empty PivotTable report area, which is where the finished PivotTable will be placed. On the right is the PivotTable Field List, which you use to build the PivotTable by adding, removing, and arranging fields, or columns. See Figure 5-29.

Figure 5-29 ▶ PivotTable report area and PivotTable Field List

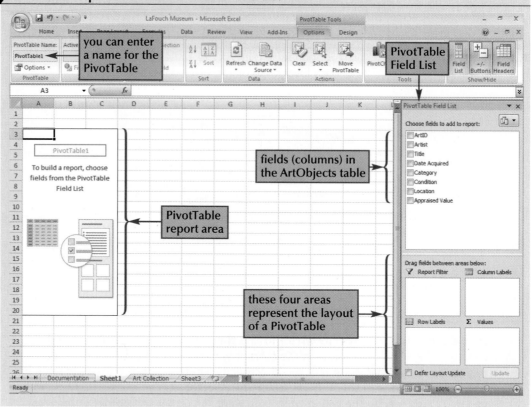

The PivotTable Field List is divided into two sections. The upper field list section displays the names of each field in the ArtObjects table. You check a field check box to add that field to the PivotTable. The lower layout section includes boxes for the four areas in which you can place fields: Report Filter, Row Labels, Column Labels, and Values. Figure 5-30 describes the function of each area.

Figure 5-30 ▶ Layout areas for a PivotTable

Layout Area	Description
Row Labels	The fields you want to display as the rows in the PivotTable. One row is displayed for each unique item in this area. You can have nested row fields.
Column Labels	The fields you want to display as columns at the top of the PivotTable. One column is displayed for each unique item in this area. You can have nested column fields.
Report Filter	A field used to filter the report by selecting one or more items, enabling you to display a subset of data in a PivotTable report.
Values	The fields you want to summarize.

Initially, selected fields with numeric data are placed in the Values area and the SUM function is used to summarize the PivotTable. Fields with nonnumeric data are placed in the Row Labels area. You can always change these default placements of fields in the PivotTable by dragging them to other layout areas to better suit your needs.

Adding Fields to a PivotTable

You need to calculate the total appraised value of art objects by location, within location by category, and within category by condition. In the PivotTable, you'll begin by adding the Location, Category, and Condition fields to appear as row labels, and the data in the Appraised Value field to be summarized. First, you will create a PivotTable summarizing Appraised Value by Location. Then, you'll expand the PivotTable report by adding the Category and Condition fields.

To add fields to the PivotTable:

▶ **1.** In the PivotTable Field List, click the **Location** check box. The Location field is added to the Row Labels box and the unique values in the Location field—Courtyard, East Pavilion, Garden, South Pavilion, and West Pavilion—appear in the PivotTable report area. See Figure 5-31.

PivotTable with the Location field items as row labels ◀ **Figure 5-31**

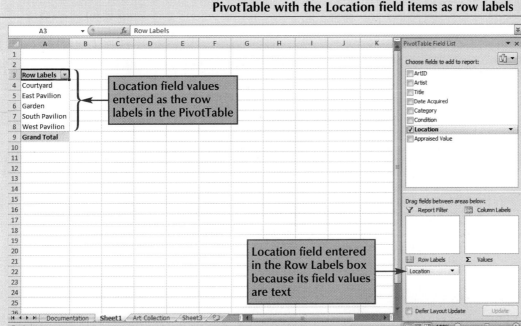

▶ **2.** Click the **Appraised Value** check box in the PivotTable Field List. The Sum of Appraised Value button appears in the Values box. The PivotTable groups the items from the ArtObjects table by Location, and calculates the total appraised value for each location. The grand total appears at the bottom of the PivotTable. See Figure 5-32.

Figure 5-32 **PivotTable of the appraised value of art objects by location**

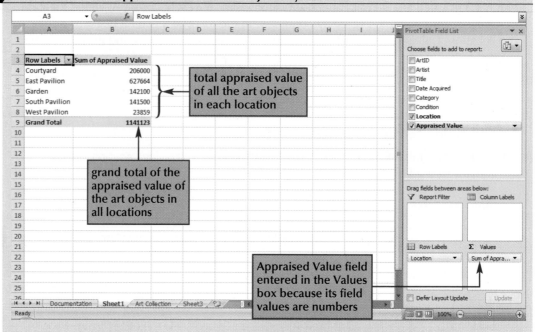

> **3.** Rename the worksheet as **Appraised Value Summary**.

By default, the PivotTable report uses the SUM function for numbers in the Values area and the COUNT function for text and other nonnumeric values. If you want a different summary function, such as average, maximum, or minimum, click the appropriate button in the Values box (in this case, the button is called Sum of Appraised Value) in the PivotTable Field List, and then click Value Field Settings. The Value Field Settings dialog box opens. You can then select the type of calculation you want from the list of available functions, and then click the OK button.

Next, you'll add the Category and Condition fields to the PivotTable.

To add the Category and Condition fields to the PivotTable:

> **1.** In the PivotTable Field List, click the **Category** check box. The Category field appears in the Row Labels box below the Location field and the unique items in the Category field are indented below each location field item in the PivotTable.

> **2.** In the PivotTable Field List, click the **Condition** check box. The Condition field appears in the Row Labels box below the Category field and its unique items are indented below the Location and Category fields already in the PivotTable. See Figure 5-33.

PivotTable with Location, Category, and Condition field items as row labels   Figure 5-33

Applying PivotTable Styles

As with worksheet cells and Excel tables, you can quickly format a PivotTable report using a preset style. You can choose from a gallery of PivotTable styles similar to Table styles. Remember that you can point to any style in the gallery to see a Live Preview of the PivotTable with that style applied. You also can modify the appearance of PivotTables using PivotTable Style Options by adding or removing Banded Rows, Banded Columns, Row Headers, and Column Headers.

Mary wants you to apply the Medium 3 Style, which makes each group in the Pivot-Table stand out and subtotals in the report easier to find.

To apply a PivotTable style to the PivotTable report:

▶ **1.** Make sure the active cell is in the PivotTable, and then click the **PivotTable Tools Design** tab on the Ribbon.

▶ **2.** In the PivotTable Styles group, click the **More** button to open the PivotTable Styles gallery.

▶ **3.** Move the pointer over each style to preview the PivotTable report with that style.

▶ **4.** Click the **Pivot Style Medium 3** style (the third style in the Medium section). The style is applied to the PivotTable.

Formatting PivotTable Value Fields

Applying PivotTable styles does not change the numeric formatting in the PivotTable. Mary wants the numbers in the PivotTable to be quickly recognized as currency. You can format cells in a PivotTable the same way as you do cells in the worksheet. You'll change the total appraised values in the PivotTable to Currency style.

To format the appraised value numbers in the PivotTable:

▶ 1. Click any cell in the **Sum of Appraised Value** column of the PivotTable report.

▶ 2. Click the **PivotTable Tools Options** tab on the Ribbon, and then, in the Active Field group, click the **Field Settings** button. The Value Field Settings dialog box opens. See Figure 5-34.

| Figure 5-34 | Value Field Settings dialog box |

Tip

You can use the Summarize by tab to change the SUM function to a different summary function, such as AVERAGE. The name in the PivotTable is updated to reflect your selection.

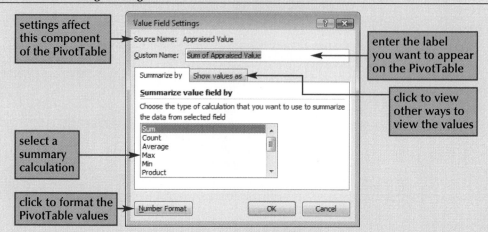

If you want to change "Sum of Appraised Value" (cell B3), the name used to describe the calculations in the PivotTable report, use the Custom Name box in the Value Field Settings dialog box.

▶ 3. Click the **Number Format** button. The Format Cells dialog box opens. This is the same dialog box you've used before to format numbers in worksheet cells.

▶ 4. Click **Currency** in the Category list, and then type **0** in the Decimal places box.

▶ 5. Click the **OK** button in each dialog box. The numbers in the PivotTable are formatted as currency with no decimal places.

With the style applied and the numbers formatted as currency, the data in the Pivot-Table is much easier to interpret.

Rearranging a PivotTable

Although you cannot change the values within a PivotTable, you can add, remove, and rearrange fields to change the PivotTable's layout. Recall that the benefit of a PivotTable is that it summarizes large amounts of data into a readable format. After you create a Piv-otTable, you can view the same data in different ways. The PivotTable Field List enables you to change, or pivot, the view of the data in the PivotTable by dragging the field buttons to different areas in the layout section.

Refer back to Mary's PivotTable sketch in Figure 5-27. As illustrated in the sketch, the Condition field items should be positioned as column labels instead of row labels in the PivotTable. You'll move the Condition field now to produce the format Mary wants.

To move the Condition field:

▶ **1.** In the layout section of the PivotTable Field List, drag the **Condition** field button from the Row Labels box to the Column Labels box. The PivotTable is rearranged so that the Condition field is a column label instead of a row label. See Figure 5-35. Each time you make a change in the PivotTable Field List, the PivotTable layout is rearranged.

PivotTable rearranged with Condition as a column label | Figure 5-35

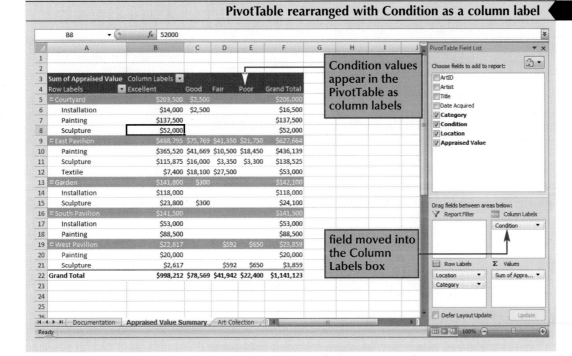

Changing the PivotTable Report Layout Options

The Compact report layout, shown in Figure 5-35, places all fields from the row area in a single column and indents the items from each field below the outer fields. This is the default layout for PivotTable reports. You can choose two other layouts. In the Outline report layout, each field in the row area takes a column in the PivotTable. By default, the outline form shows the subtotals for each group at the top of every group. The Tabular report layout displays one column for each field and leaves space for column headers. A total for each group appears at the bottom of each group. You can find these report layout options on the PivotTable Tools Design tab in the Layout group. Mary asks you to show her how the PivotTable looks in these alternative layouts so she can select the one she prefers.

To display the PivotTable in Outline and Tabular layouts:

▶ **1.** Click the **PivotTable Tools Design** tab on the Ribbon.

▶ **2.** In the Layout group, click the **Report Layout** button, and then click **Show in Outline Form**. The PivotTable layout changes. See Figure 5-36.

Figure 5-36 **Outline PivotTable report layout**

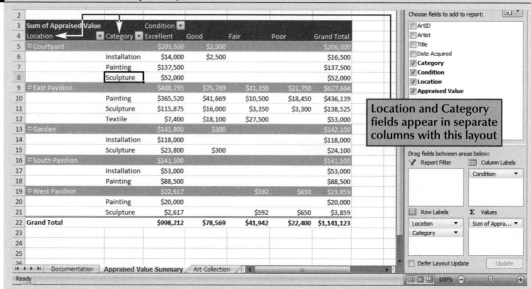

Next, you'll review the Tabular report layout.

▶ **3.** In the Layout group, click the **Report Layout** button, and then click **Show in Tabular Form**. The PivotTable layout changes. See Figure 5-37.

Figure 5-37 **Tabular PivotTable report layout**

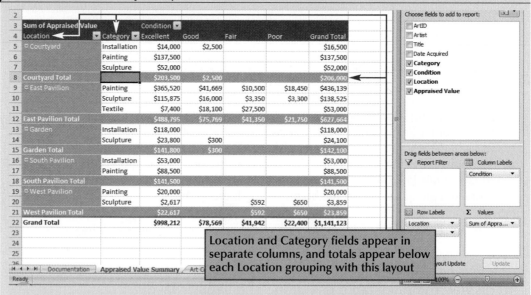

Mary prefers the original layout, the Compact form.

▶ **4.** In the Layout group, click the **Report Layout** button, and then click **Show in Compact Form**.

Adding a Report Filter to a PivotTable

You can drag a field to the Report Filter area to create a filtered view of the PivotTable report. A **report filter** allows you to filter the PivotTable to display summarized data for one or more field items or all field items in the Report Filter area. For example, creating a report filter for the Location field allows you to view or print the total appraised value for all locations or for specific locations such as the Courtyard.

You will add a report filter for the Location field to see if displaying the information in this way adds value to the report.

To add a report filter for the Location field:

▶ **1.** Drag the **Location** button from the Row Labels box to the Report Filter box. The Report Filter field item shows All to indicate that the PivotTable report displays all the summarized data associated with the Location field. See Figure 5-38.

PivotTable with the Location report filter applied ◄ Figure 5-38

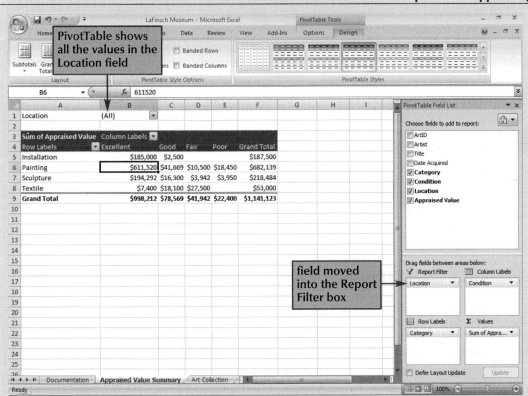

Next, you'll change the summarized report to show only art objects in the East Pavilion.

Tip

If you want to filter more than one location at a time, you can click the Select Multiple Items check box to add a check box next to each item. You could then choose multiple items from the list.

▶ **2.** Click the **report filter arrow** in cell B1. A filter menu opens, showing the field items displayed.

Mary wants you to filter by a single item.

▶ **3.** Click **East Pavilion** in the filter menu, and then click the **OK** button. The Pivot-Table displays the total appraised value of art objects located in the East Pavilion only. The report filter arrow changes to an icon to indicate the PivotTable is currently filtered. See Figure 5-39.

Figure 5-39 | **Report filter view for art objects in the East Pavilion**

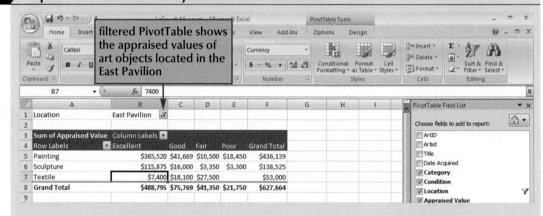

After reviewing the PivotTable, Mary decides she prefers the previous layout.

▶ **4.** In the PivotTable Field List, drag the **Location** button from the Report Filter box to the top of the Row Labels box. The Location field is positioned above the Category field, and the PivotTable returns to its previous layout.

Trouble? If the PivotTable report is arranged differently, the Location field is not the top field in the Row Labels box. Drag the Location button in the Row Labels box above the Category button.

Filtering PivotTable Fields

Filtering a field lets you focus on a subset of items in that field. You can filter field items in the PivotTable by clicking the field arrow button in the PivotTable that represents the data you want to hide and then uncheck the check box for each item you want to hide. To show hidden items, you click the field arrow button and check the check box for the item you want to show.

Mary wants to focus her analysis on art objects in excellent, good, and fair condition. She asks you to remove art objects in poor condition from the PivotTable. You will hide the art objects in poor condition from the PivotTable report.

To filter the Condition field items from the PivotTable:

▶ **1.** In the PivotTable, click the **Column Labels filter arrow**. The Filter menu displays the list of items in the Condition field.

▶ **2.** Click the **Poor** check box to remove the check mark. The Select All check box is deselected as well.

▶ **3.** Click the **OK** button. The Poor column is removed from the PivotTable. The PivotTable includes only art objects in excellent, good, and fair condition. See Figure 5-40.

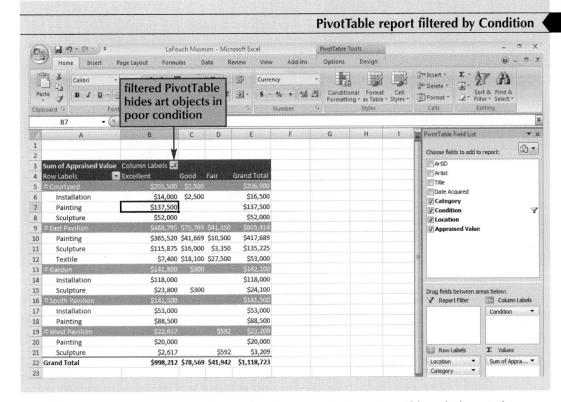

The report contains the art objects data Mary wants to review. Although the art objects in poor condition are hidden, you can show them again by clicking the Column Labels arrow and checking the Poor check box.

Collapsing and Expanding Items

You can expand and collapse items in the row labels of the PivotTable to view fields at different levels of detail. The Expand and Collapse buttons identify where more details exist. The Expand button indicates you can show more details for that item, and the Collapse button indicates you can hide details for that item. The lowest level of the hierarchy does not have Expand and Collapse buttons because there is no data to expand or collapse. These buttons are helpful when you have complex PivotTables where you want to switch quickly between a detailed view and an overview.

Mary wants to see the total appraised value for each location without the Category items in the PivotTable. She asks you to collapse the level of detail so that only the Location items are showing. Currently, all items are expanded.

To collapse the Courtyard items in the PivotTable:

▶ **1.** Point to the **Collapse** button ⊟ next to Courtyard until the pointer changes to ⍩, and then click the **Collapse** button ⊟ next to Courtyard. The detail items below Courtyard are hidden, and the Collapse button changes to an Expand button.

▶ **2.** Click the **Collapse** button ⊟ next to East Pavilion, Garden, South Pavilion, and West Pavilion. The details for these four locations are hidden, and only the Location items are displayed. The PivotTable provides a higher level summary without displaying the Category details. See Figure 5-41.

Figure 5-41 | PivotTable with all locations collapsed and categories hidden

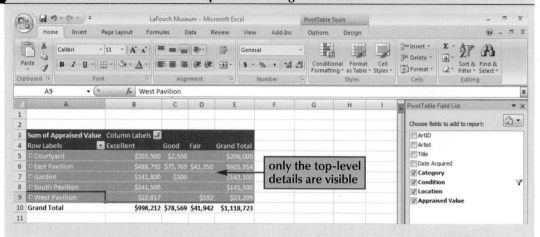

You can collapse or expand all level of detail in a PivotTable at one time. You'll do this to return to the original level of detail.

To expand all items in the PivotTable:

► 1. Click the **PivotTable Tools Options** tab on the Ribbon. The Active Field group has buttons for expanding or collapsing all the details at one time.

► 2. In the Active Field group, click the **Expand Entire Field** button. The detail items for all levels reappear. The lowest level of the hierarchy does not have Expand and Collapse buttons.

Sorting PivotTable Fields

Mary thinks the PivotTable would be more informative if the appraised values in each location were sorted in descending order. You can sort a PivotTable field either by its own items, for example alphabetizing fields such as Location and Category, or on the values in the body of the PivotTable. To sort a PivotTable field, you can use any of the Sort buttons on the Options tab to sort the information in a PivotTable report. These options are similar to the sort options you used earlier in the tutorial.

Mary wants you to sort the PivotTable so that the location with the highest total appraised value is displayed first. You need to sort the PivotTable values in descending order.

To sort the PivotTable to display the Location values in descending order based on their total appraised value amounts:

► 1. Click cell **E5**, which contains the Grand Total for Courtyard. This is the field total you want to sort.

2. In the Sort group on the PivotTable Tools Options tab, click the **Sort Largest to Smallest** button . The Location field is sorted based on the total appraised value for each location. Note, for example, that the East Pavilion location appears first in the PivotTable because it has the highest total appraised value, $605,914. The Courtyard location appears next because it has the second highest total appraised value, $206,000, and so on. See Figure 5-42.

PivotTable results sorted by Location | **Figure 5-42**

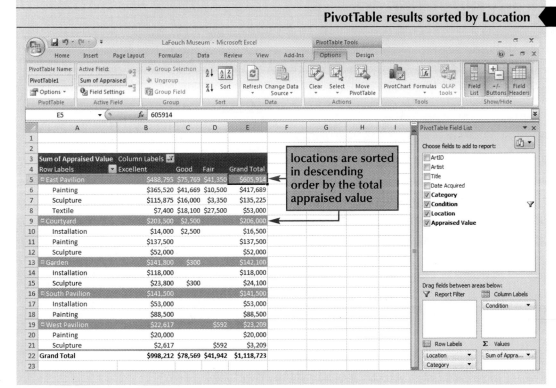

locations are sorted in descending order by the total appraised value

Adding a Second Value Field to a PivotTable

You can expand a PivotTable to create a more informative table by adding fields to the Values layout area. For example, Mary believes that a more accurate presentation of the art objects would include the number of objects corresponding to the total value in each cell of the PivotTable. Adding the Title field to the Values box would count the number of art objects in each location-category-condition combination (because the title is a nonnumeric field). Mary thinks the additional information will be useful during her meeting with the board of directors. You will add the Title field to the PivotTable.

To drag and drop the Title field to the Values box:

1. In the PivotTable Field List, drag **Title** from the field list to immediately below the Sum of Appraised Value button in the Values box. The PivotTable displays the number of art objects as well as the total appraised value. The Values box in the layout area includes a second button, Count of Title, and fields from the Values box are added to the Column Labels box. See Figure 5-43.

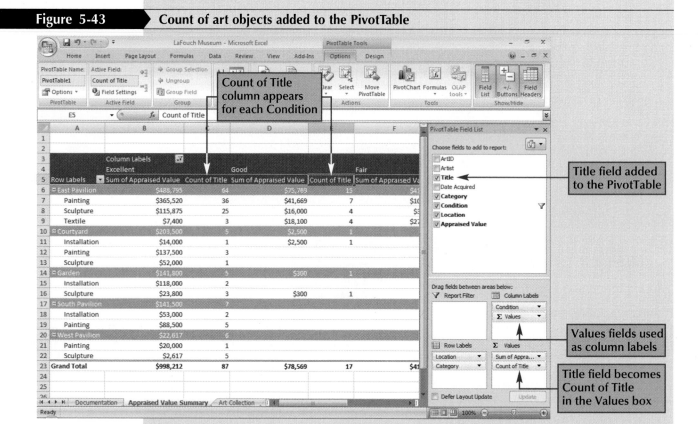

Figure 5-43 **Count of art objects added to the PivotTable**

Part of the PivotTable is hidden behind the PivotTable Field List. You'll hide the Pivot-Table Field List so you can view more of the PivotTable.

▶ **2.** In the Show/Hide group on the PivotTable Tools Options tab, click the **Field List** button. The PivotTable Field List disappears.

Next, you'll change the "Count of Title" label to "Count."

▶ **3.** In the PivotTable, click any of the **Count of Title** labels.

Tip

You can also rename a value label by typing the new text directly in any cell where the value label appears in the PivotTable.

▶ **4.** In the Active Field group on the PivotTable Tools Options tab, click the **Field Settings** button. The Value Field Settings dialog box opens.

▶ **5.** In the Custom Name box, type **Count**, and then click the **OK** button. The Count label appears in the PivotTable instead of Count of Title.

Removing a Field from a PivotTable

The PivotTable report with the Count looks cluttered and is difficult to read. Mary asks you to remove the Count field. If you want to remove a field from a PivotTable, you click the field's check box in the PivotTable Field List. Removing a field from the PivotTable has no effect on the underlying Excel table. You will remove the Title field from the PivotTable.

To remove the Title field from the PivotTable:

▶ **1.** In the Show/Hide Group on the PivotTable Tools Options tab, click the **Field List** button. The PivotTable Field List is displayed.

▶ **2.** Click the **Title** check box in the field area. The Count column is removed from the PivotTable, which returns to its previous layout. The Title field is still in the ArtObjects table.

The PivotTable is almost complete. Mary asks you to improve the appearance of the PivotTable by removing the field headers (Row Labels and Column Labels) and hiding the Expand/Collapse buttons.

To hide field headers and the Expand/Collapse buttons from the PivotTable:

▶ **1.** In the Show/Hide group on the PivotTable Tools Options tab, click the **+/- Buttons** button. The Expand/Collapse buttons disappear from the PivotTable.

▶ **2.** In the Show/Hide group, click the **Field Headers** button. The headers Column Labels and Row Labels are hidden. See Figure 5-44.

PivotTable without field headers and Expand/Collapse buttons ◀ **Figure 5-44**

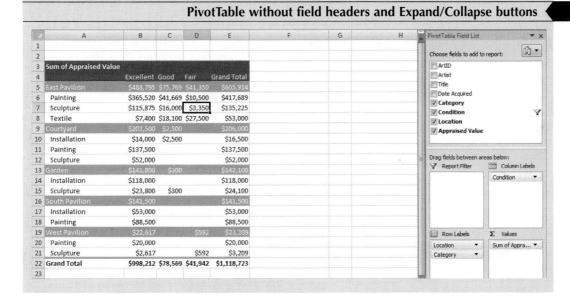

Refreshing a PivotTable

Mary just learned that the art object Dancing in the Light by Cridler has been reappraised and its value is now $4,000 (its value is currently listed as $1,000). You cannot change the data directly in the PivotTable. Instead, you must edit the Excel table, and then **refresh**, or update, the PivotTable to reflect the current state of the art objects list.

You'll edit the record for Dancing in the Light in the ArtObjects table. This sculpture is located in the East Pavilion and is in fair condition. This one change will affect the Pivot-Table in several locations. For example, currently the Total value of objects in the East Pavilion is $605,914; the sculptures in the East Pavilion are valued at $135,225; and sculptures in the East Pavilion in fair condition are valued at $3,350. After you update the appraised value of this art object in the Excel table, all these values in the PivotTable will increase by $3,000.

To update the ArtObjects table:

▶ 1. Switch to the **Art Collection** worksheet, and then find **Cridler, Dancing in the Light** (ArtID 73).

▶ 2. Click the record's Appraised Value cell, and then enter **4000**. The sculpture's value is updated in the table. You'll return to the PivotTable report to see the effect of this change on its values.

▶ 3. Switch to the **Appraised Value Summary** worksheet. The appraised value totals for the East Pavilion are still $605,914, $135,225, and $3,350, respectively.

   The PivotTable is not updated when the data in its source table is updated, so you need to refresh the PivotTable manually.

▶ 4. Click any cell in the PivotTable.

▶ 5. Click the **PivotTable Tools Options** tab on the Ribbon, and then, in the Data group, click the **Refresh** button. The PivotTable report is updated. The appraised value totals are now $608,914, $138,225, and $6,350. See Figure 5-45.

| Figure 5-45 | Refreshed PivotTable |

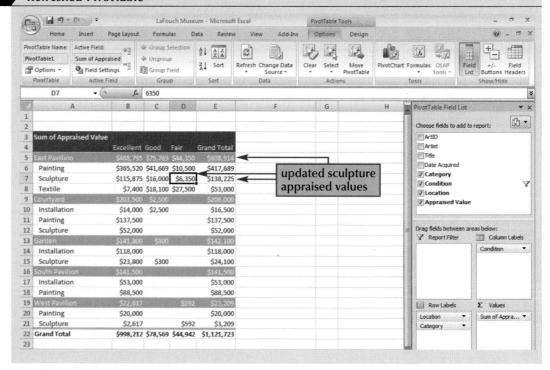

Mary is satisfied with the final version of the PivotTable report.

Grouping PivotTable Items

When a field contains numbers, dates, or times, you can combine items in the rows of a PivotTable and combine them into groups automatically. Mary thinks another PivotTable, one displaying the number of objects acquired each year, would be of interest to the board of directors. This report involves using the Date Acquired field as a row label and ArtID (or other field) as the value field. When using a date field as a row label in a PivotTable, each date initially appears as a separate item. Typically, you want to analyze date data by month, quarter, or year. To do that, you need to group the data in the Date Acquired field. Grouping items combines dates into larger groups such as months, quarters, or years, so that the PivotTable can include the desired level of summarization. You can also group numeric items, typically into equal ranges. For example, you can calculate the number of art objects in appraised value groups based on increments of any amount you specify (for example, 1–25,000, 25,001–50,000, and so on).

You'll add a second PivotTable in a new worksheet.

To create the PivotTable based on the Date Acquired field:

▶ **1.** Switch to the **Art Collection** worksheet, and then click any cell in the Excel table. The table is active.

▶ **2.** Click the **Insert** tab on the Ribbon, and then, in the Tables group, click the **PivotTable** button. The Create PivotTable dialog box opens.

▶ **3.** Verify that the Table/Range box shows **ArtObjects** and the **New Worksheet** option button is selected, and then click the **OK** button. The PivotTable report area and PivotTable Field List appear in a new worksheet.

▶ **4.** In the PivotTable Field List, click the **Date Acquired** check box. The Date Acquired field appears in the Row Labels box. Each unique date appears in the PivotTable report area. Mary wants each year to appear as a row label. You will correct that shortly.

Next, you'll add the ArtID field to the PivotTable.

▶ **5.** Click the **ArtID** check box in the PivotTable Field List. The Sum of ArtID appears in the Values box in the layout area, because the ArtID field contains numeric data. See Figure 5-46.

| Figure 5-46 | PivotTable with Sum of ArtID for each date |

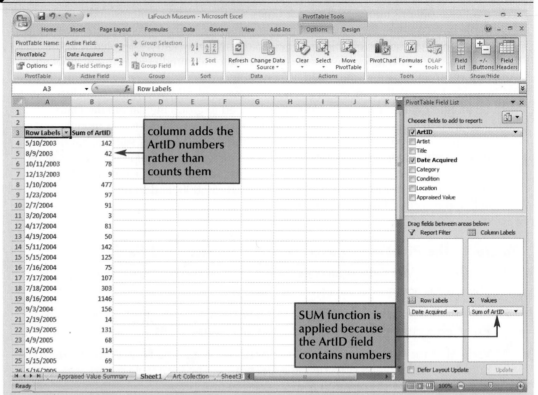

The PivotTable includes the sum of ArtIDs instead of a count of art objects, as Mary requested. This occurs because fields that contain numbers placed in the Values area are summed. Adding all the ArtIDs together to get a total is meaningless; you need to count the number of ArtIDs in each year. To do this, you need to change the SUM function to the COUNT function so Excel will *count* the number of objects in each group.

► **6.** Click any value in the **Sum of ArtID** column, and then, in the Active Field group on the PivotTable Tools Options tab, click the **Field Settings** button. The Value Field Settings dialog box opens.

► **7.** Click **Count** in the Summarize value field by box, and then type **Count** in the Custom Name box. The label indicating the type of summary in the PivotTable will be changed to Count.

► **8.** Click the **OK** button. The dialog box closes and the PivotTable report displays the number of art objects acquired by date. See Figure 5-47.

PivotTable report with count ◄ **Figure 5-47**

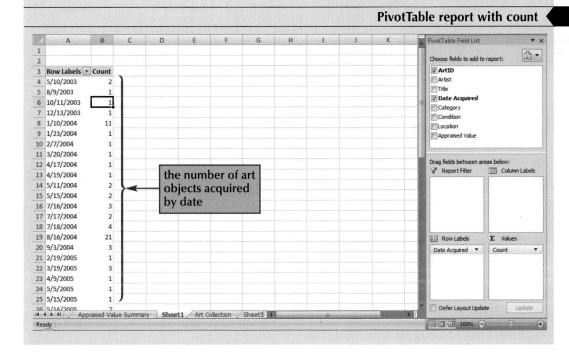

the number of art objects acquired by date

Grouping Date Fields

The layout of this PivotTable is not what Mary would like. Mary wants a count of acquisitions by year, not by date. You can group a range of dates into periods such as months, quarters, or years using the Group Fields command. Mary wants to group the Date Acquired dates by year.

To group Date Acquired by year:

▶ **1.** Click any date value in the Row Labels column of the PivotTable, and then, in the Group group on the PivotTable Tools Options tab, click the **Group Field** button. The Grouping dialog box opens.

▶ **2.** Click **Months** to deselect it, and then click **Years** to select it. See Figure 5-48.

Grouping dialog box ◄ **Figure 5-48**

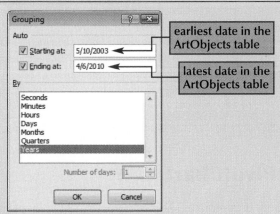

earliest date in the ArtObjects table

latest date in the ArtObjects table

> **3.** Click the **OK** button. The PivotTable report is grouped by year, displaying the number of art acquisitions in each year. See Figure 5-49.

Figure 5-49 PivotTable report of annual acquisitions

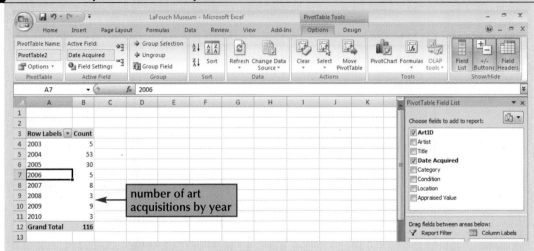

number of art acquisitions by year

> **4.** Rename the worksheet as **Acquired By Year**.

InSight | **Creating Different Types of PivotTable Reports**

This tutorial only touched the surface of the variety of PivotTable reports you can create. Here are a few more examples:

- Most PivotTable summaries are based on numeric data, but PivotTables can also contain only nonnumeric data. You cannot add nonnumeric data, so you must use the COUNT function to produce summaries. For example, you could count the number of art objects by Location and Category.
- You can use PivotTables to combine items into groups. Items that appear as row labels or column labels can be grouped. If items are numbers or dates, they can be grouped automatically using the Grouping dialog box or manually using the Ctrl key to select items in a group and choosing Group from the shortcut menu. For example, you can manually combine the Courtyard and Garden locations into an Outdoor group and combine the three pavilion locations into an Indoor group and then provide counts or total appraised values by these groups within the PivotTable. Being able to combine categories that aren't part of your original data with the grouping feature gives you flexibility to summarize your PivotTables in a way that meets your analysis requirements.
- You can develop PivotTables using the value filter, which allows you to filter one of your row or column fields in the PivotTable based on numbers that appear in the Values area of the PivotTable. For example, a PivotTable can show the total value of art objects for each artist and be filtered to display only artists whose total is greater than $25,000. Filtering provides you with a more precise way to view the PivotTable results by enabling you to include or remove data from the report.

Creating a PivotChart

Now that the PivotTable is complete, Mary asks you to add a PivotChart next to the PivotTable. A **PivotChart** is a graphical representation of the data in a PivotTable. A

PivotChart allows you to interactively add, remove, filter, and refresh data fields in the PivotChart similar to working with a PivotTable. PivotCharts can have all the same formatting as other charts, including layouts and styles. You can move and resize chart elements, or change formatting of individual data points.

Mary asks you to prepare a clustered column chart next to the new PivotTable report. You can create a PivotChart from the PivotTable.

To create the PivotChart:

▶ **1.** Click any cell in the PivotTable, and then, in the Tools group on the PivotTable Tools Options tab, click the **PivotChart** button. The Insert Chart dialog box opens.

▶ **2.** Click the **Clustered Column** chart (the first chart in the first row of the Column section), if necessary, and then click the **OK** button. A PivotChart appears next to the PivotTable along with the PivotChart Filter Pane, which you use to filter the data shown in the PivotChart.

▶ **3.** Close the PivotTable Field List, and then move the PivotChart Filter Pane to the right of the PivotChart.

Because the PivotChart has only one series, you do not need a legend.

▶ **4.** In the PivotChart, click the **legend** to select it, and then press the **Delete** key. The legend is removed from the PivotChart.

Next, you'll modify the chart title.

▶ **5.** Right-click the **chart title**, and then click **Edit Text**. The insertion point appears in the title so you can edit it.

▶ **6.** Select the title, type **Number Acquired By Year** as the new title, and then click the **chart area** to deselect the title.

▶ **7.** Move the PivotChart so its upper-left corner is in cell D3. The PivotChart is aligned with the PivotTable. See Figure 5-50.

Tip

You can also create a Pivot-Chart based directly on the Excel table, in which case both a PivotTable and a PivotChart are created.

PivotChart added to the PivotTable report | **Figure 5-50**

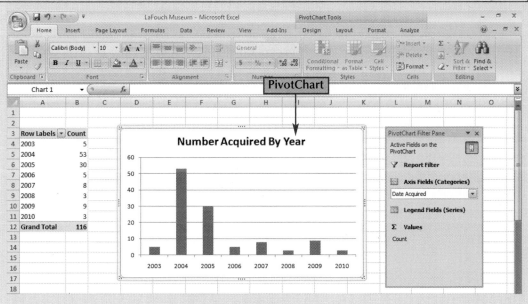

The PivotChart Tools contextual tabs enable you to manipulate and format the selected PivotChart the same way as an ordinary chart. A PivotChart and its associated PivotTable are linked. When you modify one, the other also changes. Mary asks you to display only art acquisitions after 2004.

To filter items in the PivotChart:

▶ **1.** Make sure the PivotChart is selected, and then, in the PivotChart Filter Pane, click the **Axis Fields (Categories) filter arrow**. The filter menu opens.

▶ **2.** Click the **<5/10/2003**, **2003**, and **2004** check boxes to remove the check marks.

▶ **3.** Click the **OK** button. The PivotChart displays only art objects acquired after 2004. The PivotTable is also filtered to display the same results.

You have completed your work on the LaFouch Museum workbook.

▶ **4.** Save your changes to the workbook, and then close it.

Mary is pleased with the PivotTable and PivotChart. Both show the number of art objects acquired by year, which will be important information for her upcoming board meeting.

Review | **Session 5.3 Quick Check**

---

1. What is the default summary function for numeric data in a PivotTable?

2. When creating a PivotTable, what do you use to lay out the fields in the PivotTable report?

3. After you update data in an Excel table, what must you do to a PivotTable based on that table?

4. Fields such as region, state, and country are most likely to appear as _____ in a PivotTable.

5. Fields such as revenue, costs, and profits are most likely to appear as _____ in a PivotTable.

6. A list of college students includes a code to indicate the student's gender (male or female) and a field to identify the student's major. Which tool, Filter or PivotTable, would you use to (a) create a list of all females majoring in history, and (b) count the number of males and females in each major?

Tutorial Summary | Review

In this tutorial, you learned how to create an Excel table, enter, edit, and delete data in the table, and then sort data. You filtered the Excel table to display only data that meets certain criteria. You used the Total row to display detailed rows along with summary results for a filtered table. You inserted subtotals into a structured range of data. Finally, you summarized a table using a PivotTable and PivotChart.

Key Terms

ascending order	field	record
category field	field name	refresh
clear	filter	report filter
column header	freeze	secondary sort field
criteria filter	header row	sort
custom list	PivotChart	sort field
data definition table	PivotTable	Total row
descending order	primary sort field	value field

| Practice | **Review Assignments** |

Practice the skills you learned in the tutorial using the same case scenario.

Data File needed for the Review Assignments: Art.xlsx

Mary has another art object that needs to be entered in the art objects list. To further understand the information in the workbook, she wants to sort the data by date acquired. She wants to filter data to retrieve all art with the word *cowboy* in the title. She wants to use a PivotTable to determine the average value of artwork for each artist. Mary has asked you to gather the information she needs for further analysis of the museum's art objects.

Complete the following:

1. Open the **Art** workbook located in the Tutorial.05\Review folder included with your Data Files, and then save the workbook as **Art Museum** in the same folder.
2. In the Documentation sheet, enter your name and the date, and then switch to the Art Collection worksheet.
3. Create an Excel table for the art objects data. Change the table style to Medium 25.
4. Rename the Excel table as **Collection**.
5. Sort the art objects by Date Acquired to display the newest objects first. Make a copy of the Art Collection worksheet, rename the copied worksheet as **Q5** (for "Question 5"), and then return to the Art Collection worksheet. (*Hint*: Ctrl + drag the sheet tab to make a copy of the worksheet.)
6. Sort art objects by Category (Z to A), Location (A to Z), Artist (A to Z) in ascending order, and by Date Acquired (showing the oldest first). Make a copy of the Art Collection worksheet, rename the copied worksheet as **Q6** (for "Question 6"), and then return to the Art Collection worksheet.
7. Filter the Collection table to produce a list of art objects with the word *Cowboy* in the title, and then redisplay all the art objects. Make a copy of the Art Collection worksheet, rename the copied worksheet as **Q7**, and then return to the Art Collection worksheet. Display all records.
8. Use the Total row to calculate the average value of objects acquired between 2006 and 2010. Change the label in the Total row from Total to **Average**. Make a copy of the Art Collection worksheet, rename the copied worksheet as **Q8**, and then return to the Art Collection worksheet. Remove the Total row.
9. Use the Subtotal command to count how many art objects there are in each Location, displaying the count in the ArtID column. Make a copy of the Art Collection worksheet, rename the copied worksheet as **Q9**, and then return to the Art Collection worksheet. Remove the subtotals.
10. Create a PivotTable to show the average value of art objects by artist. Format the Value column.
11. Sort the PivotTable showing the artist with highest average value first.
12. Rename the PivotTable sheet as **Q10-15 Artist Summary**.
13. Modify the PivotTable to include Category as a Report filter field, and then filter the report so the average by Artist is based on Paintings.
14. Insert a new record in the Collection Excel table, and then enter the following data:
    ArtID #: **118**   Category: **Painting**
    Artist: **Abonti**   Condition: **Excellent**
    Title: **Trouble Ahead**   Location: **Garden**
    Date Acquired: **4/15/2010**   Appraised Value: **1200**
15. Refresh the PivotTable.
16. Save and close the workbook. Submit the finished workbook to your instructor, either in printed or electronic form, as requested.

| Apply | **Case Problem 1** |

Use the skills you learned to analyze and summarize donation data for a zoo.

Data File needed for this Case Problem: Pledges.xlsx

Hewart Zoo   Marvis Chennard is the director of fund-raising for the Hewart Zoo. The zoo relies on donations to fund operations, temporary exhibits, and special programs. Marvis created an Excel table to track information about donors and their pledges. Marvis asks you to analyze the data in the list.

Complete the following:

1. Open the **Pledges** workbook located in the Tutorial.05\Case1 folder included with your Data Files, and then save the workbook as **Zoo Pledges** in the same folder.
2. In the Documentation worksheet, enter the date and your name, and then switch to the Pledges worksheet.
3. Create an Excel table, and then rename the table as **PledgeData**.
4. Sort the data in ascending order by Donor Type and Fund Name, and in descending order by Amt Pledged (largest first). Make a copy of the Pledges worksheet, rename the copied worksheet as **Q4** (for "Question 4"), and then return to the Pledges worksheet. (*Hint*: Ctrl + drag the sheet tab to make a copy of the worksheet.)
5. Filter the data to display Individual donors whose Amt Owed is over zero. Sort the filtered data by Pledge Date, with the oldest date displayed first. Make a copy of the Pledges worksheet, rename the copied worksheet as **Q5** (for "Question 5"), and then return to the Pledges worksheet. Display all records.
6. Filter the data to display records that have a Pledge Date in October through December. Sort the filtered data by Amt Pledged (largest first). Make a copy of the Pledges worksheet, rename the copied worksheet as **Q6**, and then return to the Pledges worksheet. Display all records.
7. Filter the data to display only records with Amt Received greater than zero. Then use the Subtotal command (SUM) to display the total Amt Received by Fund Name. Make a copy of the Pledges worksheet, rename the copied worksheet as **Q7**, and then return to the Pledges worksheet. Remove the subtotals.
8. Create a PivotTable that displays the total and average Amt Owed by each Donor Type and Fund Name. Place the PivotTable in a new worksheet. Select an appropriate report layout and format, and rename the worksheet with a descriptive name.
9. Using Figure 5-51 as a guide, create a PivotTable on a new worksheet that shows the Amt Pledged by month and Fund Name. Format the PivotTable appropriately, and then rename the worksheet with a descriptive name. Print the PivotTable report.

| Figure 5-51 |

	A	B	C	D	E	F
1						
2						
3	Sum of Amt Pledged	Column Labels				
4	Row Labels	Bird Sanctuary	General Support	Kids Zoo	ZooMobile	Grand Total
5	Jan		$1,000	$100		$1,100
6	Feb			$1,100	$150	$1,250
7	Mar			$100	$1,000	$1,100
8	Apr	$75	$500	$425		$1,000
9	Jun			$1,000	$50	$1,050
10	Jul	$1,000	$1,000			$2,000
11	Sep	$100	$25	$250	$150	$525
12	Oct	$200	$200			$400
13	Nov		$250			$250
14	Dec			$150	$750	$900
15	Grand Total	$1,375	$2,975	$3,125	$2,100	$9,575

10. Add the following data to the Pledge table, and then update the PivotTable you created in Step 9.

Pledge #	Donor Name	Donor Type	Fund Name	Pledge Date	Amt Pledged
2129	**Elliot Anderson**	**Individual**	**Kids Zoo**	**12/31/2010**	**1000**

11. Save and close the workbook. Submit the finished workbook to your instructor, either in printed or electronic form, as requested.

Apply	**Case Problem 2**

Use the skills you learned to analyze and summarize expenditure data for a farm.

Data File needed for this Case Problem: Ring.xlsx

Ring Family Farm Fred and Alesia Ring own a small family farm just outside Abita Springs, Louisiana. The couple wants to better organize their financial records for their accountant. They created an Excel workbook to record the various expenses associated with farming. Typical expenses include those associated with hay production (seed, fertilizer, and irrigation), animal husbandry, fence maintenance, veterinary services, self-administered medicines, vehicles and maintenance, and so forth. The workbook includes categories associated with these expenses as well as an area to record how much is spent, the purpose of the expenditure, the check number, and the date paid.

Complete the following:

1. Open the **Ring** workbook located in the Tutorial.05\Case2 folder included with your Data Files, and then save the workbook as **Ring Farm** in the same folder.
2. Insert a new worksheet. Enter the company name, your name, the date, and a purpose statement in the worksheet, and then rename the worksheet as **Documentation**.
3. Create an Excel table in the Expenditures worksheet, and then rename the table as **Checkbook**.
4. Replace the Category code Farm in each record with the more descriptive Category code **Payroll**.
5. Sort the Checkbook table in ascending order by Category, then by Description, and then by Date Paid (newest first). Make a copy of the Expenditures worksheet, rename the copied worksheet as **Q5** (for "Question 5"), and then return to the Expenditures worksheet. (*Hint*: Ctrl + drag the sheet tab to make a copy of the worksheet.)
6. Filter the Checkbook table to display all expenditures for Equipment and Repairs in December, and then sort by Amount (smallest first). Make a copy of the Expenditures worksheet, rename the copied worksheet as **Q6** (for "Question 6"), and then return to the Expenditures worksheet. Display all records.
7. Filter the Checkbook table to display all checks that include the word **vet** in the description. Include the total Amount at the bottom of the table. Make a copy of the Expenditures worksheet, rename the copied worksheet as **Q7**, and then return to the Expenditures worksheet. Remove the filter and totals.
8. Use conditional formatting to apply a Yellow Fill with Dark Yellow text to all Outstanding checks. (*Hint:* "Yes" appears in the Outstanding column.) Make a copy of the Expenditures worksheet, rename the copied worksheet as **Q8**, and then return to the Expenditures worksheet.
9. Use the Subtotal command to display total Amount for each Category, displaying the subtotal in the Amount column. Make a copy of the Expenditures worksheet, rename the copied worksheet as **Q9**, and then return to the Expenditures worksheet. Remove all subtotals.

10. Create a PivotTable that summarizes expenditures by Category and month. Place the PivotTable in a new worksheet. Format the PivotTable appropriately, choose a layout, and then rename the worksheet with a descriptive name.

11. Insert a PivotChart with the Clustered Column chart type on the same sheet as the PivotTable.

EXPLORE 12. Create the PivotTable shown in Figure 5-52 in a new worksheet. Sort the Amount column in descending order. (*Hint:* Check the Show values as tab in the Value Field Setting dialog box to calculate percent of total.)

Figure 5-52

	A	B	C
1			
2			
3		Values	
4	Row Labels ▼	Sum of Amount	Pct of Total
5	Equipment	$6,575.00	37.0%
6	Payroll	$2,638.27	14.9%
7	Vet	$2,320.57	13.1%
8	Repairs	$2,003.44	11.3%
9	Feed	$2,002.24	11.3%
10	Medicine	$1,249.32	7.0%
11	Administration	$958.09	5.4%
12	Grand Total	$17,746.93	100.0%

13. Save and close the workbook. Submit the finished workbook to your instructor, either in printed or electronic form, as requested.

Apply | Case Problem 3

Use the skills you learned to analyze and summarize loan data for a bank.

Data File needed for this Case Problem: CustLoans.xlsx

High Desert Bank   Eleanor Chimayo, loan manager for High Desert Bank, is getting ready for the bank's quarterly meeting. Eleanor is expected to present data on the status of different types of loans within three New Mexican cities. Eleanor asks you to summarize and analyze the data for her presentation.

Complete the following:

1. Open the **CustLoans** workbook located in the Tutorial.05\Case3 folder included with your Data Files, and then save the workbook as **High Desert Bank** in the same folder.

2. In the Documentation sheet, enter the date and your name.

3. In the Loans worksheet, create an Excel table, and then rename the table as **LoanData**.

4. Format the Amount and Interest Rate fields so it is clear that these fields contain dollars and percentages.

5. Change the table style to one of your choice.

EXPLORE 6. To the right of the Type column, insert a new column named **Monthly Payment**. Use the PMT function to calculate the monthly payment for each loan. Adjust the formula so each loan is displayed as a positive amount and improve the formatting.

7. Sort the loan data in ascending order by Type, within Type by City, and within City by Last Name.

8. Use conditional formatting to display loans above average using a format that highlights these loans. Make a copy of the Loans worksheet, rename the copied worksheet as **Q3–8**, for ("Question 3–8"), and then return to the Loans worksheet. (*Hint:* Ctrl + drag the sheet tab to make a copy of the worksheet.)

9. Filter the LoanData table to display loans made during March and April of 2010. Include the number of loans, total amount of loans, and average monthly payment for the filtered data at the bottom of the table. Make a copy of the Loans worksheet, rename the copied worksheet as **Q9**, for ("Question 9"), and then return to the Loans worksheet. Then remove the total loans and show all records.

10. Sort the loans in ascending order by City; then by Type of loan; and then by Amount of loan (largest loan first). Insert subtotals (Average) for loan Amount and Monthly Payment by City. Include your name in a custom footer. Make a copy of the Loans worksheet, rename the copied worksheet as **Q10**, and then return to the Loans worksheet. Remove the subtotals.

11. Create a PivotTable that displays the number (Count) and average loan by Type and City. Place the PivotTable in a new worksheet. Remove the Other loan type from the PivotTable. Format the PivotTable appropriately. Rename the PivotTable worksheet as **Q11 Loans-Type And City**.

✦ EXPLORE 12. Create a second PivotTable, shown in Figure 5-53, in a new worksheet. The PivotTable shows three calculations: Number of Loans, total loans (Loan Amount), and total monthly payments (Payment) categorized by Type of loan. Insert a report filter based on Loan Date, grouped so you can filter by month. Filter the PivotTable report for March and April. Rename the PivotTable worksheet as **Q12 Loans-Type and Loan Date**.

Figure 5-53

	A	B	C	D
1	Loan Date	(Multiple Items) ▾		
2				
3		Number of Loans	Loan Amount	Payment
4	Car	5	$157,000	$3,681.77
5	Mortgage	5	$929,000	$7,890.77
6	Other	2	$35,000	$860.49
7	Grand Total	12	$1,121,000	$12,433.03

13. Save and close the workbook. Submit the finished workbook to your instructor, either in printed or electronic form, as requested.

Challenge | Case Problem 4

Explore how to summarize data from a department store by creating more complex subtotals, PivotTables, and PivotCharts.

Data File needed for this Case Problem: Bowls.xlsx

Bowls Department Stores Bowls Department Stores, with corporate headquarters in Portland, Oregon, operates department stores in midsize towns in selected northwestern areas. Although the organization maintains a large computer system for its accounting operations, the sales department often downloads data to complete additional analysis of its operations. Daniel Partner, analyst for the corporate sales department, regularly downloads data by territories and product areas including automotive, electronics, garden centers, and sporting goods. He often presents reports based on his analysis of sales by product areas and territory, best and worst performing product group-periods, and total sales for certain regions and product groups. He asks you to help him compile and summarize the data.

Complete the following:

1. Open the **Bowls** workbook located in the Tutorial.05\Case4 folder included with your Data Files, and then save the workbook as **Bowls Stores** in the same folder.

2. In the Documentation sheet, enter the date and your name and an appropriate purpose statement.

3. In the SalesData worksheet, create an Excel table. Rename the table as **ProductSales**. Format the Sales column in the Currency number format with no decimal places.

4. Sort the table in ascending order by Territories, then by Product Group, then by Year, and then by Month. Month should be sorted in Jan, Feb, Mar, ... order, not alphabetically. Make a copy of the SalesData worksheet, rename the copied worksheet as **Q4**, for ("Question 4"), and then return to the SalesData worksheet. (*Hint*: Ctrl + drag the sheet tab to make a copy of the worksheet.)

⊕ EXPLORE

5. Display records for Automotive and Electronic products in 2010, excluding sales in Vancouver. Sort this data by Sales in descending order. Add a Total row and calculate the average sales for the filtered data. Change the label in the Total row to **Average**. Insert a new worksheet and copy this filtered data to the new worksheet. Split the worksheet into two panes. The top pane displays all the rows but the last row on your screen. The bottom pane displays the Total row. (*Hint:* Click the Split button in the Window group on the View tab.) Rename the new worksheet as **Q5 Auto Electronic**. Return to the SalesData worksheet, remove the Total row, and display all the records.

⊕ EXPLORE

6. Display subtotals for sales (Sum) by Year, Month (Jan, Feb, Mar, ...), and Territory. Make a copy of the SalesData worksheet, rename the copied worksheet as **Q6**, for ("Question 6"), and then return to the SalesData worksheet. Remove the subtotals.

7. Display the five lowest periods based on sales. Assume each row represents a period. Sort the Sales so lowest sales appears first. Insert a new worksheet and copy this filtered data to the new worksheet. Rename the new worksheet as **Q7 Lowest Periods**. Return to the SalesData worksheet, and then display all the records.

⊕ EXPLORE

8. Create a PivotTable similar to the one shown in Figure 5-54, displaying percentage of sales by Product Group, Territories, and Year. Omit the columnar grand totals. Use a tabular layout, inserting subtotals at the bottom of each Product Group and excluding the Sporting product group. Rename the worksheet as **Q8 Percent of Sales**.

Figure 5-54

	A	B	C	D
1				
2				
3	**Pct of Sales**		**Year** ▾	
4	**Product Group** ⊽	**Territories** ▾	**2009**	**2010**
5	⊟ **Automotive**	Oregon	10.05%	8.85%
6		Vancouver	7.32%	9.71%
7		Washington	6.88%	9.94%
8	**Automotive Total**		**24.25%**	**28.50%**
9	⊟ **Electronics**	Oregon	7.53%	8.67%
10		Vancouver	7.61%	6.88%
11		Washington	8.05%	9.22%
12	**Electronics Total**		**23.20%**	**24.78%**
13	⊟ **Gardening**	Oregon	8.19%	6.85%
14		Vancouver	8.46%	5.89%
15		Washington	9.77%	9.91%
16	**Gardening Total**		**26.42%**	**22.66%**
17	⊟ **Houseware**	Oregon	6.86%	5.01%
18		Vancouver	8.20%	7.67%
19		Washington	11.07%	11.39%
20	**Houseware Total**		**26.14%**	**24.07%**
21	**Grand Total**		**100.00%**	**100.00%**

⊕ EXPLORE

9. Using Figure 5-55 as a guide, create a PivotChart of total Sales By Product Group. Create a second PivotChart of total Sales By Territory in the same worksheet. Include only the PivotCharts in the worksheet. Rename the worksheet as **Q9 PivotCharts**.

Figure 5-55

10. Using Figure 5-56 as a guide, create a PivotTable to show four calculations: minimum, maximum, average, and total Sales categorized by Territories and Product Group and filtered by Year. Display the results for 2010. Rename the worksheet as **Q10 Statistical Summary**.

Figure 5-56

	A	B	C	D	E	F
1	Year	2010				
2						
3			**Values**			
4	**Territories**	**Product Group**	**Average**	**Sum**	**Minimum**	**Maximum**
5	⊟Oregon	Automotive	$ 50,196	$ 602,354	$ 1,825	$ 98,358
6		Electronics	$ 49,175	$ 590,099	$ 7,164	$ 95,985
7		Gardening	$ 38,859	$ 466,305	$ 5,396	$ 95,795
8		Houseware	$ 28,428	$ 341,139	$ 3,374	$ 64,982
9		Sporting	$ 70,243	$ 842,910	$ 26,643	$ 91,786
10	**Oregon Total**		**$ 47,380**	**$2,842,807**	**$ 1,825**	**$ 98,358**
11	⊟Vancouver	Automotive	$ 55,074	$ 660,886	$ 865	$ 99,526
12		Electronics	$ 39,033	$ 468,391	$ 2,141	$ 98,044
13		Gardening	$ 33,419	$ 401,027	$ 467	$ 97,793
14		Houseware	$ 43,473	$ 521,678	$ 4,046	$ 80,035
15		Sporting	$ 60,199	$ 722,385	$ 29,824	$ 94,129
16	**Vancouver Total**		**$ 46,239**	**$2,774,367**	**$ 467**	**$ 99,526**
17	⊟Washington	Automotive	$ 56,359	$ 676,304	$ 3,893	$ 99,258
18		Electronics	$ 52,307	$ 627,680	$ 15,485	$ 84,624
19		Gardening	$ 56,206	$ 674,471	$ 5,507	$ 94,166
20		Houseware	$ 64,579	$ 774,942	$ 27,164	$ 94,725
21		Sporting	$ 63,189	$ 758,272	$ 17,919	$ 90,879
22	**Washington Total**		**$ 58,528**	**$3,511,669**	**$ 3,893**	**$ 99,258**
23	**Grand Total**		**$ 50,716**	**$9,128,843**	**$ 467**	**$ 99,526**

11. Save and close the workbook. Submit the finished workbook to your instructor, either in printed or electronic form, as requested.

Research	**| Internet Assignments**

Use the Internet to find and work with data related to the topics presented in this tutorial.

The purpose of the Internet Assignments is to challenge you to find information on the Internet that you can use to work effectively with this software. The actual assignments are updated and maintained on the Course Technology Web site. Log on to the Internet and use your Web browser to go to the Student Online Companion for New Perspectives Office 2007 at **www.course.com/np/office2007**. Then navigate to the Internet Assignments for this tutorial.

Assess	**| SAM Assessment and Training**

If you have a SAM user profile, you may have access to hands-on instruction, practice, and assessment of the skills covered in this tutorial. Log in to your SAM account (**http://sam2007.course.com**) to launch any assigned training activities or exams that relate to the skills covered in this tutorial.

Review	**| Quick Check Answers**

Session 5.1

1. To keep, or freeze, rows and columns so that they don't scroll out of view as you move around the worksheet. Freezing the rows and columns that contain headings makes understanding the data in each record easier.
2. Filter arrows appear in the column headers, a table style format is applied to the table, and the Table Tools Design contextual tab appears on the Ribbon.
3. sort fields
4. Sort by year of graduation and then by last name.
5. Enter the data for the new record in the row immediately following the last row of data in the table.
6. Create a custom list.
7. descending (Newest to Oldest)

Session 5.2

1. You must first sort the data for which you want to calculate subtotals, because subtotals are inserted whenever the value in the specified field changes.
2. Filter the table to show only the finance department, and then use the AVERAGE function in the Total row.
3. Click the Major filter arrow, and then check only the Accounting and Finance check boxes. Click the GPA filter arrow, point to Number Filters, click Greater Than, and then enter the value 3.0 in the Greater Than dialog box to specify the condition for a GPA greater than 3.0.

4. Click the Level Outline buttons.
5. True
6. Multiselect
7. Click the Gender filter arrow, and check only the Female check box. Insert the Total row, click the arrow that appears to the right of the total for the Salary column, and then click Average in the list of functions.

Session 5.3

1. SUM
2. PivotTable Field List box
3. refresh the PivotTable
4. rows labels, column labels, or report filters
5. values
6. (a) Filter; (b) PivotTable

Ending Data Files

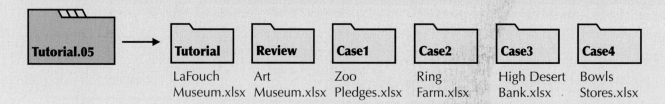

Tutorial.05	→	Tutorial	Review	Case1	Case2	Case3	Case4
		LaFouch Museum.xlsx	Art Museum.xlsx	Zoo Pledges.xlsx	Ring Farm.xlsx	High Desert Bank.xlsx	Bowls Stores.xlsx

Objectives

Managing Multiple Worksheets and Workbooks

Summarizing Ticket Sales

Case | Global Travel

Global Travel, a member-owned organization, provides a variety of services ranging from travel assistance to insurance programs to discounted vacation packages. Global Travel also offers special services and discounts to one-time entertainment events. Global Travel purchases tickets to selected theme and amusement parks to resell to its members, particularly those with families. Each local office of Global Travel markets and sells these tickets to its members. Theme and amusement park sales account for more than 10 percent of Global Travel's sales. Rhohit Gupta, accountant for Global Travel in New Mexico, is responsible for tracking ticket sales within the state and preparing an analysis for the corporate controller. Rhohit asks you to create a summary report that shows the quarterly sales in New Mexico for the past year. He already entered each quarter's values in separate worksheets, but wants you to "roll up" all the information in the four quarterly worksheets into one summary worksheet.

Rhohit reports to Alvin Alton, controller for Global Travel. Alvin already received workbooks from Colorado and Utah. After Alvin receives the New Mexico workbook, he will create a workbook that summarizes the annual totals from each state workbook in the Southwest region. He asks for your help with this.

Starting Data Files

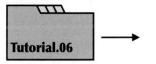

Tutorial.06 →

Tutorial
Colorado.xlsx
NM.xlsx
Sales 2010.docx
TravelTotals.xlsx
Utah.xlsx

Review
Idaho.xlsx
NW Totals 2010.xlsx
NW Travel.xltx
OR.xlsx
Washington.xlsx

Case1
Cafe.xlsx

Case2
Carson.xlsx
Reno.xlsx
Vegas.xlsx

Case3
InBurger.xlsx

Case4
Europe.xlsx
North America.xlsx
Pluto Template.xltx
South America.xlsx

Session 6.1

Using Multiple Worksheets

Workbook data is often placed in several worksheets. Using multiple worksheets makes it easier to group and summarize data. For example, a company such as Global Travel with branches in different geographic regions can place sales information for each region in separate worksheets. Rather than scrolling through one large and complex worksheet that contains data for all regions, users can access sales information for a specific region simply by clicking a sheet tab in the workbook.

Multiple worksheets enable you to place summarized data first. Managers interested only in an overall picture can view the first worksheet of summary data without looking at the details available in the other worksheets. Others, of course, might want to view the supporting data in the individual worksheets that follow the summary worksheet. In the case of Global Travel, Rhohit used separate worksheets to summarize the number of tickets sold and sales in dollars for the New Mexico branch offices for each quarter of the 2010 fiscal year. You will open Rhohit's workbook and review the current information.

To open and review the Global Travel workbook:

1. Open the **NM** workbook located in the **Tutorial.06\Tutorial** folder included with your Data Files, and then save the workbook as **New Mexico** in the same folder.

2. In the **Documentation** worksheet, enter your name and the current date.

3. Switch to the **Quarter 1** worksheet, and then view the number of tickets sold and sales for the first quarter of the year. See Figure 6-1.

Figure 6-1 | Quarter 1 worksheet for Global Travel—New Mexico

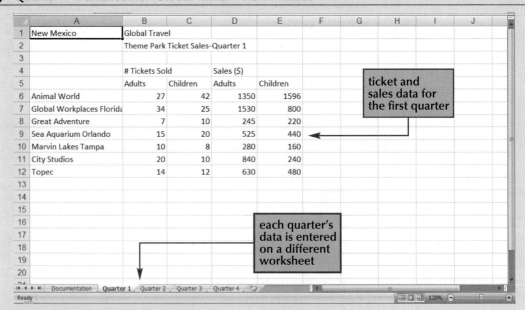

4. Review the **Quarter 2**, **Quarter 3**, and **Quarter 4** worksheets. The layout for all four worksheets is identical.

Grouping Worksheets

Rhohit didn't enter any formulas in the workbook. You need to enter formulas to calculate the total number of tickets and sales for each column (B through E) in all four worksheets. Rather than retyping the formulas in each worksheet, you can enter them all at once by creating a worksheet group. A **worksheet group** is a collection of two or more selected worksheets. When worksheets are grouped, everything you do to the active worksheet also affects the other worksheets in the group. For example, you can:

Tip

If a worksheet group includes all the worksheets in a workbook, you can edit only the active worksheet.

- Enter data and formulas in cells in one worksheet to enter the data and formulas in the same cells in all the worksheets in the group.
- Apply formatting to the active worksheet to format all the worksheets in the group, including changing row heights or column widths and applying conditional formatting.
- Edit data or formulas in worksheet to edit the data and formulas in the same cells in all the worksheets in the group. Commands such as insert rows and columns, delete rows and columns, and find and replace can also be used with a worksheet group.
- Set the page layout options in one worksheet to apply the settings to all the worksheets in the group, such as orientation, scaling to fit, and inserting headers and footers.
- Apply view options such as zooming, showing and hiding worksheets, and so forth to all worksheets in the group.
- Print all the worksheets in the worksheet group at the same time.

   Worksheet groups save you time because you can perform an action once, yet affect multiple worksheets. A worksheet group, like a range, can contain adjacent or nonadjacent worksheets.

Grouping and Ungrouping Worksheets | Reference Window

- To select an adjacent group, click the sheet tab of the first worksheet in the group, press and hold the Shift key, and then click the sheet tab of the last worksheet in the group.
- To select a nonadjacent group, click the sheet tab of one worksheet in the group, press and hold the Ctrl key, and then click the sheet tabs of the remaining worksheets in the group.
- To ungroup the worksheets, click the sheet tab of a worksheet not in the group (or right-click the sheet tab of one worksheet in the group, and then click Ungroup Sheets on the shortcut menu).

Entering Formulas in a Worksheet Group

In the travel workbook, you'll select an adjacent range of worksheets: the Quarter 1 worksheet through the Quarter 4 worksheet.

To group the quarterly worksheets:

1. Click the **Quarter 1** sheet tab to make the worksheet active. This is the first worksheet you want to include in the group.

2. Press and hold the **Shift** key, and then click the **Quarter 4** sheet tab. This is the last worksheet you want to include in the group.

3. Release the **Shift** key. The sheet tabs for Quarter 1 through Quarter 4 are white, indicating they are all selected. The text *[Group]* appears in the title bar to remind you that a worksheet group is selected in the workbook. See Figure 6-2.

Tip

If you cannot see the sheet tab of a worksheet you want to include in a group, use the sheet navigation controls to display it.

Figure 6-2 | **Grouped worksheets**

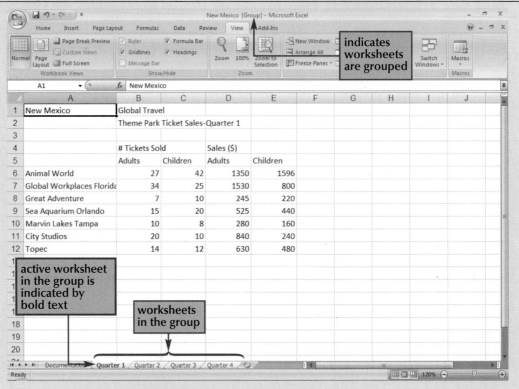

With the quarterly sheets grouped, you can enter the formulas to calculate the total number of tickets sold and total sales. When you enter a formula in the active worksheet (in this case, the Quarter 1 worksheet), the formula is entered in the same cells in all the worksheets in the group. The grouped worksheets must have the exact same organization and layout (rows and columns) for this to work. Otherwise, any formulas you enter in the active sheet will be incorrect in the other worksheets in the group and could overwrite existing data.

To enter the same formulas in all the worksheets in the group:

▶ 1. Click cell **B13**. You want to enter the formula in cell B13 in each of the four grouped worksheets.

▶ 2. In the Editing group on the Home tab, click the **Sum** button Σ, and then press the **Enter** key. The formula =SUM(B6:B12) is entered in the cell and adds the total number of adult tickets sold in the quarter, which is 127.

   You will copy the formula to add the total number of children's tickets sold, the total adult ticket sales, and the total children's ticket sales.

▶ 3. Copy the formula in cell B13 to the range **C13:E13**.

▶ 4. In cell A13, enter **Totals**, and then, in the Alignment group on the Home tab, click the **Increase Indent** button. The label shifts to the right.

   The formulas and label you entered in the Quarter 1 worksheet were entered in the Quarter 2, 3, and 4 worksheets at the same time.

▶ 5. Click the **Quarter 2** sheet tab, and then click cell **B13**. The value 174 appears in the cell and the formula =SUM(B6:B12), which adds the number of adult tickets sold in Quarter 2, appears in the formula bar.

▶ **6.** Click the **Quarter 4** sheet tab, and then click cell **B13**. The value 177 appears in the cell, and the same formula used in cell B13 in the Quarter 1 and Quarter 2 worksheets appears in the formula bar. See Figure 6-3.

Formulas entered in all worksheets in the group | Figure 6-3

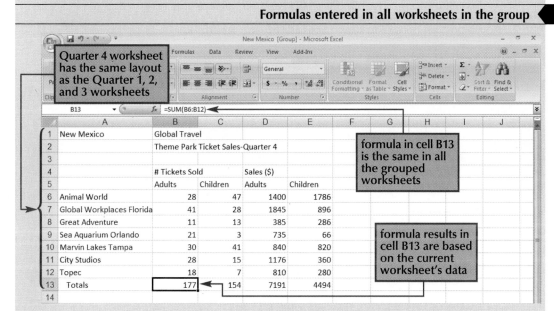

Quarter 4 worksheet has the same layout as the Quarter 1, 2, and 3 worksheets

formula in cell B13 is the same in all the grouped worksheets

formula results in cell B13 are based on the current worksheet's data

B13   *fx* =SUM(B6:B12)

	A	B	C	D	E	F	G	H	I	J
1	New Mexico	Global Travel								
2		Theme Park Ticket Sales-Quarter 4								
3										
4		# Tickets Sold		Sales ($)						
5		Adults	Children	Adults	Children					
6	Animal World	28	47	1400	1786					
7	Global Workplaces Florida	41	28	1845	896					
8	Great Adventure	11	13	385	286					
9	Sea Aquarium Orlando	21	3	735	66					
10	Marvin Lakes Tampa	30	41	840	820					
11	City Studios	28	15	1176	360					
12	Topec	18	7	810	280					
13	Totals	177	154	7191	4494					
14										

▶ **7.** Click the **Quarter 1** sheet tab to redisplay the Quarter 1 results.

Editing Grouped Worksheets | InSight

When you enter, edit, or format cells in a worksheet group, the changes you make to one worksheet are automatically applied to the other worksheets in the group. For example, if you delete a value from one cell, the value in that cell in all the worksheets in the group is also deleted. Be cautious when editing the contents of a worksheet when it is part of a group. Also, remember to ungroup the worksheet group after you finish entering data, formulas, and formatting. Otherwise, changes you intend to make to a cell or range in one worksheet will be made to all the worksheets in the worksheet group, potentially producing incorrect results.

Formatting a Worksheet Group

Now that you've applied a common set of formulas to the quarterly worksheets, you can format them. As with inserting formulas and text, any formatting changes you make to a single sheet in a group are applied to all sheets.

To apply the same formatting to all the worksheets in the group:

▶ **1.** Bold the text in the nonadjacent range **A1:B2;A6:A13;B4:E5**.

▶ **2.** Increase the width of column A to **24**.

▶ **3.** Merge and center each of the ranges **B1:E1**, **B2:E2**, **B4:C4**, and **D4:E4**.

▶ **4.** Center the text in the range **B5:E5**.

5. Apply the **Comma Style** number format with no decimal places to the range B6:C13. No change is visible because all the numbers are less than 1000.

6. Apply the **Accounting** number format with no decimal places to the range D6:E13 so the values appear with a dollar sign and no decimal places.

7. Add a bottom border to the ranges **B5:E5** and **B12:E12**.

8. Click cell **A1**. All the worksheets in the group are formatted. See Figure 6-4.

Figure 6-4 ▶ **Formatting applied to the worksheet group**

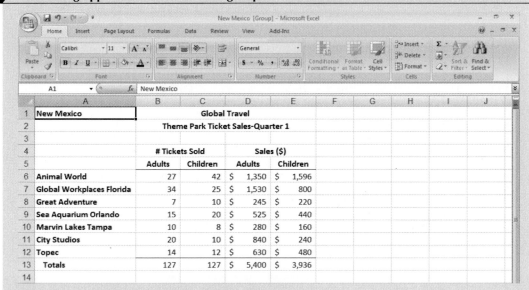

9. Click each sheet tab in the worksheet group to view the formatting changes, and then click the **Quarter 1** sheet tab.

Ungrouping Worksheets

You can ungroup the quarterly worksheets so you can work in each worksheet separately. When you ungroup the worksheets, each worksheet functions independently again. If you forget to ungroup the worksheets, any changes you make in one worksheet will be applied to all the worksheets in the group.

To ungroup the quarterly worksheets:

1. Click the **Documentation** sheet tab. The worksheets are ungrouped and the text *[Group]* is removed from the Excel title bar.

2. Verify that the worksheets are ungrouped and the word *[Group]* no longer appears in the title bar.

Tip

To ungroup worksheets, you can also right-click any sheet tab in the worksheet group, and then click Ungroup Sheets on the shortcut menu.

Copying Worksheets

Next, you'll create the Summary worksheet to provide an overall picture of the data included in the detailed quarterly worksheets. The Summary worksheet needs the same formatting and structure as the quarterly worksheets. To ensure consistency among worksheets, you will copy the Quarter 1 worksheet, and then modify its contents. The fastest way to copy an entire worksheet or worksheet group is to press and hold the Ctrl key as you drag and drop the sheet tab to another location in the workbook. A number in parentheses is added to the copy's sheet tab to distinguish it from the original worksheet. You will use this method to create the Summary worksheet.

> **Tip**
>
> To move a worksheet or worksheet group to another location in the same workbook, select the worksheets and then drag and drop them by the selected sheet tabs.

Copying Worksheets to Another Workbook | Reference Window

- Select the sheet tabs of the worksheets you want to copy.
- Right-click the sheet tabs, and then click Move or Copy on the shortcut menu.
- In the Move or Copy dialog box, select the worksheets you want to move or copy to another workbook.
- Click the To book arrow, and then click an existing workbook name or (new book) to create a new workbook for the worksheets.
- Click the Create a copy check box to insert a check mark if you want to copy the worksheets to another workbook, leaving the originals in the current workbook; uncheck the Create a copy check box to move the worksheets.
- Click the OK button.

You'll copy the Quarter 1 worksheet to the beginning of the workbook, and then modify the new copy to create the Summary worksheet.

To copy the Quarter 1 worksheet and create the Summary worksheet:

▶ 1. Click the **Quarter 1** sheet tab, press and hold the **Ctrl** key, drag the worksheet to the left of the Documentation sheet, and then release the **Ctrl** key. An identical copy of the Quarter 1 worksheet appears in the new location. The sheet tab shows *Quarter 1 (2)* to indicate that this is the copied sheet.

▶ 2. Rename the copied worksheet as **Summary**.

▶ 3. Move the Summary worksheet between the Documentation worksheet and the Quarter 1 worksheet.

   You will modify the Summary worksheet.

▶ 4. In cell A2, enter **2010**. This is the year to which the summary refers.

▶ 5. In cell B2, enter **Theme Park Ticket Sales-Total**. The new title reflects this worksheet's content.

   The range B6:E12 should add the results for the entire year. You need to delete the Quarter 1 sales, which were copied from the Quarter 1 worksheet.

▶ 6. Select the range **B6:E12**, and then press the **Delete** key. The Quarter 1 sales data is removed, but the formatting remains intact and will apply to the sales data for all four quarters that you will enter shortly.

Referencing Cells and Ranges in Other Worksheets

The Summary worksheet will show the total sales for all four quarters, which are stored in separate worksheets. When you use multiple worksheets to organize related data, you can reference a cell or range in another worksheet in the same workbook. You'll do this to create the sales totals for the entire year.

To reference a cell or range in a different worksheet, you precede the cell or range reference with the worksheet name followed by an exclamation mark. The syntax is as follows:

```
=SheetName!CellRange
```

In this formula, *SheetName* is the worksheet's name as listed on the sheet tab and *CellRange* is the reference for the cell or range in that worksheet. An exclamation mark (!) separates the worksheet reference from the cell or range reference. For example, to enter a formula in the Summary worksheet that references cell D10 in the Quarter1 worksheet, you would enter the following formula:

```
=Quarter1!D10
```

If the worksheet name contains spaces, you must enclose the sheet name in single quotation marks. For example, the reference for the *Quarter 1* worksheet is *'Quarter 1'!D10*. You can use these references to create formulas that reference cells in different locations in different worksheets. For example, to add sales from two worksheets—cell E12 in the Quarter 1 worksheet and cell D12 in the Quarter 2 worksheet—you would enter the following formula:

```
='Quarter 1'!E12+'Quarter 2'!D12
```

Reference Window | **Entering a Formula That References Another Worksheet**

- Click the cell where you want to enter the formula.
- Type = and enter the formula. To insert a reference from another worksheet, click the sheet tab for the worksheet, and then click the cell or select the range you want to reference.
- When the formula is complete, press the Enter key.

Rhohit wants you to enter a formula in cell A2 in each quarterly worksheet that displays the fiscal year from cell A2 in the Summary worksheet. All four quarterly worksheets will use the formula *=Summary!A2* to reference the fiscal year in cell A2 of the Summary sheet. You could type the formula directly in the cell, but it is faster and more accurate to use the point-and-click method to enter references to other worksheets.

To enter a formula in the quarterly worksheets that references the Summary worksheet:

1. Click the **Quarter 1** sheet tab, press and hold the **Shift** key, and then click the **Quarter 4** worksheet. The Quarter 1 through Quarter 4 worksheets are grouped.

2. Click cell **A2**. This is the cell in which you want to enter the formula to display the fiscal year.

3. Type **=** to begin the formula, click the **Summary** sheet tab, click cell **A2**, and then press the **Enter** key. The reference to cell A2 in the Summary worksheet is entered in the formula in the grouped worksheets.

4. In the Quarter 1 worksheet, click cell **A2**. The formula *=Summary!A2* appears in the formula bar and 2010 appears in the cell. See Figure 6-5.

Formula with a worksheet reference | **Figure 6-5**

cell displays the contents of cell A2 from the Summary worksheet

formula references cell A2 in the Summary worksheet

A2   ƒx =Summary!A2

	A	B	C	D	E	F	G	H	I	J
1	New Mexico			Global Travel						
2	2010		Theme Park Ticket Sales-Quarter 1							
3										

▶ **5.** In each worksheet, verify that the formula =*Summary!A2* appears in the formula bar and 2010 appears in cell A2.

    Rhohit wants to use a more descriptive label in cell A2.

▶ **6.** Switch to the **Summary** worksheet. The quarterly worksheets are ungrouped.

▶ **7.** In cell A2, enter **Fiscal Year - 2010**.

▶ **8.** Verify that the label in cell A2 changed in the Quarter 1 through Quarter 4 worksheets.

Using 3-D References to Add Values Across Worksheets

You need to calculate the number of tickets sold and the total sales for each theme park for the year and display the totals for the fiscal year in the Summary worksheet. To calculate the totals for the year, you can add the results from each quarterly worksheet and place the sum in the Summary worksheet. For example, in cell B6 of the Summary worksheet, you can enter the formula:

```
='Quarter 1'!B6+'Quarter 2'!B6+'Quarter 3'!B6+'Quarter 4'!B6
```

This formula calculates the number of Adult tickets sold to Animal World by adding the values in cell B6 in each of the quarterly worksheets. Continuing this approach for the entire worksheet is time consuming and error prone. There is an easier way.

    When two or more worksheets have *identical* row and column layouts, as do the quarterly worksheets in the New Mexico workbook, you can enter formulas with 3-D references to summarize those worksheets in another worksheet. A **3-D reference** refers to the *same* cell or range in multiple worksheets in the same workbook. The reference specifies not only the range of rows and columns, but also the range of worksheet names in which the cells appear. The general syntax of a 3-D cell reference is as follows:

WorksheetRange!CellRange

WorksheetRange is the range of worksheets you want to reference and is entered as *FirstSheetName:LastSheetName* with a colon separating the first and last worksheets in the worksheet range. *CellRange* is the same cell or range in each of those worksheets that you want to reference. An exclamation mark (!) separates the worksheet range from the cell or range.

    For example, the formula =*SUM(Quarter1:Quarter4!E13)* adds the values in cell E13 in the worksheets between Quarter1 and Quarter4, including Quarter1 and Quarter4. If worksheets named *Quarter1, Quarter2, Quarter3,* and *Quarter4* are included in the workbook, the worksheet range *Quarter1:Quarter4* references all four worksheets. Although *Quarter2* and *Quarter3* aren't specifically mentioned in this 3-D reference, all worksheets positioned within the starting and ending names are included in the calculations.

InSight	**Managing 3-D References**

The results of a formula using a 3-D reference reflect the current worksheets in the worksheet range. If you move a worksheet outside the referenced worksheet range or remove a worksheet from the workbook, the formula results will change. For example, consider a workbook with four worksheets named *Quarter1, Quarter2, Quarter3, and Quarter4.* If you move the Quarter3 worksheet after the Quarter4 worksheet, the worksheet range *Quarter1:Quarter4* includes only the Quarter1, Quarter2, and Quarter4 worksheets. Similarly, if you insert a new worksheet or move an existing worksheet within the worksheet range, the formula results reflect the change. To continue the example, if you insert a Quarter5 worksheet before the Quarter4 worksheet, the 3-D reference *Quarter1:Quarter4* includes the Quarter5 worksheet.

When you create a formula, make sure that the 3-D cell reference reflects the appropriate worksheets. Also, if you later insert or delete a worksheet within the 3-D reference, be aware of how doing so will affect the formula results.

3-D references are used in formulas that contain Excel functions, including SUM, AVERAGE, COUNT, MAX, MIN, STD, and VAR. You enter a 3-D reference either by typing the reference directly in the cell or by using your mouse to select first the sheet range, and then the cell or cell range.

Reference Window	**Entering a Function That Contains a 3-D Reference**

- Click the cell where you want to enter the formula.
- Type = to begin the formula, type the name of the function, and then type (to indicate the beginning of the argument.
- Click the sheet tab for the first worksheet in the worksheet range, press and hold the Shift key, and then click the tab for the last worksheet in the worksheet range.
- Select the cell or range to reference, and then press the Enter key.

In the New Mexico workbook, you'll use 3-D references in the Summary worksheet to add the total number of tickets sold and sales for the year.

You will begin by entering a formula to add the number of tickets sold to adults for the Animal World theme park in all four quarters of the year. Then, you'll copy this formula to calculate the tickets sold to adults and children for each theme park as well as the sales generated.

To enter a formula with the 3-D reference to the quarterly worksheets:

▶ 1. In the Summary sheet, click cell **B6**, and then type **=SUM(** to begin the formula. A ScreenTip shows the SUM function syntax.

You'll enter a 3-D reference to cell B6 in the four quarterly worksheets.

▶ 2. Click the **Quarter 1** sheet tab, press and hold the **Shift** key, click the **Quarter 4** sheet tab, and then release the **Shift** key. The worksheet range is selected and added to the SUM function as *'Quarter 1:Quarter 4'*. Single quotation marks appear around the worksheet range because the worksheet names include spaces.

3. In the Quarter 1 worksheet, click cell **B6**. The cell is selected and added to the function. See Figure 6-6.

3-D reference added to the SUM function ◀ **Figure 6-6**

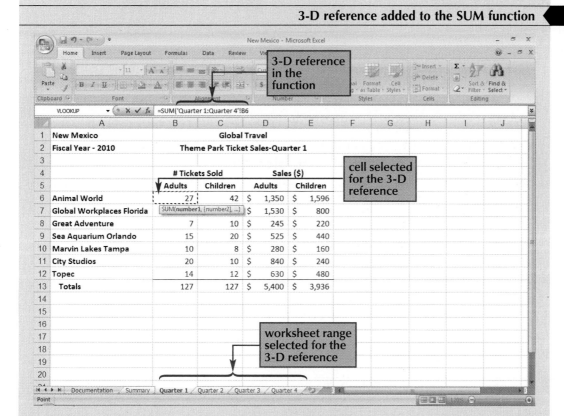

4. Press the **Enter** key to complete the formula, and then, in the Summary worksheet, click cell **B6**. The completed formula =SUM('Quarter 1:Quarter 4'!B6) appears in the formula bar, and 116—the total number of tickets for Animal World sold to adults in 2010—appears in cell B6.

You'll repeat the process to enter a 3-D reference in cell C6 that adds the total number of tickets sold to children for Animal World in 2010.

5. In the Summary worksheet, click cell **C6**, and then type **=SUM(** to begin the formula.

6. Click the **Quarter 1** sheet tab, press and hold the **Shift** key, click the **Quarter 4** sheet tab, and then release the **Shift** key. The quarterly worksheets are grouped.

7. In the Quarter 1 worksheet, click cell **C6** to select the cell, and then press the **Enter** key to complete the formula and return to the Summary worksheet.

8. In the Summary worksheet, click cell **C6**. The following formula appears in the formula bar: =SUM('Quarter 1:Quarter 4'!C6). Also, the value 175—the total number of tickets sold to children for Animal World in 2010—appears in cell C6.

In cells D6 and E6, you'll enter the SUM function with a 3-D reference to calculate the total revenue from tickets sales for Animal World.

9. In the Summary worksheet, click cell **D6**, type **=SUM(** to begin the formula, group the **Quarter 1** through **Quarter 4** worksheets, click cell **D6**, and then press the **Enter** key. The SUM function with a 3-D reference to cell D6 in the quarterly worksheets is entered. The completed formula is =SUM('Quarter 1:Quarter 4'!D6) and the total revenue from ticket sales to adults for Animal World in 2010 is $5,800.

▶ **10.** In the Summary worksheet, click cell **E6**, then enter the SUM function formula with a 3-D reference to cell **E6** in the quarterly worksheets. The completed formula is *=SUM('Quarter 1:Quarter 4'!E6)* and the total revenue from ticket sales to children for Animal World in 2010 is $6,650.

Instead of entering the SUM function to create the totals for the remaining theme parks, you can copy the formulas to the rest of the range. You copy formulas with 3-D references the same way you copy other formulas—using copy and paste or AutoFill. You'll copy the formulas in the range B6:E6 to the range B7:E12 so you can calculate the total ticket sales and revenue in 2010 for the remaining theme parks.

To copy the formulas with 3-D cell references:

▶ **1.** Select the range **B6:E6**. This range contains the SUM functions with the 3-D references you already entered.

▶ **2.** Drag the fill handle down over the range **B7:E12**. The formulas are copied for the rest of the theme park rows. The Auto Fill Options button appears below the copied range.

▶ **3.** Below cell E12, click the **Auto Fill Options** button [icon], and then click the **Fill Without Formatting** option button. You don't want to copy the formatting in this case because you want to keep the bottom border formatting in the range B12:E12. The total values for the year appear in the range.

▶ **4.** Click cell **B6** to deselect the range. See Figure 6-7.

Figure 6-7 **Summary worksheet with all the 3-D reference formulas**

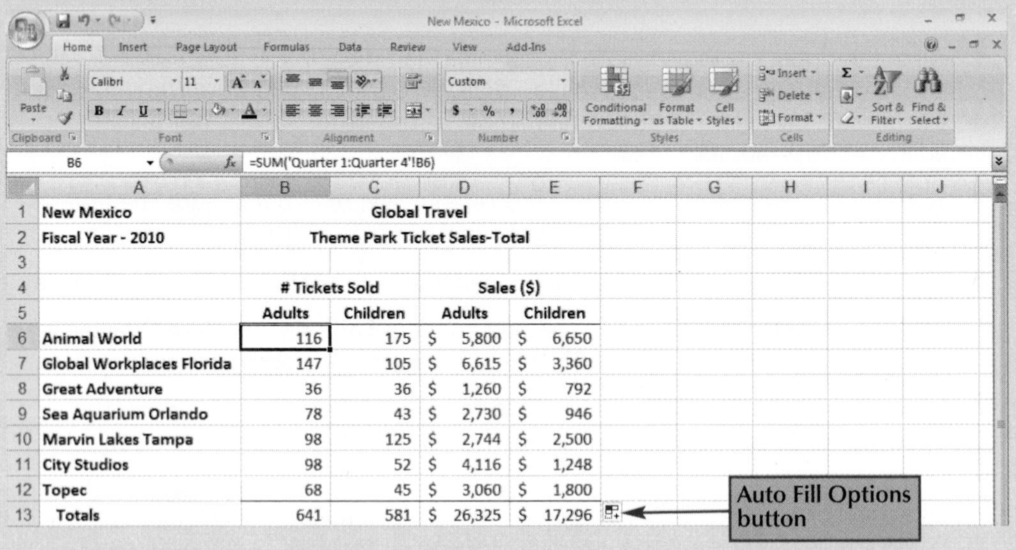

The Summary worksheet now shows the totals for the year 2010 in New Mexico for each theme park as well as statewide totals.

Rhohit discovered an error in the ticket sales data. Sea Aquarium Orlando sold 17 adult tickets in Quarter 1, not 15. One benefit of summarizing data using 3-D reference formulas, like any other formula, is that if you change the value in one worksheet, the results of formulas that reference that cell reflect the change. You will correct the number of tickets sold for Sea Aquarium Orlando in Quarter 1.

To change a value in the Quarter 1 worksheet:

▶ **1.** In the Summary worksheet, note that 78 adult tickets were sold for Sea Aquarium Orlando in 2010 and 641 total adult tickets were sold.

▶ **2.** Switch to the **Quarter 1** worksheet, and then, in cell B9, enter **17**. The total adult tickets sold in Quarter 1 is now 129.

The results in the Summary worksheet are also updated because of the 3-D references in the formulas.

▶ **3.** Switch to the **Summary** worksheet. The total number of tickets sold to adults for Sea Aquarium Orlando in 2010 is now 80, and the total number of tickets sold to adults for all theme parks in 2010 is now 643. See Figure 6-8.

Summary worksheet with updated ticket data ◀ Figure 6-8

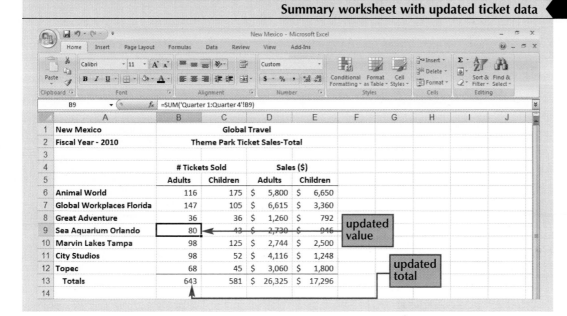

Printing a Worksheet Group

The Summary worksheet is complete and accurate. Rhohit asks you to print the five Ticket Sales worksheets to include in his report. He wants the same setup on each page. Recall that you set up the page layout and print area separately for each worksheet using the Page Layout tab on the Ribbon. Because the layout will be the same for all the quarterly worksheets in the New Mexico workbook, you can speed the page layout setup by creating a worksheet group before using the Page Setup dialog box. You will set up the worksheet group to print the report centered horizontally on the page with the name of the worksheet in the header and your name and the date in the footer.

To print the Summary and quarterly worksheets with a custom header and footer:

▶ **1.** Select the **Summary** worksheet through the **Quarter 4** worksheet. The five worksheets are grouped.

▶ **2.** Click the **Page Layout** tab on the Ribbon, and then, in the Page Setup group, click the Dialog Box Launcher. The Page Setup dialog box opens with the Page tab active.

▶ **3.** Click the **Margins** tab, and then click the **Horizontally** check box to insert a check mark. The printed content will be centered horizontally on the page.

▶ **4.** Click the **Header/Footer** tab, click the **Custom Header** button to open the Header dialog box, click in the **Center section** box, click the **Insert Sheet Name** button 🔲 to add the code *&[Tab]* in the section box to insert the sheet tab name in the center section of the header, and then click the **OK** button. A preview of the header appears in the upper portion of the dialog box.

▶ **5.** Click the **Custom Footer** button to open the Footer dialog box, type your name in the Left section box, click in the Right section box, click the **Insert Date** button 🔲 to add the code *&[Date]* in the section box to insert the current date in the right section of the footer, and then click the **OK** button.

▶ **6.** Click the **Print Preview** button. The Summary worksheet, the first worksheet in the group, appears in Print Preview. See Figure 6-9.

Figure 6-9 ▶ **Print Preview of the worksheet group**

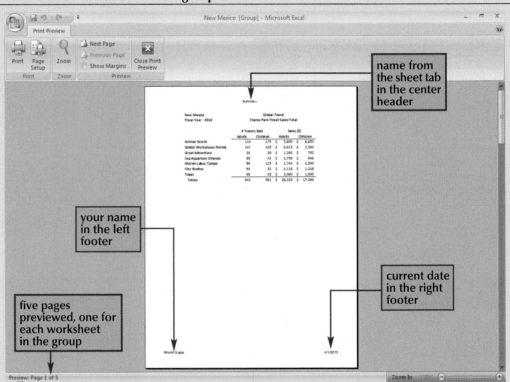

▶ **7.** In the Preview group on the Print Preview tab, click the **Next Page** button four times to view the other four worksheets in the group. Each page has the same page layout but the header shows the sheet tab names.

Trouble? If only one page appears in the Print Preview window, the worksheets are not grouped. Close the Print Preview window and repeat Steps 1 through 7.

▶ **8.** In the Preview group on the Print Preview tab, click the **Close Print Preview** button to close the Print Preview window without printing the worksheet group, unless you are instructed to print. In that case, in the Print group on the Print Preview tab, click the **Print** button.

▶ **9.** Switch to the **Documentation** sheet to ungroup the worksheets, and then switch to the **Summary** worksheet.

You have consolidated the data in Global Travel's New Mexico workbook in a Summary sheet, which will help Rhohit and the corporate controller to quickly see the totals for the theme park sales. Next, you will help the corporate controller to determine the annual totals for all of Global Travel's southwest locations—New Mexico, Utah, and Colorado.

Session 6.1 Quick Check | Review

1. What is a worksheet group?
2. How do you select an adjacent worksheet group? How do you select a nonadjacent worksheet group? How do you deselect a worksheet group?
3. What formula would you enter in the Summary worksheet to reference cell A10 in the Quarter 2 worksheet?
4. What is the 3-D cell reference to cell A10 in the adjacent Summary 1, Summary 2, and Summary 3 worksheets?
5. Explain what the formula *MAX(Sheet1:Sheet4!B1)* calculates.
6. If you insert a new worksheet (named *Sheet5*) after Sheet4, how would you change the formula in Question 5 to include Sheet5 in the calculation? How would you change the formula in Question 5 to include Sheet5 in the calculation if Sheet5 were positioned before Sheet4?
7. How do you apply the same printing page layout to all the worksheets in a workbook?

Session 6.2

Linking Workbooks

Alvin Alton, controller for Global Travel, has workbooks from the Colorado and Utah accountants similar to the one that you helped Rhohit prepare. Alvin now has three travel workbooks (named New Mexico, Colorado, and Utah), which contain the number of tickets sold and sales for the year 2010. Alvin wants to create a company-wide workbook that summarizes the annual totals from each state workbook.

If while creating formulas in one workbook you need to reference data located in one or more other workbooks, you must create a link between the workbooks. A **link** is a connection between the files that allows data to be transferred from one file to the other. When two files are linked, the **source file** is the workbook that contains the data, and the **destination file** (sometimes referred to as the *dependent* file) is the workbook that receives the data. In this case, as illustrated in Figure 6-10, the New Mexico, Utah, and Colorado workbooks are the *source* files because they contain the data from the three states. The Totals 2010 workbook is the *destination* file because it receives the data from the three state workbooks to calculate the company totals for 2010. Creating a link in the Totals 2010 workbook to the three state workbooks means the Totals 2010 workbook will always have access to the most recent information in the state workbooks, because it can be updated whenever any of the state workbook values change.

| Figure 6-10 | Source and destination files |

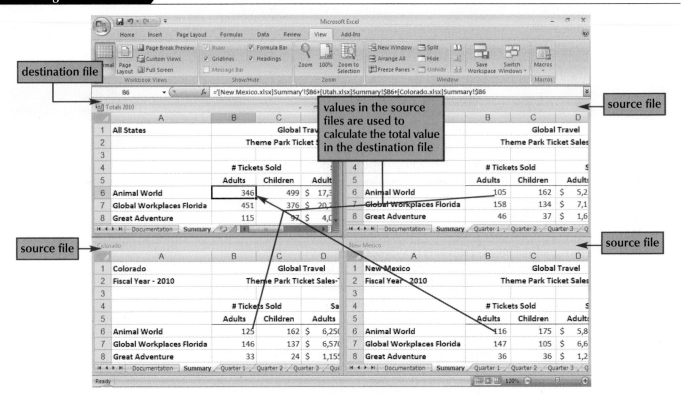

To create the link between destination and source files, you need to insert a formula in the Totals 2010 workbook that references a specific cell or range in the three state workbooks. Because the formula will contain a reference to a cell or range in a worksheet in another workbook, that reference is called an **external reference**. The syntax of an external reference is the following:

```
[WorkbookName]WorksheetName!CellRange
```

WorkbookName is the filename of the workbook (including the file extension) enclosed in square brackets. *WorksheetName* is the name of the worksheet that contains the data followed by an exclamation mark. *CellRange* is the cell or range that contains the data. For example, if you were to create a formula in one workbook to reference cell B6 in the Summary worksheet of the Colorado.xlsx workbook, you would enter the following formula:

```
=[Colorado.xlsx]Summary!B6
```

If the workbook name or the worksheet name contains one or more spaces, you must enclose the entire workbook name and worksheet name in single quotation marks. For example, to reference cell B6 in the Summary worksheet of the New Mexico.xlsx workbook, you would enter the following formula:

```
='[New Mexico.xlsx]Summary'!B6
```

Tip

When you use the point-and-click method to build formulas with external references, Excel enters all of the required punctuation, including quotation marks.

When the source and destination workbooks are stored in the same folder, you need to include only the workbook name in the external reference. However, when the source and destination workbooks are located in different folders, the workbook reference must include the file's complete location (also called the path). For example, if the destination file is stored in C:\TicketSales and the source file is stored in C:\TicketSales\Domestic Sales, the complete reference in the destination file would be:

```
='C:\TicketSales\Domestic Sales\[New Mexico.xlsx]Summary'!B6
```

The single quotation marks start at the beginning of the path and end immediately before the exclamation mark.

Understanding When to Link Workbooks | InSight

Linking workbooks is useful in many instances. The following are several examples of when to use linked workbooks:

- Separate workbooks have the same purpose and structure. For example, you can use related workbooks for different stores, branch offices, or departments with the same products or expenditure types and reporting periods (weekly, monthly, quarterly).
- A large worksheet has become unwieldy to use. You can break the large worksheet into smaller workbooks for each quarter, division, or product.
- A summary worksheet consolidates information from different workbook files. The linked workbooks enable you to more quickly and accurately summarize the information, and you know the summary worksheet contains the most current information if the information is later updated.
- Source workbooks you receive from another person or group are continually updated. With linked workbooks, you can replace an outdated source workbook and the destination workbook will then reflect the latest information without you having to modify the formulas.

Navigating and Arranging Multiple Workbooks

You'll combine the three state worksheets into one regional summary. You'll open all the workbooks you need to reference. Then, you'll switch between them to make each Summary worksheet the active sheet in preparation for creating the external references.

To open and switch between the workbooks needed to create the regional summary:

▶ **1.** If you took a break after the previous session, make sure the New Mexico workbook is open and the Summary worksheet is active.

▶ **2.** Open the **TravelTotals** workbook located in the **Tutorial.06\Tutorial** folder included with your Data Files, and then save the workbook as **Totals 2010** in the same folder.

▶ **3.** Enter your name and the current date in the Documentation sheet, and then make the **Summary** worksheet active.

▶ **4.** Open the **Utah** and **Colorado** workbooks located in the **Tutorial.06\Tutorial** folder included with your Data Files. Each open workbook has a button on the taskbar, but only one workbook is active.

▶ **5.** Click the **View** tab on the Ribbon, and then, in the Window group, click the **Switch Windows** button to open a list of all the workbooks currently open.

▶ **6.** Click **Utah** to make that the active workbook, and then make the **Summary** sheet active.

▶ **7.** In the Window group on the View tab, click the **Switch Windows** button, click **Colorado** to switch to the Colorado workbook, and then make the **Summary** worksheet active.

▶ **8.** Make the **Totals 2010** workbook the active workbook.

You'll need to move between open workbooks when you create the external reference formulas in the Totals 2010 workbook. Although you can use the Switch Windows button in the Window group on the View tab to change which workbook is active, you might find it easier to click the taskbar button for the workbook you want to make active.

Reference Window | **Arranging Workbooks**

- In the Window group on the View tab, click the Arrange All button.
- Select the desired option for arranging the workbook: Tiled, Horizontal, Vertical, or Cascade.
- When arranging multiple workbooks, uncheck the Windows of active workbook option unless you are arranging worksheets within one workbook.
- Click the OK button.

You might also want to display all the open workbooks on your screen at the same time. This way, you can easily click among the open workbooks to create links without having to continually change the active workbook. You can choose to arrange multiple open workbooks in one of four layouts:

- **Tiled** divides the open workbooks evenly on the screen.
- **Horizontal** divides the open workbooks into horizontal bands.
- **Vertical** divides the open workbooks into vertical bands.
- **Cascade** layers the open workbooks on the screen.

Currently, four workbooks are open but only one is visible. You'll arrange the workbooks using the tiled arrangement.

To tile the open workbooks:

▶ **1.** In the Window group on the View tab, click the **Arrange All** button. The Arrange Windows dialog box opens so you can select the layout arrangement you want.

▶ **2.** Click the **Tiled** option button, if necessary. The Tiled option arranges the four Global Travel workbooks evenly on the screen.

▶ **3.** Click the **OK** button. The four open workbooks appear in a tiled layout. See Figure 6-11. Totals 2010 is the active workbook (you might have a different workbook active). In the tiled layout, the active workbook has darker text in the title bar and includes scroll bars.

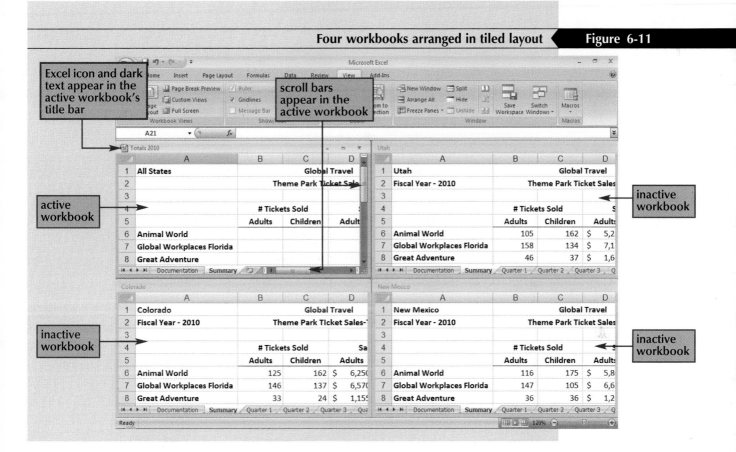

Four workbooks arranged in tiled layout ◀ **Figure 6-11**

Creating External Reference Formulas

You need to enter the external reference formulas in the Totals 2010 workbook to create a set of linked workbooks and be able to summarize the states' totals into one workbook for Alvin. The process for entering a formula with an external reference is the same as entering any other formula using references within the same worksheet or workbook. You can enter the formulas by typing them or using the point-and-click method. In most situations, you will use the point-and-click method to switch between the source files and destination files so that Excel enters the references to the workbook, worksheet, and cell using the correct syntax.

You'll start by creating the formula that adds the total number of adult tickets to Animal World sold in New Mexico, Utah, and Colorado. You cannot use the SUM function with 3-D references here because you are referencing multiple workbooks.

To create the external reference formula to total adult tickets for Animal World:

▶ **1.** In the Summary worksheet in the Totals 2010 workbook, click cell **B6**, and then type **=** to begin the formula.

▶ **2.** Click anywhere in the **New Mexico** workbook, and then, in the Summary worksheet, click cell **B6**. The external reference to cell B6 in the Summary worksheet of the New Mexico workbook—'[New Mexico.xlsx]Summary'!$B$6—is added to the formula in the Totals 2010 workbook. See Figure 6-12.

Figure 6-12 | External reference entered in formula

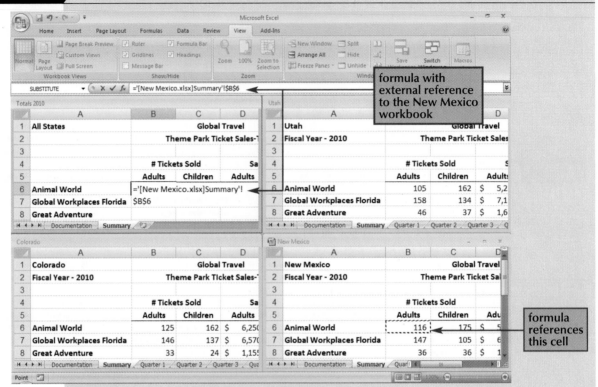

▶ **3.** Type **+**. The Totals 2010 workbook becomes active and you can continue entering the formula. You need to create an external reference to the Utah workbook.

▶ **4.** Click anywhere in the **Utah** workbook, click cell **B6** in the Summary worksheet, and then type **+**. The formula in the Totals 2010 workbook includes the external reference to the cell that has the total number of adult tickets to Animal World sold in Utah. The formula links two state workbooks to the Totals 2010 workbook.

Next, you'll create the external reference to the Colorado workbook.

▶ **5.** Click anywhere in the **Colorado** workbook, click cell **B6** in the Summary worksheet, and then press the **Enter** key. The formula with three external references is entered in the Summary sheet in the Totals 2010 workbook.

▶ **6.** In the Totals 2010 workbook, in the Summary sheet, click cell **B6**. The complete formula appears in the formula bar and the formula results appear in cell B6, showing that 346 adult tickets to Animal World were sold in the three states: 116 in New Mexico, 105 in Utah, and 125 in Colorado. See Figure 6-13.

Complete formula with external references ◄ **Figure 6-13**

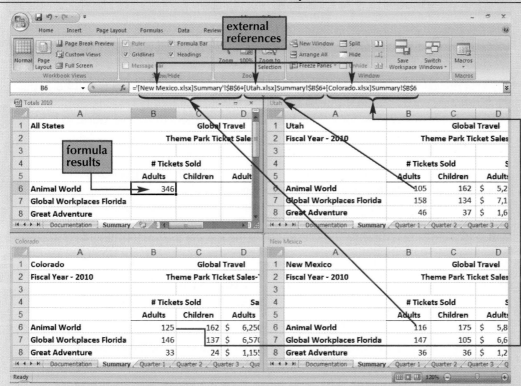

Trouble? If 346 doesn't appear in cell B6 in the Summary sheet in the Totals 2010 workbook, you might have clicked an incorrect cell for an external reference in the formula. Repeat Steps 1 through 6 to correct the formula.

You'll use the same process to enter the external reference formula for cell C6, which is the number of children's tickets to Animal World sold in the three states. Then you'll do the same to create the formulas to calculate the total sales from all three states.

To create the remaining external reference formulas:

► **1.** In the Totals 2010 workbook, in the Summary worksheet, click cell **C6**, and then type **=** to begin the formula.

► **2.** Click the **New Mexico** workbook, click cell **C6** in the Summary worksheet, and then type **+**. The formula in the Totals 2010 includes the external reference to cell C6 in the Summary worksheet in the New Mexico workbook.

► **3.** Click the **Utah** workbook, click cell **C6** in the Summary worksheet, and then type **+**. The formula includes an external reference to cell C6 in the Summary worksheet in the Utah workbook.

► **4.** Click the **Colorado** workbook, click cell **C6** in the Summary worksheet, and then press the **Enter** key. The external reference formula is complete.

► **5.** In the Totals 2010 workbook, click cell **C6** in the Summary sheet. Cell C6 displays 499, the total children's tickets sold to Animal World, and the following formula appears in the formula bar: ='[New Mexico.xlsx]Summary'!$C$6+ [Utah.xlsx]Summary!$C$6+[Colorado.xlsx]Summary!$C$6.

Next, you'll enter the external reference formulas in cells D6 and E6 to add the total sales from adult and children's tickets to Animal World.

▶ 6. Use the same procedure in Steps 1 through 4 to enter the formula in cell **D6** in the Summary worksheet in the Totals 2010 workbook. The formula results displayed in cell D6 are 17300—the total sales from adult tickets to Animal World in New Mexico, Utah, and Colorado.

▶ 7. Use the same procedure in Steps 1 through 4 to enter the formula in cell **E6** in the Summary worksheet in the Totals 2010 workbook. The formula results displayed in cell E6 are 18962—the total sales from children's tickets to Animal World in New Mexico, Utah, and Colorado.

You need to enter the remaining formulas for the six other theme parks (rows 7 to 12). Rather than creating the rest of the external reference formulas manually, you can copy the formulas in row 6 to rows 7 through 12. The formulas created using the point-and-click method contain absolute references. Before you copy the formula to other cells, you need to change the formulas to mixed references because the rows in the formula need to change.

To edit the external reference formulas to use mixed references:

▶ 1. Maximize the Totals 2010 workbook. The Totals 2010 workbook fills the program window. The other workbooks are still open but are not visible.

▶ 2. In the Summary worksheet, double-click cell **B6** to enter editing mode and display the formula in the cell.

▶ 3. Click in the first absolute reference in the formula, and then press the **F4** key twice to change the absolute reference $B$6 to the mixed reference $B6.

▶ 4. Edit the other two absolute references in the formula to be mixed references with absolute column references and relative row references.

▶ 5. Press the **Enter** key. The formula is updated to include mixed references, but the formula results aren't affected. Cell B6 still displays 346, which is correct.

▶ 6. Edit the formulas in cells C6, D6, and E6 to change the absolute references to the mixed references $C6, $D6, and $E6, respectively. The formulas are updated, but the cells in the range C6:D6 still correctly display 499, 17300, and 18962, respectively.

Tip

You can also create the mixed reference by deleting the $ from the row references in the formula.

With the formulas corrected to include mixed references, you can now copy the external reference formulas in cells B6:E6 to the other rows.

To copy the formulas to rows 7 through 12 and total the column values:

▶ 1. Select the range **B6:E6**, and then drag the fill handle to select the range **B7:E12**. The formulas are copied to the rest of the range B7:E12 and the formula results appear in the cells. The Auto Fill Options button appears in the lower-right corner of the selected range.

Next, you'll enter the SUM function to total the values in each column.

▶ 2. In cell B13, enter the SUM function to add the range **B6:B12**. A total of 2035 adult tickets were sold for all theme parks.

▶ 3. Copy the formula in cell B13 to the range **C13:E13**. The totals are 1855, 81889, and 55704, respectively.

▶ 4. Format cells D6:E13 with the **Accounting** number format with no decimal place.

▶ **5.** Format the range B12:E12 with a bottom border, and then click cell **A1** to deselect the range. See Figure 6-14.

Completed formulas in the Summary worksheet in the Totals 2010 workbook ◀ **Figure 6-14**

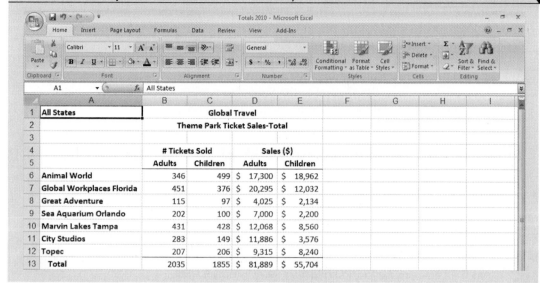

	A	B	C	D	E	F	G	H	I
1	All States		Global Travel						
2			Theme Park Ticket Sales-Total						
3									
4		# Tickets Sold		Sales ($)					
5		Adults	Children	Adults	Children				
6	Animal World	346	499	$ 17,300	$ 18,962				
7	Global Workplaces Florida	451	376	$ 20,295	$ 12,032				
8	Great Adventure	115	97	$ 4,025	$ 2,134				
9	Sea Aquarium Orlando	202	100	$ 7,000	$ 2,200				
10	Marvin Lakes Tampa	431	428	$ 12,068	$ 8,560				
11	City Studios	283	149	$ 11,886	$ 3,576				
12	Topec	207	206	$ 9,315	$ 8,240				
13	Total	2035	1855	$ 81,889	$ 55,704				

Alvin is pleased; the regional summary results match the executive team's expectations.

Managing Linked Workbooks | InSight

As you work with a linked workbook, you might need to replace a source file or change where you stored the source and destination files. However, replacing or moving a file can affect the linked workbook. Keep in mind the following guidelines to manage your linked workbooks. If you rename a source file, the destination workbook won't be able to find it. A dialog box opens, indicating "This workbook contains one or more links that cannot be updated." You click the Continue button to open the workbook with the most recent values, or you click the Change Source button in the Edit Links dialog box to specify the new name of that linked source file.

If you move a source file to a different folder, the link breaks between the destination and source files. Click the Change Source button in the Edit Links dialog box to specify the new location of the linked workbook.

If you receive a replacement source file, you can replace the original source file with the replacement file with no additional corrections.

If you receive a destination workbook but the source files are not included, Excel will not be able to find the source files, and a dialog box opens with the message "This workbook contains one or more links that cannot be updated." Click the Continue button to open the workbook with the most recent values, or click the Break button in the Edit Links dialog box to replace the external references with current values.

If you change the name of a destination file, you can open the destination file using a new name without making any corrections.

Updating Linked Workbooks

Rhohit calls Alvin to tell him of an incorrect value in the New Mexico workbook. The Animal World children's sales amount for Quarter 4 should be $2,786 not $1,786, which is currently in the file. Alvin asks you to change the value in the New Mexico workbook. How will a change to a value in any of the source workbooks affect the destination workbook?

When workbooks are linked, it is important that the data in the destination file accurately reflects the contents of the source file. When data in the source file changes, you want the destination file to reflect the changes. If both the source and destination files are open when you make a change, the destination file is updated automatically. If the destination file is closed when you make a change in the source file, you choose whether to update the link to display the current values when you open the destination file or continue to display the older values from the destination file.

You have both the source and destination files open. You will increase the value of Animal World children's sales for Quarter 4 in the New Mexico workbook by $1,000. This change will increase the amount in the Summary worksheet of the New Mexico workbook and the regional total in the Totals 2010 workbook.

To change the value in the source workbook with the destination file open:

▶ 1. Switch to the **New Mexico** workbook, and then make the **Quarter 4** worksheet active. You'll update the value of the Animal World children's dollar amount in this worksheet.

▶ 2. In cell E6, enter **2786**. The Animal World children's sales are updated.

▶ 3. Switch to the **Summary** worksheet in the New Mexico workbook, and then verify that the total Animal World children's sales is now $7,650.

   Next, you'll check the regional total.

▶ 4. Switch to the **Totals 2010** workbook, and then, in the Summary worksheet, verify that the value in cell E6 is $19,962 and the total dollar amount from sales of children's tickets is $56,704, reflecting the new value you entered in the New Mexico workbook. Because both the destination and source files are open, Excel updated the destination file automatically.

▶ 5. Save the New Mexico and Totals 2010 workbooks, and then close the Utah, Colorado, and Totals 2010 workbooks. The New Mexico workbook remains open.

Opening Destination Workbooks with Source Workbooks Closed

When you save a workbook that contains external reference formulas, such as Totals 2010, Excel stores the most recent results of those formulas in the destination file. Source files, such as the New Mexico, Colorado, and Utah workbooks, are often updated while the destination file is closed. In that case, the values in the destination file are not updated at the same time the source files are updated. When you open the destination file again it contains the old values in the cells containing external reference formulas. Therefore, some of the values in the edited source workbooks are different from the values in the destination workbook. How do you update the destination workbook?

When you open a workbook with external reference formulas (the destination file), as part of the Excel security system that attempts to protect against malicious software, links to other workbooks cannot be updated without your permission. As a result, a Security Warning appears in the Message Bar immediately below the Ribbon, notifying you that the automatic update of links has been disabled. If you "trust" the provider of the source file(s), you can choose to "Enable this content," which allows the external reference formulas to function and updates the links in the destination workbook. If you do not "trust" the provider of the source files or do not want the destination file updated at that time, do not select "Enable this content." The old values in the destination workbook are displayed and the links to the source files remain disabled.

Tip

To change the default behavior of disabling automatic links, click the Office Button, click the Excel Options button, and then click Advanced. In the General section, uncheck the Ask to update automatic links check box, and then click the OK button.

Rhohit informs Alvin that the New Mexico workbook needs a second correction. Great Adventure adult sales in Quarter 4 are $435 not $385, which is the value currently in the New Mexico workbook. You will increase the amount of the Great Adventure adult sales in Quarter 4 by $50. As a result, sales in the Summary sheet of the New Mexico workbook and the regional total in the Totals 2010 workbook will both increase by $50.

Alvin asks you to open the New Mexico workbook, correct the value in the cell, and then save the workbook. You'll edit the source file, the New Mexico workbook, while the destination file is closed.

To update the source workbook with the destination file closed:

▶ **1.** In the New Mexico workbook, make the **Quarter 4** worksheet active.

▶ **2.** In cell D8, enter **435**. The total sales for adults in Quarter 4 increases to $7,241.

▶ **3.** Switch to the **Summary** worksheet. The total sales for 2010 in cell D8 is $1,310 and total adult sales is $26,375. See Figure 6-15.

Summary worksheet with revised Quarter 4 sales for Great Adventure ◀ **Figure 6-15**

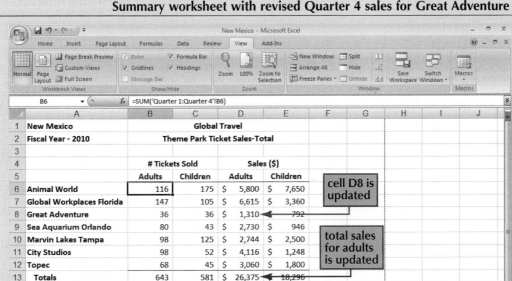

▶ **4.** Save and close the New Mexico workbook.

Now you'll open the destination file (the regional workbook) to see if the total is automatically updated.

▶ **5.** Open the **Totals 2010** workbook, and then switch to the **Summary** worksheet. The value in cell D8 has *not* changed; it still is $4,025. A Security Warning message appears in the Message Bar, indicating that automatic update of links has been disabled. See Figure 6-16.

> ### Tip
> When the destination file is open and the source files are closed, the complete file path is included as part of the external reference formula that appears in the formula bar.

Security Warning in the Message Bar ◀ **Figure 6-16**

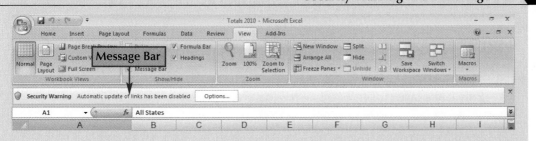

You want the current values in the source files to appear in the destination workbook.

▶ **6.** Click the **Options** button in the Message Bar. The Microsoft Office Security Options dialog box opens. See Figure 6-17.

Figure 6-17 Microsoft Office Security Options dialog box

▶ **7.** Click the **Enable this content** option button, and then click the **OK** button. The values in the destination file are updated. The sales in cell D8 of the Totals 2010 workbook increase to $4,075 and the total in cell D13 increases to $81,939.

▶ **8.** Save the workbook.

Managing Links

After the fiscal year audit is completed and there are no more revisions to the source workbooks, Alvin will archive the summary workbook as part of his year-end backup process, and he'll move the files to an off-site storage location. He will make a copy of the Totals 2010 workbook and name it *Audited 2010*. Using the copy, he will break the links using the Break Links command in the Edit Links dialog box, which converts all external reference formulas to their most recent values.

To save a copy of the Totals 2010 workbook and open the Edit Links dialog box:

▶ **1.** Click the **Office Button** , and then click **Save As**. The Save As dialog box opens.

▶ **2.** Change the filename to **Audited 2010**, make sure the save location is the **Tutorial.06\ Tutorial** folder included with your Data Files, and then click the **Save** button. The Totals 2010 workbook closes and the Audited 2010 workbook remains open.

▶ **3.** Click the **Data** tab on the Ribbon, and then, in the Connections group, click the **Edit Links** button. The Edit Links dialog box opens. See Figure 6-18.

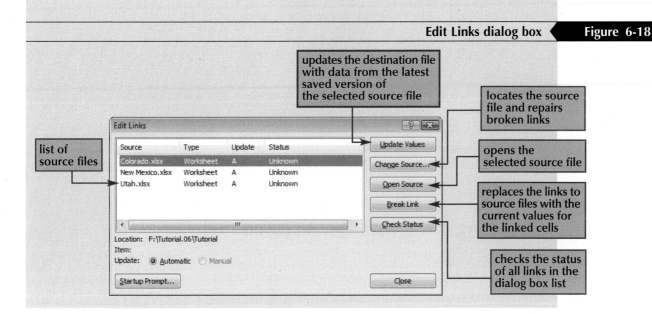

Edit Links dialog box ◀ **Figure 6-18**

The Edit Links dialog box lists all of the files the destination workbook is linked to so that you can update, change, open, or remove the links. You can see that the destination workbook, Audited 2010, has links to the Colorado, New Mexico, and Utah workbooks. The dialog box shows the following information about each link:

- **Source**. The file the link points to. The Audited 2010 workbook contains three links pointing to the workbooks New Mexico.xlsx, Colorado.xlsx, and Utah.xlsx.
- **Type**. The type of each source file. In this case, the type is an Excel worksheet but it could also be a Word document, PowerPoint presentation, or some other type of file.
- **Update**. The way values are updated from the source file. The letter *A* indicates the link is updated automatically when you open the workbook or when both the source and destination files are open simultaneously. The letter *M* indicates the link must be updated manually by the user. You can set a link to update manually when you want to see the older data values before updating to the new data. Click the Update Values button in the Edit Links dialog box if the Update option is set to *M* and you want to see the new data values.
- **Status**. Whether Excel successfully accessed the link and updated the values from the source document (Status is OK), or Excel has not attempted to update the links in this session (Status is Unknown). The status of the three links in the Audited 2010 workbook is Unknown.

You'll break the links so the Audited 2010 workbook contains only the updated values (and is no longer affected by changes in the source files). Then you'll save the Audited 2010 workbook for Alvin to archive. This allows Alvin to store a "snapshot" of the data at the end of the fiscal year.

To convert all external reference formulas to their current values:

▶ **1.** Click the **Break Link** button. A dialog box opens, alerting you that breaking links in the workbook permanently converts formulas and external references to their existing values.

▶ **2.** Click the **Break Links** button. No links appear in the Edit Links dialog box.

▶ **3.** Click the **Close** button. The Audited 2010 workbook now contains values instead of formulas with external references.

Tip

When you use the Break Link button, you cannot undo that action. To restore the links, you must reenter the external reference formulas.

You'll examine the worksheet to see how the links (external reference formulas) were converted to values.

▶ **4.** Click cell **B6**. The value 346 appears in the cell and the formula bar; the external reference formula was replaced with the data value. All cells in the range B6:E12 contain values rather than external reference formulas.

▶ **5.** Save and close the Audited 2010 workbook.

You have two workbooks. The Totals 2010 workbook has external reference formulas, and the Audited 2010 workbook has current values. The Audited 2010 workbook will be stored in Global Travel's off-site storage.

Creating an Excel Workspace

Alvin has four workbooks containing data for the ticket sales. Usually, he'll need to access only one workbook at a time, but occasionally he'll want to access all of the workbooks. If Alvin could open all the workbooks at once, he would save time, and, more important, not have to remember all the filenames and folder locations.

To open multiple workbooks at one time, you need to create a workspace. A **workspace** is an Excel file that saves information about all of the currently opened workbooks, such as their locations, window sizes, zoom magnifications, and other settings. The workspace does not contain the workbooks themselves—only information about them. To use that set of workbooks, you can open the workspace file. Excel then opens the workbooks and settings in the same configuration they were in when you saved the workspace file. Even if a workbook is included in a workspace file, you can still open that workbook separately.

You will create a workspace file for Alvin that includes the four workbooks in a cascade layout, which arranges the open workbooks so that they overlap each other with all the title bars visible. Alvin prefers this layout, because he can see more of the active workbook.

Tip

Because the workspace file contains only the location and name of each file, not the actual workbooks and worksheets, you cannot copy only the workspace file to another computer. Instead, you need to also copy the workbook files.

To create the Theme Parks workspace file:

▶ **1.** Open the **Colorado**, **New Mexico**, **Utah**, and **Totals 2010** workbooks located in the **Tutorial.06\Tutorial** folder included with your Data Files. Four workbooks are open.

▶ **2.** Make sure the **Summary** worksheet is the active worksheet in each workbook.

▶ **3.** Switch to the **Totals 2010** workbook.

▶ **4.** Click the **View** tab on the Ribbon, and then, in the Window group, click the **Arrange All** button. The Arrange Windows dialog box opens.

▶ **5.** Click the **Cascade** option button, and then click the **OK** button. The four workbooks overlap each other, with the title bars visible. See Figure 6-19.

Workbooks arranged in the cascade layout | Figure 6-19

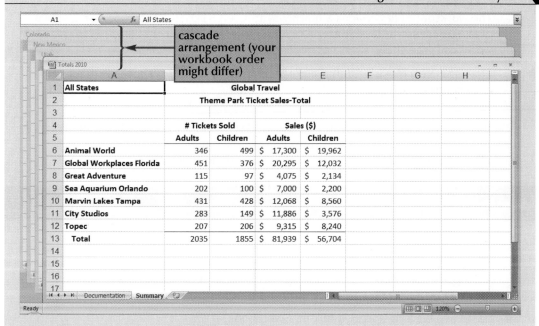

| A1 | | fx | All States | | | | | |

cascade arrangement (your workbook order might differ)

Colorado
New Mexico
Utah
Totals 2010

	A				E	F	G	H
1	All States		Global Travel					
2			Theme Park Ticket Sales-Total					
3								
4		# Tickets Sold		Sales ($)				
5		Adults	Children	Adults	Children			
6	Animal World	346	499	$ 17,300	$ 19,962			
7	Global Workplaces Florida	451	376	$ 20,295	$ 12,032			
8	Great Adventure	115	97	$ 4,075	$ 2,134			
9	Sea Aquarium Orlando	202	100	$ 7,000	$ 2,200			
10	Marvin Lakes Tampa	431	428	$ 12,068	$ 8,560			
11	City Studios	283	149	$ 11,886	$ 3,576			
12	Topec	207	206	$ 9,315	$ 8,240			
13	Total	2035	1855	$ 81,939	$ 56,704			
14								
15								
16								
17								

Documentation | Summary

Ready 120%

6. In the Window group on the View tab, click the **Save Workspace** button. The Save Workspace dialog box opens and functions similarly to the Save As dialog box.

7. Type **Theme Parks** in the File name box, verify that **Workspaces** is selected in the Save as type box, verify that the save location is the **Tutorial.06\Tutorial** folder, and then click the **Save** button. A dialog box might open, prompting you to save your changes to the open workbook files, if you haven't already done so.

8. If prompted to save changes, click the **Yes** button. The Theme Parks workspace file is saved. The workspace file has the file extension .xlw.

You will test the workspace file you created to make sure it opens all four Global Travel workbooks.

To test the Theme Parks workspace file:

1. Close all four workbooks.

2. Click the **Office Button** , and then click **Open**. The Open dialog box opens, displaying the Tutorial.06\Tutorial folder. The icon for the Theme Parks workspace file is different from the Excel workbook file icon.

3. Click **Theme Parks** in the list of files, and then click the **Open** button. The four travel workbooks open and are arranged in a cascade layout, the same layout in which you saved them. You can then work with the workbooks as usual

▶ **4.** Click the **Colorado** workbook title bar to bring it to the front of the cascaded workbooks. Colorado is now the active workbook.

The workspace file provides a quick way to open a series of workbooks in a specific display. Because it doesn't actually contain the workbooks, you must close each workbook separately, saving as needed.

▶ **5.** Close the New Mexico, Utah, Colorado, and Totals 2010 workbooks without saving any changes.

In this session, you worked with multiple worksheets and workbooks, summarizing data and linking workbooks. This ensures that the data in the summary workbook is accurate and remains updated with the latest data in the source files.

Review | **Session 6.2 Quick Check**

1. What is the external reference to the range A1:A10 in the Sales Info worksheet in the Product Report workbook located in the Reports folder on drive D?
2. What is a source file?
3. What is a destination file?
4. Name two ways to update a link in a workbook.
5. How would you determine to what workbooks a destination file is linked?
6. What is a workspace file?
7. Explain how workspace files can help you organize your work.

Session 6.3

Creating a Hyperlink

Alvin has written an executive memo summarizing the results for 2010. He wants to give members of the executive team at Global Travel easy access to the memo by including a hyperlink from his workbook to the memo.

Inserting a Hyperlink

You can insert a hyperlink directly in a workbook file. A **hyperlink** is a link in a file, such as a workbook, to information within that file or another file. The hyperlinks are usually represented by colored words with underlines or images. When you click a hyperlink, the computer switches to the file or portion of the file referenced by the hyperlink. Although hyperlinks are most often found on Web pages, they can also be placed in a worksheet and used to quickly jump to a specific cell or range within the active worksheet, another worksheet, or another workbook. Hyperlinks can also be used to jump to other files, such as a Word document or a PowerPoint presentation, or sites on the Web.

To use a hyperlink, you click the text inside the cell that contains the link. If you click white space in the cell or any text that flows into an adjacent cell, the hyperlink does not work.

Inserting a Hyperlink | Reference Window

- Select the text, graphic, or cell in which you want to insert the hyperlink.
- In the Links group on the Insert tab, click the Hyperlink button.
- To link to a file or Web page, click Existing File or Web Page in the Link to list, and then select the file or Web page from the Look in box.
- To link to a location in the current workbook, click Place in This Document in the Link to list, and then select the worksheet, cell, or range in the current workbook.
- To link to a new document, click Create New Document in the Link to list, and then specify the filename and path of the new document.
- To link to an e-mail address, click E-mail Address in the Link to list, and then enter the e-mail address of the recipient and a subject line for the e-mail message.
- Click the OK button.

Alvin wrote a memo summarizing the sales results for New Mexico, Utah, and Colorado in 2010. He wants the Totals 2010 workbook to include a link to this memo that points to the Word document Sales 2010.docx located in the Tutorial.06\Tutorial folder included with your Data Files.

To insert a hyperlink into the Totals 2010 workbook:

▶ 1. Open the Totals 2010 workbook located in the **Tutorial.06\Tutorial** folder included with your Data Files.

▶ 2. Switch to the **Documentation** worksheet, and then click cell **A12**. You want to create the hyperlink in this cell.

▶ 3. Click the **Insert** tab on the Ribbon, and then, in the Links group, click the **Hyperlink** button. The Insert Hyperlink dialog box opens with the Existing File or Web Page button selected in the Link to bar and the Current Folder displayed in the Look in area. You use this dialog box to define the hyperlink. See Figure 6-20.

Insert Hyperlink dialog box ◀ **Figure 6-20**

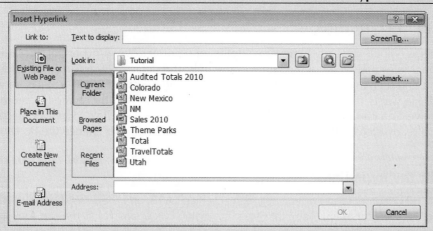

Trouble? If either the Existing File or Web Page option or the Current Folder option is not selected, select it before continuing.

▶ 4. Click the **Text to display** box, and then type **Click here to read Executive Memo**. This is the hyperlink text that will appear in cell A12 in the Documentation sheet.

▶ 5. Click the **Sales 2010** Word document in the list of files, and then click the **OK** button. As shown in Figure 6-21, the hyperlink text is in underlined blue font, indicating that the text within the cell is a hyperlink.

Figure 6-21 **Hyperlink to the Sales 2010 document**

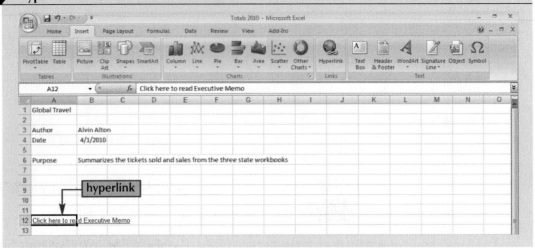

You will test the hyperlink that you just created to ensure it works correctly. To use a hyperlink, you click the text inside the cell that contains the link.

To jump to the hyperlink:

1. Point to cell **A12** until you see 🖑, and then click the hyperlink. The Sales 2010 document opens in Word.

   Trouble? If the hyperlink doesn't work, you might have clicked the text that over-flows cell A12. Point to the text within cell A12, and then click the hyperlink.

2. Click the **Close** button ☒ on the Word title bar to close the document and exit Word. The Documentation sheet in the Totals 2010 workbook is active. The color of the hyperlink in cell A12 changed to indicate that you have used the link.

Editing a Hyperlink

ScreenTips, which appear whenever you place the pointer over a hyperlink, provide additional information about the target of the link. The default ScreenTip is the folder location and filename of the file you will link to. Alvin doesn't think that this is very helpful. He wants you to change the ScreenTip for the link you just created to be more descriptive. You can insert a ScreenTip when you create a hyperlink. However, because you've already created this hyperlink, you'll edit the hyperlink to change the ScreenTip.

To edit the hyperlink:

1. In the Documentation worksheet, right-click cell **A12**, and then click **Edit Hyperlink** on the shortcut menu. The Edit Hyperlink dialog box opens; it has the same layout and information as the Insert Hyperlink dialog box.

2. Click the **ScreenTip** button. The Set Hyperlink ScreenTip dialog box opens.

3. Type **Click to view sales analysis for 2010** in the ScreenTip text box, and then click the **OK** button.

4. Click the **OK** button to close the Edit Hyperlink dialog box.

5. Point to cell **A12**, confirm that the ScreenTip *Click to view sales analysis for 2010* appears just below the cell, and then save and close the Totals 2010 workbook.

Tip

You can keep the text of a hyperlink but remove the functioning link by clicking Remove Hyperlink on the shortcut menu.

Alvin agrees that the ScreenTip is a useful addition to the hyperlink. If you want to remove a hyperlink, right-click the cell containing the hyperlink and then click Clear Contents on the shortcut menu to delete the hyperlink and text.

Creating Templates

The three state workbooks for 2010 have the same format. Alvin wants to use this workbook format for data collection and analysis for next year. One approach to accomplish this goal is to open one of the state workbooks, save it with a new name, and then replace the 2010 values with blank cells. Alvin is reluctant to use that approach because he might forget to change the filename and inadvertently overwrite the previous year's figures with blank cells when he saves the workbook. A better alternative is to have an Excel workbook that Alvin can open with the labels, formats, and formulas already built into it. Such a workbook is called a **template**. You use the template workbook as a model from which you create new workbooks.

When you use a template to create a new workbook, a copy of the template opens that includes text (row and column labels), formatting, and formulas from the template. Any changes or additions you make to the new workbook do not affect the template file. The original template retains its formatting and formulas, and the next time you open a workbook based on the template, those original settings will still be present.

There are several advantages to creating and using templates:

- Templates save you time entering formulas and formatting when you need to create several workbooks with similar features.
- Templates help you standardize the appearance and content of workbooks.
- Templates prevent you from accidentally saving new data in an old file if you use the Save command instead of the Save As command when basing a new workbook on an existing workbook.

Using Excel Templates | InSight

Excel has many templates available. Some are automatically installed on your hard disk when you install Excel, and others are available from the Microsoft Office Online Web site. In fact, the blank Book1 workbook that opens when you start Excel is based on the **default template**. The default template contains no text or formulas, but it includes all the formatting available in every new workbook: General number format applied to numbers, Calibri 11-point font, labels aligned to the left side of a cell, values and the formula results aligned to the right side of a cell, column width set to 8.43 characters, three worksheets inserted in the workbook, and so forth.

You can also download templates from the Microsoft Office Online Web site. These templates provide commonly used worksheet formats, saving you from "reinventing the wheel." Some of the task-specific templates available from the Microsoft Office Online Web site include the following:

- **Family Budget**. This template builds projections and actual expenditures for items such as housing, transportation, and insurance.
- **Inventory List**. This template tracks the cost and quantity reorder levels of inventory.
- **Team Roster**. This template lists each player's name, phone number, e-mail address, and so forth.
- **Time sheet**. This template creates an online time card to track employees' work hours.

If you need to create the same type of workbook repeatedly, it's a good idea to use a template to both save time and to ensure consistency in the design and content of the workbooks you create.

Creating a Workbook Based on an Existing Template

To see how templates work, you'll create a new workbook based on one of the Excel templates provided by Microsoft.

Reference Window | **Creating a Workbook Based on a Template**

- Click the Office Button, and then click New.
- In the Templates pane, click a template category for the type of workbook you want to create.
- In the center pane, click the template you want to use, and then click the Download button.
- Click the Continue button to let Microsoft verify your software.
- Save the workbook with a new filename.

You'll download the Time card template. **Note:** You need an Internet connection to complete the following set of steps; if you don't have an Internet connection, you should read but not complete the steps involving creating and using the online template.

To create a workbook based on a Microsoft Office Online template:

▶ **1.** Click the **Office Button** ⊞, and then click **New**. The New Workbook dialog box opens. The left pane lists the Microsoft Office Online template categories.

▶ **2.** Click **Time sheets**. A gallery of Time sheet templates appears in the center pane. The right pane shows a preview of the selected template.

▶ **3.** Scroll down the center pane until you see Time card, and then click the **Time card** thumbnail image. A preview of the worksheet based on the template appears in the right pane. See Figure 6-22.

Figure 6-22 ▶ **Preview of the Time card template**

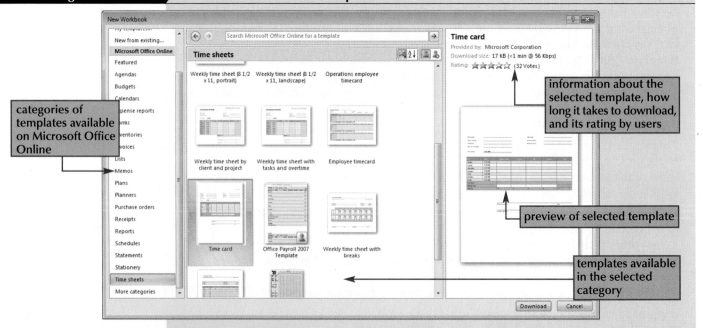

categories of templates available on Microsoft Office Online

information about the selected template, how long it takes to download, and its rating by users

preview of selected template

templates available in the selected category

▶ **4.** Click the **Download** button. The Microsoft Office Genuine Advantage dialog box opens. Before you can access the templates on Microsoft Office Online, Microsoft verifies that you have an authentic copy of the software.

▶ **5.** Click the **Continue** button to verify the copy of Microsoft Office on your computer. The Time card template opens. See Figure 6-23.

Workbook created from the Time card template | **Figure 6-23**

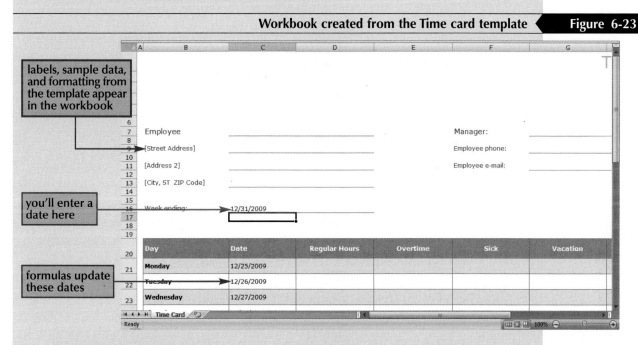

labels, sample data, and formatting from the template appear in the workbook

you'll enter a date here

formulas update these dates

Trouble? If the Microsoft Office Genuine Advantage dialog box indicates that the software installed on your computer is not genuine, then Microsoft was not able to validate your software. Click the Resolve Later button, and ask your instructor or technical support person for help.

The workbook based on the Time card template shows the name *Time card1* in the title bar, not *Time card*. Just as a blank workbook that you open is named sequentially, *Book1*, *Book2*, and so forth, a workbook based on a specific template always displays the name of the template followed by a sequential number. Any changes or additions to data, formatting, or formulas you make in this workbook affect only the new workbook you are creating and not the template (in this case, the Time card template). If you want to save your changes, you must save the workbook in the same way as you would save any new workbook.

Look at the labels and formatting already included in the Time Card worksheet. Some cells have descriptive labels, others are blank so you can enter data in them, and still other cells contain formulas where calculations for total hours worked each day and pay category will be automatically displayed as data is entered.

You'll enter data for Ed Hoot, the student assisting Alvin, in the worksheet based on the Time card template.

To enter data in the workbook based on the Time card template:

▶ **1.** In cell C7, enter **Ed Hoot**.

▶ **2.** In cell C16, enter **3/21/2010**. The dates in cells C21:C27 are automatically updated to reflect the week you specify.

> **3.** In cell D21, enter **8**. This is the total regular hours Ed worked on Monday. Totals appear in cells H21, D28, and H28 because formulas are already entered into these cells. Cell H21 shows 8 hours worked that day, cell D28 shows 8 regular hours worked that week, and cell H28 shows 8 hours total worked that week.
>
> **4.** In cell D22, enter **8** as the total regular hours Ed worked on Tuesday, and then, in cell E22, enter **2** as the total overtime hours Ed worked on Tuesday. The totals are updated to show 10 hours worked that day, 16 regular hours worked that week, 2 overtime hours worked that week, and 18 total hours worked that week.
>
> Next, you'll enter the regular hourly pay rate.
>
> **5.** In cell D29, enter **10**. The Total pay amounts in cells D30 and H30 are updated to show $160 total pay.
>
> Next, you'll enter the overtime hourly pay rate.
>
> **6.** In cell E29, enter **15**. The Total pay amounts are updated to show $160 total pay for regular hours, $30 total pay for overtime hours, and $190 total pay for the week ending 3/21/2010.
>
> **7.** Save the workbook as **Hoot Time Card** in the **Tutorial.06\Tutorial** folder included with your Data Files. The Hoot Time Card workbook, like any other workbook, is saved with the .xlsx file extension. It does not overwrite the template file.
>
> **8.** Close the workbook.

Each day Ed Hoot works at Global Travel, he or his supervisor can open the Hoot Time Card workbook just like any other workbook and enter his hours worked for the day. The total hours and pay are automatically updated. You can see how useful templates with formulas to produce a weekly time card that is fully formatted.

Having completed the New Mexico workbook according to Alvin's specifications, you have the basis for a template that can be used for similar projects. Instead of using one of the Excel templates, you can use the New Mexico workbook to create your own template file. Then, Alvin can create new workbooks based on that template and distribute them to the accountants preparing the state workbooks.

Creating a Custom Workbook Template

A **custom template** is a workbook template you create that is ready to run with the formulas for all calculations included as well as all formatting. Usually, the template is set up so a user enters the data and sees results immediately. A template can use any Excel feature, including formulas, charts, data validation, cell protection, macros, and so forth. In other words, a template includes everything but the data.

To create a template from an existing workbook, you need to be sure that all the formulas work as intended, the numbers and text are entered correctly, and the worksheet is formatted appropriately. Next, you need to remove any values and text that will change in each workbook created from the custom template. Be careful not to delete the formulas. Finally, you need to save the workbook using the Excel template file format. You can store template files in any folder, although if you store the file in the Templates folder, your custom templates are available when you click Templates in the New Workbook dialog box. If you don't save the template to the Templates folder, you can save it to another location.

Tip

You might find it helpful to replace variable data values with spaces, and apply a background color to cells in which you want data entered to differentiate them from other cells in the worksheet.

Creating a Custom Template | Reference Window

- Prepare the workbook: enter values, text, and formulas as needed; apply formatting; and replace data values with zeros or blank cells.
- Click the Office Button, and then click Save As.
- In the File name box, enter the template name.
- Click the Save as type button, and then click Excel Template.
- Save the file in the Templates folder or select an alternative folder location.
- Click the Save button.

Alvin wants you to use the New Mexico workbook as the basis for creating a custom template. You'll reopen the workbook and clear the data values in the worksheets, leaving all of the formulas intact. After completing these modifications, you will save the workbook as a template.

To replace the data values in the New Mexico workbook:

▶ 1. Open the **New Mexico** workbook located in the **Tutorial.06\Tutorial** folder included with your Data Files.

▶ 2. Group the **Quarter 1** through **Quarter 4** worksheets. All the worksheets are grouped except the Summary and Documentation worksheets.

▶ 3. Select the range **B6:E12**. This range includes the specific ticket and sales data for each theme park. You want to delete these values.

▶ 4. Click the **Home** tab on the Ribbon, in the Editing Group click the **Clear** button 2 ▾, and then click **Clear Contents**. The data values are cleared from the selected range in each of the quarterly worksheets, but the formulas and formatting remain intact. The cleared cells are blank. The range B13:E13 displays dashes, representing zeros, where there are formulas.

You'll apply a color to the range where you want users to enter data, the range B6:E12.

▶ 5. In the Font group on the Home tab, click the **Fill Color button arrow** ▾, and then click **Orange** (the third color in the Standard Colors section of the Fill Color gallery). The selected range has an orange fill to indicate where to enter quarterly data for the number of tickets sold and the sales amount.

▶ 6. In cell A1, enter **=Summary!A1**. This formula inserts the contents of cell A1 in the Summary worksheet into cell A1 in the quarterly worksheets. The text "New Mexico" is still displayed because that's the text currently in cell A1 in the Summary worksheet.

▶ 7. Switch to the **Summary** worksheet. The quarterly worksheets are ungrouped, and dashes, representing zeros, appear in the cells in the range B6:E13, which contain formulas.

▶ 8. In cell A1, enter **Enter state name here**, and then, in cell A2, enter **Enter Fiscal Year – yyyy**. This text will remind users to enter the correct state name and year. See Figure 6-24.

Figure 6-24 | **Worksheet with formatting and formulas but no data**

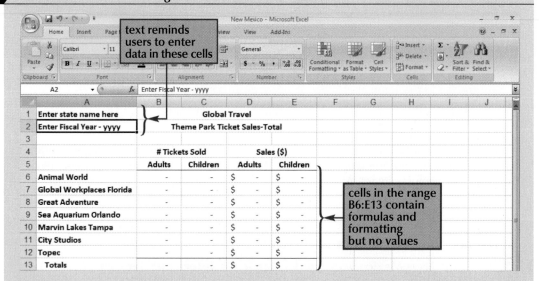

9. Switch to the **Documentation** worksheet, delete your name and the date from the range **B3:B4**, enter **Theme park ticket sales** in cell B6, and then click cell **A1**. The Documentation sheet is updated to reflect the purpose of the workbook.

The workbook is ready to save in template format. It no longer contains any specific data, but the formulas and formatting will still be in effect when new data is entered.

To save the workbook as a template:

1. Click the **Office Button** ⓐ, and then click **Save As**. The Save As dialog box opens.

2. Type **Travel Template** in the File name box.

3. Click the **Save as type** button, and then click **Excel Template**. The Address bar displays the Templates folder, which is where custom template files are often stored. Excel, by default, looks for template files in this folder. However, you can store templates in other folders as well. Because you might not have access to the Templates folder, you will save the template file with your other Data Files.

4. Navigate to the **Tutorial.06\Tutorial** folder included with your Data Files, and then click the **Save** button.

5. Close the Travel Template workbook template.

Alvin will use the Travel Template file to create the workbooks to track next year's sales for each state and then distribute the workbooks via e-mail to each accountant. By basing these new workbooks on the template file, he has a standard workbook with identical formatting and formulas for each accountant to use. He also avoids the risk of accidentally changing the workbook containing the 2010 data when preparing for 2011. All template files have the .xltx extension. This extension differentiates template files from workbook files, which have the .xlsx extension. After you have saved a workbook in a template format, you can make the template accessible to other users.

Creating a New Workbook from a Template

After you have saved a template in the Templates folder, you open the New Workbook dialog box and go to the My Templates folder to select the template you want to use. If you don't save the template to the Templates folder, the New from existing button enables you to create a new workbook from a template, much like creating a workbook based on a template found in the Templates folder.

You will use the latter approach to create a workbook from the Travel Template file because you saved the template in your Tutorial.06\Tutorial folder. Alvin asks you to test the process of creating the workbook before the state workbooks are distributed to the accountants.

To create a new workbook based on the Travel Template template:

▶ 1. Click the **Office Button** 🔘, and then click **New**. The New Workbook dialog box opens.

▶ 2. Click **New from existing** in the Templates pane. The New from Existing Workbook dialog box opens, with All Excel Files displayed. This dialog box differs from the Open dialog box in two ways. First, instead of opening the actual workbook, it opens a copy of it. Second, when you save the workbook, it adds a number to the end of the filename and opens the Save As dialog box, which makes it very difficult to overwrite the original file.

▶ 3. Click **Travel Template** in the **Tutorial.06\Tutorial** folder included with your Data Files, and then click the **Create New** button. A copy of the Travel Template workbook opens named *Travel Template1* to indicate this is the first copy of the Travel Template workbook created during the current Excel session.

▶ 4. Click the **Summary** sheet tab, and then, in cell **A1**, enter **New Mexico** and in cell **A2**, enter **Fiscal Year - 2011**.

▶ 5. Switch to the **Quarter 1** worksheet. The text "New Mexico" appears in cell A1, and the text "Fiscal Year - 2011" appears in cell A2.

You'll enter test data in the data area (which has an orange background fill color).

▶ 6. Click cell **B6**, type **120**, click cell **C6**, type **150**, click **D6**, type **3000**, click **E6**, type **2850**, and then press the **Enter** key. The range B13:E13 shows the totals of each column because these cells contain formulas to sum each column.

▶ 7. Click cell **B7**, type **180**, click cell **C7**, type **200**, click **D7**, type **3500**, click **E7**, type **3150**, and then press the **Enter** key. The range B13:E13 is updated because these cells contain formulas to sum each column. See Figure 6-25.

Tip

The worksheet that is active when you create, save, and close a template workbook is the active worksheet when you create a new workbook based on the template. In this case, the Documentation sheet is active.

Figure 6-25 | **New workbook based on Travel Template**

formulas display the state name and year you entered in the Summary worksheet

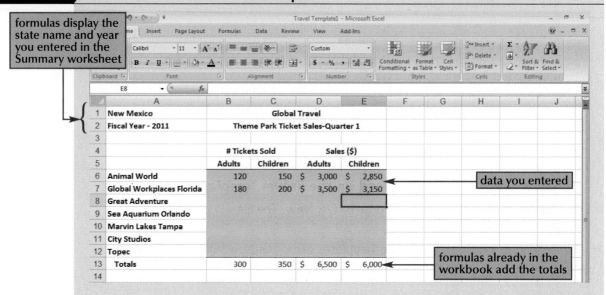

data you entered

formulas already in the workbook add the totals

▶ **8.** Switch to the **Summary** worksheet. Totals appear in the ranges B6:E7 and B13:E13 as a result of the formulas in this worksheet. See Figure 6-26.

Figure 6-26 | **Summary worksheet after data is entered**

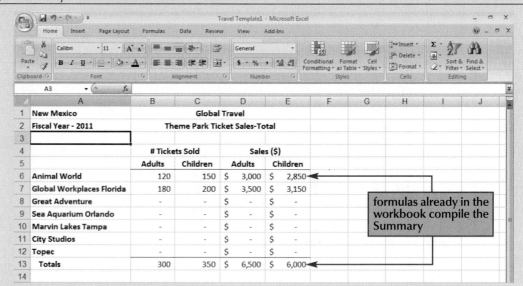

formulas already in the workbook compile the Summary

▶ **9.** Save the workbook as **New Mexico 2011** in the **Tutorial.06\Tutorial** folder included with your Data Files. The copy of the template is saved as a workbook with the .xlsx extension. The original template file is not changed.

▶ **10.** Close the workbook.

Alvin asks you to add data to the Quarter 2, Quarter 3, and Quarter 4 worksheets to verify that the Summary worksheet is correctly adding numbers from the four worksheets.

To test the New Mexico 2011 workbook:

▶ 1. Open the **New Mexico 2011** workbook located in the **Tutorial.06\Tutorial** folder included with your Data Files.

▶ 2. Group the **Quarter 2**, **Quarter 3**, and **Quarter 4** worksheets. You'll enter test values in the range B6:C6 so that each quarterly worksheet contains data.

▶ 3. In cell B6, enter **120**, and then, in cell C6, enter **150**.

▶ 4. Switch to the **Summary** worksheet. The total in cell B6 is 480 and the total in cell C6 is 600. The formulas in the Summary worksheet correctly add values from all the quarterly worksheets. So, Alvin knows that the template workbook is functioning as intended.

▶ 5. Save and close the workbook.

Alvin will use the custom template to create and distribute new state workbooks to each accountant for the next fiscal year.

Saving a Workbook as a Web Page

Alvin wants you to store the summary of the annual company-wide Theme Park Ticket Sales report you helped him create on the company's intranet which is a computer network, based on Internet technology, that is designed to meet the internal needs for sharing information within an organization.

You can convert Excel workbooks, worksheets, or ranges into Web pages that can be placed on the Web to be viewed by others. Excel allows you to create a Web page where users can scroll through the contents of an Excel workbook and switch between worksheets, but cannot make any changes to the data or formatting displayed on the Web page. When you save a worksheet as a Web page, Excel converts the contents of the worksheet into **HTML** (Hypertext Markup Language), which is a language used to write Web pages.

You can save an Excel workbook, a worksheet, or an item in a worksheet as a Web page and make it available to viewers via the Internet or an intranet. Alvin wants to make the company-wide results available to the executive team, so he needs you to create a Web page of the Totals 2010 Summary worksheet.

You use the Save As dialog box to create a Web page based on a workbook, a single worksheet, or a range within a worksheet. When you save a workbook as a Web page, you can save the workbook in one of two formats. The Web Page format saves the worksheet as an HTML file and creates a folder that stores the supporting files, such as a file for each graphic and worksheet that is included on the Web page. The Single File Web Page format saves all the elements of the Web page including text and graphics into a single file in the MHTML (Multipurpose Internet Mail Extension HTML) format.

Accessing Workbooks on the Web Interactively		InSight

In Excel 2007, if you want to publish interactive versions of your workbook or items from the worksheet as a Web page with spreadsheet functionality, you need to use a component of Microsoft Office Share-Point Server called Excel Services. This component lets users access all or part of the workbook in browsers interactively. Users can sort and filter an Excel table, use PivotTables for data analysis, and perform what-if analysis from a Web browser. To learn more, search the Excel Help system for "publish a workbook to Excel Services."

Reference Window | **Saving a Workbook, Worksheet, or Range as a Web Page**

- Click the Office Button, and then click Save As.
- Click the Save as type button, and then click Web Page or Single File Web Page.
- Click the Publish button.
- Click the Choose arrow, and select which portion of the workbook you want to publish as a Web page.
- Click the Change button to change the title of the Web page.
- Click the Browse button to change the filename and location for the Web page.
- Check or clear the AutoRepublish every time this workbook is saved check box.
- Check or clear the Open published web page in browser check box.
- Click the Publish button.

First, you will create and test the Web page on your hard drive. You will open the Save As dialog box, and then choose the Web Page file format, because it is the standard format the company uses for its Web pages, to create the Web page for the regional 2010 results.

After previewing your work offline, Alvin will "publish" the Web page by putting all of the files (both HTML files and graphic files) on the Web server that hosts the Global Travel site.

To start creating the Web page:

1. Open the **Totals 2010** workbook located in the **Tutorial.06\Tutorial** folder included with your Data Files.

2. Click the **Office button** , and then click **Save As**. The Save As dialog box opens.

3. Click the **Save as type** button, and then click **Web Page**. The area below the Save as type box expands to display several Web-based options. See Figure 6-27.

Figure 6-27 ▶ **Expanded Save As dialog box**

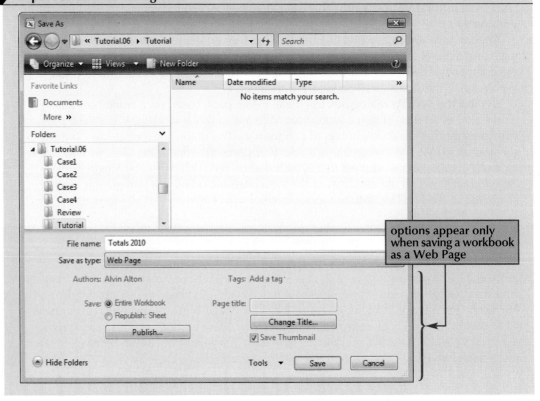

options appear only when saving a workbook as a Web Page

Setting the Page Title

Web pages usually have a page title that appears in the title bar of the Web browser. If a page title is not entered, the browser will display the page's file path and filename. Alvin wants the Web page title to clearly indicate to the executive team the purpose of the report. You'll enter a descriptive page title.

To specify the page title:

▶ **1.** Click the **Change Title** button. The Set Page Title dialog box opens.

▶ **2.** Type **Global Travel Theme Park Ticket Sales - 2010** in the Page title text box, and then click the **OK** button. The page title you just typed appears in the Page title box at the bottom of the Save As dialog box.

The next step in setting up the page for publishing on the Web is to choose which elements of the workbook to include in the Web page.

Setting the Web Page Options

You can specify which elements to include as part of the Web page. You can select the entire workbook, a specific worksheet in the workbook, a range of cells, or previously published items (which are items already on the Web server) that you are modifying. In this case, Alvin wants to include only the contents of the Summary worksheet.

To select the Summary worksheet for the Web page:

▶ **1.** In the Save As dialog box, click the **Publish** button. The Publish as Web Page dialog box opens. See Figure 6-28.

Publish as Web Page dialog box | Figure 6-28

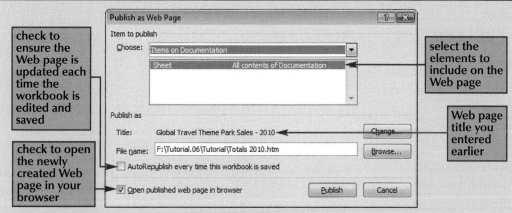

You'll specify the Summary worksheet as the item to include on the Web page.

▶ **2.** Click the **Choose** arrow, and then click **Items on Summary**. Items on Summary appears in the Choose box and the Summary worksheet is the active sheet in the workbook behind the dialog box.

In the Publish as section of the Publish as Web Page dialog box, you can also change the Web page title, browse to find the folder where you want to publish the Web page and assign or change the filename, enable automatic republishing of the Web page every time a change is saved to the workbook so the Web page always matches the source workbook, and immediately view the Web page in a browser.

The default filename for a Web page is based on the workbook's filename, which, in this case, is *Totals 2010.htm*. Alvin wants the name to conform to the company style. For consistency in naming company-related Web pages, he will name the file *Web Totals 2010.htm*. The extension .htm refers to an HTML file. You will change the filename.

To specify a filename for the Web page:

▶ 1. Click the **Browse** button. The Publish As dialog box opens.

▶ 2. Verify that the **Tutorial.06\Tutorial** folder is selected, and then type **Web Totals 2010** in the File name box.

▶ 3. Click the **OK** button. The filename appears in the Publish as Web Page dialog box.

▶ 4. Make sure the **Open published web page in browser** check box is checked so the Web page will open in a browser as soon as you complete these steps.

▶ 5. Click the **Publish** button. Excel creates the Web page based on the contents of the Summary worksheet and opens the page in your browser. You don't need an Internet connection to see the Web page, because the HTML file is stored locally on your computer. The page title *Global Travel Theme Park Sales - 2010* appears in the browser's title bar, tab, and as a heading above the information from the worksheet. See Figure 6-29.

| Figure 6-29 | **Web page based on the Summary worksheet** |

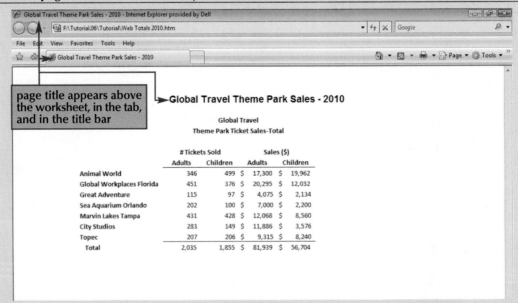

▶ 6. Close your Web browser, and then close the Totals 2010 workbook without saving.

The Web page provides a concise summary of the Global Travel ticket sales. Alvin will complete the process by uploading the Web page you created to the company's intranet later on.

Session 6.3 Quick Check | Review

1. How do you insert a hyperlink into a worksheet cell?
2. True or False? A hyperlink in a worksheet cell can be used to jump to another worksheet in the same workbook.
3. What is a template?
4. What is an advantage of using a custom template rather than simply using the original workbook file to create a new workbook?
5. How do you save a file as a template?
6. What are the two different types of Web page file formats available?

Tutorial Summary | Review

In this tutorial, you worked with multiple worksheets and workbooks. You learned how to create a worksheet group and then edit multiple worksheets at once. You consolidated information in multiple worksheets using 3-D references. You also set up grouped worksheets for printing. You linked workbooks using external references. You created an Excel workspace file and explored the advantages of using workspace files when you need to work with multiple workbooks that are related to one project or goal. You added a hyperlink to a worksheet. You learned about Excel templates and created a custom template from an existing worksheet. Finally, you converted a worksheet into a Web page.

Key Terms

3-D reference
custom template
default template
destination file
external reference
HTML (Hypertext Markup
    Language)

hyperlink
link
ScreenTip
source file

template
worksheet group
workspace

| Practice | | **Review Assignments** |

Practice the skills you learned in the tutorial using the same case scenario.

Data Files needed for the Review Assignments: OR.xlsx, Idaho.xlsx, Washington.xlsx, NW Totals 2010.xlsx, NW Travel.xltx

Elaine Dennerson, accountant for Global Travel in Oregon, needs your help. Global Travel has added Oregon to the Northwest territory, which already includes Washington and Idaho. She asks you to complete the Summary worksheet in the Oregon workbook and enter the formulas in the regional workbook, NW Totals 2010, to summarize the Northwest states' totals into one workbook.

Complete the following:

1. Open the **OR** workbook located in the Tutorial.06\Review folder included with your Data Files, and then save the workbook as **Oregon** in the same folder.

2. In the Documentation sheet, enter your name and the current date, and then review the worksheets in the workbook.

3. Create a worksheet group that contains the Qtr 1 through Qtr 4 worksheets.

4. In the worksheet group, insert formulas to total each column. Format each worksheet to match other state quarterly workbooks. Bold the range A1:B2;A6:A13;B4:E5. Merge and center the ranges B1:E1, B2:E2, B4:C4, and D4:E4. Format the range A6:A12 in italic. Add a top and double bottom border to the range B13:E13. Add a fill color to the range B1:E2 using the Orange theme color. Apply the Accounting number format with no decimal places to the range D6:E13. Ungroup the worksheets.

5. Make a copy of the Qtr 1 worksheet, name it **Summary**, and place it immediately after the Documentation worksheet. Remove the data from the range B6:E12. Change the heading in cell B2 to **Theme Park Ticket Sales-Total**. In cell A2, enter the label **Fiscal Year – 2010**.

6. In worksheets Qtr 1 through Qtr 4, enter formulas to reference the labels in cells A1 and A2 of the Summary worksheet.

7. In the Summary worksheet, create 3-D reference formulas to calculate annual totals for theme park tickets sold and sales.

8. Prepare all worksheets except the Documentation sheet for printing. Display the name of the workbook and the name of the worksheet on separate lines in the right section of the header. Display your name and the date on separate lines in the right section of the footer. Preview the worksheets.

9. Ungroup the worksheets and save the workbook.

10. Open the regional **NW Totals 2010** workbook located in the Tutorial.06\Review folder included with your Data Files, and then enter the external reference formulas in the NW Totals 2010 workbook to create a set of linked workbooks to summarize the states' totals into one workbook.

11. In the NW Totals 2010 workbook, switch to the Documentation sheet. In the range A10:A12, enter the name of each state. Create hyperlinks from each state label to the corresponding workbook (Idaho, Oregon, and Washington). Test each hyperlink.

12. Create a workspace with the following four workbooks in a tiled layout: Idaho, Oregon, Washington, and NW Totals 2010. Make the Summary worksheet in each workbook the active worksheet, and make the NW Totals 2010 workbook the active workbook. Save the workspace as **NW Workspace**.

13. Create a new workbook based on the **NW Travel** template, which is located in the Tutorial.06\Review folder included with your Data Files. Save the workbook as **Oregon 2011** in the same folder. In the Summary worksheet, enter **Oregon** in cell A1 and **Fiscal Year – 2011** in cell A2. In the Qtr 1 worksheet, enter **1000** in each cell of the range B6:C12. In the Qtr 2 worksheet, enter **2000** in each cell of the range B6:C12. Confirm that the values entered in this step were correctly totaled in the Summary worksheet. Save the Oregon 2011 workbook.

14. Create a Web page of the entire Oregon workbook, which you created in Steps 2 through 9. Add a title. Include all worksheets in the workbook. Use the Web Page format and name the Web page as **Web Oregon 2010**.

15. Close all the workbooks. Submit the finished workbooks to your instructor, either in printed or electronic form, as requested.

Apply	**Case Problem 1**

Use the skills you learned to summarize quarterly sales data for a coffee retailer.

Data File needed for this Case Problem: Cafe.xlsx

Java Café Java Café currently has three stores in the Southwest: Tempe, Arizona; Las Cruces, New Mexico; and Austin, Texas. Jayne Mitchell manages the three stores and uses Excel to summarize sales data from these stores. She asks you to total the sales by product group and store for each quarter and then format each worksheet. Jayne also needs you to add another worksheet to calculate Summary sales for the stores and product groups.

Complete the following:

1. Open the **Cafe** workbook located in the Tutorial.06\Case1 folder included with your Data Files, and then save the workbook as **Java Cafe** in the same folder.

2. In the Documentation sheet, enter your name and the current date, and then switch to the Quarter 1 worksheet.

3. For each quarter, calculate the total sales for each product group and store, and then improve the formatting of the quarterly worksheets using the formatting of your choice.

4. Insert a new worksheet between the Documentation and Quarter 1 worksheets. Rename this as worksheet **Summary Sales**. Its appearance should be identical to the quarterly worksheets.

5. In the range B5:E7 of the Summary Sales worksheet, insert the formulas that add the sales in the corresponding cells of the four quarterly worksheets. Calculate the totals for each product group and store.

6. Set up the Summary Sales and four quarterly worksheets for printing. Each worksheet should be centered horizontally with the name of the worksheet centered in the header, and your name and the date placed on separate lines in the right section of the footer.

7. Save the Java Cafe workbook, and then remove the sales data, but not the formulas, from each of the quarterly worksheets.

8. Return to cell A1 of the Documentation sheet, and then save the workbook as an Excel template with the name **Java Template** in the Tutorial.06\Case1 folder included with your Data Files.

9. Use the Java Template template you created to create a new workbook. Name the workbook as **Java Cafe 2011**. In the range B5:E7 of all four quarterly worksheets, enter **1**. Save the workbook.

10. Create a Web page of the **Java Cafe** workbook in the Web Page format with the file-name **Web Java**. Add an appropriate title. Include all worksheets in the workbook. Preview the file in your Web browser, and then close it.

11. Close the workbook. Submit the finished workbooks to your instructor, either in printed or electronic form, as requested.

Create	**Case Problem 2**

Create linked work-books to summarize sales data for a car dealership.

Data Files needed for this Case Problem: Carson.xlsx, Reno.xlsx, Vegas.xlsx

Ute Auto Sales & Services   Hardy Ute is founder and operator of Ute Auto Sales & Ser-vices with dealerships in Las Vegas, Reno, and Carson City, Nevada. His dealerships sell new and used cars, SUVs, minivans, and trucks as well as service customers' vehicles. To analyze sales and service at each of his three dealerships, Hardy asks his staff to prepare a regular report. Hardy wants the report to show the unit and dollar sales of new and used vehicles by type. In addition, he wants to see if his service business is bringing in the revenue that he anticipates.

Complete the following:

1. Open the **Carson** workbook located in the Tutorial.06\Case2 folder included with your Data Files, and then save the workbook as **UTE Carson City** in the same folder.

2. In the Documentation sheet, enter your name and the current date, and then switch to the Quarter 1 worksheet.

3. For each quarter, calculate the totals in the range B10:G10, and then improve the formatting of the quarterly worksheets using the formatting of your choice.

4. Insert a new worksheet between the Documentation and Quarter 1 worksheets. Rename this worksheet **Summary**. Format the worksheet identically to any of the quarterly worksheets except leave the range B6:G9 blank.

5. In the range B6:G9 of the Summary worksheet, insert the formulas that add the sales in the corresponding cells of the four quarterly worksheets.

6. Prepare the five sales worksheets for printing. Page setup should include the following: centered horizontally, the name of the worksheet centered in the header, and your name and the date placed on separate lines in the right section of the footer.

7. Save your changes to the workbook and close the workbook.

8. Open the **Reno** workbook located in the Tutorial.06\Case2 folder included with your Data Files, and then save the workbook as **UTE Reno**. Repeat Steps 2 through 7 for this workbook.

9. Open the **Vegas** workbook located in the Tutorial.06\Case2 folder, and then save the workbook as **UTE Vegas**. Repeat Steps 2 through 7 for this workbook.

10. Create a new workbook and use Figure 6-30 as a guide as you summarize the three dealerships' workbooks. Save the workbook as **UTE Summary**.

Figure 6-30

	A	B	C	D	E	F	G
1				Ute Auto Sales & Services			
2				Sales - All Dealers			
3							
4			New		Pre-owned		Service
5		Units	Sales ($)	Units	Sales ($)	Units	Sales ($)
6	Cars	733 $	14,940,828	203 $	1,476,397	5405 $	1,058,958
7	SUVs	288 $	7,979,268	76 $	478,632	1798 $	492,525
8	Vans	166 $	3,928,990	87 $	750,758	1007 $	328,662
9	Trucks	113 $	1,639,386	64 $	341,907	691 $	117,874
10	Totals	1300 $	28,488,472	430 $	3,047,694	8901 $	1,998,019

11. Use the Web Page format to create a Web page based on the Summary worksheet in the UTE Summary workbook. Change the page title to **UTE Auto Sales & Services**. Open the Web page using your browser. Name the file **UTE Web Page**.

12. Use the UTE Carson City workbook to create an Excel template with the name **UTE Template** in the Tutorial.06\Case2 folder included with your Data Files. Add appropriate formatting of your choice.

13. Create a new workbook using the UTE Template. Add appropriate test data for Quarter 1. Save the workbook as **Carson City 2011** in the Tutorial.06\Case2 folder included with your Data Files.

14. Close the workbook. Submit the finished workbooks to your instructor, either in printed or electronic form, as requested.

Create | **Case Problem 3**

Create linked workbooks to summarize sales data for a specialty soft drink producer.

Data File needed for this Case Problem: InBurger.xlsx

Infusion Blend Micki Goldstein, a sales representative for a specialty soft drink producer, Infusion Blend, has Florida as her territory where she is based out of Tampa. Her job takes her around the state where she meets and presents her product offerings to store managers from major supermarket chains to the small mom-and-pop corner markets. Although she does not personally make the deliveries, she often works closely with the delivery staff to assure quality service to her customers.

Micki must report her sales progress to her regional manager in Atlanta, Georgia. These reports include the overall sales volume, the types of products sold, locations, and stores into which the products were delivered. For the larger markets, she must prepare a separate workbook for each chain store.

Complete the following:

1. Open the **InBurger** workbook located in the Tutorial.06\Case3 folder included with your Data Files, and then save the workbook as **InBurger 2010** in the same folder.

2. In the Documentation sheet, enter your name and the current date, and then switch to the January worksheet.

3. For each month (January through December), enter formulas to calculate the total sales for each product and store, and then improve the formatting of the monthly worksheets using the formatting of your choice.

4. Insert a new worksheet between the Documentation and January worksheets. Rename this worksheet **YTD Summary**. Format this worksheet identically to the monthly worksheets except leave the range B6:G11 blank.

5. Use 3-D reference formulas to add the cases sold from January through December. For example, in cell B6, the product Popgo sold in the Elteron store equals 1335 cases.

6. Insert formulas that add the total cases sold by product in column G and total cases sold by store in row 12. Calculate the Summary total for all products.

⊕ **EXPLORE**　7. Insert a new worksheet following the Documentation worksheet. Rename this worksheet as **Annual Recap**. Using Figure 6-31 as a guide, create three separate summaries on this worksheet: by Products, Store, and Month.

　　a. Insert formulas that add the total cases sold of each product in the range C7:C12 (column G in the monthly worksheets). Calculate totals for all products.

　　b. Insert formulas that add the total cases sold at each store in the range G7:G11 (row 12 in the monthly worksheets). Calculate totals for all stores.

　　c. Insert formulas that add the total cases sold each month in the range K7:K18 (cell G12 in each worksheet). Calculate totals for all months.

Figure 6-31

	A	B	C	D	E	F	G	H	I	J	K	L
1						In Burger's Sales by Store and Product						
2							Cases Sold					
3												
4												
5			Breakdown by Products				Breakdown by Store				Breakdown by Month	
6		Products	Cases Sold	Percent		Store	Cases Sold	Percent		Store	Cases Sold	Percent
7		Popgo	7,065	31%		Elteron	4,700	20%		January	8,975	39%
8		Diet Popgo	4,760	21%		Mesa	4,600	20%		February	7,120	31%
9		Mt. Spring	3,360	15%		Franklin	4,700	20%		March	3,905	17%
10		Red Burst	1,675	7%		Grant	4,625	20%		April	2,980	13%
11		Dr Selsa	3,135	14%		Grover	4,355	19%		May	0	0%
12		Sun Maid	2,985	13%		Totals	22,980			June	0	0%
13		Totals	22,980							July	0	0%
14										August	0	0%
15										September	0	0%
16										October	0	0%
17										November	0	0%
18										December	0	0%
19										Totals	22,980	

8. Insert formulas in columns D, H, and L to calculate the percentage of products, stores, and months, respectively.

9. Results for the month of May are shown in Figure 6-32. Enter this data into the May worksheet.

Figure 6-32

	A	B	C	D	E	F	G
1	In Burger's Sales by Store and Product						
2	Cases Sold						
3							
4				Stores			
5	Products	Elteron	Mesa	Franklin	Grant	Grover	Totals
6	Popgo	515	545	560	670	510	2,800
7	Diet Popgo	435	445	435	430	410	2,155
8	Mt. Spring	235	275	240	240	205	1,195
9	Red Burst	125	125	150	150	325	875
10	Dr Selsa	160	145	150	160	125	740
11	Sun Maid	325	240	175	245	225	1,210
12	Totals	1,795	1,775	1,710	1,895	1,800	8,975

10. In the Documentation sheet, in the range A8:A19, type the months **January** through **December**. Create hyperlinks from each cell to its corresponding worksheet. Test the hyperlinks.

11. Save and close the workbook. Submit the finished workbook to your instructor, either in printed or electronic form, as requested.

Challenge | Case Problem 4

Explore using worksheet groups, 3-D references, external references, workspaces, and templates to summarize data for a pharmaceutical manufacturer.

Data Files needed for this Case Problem: Europe.xlsx, North America.xlsx, South America.xlsx, PlutoTemplate.xltx

Pluto Pharmaceuticals Pluto Pharmaceuticals is a multinational manufacturer of health-care products. The chief financial analyst, Kevin Cross, asks you to prepare the first quarter revenue summary for three global regions based on workbooks from the regions of North America, South America, and Europe. Each workbook has monthly worksheets displaying forecasted and actual revenues of the major product groups for the first quarter. Kevin wants you to calculate the difference between forecasted and actual sales (Difference) and the percent change between forecasted and actual sales (% Change). He also wants you to summarize each workbook, reporting the quarterly forecasted and actual totals for revenues in a new worksheet. After you have added this information to each workbook, Kevin wants you to consolidate the information from the three regional workbooks, reporting in a single workbook the summarized information for each region.

Complete the following:

1. Open the **Europe**, **North America**, and **South America** regional revenue workbooks located in the Tutorial.06\Case4 folder included with your Data Files. Save the Europe workbook as **PlutoEU**, the North America workbook as **PlutoNA**, and the South America workbook as **PlutoSA** in the same folder. In the Documentation sheet in each regional revenue workbook, enter your name and the date.

2. Each regional workbook contains a Documentation sheet, a first quarter summary worksheet, and three monthly worksheets. Complete the monthly worksheets in each region's workbook by doing the following:
   - Calculate the difference for each product group: Actual–Forecast.
   - Calculate the % change for each product group: Difference/Forecast.
   - Calculate the total revenue for the Forecast, Actual, and Difference columns, and then calculate the total % Change.
   - Format the numbers to improve the appearance of the worksheets.

3. In each workbook, complete the Quarter 1 worksheet by first summarizing the forecasted and actual totals for product groups for the first three months of the year, then calculating the difference and the % change, and, finally, summarizing the forecasted, actual, difference, and % change values for the quarter. (*Hint:* The Total Revenue % change (cell E10) is not the sum of the column; it is the percent change between the forecasted and actual totals.) Use Figure 6-33 as a guide as you complete the worksheet.

Figure 6-33

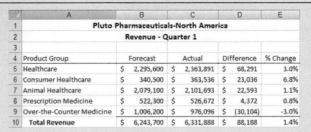

	A	B	C	D	E
1		Pluto Pharmaceuticals-North America			
2		Revenue - Quarter 1			
3					
4	Product Group	Forecast	Actual	Difference	% Change
5	Healthcare	$ 2,295,600	$ 2,363,891	$ 68,291	3.0%
6	Consumer Healthcare	$ 340,500	$ 363,536	$ 23,036	6.8%
7	Animal Healthcare	$ 2,079,100	$ 2,101,693	$ 22,593	1.1%
8	Prescription Medicine	$ 522,300	$ 526,672	$ 4,372	0.8%
9	Over-the-Counter Medicine	$ 1,006,200	$ 976,096	$ (30,104)	-3.0%
10	Total Revenue	$ 6,243,700	$ 6,331,888	$ 88,188	1.4%

4. Format the Quarter 1 sheet for each regional workbook with the same formatting used for the monthly worksheets, and then save the workbooks.

5. Create a new workbook, and save it as **Pluto Summary** in the Tutorial.06\Case4 folder included with your Data Files. Rename the Sheet1 worksheet as **Documentation**, and in column A enter the same labels used in the Documentation sheets in the other workbooks. In column B, enter **Corporate** as the region, enter your name as the author and the current date as the date created, and then enter **To report on revenue for all regions** as the purpose. Format the Documentation sheet to match the Documentation worksheet formatting in the PlutoNA, PlutoSA, and PlutoEU workbooks.

6. Switch to the Sheet2 worksheet, and then use Figure 6-34 as a guide to enter the text shown. Enter formulas to total the forecasted and actual revenue for each product group. Compute the difference and % change for each product group. Include the totals for the Forecast, Actual, and Difference columns, and calculate the % Change for the total revenue for the quarter. Rename the worksheet as **Quarter 1**.

Figure 6-34

	A	B	C	D	E
1	Pluto Pharmaceuticals-Corporate				
2	Revenue - Quarter 1				
3					
4	Product Group	Forecast	Actual	Difference	% Change
5	Healthcare	$ 5,670,800	$ 5,913,673	$ 242,873	4.3%
6	Consumer Healthcare	$ 1,210,500	$ 1,250,000	$ 39,500	3.3%
7	Animal Healthcare	$ 4,632,300	$ 4,662,070	$ 29,770	0.6%
8	Prescription Medicine	$ 1,432,900	$ 1,507,357	$ 74,457	5.2%
9	Over-the-Counter Medicine	$ 2,707,600	$ 2,657,288	$ (50,312)	-1.9%
10	Total Revenue	$ 15,654,100	$ 15,990,388	$ 336,288	2.1%

EXPLORE

7. Insert a bar chart that compares the actual and forecast sales by product group. The chart is similar to Figure 6-35. Place the chart beneath the data you entered in the Quarter 1 worksheet. Change the axis so the sales are displayed in millions of dollars.

Figure 6-35

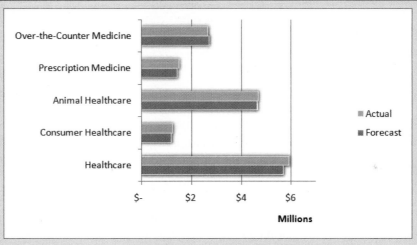

8. Prepare the three regional and corporate workbooks for printing. On each page, include the worksheet name in the center section of the header and your name in the left section of the footer.

9. Create a workspace that opens with the Quarter 1 worksheet active in each work-book using a horizontal layout for the four workbooks, and then save it as **Quarter1 Files** in the Tutorial.06\Case4 folder included with your Data Files.

10. Open the **Pluto Summary** workbook located in the Tutorial.06\Case4 folder included with your Data Files, and then save the workbook as **Pluto Yearend** in the same folder. For year-end backup, break the links in the Pluto Yearend workbook.

EXPLORE

11. You receive a new source file to substitute for the original source file. The new source file has a different name.

    a. Open the **Pluto Summary** workbook, and then save the workbook as **Pluto Summary Test**. Close the workbook.

b. Open the **PlutoNA** workbook, and then save the workbook as **PlutoNorth**. In the PlutoNorth workbook in the March worksheet, change the actual healthcare revenue in cell C5 to **$863,298**. Save and close the PlutoNorth workbook.

c. Open the **Pluto Summary Test** workbook, and change the link to the source workbook from PlutoNA to **PlutoNorth**. (*Hint:* Use the Edit Links dialog box.) Save and close the Pluto Summary Test workbook.

⊕ EXPLORE 12. Update the source program but not the destination file.

a. Open the **PlutoEU** workbook, and then save the workbook as **PlutoEurope**.

b. Open the **Pluto Summary Test** workbook, and change the link to the source workbook from PlutoEU to **PlutoEurope**. Note the actual total revenue in the Quarter 1 worksheet (cell C10). Close the Pluto Summary Test workbook.

c. In the PlutoEurope workbook, switch to the March worksheet and change the actual animal healthcare revenue in cell C7 to **$275,569**. Save and close the PlutoEurope workbook.

d. Open the **Pluto Summary Test** workbook but keep the automatic update of the links disabled. How does this affect the Quarter 1 total actual revenue (cell C10) in the Pluto Summary Test workbook (compare the current value to the value you noted in Step b)?

e. Use the Edit Links dialog box to update the Pluto Summary Test workbook. How does this affect the Quarter 1 total actual revenue (cell C10) in the Pluto Summary Test workbook (compare the current value to the value you noted in Step d)?

⊕ EXPLORE 13. Modify the template named **PlutoTemplate** located in the Tutorial.06\Case4 folder. Make the following two changes to the template, and then save the modified template as **PlutoTemplateRevised**.

a. Instead of column E displaying #DIV/0! in all sheets, change the formula in column E to display 0% when no values are entered in column B (Forecast).

b. Apply a fill color of your choice to the range B5:C9 in the monthly worksheets to identify where to enter data.

14. Create a new workbook from the modified PlutoTemplateRevised template. Enter **$500,000** in the range B5:B9 of each monthly worksheet. Enter **$550,000** in the range C5:C9 of each monthly worksheet. Save the workbook as **Pluto2011**.

15. Save and close all the workbooks. Submit the finished workbooks to your instructor, either in printed or electronic form, as requested.

Research | Internet Assignments

Use the Internet to find and work with data related to the topics presented in this tutorial.

The purpose of the Internet Assignments is to challenge you to find information on the Internet that you can use to work effectively with this software. The actual assignments are updated and maintained on the Course Technology Web site. Log on to the Internet and use your Web browser to go to the Student Online Companion for New Perspectives Office 2007 at **www.course.com/np/office2007**. Then navigate to the Internet Assignments for this tutorial.

Review | **Quick Check Answers**

Session 6.1

1. A worksheet group is a collection of two or more worksheets that have been selected.
2. To select an adjacent group of worksheets, click the first sheet tab, press and hold the Shift key, and then click the sheet tab of the last worksheet in the range. To select a nonadjacent group of worksheets, click the sheet tab of one of the worksheets in the group, press and hold the Ctrl key, and then click the sheet tabs of the remaining worksheets in the group. Deselect a worksheet group by either clicking the sheet tab of a worksheet not in the group or right-clicking one of the sheet tabs in the group and clicking Ungroup Sheets on the shortcut menu.
3. ='Quarter 2'!A10
4. 'Summary 1:Summary 3'!A10
5. the maximum value found in cell B1 of all worksheets from Sheet1 to Sheet4
6. MAX(Sheet1:Sheet5!B1); if Sheet5 were positioned before Sheet4, then MAX(Sheet1: Sheet4!B1) includes Sheet5.
7. Select a worksheet group that consists of all sheets in the workbook, click the Page Layout tab, and then select the page layout specification that you want to apply to all worksheets in the group.

Session 6.2

1. 'D:\Reports\[Product Report]Sales Info'!A1:A10
2. The source file is the file that contains the data values you want to link to.
3. The destination file receives the value(s) from the source file.
4. If both the destination and source files are open, Excel will update the link automatically when you update a value in the source file; when you open the destination file, click the Options button in the Message Bar, click the Enable this content option button, and then click the OK button.
5. In the Connections group on the Data tab, click the Edit Links button to open the Edit Links dialog box. The linked workbooks are listed in the dialog box.
6. A workspace file is a file containing information about all opened workbooks, including their locations, window sizes, and screen positions.
7. By opening a workspace file, you open all workbooks defined in the workspace. Using a workspace helps you organize projects that might involve several workbooks.

Session 6.3

1. Click the cell in which you want to insert the hyperlink, and then in the Links group on the Insert tab, click the Hyperlink button. Type the hyperlink text in the Insert Hyperlink dialog box.

2. True

3. A template is a workbook that contains specific content and formatting that you can use as a model for other similar workbooks.

4. A user can modify the contents of a workbook based on a template without changing the template file itself. The next time a new workbook is created based on a template, the workbook opens with all the original properties intact. If you use the workbook file to create a new workbook, you first must delete the values from cells that you want to change and then use the Save As dialog box to assign a new filename to the workbook.

5. Click the Office Button, click Save As, click the Save as type button, click Template, type a filename for the template, and then click the Save button.

6. Web Page; Single File Web Page

Ending Data Files

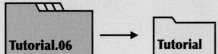

Tutorial.06 → **Tutorial**

Audited 2010.xlsx
Colorado.xlsx
Hoot Time Card.xlsx
New Mexico.xlsx
New Mexico 2011.xlsx
Sales 2010.docx
Theme Parks.xlw
Totals 2010.xlsx
Travel Template.xltx
Utah.xlsx
Web Totals 2010.htm

Review

Idaho.xlsx
NW Totals 2010.xlsx
NW Travel.xltx
NW Workspace.xlw
Oregon.xlsx
Oregon 2011.xlsx
Washington.xlsx
Web Oregon 2010.htm
📁 **Web Oregon 2010_files**

Case1

Java Cafe.xlsx
Java Cafe 2011.xlsx
Java Template.xltx
Web Java.htm

Case2

Carson City 2011.xlsx
UTE Carson City.xlsx
UTE Reno.xlsx
UTE Summary.xlsx
UTE Template.xltx
UTE Vegas.xlsx
UTE Web Page.htm

Case3

InBurger 2010.xlsx

Case4

Pluto 2011.xlsx
Pluto Summary.xlsx
Pluto Summary Test.xlsx
Pluto Yearend.xlsx
PlutoEU.xlsx
PlutoEurope.xlsx
PlutoNA.xlsx
PlutoNorth.xlsx
PlutoSA.xlxs
PlutoTemplateRevised.xltx
Quarter1 Files.xlw

Objectives

Session 7.1
- Evaluate a single condition using the IF function
- Evaluate multiple conditions using the AND function
- Calculate different series of outcomes by nesting IF functions
- Test whether one or more conditions are true with the OR function

Session 7.2
- Return values from a table with the VLOOKUP function
- Check for duplicate values using conditional formatting
- Check for data entry errors using the IFERROR function
- Summarize data using the COUNTIF, SUMIF, and AVERAGEIF functions
- Review the COUNTIFS, SUMIFS, and AVERAGEIFS functions

Session 7.3
- Use advanced filters
- Summarize data using Database functions

Using Advanced Functions, Conditional Formatting, and Filtering

Reviewing Employee Data

Case | Talent Tracs

Rita Corvales founded Talent Tracs, a software development company for the music and entertainment industry located in Austin, Texas. Talent Tracs sells EasyTracs, a software program that matches venues with artists and then schedules the performances. As the company's reputation grew, the business expanded rapidly. Today, Talent Tracs has nearly 100 employees, ranging from software developers to online customer relations staff. Rita uses Excel to track basic employee information such as each employee's name, gender, birth date, hire date, health plan, job status, pay type (hourly or salaried), pay grade, and annual salary.

Rita needs to review and manage the information about her company's employees on a regular basis. For example, she needs to track employee enrollment and costs in the benefit programs offered by the company. She also wants to calculate each employee's life insurance premium and how much the company contributes to each employee's 401(k) retirement account and health plan. And Rita needs to calculate the amount Talent Tracs spends on bonuses, which are based on employee pay grades and performance.

To provide Rita with the information she needs, you'll use a variety of Excel functions, filters, and conditional formatting.

Starting Data Files

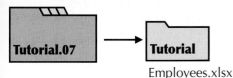

Tutorial.07 → Tutorial

Tutorial	Review	Case1	Case2	Case3	Case4
Employees.xlsx	Tracs.xlsx	Modem.xlsx	Leave.xlsx	M-Fresh.xlsx	Rock Island.xlsx

Session 7.1

Working with Logical Functions

The Talent Tracs compensation package includes salary, bonuses, and benefits. Right now, Rita wants to focus on three types of benefits: life insurance, retirement savings, and healthcare. Employees can choose to purchase additional supplemental life insurance coverage equal to their annual base salary times the insurance premium rate. The 401(k) retirement savings plan matches eligible employees' contributions, dollar for dollar, up to 3 percent of their salary. Employees can select a PPO or HMO health plan for families or individuals, or they can opt out of the health plan by providing evidence of other health-care coverage.

Rita created a workbook that contains descriptive data for employees and their benefits. You will open this workbook now and review the employee information.

To open the Employees workbook:

▶ 1. Open the **Employees** workbook located in the **Tutorial.07\Tutorial** folder included with your Data Files, and then save the workbook as **Talent Tracs** in the same folder.

▶ 2. In the Documentation worksheet, enter your name and the current date.

▶ 3. Switch to the **Employee Data** worksheet. See Figure 7-1.

Figure 7-1   Employee Data worksheet

M91   ƒx =DATEDIF([Hire Date],$AE$2,"y")

	ID	Last Name	Hire Date	Birth Date	Sex	Location	Job Status	Add Life Ins	Pay Grade	Pay Type	Annual Salary	Health Plan	Years Service
2	1024	Hovey	8/28/2008	9/6/1966	M	Austin	FT	Y	3	S	$ 85,000	HMOF	1
3	1025	Overton	5/24/2004	2/15/1986	F	Home	FT	N	2	S	$ 40,000	HMOF	6
4	1026	Fetherston	4/24/2009	9/24/1968	M	New Orleans	FT	Y	2	S	$ 37,244	HMOF	1
5	1027	Lebrun	7/18/2008	8/9/1959	F	Austin	FT	N	3	S	$ 80,000	None	1
6	1028	Hanson	8/21/2009	7/15/1950	M	Austin	FT	Y	3	S	$ 65,000	None	0
7	1029	Philo	3/5/2009	5/2/1958	M	New Orleans	FT	Y	3	S	$125,000	PPOI	1
8	1030	Stolt	3/1/2007	12/7/1977	M	New Orleans	FT	N	3	S	$ 95,000	HMOI	3
9	1031	Akhalaghi	12/8/2009	12/4/1961	M	Austin	FT	N	2	S	$ 36,000	None	0
10	1032	Vankeuren	8/11/2005	1/10/1959	F	Austin	PT	N	1	H	$ 33,508	PPOF	4
11	1033	Mccorkle	6/12/2003	1/30/1942	F	Nashville	FT	N	1	H	$ 21,840	None	7
12	1034	Nightingale	5/4/2006	8/27/1989	M	Nashville	FT	N	1	H	$ 25,792	PPOF	4
13	1035	Croasdale	12/18/2009	1/6/1968	F	Austin	FT	N	1	H	$ 32,011	PPOI	0
14	1036	Lambrechts	5/4/2005	4/28/1958	F	Nashville	FT	Y	1	H	$ 23,920	HMOF	5
15	1037	Palmer	11/26/1998	10/4/1971	F	Austin	FT	Y	1	H	$ 32,011	None	11
16	1038	Tetreault	2/22/2002	1/4/1960	F	Nashville	FT	Y	1	H	$ 21,840	PPOI	8
17	1039	Cugini	12/4/2009	1/16/1970	F	Austin	FT	Y	2	S	$ 55,000	PPOF	0
18	1040	Dash	10/12/2009	12/2/1985	M	Nashville	FT	Y	2	S	$ 65,000	HMOF	0
19	1041	Donnelly	12/4/2009	5/9/1959	F	New Orleans	FT	Y	3	S	$125,000	HMOF	0

Documentation | Employee Data | Employee Summary | Lookup Tables

Ready   120%

The Employee Data worksheet contains an Excel table of employee data. Rita entered each employee's ID, last name, hire date, birth date, gender, location, job status (FT for full-time, PT for part-time, or CN for paid consultant), additional life insurance coverage (Y for Yes, N for No), pay grade (1, 2, or 3), and pay type (S for Salaried, H for Hourly). The worksheet also includes the employee's annual salary, the type of health plan the employee selected (HMOF for HMO-Family, HMOI for HMO-Individual, PPOF for PPO-Family, PPOI for PPO-Individual, or None), and the number of years the employee has worked at Talent Tracs (Years Service). Rita stores the employees' additional personal information, including home address, phone numbers, Social Security numbers, and so forth, in another workbook.

Creating Fields in a Table | InSight

Keep the following guidelines in mind when creating fields in an Excel table:

- **Create fields that require the least maintenance.** For example, fields such as Hire Date and Birth Date require no maintenance because their values do not change, unlike fields such as Age and Years of Service, whose values change each year. If you need to track information such as the specific age or years of service, a best practice is to use calculations to determine these values based on values in the Hire Date and Birth Date fields.
- **Store the smallest unit of data possible in a field.** For example, use three separate fields for City, State, and Zip Code rather than one field. Using separate fields for each unit of data enables you to sort or filter each field. If you want to display data from two or more fields in one column, you can use a formula to reference the City, State, and Zip Code fields. For example, you can use the concatenation operator (the ampersand) to combine the city, state, and zip code in one cell as follows: =C2 & D2 & E2.
- **Apply a text format to fields with numerical text data.** For example, formatting fields such as Zip Code and Social Security Number as text ensures that leading zeros are stored as part of the data. Otherwise, the zip code 02892 is stored as a number and displayed as 2892, which is not the intended result.

Rita formatted the data as an Excel table to take advantage of the additional analysis and organization tools available for Excel tables. Rita asks you to replace the default name for the Excel table with a more descriptive name.

To rename the Excel table:

▶ **1.** Make sure cell **A1** (the first cell in the Excel table) is the active cell, and then click the **Table Tools Design** tab on the Ribbon.

▶ **2.** In the Properties group, select **Table1** in the Table Name box, type **Employee**, and then press the **Enter** key. The Excel table is now named *Employee*.

Next, you'll insert formulas that calculate each employee's additional life insurance premium (if any), 401(k) cost, health plan cost, and bonus amount. After you calculate those values, Rita wants you to summarize that information in the Employee Summary worksheet, so she can quickly see the impact of the compensation and benefits package on the company.

Whenever you enter a formula into an empty table column, Excel automatically fills the rest of that table column with the formula. This is referred to as a **calculated column**. If you need to modify the formula in a calculated column, you edit the formula in one cell of the column and the formulas in that table column are also modified. If you edit a cell in a calculated column so it is no longer consistent with the other formulas in the column (such as replacing a formula with a value), a green triangle appears in the upper-left corner of the cell, making the inconsistency easy to see. After a calculated column contains an inconsistency, any other edits you make to that column are no longer automatically applied to the rest of the cells in that column because Excel does not overwrite custom values.

Tip

Calculated columns work only in Excel tables. To achieve the same results in a range of data, you must copy and paste the formula or use the AutoFill feature.

You'll start by calculating the additional life insurance premiums. This amount depends on whether an employee has elected additional life insurance coverage. So, you'll need to enter a formula that includes the IF function to determine the amount of the premium.

Using the IF Function

In many situations, the value you store in a cell depends on certain conditions. Consider the following examples:

- An employee's gross pay depends on whether that employee worked overtime.
- An income tax rate depends on the taxpayer's adjusted taxable income.
- A shipping charge depends on the size of an order.

To evaluate these types of conditions in Excel, you use the IF function. Recall that the IF function is a logical function that evaluates a condition (a logical test), and then returns one value if the condition is true and another value if the condition is false. The IF function has the following syntax:

IF(*logical_test*, *value_if_true*, [*value_if_false*])

In this function, *logical_test* is a condition such as A5="Yes" that is either true or false, *value_if_true* is the value displayed in the cell if the logical test is true, and *value_if_false* is the value displayed in the cell if the logical test is not true. Although the *value_if_false* argument is optional, you should usually include it so the IF function covers both possibilities.

You use the IF function to create a conditional statement such as =IF(A5="Yes",C5+B5,B5–C5). The first argument, the *logical_test* A5="Yes", is always performed first and has a result that is either true or false. If the *logical_test* is true, the *value_if_true*, C5+B5, is calculated next and its value is displayed in the cell. If the *logical_test* is false, the *value_if_false*, B5–C5, is calculated next and its value is displayed in the cell. The IF function results in only one value—either the *value_if_true* or the *value_if_false*; the other is ignored.

Talent Tracs employees can purchase additional life insurance coverage equal to the employee's annual salary multiplied by the premium rate (.001). Rita created the flowchart shown in Figure 7-2, which illustrates the logic for calculating an employee's additional life insurance premium. The flowchart shows that if the employee elected additional life insurance (Add Life Ins = "Y" is True), then the premium is calculated using the formula Salary*.001. If the employee did not elect additional life insurance (Add Life Ins = "Y" is False), then the premium is 0.

Flowchart with logic for the additional life insurance premium ◄ **Figure 7-2**

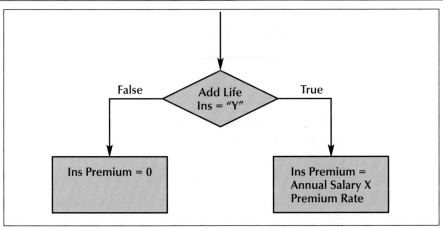

You will add a column in the Employee table to display the life insurance premium. Then, you'll enter a formula with an IF function to calculate the life insurance premium employees will pay if they select additional life insurance coverage.

To calculate the life insurance premium using an IF function:

▸ **1.** In cell N1, enter **Life Ins Premium**. The Excel table expands to include this column and applies the table formatting to all the rows in the new column.

▸ **2.** Make sure cell **N2** is the active cell, and then, on the formula bar, click the **Insert Function** button f_x. The Insert Function dialog box opens.

▸ **3.** Click **Logical** in the Or select a category list, click **IF** in the Select a function box, and then click the **OK** button. The Function Arguments dialog box for the IF function opens. You will use this dialog box to enter the values for the IF function arguments.

▸ **4.** In the Logical_test argument box, type **H2="Y"** and then press the **Tab** key. This sets the logical test to evaluate whether the employee wants additional life insurance, indicated by Y for Yes or N for No in cell H2. *TRUE* appears to the right of the Logical_test argument box, indicating the result for the employee in row 2 is true. That is, the employee wants additional life insurance.

▸ **5.** In the Value_if_true argument box, type **K2*0.001**. This argument specifies that if the condition is true (the employee wants additional life insurance), the result of the employee's current salary (listed in cell K2) is multiplied by 0.1% and appears in cell N2. The value to the right of the Value_if_true argument box is 85, which is the premium the employee in row 2 will pay for additional life insurance if the condition is true.

▸ **6.** In the Value_if_false argument box, type **0**. This argument specifies that if the condition is false (the employee does not want additional life insurance), 0 appears in cell N2. The value to the right of the Value_if_false argument box is 0, which is the value that appears in cell N2 if the condition is false. See Figure 7-3.

Tip

Testing for text values is not case-sensitive. So the conditions H2="Y" and H2="y" return the same value.

| Figure 7-3 | Function Arguments dialog box for IF function |

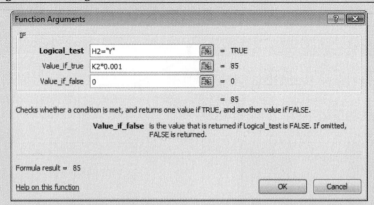

Tip

Click the top portion of the column header in an Excel table (not the worksheet column heading) to select the column data but not the header; double-click to select the entire column including the column header.

▶ **7.** Click the **OK** button. The formula =IF(H2="Y",K2*0.001,0) appears in the formula bar, and the value 85 appears in cell N2 because the condition is true. The results are automatically copied to all rows in column N of the table.

▶ **8.** Point to the top of cell **N1** until the pointer changes to ↓, and then click to select the range N2:N101. The data in the Life Ins Premium column is selected, but not the column header.

▶ **9.** Format the selected range N2:N101 with the **Accounting** number format with **2** decimal places. The Life Ins Premium column shows the premiums employees will pay for additional life insurance, formatted as currency. See Figure 7-4.

| Figure 7-4 | Life Ins Premium column added to the Employee table |

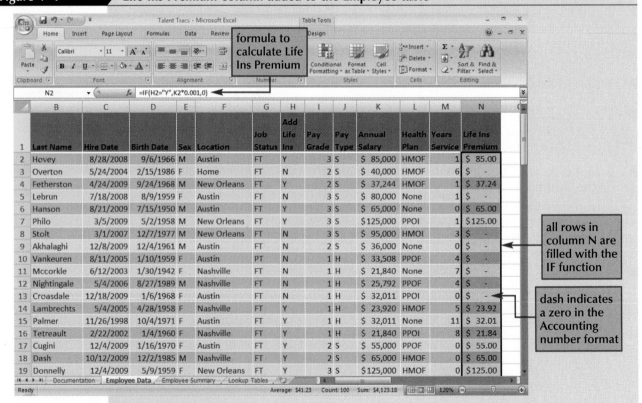

Using the And Function

Employees are eligible for the 401(k) benefit if they are full-time (FT in Job Status) *and* have worked for the company for one or more years (1 or greater in Years Service). As long as *both* conditions are true, the company contributes an amount equal to 3 percent of the employee's salary to the employee's 401(k). If neither condition is true or if only one condition is true, the employee is not eligible for the 401(k) benefit and the company's contribution is 0. Rita outlined these eligibility conditions in the flowchart shown in Figure 7-5.

Flowchart illustrating logic for the 401(k) benefit   Figure 7-5

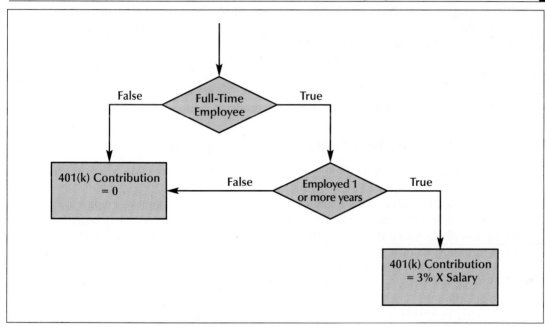

The IF function evaluates a single condition; however, you often need to test two or more conditions and determine whether *all* conditions are true. You can do this with the AND function. The **AND function** is a logical function that returns a TRUE value if all the logical conditions are true and a FALSE value if any or all of the logical conditions are false. The syntax of the AND function is as follows:

```
AND(logical1 [,logical2]...)
```

In this function, *logical1* and *logical2* are conditions that can be either true or false. If all of the logical conditions are true, the AND function returns the logical value TRUE; otherwise, the function returns the logical value FALSE. You can include up to 255 logical conditions in the AND function, but keep in mind that *all* the logical conditions listed in the AND function must be true for the AND function to return a TRUE value.

To calculate the contribution amount for each employee to the 401(k) plan, you need to use the AND function along with the IF function. You use the AND function to test whether each employee in the Employee table fulfills the eligibility requirements, as shown in the following formula:

```
=AND(G2="FT",M2>=1)
```

This formula tests whether the value in cell G2 (the job status for the first employee) is equal to FT (the abbreviation for full-time) and whether the value in cell M2 (the years of service for the first employee) is greater than or equal to 1 (indicating one or more years of employment at Talent Tracs). Therefore, if the employee is a full-time employee (G2="FT") *and* has worked one or more years at Talent Tracs (M2>=1), the AND function returns the value TRUE; otherwise, the AND function returns the value FALSE.

The AND function, however, does not calculate how much Talent Tracs will contribute to the employee's 401(k) plan. To determine whether an employee is eligible *and* to calculate the amount of the 401(k) contribution, you need to insert the AND function within an IF function, as shown in the following formula:

```
=IF(AND(G2="FT",M2>=1),K2*0.03,0)
```

The first argument of the IF function, =IF(AND(G2="FT",M2>=1), uses the AND function to determine if the employee is eligible for a 401(k) contribution. If the employee is eligible, the logical test AND(G2="FT",M2>=1) returns the logical value TRUE and the formula in the value_if_true argument of the IF function multiplies the employee's annual salary by 0.03 (K2*0.03). If one or both conditions are false, the logical test AND(G2="FT",M2>=1) returns the logical value FALSE, and the IF function displays the value 0.

You'll insert a new column in the Employee table, and then enter the formula to calculate the 401(k) contribution using structured references.

Using Structured References with Excel Tables

When you create a formula that references all or parts of an Excel table, you can replace the specific cell or range address with a **structured reference**, the actual table name or column header. The table name is Table1, Table2, and so forth unless you entered a more descriptive table name, as you did for the Employee table. Column headers provide a description of the data entered in each column. Structured references make it easier to create formulas that use portions or all of an Excel table because the names or headers are usually simpler to identify than cell addresses. For example, in the Employee table, the table name *Employee* refers to the range A2:N101, which is the range of data in the table excluding the header row and Total row. When you want to reference an entire column of data in a table, you create a column qualifier, which has the following syntax:

```
Tablename[qualifier]
```

The *Tablename* is the name entered in the Table Name box in the Properties group on the Table Tools Design tab. The *qualifier* is the column header enclosed in square brackets. For example, the structured reference *Employee[Annual Salary]* references the annual salary data in the range K2:K101 of the Employee table. You use structured references in formulas, as shown in the following formula:

```
=SUM(Employee[Annual Salary])
```

This formula adds the annual salary data in the range K2:K101 of the Employee table. In this case, *[Annual Salary]* is the column qualifier.

When you create a calculated column, as you did to calculate life insurance premiums in the Employee table, you can use structured references to create the formula. A formula that includes a structured reference can be fully qualified or unqualified. In a fully qualified structured reference, the table name precedes the column qualifier. In an unqualified structured reference, only the column qualifier appears in the reference. For example, you could have used either of the following formulas with structured references to calculate Life Ins Premium in the calculated column you added to the Employee table (the first formula is unqualified, and the second is fully qualified):

```
=IF([Add Life Ins]="Y",[Annual Salary]*001,0)
=IF(Employee[Add Life Ins]="Y",Employee[Annual Salary]*.001,0)
```

Tip

If you are not sure of a table's name, click in the table, click the Table Tools Design tab on the Ribbon, and then check the Table Name box in the Properties group.

If you are creating a calculated column or formula within an Excel table, you can use the unqualified structured reference in the formula. If you use a structured reference outside the table or in another worksheet to reference an Excel table or portion of the table, you need to use a fully qualified reference.

In addition to referencing a specific column in a table by its column header, you can also reference other portions of a table, such as the header row or Total row. Figure 7-6 lists the special item qualifiers needed to reference these table portions in the formula.

Special item qualifiers for structured references | Figure 7-6

Qualifier	References	Example of Structured Reference
#All	The entire table, including column headers, data, and Total row if displayed	=Employee[#All]
#Data	The data in the table	=Employee[#Data]
#Headers	The header row in the table	=Employee[#Headers]
#Totals	The Total row in the table; if the Total row is hidden, then an error is returned	=Employee[#Totals]
#ThisRow	The current row in the specified column of the table	=Employee[[#ThisRow],[Column Header]]

You'll use structured references to calculate the 401(k) contributions for Talent Tracs.

To enter a formula with IF and AND functions to calculate 401(k) contributions:

▶ **1.** In cell O1, enter **401(k)** as the column header. The Excel table expands to include the new column, and cell O2 is the active cell.

▶ **2.** In cell O2, type **=I**. A list of valid function names opens scrolled to the I entries.

▶ **3.** Double-click **IF**. The first part of the formula with the IF function, =IF(, appears in the cell and the formula bar with the insertion point placed directly after the opening parenthesis so you can continue typing the formula. The syntax of the IF function appears in a ScreenTip below cell O2. See Figure 7-7.

Tip

You can also insert the selected function in the list by pressing the Tab key.

IF function ScreenTip | Figure 7-7

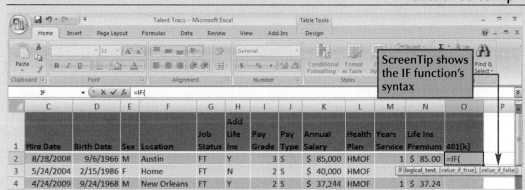

Next, you'll enter the AND function as the logical test for the IF function.

▶ **4.** Type **A** to open the function list scrolled to the A entries, and then double-click **AND**. The first part of the AND function is added to the formula, and =IF(AND(appears in the cell and the formula bar. The syntax of the AND function appears in a ScreenTip below cell O2.

Trouble? If a function other than the AND function appears in cell O2, you probably double-clicked a different function name. Press the Backspace key to delete the incorrect function name and redisplay the list of function names. When you see the AND function, double-click the name.

You'll enter the logical conditions for the AND function using structured references.

▶ **5.** Type **[** to display a list of all the column headers in the Employee table. You want to enter the Job Status column for the first logical condition. See Figure 7-8.

Figure 7-8 | **List of column qualifiers**

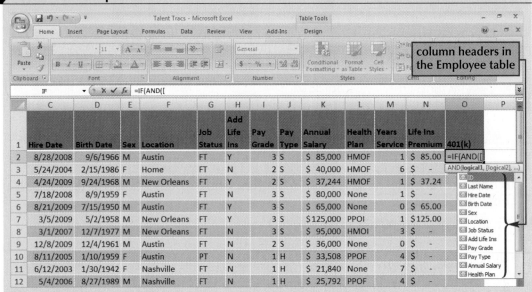

▶ **6.** Double-click **Job Status**, and then type **]** to enter the structured reference for column G, which is the Job Status column. A blue box surrounds the Job Status data and [Job Status] is colored blue in the formula =IF(AND([Job Status] in the cell. This is the first part of the logical condition for the AND function, which is job status is full-time.

▶ **7.** Type **="FT",** (including the comma) to complete the first logical condition. The first logical condition states that the content in the Job Status cell must equal FT.

▶ **8.** Type **[** to begin the second logical condition, double-click **Years Service** in the list, and then type **]**. The structured reference for cell O2, which is years of service for the first employee, is entered in the formula. A green box surrounds the Years Service data and the structured reference is colored green in the formula.

▶ **9.** Type **>=1),** to complete the second logical condition. The second logical condition states that the content in the Years Service cell must be greater than or equal to 1. The complete logical expression for the IF function, =IF(AND([Job Status]="FT",[Years Service]>=1), appears in the cell and the formula bar. The ScreenTip shows the syntax of the IF function again, because you are ready to enter the value_if_true argument and the value_if_false argument.

▶ **10.** Type **[** to open the list of column headers, double-click **Annual Salary**, and then type **]*0.03,** to complete the value_if_true argument using a structured reference. The Annual Salary data appears in a purple box, and the structured reference in the formula is purple. If the employee is eligible for the 401(k) contribution, as determined by the AND function, then the amount in the Annual Salary cell for the employee is multiplied by 3%.

You'll complete the formula by entering the value_if_false argument.

▶ **11.** Type **0)** for the value_if_false argument, and then press the **Enter** key. The formula is entered in cell O2 and copied to the rest of the 401(k) column in the table. If the employee is not eligible for the 401(k) contribution, as determined by the AND function, then 0 is entered in the 401(k) cell. In this case, cell O2 displays the value 2550, which is the result of multiplying the employee's annual salary of $85,000 by 3 percent, because the employee in row 2 meets both conditions of the logical test (job status is full-time and years of service is 1 year). See Figure 7-9.

Formula using IF and AND functions to calculate 401(k) ◀ **Figure 7-9**

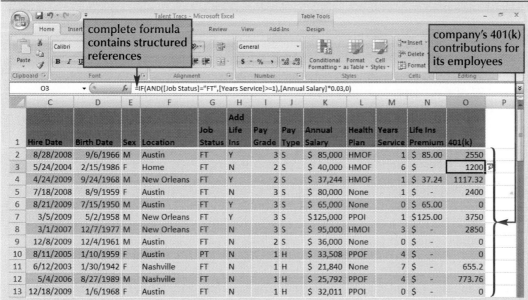

Cell O3 formula: `=IF(AND([Job Status]="FT",[Years Service]>=1),[Annual Salary]*0.03,0)`

	C	D	E	F	G	H	I	J	K	L	M	N	O	P
1	Hire Date	Birth Date	Sex	Location	Job Status	Add Life Ins	Pay Grade	Pay Type	Annual Salary	Health Plan	Years Service	Life Ins Premium	401(k)	
2	8/28/2008	9/6/1966	M	Austin	FT	Y	3	S	$ 85,000	HMOF	1	$ 85.00	2550	
3	5/24/2004	2/15/1986	F	Home	FT	N	2	S	$ 40,000	HMOF	6	$ -	1200	
4	4/24/2009	9/24/1968	M	New Orleans	FT	Y	2	S	$ 37,244	HMOF	1	$ 37.24	1117.32	
5	7/18/2008	8/9/1959	F	Austin	FT	N	3	S	$ 80,000	None	1	$ -	2400	
6	8/21/2009	7/15/1950	M	Austin	FT	Y	3	S	$ 65,000	None	0	$ 65.00	0	
7	3/5/2009	5/2/1958	M	New Orleans	FT	Y	3	S	$125,000	PPOI	1	$125.00	3750	
8	3/1/2007	12/7/1977	M	New Orleans	FT	N	3	S	$ 95,000	HMOI	3	$ -	2850	
9	12/8/2009	12/4/1961	M	Austin	FT	N	2	S	$ 36,000	None	0	$ -	0	
10	8/11/2005	1/10/1959	F	Austin	PT	N	1	H	$ 33,508	PPOF	4	$ -	0	
11	6/12/2003	1/30/1942	F	Nashville	FT	N	1	H	$ 21,840	None	7	$ -	655.2	
12	5/4/2006	8/27/1989	M	Nashville	FT	N	1	H	$ 25,792	PPOF	4	$ -	773.76	
13	12/18/2009	1/6/1968	F	Austin	FT	N	1	H	$ 32,011	PPOI	0	$ -	0	

Callouts: "complete formula contains structured references"; "company's 401(k) contributions for its employees"

Trouble? If a dialog box opens, indicating that your formula contains an error, you might have omitted a comma, a square bracket, or a parenthesis. Edit the formula as needed to ensure the complete formula is =IF(AND([Job Status]="FT",[Years Service]>=1),[Annual Salary]*0.03,0), and then press the Enter key.

▶ **12.** Point to the top of cell **O1** until the pointer changes to ⬇, click to select the 401(k) data values, and then format the range using the **Accounting** number format with **2** decimal places.

| InSight | | **Using the DATEDIF Function** |

The column Years Service was calculated using the DATEDIF function. The **DATEDIF function** calculates the difference between two dates and shows the result in months, days, or years. The DATEDIF function has the following syntax:

```
DATEDIF(Date1,Date2,Interval)
```

In this function, *Date1* is the earliest date, *Date2* is the latest date, and *Interval* is the unit of time the DATEDIF function will use in the result. You specify the *Interval* with one of the following interval codes:

Interval Code	Meaning	Description
"m"	Months	The number of complete months between Date1 and Date2
"d"	Days	The number of complete days between Date1 and Date2
"y"	Years	The number of complete years between Date1 and Date2

Thus, the formula to calculate years of service at Talent Tracs in complete years is:

```
=DATEDIF(C2,$AE$2,"y")
```

The earliest date is located in cell C2, the Hire Date. The latest date is in cell $AE$2, which shows the date used to compare against the Hire Date, the Years Service as of a cut-off date. The Interval is "y" to indicate you want to display the number of complete years between these two dates.

Note that the DATEDIF function is undocumented in Excel, but it has been available since Excel 97. If you want to learn more about this function, use your favorite search engine to search the Web for *DATEDIF function in Excel*.

Creating Nested IF Functions

The IF function tests for only two outcomes. However, many situations involve a series of outcomes. For example, Talent Tracs pays three levels of employee bonuses. Each bonus is based on the employee's pay grade, which is a system Talent Tracs uses to group jobs based on difficulty and responsibility. Talent Tracs has three pay grade codes (1, 2, and 3). Pay grade 1 has a starting bonus of $2,500, pay grade 2 has a starting bonus of $5,000, and pay grade 3 has a starting bonus of $7,500. Supervisors can increase or decrease these amounts based on the employee's performance. The IF function can choose between only two outcomes; it cannot choose between three outcomes. However, you can nest IF functions to allow for three or more outcomes. A **nested IF function** is when one IF function is placed inside another IF function to test an additional condition. You can nest more than one IF function. In this case, you need to nest three IF functions to calculate the different series of outcomes for the employee bonuses.

Rita created a flowchart to illustrate the logic for determining bonus awards, shown in Figure 7-10. She used different colors to identify each nested IF function. The flowchart shows that if the employee has a pay grade equal to 1, then the bonus equals $2,500 and the IF function is finished (the green portion of the flowchart). If the pay grade is not equal to 1, then the second IF function (shown in blue) is evaluated. If the employee has a pay grade equal to 2, then the bonus equals $5,000 and the IF function is finished. If the pay grade is not equal to 2, then the third IF function (shown in gray) is evaluated. If the employee has a pay grade equal to 3, then the bonus equals $7,500 and the IF function is finished. If the pay grade is not equal to 3, then the message "Invalid pay grade" (shown in dark yellow) is entered in the cell.

Flowchart illustrating the logic to determine the bonus amount | **Figure 7-10**

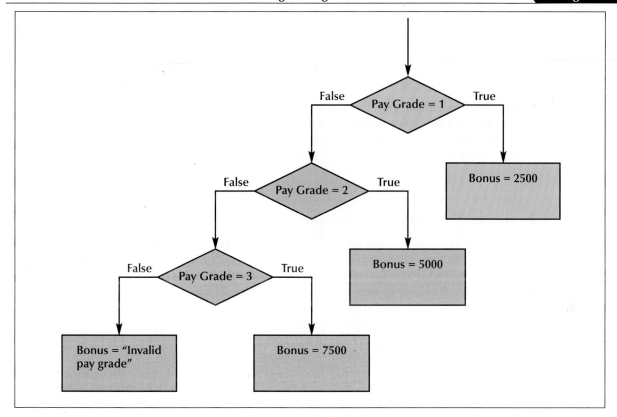

Next, you need to convert Rita's flowchart into a formula. The complete formula is as follows:

```
=IF([Pay Grade]=1,2500,IF([Pay Grade]=2,5000, IF([Pay Grade]=3,
7500,"Invalid pay grade")))
```

The first IF function (shown in green in the flowchart and the formula) tests whether the value in the current Pay Grade cell is equal to 1. If the condition ([Pay Grade]=1) is true, the formula enters 2500 in the Bonus cell. The second IF function (shown in blue in the flowchart and the formula) is executed only if Pay Grade is equal to 1 is false. If the value in the current Pay Grade cell is equal to 2, then the formula returns 5000 in the Bonus cell. The third IF function (shown in gray in the flowchart and the formula) is executed only if [Pay Grade]=2 is false. If the value in the current Pay Grade cell is equal to 3, then the formula returns 7500 in the Bonus cell. If the current value of Pay Grade is not equal to 3, then the message "Invalid pay grade" is entered in the Bonus cell (shown in dark yellow in the flowchart and the formula).

Next, you'll add a column to the Employee table to track the bonus and enter the formula to calculate the bonus amount. Rita mentions that the bonus amounts for each pay grade are not yet final. To make the bonus calculation more flexible, she stored the three bonus amounts (2500, 5000, 7500) in cells Y2, Y3, and Y4 of the Employee Data worksheet. You will reference these cells as you build the formula to calculate the employee bonus. This approach enables you to quickly update the calculated bonus amounts, by changing the values in cells Y2, Y3, and Y4, without having to edit the bonus formula.

To enter nested IFs to calculate employee bonuses:

▶ **1.** In cell P1, enter **Bonus**. A new column with the column header Bonus is added to the Employee table, and cell P2 is the active cell.

▶ **2.** In cell P2, type **=I**, and then double-click **IF**. The beginning of the formula =IF(appears in the cell and formula bar. The syntax of the IF function appears in a ScreenTip below cell P2.

▶ **3.** Type **[** to open a list of all the column headers in the Employee table, double-click **Pay Grade**, type **]** to complete the column qualifier, and then type **=1,$Y$2,** to complete the first logical condition. This condition states that if the logical condition [Pay Grade]=1 is true, then the value stored in cell Y2 (which contains the 2500 bonus) is displayed.

   Next, you'll nest a second IF function inside the first IF function.

▶ **4.** Type **IF** and then press the **Tab** key to select the IF function.

▶ **5.** Type **[p**, press the **Tab** key to enter Pay Grade for the structured reference, type **]** to complete the column qualifier, and then type **=2,$Y$3,** to enter the rest of the first nested IF function. The partial formula IF([Pay Grade]=1,$Y$2,IF([Pay Grade]=2,$Y$3 appears in the cell. The second IF function, IF([Pay Grade]=2,$Y$3, is complete and is executed if the logical condition [Pay Grade]=1 is false. If the condition [Pay Grade]=2 is true, the value stored in cell Y3 (which contains 5000) is displayed.

   Next, you'll enter a third IF function inside the second IF function.

▶ **6.** Type **IF([Pay Grade]=3, $Y$4,"Invalid pay grade")))**. The formula is complete. The third IF function is executed only if an employee's pay grade is neither 1 nor 2. If the condition [Pay Grade]=3 is true, the value stored in cell Y4 is displayed. If the Pay Grade cell is not equal to 3, then the message "Invalid pay grade" is displayed in the cell instead of the bonus amount.

▶ **7.** Press the **Enter** key. The value 7500 appears in the cell because this employee has a pay grade of 3. The bonus formula is automatically copied to all other rows in the Bonus column. The references to cells Y2, Y3, and Y4 are absolute references and do not change as you move from cell to cell in the Bonus column.

   Trouble? If a dialog box opens, indicating that the name you typed is invalid, you might have omitted a square bracket around [Pay Grade] or made a typing error. Click the OK button. The section of the formula that appears to have a problem is highlighted in the formula bar. Compare the formula you typed to =IF([Pay Grade]=1,$Y$2,IF([Pay Grade]=2,$Y$3, IF([Pay Grade]=3,$Y$4,"Invalid pay grade"))) and edit the formula as needed to correct the problem.

▶ **8.** Format the Bonus values in the **Accounting** number format with no decimals. See Figure 7-11.

Tip

You can type an apostrophe to the left of the = sign to convert the formula to text, and then make the corrections to the text, saving you from retyping a long formula. After you correct the formula, delete the apostrophe to test the formula again.

Nested IF functions calculating the employee bonus amounts | Figure 7-11

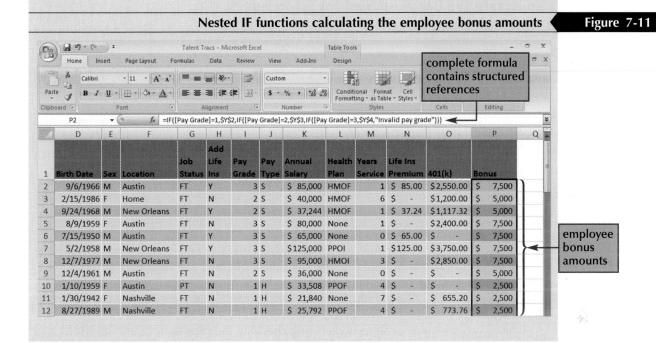

Checking Formulas for Matching Parentheses | InSight

You should verify that you enclosed the correct argument, function, or term within the parentheses of the formula you are creating. This is especially important when you develop a complex formula that includes many parentheses, because it's easy to lose track of how many closing parenthesis marks you need, particularly at the end of a complex formula. Excel color-codes the parentheses so you can quickly determine whether you have complete pairs of them. You can also verify that the formula includes matching pairs of parentheses by selecting the cell with the formula and then clicking in the formula bar. Press the right arrow key to move the insertion point through the formula one character at a time. When the insertion point moves across one parenthesis, its pair is also highlighted briefly. This color coding helps you make sure that all parentheses in a formula are part of a pair (opening and closing parentheses), which helps to ensure the accuracy of the formula and the results it produces.

You'll scroll the Bonus column to verify that all the bonus amounts were assigned correctly.

To check for invalid pay grade messages in the Employee table:

▶ **1.** Scroll the Bonus column. Cell P31 displays the message, "Invalid pay grade." Rita tells you the correct pay grade for this employee is 3.

▶ **2.** In cell I31 (row 31 of the Pay Grade column), enter **3**. The invalid pay grade code entry is removed and the correct bonus amount, $7,500, is displayed.

▶ **3.** AutoFit the column width of the Bonus column.

The executive team increased the bonus for employees in pay grade 1 from $2,500 to $2,750. Rita asks you to update the bonus amount for pay grade 1 so the employee bonuses will be current.

> ## To update the Bonus amount for pay grade 1:
>
> ▶ **1.** In cell Y2, enter **2750**.
>
> ▶ **2.** Scroll to the Bonus column and observe that all employees with a pay grade equal to 1 now show a bonus amount equal to $2,750.

Exploring the OR Function

The **OR function** is a logical function that returns a TRUE value if any of the logical conditions are true and a FALSE value if all the logical conditions are false. The syntax of the OR function is as follows:

```
OR(logical1 [,logical2,]...)
```

In this function, *logical1* and *logical2* are conditions that can be either true or false. If any of the logical conditions are true, the OR function returns the logical value TRUE; otherwise, the function returns the logical value FALSE. You can include up to 255 logical conditions in the OR function. However, keep in mind that *if any* logical condition listed in the OR function is true, the OR function returns a TRUE value.

Talent Tracs' executive team is considering changing the criteria to determine which employees receive a bonus. They are considering excluding employees who have worked at Talent Tracs for less than one year or employees who earn more than $100,000 and have other compensation packages.

The OR function can be nested within the IF function to determine employees who are not eligible for a bonus under the proposed criteria and assign a 0 bonus for those employees. The modified formula to calculate the bonus is as follows:

```
=IF(OR([Years Service]<1,[Annual Salary]>100000),0, IF([Pay Grade]=
1,$T$1,IF([Pay Grade]=2,$T$2, IF([Pay Grade]=3,$T$3,"Invalid pay
grade"))))
```

This formula uses the OR function to test whether the current cell for Years Service is less than 1 and also whether the current cell for Annual Salary is greater than 100,000 (shown in red). If either condition or both conditions are true, the OR function returns a TRUE value and 0 is entered in the Bonus cell. If both conditions are false, the OR function returns a FALSE value and determines the bonus for the employee using the nested IF functions you just entered to calculate bonuses based on the pay grade (shown in blue).

In this session, you used the IF and AND functions to calculate the additional life insurance premium and 401(k) benefits for Talent Tracss' employees. You also used nested IF functions to calculate the employee bonuses. Next, Rita needs to calculate health plan costs and the employee recognition award for each employee. She also wants to ensure the validity of data entered into the Employee table and then summarize the results in the Employee Summary worksheet. You'll complete these tasks in the next sessions.

Session 7.1 Quick Check | Review

1. What changes occur in an Excel table's appearance and size after you enter the new column header *Phone*?

2. What term describes the following behavior in Excel: Whenever you enter a formula in an empty column of an Excel table, Excel automatically fills the column with the same formula.

3. An Excel worksheet stores the cost per meal in cell C5, the number of attendees in cell C6, and the total cost of meals in cell C7. What IF function would you enter in cell C7 to calculate the total cost of meals (cost per meal times the number of attendees) with a minimum cost of $10,000?

4. True or False? The AND function is a logical function that returns a TRUE value if any of the logical conditions are true and a FALSE value if all of the logical conditions are false.

5. Write the formula that displays the label *Outstanding* if the amount owed (cell J5) is above 0 and the transaction date (cell D5) is before 3/15/2008, but otherwise leaves the cell blank.

6. When you create a formula that references all or part of an Excel table, you can replace the specific cell or range address with the actual table name or column header name. What are these references called?

7. What are you creating when you include one IF function inside another IF function?

Session 7.2

Using Lookup Tables and Functions

At Talent Tracs, all employees are eligible for the company's health plan. Employees can choose one of four health plans: an HMO for individuals (HMOI), an HMO for families (HMOF), a PPO for individuals (PPOI), and a PPO for families (PPOF). Each health plan has a different monthly premium, and Talent Tracs pays the entire amount. If an employee shows evidence of coverage elsewhere, there is no health plan cost. Figure 7-12 shows the HealthPlanRates table that Rita created with the cost per employee for the different available health plans.

HealthPlanRates table   Figure 7-12

	Plan	Monthly Premium
4	HMOF	$ 1,500
5	HMOI	$ 875
6	PPOF	$ 1,650
7	PPOI	$ 950
8	None	$ -

Rita created a flowchart to explain the logic for determining health plan costs, as shown in Figure 7-13. The flowchart shows that if the employee chooses the HMO for Family health plan (Health Plan=HMOF), then Talent Tracs pays $1500 per month (Health Plan Cost=1500) and the IF function is finished. If the employee chooses the HMO for Individual health plan (Health Plan=HMOI), then Talent Tracs pays $875 per month (Health Plan Cost=875) and the IF function is finished. If the employee chooses the PPO for Family health plan (Health Plan=PPOF), then Talent Tracs pays $1650 per month (Health Plan Cost=1650) and the IF function is finished. If the employee chooses the PPO for Individual health plan (Health Plan=PPOI), then Talent Tracs pays $950 per month (Health Plan Cost=950) and the IF function is finished. If the employee chooses none of the health plans (Health Plan=None), then Talent Tracs pays $0 per month (Health Plan Cost=0), and the IF function is finished.

Figure 7-13   **Flowchart illustrating the logic of calculating health plan costs**

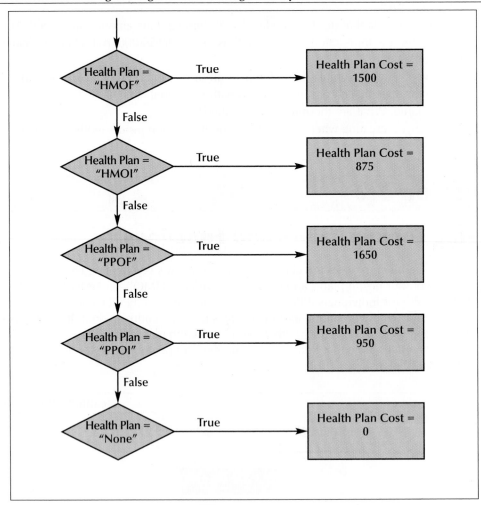

You could calculate these health plan costs using several nested IF functions. However, an easier approach is to use a lookup table. A **lookup table** is a table that organizes data you want to retrieve into different categories, such as each health plan code. The categories for the lookup table, called **compare values**, are located in the table's first column or row. To retrieve a particular value from the table, a **lookup value** (the value you are trying to find) needs to match the compare values. When the lookup value matches a particular compare value, a value from an appropriate column (or row) in the lookup table is returned to the cell in which the lookup formula is entered or used as part of a more complex formula.

You can use the HealthPlanRates table shown in Figure 7-12 that Rita created in the Lookup Tables worksheet as a lookup table. For example, the health plan cost for each eligible employee is based on the plan the employee selected. The lookup value is the employee's health plan code, which is entered in column L of the Employee table. The compare values come from the first column of the HealthPlanRates table, which is in the range B4:C8 in the Lookup Tables worksheet. To retrieve the monthly cost for an employee, Excel moves down the first column in the lookup table (HealthPlanRates) until it finds the health plan code that matches (is equal to) the lookup value. Then, it moves to the second column in the lookup table to locate the monthly cost, which is displayed in the cell where the lookup formula is entered or used as part of a calculation.

To retrieve correct values from the lookup table, you use either the VLOOKUP or HLOOKUP function. VLOOKUP and HLOOKUP functions search a lookup table and, based on what you entered, retrieve the appropriate value from that table. The **VLOOKUP** (vertical lookup) **function** searches vertically down the lookup table and is used when the compare values are stored in the first column of the lookup table. The **HLOOKUP** (horizontal lookup) **function** searches horizontally across the lookup table and is used when the compare values are stored in the first row of the lookup table.

The HealthPlanRates table's compare values are in the first column, so you will use the VLOOKUP function. The HLOOKUP function works similarly. The VLOOKUP function has the following syntax:

```
VLOOKUP(lookup_value, table_array, col_index_num, [range_lookup])
```

In this function, *lookup_value* is the value you want to use to search the first column of the lookup table; *table_array* is the cell reference of the lookup table or its table name, *col_index_num* is the number of the column in the lookup table that contains the value you want to return, and *range_lookup* indicates whether the compare values are a range of values (sometimes referred to as an approximate match) or an exact match. When you use a range of values (such as in a tax rate table), you set the *range_lookup* value to TRUE; when you want the *lookup_value* to exactly match a value in the first column of the *table_array* (such as in the HealthPlanRates table), you set the *range_lookup* value to FALSE. The *range_lookup* argument is optional; if you don't include a *range_lookup* value, the value is considered TRUE (an approximate match).

Looking Up an Exact Match

You'll use the VLOOKUP function to calculate the annual health plan cost for Talent Tracs. You'll use the VLOOKUP function because you want to search the values in the first column of the lookup table. You can use range references or structured references when you create the formula for the annual health plan cost for an employee from the HealthPlanRates table shown earlier in Figure 7-12, as follows (the first formula uses range references, and the second formula uses structured references):

```
=VLOOKUP(L2,'Lookup Tables'!$B$4:$C$8,2,FALSE)*12
=VLOOKUP([HealthPlan],HealthPlanRates,2,FALSE)*12
```

The formula uses the VLOOKUP function to search for the code in the Health Plan column (column L) of the Employee table in the first column of the lookup table (the HealthPlanRates table in the range B4:C8 in the Lookup Tables worksheet), and then return the value in the second column of the HealthPlanRates lookup table, which shows the monthly cost. This value is then multiplied by 12 to return the annual cost. The formula uses FALSE as the *range_lookup* argument because you want the lookup value to exactly match a value in the first column of the HealthPlanRates table.

To use the VLOOKUP function in the Employee table to find an exact match in the HealthPlanRates table:

▶ **1.** If you took a break after the previous session, make sure the Talent Tracs workbook is open and the Employee Data worksheet is active.

▶ **2.** In cell Q1, enter **Health Cost**. The table expands to include the new column and the table's formatting is applied to all rows in the new column.

▶ **3.** Make sure cell **Q2** is the active cell, and then click the **Insert Function** button f_x on the formula bar. The Insert Function dialog box opens.

▶ **4.** Click the **Or select a category** arrow, click **Lookup & Reference**, and then double-click **VLOOKUP** at the bottom of the function list. The Function Arguments dialog box opens.

▶ **5.** Drag the Function Arguments dialog box below row 2 to make it easier to see the column headers.

▶ **6.** In the Lookup_value argument box, enter **L2**. The *lookup_value* is the employee's health plan code, which is located in column L.

Next, you'll enter the *table_array* argument, which is equal to the range containing the HealthPlanRates table located in the Lookup Tables worksheet.

▶ **7.** Click the Table_array argument **Collapse** button to shrink the dialog box to show only the Table_array argument box, switch to the **Lookup Tables** worksheet, select the range **B4:C8** (the HealthPlanRates table), and then click the **Expand** button to return the dialog box to its full size. The table name *HealthPlanRates* appears in the Table_array argument box. If the HealthPlanRates data was entered in a range of cells instead of an Excel table, the table_array would be *'Lookup Tables'!B4:B8*, and you would need to change the range to absolute references *'Lookup Tables'!$B$4:$B$8* so the formula would copy correctly to other cells.

▶ **8.** In the Col_index_num argument box, enter **2**. The number 2 indicates the monthly cost is stored in the second column of the HealthPlanRates lookup table. When entering the col_index_num value, be sure to enter the number that corresponds to the column's position within the lookup table, rather than its column letter.

▶ **9.** In the Range_lookup argument box, enter **FALSE**. This sets the function to find an exact match in the lookup table. See Figure 7-14.

Tip

If you see *#NAME?* or *#VALUE!* as the result of a VLOOKUP formula, you might have entered a letter for the col_index_num instead of a number.

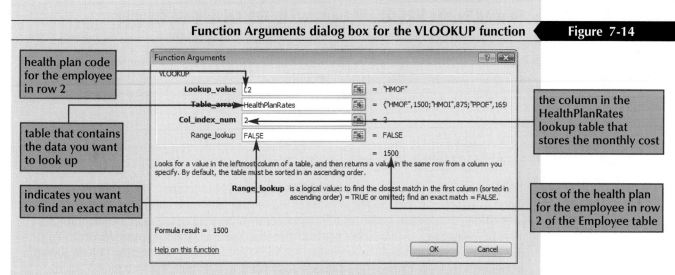

Function Arguments dialog box for the VLOOKUP function ◀ **Figure 7-14**

10. Click the **OK** button. The dialog box closes and the result 1500 appears in cell Q2. The formula *VLOOKUP(L2,HealthPlanRates,2,FALSE)* appears in the formula bar. The remaining rows in the Health Cost column are filled with the VLOOKUP function. If a value in column L does not match a value in the first column of the HealthPlanRates table, there is not an exact match and #N/A appears in the cell, as you'll see shortly.

11. Format the Health Cost values in the **Accounting** number format with no decimal places. Recall that a dash indicates a 0 in the Accounting number format. See Figure 7-15.

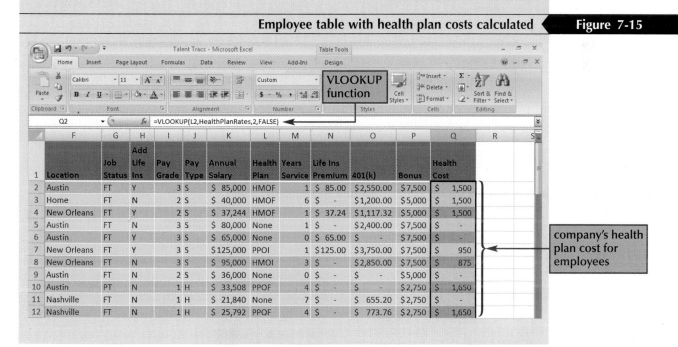

Employee table with health plan costs calculated ◀ **Figure 7-15**

The health plan costs in the Employee table are monthly amounts rather than annual. You need to modify the formula in the Health Cost column to reflect the annual amounts. Because the formula is in a calculated table column, you need to make the change in only one cell and the change will automatically be copied to all the cells in the column.

To modify the VLOOKUP function in the calculated column:

▶ **1.** Double-click cell **Q2** to enter editing mode and display the formula in the cell.

▶ **2.** Click at the end of the formula, type ***12** to multiply the monthly amount by 12, and then press the **Enter** key. The amount in cell Q2 changes to $18,000 and all the other cells in the column are updated with the revised formula and display the annual cost.

Looking Up an Approximate Match

The previous table lookup used the HealthPlanRates table to return a value only if Excel found an exact match in the first column of the lookup table. The categories in the first column or row of a lookup table can also represent a range of values. As part of Talent Tracs 10-year anniversary, management plans to give employee recognition awards based on the number of years individuals have worked for Talent Tracs. Rita developed the criteria shown in Figure 7-16 to summarize how the company plans to distribute the recognition award.

Figure 7-16 ▶ **Recognition award distribution based on years of service**

Years of Service	Award
>=0 years and < 1 year	0
>=1 year and <3 years	100
>=3 years and <5 years	200
>=5 years and <7 years	300
7 years or more	500

In the recognition awards table, you are not looking for an *exact match* for the lookup value. Instead, you need to use an *approximate match* lookup, which determines whether the lookup value falls within a range of values. You want to use the table lookup to determine what service range an employee falls into and then return the recognition award based on the appropriate row. To accomplish this, you must rearrange the first column of the lookup table so each compare value (row) in the table represents the low end of the category range. Rita followed this format when she created the Recognition lookup table as shown in Figure 7-17.

Figure 7-17 ▶ **Recognition award table converted to a lookup table**

	F	G	H	I
1				
2				
3		Years of Service	Recognition Award	
4		0	$ -	
5		1	$ 100	
6		3	$ 200	
7		5	$ 300	
8		7	$ 500	
9				

To determine whether a lookup value falls within a range of values in the revised lookup table, Excel searches the first column of the table until it locates the largest value that is still less than the lookup value. Then, Excel moves across the table to retrieve the appropriate row. For example, an employee working at Talent Tracs for six years would receive a $300 employee recognition award.

Setting Up an Approximate Match Lookup Table | InSight

When a lookup table is used with a range of values, the compare values must be sorted in alphabetical order if they are text, and low-to-high order if they are numbers. When the compare values are arranged in a different order, Excel cannot retrieve the correct results. In this case, the VLOOKUP function seems incorrect, but the real problem is how the lookup table is organized. The setup of the lookup table in an approximate match is critical for a VLOOKUP formula to work as intended.

Consider the following example, in which an instructor uses Excel to calculate grades. The instructor assigns final grades based on the grading policy shown below, on the left. To set up the lookup table correctly, the leftmost column in the lookup table must represent the lower end of the range for each category *and* the lookup table must be sorted in ascending order based on the value in the first column. Otherwise, Excel cannot retrieve the correct result. Following this structure, the lookup table for the instructor's grading policy would be arranged as shown below, on the right.

Grading Policy			Lookup Table	
Score	**Grade**		**Score**	**Grade**
90–100	A		0	F
80–89	B		60	D
70–79	C		70	C
60–69	D		80	B
0–59	F		90	A

If a VLOOKUP or HLOOKUP function with an approximate match doesn't return the values you expected, first confirm that you entered the formula correctly. Then, verify that the lookup table has the proper arrangement.

You'll create the formula in the Employee table to determine the recognition award for each employee. You will use an approximate match VLOOKUP formula because the years of service in the lookup table has a range of values.

To insert an approximate match VLOOKUP formula:

▸ 1. In cell R1, enter **Award**. A new column is added to the table.

▸ 2. In cell R2, type **=V** and then double-click **VLOOKUP**. The start of the formula =VLOOKUP(appears in the cell and formula bar.

▸ 3. Type **[** to open a list of all the column headers in the Employee table, scroll down and double-click **Years Service**, and then type **]**, to complete the entry for the first argument of the VLOOKUP function.

▸ 4. Type **R** and then double-click **Recognition** to enter the second argument, the lookup table. *Recognition* is the name of the Excel table in the range G4:H8 in the Lookup Tables worksheet.

▸ 5. Type **,2)** to complete the VLOOKUP formula. The number 2 indicates the column number in the Recognition lookup table where the award amount is stored. You did not enter the optional fourth argument in the VLOOKUP formula; Excel assumes the value to be TRUE and uses an approximate match table lookup.

Tip

You can also enter a column header in a formula by starting to type the name of the column header until it is highlighted in the list, and then pressing the Tab key.

▶ **6.** Press the **Enter** key. Each cell in the calculated column Award is filled. The employee in row 2 has 1 year of service and will receive a recognition award of $100. The employee in row 3 has 6 years of service and will receive an award of $300. This second employee is a good illustration of the approximate match lookup, because 6 is not equal to a value in the first column of the lookup table. Instead, it falls within two values in the table. See Figure 7-18.

Figure 7-18 **Recognition award column**

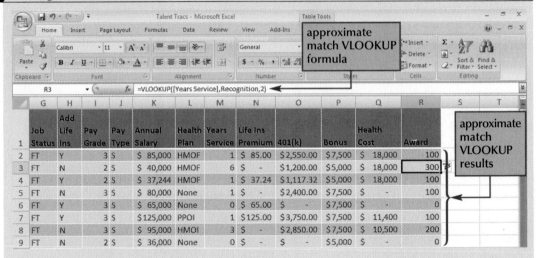

▶ **7.** Format the Award values in the **Accounting** number format with no decimals places, and then AutoFit the column width.

Checking for Data Entry Errors

Rita believes the current data in the Employee table is accurate, but she is concerned that invalid data could be entered into the table. She wants to use conditional formatting and the IFERROR function to help reduce data entry errors.

Reference Window | **Highlighting Duplicate Records with a Custom Format**

- Select the column you want to search for duplicates.
- In the Styles group on the Home tab, click the Conditional Formatting button, point to Highlight Cells Rules, and then click Duplicate Values.
- Click the values with arrow, and then click Custom Format.
- In the Format Cells dialog box, set the formatting you want to use.
- Click the OK button in each dialog box.

Highlighting Duplicate Values with Conditional Formatting

Conditional formatting changes a cell's formatting when its contents match a specified condition. You've already used conditional formatting to add data bars that indicate the relative values in a range and to add highlights to cells based on their values for emphasis. Now you'll use conditional formatting to highlight duplicate values in a column of data. Duplicate value highlighting helps verify that columns of data have unique entries, such as the employee ID column in the Employee table. Rita wants you to change the background color of records that have duplicate employee IDs to red. This alert will help Rita ensure that each employee is entered in the table only once.

To highlight duplicate records in the Employee table:

▶ 1. Scroll to column A, point to the top of cell **A1** until the pointer changes to ⬇, and then click the top of cell **A1** just below the column header. Rows 2 through 101 in the ID column are selected.

▶ 2. Click the **Home** tab on the Ribbon, and then, in the Styles group, click the **Conditional Formatting** button.

▶ 3. Point to **Highlight Cells Rules**, and then click **Duplicate Values**. The Duplicate Values dialog box opens.

▶ 4. Click the **values with** arrow to display a list of formatting options, and then click **Custom Format** to create a format that is not in the list. The Format Cells dialog box opens. You'll change the background fill color to red.

▶ 5. Click the **Fill** tab, and then, in the Background Color palette, click **Red** (the second color in the last row).

▶ 6. Click the **OK** button in the Format Cells dialog box, and then click the **OK** button in the Duplicate Values dialog box. Any duplicate values in the ID column are in a red cell.

▶ 7. Scroll the table to see if any duplicate values are found.

No duplicate records are found in the Employee table. You need to test the conditional format to make sure it works as intended. As you build a formula, you should test all situations to verify how the formula performs in each case. In this case, you should test the column both with duplicate values and without duplicate values. You'll intentionally change the ID of the last record from 1123 to 1024, which is the ID of the first employee, to confirm the duplicate IDs are formatted in red cells. Then, you will return the ID to its original value and confirm that the duplicate highlighting is removed.

To test that the duplicate value conditional format works correctly:

▶ 1. Click in the **Name** box, type **A101**, and then press the **Enter** key. The active cell moves to the last record in the Employee table.

▶ 2. In cell A101, enter **1024**. The ID changes from 1123 to 1024 and red fills this cell because it has a duplicate ID. See Figure 7-19.

Duplicate record highlighted   ◀   **Figure 7-19**

	A	B	C	D	E	F	G	H	I	J	K	L	M	N
99	1121	Winters	2/14/2002	3/1/1953	F	Nashville	FT	N	1	H	$ 33,800	PPOF	8	$ -
100	1122	Wang	8/24/1998	8/11/1966	F	Austin	FT	N	1	H	$ 35,048	PPOI	11	$ -
101	1024	Harrison	6/19/2009	11/25/1963	M	Austin	FT	N	2	S	$ 41,000	PPOF	1	$ -
102														
103														

▶   **3.** Press the **Ctrl+Home** keys to move to the top of the table. Cell A2 also has a red background fill because it has the same ID you entered in cell A101. Excel identified the duplicate records.

Sometimes you might find that the built-in conditional formatting rules do not fit your needs. In these cases, you can create a conditional formatting rule based on a formula that uses a logical expression to describe the condition you want. For example, you can create a formula that uses conditional formatting to compare cells in different columns or to highlight an entire row.

When you create the formula, keep in mind the following guidelines:

- The formula must start with an equal sign.
- The formula must be in the form of a logical test that results in a true or false value.
- In most cases, the formula should use relative references and point to the first row of data in the table. If the formula references a cell or range outside the table, use an absolute reference.
- After you create the formula, enter test values to ensure the conditional formatting works in all situations that you intended.

For example, to use conditional formatting to highlight whether the Hire Date entered in column C is less than the Birth Date entered in column D (which would indicate a data entry error), you need to enter a formula that applies conditional formatting that compares cells in different columns of a table. Do the following:

1. Select the range you want to format (in this case, the Hire Date column).
2. Click the Conditional Formatting button in the Styles group on the Home tab, and then click New Rule.
3. In the Select a Rule Type box, click the "Use a formula to determine which cells to format" rule.
4. In the Format values where this formula is true box, enter the appropriate formula (in this case, =C2<D2).
5. Click the Format button to open the Format Cells dialog box, and select the formatting you want to apply.
6. Click the OK button in each dialog box.

Another example is to highlight the entire row if an employee has 10 or more years of service. In this case, you would select the range of data, such as A2:R101, and enter =M$2>10 in the Format values where this formula is true box. The other steps remain the same.

The red background fill makes the text difficult to read. Rita asks you to use yellow as the fill color to better contrast with the black text. After you apply a conditional format, you can modify it from the Conditional Formatting Rules Manager dialog box.

Using the Conditional Formatting Rules Manager

Each time you create a conditional format, you are defining a conditional formatting rule. A **rule** specifies the type of condition (such as formatting cells greater than a specified value), the type of formatting when that condition occurs (such as light red fill with dark red text), and the cell or range the formatting is applied to. You can edit existing conditional formatting rules from the Conditional Formatting Rules Manager dialog box. You'll use this dialog box to edit the rule that specifies the formatting applied to duplicate values in the ID column of the Employee table.

To change the duplicate values background fill color to yellow:

▶ **1.** In the Styles group on the Home tab, click the **Conditional Formatting** button, and then click **Manage Rules**. The Conditional Formatting Rules Manager dialog box opens, listing all the formatting rules for the current selection, which, in this case, is the Employee table.

▶ **2.** Verify that the Show formatting rules for box displays **This Table**. All the rules currently in effect in the Employee table are displayed. You can add new rules and edit or delete existing rules. You also can control which formatting rules are displayed in the dialog box, such as all rules in a specific worksheet or table. See Figure 7-20.

Conditional Formatting Rules Manager dialog box Figure 7-20

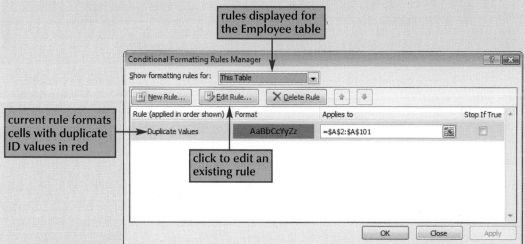

rules displayed for the Employee table

current rule formats cells with duplicate ID values in red

click to edit an existing rule

You want to change the Duplicate Values rule to use a yellow background fill color for duplicate entries in the ID column.

▶ **3.** Click **Duplicate Values** in the Rule list to select the rule, and then click the **Edit Rule** button. The Edit Formatting Rule dialog box opens. See Figure 7-21.

Edit Formatting Rule dialog box Figure 7-21

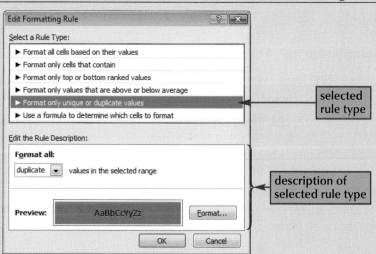

selected rule type

description of selected rule type

▶ **4.** Click the **Format** button. The Format Cells dialog box opens.

▶ **5.** Click the **Fill** tab, if necessary, and then click **Yellow** in the Background Color palette (the fourth color in the last row).

6. Click the **OK** button in each dialog box. The duplicate records in the table are now formatted with a yellow background color. See Figure 7-22.

Figure 7-22 **Revised conditional format for duplicate records**

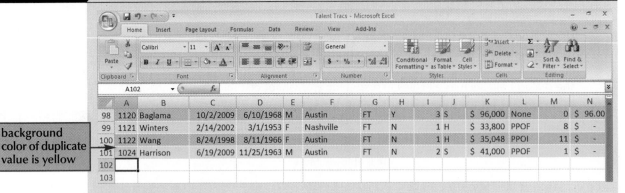

background color of duplicate value is yellow

	A	B	C	D	E	F	G	H	I	J	K	L	M	N
98	1120	Baglama	10/2/2009	6/10/1968	M	Austin	FT	Y		3 S	$ 96,000	None	0	$ 96.00
99	1121	Winters	2/14/2002	3/1/1953	F	Nashville	FT	N		1 H	$ 33,800	PPOF	8	$ -
100	1122	Wang	8/24/1998	8/11/1966	F	Austin	FT	N		1 H	$ 35,048	PPOI	11	$ -
101	1024	Harrison	6/19/2009	11/25/1963	M	Austin	FT	N		2 S	$ 41,000	PPOF	1	$ -
102														
103														

The cell text is easier to read on the yellow background. You can filter the duplicate records by color. This enables you to view only records that are duplicates, because they are in the yellow background.

To filter duplicate records by color:

1. Click the **Data** tab on the Ribbon, and then, in the Sort & Filter group, click the **Filter** button. Filter arrows appear on the column headers.

2. Click the **ID** filter arrow to open the Filter menu, and then point to **Filter by Color** to display the Filter by Cell Color palette.

3. Click the **yellow** color. The filter is applied and only records with a yellow cell color (duplicate records) are displayed.

You'll redisplay all records.

4. Click the **ID** filter arrow to open the Filter menu, and then click **Clear Filter From "ID"**. The filter is removed and all of the records are displayed.

5. In the Sort & Filter group on the Data tab, click the **Filter** button to remove the filter arrows from the column headers.

Tip

You can also sort records by color. Click the filter arrow to open the Filter menu, and then click Sort by Color.

You'll correct the duplicate ID in cell A101 by entering the employee's actual ID number.

To correct the duplicate ID:

1. In cell A101, enter **1123**. The employee's ID is updated and the conditional formatting is removed because the value in the ID column is no longer a duplicate. However, the conditional formatting is still active. This rule will apply to any new records that Rita adds to the Employee table, which will help her to ensure that each employee has only one record in the table.

2. Scroll to the top of the Employee table, and verify that the conditional formatting no longer appears in cell A2.

3. Click cell **A1**.

The Duplicate Values rule enables you to verify that each entry in the ID column is unique, but it doesn't ensure that each unique value is accurate. Excel uses error values to help you find incorrectly entered data.

Using the IFERROR Function

Only five codes are used for the Health Plan column—PPOI, PPOF, HMOI, HMOF, and None. Rita wants to make sure that only these five valid codes are entered in the Health Plan column because the formula in the Health Cost column requires a valid health plan code. For instance, entering an inaccurate health plan code for an employee, such as HMOG instead of HMOF, would result in the error value (#N/A) in the Health Cost cell because the VLOOKUP function cannot find the invalid code in the HealthPlanRates lookup table.

Error values such as #DIV/0!, #N/A, and #VALUE! indicate that some element in a formula or a cell referenced in a formula is preventing Excel from returning a calculated value. An error value begins with a number sign (#) followed by an error name, which indicates the type of error. Figure 7-23 describes common error values you might see in workbooks.

Excel error values ◀ **Figure 7-23**

Error Value	Description of Error
#DIV/0!	The formula or function contains a number divided by 0.
#NAME?	Excel doesn't recognize text in the formula or function, such as when the function name is misspelled.
#N/A	A value is not available to a function or formula, which can occur when an invalid value is specified in the LOOKUP function.
#NULL!	A formula or function requires two cell ranges to intersect, but they don't.
#NUM!	Invalid numbers are used in a formula or function, such as text entered in a function that requires a number.
#REF!	A cell reference used in a formula or function is no longer valid, which can occur when a cell used by the function was deleted from the worksheet.
#VALUE!	The wrong type of argument is used in a function or formula, which can occur when you supply a range of values to a function that requires a single value.

These error value messages are not particularly meaningful or helpful, so Rita wants you to display a more descriptive message when Excel detects an error value. If a record includes an invalid health plan code, #N/A appears in the corresponding Health Cost cell because the VLOOKUP function doesn't find a value in the first column of the lookup table and cannot return a value. The IFERROR function enables you to display a more descriptive message that helps users fix the problem rather than adding confusion, as error values often do. The **IFERROR function** can determine if a cell contains an error value and display the message you choose rather than the default error value. The IFERROR function has the following syntax:

```
IFERROR(expression,valueIfError)
```

In this function, *expression* is the formula you want to check for an error and *valueIfError* is the message you want displayed if Excel detects an error in the formula you are checking. If Excel does not detect an error, the result of the *expression* is displayed.

The IFERROR function enables you to easily find and handle formula errors. For example, you can enter the following formula to determine whether an invalid code was entered in the Health Plan column of the Employee table:

```
=IFERROR(VLOOKUP(L2,HealthPlanRates,2,False)*12,"Invalid code")
```

Based on this formula, if the value in cell L2 is HMOF, the result of the VLOOKUP formula is $1,500 (a value from the HealthPlanRates table), and then the first argument in the IFERROR function (shown in blue) is executed. On the other hand, if cell L2 has an invalid Health Plan code, such as HMOG, the VLOOKUP function returns the error value #N/A, and then the second argument in the IFERROR function (shown in red) is executed, and the message "Invalid code" is displayed. You will scan the Health Cost column to verify that all employees have been assigned a health cost to determine if the formula calculating the health costs is working correctly.

To check for an error value in the Health Cost column:

▸ **1.** Scroll to row 54 of the Health Cost column to see the error value #N/A in cell Q54. See Figure 7-24.

Figure 7-24 ▸ **Error value in Health Cost column**

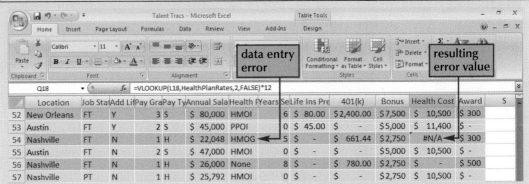

▸ **2.** In row 54 in the Health Plan column, observe that the Health Plan code is HMOG, which is an invalid code.

Rita asks you to modify the formulas in the Health Cost column to display a more descriptive error message. She wants the message "Invalid code" to appear rather than the error value. The IFERROR function will check for errors in the formula, and display the error message you create rather than the error value if it finds an error.

You'll nest the VLOOKUP function within the IFERROR function to display the message "Invalid code" in the Health Cost column if Excel detects an error value.

To nest the VLOOKUP function within the IFERROR function:

▸ **1.** Double-click cell **Q54** to enter editing mode. The formula =VLOOKUP(L54, HealthPlanRates,2,FALSE)*12 appears in the cell and the formula bar.

   You'll nest this formula within the IFERROR function.

▸ **2.** Click to the right of = (the equal sign), and then type **IFERROR(** to begin entering the IFERROR function. The first argument in the IFERROR function is the formula you want to use if no error value is found; this is the VLOOKUP formula already entered in the cell.

▸ **3.** Move the insertion point to the right of the VLOOKUP formula, and then type **,"Invalid code")** to add the text you want to display if an error is found.

▸ **4.** Press the **Enter** key, and then click cell **Q54**. The error message "Invalid code" appears in cell Q54, and the revised formula is automatically copied to all cells in the column. See Figure 7-25.

Figure 7-25

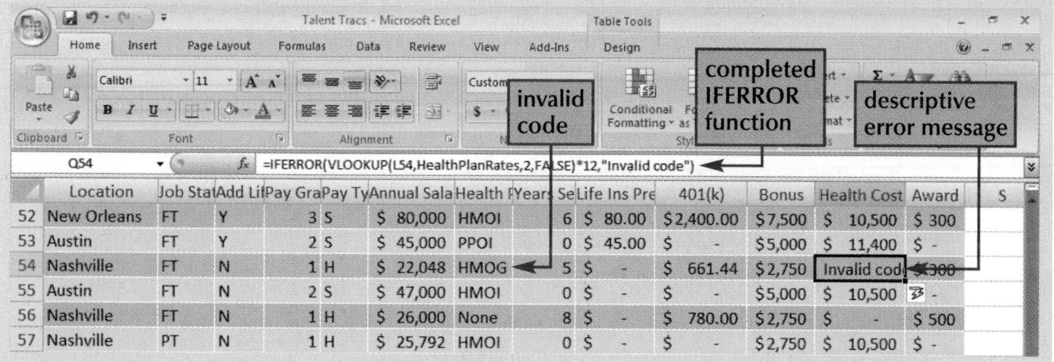

5. In cell L54 (Health Plan), enter **HMOF**. You entered a valid Health Plan code, so the Health Cost value $18,000 appears in cell Q54.

6. Scroll to the top of the table, click cell **Q2**, and observe in the formula bar that the IFERROR formula was copied to this cell.

Tip

You can change a formula in any row of an Excel table (it doesn't have to be the first row) and all values in the column will be updated with the new formula.

Summarizing Data Conditionally

The COUNT function tallies the number of data values in a range, the SUM function adds the values in a range, and the AVERAGE function calculates the average of the values in a range. However, sometimes you need to calculate a conditional count, sum, or average using only those cells that meet a particular condition. In those cases, you need to use the COUNTIF, SUMIF, and AVERAGEIF functions. Rita wants you to create a report that shows the number, total, and average salaries for employees in Austin, New Orleans, and Nashville as well as for employees who work from home.

Using the COUNTIF Function

You can calculate the number of cells in a range that match criteria you specify using the **COUNTIF function**, which is sometimes referred to as a **conditional count**. The COUNTIF function has the following syntax:

```
COUNTIF(range, criteria)
```

In this function, *range* is the range of cells you want to count and *criteria* is an expression that defines which cells to count. Rita wants to know how many employees are located in Austin. You can use the COUNTIF function to find this answer, because you want a conditional count (a count of employees who meet a specified criterion; in this case, "employees located in Austin"). The location information is stored in column F of the Employee table. To count the number of employees in Austin, you can use either one of the following formulas (the first uses cell references, and the second uses fully qualified structured references):

```
=COUNTIF('Employee Data'!F2:F101,"Austin")
=COUNTIF(Employee[Location],"Austin")
```

With either formula, Excel counts all the cells in the Location column of the Employee table that contain the text "Austin". Because Austin is a text string, you must enclose it within quotation marks. Numeric criteria are not enclosed in quotes. You will enter this formula using the COUNTIF function in the Employee Summary worksheet.

Tip

You can use structured references or cell and range addresses to reference cells within an Excel table. If an Excel table has not been created for a range of data, you must use cell and range addresses.

To use the COUNTIF function to count employees located in Austin:

▶ **1.** Switch to the **Employee Summary** worksheet. You will enter a formula using worksheet and range references to calculate the number of employees who work in Austin.

▶ **2.** Click cell **C4**, type **=COU**, and then double-click **COUNTIF**. The beginning of the formula, =COUNTIF(, appears in the cell and the formula bar.

▶ **3.** Type **'Employee Data'!F2:F101,** to enter the range to search. In this case, 'Employee Data'!F2:F101 refers to all data values in the range F2:F101 (Location column) of the Employee Data worksheet.

▶ **4.** Type **B4)** to finish the formula. Cell B4, which contains the value Austin, is the criteria. The formula =COUNTIF('Employee Data'!F2:F101,B4) appears in the cell and the formula bar.

▶ **5.** Press the **Enter** key. The value 57 appears in cell C4, indicating the company has 57 employees in Austin.

You will enter a similar formula using structured references to calculate the number of employees who work from home.

To use structured references to enter the COUNTIF function:

▶ **1.** In cell C5, type **=COU**, and then double-click **COUNTIF**. The beginning of the formula, =COUNTIF(, appears in the cell and the formula bar.

▶ **2.** Type **E** and then double-click **Employee**.

▶ **3.** Type **[** to open the list of column headers, double-click **Location**, and then type **],** to complete the first argument of the COUNTIF function. In this formula, the structured reference Employee [Location] refers to the data values in the Location column (F2:F101) of the Employee table.

▶ **4.** Type **B5)**. Cell B5 stores the value Home, which is the criterion. The formula =COUNTIF(Employee[Location],B5) appears in the cell and formula bar.

▶ **5.** Press the **Enter** key. The formula results indicate that 7 employees work from home.

Next, you'll copy the formula in cell C5 to cells C6 and C7.

To copy the COUNTIF function:

▶ **1.** Copy the formula in cell **C5** and then paste the formula in cells **C6** and **C7** to calculate the number of employees for Nashville (cell B6) and New Orleans (cell B7). The formula results show that Talent Tracs has 21 employees working in Nashville and 15 employees working in New Orleans.

▶ **2.** In cell C8, enter a formula with the SUM function to calculate the total number of employees working at Talent Tracs. The formula results show that Talent Tracs has a total of 100 employees.

Using the SUMIF Function

The SUMIF function is similar to the COUNTIF function. You can add the values in a range that meet criteria you specify using the **SUMIF function**, which is also called a **conditional sum**. The syntax of the SUMIF function is:

```
SUMIF(range, criteria[, sum_range])
```

In this formula, *range* is the range of cells that you want to filter before calculating a sum, *criteria* is the condition used in the range to filter the table, and *sum_range* is the range of cells that you want to add. The *sum_range* argument is optional; if you omit it, Excel will add the values specified in the *range* argument. For example, if you want to add the salaries for all employees with salaries greater than $50,000, you do not use the optional third argument.

Rita wants to know the total salaries paid to employees at each location. She can use the SUMIF function to do this, because she wants to conditionally add salaries of employees at a specified location. Each employee's location is recorded in column F of the Employee Data worksheet, and the salary data is stored in column K. The formula to calculate this value is as follows (the first uses cell references, and the second uses fully qualified structured references):

```
=SUMIF('Employee Data'!F2:F101,"Austin",'Employee Data'!K2:K101)
=SUMIF(Employee[Location],"Austin",Employee[Annual Salary])
```

This formula states that employees whose location is "Austin" will have their salary values added to the total. You will insert this formula using the SUMIF function into the Employee Summary worksheet.

To use the SUMIF function:

▶ 1. In cell D4, enter **=SUMIF('Employee Data'!F2:F101,B4,'Employee Data'!K2:K101)**. The value $3,969,426—the total salaries paid to employees in Austin—appears in cell D4. The first argument specifies to use the range F2:F101 from the Employee Data worksheet (Location column) to filter the employee data. The second argument specifies that the criterion is equal to the value in cell B4 (Austin). The third argument indicates that the Annual Salary column, the range K2:K101 in the Employee Data worksheet, is used to add the filtered rows.

You will enter the formula to calculate the total salaries for employees working from home using structured references.

▶ 2. In cell D5, enter **=SUMIF(Employee[Location],B5,Employee[Annual Salary])**. Talent Tracs pays $236,313 per year to employees working from home. The first argument uses the structured reference Employee[Location] to specify you want to use the cells in the Location column to filter the employee data. The second argument specifies that the criterion is equal to the value in cell B5 (Home). The third argument uses the structured reference Employee[Annual Salary] to indicate that the Annual Salary column will be used to add the filtered rows.

▶ 3. Copy the SUMIF formula in cell D5 to the range **D6:D7**. The total salaries per year for employees working in Nashville (from cell B6) is $587,833. The total salaries per year for employees working in New Orleans (from cell B7) is $1,570,994.

▶ 4. In cell D8, use the SUM function to calculate the total of all salaries. The total salaries of all Talent Tracs employees is $6,364,566.

> **5.** If necessary, format the range D4:D8 in the **Accounting** number format with no decimal places.

Using the AVERAGEIF Function

The AVERAGEIF function works in the same way as the SUMIF function. You use the **AVERAGEIF function** to calculate the average of values in a range that meet criteria you specify. The syntax of the AVERAGEIF function is:

```
AVERAGEIF(range,criteria[,average_range])
```

In this function, *range* is the range of cells that you want to filter before calculating the average, *criteria* is the condition used in the range to filter the table, and *average_range* is the range of cells that you want to average. The *average_range* argument is optional; if you omit it, Excel will average the values specified in the *range* argument.

Rita wants to know the average salaries paid to employees at each location. Each employee's location is recorded in column F of the Employee Data worksheet, and the salary data is stored in column K. The formula to calculate this value is as follows (the first formula uses cell references, and the second uses fully qualified structured references):

```
=AVERAGEIF('Employee Data'!F2:F101,"Austin",'Employee Data'!K2:K101)
=AVERAGEIF(Employee[Location],"Austin",Employee[Annual Salary])
```

This formula states that any employee whose location is "Austin" will have his or her salary included in the average. You will enter this formula using the AVERAGEIF function into the Employee Summary worksheet.

To use the AVERAGEIF function:

> **1.** In cell E4, enter **=AVERAGEIF(Employee[Location],B4,Employee[Annual Salary])**. The value 69,639—the average salary paid to employees in Austin—appears in the cell. The first argument indicates that you want to use the cells in the Location column to filter the employee data. The second argument specifies that the criterion to filter the location column is equal to the value in cell D4 (Austin). The third argument indicates that the Annual Salary column will be used to average the filtered rows.
>
> You will enter the formula to calculate the average salaries for employees working at Home, Nashville, and New Orleans.

> **2.** Copy the formula in cell E4 to the range **E5:E7**. Talent Tracs pays an average of $33,759 to employees working at home, $27,992 to employees working in Nashville, and $104,733 to employees working in New Orleans.
>
> Next, you will calculate the average salary at Talent Tracs by dividing the total salaries at Talent Tracs by the number of employees at the company.

> **3.** In cell E8, enter **=D8/C8**. The average salary for all employees is $63,646.

> **4.** If necessary, format the range E4:E8 in the **Accounting** number format with no decimal places.

> **5.** Add a bottom border to the range C7:E7. See Figure 7-26.

Salary analysis of employees by location | **Figure 7-26**

As Rita enters new employees or edits the location or annual salary values of current employees, the values in the Employee Summary worksheet will be automatically updated because the formulas reference the Employee table.

Summarizing Data Using the COUNTIFS, SUMIFS, and AVERAGEIFS Functions

The COUNTIFS, SUMIFS, and AVERAGEIFS functions are similar to the COUNTIF, SUMIF, and AVERAGEIF functions except with the latter functions you can specify only one condition to summarize the data, whereas the former functions enable you to summarize the data using several conditions.

The **COUNTIFS function** counts the number of cells within a range that meet multiple criteria. Its syntax is as follows:

```
COUNTIFS(criteria_range1,criteria1[,criteria_range2,criteria2...])
```

In this function, *criteria_range1, criteria_range2*, represents up to 127 ranges (columns of data) in which to evaluate the associated criteria, and *criteria1, criteria2* and up to 127 criteria in the form of a number, expression, cell reference, or text define which cells will be counted. Criteria can be expressed as a number such as 50 to find a number equal to 50, ">10000" to find an amount greater than 10000, "FT" to find a text value equal to FT, or B4 to find the value equal to the value stored in cell B4. Each cell in a range is counted only if all of the corresponding criteria specified in the COUNTIFS function are true.

For example, to count the number of full-time employees (FT) who are female (F) and earn more than $50,000, you can use the following function:

```
=COUNTIFS(Employee[Job Status],"FT",Employee[SEX],"F",Employee
[Annual Salary],">50000")
```

This function counts the full-time employees using the argument combination Employee [Job Status],"FT", that are female using the arguments Employee[Sex],"F", and have a salary greater than 50,000 using the arguments Employee[Annual Salary],">50000".

The SUMIFS and AVERAGEIFS functions have a slightly different syntax. The **SUMIFS function** adds values in a range that meet multiple criteria using the following syntax:

```
SUMIFS(sum_range,criteria_range1,criteria1[,criteria_range2,
criteria2...])
```

In the SUMIFS function, *sum_range* is the range you want to add; *criteria_range1*, *criteria_range2*, represent up to 127 ranges (columns of data) in which to evaluate the associated criteria; and *criteria1*, *criteria2* and so on up to 127 criteria in the form of a number, expression, cell reference, or text define which cells will be added.

For example, to calculate the total salary paid to full-time (FT) employees hired after 2007 who are living in Austin, you can use the following SUMIFS function:

```
=SUMIFS(Employee[Annual Salary],Employee[Location],"Austin",
Employee[Hire Date],">=1/1/2008",Employee[Job Status],"FT")
```

This function adds the salaries (Employee[Annual Salary]) of employees located in Austin using the argument combination Employee[Location],"Austin", having a hire date on or later than 1/1/2008 using the arguments Employee[Hire Date],">=1/1/2008", and are full-time employees using arguments Employee [Job Status],"FT".

The **AVERAGEIFS function** calculates the average of values within a range of cells that meet multiple conditions. Its syntax is as follows:

```
AVERAGEIFS(average_range,criteria_range1,criteria1[,criteria_range2,
criteria2...])
```

In this function, *average_range* is the range to average; *criteria_range1*, *criteria_range2*, represent up to 127 ranges in which to evaluate the associated criteria; and *criteria1*, *criteria2* and so on up to 127 criteria in the form of a number, expression, cell reference, or text define which cells will be averaged.

For example, to calculate the average salary paid to males (M) who have worked at Talent Tracs for more than 5 years, you can use the following AVERAGEIFS function:

```
=AVERAGEIFS(Employee[Annual Salary],Employee[Sex],"M", Employee[Years
Service],">5")
```

This function averages the salaries (Employee[Annual Salary]) of male employees using the arguments Employee[Sex],"M", having more than 5 years of service using the arguments Employee[Years Service],">5".

In this session, you used the VLOOKUP function to calculate the health plan cost and employee recognition award. You used conditional formatting to identify duplicate employee IDs and the IFERROR function to help you correct errors. You used functions and features that deal with conditional situations. In the next session, you will use advanced filtering techniques to find potential candidates for a new full-time position and Database functions to prepare a report on the number of employees in each health plan who are classified as salaried and hourly.

Review | **Session 7.2 Quick Check**

1. Explain the difference between an exact match and approximate match table lookup.
2. A customers table includes name, street address, city, state abbreviation, and zip code. A second table includes state abbreviations and state names from all 50 states. You need to add a new column to the customers table with the state name. What is the most appropriate function to use to display the state name in this new column?
3. Would you apply the duplicate value conditional formatting rule to a table column of last names? Why or why not?

4. In cell D5, the error value #DIV/0! is displayed when you divide by 0. Use the IFERROR function with the formula =C5/C25 so instead of the error value #DIV/0!, you display the message "Dividing by 0" in the cell.

5. Explain what the formula =COUNTIF(Employee[SEX],"F") calculates.

6. Explain what the formula =AVERAGEIF(Employee[Pay Type],"H",(Employee[Salary]) calculates.

7. If you receive a worksheet that includes conditional formatting, which dialog box would you use to find out the criteria for the formatting?

Session 7.3

Using Advanced Filtering

Talent Tracs is growing rapidly and management plans to hire additional full-time employees. Rita wants to give first preference to part-time employees and consultants currently working for the company. She asks you to create a list of individuals who meet the following criteria:

- Consultants who have worked for Talents Tracs for more than three years earning less than $55,000

  or

- Part-time employees who have worked for Talent Tracs for two or more years

You need to use advanced filtering features to retrieve the list of individuals Rita wants. Advanced filtering enables you to perform OR conditions across multiple fields, such as the criteria Rita wants you to use to find eligible candidates within the company for the new full-time positions. You can also use advanced filtering to create complex criteria using functions and formulas. For example, if Rita wants to find all female salaried employees whose salary falls below the median salary for all employees, she could use advanced filtering.

Advanced filtering, similar to filtering, displays a subset of the rows in a table or range of data. The primary difference is that you specify criteria in a range outside the data you want to filter. So, before you can use advanced filters, you need to create a criteria range. The **criteria range** is an area in a worksheet, separate from the range of data or Excel table, used to specify the criteria for the data to be displayed after the filter is applied to the table. The criteria range consists of a header row that lists one or more field names from the table's header row and at least one row of the specific filtering criteria for each field. A criteria range must include at least two rows. The first row must contain field names (column headers). All other rows consist of the criteria. Figure 7-27 shows the criteria range you will create to display the eligible candidates within the company for the new full-time positions.

| Figure 7-27 | Criteria range above Excel table |

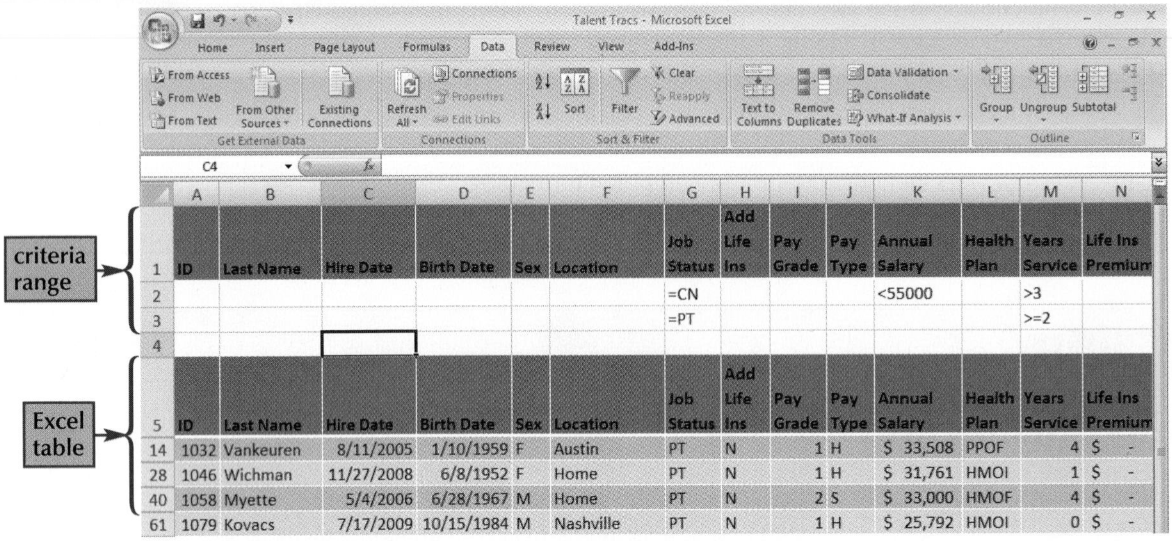

To create a criteria range, you need to specify the condition for each criterion. Text, numeric, and date conditions each use different syntax. Figure 7-28 lists the type of condition, corresponding syntax, and an example for each criterion. For example, to develop a criteria range to filter employees whose annual salaries (numeric data) are greater than (condition) 50,000, the top row of the criteria range contains the column header from the Employee table, Annual Salary, and the second row contains the criterion >50000.

| Figure 7-28 | Types of conditions |

Condition	Text Data		Numeric Data		Date Data	
	Syntax	Sample Last Name	Syntax	Sample Annual Salary	Syntax	Sample Hire Date
Exact match	="=text string"	="=Stolt"	value	50000	mm/dd/yyyy	1/3/2010
Begins with	text string	S	does not apply		does not apply	
Greater than	>text string	>S	>value	>50000	>mm/dd/yyyy	>12/31/2009
Greater than or equal to	>=text string	>=S	>=value	>=50000	>= mm/dd/yyyy	>=1/1/2010
Less than	< text string	<S	<value	<50000	<mm/dd/yyyy	<1/1/2010
Less than or equal to	<= text string	<=S	<=value	<=50000	<=mm/dd/yyyy	<=12/31/2009
Between (beginning and ending points must be in separate cells)	>=beginning text string	>=Sa	>= beginning value	>=50000	> beginning mm/dd/yyyy	>=4/1/2010
	<=ending text string	<=Sm	<= ending value	<=60000	< ending mm/dd/yyyy	<=4/30/2010

Understanding Criteria Ranges

The criteria range specifies which records from the Excel table will be included in the filtered data. The following examples illustrate multiple criteria conditions. Criteria placed on the same row are considered connected with the logical operator AND. That means all criteria in the same row must be met before a record is included in the filtered table. Figure 7-29 shows an AND criteria range to retrieve all employees from Nashville who are earning more than $55,000.

Example of AND criteria range   **Figure 7-29**

	F	G	H	I	J	K
1	Location	Job Status	Add Life Ins	Pay Grade	Pay Type	Annual Salary
2	="=Nashville"					>55000
3						

Specifying the equality comparison operator (exact match) for a text string in the criteria range, as in the Location field in Figure 7-29, is not intuitive. When you type a formula in a cell, the equal sign indicates that a formula follows. If you want to indicate the equality comparison operator within the criteria range, you must type the criteria using the following syntax:

    ="=entry"

In this syntax, *entry* is the text or value you want to find.

Criteria placed on separate rows are treated as the logical operator OR. That means records that meet all the criteria on either row in the criteria range will be displayed. Figure 7-30 shows the criteria range to retrieve female employees or employees who are working in Austin.

Example of OR criteria range   **Figure 7-30**

	E	F	G	H	I	J
1	Sex	Location	Job Status	Add Life Ins	Pay Grade	Pay Type
2	="=F"					
3		="=Austin"				
4						

To specify criteria between a range of values in the same field, you use the same field name repeated in separate cells within the same row to match a range of values (BETWEEN criteria). Figure 7-31 shows the criteria range to retrieve all employees who were hired between 1/1/2005 and 12/31/2008.

Example of BETWEEN criteria range   **Figure 7-31**

	B	C	D	E	F	G
1	Hire Date	Hire Date	Birth Date	Sex	Location	Job Status
2	>=1/1/2005	<=12/31/2008				
3						

You can also set up criteria to find records that begin with a group of characters. Figure 7-32 shows the criteria range that retrieves all records with a location that begin with *Home*. This criteria range would retrieve Talent Tracs employees working in Homewood, Illinois, along with those working from Home. If you want more precise results, you need to use the exact match criteria. The exact match criteria would be entered as ="=Home" and only employees working from Home would be retrieved.

Figure 7-32 **Example of BEGINS WITH criteria range**

	F	G	H	I	J	K
1	Location	Job Status	Add Life Ins	Pay Grade	Pay Type	Annual Salary
2	Home					
3						

Tip

Because the field names in the criteria range must exactly match the field names in the Excel table or range except for capitalization, you should copy and paste the field names instead of retyping them.

Creating a Criteria Range

Typically, you place a criteria range above the Excel table to keep it separate from the table. If you place a criteria range next to the Excel table, the criteria might be hidden when the advanced filtering cause rows to be hidden. You can also place a criteria range in a separate worksheet, particularly if you need to enter several criteria ranges in different cells to perform calculations based on various sets of filtered records.

You will place the criteria range in rows 1 to 4 of the Employee Data worksheet to make it easier to locate.

To create the criteria range to find eligible candidates for full-time positions:

▶ 1. Switch to the **Employee Data** worksheet, and then click cell **A1**.

You'll insert four blank rows above the Excel table in which to place the criteria range.

▶ 2. Select rows **1** through **4**, right-click the selected row headings, and then click **Insert** on the shortcut menu. Four rows are added at the top of the worksheet.

Next, you'll copy the column headers from the Excel table into row 1.

▶ 3. Point to the left side of cell **A5** until the pointer changes to ➡, and then click the mouse button. The column headers in row 5 are selected.

▶ 4. Click the **Home** tab on the Ribbon, if necessary, and then, in the Clipboard group, click the **Copy** button 🔲. The field names are copied to the Clipboard.

▶ 5. Click cell **A1**, and then, in the Clipboard group on the Home tab, click the **Paste** button. The field names for the criteria range appear in row 1.

In row 2, you will enter an AND criteria range with the criteria for consultants (code CN) who earn less than $55,000 and have worked at Talent Tracs for more than three years.

▶ 6. In cell G2, enter **="=CN"**. The condition =CN is displayed, which specifies the criteria to retrieve all consultants, employees with Pay Status code equal to CN.

▶ 7. In cell K2, enter **<55000**. This condition specifies the criteria to retrieve all employees who have salaries less than $55,000.

▶ 8. In cell M2, enter **>3**. This condition specifies the criteria to retrieve all employees with more than three years of service.

The criteria in row 2 selects all employees who are consultants and who earn less than $55,000 and have more than three years service at Talent Tracs. Next, you will enter the criteria for part-time employees working more than two years.

▶ 9. In cell **G3**, enter **="=PT"**; and then, in cell **M3**, enter **>=2**. The criteria in row 3 selects all employees who are part-time (Job Status is equal to PT) and who have two or more years service at Talent Tracs (Years Service is greater than or equal to 2). See Figure 7-33.

Criteria range ◄ Figure 7-33

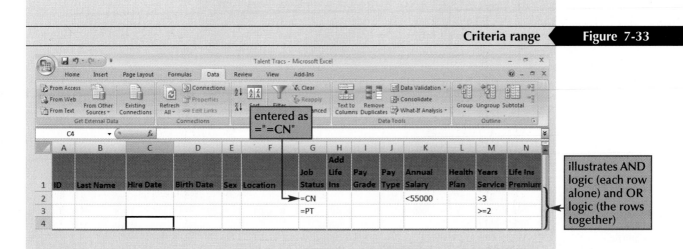

illustrates AND logic (each row alone) and OR logic (the rows together)

Now that the criteria range is established, you can use the Advanced Filter command to filter the Employee table. You can filter the records in their current location by hiding rows that don't match your criteria, as you have done with the Filter command. Or, you can copy the records that match your criteria to another location in the worksheet. Rita wants you to filter the records in their current location.

To filter the Employee table in its current location:

▶ **1.** Click any cell in the Employee table to make the table active.

▶ **2.** Click the **Data** tab on the Ribbon, and then, in the Sort & Filter group, click the **Advanced** button. The Advanced Filter dialog box opens.

▶ **3.** Make sure the **Filter the list, in-place** option button is selected and the range **$A$5:$R$105** appears in the List range box. The range $A$5:$R$105 is the current location of the Employee table, which is the table you want to filter.

   Trouble? If the List range displays $A$5:$L$105, you need to edit the range to $A$5:$R$105 to include the entire table.

▶ **4.** Type **$A$1:$R$3** in the Criteria range box. This is the range in which you entered the criteria range. See Figure 7-34.

Advanced Filter dialog box ◄ Figure 7-34

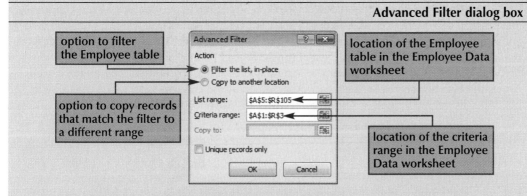

option to filter the Employee table

option to copy records that match the filter to a different range

location of the Employee table in the Employee Data worksheet

location of the criteria range in the Employee Data worksheet

▶ **5.** Click the **OK** button, and then scroll to the top of the worksheet. The list is filtered in its current location, and nine employee records match the criteria, as indicated in the status bar. See Figure 7-35.

| Figure 7-35 | Filtered Employee table |

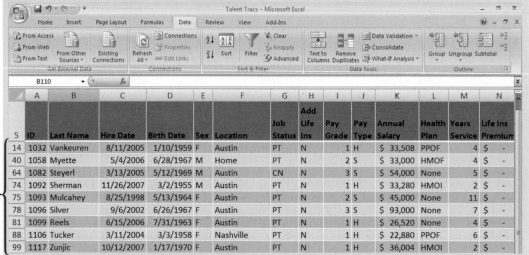

nine employees are eligible to apply for the full-time positions

5	ID	Last Name	Hire Date	Birth Date	Sex	Location	Job Status	Add Life Ins	Pay Grade	Pay Type	Annual Salary	Health Plan	Years Service	Life Ins Premium
14	1032	Vankeuren	8/11/2005	1/10/1959	F	Austin	PT	N	1	H	$ 33,508	PPOF	4	$ -
40	1058	Myette	5/4/2006	6/28/1967	M	Home	PT	N	2	S	$ 33,000	HMOF	4	$ -
64	1082	Steyerl	3/13/2005	5/12/1969	M	Austin	CN	N	3	S	$ 54,000	None	5	$ -
74	1092	Sherman	11/26/2007	3/2/1955	M	Austin	PT	N	1	H	$ 33,280	HMOI	2	$ -
75	1093	Mulcahey	8/25/1998	5/13/1964	F	Austin	PT	N	2	S	$ 45,000	None	11	$ -
78	1096	Silver	9/6/2002	6/26/1967	F	Austin	PT	N	3	S	$ 93,000	None	7	$ -
81	1099	Reels	6/15/2006	7/31/1963	F	Austin	PT	N	1	H	$ 26,520	None	4	$ -
88	1106	Tucker	3/11/2004	3/3/1958	F	Nashville	PT	N	1	H	$ 22,880	PPOF	6	$ -
99	1117	Zunjic	10/12/2007	1/17/1970	F	Austin	PT	N	1	H	$ 36,004	HMOI	2	$ -

Trouble? If no records appear in the filtered table, the list range or criteria range might be incorrect. Click the Clear button in the Sort & Filter group on the Data tab, and then repeat Steps 1 through 5, making sure the list range is $A$5:$R$105 and the criteria range is $A$1:$R$3 in the Advanced Filter dialog box.

After providing the list of eligible employees to Rita, you remove the filter to display all the records in the Employee table.

To show all the records in the Employee table:

1. In the Sort & Filter group on the Data tab, click the **Clear** button. All the records in the Employee table reappear.

| InSight | **Copying Filtered Records to a New Location** |

The Advanced Filtering command does more than filter data in a range or an Excel table. You can also copy data in a table to another worksheet location. If you want to filter the data and then copy the filtered data to a different location, you select the Copy to another location option button in the Action section of the Advanced Filter dialog box and specify the first cell of the range where you want to copy the filtered records in the Copy to box. Excel copies the filtered records to the location beginning at the cell you specified in the Copy to box. All cells below this cell will be cleared when the Advanced Filter is applied.

The Advanced Filtering command offers many advantages, allowing you to copy the following:

- All the columns from the original table in their current order to another worksheet location.
- A subset of columns from the original table to another worksheet location.
- A subset or all the columns from the original table and change the sequence of columns in the new worksheet location.
- A unique list of values from the original table into another worksheet location. For example, you can obtain a unique list of customer names from a table of invoices where customer names are repeated many times.

Using Database Functions to Summarize Data

Functions that perform summary data analysis (SUM, AVERAGE, COUNT, and so on) on a table of values based on criteria that you set are called the **Database functions**, or **Dfunctions**. Figure 7-36 lists the Database functions. Although the SUMIF, AVERAGEIF and COUNTIF functions, the Total row feature of an Excel table, and PivotTables often can achieve the same results as Database functions and are considered simpler to use, some situations call for Database functions. For example, the type of summary analysis, the placement of the summary results, or the complexity of the criteria might require that you use Database functions.

Database functions ◄ **Figure 7-36**

Function Name	Description
DAVERAGE	Returns the average of the values that meet specified criteria
DCOUNT	Returns the number of cells containing numbers that meet specified criteria
DCOUNTA	Returns the number of nonblank cells that meets specified criteria
DMAX	Returns the maximum value in search column that meets specified criteria
DMIN	Returns the minimum value in search column that meets specified criteria
DSTDEV	Returns the estimate of standard deviation based on a sample of entries that meet the specified criteria
DSUM	Returns the sum of the values in the summary column that meets specified criteria

Rita wants you to provide a report summarizing the number of salaried and hourly workers by health plan. Rita's request combines the HMOF and HMOI codes into one group on the report and the PPOF and PPOI codes into another group. You must set up a criteria range to retrieve the appropriate records for each calculation. As a result, a Dfunction becomes a good approach for solving Rita's request.

Dfunctions use a criteria range to specify the records to summarize. In a Dfunction, the criteria range is used as one of the arguments of the function. Any Dfunction has the following general syntax:

```
DfunctionName(table range, column to summarize, criteria range)
```

In this syntax, *table range* refers to the cells where the data to summarize is located, including the column header, *column to summarize* is the column name of the field you want to summarize, and *criteria range* is the range where the criteria that determines which records are used in the calculation is specified.

You will use Dfunctions to complete the Employee Summary worksheet, summarizing the number of salaried and hourly employees covered by HMO and PPO health plans. First, you will set up a separate criteria range for each cell in the report, excluding totals for rows and columns. Although the criteria range often includes all fields from the table, even those that are not needed to select records, you do not have to include all field names from the table when setting up a criteria range. In setting up the criteria range to use with the Database functions, you will use only the fields needed to specify the criteria.

You will create six criteria ranges to complete the Health Plan Count report.

To establish criteria ranges for the Health Plan Count report:

▶ **1.** Switch to the **Employee Summary** worksheet. The column headers for the criteria range have already been copied from the Employee Data worksheet.

You'll set up the criteria for salaried employees who have selected HMOs, PPOs, and No Plan.

▶ **2.** In cell G15, enter **HMO**, and then, in cell H15, enter **S**. You entered *begins with* criteria (HMO) to find all HMOs (HMOI and HMOF). The code for salaried employees is S and because only S or H codes are used in the Pay Type column, you used the *begins with* criteria to find salaried employees. The criteria range for salaried employees electing either HMO plan is complete.

▶ **3.** In cell J15, enter **PPO** as the *begins with* criteria to find all PPOs (PPOI and PPOF), and then, in cell K15, enter the *begins with* criteria **S** to find salaried employees. The criteria range for salaried employees electing either PPO plan is complete.

▶ **4.** In cell M15, enter the *begins with* criteria **None**, and then, in cell N15, enter the *begins with* criteria **S** to find salaried employees. The criteria range for salaried employees with no plan is complete.

You'll set up the criteria for Hourly HMOs, Hourly PPOs, and Hourly No Plan.

▶ **5.** In cell G20, enter the *begins with* criteria **HMO** to find all HMOs (HMOI and HMOF), and then, in cell H20, enter the *begins with* criteria **H** to find hourly employees. The criteria range for hourly employees electing an HMO plan is complete.

▶ **6.** In cell J20, enter the *begins with* criteria **PPO** to find all PPOs (PPOI and PPOF), and then, in cell K20, enter the *begins with* criteria **H** to find hourly employees. The criteria range for hourly employees electing a PPO plan is complete.

▶ **7.** In cell M20, enter the *begins with* criteria **None**, and then, in cell N20, enter the *begins with* criteria **H** to find hourly employees. The criteria range for hourly employees with no plan is complete. See Figure 7-37.

| Figure 7-37 | Criteria range for report |

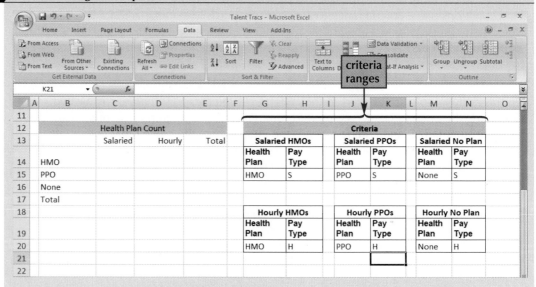

The criteria ranges are complete, so you can enter the formulas to finish the Health Plan Count report for Rita. You will enter the DCOUNT function six times. In each function, the first two arguments are identical. The third argument, the criteria range, is different for each function so that you can count a different subset of employees each time.

To enter the first DCOUNT function:

▶ **1.** In cell C14, type **=D** and double-click **DCOUNT**. The beginning of the formula, =DCOUNT(, appears in the cell and the formula bar.

▶ **2.** Type **Em** and then press the **Tab** key to enter Employee in the first argument. Employee references only the data in the Employee table.

▶ **3.** Type **[#** to open the list of special Item qualifiers, press the **Tab** key to enter #All, and then type **],** to complete the first argument, Employee[#All],. The special qualifier [#All] indicates you want to reference the column headers as well as the data.

▶ **4.** Type **"ID",** to specify the field in the Employee table that you want to count. The second argument, ID, shows the column whose cells will be counted. The field name must be within quotation marks.

▶ **5.** Type **G14:H15)** to complete the formula. The third argument G14:H15 references the criteria range that determines which cells in the ID column to count.

▶ **6.** Press the **Enter** key, and then click cell **C14**. There are 32 salaried employees electing either HMO plan. The formula =DCOUNT(Employee[#All],"ID",G14:H15) appears in the formula bar.

You'll repeat this process to finish the Health Plan Count report. The DCOUNT function is the same for each of the remaining counts, except the third argument reflects the appropriate criteria range that you entered in the Employee Summary worksheet.

To enter the remaining DCOUNT functions for the Health Plan Count report:

▶ **1.** In cell C15, enter **=DCOUNT(Employee[#All],"ID",J14:K15)**. This DCOUNT function calculates the number of salaried employees electing either PPO plan. The formula is identical to the first DCOUNT function you entered except the criteria range J14:K15 specifies the criteria to retrieve salaried employees electing either PPO plan. There are 15 in this category.

▶ **2.** In cell C16, enter **=DCOUNT(Employee[#All],"ID",M14:N15)**. This DCOUNT function calculates the number of salaried employees with no health plan. Again, the formula is identical to the other DCOUNT functions you entered except the criteria range M14:N15 specifies the criteria to retrieve salaried employees with no health plan. There are 18 employees in this category.

▶ **3.** In cell D14, enter **=DCOUNT(Employee[#All],"ID",G19:H20)** to calculate the number of hourly HMO employees. The formula is identical to the other DCOUNT functions you entered except the criteria range G19:H20 specifies the criteria to retrieve hourly employees electing either HMO plan. There are 13 in this category.

▶ **4.** In cell D15, enter **=DCOUNT(Employee[#All],"ID",J19:K20)** to calculate the number of hourly PPO employees. The criteria range references the criteria range J19:K20, which retrieves hourly workers electing either PPO plan. There are 14 employees in this category.

▶ **5.** In cell D16, enter **=DCOUNT(Employee[#All],"ID",M19:N20)** to calculate the number of hourly employees with no plan. The criteria range references the range M19:N20, which retrieves hourly workers with no health plan. There are 8 in this category.

▶ **6.** In cells C17 and D17, enter the SUM function to calculate totals for each column.

▶ **7.** In the range E14:E17, use the SUM function to total each row.

▶ **8.** Add a bottom border to the range C16:E16, and then click cell **C18** to deselect the report. See Figure 7-38.

Figure 7-38	Health Plan Count report

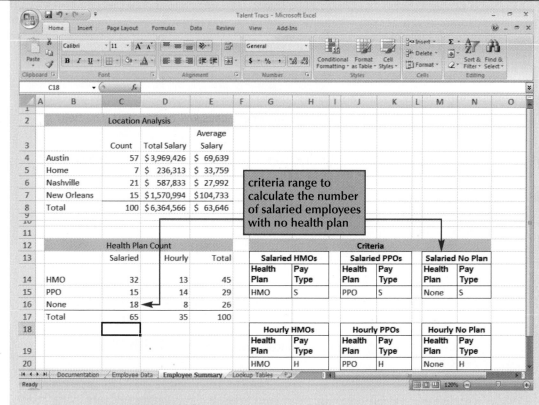

▶ **9.** Save the workbook, and then close it.

The Health Plan Count report provides Rita with useful information as she goes into a meeting to plan Talent Tracs' healthcare coverage for future years.

Session 7.3 Quick Check | Review

1. Describe in words the following criteria range:

   Sex   Salary Class
   ="=M"   ="=H"

2. Create a criteria range to retrieve employees located in either Austin or New Orleans. The column name is Location.

3. Describe in words the following criteria range:

   Annual Salary   Annual Salary
   <25000
                   >=100000

4. After an Advanced Filter command has filtered records, how do you redisplay all the records in the table?

5. Explain the function: =DSUM(Employee[#All],"Annual Salary",T1:U2)

   The following criteria range appears in the range T1:U2:
   Sex   Hire Date
   M   >=1/1/2010

6. Why would you use the structured reference Employee[#All] in Quick Check 5 instead of Employee?

7. Rewrite the DSUM function in Quick Check 5 using range addresses instead of structured references. The employee data is found in the Employee Data worksheet in the range A5:R105. The DSUM function is entered in the Employee Summary worksheet.

Tutorial Summary | Review

In this tutorial, you used the Logical functions IF, AND, and OR, and you nested one IF function inside another IF function. You used the VLOOKUP function to look up data in a table. You used conditional formatting and the IFERROR function to locate and fix data entry errors. You also used the COUNTIF, SUMIF, and AVERAGEIF functions to calculate counts, sums, and averages based on search criteria. You filtered a table using more advanced filtering criteria. Finally, you used Database functions to summarize a table based on specified criteria.

Key Terms

AND function	criteria range	nested IF function
AVERAGEIF function	Database function	OR function
AVERAGEIFS function	DATEDIF function	rule
calculated column	Dfunction	structured reference
compare value	error value	SUMIF function
conditional count	HLOOKUP function	SUMIFS function
conditional sum	IFERROR function	VLOOKUP function
COUNTIF function	lookup table	
COUNTIFS function	lookup value	

| Practice | **Review Assignments** |

Practice the skills you learned by using the Employee Data worksheet to test alternative calculations.

Data File needed for the Review Assignments: Tracs.xlsx

Rita suggests you try some alternative calculations for bonuses and benefits. Complete the following:

1. Open the **Tracs** workbook located in the Tutorial.07\Review folder included with your Data Files, save the workbook as **Tracs Employees** in the same folder, and then, in the Documentation sheet, enter the date and your name.

2. In the Employee Data worksheet, rename the Excel table as **EmpData**.

3. Employees who want additional coverage (Add Life Ins) pay 0.1% premium rate times annual salary. For employees who do not elect additional coverage, enter 0 in the life Ins Premium column. The life insurance premiums are entered in cell Z9. Calculate the life insurance premiums using an IF function and include a reference to cell Z9 to obtain the life insurance rate.

4. All full-time (Job Status) employees over the age of 30 (Age in column N) are eligible for the 401(k) benefit. Use the IF and AND functions to calculate the 401(k) benefit as 3% of annual salary. If the employee is not eligible, enter 0. In the formula you create, include a reference to cell Z10 to obtain the 401(k) matching percent rate (3%).

5. Calculate Bonus assuming it is available to all employees with 1 or more years of service (Years Service). Employees with pay grade 1 receive $3,000 (cell Z6), pay grade 2 receive $6,000 (cell Z7), and pay grade 3 receive $8,000 (cell Z8). For employees not eligible for a bonus, display the label **NE**. For pay grades not equal to 1, 2, or 3, display the message **Invalid pay grade**. Use nested IF functions to calculate the bonus.

6. Change the format color of the duplicate value conditional formatting rule to Green (sixth color in the last row of the color palette) using the Conditional Formatting Rules Manager dialog box.

7. Calculate the health plan cost using the HLOOKUP function to do an exact match lookup. The layout of Health Plan Rates data ($B$2:$F$3) in the Lookup Tables worksheet has been revised to work with the HLOOKUP function. Use the range address reference in the HLOOKUP function to reference Health Plan Rates data.

8. Modify the calculation of the recognition award (Award) to incorporate the IFERROR function. Display the message **Invalid hire date**.

9. Change the hire date in cell C12 from 3/1/2007 to **#/1//2007** (note that you are entering a date with an intentional error). Insert a comment in cell S12 describing what appears in row 12 of the Years Service, Bonus, and Award columns. After entering the comment, change the date in cell C12 to **3/1/2007**.

10. Complete the criteria range located in the range A1:S3 of the Employee Data worksheet so you can use advanced filtering to display all part-time (PT) employees working in Austin as well as full-time (FT) employees working at home and earning $40,000 or more.

11. Use the COUNTIF count and AVERAGEIF functions to complete the Gender Summary report in the range B4:D5 of the Reports worksheet.

12. Use the Database function to calculate the average salary by Sex (F or M) and Pay Type (S or H). Enter the criteria in the ranges J12:K12, M12:N12, J17:K17, and M17:N17 in the Reports worksheet, and then use the DAVERAGE function to complete the report found in the range B11:D13 of the Reports worksheet.

13. Save and close the workbook. Submit the finished workbook to your instructor, either in printed or electronic form, as requested.

Apply | **Case Problem 1**

Apply the skills you learned to analyze and summarize monthly sales data for a computer supply store.

Data File needed for this Case Problem: Modem.xlsx

PC-Market Distribution   Linda Klaussen works for PC-Market Distribution, a computer supply store. She needs your help in designing an Excel workbook to enter purchase order information. She has already entered the product information on PC-Market's line of modems. She wants you to insert a lookup function to look up data from the product table. The company also supports three shipping options that vary in price. She wants the purchase order worksheet to be able to calculate the total cost of the order, including the type of shipping the customer requests. She also wants to use advanced filtering to copy data on all modems under $50 to a new worksheet to review prices of the inexpensive items. Finally, she wants to calculate average prices for each category of modems using a Database function.

Complete the following:

1. Open the **Modem** workbook located in the Tutorial.07\Case1 folder included with your Data Files, save the workbook as **PC Modem** in the same folder, and then, in the Documentation worksheet, enter the date and your name.

2. In the Purchase Order worksheet, Product ID numbers will be entered in cell B5. Create three lookup functions: the first to display the product type in cell C7, the second to display the model name in cell C8, and the third to display the price in cell C9. Product information is displayed in the Product List worksheet.

3. If an incorrect product ID number is entered in cell B5, then cells C7, C8, and C9 will display the #N/A error value. Linda wants these cells to display the message **Product ID not found** if the ID entered is not found.

4. Enter one of three shipping options offered by PC-Market (Standard, Express, Overnight) in cell B15. Set up an area in the range D40:E42 to store Standard shipping costs $9.50, Express shipping costs $14.50, and Overnight shipping costs $18.50. Use IF functions to display the costs of the shipping in cell C17. If an invalid shipping option is entered in cell B15, then **Invalid Shipping option** should appear in cell C17. If the Shipping option, cell B15, is blank, then cell C17 should be blank. (*Hint:* The IF functions should reference the cells in the range D40:E42.)

5. Display the total cost of the product (price times quantity) plus shipping in cell C19. If the cell equals an error value (#Value!), display the message **Check Product ID, Quantity, or Shipping option**.

6. Test the worksheet using a product ID number of **1050**, quantity **2**, and the **Express** shipping option.

7. On the Product List worksheet use advanced filtering to display all 56K Desktop modems (Type) with a price under $50 or Modem Card (Type) over $200. Make sure the values in all the columns are visible. Make a copy of the Product List worksheet, rename the copied worksheet **Q7 Advanced Filter** and then return to the Product List worksheet. Display all the records.

8. In the Summary worksheet, use appropriate functions to determine the average modem price and count for each modem type.

9. Save and close the workbook. Submit the finished workbook to your instructor, either in printed or electronic form, as requested.

| Apply | | Case Problem 2 |

Apply the skills you learned by creating a worksheet that tracks the amount of vacation time and family leave to which an employee is entitled.

Data File needed for this Case Problems: Leave.xlsx

Town of Baltic Administrative Office Alan Welton, HR Generalist, at the Town of Baltic Administrative Office in Baltic, Indiana, has a workbook that tracks the amount of vacation time and family leave used by each employee in the town. Alan needs to calculate how much vacation and family leave each employee is eligible for. Then, he can subtract the amount they have already used from that amount. He also wants to calculate the total number of vacation and family leave days used by all employees, as well as the total number of days remaining. The eligibility requirements for the different vacation and family leave plans are as follows:

For vacation:
- 15 days for full-time employees who have worked 4 or more years
- 10 days for full-time employees who have worked 2 years but less than 4 years
- 5 days for full-time employees who have worked 1 year but less than 2 years
- 0 days for everyone else

For family leave:
- 5 days for full-time employees who have worked 1 or more years
- 3 days for full-time employees who have worked less than 1 year or for part-time employees who have worked more than 1.5 years
- 0 days for everyone else

Use these eligibility requirements to calculate the available vacation and family leave time for each employee.

Complete the following:

1. Open the workbook **Leave** located in the Tutorial.07\Case2 folder included with your Data Files, save the workbook as **Baltic Leave** in the same folder, and then enter the date and your name in the Documentation worksheet.
2. In the LeaveData worksheet, create an Excel table from the range A5:J107, name the Excel table as **Leave**, and then remove the filter arrows. Set the column width for columns B through J to **10**.
3. Calculate Years Employed in column D. Use Date Hired and current date (assume 7/1/2010, which is stored in cell Z6) and express length of time employed in years. Use the formula (current date – date hired)/365.
4. In column E, enter a formula using nested IF and AND functions to determine the number of vacation days (based on the vacation rules described previously) each employee is eligible for based on the employee's job status in column B and on the Length of Time Employed in column D.
5. Subtract the amount of vacation used from the available vacation time, displaying the remaining vacation time in column G for all employees.
6. In column H, enter a formula to determine each employee's total family leave time (based on the family leave rules described previously). (*Hint*: Use nested IF, AND, and OR functions.)
7. To determine the remaining family time, subtract the used portion of the family leave from their total family leave and display the results in column J.

⊕ **EXPLORE**

8. In the Leave Summary worksheet, use a function to calculate the total number of employees eligible for the different vacation leave plan. (*Hint*: An employee who is eligible for the 15-day vacation leave will have the value 15 in column E of the Leave Data worksheet.)

9. Enter formulas in the Vacation Leave Summary report to calculate the total number of vacation days and days remaining for each vacation plan.

10. Calculate the total number of employees, total days, and days remaining in row 8 of the report you started in Step 9.

11. Use advanced filtering to display all full-time employees with five remaining family leave days as well as all part-time employees with three remaining family leave days. Make a copy of the Leave Data worksheet, rename the copied worksheet **Q11 Advanced Filter**, and then return to the Leave Data worksheet. Clear the filter.

12. Save and close the workbook. Submit the finished workbook to your instructor, either in printed or electronic form, as requested.

| Challenge | Case Problem 3 |

Create reports for a water company based on different billing plans.

Data File needed for this Case Problem: M-Fresh.xlsx

M-Fresh Water Company   A small independent water company in Miami, Oklahoma, M-Fresh Water Company provides water to its commercial customers throughout the region, delivering the supply of water through pipelines, on-demand storage tanks, and bottles. Customers of M-Fresh Water range from government offices to nonprofit organizations to commercial retail shops and markets. Town regulations indicate that the latter group of commercial customers is taxed on their usage, whereas nonprofit and government offices are not. Furthermore, M-Fresh Water will, from time to time, choose to waive a water bill based on its charitable giving policy.

Dawes Cado is in charge of the billing system that must take into account these business rules and ensure accurate and on-time billing, which is completed each quarter. Complete the following:

1. Open the **M-Fresh** workbook located in the Tutorial.07\Case3 folder included with your Data Files, save the workbook as **Water Bills** in the same folder, and then enter the date and your name in the Documentation worksheet.

2. In the Quarterly Data worksheet, create an Excel table for the range A1:G73. Name the table as **WaterData**. Remove the filter arrows. Format the Gal Used data in the Comma Style number format with no decimal places. Add the following three columns to the table: **Water Bill**, **Tax**, and **Total Bill**.

3. Calculate the Water Bill based on the following rules:
   - If a customer's bill is waived, place 0 in the Water Bill column.
   - Gal Used (gallons used) must be greater than 25,000 gallons during the quarter; otherwise, the water bill is 0.
   - For all other accounts, the billing rate varies based on the type of customer. The billing rate is $3, $2, or $1.50 per *thousand* gallons used depending on the type of customer (see the Billing Rate worksheet). For example, a commercial customer using 75,000 gallons has a water bill of $225(75×$3), whereas a government customer using 100,000 gallons pays $150(100×$1.50). A commercial customer using 15,000 gallons has a water bill of 0.

4. Calculate Tax based on the following rule: If a customer is taxable, then multiply the water bill times 3.5%; otherwise, the tax is 0. (Tax rate is stored in cell T1.)

5. Calculate the Total Bill amount using the following formula: *Water Bill + Tax*.

6. Improve the formatting of the number fields, and then insert totals for GalUsed (average) and Total bill (sum). Make a copy of the Quarterly Data worksheet, rename the copied worksheet **Q2-6** and then return to the Quarterly Data worksheet.

7. Use conditional formatting to highlight the top 15% of customers based on the total bill. Use appropriate formatting. Filter the bills so only the top 15% are displayed. Sort the largest first. Make a copy of the Quarterly Data worksheet, rename the copied worksheet **Q7** and then return to the Quarterly Data worksheet. Display all records.

8. Insert a new worksheet and then create the Water Usage and Billing By Type of Customer report (shown in Figure 7-39). Rename the worksheet as **Q8 Billing Summary**. Use conditional IF functions to prepare the report.

Figure 7-39

	A	B	C	D	E	F
1						
2						
3						
4		Customer Type	Nbr Customers	Avg Gals Used	Total Billed	
5		Commercial	37	322,437	$ 37,043.12	
6		Non-profit	11	87,661	$ 224.18	
7		Government	24	774,532	$ 27,901.44	
8		Total	72	437,267	$ 65,168.74	
9						
10						

⊕EXPLORE 9. Make a copy of the Quarterly Data worksheet, rename the copied worksheet **Q9-10**. Management is considering eliminating the 25,000 gallon cutoff and bill waivers. In the Quarterly Data worksheet use advanced filtering to copy all data for waived customers or customers using 25,000 gallons or less to row 101 in the Q9-10 worksheet.

⊕EXPLORE 10. Use the data you retrieved from Step 9 to calculate the lost revenue from waived bills and customers with water usage below 25,000. Assume for the purposes of the analysis that all water usage (25,000 gallon cutoff no longer exists) will be billed. Prepare a report.

⊕EXPLORE 11. You want to know how many businesses are either churches, schools, or clinics. Use the COUNTIF function to complete the report in a new worksheet named **Q11 Type Institution**. (*Hint:* Use Help to research using the wildcard characters as part of your criteria.)

12. Save and close the workbook. Submit the finished workbook to your instructor, either in printed or electronic form, as requested.

Create | **Case Problem 4**

Create a worksheet that compiles and summarizes reports for a newspaper.

Data File needed for this Case Problem: Rock Island.xlsx

Rock Island Home Sales Tim Derkson, reporter for Rock Island Times, in Rock Island, Illinois, is compiling a quarterly real estate sales analysis for his newspaper. He obtained data on home sales from the local real estate association and county records. He asked you to help design a worksheet that will display summary information on the home sales in Rock Island. Tim has already set up and formatted a workbook, but he wants you to insert the correct formulas. Tim stored the housing data in the Home Data worksheet. He wants to use the Home Summary worksheet to search for information about the homes.

Complete the following:

1. Open the **Rock Island** workbook located in the Tutorial.07\Case4 folder included with your Data Files, save the workbook as **Home Sales** in the same folder, and then, in the Documentation worksheet, enter the date and your name.

2. In the Home Sales Data worksheet, create an Excel table in the range A6:K123. Remove the filter arrows. Name the Excel table as **SalesData**.

3. Using the Date Sold and Date Listed columns, add a calculated column named **Days on Market**, which is the difference between these two dates. (*Hint:* You might need to format this column in the General number format.)

⊕ EXPLORE 4. Use conditional formatting to highlight records where the sales price was above the asking price. Add appropriate formatting. (*Hint:* Create a new rule using the formula rule type and build a conditional statement to compare first data row between the two columns of interest.) Make a copy of the Home Sales Data worksheet, rename the copied worksheet **Q3-4**, and then return to the Home Sales Data worksheet.

5. Insert a new worksheet, and then rename it as **Q5-6 Sales Summary**. Create a report on Overall Home Sales based on Sales Price, using Figure 7-40 as a guide.

Figure 7-40

	A	B	C	D	E	F	G
1				**Rock Island Home Sales**			
2				**Overall Data**			
3							
4			**Number Sold**	**Average Sales Price**	**Highest Sales Price**	**Lowest Sales Price**	
5			117	$ 100,461.54	$ 215,000	$ 51,000	
6							

⊕ EXPLORE 6. Below the report, create a report on Home Sales based on Sales Price and broken down by Type of Home. Figure 7-41 shows the output. Use conditional IF functions for Number Sold and Average Sales Price and database functions (DMAX and DMIN) to calculate the highest and lowest price.

Figure 7-41

7			By Type of Home		
8					
9	Type	Number Sold	Average Sales Price	Highest Sales Price	Lowest Sales Price
10	Condo	23	$ 90,347.83	$ 182,500	$ 53,000
11	Ranch	46	$ 91,842.39	$ 193,500	$ 51,000
12	Victorian	48	$113,567.71	$ 215,000	$ 51,750
13					

7. In the Home Sales Data worksheet use Advanced Filtering to display all homes that were:

- On the market more than 150 days and 25 or more years old

OR

- Have more than 2 bedrooms and 1.5 or more bathrooms

Sort the filtered data by Days on Market in descending order. Make a copy of the Home Sales Data worksheet, rename the copied worksheet **Q7 Advanced Filter** and then return to the Home Sales Data worksheet. Display all records.

⊕EXPLORE 8. Insert a new worksheet. Rename the worksheet as **Q8-9 DaysOnMarket**. Create a PivotTable to create a report with the information in Figure 7-42.

Figure 7-42

4		Values	
5	Days	Number Sold	Avg Sales Price
6	1-100	31	$ 94,451.61
7	101-200	27	$ 106,879.63
8	201-300	37	$ 103,939.19
9	301-400	22	$ 95,204.55
10	Grand Total	117	$ 100,461.54

⊕EXPLORE 9. In a separate section of the same Q8-9 DaysOnMarket worksheet, use Database functions and complete the criteria ranges to create the report shown in Figure 7-43, which provides the same information as the report you created in Step 8.

Figure 7-43

15	Days	Number Sold	Avg Sales Price
16	1-100	31	$ 94,451.61
17	101-200	27	$ 106,879.63
18	201-300	37	$ 103,939.19
19	301-400	22	$ 95,204.55
20	Total	117	$ 100,461.54

10. Display the Total row in the SalesData table. In this row, display a count of homes sold, average taxes, average asking price, average sales price, and average days on market. Make a copy of the Home Sales Data worksheet, rename the copied worksheet **Q10-11 Home Sales Data** and then return to the Home Sales worksheet.

⊕ EXPLORE   11. In the Q10-11 Home Sales Data worksheet, split the Home Sales Data worksheet so the top section shows all the Home Data table. The bottom section is the last one or two rows on your screen, which displays the Total row. (*Hint:* Use Excel Help to find information on how to split the window.)

12. Save and close the workbook. Submit the finished workbook to your instructor, either in printed or electronic form, as requested.

| Research | **Internet Assignments** |

Use the Internet to find and work with data related to the topics presented in this tutorial.

The purpose of the Internet Assignments is to challenge you to find information on the Internet that you can use to work effectively with this software. The actual assignments are updated and maintained on the Course Technology Web site. Log on to the Internet and use your Web browser to go to the Student Online Companion for New Perspectives Office 2007 at **www.course.com/np/office2007**. Then navigate to the Internet Assignments for this tutorial.

| Assess | **SAM Assessment and Training** |

If you have a SAM user profile, you may have access to hands-on instruction, practice, and assessment of the skills covered in this tutorial. Log in to your SAM account (**http://sam2007.course.com**) to launch any assigned training activities or exams that relate to the skills covered in this tutorial.

| Review | **Quick Check Answers** |

Session 7.1

1. The table style is applied to all rows in the new column; the range of the Excel table expands to include the new column (Phone). All features that apply to other columns in the table apply to the Phone column, too.
2. calculated column
3. In cell C7, enter = IF(C5*C6 > 10000,C5*C6,10000).
4. False
5. =IF(AND(J5>0,D5<3/15/2008),"Outstanding","")
6. structured references
7. nested IF

Session 7.2

1. An exact match compares the lookup value to the compare value. They must be equal for a value to be returned from the lookup table. An approximate match also compares the lookup value to the compare value. The two values do not have to be equal, just fall within a range of values for Excel to return a value from the lookup table.
2. VLOOKUP function
3. No, duplicate last names do not mean the data in the Last Name column is a duplicate.
4. =IFERROR(C5/C25,"Dividing by 0")
5. counts the number of females in the Employee table

6. Calculate the average salary for all hourly employees.
7. Conditional Formatting Rules Manager dialog box

Session 7.3

1. retrieve all male employees classified as hourly
2. Location
   ="=Austin"
   ="=New Orleans"
3. retrieve employees earning less than 25,000 or 100,000 or more in annual salary
4. Clear command
5. sum the annual salaries of all males hired on 1/1/2010 or later
6. The structured reference to Employee includes only the data in an Excel table, whereas Employee[#ALL] includes the header and total row. The DSUM function's first argument must reference the header row.
7. =DSUM('Employee Data'!A5:R105,"Annual Salary",T1:U2)

Ending Data Files

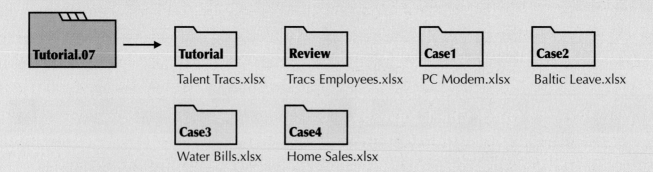

Tutorial.07 →

Tutorial
Talent Tracs.xlsx

Review
Tracs Employees.xlsx

Case1
PC Modem.xlsx

Case2
Baltic Leave.xlsx

Case3
Water Bills.xlsx

Case4
Home Sales.xlsx

Developing an Excel Application

Creating an Invoice

Case | Eugene Community Theatre

Ellen Jefferson, business manager for the Eugene Community Theatre in Eugene, Oregon, is automating several processes for the theatre's business office. Each year, the theatre mails a brochure to patrons and other interested individuals showcasing the upcoming seasons' offerings. Then, theatre-goers make their selections and mail in the order form. Ellen wants to automate the process of invoicing, capturing the order, calculating the charges, and printing an invoice. She also wants the invoice system to reflect specific requests for tickets (number, series, and location in theatre).

Many of these tasks can be accomplished in Excel. But without validating data entry, protecting cells with formulas from accidental deletion, and reducing repetitious keystrokes and mouse clicks, Ellen realizes too many opportunities for errors exist. In addition, the theatre, as a nonprofit organization, relies on numerous volunteers who have varying degrees of computer experience and skill. To accommodate these varying skill levels and reduce potential errors, Ellen wants to create a custom interface for this project that does not rely exclusively on the Ribbon, galleries, and so forth. You'll help Ellen create a unique Excel application that can resolve these issues and help ensure accurate data entry.

Starting Data Files

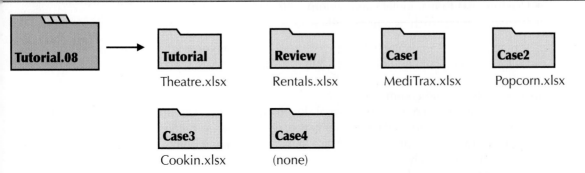

Tutorial.08 →	Tutorial	Review	Case1	Case2
	Theatre.xlsx	Rentals.xlsx	MediTrax.xlsx	Popcorn.xlsx
	Case3	Case4		
	Cookin.xlsx	(none)		

Session 8.1

Planning an Excel Application

An **Excel application** is a spreadsheet written or tailored to meet the user's specific needs. Applications typically include the following:

- Reports and/or charts designed to aid understanding and produce insights
- A way to enter and edit data, often controlling the type of values that can be entered and where data can be entered
- An interface that assists the user, ranging from buttons for executing specific tasks to customizing the entire Excel interface with custom tabs, menus, and toolbars
- Clearly written instructions and documentation

Ellen sketched the application she wants you to create, which is shown in Figure 8-1. She wants to be able to easily print the invoice and transfer the invoice items to another worksheet. In addition, she wants volunteers to be able to enter data for a season ticket in a specific area of the worksheet reserved for input. The application would use this data to automatically generate and print the invoice. To keep the process simple, she also wants users to be able to click buttons to print a single invoice, print the entire worksheet, and transfer the data from one worksheet to another.

| Figure 8-1 | Ellen's sketch of the Excel application for invoicing |

Application planning includes designing how the worksheet(s) will be organized. You can include different sections for each function, depending on the complexity of the project. For example, you could include separate sections to:

- Enter and edit data (even setting what types of values can be entered and where a user can enter data)
- Store data after it has been entered
- Use formulas to manipulate and perform calculations on data
- Prepare outputs, such as reports and charts

An application's interface helps others use it. For example, you can have separate sections for inputting data and displaying outputs. You can create special buttons for performing specific tasks. You can also change the entire Excel interface by adding custom menus, toolbars, and commands.

An application often includes internal documentation in a Documentation worksheet as well as comments to explain cell contents and provide instructions. It can also include a set of clearly written instructions. All of these help you and others use the workbook correctly and accurately.

You'll open the workbook Ellen created and complete the application.

To open and review the Theatre workbook:

▶ **1.** Open the **Theatre** workbook located in the **Tutorial.08\Tutorial** folder included with your Data Files, and then save the workbook as **Community Theatre** in the same folder.

▶ **2.** In the Documentation sheet, enter the current date and your name.

▶ **3.** Review the contents of the workbook, and then switch to the **Invoice** worksheet. See Figure 8-2.

Initial Invoice worksheet ◀ Figure 8-2

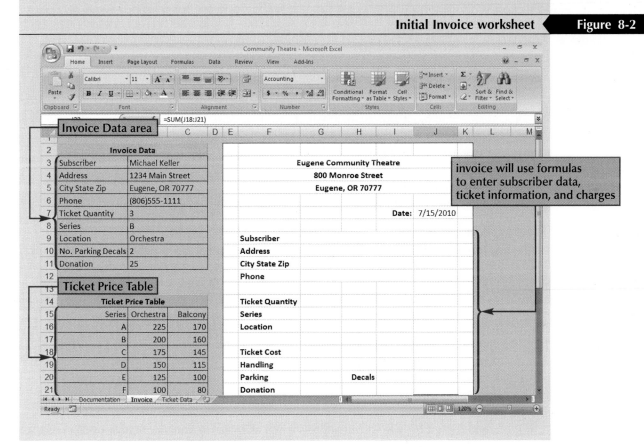

In addition to the Documentation worksheet, the Community Theatre workbook includes two other worksheets: Invoice and Ticket Data.

The Invoice worksheet contains input, output, and transfer data sections. The input section is divided into the following three areas:

- Invoice Data contains items that change for each request, such as the subscriber name, address, phone number, ticket quantity, series, location of seats, and so forth.
- Ticket Price Table contains the pricing table for all tickets for the upcoming season.
- Invoice Constants contains charges for items that will not change during the upcoming theatre season, such as the cost for parking ($15/decal) and the handling charge ($8/invoice).

The output section contains formulas and labels used to generate the invoice based on data in the input section. The invoice in the output section will be printed. The transfer data section gathers selected data from the invoice in one area before the data is transferred to the Ticket Data worksheet for storage. The transfer data section makes it simpler to move the data to the Ticket Data worksheet.

> **Tip**
>
> Larger and more complex applications often place the input and output sections in separate worksheets.

Naming Cells and Ranges

In the Invoice worksheet, the range B3:B11 contains the data values for each request for season tickets. As you can see, this range includes many variables. It will be simpler to remember where different data is stored by assigning a descriptive name to each cell or range rather than using its cell address. For example, the name *Customer* is easier to remember than cell B3. Assigning names to cells or ranges makes building an application more intuitive and easier to document. Ellen asks you to name the cells in the input section.

Creating Defined Names

So far, you have referred to a cell or range by its cell and range address except when you entered formulas within an Excel table. Cell and range references do not indicate what data is stored in those cells. Instead, you can assign a meaningful, descriptive name to a cell or range. A **defined name** (often called simply a **name**) is a word or string of characters associated with a single cell or a range. For example, if the range D1:D100 contains sales data for 100 transactions, you can define the name *Sales* to refer to the range of sales data.

You can use a defined name to quickly navigate within a workbook to the cell with defined name. You can also create more descriptive formulas by using defined names in formulas instead of cell or range references. For example, the defined name *Sales* can replace the range reference D1:D100 in a formula to calculate average sales, as follows (the first formula uses a range reference, the second formula uses a defined name):

```
=AVERAGE(D1:D100)
=AVERAGE(Sales)
```

When you define a name for a cell or range, keep in mind the following rules:

- The name must begin with a letter or _ (an underscore).
- The name can include letters and numbers as well as periods and underscores, but not other symbols or spaces. To distinguish multiword names, use an underscore between the words or capitalize the first letter of each word. For example, the names *Net_Income* or *NetIncome* are valid, but *Net Income* and *Net-Income* are not.
- The name cannot be a valid cell address (such as *FY2010*), function name, or reserved word (such as *Print_Area*).
- The name can include as many as 255 characters, although short, meaningful names of 5 to 15 characters are more practical.
- The name is not case-sensitive. For example, *Sales* and *SALES* are the same name and refer to the same cell or range.

Saving Time with Defined Names | InSight

Defined names have several advantages over cell references, especially as a worksheet becomes longer and more complex. Some advantages include:

- Names, such as *TaxRate* and *TotalSales*, are more descriptive than cell references, making it easier to remember a cell or range's content.
- Names can be used in formulas, making it easier for users to understand the calculations being performed. For example, *=GrossPay–Deductions* is more understandable than *=C15–C16*.
- When you move a named cell or range within a worksheet, its name moves with it. Any formulas that contain the name automatically reference the new location.
- In a formula, a named cell or range is the same as using the cell or range's absolute reference. So, if you move a formula that includes a defined name, the reference remains pointed to the correct cell or range.

By using defined names, you'll often save time and have a better understanding of what a formula is calculating.

Creating a Name for a Cell or Range | Reference Window

- Select the cell or range to which you want to assign a name.
- Click in the Name box on the formula bar, type the name, and then press the Enter key (or in the Defined Names group on the Formulas tab, click the Define Name button, type a name in the Name box, and then click the OK button).

or

- Select the range with labels and blank cells in the top row or first column to which you want to assign a name.
- In the Defined Names group on the Formulas tab, click the Create from Selection button.
- Specify whether to create the ranges based on the top row, bottom row, left column, or right column in the list.
- Click the OK button.

The fastest way to create a defined name is to use the Name box. You'll use the Name box to define names for the cells that contain the handling costs and the parking fee. Then, you'll define a name for the Ticket Price Table, which you will use in a formula later in the tutorial.

To use the Name box to name the invoice constants and the Ticket Price Table:

▶ 1. Click cell **B24** to make it active, and then click the **Name box**. The cell reference for the active cell, B24, is selected in the Name box.

▶ 2. Type **HandlingCost**, and then press the **Enter** key. Cell B24 remains active, and the name *HandlingCost* appears in the Name box instead of the cell reference.

   Trouble? If the label *HandlingCost* appears in cell B24, you probably did not click the Name box before typing the name. On the Quick Access Toolbar, click the Undo button, and then repeat Steps 1 and 2.

▶ 3. Click cell **B25** to make it active, click the **Name box** to select the cell reference, type **ParkingFee**, and then press the **Enter** key. Cell B25 remains active, and the name *ParkingFee* appears in the Name box instead of the cell reference. See Figure 8-3.

| Figure 8-3 | Defined name for cell B25 |

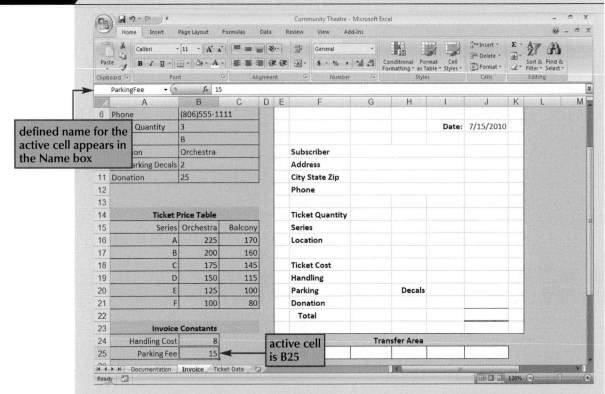

> **4.** Select the range **A16:C21**. The cell reference for the active cell in the range appears in the Name box.

> **5.** Click the **Name box**, type **TicketPrices**, and then press the **Enter** key. The name *TicketPrices* is assigned to the range A16:C21.

> **6.** Select the range **F25:J25**, click the **Name box**, type **TransferArea**, and then press the **Enter** key. The name *TransferArea* is assigned to the range F25:J25.

The Name box, as the title implies, displays all of the names in a workbook. You can select a name in the Name box to quickly select the cell or range referenced by the name. You'll view the defined names you added to the workbook.

To select cells and ranges with the Name box:

> **1.** Click the **Name box** arrow to open a list of defined names in the workbook. Four names appear in the list: *HandlingCost*, *ParkingFee*, *TicketPrices*, and *TransferArea*.

> **2.** Click **ParkingFee**. The active cell moves to cell B25.

> **3.** Click the **Name box** arrow, and then click **TicketPrices**. The range A16:C21 is selected in the worksheet, and cell A16 is the active cell.

Ellen wants to define names to each cell in the Invoice Data area. You can quickly define names without typing them if the data is organized in a tabular format with labels in the first or last column or top or bottom row. The names are based on the row or column labels. Any blanks or parentheses in the row or column labels are changed to an underscore (_) in the defined name.

You will create names for the Invoice Data area, using the labels in the range A3:A11.

To create defined names by selection for the Invoice Data area:

▶ **1.** Select the range **A3:B11**. In this range, column A contains the labels you want to use as the defined names and column B contains the cells you want to name.

▶ **2.** Click the **Formulas** tab on the Ribbon, and then, in the Defined Names group, click the **Create from Selection** button. The Create Names from Selection dialog box opens. See Figure 8-4.

Create Names from Selection dialog box ◀ Figure 8-4

check the location with the names for the defined names

labels in the left column (column A) defined as names for the adjacent cells

▶ **3.** Click the **Top row** check box to remove the check mark, and then verify that the **Left column** check box contains a check mark. The labels in the left column will be used to create the defined names.

▶ **4.** Click the **OK** button. Each cell in the range B3:B11 is named based on its label in column A.

Although you can use the Name box to verify the names were created, the Name Manager dialog box lists all of the names currently defined in the workbook, including Excel table names. You can also use the Name Manager dialog box to a create new names, edit or delete existing names, and filter the list of names.

To use the Name Manager dialog box to edit and delete defined names:

▶ **1.** In the Defined Names group on the Formulas tab, click the **Name Manager** button. The Name Manager dialog box opens, listing the nine defined names based on the labels in the range A3:A11 in the Invoice Data area as well as the four names you defined with the Name box. See Figure 8-5.

Tip

The Name Manager dialog box also lists Excel table names.

| Figure 8-5 | Name Manager dialog box |

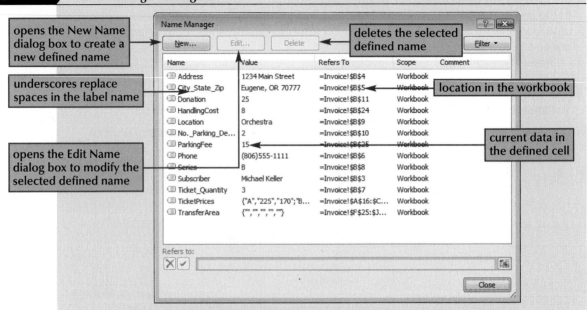

opens the New Name dialog box to create a new defined name

underscores replace spaces in the label name

opens the Edit Name dialog box to modify the selected defined name

deletes the selected defined name

location in the workbook

current data in the defined cell

The name *No._Parking_Decals* is too long, so you'll change it to *Decals*.

▶ **2.** Click **No._Parking_Decals** in the Name list, and then click the **Edit** button. The Edit Name dialog box opens. See Figure 8-6.

| Figure 8-6 | Edit Name dialog box |

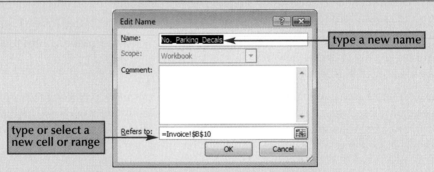

type a new name

type or select a new cell or range

▶ **3.** In the Name box, type **Decals**, and then click the **OK** button. The edited name appears in the list.

Ellen decides the name *TransferArea* is not needed.

▶ **4.** Click **TransferArea**, and then click the **Delete** button. A dialog box opens, confirming that you want to delete the selected name.

▶ **5.** Click the **OK** button. The name is removed from the list.

▶ **6.** Click the **Close** button. The Name Manager dialog box closes.

When a workbook contains many defined names, it can be helpful to list all of the defined names and their corresponding cell addresses as part of the workbook's documentation. You can generate a list of names using the Paste Names command.

To create a list of defined names in the Documentation worksheet:

▶ **1.** Switch to the **Documentation** worksheet.

▶ **2.** Click in cell **A12**, type **Defined Names**, and then press the **Enter** key. The heading for the list of defined names appears in cell A12, and cell A13 is the active cell.

▶ **3.** In the Defined Names group on the Formulas tab, click the **Use in Formula** button. The list includes all the defined names in the workbook followed by the Paste Names command.

▶ **4.** Click **Paste Names**. The Paste Name dialog box opens. You can paste any selected name, or you can paste the entire list of names.

▶ **5.** Click the **Paste List** button. The defined names and their associated cell references are pasted into the range A13:B24.

▶ **6.** Adjust the column widths of columns A and B to display all the defined names data, if necessary, and then deselect the range. See Figure 8-7.

Defined names in the Community Theatre workbook ◄ **Figure 8-7**

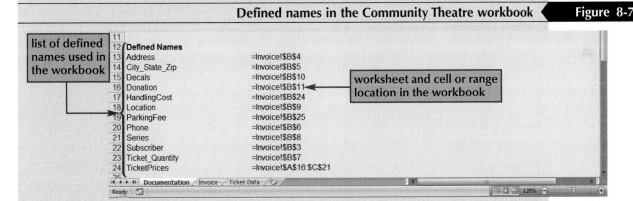

▶ **7.** Switch to the **Invoice** worksheet.

If you edit a defined name or add a new defined name, the list of defined names and their addresses in the Documentation worksheet is not updated. You must paste the list again to update the names and locations. Usually, it is a good idea to wait until the workbook is complete before pasting defined names in the Documentation worksheet.

Entering Formulas with Defined Names

Ellen already entered the TODAY function in cell J7 to ensure the current date always appears on the invoice. You'll enter the remaining formulas needed to generate the invoice. You'll start by entering formulas to display the subscriber's name and address in the invoice. Ellen entered sample subscriber data in the input section of the Invoice worksheet so you can test the formulas as you enter them.

To enter formulas to display the subscriber's name and address:

▶ **1.** In cell G9, enter **=B3**. Michael Keller, the subscriber's name in the sample data, appears in the cell.

▶ **2.** In cell G10, enter **=B4**. The subscriber's address, 1234 Main Street, appears in the cell.

► **3.** Click cell **G10**. The formula =B4 appears in the formula bar.

You entered these formulas using cell addresses rather than defined names. Although you defined names for cells B3 and B4, the names do not automatically replace the cell addresses in the formula. Because defined names make formulas simpler to enter and understand, you will use the named cells and ranges as you enter the remaining formulas.

As you type a defined name in a formula, the Formula AutoComplete box lists items that match the letters you typed. You can type the entire name, double-click the name in the Formula AutoComplete box, or press the Tab key to enter the selected name.

To type defined names in formulas:

► **1.** In cell G11, enter **=City_State_Zip**.

► **2.** Click cell **G11**. The data from cell B5 appears in the cell, and the formula with the defined name, =City_State_Zip, appears in the formula bar.

► **3.** In cell G12, enter **=Phone**, and then click cell **G12**. The sample data from cell B6 appears in the cell, the formula with the defined name, =Phone, appears in the formula bar.

You can also use the point-and-click method to create a formula with defined names. When you click a cell or select a range, Excel substitutes the defined name for the cell reference in the formula. You'll use this method to enter formulas that display the ticket quantity, series, and theatre location from the input area in the invoice.

To enter formulas with defined names using the point-and-click method:

► **1.** Click cell **I14**, type **=**, and then click cell **B7**. The formula uses the defined name *Ticket_Quantity* rather than the cell reference B7.

► **2.** Press the **Enter** key. The number 3, indicating the number of tickets the subscriber ordered, appears in cell I14.

► **3.** In cell I15, type **=**, and then click cell **B8**. The formula uses the defined name *Series* rather than the cell reference B8.

► **4.** Press the **Enter** key. The letter B, indicating the series the subscriber selected, appears in cell I15.

Next, you'll move the subscriber's preferred location to the invoice.

> **5.** In cell I16, type **=**, click **B9**, and then click the **Enter** button ✔ on the formula bar. Orchestra, the location the subscriber selected, appears in cell I16, and the formula with the defined name, =Location, appears in the formula bar. See Figure 8-8.

Formula with a defined name　　**Figure 8-8**

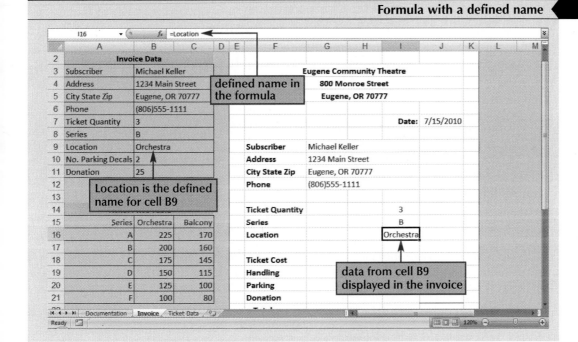

Next, you will enter the formula to calculate the ticket cost to the subscriber. You need to combine two VLOOKUP functions within an IF function to create the formula to calculate ticket costs. The VLOOKUP functions will find the ticket price. The lookup value is the Series the subscriber selects (A, B, C, D, E, or F). Recall that the lookup value searches the first column of the lookup table to find the appropriate row. In this case, the lookup table is the Ticket Price Table (the range you earlier named *TicketPrices*) which has two columns of ticket prices. Column 2 of the table lists the prices for the Orchestra and column 3 of the table lists the prices for the Balcony. The column used to return the ticket prices depends on the Location the subscriber selected. You need to use an IF function to determine whether to search the second or third column for the ticket price.

To enter the formula to determine ticket cost:

▶ 1. In cell J18, enter **=IF(Location="Orchestra",VLOOKUP(Series,TicketPrices, 2,FALSE),VLOOKUP(Series,TicketPrices,3,FALSE))*Ticket_Quantity**. The ticket cost based on the sample subscriber data is $600. The first argument of the IF function, *Location="Orchestra"*, determines which VLOOKUP formula to use—the one returning a value from column 2 (Orchestra) in the TicketPrices table or the one returning a value from column 3 (Balcony) in the TicketPrices table. The second argument, *VLOOKUP(Series,TicketPrices,2,FALSE)*, uses the VLOOKUP function to find a ticket price for a seat in the Orchestra. The first argument of the VLOOKUP function, *Series*, is the defined name that stores the Series code (A, B, C, and so on) used to look up a value in the second argument, *TicketPrices* (range A16:C21). The third argument, *2*, returns a ticket price from the second column (Orchestra) of the TicketPrices table. The fourth argument, *FALSE,* indicates an exact match lookup. The second VLOOKUP function is identical except the third argument has a value of 3, which returns a ticket price from the third column (Balcony) of the TicketPrices table. The final part of the formula, **Ticket_Quantity*, multiplies the ticket price by the number of tickets to calculate the ticket cost.

Trouble? If #Name? or #Value? appears in the cell J18, you might have entered the formula incorrectly. Click cell J18, compare the formula you entered with the formula in Step 1, and then edit the formula in the formula bar as needed. Also, make sure the references in your defined names are correct (see Figure 8-7).

▶ 2. Click cell **J18**, and then click the **Expand Formula Bar** button ⌄ on the right side of the formula bar. The entire formula is visible in the expanded formula bar. The IF function determines which column in the TicketPrices range to use to return the ticket price. If Location in the invoice data area is Orchestra, then the condition Location="Orchestra" is TRUE and the VLOOKUP function returns a ticket price from column 2. If the subscriber requests the Balcony location, then the VLOOKUP function searches column 3 for the ticket price. The price for one ticket, as determined by the IF and VLOOKUP functions, is multiplied by the ticket quantity to calculate the total ticket cost for this transaction. See Figure 8-9.

Figure 8-9	Formula to calculate the ticket cost

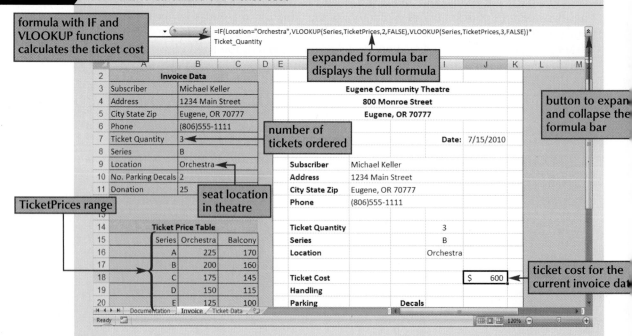

3. Click the **Collapse Formula Bar** button ⌃ on the formula bar. The formula bar returns to its usual height.

You'll enter the remaining formulas needed to complete the invoice.

To enter the remaining formulas in the invoice:

▶ 1. In cell J19, enter **=HandlingCost**. The handling cost is $8, which is the amount in cell B24 in the Invoice Constants area.

▶ 2. In cell I20, enter **=Decals**. The number of parking decals ordered is 2, which is the number listed in cell B10 in the Invoice Data area.

▶ 3. In cell J20, enter **=Decals*ParkingFee**. The parking cost is $30, which is the number of decals listed in cell B10 multiplied by the parking fee in cell B25. You can see how the defined names make entering this calculation faster and the formula easier to understand.

▶ 4. In cell J21, enter **=Donation**. The donation amount is $25, which is listed in cell B11.

▶ 5. In cell J22, enter **=SUM(J18:J21)**. The SUM function adds all the costs to determine the total invoice amount of $663. See Figure 8-10.

| Invoice with all formulas entered | Figure 8-10 |

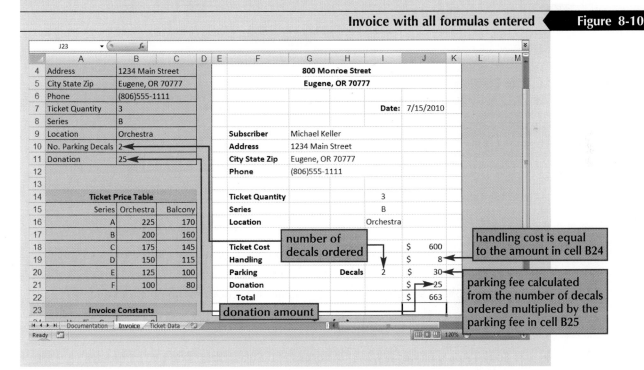

Adding Defined Names to Existing Formulas

Sometimes, you might name cells after creating formulas in the worksheet. Other times, you might not use the defined names when you create formulas (as with the first two formulas you created in the invoice for the subscriber name and address). Recall that defined names are not automatically substituted for the cell addressess in a formula. However, you can replace cell addresses in existing formulas with their defined names to make the formulas more understandable.

Tip

If a formula uses a defined name that doesn't exist, #NAME? appears in the cell. Verify the defined name is spelled correctly and that the name wasn't deleted from the worksheet.

You'll change the two formulas you created to display the subscriber name and address in the invoice to use defined names instead of cell references.

To add defined names to existing formulas in the invoice:

1. In the Defined Names group on the Formulas tab, click the **Define Name** button arrow, and then click **Apply Names**. The Apply Names dialog box appears. See Figure 8-11.

Figure 8-11 ▶ Apply Names dialog box

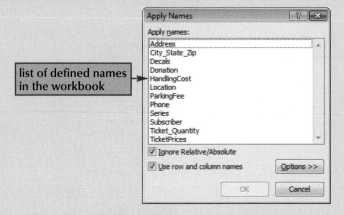

list of defined names in the workbook

You want to select only the two names you need for the existing formulas with cell references.

2. If any name is selected in the Apply names list, click that name to deselect it.

Now that no names are selected in the Apply names list, you will select the names you want to apply to the formulas.

3. In the Apply names list, click **Address** and **Subscriber**. The two names are selected.

4. Click the **OK** button. The two selected names are applied to the formulas.

5. Click cell **G9** and verify that the formula changed to =Subscriber, and then click cell **G10** and verify that the formula changed to =Address.

Ellen wants to store the following items in the Ticket Data worksheet: subscriber name, transaction date, ticket quantity, ticket cost, and total amount owed from the invoice. Displaying these data items in the Transfer Area enables you to copy and paste all the items to the Ticket Data worksheet at once. You'll enter formulas to display the appropriate items in this section of the worksheet.

To enter formulas to display data in the Transfer Area:

▶ **1.** In cell F25, enter **=Subscriber**. The formula displays the subscriber name in this cell.

▶ **2.** In cell G25, enter **=J7**. The formula displays the current date.

▶ **3.** In cell H25, enter **=I14**. The formula displays the number of tickets.

▶ **4.** In cell I25, enter **=J18**. The formula displays the ticket cost.

▶ **5.** In cell J25, enter **=J22**. The formula displays the total cost.

The worksheet contains all the formulas to create the invoice based on the subscriber information. Because Ellen relies on volunteers to enter season ticket requests into the worksheet and print invoices, she wants to be sure the values entered are correct. You will continue to work on Ellen's application by creating validation checks, which are designed to prevent users from inserting incorrect data values. You will also protect cells so that volunteers cannot accidentally overwrite or delete the formulas. You'll do both of these tasks in the next session.

Session 8.1 Quick Check | Review

1. What is a defined name? Give two advantages of using names in workbooks.
2. Describe three ways to create a name.
3. Which of the following is a valid defined name?
   a. Annual_Total
   b. 3rdQtr
   c. Annual total
4. How can you quickly select a cell or range using its name?
5. In the Report workbook, the Expenses name refers to a list of expenses stored in the range D2:D100. Currently the total expenses are calculated with the formula =SUM(D2:D100). Change this formula to use the defined name.
6. True or False? If you define names for a range referenced in an existing formula, you cannot change the formula to use the new name.

Session 8.2

Validating Data Entry

To ensure that correct data is entered and stored in a worksheet, you can use **data validation** to create a set of rules that determine what users can enter in a specific cell or range. Each **validation rule** defines criteria for the data that can be stored in a cell or range. You can specify the type of data allowed (for example, whole numbers, decimals, dates, time, text, and so forth) as well as a list or range of acceptable values (for example, the condition codes *Excellent*, *Good*, *Fair*, and *Poor*, or integers between 1 and 100).

You can also add messages for the user to that cell or range. An **input message** appears when the cell becomes active and can be used to specify the type of data the user should enter in that cell. An **error alert message** appears if a user tries to enter a value in the cell that does not meet the validation rule.

Reference Window | **Validating Data**

- In the Data Tools group on the Data tab, click the Data Validation button.
- Click the Settings tab.
- Click the Allow arrow, click the type of data allowed in the cell, and then enter the validation criteria for that data.
- Click the Input Message tab, and then enter a title and text for the input message.
- Click the Error Alert tab, and then, if necessary, click the Show error alert after invalid data is entered check box to insert a check mark.
- Select an alert style, and then enter the title and text for the error alert message.
- Click the OK button.

Specifying a Data Type and Acceptable Values

Ellen wants you to add three validation rules to the workbook to help ensure that volunteers enter the correct values in the designated range of the Invoice worksheet. These three rules are:

- The Ticket Quantity value in cell B7 should be between 1 and 19. In previous years, 19 was the maximum number of tickets purchased in any invoice transaction.
- The Series value in cell B8 is one of the following: A, B, C, D, E, or F.
- The Location value in cell B9 is either Orchestra or Balcony.

These validation rules will help ensure that the invoice is completed accurately.

Each of these rules specifies the type of values allowed and the validation criteria used when entering a value in a cell. For example, the first rule allows a range of numbers, the second and third rules allow only the values in a list. When you create a data validation rule, you specify what types of values you want to allow as well as the validation criteria. Figure 8-12 describes the types of values you can allow.

Tip

Each cell can have only one validation rule. Creating a second validation rule for a cell replaces the existing rule.

Figure 8-12 | **Allow options for the validation criteria**

Value Type	Cell Accepts
Any value	Any number, text, or date; removes any existing data validation.
Whole number	Integers only; you can specify the range of acceptable integers.
Decimal	Any type of number; you can specify the range of acceptable numbers.
List	Any value in a range or entered in the Data Validation dialog box separated by commas.
Date	Dates only; you can specify the range of acceptable dates.
Time	Times only; you can specify the range of acceptable times.
Text length	Text limited to a specified number of characters.
Custom	Values based on the results of a logical formula.

You will define the validation rule for the number of season tickets.

To specify a whole number range validation rule for the number of tickets:

1. If you took a break after the previous session, make sure the Community Theatre workbook is open and the Invoice worksheet is active.

2. Click cell **B7**. This is the first cell for which you will enter a validation rule.

▶ **3.** Click the **Data** tab on the Ribbon, and then, in the Data Tools group, click the **Data Validation** button. The Data Validation dialog box opens. It contains three tabs: Settings, Input Message, and Error Alert. You use the Settings tab to enter the validation rule for the active cell.

Cell B7, the number of tickets, requires an integer that is greater than 0 and less than 20.

▶ **4.** On the Settings tab, click the **Allow** arrow, and then click **Whole number**. This option specifies that the number must be an integer. The Data Validation dialog box expands to display the options specific to whole numbers. The Ignore blank check box is checked, which means the validation rule is not applied when the cell is empty. If you uncheck the option, users are required to make an entry in the cell.

▶ **5.** If necessary, click the **Data** arrow, and then click **between**. The dialog box reflects the selected criteria.

▶ **6.** Click the **Minimum** box, and then type **1** to specify the smallest value a user can enter.

▶ **7.** Press the **Tab** key to move to the Maximum box, and then type **19** to specify the largest value a user can enter. See Figure 8-13.

Settings tab in the Data Validation dialog box ◀ **Figure 8-13**

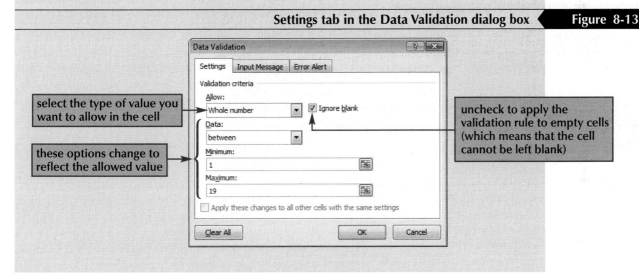

select the type of value you want to allow in the cell

these options change to reflect the allowed value

uncheck to apply the validation rule to empty cells (which means that the cell cannot be left blank)

Validating Existing Data | InSight

Validation rules come into play only during data entry. If you add validation rules to a workbook that already contains data with erroneous values, Excel does not determine if any existing data is invalid. Instead, you can use the Circle Invalid Data command to help identify invalid data that is already in the workbook. (You'll learn about the Circle Invalid Data command later in this tutorial.)

Specifying an Input Message

One way to reduce the chance of a data-entry error is to display an input message when a user makes the cell active. An input message provides additional information about the type of data allowed for that cell. Input messages appear as ScreenTips next to the cell when the cell is selected. You can add an input message to a cell even if you don't set up a rule to validate the data in that cell.

Before a user enters values into the input section of the workbook, Ellen wants them to see the acceptable data values that can be entered in the cell. You will create an input message for cell B7, where users enter the ticket quantity. The input message will help minimize the chance of a volunteer entering an incorrect value.

To create an input message for the ticket quantity cell:

▶ **1.** In the Data Validation dialog box, click the **Input Message** tab. You enter the input message title and text on this tab.

▶ **2.** Verify that the **Show input message when cell is selected** check box contains a check mark. If you uncheck this option, you cannot enter a new input message and any existing input message will not be displayed.

▶ **3.** Click in the **Title** box, and then type **Number of Tickets**. This title will appear in bold at the top of the ScreenTip above the text of the input message.

▶ **4.** Press the **Tab** key to move the insertion point to the Input message box, and then type **Enter the number of tickets purchased**. This text will appear in the Screen-Tip when the cell becomes active. See Figure 8-14.

Figure 8-14 | Input Message tab in the Data Validation dialog box

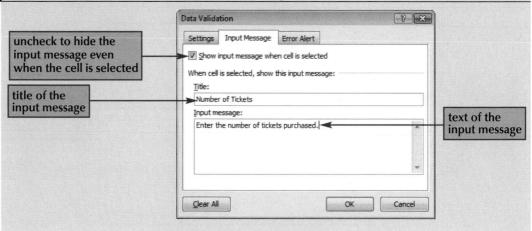

uncheck to hide the input message even when the cell is selected

title of the input message

text of the input message

Specifying an Error Alert Style and Message

Ellen wants to display an error alert message if a volunteer enters data that violates the validation rule. The three error alert styles are Stop, Warning, and Information. The style of the error alert determines what happens after a user attempts to make an invalid entry. The Stop alert prevents the entry from being stored in the cell. The Warning alert prevents the entry from being stored in the cell, unless the user overrides the rejection and decides to continue using the data. The Information alert accepts the data value entered, but allows the user to choose to cancel the data entry.

Although ticket quantities between 1 and 19 are the norm for the theatre, occasionally a subscriber wants to purchase 20 or more tickets, and those entries should be allowed. To account for this possibility, you will create a Warning error alert that appears when a user enters a value greater than 20 or less than 1 for the number of tickets purchased. The user can verify the number entered. If the entry is correct, the user can accept the entry. If the entry is incorrect, the user can reenter a correct number.

You'll enter the Warning error alert message for the ticket quantity cell.

To create the Warning error alert message for the ticket quantity cell:

▶ 1. In the Data Validation dialog box, click the **Error Alert** tab. You use this tab to select the type of error alert and enter the message you want to appear.

▶ 2. Make sure that the **Show error alert after invalid data is entered** check box is checked. If unchecked, the error alert won't appear when an invalid value is entered in the cell.

▶ 3. Click the **Style** arrow, and then click **Warning**. This style allows the user to accept the invalid value, return to the cell and reenter a valid value, or cancel the data entry and restore the previous value to the cell.

▶ 4. Click in the **Title** box, and then type **Number of Tickets Invalid?**. This text will appear as the title of the error alert message box.

▶ 5. Press the **Tab** key to move the insertion point to the Error message box, and then type **You have entered a value less than 1 or greater than 19. Check the number you entered. If it is correct, click Yes. If it is incorrect, click No. If you are not sure, click Cancel.** (including the period). See Figure 8-15.

Tip

You might hide the input and error alert messages when only experienced users will enter data in the workbook. Because the messages are not deleted, you can show them again if a new user will enter data in the workbook.

Error Alert tab in the Data Validation dialog box ◀ **Figure 8-15**

▶ 6. Click the **OK** button. The input message appears below cell B7. See Figure 8-16.

Input message for cell B7 ◀ **Figure 8-16**

The built-in data validation rules are adequate for most simple needs. Sometimes, however, those rules just don't fit your specific worksheet. In those cases, you need to create a custom validation rule that includes a formula. To create a custom validation rule, open the Data Validation dialog box. On the Settings tab, click the Allow arrow, and then click Custom. You can then create the data validation formula.

The formula you specify must be in the form of a condition that returns either True or False. If True is returned, the data entered is considered valid and accepted. If False is returned, the entry is considered invalid and an error alert message is displayed. Consider the following two data validation examples.

The first example uses data validation to prevent the entry of dates that fall on Saturday or Sunday. The WEEKDAY function returns a number (1 to 7) for the date entered in the cell, and then you create a formula to display an error alert if values of 1 (Sunday) or 7 (Saturday) are detected. Assuming the date is entered in cell B2, the following formula returns False if either Saturday or Sunday is entered in cell B2:

```
=AND(WEEKDAY(B2)<>1,WEEKDAY(B2)<>7)
```

The second example uses data validation to ensure all product codes begin with the letter C. To prevent any letter except a C as the first character entered in cell A2, you would use the LEFT function to extract the first character in the cell. The following formula returns True if the first character entered in cell A2 begins with a C; otherwise, an error alert message is displayed:

```
=LEFT(A2,1) = "C"
```

Creating a List Validation Rule

You can use the data validation feature to restrict a cell to accept only entries that are on a list you create. You can create the list of valid entries in the Data Validation dialog box, or you can use a list of valid entries in a single column or row. You will enter the validation rule for the Series being requested, which is one of six values (A, B, C, D, E, and F).

To restrict the Series values to a list of entries you create:

1. Click cell **B8**. Users will enter the series data in this cell.

2. In the Data Tools group on the Data tab, click the **Data Validation** button to open the Data Validation dialog box, and then click the **Settings** tab.

3. Click the **Allow** arrow, and then click **List**. The dialog box expands to display the Source box. You can enter values directly in the Source box separated by commas, or you can select a range of valid entries in the worksheet.

4. Click the **Collapse** button 🔝 next to the Source box so you can see the entire worksheet.

5. Select the range **A16:A21**, which lists the valid six entry values in a row, and then click the **Expand** button 🔲. The Data Validation dialog box returns to its full size. Next, you'll enter an input message.

6. Click the **Input Message** tab, click in the **Title** box, and then type **Series** to enter the title of the input message.

7. Click in the Input message box, and then type **Click the arrow and select one of the choices listed.** to enter the text of the input message.

8. Click the **Error Alert** tab, and then verify that **Stop** appears in the Style box. You want to prevent a user from entering a value that is not included in the list of values you specified.

▶ **9.** In the Title text box, type **Invalid Series**, and then in the Error message box, type **An invalid series has been entered. Click Retry. Press the Esc key, and click the arrow to the right of cell B8. Select A, B, C, D, E, or F.** (including the period). This is the title and text for the error alert message.

▶ **10.** Click the **OK** button. An arrow appears to the right of cell B8 and the input message appears in a ScreenTip.

You need to enter a third data validation rule for cell B9, which indicates the subscriber's choice of location. You will create another list validation rule that allows a user to select either Orchestra or Balcony. You will also create an error alert message.

To create a drop-down list for the Location field:

▶ **1.** Click cell **B9**, and then, in the Data Tools group on the Data tab, click the **Data Validation** button. The Data Validation dialog box opens.

▶ **2.** Click the **Settings** tab, select **List** in the Allow box, and then set the Source box for the range **B15:C15**. This range contain the two values you want to allow users to select for the location.

▶ **3.** Click the **Input Message** tab, type **Location** in the Title box, and then type **Click the arrow and select Orchestra or Balcony** in the Input message box.

▶ **4.** Click the **Error Alert** tab, verify that **Stop** is in the Style box, type **Invalid Location** in the Title box, and then type **An invalid location has been entered. Click Retry, press Esc, and click the arrow to the right of cell B9. Select Orchestra or Balcony.** (including the period) in the Error message box.

▶ **5.** Click the **OK** button. The data validation rule is complete.

You will test the validation feature you've just created by entering incorrect values that violate the validation rules.

To test the data validation rules:

▶ **1.** Click cell **B7**. The input message appears in a ScreenTip, indicating the type of data allowed in the cell. You will enter an invalid value to test the validation rule for the Ticket Quantity field.

▶ **2.** Type **30**, and then press the **Tab** key. The Number of Tickets Invalid? message box opens, informing you that the value you entered might be incorrect. The entry 30 is incorrect; you'll enter a valid number.

▶ **3.** Click the **No** button, type **3** in cell B7, and then press the **Enter** key. The data is entered in cell B7. Cell B8 is the active cell and the input message for Series appears.

You will select a value for the Series using the list.

▶ **4.** Click the arrow to the right of cell B8, and then click **C**. The value is accepted.

The only way an error occurs in cells that have a list validation is if an incorrect entry is *typed* in the cell. You'll try that method.

▶ **5.** In cell B8, enter **G**. The Invalid Series message box opens.

▶ **6.** Click the **Retry** button to close the message box, press the **Esc** key to clear the current value from the cell, and then click the arrow to the right of cell B8 and select **B**. The value is accepted.

Next, you will enter the Location value. You should use the arrow to select an option but you'll intentionally type an invalid entry.

▶ **7.** In cell B9, enter **Mezzanine**. The Invalid Location message box opens, indicating that the Location must be Orchestra or Balcony.

▶ **8.** Click the **Retry** button, press the **Esc** key, click the arrow to the right of cell B9, and then click **Orchestra**. The value is accepted. The three validation rules you entered work as you intended.

Drawing Circles Around Invalid Data

Data validation prevents users from entering invalid data into a cell. It does not verify data that was already entered into a worksheet before the validation criteria were applied. To ensure the entire workbook contains valid data, you need to also verify any data previously entered in the workbook. You can use the Circle Invalid Data command to find and mark cells that contain invalid data. Red circles appear around any data that does not meet the validation criteria, making it simple to scan a worksheet for errors. After you correct the data in a cell, the circle disappears.

To display circles around invalid data, you must perform the following steps:

1. Apply validation rules to existing data.
2. In the Data Tools group on the Data tab, click the Data Validation button arrow, and then click Circle Invalid Data. Red circles appear around cells that contain invalid data.
3. To remove the circle from a single cell, enter valid data in the cell.
4. To hide all circles, in the Data Tools group on the Data tab, click the Data Validation button arow, and then click Clear Validation Circles.

To ensure an error-free workbook, you should use the Circle Invalid Data command to verify data entered before you set up the validation criteria or to verify data in a workbook you inherited from someone else, such as a coworker.

Protecting a Worksheet and Workbook

Another way to reduce data-entry errors is to limit access to certain parts of the workbook. When you **protect** a workbook, you limit the ability users have to make changes to the file. For example, you can prevent users from changing formulas in a worksheet, or you can keep users from deleting worksheets or inserting new ones. You can even keep users from viewing the formulas used in the workbook.

To further help the volunteers work error-free, Ellen wants to protect the contents of the Invoice and Ticket Data worksheets. She wants users to have access only to the range B3:B11, where new season request data are entered. She wants to prevent users from editing the contents of any cells in the Ticket Data worksheet.

Locking and Unlocking Cells

Every cell in a workbook has a **locked property** that determines whether changes can be made to that cell. The locked property has no impact as long as the worksheet is unprotected. However, after you protect a worksheet, the locked property controls whether the cell can be edited. You unlock a cell by turning off the locked property. By default, the locked property is turned on for each cell, and worksheet protection is turned off.

So, unless you unlock cells in a worksheet *before* protecting the worksheet, all of the cells in the worksheet will be locked, and you won't be able to make any changes in the worksheet. Usually, you will want to protect the worksheet, but leave some cells unlocked. For example, you might want to lock cells that contain formulas and formatting so they cannot be changed, but unlock cells in which you want to enter data.

To protect some—but not all—cells in a worksheet, you first turn off the locked property of cells in which data can be entered. Then, you protect the worksheet to activate the locked property for the remaining cells.

In the Invoice worksheet, you want users to be able to enter data in the range B3:B11 but not any other cell in the worksheet. To do this, you must unlock the cells in the range B3:B11.

To unlock the cells in the range B3:B11:

▶ 1. In the Invoice worksheet, select the range **B3:B11**. You want to unlock the cells in this range before you protect the worksheet.

▶ 2. Click the **Home** tab on the Ribbon, and then, in the Font group, click the **Dialog Box Launcher**. The Format Cells dialog box opens with the Font tab active.

▶ 3. Click the **Protection** tab, and then click the **Locked** check box to remove the check mark.

▶ 4. Click the **OK** button, and then click cell **A1** to deselect the highlighted cells. The cells in the range B3:B11 are unlocked.

Protecting a Worksheet

When you set up worksheet protection, you specify which actions are still available to users in the protected worksheet. For example, you can choose to allow users to insert new rows or columns or to delete rows and columns. You can limit the user to selecting only unlocked cells or allow the user to select any cell in the worksheet. These choices remain active as long as the worksheet is protected.

A protected worksheet can always be unprotected. You can also add a password to the protected worksheet that users must enter in order to turn off the protection. If you are concerned that users will turn off protection and make changes to formulas you should use a password; otherwise, it's probably best to not specify a password.

Tip

You can password-protect ranges of cells by selecting the ranges and clicking the Allow Users to Edit Ranges button in the Changes group on the Review tab. Specify a name for the selected cells and provide a password to protect the values in the range. Range passwords become active only when the worksheet is protected.

Protecting a Worksheet | Reference Window

- Select the cell or range you want to unlock.
- In the Font group on the Home tab, click the Dialog Box Launcher.
- In the Format Cells dialog box, click the Protection tab, click the Locked check box to remove the check mark, and then click the OK button.
- In the Changes group on the Review tab, click the Protect Sheet button.
- Enter a password (optional).
- Select all of the actions you want to allow users to take when the worksheet is protected.
- Click the OK button.

Ellen wants to protect the Invoice and Ticket Data worksheets, but she doesn't want a password specified. You will enable worksheet protection that will allow users to select any cell in those worksheets, but enter data only in the unlocked cells.

To protect the Invoice and Ticket Data worksheets:

▶ **1.** Click the **Review** tab on the Ribbon, and then, in the Changes group, click the **Protect Sheet** button. The Protect Sheet dialog box opens, as shown in Figure 8-17.

Figure 8-17   **Protect Sheet dialog box**

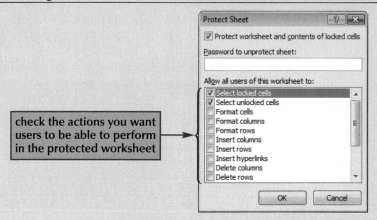

check the actions you want
users to be able to perform
in the protected worksheet

Tip

Keep passwords in a safe place. Remember, passwords are case sensitive. If you forget the password, it is very difficult to remove the worksheet protection.

You will leave the Password box blank because you do not want to use a password. By default, users can select locked and unlocked cells, which are all cells in the worksheet, but they can enter or edit values only in unlocked cells. Ellen wants the volunteers to be able to perform these actions.

▶ **2.** Click the **OK** button. The Protect Sheet dialog box closes.

You'll test the protection by trying to edit a locked cell and then an unlocked cell in the Invoice worksheet.

▶ **3.** Click cell **I14**, and then type **8**. As soon as you press any key, a dialog box opens, indicating that the cell is protected and cannot be modified.

▶ **4.** Click the **OK** button.

▶ **5.** Click cell **B7**, type **8**, and then press the **Enter** key. The ticket quantity is updated because you allowed editing in the range B3:B11. A user can enter and edit values in these cells. Although users can select any cell in the worksheet, they cannot make an entry in any other cell.

▶ **6.** On the Quick Access Toolbar, click the **Undo** button 🔁 to return the Ticket Quantity to 3.

Next, you will protect all of the cells in the Ticket Data worksheet.

▶ **7.** Switch to the **Ticket Data** worksheet.

▶ **8.** In the Changes group on the Review tab, click the **Protect Sheet** button to open the Protect Sheet dialog box, and then click the **OK** button to accept the default set of user actions.

You will test to see what would happen if someone tried to edit one of the cells in the Ticket Data worksheet.

9. Click cell **A2** and type **B**. A dialog box opens, indicating that the cell is protected and cannot be modified. All the cells in this worksheet are protected because no cells have been unlocked.

10. Click the **OK** button to close the dialog box.

Protecting a Workbook

The contents of the Invoice and Ticket Data worksheets, with the exception of the range B3:B11 in the Invoice worksheet, cannot be changed. However, worksheet protection applies only to the contents of the worksheet, not to the worksheet itself. So, a theatre volunteer could inadvertently rename or delete the protected worksheet. To keep the worksheets themselves from being modified, you need to protect the workbook.

You can protect both the structure and the windows of the workbook. Protecting the structure prohibits users from renaming, deleting, hiding, or inserting worksheets. Protecting the windows prohibits users from moving, resizing, closing, or hiding parts of the Excel window. The default is to protect only the structure of the workbook, not the windows used to display it. You can also add a password; however, the same guideline is true here as for protecting worksheets. Add a password only if you are concerned that others might unprotect the workbook and modify it. If you add a password, keep in mind that it is case sensitive and you cannot unprotect the workbook without it.

| **Protecting a Workbook** | | Reference Window |

- In the Changes group on the Review tab, click the Protect Workbook button.
- Click the check boxes to indicate whether you want to protect the workbook's structure, windows, or both.
- Enter a password (optional).
- Click the OK button.

Ellen doesn't want users to be able to change the structure of the workbook, so you will set protection for the workbook structure, but not the window.

To protect a workbook:

1. In the Changes group on the Review tab, click the **Protect Workbook** button. The Protect Structure and Windows dialog box opens. You can choose to protect the structure, protect the windows, or both. See Figure 8-18.

Protect Structure and Windows dialog box ◄ **Figure 8-18**

2. Make sure the **Structure** check box is checked, the Windows check box is unchecked, and the Password box is blank.

3. Click the **OK** button to protect the workbook without specifying a password.

> **4.** Right-click the **Ticket Data** sheet tab, on the shortcut menu, notice that the Insert, Delete, Rename, Move or Copy, Tab Color, Hide, and Unhide commands are gray, indicating that the options that modify the worksheets are no longer available for the Ticket Data worksheet.

> **5.** Press the **Esc** key to close the shortcut menu.

Unprotecting a Worksheet

Ellen is pleased with the different levels of protection that can be applied to the worksheet. At this point, you still have a lot of editing to do in the Invoice worksheet, so you'll turn off worksheet protection in that worksheet. Later, when you've completed your modifications, Ellen can turn worksheet protection back on.

To turn off worksheet protection for the Invoice worksheet:

Tip

You can also remove workbook protection; in the Changes group on the Review tab, click the Unprotect Workbook button.

> **1.** Switch to the **Invoice** worksheet.

> **2.** In the Changes group on the Review tab, click the **Unprotect Sheet** button. Worksheet protection is removed from the Invoice worksheet. The button changes back to the Protect Sheet button. If you had assigned a password when you protected the worksheet, you would have had to enter the password to remove worksheet protection.

Adding Worksheet Comments

Providing documentation is important for a successful application. In addition to including a documentation sheet that provides an overview of the workbook, you used defined names instead of cell addresses to make it easier to write and understand formulas and then you pasted a list of these names in the worksheet for you and others to see. You also used input messages to assist with data validation. Another source of documentation you can use in a workbook is comments. A **comment** is a text box that is attached to a specific cell in a worksheet. Comments are often used in workbooks to: (a) explain the contents of a particular cell, such as a complex formula, (b) provide instructions to users, and (c) share ideas and notes from several users collaborating on a project.

Reference Window | **Inserting a Comment**

- Click the cell to which you want to attach a comment.
- Right-click the cell, and then click Insert Comment on the shortcut menu (or in the Comments group on the Review tab, click the New Comment button).
- Type the comment into the comment box.

Ellen wants you to insert a brief note about entering data from the order form into the input section in cell A2 and a note explaining how the IF and VLOOKUP functions are used to determine the cost of theatre tickets in cell J18.

To insert comments in cells A2 and J18:

▶ 1. In the Invoice worksheet, right-click cell **A2**, and then click **Insert Comment** on the shortcut menu. A text box opens to the right of cell A2. The user name for your installation of Excel appears in bold at the top of the box. A small red triangle appears in the upper-right corner of the cell.

▶ 2. Type **Enter all data from the order form into cells B3 through B12** in the text box. An arrow points from the text box to cell A2 which contains the comment. Selection handles appear around the text box, which you can use to resize the box; you can drag the text box by its hatched border to move the comment to a new location in the worksheet. See Figure 8-19.

Comment added to cell A2 | **Figure 8-19**

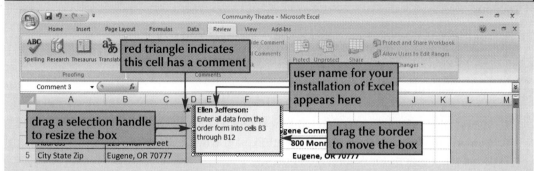

▶ 3. Click cell **B12** to hide the comment. The comment disappears. A small red triangle remains in the upper-right corner of cell A2 to indicate this cell contains a comment.

The comment in cell A2 should reference the range B3:B11. You'll edit the comment.

▶ 4. Click cell **A2**, and then, in the Comments group on the Review tab, click the **Edit Comment** button. The text box appears with the insertion point at the end of the comment text.

▶ 5. In the text box, change B12 to **B11**.

▶ 6. Click any cell to hide the text box, and then point to cell **A2** to view the edited comment.

Next, you'll add a comment to cell J18.

▶ 7. Click cell **J18**, and then, in the Comments group on the Review tab, click the **New Comment** button. A comment box opens to the right of cell J18.

▶ 8. Type **This IF function determines whether to use a VLOOKUP function referencing column 2 or 3 of the Ticket Price table** in the text box.

▶ 9. Drag the lower-right selection handle down to increase the size of the text box to fit the comment.

▶ 10. Click cell **I17** to hide the comment. A small red triangle remains in the upper-right corner of cell J18 to indicate it contains a comment.

▶ 11. Point to cell **J18** to see the comment.

Ellen decides that the volunteers don't need to know how the ticket cost is calcuated. You'll delete the comment in cell J18.

Tip

To keep an active cell's comment on screen, in the Comments group on the Review tab, click the Show/ Hide Comment button. Click the button again to hide the active cell's comment. To show or hide all the comments in a worksheet, click the Show All Comments button.

▶ **12.** Click cell **J18**, and then, in the Comments group on the Review tab, click the **Delete** button. The comment is deleted, and the red triangle in the upper-right corner of cell J18 is removed.

In this session, you used data validation to help ensure that all values entered in the Invoice worksheet are accurate. You created validation rules that included input messages and error alert messages. You learned how to protect and unprotect both the worksheet and the workbook. In addition, you learned how to use comments to add notes to specific cells in the workbook. In the next session, you'll automate some of the steps in the application by recording macros.

Review	**Session 8.2 Quick Check**

1. How do you turn on data validation for a specified cell?
2. How do you specify an input message for a cell?
3. Describe the three types of error alert messages Excel can display when a user violates a validation rule.
4. What is a locked cell?
5. What is the difference between worksheet protection and workbook protection?
6. Can you rename a protected worksheet? Explain why or why not.
7. What are the steps for editing a comment?

Session 8.3

Working with Macros

Ellen needs to print the entire Invoice worksheet, which includes the input area, transfer area, and invoice, for her paper files. In addition, she needs to print only the invoice to send to the season subscriber. Each printout has different custom headers and footers. In addition, data from the invoice needs to be transferred to the Ticket Data worksheet. Ellen wants to simplify these tasks so volunteers don't need to repeat the same actions for each subscriber order and also to reduce the possibility of errors being introduced during the repetitive process.

You can automate any task you perform repeatedly with a macro. A **macro** is a series of stored commands that can be run whenever you need to perform the task. For example, you can create a macro to print a worksheet, insert a set of dates and values, or import data from a text file and store it in Excel. Macros perform repetitive tasks more quickly than you can. And, after the macro is created, you can be assured that no mistakes will occur from performing the same task over and over again.

To create and run macros, you need to use the Developer tab. By default, this tab is not displayed on the Ribbon, so you'll display it. The Developer tab has three groups: one for code, one for controls, and one for XML. You'll use the Code group when working with macros.

To display the Developer tab on the Ribbon:

▶ **1.** If you took a break after the previous session, make sure the Community Theatre workbook is open and the Invoice worksheet is active.

▶ **2.** Look for the **Developer** tab on the Ribbon. If you see the Developer tab, continue with Step 5. If you do not see the Developer tab, continue with Step 3.

3. Click the **Office Button** 🔘, and then click the **Excel Options** button. The Excel Options dialog box opens with the Popular options displayed. See Figure 8-20.

Popular category in the Excel Options dialog box ◀ Figure 8-20

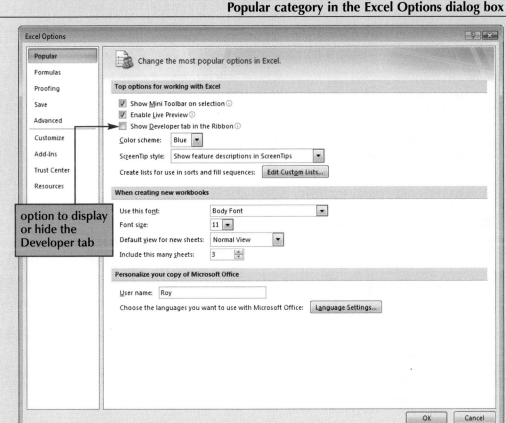

4. In the Top options for working with Excel section, click the **Show Developer tab in the Ribbon** check box to insert a check mark, and then click the **OK** button. The Developer tab appears on the Ribbon.

5. Click the **Developer** tab. See Figure 8-21.

Developer tab on the Ribbon ◀ Figure 8-21

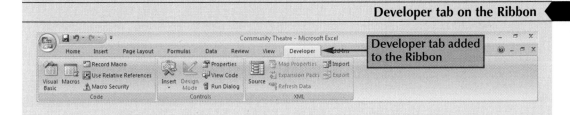

Protecting Against Macro Viruses

In recent years, viruses have been attached as macros to files created in Excel and other Office programs. When unsuspecting users opened these infected workbooks, Excel automatically ran the attached virus-infected macro. **Macro viruses** are a type of virus that uses a program's own macro programming language to distribute the virus. Most macro viruses are not harmful and do not affect data in any way. For example, one macro virus changed the title bar text from *Microsoft Excel* to *Microsofa Excel*. Occasionally, macro viruses are destructive and can modify or delete files that may not be recoverable. Because it is possible for a macro to contain a virus, Microsoft Office 2007 provides several options from which you can choose to set a security level you feel comfortable with.

Macro Security Settings

The **macro security settings** control what Excel will do about macros in a workbook when you open that workbook. For example, one user may choose to run macros only if they are "digitally signed" by a developer who is on a list of trusted sources. Another user might want to disable all macros in workbooks and see a notification when a workbook contains macros. The user can then elect to enable the macros. Excel has four macro security settings, as described in Figure 8-22.

Figure 8-22   **Macro security settings**

Setting	Description
Disable all macros without notification	All macros in all workbooks are disabled and no security alerts about macros are displayed. Use this setting if you don't want macros to run.
Disable a macro with notification	All macros in all workbooks are disabled, but security alerts appear when the workbook contains a macro. Use this default setting to choose on a case-by-case basis whether to run a macro.
Disable all macros except digitally signed macros	The same as the *Disable a macro with notification* setting except any macro signed by a trusted publisher runs if you have already trusted the publisher. Otherwise, security alerts appear when a workbook contains a macro.
Enable all macros	All macros in all workbooks run. Use this setting temporarily in such cases as when developing an application that contains macros. This setting is not recommended for regular use.

You set macro security in the Trust Center using the Security dialog box. The **Trust Center** is a central location for all the security settings in Office 2007. By default, all potentially dangerous content, such as macros and workbooks with external links, is blocked without warning. If content is blocked, the Message Bar (also called the trust bar), located under the Ribbon, appears, notifying you that some content was disabled. You can click the Message Bar to open a dialog box with all of the disabled content and options for enabling or disabling that content.

In Office 2007 you can define a set of locations (file path) where you can place files you consider trustworthy. This feature is known as *Trusted Locations*. Any workbook opened from a trusted location is considered "safe" and content such as macros will work without having to respond to additional security questions to use the workbook.

Setting Macro Security in Excel | Reference Window

- In the Code group on the Developer tab, click the Macro Security button.
- Click the option button for the security setting you want.
- Click the OK button.

or

- Click the Office Button, and then click the Excel Options button.
- Click the Trust Center category, and then click the Trust Center Settings button.
- Click the Macro Settings category, and then select the option button for the security setting you want.
- Click the OK button.

Ellen wants some protection against macro viruses, so she suggests you set the security level to *Disable all macros with notification*. When you open a file with macros, the macros will be disabled and a security alert will appear, allowing you to activate the macros if you believe the workbook comes from a trusted source.

To set the macro security level:

▶ **1.** In the Code group on the Developer tab, click the **Macro Security** button. The Trust Center dialog box opens with the Macro Settings category displayed.

▶ **2.** In the Macro Settings section, click the **Disable all macros with notification** option button if it is not selected. See Figure 8-23.

Macro Settings in the Trust Center dialog box ◀ Figure 8-23

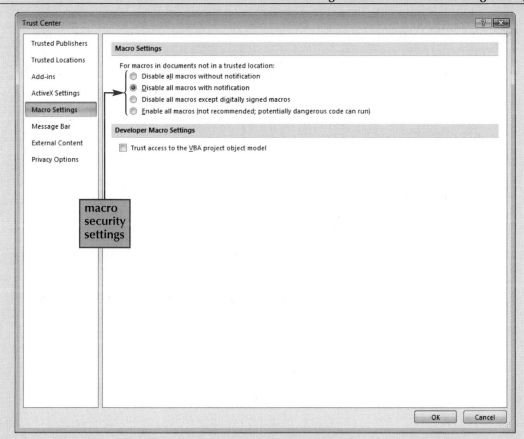

▶ **3.** Click the **OK** button.

Each time you open a workbook that contains a macro that the Trust Center detects, the macro is disabled and a Message Bar appears below the Ribbon with the Security Warning that macros have been disabled. Click the Options button to open a security dialog box with the option to enable the macro or leave it disabled. If you developed the workbook or trust the person who sent you the workbook, click the Enable this content option button to run the macros in the workbook.

InSight		**Using Digital Signatures with Macros**

A **digital signature** is like a seal of approval. It's often used to identify the author of a workbook that contains macros. You add a digital signature as the last step before you distribute a file. Before you can add a digital signature to a workbook, you need to obtain a digital ID (also called a digital certificate) that proves your identity. Digital certificates are typically issued by a certificate authority. After you have a digital certificate, do the following to digitally sign a workbook:

1. Click the Office Button, point to Prepare, and then click Add a Digital Signature to open the Sign dialog box.
2. Click in the Purpose for signing this document box, and then type a reason why you are adding a digital signature to this workbook.
3. Click the Sign button. The invisible digital signature does not appear within the workbook, but users will see the Signatures button on the status bar.

By digitally signing a workbook that contains a macro you intend to publicly distribute, you assure others of two things: (1) the identity of the creator of the macro, and (2) the macro has not been altered since the digital signature was created.

When you open a digitally signed file, you can see who the author is and decide whether the information in the file is authentic and you trust that the macros in the workbook are safe to run.

The digital signature is removed any time a file is saved after the signature has been added to the file. Therefore, no one (including the original workbook author) can open a digitally signed file, make changes to the workbook, save the workbook, and then send the file to another user with the digital signature intact. The original author must digitally resign the modified workbook.

Recording a Macro

You can create an Excel macro in one of two ways: You can use the macro recorder to record keystrokes and mouse actions as you perform them, or you can enter a series of commands in the **Visual Basic for Applications (VBA)** programming language. The macro recorder can record only those actions you perform with the keyboard or mouse. The macro recorder is a good choice for creating simple macros. For more sophisticated macros, you might need to write VBA code directly in the Visual Basic Editor.

For Ellen's application, the tasks you need to perform can all be done with the keyboard and the mouse, so you will use the macro recorder to record the three macros. One macro will show the invoice in Print Preview, a second macro will show the entire Invoice worksheet in Print Preview, and a third macro will transfer data from the Invoice worksheet to the Ticket Data worksheet.

Planning and Recording a Macro | InSight

Advance planning and practice help to ensure you create an error-free macro. First, decide what you want to accomplish. Then, consider the best way to achieve those results. Next, practice the keystrokes and mouse actions before you actually record the macro. This may seem like extra work, but it reduces the chance of error when you actually record the macro. As you set up the macro, consider the following:

- Choose a descriptive name that helps you recognize the macro's purpose.
- Weigh the benefits of selecting a shortcut key against its drawbacks. Although a shortcut key is an easy way to run a macro, you are limited to one-letter shortcuts, which can make it difficult to remember the purpose of each shortcut key. In addition, the macro shortcut keys will override the standard Office shortcuts for the workbook.
- Store the macro with the current workbook unless the macro can be used with other workbooks.
- Include a description that provides an overview of the macro and perhaps your name and contact information.

Ellen provides you with an outline of the actions needed for the macro to show the invoice in Print Preview. These are:

1. Set the print area (E2:J23).
2. Define the Page Layout setting with the custom heading I N V O I C E.
3. Display the invoice in Print Preview.
4. Close the Print Preview window.
5. Make cell B3 the active cell.

Each macro must have a unique name that begins with a letter. The macro name can be up to 255 characters, including letters, numbers, and the underscore symbol. The macro name cannot include spaces or special characters. It is helpful to use a descriptive name that describes the macro's purpose. You can assign a shortcut key to run the macro directly from the keyboard. You can also add a description of the macro. Finally, a macro needs to be stored somewhere. By default, the macro is stored in the current workbook, making the macro available in only that workbook when it is open. Another option is to store the macro in the **Personal Macro workbook**, a hidden workbook named *Personal.xlsb* that opens whenever you start Excel, making the macro available anytime you use Excel. The Personal Macro workbook stores commonly used macros that apply to many workbooks. It is most convenient for users on stand-alone computers. Finally, you can store the macro in a new workbook. Keep in mind, the new workbook must be open to use the macro. For example, an accountant might store a set of macros that help with end-of-the-month tasks in a separate workbook.

Recording a Macro | Reference Window

- In the Code group on the Developer tab, click the Record Macro button.
- Enter a name for the macro, and specify the location to store the macro.
- Specify a shortcut key (optional).
- Enter a description of the macro (optional).
- Click the OK button to start the macro recorder.
- Perform the tasks you want to automate.
- Click the Stop Recording button.

For Ellen's application, you'll record a macro named *PrintPreviewInvoice*, assigned a keyboard shortcut, with a description, stored in the Community Theatre workbook. Macro shortcut keys are used to run a macro. Assigning a shortcut key overrides the default Office shortcut for the open workbook. Therefore, pressing the Ctrl+p keys runs the PrintPreviewInvoice macro, overriding the default Office 2007 shortcut for printing a selected area. Some people find macro shortcut keys a quick way to run a macro; others dislike them because they lose the original function of the shortcut key. It's a personal preference.

You'll start the macro recorder.

To start the macro recorder:

▶ **1.** In the Code group on the Developer tab, click the **Record Macro** button. The Record Macro dialog box opens. The Macro name box displays a default name for the macro that consists of the word *Macro* followed by a number that is one greater than the number of macros already recorded in the workbook during the current Excel session. See Figure 8-24.

Figure 8-24 ▶ **Record Macro dialog box**

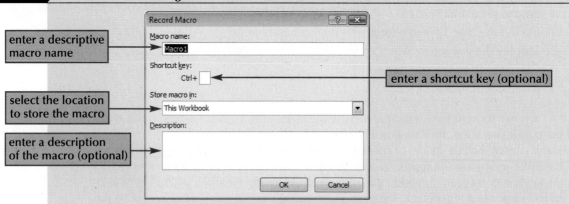

enter a descriptive macro name

enter a shortcut key (optional)

select the location to store the macro

enter a description of the macro (optional)

▶ **2.** In the Macro name box, type **PrintPreviewInvoice** to change the default name to a more descriptive one, and then press the **Tab** key.

▶ **3.** In the Shortcut key box, type **p** to set Ctrl+p as the shortcut to run the macro from the keyboard, and then press the **Tab** key.

▶ **4.** Verify that **This Workbook** appears in the Store macro in box to store the macro in the Community Theatre workbook, and then press the **Tab** key.

▶ **5.** In the Description box, type **Created 7/15/2010. Print Preview of invoice area: range E2:K23.** (including the period) to enter notes about the macro.

▶ **6.** Click the **OK** button. The workbook enters macro record mode. The Record Macro button in the Code group on the Developer tab changes to the Stop Recording button, which also appears on the status bar.

From this point on, every mouse click and keystroke you perform will be recorded and stored as part of the PrintPreviewInvoice macro. For that reason, it's very important to follow the instructions in the next steps precisely. Take your time as you perform each step, reading the entire step carefully first. After you finish recording the keystrokes, you click the Stop Recording button to turn off the macro recorder.

To record the PrintPreviewInvoice macro:

▶ 1. Click the **Page Layout** tab on the Ribbon.

▶ 2. Click cell **E2**, press and hold the **Shift** key, click cell **K23**, and then release the Shift key to select the range E2:K23. This range contains the invoice area.

▶ 3. In the Page Setup group, click the **Print Area** button, and then click **Set Print Area**. The invoice area is set as the print area. Next, you'll insert a custom header.

▶ 4. In the Page Setup group, click the **Dialog Box Launcher** to open the Page Setup dialog box, click the **Header/Footer** tab, click the **Custom Header** button to open the Header dialog box, click in the **Center section** box, type **I N V O I C E**, and then click the **OK** button.

▶ 5. Click the **Margins** tab, verify that the **Horizontally** check box is checked to center the invoice on the page.

▶ 6. Click the **Print Preview** button. The invoice appears in Print Preview. Next, you will close the Print Preview window and set cell B3 as the active cell.

▶ 7. Click the **Close Print Preview** button to return to Normal view. Although this step is not intuitive, you need to close Print Preview before you can continue recording the macro or stop recording the macro. When you run the macro, Excel will automatically stop at the point where the Print Preview window opens to give the user the option of printing or closing Print Preview without printing.

▶ 8. In the Invoice worksheet, click cell **B3**. You've completed all the steps in the PrintPreviewInvoice macro. You'll turn off the macro recorder.

▶ 9. Click the **Stop Recording** button 🔲 on the status bar. The button changes to the Record macro button.

Trouble? If you made a mistake while recording the macro, close the Community Theatre workbook without saving your changes. Reopen the workbook, and then repeat all the steps beginning with the "To start the macro recorder" steps.

Trouble? If you need to save your work before completing the tutorial, read pages EX 439–440 to learn how to save a workbook with macros.

> **Tip**
>
> You can also turn off the macro recorder by clicking the Stop Recording button in the Code group on the Developer tab.

Running a Macro

Next, you'll test the macro to ensure it works as intended. To run the macro you created, you can either use the shortcut key you specified or select the macro in the Macro dialog box and click the Run button.

Running a Macro | Reference Window

- Press the shortcut key assigned to the macro.

or

- In the Code group on the Developer tab, click the Macros button.
- Select the macro from the list of macros, and then click the Run button.

To run the PrintPreviewInvoice macro:

▶ **1.** Click the **Developer** tab on the Ribbon, and then, in the Code group, click the **Macros** button. The Macro dialog box opens, as shown in Figure 8-25. This dialog box lists all of the macros in the open workbooks. You can select a macro, and then run it, edit the macro with VBA, run the macro one step at a time so you can determine in which step an error occurs, or delete it.

Figure 8-25 ▶ Macro dialog box

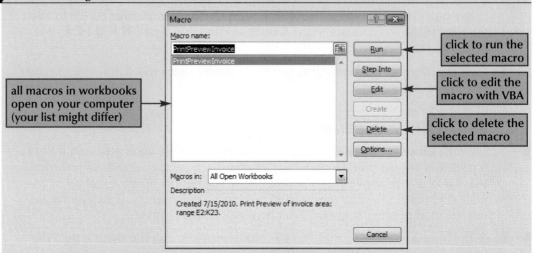

- all macros in workbooks open on your computer (your list might differ)
- click to run the selected macro
- click to edit the macro with VBA
- click to delete the selected macro

▶ **2.** Verify that **PrintPreviewInvoice** is selected in the list, and then click the **Run** button. The PrintPreviewInvoice macro runs and the invoice appears in Print Preview. You can now print the invoice or close Print Preview without printing. Notice that the PrintPreviewInvoice macro did not run very quickly and caused some screen flicker. You will fix this later in the tutorial.

Trouble? If the PrintPreviewInvoice macro did not run properly, you might have made a mistake in the steps while recording the macro. Click the Close Print Preview button in the Preview group on the Print Preview tab. Click the Developer tab, and then, in the Code group, click the Macros button. Select the PrintPreviewInvoice macro and then click the Delete button. Click the OK button to confirm the deletion, and then repeat all the steps beginning with the "To start the macro recorder" steps.

▶ **3.** In the Preview group on the Print Preview tab, click the **Close Print Preview** button. The workbook returns to Normal view and cell B3 is the active cell. The macro works correctly. If you had printed the invoice, the Print Preview window would automatically close after the invoice printed.

Next, you will test the shortcut keys you used for the PrintPreviewInvoice macro.

▶ **4.** Press the **Ctrl+p** keys. The PrintPreviewInvoice macro runs. The invoice is displayed in the Print Preview window.

You will not print the invoice.

▶ **5.** In the Preview group, click the **Close Print Preview** button. The worksheet returns to Normal view and cell B3 is the active cell. As an alternative, you could select the Print command on the Print Preview tab to print the invoice. After printing the invoice, the worksheet would return to Normal view and cell B3 would be the active cell.

Trouble? If your macro doesn't end on its own, you need to end it. Press the Ctrl+Break keys to stop the macro from running.

How Edits Can Affect Macros | InSight

Be careful when making seemingly small changes to your workbook, as these can have a great impact on your macros. If a runtime error (an error that occurs while running a macro) appears when you run a macro that has worked in the past, some part of the macro code no longer makes sense to Excel. For example, simply adding a space to a worksheet name can affect a macro that references the worksheet. If you recorded a macro that referenced a worksheet named *TicketData* (no spaces in the name) that you later changed to *Ticket Data* (space added to the name), the macro no longer works because the TicketData worksheet no longer exists. You can record the macro again, or you could edit the macro in VBA changing *TicketData* to *Ticket Data*.

Next, you'll record the macro to print the entire worksheet. The steps will be similar to the first macro, except that you'll set the print area to A1:K25, display *OFFICE COPY* as the custom header, display Ellen's name and title in the left section of the custom footer, and scale the worksheet to fit on one page. For this macro, you'll use the Ctrl+s shortcut keys.

To record the PrintPreviewEntireSheet macro:

▶ 1. On the status bar, click the **Record Macro** button 🔲. The Record Macro dialog box opens.

▶ 2. In the Macro name box, type **PrintPreviewEntireSheet** to enter a descriptive name, and then press the **Tab** key.

▶ 3. In the Shortcut key box, type **s**, and then press the **Tab** key twice. The This Workbook option appears in the Store macro in box.

▶ 4. In the Description box, type **Created 7/15/2010. Print Preview of entire worksheet area: range A1:K25**, and then click the **OK** button. The macro recorder is on.

▶ 5. Click the **Page Layout** tab on the Ribbon.

▶ 6. In the Invoice worksheet, select the range **A1:K25**, in the Page Setup group, click the **Print Area** button, and then click **Set Print Area**.

▶ 7. In the Page Setup group, click the **Dialog Box Launcher** to open the Page Setup dialog box, click the **Header/Footer** tab, click the **Custom Header** button, select the text in the Center section box, type **O F F I C E   C O P Y**, and then click the **OK** button.

▶ 8. Click the **Custom Footer** button, click in the **Left section** box, type **Ellen Jefferson, Business Manager**, and then click the **OK** button.

▶ 9. Click the **Page** tab in the Page Setup dialog box, in the Scaling section, click the **Fit To** option button, and then confirm that **1** appears in both Fit to boxes.

▶ 10. Click the **Print Preview** button to display the invoice in Print Preview.

▶ 11. Click the **Close Print Preview** button, and then click cell **B3**.

▶ 12. Click the **Stop Recording** button 🔲 on the status bar. The button changes to the Record Macro button, and the macro recorder is turned off.

You'll use the shortcut key method to test both the PrintPreviewEntireSheet and PrintPreviewInvoice macros.

To test the PrintPreviewEntireSheet and PrintPreviewInvoice macros:

▶ **1.** Press the **Ctrl+s** keys. The PrintPreviewEntireSheet macro runs.

▶ **2.** In the Preview group on the Print Preview tab, click the **Close Print Preview** button. The worksheet returns to Normal view and cell B3 is the active cell. The PrintPreviewEntireSheet macro was successful.

Trouble? If the PrintPreviewEntireSheet macro did not run properly, you might have made a mistake in the steps while recording it. Click the Close Print Preview button in the Preview group on the Print Preview tab. Click the Developer tab, and then, in the Code group, click the Macros button. Select the PrintPreviewEntireSheet macro, and then click the Delete button to remove the macro. Click the OK button to confirm the deletion, and then repeat all the steps beginning with the "To record the PrintPreviewEntireSheet macro" to record and test the macro again.

Next, you'll run the PrintPreviewInvoice macro.

▶ **3.** Press the **Ctrl+p** keys. The PrintPreviewInvoice macro runs.

▶ **4.** In the Preview group on the Print Preview tab, click the **Close Print Preview** button.

Creating the TransferData Macro

You need to record one more macro. The data you entered earlier in the input section of the Invoice worksheet was never added to the Ticket Data worksheet. Ellen wants to add this data from the purchase of season tickets to the next available blank row in the Ticket Data worksheet. The macro that you'll create will fix that problem. The actions of this macro will be as follows:

- Switch to the Ticket Data worksheet.
- Turn off worksheet protection in the Ticket Data worksheet.
- Switch to the Invoice worksheet.
- Select and copy the Transfer Area to the Clipboard.
- Switch to the Ticket Data worksheet.
- Go to cell A1, and then go to last row in ticket data table.
- Turn on Relative References. The Relative Reference button controls how Excel records the act of selecting a range in the worksheet. By default, the macro will select the same cells regardless of which cell is first selected because the macro records a selection using absolute cell references. If you want a macro to select cells regardless of the position of the active cell when you run the macro, set the macro recorder to record relative cell references.
- Move down one row.
- Turn off Relative References.
- Paste values to the Ticket Data worksheet.
- Go to cell A1.
- Turn on worksheet protection.
- Switch to the Invoice worksheet, and go to cell A1.

Ellen wants you to name this new macro *TransferData*. You'll assign the Ctrl+t keys as the shortcut.

To record the TransferData macro:

▶ 1. Click the **Record Macro** button 📇 on the status bar to open the Record Macro dialog box, type **TransferData** in the Macro name box, type **t** in the Shortcut key box, type **Created 7/15/2010. Copy values in the transfer area in the Invoice worksheet to Ticket Data worksheet** in the Description box, and then click the **OK** button. The macro recorder is on.

▶ 2. Click the **Ticket Data** sheet tab, click the **Review** tab on the Ribbon, and then, in the Changes group, click the **Unprotect Sheet** button to turn off protection.

▶ 3. Click the **Invoice** sheet tab, and then select the range **F25:J25** in the Transfer Area.

▶ 4. Click the **Home** tab on the Ribbon, and then, in the Clipboard group, click the **Copy** button 📋.

▶ 5. Click the **Ticket Data** sheet tab, click cell **A1**, and then press the **End+↓** keys to go to the last row with values.

▶ 6. Click the **Developer** tab on the Ribbon, and then, in the Code group, click the **Use Relative References** button. Relative references are on so you don't always go to row 5 in the Ticket Data worksheet

▶ 7. Click the **↓** key to move to the first blank cell in the worksheet.

▶ 8. In the Code group on the Developer tab, click the **Use Relative References** button. The Use Relative References button is toggled off.

▶ 9. Click the **Home** tab on the Ribbon, in the Clipboard group, click the **Paste button arrow**, and then click **Paste Values**. This option pastes the values in the transfer area to the data area rather than the formulas entered in the transfer area.

   Trouble? If #REF! appears in row 6 of the Ticket Data worksheet, you clicked the Paste button instead of the Paste Values button. Stop recording the macro. Delete the macro and begin recording the macro again.

▶ 10. Click cell **A1**, click the **Review** tab on the Ribbon, click the **Protect Sheet** button, and then click the **OK** button.

▶ 11. Click the **Invoice** sheet tab, and then click cell **B3**.

▶ 12. Click the **Stop Recording** button 📇 on the status bar. The macro recorder turns off.

You've completed recording the TransferData macro. Next, you'll test whether it works. Ellen has a new season ticket request to add to the worksheet. You'll enter this data as you test the TransferData macro.

To test the TransferData macro:

▶ 1. Enter the following data into the range B3:B11, pressing the **Enter** key after each entry.

   Kate Holland
   186 Pinetop Drive
   Eugene, OR 70777
   (888) 555–1234
   2 tickets, D series, Balcony
   1 decal, 40 donation

You'll print preview the invoice, and then you'll use the macro to transfer the data.

▶ **2.** Press the **Ctrl+p** keys to display the invoice in Print Preview, and then in the Preview group on the Print Preview tab, click the **Close Print Preview** button.

▶ **3.** Press the **Ctrl+t** keys. The TransferData macro runs and the data transfers to the Ticket Data worksheet.

▶ **4.** Switch to the **Ticket Data** worksheet, verify the data for Kate Holland transferred, and then switch to the **Invoice** worksheet.

Fixing Macro Errors

If a macro does not work correctly, you can fix it. Sometimes, you'll find a mistake when you test a macro you just created. Other times, you might not discover that error until later. No matter when you find an error in a macro, you have the following options:

• Rerecord the macro using the same macro name.
• Delete the recorded macro, and then record the macro again.
• Run the macro one step at a time to locate the problem, and then use one of the previous methods to correct the problem.

You can delete or edit a macro by opening the Macro dialog box (shown earlier in Figure 8-25), selecting the macro from the list, and then clicking the appropriate button. To rerecord the macro, simply restart the macro recorder and enter the same macro name you used earlier. Excel overwrites the previous version of the macro.

Working with the Macro Editor

Ellen is concerned about the flickering screen activity that occurs when the PrintPreview-Invoice macro is running. She thinks that this might be disconcerting to some volunteers. Eric Dean, an Office application developer, says you can speed up the macro and eliminate the flicker using a simple VBA command.

Reference Window | **Editing a Macro**

• In the Code group on the Developer tab, click the Macros button, select the macro in the Macro name list, and then click the Edit button (or in the Code group on the Developer tab, click the Visual Basic button).
• Use the Visual Basic Editor to edit the macro code.
• Click File on the menu bar, and then click Close and Return to Microsoft Excel.

To view the code of the PrintPreviewInvoice macro, you need to open the **Visual Basic Editor**, which is a separate application that works with Excel and all of the Office programs to edit and manage VBA code. You can access the Visual Basic Editor through the Macro dialog box.

To view the code for the PrintPreviewInvoice macro:

▶ 1. Click the **Developer** tab on the Ribbon, and then, in the Code group, click the **Macros** button. The Macro dialog box opens.

▶ 2. Click **PrintPreviewInvoice** in the Macro name list, and then click the **Edit** button. The Visual Basic Editor opens as a separate program, consisting of several windows. The Code window contains the VBA code generated by the macro recorder. See Figure 8-26.

Code window in the Visual Basic Editor **Figure 8-26**

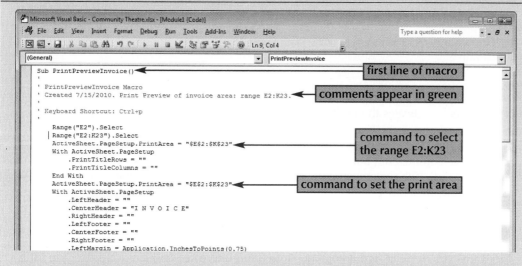

Trouble? The number of windows and their contents will differ, depending on how your computer is configured. At this point, you can ignore all other windows aside from the Code window.

▶ 3. If the Code window is not maximized, click the **Maximize** button on the Code window title bar.

Understanding the Structure of Macros

The VBA code in the Code window lists all of the actions you performed when recording the PrintPreviewInvoice macro. In VBA, macros are called **sub procedures**. Each sub procedure begins with the keyword *Sub* followed by the name of the sub procedure and a set of parentheses. In this example, the code begins with:

```
Sub PrintPreviewInvoice()
```

which provides the name of this sub procedure, *PrintPreviewInvoice*—the name you gave the macro. The parentheses are used to include any arguments in the procedure. These arguments pass information to the sub procedure and have roughly the same purpose as the arguments in an Excel function. If you write your own VBA code, sub procedure arguments are an important part of the programming process, but they are not used when you create macros with the macro recorder.

Following the Sub PrintPreviewInvoice() statement are comments about the macro, taken from the description you entered in the Record New Macro dialog box. Each line appears in green and is preceded by an apostrophe ('). The apostrophe indicates that the line is a comment and does not include any actions Excel needs to perform.

After the comments is the body of the macro, a listing of all of the commands performed by the PrintPreviewInvoice macro as written in the language of VBA. Your list of commands might look slightly different, depending on the exact actions you performed when recording the macro. Even though you might not know VBA, some of the commands are easy to interpret. Near the top of the PrintPreviewInvoice macro, you should see the command:

```
Range("E2:K23").Select
```

This command tells Excel to select the range E2:K23. The next command is:

```
ActiveSheet.PageSetup.PrintArea= $E$2:$K$23
```

This command sets the range E2:K23 as the print area. At the bottom of the macro is the statement:

```
End Sub
```

This statement indicates the end of the PrintPreviewInvoice sub procedure.

A Code window can contain several sub procedures, with each procedure separated from the others by the *Sub ProcedureName()* statement at the beginning, and the *End Sub* statement at the end. Sub procedures are organized into **modules**. As shown in Figure 8-26, all of the macros that have been recorded are stored in the Module1 module (your window may differ).

Writing a Macro Command

Eric wants you to insert two commands into the PrintPreviewInvoice sub procedure to hide the actions of the macro as it runs. The first command, which needs to be inserted directly after the *Sub PrintPreviewInvoice()* statement, is:

```
Application.ScreenUpdating = False
```

This command turns *off* Excel's screen updating, keeping any actions that run in the macro from being displayed on the screen. The second command, which needs to be inserted before the *End Sub* statement, is:

```
Application.ScreenUpdating = True
```

This command turns Excel's screen updating back on, enabling the user to see the final results of the macro after it has completed running.

You must enter these commands exactly. VBA will not be able to run a command if you mistype a word or omit part of the statement. The Visual Basic Editor provides tools to assist you in writing error-free code. As you type a command, the editor will provide pop-up windows and text to help you insert the correct code.

To insert the new commands into the macro:

▶ 1. At the top the Code window, click the end of the Sub PrintPreviewInvoice () statement and then press the **Enter** key. A new blank line appears under the statement.

▶ 2. Press the **Tab** key, and then type **Application.** (including the period, but no spaces). A list box opens with possible keywords you could type at this point in the command. You can either scroll down the list or continue typing the command yourself.

> **3.** Type **ScreenUpdating =**. As you type the equal sign, another list box opens with two possible choices: True or False. This instruction eliminates the screen refreshing (updating) which causes the screen flickering.

> **4.** Type **False** to turn off the screen updating feature of Excel, and then press the **Enter** key. Figure 8-27 shows the new command inserted into the sub procedure.

Command inserted in the PrintPreviewInvoice macro ◀ **Figure 8-27**

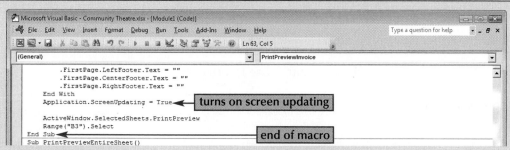

Next, you'll insert a command at the end of the sub procedure to turn screen updating back on.

> **5.** Scroll down the Code window to view the end of the PrintPreviewInvoice sub procedure.

> **6.** Click three lines above the End Sub statement at the end of the End With statement to position the insertion point, and then press the **Enter** key. A new blank line appears below the End With statement.

> **7.** Type **Application.ScreenUpdating = True** and then press the **Enter** key. The command appears in the macro. See Figure 8-28.

Second command added to the PrintPreviewInvoice macro ◀ **Figure 8-28**

> **8.** Click **File** on the menu bar, and then click **Close and Return to Microsoft Excel**. The Visual Basic Editor closes, and the Community Theatre workbook is redisplayed.

To return to the Visual Basic Editor, you can select a macro in the Macro dialog box and click the Edit button again, or you can click the Visual Basic button in the Code group on the Developer tab.

Eric suggests that you test the macro. You'll check to see whether the commands to turn off the screen updating feature make the macro run more smoothly.

To test the edited PrintPreviewInvoice macro:

> **1.** Press the **Ctrl+p** keys. The PrintPreviewInvoice macro runs faster and without the flicker.

▶ **2.** In the Preview group on the Print Preview tab, click the **Close Print Preview** button. The worksheet returns to Normal view.

Ellen is pleased with the change you made to the macro. She thinks it runs more smoothly and will be less distracting to the theatre's volunteers.

Creating Macro Buttons

Another way to run a macro is to assign it to a button placed directly on the worksheet. Ellen wants you to add three macro buttons to the Invoice worksheet, one for each of the macros you've created. Macro buttons are often a better way to run macros than shortcut keys. Clicking a button (with a descriptive label) is often more intuitive and simpler for users than trying to remember different combinations of keystrokes.

Reference Window | **Creating a Macro Button**

- In the Controls group on the Developer tab, click the Insert button.
- In the Form Controls section, click the Button (Form Control) tool, click the worksheet where you want the macro button to be located, drag the pointer until the button is the size and shape you want, and then release the mouse button.
- In the Assign Macro dialog box, select the macro you want to assign to the button, and then, with the button still selected, type a new label.

You'll add the three macro buttons to the Invoice worksheet.

To insert a button on the worksheet:

▶ **1.** If necessary, scroll to the right so columns **L**, **M**, and **N** are completely visible.

▶ **2.** In the Controls group on the Developer tab, click the **Insert** button. The Form Controls appear, with a variety of objects that can be placed in the worksheet. You'll insert the Button form control. See Figure 8-29.

Figure 8-29 ▶ **Form Controls**

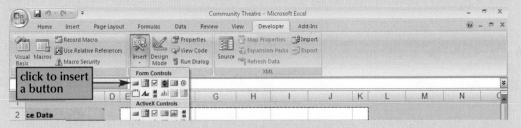

Trouble? If the Insert command is unavailable, the worksheet is protected. Click the Review tab on the Ribbon, in the Changes group, click the Unprotect Sheet button to unprotect the Invoice worksheet, and then repeat Step 2.

▶ **3.** In the Form Controls section, click the **Button (Form Control)** tool ▣, and then point to cell **L3**. The pointer changes to ┼.

▶ **4.** Click and drag the pointer over the range **L3:M4**, and then release the mouse button. A button appears on the worksheet, and the Assign Macro dialog box opens with the button's default name in the Macro name box. See Figure 8-30.

Assign Macro dialog box | **Figure 8-30**

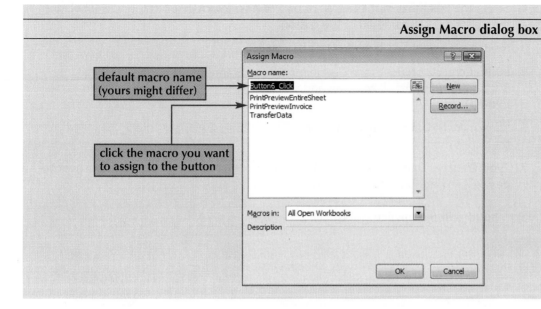

From the Assign Macro dialog box, you can assign a macro to the button. Ellen wants you to assign the PrintPreviewInvoice macro to this new button.

To assign a button to the PrintPreviewInvoice macro:

▶ **1.** Click **PrintPreviewInvoice** in the list of macros, and then click the **OK** button. The PrintPreviewInvoice macro is assigned to the selected button.

You will change the default label on the button to a descriptive one that indicates which macro will run when the button is clicked.

▶ **2.** With the selection handles still displayed around the button, select the label text, and then type **Preview Invoice** (do not press the Enter key). The new label replaces the default label.

Trouble? If no selection handles appear around the button, the button is not selected. Right-click the button, and then click Edit Text to place the insertion point within the button, and then repeat Step 2.

Trouble? If you pressed the Enter key after entering the label on the button, you created a new line in the button. Press the Backspace key to delete the line, and then continue with Step 3.

▶ **3.** Click any cell in the worksheet to deselect the macro button.

At this point, if you click the Preview Invoice button, the PrintPreviewInvoice macro will run. Before you test the Preview Invoice button, you will add the other buttons.

To add the remaining macro buttons to the Invoice worksheet:

▶ **1.** In the Controls group on the Developer tab, click the **Insert** button to display the Form Controls, and then click the **Button (Form Control)** tool ▣ .

▶ **2.** Point to cell **L6**, click and drag the pointer over the range **L6:M7**, and then release the mouse button. The Assign Macro dialog box opens.

▶ **3.** Select **PrintPreviewEntireSheet** in the Macro name list, and then click the **OK** button. The selected macro button appears in the Invoice worksheet.

> **4.** Select the label text in the button, type **Preview Worksheet** as the new label, and then click any cell to deselect the button.
>
> Next, you'll insert the Transfer Data button.
>
> **5.** In the Controls group on the Developer tab, click the **Insert** button, click the **Button (Form Control)** tool ▦, and then drag the pointer over the range **L9:M10**.
>
> **6.** Click **TransferData** in the Macro name list in the Assign Macro dialog box, and then click the **OK** button.
>
> **7.** Type **Transfer Data** as the button label, and then click any cell in the worksheet to deselect the button. See Figure 8-31.

| Figure 8-31 | Macro buttons in the Invoice worksheet |

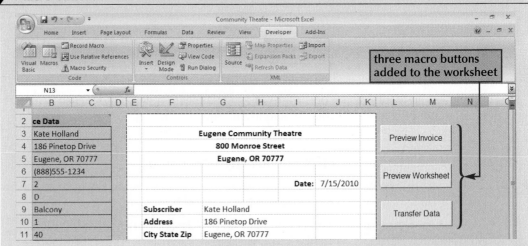

Tip

To move or resize a macro button, right-click the button to select it, press the Esc key to close the shortcut menu, and then drag a selection handle to resize the button or drag the selection border to move the button.

Trouble? If the macro buttons on your screen do not match the size and location of the buttons shown in the figure, right-click a button to select it, press the Esc key to close the shortcut menu, and then resize or reposition the button on the worksheet.

You have completed the application so you will reset worksheet protection.

> **8.** Click the **Review** tab on the Ribbon, in the Changes group click the **Protect Sheet** button to open the Protect Sheet dialog box, and then click the **OK** button to turn on worksheet protection.

Next, you will test the macro buttons to verify that they run the macros. Ellen received another subscriber order. You will use the new macro buttons as you enter this data.

To test the macro buttons:

> **1.** In the range **B3:B11**, enter the following subscriber order:
>
> **George Zidane**
> **105 Central Ave.**
> **Eugene, OR 70777**
> **(808) 685–1111**
> **3 tickets, E series, Balcony**
> **2 parking decals, 30 donation**

▶ **2.** Click the **Preview Invoice** button to display the current invoice in Print Preview, and then close Print Preview to return to the Invoice worksheet.

▶ **3.** Click the **Preview Worksheet** button to display the Invoice worksheet in Print Preview. The flickering occurs as this macro runs because you did not edit the code in the PrintPreviewEntireSheet macro.

▶ **4.** Close Print Preview without printing.

▶ **5.** Click the **Transfer Data** button to transfer data to the Ticket Data worksheet. Excel inserts the new transaction in the table.

▶ **6.** Switch to the **Ticket Data** worksheet, and verify the data was transferred. See Figure 8-32.

Ticket Data worksheet with new transaction record ◀ Figure 8-32

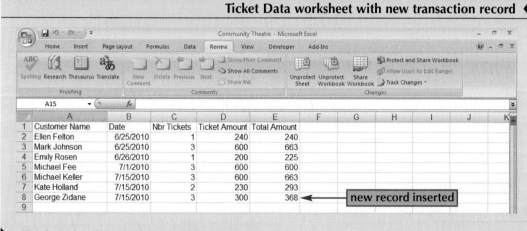

▶ **7.** Switch to the **Documentation** sheet.

Saving Workbooks with Macros

You've completed your work on the Excel application, so you will save and close the workbook and then exit Excel.

To save a workbook with a macro:

▶ **1.** On the Quick Access Toolbar, click the **Save** button 🔲. A dialog box opens, indicating that the workbook you are trying to save contains features that cannot be saved in a macro-free workbook. See Figure 8-33. The default Excel workbook (.xlsx file extension) does not allow macros to be stored as part of the file. If you click the Yes button, this workbook will be saved as a macro-free workbook, which means the macros you created will be lost.

Dialog box with macro warning ◀ Figure 8-33

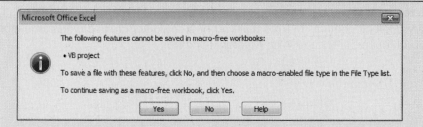

You want to include the macros in the file. To do this, you have to save the workbook as a new file; one that allows macros to be saved as part of the file.

▶ **2.** Click the **No** button. The Save As dialog box opens.

▶ **3.** In the File name box, type **Theatre With Macros** so you can easily determine which workbook contains macros.

The default Excel Workbook, which is a macro-free workbook, has the .xlsx file extension. You need to change this to a macro-enabled workbook, which has the .xlsm file extension.

▶ **4.** Click the **Save as type** button, and then click **Excel Macro-Enabled Workbook**.

▶ **5.** Click the **Save** button. The workbook is saved with the macros.

Minimize the Ribbon

Now that the application is complete, Ellen wants to provide more screen space for the input and output sections of the worksheet. You can minimize the Ribbon to make more space for the worksheet. When the Ribbon is minimized all that is displayed is the Quick Access Toolbar and the tab names. To access any command from the Ribbon, click the desired tab. The Ribbon expands to show all the groups and buttons on the tab.

To minimize the Ribbon:

▶ **1.** Double-click any tab on the Ribbon. The Ribbon is minimized. See Figure 8-34.

Figure 8-34	Minimized Ribbon

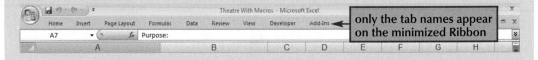

only the tab names appear on the minimized Ribbon

▶ **2.** Click the **Home** tab to view all buttons and toolbars for this tab. You can click any other tabs on the Ribbon to display their options. After you click any button on the Ribbon or a cell in the worksheet, the Ribbon returns to its minimized state.

▶ **3.** Close the workbook.

Opening a Workbook with Macros

What happens when you open a file with macros, Excel checks the opening workbook to see if it contains a macro. The response you see is based on the security level set on the computer. Ellen has disabled all macros with notification. So, all macros are disabled upon opening the workbook, but a security alert provides her with the option to enable the macros so they can be run or open the workbook with the macros disabled. If you know a workbook contains macros that you or a coworker created, you can enable them. You'll open the Theatre With Macros workbook.

To open the Community Theatre workbook that contains macros:

▶ **1.** Open the **Theatre With Macros** workbook. The workbook opens, and a Message Bar appears below the Ribbon indicating the macros have been disabled. See Figure 8-35. Although the workbook is open you must complete one more step to use the macros.

Security alert appears when opening a workbook with macros | Figure 8-35

▶ **2.** In the Message Bar, click the **Options** button to open the Microsoft Office Security Options dialog box. See Figure 8-36.

Microsoft Office Security Options dialog box | Figure 8-36

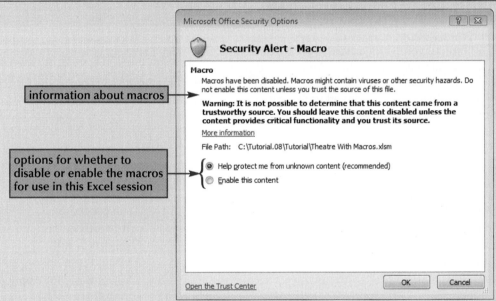

▶ **3.** Click the **Enable this content** option button, and then click the **OK** button. The macros in the workbook are available for use. If you selected the recommended option, Help protect me from unknown content, the macros would remain disabled and unavailable during the current session. The other features of the workbook would still be available.

▶ **4.** Click the **Invoice** sheet tab. The Ribbon is still minimized. It will remain minimized in Excel on this computer until you maximize the Ribbon.

▶ **5.** Double-click any tab to maximize the Ribbon, and then close the workbook without saving the changes.

Finally, you'll remove the Developer tab from the Ribbon.

▶ **6.** Click the **Office Button** 🔘, and then click the **Excel Options** button to open the Excel Options dialog box.

▶ **7.** In the Popular section, click the **Show Developer tab in the Ribbon** check box to remove the check mark, and then click the **OK** button. The Developer tab is hidden from the Ribbon.

Ellen is pleased with the ease of the interface for the community theatre workbook. The workbook protection and macros will streamline the data entry process for the theatre volunteers.

Review | **Session 8.3 Quick Check**

1. Discuss two ways of creating a macro.
2. How do you identify a comment in the Visual Basic code?
3. What are the three places in which you can store a macro?
4. What are the steps you follow to delete a macro?
5. What are the steps you follow to edit a macro?
6. How do you insert a macro button into your worksheet?

Review | **Tutorial Summary**

In this tutorial, you learned how to create data validation rules that help guide users as they input data into a worksheet. You learned how to define names to make formulas easier to understand. You also learned how to protect the contents of worksheets, the worksheets themselves, and workbooks. Finally, you learned how to automate a series of actions by creating macros.

Key Terms

comment	locked property	protect worksheet
data validation	macro	sub procedure
defined name	macro security settings	Trust Center
digital signature	maco virus	validation rule
error alert message	module	Visual Basic Editor
Excel application	name	Visual Basic for Applications
input message	Personal Macro workbook	(VBA)

| Practice | **Review Assignments** |

Practice the skills you learned in the tutorial to create a workbook with macros for a car rental company.

Data File needed for the Review Assignments: Rentals.xlsx

Ellen's student intern, Mark, did such a good job helping her with the Community Theatre application that she recommended him to a friend who has a similar project. Ellen's friend needs to create an invoice system for his new car rental company, Eugene Discount Car Rental.

Complete the following:

1. Open the **Rentals** workbook located in the Tutorial.08\Review folder included with your Data Files, and then save the workbook as **Discount Rental** in the same folder.
2. Enter the current date and your name in the Documentation sheet.
3. In the Customer worksheet, define names for cells using the following information:

Cell	Defined Name	Cell	Defined Name
B4	**Customer**	H9	**ChargePerDay**
B5	**TypeCar**	H10	**ChargePerMile**
B6	**DaysRented**	A12:C16	**RentalRates**
B7	**MilesDriven**	B19	**SalesTaxRate**

4. Create the validation rules for cells B5, B6, and B7 shown in Figure 8-37.

Figure 8-37

Cell	Settings	Input Message	Error Alert
B5	List Source (A12:A16)	Enter an appropriate title and message	Style: Stop Title: Invalid Type Message: Enter an appropriate message
B6	Integers >0 and <30	Enter an appropriate title and message	Style: Warning Title: Warning Days Rented Message: Enter an appropriate message
B7	Integers >0 and <=5000	Enter an appropriate title and message	Style: Warning Title: Warning Miles Message: Enter an appropriate message

5. Enter the following formulas, using the defined names you created in Step 3, to calculate the Rental Bill:
   - Cell F6 is equal to the value in cell B4.
   - Cell F7 is equal to the value in cell B5.
   - Cell F9 is equal to the value in cell B6.
   - Cell F10 is equal to the value in cell B7.
   - Cell H9 is equal to charge per day, which depends on the type of car entered in cell B5 and the rate table. (*Hint:* Use the VLOOKUP function.)
   - Cell H10 is equal to the charge per mile, which depends on the type of car rented in cell B5 and the rate table. (*Hint:* Use the VLOOKUP function.)
   - Cell F12 is equal to the Rental Amount, which equals the days rented multiplied by the charge per day plus the miles driven multiplied by the charge per mile.
   - Cell F13 is equal to Sales Tax Rate times Rental Amount.
   - Cell F14 is equal to Rental Amount plus Sales Tax.
   - Use the IFERROR function in cells H9, H10, F12, F13, and F14 to test for an error value. If an error value is found, display a blank; otherwise, use the appropriate formula.

6. Test the worksheet using the data: **Myles Fast**, **Intermediate**, **4**, **450**.

7. Protect the worksheet so a user can enter data only in the range B4:B7. Do not use a password to enable protection. Save the workbook.

   Note: In the following steps, you'll be creating two macros. Save your workbook before recording each macro. That way, if you make a mistake in recording the macro, you can close the workbook without saving the changes, and then reopen the workbook and try again. Be sure to read the list of tasks before you begin recording them.

8. Remove worksheet protection from the Customer worksheet.

9. Create a macro named **PrintPreviewBill** with the shortcut key **Ctrl+p** that displays only the bill portion of the worksheet in the range E3:H15 in Print Preview, centers the bill horizontally on the page and shows your name in the right footer of the printout. Create a macro button, assign the PrintPreviewBill macro to the button, and then change the default label to **Preview Bill**.

10. Create a macro named **ClearInputs** with the shortcut key **Ctrl+c** that clears the data in the rental inputs section of the worksheet (range B4:B7). Create a macro button, assign the ClearInputs macro to the button, and then change the label to **Clear**.

11. Turn protection on in the Customer worksheet.

12. Test the macro using the data: **Eddie Elders**, **Intermediate**, **3** days, **2000** miles.

13. Use the Preview Bill macro button to preview the customer bill for Ed Elders.

14. Use the Clear macro button to remove the rental data.

15. In the Documentation worksheet, use the Paste List command to document the defined names and their locations.

16. Save the workbook with the name **Rentals With Macros** in the macro-enabled workbook format, and then close it. Submit the finished workbook to your instructor, either in printed or electronic form, as requested.

| Apply | **Case Problem 1** |

Apply the skills you learned to create, edit, and run macros to produce monthly reports.

Data File needed for this Case Problem: MediTrax.xlsx

MediTrax Controls MediTrax Controls, a U.S. subsidiary of a European multinational corporation, is testing an HVAC system designed to eliminate large temperature variances in its medical storage rooms. Lisa Goodman is a product tester for MediTrax, and each week, she records 25 temperature readings, five samples each day, in an Excel workbook. At the end of the month, Lisa sends the results to the parent company's Quality Department. Because many repetitive steps occur in developing the output requested by the parent company, Lisa asks you to create a macro to speed the creation of the report and reduce chances for error.

Complete the following:

1. Open the **MediTrax** workbook located in the Tutorial.08\Case1 folder included with your Data Files, and then save the workbook as **MediTrax Controls** in the same folder.

2. In the Documentation sheet, enter your name and the current date, and then review all the worksheets in the workbook. Make Week 1 the active worksheet.

3. Create a macro to convert the worksheet to the one shown in Figure 8-38. Name the macro **ConvertData** and assign the shortcut key **Ctrl+d** to run the macro. The macro performs the following steps:

   a. Formats the dates in the Date column using the date format type (3/14/2001).

   b. Formats the times in the Time column so they are displayed in 24-hour notation (format type 13:30).

   c. Types the title **Celsius** in cell D1.

   d. Converts the Fahrenheit temperatures to Celsius by entering the following formula in cell D2 and then copying down the column: **=5/9*(C2–32)**

   e. Formats the cells in column D using the Number format to 1 decimal place.

   f. Bolds the column heading and resizes the column to fully display "Fahrenheit."

   g. Places the label **Average** in cell A27, computes the average Celsius temperature for the week in cell D27 and bolds the row.

   h. Makes cell F1 the active cell.

   i. Uses Print Preview to view the results centered horizontally on the page with the worksheet name in the center header and your name in the right footer.

   j. Closes Print Preview.

   k. Stops recording the macro.

Figure 8-38

	A	B	C	D	E	F	G	H	I	J	K	L
1	Date	Time	Fahrenheit	Celsius								
2	4/1/2010	1:05	60.5	15.8								
3	4/1/2010	2:02	64.5	18.1								
4	4/1/2010	6:42	63.8	17.7								
5	4/1/2010	14:45	61.1	16.2								
6	4/1/2010	21:12	60.2	15.7								
7	4/2/2010	1:33	61.2	16.2								
8	4/2/2010	2:25	62.9	17.2								
9	4/2/2010	6:12	64.4	18.0								
10	4/2/2010	15:35	62.3	16.8								
11	4/2/2010	20:32	61.9	16.6								
12	4/3/2010	1:56	63.9	17.7								
13	4/3/2010	2:51	60.6	15.9								
14	4/3/2010	6:55	62.6	17.0								
15	4/3/2010	14:30	64.5	18.1								
16	4/3/2010	22:18	63.2	17.3								
17	4/4/2010	1:32	62.6	17.0								
18	4/4/2010	2:58	62.7	17.1								
19	4/4/2010	7:05	62.4	16.9								
20	4/4/2010	14:12	63.5	17.5								
21	4/4/2010	21:45	62.6	17.0								
22	4/5/2010	1:22	64.8	18.2								
23	4/5/2010	2:18	62.4	16.9								
24	4/5/2010	6:50	61.9	16.6								
25	4/5/2010	13:59	63.4	17.4								
26	4/5/2010	22:03	64.2	17.9								
27	**Average**			**17.1**								
28												

Documentation | Week 1 | Week 2 | Week 3

4. Switch to the Week 2 worksheet and test the macro using the shortcut key.

5. Edit the macro so screen updating is turned off while the macro is running and turned on when the macro ends.

6. Switch to the Week 3 worksheet and test the revised macro using the shortcut key.

7. Save the workbook as **MTC With Macros** as an Excel Macro-Enabled workbook, and then close it. Submit the finished workbook to your instructor, either in printed or electronic form, as requested.

Apply | **Case Problem 2**

Apply the skills you've learned to define data validation rules, name cells, set worksheet protection, and create macros in a profit analysis workbook.

Data File needed for this Case Problem: Popcorn.xlsx

Seattle Popcorn   Seattle Popcorn is a small company located in Tacoma, Washington, that produces gourmet popcorn distributed in the Northwest. Steve Wilkes has developed a workbook that will allow him to perform a profit analysis for the company. Using this workbook, he wants to create formulas to determine the break-even point for the company—the sales volume needed so that revenues will match the anticipated monthly expenses. Three factors determine the break-even point: the sales price of each unit of Seattle Popcorn, the variable manufacturing cost to the company for each unit, and the fixed expenses (salaries, rent, insurance, and so on) that the company must pay each month. Steve wants to be able to explore a range of possible values for each of these factors, as follows:

- The sales price of each unit of Seattle Popcorn can vary from $5 to $15 (in whole numbers).
- The variable manufacturing cost of each unit can vary from $5 to $15 (in whole numbers).
- The fixed monthly expense for the company can vary from $15,000 to $30,000 (in whole numbers).

Figure 8-39 shows a preview of the application you'll create for Steve.

Figure 8-39

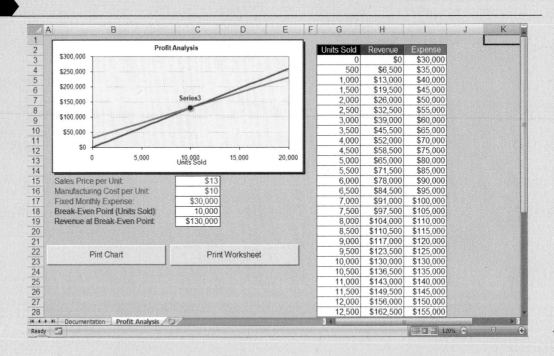

Complete the following:

1. Open the **Popcorn** workbook located in the Tutorial.08\Case2 folder included with your Data Files, and then save the workbook as **Seattle Popcorn** in the same folder. Enter the date and your name in the Documentation sheet.
2. Switch to the Profit Analysis worksheet, and then define the following names: in cell C15 **PricePerUnit**, in cell C16 **CostPerUnit**, and in cell C17 **MonthlyExpenses**.

3. In the range H3:H43, enter a formula using defined names to calculate the revenue, which is determined by the units sold multiplied by the price per unit. In the range I3:I43, enter a formula using defined names to calculate the expenses, which are determined by the units sold multiplied by the cost per unit plus the fixed monthly expense.

4. In cell C18, enter a formula to calculate the break-even point, which is determined by the fixed monthly expense divided by the difference between the price per unit and the cost per unit. Use the IFERROR function to display a blank cell instead of an error value.

5. In cell C19, enter a formula to calculate the revenue at the break-even point, which is determined by the break-even point multiplied by the sale price per unit. Use the IFERROR function to display a blank cell instead of an error value.

6. Create the validation rules for cells C15, C16, and C17, as shown in Figure 8-40.

Figure 8-40

Cell	Settings	Input Message	Error Alert
C15	Integers from 5 to 15	Enter an appropriate title and message	Title: Sales Price Warning Style: Warning Message: Enter an appropriate message
C16	Integers from 5 to 15	Enter an appropriate title and message	Title: Cost Warning Style: Warning Message: Enter an appropriate message
C17	Integers from 15000 to 30000	Enter an appropriate title and message	Title: Fixed Monthly Expense Warning Style: Warning Message: Enter an appropriate message

7. Protect the worksheet so the user can enter data only in cells C15, C16, and C17. Everything else in the worksheet should remain locked.

8. Enter the following values in the worksheet to determine how many units Seattle Popcorn must sell each month in order to break even:
   * Sales Price per Unit = **$13**
   * Manufacturing Cost per Unit = **$10**
   * Fixed Monthly Expense = **$30,000**

   Note: In the following steps, you'll create two macros. Save your workbook before recording each macro. That way, if you make a mistake while recording the macro, you can close the workbook without saving the changes, and then reopen it and try again. Also, read the list of tasks before you begin recording them.

9. Create a macro named **PrintChart** with the shortcut key **Ctrl+a** that performs the following tasks:
   a. Print Preview the chart and input/output area (range A1:E20) in landscape orientation, centered horizontally on the page, and with the text **Break-even Analysis** in the center header, and your name and date in the right footer.
   b. Closes Print Preview and then makes cell A1 the active cell.

10. Test the PrintChart macro by pressing the Ctrl+a keys. If the macro doesn't work, close the workbook without saving your changes, reopen the workbook, and record the macro again.

11. Create a button in the range A22:B23, assign the PrintChart macro to the button, and change the default label to a more descriptive one.

12. Edit the PrintChart macro so screen updating is turned off while the macro is running and turned on when the macro ends.

13. Run the PrintChart macro again to test the button and verify that screen updating is turned off while the macro is running and on when the macro ends.

14. Create a macro named **PrintWorksheet** with shortcut key **Ctrl+b** that performs the following tasks:

    a. Print Preview the entire worksheet on one page with text **Profit Analysis** in the center header and your name and date in the right footer.

    b. Closes Print Preview, and then makes cell A1 the active cell.

15. Test the PrintWorksheet macro by pressing the Crtl+b keys. If the macro doesn't work, close the workbook without saving your changes, reopen the workbook, and record the macro again.

16. Create a button in the range C22:E23, assign the PrintWorksheet macro to the button, and then change the default label to a more descriptive one.

17. Edit the macro so screen updating is turned off while the macro is running and turned on when the macro ends.

18. Run the PrintWorksheet macro again to test the button and verify that screen updating is turned off while the macro is running and on when the macro ends.

19. Save the workbook as **SP With Macros**, and then close it. Submit the finished workbook to your instructor, either in printed or electronic form, as requested.

Apply	**Case Problem 3**

Apply the skills you learned to design an Excel workbook for use as a data entry form.

Data File needed for this Case Problem: Cookin.xlsx

Cookin Good   Cookin Good is a company that sells specialized home cooking products. The company employs individuals to organize "Cookin Good Parties" in which the company's products are sold. Cleo Benard is responsible for entering sales data from various Cookin Good Parties. She wants to design an Excel workbook to act as a data entry form. She has already created the workbook, but she needs your help in setting up data validation rules, creating a table lookup, and writing the macros to enter the data.

Complete the following:

1. Open the **Cookin** workbook located in the Tutorial.08\Case3 folder included with your Data Files, save the workbook as **Cookin Good** in the same folder. Enter your name and the date in the Documentation sheet, and then switch to the Sales Form worksheet.

2. Create appropriate defined names for each cell in the range C3:C8. Assign the name **ProductInfo** to the range E4:G15.

3. In the Sales Form worksheet, create the following validation rules:

    a. Cell C3 for which the criteria allows only one of five regions (represented by the numbers 1, 2, 3, 4, and 5) to be entered. Enter an appropriate input message and error alert.

    b. Cell C4 for which the criteria provides the list of 12 products (found in range E4:E15). Enter an appropriate input message and error alert.

    c. Cell C7 for which the criteria allows only positive numbers to be entered as the number of units sold. Enter an appropriate input message and error alert.

4. Use a Lookup function to have the product name and price automatically entered into the sales form when the ProductID is entered. (*Hint:* Cells should be blank if an error value appears in a cell.)

5. Enter a formula that automatically calculates the total sale for the order, which is determined by the number of units sold multiplied by the price of the product.

6. Prevent users from selecting any cell in the Sales Form worksheet other than cells C3, C4, and C7, and then protect all of the worksheets in the workbook, except for the Documentation sheet.

7. Test the data entry form by entering the following new record: Region = **1**, Product ID = **CW**, Units Sold = **5**.

8. Save the workbook, and then create a macro named **AddData** with the shortcut key **Ctrl+d** that performs the following tasks:

   a. In the Sales Form worksheet, copy the values in the range C3:C8. (*Hint:* You'll paste later in the macro.)

   b. Switch from the Sales Form worksheet to the Sales Record worksheet. Click cell A1.

   c. Turn on Relative References. Use the arrow keys to locate the last used row in the table.

   d. Use an arrow key to move to the next row. Turn off Relative References.

   e. Paste the copied values from Step A into the blank row. (*Hint:* Use the Paste Special command to paste transposed values, Values option, Transpose check box.)

   f. Switch to the Sales Table worksheet, click inside the PivotTable and refresh the contents of the PivotTable to include the new data.

   g. Switch to the Sales Form and clear the values in cells C3, C4, and C7 of the Sales Form worksheet. Make C3 the active cell.

   h. Stop Recording.

9. Create a button in the range C11:C12 on the Sales Form worksheet and assign the AddData macro to the button. Change the button label to **Transfer Sales Data**.

10. Test the data entry form and AddData macro by entering the following new records:

Region	Product ID	Units Sold
3	**HR**	7
4	**OEG**	3

11. Create a macro named **ViewTable** with the **Ctrl+t** shortcut key that displays the contents of the Sales Table worksheet.

12. Create a macro named **ViewChart** with the **Ctrl+c** shortcut key that displays the Sales Chart worksheet.

13. Create a macro named **ViewForm** with the **Ctrl+f** shortcut key that displays the Sales Form worksheet. Test each macro using its shortcut keys.

14. In the Documentation sheet, create three macro buttons to view the Sales Table (Step 11), the Sales Chart (Step 12), and the Sales Form (Step 13). Insert the macro buttons below row 9. Change the labels on the buttons to be more descriptive.

⊕ EXPLORE 15. Sales Table displays the Total product sales in each region. Change the display so the values in the cell are percentage of the total (Field Setting). You can return the original value by choosing Normal.

16. Save the workbook as **CG With Macros**, and then close it. Submit the finished workbook to your instructor, either in printed or electronic form, as requested.

| Create | **Case Problem 4** |

Go beyond what you've learned to define names, apply worksheet protection, and create macros to prepare an invoice.

There are no Data Files needed for this Case Problem.

Alia's Senior Living Supplies   Alia Moh for years had been touched by the needs of the senior population she was serving, thinking that if people had just a little help, they might not end up at her hospital. Ultimately, she left her job at a local hospital in Chicago to establish Alia's Senior Living Supplies, which supplies products and services designed for seniors. Products offered by Alia on her Web site range from safety step ladders, doorknob grippers, skid resistant surfaces, to wheelchair ponchos.

Finding these uniquely designed products a great help in their day-to-day lives, a large following of clients regularly purchase from Alia. To be sure her company stays in business, Alia must assure timely receipt of payments from her growing client base. She wants a billing/invoicing system to expedite that work. Figure 8-41 shows the finished application she asks you to create.

Figure 8-41

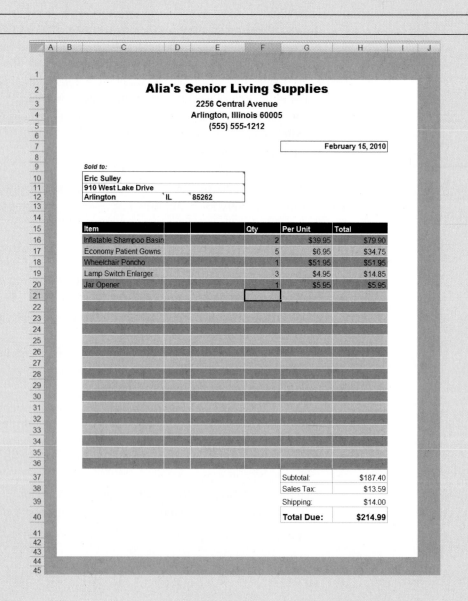

Complete the following:

1. Open a new workbook, and save it as **AliasSupplies** in the Tutorial.08\Case4 folder included with your Data Files.
2. Rename the first sheet **Documentation** and then enter the company name, your name, the current date, and a purpose statement. Rename the second sheet **Invoice**. Rename the third sheet **Product Pricing And Shipping**.
3. Review Figures 8-42 and 8-43, and the steps below before you begin to enter the tables, labels, and formulas to build the invoice. First, enter the data for Product Pricing (shown in Figure 8-42) and Shipping costs (shown in Figure 8-43) in the Product Pricing And Shipping worksheet. Next, follow Steps a through n and Figure 8-41 to build the invoice. Use defined names and structured referencing to assist in creating formulas.
   a. Current date in cell G7 (merged with H7).
   b. Insert comments as a reminder as to what data is to be entered in cells C10, C11, C12, D12, and E12.
   c. Adjust the column widths so column A is 2.57; column B is 6.14; column C is 20.86; Column D is 6.14; column E is 13.57; column F is 8.71; column G is 12.71; column H is 13.71; and column I is 7.29.
   d. Insert the column headers in row 15.
   e. Create an Excel table in the range C15:H36. Remove the filter arrows and format cells G7 and the range G40:H40 as bold.
   f. Use defined names wherever appropriate.
   g. Item column (the range C16:C36): User looks up Item using a list. Use the Product Pricing table, shown in Figure 8-42, for the Item.

Figure 8-42

	A	B
1	**Product Pricing**	
2		
3	Adjustable Home Bed Rail	89.95
4	Bed Cane	81.95
5	Doorknob Gripper	4.95
6	Easy Grip Utensils	32.95
7	Economy Patient Gowns	6.95
8	Full-page Magnifier	4.99
9	Giant TV Remote	34.95
10	Inflatable Shampoo Basin	39.95
11	Jar Opener	5.95
12	Lamp Switch Enlarger	4.95
13	Medication Dispenser	135.95
14	No Rinse Shampoo	34.95
15	Tilting Overbed Table	114.95
16	Trolley Walker	139.95
17	Wheelchair Poncho	51.95

   h. Qty column: User enters the quantity ordered. Issue an error alert warning message if the quantity is above 50.
   i. Per Unit column: Based on a table lookup in the Product Pricing table based on value selected in Item column (refer to Figure 8-42).
   j. Total column: Qty × Per Unit.
   k. Subtotal (cell H37): Sum of Total column. Format this cell appropriately.
   l. Sales tax: 7.25% of subtotal in cell H38 if the customer state is IL; otherwise, sales tax is 0. Format this cell appropriately.
   m. Shipping costs: If subtotal is $200 or more, no shipping cost; otherwise, look up shipping cost (refer to Figure 8-43) based on the subtotal in cell H37. Format this cell appropriately.

Figure 8-43

Subtotal amount	Shipping cost
0–54.99	5.95
55–99.99	8.25
100–149.99	11.50
150–199.99	14.00

    n. Total Due = Subtotal + Sales Tax + Shipping. Format this cell appropriately.

4. Protect the worksheet so a user can enter data in cells C10, C11, C12, D12, E12, items (C16:C36), and Qty (F16:F36) but not in any other cells. Do not use a password.

5. Create a macro named **PrintInvoice** that prints the Invoice. Assign the **Ctrl+p** shortcut key to this macro. Center the worksheet horizontally and fit it on 1 printed page. The heading has the label **I N V O I C E**. Attach a button and place it on the worksheet (column K) that is assigned to the PrintInvoice macro. Assign a descriptive name to the macro button.

6. Create a macro named **ClearInputs** that deletes the values from cells C10, C11, C12, D12, E12, items in the range C16:C36, and quantities in the range F16:F36. Assign the **Ctrl+c** shortcut key to this macro. Attach a button and place it on the worksheet (column K) that is assigned to the ClearInputs macro. Assign a descriptive name to the macro button.

7. In the Documentation sheet, paste a list of defined names with location, and list of macro names, shortcut keys, and purpose.

8. Test the worksheet using the data in Figure 8-40.

9. Use the PrintInvoice macro button to print the bill for the data you entered in Step 8, and then use the ClearInputs macro button to remove the input data.

10. Save the workbook as **Alia With Macros**, and then close it. Submit the finished workbook to your instructor, either in printed or electronic form, as requested.

Research | Internet Assignments

Use the Internet to find and work with data related to the topics presented in this tutorial.

The purpose of the Internet Assignments is to challenge you to find information on the Internet that you can use to work effectively with this software. The actual assignments are updated and maintained on the Course Technology Web site. Log on to the Internet and use your Web browser to go to the Student Online Companion for New Perspectives Office 2007 at **www.course.com/np/office2007**. Then navigate to the Internet Assignments for this tutorial.

Assess | SAM Assessment and Training

If you have a SAM user profile, you may have access to hands-on instruction, practice, and assessment of the skills covered in this tutorial. Log in to your SAM account (**http://sam2007.course.com**) to launch any assigned training activities or exams that relate to the skills covered in this tutorial.

Session 8.1

1. A descriptive word or characters assigned to a cell or range. Defined names make interpreting formulas easier. If you move a cell or range with a defined name to a different location, any formula using that named range reflects the new location.
2. any three of the following: Name box, New Name dialog box, Create Names from Selection dialog box, and Name Manager dialog box
3. (a) Annual_Total
4. Click Name box arrow, and then click the defined name
5. =SUM(Expenses)
6. False

Session 8.2

1. Select the cell, click the Data tab on the Ribbon, and then, in the Data Tools group, click the Data Validation button.
2. Select the cell, open the Data Validation dialog box, click the Input Message tab, and then enter the input message title and text.
3. The *Stop* alert prevents the user from storing the data in the cell; the *Warning* alert rejects the invalid data but allows the user to override the rejection; and the *Information* alert accepts the invalid data but allows the user to cancel the data entry.
4. A locked cell prohibits data entry when the worksheet is protected.
5. Worksheet protection controls the user's ability to edit cells within the worksheet. Workbook protection controls the user's ability to change the structure of the workbook (including worksheet names) and the format of the workbook window.
6. Yes, as long as the structure of the workbook is not protected.
7. Select the cell with a comment. In the Comments group on the Review tab, click the Edit Comment button, edit the comment in the text box, and then click any cell.

Session 8.3

1. Use the macro recorder to record the exact keystrokes and commands you want the macro to run, or write the macro code directly in the Visual Basic Editor with VBA macro language.
2. A line that begins with an apostrophe is treated as a comment; the line of a comment is green.
3. You can store a macro in the current workbook, in a new workbook, or in the Personal Macro workbook, which is available whenever you use Excel.
4. Click Developer tab, in the Code group click Macros to open the Macros dialog box, select the macro from the list of macros, and then click the Delete button.
5. Click the Developer tab on the Ribbon, in the Code group, click the Macros button to open the Macro dialog box, select the macro from the list of macros, and then click the Edit button.
6. If the worksheet is protected, unprotect the worksheet. In the Controls group on the Developer tab, click the Insert button to display the Form Controls toolbar. Click the Button (Form Control) tool, and then draw the button image on the worksheet. Assign a macro and label to the button.

Ending Data Files

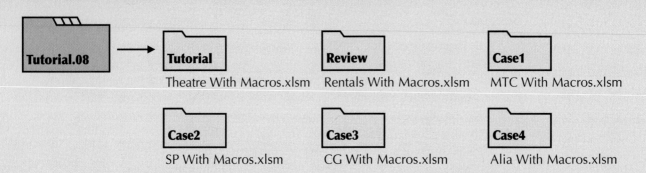

Theatre With Macros.xlsm   Rentals With Macros.xlsm   MTC With Macros.xlsm

SP With Macros.xlsm   CG With Macros.xlsm   Alia With Macros.xlsm

Reality Check

Excel can be a useful program for tracking information about many everyday activities, such as

- Organizations you belong to/participate in
- Collections
- Hobbies
- Community work
- Social events
- Sports records and statistics

In this exercise, you need to select an area that fits your interests and create an application in Excel to track information related to your area of interest, using the Excel skills and features presented in Tutorials 5 through 8.

Note: Please be sure *not* to include any personal information of a sensitive nature in any worksheets you create to submit to your instructor. Later, you can update the worksheets with such information for your own personal use.

1. Plan the organization of your workbook—what information related to your area of interest do you want to track; what fields do you need to enter; how will you organize the data; what calculations will you need to perform; how do you want to format the information, and so on.
2. Create a Documentation worksheet that includes your name, the date, and the purpose of your workbook. Format it appropriately.
3. Set up multiple worksheets to record your data on (for example, a budget for each event could be a separate worksheet). Use a worksheet group to enter labels and other nonvariable text, formatting, and formulas in the worksheets.
4. Apply validity checks to improve the accuracy of data entry.
5. Create a summary worksheet that consolidates the information from these worksheets.
6. Create an Excel table to track data. Enter an appropriate table name, column headers, and formulas. Format the table attractively. Add records to the table. Insert a Total row in the table with an appropriate summary calculation (SUM, COUNT, etc.).
7. Add a calculated column to the table with an appropriate function (such as an IF function, an AND function, and so on).
8. In a worksheet with a range of data, define names for cells and ranges. Convert the existing formulas in that worksheet to use the defined names.
9. Paste a list of defined names as documentation in the Documentation sheet.
10. Check for duplicate values using conditional formatting.
11. Check for data entry errors using the IFERROR function.
12. Sort the data as needed.
13. Use a filter to answer a specific question about the data. Add a comment to explain how the data was filtered and what question it answers.
14. Create an advanced filter using a criteria range, such as a filter to determine which events have food costs less than $100.

15. Use a PivotTable to analyze data in the workbook. Format, filter, and sort the PivotTable appropriately. Add a comment to explain what you learned from the PivotTable.

16. Plan and record an appropriate macro. Assign the macro to a button. Save the workbook in macro enabled format.

17. Prepare the workbook for printing. Include headers and footers that indicate the filename of your workbook, the workbook's author, and the date on which the workbook is printed. If a printed worksheet will extend across several pages, repeat appropriate print titles across all of the pages and include page numbers and the total number of pages on each printed page.

18. Save the workbook. Submit the completed workbook to your instructor, in printed or electronic form, as requested.

Objectives

- Open a workbook in Compatibility Mode
- Use the LEN function to determine the number of characters in a cell
- Use the LEFT function to extract a series of characters from a text string
- Use the Paste Values command
- Use the PROPER function to convert the case of a text string
- Use the Concatenation operator to join several text strings into one text string
- Use the Text to Columns command to separate multiple pieces of data in one column into separate columns
- USE the UPPER function to convert text to uppercase
- Use the SUBSTITUTE function to replace characters in a text string
- Use a special format for phone number
- Create custom formats for numbers and dates

Working with Text Functions and Creating Custom Formats

Cleaning Data in a Spreadsheet

Case | Zeus Engineering

Growth in the town of Bayville has strained the capacity of local roads. Traffic increases have created delays, vehicular hazards, and pedestrian safety concerns. To address these issues, the town has contracted Zeus Engineering to develop a Transportation Improvement Program (TIP).

Myron Londale, traffic analyst at Zeus Engineering, will analyze data on private homes and commercial buildings located along the route being analyzed. He received the data from the Bayville Assessor's office, which transferred the data to Excel. Before Myron begins his analysis, he needs to "clean" the data, and has asked for your help.

Starting Data Files

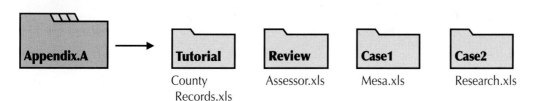

Appendix.A → Tutorial   Review   Case1   Case2

County   Assessor.xls   Mesa.xls   Research.xls
Records.xls

Opening and Saving Workbooks Created in Earlier Versions of Excel

The workbook Myron received from the Bayville Assessor's office was created in an earlier version of Excel. When you open a workbook that was created in an earlier version of Excel, Excel 2007 opens the workbook in **Compatibility Mode**. The words *[Compatibility Mode]* appear in the title bar, indicating the file is not in the latest Excel format. You can work in Compatibility Mode, which keeps the workbook in the older file format and makes the workbook accessible for users who do not have the current version of Excel installed. However, to have access to all the latest features and tools in Excel 2007, the workbook must be converted to the current file format, which has the file extension.xlsx. This is the file format you have used to save all workbooks in this book.

Myron wants to use Excel tables to manage and analyze the data. Because tables are a new feature in Excel 2007, Myron asks you to open the current workbook and convert it to the current file format. You can tell when a workbook has been saved in the current file format, because its file extension changes from .xls to .xlsx.

To save the County Records workbook in the Excel 2007 file format:

▶ **1.** Open the **County Records** workbook located in the **Appendix.A\Tutorial** folder included with your Data Files. The workbook opens in Compatibility Mode, because the workbook was created in an earlier version of Excel. See Figure A-1.

| Figure A-1 | Workbook in Compatibility Mode |

▶ **2.** Click the **Office Button** , and then click **Save As**. The Save As dialog box opens.

▶ **3.** Type **Bayville County** in the File name box.

The Save as type box shows that the current file format is Excel 97-2003 Workbook, which is the earlier file format. You'll change this to the latest file format.

▶ **4.** Click the **Save as type** button, and then click **Excel Workbook**. This is the file format for Excel 2007.

▶ **5.** Click the **Save** button. The workbook is saved with the new name and file type.

The workbook remains in Compatibility Mode, as you can see from the title bar. You can continue to work in Compatibility Mode, or you can close and then reopen the workbook in the new file format.

To open the Bayville County workbook in the Excel 2007 file format:

▶ **1.** Close the Bayville County workbook.

▶ **2.** Open the **Bayville County** workbook. The words *[Compatibly Mode]* no longer appear on the title bar, indicating the workbook is in the Excel 2007 file format.

▶ **3.** In the Documentation sheet, enter your name and the current date.

The Data worksheet contains data obtained from the county assessor's office. Myron wants you to convert this data to an Excel table.

To create an Excel table from the county records:

▶ **1.** Switch to the **Data** worksheet.

▶ **2.** Click the **Insert** tab on the Ribbon, and then, in the Tables group, click the **Table** button. The Create Table dialog box opens with the data in the range A1:H51 selected.

▶ **3.** Click the **OK** button to create the Excel table.

▶ **4.** In the Properties group on the Table Tools Design tab, type **TIPData** in the Table Name box to rename the table.

▶ **5.** Click the **Data** tab on the Ribbon, and then in the Sort & Filter group, click the **Filter** button. The filter arrows are removed from the column headers.

▶ **6.** Click any cell in the Excel table.

Using Text Functions

If you receive a workbook from a coworker or obtain data from other software packages, you often have to edit (sometimes referred to as *clean* or *scrub*) and manipulate the data before it is ready to use. Many Text functions help users edit and correct the text values in their workbooks. Text values, also referred to as a *text string* or *string*, contain one or more characters and can include spaces, symbols, and numbers as well as uppercase and lowercase letters. For example, Text functions are used to return the number of characters, remove extra spaces, and change the case of text strings. Figure A-2 reviews some of the common Text functions available in Excel.

Text functions ◄ **Figure A-2**

Function	Syntax	Description	Example
LEFT	LEFT(text,nbr chars)	Returns a specified number of characters at the left of the string	=LEFT("Michael",3) returns Mic
RIGHT	RIGHT(text,nbr chars)	Returns a specified number of characters at the right of the string	=RIGHT("Michael",3) returns ael
MID	MID(text,start nbr, nbr chars)	Returns a specified number of characters from a string, starting at a position you specify	=MID("Net Income"),5,3) returns Inc
UPPER	UPPER(text)	Converts all lowercase characters in a string to uppercase	=UPPER("kim") returns KIM
LOWER	LOWER(text)	Converts all uppercase characters in a string to lowercase	=LOWER("KIM") returns kim
PROPER	PROPER(text)	Capitalizes first letter of each word in a string	=PROPER("JASON BAKER") returns Jason Baker
LEN	LEN(text)	Returns the number of characters in a string	=LEN("Judith Tinker") returns 13
SEARCH	SEARCH(find_text, within_text, start_nbr)	Returns the number of the character at which the find_text is first found reading from left to right	=SEARCH("Main", "1234 Main St",1) returns 6
TEXT	TEXT((value, format_text_code)	Formats numbers within text using a specific number format	="Total Revenue" & TEXT(SUM(D5:D75),"$#,0.00")
TRIM	TRIM(text)	Remove all spaces from a string except for single spaces between words	=TRIM(" Mary Eck") returns Mary Eck

The Zip column includes zip codes in both 5-digit and 10-digit formats. Myron wants only the 5-digit component of the zip code. You will use the LEN and LEFT functions to convert all of the zip codes to the shorter format.

Using the LEN function

First, you need to determine how many characters are in each cell of the Zip column. The **LEN function** returns the number of characters (length) of the specified string. The syntax for the LEN function is:

LEN(*text*)

In this function, *text* is a string constant or cell address containing a text string. For example, cell D4 stores the text value *Narragansett, ri* so the formula =LEN(D4) returns the value 16, the number of characters, including spaces, in *Narragansett, ri.*

The LEN function will be nested inside an IF function to test whether the length of the zip code is equal to 10. If the length is equal to 10, you will use the LEFT function to display the first 5 digits of the zip code; otherwise, the entire contents of the cell will be displayed.

Using the LEFT Function

The **LEFT function** returns a specified number of characters from the beginning of the string. The syntax for the LEFT function is:

LEFT(*text, number of characters*)

In this function, *text* is a string constant or cell address, and *number of characters* indicates the number of characters from the beginning of the string that you want to return. For example, to extract the 5-digit zip code from the zip code 92975-0999 stored in cell G3, you use the following LEFT function to return 92975:

=LEFT(G3,5)

You can use the IF function to display a 5-digit zip code. The IF function uses the LEN function to test whether the zip code has 10 digits. If true (the zip code is 10 digits), the LEFT function displays the first 5 digits in the cell. If false (the code is not 10 digits), all the digits in the cell are displayed. You'll enter the following formula to display the first five digits from the Zip column:

=IF(LEN([Zip]) = 10, LEFT([Zip],5),[Zip])

You'll insert a new column to the left of the Phone column in which to display the results.

To extract the 5-digit zip code from the Zip column:

1. Click cell **F2**. You'll insert the table column to the left of this column.

2. Click the **Home** tab on Ribbon, in the Cells group, click the **Insert button arrow**, and then click **Insert Table Columns to the Left**. A new column named *Column1* is inserted with the same formatting as the column to its left. The new column is formatted in the Text number format, which is the same format as the Zip column (column E).

   You cannot enter a formula in a cell formatted as Text. You'll convert the new column to General number format.

3. Select the range **F2:F51**, and then, in the Number group on the Home tab, click the **Number Format** box arrow and click **General**.

   Now, you can insert the formula in cell F2.

4. Click cell **F2**, type **=I** and then double-click **IF** to start the formula.

5. Type **L** and then double-click **LEN**. The LEN function is nested in the IF function.

▶ **6.** Type **[** to begin the column specifier, double-click **Zip**, and then type **])** to complete the LEN function.

▶ **7.** Type **=10,** to complete the first argument of the IF function. The logical test *LEN([Zip])=10* tests whether the number of characters in the current cell of the Zip column equals 10.

▶ **8.** Type **L** and double-click **LEFT** to begin the second argument of the IF function.

▶ **9.** Type **[** to begin the column specifier, double-click **Zip**, and then type **],5),** to complete the second argument. If LEN([Zip])=10 is true, LEFT([ZIP],5) displays the first five characters from the value in the cell.

▶ **10.** Type **[** to begin the column specifier, double-click **Zip**, and then type **])** to enter the third argument. If LEN([Zip])=10 is false, [Zip] displays all the characters from the value in the cell. The complete formula =IF(LEN([Zip])=10,LEFT([Zip],5),[Zip]) appears in the cell and formula bar.

▶ **11.** Press the **Enter** key. Each cell in column F displays the 5-digit zip code. See Figure A-3.

Table column displays 5-digit zip codes ◀ **Figure A-3**

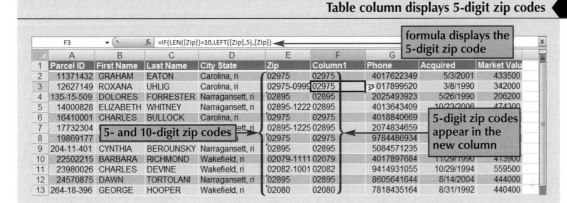

You now have two columns with zip codes (column E and F). You need to keep only the column that displays the 5-digit zip code. However, the data in column F is dependent on column E. If you delete column E, column F displays the error value #REF!. Therefore, before you delete column E, you need to convert the data in column F, which is based on a formula, to values. The easiest way to do that is to copy and paste the formula results, but not the actual formula, to a new column using the Paste Values command. Then, you can delete columns E and F.

To convert the 5-digit zip code formula results to values:

▶ **1.** Click cell **G2**, in the Cells group on the Home tab, click the **Insert button arrow**, and then click **Insert Table Columns to the Left**. A new column named Column 2 is inserted to the left of the Phone column.

▶ **2.** Select the range **F2:F51**, which contains the formula results you want to convert to values.

▶ **3.** In the Clipboard group on the Home tab, click the **Copy** button 🗎.

▶ **4.** Click cell **G2**, in the Clipboard group, click the **Paste button arrow**, and then click **Paste Values**. The values from Column 1 are pasted into Column 2.

▶ **5.** Press the **Esc** key, and then click cell **F2**. The formula appears in the formula bar and the formula results appear in the cell.

▶ **6.** Click cell **G2**. Both the formula bar and the cell display values because you pasted the range using the Paste Values command.

You no longer need columns E and F, so you will delete them.

▶ **7.** Select columns E and F, right-click the selected columns, and then click **Delete**. The two columns are removed.

▶ **8.** In cell E1, enter **Zip**. Column E, which stores the 5-digit zip code values, now has a descriptive column header.

Using the Proper Function

Myron wants to capitalize the first letter of each name in the First Name and Last Name columns. The **PROPER function** converts the first letter of each word in a text string to uppercase, capitalizes any letter in a text string that does not follow another letter, and changes all other letters to lowercase. The syntax of the PROPER function is:

PROPER(text)

In this function *text* is a string constant or contents of a cell. For example, the following formula changes the word *BOOTH* to *Booth*:

=PROPER("BOOTH")

Joining Text Using the Concatenation Operator

Myron wants to combine the First Name and Last Name columns into one column named Owner. You need to use the concatenation operator (&, an ampersand) to do this. **Concatenation** describes what happens when you join the contents of two or more cells. The syntax of the concatenation operator is as follows:

Value1 & Value2 [& Value3 …]

where & (the ampersand) operator joins (or concatenates) two or more string constants, cells, or expressions to produce a single string. For example, if cell B2 contains the last name *Eaton* and cell C2 contains the first name *Graham*, and you want to combine these cells' contents to display the full name in cell D2, you can use the following formula to join the contents of the two cells (last name and first name):

=B2 & C2

However, this formula returns *EatonGraham* in cell D2. To include a comma and a space between the two names, you must change the formula to the following:

=B2 & ", " & C2

This formula uses two concatenation operators and a string constant (a comma and a space enclosed in quotation marks) to display *Eaton, Graham*.

You need to combine the PROPER function and the concatenation operator as shown in the following formula:

=PROPER(B2) & ", " & PROPER(C2)

This formula capitalizes the first letter in the First Name and Last Name columns and combines them into one column named *Owner*.

To enter the formula to change the names to standard capitalization and combine them in one column:

▶ 1. Click cell **D2**, in the Cells group on the Home tab, click the **Insert button arrow**, and then click **Insert Table Columns to the Left**. A new column named *Column1* is inserted to the left of the City State column.

▶ 2. In cell D2, type **=PR**, and then double-click **PROPER**. The beginning of the formula, =PROPER(, appears in the cell and the formula bar.

▶ 3. Type **[** to begin the column specifier, double-click **Last Name**, and then type **])** to complete the PROPER function that converts the last name to upper and lowercase letters.

▶ 4. Type **& ", "** to join the contents of cell D2 with a comma and space.

▶ 5. Type **& PR** and then double-click **PROPER** to begin the second PROPER function.

▶ 6. Type **[** to begin the column specifier, double-click **First Name**, and then type **])** to complete the second PROPER function. The complete formula =PROPER([Last Name]) & ", " & PROPER([First Name]) appears in the cell and the formula bar.

▶ 7. Press the **Enter** key. Each cell in column D displays the owner's name in the form *Last name, First name* with the first letter of each name capitalized. See Figure A-4.

Owner's names displayed in one column ◀ **Figure A-4**

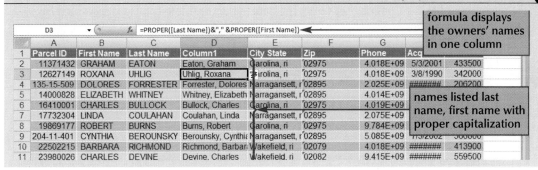

Now that the owners' names data is stored in column D, you no longer need the data in column B (Last Name) and column C (First Name). Because the results in column D are based on a formula, you need to convert the formula in column D to values before you delete columns B and C.

To paste the formula results as values and delete the original data:

▶ 1. Click cell **E2**, in the Cells group on the Home tab, click the **Insert button arrow**, and then click **Insert Table Columns to the Left**. A new column named *Column2* is added to the table.

▶ 2. Select the range **D2:D51**. You want to copy this range and paste the values to Column2.

▶ 3. In the Clipboard group on the Home tab, click the **Copy** button.

▶ 4. Click cell **E2**, in the Clipboard group, click the **Paste button arrow**, and then click **Paste Values**.

▶ 5. Press the **Esc** key, and then AutoFit column E so you can see the owners' full names.

▶ 6. In cell E1, enter **Owner** as the column header.

▶ 7. Select columns **B**, **C**, and **D**, right-click the selected columns, and then click **Delete** on the shortcut menu. The three columns are deleted. Column B, the Owner column, remains in the Excel table.

Using the Text to Columns Command

Myron wants you to split the city and state data into different columns. When multiple data is stored in one cell, you can separate each piece of data into a separate column using the Text to Columns command. You select what **delimits**, or separates, the data, such as a tab, a semicolon, a comma, or a space.

To split the city and state data into separate columns:

▶ **1.** Click cell **D2**, in the Cells group on the Home tab, click the **Insert button arrow**, and then click **Insert Table Columns to the Left**. A new column named *Column1* is inserted to the left of the Zip column.

▶ **2.** Select the range **C2:C51**. These cells contain the values you want to split.

▶ **3.** Click the **Data** tab on the Ribbon, and then, in the Data Tools group, click the **Text to Columns** button. The Convert Text to Columns Wizard - Step 1 of 3 dialog box opens. You select how the data is organized in this step—delimited or a fixed width.

▶ **4.** In the Original data type area, verify that the **Delimited** option button is selected, and then click the **Next** button. The Convert Text to Columns Wizard - Step 2 of 3 dialog box opens. You select the delimiter character in this step.

▶ **5.** Click any check box with a check mark in the Delimiters section to remove the check mark, and then click the **Comma** check box. The data in the City State column is separated by a comma. The Data preview box shows the City and State data in separate columns. See Figure A-5.

| **Figure A-5** | **Convert Text to Columns Wizard - Step 2 of 3 dialog box** |

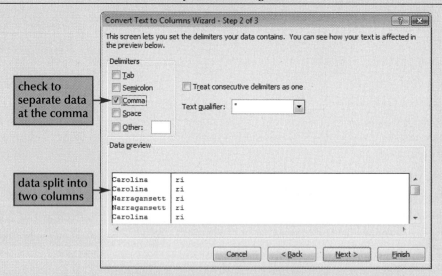

▶ **6.** Click the **Next** button. The Convert Text to Columns Wizard - Step 3 of 3 dialog box opens so you can set the data format for each column. The Data preview box shows that each column is set to the General number format. You'll leave this format.

▶ **7.** Click the **Finish** button. The cities remain in column C and the states move to column D.

▶ **8.** In cell C1, enter **City**. In cell D1, enter **State**. See Figure A-6.

City and state in separate columns ◀ **Figure A-6**

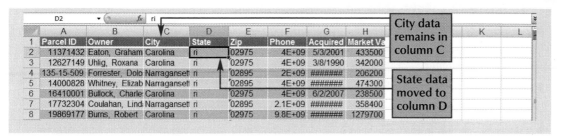

Using the UPPER Function to Convert Case

The state abbreviations in column D are all lowercase. Myron wants to capitalize them. The **UPPER function** converts all letters of each word in a text string to uppercase. The syntax of the UPPER function is:

UPPER(text)

In this function, *text* is a string constant or contents of a cell. For example, the following formula returns RI:

=UPPER("ri")

You'll enter the UPPER function now.

Tip

You can convert cell contents to all lowercase by using the LOWER function.

To enter the UPPER function to capitalize the state abbreviations:

▶ **1.** Click cell **E2**, and then click the **Home** tab on Ribbon.

▶ **2.** In the Cells group, click the **Insert button arrow**, and then click **Insert Table Columns to the Left**. A new column named *Column1* is inserted to the left of the Zip column.

▶ **3.** In cell E2, type **=U**, and then double-click **UPPER**. The beginning of the formula, =UPPER(, appears in the cell and the formula bar.

▶ **4.** Type **[** to begin the column specifier, double-click **State**, and then type**])**. The formula =UPPER([STATE]) appears in the formula bar.

▶ **5.** Press the **Enter** key. The state abbreviation appears in all uppercase in column E. See Figure A-7.

UPPER function converts the state abbreviations to uppercase ◀ **Figure A-7**

	A	B	C	D	E	F	G	H	I
1	Parcel ID	Owner	City	State	Column1	Zip	Phone	Acquired	Market Va
2	11371432	Eaton, Graham	Carolina	ri	RI	02975	4E+09	5/3/2001	433500
3	12627149	Uhlig, Roxana	Carolina	ri	RI	02975	4E+09	3/8/1990	342000
4	135-15-509	Forrester, Dolo	Narraganset	ri	RI	02895	2E+09	######	206200
5	14000828	Whitney, Elizab	Narraganset	ri	RI	02895	4E+09	######	474300
6	16410001	Bullock, Charle	Carolina	ri	RI	02975	4E+09	6/2/2007	238500
7	17732304	Coulahan, Lind	Narraganset	ri	RI	02895	2.1E+09	######	358400
8	19869177	Burns, Robert	Carolina	ri	RI	02975	9.8E+09	######	1279700
9	204-11-401	Berounsky, Cyr	Narraganset	ri	RI	02895	5.1E+09	7/5/2002	566800
10	22502215	Richmond, Bar	Wakefield	ri	RI	02079	4E+09	######	413900
11	23980026	Devine, Charle	Wakefield	ri	RI	02082	9.4E+09	######	559500

E3 — =UPPER([State])

UPPER function formula converts cell contents to uppercase

state abbreviations are capitalized

You need to keep only the data in column E. Because the results of column E are based on a formula, you again need to convert the formula in column E to values before you delete columns D and E.

To paste the state abbreviations as values:

▶ 1. Click cell **F2**. In the Cells group on the Home tab, click the **Insert button arrow**, and then click **Insert Table Columns to the Left**. A new column named Column2 is inserted to the left of column E.

▶ 2. Select the range **E2:E51**. You want to copy and paste these values to Column2.

▶ 3. In the Clipboard group on the Home tab, click the **Copy** button.

▶ 4. Click cell **F2**, in the Clipboard group, click the **Paste button arrow**, and then click **Paste Values**.

▶ 5. Select columns **D** and **E**, right-click the selected columns, and then click **Delete** on the shortcut menu. The two columns are deleted. Column D remains in the Excel table.

▶ 6. In cell D1, enter **State**. The column is renamed with a more descriptive header.

Using the SUBSTITUTE Function

The entries in Parcel ID, column A, are inconsistent. Sometimes they are an 8-digit value, other times hyphens separate the components of the Parcel (Book No., Map No., and Parcel No.). Myron wants you to remove the hyphens from the Parcel ID. The **SUBSTITUTE function** replaces existing text with new text in a text string. The SUBSTITUTE function has the following syntax:

SUBSTITUTE (*text,old_text,new_text,instance_num*)

In this function, *text* is a string constant or reference to a cell containing text you want to replace, *old_text* is the existing text you want to replace, *new_text* is the text you want to replace *old_text* with, and *instance_num* specifies which occurrence of *old_text* you want to replace. If you omit *instance_num*, every instance of *old_text* is replaced. For example, the following formula returns 16445890:

=SUBSTITUTE("164-45-890","-","").

You'll enter the formula to remove the hyphens from the Parcel ID data.

To remove hyphens from the Parcel ID data:

▶ 1. Click cell **B2**. In the Cells group on the Home tab, click the **Insert button arrow**, and then click **Insert Table Columns to the Left**. A new column named Column1 is inserted to the left of the Owner column.

▶ 2. Click the **Insert Function** button on the formula bar. The Insert Function dialog box opens.

▶ 3. Click the **Or select a category** arrow, click **Text** to display the Text functions, and then double-click **SUBSTITUTE** in the Select a function box. The Function Arguments dialog box opens.

▶ 4. In the Text argument box, type **A2**. The text in cell A2 is displayed.

▶ 5. In the Old_text argument box, type **"-"**. The hyphen is the text you want to remove.

▶ 6. In the New_text argument box, type **""**. You want to replace the old text with nothing. You do not need to enter anything in the Instance_num argument box because you want to replace every instance of a hyphen.

7. Click the **OK** button. All of the Parcel IDs are changed to 8-digit numbers. The hyphens were replaced with an empty string (a blank or nothing). See Figure A-8.

SUBSTITUTE function removed hyphens from the Parcel IDs   Figure A-8

B2   fx =SUBSTITUTE(A2,"-","")

	A	B	C	D	E	F	G	H	I
	Parcel ID	Column1	Owner	City	State	Zip	Phone	Acquired	Market V
2	11371432	11371432	Eaton, Grah	Carolina	RI	02975	4E+09	5/3/2001	433500
3	12627149	12627149	Blig, Roxar	Carolina	RI	02975	4E+09	3/8/1990	342000
4	135-15-509	13515509	Forrester, D	Narragans	RI	02895	2E+09	######	206200
5	14000828	14000828	Whitney, Eli	Narragans	RI	02895	4E+09	######	474300
6	16410001	16410001	Bullock, Cha	Carolina	RI	02975	4E+09	6/2/2007	238500
7	17732304	17732304	Coulahan, L	Narragans	RI	02895	2.1E+09	######	358400
8	19869177	19869177	Burns, Robe	Carolina	RI	02975	9.8E+09	######	1279700
9	204-11-401	20411401	Berounsky,	Narragans	RI	02895	5.1E+09	7/5/2002	566800
10	22502215	22502215	Richmond, E	Wakefield	RI	02079	4E+09	######	413900
11	23980026	23980026	Devine, Cha	Wakefield	RI	02082	9.4E+09	######	559500
12	24570875	24570875	Tortolani, D	Narragans	RI	02895	8.6E+09	######	444000
13	264-18-396	26418396	Hooper, Ge	Wakefield	RI	02080	7.8E+09	######	440400

formula converts the Parcel IDs to 8 digits

all IDs are numbers only

original IDs sometimes include hyphens

After you convert the formula in column B to values, you can delete columns A and B.

To paste the Parcel ID column as values:

1. Click cell **C2**. In the Cells group on the Home tab, click the **Insert button arrow**, and then click **Insert Table Columns to the Left**. A new column named *Column2* is inserted to the left of the Owner column.

2. Select the range **B2:B51**. You want to copy this range and paste the values in Column2.

3. In the Clipboard group on the Home tab, click the **Copy** button.

4. Click cell **C2**. In the Clipboard group, click the **Paste button arrow**, and click **Paste Values**.

5. Select columns **A** and **B**, right-click the selected columns, and then click **Delete** on the shortcut menu. The two columns are deleted. Column A, the Parcel ID column, remains in the Excel table.

6. In cell A1, enter **Parcel ID**.

7. AutoFit the Parcel ID, Owner, State, City, Zip, Phone, Acquired, and Market Value columns.

You have cleaned all of the data in the worksheet. Myron can more easily work with the data in this arrangement.

Adding Special and Custom Formatting

Now that the data in the workbook is clean, Myron wants you to apply the following formatting to the data:

- Display the phone number using the common format of area code in parentheses and a hyphen between the prefix and the last four digits.
- Display the market values in thousands, so that a value such as 456600 is displayed as 457.
- Display the acquired date with the name of the month followed by the year (for example, 6/12/2005 is displayed as June, 2005).

These formatting changes will make the data easier to understand and use.

Using Special Formats

Four commonly used formats, referred to as Special formats, are available. They include two zip code formats (5-digit and 10-digit), a phone number format (with area code in parentheses and hyphen between the prefix and the last four digits), and a social security number format. Using these Special formats allows you to type a number without punctuation, yet still display that number in its common format.

To format the phone number with the Phone Number format:

▶ **1.** Select the range **F2:F51**.

▶ **2.** In the Numbers group on the Home tab, click the **Dialog Box Launcher**. The Format Cells dialog box opens with the Number tab active.

▶ **3.** In the Category list, click **Special**. Four special formats appear in the Type list: Zip Code, Zip Code + 4, Phone Number, and Social Security Number.

▶ **4.** In the Type list, click **Phone Number**, and then click the **OK** button. The phone numbers are formatted in a standard phone number format.

Creating Custom Formats

Excel supplies a generous collection of formats and styles to improve the appearance and readability of your documents. However, sometimes you still will not be able to find formats and styles to accommodate a specific requirement. In these cases, you can create your own formats, called **custom formats**. Custom formats use **format codes**, a series of symbols, to describe exactly how Excel should display a number, date, time, or text string. You can use format codes to display text strings and spaces, and determine how many decimal places to display in a cell.

Working with Numeric Format Codes

Each number is composed of digits. In displaying these digits, Excel makes special note of **insignificant zeros**, which are zeros whose omission from the number does not change the number's value. For example, the number 0.1 is displayed in the General number format but changes to 0.10 when the cell is formatted as a number. To format a value, Excel uses the **placeholders** shown in Figure A-9 to represent individual digits.

Description of digit placeholders ◀ **Figure A-9**

Placeholder	Description
#	Displays only significant digits; insignificant zeros are omitted.
0 (zero)	Displays significant digits as well as insignificant zeros.
?	Replaces insignificant zeros with spaces on either side of the decimal point so that decimal points align when formatted with a fixed-width font, such as Courier.

A custom format can use combinations of these placeholders. For example, the custom format #.00 displays the value 8.9 as 8.90. If a value has more digits than placeholders in the custom format, Excel rounds the value to match the number of placeholders. Thus, the value 8.938 formatted with the custom format #.## is displayed as 8.94. Figure A-10 shows how the same series of numbers appear with different custom number formats.

Examples of digit placeholders   **Figure A-10**

| Value in Cell | Custom Formats | | | |
	#.##	0.00	?.??	#.#0
0.57	.57	0.57	.57	.57
123.4	123.4	123.40	123.4	123.40
3.45	3.45	3.45	3.45	3.45
7.891	7.89	7.89	7.89	7.89
5.248	5.25	5.25	5.25	5.25

In addition to digit placeholders, number formats also include separators, such as the decimal point separator (.), the thousands separator (,), and the fraction separator (/). The thousands separator can be used to separate the number in groups of one thousand, but it can also be used to scale a number by a multiple of one thousand.

The fraction separator displays decimal values as fractions. The general syntax is *placeholder/placeholder*, where *placeholder* is one or more of the custom format placeholders discussed above. Excel displays the fraction that best approximates the decimal value. You can also specify the denominator for the fraction to convert the decimals to halves, quarters, and so forth. Figure A-11 provides examples of the thousands separator and the fraction separator.

Examples of thousands separator and fraction separator   **Figure A-11**

Value in Cell	Custom Format	Appearance
12000	#,###	12,000
12000	#,	12
12200000	0.0,,	12.2
5.4	# #/#	5 2/5

All of the numeric format codes can be combined in a single custom format, providing you with great control over data's appearance. If you don't specify a numeric code for data values, Excel uses the General format code, which applies a general numeric format to the data values. The General format hides all insignificant zeros.

Myron wants you to display the market value of the properties to the nearest thousand. You will create the custom format #.###, to display the market values to the nearest thousands.

To create a custom format for the market values to the nearest thousands:

▶ **1.** Select the range **H2:H51**.

▶ **2.** In the Number group on the Home tab, click the **Dialog Box Launcher**. The Format Cells dialog box opens with the Number tab active.

You will enter a custom format to display the numbers to the nearest thousand.

▶ **3.** Click **Custom** in the Category box.

▶ **4.** In the Type box, double-click **General** to select it, and then type **#,###,** as the custom format code. See Figure A-12.

Figure A-12 ▶ **Custom category on the Number tab**

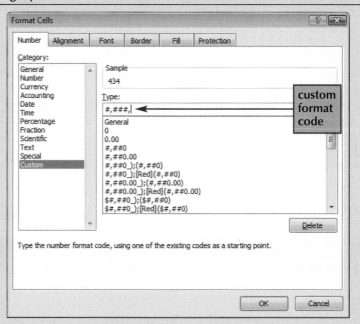

▶ **5.** Click the **OK** button. The market values are displayed to the nearest thousand.

Next, you'll enter a comment in cell H1 to explain how the values are displayed.

▶ **6.** Right-click cell **H1**, and then click **Insert Comment** on the shortcut menu. A comment box appears next to the cell.

▶ **7.** Type **market values are rounded to nearest thousand**, and then click any cell to close the comment box.

▶ **8.** Point to cell **H1**. The comment appears.

Formatting Dates

When you have dates, times, or both in a workbook, you can use a predefined date and time format to display this information in a readable format. Although the predefined time and date formats are usually fine, you can also create your own custom date formats. Figure A-13 describes the format codes used for dates and times.

Date and Time format codes ◀ **Figure A-13**

Symbol	To Display
m	Months as 1 through 12
mm	Months as 01 through 12
mmm	Months as Jan through Dec
mmmm	Months as January through December
d	Days as 1 through 31
dd	Days as 01 through 31
ddd	Days as Sun through Sat
dddd	Days as Sunday through Saturday
yy	Years as 00 through 99
yyyy	Years as 1900 through 9999
h	Hours as 1 through 24
mm	Minutes as 01 through 60 (when immediately following h, mm signifies minutes; otherwise, months)
ss	Seconds as 01 through 60

Myron wants the date values in the Acquired column to show the name of the month followed by the year (for example, July, 2010). You need to apply the custom format code *mmmm, yyyy* to do this.

To apply a custom date format to the Acquisition dates:

▶ **1.** Select the range **G2:G51**.

▶ **2.** In the Number group on the Home tab, click the **Dialog Box Launcher**. The Format Cells dialog box opens with the Number tab active.

▶ **3.** Click **Custom** in the Category box.

▶ **4.** In the Type box, select the current format, and then type **mmmm, yyyy**. The Sample box shows an example of the custom format you entered.

▶ **5.** Click the **OK** button, and then click cell **A1** to deselect the range. See Figure A-14.

Final formatted workbook ◀ **Figure A-14**

	A	B	C	D	E	F	G	H	I	J
	A1	▾	fx	Parcel ID						
1	Parcel ID	Owner	City	State	Zip	Phone	Acquired	Market Value		
2	11371432	Eaton, Graham	Carolina	RI	02975	(401) 762-2349	May, 2001	434		
3	12627149	Uhlig, Roxana	Carolina	RI	02975	(401) 789-9520	March, 1990	342		
4	13515509	Forrester, Dolores	Narragansett	RI	02895	(202) 549-3923	May, 1990	206		
5	14000828	Whitney, Elizabeth	Narragansett	RI	02895	(401) 364-3409	October, 2006			
6	16410001	Bullock, Charles	Carolina	RI	02975	(401) 884-0669	June, 2007			
7	17732304	Coulahan, Linda	Narragansett	RI	02895	(207) 483-4659	April, 1998			
8	19869177	Burns, Robert	Carolina	RI	02975	(978) 448-6934	October, 2003	1,250		
9	20411401	Berounsky, Cynthia	Narragansett	RI	02895	(508) 457-1235	July, 2002	567		
10	22502215	Richmond, Barbara	Wakefield	RI	02079	(401) 789-7684	November, 1990	414		
11	23980026	Devine, Charles	Wakefield	RI	02082	(941) 493-1055	October, 1994	560		

dates with the custom format

▶ **6.** Save the workbook.

Any custom format you create is stored in the workbook, and you can apply the custom format to any other cell or range in the workbook. However, you can use a custom format only in the workbook in which it was created. If you want to use the custom formats you created for the Bayville County workbook in another workbook, you need to reenter them.

InSight | **Storing Dates and Time in Excel**

Excel stores dates and times as a number representing the number of days since January 0, 1900 plus a fractional portion of a 24-hour day. This is called a **serial date**, or serial date-time.

Dates The integer portion of the number is the number of days since January 0, 1900. For example, the date 1/1/2010 is stored as 40,179, because 40,179 days have passed since January 0, 1900. The number 1 is the serial date for 1/1/1900.

Times The decimal portion of the number is the fraction of a 24-hour day that has passed. For example, 6:00 AM is stored as 0.25, which is 25% of a 24-hour day. Similarly, 6 PM is stored as 0.75, which is 75% of a 24-hour day.

Any date and time can be stored as the sum of the date and the time. For example, 3 PM on 1/1/2010 is stored in Excel as 40,179.625.

As an experiment, enter 1/1/2010 in cell A1 of a new worksheet. Change the format in the cell to General. The value appears as 40179. Change the format to a Short Date format to see the value displayed as 1/1/2010.

Using the Compatibility Checker

Myron needs to travel to Seattle while continuing to work on this project. Although all of the desktop computers at Zeus Engineering have Excel 2007 installed, Myron's notebook computer hasn't yet been upgraded. Myron asks you to make a copy of the current workbook, converting it to a format Excel 2003 can read. When you save an Excel 2007 formatted workbook to an earlier format, the **Compatibility Checker** alerts you to any features that are not supported by earlier versions of Excel.

To convert an Excel 2007 workbook to an earlier Excel file format:

▶ 1. Click the **Office Button** 🔘, and then click **Save As**. The Save As dialog box opens.

▶ 2. In the File Name box, change the filename to **Bayville County 2003**.

▶ 3. Click the **Save as type** button, and then click **Excel 97-2003 Workbook**. This is the earlier Excel file format you want to use.

▶ 4. Click the **Save** button. The Microsoft Office Excel – Compatibility Checker dialog box opens, alerting you to features not supported by earlier versions of Excel. See Figure A-15.

Figure A-15 ▶ **Compatibility Checker**

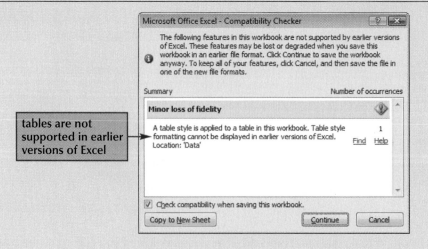

tables are not supported in earlier versions of Excel

▶ **5.** Read the message, and then click the **Continue** button. The workbook is saved in the earlier file format with the file extension .xls.

▶ **6.** Close the workbook.

The workbook data is clean and formatted in the best way for Myron. He'll analyze this data as he comes up with a proposal to address Bayville's traffic concerns.

Appendix Summary | Review

In this appendix, you used a variety of Text functions, the concatenation operator, and the Text to Column command. You created a custom format to round numbers to the nearest thousands. Finally, you created a custom format code to display dates as a month and year.

Key Terms

Compatibility Checker	format code	PROPER function
Compatibility Mode	insignificant zero	serial date (or serial date-
concatenation	LEFT function	time)
custom format	LEN function	SUBSTITUTE function
delimit	placeholder	UPPER function

Practice	**Review Assignments**

Practice the skills you learned in the appendix using the same case scenario.

Data File needed for the Review Assignments: Assessor.xls

As part of the Transportation Improvement Program (TIP) study, Myron Londale, traffic analyst at Zeus Engineering, obtained a second workbook from the Bayville Assessor's Office containing data on private homes and commercial buildings located along the route being reviewed. The assessor's office was able to transfer the data requested by Zeus Engineering to Excel. Before Myron begins his analysis, he asks you to clean and format the data.

Complete the following:

1. Open the **Assessor** workbook located in the Appendix.A\Review folder included with your Data Files, and then save the workbook in the Excel 2007 format as **Owners** in the same folder.
2. Insert a new worksheet. Enter your name, the date, and a purpose statement in the worksheet, and then rename the worksheet as **Documentation**.
3. Create an Excel table for the data in the range A1:G5.
4. Use the Text to Columns command to split the Owner column into two columns named **Last Name** and **First Name**. Insert a blank column to the left of column C to store the first name and leave the last name in column B.
5. In cell I1, enter the column header **Status**. In the Status column, use the IF and LEFT functions to display the word **Discard** if the address is a PO Box; otherwise, leave the cell blank.
6. In cell J1, enter the column header **Twn**. In cell J2, enter a formula to convert the data in the Town column to proper case.
7. In cell K1, enter the column header **St**. In column K, enter a formula to convert the data in the State column to uppercase.
8. In cell L1, enter the column header **Town State**. In column L, combine the town and state data into one column using the format *town, state*.
9. Format the data in the SSN column (column A) with the special Social Security number format.
10. Save and close the workbook. Submit the finished workbook to your instructor, either in printed or electronic form, as requested.

Apply	**Case Problem 1**

Apply the skills you learned to clean and format membership data.

Data File needed for this Case Problem: Mesa.xls

Mesa Senior Center   Elliot Turner, director of the Mesa Senior Center, has begun compiling a list of its members. He's asked you to clean and format the data in the worksheet before he continues working on the project.

Complete the following:

1. Open the **Mesa** workbook located in the Appendix.A\Case1 folder included with your Data Files, and then save the workbook as **Senior Center** in the same folder.
2. Insert a new worksheet. Enter your name and the date in the worksheet, and then rename the worksheet as **Documentation**.

3. In the Members worksheet, apply the special Social Security Number format to the data in the SSN column.

4. Split the Name data into two columns. Store the first name in column B and the last name in column C. Change the column headers to **First Name** (column B) and **Last Name** (column C).

5. Insert two columns to the left of the City column. In column D, apply the proper case to the first name data, and change the column header to **F Name**. In column E, apply the proper case to the last name data, and change the column header to **L Name**.

6. In the Member Since column, apply a custom format that displays only the year.

7. Split the CSZ column into three columns named **City**, **State**, and **Zip**.

8. Sort the data by City and then within City by L Name.

9. Name column J as **UniqueID**. Instead of using Social Security numbers as the unique identifier, the senior center is considering using an ID of the first three letters of the last name (L Name) followed by the first letter of first name (F Name). If the last name is fewer than three characters, the letter Z replaces each missing character. Use the LEN and LEFT functions and the concatenation operator to display the proposed Unique ID.

10. Save the workbook. Submit the finished workbook to your instructor, either in printed or electronic form, as requested.

Apply	**Case Problem 2**

Apply the skills you learned to calculate overhead allocation.

Data File needed for this Case Problem: Research.xls

Steuben Institute   Every two weeks Elli Pjster processes payroll information for employees whose salaries are paid fully or partially from research grants. She downloads an Excel workbook from the Institute's Research and Grant Accounting system to calculate overhead. The overhead rate varies depending on the research grant. Overhead is calculated by multiplying the employee salary by the overhead rate of the grant that funds the employee. She asks you to clean and format the data in the worksheet.

Complete the following:

1. Open the **Research** workbook located in the Appendix.A\Case2 folder included with your Data Files, and then save the workbook in the Excel 2007 file format as **Grants** in the same folder.

2. Insert a new worksheet, enter the company name, your name, the date, and a purpose statement in the worksheet, and then rename the worksheet as **Documentation**.

3. In the Pay Period worksheet, create an Excel table for the data in the range A1:C51. Hide the filter arrows.

4. Split the data in column A into separate columns for the first name and the last name. Change the column headers to **First Name** and **Last Name**. AutoFit the two columns, and then sort the table by the Last Name data.

⊕ EXPLORE   5. Use the MID function to extract the grant number from the ChartString column and display it in column E. Name the new column **Grant Nbr**. The Grant Nbr is a four-digit number that begins in position ten of the ChartString column. (*Hint:* Research the MID function in the Help system.)

6. In the column to the right of the Grant Nbr column (column F), enter a VLOOKUP function to find the grant number in the lookup table in the Overhead Rates worksheet and display the grant name from column 2. Name the column header in cell F1 **Grant Name**. AutoFit the column.

7. In column G enter the formula to calculate overhead, which is the Overhead Rate located in the third column of the Overhead Rates worksheet multiplied by Salary. You need to use a VLOOKUP function to find the correct overhead rate for the grant. Name the column **Overhead**.

8. Format the Salary and Overhead columns in the Accounting number format with two decimals place.

9. Save and close the workbook. Submit the finished workbook to your instructor, either in printed or electronic form, as requested.

Ending Data Files

Appendix.A → **Tutorial**

Bayville County.xlsx
Bayville County 2003.xls

Review

Owners.xlsx

Case1

Senior Center.xlsx

Case2

Grants.xlsx

Objectives

- Learn about methods of integration using Office programs
- Link an Excel worksheet to a Word document
- Update a linked object
- Embed an object
- Modify an embedded object

Integrating Excel with Other Windows Programs

Creating Integrated Documents

Case | Metro Zoo

Marvin Hall is the director of Metro Zoo. Each year, he sends out a financial report to the zoo's supporters and contributors. Marvin stores the financial data in an Excel workbook, and he uses Word to create a letter that includes data from Excel. Marvin wants to be able to copy the Excel data and insert it directly into the Word document. He also wants to tie the two documents together, so that if he updates the financial information in the Excel workbook, the report in the Word document will be automatically updated as well.

Marvin asks you to help him integrate his Excel data into his Word document and link the files, so that the data in the report is automatically updated each time Marvin modifies the workbook.

Starting Data Files

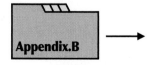

Appendix.B →

Tutorial

MZoo.xlsx
Zoo Letter.docx

Review

Sales Memo.docx
State Sales.xlsx

Case1

Event.docx
Quote.xlsx

Case2

Request.docx
Usage.xlsx

Methods of Integration

Excel is part of a suite of programs called Microsoft Office. In addition to Excel, the Office programs include Word, a word-processing program; Access, a database management program; PowerPoint, a presentation and slide show program; Outlook, a personal information manager; and Publisher, a program for creating desktop publishing projects. All of these programs share a common interface and can read each other's file formats.

Occasionally, you will create a file that relies on data from more than one program. This type of file is called a **compound file**. The **source file** (or files) supplies the data to be shared. The **destination file** (or files) displays the data from the source file (or files). Compound files are easy to create in Office because of the tight integration of the Office programs. At Metro Zoo, Marvin needs to create a letter using Word that incorporates information from an Excel workbook that contains financial data as well as a chart.

There are three ways to insert data from one program into another program: copying and pasting, linking, and embedding. Each of these techniques can be used to create a compound file. Figure B-1 describes each of these methods, and provides examples of when each method is appropriate.

Figure B-1	Integration methods

Method	Description	Use When
Copying and pasting	Inserts an object into a file	You want to exchange the data between the two files only once, and it doesn't matter if the data changes.
Linking	Displays an object in the destination file but doesn't store it there—only the location of the source file is stored in the destination file	You want to use the same data in more than one file, and you need to ensure that the data will be current and identical in each file. Any changes you make to the source file will be reflected in the destination file(s).
Embedding	Displays and stores an object in the destination file	You want the source data to become a permanent part of the destination file, or the source data will no longer be available to the destination file. Any changes you make to either the destination file or the source file do not affect the other.

Copying and Pasting Data

You can copy text, values, cells and ranges, or even charts and graphics from one program and paste it in another program using the Windows copy and paste features. The item being copied and pasted is referred to as an **object**. When you paste an object from the source file into the destination file, you are inserting the object so that it is part of the destination file. The **pasted object** is static, having no connection to the source file. If you want to change the pasted object, you must do so in the destination file. For example, a range of cells pasted into a Word document can be edited only within the Word document. Any changes made in the original Excel workbook have no impact on the Word document. For this reason, pasting is used only for one-time exchanges of information.

Object Linking and Embedding

If you want to create a live connection between two files, so that changes in the source file are automatically reflected in the destination file, you must use object linking and embedding. **Object linking and embedding (OLE)** refers to the technology that allows you to copy and paste objects, such as graphic files, cell and ranges, or charts, so that information about the program that created the object is included with the object itself.

The objects are inserted into the destination file as either linked objects or embedded objects. A **linked object** is actually a separate file that is linked to the source file. If you make a change to the source file, the destination file can automatically reflect the change. On the other hand, an **embedded object** is stored in the destination file (Word, in this example) and is no longer part of the source file. In the case of Office programs, embedded objects include their Ribbon, tabs, and buttons. This means you can edit an Excel worksheet or chart embedded in a Word document using Excel tools and commands to modify the worksheet or chart content. Because embedded objects have no link to the source file, changes made to the embedded object are not reflected in the source file.

Thus, the main difference between linked and embedded objects lies in where the data is stored and how the data is updated after being inserted into the destination file. Figure B-2 illustrates the difference between linking and embedding.

Embedding contrasted with linking | **Figure B-2**

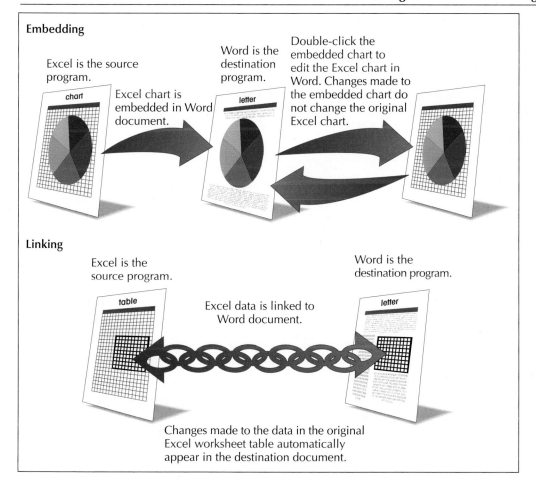

Embedding

Excel is the source program.

Excel chart is embedded in Word document.

Word is the destination program.

Double-click the embedded chart to edit the Excel chart in Word. Changes made to the embedded chart do not change the original Excel chart.

Linking

Excel is the source program.

Excel data is linked to Word document.

Word is the destination program.

Changes made to the data in the original Excel worksheet table automatically appear in the destination document.

Linking Excel and Word Files

Marvin asks you to insert the financial data stored in a workbook into a letter he has been writing to Metro Zoo's supporters. He is still working on the details of the financial report, and he might need to edit some of the values in the workbook. Rather than pasting the data each time he modifies the report, Marvin wants you to create a link between his Excel workbook and his Word document, so that any changes he makes to the workbook are automatically reflected in the letter. You will open both files and link the Excel data to the Word document.

To open Marvin's two files:

© **1.** Open the **MZoo** Excel workbook located in the **Appendix.B\Tutorial** folder included with your Data Files, and then save the workbook as **Metro Zoo** in the same folder.

© **2.** In the Documentation sheet, enter your name and the current date.

© **3.** Open the **Zoo Letter** Word document located in the **Appendix.B\Tutorial** folder included with your Data Files, and then save the document as **Metro Zoo Ltr** in the same folder.

© **4.** Return to the **Metro Zoo** workbook, and then switch to the **Financial Summary** worksheet.

The financial data Marvin wants to display in his letter is stored in the range A2:D17 of the Financial Summary worksheet. To transfer that data, you'll copy the range in the workbook and then paste the data as a link in the Word document.

To copy and paste a link:

© **1.** Select the range **A2:D17**.

© **2.** In the Clipboard group on the Home tab, click the **Copy** button 🗐.

© **3.** Return to the **Metro Zoo Ltr** document, and then click the paragraph mark below the letter's second paragraph (below the sentence that reads "Below are Metro Zoo's revenues and expenses for the past two years"). See Figure B-3.

Figure B-3 ▶ **Metro Letter document**

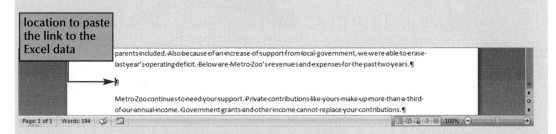

location to paste the link to the Excel data

Trouble? If your document does not show paragraph marks at the end of each paragraph, you need to show the nonprinting characters. In the Paragraph group on the Home tab, click the Show/Hide button.

© **4.** In the Clipboard group on the Home tab, click the **Paste button arrow**, and then click **Paste Special**. The Paste Special dialog box opens. The Paste link option enables you to paste data in several different formats. The default format is to insert the data as a Word table using HTML (Hypertext Markup Language). You could also paste the data as a graphic image, unformatted text, or an embedded worksheet object. See Figure B-4.

Paste Special dialog box ◀ **Figure B-4**

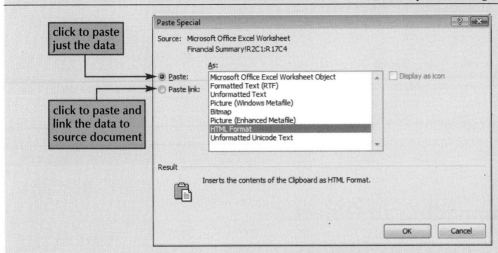

5. Click the **Paste link** option button, and then click **Microsoft Office Excel Worksheet Object**.

6. Click the **OK** button. Word places a link (the location of the source file) to the Excel object within the Word document so the financial data is linked to the Excel workbook. A representation of the financial data is displayed in the Word document, as shown in Figure B-5.

Financial data pasted into the Metro Zoo Ltr document ◀ **Figure B-5**

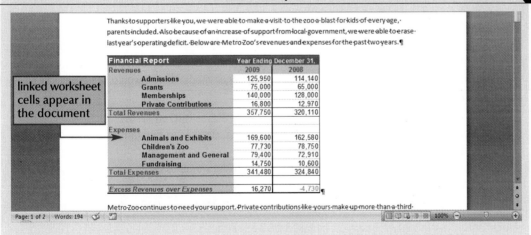

Tip

You can edit and format this table using any of the Word formatting features.

Updating a Linked Object

When an object is linked, the linked objects are updated automatically. This means that Word updates the linked information every time you open the Word document or any time the Excel source file changes while the Word document is open.

Marvin finished reviewing the financial summary in the Metro Zoo workbook. He finds a data-entry error in the report. A $2500 overstatement of a government grant to Metro Zoo was entered in error. You need to correct the total amounts of grants. You can update the linked data without having to paste the data again.

To update the linked data:

© **1.** Return to the **Metro Zoo** workbook, and then press the **Esc** key to deselect the range A2:D17.

© **2.** In cell C5 enter **72500**. The correct value for the government grants is inserted.

© **3.** Switch to the **Metro Zoo Ltr** document to verify that the value of the grant changed, reflecting the current value in the Metro Zoo workbook.

Trouble? If the link doesn't update automatically, right-click the table and click Update Link on the shortcut menu.

Embedding an Object

Marvin also wants the letter to include the pie chart in the Metro Zoo workbook that details the source of Metro Zoo's revenue. Marvin is confident that the financial summary is correct and requires no further edits. Therefore, you don't need to create a link between Marvin's letter and the workbook's chart. Instead, Marvin wants to embed the chart in the letter. Then, he will be able to use the Excel chart-editing tools directly from the Word document, if he chooses to modify the chart's appearance before printing the letter. You will embed the Revenue chart in the document.

To embed an Excel chart in a Word document:

© **1.** Switch to the **Metro Zoo** workbook, and then click the **Revenues** chart to select it.

© **2.** In the Clipboard group on the Home tab, click the **Copy** button 🔳.

© **3.** Switch to the **Metro Zoo Ltr** document, and then click the paragraph mark above the letter's next to last paragraph (above the sentence that reads "If you would like to learn more about the Metro Zoo...").

© **4.** In the Clipboard group on the Home tab, click the **Paste button arrow**, and then click **Paste Special**. The Paste Special dialog box opens, displaying two format options for charts in the As box. You can choose to paste the chart as an Excel chart object; or you can choose to paste the chart as a graphic object. Marvin wants to be able to use the Excel chart-editing tools, so you'll choose the first option.

© **5.** Verify that the **Paste** option button is selected, click **Microsoft Office Excel Chart Object**, and then click the **OK** button. Excel places a copy of the chart as an embedded object into the letter. See Figure B-6.

Figure B-6 ▷ Chart embedded in the Metro Zoo Letter document

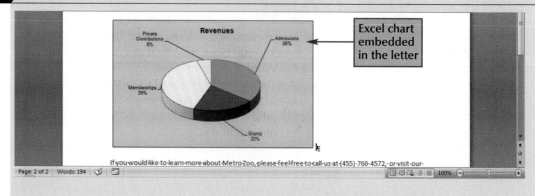

Modifying an Embedded Object

Embedded objects such as the chart become part of the Word document after they are inserted; they are no longer linked to the source file. For example, if you change the chart in the source file, the embedded object in Word does not change. Conversely, if you change the embedded object in Word, the source file is not modified.

After viewing the contents of the chart, Marvin wants you to change the chart's title from "Revenues" to "Revenues for 2009." You can do this by editing the chart within Word. Recall that when you make changes to an embedded object, those changes will not be reflected in the object in the source file. You will change the title of the chart that is embedded in the letter.

To edit the embedded chart:

© **1.** Double-click the embedded chart in the Metro Zoo Letter document, and then click anywhere within the chart. The hatch-marked border appears around the chart, and the embedded object appears in an Excel workbook window, as shown in Figure B-7. Also, notice that the Ribbon shows the Excel tabs and buttons.

Embedded chart selected for editing   **Figure B-7**

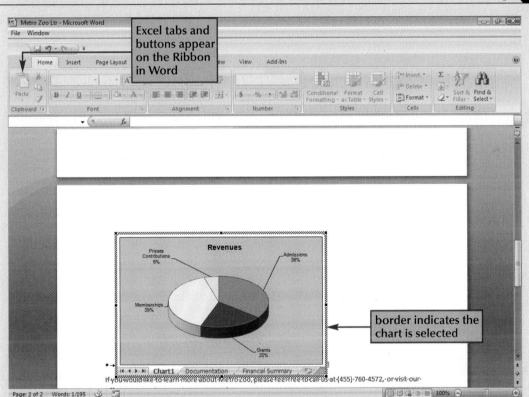

You can edit the object using the Excel chart-editing tools within Word.

© **2.** Click the **Title object** and change the title to **Revenues for 2009**. The chart title is updated.

© **3.** Click outside the chart to deselect it. See Figure B-8.

Figure B-8 **Embedded chart updated with new chart title**

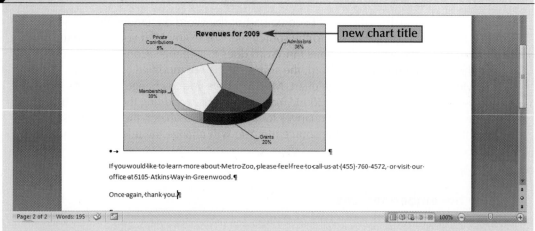

Your work on both the Metro Zoo workbook and the Metro Zoo Letter document are complete. You can save your changes and then exit the programs.

4. Save and close the Metro Zoo Ltr document, and then exit Word.

5. Return to the **Metro Zoo** workbook, and verify that the revenue chart title remains *Revenues*. The title was not updated to *Revenues for 2009* because you edited the embedded chart, which is not linked to the Excel workbook.

6. Save and close the Metro Zoo workbook, and then exit Excel.

You may have noticed in Figure B-8 that the embedded object included not just the chart sheet for the revenue statement, but also the other worksheets in the workbook. You could have selected one of the other worksheets in the workbook and displayed that information in place of the chart. This highlights one disadvantage of embedded objects: They tend to greatly increase the size of the destination file. The Metro Zoo Letter document now contains both the original letter and the Metro Zoo workbook. For this reason, you should embed objects only when file size is not an issue.

Appendix Summary | Review

In this appendix, you examined the different methods for sharing data between Office programs. You learned how to copy data from Excel to Word using pasting and linking. You saw how changes to the data in an Excel workbook are updated automatically in a linked Word document. You also learned how to embed an Excel chart within a Word document, making Excel tools available in Word.

Key Terms

compound file
destination file
embedded object
linked object

object
object linking and
    embedding (OLE)

pasted object
source file

Practice	**Review Assignments**

Practice the skills you learned in the appendix.

Data Files needed for the Review Assignments: State Sales.xlsx, Sales Memo.docx

Happy Morning Farms Cassie Meyers is product manager for a line of breakfast cereals at Happy Morning Farms. Cassie is waiting for one number to complete her sales report for next week's Operations Management Team (OMT) meeting. As she is working on the report, she receives an urgent call from the Chicago sales representative, asking her to come to Chicago immediately to deal with a customer problem that requires management attention. Cassie plans to complete her sales report while she is in Chicago. After she finishes the report, she will e-mail it to John Styles, a colleague, who will represent her at the meeting.

Complete the following:

1. Open the **State Sales** workbook located in the Appendix.B\Review folder included with your Data Files, and then save the workbook as **State Sales Embed** in the same folder.
2. In the Documentation sheet, enter the date and your name, and then switch to the Sales Data worksheet.
3. Open the **Sales Memo** document located in the Appendix.B\Review folder, and then save the document as **Sales Memo Embed** in the same folder.
4. Return to the State Sales Embed workbook, and then copy the range A1:C24 in the Sales Data worksheet.
5. Return to the Sales Memo Embed document, and embed the worksheet data you copied at the end of the memo.
6. Save the Sales Memo Embed document. Close the State Sales Embed workbook.
7. Update the Word document by entering the Iowa sales for this month, which are $42.1 (omit the 000). Do not open the Excel workbook.
8. Save and close the Sales Memo Embed document.
9. Open the **State Sales** workbook located in the Appendix.B\Review folder included with your Data Files, and then save the workbook as **State Sales Link** in the same folder.
10. In the Documentation sheet, enter the date and your name, and then switch to the Sales Data worksheet.
11. Open the **St Memo** document located in the Appendix.B\Review folder, and then save the document as **Sales Memo Link** in the same folder.
12. Return to the State Sales Link workbook, and then copy the range A1:C24 in the Sales Data worksheet.
13. Return to the Sales Memo Link document, and then paste the selected range as a link at the end of the memo. Save the Word document.
14. Update the State Sales Link workbook by entering the Iowa sales for this month, which are $42.1 (omit the 000).
15. Save and close the Sales Memo Link document.
16. Open both the **State Sales Embed** and **State Sales Link** workbooks. Scroll to cell C10, sales for Iowa, in each worksheet. Using the results in these cells, explain the differences between object linking and embedding.
17. Close all files. Submit the finished workbooks and documents to your instructor, either in printed or electronic form, as requested.

Apply	**Case Problem 1**

Apply the skills you learned by inserting Excel objects into a Word document.

Data Files needed for this Case Problem: Quote.xlsx, Event.docx

Kirk Harbor Inn   Ellen Felton is events coordinator at Kirk Harbor Inn, which is located on Cape Cod. She schedules weddings, conferences, engagements, and so forth at this waterfront Victorian inn. She constantly is sending quotes to potential clients and asks you to assist her in linking the workbook she developed to the letter she sends to potential clients.

Complete the following:

1. Open the **Quote** workbook located in the Appendix.B\Case1 folder included with your Data Files, and then save the workbook as **Harbor Quote** in the same folder.
2. In the Documentation sheet, enter the date and your name, and then switch to the Quote worksheet.
3. Open the **Event** document located in the Appendix.B\Case1 folder, and then save the document as **Event Planner** in the same folder.
4. Return to the Harbor Quote workbook, and then copy the range B2:H20 in the Quote worksheet.
5. Return to the Event Planner document, and then paste the selected range as a link below the sentence "Here are the details."
6. Ellen's client requests two changes: move the wedding to the Salon room and change the number of guests to 160. Make these changes in the Harbor Quote workbook, and then verify that the Harbor Quote document is updated. (*Hint:* You might need to right-click the mouse and click Update Link.)
7. Save and close the Harbor Quote and Event Planner files. Submit the finished workbook and document to your instructor, either in printed or electronic form, as requested.

Apply	**Case Problem 2**

Apply the skills you learned by inserting Excel objects into a Word document.

Data Files needed for this Case Problem: Usage.xlsx, Request.docx

Bright Light   Peter Skinner is writing a letter to the state government to report on the Shelter and meal programs used at Bright Light. He has data in an Excel workbook and needs to incorporate the data into the letter he is composing in Word. Because the report will also include projections for the upcoming year, which he might modify, Peter wants to create a link between the information in the Excel workbook and the Word document. He also wants to embed in the Word document a chart that he has created in his workbook. He asked you to help link the two files.

Complete the following:

1. Open the **Usage** workbook located in the Appendix.B\Case2 folder included with your Data Files, and then save the workbook as **Bright Usage** in the same folder.
2. In the Documentation sheet, enter the date and your name, and then switch to the Shelter Usage worksheet.
3. Open the **Request** document located in the Appendix.B\Case2 folder, and then save the document as **Bright Request** in the same folder.
4. Return to the Bright Usage workbook, and then copy the range A2:G9 in the Shelter Usage worksheet.
5. Return to the Bright Request document, and then paste the selected range as a link below the first paragraph of Peter's letter. (*Hint:* If necessary, display the paragraph marks in the Word document.)

6. Peter discovered that the number of client days in the domestic abuse shelter in December 2010 was actually 75, not 72. Make this change in the Bright Usage work-book, and then verify that the Bright Request document is automatically updated. (*Hint*: If necessary, use the Update Link command on the shortcut menu to see the change.)

⊕ **EXPLORE**

7. Copy the Projected Usage chart from the Shelter Usage worksheet, and then embed the chart below the second paragraph in Peter's letter (do not link the chart).

8. Edit the embedded chart, changing the background color of the plot area from yellow to white.

9. Save and close the Bright Request and Bright Usage files. Submit the finished work-book and document to your instructor, either in printed or electronic form, as requested.

Ending Data Files

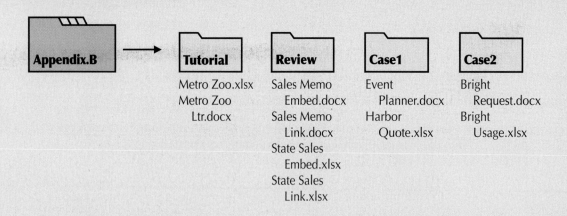

| Appendix.B | → | Tutorial | Review | Case1 | Case2 |

Tutorial
Metro Zoo.xlsx
Metro Zoo
  Ltr.docx

Review
Sales Memo
  Embed.docx
Sales Memo
  Link.docx
State Sales
  Embed.xlsx
State Sales
  Link.xlsx

Case1
Event
  Planner.docx
Harbor
  Quote.xlsx

Case2
Bright
  Request.docx
Bright
  Usage.xlsx

Objectives

Session 5.1
- Review table and object naming standards
- Use the Like, In, Not, and & operators in queries
- Filter data using an AutoFilter
- Use the IIf function to assign a conditional value to a calculated field in a query
- Create a parameter query

Session 5.2
- Use query wizards to create a crosstab query, a find duplicates query, and a find unmatched query
- Create a top values query

Session 5.3
- Modify table designs using lookup fields, input masks, and data validation rules
- Identify object dependencies
- Review a Memo field's properties
- Designate a trusted folder

Creating Advanced Queries and Enhancing Table Design

Making the Panorama Database Easier to Use

Case | Belmont Landscapes

After graduating with a university degree in Landscape Architecture and then working for a firm that provides basic landscape services to residential customers, Oren Belmont started his own landscape architecture firm in Holland, Michigan. Belmont Landscapes specializes in landscape designs for residential and commercial customers and numerous public agencies. The firm provides a wide range of services—from site analyses and feasibility studies, to drafting and administering construction documents—for projects of various scales. Oren's company developed the Panorama database of customer, contract, and invoice data; and the employees use Microsoft Office Access 2007 (or simply Access) to manage it. The Panorama database contains tables, queries, forms, and reports that Sarah Fisher, office manager, and Taylor Sico, marketing manager, use to track customers and their landscape projects.

Oren, Sarah, and Taylor are interested in taking better advantage of the power of Access to make the database easier to use and to create more sophisticated queries. For example, Taylor wants to obtain lists of employers in certain cities, and Sarah needs a summarized list of invoice amounts by city. Sarah wants to change the design of the Customer and Contract tables. In this tutorial, you'll modify and customize the Panorama database to satisfy these requirements.

Starting Data Files

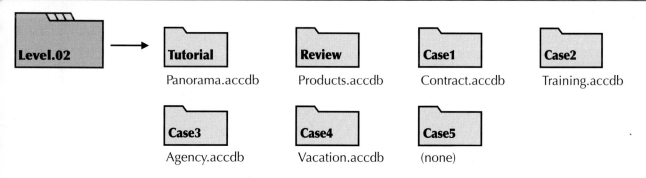

Level.02 → Tutorial
Panorama.accdb

Review
Products.accdb

Case1
Contract.accdb

Case2
Training.accdb

Case3
Agency.accdb

Case4
Vacation.accdb

Case5
(none)

Session 5.1

Reviewing the Panorama Database

Tip

Read the Microsoft Access Naming Conventions section in the appendix titled "Relational Databases and Database Design" for more information about naming conventions.

Sarah and her staff had no previous database experience when they created the Panorama database using the wizards and other easy-to-use Access tools. As business continued to grow at Belmont Landscapes, Sarah convinced Oren that they needed to hire a computer expert to further enhance the Panorama database, and they hired Lucia Perez, who has a business information systems degree and nine years of experience developing database systems. Lucia spent a few days reviewing the Panorama database, and she decided to implement simple naming standards for the objects and field names in the database to make her future work easier.

Before implementing the enhancements for Sarah and Taylor, you'll review the naming changes Lucia made to the object and field names in the Panorama database.

To review the object naming standards in the Panorama database:

▶ 1. Make sure you have created your copy of the Access Data Files, and that your computer can access them.

Trouble? If you don't have the Access Data Files, you need to get them before you can proceed. Your instructor will either give you the Data Files or ask you to obtain them from a specified location (such as a network drive). In either case, make a backup copy of the Data Files before you start so that you will have the original files available in case you need to start over. If you have any questions about the Data Files, see your instructor or technical support person for assistance.

▶ 2. Start Access, and then open the **Panorama** database in the Level.02\Tutorial folder provided with your Data Files.

Trouble? If the Security Warning is displayed below the Ribbon, click the Options button next to the Security Warning. In the dialog box that opens, click the "Enable this content" option button, and then click the OK button.

The Navigation Pane displays the objects grouped by object type, as shown in Figure 5-1. Lucia added prefix tags to the object names—a tbl prefix tag for tables, a qry prefix tag for queries, a frm prefix tag for forms, and a rpt prefix tag for reports. Using object prefix tags, you can readily identify the object type, even when the objects have the same base name—for instance, tblContract, frmContract, and rptContract. In addition, Lucia removed spaces from the object names based on her experience with other database management systems, such as SQL Server and Oracle, that do not permit spaces in object and field names. If Belmont Landscapes needs to upscale to one of these other database management systems in the future, Lucia will have to do less work to make the transition.

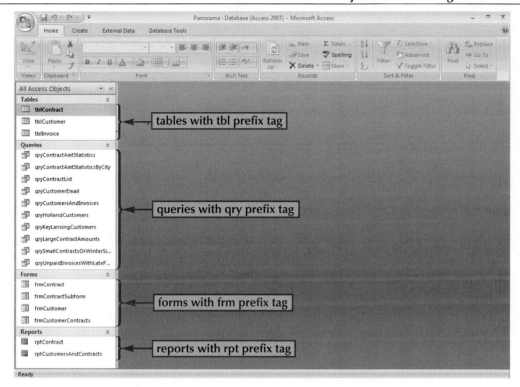

Next, you'll review the naming changes Lucia made to the tables by opening the tblContract table in Datasheet view and then in Design view.

To review the field naming standards in the tblContract table:

▶ **1.** In the Tables group on the Navigation Page, double-click **tblContract** to open the tblContract table in Datasheet view.

Notice that each column heading name contains spaces. You need to review the table in Design view to see Lucia's changes.

▶ **2.** In the Views group on the Home tab, click the **View** button. The table is displayed in Design view with the ContractNum field selected. See Figure 5-2.

| Figure 5-2 | Panorama database field names and Caption property settings |

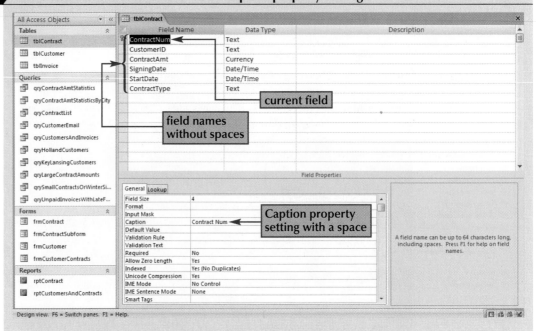

Notice that Lucia removed the spaces from each of the six field names. If the field names do not contain spaces, why do the column headings in Datasheet view contain spaces? Lucia set the Caption property for the ContractNum field to Contract Num, and she set the Caption property for the other five fields in a similar way. The **Caption property** for a field specifies its column heading value in datasheets and its label value in forms and reports. If you don't set the Caption property, Access uses the field name as the default column heading name and the default label name. Using the Caption property, you can use field names without spaces as a standard, while providing the users with more readable names on their queries, forms, and reports.

Now that you've reviewed Lucia's database changes, you'll create the queries that Sarah and Taylor need.

Using a Pattern Match in a Query

You are already familiar with queries that use an exact match or a range of values (for example, queries that use the >= or < comparison operators) to select records. Access provides many other operators for creating select queries. These operators let you create more complicated queries that are difficult or impossible to create with exact match or range of values selection criteria.

Sarah and Taylor created a list of questions they want to answer using the Panorama database:

• Which customers have the 616 area code?
• What is the customer information for customers located in Holland, Rockford, or Saugatuck?
• What is the customer information for all customers *except* those located in Holland, Rockford, or Saugatuck?
• What is the customer and contract information for contracts that have values of less than $10,000 or that were signed during the winter *and* are located in Grand Rapids or East Grand Rapids?

- What are the names of Belmont Landscapes' customers? The customer name is either the company name for nonresidential customers or the last and first names for residential customers.
- What is the customer information for customers in a particular city? For this query, the user needs to be able to specify the city.

Next, you will create the queries necessary to answer these questions. Taylor wants to view the records for all customers located in the 616 area code. She plans to travel to this area next week and wants to contact customers ahead of time to schedule appointments. To answer Taylor's question, you can create a query that uses a pattern match. A **pattern match** selects records with a value for the designated field that matches the pattern of the simple condition value, in this case, customers with the 616 area code. You do this using the Like comparison operator.

The **Like comparison operator** selects records by matching field values to a specific pattern that includes one or more of these wildcard characters: asterisk (*), question mark (?), and number symbol (#). The asterisk represents any string of characters, the question mark represents any single character, and the number symbol represents any single digit. Using a pattern match is similar to using an exact match, except that a pattern match includes wildcard characters.

To create the query, you must first place the tblCustomer table field list in the Query window in Design view.

To create the new query in Design view:

▶ 1. Close the **tblContract** table, and then click the **Shutter Bar Open/Close Button** `«` at the top of the Navigation Pane to close it.

▶ 2. Click the **Create** tab on the Ribbon and then, in the Other group on the Create tab, click the **Query Design** button. Access opens the Show Table dialog box on top of the Query window in Design view.

▶ 3. Click **tblCustomer** in the Tables list box, click the **Add** button, and then click the **Close** button. Access places the tblCustomer table field list in the Query window and closes the Show Table dialog box.

▶ 4. Double-click the **title bar** of the tblCustomer field list to highlight all the fields, and then drag the highlighted fields to the first column's Field text box in the design grid. Access places each field in a separate column in the design grid, in the same order that the fields appear in the table. See Figure 5-3.

Tip

You can also double-click a table name to add the table's field list to the Query window.

Figure 5-3 **Adding the fields for the pattern match query**

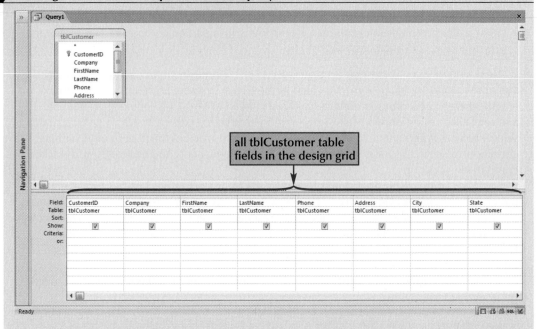

Trouble? If tblCustomer.* appears in the first column's Field text box, you dragged the * from the field list instead of the highlighted fields. Press the Delete key, and then repeat Step 4.

Now you will enter the pattern match condition Like "616*" for the Phone field. Access will select records with a Phone field value of 616 in positions one through three. The asterisk wildcard character specifies that any characters can appear in the remaining positions of the field value.

To specify records that match the specified pattern:

▶ **1.** Click the **Phone Criteria** text box, and then type **Like "616*"**. See Figure 5-4.

Figure 5-4 **Record selection based on matching a specific pattern**

Tip

If you omit the Like operator, Access automatically adds it when you run the query.

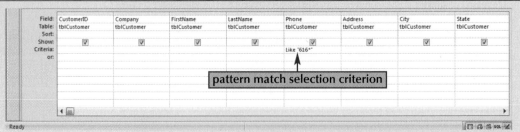

Now you can save the query.

▶ **2.** Click the **Save** button on the Quick Access Toolbar to open the Save As dialog box.

▶ **3.** Type **qry616AreaCode** in the Query Name text box, and then press the **Enter** key. Access saves the query with the specified name and displays the name on the query tab.

▶ **4.** In the Results group on the Query Tools Design tab, click the **Run** button. The query results display the 24 records with the area code 616 in the Phone field. See Figure 5-5.

tblCustomer table records for area code 616 ◄ Figure 5-5

qry616AreaCode

Customer ID	Company	First Name	Last Name	Phone	Address	City	State
11001		Sharon	Maloney	6168663901	49 Blackstone Dr	Rockford	MI
11004		Amber	Sullivan	6168669111	2807 Fairview Dr	Rockford	MI
11005		Owen	Hawes	6163920622	102 Pineview Rd	Holland	MI
11012	Grand Rapids Engineering Dept	Anthony	Rodriguez	6164549801	225 Summer St	Grand Rapids	MI
11014		Amol	Mehta	6163961972	54 Lakeshore Ave	Holland	MI
11015		John	Weiss	6166377783	456 Winchester St	South Haven	MI
11030	Finn's on the Waterfront	Devin	Finnerty	6163931228	78 E 8th St	Holland	MI
11031	Happy Haven Day Care	Kathy	Rowe	6168424603	29 Graham's Ln	Grand Haven	MI
11040	RiverView Development Company	Susan	Darcy	6169880777	144 E Tower Ave	Grand Rapids	MI
11043	Monroe State College	Rachel	Kirk	6169881320	40 Monroe St	Grand Rapids	MI
11048		Olivia	Pappas	6166376591	4 N Orchard St	South Haven	MI
11053		Hwan	Tang	6163968401	283 Cottrell St	Holland	MI
11054	Gilded Goose Gift Shop	Taylor	Wilson	6163553989	258 Briar Ln	Holland	MI
11059	G. R. Neighborhood Development Corp	Matthew	Fraser	6163920015	8045 Jefferson Ave	Grand Rapids	MI
11060		Jerome	Smith	6169493862	75 Hillcrest St	East Grand Rapids	MI
11065	Town of Holland	Amber	Ward	6163930403	24 Prospect St	Holland	MI
11068	Grand Rapids Housing Authority	Jessica	Ropiak	6164544002	5230 Fulton St	Grand Rapids	MI
11070	Legacy Companies, LTD	Michael	Faraci	6164567093	250 Market Ave	Grand Rapids	MI
11079	Dept. of Neighborhood Development	Sarah	Russell	6169403380	722 Beechwood Dr	East Grand Rapids	MI
11080	Three Tulips Café	Jan	Van Dousen	6163924629	249 W 11th St	Holland	MI
11084		Cathy	DeSantis	6168664882	78 Spring St	Rockford	MI
11085		Edward	Phillips	6166375408	39 Water St	South Haven	MI
11088	Weston Community Parks Foundation	Sam	Kervin	6164543327	333 Pearl St	Grand Rapids	MI
11090	Lily's Boutique	Lily	Shaw	6168425361	751 E Maple St	Grand Haven	MI

Record: I◄ ◄ 1 of 24 ► ►I ►▣ 🍋 No Filter | Search   ◄

Ready

Note that Lucia removed the hyphens from the Phone field values; for example, 6168663901 in the first record used to be 616-866-3901. You'll modify the Phone field later in this tutorial to format its values with hyphens.

▶ **5.** Close the qry616AreaCode query.

Next, Sarah asks you to create a query that displays information about customers in Holland, Rockford, or Saugatuck. She wants a printout of the customer data for her administrative aide, who will contact these customers. To produce the results Sarah wants, you'll create a query using a list-of-values match.

Using a List-of-Values Match in a Query

A **list-of-values match** selects records whose value for the designated field matches one of two or more simple condition values. You could accomplish this by including several Or conditions in the design grid, but the In comparison operator provides an easier and clearer way to do this. The **In comparison operator** lets you define a condition with a list of two or more values for a field. If a record's field value matches one value from the list of defined values, then Access selects and includes that record in the query results.

To display the information Sarah requested, you want to select records if their City field value equals Holland, Rockford, or Saugatuck. These are the values you will use with the In comparison operator. Sarah wants the query to contain the same data as the qry616AreaCode query, so you'll make a copy of that query and modify it.

To create the query using a list-of-values match:

▶ **1.** Open the Navigation Pane, then in the Queries group on the Navigation Page, right-click **qry616AreaCode**, and then click **Copy** on the shortcut menu.

▶ **2.** In the Clipboard group on the Home tab, click the **Paste** button, type **qryHollandRockfordSaugatuckCustomers** in the Query Name text box, and then press the **Enter** key.

To modify the copied query, you need to open it in Design view.

▶ **3.** In the Queries group on the Navigation Pane, right-click **qryHollandRockfordSaugatuckCustomers** to select it and display the shortcut menu.

▶ **4.** Click **Design View** on the shortcut menu to open the query in Design view, and then close the Navigation Pane.

You need to delete the existing condition from the Phone field.

▶ **5.** Click the **Phone Criteria** text box, press the **F2** key to highlight the entire condition, and then press the **Delete** key to remove the condition.

Now you can enter the criteria for the new query using the In comparison operator. When you use this operator, you must enclose the list of values you want to match within parentheses and separate the values with commas. In addition, for fields defined using the Text data type, you enclose each value in quotation marks, although Access adds the quotation marks if you omit them. When using the In comparison operator for fields defined using the Number or Currency data type, you don't enclose the values in quotation marks.

▶ **6.** Right-click the **City Criteria** text box to open the shortcut menu, click **Zoom** to open the Zoom dialog box, and then type **In ("Holland","Rockford", "Saugatuck")**. See Figure 5-6.

Figure 5-6	Record selection based on matching field values to a list of values

Tip

After clicking in a text box, you can also open the Zoom dialog box for that text box by holding down the Shift key and pressing the F2 key.

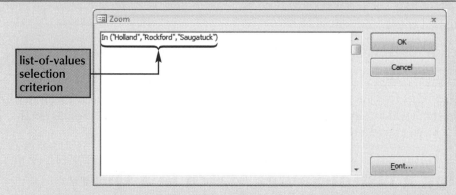

list-of-values
selection
criterion

▶ **7.** Click the **OK** button to close the Zoom dialog box, and then save and run the query. Access displays the recordset, which shows the 13 records with Holland, Rockford, or Saugatuck in the City field.

▶ **8.** Close the query.

Sarah asks her assistant to contact Belmont Landscapes customers who are not in Holland, Rockford, and Saugatuck. You can provide Sarah with this information by creating a query with the Not logical operator.

Using the Not Operator in a Query

The **Not logical operator** negates a criterion or selects records for which the designated field does not match the criterion. For example, if you enter Not "Holland" in the Criteria text box for the City field, the query results show records that do not have the City field value Holland, that is, records of all customers not located in Holland.

To create Sarah's query, you will combine the Not logical operator with the In comparison operator to select customers whose City field value is not in the list ("Holland", "Rockford","Saugatuck"). The qryHollandRockfordSaugatuckCustomers query has the fields that Sarah needs to see in the query results. Sarah doesn't need to keep the qryHollandRockfordSaugatuckCustomers query, so you'll rename and then modify the query.

To create the query using the Not logical operator:

1. Open the Navigation Pane, then in the Queries group on the Navigation Page, right-click **qryHollandRockfordSaugatuckCustomers**, and then click **Rename** on the shortcut menu.

2. Position the insertion point after "qry," type **Non**, and then press the **Enter** key. The query name is now qryNonHollandRockfordSaugatuckCustomers.

3. Open the **qryNonHollandRockfordSaugatuckCustomers** query in Design view, and then close the Navigation Pane.

   You need to change the existing condition in the City field to add the Not logical operator.

4. Click the **City Criteria** text box, open the Zoom dialog box, click at the beginning of the expression, type **Not**, and then press the **spacebar**. See Figure 5-7.

You can rename any object type, including tables, in the Navigation Pane using the Rename command on the shortcut menu.

Record selection based on not matching a list of values **Figure 5-7**

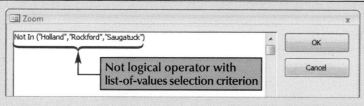

5. Click the **OK** button, and then save and run the query. The recordset displays only those records with a City field value that is not Holland, Rockford, or Saugatuck. The recordset includes a total of 29 customer records.

6. Scroll down the datasheet to make sure that no Holland or Rockford or Saugatuck customers appear in your results.

   Now you can close and delete the query, because Sarah does not need to run this query again.

7. Close the query, and then open the Navigation Pane.

8. Right-click **qryNonHollandRockfordSaugatuckCustomers**, click **Delete** on the shortcut menu, and then click the **Yes** button when asked to confirm the query deletion. The query is permanently deleted from the database.

You can delete any object type, including tables, in the Navigation Pane using the Delete command on the shortcut menu.

You now are ready to answer Taylor's question about Grand Rapids or East Grand Rapids customers that signed contracts for less than $10,000 or that signed contracts during the winter.

Using an AutoFilter to Filter Data

Taylor wants to view the customer last and first names, company names, cities, contract amounts, signing dates, and contract types for customers in Grand Rapids or East Grand Rapids that have signed contracts for less than $10,000 or that signed contracts during the winter. The qrySmallContractsOrWinterSignings query contains the same fields Taylor wants to view. This query also uses the Or logical operator to select records if the ContractAmt field value is less than $10,000 or if the SigningDate field value is between 1/1/2011 and 3/1/2011. These are two of the conditions needed to answer Taylor's question. You could modify the qrySmallContractsOrWinterSignings query in Design view to further restrict the records selected to customers located only in Grand Rapids and East Grand Rapids. However, you can use the AutoFilter feature to choose the city restrictions faster and more flexibly. You previously used the AutoFilter feature to sort records, and you previously used Filter By Form and Filter By Selection to filter records. Now you'll show Taylor how to use the AutoFilter feature to filter records.

To filter the records using an AutoFilter:

▶ **1.** Open the **qrySmallContractsOrWinterSignings** query in Design view, and then close the Navigation Pane.

The *<10000* condition for the ContractAmt field selects records whose contract amounts are less than $10,000, and the *Between #1/1/2011# And #3/1/2011#* condition for the SigningDate field selects records whose contracts were signed during the first two months of 2011. Because the conditions are in two different rows, the query uses the Or logical operator. If you wanted to answer Taylor's question in Design view, you would add a condition for the City field, using either the Or logical operator—*"Grand Rapids" Or "East Grand Rapids"*—or the In comparison operator—*In ("Grand Rapids","East Grand Rapids")*. You'd place this condition for the City field in both the Criteria row and in the or row. The query recordset would include a record only if both conditions in either row are satisfied.

Instead, you'll show Taylor how to choose the information she wants using an AutoFilter.

▶ **2.** Run the query, and then click the **arrow** on the City column heading to display the AutoFilter menu. See Figure 5-8.

| Figure 5-8 | Using an AutoFilter to filter records in the query recordset |

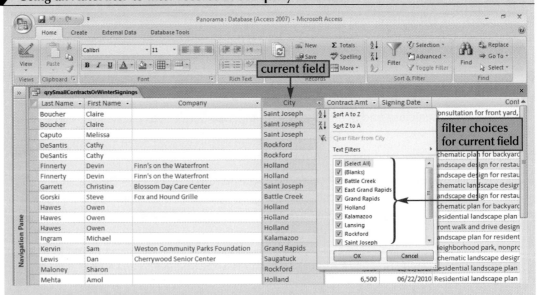

The AutoFilter menu lists all City field values that appear in the recordset. A check mark next to an entry indicates that records with that City field value appear in the recordset. To filter for selected City field values, you uncheck the cities you don't want selected and leave checked the cities you do want selected. You can click the "(Select All)" check box to select or deselect all field values. The "(Blanks)" entry includes null values when checked and excludes null values when unchecked. (Recall that a null field value is the absence of a value for the field.)

3. Click the **(Select All)** check box to deselect all check boxes, click the **East Grand Rapids** check box, and then click the **Grand Rapids** check box.

   The two check boxes indicate that the AutoFilter will include only East Grand Rapids and Grand Rapids City field values.

4. Click the **OK** button. Access displays the four records for customers in East Grand Rapids and Grand Rapids with small contract amounts or with winter signing dates. See Figure 5-9.

Using an AutoFilter to filter records in the query recordset | Figure 5-9

You click the Toggle Filter button in the Sort & Filter group on the Home tab to remove the current filter and display all records in the query. If you click the Toggle Filter button a second time, you reapply the filter.

5. In the Sort & Filter group on the Home tab, click the **Toggle Filter** button. Access removes the filter, and all 31 records appear in the recordset.

6. Click the **Toggle Filter** button. Access applies the City filter, displaying the four records for customers in East Grand Rapids and Grand Rapids.

   Taylor knows how to use the AutoFilter feature and has the information she needs. You can close the query without saving your query design changes.

7. Close the query without saving the query design changes.

Sarah wants to view all fields from the tblCustomer table, along with the customer name. The customer name is either the company name for nonresidential customers or the last and first names for residential customers.

Assigning a Conditional Value to a Calculated Field

Records for residential customers have nonnull FirstName and LastName field values and null Company field values in the tblCustomer table, while records for all other customers have nonnull values for all three fields. Sarah wants to view records from the tblCustomer table in order by the Company field value, if it's nonnull, and at the same time in order by the LastName and then FirstName field values, if the Company field value is null. To produce the information for Sarah, you need to create a query that includes all fields from the tblCustomer table and then add a calculated field that will display the customer name—either the Company field value or the LastName and FirstName field values, separated by a comma and a space.

To combine the LastName and FirstName fields, you'll use the expression *LastName & ", " & FirstName*. The **& (ampersand) operator** is a concatenation operator that joins text expressions. If the LastName field value is Maloney and the FirstName field value is Sharon, for example, the result of the expression is *Maloney, Sharon*.

To display the correct customer value, you'll use the IIf function. The **IIf (Immediate If) function** assigns one value to a calculated field or control if a condition is true, and a second value if the condition is false. The IIf function has three parts: a condition that is true or false, the result when the condition is true, and the result when the condition is false. Each part of the IIf function is separated by a comma. The condition you'll use is *IsNull(Company)*. The **IsNull function** tests a field value or an expression for a null value; if the field value or expression is null, the result is true; otherwise, the result is false. The expression *IsNull(Company)* is true when the Company field value is null, and is false when the Company field value is not null.

For the calculated field, you'll enter *IIf(IsNull(Company),LastName & ", " & FirstName,Company)*. You interpret this expression as: If the Company field value is null, then set the calculated field value to the concatenation of the LastName field value and the text string ", " and the FirstName field value. If the Company field value is not null, then set the calculated field value to the Company field value.

Now you are ready to create Sarah's query to display the customer name.

To create the query to display the customer name:

▶ 1. Click the **Create** tab on the Ribbon and then, in the Other group on the Create tab, click the **Query Design** button to open the Show Table dialog box on top of the Query window in Design view.

▶ 2. Click **tblCustomer** in the Tables list box, click the **Add** button, and then click the **Close** button to place the tblCustomer table field list in the Query window and close the Show Table dialog box.

Sarah wants all fields from the tblCustomer table to appear in the query recordset and the new calculated field to appear in the first column.

▶ 3. Double-click the **title bar** of the tblCustomer field list to highlight all the fields, and then drag the highlighted fields to the second column's Field text box in the design grid. Access places each field in a separate column in the design grid starting with the second column in the design grid, in the same order that the fields appear in the table.

Trouble? If you accidentally drag the highlighted fields to the first column in the design grid, click the CustomerID Field text box, and then click the Insert Columns button in the Query Setup group on the Query Tools Design tab. Continue with Step 4.

Tip

After clicking in a text box, you can also open the Expression Builder dialog box for that text box by holding down the Ctrl key and pressing the F2 key.

▶ 4. Right-click the blank Field text box to the left of the CustomerID field, and then click **Build** on the shortcut menu to open the Expression Builder dialog box.

Sarah wants to use "Customer" as the name of the calculated field, so you'll type that name, followed by a colon, and then you'll choose the IIf function.

▶ 5. Type **Customer:** and then press the **spacebar**. Be sure you type the colon following Customer.

▶ 6. Double-click **Functions** in the left column, click **Built-In Functions** in the left column, scroll down the middle column and click **Program Flow**, click **IIf** in the right column, and then click the **Paste** button. Access adds the IIf function with four placeholders to the right of the calculated field name in the expression box. See Figure 5-10.

Pasted IIf function for the calculated field ◀ **Figure 5-10**

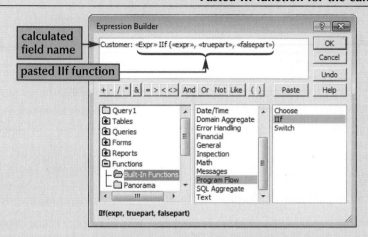

The expression you will create does not need the leftmost placeholder, <<Expr>>, so you'll delete it. You'll replace the second placeholder (<<expr>>) with the condition using the IsNull function, the third placeholder (<<truepart>>) with the expression using the & operator, and the fourth placeholder (<<falsepart>>) with the Company field name.

▶ **7.** Click **<<Expr>>** in the expression box, and then press the **Delete** key to delete the first placeholder.

▶ **8.** Click **<<expr>>** in the expression box, click **Inspection** in the middle column, click **IsNull** in the right column, click the **Paste** button, click **<<varexpr>>** in the expression box, and then type **Company**. You've completed the entry of the condition in the IIf function. See Figure 5-11.

After entering the condition for the calculated field's IIf function ◀ **Figure 5-11**

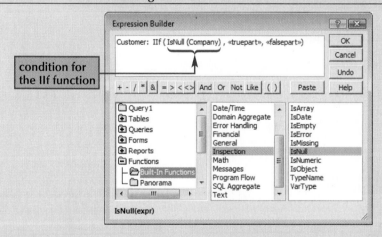

Instead of typing the field name of Company in the previous step, you could have double-clicked Tables in the left column, clicked tblCustomer, and then pasted Company.

Now you'll replace the fourth placeholder and then the third placeholder.

▶ **9.** Click **<<falsepart>>** and then type **Company**.

▶ **10.** Click **<<truepart>>**, and then type **LastName & ", " & FirstName** to finish creating the calculated field. Be sure you type a space after the comma within the quotation marks. See Figure 5-12.

| Figure 5-12 | The completed calculated field |

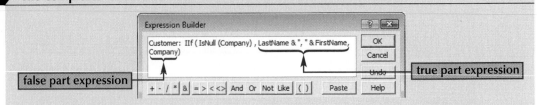

Sarah wants the query sorted in ascending order by the Customer calculated field.

To sort, save, and run the query:

▶ 1. Click the **OK** button in the Expression Builder dialog box to close it.

▶ 2. Click the right side of the **Customer Sort** text box to display the sort order options, and then click **Ascending**. The query will display the records in alphabetical order based on the Customer field values.

The calculated field name of Customer consists of a single word, so you do not need to set the Caption property for it. However, you'll review the properties for the calculated field by opening the property sheet for it.

▶ 3. In the Show/Hide group on the Query Tools Design tab, click the **Property Sheet** button. The property sheet opens and displays the properties for the Customer calculated field. See Figure 5-13.

| Figure 5-13 | Property sheet for the Customer calculated field |

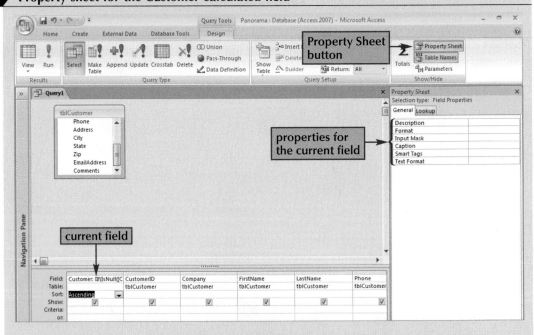

Among the properties for the calculated field, which is the current field, is the Caption property. Leaving the Caption property set to null means that the column name for the calculated field in the query recordset will be Customer, which is the calculated field name. The Property Sheet button is a toggle, so you'll click it again to close the property sheet.

▶ 4. Click the **Property Sheet** button to close the property sheet.

5. Save the query as **qryCustomersByName**, run the query, and then resize the Customer column to its best fit. Access displays all records from the tblCustomer table in alphabetical order by the Customer field. See Figure 5-14.

Completed query displaying the Customer calculated field — Figure 5-14

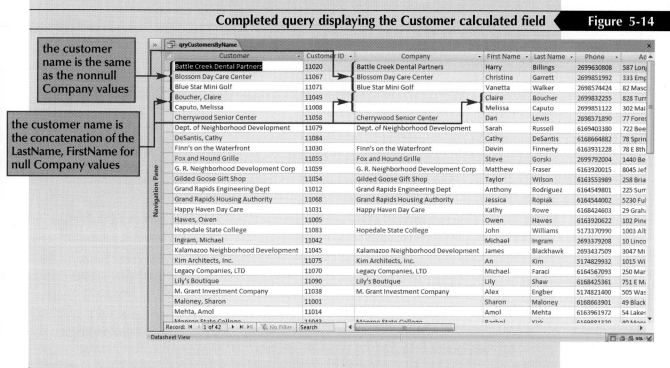

the customer name is the same as the nonnull Company values

the customer name is the concatenation of the LastName, FirstName for null Company values

6. Save and close the query.

You are now ready to create the query to satisfy Sarah's request for information about customers in a particular city.

Creating a Parameter Query

Sarah's next request is for records in the qryCustomersByName query for customers in a particular city. For this query, she wants to specify the city, such as Battle Creek or Holland, when she executes the query.

To create this query, you will copy, rename, and modify the qryCustomersByName query. You could create a simple condition using an exact match for the City field, but you would need to change it in Design view every time you run the query. Alternatively, Sarah or a member of her staff could filter the qryCustomersByName query for the city records they want to view. Instead, you will create a parameter query. A **parameter query** displays a dialog box that prompts the user to enter one or more criteria values when the query is run. In this case, you want to create a query that prompts for the city and selects only those customer records with that City field value from the table. You will enter the prompt in the Criteria text box for the City field. When Access runs the query, it will open a dialog box and prompt you to enter the city. Access then creates the query results, just as if you had changed the criteria in Design view.

- Create a select query that includes all fields to appear in the query results. Also choose the sort fields and set the criteria that do not change when you run the query.
- Decide which fields to use as prompts when the query runs. In the Criteria text box for each of these fields, type the prompt you want to appear in a message box when you run the query, and enclose the prompt in brackets.

Now you can copy and rename the qryCustomersByName query, and then change its design to create the parameter query.

To create the parameter query based on an existing query:

▶ **1.** Open the Navigation Pane, copy and then paste the qryCustomersByName query, renaming it **qryCustomersByNameParameter**.

▶ **2.** Open the **qryCustomersByNameParameter** query in Design view, and then close the Navigation Pane.

Next, you must enter the criteria for the parameter query. In this case, Sarah wants the query to prompt users to enter the city for the customer records they want to view. So, you need to enter the prompt in the Criteria text box for the City field. Brackets must enclose the text of the prompt.

▶ **3.** Click the **City Criteria** text box, type **[Enter the city:]** and then press the **Enter** key. See Figure 5-15.

| Figure 5-15 | Specifying the prompt for the parameter query |

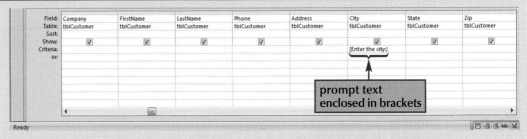

Field:	Company	FirstName	LastName	Phone	Address	City	State	Zip
Table:	tblCustomer	tblCustomer	tblCustomer	tblCustomer	tblCustomer	tblCustomer	tblCustomer	tblCustomer
Sort:								
Show:	✓	✓	✓	✓	✓	✓	✓	✓
Criteria:						[Enter the city:]		
or:								

prompt text enclosed in brackets

▶ **4.** Save and run the query. Access displays a dialog box prompting you for the name of the city. See Figure 5-16.

| Figure 5-16 | Enter Parameter Value dialog box |

Tip

You must enter a value so that it matches the spelling of a City field value in the table, but you can enter the value in either lower-case or uppercase letters.

enter value here → [ ]

prompt

The bracketed text you specified in the Criteria text box of the City field appears above a text box, in which you must type a City field value. Sarah wants to see all customers in Holland.

▶ **5.** Type **Holland**, press the **Enter** key, and then scroll to the right, if necessary, to display the City field values. The recordset displays the data for the seven customers in Holland. See Figure 5-17.

Results of the parameter query **Figure 5-17**

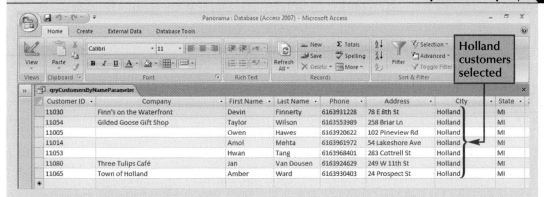

Sarah asks what happens if she doesn't enter a value in the dialog box when she runs the qryCustomersByNameParameter query. You can run the query again to show Sarah the answer to her question.

6. Switch to Design view, and then run the query. The Enter Parameter Value dialog box opens.

   If you click the OK button or press the Enter key, you'll run the parameter query without entering a value for the City field criterion.

7. Click the **OK** button. Access displays no records in the query results.

When you run the parameter query and enter Holland in the dialog box, Access runs the query the same way as if you had entered *"Holland"* in the City Criteria text box in the design grid by displaying all Holland customer records. When you do not enter a value in the dialog box, Access runs the query the same way as if you had entered *null* in the City Criteria text box. Because none of the records has a null City field value, Access displays no records. Sarah asks if there's a way to display records for a selected City field value when she enters its value in the dialog box and to display all records when she doesn't enter a value.

InSight | Creating a More Flexible Parameter Query

Most users want parameter queries to display the records that match their entered parameter value or to display all records when they don't enter a parameter value. To provide this functionality, you can change the Criteria text box in the design grid for the specified column. For example, you could change an entry for a City field from *[Enter the city:]* to *Like [Enter the city:] & "*"*. That is, you can prefix the Like operator to the original criterion and concatenate the criterion to a wildcard character. When you run the parameter query with this new entry, Access will display one of the following recordsets:

- If you enter a specific City field value in the dialog box, such as Saugatuck, the entry is the same as *Like "Saugatuck" & "*"*, which becomes *Like "Saugatuck*"* after the concatenation operation. That is, Access selects all records whose City field values have Saugatuck in the first nine positions and any characters in the remaining positions. If the table on which the query is based contains records with City field values of Saugatuck, Access displays only those records. However, if the table on which the query is based also contains records with City field values of Saugatuck City, then Access would display both the Saugatuck and the Saugatuck City records.
- If you enter a letter in the dialog box, such as S, the entry is the same as *Like "S*"*, and the recordset displays all records with City field values that begin with the letter S.
- If you enter no value in the dialog box, the entry is the same as *Like Null & "*"*, which becomes *Like "*"* after the concatenation operation, and the recordset displays all records.

Now you'll modify the parameter query to satisfy Sarah's request and test the new version of the query.

To modify and test the parameter query:

▶ **1.** Switch to Design view.

▶ **2.** Click the **City Criteria** text box, and then open the Zoom dialog box.

You'll use the Zoom dialog box to modify the value in the City Criteria text box.

▶ **3.** Click to the left of the expression in the Zoom dialog box, type **Like**, press the **spacebar**, press the **End** key, press the **spacebar**, and then type **& "*"**. See Figure 5-18.

| Figure 5-18 | Modified City Criteria value in the Zoom dialog box |

Now you can test the modified parameter query.

▶ **4.** Click the **OK** button to close the Zoom dialog box, save your query design changes, and then run the query.

First, you'll test the query to display customers in Saugatuck.

▶ **5.** Type **Saugatuck**, and then press the **Enter** key. The recordset displays the data for the three customers in Saugatuck.

Now you'll test the query without entering a value when prompted.

▶ **6.** Switch to Design view, run the query, and then click the **OK** button. The recordset displays all 42 original records from the tblCustomer table.

Finally, you'll test the query and enter S in the dialog box.

▶ **7.** Switch to Design view, run the query, type **S**, and then press the **Enter** key. The recordset displays the 10 records for customers in Saint Joseph, Saugatuck, and South Haven.

▶ **8.** Close the query.

▶ **9.** If you are not continuing on to the next session, close the Panorama database, and then exit Access, clicking the **Yes** button if you are prompted to confirm that you want to exit Access and to empty the Clipboard.

The queries you created will make the Panorama database easier to use. In the next session, you will create a top values query and use query wizards to create three additional queries.

Session 5.1 Quick Check | Review

1. You use the _____ property to specify how a field name appears in datasheet column headings and in form and report labels.
2. Which comparison operator selects records based on a specific pattern?
3. What is the purpose of the asterisk (*) in a pattern match query?
4. When do you use the In comparison operator?
5. How do you negate a selection criterion?
6. The _____ function returns one of two values based on whether the condition being tested is true or false.
7. When do you use a parameter query?

Session 5.2

Creating a Crosstab Query

Oren wants to analyze his company's invoices by city, so he can view the paid and unpaid contract amounts for all customers located in each city. He asks you to create a crosstab query using the Crosstab Query Wizard to provide the information he needs.

A **crosstab query** performs aggregate function calculations on the values of one database field and displays the results in a spreadsheet format. Recall that an aggregate function performs an arithmetic operation on selected records in a database. Figure 5-19 lists the aggregate functions you can use in a crosstab query. A crosstab query can also display one additional aggregate function value that summarizes the set of values in each row. The crosstab query uses one or more fields for the row headings on the left and one field for the column headings at the top.

Figure 5-19 ▶ **Aggregate functions used in crosstab queries**

Aggregate Function	Definition
Avg	Average of the field values
Count	Number of the nonnull field values
First	First field value
Last	Last field value
Max	Highest field value
Min	Lowest field value
StDev	Standard deviation of the field values
Sum	Total of the field values
Var	Variance of the field values

Figure 5-20 shows two query recordsets—the top recordset (qryCustomersAndInvoices) is from a select query and the bottom recordset (qryCitiesAndInvoicesCrosstab) is from a crosstab query based on the select query.

Figure 5-20 ▶ **Comparing a select query to a crosstab query**

qryCustomersAndInvoices

Customer ID	Company	First Name	Last Name	City	Invoice Amt	Invoice Paid
11001		Sharon	Maloney	Rockford	$1,500.00	☑
11001		Sharon	Maloney	Rockford	$2,500.00	☑
11027		Karen	O'Brien	Lansing	$300.00	☑
11005		Owen	Hawes	Holland	$1,500.00	☑
11012	Grand Rapids Engineerin	Anthony	Rodriguez	Grand Rapids	$2,250.00	☑
11055	Fox and Hound Grille	Steve	Gorski	Battle Creek	$1,500.00	☑
11055	Fox and Hound Grille	Steve	Gorski	Battle Creek	$2,000.00	☑
11055	Fox and Hound Grille	Steve	Gorski	Battle Creek	$2,000.00	☑
11055	Fox and Hound Grille	Steve	Gorski	Battle Creek	$1,000.00	☑
11040	RiverView Development Company	Susan	Darcy	Grand Rapids	$4,500.00	☑
11040	RiverView Development Company	Susan	Darcy	Grand Rapids	$3,000.00	☑
11040	RiverView Development Company	Susan	Darcy	Grand Rapids	$12,000.00	☐
11040	RiverView Development Company	Susan	Darcy	Grand Rapids	$8,500.00	☐
11043	Monroe State College	Rachel	Kirk	Grand Rapids	$4,500.00	☑
11043	Monroe State College	Rachel	Kirk	Grand Rapids	$12,000.00	☑
11043	Monroe State College	Rachel	Kirk	Grand Rapids	$5,500.00	☑
11070	Legacy Companies, LTD	Michael	Faraci	Grand Rapids	$9,000.00	☑
11070	Legacy Companies, LTD	Michael	Faraci	Grand Rapids	$20,000.00	☑
11070	Legacy Companies, LTD	Michael	Faraci	Grand Rapids	$10,000.00	☐
11083	Hopedale State College	John	Williams	East Lansing	$4,000.00	☑
11083	Hopedale State College	John	Williams	East Lansing	$8,000.00	☑
11083	Hopedale State College	John	Williams	East Lansing	$3,500.00	☑
11038	M. Grant Investment Company	Alex	Engber	Lansing	$35,000.00	☑
11038	M. Grant Investment Company	Alex	Engber	Lansing	$10,000.00	☐
11038	M. Grant Investment Company	Alex	Engber	Lansing	$70,000.00	☐

individual Lansing records

Lansing records with paid invoice

Lansing records with unpaid invoice

Comparing a select query to a crosstab query (continued) ◀ **Figure 5-20**

paid invoices

unpaid invoices

one row for Lansing invoice amounts

qryCitiesAndInvoicesCrosstab			
City	Total Of InvoiceAmt	Paid	Unpaid
Battle Creek	$272,250.00	$10,250.00	$262,000.00
East Grand Rapids	$141,500.00	$6,500.00	$135,000.00
East Lansing	$34,500.00	$31,500.00	$3,000.00
Grand Haven	$15,750.00	$5,250.00	$10,500.00
Grand Rapids	$416,050.00	$118,250.00	$297,800.00
Holland	$146,050.00	$43,500.00	$102,550.00
Kalamazoo	$371,500.00	$52,000.00	$319,500.00
Lansing	$263,800.00	$62,800.00	$201,000.00
Rockford	$9,000.00	$4,000.00	$5,000.00
Saint Joseph	$34,625.00	$11,125.00	$23,500.00
Saugatuck	$45,500.00	$21,000.00	$24,500.00
South Haven	$13,050.00	$7,050.00	$6,000.00

The qryCustomersAndInvoices query, a select query, joins the tblCustomer, tblContract, and tblInvoice tables to display selected data from those tables for all invoices. The qryCitiesAndInvoicesCrosstab query, a crosstab query, uses the qryCustomersAndInvoices query as its source query and displays one row for each unique City field value. The City column in the crosstab query identifies each row. The crosstab query uses the Sum aggregate function on the InvoiceAmt field to produce the displayed values in the Paid and Unpaid columns for each City row. An entry in the Total Of InvoiceAmt column represents the total of the Paid and Unpaid values for the City field value in that row.

Tip

Microsoft Office Access Help provides more information on creating a crosstab query without using a wizard.

The quickest way to create a crosstab query is to use the **Crosstab Query Wizard**, which guides you through the steps for creating one. You could also change a select query to a crosstab query in Design view using the Crosstab button in the Query Type group on the Query Tools Design tab.

Reference Window | **Using the Crosstab Query Wizard**

- In the Other group on the Create tab, click the Query Wizard button.
- In the New Query dialog box, click Crosstab Query Wizard, and then click the OK button.
- Complete the Wizard dialog boxes to select the table or query on which to base the crosstab query, select the row heading field (or fields), select the column heading field, select the calculation field and its aggregate function, and enter a name for the crosstab query.

The crosstab query you will create, which is similar to the one shown in Figure 5-20, has the following characteristics:

- The qryCustomersAndInvoices query in the Panorama database is the basis for the new crosstab query. The base query includes the CustomerID, Company, FirstName, LastName, City, InvoiceAmt, and InvoicePaid fields.
- The City field is the leftmost column in the crosstab query and identifies each crosstab query row.
- The values from the InvoicePaid field, which is a Yes/No field, identify the rightmost columns of the crosstab query.
- The crosstab query applies the Sum aggregate function to the InvoiceAmt field values and displays the resulting total values in the Paid and Unpaid columns of the query results.
- The grand total of the InvoiceAmt field values appears for each row in a column with the heading Total Of InvoiceAmt.

You are now ready to create the crosstab query for Oren.

To start the Crosstab Query Wizard:

▶ 1. If you took a break after the previous session, make sure that the Panorama database is open and the Navigation Pane is closed.

   Trouble? If the Security Warning is displayed below the Ribbon, click the Options button next to the Security Warning. In the dialog box that opens, click the "Enable this content" option button, and then click the OK button.

▶ 2. Click the **Create** tab on the Ribbon and then, in the Other group on the Create tab, click the **Query Wizard** button. The New Query dialog box opens.

▶ 3. Click **Crosstab Query Wizard**, and then click the **OK** button. The first Crosstab Query Wizard dialog box opens.

You'll now use the Crosstab Query Wizard to create the crosstab query for Oren.

To finish the Crosstab Query Wizard:

▶ 1. Click the **Queries** option button in the View section to display the list of queries in the Panorama database, and then click **Query: qryCustomersAndInvoices**. See Figure 5-21.

Choosing the query for the crosstab query ◄ **Figure 5-21**

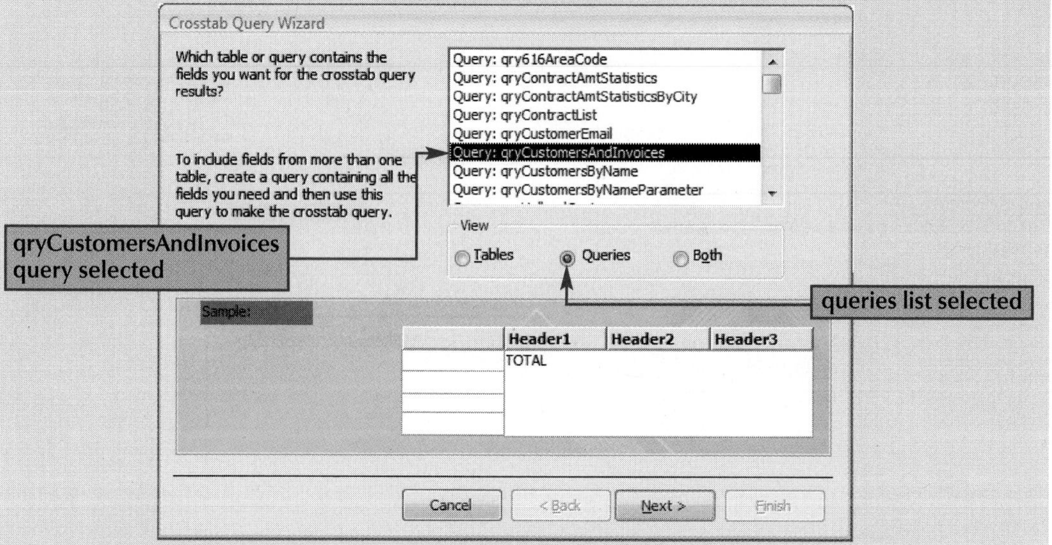

2. Click the **Next** button to open the next Crosstab Query Wizard dialog box, in which you choose the field (or fields) for the row headings. Because Oren wants the crosstab query to display one row for each unique City field value, you will select that field for the row headings.

3. In the Available Fields list box, click **City**, and then click the [>] button to move the City field to the Selected Fields list box.

4. Click the **Next** button to open the next Crosstab Query Wizard dialog box, in which you select the field values that will serve as column headings. Oren wants to see the paid and unpaid total invoice amounts, so you need to select the InvoicePaid field for the column headings.

5. Click **InvoicePaid** in the list box, and then click the **Next** button.

    In the Crosstab Query Wizard dialog box that appears next, you choose the field that will be calculated for each row and column intersection and the function to use for the calculation. The results of the calculation will appear in the row and column intersections in the query results. Oren needs to calculate the sum of the InvoiceAmt field value for each row and column intersection.

6. Click **InvoiceAmt** in the Fields list box, click **Sum** in the Functions list box, and then make sure that the **Yes, include row sums** check box is checked. The "Yes, include row sums" option creates a column showing the overall totals for the values in each row of the query recordset. See Figure 5-22.

Tip

When you select a field, Access changes the sample crosstab query in the dialog box to illustrate your choice.

Figure 5-22 Completed crosstab query design

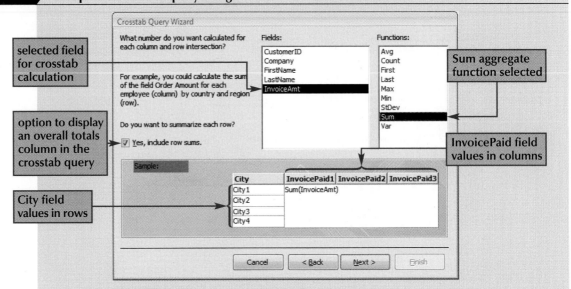

▶ 7. Click the **Next** button to open the final Crosstab Query Wizard dialog box, in which you choose the query name.

▶ 8. Click in the text box, delete the underscore character so that the query name is qryCustomersAndInvoicesCrosstab, be sure the option button for viewing the query is selected, and then click the **Finish** button. Access saves the crosstab query, and then displays the query recordset.

▶ 9. Resize all the columns in the query recordset to their best fit, and then click the City field value in the first row (**Battle Creek**). See Figure 5-23.

Figure 5-23 Crosstab query recordset

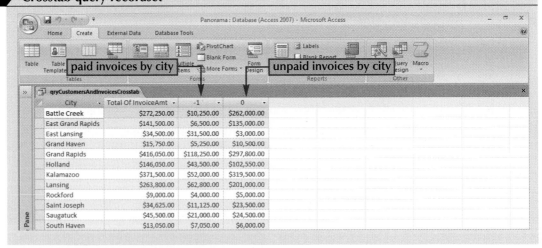

The query recordset contains one row for each City field value. The Total Of InvoiceAmt column shows the total invoice amount for the customers in each city. The columns labeled -1 and 0 show the total paid (-1 column) and unpaid (0 column) invoice amounts for customers in each city. Because the InvoicePaid field is a Yes/No field, by default, Access displays field values in datasheets, forms, and reports in a check box (either checked or unchecked), but stores a checked value in the database as a -1 and an unchecked value as a zero. Instead of displaying check boxes, the crosstab query displays the stored values as column headings.

Oren wants you to change the column headings of -1 to Paid and of zero to Unpaid. You'll use the IIf function to change the column headings, using the expression *IIf (InvoicePaid,"Paid","Unpaid")*—if the InvoicePaid field value is true (because it's a Yes/No field or a True/False field), or is checked, use Paid as the column heading; otherwise, use Unpaid as the column heading.

Tip

Because the InvoicePaid field is a Yes/No field, the condition *InvoicePaid* is the same as the condition *InvoicePaid = −1*, which uses a comparison operator and a value. For all data types except Yes/No fields, you must use a comparison operator in a condition.

To change the crosstab query column headings:

▶ **1.** Click the **Home** tab on the Ribbon, and then switch to Design view. The design grid has four entries. See Figure 5-24.

Crosstab query in the design grid ◀ **Figure 5-24**

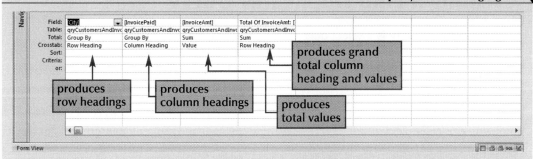

From left to right, the City entry produces the row headings in the crosstab query, the InvoicePaid entry produces the column headings, the InvoiceAmt entry produces the totals in each row/column intersection, and the Total Of InvoiceAmt entry produces the row total column heading and total values. Each field name is enclosed in brackets.

You need to replace the Field text box value in the second column with the IIf function expression to change the -1 and zero column headings to Paid and Unpaid. You can type the expression directly in the text box, use Expression Builder to create the expression, or type the expression in the Zoom dialog box. You'll use the last method.

▶ **2.** Click the **InvoicePaid Field** text box, and then open the Zoom dialog box.

▶ **3.** Delete the highlighted expression, and then type **IIf (InvoicePaid,"Paid", "Unpaid")** in the Zoom dialog box. See Figure 5-25.

IIf function for the crosstab query column headings ◀ **Figure 5-25**

▶ **4.** Click the **OK** button, and then save and run the query. Access displays the complete crosstab query with Paid and Unpaid as column headings.

You can now close the completed query.

▶ **5.** Close the query, and then open the Navigation Pane.

Tip

If you point to an object in the Navigation Pane, a ScreenTip displays the full object name.

In the Navigation Pane, Access displays objects alphabetically by object type with tables appearing first and then queries, forms, and reports. Access displays some types of queries separately from select queries; for example, crosstab queries appear before select queries. Access uses unique icons to represent different types of queries. The crosstab query icon appears in the Queries list to the left of the qryCustomersAndInvoicesCrosstab query. This icon looks different from the icon that appears to the left of the other queries, which are all select queries.

Next, Oren wants to identify any contracts that have the same start dates as other contracts, because these are the ones that might have potential scheduling difficulties. To find the information Oren needs, you'll create a find duplicates query.

Creating a Find Duplicates Query

A **find duplicates query** is a select query that finds duplicate records in a table or query. You can create this type of query using the **Find Duplicates Query Wizard**. A find duplicates query searches for duplicate values based on the fields you select as you answer the Wizard's questions. For example, you might want to display all employers that have the same name, all students who have the same phone number, or all products that have the same description. Using this type of query, you can locate duplicates to avert potential problems (for example, you might have inadvertently assigned two different numbers to the same product), or you can eliminate duplicates that cost money (for example, you could send just one advertising brochure to all customers having the same address).

You can meet Oren's request by using the Find Duplicates Query Wizard to display records for contracts that have the same start dates in the tblContract table.

Reference Window | **Using the Find Duplicates Query Wizard**

- In the Other group on the Create tab, click the Query Wizard button.
- Click Find Duplicates Query Wizard, and then click the OK button.
- Complete the Wizard dialog boxes to select the table or query on which to base the query, select the field (or fields) to check for duplicate values, select the additional fields to include in the query results, enter a name for the query, and then click the Finish button.

You'll use the Find Duplicates Query Wizard to create and run a new query to display duplicate start dates in the tblContract table.

To create the query using the Find Duplicates Query Wizard:

▶ 1. Close the Navigation Pane, click the **Create** tab on the Ribbon and then, in the Other group on the Create tab, click the **Query Wizard** button to open the New Query dialog box.

▶ 2. Click **Find Duplicates Query Wizard**, and then click the **OK** button. The first Find Duplicates Query Wizard dialog box opens. In this dialog box, you select the table or query on which to base the new query. You'll use the tblContract table.

▶ 3. Click **Table: tblContract** (if necessary), and then click the **Next** button. Access opens the next Find Duplicates Query Wizard dialog box, in which you choose the fields you want to check for duplicate values.

4. In the Available fields list box, click **StartDate**, click the ⟨ > ⟩ button to select the StartDate field as the field to check for duplicate values, and then click the **Next** button. In the next Find Duplicates Query Wizard dialog box, you select the additional fields you want displayed in the query results.

Oren wants all remaining fields to be included in the query results.

5. Click the ⟨ >> ⟩ button to move all fields from the Available fields list box to the Additional query fields list box, and then click the **Next** button. Access opens the final Find Duplicates Query Wizard dialog box, in which you enter a name for the query. You'll use qryDuplicateContractStartDates as the query name.

6. Type **qryDuplicateContractStartDates** in the text box, be sure the option button for viewing the results is selected, and then click the **Finish** button. Access saves the query, and then displays the 10 records for contracts with duplicate start dates. See Figure 5-26.

Query recordset for contracts with the same start dates ⟨ **Figure 5-26**

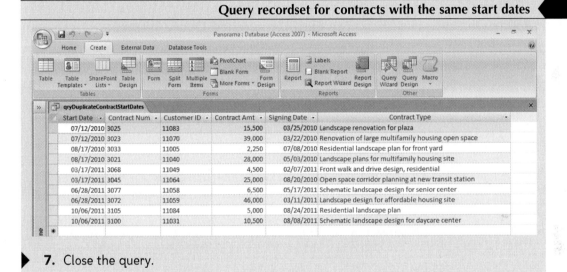

7. Close the query.

Oren now asks you to find the records for customers with no contracts. These are customers who had contracts in the past, but who have chosen not to sign a contract with Belmont Landscapes in the past year. Oren wants to contact these customers to see if there are any services that the company might be able to furnish. To provide Oren with this information, you need to create a find unmatched query.

Creating a Find Unmatched Query

A **find unmatched query** is a select query that finds all records in a table or query that have no related records in a second table or query. For example, you could display all customers who have not signed recent contracts or all students who are not currently enrolled in classes. Such a query provides information for Oren to solicit business from the inactive customers and for a school administrator to contact the students to find out their future educational plans. You can use the **Find Unmatched Query Wizard** to create this type of query.

Reference Window | **Using the Find Unmatched Query Wizard**

- In the Other group on the Create tab, click the Query Wizard button.
- Click Find Unmatched Query Wizard, and then click the OK button.
- Complete the Wizard dialog boxes to select the table or query on which to base the new query, select the table or query that contains the related records, specify the common field in each table or query, select the additional fields to include in the query results, enter a name for the query, and then click the Finish button.

Oren wants to know which customers have no open contracts. These customers are inactive, and he will contact them to determine their interest in doing further business with Belmont Landscapes. To create a list of inactive customers, you'll use the Find Unmatched Query Wizard to display only those records from the tblCustomer table with no matching CustomerID field value in the tblContract table.

To create the query using the Find Unmatched Query Wizard:

▶ **1.** In the Other group on the Create tab, click the **Query Wizard** button to open the New Query dialog box.

▶ **2.** Click **Find Unmatched Query Wizard**, and then click the **OK** button. The first Find Unmatched Query Wizard dialog box opens. In this dialog box, you select the table or query on which to base the new query. You'll use the qryCustomersByName query.

▶ **3.** Click the **Queries** option button in the View section to display the list of queries, click **Query: qryCustomersByName** in the list box to select this query, and then click the **Next** button to open the next Find Unmatched Query Wizard dialog box, in which you choose the table that contains the related records. You'll select the tblContract table.

▶ **4.** Click **Table: tblContract** in the list box (if necessary), and then click the **Next** button to open the next dialog box, in which you choose the common field for both tables. See Figure 5-27.

Figure 5-27 **Selecting the common field**

Tip

If the two objects you selected for the find unmatched query have a one-to-many relationship defined in the Relationships window, the Matching fields box will join the two correct fields automatically.

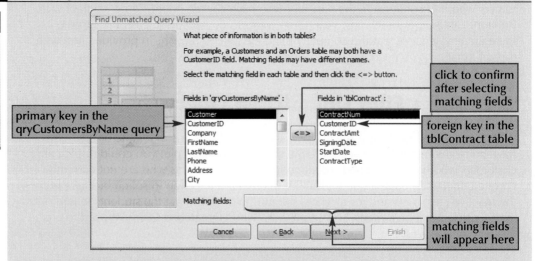

The common field between the query and the table is the CustomerID field. You need to click the common field in each list box, and then click the symbol between the two list boxes to join the two objects. The Matching fields box then will display CustomerID <=> CustomerID to indicate the joining of the two matching fields.

▶ **5.** Click **CustomerID** in the Fields in 'qryCustomersByName' list box, click **CustomerID** in the Fields in 'tblContract' list box, click the `<=>` button to connect the two selected fields, and then click the **Next** button to open the next Find Unmatched Query Wizard dialog box, in which you choose the fields you want to see in the query recordset. Oren wants the query recordset to display all available fields.

▶ **6.** Click the `>>` button to to move all fields from the Available fields list box to the Selected fields list box, and then click the **Next** button to open the final dialog box, in which you enter the query name.

▶ **7.** Type **qryInactiveCustomers**, be sure the option button for viewing the results is selected, and then click the **Finish** button. Access saves the query and then displays two records in the query recordset. See Figure 5-28.

Query recordset displaying customers without contracts Figure 5-28

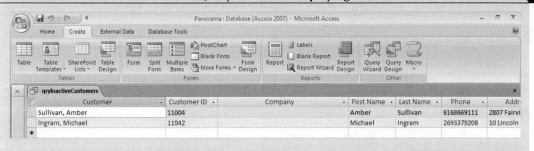

The query recordset includes information for the two inactive customers. Oren will use this information to contact these customers to see if they have any current or future landscaping needs.

▶ **8.** Close the query.

Next, Oren wants Taylor to contact those customers who have the highest contract amounts to make sure that Belmont Landscapes is providing satisfactory service. To display the information Taylor needs, you will create a top values query.

Creating a Top Values Query

Whenever a query displays a large group of records, you might want to limit the number to a more manageable size by displaying, for example, just the first 10 records. The **Top Values property** for a query lets you limit the number of records in the query results. For the Top Values property, you can click one of the preset values from a list, or enter either an integer (such as 15, to display the first 15 records) or a percentage (such as 20%, to display the first fifth of the records) to find a specific number of records.

Suppose you have a select query that displays 45 records. If you want the query recordset to show only the first five records, you can change the query by entering a Top Values property value of either 5 or 10%. If the query contains a sort and the last record that Access can display is one of two or more records with the same value for the primary sort field, Access displays all records with that matching key value.

Creating a Top Values Query | Reference Window

- Create a select query with the necessary fields and sorting and selection criteria.
- In the Query Setup group on the Query Tools Design tab, enter the number of records (or percentage of records) you want selected in the Return (Top Values) text box.

Taylor wants to view the same data that appears in the qryLargeContractAmounts query for customers with the highest 25% contract amounts. You will modify the query and then use the Top Values property to produce this information for Taylor.

Tip

Based on the number or percentage you enter, a top values query selects that number or percentage of records starting from the top of the recordset. Thus, you usually include a sort in a top values query to display the records with the highest or lowest values for the sorted field.

To set the Top Values property for the query:

1. Open the Navigation Pane, open the **qryLargeContractAmounts** in Datasheet view, and then close the Navigation Pane. Access displays 22 records, all with ContractAmt field values greater than $25,000, sorted in descending order by the ContractAmt field.

2. Click the **Home** tab, and then switch to Design view.

3. In the Query Setup group on the Query Tools Design tab, click the **Return** arrow (with the ScreenTip "Top Values"), and then click **25%**. See Figure 5-29.

Figure 5-29	Creating the top values query

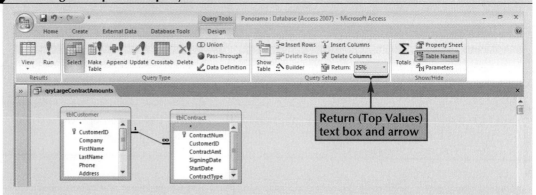

If the number or percentage of records you want to select, such as 15 or 20%, doesn't appear in the Top Values list, you can type the number or percentage in the Return text box.

4. Run the query. Access displays six records in the query recordset; these records represent the customers with the highest 25% contract amounts (25% of the original 22 records). See Figure 5-30.

Figure 5-30	Top values query recordset

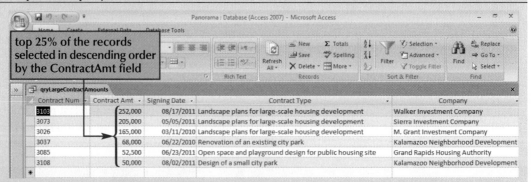

Because Taylor won't need to run this query again, you won't save it.

5. Close the query without saving it.

6. If you are not continuing on to the next session, close the Panorama database, and then exit Access, clicking the **Yes** button if you are prompted to confirm that you want to exit Access and to empty the Clipboard.

Oren and Taylor will use the information provided by the queries you created to analyze the business and to contact customers. In the next session, you will enhance the tblCustomer and tblContract tables.

Session 5.2 Quick Check | Review

1. What is the purpose of a crosstab query?
2. What are the four query wizards you can use to create a new query?
3. What is a find duplicates query?
4. What does a find unmatched query do?
5. What happens when you set a query's Top Values property?
6. What happens if you set a query's Top Values property to 2 and the first five records have the same value for the primary sort field?

Session 5.3

Creating a Lookup Field

The tblContract table in the Panorama database contains information about the contracts Belmont Landscapes has signed with its customers. Sarah wants to make entering data in the table easier for her staff. In particular, data entry is easier if they do not need to remember the correct CustomerID field values for each customer. Because the tblCustomer and tblContract tables have a one-to-many relationship, Sarah asks you to change the tblContract table's CustomerID field, which is a foreign key to the tblCustomer table, to a lookup field. A **lookup field** lets the user select a value from a list of possible values. For the CustomerID field, the user will be able to select a customer's ID number from the list of customer names in the qryCustomersByName query rather than having to remember the correct CustomerID field value. Access will store the CustomerID in the tblContract table, but both the customer name and the CustomerID field value will appear in Datasheet view when entering or changing a CustomerID field value. This arrangement makes entering and changing CustomerID field values easier for the user and guarantees that the CustomerID field value is valid. You use a **Lookup Wizard field** in Access to create a lookup field in a table.

Sarah asks you to change the CustomerID field in the tblContract table to a lookup field. You begin by opening the Panorama database and then opening the tblContract table in Design view.

To change the CustomerID field to a lookup field:

▶ 1. If you took a break after the previous session, make sure that the Panorama database is open.

   Trouble? If the Security Warning is displayed below the Ribbon, click the Options button next to the Security Warning. In the dialog box that opens, click the "Enable this content" option button, and then click the OK button.

▶ 2. If necessary, open the Navigation Pane, and then open the **tblContract** table in Design view.

> **3.** Click the right side of the **Data Type** text box for the CustomerID field to display the list of data types, and then click **Lookup Wizard**. A message box appears, warning you to delete the relationship between the tblCustomer and tblContract tables if you want to make the CustomerID field a lookup field. See Figure 5-31.

Figure 5-31	Warning message for an existing table relationship

Access will use the lookup field to form the one-to-many relationship between the tblCustomer and tblContract tables, so you don't need the relationship you previously defined between the two tables.

> **4.** Click the **OK** button, close the tblContract table, and then click the **No** button when asked if you want to save the table design changes.
>
> **5.** Click the **Database Tools** tab on the Ribbon, and then, in the Show/Hide group on the Database Tools tab, click the **Relationships** button to open the Relationships window.
>
> **6.** Right-click the join line between the tblCustomer and tblContract tables, click **Delete**, and then click the **Yes** button to confirm the deletion.
>
> **Trouble?** If the Delete command does not appear on the shortcut menu, click a blank area in the Relationships window to close the shortcut menu, and then repeat Step 6.
>
> **7.** Close the Relationships window.

Now you can resume changing the CustomerID field to a lookup field.

To finish changing the CustomerID field to a lookup field:

> **1.** Open the **tblContract** table in Design view.
>
> **2.** Click the right side of the **Data Type** text box for the CustomerID field, and then click **Lookup Wizard**. The first Lookup Wizard dialog box opens.
>
> This dialog box lets you specify a list of allowed values for the CustomerID field in a record in the tblContract table. You can specify a table or query from which users select the value, or you can enter a new list of values. You want the CustomerID values to come from the qryCustomersByName query.
>
> **3.** Make sure the option for looking up the values in a table or query is selected, and then click the **Next** button to display the next Lookup Wizard dialog box.
>
> **4.** Click the **Queries** option button in the View section to display the list of queries, click **Query: qryCustomersByName**, and then click the **Next** button to display the next Lookup Wizard dialog box. See Figure 5-32.

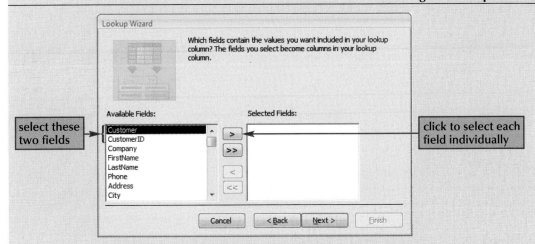

This dialog box lets you select the lookup fields from the qryCustomersByName query. You need to select the CustomerID field because it's the common field that links the query and the tblContract table. You also must select the Customer field because Sarah wants the user to be able to select from a list of customer names when entering a new contract record or changing an existing CustomerID field value.

5. Click **Customer** (if necessary), click the ⟩ button to move the Customer field to the Selected Fields list box, click **CustomerID** (if necessary), click the ⟩ button to move the CustomerID field to the Selected Fields list box, and then click the **Next** button to display the next Lookup Wizard dialog box. This dialog box lets you choose a sort order for the list box entries. Sarah wants the entries to appear in ascending Customer order. Note that ascending is the default sort order.

6. Click the **1** arrow, click **Customer**, and then click the **Next** button to open the next dialog box.

In this dialog box, you can adjust the widths of the lookup columns. Note that when you resize a column to its best fit, Access resizes the column so that the widest column heading and the visible field values fit the column width. However, some field values that aren't visible in this dialog box might be wider than the column width, so you must scroll down the column to make sure you don't have to repeat the column resizing.

7. Click the **Customer** column selector, press and hold down the **Shift** key, click the **CustomerID** column selector to select both columns, release the **Shift** key, and then place the pointer on the right edge of the CustomerID field column heading. When the pointer changes to a ↔ shape, double-click to resize the columns to their best fits, and then scroll down the columns, and repeat the resizing as necessary. When you are finished, press **Ctrl + Home** to scroll back to the top of the Customer column. See Figure 5-33.

Figure 5-33 **Adjusting the widths of lookup columns**

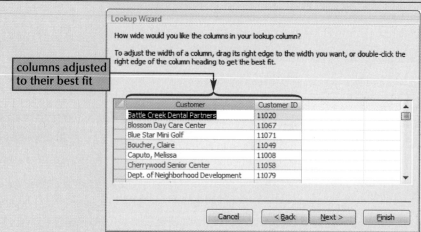

columns adjusted to their best fit

▶ 8. Click the **Next** button.

In the dialog box that appears next, you select the field you want to store in the table. You'll store the CustomerID field in the tblContract table, because it's the foreign key to the tblCustomer table.

▶ 9. Click **CustomerID** in the Available Fields list box, and then click the **Next** button.

In the dialog box that appears next, you specify the field name for the lookup field. Because you'll be storing the CustomerID field in the table, you'll accept the default field name, CustomerID.

▶ 10. Click the **Finish** button, and then save the table.

The Data Type value for the CustomerID field is still Text because this field contains text data. However, when you update the field, Access uses the CustomerID field value to look up and display in the tblContract table datasheet both the Customer and CustomerID field values from the qryCustomersByName query.

In reviewing contracts recently, Sarah noticed that the CustomerID field value stored in the tblContract table for contract number 3030 is incorrect. She asks you to test the new lookup field to select the correct code. To do so, you need to switch to Datasheet view.

To change the CustomerID field value:

▶ 1. Switch to Datasheet view, and then resize the **CustomerID** column to its best fit.

Notice that the Customer ID column displays Customer field values, even though it's the CustomerID field values that are stored in the table.

▶ 2. For Contract Num 3030, click **Lily's Boutique** in the Customer ID column, and then click the **arrow** to display the list of Customer and CustomerID field values from the qryCustomersByName query. See Figure 5-34.

List of Customer and CustomerID field values ◄ **Figure 5-34**

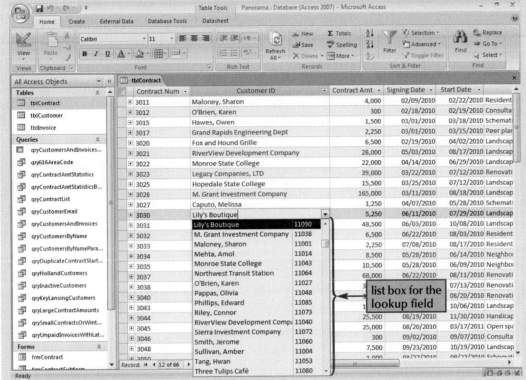

The customer for contract 3030 is Michael Ingram, so you need to select his entry in the list box to change the CustomerID field value.

▶ **3.** Scroll up the list box, and then click **Ingram, Michael** to select that value to display in the datasheet and to store the CustomerID field value of 11042 in the table. The list box closes and "Ingram, Michael" appears in the Customer ID text box.

▶ **4.** Save and close the tblContract table.

Sarah wants you to make changes to the design of the tblCustomer table, so you'll open the table in preparation for the changes.

▶ **5.** Open the **tblCustomer** table in Datasheet view, and then close the Navigation Pane.

Sarah asks you to change the appearance of the Phone field in the tblCustomer table to a standard telephone number format.

Using the Input Mask Wizard

The Phone field in the tblCustomer table is a 10-digit number that's difficult to read because it appears with none of the special formatting characters usually associated with a telephone number. For example, the Phone field value for Sharon Maloney, which appears as 6168663901, would be more readable in any of the following formats: 616-866-3901, 616.866.3901, 616/866-3901, or (616) 866-3901. Sarah asks you to use the (616) 866-3901 style for the Phone field.

Sarah wants the parentheses and hyphens to appear as literal display characters whenever users enter Phone field values. A **literal display character** is a special character that automatically appears in specific positions of a field value; users don't need to type literal display characters. To include these characters, you need to create an **input mask**, a pre-defined format used to enter and display data in a field. An easy way to create an input mask is to use the **Input Mask Wizard**, an Access tool that guides you in creating a pre-defined format for a field. You must use the Input Mask Wizard in Design view.

To use the Input Mask Wizard for the Phone field:

▶ **1.** Switch to Design view, and then click the **Phone Field Name** text box to make that row the current row and to display its Field Properties options.

▶ **2.** Click the **Input Mask** text box in the Field Properties pane. A Build button [...] appears to the right of the Input Mask text box.

▶ **3.** Click the **Build** button [...] next to the Input Mask text box. The first Input Mask Wizard dialog box opens. See Figure 5-35.

Figure 5-35 ▶ **Input Mask Wizard dialog box**

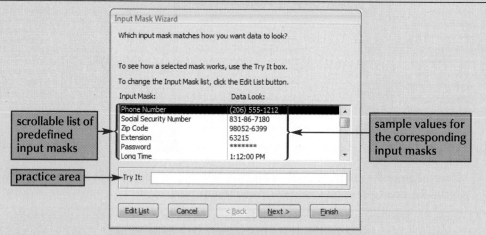

You can scroll the Input Mask list box, select the input mask you want, and then enter representative values to practice using the input mask.

▶ **4.** If necessary, click **Phone Number** in the Input Mask list box to select it.

▶ **5.** Click the far left side of the **Try It** text box. (___) ___-____ appears in the Try It text box. As you type a phone number, Access replaces the underscores, which are placeholder characters.

Trouble? If your insertion point is not immediately to the right of the left parenthesis, press the ← key until it is.

▶ **6.** Type **9876543210** to practice entering a sample phone number. The input mask formats the typed value as (987) 654-3210.

▶ **7.** Click the **Next** button. The next Input Mask Wizard dialog box opens. In it, you can change the input mask and placeholder character. Because you can change an input mask easily after the Input Mask Wizard finishes, you'll accept all wizard defaults.

▶ **8.** Click the **Finish** button. The Input Mask Wizard creates the phone number input mask, placing it in the Input Mask text box for the Phone field. See Figure 5-36.

Phone number input mask created by the Input Mask Wizard ◀ **Figure 5-36**

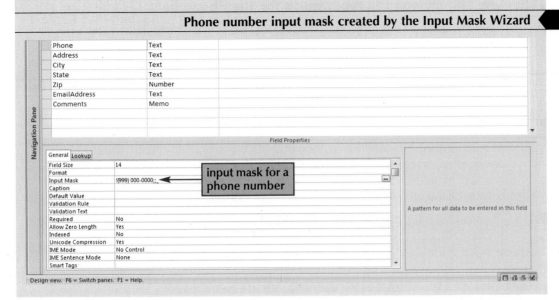

The characters used in a field's input mask restrict the data you can enter in the field, as shown in Figure 5-37. Other characters, such as the left and right parenthesis in the phone number input mask, that appear in an input mask are literal display characters.

Input mask characters ◀ **Figure 5-37**

Input Mask Character	Description
0	Digit only must be entered. Entry is required.
9	Digit or space can be entered. Entry is optional.
#	Digit, space, or a plus or minus sign can be entered. Entry is optional.
L	Letter only must be entered. Entry is required.
?	Letter only can be entered. Entry is optional.
A	Letter or digit must be entered. Entry is required.
a	Letter or digit can be entered. Entry is optional.
&	Any character or a space must be entered. Entry is required.
C	Any character or a space can be entered. Entry is optional.
>	All characters that follow are displayed in uppercase.
<	All characters that follow are displayed in lowercase.
"	Enclosed characters treated as literal display characters.
\	Following character treated as a literal display character. This is the same as enclosing a single character in quotation marks.
!	Input mask is displayed from right to left, rather than the default of left to right. Characters typed into the mask always fill in from left to right.
;;	The character between the first and second semicolon determines whether to store in the database the literal display characters. If left blank or a value of 1, do not store the literal display characters. If a value of 0, store the literal display characters. The character following the second semicolon is the placeholder character that will appear in the displayed input mask.

Sarah wants to view the Phone field with the default input mask before you change it for her.

To view and change the input mask for the Phone field:

▶ **1.** Save the table, and then switch to Datasheet view. The Phone field values now have the format specified by the input mask.

Sarah decides that she would prefer to omit the parentheses around the area codes and use only hyphens as separators in the displayed Phone field values, so you'll change the input mask in Design view.

▶ **2.** Switch to Design view.

The input mask changed from !(999) 000-0000;;_ to !\(999") "000\-0000;;_. The backslash character (\) causes the character that follows it to appear as a literal display character. Characters enclosed in quotation marks also appear as literal display characters. (See Figure 5-37.)

▶ **3.** Change the input mask to **999\-000\-0000;;_** in the Input Mask text box for the Phone field, and then press the **Tab** key.

Because you've modified a field property, the Property Update Options button appears to the left of the Input Mask property.

▶ **4.** Click the **Property Update Options** button, and then click **Update Input Mask everywhere Phone is used**. The Update Properties dialog box opens. See Figure 5-38.

Tip

If you omit the backslashes preceding the hyphens, Access will automatically insert them when you press the Tab key. However, Access doesn't add backslashes automatically for other literal display characters, such as periods and slashes, so it's best to always include the backslashes.

Figure 5-38	Update Properties dialog box

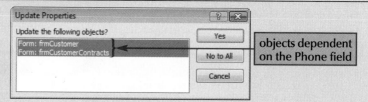

objects dependent on the Phone field

Because the frmCustomer and frmCustomerContracts forms display Phone field values from the tblCustomer table, Access will automatically change the Phone field's Input Mask property in these objects to your new input mask. This capability to update field properties in objects automatically when you modify a table field property is called **property propagation**. Although the Update Properties dialog box displays no queries, property propagation also does occur with queries automatically. Property propagation is limited to field properties such as the Decimal Places, Description, Format, and Input Mask properties.

▶ **5.** Click the **Yes** button, save the table, and then switch to Datasheet view. The Phone field values now have the format Sarah requested. See Figure 5-39.

Figure 5-39	After changing the Phone field input mask

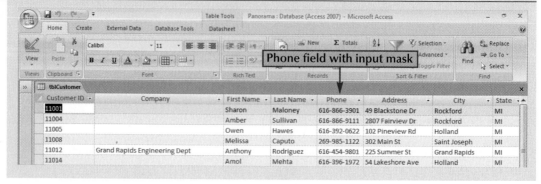

Because Sarah wants her staff to store only standard 10-digit U.S. phone numbers for customers, the input mask you've created will enforce the standard entry and display format that Sarah desires.

Understanding When to Use Input Masks | InSight

An input mask is appropriate for a field only if all field values have a consistent format. For example, you can use an input mask with hyphens as literal display characters to store U.S. phone numbers in a consistent format of 987-654-3210. However, a multinational company would not be able to use an input mask to store phone numbers from all countries, because international phone numbers do not have a consistent format. For another example, U.S. zip codes have a consistent format, and you could use an input mask of 00000#9999 to enter and display U.S. zip codes such as 98765 and 98765-4321, but you could not use an input mask if you need to store and display foreign postal codes in the same field. If you need to store and display phone numbers, zip/postal codes, and other fields in a variety of formats, it's best to define them as Text fields without an input mask and let users enter field values and the literal display characters.

After the change to the Phone field's input mask, Access gave you the option to update, selectively and automatically, the Phone field's Input Mask property in other objects in the database. Sarah asks if there's an easy way to determine which objects are affected by changes made to other objects. To show Sarah how to determine the dependencies among objects in an Access database, you'll open the Object Dependencies pane.

Identifying Object Dependencies

An **object dependency** exists between two objects when a change to the properties of data in one object affects the properties of data in the other object. Dependencies between Access objects (tables, queries, forms, and so on) can occur in various ways. For example, the tblContract and tblInvoice tables are dependent on each other because they have a one-to-many relationship. As another example, because the tblContract table uses the qryCustomersByName query to obtain the Customer field to display along with the CustomerID field, these two tables have a dependency. Any query, form, or other object that uses fields from the tblCustomer table is dependent on the tblCustomer table. Any form or report that uses fields from a query is directly dependent on the query and is indirectly dependent on the tables that provide the data to the query. Large databases contain hundreds of objects, so it would be useful to have a way to view the dependencies among objects easily before you attempt to delete or modify an object. The **Object Dependencies pane** displays a collapsible list of the dependencies among the objects in an Access database; you click the list's expand indicators to show or hide different levels of dependencies. Next, you'll open the Object Dependencies pane to show Sarah the object dependencies in the Panorama database.

To open and use the Object Dependencies pane:

▶ **1.** Click the **Database Tools** tab on the Ribbon, and then, in the Show/Hide group, click the **Object Dependencies** button to open the Object Dependencies pane, and then drag the left edge of the pane to the left until the horizontal scroll bar at the bottom of the pane disappears. See Figure 5-40.

Figure 5-40 **After opening the Object Dependencies pane**

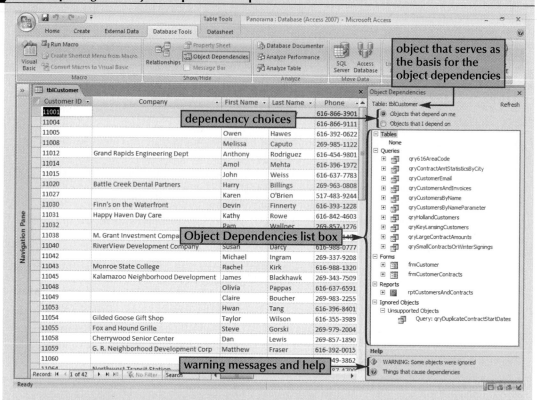

Trouble? If the "Objects that depend on me" option button is not selected, click the option button to select it.

The Object Dependencies list box displays the objects that depend on the tblCustomer table, the object name that appears at the top of the pane. If you change the design of the tblCustomer table, the change might affect objects in the list box. Changing a property for a field in the tblCustomer table that's also used by another listed object affects that other object. If the other object does not use the field you are changing, that other object is not affected.

Objects listed in the Ignored Objects portion of the pane might, or might not, have an object dependency with the tblCustomer table, and you'd have to review them yourself. The Help section at the bottom of the pane displays links for further information about object dependencies.

▶ **2.** Click the **frmCustomer** link in the Object Dependencies pane. The frmCustomer form opens in Design view. All the fields in the form are fields from the tblCustomer table, which is why the form has an object dependency with the table.

▶ **3.** Switch to Form view for the frmCustomer form. Note that the Phone field values are displayed using the input mask you applied to the field in the tblCustomer table. This change propagated from the table to the form.

▶ **4.** Close the frmCustomer form, open the **tblContract** table in Datasheet view, and then click the **Refresh** link near the top of the Object Dependencies pane. The Object Dependencies list box now displays the objects that depend on the tblContract table.

▶ **5.** Click the **Objects that I depend on** option button near the top of the pane to view the objects that affect the tblContract table.

▶ **6.** Click the **expand indicator** ⊞ for the qryCustomersByName query in the Object Dependencies pane. The list expands to display all the tblCustomer table, which is another table that the query depends upon.

▶ **7.** Close the tblContract table, close the Object Dependencies pane, and then close the Navigation Pane.

Sarah now better understands object dependencies and how to identify them by using the Object Dependencies pane.

Defining Data Validation Rules

Sarah wants to limit the entry of Zip field values in the tblCustomer table to Michigan zip codes because Belmont Landscapes customers are located only in Michigan. In addition, Sarah wants to make sure that a SigningDate field value entered in a tblContract table record is chronologically earlier than the StartDate field value in the same record. She's concerned that typing errors might produce incorrect query results and cause other problems. To provide these data-entry capabilities, you'll set field validation properties for the Zip field in the tblCustomer table and set table validation properties in the tblContract table.

Defining Field Validation Rules

To prevent a user from entering an incorrect value in the Zip field, you can create a **field validation rule** that verifies a field value by comparing it to a constant or a set of constants. You create a field validation rule by setting the Validation Rule and the Validation Text field properties. The **Validation Rule property** value specifies the valid values that users can enter in a field. The **Validation Text property** value will be displayed in a dialog box if the user enters an invalid value (in this case, a value other than a Michigan zip code). After you set these two Zip field properties in the tblCustomer table, Access will prevent users from entering an invalid Zip field value in the tblCustomer table and in all current and future queries and forms that include the Zip field.

You'll now set the Validation Rule and Validation Text properties for the Zip field in the tblCustomer table. Michigan zip codes must be between 48000 and 49999.

To create and test a field validation rule for the Zip field:

▶ **1.** Switch to Design view for the tblCustomer table, and then click the **Zip Field Name** text box to make that row the current row.

To make sure that the only values entered in the Zip field are between 48000 and 49999, you'll specify a range of valid values in the Validation Rule text box. The Zip field is a Number field, so you can use this numeric range test.

▶ **2.** In the Field Properties pane, click the **Validation Rule** text box, type **>=48000 And <=49999**, and then press the **Tab** key.

Instead of using the range of values test, you could also use the equivalent *Between 48000 And 49999*.

You can set the Validation Text property to a value that appears in a dialog box that opens if a user enters a value not listed in the Validation Rule text box.

▶ **3.** Type **Michigan zip codes must be between 48000 and 49999** in the Validation Text text box. See Figure 5-41.

Tip

Using the numeric range test with a Text field isn't allowed; you'll get an error message. Also, enclosing the numbers in quotation marks for a Text field range test will eliminate the error message but will yield unpredictable results.

| Figure 5-41 | **Validation properties for the Zip field** |

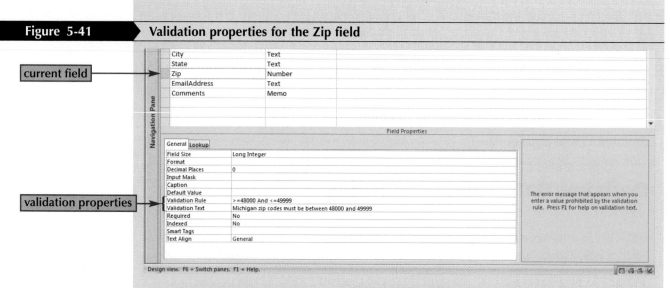

current field

validation properties

You can now save the table design changes and then test the validation properties.

▶ **4.** Save the table, and then click the **Yes** button when asked if you want to test the existing Zip field values in the tblCustomer table against the new validation rule.

Access tests the existing records in the tblCustomer table against the validation rule. If any record violates the rule, you are prompted to continue testing or to revert to the previous Validation Rule property setting. Next, you'll test the validation rule.

▶ **5.** Switch to Datasheet view, and then scroll the table to the right until the Zip field is visible.

▶ **6.** Double-click **49341** in the first row's Zip field text box, type **54321**, and then press the **Tab** key. A dialog box opens containing the message "Michigan zip codes must be between 48000 and 49999," which is the Validation Text property setting you created in Step 3.

▶ **7.** Click the **OK** button, and then press the **Esc** key. The first row's Zip field value again has its original value, 49341.

▶ **8.** Close the tblCustomer table.

Now that you've finished entering the field validation rule for the Zip field in the tblCustomer table, you'll enter the table validation rule for the date fields in the tblContract table.

Defining Table Validation Rules

To make sure that a user enters a SigningDate field value in the tblContract table that is chronologically earlier than the record's StartDate field value, you can create a **table validation rule** that compares one field value in a table record to another field value in the same record to verify their relative accuracy. Once again, you'll use the Validation Rule and Validation Text properties, but this time you'll set these properties for the table instead of for an individual field.

You'll now set the Validation Rule and Validation Text properties to compare the SigningDate and StartDate field values in the tblContract table.

To create and test a table validation rule in the tblContract table:

▶ **1.** Open the Navigation Pane, open the **tblContract** table in Design view, and then, in the Show/Hide group on the Table Tools Design tab, click the **Property Sheet** button to open the property sheet for the table.

To make sure that each SigningDate field value is chronologically earlier than, or less than, each StartDate field value, you'll compare the two field values in the Validation Rule text box.

▶ **2.** In the property sheet, click the **Validation Rule** text box, type **[SigningDate]<[StartDate]**, and then press the **Tab** key.

▶ **3.** Type **The signing date must be earlier than the start date** in the Validation Text text box. See Figure 5-42.

Tip

Make sure you type the brackets to enclose the field names. If you omit the brackets, Access automatically inserts quotation marks around the field names, in effect treating the field names as field values, and the table validation rule will not work correctly.

Setting table validation properties ◀ **Figure 5-42**

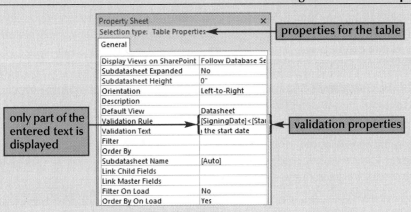

You can now test the validation properties.

▶ **4.** Close the property sheet, save the table, and then click the **Yes** button when asked if you want to test the existing dates in the tblContract table against the new validation rule.

▶ **5.** Close the Navigation Pane, switch to Datasheet view, click the Signing Date column value in the first record, click the **date picker** icon to the right of the date, click **27** in the calendar control to change the date to 2/27/2010, press the **Tab** key to advance to the Start Date column, and then press the **Tab** key two more times to complete your changes to the record. A dialog box opens containing the message "The signing date must be earlier than the start date," which is the Validation Text property setting you entered in Step 3.

Unlike field validation rule violations, which Access detects immediately after you finish your field entry and advance to another field, Access detects table validation rule violations when you finish all changes to the current record and advance to another record.

▶ **6.** Click the **OK** button, and then press the **Esc** key to undo your change to the Signing Date column value.

▶ **7.** Close the tblContract table.

Based on a request from Sarah, Lucia added a Memo field to the tblCustomer table, and now you'll review Lucia's work.

Working with Memo Fields

You use a Memo field for long comments and explanations. Text fields are limited to 255 characters, but Memo fields can hold up to 65,535 characters. In addition, Text fields limit you to plain text with no special formatting, but you can define Memo fields either to store plain text similar to Text fields or to store rich text, which you can selectively format with options such as bold, italic, and different fonts and colors.

You'll review the Memo field, named Comments, that Lucia added to the tblCustomer table.

To review the Memo field in the tblCustomer table:

1. Open the Navigation Pane, open the **tblCustomer** table in Datasheet view, and then close the Navigation Pane.

   If you scroll to the right to view the Comments field, you'll no longer be able to identify which customer applies to a row because the Company, First Name, and Last Name columns will be hidden. You'll freeze those three columns so they remain visible in the datasheet as you scroll to the right.

2. Click the **Company** column selector, press and hold down the **Shift** key, click the **Last Name** column selector, and then release the **Shift** key to select the Company, First Name, and Last Name columns.

3. In the Records group on the Home tab, click the **More** button, and then click **Freeze**. The three selected columns shift to the left and are now the three leftmost columns in the datasheet.

4. Scroll to the right until you see the Comments column. Notice that the Company, First Name, and Last Name columns, the three leftmost columns, remain visible. See Figure 5-43.

Figure 5-43	Freezing three datasheet columns

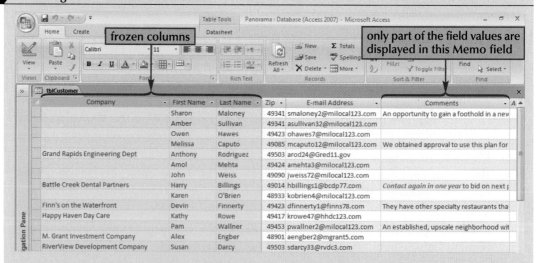

The Comments column is a Memo field that Belmont Landscapes staff members use to store notes, explanations, and other commentary about the customer. Notice that the Comments field value for Battle Creek Dental Partners displays rich text, using a bold, italic, and blue font. The Comments field values are partially hidden because the datasheet column is not wide enough. You'll view the first record's Comments field value in the Zoom dialog box.

▶ **5.** Click the **Comments** text box for the first record, hold down the **Shift** key, press the **F2** key, and then release the **Shift** key. The Zoom dialog box displays the entire Comments field value.

▶ **6.** Click the **OK** button to close the Zoom dialog box.

Table Datasheet Row and Column Resizing for Memo Fields | InSight

For Memo fields that contain many characters, you can widen the column to view more of its contents by dragging the right edge of the field's column selector to the right or by using the Column Width command when you click the More button in the Records group on the Home tab. However, increasing the column width reduces the number of other columns you can view at the same time. Further, for Memo fields containing thousands of characters, you can't widen the column enough to be able to view the entire contents of the field at one time across the width of the screen. Therefore, increasing the column width of a Memo field seldom makes sense.

Alternatively, you can increase the row height of a datasheet by dragging the bottom edge of a row selector down or by using the Row Height command when you click the More button in the Records group on the Home tab. Increasing the row height causes the text in a Memo field to wrap to the next line, so that you can view multiple lines at one time. Once again, however, for Memo fields containing thousands of characters, you can't increase the row height enough to ensure viewing the entire contents of the field at one time on screen. In addition, you'd view fewer records at one time, and the row height setting for a table propagates to all queries that have an object dependency with the table. Thus, you shouldn't increase the row height of a table datasheet to accommodate a Memo field.

What is the best way to view the contents of Memo fields that contain a large number of characters? It is best to use the Zoom dialog box in a datasheet, or to use a large scrollable text box on a form.

Now you'll review the property settings for the Comments field Lucia added to the tblCustomer table.

To review the property settings of the Memo field:

▶ **1.** Save the table, switch to Design view, click the **Comments Field Name** text box to make that row the current row, and then scroll to the bottom of the list of properties in the Field Properties pane.

▶ **2.** Click the **Text Format** text box in the Field Properties pane, and then click its **arrow**. The list of available text formats appears in the list box. See Figure 5-44.

Figure 5-44 ▶ **Viewing the properties for a Memo field**

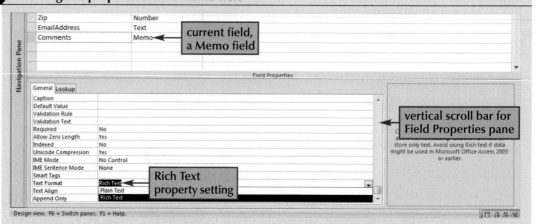

Lucia set the **Text Format property** to Rich Text, which lets you format the datasheet field contents using the options in the Font group on the Home tab. The default Text Format property setting for a Memo field is Plain Text, which doesn't allow text formatting.

▶ 3. Click the **arrow** on the Text Format text box to close the list, and then click the **Append Only** text box.

The **Append Only property**, which appears at the bottom of the list of properties, tracks the changes that you make to a Memo field. The default setting of No lets you edit the Memo field value in a normal way. Setting this property to Yes also lets you edit the Memo field value in a normal way but, additionally, causes Access to keep a historical record of all versions of the Memo field value. You can view each version of the field value, along with a date and time stamp of when each version change occurred.

You've finished your review of the Memo field, so you can close the table.

▶ 4. Close the tblCustomer table.

When employees at Belmont Landscapes open the Panorama database, a Security Warning appears below the Ribbon, and they must "enable this content" in the database before beginning their work. Sarah asks if you can eliminate this extra step when employees open the database.

Designating a Trusted Folder

A database is a file, and files can contain malicious instructions that can damage other files on your computer or files on other computers on your network. Unless you take special steps, Access treats every database as a potential threat to your computer. One such special step is to designate a folder as a trusted folder. A **trusted folder** is a folder on a drive or network that you designate as trusted and where you place databases you know are safe. When you open a database located in a trusted folder, Access treats it as a safe file and no longer displays a Security Warning. You can also place files used with other Microsoft Office programs, such as Word documents and Excel workbooks, in a trusted folder to eliminate warnings when you open them.

Because the Panorama database does not contain harmful instructions, you'll set up a trusted folder in which to store it to eliminate the Security Warning when a user opens the database.

To designate a trusted folder:

▶ 1. Click the **Office Button** , and then click the **Access Options** button. The Access Options dialog box opens.

▶ 2. In the left section of the dialog box, click **Trust Center**, click the **Trust Center Settings** button in the window on the right to open the Trust Center dialog box, and then in the left section, click **Trusted Locations**. The trusted locations for your installation of Access and other options are displayed on the right. See Figure 5-45.

Designating a trusted folder ◀ **Figure 5-45**

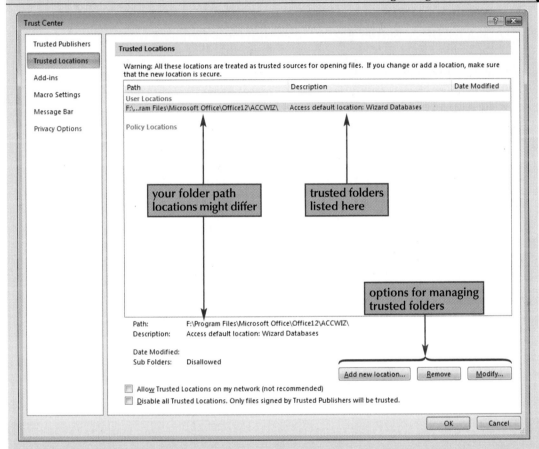

Existing trusted locations appear in the list at the top; and options to add, remove, and modify trusted locations appear at the bottom.

Trouble? Check with your instructor before adding a new trusted location. If your instructor tells you not to select this option, skip to Step 5.

▶ 3. Click the **Add new location** button to open the Microsoft Office Trusted Location dialog box, click the **Browse** button, navigate to the Level.02\Tutorial folder where your Data Files are stored, and then click the **OK** button.

You can also choose to designate subfolders of the selected location as trusted locations, but you won't select this option.

▶ 4. Click the **OK** button. Access adds the Level.02\Tutorial folder to the list of trusted locations.

▶ 5. Click the **OK** button to close the Trust Center dialog box, and then click the **OK** button to close the Access Options dialog box.

To show Sarah that adding the trusted location eliminates the Security Warning, you need to close and then open the database. You've created several queries and completed several table design changes, so you should compact and repair the Panorama database when you reopen it. Lucia doesn't use the Compact on Close option with the Panorama database, because it's possible to lose the database if there's a computer malfunction when the Compact on Close operation runs. As a precaution, you'll make a backup copy of the database before you reopen it. Making frequent backup copies of your critical files safeguards your data from hardware and software malfunctions, which can occur at any time.

To copy, open, and compact and repair the Panorama database:

1. Click the **Office Button** ⊙, and then click **Close Database** to close the Panorama database.

2. Make a backup copy of the Panorama database, preferably to a USB drive or other external medium, using a filename of Copy of Panorama_date, where *date* is the current date in the format 2010_02_15, for example, if you made the backup on February 15, 2010.

3. Make sure the Access window is the active window, and then click **C:\Level.02\ ... \Panorama** in the Open Recent Database pane of the Getting Started window. The database opens, and no Security Warning appears below the Ribbon because the database is located in the trusted location you designated.

   Next, you'll compact and repair the database.

4. Click the **Office Button** ⊙, point to **Manage**, and then click **Compact and Repair Database**.

   You've finished the work requested by Belmont Landscapes, so you can close the database and exit Access.

5. Close the Panorama database and then exit Access, clicking the **Yes** button if you are prompted to confirm that you want to exit Access and empty the Clipboard.

> **Tip**
>
> The date the database was last opened appears below the filename in the Open Recent Database pane.

You've completed the table design changes to the Panorama database that will make working with it easier and more accurate.

Review | Session 5.3 Quick Check

1. What is a lookup field?
2. A(n) _____ is a predefined format you use to enter and display data in a field.
3. What is property propagation?
4. Define the Validation Rule property, and give an example of when you would use it.
5. Define the Validation Text property, and give an example of when you would use it.
6. Setting a Memo field's Text Format property to _____ lets you format its contents.
7. A(n) _____ folder is a location in which you can place safe databases.

In this tutorial, you built on your earlier work with simple queries by learning how to use pattern and list-of-values matches, the Not operator, the & operator, and the IIf function. You also learned how to create parameter, crosstab, find duplicates, find unmatched, and top values queries. You enhanced the design of tables by creating lookup fields and input masks and by defining field and table validation rules. You also learned how to identify object dependencies, work with Memo fields, and designate trusted folders.

Key Terms

& (ampersand) operator
Append Only property
Caption property
crosstab query
Crosstab Query Wizard
field validation rule
find duplicates query
Find Duplicates Query
    Wizard
find unmatched query
Find Unmatched Query
    Wizard
IIf (Immediate If) function

In comparison operator
input mask
Input Mask Wizard
IsNull function
Like comparison operator
list-of-values match
literal display character
lookup field
Lookup Wizard field
Not logical operator
Object Dependencies pane
object dependency

parameter query
pattern match
property propagation
SQL (Structured Query
    Language)
table validation rule
Text Format property
Top Values property
trusted folder
Validation Rule property
Validation Text property

| Practice | **Review Assignments** |

Practice the skills you learned in the tutorial using the same case scenario.

Data File needed for the Review Assignments: Products.accdb

In the Review Assignments, you'll create several new queries and enhance the table design in a database that contains information about the suppliers that Belmont Landscapes works with on its landscape design projects. Complete the following steps:

1. Open the **Products** database, which is located in the Level.02\Review folder provided with your Data Files.
2. Modify the first record in the **tblCompany** table datasheet by changing the ContactFirstName and ContactLastName field values to your first and last names. Close the table.
3. Create a query to find all records in the tblCompany table in which the City field value starts with the letter H. Display all fields in the query recordset, and sort in ascending order by CompanyName. Save the query as **qryHSelectedCities**, run the query, and then close it.
4. Make a copy of the qryHSelectedCities query using the new name **qryOtherSelectedCities**. Modify the new query to find all records in the tblCompany table in which the City field values are not Lansing, Rockford, or Zeeland. Save and run the query, and then close it.
5. Create a query to find all records from the tblProduct table in which the Color field value is Black, White, or Grey. Use a list-of-values match for the selection criteria. Display all fields in the query recordset, and sort in descending order by Price. Save the query as **qrySelectedColors**, run the query, and then close it.
6. Create a query to display all records from the tblCompany table, selecting the CompanyName, City, and Phone fields, and sorting in ascending order by CompanyName. Add a calculated field named **ContactName** as the first column that concatenates the ContactFirstName, a space, and the ContactLastName. Set the Caption property for the ContactName field to **Contact Name**. Save the query as **qryCompanyContacts**, run the query, resize the Contact Name column to its best fit, and then save and close the query.
7. Create a parameter query to select the tblProduct table records for a Color field value that the user specifies. If the user doesn't enter a Color field value, select all records from the table. Display the ProductType, Price, Color, and DiscountOffered fields in the query recordset, sorting in ascending order by Price. Save the query as **qryColorParameter**. Run the query and enter no value as the Color field value, and then run the query again and enter **Wood** as the Color field value. Close the query.
8. Create a find duplicates query based on the tblProduct table. Select ProductType as the field that might contain duplicates, and select the ProductID, CompanyID, Price, and DiscountOffered fields as additional fields in the query recordset. Save the query as **qryDuplicateProductTypes**, run the query, and then close it.
9. Create a find unmatched query that finds all records in the tblCompany table for which there is no matching record in the tblProduct table. Display the CompanyID, CompanyName, City, Phone, ContactFirstName, and ContactLastName fields from the tblCompany table in the query recordset. Save the query as **qryCompaniesWithoutMatchingProducts**, run the query, and then close it.
10. Make a copy of the qryPricesWithDiscountAmounts query using the new name **qryTopPricesWithDiscountAmounts**. Modify the new query to use the Top Values property to select the top 25% of records. Save and run the query, and then close it.

11. In the **tblProduct** table, change the CompanyID field to a lookup field. Select the CompanyName and CompanyID fields from the tblCompany table, sort in ascending order by the CompanyName field, do not hide the key column, make sure the Company Name column is the leftmost column, resize the lookup columns to their best fit, select CompanyID as the field to store in the table, and accept the default label for the lookup column. View the tblProduct table datasheet, resize the Company ID column to its best fit, test the lookup field without changing a value permanently, and then save and close the table.

12. Use the Input Mask Wizard to add an input mask to the Phone field in the **tblCompany** table. The ending input mask should use periods as separators, as in 987.654.3210 with only the last seven digits required; do not store the literal display characters if you are asked to do so. Update the Input Mask property everywhere the Phone field is used. Test the input mask by typing over an existing Phone field value, being sure not to change the value by pressing the Esc key after you type the last digit in the Phone field.

13. Add a Memo field named **CompanyComments** as the last field in the tblCompany table. Set the Caption property to **Company Comments** and the Text Format property to Rich Text. In the table datasheet, resize the new column to its best fit, and then add your city and state in bold, italic font to the Memo field in the first record. Save and close the tblCompany datasheet.

14. Designate the Level.02\Review folder as a trusted folder. (*Note:* Check with your instructor before adding a new trusted location.)

15. Close the Products database without exiting Access, make a backup copy of the database, open the **Products** database, compact and repair the database, close the database, and then exit Access.

| Apply | **Case Problem 1** |

Use the skills you learned in the tutorial to work with the data contained in a database for a small music school.

Data File needed for this Case Problem: Contract.accdb

Pine Hill Music School Yuka Koyama owns and runs the Pine Hill Music School in Portland, Oregon. She and the qualified teachers who work for her offer instruction in voice, violin, cello, guitar, percussion, and other instruments. Yuka created an Access database named Contract to store data about students, teachers, and contracts. You'll help Yuka create several new queries and make design changes to the tables. Complete the following:

1. Open the **Contract** database, which is located in the Level.02\Case1 folder provided with your Data Files.

2. Change the first record in the **tblStudent** table datasheet so the First Name and Last Name columns contain your first and last names. Close the table.

3. Create a query to find all records in the tblStudent table in which the Phone field value begins with 541. Display the FirstName, LastName, City, and Phone fields in the query recordset; and sort in ascending order by LastName. Save the query as **qry541AreaCodes**, run the query, and then close it.

4. Make a copy of the qryCurrentLessons query using the new name **qrySelectedLessons**. Modify the new query to delete the existing condition for the ContractEndDate field and to include a list-of-values criterion that finds all records in which the LessonType field value is Cello, Flute, or Violin. Save and run the query, and then close it.

5. Create a query to find all records in the tblStudent table in which the City field value is not equal to Portland. Display the FirstName, LastName, City, and Phone fields in the query recordset; and sort in ascending order by City. Save the query as **qryNonPortland**, run the query, and then close it.

6. Create a query to display all records from the tblTeacher table, selecting all fields, and sorting in ascending order by LastName and then in ascending order by FirstName. Add a calculated field named **TeacherName** as the second column that concatenates FirstName, a space, and LastName for each teacher. Set the Caption property for the TeacherName field to **Teacher Name**. Do not display the FirstName and LastName fields in the query recordset. Save the query as **qryTeacherNames**, run the query, resize the Teacher Name column to its best fit, and then save and close the query.

7. Create a parameter query to select the tblContract table records for a LessonType field value that the user specifies. If the user doesn't enter a LessonType field value, select all records from the table. Include all fields from the tblContract table in the query recordset. Save the query as **qryLessonTypeParameter**. Run the query and enter no value as the LessonType field value, and then run the query again and enter **Guitar** as the LessonType field value. Close the query.

⊕ EXPLORE

8. Create a crosstab query based on the tblContract table. Use the LessonType field values for the row headings, the LessonLength field values for the column headings, and the count of the ContractID field values as the summarized value, and include row sums. Save the query as **qryLessonTypeCrosstab**. Change the column heading for the row sum column to **Total Number of Lessons**, and change the column headings for the [LessonLength] columns to **Number of 30-Minute Lessons** and **Number of 60-Minute Lessons**. Resize the columns in the query recordset to their best fit, and then save and close the query.

9. Create a find duplicates query based on the tblContract table. Select StudentID and LessonType as the fields that might contain duplicates, and select all other fields in the table as additional fields in the query recordset. Save the query as **qryMultipleLessonsForStudents**, run the query, and then close it.

10. Create a find unmatched query that finds all records in the tblStudent table for which there is no matching record in the tblContract table. Display all fields from the tblStudent table in the query recordset. Save the query as **qryStudentsWithoutContracts**, run the query, and then close it.

11. In the **tblContract** table, change the TeacherID field data type to Lookup Wizard. Select the TeacherName and TeacherID fields from the qryTeacherNames query, sort in ascending order by TeacherName, resize the lookup columns to their best fit, select TeacherID as the field to store in the table, and accept the default label for the lookup column. View the tblContract table datasheet, resize the TeacherID column to its best fit, and then save and close the table.

12. Use the Input Mask Wizard to add an input mask to the Phone field in the **tblStudent** table. The ending input mask should use periods as separators, as in 987.654.3210 with only the last seven digits required; do not store the literal display characters if you are asked to do so. Update the Input Mask property everywhere the Phone field is used. Test the input mask by typing over an existing Phone field value, being sure not to change the value permanently by pressing the Esc key after you type the last digit in the Phone field.

13. Define a field validation rule for the Gender field in the tblStudent table. Acceptable field values for the Gender field are M or F. Use the message "Gender values must be M or F" to notify a user who enters an invalid Gender field value. Save your table changes, test the field validation rule for the Gender field, making sure any tested field values are the same as they were before your testing, and then close the table.

14. Define a table validation rule for the **tblContract** table to verify that ContractStartDate field values precede ContractEndDate field values in time. Use an appropriate validation message. Save your table changes, test the table validation rule, making sure any tested field values are the same as they were before your testing, and then close the table.

15. Designate the Level.02\Case1 folder as a trusted folder. (*Note:* Check with your instructor before adding a new trusted location.)

16. Close the Contract database without exiting Access, make a backup copy of the database, open the **Contract** database, compact and repair the database, close the database, and then exit Access.

Apply	**Case Problem 2**

Apply what you learned in the tutorial to work with the data for a new business in the health and fitness industry.

Data File needed for this Case Problem: Training.accdb

Parkhurst Health & Fitness Center Martha Parkhurst owns and operates the Parkhurst Health & Fitness Center in Richmond, Virginia. The center offers the usual weight training equipment and fitness classes and also offers specialized programs designed to meet the needs of athletes who participate in certain sports or physical activities. Martha created the Training database to maintain information about the members who have joined the center and the types of programs offered. To make the database easier to use, Martha wants you to create several queries and to make changes to its table design. Complete the following steps:

1. Open the **Training** database, which is located in the Level.02\Case2 folder provided with your Data Files.

2. Modify the first record in the **tblMember** table datasheet by changing the First Name and Last Name column values to your first and last names. Close the table.

3. Create a query to find all records in the tblProgram table in which the MonthlyFee field value is 20, 30, or 40. Use a list-of-values match for the selection criterion, and include all fields from the table in the query recordset. Sort the query in descending order by the ProgramID field. Save the query as **qrySelectedPrograms**, run the query, and then close it.

4. Make a copy of the qrySelectedPrograms query using the new name **qrySelectedProgramsModified**. Modify the new query to find all records in the tblProgram table in which the MonthlyFee field value is not 20, 30, or 40. Save and run the query, and then close it.

5. Create a query to display all records from the tblMember table, selecting the LastName, FirstName, Street, and Phone fields, and sorting in ascending order by LastName and then in ascending order by FirstName. Add a calculated field named **MemberName** as the first column that concatenates FirstName, a space, and LastName. Set the Caption property for the MemberName field to **Member Name**. Do not display the FirstName and LastName fields in the query recordset. Create a second calculated field named **CityLine**, inserting it between the Street and Phone fields. The CityLine field concatenates City, a space, State, two spaces, and Zip. Set the Caption property for the CityLine field to **City Line**. Save the query as **qryMemberNames**, run the query, resize all columns to their best fit, and then save and close the query.

⊕ EXPLORE

6. Create a query to display all matching records from the tblProgram and tblMember tables, selecting the ProgramType and MonthlyFee fields from the tblProgram table, and the FirstName and LastName fields from the tblMember table. Add a calculated field named **MonthlyFeeStatus** as the last column that equals Active if the MembershipStatus field is equal to Active and equals Not Active otherwise. Set the Caption property for the calculated field to **Monthly Fee Status**. Save the query as **qryMonthlyFeeStatus**, run the query, resize all columns to their best fit, and then save and close the query.

7. Make a copy of the qryRichmondOnHold query using the new name **qryRichmondAndChesterActive**. Modify the new query to select all records in which the City field value is Richmond or Chester and the MembershipStatus field value is Active. Save and run the query, and then close the query.

8. Create a parameter query to select the tblMember table records for a City field value that the user specifies. If the user doesn't enter a City field value, select all records from the table. Display all fields from the tblMember table in the query recordset. Save the query as **qryMemberCityParameter**. Run the query and enter no value as the City field value, and then run the query again and enter **Ashland** as the City field value. Close the query.

9. Create a crosstab query based on the qryMonthlyFeeStatus query. Use the ProgramType field values for the row headings, the MonthlyFeeStatus field values for the column headings, the sum of the MonthlyFee field values as the summarized value, and include row sums. Save the query as **qryMonthlyFeeCrosstab**, resize the columns in the query recordset to their best fit, and then save and close the query.

10. Create a find duplicates query based on the tblMember table. Select ExpirationDate as the field that might contain duplicates, and select all other fields in the table as additional fields in the query recordset. Save the query as **qryDuplicateMemberExpirationDates**, run the query, and then close it.

11. Create a find unmatched query that finds all records in the tblProgram table for which there is no matching record in the tblMember table. Select all fields from the tblProgram table. Save the query as **qryProgramsWithoutMembers**, run the query, and then close it.

12. Create a new query based on the tblMember table. Display the FirstName, LastName, Phone, ExpirationDate, MembershipStatus, and ProgramID fields in the query recordset. Sort in ascending order by the ExpirationDate field, and then use the Top Values property to select the top 25% of records. Save the query as **qryUpcomingExpirations**, run the query, and then close it.

⊕ EXPLORE

13. Use the Input Mask Wizard to add an input mask to the JoinDate field in the **tblMember** table. Select the Short Date input mask, and then modify the default Short Date input mask by changing the two slashes to dashes. Next type **mm-dd-yyyy** in the Format property text box for the JoinDate field to specify the date format. Test the input mask by typing over an existing Join Date column value, being certain not to change the value by pressing the Esc key after you type the last digit in the Join Date column. Finally, repeat the same procedure to add the same input mask and Format property setting to the ExpirationDate field, and then save and close the table.

14. Define a field validation rule for the MonthlyFee field in the **tblProgram** table. Acceptable field values for the MonthlyFee field are values between 15 and 55. Enter the message **Value must be between 15 and 55, inclusive** so it appears if a user enters an invalid MonthlyFee field value. Save your table changes and then test the field validation rule for the MonthlyFee field; be certain the field values are the same as they were before your testing.

15. Define a table validation rule for the **tblMember** table to verify that JoinDate field values precede ExpirationDate field values in time. Use an appropriate validation message. Save your table changes, test the table validation rule, making sure any tested field values are the same as they were before your testing.

16. Add a Memo field named **MemberComments** as the last field in the tblMember table. Set the Caption property to **Member Comments** and the Text Format property to Rich Text. In the table datasheet, resize the new column to its best fit, and then add a comment in the Memo field in the first record about the types of physical activities you pursue, formatting the text with blue, italic font. Save your table changes, and then close the table.

17. Designate the Level.02\Case2 folder as a trusted folder. (*Note:* Check with your instructor before adding a new trusted location.)

18. Close the Training database without exiting Access, make a backup copy of the database, open the **Training** database, compact and repair the database, close the database, and then exit Access.

Challenge	**Case Problem 3**

Apply the skills you've learned, and explore some new skills, to work with a database that contains data about an agency that recycles household goods.

Data File needed for this Case Problem: Agency.accdb

Rossi Recycling Group   The Rossi Recycling Group is a not-for-profit agency in Salina, Kansas that provides recycled household goods to needy people and families at no charge. Residents of Salina and surrounding communities donate cash and goods, such as appliances, furniture, and tools, to the Rossi Recycling Group. The group's volunteers then coordinate with local human services agencies to distribute the goods to those in need. The Rossi Recycling Group was established by Mary and Tom Rossi, who live on the outskirts of Salina on a small farm. Mary and Tom organize the volunteers to collect the goods and store the collected items in their barn for distribution. Tom has created an Access database to keep track of information about donors, their donations, and the human services agencies. He wants you to create several queries and to make changes to the table design of the database. To do so, you'll complete the following steps:

1. Open the **Agency** database, which is located in the Level.02\Case3 folder provided with your Data Files.

2. Modify the first record in the **tblDonor** table datasheet by changing the Title, First Name, and Last Name column values to your title and name. Close the table.

3. Create a query to find all records in the tblDonation table in which the AgencyID field value starts with either the letter R or the letter W. Display all fields in the query recordset, and sort in descending order by DonationValue. Save the query as **qryROrWAgencyDonations**, run the query, and then close it.

4. Make a copy of the qryAgenciesByCity query using the new name **qryNonSalinaAgencies**. Modify the new query to select all records in which the City field value is not Salina. Save and run the query, and then close it.

EXPLORE

5. The existing qryDonationsAfterPickupCharge query displays the DonorID, AgencyName, DonationDescription, and DonationValue fields for all donations that require a pickup, along with the NetDonation calculated field that displays the results of subtracting $8.75 from the DonationValue field value. Make a copy of the qryDonationsAfterPickupCharge query using the new name **qryNetDonations**. Modify the new query to select *all* records, to display the PickupRequired field, and to sort only in descending order by NetDonation. Also, change the NetDonation calculated field to subtract the delivery charge of $8.75 from the DonationField value when a pickup is required and to otherwise use the DonationValue field value. Save and run the query, and then close it.

6. Create a query to display all records from the tblAgency table, selecting all the fields except the ContactFirstName and ContactLastName fields, and sorting in ascending order by AgencyName. Add a calculated field named **ContactName** as the third column that concatenates ContactFirstName, a space, and ContactLastName. Set the Caption property for the ContactName field to **Contact Name**. Save the query as **qryAgencyContactNames**, run the query, resize the new column to its best fit, and then save and close the query.

7. Create a parameter query to select the tblDonation table records for a DonationDesc (donation description) field value that the user specifies. If the user doesn't enter a DonationDesc field value, select all records from the table. Display all fields from the tblDonation table in the query recordset, and sort in ascending order by DonationValue. Save the query as **qryDonationDescParameter**. Run the query and enter no value as the DonationDesc field value, and then run the query again and enter **Cash** as the DonationDesc field value. Close the query.

EXPLORE

8. Create a crosstab query based on the qryNetDonations query. Use the AgencyName field values for the row headings, the PickupRequired field values for the column headings, and the sum of the NetDonation field values as the summarized value, and include row sums. Save the query as **qryNetDonationsCrosstab**. Change the column headings for the two rightmost columns to **No Pickup** and **Pickup Required**. Change the format of the displayed values to Standard with two decimal places. Resize the columns in the query recordset to their best fit, and then save and close the query.

9. Create a find duplicates query based on the qryNetDonations query. Select DonorID and AgencyName as the fields that might contain duplicates, and select the remaining fields in the query as additional fields in the query recordset. Save the query as **qryMultipleDonorDonations**, run the query, and then close it.

10. Create a find unmatched query that finds all records in the tblDonor table for which there is no matching record in the tblDonation table. Select all fields from the tblDonor table in the query recordset. Save the query as **qryDonorsWithoutDonations**, run the query, and then close it.

EXPLORE

11. Make a copy of the qryNetDonations query using the new name **qryTopNetDonations**. Modify the new query by using the Top Values property to select the top 40% of the records. Save and run the query, and then close the query.

12. Use the Input Mask Wizard to add an input mask to the Phone field in the **tblDonor** table. The ending input mask should use hyphens as separators, as in 987-654-3210, with only the last seven digits required; do not store the literal display characters if you are asked to do so. Update the Input Mask property everywhere the Phone field is used. Test the input mask by typing over an existing Phone field value, being sure not to change the value permanently by pressing the Esc key after you type the last digit in the Phone field. Close the table.

13. Designate the Level.02\Case3 folder as a trusted folder. (*Note:* Check with your instructor before adding a new trusted location.)

14. Close the Agency database without exiting Access, make a backup copy of the database, open the **Agency** database, compact and repair the database, close the database, and then exit Access.

| Challenge | **Case Problem 4** |

Apply the skills you've learned, and explore some new skills, to work with the data for a luxury property rental company.

Data File needed for this Case Problem: Vacation.accdb

GEM Ultimate Vacations   Griffin and Emma MacElroy own and operate their own agency, GEM Ultimate Vacations, which specializes in locating and booking luxury rental properties in Europe and Africa. To track their guests, properties, and reservations, they created the Vacation database. Griffin and Emma want you to create several queries and to make changes to the table design. To do so, you'll complete the following steps:

1. Open the **Vacation** database, which is located in the Level.02\Case4 folder provided with your Data Files.

2. Modify the first record in the **tblGuest** table datasheet by changing the First Name and Last Name column values to your first and last names.

3. Create a query to find all records in the tblProperty table in which the PropertyName field value starts with the word Chateau. Display all fields except the Description field in the query recordset. Save the query as **qryChateauProperties**, run the query, and then close it.

4. Make a copy of the qryChateauProperties query using the new name **qryNonChateauProperties**. Modify the new query to find all records in the tblProperty table in which the PropertyName field value starts with a word other than Chateau, and sort in ascending order by PropertyName. Save and run the query, and then close it.

5. Create a query to find all records in the tblGuest table in which the City field value is Aurora, Chicago, or Crown Point. Use a list-of-values match for the selection criterion, and display all fields from the tblGuest table in the query recordset. Save the query as **qrySelectedGuests**, run the query, and then close it.

⊕ EXPLORE

6. Create a query to select all records from the tblProperty table with nightly rates of $1,700 or $2,000 in France or Italy. Display all fields except the Description field in the query recordset. Save the query as **qryFranceItalySelectedProperties**, run the query, and then close it.

7. Create a parameter query to select the tblProperty table records for a Country field value that the user specifies. If the user doesn't enter a Country field value, select all records from the table. Display all fields from the tblProperty table in the query recordset, and sort in ascending order by PropertyName. Save the query as **qryCountryParameter**. Run the query and enter no value as the Country field value, and then run the query again and enter **Scotland** as the Country field value. Close the query.

8. Create a query that contains all records from the tblGuest table and all matching records from the tblReservation table. Display all fields from the tblGuest table and all fields except GuestID from the tblReservation table. Save the query as **qryGuestsAndReservations**, run the query, and then close it. Create a crosstab query based on the qryGuestsAndReservations query. Use the City field values for the row headings, the People field values for the column headings, and the sum of the RentalRate field as the summarized value, and include row sums. Save the query as **qryReservationsCrosstab**, resize the columns in the query recordset to their best fit, and then save and close the query.

9. Create a find duplicates query based on the tblProperty table. Select Location and Country as the fields that might contain duplicates, and select the remaining fields in the table as additional fields in the query recordset. Save the query as **qryDuplicateLocations**, run the query, and then close it.

10. Create a find unmatched query that finds all records in the tblGuest table for which there is no matching record in the tblReservation table. Display the GuestFirstName, GuestLastName, City, and Phone fields from the tblGuest table in the query recordset. Save the query as **qryGuestsWithoutReservations**, run the query, and then close it.

⊕ EXPLORE 11. Modify the **qryTopRentalCost** query to use the Top Values property to select the top 30% of the records. Save and run the query, and then close it.

12. In the **tblReservation** table, change the PropertyID field data type to Lookup Wizard. Select the PropertyID, PropertyName, and Location fields from the tblProperty table, sort in ascending order by PropertyName, do not hide the key column, resize the lookup columns to their best fit, select PropertyID as the field to store in the table, and accept the default label for the look up column. View the tblReservation datasheet, resize the PropertyID column to its best fit, test the lookup field without changing a field value permanently, and then close the table.

⊕ EXPLORE 13. Open the **tblGuest** table in Design view. Change the StateProv field data type to Lookup Wizard using a list of values that you enter. In the Lookup Wizard dialog box, create two columns and type the following pairs of values: **Illinois** and **IL**, **Indiana** and **IN**, and **Ontario** and **ON**. Resize the lookup columns to their best fit, select Col2 as the field to store in the table, and accept the default label for the lookup column. View the tblGuest table datasheet, resize the lookup column to its best fit, test the lookup field without changing permanently field values, and then save and close the table.

⊕ EXPLORE 14. Define a field validation rule for the Bedrooms field in the **tblProperty** table. Acceptable field values for the Bedrooms field are values between 3 and 25, including those two values. Display the message **Value must be between 3 and 25** when a user enters an invalid Bedrooms field value. Save your table changes and then test the field validation rule for the Bedrooms field; be certain the field values are the same as they were before your testing.

15. Define a table validation rule for the **tblReservation** table to verify that StartDate field values precede EndDate field values in time. Use an appropriate validation message. Save your table changes, test the table validation rule, making sure any tested field values are the same as they were before your testing, and then close the table.

16. Designate the Level.02\Case4 folder as a trusted folder. (*Note:* Check with your instructor before adding a new trusted location.)

17. Close the Vacation database without exiting Access, make a backup copy of the database, open the **Vacation** database, compact and repair the database, close the database, and then exit Access.

| Create | **Case Problem 5** |

Work with the skills you've learned, and explore some new skills, to create a database for an Internet service provider.

There are no Data Files needed for this Case Problem.

Always Connected Everyday Chris and Pat Dixon own and manage Always Connected Everyday (ACE), a successful Internet service provider (ISP) in your area. ACE provides Internet access to residential and business customers and offers a variety of access plans, from dial-up and DSL to wireless. Figure 5-46 shows the pricing options for the access plans ACE offers.

Figure 5-46

Access Plan	Monthly	Annually	Setup Fee
Dial-up limited	$9.95		
Dial-up no e-mail	$14.95	$149.50	
Dial-up unlimited	$19.95	$199.50	
DSL pro	$29.95		$69.00
DSL turbo	$49.95		$69.00
DSL business	$89.95		$129.00
Wireless city economy	$39.95		$99.00
Wireless city basic	$49.95		$99.00
Wireless city advanced	$64.95		$109.00
Wireless city business	$99.95		$199.00
Wireless rural basic	$59.95		$109.00

Dial-up plans are available in all communities served by ACE, and DSL and wireless access are limited by a customer's proximity to DSL phone lines or wireless towers. Within each type of service—dial-up, DSL, and wireless—ACE offers low-cost plans with either slower access speeds or fewer capabilities and more expensive plans with either higher access speeds or greater service and features.

Chris and Pat need you to create a database to track their plans, customers, and service calls. The process of creating a complete database—including all fields, tables, relationships, queries, forms, and other database objects—for ACE is an enormous undertaking. You will start with just a few database components, and then you will create additional objects and functionality in subsequent tutorials.

Complete the following steps to create the database and its initial objects:

1. Read the appendix titled "Relational Databases and Database Design" at the end of this book.
2. If you are not familiar with ISPs, use your Web browser to find out more about them, so that you know common terminology and offerings.
3. The initial database structure includes the following tables and fields:
   a. The **tblAccessPlan** table includes the fields shown in Figure 5-46, along with a primary key field, which you can define as an AutoNumber field.
   b. The **tblCustomer** table includes a unique customer account number; an optional company name; and first name, last name, address, city, state, zip, phone, access plan ID (foreign key), next billing date, and e-mail address for the customer; and the customer's user ID and password for accessing ACE's Web site.

4. Building on Step 3, for each field, determine and set its attributes, such as data type, field size, and validation rules.

5. Create the database structure using Access. Use the database name **ACE**, and save the database in the Level.02\Case5 folder provided with your Data Files. Create the tables with their fields, following the naming standards used in this tutorial. Be sure to set each field's properties correctly, including the Caption property. Select a primary key for each table, use an input mask for one field, and then define the relationships between the tables.

6. For each table, create a form that you'll use to view, add, edit, and delete records in that table.

7. For tables with one-to-many relationships, create a form with a main form for the primary table and a subform for the related table.

8. Design test data for each table in the database. Your tblCustomer table should contain at least 15 records. Make sure your test data covers common situations. For example, your test data should include at least two access plans with multiple customers using the plans; at least two access plans with no customers using it; multiple cities, phone prefixes, and next billing dates; residential customers with no company names; and commercial customers with company names and the first and last names of the company's contact. Use your first and last names for the first record in the tblCustomer table.

9. Add the test data to your tables using the forms you created in Steps 6 and 7.

10. Open each table datasheet, and resize all datasheet columns to their best fit.

11. For the foreign key field in the tblCustomer table, change the field's data type to Lookup Wizard, including both the foreign key and its description as lookup columns. If necessary, resize the lookup column in the table datasheet.

12. Create a query named **qryCustomerNames** that contains all the fields from the tblCustomer table. Add a calculated field named **CustomerName** as the first column that is either the company name or the concatenation of the last name, a comma, a space, and the first name; set its Caption property to **Customer Name**. Sort in ascending order by CustomerName.

13. Create one parameter query, one crosstab query, and one find unmatched query, and save them using appropriate object names.

14. Designate the Level.02\Case5 folder as a trusted folder. (*Note:* Check with your instructor before adding a new trusted location.)

15. Close the ACE database without exiting Access, make a backup copy of the database, open the **ACE** database, compact and repair the database, close the database, and then exit Access.

Research | **Internet Assignments**

Use the Internet to find and work with data related to the topics presented in this tutorial.

The purpose of the Internet Assignments is to challenge you to find information on the Internet that you can use to work effectively with this software. The actual assignments are updated and maintained on the Course Technology Web site. Log on to the Internet and use your Web browser to go to the Student Online Companion for New Perspectives Office 2007 at **www.course.com/np/office2007**. Then navigate to the Internet Assignments for this tutorial.

Review | **Quick Check Answers**

Session 5.1

1. Caption
2. Like
3. a wildcard that represents any string of characters in a pattern match query
4. to define a condition with two or more values
5. Use the Not logical operator to negate a condition.
6. IIf (or Immediate If)
7. when you want to prompt the user to enter the selection criterion when the query runs

Session 5.2

1. It performs aggregate function calculations on the values of one database field and displays the results in a spreadsheet format.
2. Simple Query Wizard, Crosstab Query Wizard, Find Duplicates Query Wizard, Find Unmatched Query Wizard
3. It finds duplicate records in a table or query based on the values in one or more fields.
4. It finds all records in a table or query that have no related records in a second table or query.
5. You limit the number of records displayed in the query results.
6. Access displays the first five records.

Session 5.3

1. A field that lets you select a value from a list of possible values
2. input mask
3. an Access feature that updates control properties in objects when you modify table field properties
4. A property that specifies the valid values that users can enter in a field. You could use this property to specify that users can enter only positive numeric values in a numeric field.
5. A property value that appears in a dialog box if a user violates the field's validation rule. You could display the message "Must be a positive integer" if the user enters a value less than or equal to zero.
6. Rich Text
7. Trusted

Ending Data Files

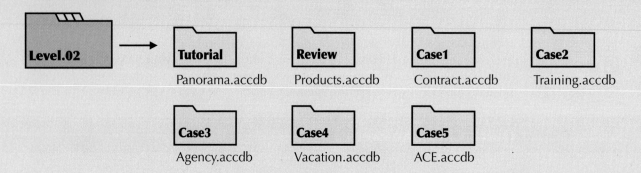

Using Form Tools and Creating Custom Forms

Creating Forms for Entering and Maintaining Contract and Invoice Data

Case | Belmont Landscapes

Oren Belmont hired Lucia Perez to enhance the Panorama database, and she initially concentrated on standardizing the table design and creating queries for Belmont Landscapes. Sarah Fisher and her staff created a few forms before Lucia's hiring, and Lucia's next priority is to work with Sarah to create new forms that will be more useful and easier to use.

In this tutorial, you will create new forms for Belmont Landscapes. In creating the forms, you will use many Access form customization features, such as adding controls and a subform to a form, using combo boxes and calculated controls, and adding color and special effects to a form. These features will make it easier for Sarah and her staff to interact with the Panorama database.

Starting Data Files

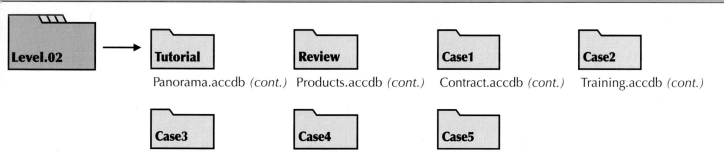

Level.02 → Tutorial
Panorama.accdb *(cont.)*

Review
Products.accdb *(cont.)*

Case1
Contract.accdb *(cont.)*

Case2
Training.accdb *(cont.)*

Case3
Agency.accdb *(cont.)*

Case4
Vacation.accdb *(cont.)*

Case5
ACE.accdb *(cont.)*

Session 6.1

Designing Forms

You've used wizards to create forms, and you've modified a form's design in Layout view to create a custom form. To create a **custom form**, you can modify an existing form in Layout view or in Design view, or you can design and create a form from scratch in Layout view or in Design view. You can design a custom form to match a paper form, to display some fields side by side and others top to bottom, to highlight certain sections with color, or to add visual effects. Whether you want to create a simple or complex custom form, planning the form's content and appearance is always your first step.

InSight		**Form Design Guidelines**

When you plan a form, you should keep in mind the following form design guidelines:
- Use forms to perform all database updates, because forms provide better readability and control than do table and query recordsets.
- Determine the fields and record source needed for each form. A form's **Record Source property** specifies the table or query that provides the fields for the form.
- Group related fields and position them in a meaningful, logical order.
- If users will refer to a source document while working with the form, design the form to match the source document closely.
- Identify each field value with a label that names the field, and align field values and labels for readability.
- Size the width of each text box to fully display the values it contains and also to provide a visual clue to users about the length of those values.
- Display calculated fields in a distinctive way, and prevent users from changing and updating them.
- Use default values, list boxes, and other form controls whenever possible to reduce user errors by minimizing keystrokes and limiting entries. A **control** is an item, such as a text box or command button, that you place in a form or report.
- Use colors, fonts, and graphics sparingly to keep the form uncluttered and to keep the focus on the data.
- Use a consistent style for all forms in a database.

Sarah and her staff had created a few forms and made table design changes before learning about proper form design guidelines. The guidelines recommend performing all database updates using forms. As a result, Belmont Landscapes won't use table or query datasheets to update the database, and Sarah asks if she should reconsider any of the table design changes you made to the Panorama database in the previous tutorial.

Changing a Lookup Field to a Text Field

The input mask and validation rule changes are important table design changes, but setting the CustomerID field to a lookup field in the tblContract table is an unnecessary change. A form combo box provides the same capability in a clearer, more flexible way. A **combo box** is a control that provides the features of a text box and a list box; it lets you choose a value from the list or type an entry. Before creating the new forms for Sarah, you'll change the data type of the CustomerID field in the tblContract table from a Lookup Wizard field to a Text field.

To change the data type of the CustomerID field:

▶ **1.** Start Access, and then open the **Panorama** database in the Level.02\Tutorial folder provided with your Data Files.

   Trouble? If the Security Warning is displayed below the Ribbon, either the Panorama database is not located in the Level.02\Tutorial folder or you did not designate that folder as a trusted folder. Make sure you opened the database in the Level.02\Tutorial folder, and make sure that it's a trusted folder.

▶ **2.** Open the Navigation Pane, open the **tblContract** table in Design view, and then close the Navigation Pane.

▶ **3.** Click the Field Name box for the CustomerID field, and then click the **Lookup** tab in the Field Properties pane. The Field Properties pane now displays the lookup properties for the CustomerID field. See Figure 6-1.

Tip

You can press the F11 key to open or close the Navigation Pane.

Lookup properties for the CustomerID field ◀ **Figure 6-1**

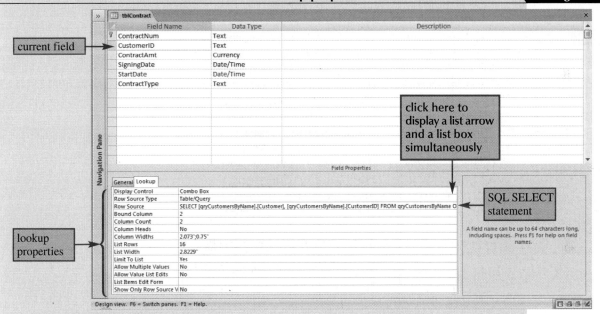

Notice the **Row Source property**, which specifies the data source for a control in a form or report or for a field in a table or query. The Row Source property is usually set to a table name, a query name, or an SQL statement. For the CustomerID field, the Row Source property is set to an SQL SELECT statement. You'll learn more about SQL later in the text.

To remove the lookup feature for the CustomerID field, you need to change the **Display Control property**, which specifies the default control used to display a field, from Combo Box to Text Box.

▶ **4.** Click the right side of the **Display Control** property box, and then click **Text Box**. All the lookup properties in the Field Properties pane disappear, and the CustomerID field changes back to a Text field without lookup properties.

▶ **5.** Click the **General** tab in the Field Properties pane and notice that the properties for a Text field still apply to the CustomerID field.

6. Save the table, switch to Datasheet view, resize the Customer ID column to its best fit, and then click one of the **CustomerID** text boxes. An arrow does not appear in the CustomerID text box because the field is no longer a lookup field.

7. Save the table, and then close the tblContract table.

Before you could change the CustomerID field in the tblContract table to a lookup field in the previous tutorial, you had to delete the one-to-many relationship between the tblCustomer and tblContract tables. Now that you've changed the data type of the CustomerID field back to a Text field, you'll view the table relationships to make sure that the tables in the Panorama database are related correctly.

To view the table relationships in the Relationships window:

1. On the Ribbon, click the **Database Tools** tab, and then in the Show/Hide group, click the **Relationships** button to open the Relationships window. See Figure 6-2.

Figure 6-2 Panorama database tables in the Relationships window

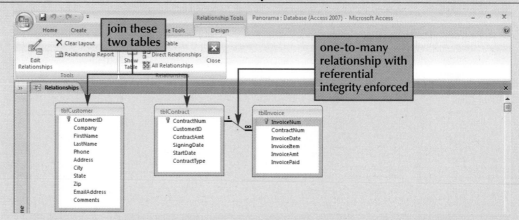

The primary tblContract table and the related tblInvoice table have a one-to-many relationship with referential integrity enforced. You need to establish a similar one-to-many relationship between the tblCustomer and tblContract tables.

2. Click **CustomerID** in the tblCustomer field list, drag it to **CustomerID** in the tblContract field list, and then release the mouse button to open the Edit Relationships dialog box.

3. Click the **Enforce Referential Integrity** check box, click the **Cascade Update Related Fields** check box, and then click the **Create** button to define the one-to-many relationship between the two tables and to close the dialog box. The join line connecting the tblCustomer and tblContract tables indicates the type of relationship (one-to-many) with referential integrity enforced (bold join line).

Sarah asks you to print a copy of the database relationships to use as a reference, and she asks if other Access documentation is available.

Printing Database Relationships and Using the Documenter

You can print the Relationships window to document the fields, tables, and relationships in a database. You can also use the **Documenter**, another Access tool, to create detailed documentation of all, or selected, objects in a database. For each selected object, the Documenter lets you print documentation, such as the object's properties and relationships, and the fields used by the object and their properties. You can use the documentation to help you understand an object and to help you plan changes to that object.

Using the Documenter | Reference Window

- Start Access and open the database you want to document.
- In the Analyze group on the Database Tools tab, click the Database Documenter button.
- Select the object(s) you want to document.
- If necessary, click the Options button to select specific documentation options for the selected object(s), and then click the OK button.
- Click the OK button, print the documentation, and then close the Object Definition window.

Next, you'll print the Relationships window and use the Documenter to create documentation for the tblContract table. Sarah will show her staff the tblContract table documentation as a sample of the information that the Documenter provides.

To print the Relationships window and use the Documenter:

▸ **1.** In the Tools group on the Design tab, click the **Relationship Report** button to open the Relationships for Panorama report in Print Preview. See Figure 6-3.

Relationships for Panorama report | Figure 6-3

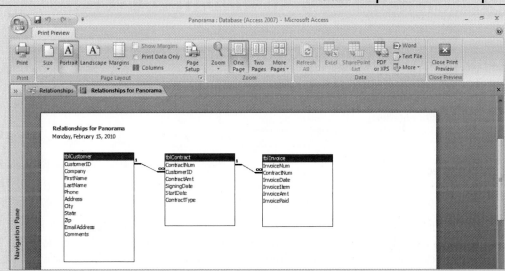

▸ **2.** In the Print group on the Print Preview tab, click the **Print** button, select your printer in the Name text box, and then click the **OK** button. Access prints the Relationships for Panorama report.

▶ **3.** Click the **Close 'Relationships for Panorama'** button ⊠ on the Relationships for Panorama tab to close the window. A dialog box opens and asks if you want to save the report. Because you can easily create the report at any time, you won't save it.

▶ **4.** Click the **No** button to close the report without saving changes, and then close the Relationships window.

Now you'll use the Documenter to create detailed documentation for the tblContract table as a sample to show Sarah.

▶ **5.** On the Ribbon, click the **Database Tools** tab. In the Analyze group, click the **Database Documenter** button, and then click the **Tables** tab (if necessary) in the Documenter dialog box. See Figure 6-4.

Figure 6-4 ▶ Documenter dialog box

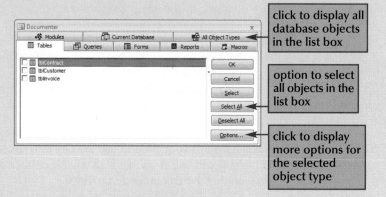

▶ **6.** Click the **tblContract** check box, and then click the **Options** button. The Print Table Definition dialog box opens. See Figure 6-5.

Figure 6-5 ▶ Print Table Definition dialog box

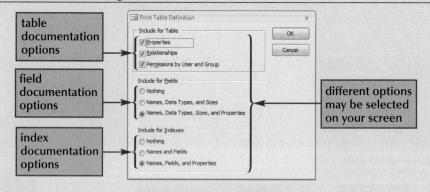

You select which documentation you want the Documenter to include for the selected table, its fields, and its indexes. Sarah asks you to include all table documentation and the second options for fields and for indexes.

▶ **7.** Make sure all check boxes are checked in the Include for Table section, click the **Names, Data Types, and Sizes** option button in the Include for Fields section (if necessary), click the **Names and Fields** option button in the Include for Indexes section (if necessary), click the **OK** button, and then click the **OK** button. The Documenter dialog box closes and the Object Definition report opens in Print Preview.

▶ **8.** In the Zoom group on the Print Preview tab, click the arrow on the **Zoom** button, and then click **Zoom 100%**.

When you need to view more of the horizontal contents of an open object, you can close the Navigation Pane. You can also minimize the Ribbon when you want to view more of the vertical contents of an open object. To minimize the Ribbon, double-click any tab on the Ribbon, or right-click a tab and then click Minimize the Ribbon. To restore the Ribbon, double-click any tab on the Ribbon, or right-click a tab and then click Minimize the Ribbon (it's a toggle option).

▶ **9.** Double-click the **Print Preview** tab on the Ribbon to minimize the Ribbon, and then scroll down the report so you can see the date at the top of the window. See Figure 6-6.

Object Definition report for the tblContract table **Figure 6-6**

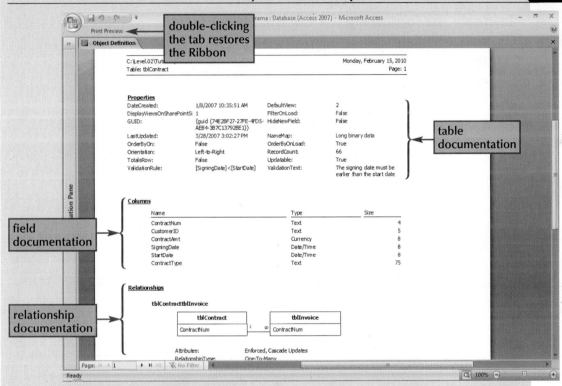

The Object Definition report displays table, field, and relationship documentation for the tblContract table.

▶ **10.** Scroll down the Object Definition report to view the remaining information in the documentation, print the documentation if your instructor asks you to do so, and then close the Object Definition report. Notice that the Navigation Pane is closed and the Ribbon is minimized.

Sarah and her staff will review the printout of the Relationships window and the documentation about the tblContract table and decide if they need to view additional documentation. Next, you'll create new forms for Sarah and her staff.

Creating Forms Using Form Tools

The Panorama database currently contains four forms: the frmContract form was created using the Form tool, the frmCustomer form was created using the Form Wizard, and the frmCustomerContracts main form and its frmContractSubform subform were created using the Form Wizard. Only the frmCustomer form is a custom form. Design changes that were made to the frmCustomer form in Layout view include changing its AutoFormat, changing its form title color and its line type, adding a picture, and moving a field.

Sarah wants to view the forms that can be created using other types of form tools, so she can determine if any of the forms would be helpful to her when updating the database.

Creating a Form Using the Datasheet Tool

The **Datasheet tool** creates a form in a datasheet format that contains all the fields in the source table or query. You'll use the Datasheet tool to create a form based on the tblContract table.

To create the form using the Datasheet tool:

Tip

When you use the Datasheet tool, the record source (either a table or query) for the form must either be open or selected in the Navigation Pane.

1. Open the Navigation Pane, and then click **tblContract** (if necessary) in the Navigation Pane.

2. Double-click the **Create** tab on the Ribbon to restore the Ribbon and to display the Create tab.

3. In the Forms group, click the **More Forms** button, and then click **Datasheet**. The Datasheet tool creates a form showing every field in the tblContract table in a datasheet format. See Figure 6-7.

| **Figure 6-7** | **Form created by the Datasheet tool** |

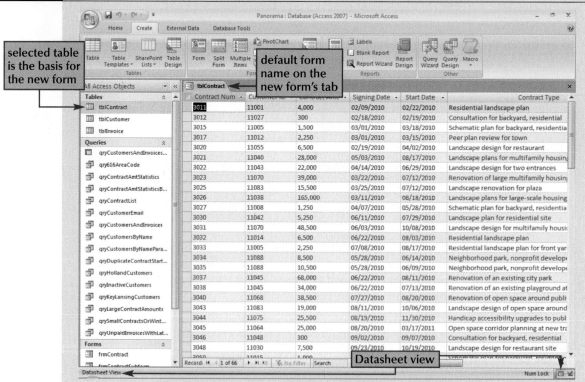

The new form displays all the records and fields from the tblContract table in Datasheet view and in the same format as a table or query recordset displayed in Datasheet view. "Datasheet View" appears on the status bar, as do two view icons, one for Datasheet view and the other for Design view. The form name, tblContract, is the same name as the table used as the basis for the form, but you should change the name when you save the form.

When working with forms, you view and update data in Form view, you view and make simple design changes in Layout view, and you make simple and complex design changes in Design view. For the form created with the Datasheet tool, you'll check the available view options.

▸ **4.** Click the **Home** tab on the Ribbon.

▸ **5.** In the Views group, click the arrow on the **View** button. See Figure 6-8.

View options for a form created by the Datasheet tool ◂ **Figure 6-8**

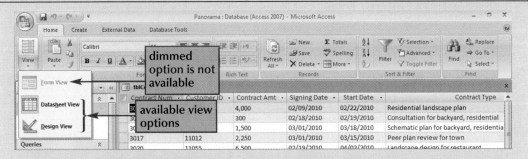

Form view is dimmed, which means that it's unavailable for this form type, and Layout view is not an option in the list. Datasheet view allows you to view and update data, and Design view is the only other view option for this form.

Sarah and her staff don't have a need for a form with a datasheet format, so you won't save it.

▸ **6.** Click the arrow on the **View** button to close the menu, and then close the form without saving it.

Next, you'll show Sarah a form created using the Multiple Items tool.

Creating a Form Using the Mulitple Items Tool

The **Multiple Items tool** creates a customizable form that displays multiple records from a source table or query in a datasheet format. You'll use the Multiple Items tool to create a form based on the tblContract table.

To create the form using the Multiple Items tool:

▸ **1.** Make sure that the tblContract table is selected in the Navigation Pane, and then click the **Create** tab on the Ribbon.

▸ **2.** In the Forms group, click the **Multiple Items** button. The Multiple Items tool creates a form showing every field in the tblContract table and opens the form in Layout view. See Figure 6-9.

Figure 6-9 | **Form created by the Multiple Items tool**

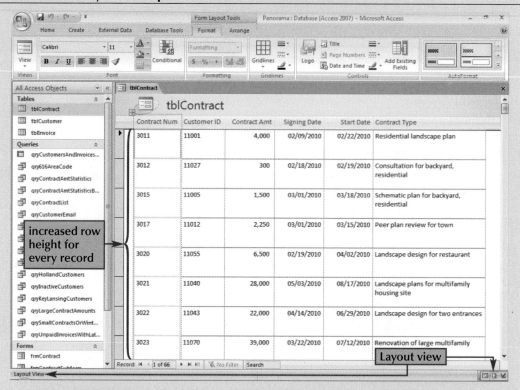

Tip

You can click one of the view buttons on the right side of the status bar to switch to another view.

The new form displays all the records and fields from the tblContract table in a format similar to a datasheet, but the row height for every record is increased compared to a standard datasheet. Unlike a form created by the Datasheet tool, which has only Datasheet view and Design view available, a Multiple Items form is a standard form that can be displayed in Form view, Layout view, and Design view, as indicated by the buttons on the right side of the status bar.

For the form created with the Multiple Items tool, you'll check the available view options.

▸ **3.** In the Views group, click the arrow on the **View** button. Form view, Layout view, and Design view are the available views for this form. See Figure 6-10.

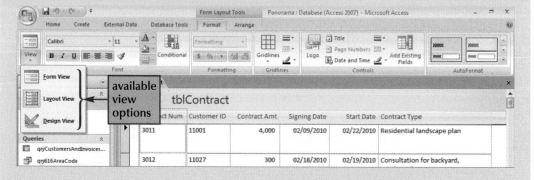

Sarah thinks this new form could be more useful than the form created by the Datasheet tool, but she doesn't have an immediate need for the form, so you won't save it.

▶ **4.** Click the arrow on the **View** button to close the menu, and then close the form without saving it.

The final form tool you'll show Sarah is the Split Form tool.

Creating a Form Using the Split Form Tool

The **Split Form tool** creates a customizable form that displays the data in a form in both Form view and Datasheet view at the same time. The two views are synchronized with each other at all times. Selecting a field in one view selects the same field in the other view. You can add, change, or delete data from either view. Typically, you'd use Datasheet view to locate a record, and then use Form view to update the record. You'll use the Split Form tool to create a form based on the tblContract table.

To create the form using the Split Form tool:

▶ **1.** Make sure that the tblContract table is selected in the Navigation Pane, and then click the **Create** tab on the Ribbon.

▶ **2.** In the Forms group, click the **Split Form** button, and then close the Navigation Pane. The Split Form tool creates a split form that opens in Layout view and displays a form with the contents of the first record in the tblContract table on the top and a datasheet of the first several records in the tblContract table on the bottom. See Figure 6-11.

Form created by the Split Form tool ◀ Figure 6-11

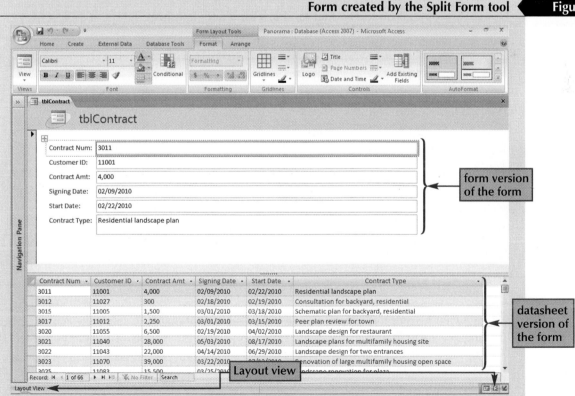

In Layout view, you can make layout and design changes to the form and layout changes to the datasheet. Sarah thinks the split form will be a useful addition to the

Panorama database, and she wants you to show her the types of design modifications that are possible with a split form.

Modifying a Split Form in Layout View

You use the Format tab on the Ribbon, as shown in Figure 6-12, to modify the format and appearance of a split form and all other form types.

Figure 6-12 | **Layout view options on the Format tab**

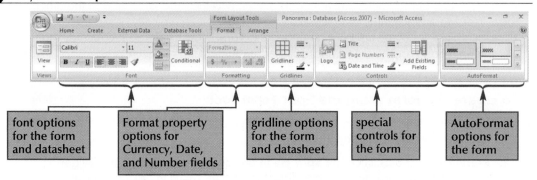

For a split form, some options on the Format tab apply to the form or the datasheet, other options apply to only the form, and the Add Existing Fields in the Controls group applies to both the form and the datasheet at the same time, as described in Figure 6-13.

Figure 6-13 | **Layout view options on the Format tab for a form and datasheet**

Group	Form Is Active	Datasheet Is Active
Font	Selected option applied to the selected labels and text boxes.	Selected option applied to every field value in the datasheet.
Formatting	Selected option applied to the selected text box, which must be a Currency, Date, or Number field.	Selected option applied to every field value in the active column, which must be a Currency, Date, or Number field.
Gridlines	Selected option applied to every label and text box in the form.	Only the options in the Gridlines list apply to the entire datasheet.
Controls	All options applied only to the form, except for the Add Existing Fields button, which applies to both the form and the datasheet.	Options do not apply in a datasheet, except for the Add Existing Fields button, which applies to both the form and the datasheet.
AutoFormat	Selected choice applied only to the form.	Not available.

Before selecting an option from the Format tab, you need to decide whether you want to modify the form or the datasheet, and then click in that object to select the object. Clicking anywhere in a datasheet selects the datasheet and also selects the column and the record you clicked. Clicking anywhere in a form selects the form. For controls in a form, you click a control to select it. To select several controls in a form, press and hold down the Shift key while clicking each control; a thicker, colored border appears around the selected controls. An option you choose from a group on the Format tab applies to all selected controls.

In previous tutorials, you've shown Sarah how to use some of the form modification options on the Format tab, and you'll use other options on this tab later in this tutorial, so you won't show her any Format tab options now. Instead, you'll show her some options on the Arrange tab. For a split form, options on the Arrange tab apply only to the form and do not apply to the datasheet.

To modify the form in Layout view:

▶ **1.** Click the **Arrange** tab on the Ribbon.

The form's label and text box controls for the fields from the tblContract table are grouped in a control layout. A **control layout** is a set of controls grouped together in a form or report, so that you can manipulate the set as a single control. For example, you can move and resize all the controls in a control layout as a group—moving or resizing one control in the control layout moves or resizes all controls in the control layout. You also can rearrange fields and their attached labels within the control layout.

All the text boxes in the control layout are the same width. The first five text boxes—from the ContractNum text box to the StartDate text box—are much wider than necessary. However, if you reduce the width of any text box in a control layout, all text boxes in the control layout are also resized. Sarah wants you to reduce the width of the first five text boxes and to move and resize the ContractType label and text box.

▶ **2.** Click the **layout selector** ⊞, which is located at the top-left corner of the Contract Num label, to select the entire control layout. An orange outline, which identifies the controls that you've selected, appears around the labels and text boxes in the form. See Figure 6-14.

Control layout selected in the form ◀ **Figure 6-14**

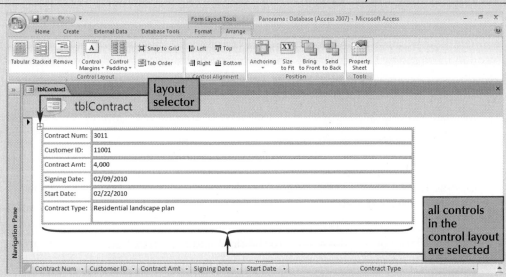

Next, you'll resize the text boxes in the control layout.

▶ **3.** Click the **ContractNum** text box (the text box that contains the value 3011) to deselect the control layout and select the ContractNum text box, hold down the **Shift** key, click each of the five text boxes below the ContractNum text box, and then release the **Shift** key to select all six text boxes in the control layout. When you resize one of the text boxes, all six selected text boxes will be resized equally.

4. Position the pointer on the right edge of the SigningDate text box until the pointer changes to a ↔ shape, click and drag to the left until the right edge is just to the right of the SigningDate field value, and then release the mouse button. You've resized all six text boxes. See Figure 6-15.

Figure 6-15 **After resizing the text boxes in the control layout**

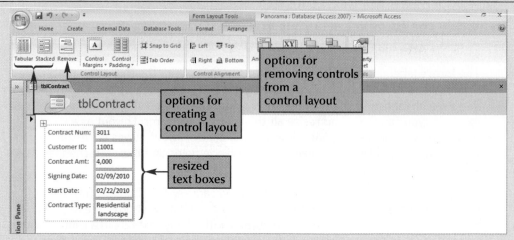

Trouble? If you resize the text boxes too far to the left, number signs appear inside the SigningDate and StartDate text boxes. Drag the right edge of the text boxes slightly to the right and repeat the process until the date values are visible inside the text boxes.

The control layout for the form is a **stacked layout**, which arranges text box controls vertically with a label to the left of each control; you click the Stacked button in the Control Layout group to place selected controls in a stacked layout. You can also choose a **tabular layout**, which arranges text box controls in a datasheet format with labels above each column; you click the Tabular button in the Control Layout group to place selected controls in a tabular layout.

You can now remove the ContractType text box and its label from the stacked layout, move the two controls, and then resize the text box.

5. Click the **ContractType** text box, and then in the Control Layout group, click the **Remove** button. An orange outline appears around the ContractType text box and its label, indicating that the two controls have been removed from the stacked layout.

6. Make sure that the ContractType text box and its label are selected, and then drag the two controls up and to the right until their tops are aligned with the top of the ContractNum controls. See Figure 6-16. (*Note:* You will resize the ContractType text box in the next step.)

7. Click the **ContractType** text box so that it's the only selected control, and then drag the right edge of the control to the right and the bottom edge of the control down to the positions shown in Figure 6-16.

After moving and resizing the ContractType controls ◀ Figure 6-16

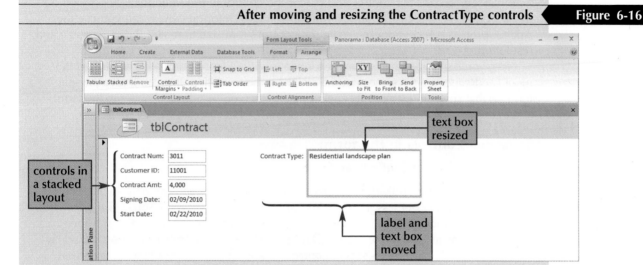

Trouble? It won't cause any problems if the two ContractType controls on your screen are in slightly different positions than the ones shown in the figure or your ContractType text box is not exactly the same size.

You do not usually need to change the default settings for the **Control Margins property**, which controls the spacing around the text inside a control, and the **Control Padding property**, which controls the spacing around the outside of a control. However, you'll show Sarah the effects of changing these properties.

▶ **8.** Click one of the controls in the stacked layout, click the **layout selector** ⊞ to select all controls in the stacked layout, click the **Control Margins** button in the Control Layout group, and then click **Medium**. The text inside the stacked layout controls moves down and to the right.

▶ **9.** Click the **Control Margins** button, click **Wide** and observe the effect of this setting on the text inside the controls, click the **Control Margins** button, click **None** and observe the effect of this setting, click the **Control Margins** button, and then click **Narrow**. Narrow is the default setting for the Control Margins property.

Narrow is also the default setting for the Control Padding property.

▶ **10.** In the Control Layout group, click the **Control Padding** button, click **Medium** and observe the change to the spacing around the controls, and then repeat for the other settings of this property, making sure you set the property to **Narrow** as your final step.

Next, you'll show Sarah how to anchor controls.

Anchoring Controls in a Form

You can design attractive forms that use the screen dimensions effectively when all the users of a database have the same sized monitors and use the same screen resolution. How do you design attractive forms when users have a variety of monitor sizes and screen resolutions? If you design a form to fit on large monitors using high screen resolutions, then only a portion of the controls in the form fit on smaller monitors with lower resolutions, forcing users to scroll the form. If you design a form to fit on small monitors with low screen resolutions, then the form is displayed on larger monitors in a small area in the upper-left corner of the screen, making the form look unattractively cramped. As a compromise, you can anchor the controls in the form. The **Anchor property** for a control automatically resizes the control and places the control in the same relative position on the screen as the screen size and resolution change. Unfortunately, when you use the Anchor property, Access doesn't scale the control's font size to match the screen size and resolution.

Next, you'll show Sarah how to anchor controls in a form. Because all monitors at Belmont Landscapes are the same size and use the same resolution, first you'll save the split form, so that you can demonstrate anchoring and then discard those changes to the form.

To anchor controls in the form:

▶ 1. Save the form as **frmContractSplit**.

You can't anchor individual controls in a control layout; you can only anchor the entire control layout as a group. You've already removed the ContractType controls from the stacked layout, so you can anchor them separately from the stacked layout. You'll remove the SigningDate and StartDate controls from the stacked layout, so you'll have three sets of controls to anchor—the stacked layout is one set, the ContractType controls are in the second set, and the SigningDate and StartDate controls make up the third set.

▶ 2. Use **Shift + Click** to select the **SigningDate** and **StartDate** text boxes, and then click the **Remove** button in the Control Layout group to remove these two controls and their labels from the stacked layout.

First, you'll anchor the selected SigningDate and StartDate controls.

▶ 3. In the Position group on the Arrange tab, click the **Anchoring** button to open the Anchoring gallery. See Figure 6-17.

| Figure 6-17 | Displaying the Anchoring gallery |

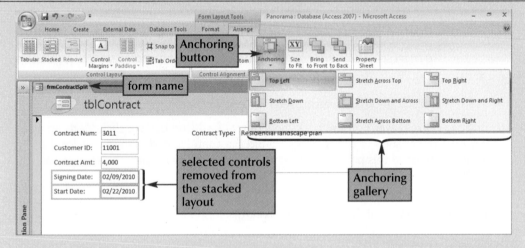

Four of the nine options in the Anchoring gallery fix the position of the selected controls in the top left (the default setting), bottom left, top right, or bottom right positions in the form. If other controls block the corner positions for controls you're anchoring for the first time, the new controls are positioned in relation to the blocking controls. The other five anchoring options resize, or stretch, and position the selected controls.

You'll anchor the SigningDate and StartDate controls in the bottom left and the ContractType controls in the top right.

4. Click **Bottom Left** in the Anchoring gallery, click the **ContractType** text box, click the **Anchoring** button, and then click **Top Right**. The SigningDate and StartDate controls shifted down, and the ContractType controls shifted to the right.

Next, you'll open the Navigation Pane, and then increase the height of the form to simulate the effect of a larger screen for the form.

5. Open the Navigation Pane. The two sets of controls on the left shift to the right, because the horizontal dimensions of the form decreased from the left, and these two sets of controls are anchored to the left in the form. The ContractType controls remain in the same position in the form.

6. Position the pointer on the border between the form and the datasheet until the pointer changes to a ╪ shape, and then drag down until you see only the column headings and the first row in the datasheet. The bottom set of controls shifts down, because it's anchored to the bottom, and the two sets of controls at the top remain in the same positions in the form. See Figure 6-18.

Anchored controls in a resized form | **Figure 6-18**

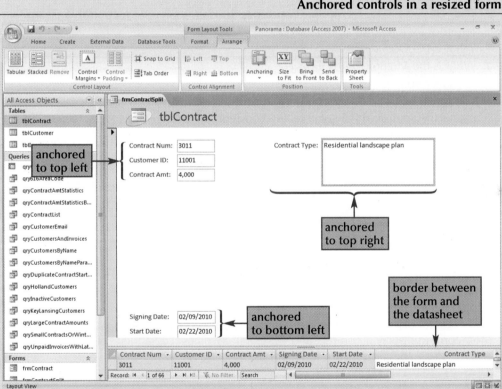

Finally, you'll show Sarah one of the anchoring options that resizes the ContractType text box as the form dimensions change.

7. Click the **ContractType** text box, click the **Anchoring** button, and then click **Stretch Down and Right**. Because the ContractType text box is already anchored to the top right, it can't stretch any more to the right, but it does stretch down to increase the height of the text box.

8. Position the pointer on the border between the form and the datasheet until the pointer changes to a ╪ shape, and then drag up until you can see several rows in the datasheet. The bottom set of controls shifts up, and the bottom edge of the ContractType text box shifts up, reducing its height.

You've finished showing Sarah Layout view changes to the split form, so you can close the form without saving the anchoring changes.

▶ **9.** Close the frmContractSplit form without saving your design changes.

▶ **10.** If you are not continuing on to the next session, close the Panorama database, and then exit Access.

You've used form wizards and form tools to create forms, and you've modified forms in Layout view. In the next session, you will continue your work with forms, concentrating on the techniques, tools, and options available in Design view.

Review | **Session 6.1 Quick Check**

1. According to the form design guidelines, which object(s) should you use to perform all database updates?
2. The _____ property specifies the data source for a control in a form or report or for a field in a table or query.
3. What is the Documenter?
4. What is the Multiple Items tool?
5. What is a split form?
6. The _____ property for a control automatically resizes the control and places the control in the same relative position on the screen as the screen's size and resolution change.

Session 6.2

Planning and Designing a Custom Form

Sarah needs a form to enter and view information about Belmont Landscapes' contracts and their related invoices. She wants the information in a single form, and she asks Lucia to design a form for her review.

After several discussions with Sarah and her staff, Lucia prepared a paper design for a custom form to display a contract and its related invoices. Lucia then used her paper design to create the form shown in Figure 6-19.

Lucia's design for the custom form ◄ Figure 6-19

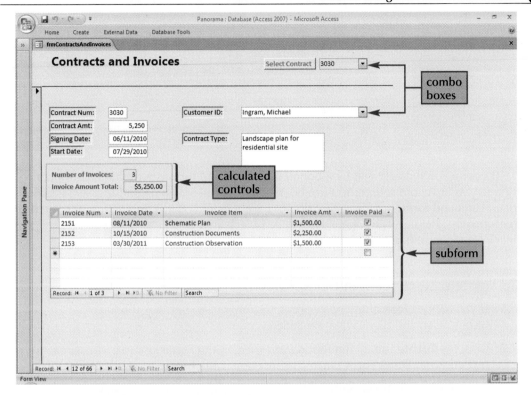

Notice that the top of the form displays a title and a combo box to select a contract record. Below these items are six field values with identifying labels from the tblContract table; these fields are the ContractNum, ContractAmt, SigningDate, StartDate, CustomerID, and ContractType fields. The CustomerID field is displayed in a combo box and the other field values are displayed in text boxes. The tblInvoice table fields appear in a subform, a separate form contained within another form. Unlike the tblContract table data, which displays identifying labels to the left of the field values in text boxes, the tblInvoice table data is displayed in datasheet format with identifying column headings above the field values. Finally, Number of Invoices and Invoice Amount Total in the main form display calculated controls based on the content of the subform.

Creating a Custom Form in Design View

To create Lucia's custom form, you could use the Form Wizard to create a basic version of the form and then customize it in Layout and Design views. However, to create Lucia's form, you would need to make many modifications to a basic form created by a wizard, so you will create the form directly in Design view. Creating forms in Design view is easy once you've done one form, and Design view allows you more control, precision, and options than creating forms in Layout view. You'll also find that you'll create forms more productively if you switch between Design view and Layout view, because some design modifications are easier to make in one of the two views than in the other view.

The Form Window in Design View

You use the Form window in Design view to create and modify forms. To create the custom form based on Lucia's design, you'll create a blank form, add the fields from the tblContract and tblInvoice tables, and then add other controls and make other form modifications.

Reference Window | **Creating a Form in Design View**

- Click the Create tab on the Ribbon.
- In the Forms group, click the Blank Form button.
- Click the Design View button on the status bar.
- Make sure the Field List pane is open, and then add the required fields to the form.
- Add other required controls to the form.
- Modify the size, position, and other properties as necessary for the fields and other controls in the form.
- Save the form.

The form you'll create will be a bound form. A **bound form** is a form that has a table or query as its record source. You use bound forms for maintaining and displaying table data. **Unbound forms** are forms that do not have a record source and are usually used for forms that help users navigate among the objects in a database. Now you'll create a blank bound form based on the tblContract table.

To create a blank form in Design view:

▶ 1. If you took a break after the previous session, make sure that the Panorama database is open and the Navigation Pane is open.

▶ 2. Click the **Create** tab on the Ribbon and then, in the Forms group on the Create tab, click the **Blank Form** button. Access opens the Form window in Layout view.

▶ 3. Click the **Design View** button on the status bar to switch to Design view, and then close the Navigation Pane. See Figure 6-20.

Figure 6-20 ▶ **Blank form in Design view**

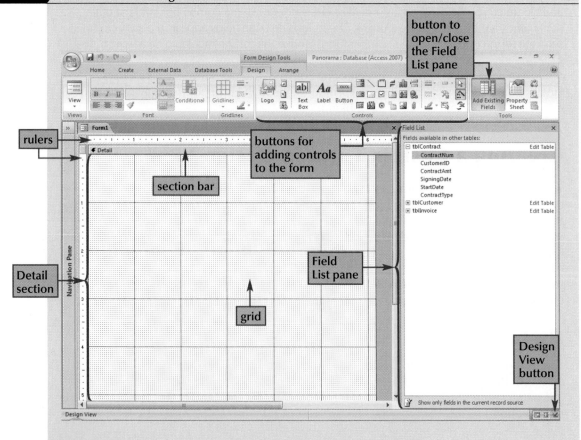

Trouble? If the Field List pane displays the "No fields available to be added to the current view" message, click the "Show all tables" link to display the tables in the Panorama database, and then click the plus sign next to tblContract in the Field List pane to display the fields in the table.

Trouble? If the tblContract table in the Field List pane is not expanded to show the fields in the table, click the plus sign next to tblContract to display the fields.

Design view contains the tools necessary to create a custom form. You create the form by placing controls in the blank form. You can place three kinds of controls in a form:

- A **bound control** is connected, or bound, to a field in the database based on the record source, or the underlying table or query. You use bound controls to display and maintain table field values.
- An **unbound control** is not connected to a field in the database. You use unbound controls to display text, such as a form title or instructions; to display lines, rectangles, and other objects; or to display graphics and pictures created using other software programs. An unbound control that displays text is called a **label**.
- A **calculated control** displays a value that is the result of an expression. The expression usually contains one or more fields, and the calculated control is recalculated each time any value in the expression changes.

To create a bound control, you add fields from the Field List pane to the Form window, and position the bound controls where you want them to appear in the form. To place other controls in a form or a report, you use the buttons in the Controls group on the Design tab; ScreenTips are available for each control in the Controls group. The buttons in the Controls group let you add to the form controls such as lines, rectangles, images, buttons, check boxes, and list boxes.

Design view for a form contains a **Detail section**, which is a rectangular area consisting of a grid with a section bar above the grid. You click the **section bar** to select the section in preparation for setting properties for the entire section. The **grid** consists of the area with dotted and solid lines that help you position controls precisely in a form. In the Detail section, you place bound controls, unbound controls, and calculated controls for your form. You can change the size of the Detail section by dragging its edges.

Rulers at the top and left edges of the Detail section define the horizontal and vertical dimensions of the form and serve as guides for placing controls in a form.

Your first task is to add bound controls to the Detail section for the six fields from the tblContract table.

Adding Fields to a Form

When you add a bound control to a form, Access adds a text box and, to its left, an attached label. The text box displays a field value from the record source. The attached label displays either the Caption property value for the field, if the Caption property value has been set, or the field name. To create a bound control, you first display the Field List pane by clicking the Add Existing Fields button in the Tools group on the Design tab. Then you double-click a field in the Field List pane to add the bound control to the Detail section. You can also drag a field from the Field List pane to the Detail section.

Next, you'll add bound controls to the Detail section for the six fields in the Field List pane. The Field List pane displays the three tables in the Panorama database, and the six fields in the tblContract table.

To add bound controls from the tblContract table to the grid:

▶ **1.** Double-click **ContractNum** in the Field List pane. Access adds a bound control in the Detail section of the form, removes the tblCustomer and tblInvoice tables from the "Fields available for this view" section of the Field List pane, and places the two tables in the "Fields available in related tables" section of the Field List pane.

▶ **2.** Repeat Step 1 for the **ContractAmt**, **SigningDate**, **StartDate**, **CustomerID**, and **ContractType** fields, in this order, in the Field List pane. Six bound controls—one for each of the six fields in the Field List pane—have been added in the Detail section of the form. See Figure 6-21.

Figure 6-21	Adding text boxes and attached labels as bound controls to a form

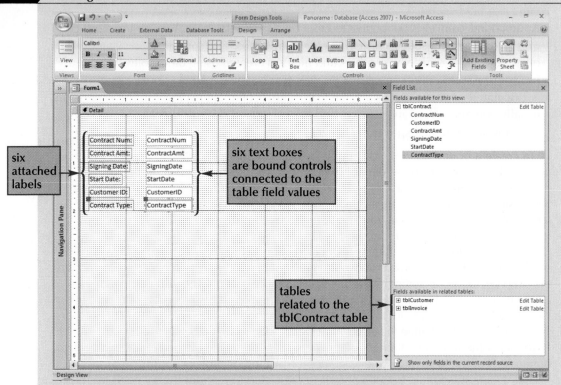

You should periodically save your work as you create a form, so you'll now save the form.

▶ **3.** Click the **Save** button 🖫 on the Quick Access Toolbar. The Save As dialog box opens.

▶ **4.** With the default name Form1 selected in the Form Name text box, type **frmContractsAndInvoices**, and then press the **Enter** key. The tab for the form now displays the form name, and the form design is saved in the Panorama database.

You've added the fields you need to the grid, so you can close the Field List pane.

▶ **5.** In the Tools group on the Design tab, click the **Add Existing Fields** button to close the Field List pane.

Creating and modifying a form in Design view might seem awkward at first. With practice you will become comfortable working with custom forms.

To design a form productively, you should keep in mind the following suggestions:

- You can click the Undo button one or more times immediately after you make one or more errors or make undesired form adjustments.
- You should back up your database frequently, especially before you create new objects or customize existing objects. If you run into difficulty, you can revert to your most recent backup copy of the database.
- You should save your form after you've completed a portion of your work successfully and before you need to perform steps you've never done before. If you're not satisfied with subsequent steps, close the form without saving the changes you made since your last save, and then open the form and perform the steps again.
- You can always close the form, make a copy of the form in the Navigation Pane, and practice with the copy.
- Adding controls, setting properties, and performing other tasks in Access in the correct way should work all the time with consistent results, but in rare instances, you might find a feature doesn't work properly. If a feature you've used succesfully doesn't work suddenly, you should save your work, close the database, make a backup copy of the database, open the database, and then compact and repair the database. Performing a compact and repair resolves most of these types of problems.

Compare your form's Detail section with Sarah's design, and notice that you need to move the ContractType bound control up and to the right. To do so, you must select and move the bound control.

Selecting, Moving, and Aligning Controls

Six text boxes now appear in the form's Detail section, one below the other. Each text box is a bound control connected to a field in the underlying table. Each text box has an attached label to its left. Each text box and attached label pair is a control in the form, and each individual text box is also a control in the form, as is each individual label. When you select a control, the control becomes outlined in orange, and eight squares, called handles, appear on its four corners and at the midpoints of its four edges. The larger handle in a control's upper-left corner is its **move handle**, which you use to move the control. You use the other seven handles, called **sizing handles**, to resize the control. When you work in Design view, controls you place in the form do not become part of a control layout, so you can individually select, move, resize, and otherwise manipulate one control without also changing the other controls. However, at any time you can select a group of controls and place them in a control layout—either a stacked layout or a tabular layout.

Reference Window | **Selecting and Moving Controls**

- Click the control to select it. To select several controls at once, press and hold down the Shift key while clicking each control. Handles appear around all selected controls.
- To move a single selected control, drag the control's move handle, which is the handle in the upper-left corner, to its new position.
- To move a group of selected controls, point to any selected control until the pointer changes to a move pointer, and then drag the group of selected controls to its new position.
- To move selected controls in small increments, press the appropriate arrow key.
- To move selected controls to the next nearest grid dot, hold down the Ctrl key and press the appropriate arrow key.

Based on Lucia's design for the custom form, you must select the ContractType bound control and move it up and to the right in the Detail section. The ContractType bound control consists of a field-value text box, labeled ContractType, and an attached label, labeled Contract Type, to its left.

To select the ContractType bound control:

1. If necessary, click the **ContractType** text box to select it. Move handles, which are the larger handles, appear on the upper-left corners of the selected text box control and its attached label. Sizing handles also appear, but only on the text box. See Figure 6-22.

| Figure 6-22 | Selecting the ContractType bound control |

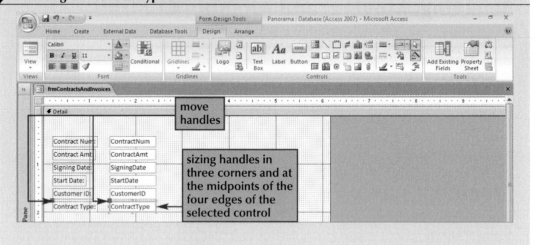

You can move a text box and its attached label together. To move them, place the pointer anywhere on the border of the text box, but not on a move handle or a sizing handle. When the pointer changes to a ⌖ shape, you can drag the text box and its attached label to the new location. As you move a control, an outline of the control moves on the rulers to indicate the current position of the control as you drag it. To move a group of selected controls, point to any selected control until the pointer changes to a ⌖ shape, and then drag the group of selected controls to its new position. You can move controls with more precision when you use the arrow keys instead of the mouse. To move selected controls in small increments, press the appropriate arrow key. To move selected controls to the next nearest grid dot, hold down the Ctrl key and press the appropriate arrow key.

You can also move either a text box or its label individually. If you want to move the text box but not its label, for example, place the pointer on the text box's move handle. When the pointer changes to a 🖑 shape, drag the text box to the new location. You use the label's move handle in a similar way to move only the label.

You'll now arrange the controls to match Lucia's design.

To move the ContractType bound control:

▶ **1.** Position the pointer on one of the edges of the ContractType text box, but not on a move handle or a sizing handle. When the pointer changes to a 🖑 shape, drag the control to the right until the left edge of the highlight on the horizontal ruler is at the 3-inch mark, drag the control up until the top of the highlight on the vertical ruler is just below the top of the SigningDate bound control, and then release the mouse button. See Figure 6-23.

After moving the ContractType bound control | Figure 6-23

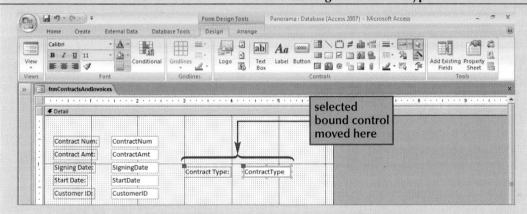

Trouble? If you need to make major adjustments to the placement of the ContractType bound control, click the Undo button on the Quick Access Toolbar one or more times until the bound control is back to its starting position, and then repeat Step 1. If you need to make minor adjustments to the placement of the ContractType bound control, use the arrow keys.

Now you need to align the ContractType and SigningDate bound controls on their top edges. If you've selected a column of controls, you can align the left edges or the right edges of the controls. If you've selected a row of controls, you can align the top edges or the bottom edges of the controls. A fifth alignment option, To Grid, aligns selected controls with the dots in the grid. You can find the five alignment options on the Arrange tab of the Ribbon or on the shortcut menu. You'll use the shortcut menu to align the two bound controls. Then you'll save the modified form and review your work in Form view.

To align the ContractType and SigningDate bound controls:

▶ **1.** Make sure the ContractType bound control is selected, hold down the **Shift** key, click the **Contract Type** label, click the **SigningDate** text box, click the **Signing Date** label, and then release the **Shift** key. This action selects the four controls; each selected control has an orange border.

▶ **2.** Right-click one of the selected controls, point to **Align** on the shortcut menu, and then click **Top**. The four selected controls are aligned on their top edges. See Figure 6-24.

Figure 6-24 — After top-aligning four controls in the Detail section

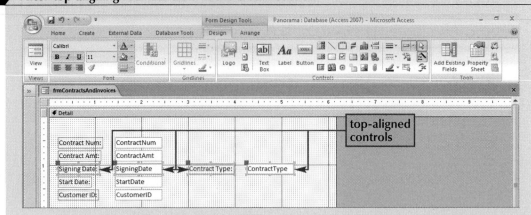

As you create a form, you should periodically save your modifications to the form and review your progress in Form view.

3. Save your form design changes, and then switch to Form view. See Figure 6-25.

Figure 6-25 — Form displayed in Form view

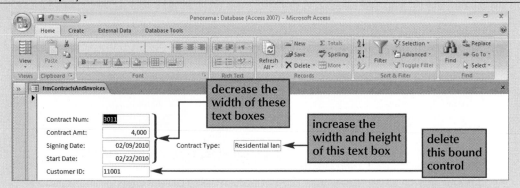

The value in the ContractType text box is not fully displayed, so you need to increase the size of the text box. The widths of the other four text boxes are wider than necessary, so you'll reduce their widths. Also, the CustomerID bound control consists of a label and a text box, but the plan for the form shows a combo box for the CustomerID positioned above the ContractType bound control. You'll delete the CustomerID bound control in preparation for adding it to the form as a combo box.

Resizing and Deleting Controls

A selected control displays seven sizing handles: four at the midpoints on each edge of the control and one at each corner except the upper-left corner. Recall that the upper-left corner displays the move handle. Positioning the pointer over a sizing handle changes the pointer to a two-headed arrow; the directions in which the arrows point indicate in which direction you can resize the selected control. When you drag a sizing handle, you resize the control. As you resize the control, a thin line appears inside the sizing handle to guide you in completing the task accurately, as do the outlines that appear on the horizontal and vertical rulers.

Resizing a Control | Reference Window

- Click the control to select it and display the sizing handles.
- Place the pointer over the sizing handle you want, and then drag the edge of the control until it is the size you want.
- To resize selected controls in small increments, hold down the Shift key and press the appropriate arrow key. This technique applies the resizing to the right edge and the bottom edge of the control.

You'll begin by deleting the CustomerID bound control. Then you'll resize the ContractType text box, which is too narrow and too short to display ContractType field values. Then you'll resize the remaining four text boxes to reduce their widths.

To delete a bound control and resize the text boxes:

▶ **1.** Switch to Design view, click an unused portion of the grid to deselect all controls, and then click the **CustomerID** text box to select it.

▶ **2.** Right-click the **CustomerID** text box to open the shortcut menu, and then click **Delete**. The label and the text box for the CustomerID bound control are deleted.

▶ **3.** Click the **ContractType** text box to select it.

▶ **4.** Place the pointer on the middle-right handle of the ContractType text box. When the pointer changes to a ↔ shape, drag the right border horizontally to the right to the 6-inch mark on the horizontal ruler.

▶ **5.** Place the pointer on the middle-bottom handle of the ContractType text box. When the pointer changes to a ↕ shape, drag the bottom border down to the 1.75-inch mark on the vertical ruler. See Figure 6-26.

> **Tip**
>
> If you want to delete a label but not its associated text box, right-click the label, and then click Delete on the shortcut menu.

After resizing the ContractType text box | **Figure 6-26**

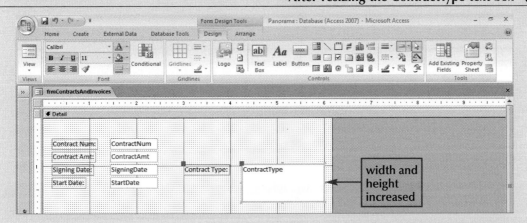

Resizing controls in Design view is a trial-and-error process, in which you resize a control in Design view, switch to Form view to observe the effect of the resizing, switch back to Design view to make further refinements to the control's size, and continue until the control is sized correctly. It's easier to resize controls in Layout view, because you can see actual field values while you resize the controls. You'll resize the other four text boxes in Layout view.

6. Switch to Layout view, and then click the **ContractNum** text box (if necessary) to select it.

7. Position the pointer on the right edge of the **ContractNum** text box. When the pointer changes to a ↔ shape, drag the right border horizontally to the left until the text box is slightly wider than the field value it contains. See Figure 6-27.

The sizes of the ContractAmt, SigningDate, and StartDate text boxes will look fine if you reduce them to have the same widths, so you'll select all three text boxes and resize them as a group.

8. Select the **ContractAmt**, **SigningDate**, and **StartDate** text boxes.

9. Position the pointer on the right edge of any of the three selected controls. When the pointer changes to a ↔ shape, drag the right border horizontally to the left until the SigningDate and StartDate text boxes are slightly wider than the field values they contain. See Figure 6-27.

Tip

If you select a control by mistake, hold down the Shift key, and then click the selected control to deselect it.

Figure 6-27 | After resizing text boxes in Layout view

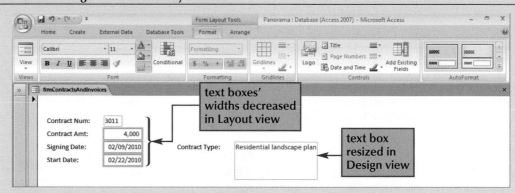

Trouble? If you resized the text boxes too far to the left, number signs will be displayed inside the SigningDate and StartDate text boxes. Drag the right edge of the text boxes slightly to the right and repeat the process until the date values are visible inside the text boxes.

10. Navigate through the first several records to make sure the five text boxes are sized properly to display the full field values. If any text box is too small, select the text box and increase its width the appropriate amount.

11. Save your form design changes, switch to Design view, and then deselect all controls by clicking in an unused portion of the grid.

InSight | Making Form Design Modifications

When you design forms and other objects, you'll find it helpful to switch frequently between Design view and Layout view. Some form modifications are easier to make in Layout view, other form modifications are easier to make in Design view, and still other form modifications can be made only in Design view. You should check your progress frequently in either Layout view or Form view, and you should save your modifications after completing a set of changes successfully.

Recall that you removed the lookup feature from the CustomerID field because a combo box provides the same lookup capability in a form. Next, you'll add a combo box for the CustomerID field to the custom form.

Adding a Combo Box to a Form

The tblCustomer and tblContract tables are related in a one-to-many relationship. The CustomerID field in the tblContract table is a foreign key to the tblCustomer table, and you can use a combo box in the custom form to view and maintain CustomerID field values more easily and accurately than using a text box. Recall that a combo box is a control that provides the features of a text box and a list box; you can choose a value from the list or type an entry.

You use the **Combo Box tool** in Design view to add a combo box to a form. If you want help when adding the combo box, you can select one of the Access Control Wizards. A **Control Wizard** asks a series of questions and then uses your answers to create a control in a form or report. Access offers Control Wizards for the Combo Box, List Box, Option Group, Command Button, Subform/Subreport, and other control tools.

You will use the Combo Box Wizard to add a combo box to the form for the CustomerID field.

To add a combo box to the form:

▶ **1.** In the Controls group on the Design tab, make sure the Use Control Wizards button ⬛ is selected.

▶ **2.** In the Controls group on the Design tab, click the **Combo Box** button 🔲 (with the ScreenTip "Combo Box (Form Control)"). After you click the Combo Box tool or most other tools in the Controls group, nothing happens until you move the pointer over the form. When you move the pointer over the form, the pointer changes to a shape that is unique for the tool with a plus symbol in its upper-left corner. You position the plus symbol in the location where you want to place the upper-left corner of the control.

You'll place the combo box near the top of the form above the ContractType bound control, and then position it more precisely after you've finished the wizard.

▶ **3.** Position the + portion of the pointer three grid dots from the top of the grid and at the 4-inch mark on the horizontal ruler, and then click the mouse button. Access places a combo box control in the form and opens the first Combo Box Wizard dialog box.

You can use an existing table or query as the source for a new combo box or type the values for the combo box. In this case, you'll use the qryCustomersByName query as the basis for the new combo box. This query includes the Customer calculated field, whose value equals the Company field value, if it's nonnull, or the concatenation of the LastName and FirstName field values in all other cases.

▶ **4.** Click the **I want the combo box to look up the values in a table or query** option button (if necessary), click the **Next** button to open the next Combo Box Wizard dialog box, click the **Queries** option button in the View group, click **Query: qryCustomersByName**, and then click the **Next** button. Access opens the third Combo Box Wizard dialog box. This dialog box lets you select the fields from the query to appear as columns in the combo box. You'll select the first two fields.

▶ **5.** Double-click **Customer** to move this field to the Selected Fields list box, double-click **CustomerID**, and then click the **Next** button. This dialog box lets you choose a sort order for the combo box entries. Sarah wants the entries to appear in ascending Customer order.

▶ **6.** Click the **arrow** for the first list box, click **Customer**, and then click the **Next** button to open the next Combo Box Wizard dialog box.

▶ **7.** Resize the columns to their best fit, scrolling down the columns to make sure all values are visible and resizing again if they're not, and then click the **Next** button.

In this dialog box, you select the foreign key, which is the CustomerID field.

▶ **8.** Click **CustomerID** and then click the **Next** button.

In this dialog box, you specify the field in the tblContract table where you will store the selected CustomerID value from the combo box. You'll store the value in the CustomerID field in the tblContract table.

▶ **9.** Click the **Store that value in this field** option button, click its **arrow**, click **CustomerID**, and then click the **Next** button.

Trouble? If CustomerID doesn't appear in the list, click the Cancel button, press the Delete key to delete the combo box, click the Add Existing Fields button in the Tools group on the Ribbon, double-click CustomerID in the Field List pane, press the Delete key to delete CustomerID, close the Field List pane, and then repeat Steps 1-9.

In this dialog box, you specify the name for the combo box control. You'll use the field name of CustomerID.

▶ **10.** Type **CustomerID** and then click the **Finish** button. The completed CustomerID combo box appears in the form.

You need to position and resize the combo box control, but first you'll change the text for the attached label from CustomerID to Customer ID with a terminating colon to match the format used for other label controls in the form. To change the text for a label control, you set the control's **Caption property** value.

Reference Window | **Changing a Label's Caption**

- Right-click the label to select it and to display the shortcut menu, and then click Properties to display the property sheet.
- If necessary, click the All tab to display the All page in the property sheet.
- Edit the existing text in the Caption text box; or click the Caption text box and press the F2 key to select the current value, and then type a new caption.
- In the Tools group on the Design tab, click the Property Sheet button to close the property sheet.

Next, you'll change the text that appears in the combo box label.

To set the Caption property value for the Customer ID label:

▶ 1. Right-click the **Customer ID** label, which is the control to the left of the CustomerID text box, to select it and to display the shortcut menu, and then click **Properties** on the shortcut menu. The property sheet for the Customer ID label opens.

▶ 2. If necessary, click the **All** tab to display all properties for the selected Customer ID label.

   Trouble? If the Selection type entry below the Property Sheet title bar is not "Label," then you selected the wrong control in Step 1. Click the Customer ID label to change to the property sheet for this control.

▶ 3. Click before the "ID" in the Caption text box, press the **spacebar**, press the **End** key, type a colon, and then press the **Tab** key to move to the next property in the property sheet. The Caption property value should now be Customer ID: and the label for the CustomerID bound control now displays Customer ID:. See Figure 6-28.

Tip

After selecting a control, you can press the F4 key to open and close the property sheet for the control.

Tip

After you've set a property value, you won't see the effects of the new setting until you select another property in the property sheet, select another control in the form, or close the property sheet.

CustomerID combo box added to the form ◀ **Figure 6-28**

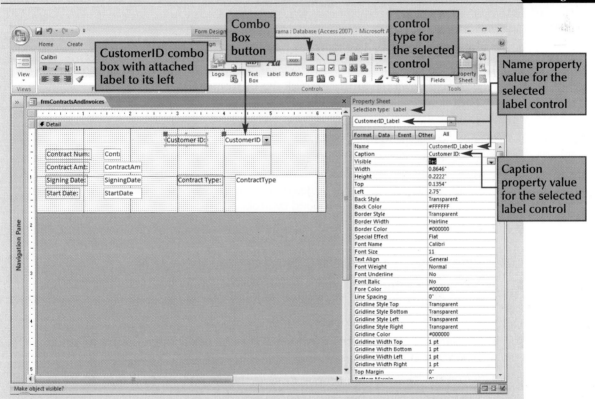

Trouble? Some property values in your property sheet, such as the Width and Top property values, might differ if your label's position slightly differs from the label position used as the basis for Figure 6-28. These differences cause no problems.

Tip

You should always check that the Selection type entry is the correct control type and the Control list box displays the correct name for the control whose properties you are changing.

The Selection type entry, which is the line below the property sheet title bar, displays the control type (Label in this case) for the selected control. Below the Selection type entry in the property sheet is the Control list box, which you can use to select another control in the form and then change its properties in the property sheet. Or you can simply click the control to change to its properties in the property sheet. The first property in the property sheet, the **Name property**, is the property that specifies the name of a control, section, or object (CustomerID_Label in this case). The Name property value is the same as the value displayed in the Control list box. For bound controls, the Name property value matches the field name. For unbound controls, Access sets the Name property to the control type (for example, Label) followed by a number (for example, Label2). For unbound controls, you can set the Name property to another, more meaningful value at any time.

▶ **4.** Close the property sheet, and then save your design changes.

Now that you've added the combo box to the form, you can view the form in Layout view, and then position the combo box and its attached label and resize the combo box. You'll need to view the form in Form view to determine any fine-tuning necessary for the width of the combo box.

To view and modify the combo box in Layout view:

▶ **1.** Switch to Layout view to view the form, and then click the **CustomerID** combo box, hold down the **Shift** key, click the **Customer ID** label, and then release the **Shift** key to select both controls.

First, you'll align the CustomerID combo box and its label with the ContractType and ContractNum bound controls. You'll move the selected controls to the right of the Contract Type label, align the Customer ID and Contract Type labels on their left edges, align the CustomerID and ContractType controls on their left edges, and then align the bottom edges of the combo box and its label with the bottom edges of the ContractNum bound control.

▶ **2.** Drag the selected controls to the right until the Customer ID label is approximately one inch to the right of the Contract Type label, making sure the two controls remain above the ContractNum bound control.

▶ **3.** Select the **Customer ID** label and the **Contract Type** label, click the **Arrange** tab on the Ribbon, and then in the Control Alignment group on the Arrange tab, click the **Left** button. The selected controls are aligned on their left edges.

▶ **4.** Repeat Step 3 to align the **CustomerID** combo box and the **ContractType** text boxes on their left edges.

▶ **5.** Select the **Contract Num** label, **ContractNum** text box, **Customer ID** label, and **CustomerID** combo box, and then in the Control Alignment group on the Arrange tab, click the **Bottom** button. The four selected controls are aligned on their bottom edges.

▶ **6.** Switch to Form view, and then click the **CustomerID** arrow to open the control's list box. See Figure 6-29.

CustomerID combo box in Form view ⟩ Figure 6-29

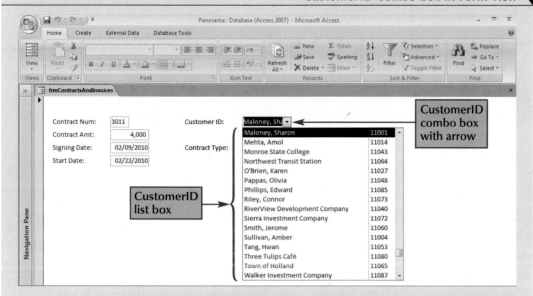

You need to widen the CustomerID combo box, so that the widest customer value in the list is displayed in the combo box. You can widen the combo box in Layout view or in Design view. Because Layout view displays live data, you'll use Layout view instead of Design view to make this change because you can determine the proper width more accurately in Layout view.

▶ **7.** Switch to Layout view, and then navigate to record 16. Weston Community Parks Foundation, which is the customer value for this record, is the widest value that is displayed in the combo box. You want to widen the combo box, so that the value in record 16 is completely visible.

▶ **8.** Make sure that only the combo box is selected, and then pointing to the right edge, widen the combo box until the entire customer value is visible. See Figure 6-30.

After resizing the CustomerID combo box in Layout view ⟩ Figure 6-30

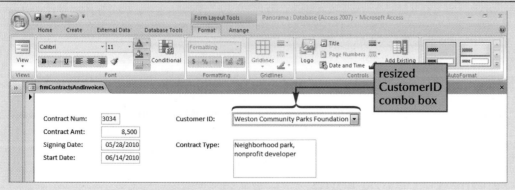

Now you'll add the title to the top of the form.

Using Form Headers and Form Footers

The **Form Header** and **Form Footer sections** let you add titles, instructions, command buttons, and other controls to the top and bottom of your form, respectively. Controls placed in the Form Header or Form Footer sections remain on the screen whenever the form is displayed in Form view or Layout view; they do not change when the contents of the Detail section change as you navigate from one record to another record.

To add either a form header or footer to your form, you must first add both the Form Header and Form Footer sections as a pair to the form. If your form needs one of these sections but not the other, you can remove a section by setting its height to zero, which is the same method you would use to remove any form section. You can also prevent a section from appearing in Form view or in Print Preview by setting its Visible property to No. The **Visible property** determines if Access displays a control or section. Set the Visible property to Yes to display the control or section, and set the Visible property to No to hide it.

You can add the Form Header and Form Footer sections as a pair to a form either directly or indirectly. The direct way to add these sections is to click the Form Header/Footer button in the Show/Hide group on the Arrange tab. This direct method is available only in Design view. The indirect way to add the Form Header and Form Footer sections in Layout view or Design view is to use one of these four buttons in the Controls group on the Design tab: the Logo button, the Title button, the Page Numbers button (Insert Page Number button in Design view), or the Date and Time button (Date & Time button in Design view). Clicking any of these four buttons causes Access to add the Form Header and Form Footer sections to the form and to place an appropriate control in the Form Header section. If you use the indirect method in Layout view, Access sets the Form Footer section's height to zero. In Design view, the indirect method creates a nonzero height Form Footer section. Note that the Page Numbers button is dimmed, and thus inactive, in Layout view. Many forms contain a title and possibly a picture, but forms rarely display a page number or the date and time, so an inactive Page Numbers button is not a problem, especially because you can add page numbers in Design view.

Tip

If you've set the Form Footer section's height to zero or set its Visible property to No and a future form design change makes adding controls to the Form Footer section necessary, you can restore the section by using the pointer to drag its bottom edge back down or by setting its Visible property to Yes.

Reference Window | Adding and Removing Form Header and Form Footer Sections

- In Design view, click the Form Header/Footer button in the Show/Hide group on the Arrange tab.

or

- In Layout view or Design view, click a button in the Controls group to add a logo, title, page numbers, or date and time to the form.
- To remove a Form Header or Form Footer section, drag its bottom edge up until the section area disappears or set the section's Visible property to No.

Lucia's design includes a title at the top of the form. Because the title will not change as you navigate through the form records, you will add the title to the Form Header section in the form.

Adding a Title to a Form

You'll add the title to Sarah's form in Layout view. When you add the title to the form in Layout view, Access adds the Form Header section to the form and places the title in the Form Header section. At the same time, Access adds the Page Footer section to the form and sets its height to zero.

To add a title to the form:

▶ 1. In the Controls group on the Format tab, click the **Title** button. Access adds the title to the form, displaying it in the upper-left corner of the form and using the form name as the title.

You need to change the title. Because the title is already selected, you can type over or edit the selected title.

▶ 2. Press the **Home** key to move to the start of the title, press the **Delete** key three times to delete the first three characters, click before the word "And," press the **spacebar**, type the letter **a**, press the **Delete** key, press the → key twice, press the **spacebar**, and then press the **Enter** key. You've changed the title to Contracts and Invoices. See Figure 6-31.

Title placed in the Form Header section ◀ Figure 6-31

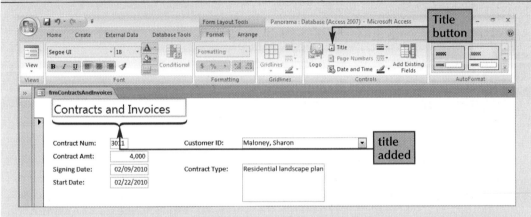

Sarah wants the title to be prominent in the form. The title is already a larger font size than the font used for the form's labels and text boxes, so you'll change the title's font weight to bold to increase its prominence.

▶ 3. Make sure the title control is still selected, and then in the Font group on the Format tab, click the **Bold** button **B**. The title is displayed in 18-point, bold text.

It is not obvious in Layout view that the title is displayed in the Form Header section, so you'll view the form design in Design view.

▶ 4. Switch to Design view, and then save your design changes. The title is displayed in the Form Header section. See Figure 6-32.

Tip

Keep in mind that a form's total height includes the heights of the Form Header, Detail, and Form Footer sections. If you set the form's total height to more than the screen size, users will need to use scroll bars to view the content of your form, which is less productive for users and isn't good form design.

Figure 6-32 | **Form Header and Form Footer sections in Design view**

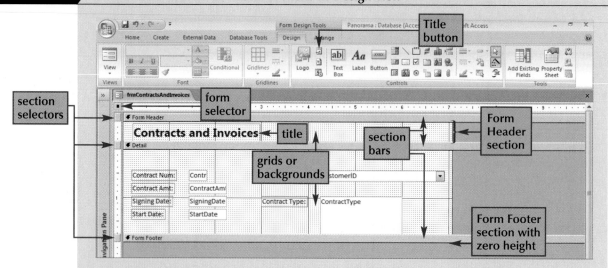

> **5.** If you are not continuing on to the next session, close the Panorama database, and then exit Access.

The form now contains a Form Header section that displays the title, a Detail section that displays the bound controls and combo box, and a Form Footer section that is set to a height of zero. Each section consists of a **section selector** and a section bar, either of which you can click to select and set properties for the entire section, and a grid or background, which is where you place controls that you want display in the form. The **form selector** is the selector at the intersection of the horizontal and vertical rulers; you click the form selector when you want to select the form and set its properties. The vertical ruler is segmented into sections for the Form Header section, the Detail section, and the Form Footer section.

So far, you've added controls to the form and modified the controls by selecting, moving, aligning, resizing, and deleting them. You've added and modified a combo box and added a title in the Form Header section. In the next session, you will continue your work with the custom form by adding a combo box to find records, adding a subform, adding calculated controls, changing form and section properties, and changing control properties.

| Review | **Session 6.2 Quick Check** |

1. What is a bound form, and when do you use bound forms?
2. What is the difference between a bound control and an unbound control?
3. The _____ consists of the dotted and solid lines that appear in the Detail section to help you position controls precisely in a form.
4. The handle in a selected object's upper-left corner is the _____ handle.
5. How do you move a selected text box and its label at the same time?
6. How do you resize a control?
7. A(n) _____ control provides the features of a text box and a list box.
8. How do you change a label's caption?
9. What is the Form Header section?

Session 6.3

Adding a Combo Box to Find Records

Most combo boxes, such as the CustomerID combo box, are used to display and update data. You can also use combo boxes to find records. You will add a combo box to the Form Header section to find a specific record in the tblContract table to display in the form.

You can use the Combo Box Wizard to add a combo box to find records in a form. However, the Combo Box Wizard provides this find option only if the form's record source is a table or query. You'll view the property sheet for the form to view the Record Source property, and you'll change the property setting, if necessary.

To add a combo box to find records to the form:

▶ **1.** If you took a break after the previous session, make sure that the Panorama database is open, the frmContractsAndInvoices form is open in Design view, and the Navigation Pane is closed.

▶ **2.** Click the **form selector** (located to the left of the horizontal ruler) to select the form, open the property sheet, and then click the **All** tab (if necessary). The property sheet displays the properties for the form. See Figure 6-33.

Property sheet settings for the form | Figure 6-33

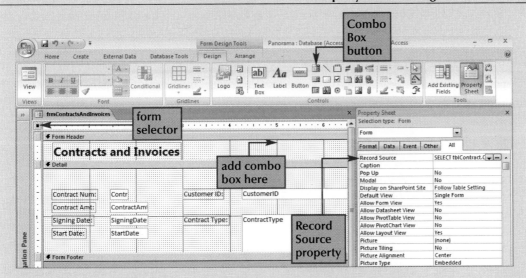

The Record Source property is set to an SQL SELECT statement. You need to change the Record Source property to a table or query, or the Combo Box Wizard will not present you with the option to find records in a form. You'll change the Record Source property to the tblContract table, because this table is the record source for all the bound controls you added to the Detail section.

▶ 3. Click the **Record Source** text box, press the **F2** key to select the entire property setting, type **tblContract**, and then close the property sheet.

You'll now use the Combo Box Wizard to add a combo box to the form's Form Header section to find a record in the tblContract table to display in the form.

▶ 4. In the Controls group on the Design tab, click the **Combo Box** button ▦ (with the ScreenTip "Combo Box (Form Control)"), position the + portion of the pointer at the top of the Form Header section and at the 5-inch mark on the horizontal ruler (see Figure 6-33), and then click the mouse button. Access places a combo box control in the form and opens the first Combo Box Wizard dialog box.

The dialog box now displays a third option to "Find a record on my form based on the value I selected in my combo box," which you'll use for this combo box. You choose the first option, which you used for the CustomerID combo box, when you want to select a value from a list of foreign key values from an existing table or query. You choose the second option when you want users to select a value from a short fixed list of values that don't change. For example, if Belmont Landscapes wanted to include a field in the tblCustomer table to classify each customer, you could use a combo box with this second option to display a list of values such as Residential, Commercial, Nonprofit, and Government.

▶ 5. Click the **Find a record on my form based on the value I selected in my combo box** option button, and then click the **Next** button to open the next dialog box. This dialog box lets you select the fields from the tblContract table to appear as columns in the combo box. You'll select the first field.

▶ 6. Double-click **ContractNum** to move this field to the Selected Fields list box, and then click the **Next** button.

▶ 7. The column is already resized properly, so click the **Next** button.

In this dialog box, you specify the name for the combo box's label. You'll use Select Contract as the label.

▶ 8. Type **Select Contract**, and then click the **Finish** button. The completed unbound combo box is displayed in the form. See Figure 6-34.

Figure 6-34   Unbound combo box added to the form

You'll align the right edges of the two combo boxes, move the attached label close to the combo box, and then align the bottoms of the combo box and its attached label with the bottom of the title in the Form Header section.

▶ **9.** Deselect all controls, select the two combo boxes (one in the Form Header section and the other in the Detail section), right-click one of the selected controls, point to **Align**, and then click **Right**. The two combo boxes are aligned on their right edges.

▶ **10.** Click the **Select Contract** label, point to the label's move handle, and then drag the label to the right until it is two grid dots to the left of the combo box.

▶ **11.** Select the combo box in the Form Header section, the **Select Contract** label, and the title, right-click one of the selected controls, point to **Align**, click **Bottom**, and then click the **Select Contract** label. The three controls are aligned on their bottom edges. See Figure 6-35.

After aligning the combo box and its label ◄ **Figure 6-35**

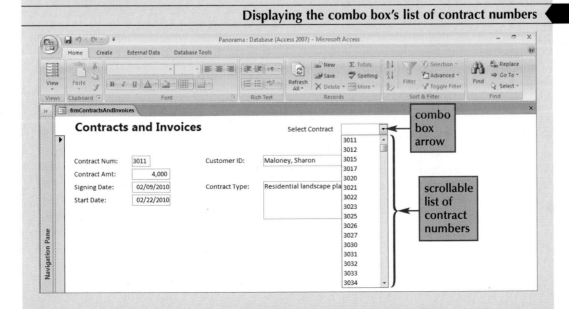

You'll save your form changes and view the new combo box in Form view.

To find contract records using the combo box:

▶ **1.** Save the form design changes, and then switch to Form view.

▶ **2.** Click the **Select Contract** combo box arrow to open the combo box's list box. See Figure 6-36.

Displaying the combo box's list of contract numbers ◄ **Figure 6-36**

▶ **3.** Scroll down the list, and then click **3073**. The current record changes from record 1 to record 41, which is the record for contract number 3073.

The form design is very plain at this point with no color, special effects, or visual contrast among the controls. Before making the form more attractive and useful, you'll add the remaining controls to the form: a subform and two calculated controls.

Adding a Subform to a Form

Lucia's design for the form includes a subform that displays the related invoices for the displayed contract. The form you've been creating is the main form for records from the primary tblContract table (the "one" side of the one-to-many relationship), and the subform will display records from the related tblInvoice table (the "many" side of the one-to-many relationship). You use the **Subform/Subreport tool** in Design view to add a subform to a form. You can add the subform on your own, or you can get help adding the subform by using the SubForm Wizard.

You will use the SubForm Wizard to add the subform for the Invoice table records to the bottom of the form. First, you'll increase the height of the Detail section to make room for the subform.

To add the subform to the form:

▶ **1.** Switch to Design view.

▶ **2.** Place the pointer on the bottom edge of the Detail section. When the pointer changes to a ➕ shape, drag the section's edge down until it is at the 4-inch mark on the vertical ruler.

▶ **3.** In the Controls group on the Design tab, make sure the Use Control Wizards tool ⚉ is selected.

▶ **4.** In the Controls group on the Design tab, click the **Subform/Subreport** button ⊞ .

▶ **5.** Position the + portion of the pointer in the Detail section at the 2.5-inch mark on the vertical ruler and at the 1-inch mark on the horizontal ruler, and then click the mouse button. Access places a subform control in the form's Detail section and opens the first SubForm Wizard dialog box.

You can use a table or query, or an existing form as the record source for a subform. In this case, you'll use the related tblInvoice table as the record source for a new subform.

To use the SubForm Wizard to add the subform to the form:

▶ **1.** Make sure the Use existing Tables and Queries option button is selected, and then click the **Next** button. Access opens the next SubForm Wizard dialog box, which lets you select a table or query as the record source for the subform and the fields from the selected table or query.

▶ **2.** Click the **Tables/Queries** arrow to display the list of tables and queries in the Panorama database, scroll to the top of the list box, and then click **Table: tblInvoice**. The Available Fields list box shows the fields in the tblInvoice table.

Tip

When you increase a section's height, you might need to go slightly beyond the desired ending position to expose the vertical ruler measurement, and then decrease the height back to the correct position.

Lucia's form design includes all fields from the tblInvoice table in the subform, except the ContractNum field, which is already placed in the Detail section of the form from the tblContract table.

▶ **3.** Click the >> button to move all available fields to the Selected Fields list box, click **ContractNum** in the Selected Fields list box, click the < button, and then click the **Next** button to open the next SubForm Wizard dialog box. See Figure 6-37.

Selecting the linking field | Figure 6-37

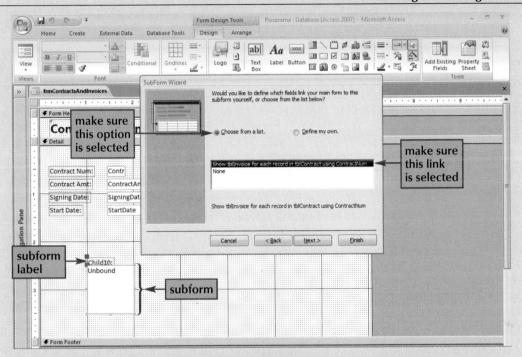

In this dialog box, you select the link between the primary tblContract table and the related tblInvoice table. The common field in the two tables, ContractNum, links the tables. Access uses the ContractNum field to display a record in the main form, which displays data from the primary tblContract table, and to select and display the related records for that contract in the subform, which displays data from the related tblInvoice table.

▶ **4.** Make sure the Choose from a list option button is selected and that the first link is highlighted, and then click the **Next** button. The next SubForm Wizard dialog box lets you specify a name for the subform.

▶ **5.** Type **frmInvoiceSubform** and then click the **Finish** button. Access increases the height and width of the subform in the form. The subform is where the related tblInvoice records will appear. The subform label appears above the subform and displays the subform name.

▶ **6.** Deselect all controls, save your form changes, switch to Form view, and then click the **ContractNum** text box to deselect the value. See Figure 6-38.

Figure 6-38 Viewing the subform in Form view

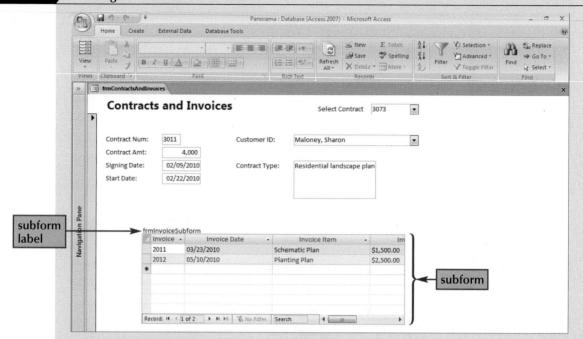

The subform displays the two invoices related to the first contract record for contract number 3011.

Trouble? If the size of the columns in your datasheet differs or the position of your subform is different, don't worry. You'll resize all columns to their best fit and move the subform later.

After viewing the form, Sarah identifies some modifications she wants you to make. The subform is not properly sized and the columns in the subform are not sized to their best fit. She wants you to resize the subform and its columns, so that all columns in the subform are entirely visible. Also, she asks you to delete the subform label, because the label is unnecessary for identifying the subform contents. You'll switch to Design view to make these changes.

To modify the subform's design:

▶ **1.** Switch to Design view. Notice that in Design view, the subform data does not appear in a datasheet format as it does in Form view. That difference causes no problem; you can ignore it.

First, you'll delete the subform label.

▶ **2.** Deselect all controls, right-click the subform label to open the shortcut menu (make sure no other controls have handles), and then click **Cut**.

Next, you'll open the subform in another window, and then resize the columns to their best fit in Datasheet view.

3. Move the pointer to the edge of the subform border, click the border's edge to select the subform (an orange border and handles appear on the subform's border when the subform is selected), position the pointer on the border and right-click the border when the pointer changes to a ⁑ shape, and then click **Subform in New Window** on the shortcut menu. The subform opens in Design view. You'll switch to Datasheet view to resize the columns to their best fit.

4. Switch to Datasheet view, and then resize all columns to their best fit, scrolling down the datasheet to resize the Invoice Item column again, as necessary.

5. Save your design changes, and then close the frmInvoiceSubform form.

Trouble? If the subform in the frmContractsAndInvoices form appears to be blank after you close the frmInvoiceSubform, don't worry. This is a temporary effect; the subform's controls do still exist.

Next, you'll move and resize the subform in Layout view, where you can more easily observe the effects of your changes.

6. Switch to Layout view, click the edge of the subform to select it, hold down the **Shift** key, click the **Start Date** label, and then release the **Shift** key. The subform and the Start Date label are selected, and you'll align the two controls on their left edges.

7. Click the **Arrange** tab on the Ribbon, and then in the Control Alignment group on the Arrange tab, click **Left**. The two controls are aligned on their left edges.

Next, you'll widen the subform on its right side.

8. Hold down the **Shift** key, click the **Start Date** label to deselect it, release the **Shift** key, leaving only the subform selected, and then drag the right edge of the subform to the right until all five datasheet columns are fully visible. See Figure 6-39.

| After moving and resizing the subform in Layout view | Figure 6-39 |

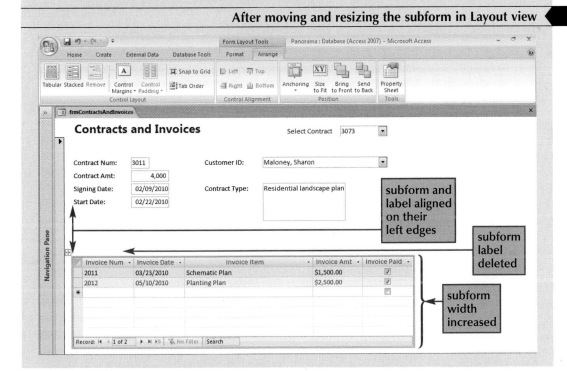

You've finished your work with the subform, and now you need to add two calculated controls to the main form. The first calculated control will display the number of invoices displayed in the subform, and the other will display the total of the invoice amounts displayed in the subform.

Displaying a Subform's Calculated Controls in the Main Form

For the invoices displayed in the subform, Lucia's form design includes calculated controls in the main form for the number of invoices and for the total of the invoice amounts for the related records displayed in the subform. To display these calculated controls in a form or report, you use the Count and Sum functions. The **Count function** determines the number of occurrences of an expression, and its general format as a control in a form or report is =Count(*expression*). The **Sum function** calculates the total of an expression, and its general format as a control in a form or report is =Sum(*expression*). The invoices and invoice amounts are displayed in the subform's Detail section, so you'll need to place calculated controls for the number of invoices and the total invoice amounts in the subform's Form Footer section. However, your design has these two calculated controls displayed in the main form, not in the subform. Fortunately, the subform appears in Datasheet view, and Form Headers and Footers do not appear in Datasheet view, so the subform's calculated controls will not appear in the subform. Although the calculated controls are not displayed in the subform, the calculations occur, and you can add calculated controls in the main form that reference the subform's calculated controls and display these values.

Adding Calculated Controls to a Subform's Form Footer Section

First, you'll open the subform in Design view in another window and add the calculated controls to the subform's Form Footer section.

To add calculated controls to the subform's Form Footer section:

▶ 1. Save your form design changes, switch to Design view, click the subform border to select the subform, right-click the border, and then click **Subform in New Window** on the shortcut menu. The subform opens in Design view. See Figure 6-40.

Figure 6-40 ▶ Subform in Design view

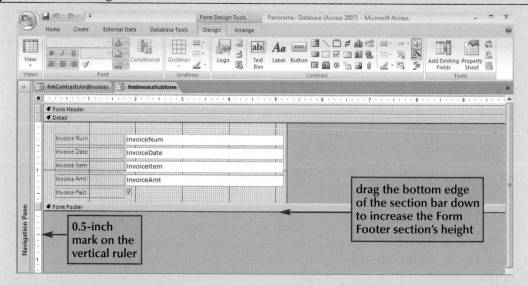

drag the bottom edge of the section bar down to increase the Form Footer section's height

0.5-inch mark on the vertical ruler

The subform's Detail section contains the tblInvoice table fields. As a subform in the main form, the fields appear as a datasheet even though the fields do not appear that way in Design view. The heights of the subform's Form Header and Form Footer sections are zero, meaning that these sections have been removed from the subform. You'll increase the height of the Form Footer section so that you can add the two calculated controls to the section.

2. Place the pointer at the bottom edge of the Form Footer section bar. When the pointer changes to a ✛ shape, drag the bottom edge of the section down to the 0.5-inch mark on the vertical ruler.

   Now you'll add the first calculated control to the Form Footer section. To create the text box for the calculated control, you use the **Text Box tool** in the Controls group on the Design tab. Because the Form Footer section is not displayed in a datasheet, you do not need to position the control precisely.

3. In the Controls group on the Design tab, click the **Text Box** button.

4. Position the + portion of the pointer near the top of the Form Footer section and at the 1-inch mark on the horizontal ruler, and then click the mouse button. Access places a text box control and an attached label control to its left in the Form Footer section.

   Next, you'll set the Name and Control Source properties for the text box. Recall that the Name property specifies the name of an object or control. Later, when you add the calculated control in the main form, you'll reference the subform's calculated control value by using its Name property value. The **Control Source property** specifies the source of the data that appears in the control; the Control Source property setting can be either a field name or an expression. You precede expressions with an equal sign to distinguish them from field names, which do not have an equal sign.

5. Open the property sheet for the text box in the Form Footer section (the word "Unbound" is displayed inside the text box), click the **All** tab (if necessary), select the entry in the Name text box, type **txtInvoiceAmtSum** in the Name text box, press the **Tab** key, type **=Sum(InvoiceAmt)** in the Control Source text box, and then press the **Tab** key. See Figure 6-41.

Setting properties for the subform calculated control ◄ | **Figure 6-41**

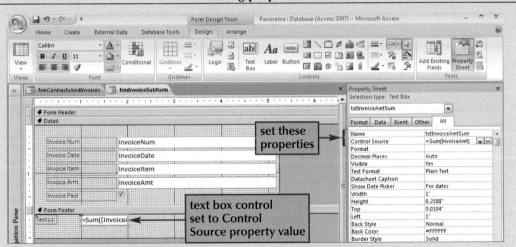

Tip

Read the Naming Conventions section in the appendix titled "Relational Databases and Database Design" for more information about naming conventions.

The calculated control's Name property setting (txtInvoiceAmtSum) follows a common naming convention: txt is a prefix tag to identify the control type (a text box), InvoiceAmt is the name for the related field, and Sum is a suffix tag to identify the control as a summary control.

You've finished creating the first calculated control, and now you'll create the other calculated control.

▶ **6.** Repeat Steps 3 through 5, positioning the + portion of the pointer near the top of the Form Footer section and at the 4-inch mark on the horizontal ruler, setting the Name property value to **txtInvoiceNumCount**, and setting the Control Source property value to **=Count(InvoiceNum)**.

When you use the Count function, you are counting the number of displayed records—in this case, the number of records displayed in the subform. Instead of using InvoiceNum as the expression for the Count function, you could use any of the other fields displayed in the subform.

You've finished creating the subform's calculated controls, so you can close the property sheet, save your subform design changes, and return to the main form.

▶ **7.** Close the property sheet, save your subform changes, and then close the subform. You return to Design view for the main form.

Next, you'll add two calculated controls in the main form to display the values of the two calculated controls from the subform.

Adding Calculated Controls to a Main Form

The subform's calculated controls now contain a count of the number of invoices and a total of the invoice amounts. You need to add two calculated controls in the main form that reference the values in the subform's calculated controls. Because it's easy to make a typing mistake with these references, you'll use Expression Builder to set the Control Source property for the two main form calculated controls.

To add a calculated control to the main form's Detail section:

▶ **1.** In the Controls group on the Design tab, click the **Text Box** button, and then add the text box and its attached label in the Detail section, clicking the + portion of the pointer at the 2-inch mark on the horizontal ruler and the 2-inch mark on the vertical ruler. Don't be concerned about positioning the control precisely, because you'll resize and move the label and text box later.

▶ **2.** Select the label and open the property sheet, set its Caption property to **Number of Invoices:**, right-click an edge of the label to open the shortcut menu, point to **Size**, and then click **To Fit**. Don't be concerned if the label now overlaps the text box.

You'll use Expression Builder to set the Control Source property for the text box.

▶ **3.** Click the text box (the word "Unbound" is displayed inside the text box) to select it, click the **Control Source** text box in the property sheet, and then click the property's **Build** button 〔...〕 to open Expression Builder.

▶ **4.** Double-click **frmContractsAndInvoices** in the left column, click **frmInvoiceSubform** in the left column, scroll down the middle column, click **txtInvoiceNumCount** in the middle column, and then click the **Paste** button. See Figure 6-42.

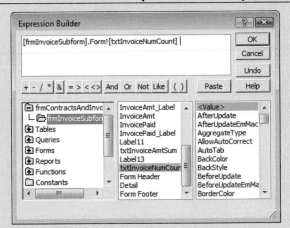

Access changed the pasted txtInvoiceNumCount to [frmInvoiceSubform].Form!
[txtInvoiceNumCount]. This expression asks Access to display the value of the
txtInvoiceNumCount control that is located in the frmInvoiceSubform form, which
is a form object.

You need to add an equal sign to the start of the expression.

5. Press the **Home** key, click the **=** button in the row of operators to the left of the
Paste button, and then click the **OK** button. Access closes the Expression Builder
dialog box and sets the Control Source property.

Next, you'll add a second text box to the main form, set the Caption property for
the label, and use Expression Builder to set the text box's Control Source property.

6. Repeat Steps 1 through 3 to add a text box to the main form, clicking the + portion of
the pointer at the 5-inch mark on the horizontal ruler and the 2-inch mark on the vertical ruler, and setting the label's Caption property to **Invoice Amount Total:**.

7. With the Expression Builder dialog box open for the new text box, click the **=** button to
insert an equal sign in the large text box, double-click **frmContractsAndInvoices** in
the left column, click **frmInvoiceSubform** in the left column, scroll down the middle
column, click **txtInvoiceAmtSum** in the middle column, and then click the **Paste**
button. Access changed the pasted txtInvoiceAmtSum to the expression
[frmInvoiceSubform].Form![txtInvoiceAmtSum].

Next, you'll save your form changes and view the form in Layout view.

8. Close the Expression Builder dialog box, close the property sheet, save your form
changes, and then switch to Layout view. See Figure 6-43.

Figure 6-43 ▶ **After adding two calculated controls**

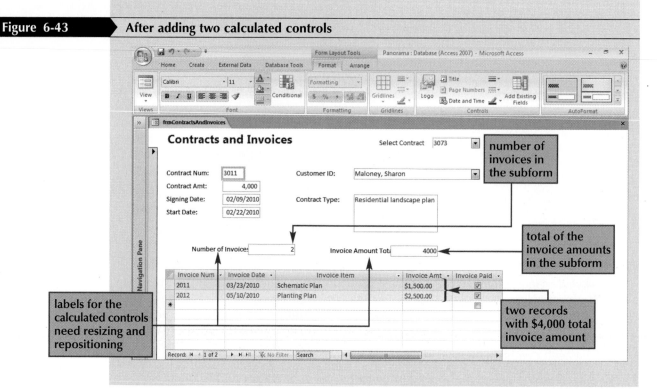

Next, you need to resize, move, and format the two calculated controls and their attached labels.

Resizing, Moving, and Formatting Calculated Controls

In addition to resizing and repositioning the two calculated controls and their attached labels, you need to change the format of the rightmost calculated control to Currency and to set the following properties for both calculated controls:

- Set the Tab Stop property to a value of No. The **Tab Stop property** specifies whether users can use the Tab key to move to a control on a form. If the Tab Stop property is set to No, users can't tab to the control.
- Set the ControlTip Text property to a value of "Calculated total number of invoices for this contract" for the leftmost calculated control and "Calculated invoice total for this contract" for the rightmost calculated control. The **ControlTip Text property** specifies the text that appears in a ScreenTip when users hold the mouse pointer over a control on a form.

InSight | **Setting Properties in the Property Sheet**

You can set many properties in the property sheet by typing a value in the property's text box, by selecting a value from the property's list box, or by double-clicking the property name. If you need to set a property by typing a long text entry, you can open the Zoom dialog box and type the entry in the dialog box. You can also use Expression Builder to help you enter expressions.

Now you'll resize, move, and format the calculated controls and their attached labels, and you'll set other properties for the calculated controls.

To modify the calculated controls and their attached labels:

▶ **1.** Right-click the rightmost calculated control, click **Properties** on the shortcut menu to open the property sheet, click the **All** tab in the property sheet (if necessary), set the Format property to **Currency**, and then close the property sheet. The value displayed in the calculated control changes from 4000 to $4,000.00.

Now you'll resize the calculated controls, adjust the positions of each label and text box pair with respect to each other, and then move the controls into their final positions in the form.

▶ **2.** Individually, reduce the widths of the two calculated controls. See Figure 6-44.

▶ **3.** Click the **Number of Invoices** label, use the arrow keys to move the label into position next to its related calculated control, repeat the process for the **Invoice Amount Total** label and its related calculated control, and then deselect all controls. See Figure 6-44.

After modifying the calculated controls and their labels ◀ **Figure 6-44**

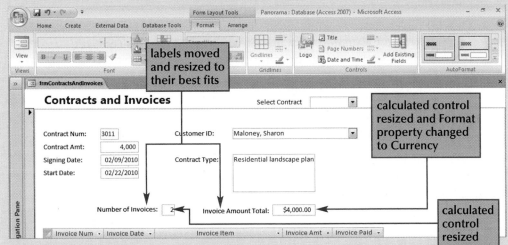

▶ **4.** Use **Shift + Click** to select the **Start Date** label and the **Number of Invoices** label, click the **Arrange** tab on the Ribbon, click the **Left** button in the Control Alignment group to align the labels on their left edges, press the **Shift** key, click the **Start Date** label to deselect it, release the **Shift** key, and then move the **Number of Invoices** label up to the position shown in Figure 6-45.

▶ **5.** Select the **Number of Invoices** label and its related calculated control, and then in the Control Alignment group, click the **Top** button to align the two controls on their top edges.

▶ **6.** Repeat Steps 4 and 5 for the **Invoice Amount Total** label and its related calculated control. See Figure 6-45.

▶ **7.** Move the bottom calculated control to the left to the position shown in Figure 6-45, align the two calculated controls on their left edges, and then deselect all controls.

Figure 6-45 | **After moving and aligning the calculated controls and their labels**

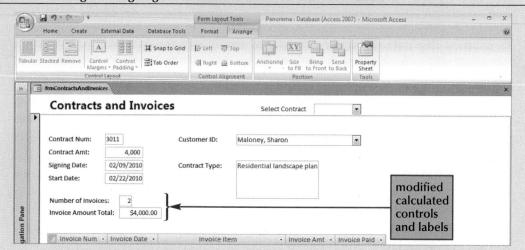

▶ **8.** Right-click the bottom calculated control, click **Properties** on the shortcut menu, click the **Other** tab in the property sheet, set the Tab Stop property to **No**, and then set the ControlTip Text property to **Calculated invoice total for this contract**.

▶ **9.** Click the top calculated control, set the Tab Stop property to **No**, set the ControlTip Text property to **Calculated total number of invoices for this contract**, close the property sheet, save your form design changes, and then switch to Form view.

▶ **10.** Click the **Number of Invoices** text box, position the pointer on the Number of Invoices text box to display its ScreenTip, click the **Invoice Amount Total** text box, and then position the pointer on the Invoice Amount Total text box to display its ScreenTip. See Figure 6-46.

Figure 6-46 | **Displaying a control's ScreenTip**

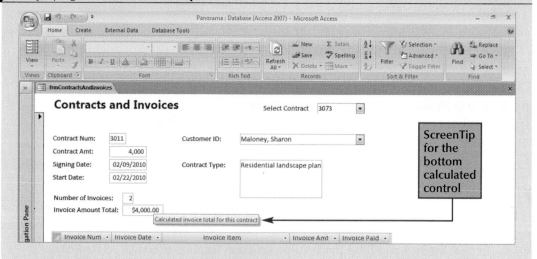

Trouble? Do not be concerned if the ScreenTips do not display on your screen.

Sarah asks you to verify that users can't update the calculated controls in the main form and that users will tab in the correct order through the controls in the form.

Changing the Tab Order in a Form

Pressing the Tab key in Form view moves the focus from one control to another. **Focus** refers to the control that is currently active and awaiting user action; focus also refers to the object and record that is currently active. The order in which you move from control to control, or change the focus, in a form when you press the Tab key is called the **tab order**. Sarah wants to verify that the tab order in the main form is top-to-bottom, left-to-right. First, you'll verify that users can't update the calculated controls.

To test the calculated controls and modify the tab order:

▶ **1.** Select **2** in the Number of Invoices text box, and then press the **8** key. The Number of Invoices value remains at 2, and a message is displayed on the status bar. See Figure 6-47.

After attempting to update a calculated control ◀ **Figure 6-47**

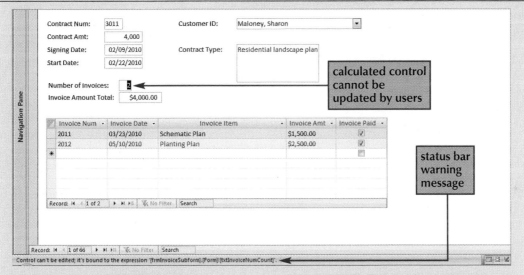

The status bar message warns you that you can't update, or edit, the calculated control because it's bound to an expression. The calculated control in the main form changes in value only when the value of the expression changes.

▶ **2.** Click the **Invoice Amount Total** text box, and then press any key. The value remains unchanged, and a message displays on the status bar, because you cannot edit a calculated control.

Next, you'll determine the tab order of the fields in the main form. Sarah wants the tab order to be down and then across.

▶ **3.** Select **3011** in the ContractNum text box, press the **Tab** key to advance to the ContractAmt text box, and then press the **Tab** key five more times to advance to the SigningDate, StartDate, ContractType, CustomerID text boxes, in order, and then to the subform.

You tab through the text boxes in a main form before tabbing through the fields in a subform. In the main form, tabbing bypasses the two calculated controls because you set their Tab Stop property to No, and you bypass the Select Contract combo box because it's an unbound control. Also, you tab through only the text boxes in a form, not the labels.

Tip

Access sets the tab order in the same order in which you add controls to a form, so you should always check the form's tab order when you create a custom form in Layout or Design view.

The tab order Sarah wants for the text boxes in the main form (top-to-bottom, left-to-right) is correct for the first four text boxes (ContractNum, ContractAmt, SigningDate, and StartDate text boxes). Then you should tab from the StartDate text box to the CustomerID text box and finally to the ContractType text box, but tabbing is reversed for the last two text boxes. The default tab order doesn't match the order Sarah wants, so you'll change the tab order. You can change the tab order in Layout view or in Design view.

▶ 4. Switch to Design view, click the **Arrange** tab on the Ribbon, and then in the Control Layout group on the Arrange tab, click the **Tab Order** button. The Tab Order dialog box opens. See Figure 6-48.

| Figure 6-48 | Changing the tab order for the main form |

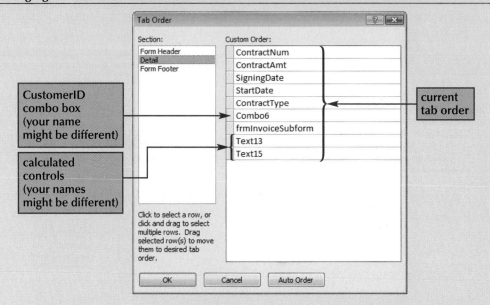

Because you did not set the Name property for the combo box control and the calculated controls, Access assigned their names: Combo6 (your name might be different) for the CustomerID combo box, Text13 (your name might be different) for the Number of Invoices calculated control, and Text15 (your name might be different) for the Invoice Amount Total calculated control. The Auto Order button lets you create a left-to-right, top-to-bottom tab order automatically, which is not the order Sarah wants. You need to move the Combo6 entry above the ContractType entry.

Tip

You should set the Name property for all your controls to meaningful names, so that you don't have to guess which control a name references in this and similar situations.

▶ 5. Click the **row selector** to the left of Combo6, and then drag the row selector above the ContractType entry. The entries are now correct in the correct order.

▶ 6. Click the **OK** button, save your form design changes, switch to Form view, and then tab through the controls in the main form to make sure the tab order is correct.

Trouble? If the tab order is incorrect, switch to Design view, click the Arrange tab on the Ribbon, click Tab Order in the Control Layout group, move appropriate entries in the Tab Order dialog box, and then repeat Step 6.

You've finished adding controls to the form, but the form is plain looking and lacks visual clues for the different controls in the form. You'll complete the form by making it more attractive and easier for Sarah and her staff to use.

Improving a Form's Appearance

The frmContractsAndInvoices form has four distinct areas: the Form Header section containing the title and the Select Contract combo box, the six bound controls in the Detail section, the two calculated controls in the Detail section, and the subform in the Detail section. To visually separate these four areas, you'll increase the height of the Form Header section, add a horizontal line at the bottom of the Form Header section, and draw a rectangle around the calculated controls.

Adding a Line to a Form

You can use lines in a form to improve the form's readability, to group related information, or to underline important values. You use the **Line tool** in Design view to add a line to a form or report.

Adding a Line to a Form or Report | Reference Window

- Display the form or report in Design view.
- In the Controls group on the Design tab, click the Line button.
- Position the pointer where you want the line to begin.
- Drag the pointer to the position for the end of the line, and then release the mouse button. If you want to ensure that you draw a straight horizontal or vertical line, hold down the Shift key before and during the drag operation.
- To make small adjustments to the line length, select the line, hold down the Shift key, and then press an arrow key. To make small adjustments in the placement of a line, select the line, hold down the Ctrl key, and then press an arrow key.

You will add a horizontal line to the Form Header section to separate the controls in the this section from the controls in the Detail section.

To add a line to the form:

▶ 1. Switch to Design view, and then drag down the bottom of the Form Header section to the 1-inch mark on the vertical ruler to make room to draw a horizontal line at the bottom of the Form Header section.

▶ 2. In the Controls group on the Design tab, click the **Line** button ◥.

▶ 3. Position the pointer's plus symbol (+) at the left edge of the Form Header section and at the 0.75-inch mark on the vertical ruler.

▶ 4. Hold down the **Shift** key, drag a horizontal line from left to right, so the end of the line aligns with the right edge of the grid in the Form Header section, release the mouse button, and then release the **Shift** key. See Figure 6-49.

Figure 6-49   **Adding a line to the form**

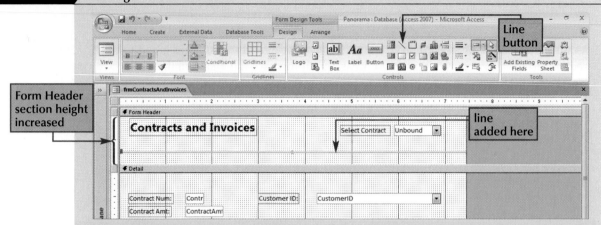

Trouble? If the line is not straight or not positioned correctly, click the Undo button on the Quick Access Toolbar, and then repeat Steps 2 through 4. If the line is not the correct length, hold down the Shift key, and press one or more of the arrow keys until the line's length is the same as that of the line shown in Figure 6-49.

▶ **5.** Drag up the bottom of the Form Header section to just below the line at the 0.75-inch mark on the vertical ruler.

▶ **6.** Save your form design changes.

Next, you'll add a Rectangle around the calculated controls in the Detail section.

Adding a Rectangle to a Form

You can use a rectangle in a form to group related controls and to separate the group from other controls. You use the **Rectangle tool** in Design view to add a rectangle to a form or report.

- Display the form or report in Design view.
- In the Controls group on the Design tab, click the Rectangle button.
- Click in the form or report to create a default-sized rectangle, or drag a rectangle in the position and size you want.

You will add a rectangle to the Detail section around the calculated controls and their labels to separate them from the subform and from the other controls in the Detail section.

To add a rectangle to the form:

▶ **1.** In the Controls group on the Design tab, click the **Rectangle** button ☐.

▶ **2.** Position the pointer's plus symbol (+) approximately two grid dots above and two grid dots to the left of the Number of Invoices label.

3. Drag a rectangle down and to the right until all four sides of the rectangle are approximately two grid dots from the two calculated controls and their labels. See Figure 6-50.

Adding a rectangle to the form | **Figure 6-50**

Trouble? If the rectangle is not sized or positioned correctly, use the sizing handles to adjust its size and the move handle to adjust its position.

Next, you'll set the thickness of the rectangle's lines.

4. In the Controls group on the Design tab, click the **Line Thickness** button ☰▼, click the line with the ScreenTip **2 pt** in the list, and then deselect the control.

Next, you'll add color and visual effects to the controls in the Detail and Form Header sections.

Modifying the Visual Effects of the Controls in a Form

Distinguishing one group of controls in a form from other groups is an important visual cue to the users of the form. For example, users should be able to distinguish the bound controls in the form from the calculated controls and from the Select Contract control in the Form Header section. You'll now modify the controls in the form to provide these visual cues. You'll start by setting font properties for the calculated control's labels.

Tip

Using one of the available AutoFormats is always an option for improving the appearance of a form, but an AutoFormat doesn't provide the control you can achieve by setting properties in Design view and in Layout view.

To modify the controls in the form:

1. Select the **Number of Invoices** label and the **Invoice Amount Total** label; in the Font group on the Design tab, click the arrow for the **Font Color** button 🅰; click the **Blue** color (row 7, column 8) in the Standard Colors palette; and then in the Font group on the Design tab, click the **Bold** button **B**. The labels' captions now use a bold, blue font.

Next, you'll set properties for the Select Contract label in the Form Header section.

▶ **2.** Select the **Select Contract** label in the Form Header section, set the label's color to **Red** (row 7, column 2 in the Standard Colors palette), and then set the font style to bold.

Next, you'll set the label's Special Effect property to a raised effect. The **Special Effect property** specifies the type of special effect applied to a control in a form or report. The choices for this property are Flat, Raised, Sunken, Etched, Shadowed, and Chiseled.

▶ **3.** In the Controls group on the Design tab, click the arrow for the **Special Effect** button ⬜, and then click **Special Effect: Raised**. The label now has a raised special effect, and the label's caption now uses a bold, red font.

Next, you'll set the Special Effect property for the bound control labels to a sunken effect.

▶ **4.** Select the **Contract Num** label, **Contract Amt** label, **Signing Date** label, **Start Date** label, **Customer ID** label, and **Contract Type** label, set the controls' Special Effect property to **Special Effect: Sunken**, and then deselect all controls.

Trouble? If setting the Sunken effect does not work, repeat Step 4 and set the selected controls' Special Effect property to Special Effect: Shadowed, and then repeat Step 4 and set the selected controls' Special Effect property to Special Effect: Sunken.

Finally, you'll set the background color of the Form Header section, the Detail section, the Select Contract combo box, and the two calculated controls. You can use the **Fill/Back Color button** in the Font group on the Design tab to change the background color of a control, section, or object (form or report).

▶ **5.** Click the Form Header's section bar, and in the Font group on the Design tab, click the arrow for the **Fill/Back Color** button 🖌; and then click the **Access Theme 2** color (row 2, column 2) in the Access Theme Colors palette. The Form Header's background color changes to the Access Theme 2 color.

▶ **6.** Click the Detail section's section bar, and in the Font Group on the Design tab, click the **Fill/Back Color** button to change the Detail section's background color to the **Access Theme 2** color.

▶ **7.** Select the **Select Contract** combo box, **Number of Invoices** text box, and the **Invoice Amount Total** text box, set the selected controls' background color to the **Access Theme 2** color, and then deselect all controls by clicking to the right of the Detail section's grid. See Figure 6-51.

Completed custom form in Design view Figure 6-51

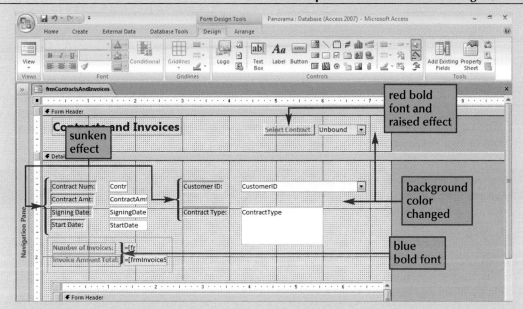

8. Switch to Form view, and then click the **ContractNum** text box to deselect the value. See Figure 6-52.

Completed custom form in Form view Figure 6-52

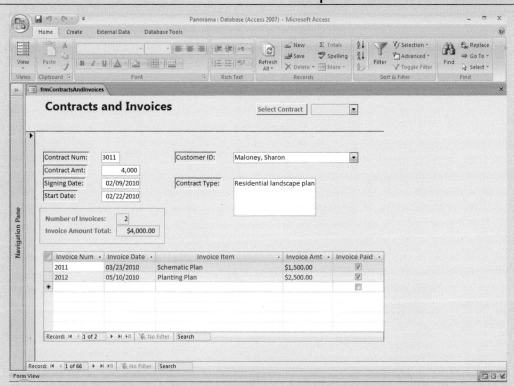

Trouble? Depending on which control has the focus in the form, the CustomerID combo box's background color might be white or it might be the background color of the Detail section.

▶ **9.** Test the form by tabbing from field to field, navigating from record to record, and using the Select Contract combo box to find records, making sure you don't change any field values and observing that the calculated controls display the correct values.

You've completed the custom form.

▶ **10.** Save your form design changes, close the form, close the Panorama database, make a backup copy of the database, open the **Panorama** database, compact and repair the database, close the database, and then exit Access.

The custom form you created will make it easier for Sarah and her staff to work with contract and invoice data in the Panorama database.

Review | **Session 6.3 Quick Check**

1. To create a combo box to find records in a form with the Combo Box Wizard, the form's record source must be a(n) _____ .
2. You use the _____ tool to add a subform to a form.
3. To calculate subtotals and overall totals in a form or report, you use the _____ function.
4. The Control Source property setting can be either a(n) _____ or a(n) _____ .
5. Explain the difference between the Tab Stop property and tab order.
6. What is focus?
7. The _____ property has settings such as Raised and Sunken.

In this tutorial, you examined general form design guidelines and learned how to use them in planning a custom form. You learned how to change a lookup field back to a Text field, to print database relationships, and to use the Documenter. You created a datasheet form, a multiple items form, and a split form, and you modified a form in Layout view. After creating a blank bound form, you learned how to add bound controls to a form, and how to select, move, align, resize, delete, and rename controls. You also learned how to add and delete form headers and footers, how to add a combo box to display and update a field and a combo box to find records, how to add a subform to a form, how to add calculated controls to a subform and a main form, and how to change the tab order in a form. Finally, you learned how to improve the visual appearance of a form.

Key Terms

Anchor property	Detail section	rulers
bound control	Display Control property	section bar
bound form	Documenter	section selector
calculated control	Fill/Back Color button	sizing handle
Caption property	focus	Special Effect property
combo box	Form Footer section	Split Form tool
Combo Box tool	Form Header section	stacked layout
control	form selector	Subform/Subreport tool
control layout	grid	Sum function
Control Margins property	label	tab order
Control Padding property	Line tool	Tab Stop property
Control Source property	move handle	tabular layout
Control Wizard	Multiple Items tool	Text Box tool
ControlTip Text property	Name property	unbound control
Count function	Record Source property	unbound form
custom form	Rectangle tool	Visible property
Datasheet tool	Row Source property	

| Practice | **Review Assignments** |

Practice the skills you learned in the tutorial using the same case scenario.

Data File needed for the Review Assignments: Products.accdb (*cont. from Tutorial 5*)

Sarah wants you to create several forms, including a custom form that displays and updates companies and the products they offer. You'll do so by completing the following:

1. Open the **Products** database located in the Level.02\Review folder provided with your Data Files.
2. Remove the lookup feature from the CompanyID field in the **tblProduct** table, and resize the Company ID column to its best fit.
3. Edit the relationship between the primary tblCompany and related tblProduct tables to enforce referential integrity and to cascade update related fields. Create the relationship report, and then save the report as **rptRelationshipsForProducts**.
4. Use the Documenter to document the qryContactList query. Select all query options; use the Names, Data Types, and Sizes option for fields; and use the Names and Fields option for indexes. Print the report produced by the Documenter.
5. Use the Datasheet tool to create a form based on the tblProduct table, and then save the form as **frmProductDatasheet**.
6. Use the Multiple Items tool to create a form based on the qryCompanyList query, and then save the form as **frmCompanyListMultipleItems**.
7. Use the Split Form tool to create a split form based on the tblProduct table, and then make the following changes to the form in Layout view.
   a. Remove the Unit control from the stacked layout, and then anchor it to the bottom left.
   b. Remove the five controls in the right column from the stacked layout, and then anchor the group to the bottom right.
   c. Remove the ProductType and Price controls from the stacked layout, move them to the top right, and then anchor them to the top right.
   d. Reduce the widths of the ProductID and CompanyID text boxes to a reasonable size.
   e. Save the modifiied form as **frmProductSplitForm**.
8. Use Figure 6-53 and the following steps to create a custom form named **frmCompaniesWithProducts** based on the tblCompany and tblProduct tables.

Figure 6-53

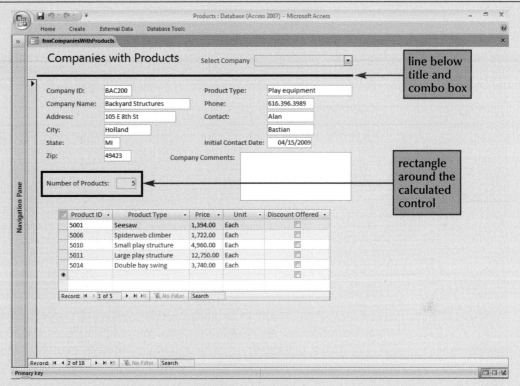

a. Place the fields from the tblCompany table at the top of the Detail section. Delete the Contact Last Name label and change the caption for the Contact First Name label to **Contact:**.

b. Move the fields into two columns in the Detail section, resizing and aligning controls, as necessary.

c. Add the title in the Form Header section.

d. Make sure the form's Record Source property is set to tblCompany, and then add a combo box in the Form Header section to find CompanyName field values. In the wizard steps, select the CompanyName and CompanyID fields, and hide the key column. Resize and move the control.

e. Add a subform based on the tblProduct table, include only the fields shown in Figure 6-53, link with CompanyID, name the subform **frmPartialProductSubform**, delete the subform label, and resize the columns in the subform to their best fit and resize and position the subform.

f. Add a calculated control that displays the number of products displayed in the subform. Set the calculated control's Tab Stop property to No, and the ControlTip Text property to **Calculated number of products**.

g. Add a line in the Form Header section, and add a rectangle around the calculated control and its label, setting the line thickness of both controls to the line style with the ScreenTip 3 pt.

h. Use the Dark Label Text font (row 1, column 3 in the Access Theme Colors palette) for all labels, and use the Background fill color (row 1, column 5 in the Access Theme Colors palette) for the sections, the calculated control, and the Select Company combo box.

i. Make sure the tab order is top-to-bottom, left-to-right for the main form text boxes.

9. Close the Products database without exiting Access, make a backup copy of the database, open the **Products** database, compact and repair the database, close the database, and then exit Access.

| Challenge | **Case Problem 1** |

Apply the skills you learned in the tutorial to create a custom form for a small music school.

Data File needed for this Case Problem: Contract.accdb (*cont. from Tutorial 5*)

Pine Hill Music School Yuka wants you to create several forms, including a custom form that displays and updates the school's music contracts with students. You'll do so by completing the following:

1. Open the **Contract** database located in the Level.02\Case1 folder provided with your Data Files.
2. Remove the lookup feature from the TeacherID field in the **tblContract** table, and then resize the Teacher ID column to its best fit.
3. Define a one-to-many relationship between the primary tblTeacher table and the related tblContract table. Select the referential integrity option and the cascade updates option for this relationship.
4. Use the Documenter to document the tblContract table. Select all table options; use the Names, Data Types, and Sizes option for fields; and use the Names and Fields option for indexes. Print the report produced by the Documenter.
5. Use the Multiple Items tool to create a form based on the qryLessonsByTeacher query, change the title to **Lessons by Teacher**, and then save the form as **frmLessonsByTeacherMultipleItems**.
6. Use the Split Form tool to create a split form based on the qryLessonsByTeacher query, and then make the following changes to the form in Layout view.
   a. Reduce the widths of all six text boxes to a reasonable size.
   b. Remove the LessonType, LessonLength, and MonthlyLessonCost controls from the stacked layout, move these three controls to the right and then to the top of the form, and then anchor them to the top right.
   c. Select the MonthlyLessonCost control and its label, and then anchor them to the bottom right.
   d. Remove the ContractEndDate control from the stacked layout, and then anchor the control to the bottom left.
   e. Change the title to **Lessons by Teacher**, and then save the modifiied form as **frmLessonsByTeacherSplitForm**.
7. Use Figure 6-54 and the following steps to create a custom form named **frmContract** based on the tblContract table.

Figure 6-54

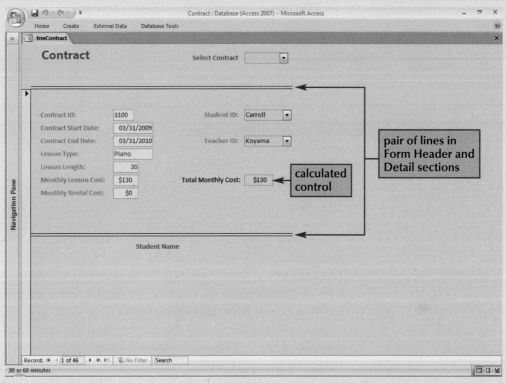

a. For the StudentID combo box, select the LastName, FirstName, and StudentID fields, in order; and sort in ascending order by the LastName field and then by the FirstName field.

b. For the TeacherID combo box, select the LastName, FirstName, and TeacherID fields, in order; and sort in ascending order by the LastName field and then by the FirstName field.

c. Make sure the form's Record Source property is set to tblContract, and then add a combo box in the Form Header section to find ContractID field values.

⊕ EXPLORE   d. Add a calculated control that displays the total of the MonthlyLessonCost and MonthlyRentalCost fields. Set the calculated control's Tab Stop property to No and format the values as currency with no decimal places.

⊕ EXPLORE   e. Add a line in the Form Header section, add a second line below it, and then add a second pair of lines near the bottom of the Detail section. Set the line thickness of all lines to the line setting with the ScreenTip 1 pt.

⊕ EXPLORE   f. Use the Label tool to add your name below the pair of lines at the bottom of the Detail section.

g. For the labels in the Details section, except for the Total Monthly Cost label and the label displaying your name, use the Red font (row 7, column 2 in the Standard Colors palette).

h. For the title, the Select Contract label, and the label displaying your name, use the Dark Red font (row 7, column 1 in the Standard Colors palette).

i. For the background color of the bound controls in the Detail section, use the Background fill color (row 1, column 5 in the Access Theme Colors palette). For the background fill color of the sections, the calculated control, and the Select Contract combo box, use the Brown 3 color (row 4, column 10 in the Standard Colors palette).

j. Make sure the tab order is top-to-bottom, left-to-right for the main form text boxes.

8. Close the Contract database without exiting Access, make a backup copy of the database, open the **Contract** database, compact and repair the database, close the database, and then exit Access.

| Create | **Case Problem 2** |

Use the skills you learned in the tutorial to work with the data for a health and fitness center and to create a custom form.

Data File needed for this Case Problem: Training.accdb (*cont. from Tutorial 5*)

Parkhurst Health & Fitness Center Martha Parkhurst wants you to create several forms, including two custom forms that display and update data in the Training database. You'll do so by completing the following:

1. Open the **Training** database located in the Level.02\Case2 folder provided with your Data Files.

2. Use the Documenter to document the qryMemberNames query. Select all query options; use the Names, Data Types, and Sizes option for fields; and use the Names and Fields option for indexes. Print the first page of the report produced by the Documenter.

3. Use the Datasheet tool to create a form based on the tblProgram table, and then save the form as **frmProgramDatasheet**.

⊕ EXPLORE

4. Create a custom form based on the qryUpcomingExpirations query. Display all fields from the query in the form. Create your own design for the form. Add a label to the bottom of the Detail section that contains your first and last names. Change the label's font so that your name appears in bold, blue text. Change the ExpirationDate text box format so that the field value displays in bold, red text. Save the form as **frmUpcomingExpirations**.

5. Use Figure 6-55 and the following steps to create a custom form named **frmProgramsAndMembers** based on the tblProgram and tblMember tables.

Figure 6-55

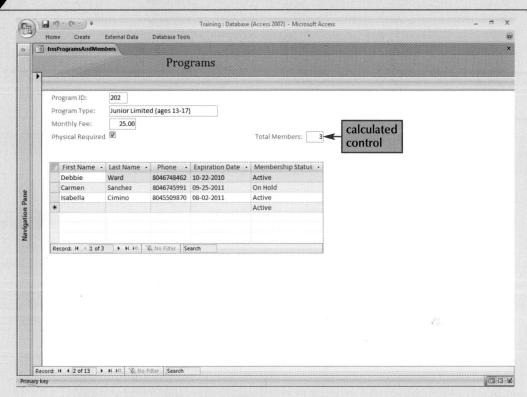

a. Selected fields from the **tblMember** table appear in a subform named **frmProgramMemberSubform**.

b. The calculated control displays the total number of records that appear in the subform. Set the calculated control's ControlTip Text property to **Total number of members in this program**. Set the calculated control's Tab Stop property to No.

c. Apply an appropriate AutoFormat to the form.

d. View the completed form.

6. Close the Training database without exiting Access, make a backup copy of the database, open the **Training** database, compact and repair the database, close the database, and then exit Access.

Create | **Case Problem 3**

Use the skills you learned in the tutorial to create forms for a recycling agency.

Data File needed for this Case Problem: Agency.accdb (*cont. from Tutorial 5*)

Rossi Recycling Group Mary Rossi asks you to create several forms, including a custom form for the Agency database so that she can better track donations for the agency. You'll do so by completing the following:

1. Open the **Agency** database located in the Level.02\Case3 folder provided with your Data Files.

2. Use the Documenter to document the tblDonor table. Select all table options; use the Names, Data Types, and Sizes option for fields; and use the Names and Fields option for indexes. Print the report produced by the Documenter.

3. Use the Multiple Items tool to create a form based on the qryDonorPhoneList query, change the title to **Donor Phone List**, and then save the form as **frmDonorPhoneListMultipleItems**.

4. Use the Split Form tool to create a split form based on the tblDonor table, and then make the following changes to the form in Layout view.
    a. Reduce the widths of all five text boxes to a reasonable size.
    b. Remove the FirstName, LastName, and Phone controls from the stacked layout, move them to the top right, and then anchor them to the top right.
    c. Change the title to **Donor**, and then save the modifiied form as **frmDonorSplitForm**.
5. Use Figure 6-56 and the following steps to create a custom form named **frmDonorDonations** based on the tblDonor and tblDonation tables.

Figure 6-56

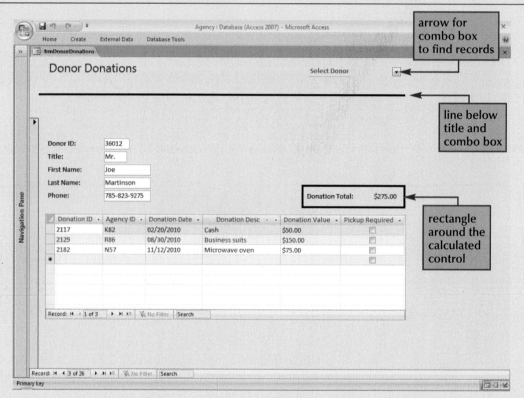

a. Add the title in the Form Header section.
b. Make sure the form's Record Source property is set to tblDonor, and then add a combo box in the Form Header section to find DonorID field values. In the wizard steps, select the DonorID field. Format the label using a bold, Red font (row 7, column 2 in the Standard Colors palette) and the Chiseled special effect.
c. Add a subform based on the tblDonation table, name the subform **frmDonorDonationSubform**, delete the subform label, and resize the columns in the subform to their best fit and resize and position the subform.

EXPLORE

    d. Add a calculated control that displays the total of the DonationValue field displayed in the subform with the Currency format. Set the calculated control's Tab Stop property to No, and the Border Style property to Transparent.

    e. Add a line in the Form Header section, and add a rectangle around the calculated control and its label, setting the line thickness of both controls to the line style with the ScreenTip 3 pt.

    f. Use the background color Aqua Blue 2 (row 3, column 9 in the Standard Colors palette) for the sections, the calculated control, and the Select Donor combo box.

    g. Make sure the tab order is top-to-bottom for the main form text boxes.

6. Close the Agency database without exiting Access, make a backup copy of the database, open the **Agency** database, compact and repair the database, close the database, and then exit Access.

| Create | **Case Problem 4** |

Use the skills you learned in the tutorial to create forms for a luxury property rental company.

Data File needed for this Case Problem: Vacation.accdb (*cont. from Tutorial 5*)

GEM Ultimate Vacations   Griffin and Emma MacElroy want you to create several forms, including a custom form that displays and updates guest and reservation data in the Vacation database. You'll do so by completing the following:

1. Open the **Vacation** database located in the Level.02\Case4 folder provided with your Data Files.

2. Remove the lookup feature from the PropertyID field in the **tblReservation** table.

3. Edit the relationship between the primary tblProperty and related tblReservation tables to enforce referential integrity and to cascade update related fields. Create the relationship report, and then save the report as **rptRelationshipsForVacation**.

4. Use the Documenter to document the qryIllinoisGuests query. Select all query options; use the Names, Data Types, and Sizes option for fields; and use the Nothing option for indexes. Print the report produced by the Documenter.

5. Use the Datasheet tool to create a form based on the qryGuestTripDates query, and then save the form as **frmGuestTripDates**.

EXPLORE

6. Create a custom form based on the qryRentalCost query. Display all fields in the form. Use your own design for the form, but use the title **Reserved Trips** in the Form Header section, and use the Label tool to add your name to the Form Header section. Save the form as **frmRentalCost**.

7. Use Figure 6-57 and the following steps to create a custom form named **frmGuestsWithReservations** based on the tblGuest and tblReservation tables.

Figure 6-57

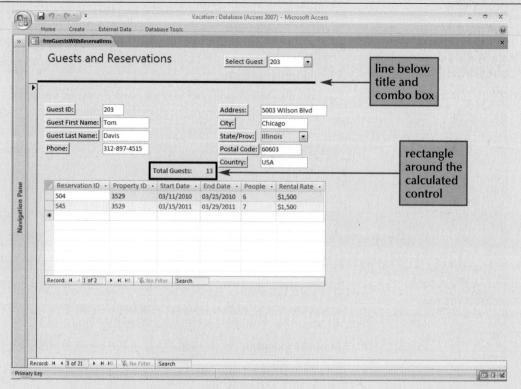

a. Add the title in the Form Header section.

b. Make sure the form's Record Source property is set to tblGuest and then add a combo box in the Form Header section to find GuestID field values.

c. Add a subform based on the tblReservation table, name the subform **frmGuestAndReservationSubform**, delete the subform label, and resize the columns in the subform to their best fit and resize and position the subform.

EXPLORE

d. Add a calculated control that displays the total of the People field displayed in the subform. Set the calculated control's Tab Stop property to No, and set the label's and calculated control's Border Style property to Transparent.

e. Add a line in the Form Header section, and add a rectangle around the calculated control and its label, setting the line thickness of both controls to the line style with the ScreenTip 3 pt.

f. Use the Background fill color (row 1, column 5 in the Access Theme Colors palette) for the sections and the calculated control.

g. Use the Raised special effect for the labels in the Detail section and the Form Header section.

h. Make sure the tab order is top-to-bottom and left-to-right for the main form text boxes.

8. Close the Vacation database without exiting Access, make a backup copy of the database, open the **Vacation** database, compact and repair the database, close the database, and then exit Access.

Create | Case Problem 5

Use the skills you learned in this tutorial to work with the data for an Internet service provider.

Data File needed for this Case Problem: ACE.accdb (*cont. from Tutorial 5*)

Always Connected Everyday Chris and Pat Dixon want you to create several forms, including a custom form that displays and updates data in the ACE database. You'll do so by completing the following:

1. Open the **ACE** database located in the Level.02\Case5 folder provided with your Data Files.
2. In Tutorial 5, you created a lookup field in the tblCustomer table. Remove the lookup feature from this field.
3. Make sure that the table relationship enforces referential integrity and cascade updates related fields. Create the relationship report, and then save the report as **rptRelationshipsForACE**.
4. Use the Documenter to document one of your forms. Select all form options and use the Names option for sections and controls. Print the report produced by the Documenter.
5. In Tutorial 5, you created forms to display and update the data in the ACE database. Review these forms, and develop a consistent design strategy that you'll use to customize all the forms. Your design strategy should include the use of combo boxes for foreign keys and for searching, calculated controls, and visual effects.
6. Using your form design strategy, customize all the forms in the ACE database.
7. Close the ACE database without exiting Access, make a backup copy of the database, open the **ACE** database, compact and repair the database, close the database, and then exit Access.

Research | Internet Assignments

Use the Internet to find and work with data related to the topics presented in this tutorial.

The purpose of the Internet Assignments is to challenge you to find information on the Internet that you can use to work effectively with this software. The actual assignments are updated and maintained on the Course Technology Web site. Log on to the Internet and use your Web browser to go to the Student Online Companion for New Perspectives Office 2007 at **www.course.com/np/office2007**. Then navigate to the Internet Assignments for this tutorial.

Assess | SAM Assessment and Training

If you have a SAM user profile, you may have access to hands-on instruction, practice, and assessment of the skills covered in this tutorial. Log in to your SAM account (**http://sam2007.course.com**) to launch any assigned training activities or exams that relate to the skills covered in this tutorial.

Review | Quick Check Answers

Session 6.1

1. forms
2. Row Source
3. An Access tool that creates detailed documentation of the objects in a database.

4. A form tool that creates a customizable form that displays multiple records from a source table or query in a datasheet format.

5. A form that displays a form's data in Form view and Datasheet view at the same time; the views are synchronized with each other at all times.

6. Anchor

Session 6.2

1. A bound form has a table or query as its record source, and is used to maintain and display table data.

2. A bound control is connected to a field in the database; an unbound control is not.

3. grid

4. move

5. Click the text box to select it, position the pointer anywhere on the border of the text box (but not on a move or sizing handle), and then drag the text box and its attached label.

6. Select the control, position the pointer on a sizing handle, and then drag the pointer in the appropriate direction until it is the desired size.

7. combo box

8. Right-click the label, click Properties on the shortcut menu, click the All tab, and then change the entry in the Caption text box.

9. The Form Header section lets you add titles, instructions, command buttons, and other controls to the top of a form. This section of the form does not change as you navigate through the records.

Session 6.3

1. table or query

2. Subform/Subreport

3. Sum

4. field name, expression

5. The Tab Stop property specifies whether users can use the Tab key to move to a control on a form. Tab order is the order in which you move from control to control, or change the focus, in a form when you press the Tab key.

6. Focus refers to the control that is currently active and awaiting user action; focus also refers to the object and record that is currently active.

7. Special Effect

Ending Data Files

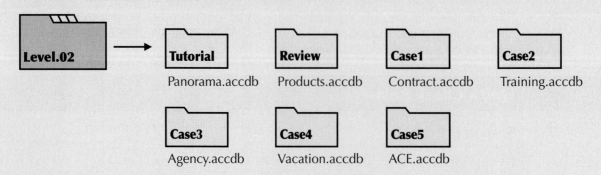

Level.02	→	Tutorial	Review	Case1	Case2
		Panorama.accdb	Products.accdb	Contract.accdb	Training.accdb

Case3	Case4	Case5
Agency.accdb	Vacation.accdb	ACE.accdb

Objectives

Session 7.1
- View, filter, and copy report information in Report view
- Modify a report in Layout view
- Modify a report in Design view

Session 7.2
- Design and create a custom report
- Sort and group data in a report
- Add, move, resize, and align controls in a report
- Add lines to a report
- Hide duplicate values in a report

Session 7.3
- Add the date, page numbers, and title to a report
- Create and modify mailing labels

Creating Custom Reports

Creating Reports with Information About Contracts and Invoices

Case | Belmont Landscapes

At a recent staff meeting, Sarah Fisher indicated that she would like to make some changes to an existing report in the database. She also requested a new report that she can use to produce a printed list of all invoices for all contracts.

In this tutorial, you will modify an existing report and create the new report for Sarah. In modifying and building these reports, you will use many Access report customization features, including grouping data, calculating totals, and adding lines to separate report sections. These features will enhance Sarah's reports and make them easier to read and use.

Starting Data Files

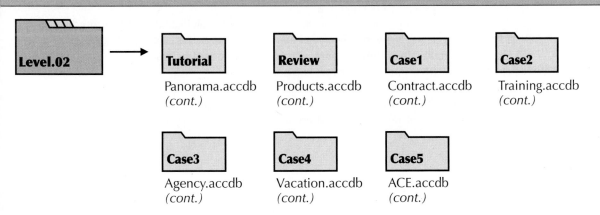

Level.02 → Tutorial
Panorama.accdb *(cont.)*

Review
Products.accdb *(cont.)*

Case1
Contract.accdb *(cont.)*

Case2
Training.accdb *(cont.)*

Case3
Agency.accdb *(cont.)*

Case4
Vacation.accdb *(cont.)*

Case5
ACE.accdb *(cont.)*

Session 7.1

Customizing Existing Reports

A report is a formatted printout (or screen display) of the contents of one or more tables in a database. Although you can format and print data using datasheets, queries, and forms, reports offer greater flexibility and provide a more professional, readable appearance. For example, the staff at Belmont Landscapes can create reports from the database for billing statements and mailing labels, but they could not use datasheets, queries, and forms for the same purposes.

Before Lucia Perez joined Belmont Landscapes to enhance the Panorama database, Sarah Fisher and her staff created two reports. Sarah used the Report tool to create the rptContract report and the Report Wizard to create the rptCustomersAndContracts report. One of Sarah's staff members modified the rptCustomersAndContracts report in Layout view by modifying the title, moving and resizing fields, changing the font color of field names, inserting a picture, and using conditional formatting to format values in the ContractAmt field that exceed $25,000 in a red font. The rptCustomersAndContracts report is an example of a custom report. When you modify a report created by the Report tool or the Report Wizard in Layout view or in Design view, or when you create a report from scratch in Layout view or in Design view, you produce a **custom report**. You need to produce a custom report whenever the Report tool or the Report Wizard cannot automatically create the specific report you need, or when you need to fine-tune an existing report to fix formatting problems or to add controls and special features.

Sarah asks Lucia to review the rptContract report, make improvements to it, and demonstrate features that Sarah's staff can use when working with reports.

Viewing a Report in Report View

You can view reports on screen in Print Preview, Layout view, Design view, and Report view. You've already viewed and worked with reports in Print Preview and Layout view, and you'll find that making modifications in Design view for reports is similar to making changes in Design view for forms. **Report view** provides an interactive view of a report. You can use Report view to view the contents of a report and to apply a filter to the data in a report. You can also copy selected portions of the report to the Clipboard and use the selected data in another program.

InSight	**Choosing the View to Use for a Report**

You can view a report on screen using Report view, Print Preview, Layout view, or Design view. Which view you choose depends on what you intend to do with the report and its data.

- Use Report view when you want to filter the report data before printing a report, or when you want to copy a selected portion of a report.
- Use Print Preview when you want to see what a report will look like when it is printed. Print Preview is the only view in which you can navigate the pages of a report, zoom in or out, and view a **multiple-column report**, which is a report that prints the same collection of field values in two or more sets across the page.
- Use Layout view when you want to modify a report while seeing actual report data.
- Use Design view when you want to fine-tune a report's design, or when you want to add lines, rectangles, and other controls that are available only in Design view.

You'll open the rptContract report in Report view and show Sarah how she can interact with the report in this view.

To interact with the rptContract report in Report view:

▶ **1.** Start Access, and then open the **Panorama** database in the Level.02\Tutorial folder provided with your Data Files.

Trouble? If the Security Warning is displayed below the Ribbon, either the Panorama database is not located in the Level.02\Tutorial folder or you did not designate that folder as a trusted folder. Make sure you opened the database in the Level.02\Tutorial folder, and make sure that it's a trusted folder.

▶ **2.** Open the Navigation Pane, scroll down the Navigation Pane (if necessary), right-click **rptContract**, click **Open** on the shortcut menu, and then close the Navigation Pane. The rptContract report opens in Report view and the Navigation Pane closes. See Figure 7-1.

Tip

Double-clicking a report name in the Navigation Pane opens the report in Report view.

Report displayed in Report view | **Figure 7-1**

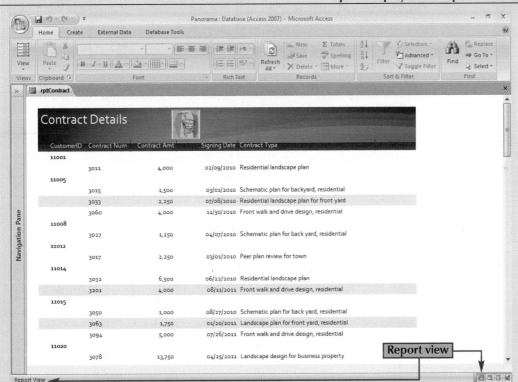

In Report view, you can view the live version of the report prior to printing it, just as you can do in Print Preview. Unlike Print Preview, you can apply filters to the report before printing it. You'll show Sarah how to apply filters to the rptContract report.

▶ **3.** In the first report detail line for Contract Num 3011, right-click **Residential landscape plan** in the Contract Type column to open the shortcut menu, and then point to **Text Filters**. A submenu of filter options for the Text field opens. See Figure 7-2.

Figure 7-2 | **Filter options for a Text field in Report view**

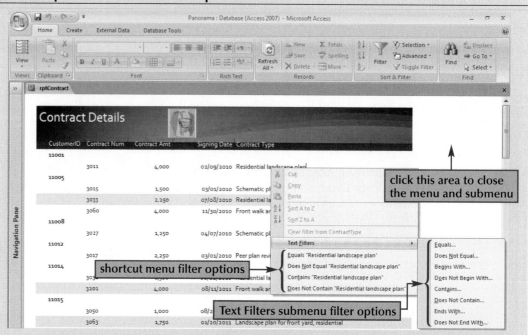

The filter options that appear on the shortcut menu depend on the selected field's data type and the selected value. Because you clicked the ContractType field value without selecting a portion of the value, the shortcut menu displays filter options—various conditions using the value "Residential landscape plan"—for the entire ContractType field value. You'll close the menus and select a portion of the ContractNum field value to show Sarah a different way of filtering the report.

4. Click an unused portion of the window (see Figure 7-2) to close the menus, and in the report detail line for Contract Num 3011, double-click **Residential** in the Contract Type column to select it, right-click **Residential**, and then point to **Text Filters** on the shortcut menu. The filter options now apply to the selected text.

Notice that the filter options on the shortcut menu include options such as "Begins With" and "Does Not Begin With," because the text you selected is at the beginning of the field value in the Contract Type column.

5. Click **Contains "Residential"** on the shortcut menu. The report content changes to display only those contracts that contain the word "residential" in the Contract Type column.

6. Double-click the word **residential** in the Contract Type column for the report detail line for Contract Num 3015 to select it, right-click **residential** to open the shortcut menu, and then point to **Text Filters**. The filter options on the shortcut menu now include the "Ends With" and "Does Not End With" options, because the text you selected is at the end of the field value in the Contract Type column.

Sarah wants to view only those contracts whose Contract Type column equals "residential landscape plan."

7. Click an unused portion of the window to close the menus, and in the report detail line for Contract Num 3011, right-click **Residential landscape plan** in the Contract Type column, and then click **Equals "Residential landscape plan"** on the shortcut menu. Only the five contracts that contain the selected phrase are displayed in the report. See Figure 7-3.

Filter applied to the report in Report view　　　　**Figure 7-3**

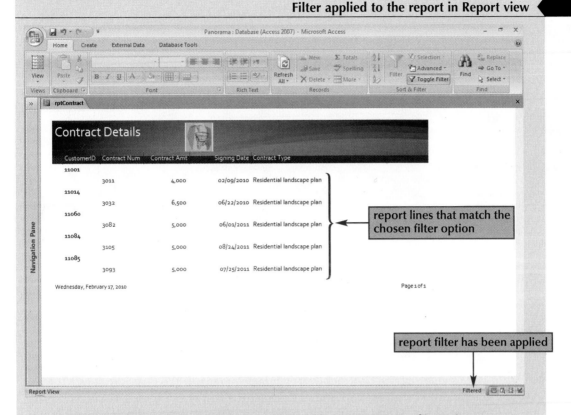

report lines that match the chosen filter option

report filter has been applied

Sarah can print the filtered report, or she can select the entire filtered report or a portion of the filtered report. Then she can copy the selection to the Clipboard and paste it into another program, such as a Word document or an Excel spreadsheet. You'll show Sarah how to copy the entire filtered report to the Clipboard.

8. Click to the left of the Contract Details title at the top of the report (but don't click in the Navigation Pane), drag down to the bottom of the report, release the mouse button to select the entire report, and then in the Clipboard group on the Home tab, point to the **Copy** button ⎘. See Figure 7-4.

Tip

To select a portion of the report instead of the entire report, click to the left of the top of the selection and drag down to the bottom of the selection.

Figure 7-4 **After selecting the entire report in Report view**

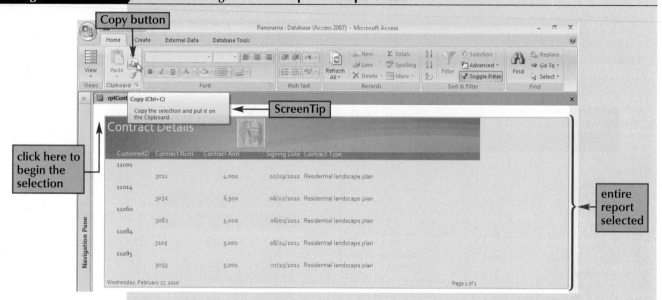

If you needed to copy the selection to the Clipboard, you would click the Copy button (see Figure 7-4). Sarah doesn't need to copy the selection, so you'll show her how to remove the filter from the report.

9. Click to the left of the Contract Details title at the top of the report to select the top portion of the report and to deselect the rest of the report, right-click **Residential landscape plan** in any report detail line in the Contract Type column, and then click **Clear filter from ContractType**. Access removes the filter and displays the complete report.

10. Scroll down the report, and notice that some field values in the Contract Type column are not fully displayed and that no grand total of the ContractAmt field values is displayed at the end of the report.

Sarah wants you to enlarge the Contract Type column in the rptContract report so that all field values are fully displayed. She also wants you to insert a space in the CustomerID column heading, remove the report's AutoFormat, format the ContractAmt field values using the Currency format, and add a grand total of the ContractAmt field values. These changes will make the report more useful for Sarah.

Enhancing and Correcting Reports Created by the Report Tool and the Report Wizard | InSight

Creating a report using the Report tool or the Report Wizard can save time, but you should review the report to determine if you need to make any of the following types of common enhancements and corrections:

- Change the report title from the report object name (with an rpt prefix and no spaces) to one that has meaning to the users.
- Reduce the widths of the date and page number controls, and move the controls so that they are not printed on a separate page.
- Review the report in Print Preview and, if the report displays excess pages, adjust the page margins and the placement of controls.
- Verify that all controls are large enough to fully display their values.

Modifying a Report in Layout View

You can make all the report changes Sarah wants in Layout view. Modifying a report in Layout view is similar to modifying a form in Layout view.

To view the report in Layout view:

▶ **1.** On the status bar, click the **Layout View** button 🔲, and then scroll to the top of the report (if necessary). See Figure 7-5.

Viewing the report in Layout view ◀ Figure 7-5

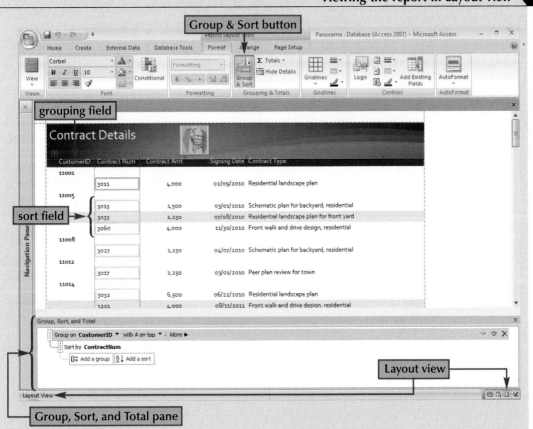

Tip

You can also switch views by right-clicking the object tab, and then clicking the view option on the shortcut menu.

Trouble? If the Group, Sort, and Total pane is not open at the bottom of the screen, click the Group & Sort button in the Grouping & Totals group on the Format tab.

Because the rptContract report has a grouping field and a sort field, the Group & Sort button is selected, and the Group, Sort, and Total pane is open at the bottom of the screen. In the **Group, Sort, and Total pane**, you can modify the report's grouping fields and sort fields, and the report calculations for the groups. A **grouping field** is a report sort field that includes a Group Header section before a group of records having the same sort field value and a Group Footer section after the group of records. A **Group Header section** usually displays the group name and the sort field value for the group. A **Group Footer section** usually displays subtotals or counts for the records in that group. The rptContract report's grouping field is the CustomerID field, which is displayed in a Group Header section that precedes the set of contracts for the customer; the grouping field does not have a Group Footer section. The ContractNum field is a secondary sort key, as shown in the Group, Sort, and Total pane.

Because you don't need to change the grouping or sort fields for the report, you'll close the pane and then make Sarah's modifications to the report.

To modify the report in Layout view:

▶ 1. In the Grouping & Totals group on the Format tab, click the **Group & Sort** button to close the Group, Sort, and Total pane.

First, you'll increase the height of the Contract Type column.

▶ 2. Scroll down the report to CustomerID 11083, which has the longest field value in the Contract Type column, click the **ContractType** field value for ContractNum 3043, move the pointer to the bottom edge of the selected value, and when the pointer changes to a ↕ shape, drag down the bottom edge to increase the height to display two lines. See Figure 7-6. After you make a resizing adjustment to the control, the portion of the report you're using as a basis for the resizing might move off the screen, and you might have to scroll back to it.

Figure 7-6	After resizing the Contract Type column

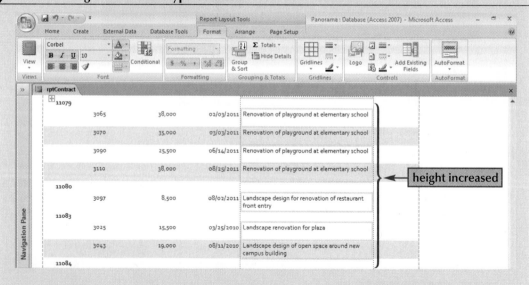

Next, you'll change the format of the field values in the Contract Amt column to Currency.

▶ **3.** Right-click any value in the Contract Amt column to open the shortcut menu, click **Properties** to open the property sheet, set the Format property to **Currency**, and then close the property sheet.

When Lucia made her initial modifications to the tables, queries, forms, and reports in the Panorama database, she failed to change the first column heading in the rptContract report to Customer ID (with a space) when she modified the report. Although Lucia had set the Caption property for the CustomerID field in the tblContract table to Customer ID before she modified the rptContract report, Caption property changes do not propagate to existing forms and reports. However, a Caption property setting propagates to all new forms and reports.

▶ **4.** Scroll to the top of the report (if necessary), double-click the **CustomerID** column heading, insert a space before "ID," and then press the **Enter** key.

Sarah intends to print the rptContract report periodically in the future, and she finds the AutoFormat at the beginning of the report distracting and unnecessary in a printed report. You'll remove the AutoFormat from the report.

▶ **5.** In the AutoFormat group on the Format tab, click the **AutoFormat** button to open the AutoFormat gallery, and then click the **None** button (row 3, column 4). The AutoFormat gallery closes, and the AutoFormat is removed from the report. See Figure 7-7.

After removing the AutoFormat from the report ◀ Figure 7-7

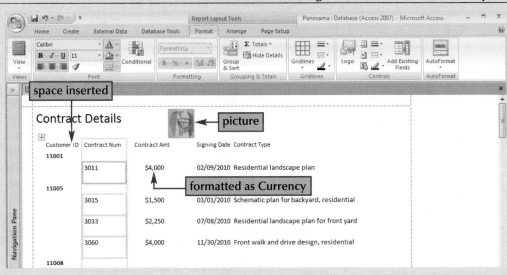

Sarah notes that the picture at the top of the report isn't needed now that you've removed the AutoFormat, so you'll delete it.

▶ **6.** Right-click the picture at the top of the report to open the shortcut menu, and then click **Delete** to remove the picture.

Removing the AutoFormat also removed the alternate background color setting in the detailed contract lines, and Sarah wants you to restore this feature.

▶ **7.** Click to the left of **3011** in the Contract Num column to select the detail lines, click the arrow on the **Alternate Fill/Back Color** button ▦ to display the gallery of available colors, and then in the Access Theme Colors palette, click the **Background** color (row 1, column 5). The Background color is applied to alternate detail lines in the report.

Sarah's last change to the report is to add a grand total of the ContractAmt field values. First, you must select the Contract Amt column or one of the values in the column.

▶ **8.** In the detail line for ContractNum 3011, click **$4,000** in the Contract Amt column, and then in the Grouping & Totals group on the Format tab, click the **Totals** button to display the Totals menu. See Figure 7-8.

Figure 7-8 | **Displaying options on the Totals menu**

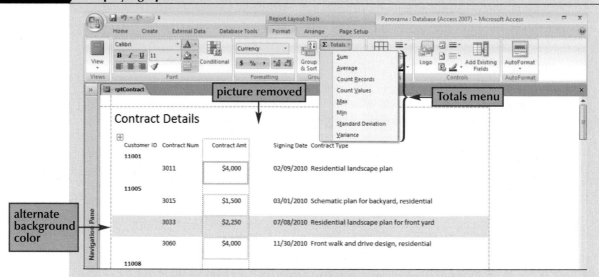

You select one of the eight aggregate functions on the Totals menu to summarize values in the selected column. To calculate and display the grand total contract amount, you'll select the Sum aggregate function.

▶ **9.** Click **Sum** on the Totals menu, and then scroll to the bottom of the report. The grand total of the ContractAmt field values ($1,758,075) is displayed at the end of the report, as are subtotals for each group of contracts for each CustomerID field value ($19,000 for the last customer). See Figure 7-9.

Figure 7-9 | **After adding subtotals and a grand total of the ContractAmt field values**

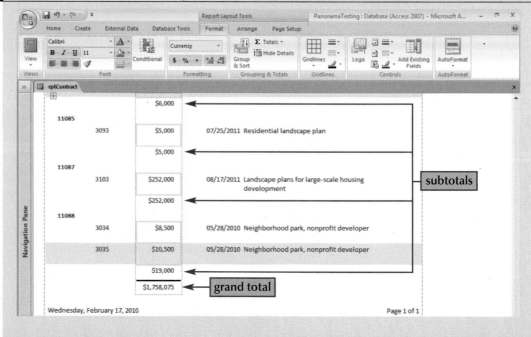

When you use an aggregate function in Layout view, Access adds the results of the function to the end of the report and adds subtotals for each grouping field. Because each customer has few contracts, Sarah asks you to remove the subtotals from the report.

10. Right-click the **$19,000** subtotal to open the shortcut menu, click **Delete** to remove the subtotals, and then scroll to the end of the report. Although you deleted the subtotals, the grand total still appears at the end of the report.

Sarah wants to review the rptContract report in Print Preview.

11. Save your report changes, switch to Print Preview, and then scroll through the report, ending on the last page of the report.

You can use the Zoom control on the status bar to zoom in or out the report view in 10% increments (click the Zoom In or Zoom Out buttons) or in variable increments (drag the Zoom slider control).

12. Click the **Zoom In** button ⊕ on the status bar to increase the zoom percentage to 110%. See Figure 7-10.

Viewing the rptContract report in Print Preview | Figure 7-10

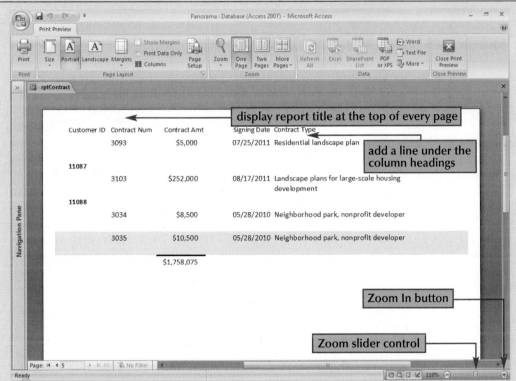

Trouble? Depending on the printer you are using, the last page of your report might differ. If so, don't worry. Different printers format reports in different ways, sometimes affecting the total number of pages and the number of records printed per page.

Sarah identifies two additional modifications she wants you to make to the report. She wants you to add a line below the column heading labels to separate them from the following detail report lines, and she wants the report title to be displayed at the top of every page, not just on the first page of the report.

Modifying a Report in Design View

Unlike the modifications you made to the report in Layout view, you can't use Layout view for Sarah's two new modifications. You must make these modifications in Design view. Design view for reports is similar to Design view for forms, which you used in Tutorial 6 to customize forms.

To view the report in Design view:

▶ **1.** Switch to display the report in Design view. See Figure 7-11.

Figure 7-11 ▶ **rptContract report in Design view**

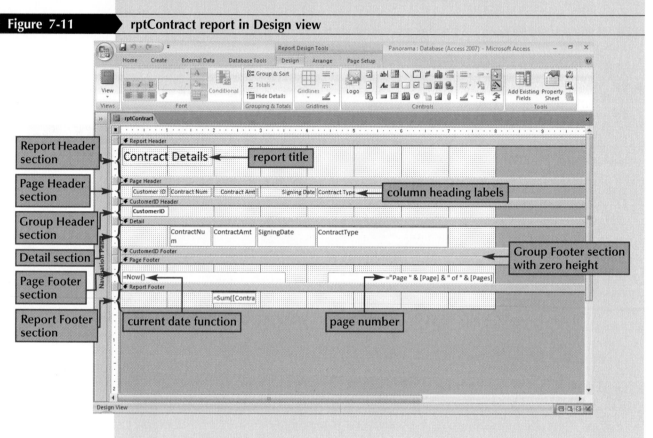

Notice that Design view for a report has most of the same components as Design view for a form. For example, Design view for forms and reports includes horizontal and vertical rulers, grids in each section, and similar buttons in groups on the Design tab.

Design view for the rptContract report displays seven sections: the Report Header section contains the report title, the Page Header section contains column heading labels, the Group Header section (CustomerID Header) contains the CustomerID grouping field, the Detail section contains the bound controls to display the field values for each record in the record source (tblContract), the Group Footer section (CustomerID Footer) has zero height and isn't displayed in the report, the Page Footer section contains the current date and the page number, and the Report Footer section contains a horizontal line above the Sum function for the grand total of the ContactAmt field values.

Each Access report can have the seven different sections described in Figure 7-12.

Access report sections ◄ **Figure 7-12**

Report Section	Description
Report Header	Appears once at the beginning of a report. Use it for report titles, company logos, report introductions, and cover pages.
Page Header	Appears at the top of each page of a report. Use it for column headings, report titles, page numbers, and report dates. If your report has a Report Header section, it precedes the first Page Header section.
Group Header	Appears before each group of records that has the same sort field value. Use it to print the group name and the field value that all records in the group have in common. A report can have up to 10 grouping levels.
Detail	Appears once for each record in the underlying table or query. Use it to print selected fields from the table or query and to print calculated values.
Group Footer	Appears after each group of records that has the same sort field value. It is usually used to print totals for the group.
Report Footer	Appears once at the end of the report. Use it for report totals and other summary information.
Page Footer	Appears at the bottom of each page of a report. Use it for page numbers and brief explanations of symbols or abbreviations. If your report has a Report Footer section, it precedes the Page Footer section on the last page of the report.

You don't have to include all seven sections in a report. When you design a report, you determine which sections to include and what information to place in each section. Figure 7-13 shows a sample report produced from the Panorama database; it includes all seven sections.

Figure 7-13 | **Sample report showing the seven sections of a report**

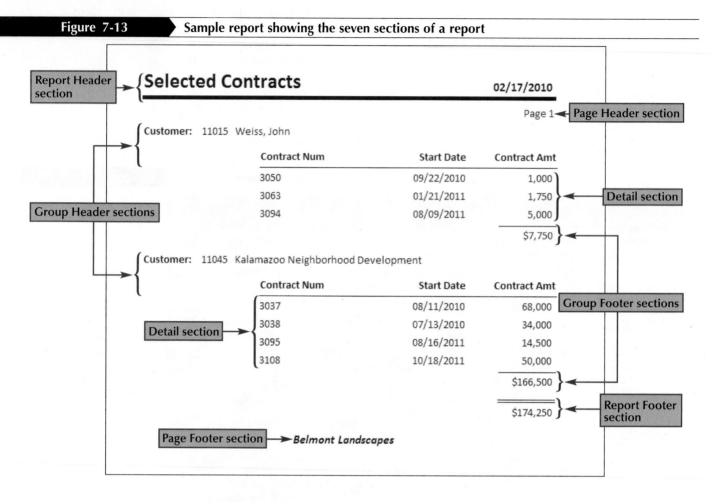

The Report tool used six of the seven report sections to create the rptContract report for Sarah. To make Sarah's changes to the report, you need to increase the height of the Page Header section, move the column heading labels down in the section, add a line under the column heading labels, cut the report title from the Report Header section and paste it in the Page Header section, move the report title, and then resize the Report Header and Page Header sections.

To modify the report in Design view:

▶ 1. Place the pointer on the bottom edge of the Page Header section. When the pointer changes to a ✛ shape, drag the section's edge down until it is at the 1-inch mark on the vertical ruler.

Before you can move the column heading labels down in the Page Header section, you need to remove them and their related text boxes from the tabular layout. Recall that a tabular layout is a control layout arranged in a datasheet format. If you don't remove all the controls from the tabular layout before moving the labels, some of the controls that remain in the tabular layout might shift position or undergo unintended property changes.

▶ 2. Use **Shift + Click** to select all five labels in the Page Header section, the **CustomerID** text box in the CustomerID Header section, the four text boxes in the Detail section, and the grand total text box in the Report Footer section, and then click the **Arrange** tab on the Ribbon. See Figure 7-14.

Labels and text boxes selected ◀ **Figure 7-14**

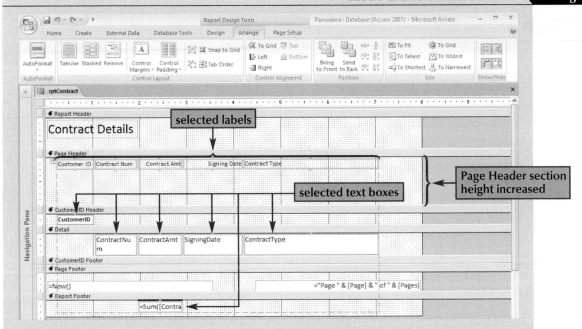

▶ **3.** In the Control Layout group on the Arrange tab, click the **Remove** button to remove all selected controls from the tabular layout.

▶ **4.** Use **Shift + Click** to deselect the **CustomerID** text box in the CustomerID Header section, the four text boxes in the Detail section, and the grand total text box in the Report Footer section, leaving only the five labels selected, and then use the ↓ key to move the labels down in the Page Header section until the tops of the labels are at the 0.625-inch mark on the vertical ruler.

Next, you'll add a line under the labels.

▶ **5.** Click to the right of the grid in the Page Header section to deselect all controls, click the **Design** tab on the Ribbon, and then in the Controls group on the Design tab, click the **Line** button ◣ .

▶ **6.** Position the pointer's plus symbol (+) at the lower-left corner of the Customer ID label in the Page Header section, hold down the **Shift** key, drag a horizontal line from left to right, so the end of the line aligns with the right edge of "Contract Type" in the Contract Type label box, release the mouse button, and then release the **Shift** key.

▶ **7.** In the Controls group on the Design tab, click the **Line Thickness** button ▤▾ , click the line with the ScreenTip **1 pt** in the list, and then deselect the control.

▶ **8.** Reduce the height of the Page Header section by dragging the bottom of the section up until it touches the bottom of the line you just added.

Finally, you'll cut the report title from the Report Header section and paste it in the Page Header section, and then remove the Report Header section.

▶ **9.** Right-click the report title in the Report Header section to open the shortcut menu, click **Cut** to delete the control and place it on the Clipboard, right-click the **Page Header** section bar to select that section and open the shortcut menu, and then click **Paste**. The report title is pasted in the upper-left corner of the Page Header section.

Tip

If you want to make sure you draw a straight horizontal or vertical line, press the Shift key before you start drawing the line and release the Shift key after you've created it.

▶ **10.** Drag the bottom of the Report Header section all the way up to the Report Header section bar to remove the section from the report. See Figure 7-15.

Figure 7-15 | **After modifying the rptContract report in Design view**

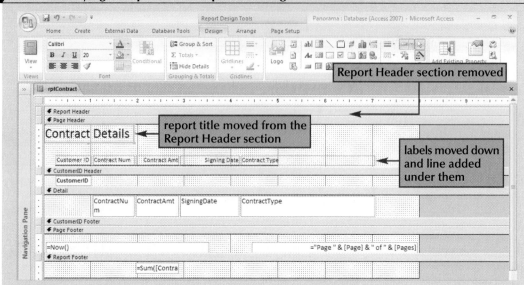

▶ **11.** Save your report changes, switch to Print Preview, and then scroll through the report, ending on the last page of the report. See Figure 7-16.

Figure 7-16 | **The modified rptContract report in Print Preview**

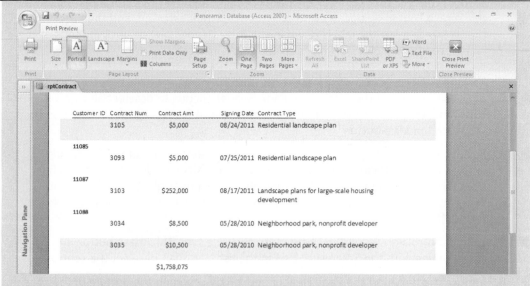

▶ **12.** Close the report.

▶ **13.** If you are not continuing on to the next session, close the Panorama database, and then exit Access.

Now that you have completed the changes to the rptContract report, you'll create a custom report for Sarah in the next session.

Session 7.1 Quick Check | Review

1. What is a custom report?
2. You can view a report in Report view. What other actions can you perform in Report view?
3. What is a grouping field?
4. Describe the seven sections of an Access report.

Session 7.2

Designing a Custom Report

Before you create a custom report, you should first plan the report's contents and appearance.

Guidelines for Designing a Report | InSight

When you plan a report, you should keep in mind the following report design guidelines:

- Determine the purpose of and record source for the report. Recall that the record source is a table or query that provides the fields for a form or report. If the report displays detailed information (a **detail report**), such as a list of all contracts, then the report will display fields from the record source in the Detail section. If the report displays only summary information (a **summary report**), such as total contracts by city, then no detailed information appears; only grand totals and possibly subtotals appear based on calculations using fields from the record source.
- Determine the sort order for the information in the report.
- Identify any grouping fields in the report.

At the same time you are designing a report, you should keep in mind the following report formatting guidelines:

- Balance the report's attractiveness against its readability and economy. Keep in mind that an attractive, readable two-page report is more economical than a report of three pages or more. Unlike forms, which usually display one record at a time in the main form, reports display multiple records. Instead of arranging fields vertically as you do in a form, you usually position fields horizontally across the page in a report. Typically, you single space the detail lines in a report. At the same time, make sure to include enough white space between columns so the values do not overlap or run together.
- Group related fields and position them in a meaningful, logical order. For example, position identifying fields, such as names and codes, on the left. Group together all location fields, such as street and city, and position them in their customary order.
- Identify each column of field values with a column heading label that names the field.
- Include the report title, page number, and date on every page of the report.
- Identify the end of a report either by displaying grand totals or an end-of-report message.
- Use few colors, fonts, and graphics to keep the report uncluttered and to keep the focus on the information.
- Use a consistent style for all reports in a database.

After working with Sarah and her staff to determine their requirements for a new report, Lucia prepared a paper design for a custom report to display invoices grouped by invoice item. Lucia then used her paper design to create the report shown in Figure 7-17.

Figure 7-17 ▶ **Lucia's design for the custom report**

The custom report will list the records for all invoices and will contain five sections:

- The Page Header section contains the report title ("Invoices by Item") centered between the current date on the left and the page number on the right. A horizontal line separates the column heading labels from the rest of the report page. From your work with the Report tool and the Report Wizard, you know that, by default, Access places the report title in the Report Header section and the date and page number in the Page Footer section. Sarah prefers the date, report title, and page number to appear at the top of each page, so you need to place this information in the custom report's Page Header section.
- The InvoiceItem field value from the tblInvoice table is displayed in a Group Header section.
- The Detail section contains the InvoiceDate, InvoiceAmt, and InvoicePaid field values from the tblInvoice table; the ContractType field value from the tblContract table; the City field value from the tblCustomer table; and the Customer calculated field value from the qryCustomersByName query. The detail records are sorted in ascending value by the InvoiceDate field.
- A subtotal of the InvoiceAmt field values is displayed below a line in the a Group Footer section.
- The grand total of the InvoiceAmt field values is displayed below a double line in the Report Footer section.

Before you start creating the custom report, you need to create a query that'll serve as the record source for the report.

Creating a Query for a Custom Report

The data for a report or form can come from a single table, from a single query based on one or more tables, or from multiple tables and/or queries. Sarah's report will contain data from the tblInvoice, tblContract, and tblCustomer tables, and from the qryCustomersByName query. You'll use the Simple Query Wizard to create a query to retrieve all the data required for the custom report and to serve as the report's record source.

Tip

For reports and forms that use data from multiple tables and/or queries, you should create a query to serve as the record source. If the report or form requirements change, you can easily add fields, including calculated fields, to the query.

To create the query using the Simple Query Wizard:

▶ 1. If you took a break after the previous session, make sure that the Panorama database is open and the Navigation Pane is closed.

▶ 2. Click the **Create** tab on the Ribbon, in the Other group on the Create tab, click the **Query Wizard** button, make sure **Simple Query Wizard** is selected, and then click the **OK** button. The first Simple Query Wizard dialog box opens.

   You need to select fields from the tblInvoice, tblContract, and tblCustomer tables, and from the qryCustomersByName query, in that order.

▶ 3. Make sure **Table: tblInvoice** is selected in the Tables/Queries box, and then move the **InvoiceItem**, **InvoiceDate**, **InvoiceAmt**, and **InvoicePaid** fields, in that order, to the Selected Fields list box.

▶ 4. Select **Table: tblContract** in the Tables/Queries box, and then move the **ContractType** field to the Selected Fields list box.

▶ 5. Select **Table: tblCustomer** in the Tables/Queries box, and then move the **City** field to the Selected Fields list box.

▶ 6. Select **Query: qryCustomersByName** in the Tables/Queries box, move the **Customer** calculated field to the Selected Fields list box, and then click the **Next** button.

▶ 7. Make sure the **Detail (shows every field of every record)** option button is selected, and then click the **Next** button to open the final Simple Query Wizard dialog box.

   After entering the query name and creating the query, you'll need to set the sort fields for the query.

▶ 8. Change the query name to **qryInvoicesByItem**, click the **Modify the query design** option button, and then click the **Finish** button.

   The InvoiceItem field will be a grouping field, which means it's the primary sort field, and the InvoiceDate field is the secondary sort field.

▶ 9. Set the InvoiceItem Sort text box to **Ascending**, set the InvoiceDate Sort text box to **Ascending**, save your query changes, and then click below the field lists and above the design grid to deselect all values. The completed query contains seven fields from three tables and one query and has two sort fields, the InvoiceItem primary sort field and the InvoiceDate secondary sort field. See Figure 7-18.

| Figure 7-18 | Finished qryInvoicesByItem query in Design view |

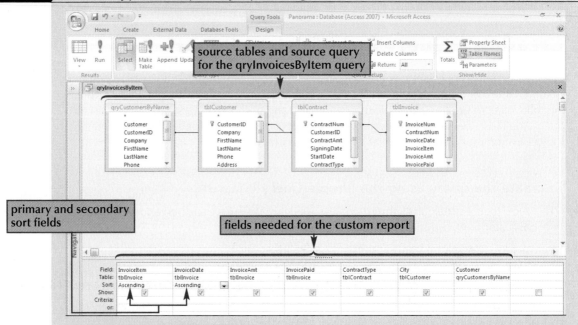

Trouble? After you've finished creating the query and close it, if you later open the query in Design view, you'll see the thicker join lines with referential integrity enforced connecting the tblCustomer and tblContract table field lists and the tblContract and tblInvoice table field lists.

Before closing the query, you'll run it to view the query recordset.

10. Run the query, which displays 172 records, and then close the query.

You'll use the qryInvoicesByItem query as the record source for Lucia's custom report.

Creating a Custom Report

You could use the Report Wizard to create the report and then modify it to match the report design. However, because you need to customize several components of the report, you will create a custom report in Layout view, and then switch between Layout and Design view to fine-tune the report. As the first step to creating the report, you need to display a blank report in Layout view.

| Reference Window | **Creating a Blank Report in Layout View** |

- Click the Create tab on the Ribbon.
- In the Reports group on the Create tab, click the Blank Report button to open a blank report in Layout view.

Making Report Design Modifications | InSight

You perform operations in Layout and Design views for reports the same as you perform operations in these views for forms. These operations become easier with practice. Remember to use the Undo button, back up your database frequently, save your report changes frequently, work from a copy of the report for complicated design changes, and compact and repair the database on a regular basis. You can also display the report in Print Preview at any time to view your progress on the report.

The record source for the report will the qryInvoicesByItem query. You'll set the record source after you create a blank report in Layout view.

To create a blank report and add bound controls in Layout view:

▶ **1.** Click the **Create** tab on the Ribbon, and then in the Reports group on the Create tab, click the **Blank Report** button. A new report opens in Layout view. In addition, the Field List pane and the Group, Sort, and Total pane open. See Figure 7-19.

Blank report in Layout view ◀ **Figure 7-19**

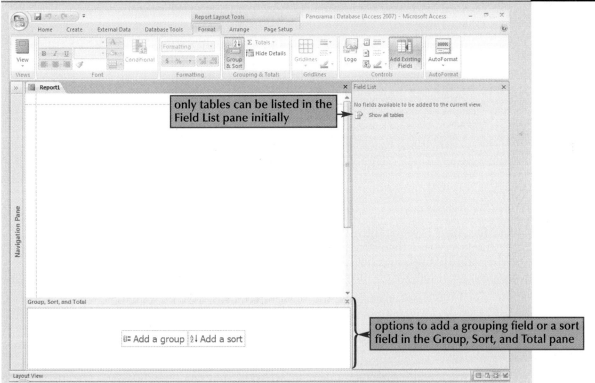

Trouble? If the Group, Sort, and Total pane is not open on your screen, click the Group & Sort button in the Grouping & Totals group on the Format tab.

▶ **2.** Click the **Arrange** tab on the Ribbon, and then in the Tools group on the Arrange tab, click the **Property Sheet** button to open the property sheet for the report.

▶ **3.** In the property sheet, click the **Record Source** arrow, click **qryInvoicesByItem**, and then close the property sheet.

▶ **4.** Click the **Format** tab on the Ribbon, and then in the Controls group on the Format tab, click the **Add Existing Fields** button to open the Field List pane. The Field List pane displays the seven fields in the qryInvoicesByItem query, which is the record source for the report.

Referring to Lucia's report design, you'll add six of the seven fields to the report in a tabular layout, which is the default control layout when you add fields to a report in Layout view.

▶ **5.** Double-click **InvoiceDate** in the Field List pane, and then in order, double-click **Customer**, **City**, **ContractType**, **InvoiceAmt**, and **InvoicePaid** in the Field List pane. The six bound controls are displayed in a tabular layout in the report. See Figure 7-20.

Figure 7-20 **After adding fields to the report in Layout view**

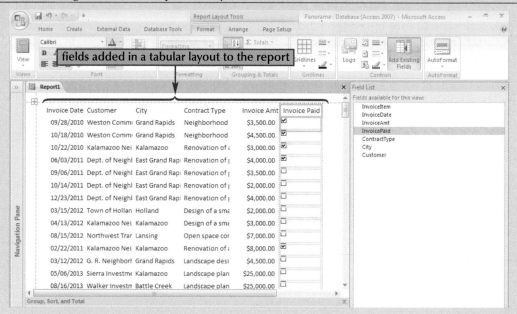

Trouble? If you add the wrong field to the report, right-click the field in the tabular layout, and then click Delete on the shortcut menu to delete it. If you add a field in the wrong order, click the field in the tabular layout, and then drag it to its correct columnar position.

You'll add the seventh field, the InvoiceItem field, as a grouping field, so you are done working with the Field List pane.

▶ **6.** Close the Field List pane, and then save the report as **rptInvoicesByItem**.

Next, you'll adjust the column widths in Layout view, and then fine-tune the adjustments and the spacing between columns later in Design view. Also, because the Invoice Amt and Invoice Paid columns are adjacent, you can change the rightmost column heading to Paid without losing any meaning and to save space.

To resize and rename columns in Layout view:

▶ **1.** Click **Customer** to select the column, and then drag the right edge of the control to increase its width. See Figure 7-21.

▶ **2.** Repeat Step 1 to increase the width of the **City** column and the **Contract Type** column. See Figure 7-21.

▶ **3.** Double-click **Invoice Paid** in the rightmost column, delete **Invoice** and the following space, and then press the **Enter** key.

▶ **4.** Drag the right edge of the **Paid** control to the left to decrease the column's width. See Figure 7-21.

After resizing and renaming columns in Layout view ◀ **Figure 7-21**

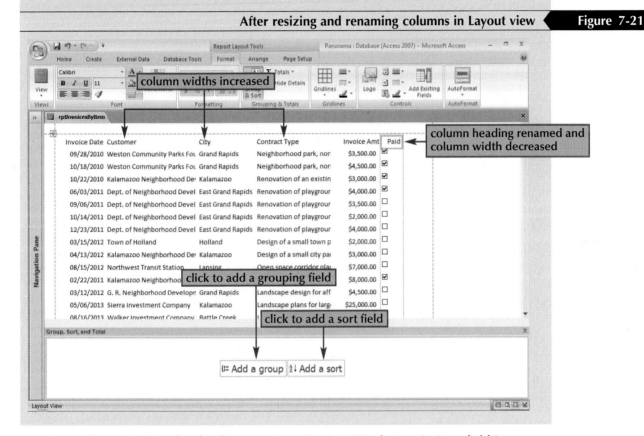

According to Lucia's plan for the report (see Figure 7-17), the InvoiceItem field is a grouping field that is displayed in a Group Header section. Subtotals for the InvoiceAmt field are displayed in a Group Footer section for each InvoiceItem field value.

Sorting and Grouping Data in a Report

Access lets you organize records in a report by sorting them using one or more sort fields. Each sort field can also be a grouping field. If you specify a sort field as a grouping field, you can include a Group Header section and a Group Footer section for the group. A Group Header section typically includes the name of the group, and a Group Footer section typically includes a count or subtotal for records in that group. Some reports have a Group Header section but not a Group Footer section, some reports have a Group Footer section but not a Group Header section, and some reports have both sections or have neither section.

You use the Group, Sort, and Total pane to select sort fields and grouping fields for a report. Each report can have up to 10 sort fields, and any of its sort fields can also be grouping fields.

Reference Window | **Sorting and Grouping Data in a Report**

- Display the report in Layout or Design view.
- If necessary, click the Group & Sort button in the Grouping & Totals group on the Format tab in Layout view or the Design tab in Design view to display the Group, Sort, and Total pane.
- To select a grouping field, click the Add a group button in the Group, Sort, and Total pane, and then click the grouping field in the list. To set additional properties for the grouping field, click the More button on the grouping field band.
- To select a sort field that is not a grouping field, click the Add a sort button in the Group, Sort, and Total pane, and then click the sort field in the list. To set additional properties for the sort field, click the More button on the sort field band.

In Lucia's report design, the InvoiceItem field is a grouping field, and the InvoiceDate field is a sort field. The InvoiceItem field value is displayed in a Group Header section, but not its label. The sum of the InvoiceAmt field values is displayed in the Group Footer section for the InvoiceItem grouping field. Next, you'll select the grouping field and the sort field and set their properties.

To select and set the properties for the grouping field and the sort field:

▶ **1.** In the Group, Sort, and Total pane, click the **Add a group** button, and then click **InvoiceItem** in the list. Access adds a Group Header section to the report with InvoiceItem as the grouping field, and adds a group band in the Group, Sort, and Total pane. See Figure 7-22.

| Figure 7-22 | After selecting InvoiceItem as a grouping field in Layout view |

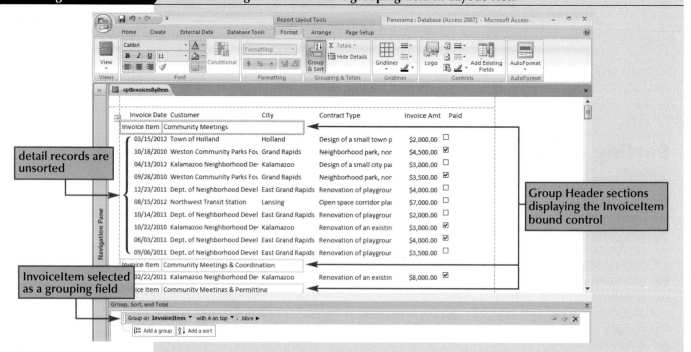

InvoiceItem is now a bound control in the report in a Group Header section that displays a field value text box and its attached label. The group band in the Group, Sort, and Total pane contains the name of the grouping field (InvoiceItem), the sort order ("with A on top" to indicate ascending), and the More option, which you click to display more options for the grouping field. You can click the "with A on top" arrow to change to descending sort order ("with Z on top").

Notice that the detail records are unsorted, and Lucia's design specifies an ascending sort on the InvoiceDate field. Next, you'll select this field as a secondary sort field; the InvoiceItem grouping field is the primary sort field.

2. In the Group, Sort, and Total pane, click the **Add a sort** button, and then click **InvoiceDate** in the list. Access displays the detail records in ascending InvoiceDate order, and adds a sort band for the InvoiceDate field in the Group, Sort, and Total pane.

Next, you'll display all the options for the InvoiceItem grouping field, and set grouping options as shown in Lucia's report design.

3. Click ⁞ to the left of the group band to select it, and then click **More** to expand the band and display all group options. See Figure 7-23.

After expanding the group band ◄ **Figure 7-23**

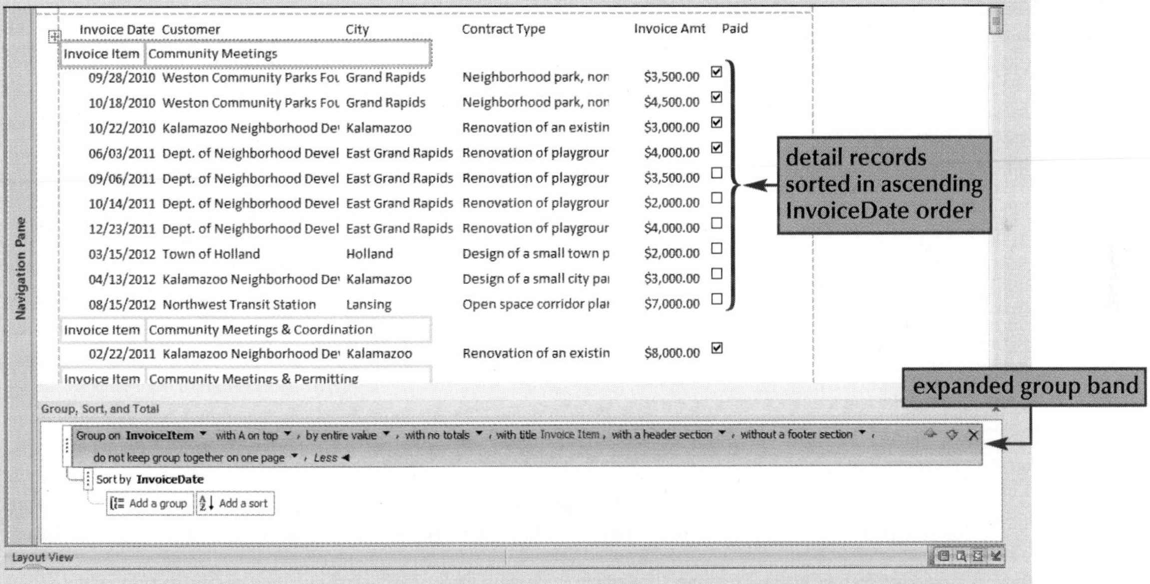

Reviewing Lucia's report design (see Figure 7-17), you need to delete the InvoiceItem label, add a Group Footer section, add a grand total and subtotals for the InvoiceAmt field values to the Group Footer section, and set the Keep Together property. The **Keep Together property** prints a group header on a page only if there is enough room on the page to print the first detail record for the group; otherwise, the group header prints at the top of the next page.

▶ **4.** In the "with title Invoice Item" option, click the **Invoice Item** link to open the Zoom dialog box, press the **Delete** key to delete the expression, and then click the **OK** button. The Invoice Item label is deleted from the report, and the option in the group band changes to "with title click to add."

▶ **5.** Click the **do not keep group together on one page** arrow, and then click **keep header and first record together on one page**.

▶ **6.** Click the **without a footer section** arrow, and then click **with a footer section**. Access adds a Group Footer section for the InvoiceItem grouping field, but the report doesn't display this new section until you add controls to it.

▶ **7.** Click the **with no totals** arrow to open the Totals menu, click the **Total On** arrow, click **InvoiceAmt**, make sure **Sum** is selected in the Type box, click the **Show Grand Total** check box, click the **Show in group footer** check box, and then click an empty area of the group band to close the menu. Access adds InvoiceAmt sub-totals to the report. See Figure 7-24.

Figure 7-24 ▶ **After setting properties in the group band**

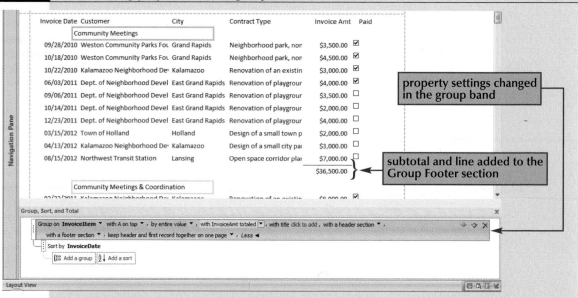

Similar to the sound form design strategy you followed in the previous tutorial, you should frequently save your report changes and review the report in Print Preview.

▶ **8.** Save your report changes, switch to Print Preview, and review every page until you reach the end of the report—noticing in particular the details of the report format and the effects of the Keep Together property. See Figure 7-25.

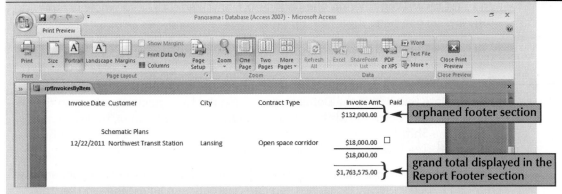

Trouble? Depending on the printer you are using, the last page of your report might differ.

The grand total of the InvoiceAmt field values is displayed at the end of the report. Also, as shown in Figure 7-25, it's possible for subtotals, which you added to the Group Footer section, to appear in an orphaned footer section. An **orphaned footer section** appears by itself at the top of a page, and the detail lines for the section appear on the previous page. When you set the Keep Together property for the grouping field, you set it to keep the group and the first detail record together on one page to prevent an **orphaned header section**, which is a section that appears by itself at the bottom of a page. To prevent both types of orphaned sections, you'll set the Keep Together property to keep the whole group together on one page.

In addition, you need to fine-tune the sizes of the text boxes in the Detail section, adjust the spacing between columns, and make other adjustments to the current content of the report design before adding a report title, the date, and page numbers to the Page Header section. You'll make most of these report design changes in Design view.

Working with Controls in Design View

Compared to Layout view, Design view gives you greater control over the placement and sizing of controls, and lets you add and manipulate many more controls, but at the expense of not being able to see live data in the controls to guide you as you make changes.

You'll switch to Design view to move and resize controls in the report.

To move and resize controls in the report:

▶ **1.** Switch to Design view. The report has five sections: the Page Header section contains the six column heading labels, the InvoiceItem Header section (a Group Header section) contains the InvoiceItem text box, the Detail section contains the six bound controls, the InvoiceItem Footer section (a Group Footer section) contains a line and the subtotal text box, and the Report Footer section contains a line and the grand total text box.

The Group, Sort, and Total pane is still open, so first you'll change the Keep Together property setting.

▶ **2.** In the Group, Sort, and Total pane, click ⋮ to the left of the group band to select it, click **More** to expand the band and display all group options, click the **keep header and first record together on one page** arrow, and then click **keep whole group together on one page**, and then close the Group, Sort, and Total pane.

You'll start improving the report by moving the InvoiceItem text box to the left in the InvoiceItem Header section and setting its font to bold.

▶ **3.** Select the **InvoiceItem** text box in the InvoiceItem Header section and the **InvoiceDate** text box in the Detail section, align the two selected controls on their left edges, hold down the **Shift** key, click the **InvoiceDate** text box to deselect it, release the **Shift** key, and then in the Font group on the Design tab, click the **Bold** button **B**. The InvoiceItem text box is displayed as bold text.

The report width is 8 inches, and Sarah will want to print the report on standard 8.5" × 11" paper, so you'll change the page orientation to landscape, and set the left and right margin widths to 1.5 inches each.

▶ **4.** Click the **Page Setup** tab on the Ribbon, and in the Page Layout group on the Page Setup tab, click the **Page Setup** button to open the Page Setup dialog box, click the **Page** tab, click the **Landscape** option button, click the **Print Options** tab, set the Top and Bottom margin properties to **0.7** and the Left and Right margin properties to **1.5**, and then click the **OK** button.

The text boxes in the Detail section are crowded together with little space between them. Your reports shouldn't have too much space between columns, but reports are easier to read when the columns are separated more than they are in the rptInvoicesByItem report. Sometimes the amount of spacing is dictated by the users of the report, but mostly it's the report designer's choice to make. First, you'll remove the Paid label and the InvoicePaid text box from the tabular layout, resize them, and move them to the right.

▶ **5.** Select the **Paid** label in the Page Header section and the **InvoicePaid** text box (it contains a check box) in the Detail section, right-click one of the selected controls to open the shortcut menu, point to **Layout**, click **Remove** to remove both controls from the tabular layout, deselect the **InvoicePaid** text box, right-click an edge of the **Paid** label to open the shortcut menu, point to **Size**, click **To Fit**, and then move the label to the right until its right edge is at the 8-inch mark on the horizontal ruler.

▶ **6.** Click the **InvoicePaid** text box in the Detail section, decrease its width until it's slightly wider than the check box inside it, and then move it to the right until the check box is centered under the Paid label. See Figure 7-26.

To move the remaining bound controls, you first need to remove them from the tabular layout.

▶ **7.** Select the **InvoiceAmt** text box and the other three controls in that column, right-click the **InvoiceAmt** text box, point to **Layout** on the shortcut menu, click **Remove**, deselect all controls except the **Invoice Amt** label in the Page Header section, right-click the **Invoice Amt** label, point to **Size** on the shortcut menu, click **To Fit**, select all controls in the column, right-click one of the selected controls, point to **Align** on the shortcut menu, click **Right**, and then move the selected controls to the right. See Figure 7-26.

▶ **8.** Refer to Figure 7-26 and repeat Step 7 for the **ContractType**, **City**, and **Customer** bound controls, in that order, but do not align the bound controls on their right edges. See Figure 7-26.

After resizing and moving controls in Design view ◄ **Figure 7-26**

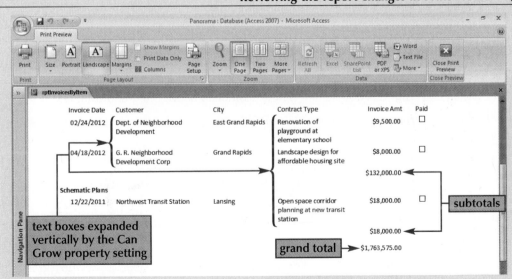

You resized the Customer and ContractType text boxes in Layout view, but you did not resize them wide enough to display the entire field value in all cases. For the Customer and ContractType text boxes, you'll set their Can Grow property to Yes. The **Can Grow property**, when set to Yes, expands a text box vertically to fit the field value when the report is printed, previewed, or viewed in Layout and Report views.

▶ **9.** Select the **Customer** and **ContractType** text boxes in the Detail section, open the property sheet, click the **Format** tab in the property sheet, scroll down the property sheet, set the Can Grow property to **Yes** (if necessary), close the property sheet, and then save your report changes.

▶ **10.** Switch to Print Preview, and review every page of the report, ending on the last page of the report. See Figure 7-27.

> **Tip**
>
> You can select two or more controls, and then set common properties for the selected controls, instead of setting them one control at a time.

Reviewing the report changes in Print Preview ◄ **Figure 7-27**

The groups stay together on one page, except for the Schematic Plan group, which has too many lines to fit on one page. The Can Grow property correctly expands the height of the Customer and ContractType text boxes. Also, the lines that were displayed above the subtotals and grand total are no longer displayed. You'll add those lines back in the report.

Adding Lines to a Report

You've used the Line tool to add lines to a form. You can also use the Line tool to add lines to a report, and you'll use the Line tool to add a single line above the subtotal control and a double line above the grand total control.

You'll switch to Design view to add the lines to the report.

To add lines to the report:

▶ **1.** Switch to Design view.

▶ **2.** In the Controls group on the Design tab, click the **Line** button ◹ , position the pointer's plus symbol (+) at the upper-left corner of the subtotal text box in the InvoiceItem Footer section, hold down the **Shift** key, drag a horizontal line from left to right, so the end of the line aligns with the upper-right corner of the subtotal text box, release the mouse button, and then release the **Shift** key.

▶ **3.** Click the **grand total** text box in the Report Footer section, and then press the ↓ key four times to move the control down slightly in the section, and then deselect all controls.

▶ **4.** In the Controls group on the Design tab, click the **Line** button ◹ , position the pointer's plus symbol (+) at the grid dot just above the upper-left corner of the grand total text box in the Report Footer section, hold down the **Shift** key, drag a horizontal line from left to right, so the end of the line aligns with the right edge of the grand total text box, release the mouse button, and then release the **Shift** key.

Next, you'll copy and paste the line in the Report Footer section, and then align the copied line into position.

▶ **5.** Right-click the selected line in the Report Footer section, and then click **Copy** on the shortcut menu.

▶ **6.** Right-click the Report Footer section bar, and then click **Paste** on the shortcut menu. A copy of the line is pasted in the upper-left corner of the Report Footer section.

▶ **7.** Press the ↓ key twice to move the copied line down slightly in the section, hold down the **Shift** key, click the original line in the Report Footer section to select both lines, release the **Shift** key, right-click the copied line, point to **Align**, and then click **Right**. A double line is now positioned above the grand total text box.

▶ **8.** Save your report changes, switch to Print Preview, and then navigate to the last page of the report. See Figure 7-28.

After adding lines to the report ◀ **Figure 7-28**

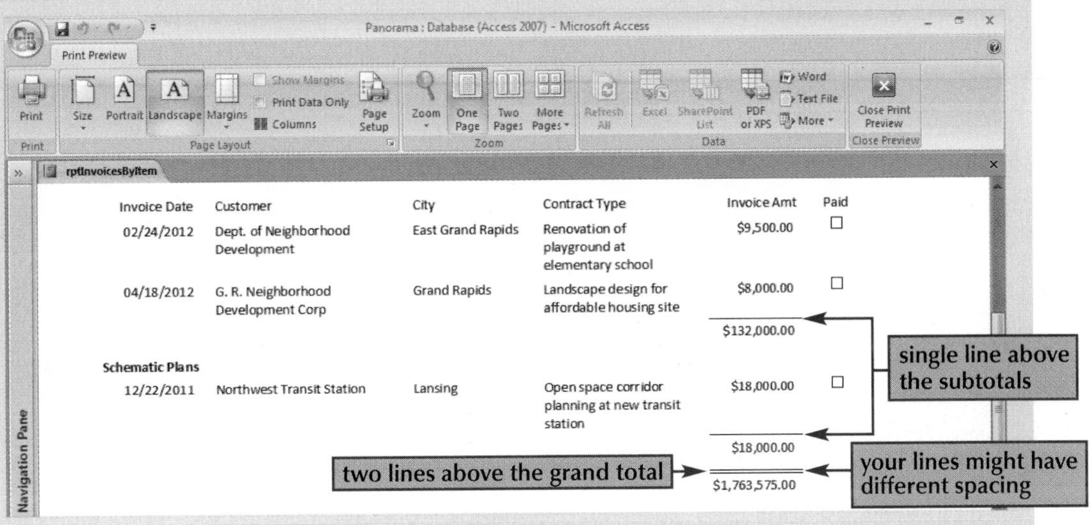

For the rptInvoicesByItem report, the InvoiceDate field is a sort field. Two or more consecutive detail report lines can have the same InvoiceDate field value. In these cases, Sarah wants the InvoiceDate field value printed for the first detail line but not for subsequent detail lines because she believes it makes the printed information easier to read.

Hiding Duplicate Values in a Report

You use the **Hide Duplicates property** to hide a control in a report when the control's value is the same as that of the preceding record in the group.

Hiding Duplicate Values in a Report	Reference Window

- Display the report in Layout or Design view.
- Open the property sheet for the field whose duplicate values you want to hide, set the Hide Duplicates property to Yes, and then close the property sheet.

Your next design change to the report is to hide duplicate InvoiceDate field values in the Detail section. This change will make the report easier to read.

To hide the duplicate InvoiceDate field values:

▶ 1. Switch to Design view, and then click below the Report Footer section to deselect all controls.

▶ 2. Open the property sheet for the **InvoiceDate** text box in the Detail section.

▶ 3. Click the **All** tab (if necessary), click the right side of the **Hide Duplicates** text box, and then click **Yes**. See Figure 7-29.

Tip

For properties in the property sheet that offer a list of choices, you can double-click the property name to cycle through the options in the list.

Figure 7-29 **Hiding duplicate field values**

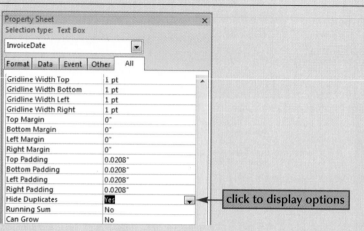

click to display options

▶ **4.** Close the property sheet, save your report changes, switch to Print Preview, navigate to the last page of the report, and then navigate back one page (if necessary) until you see the two invoice records for 08/25/2011. The InvoiceDate value is hidden for the second of the two consecutive records with a 08/25/2011 date. See Figure 7-30.

Figure 7-30 **Report in Print Preview with hidden duplicate values**

hidden duplicate value

▶ **5.** If you are not continuing on to the next session, close the Panorama database, and then exit Access.

You have completed the Detail section of the custom report. In the next session, you will complete the custom report according to Lucia's design by adding controls to the Page Header section.

Session 7.2 Quick Check | Review

1. What is a detail report? a summary report?
2. The _____ property prints a group header on a page only if there is enough room on the page to print the first detail record for the group; otherwise, the group header prints at the top of the next page.
3. A(n) _____ section appears by itself at the top of a page, and the detail lines for the section appear on the previous page.
4. The _____ property, when set to Yes, expands a text box vertically to fit the field value when a report is printed, previewed, or viewed in Layout and Report views.
5. Why might you want to hide duplicate values in a report?

Session 7.3

Adding the Date to a Report

According to Lucia's design, the rptInvoicesByItem report includes the date in the Page Header section, along with the report title, the page number, the column heading labels, and a line under the labels.

Placing the Report Title, Date, and Page Number in the Page Header Section | InSight

When you use the Report tool or the Report Wizard to create a report, the report title is displayed in the Report Header section and the page number is displayed in the Page Footer section. However, the date (and time) is displayed in the Report Header section when you use the Report tool and in the Page Footer section when you use the Report Wizard. Because you should create reports that display controls in consistent positions, you have to move the date control for reports created by the Report tool or by the Report Wizard so the date is displayed in the same section for all reports.

Although company standards vary, a common report standard places the report title, date, and page number on the same line in the Page Header section. Using one line saves vertical space in the report compared to placing some controls in the Page Header section and others in the Page Footer section. Placing the report title in the Page Header section, instead of in the Report Header section, allows users to identify the report title on any page without having to turn to the first page.

To add the date to a report, you can click the Date & Time button in the Controls group on the Ribbon, and Access will insert the Date function in a text box without an attached label at the right edge of the Report Header section. The **Date function** returns the current date. The format of the Date function is =Date(). The equal sign (=) indicates that what follows it is an expression; Date is the name of the function; and the empty set of parentheses indicates a function rather than simple text.

Reference Window | **Adding the Date and Time to a Report**

- Display the report in Layout or Design view.
- In the Controls group on the Design tab in Design view, or on the Format tab in Layout view, click the Date & Time button to open the Date and Time dialog box.
- To display the date, click the Include Date check box, and then click one of the three date option buttons.
- To display the time, click the Include Time check box, and then click one of the three time option buttons.
- Click the OK button.

According to Lucia's design for the report, the date appears at the left edge of the Page Header section, so you'll need to add the date to the report, and then cut the date from the Report Header section and paste it into the Page Header section.

To add the date to the Page Header section:

1. If you took a break after the previous session, make sure that the Panorama database is open, that the rptInvoicesByItem report is open in Print Preview, and that the Navigation Pane is closed.

   You can add the current date in Layout or Design view. Because you can't cut and paste controls between sections in Layout view, you'll add the date in Design view. First, you'll move the column heading labels down in the Page Header section to make room for the controls you'll be adding above them.

2. Switch to Design view, increase the height of the Page Header section until the bottom edge of the section is at the 1-inch mark on the vertical ruler, select all six labels in the Page Header section, and then use the ↓ key to move the labels down until the tops of the labels are at the 0.5-inch mark on the vertical ruler.

   Lucia's report design has a horizontal line under the labels that you'll add next.

3. In the Controls group on the Design tab, click the **Line** button ╲ , position the pointer's plus symbol (+) at the lower-left corner of the Invoice Date label in the Page Header section, hold down the **Shift** key, drag a horizontal line from left to right so the end of the line aligns with the right edge of the Paid label, release the mouse button, and then release the **Shift** key.

4. Reduce the height of the Page Header section by dragging the bottom of the section up until it touches the bottom of the line you just added.

5. In the Controls group on the Design tab, click the **Date & Time** button 📅 to open the Date and Time dialog box, make sure the **Include Date** check box is checked and the **Include Time** check box is unchecked, and then click the third date option button. See Figure 7-31.

Completed Date and Time dialog box ◀ Figure 7-31

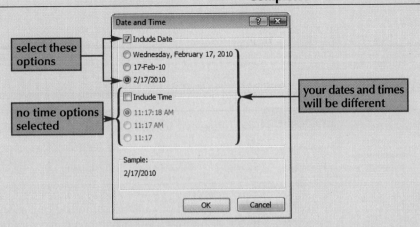

6. Click the **OK** button. The Date function is added to the Report Header section. See Figure 7-32.

Date function added to the Report Header section ◀ Figure 7-32

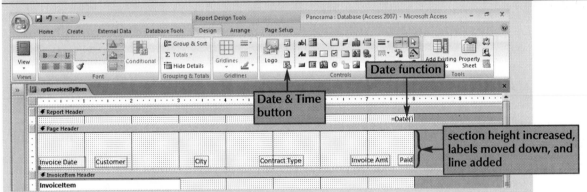

The default size for the Date function text box must accommodate long dates and long times, so the text box is much wider than needed for the date that'll appear in the custom report. You'll decrease its width before moving it to the Page Header section.

7. Click the **Date function** text box, decrease its width from the left to one inch total, right-click an edge of the Date function text box to open the shortcut menu, click **Cut** to delete the control, right-click the **Page Header** section bar to select that section and open the shortcut menu, and then click **Paste**. The Date function text box is pasted in the upper-left corner of the Page Header section.

8. Save your report changes, and then switch to Print Preview to view the date in the Page Header section. See Figure 7-33.

Tip

When you print, preview, or view the report in Report or Layout view, the current date is displayed instead of the Date function that appears in the text box in Design view.

Figure 7-33 **Viewing the date in Print Preview**

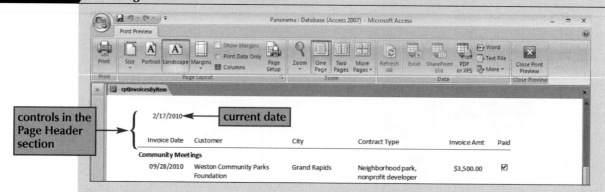

Trouble? Your year might appear with two digits instead of four digits as shown in Figure 7-33. Your date format might also differ, depending on your computer's date settings. These differences do not cause any problems.

You'll left-align the date in the text box in Design view.

▶ **9.** Switch to Design view, make sure the Date function text box is selected, and then in the Font group on the Design tab, click the **Align Text Left** button ▤.

You are now ready to add page numbers to the Page Header section.

Adding Page Numbers to a Report

You can display page numbers in a report by including an expression in the Page Header or Page Footer section. You can click the Insert Page Number button in the Controls group in Layout or Design view to add a page number expression to a report. The inserted page number expression automatically displays the correct page number on each page of a report.

Reference Window | **Adding Page Numbers to a Report**

- Display the report in Layout or Design view.
- In the Controls group on the Design tab in Design view, or on the Format tab in Layout view, click the Insert Page Number button to open the Page Numbers dialog box.
- Select the format, position, and alignment options you want.
- Select whether you want to display the page number on the first page.
- Click the OK button to place the page number expression in the report.

Lucia's design shows the page number displayed on the right side of the Page Header section, on the same line with the date.

To add page numbers in the Page Header section:

▶ **1.** In the Controls group on the Design tab, click the **Insert Page Number** button ▣. The Page Numbers dialog box opens.

You use the Format options to specify the format of the page number. Sarah wants page numbers to appear as Page 1, Page 2, and so on. This is the Page N format option. You use the Position options to place the page numbers at the top of the page in the Page Header section or at the bottom of the page in the Page Footer section. Lucia's design shows page numbers at the top of the page.

▶ 2. Make sure that the **Page N** option button in the Format section and that the **Top of Page [Header]** option button in the Position section are both selected.

The report design shows page numbers at the right side of the page. You can specify this placement in the Alignment list box.

▶ 3. Click the **Alignment** arrow, and then click **Right**.

▶ 4. Make sure the **Show Number on First Page** check box is checked, so the page number prints on the first page and all other pages as well. See Figure 7-34.

Completed Page Numbers dialog box | Figure 7-34

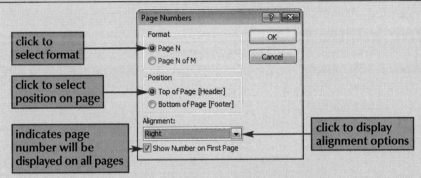

click to select format

click to select position on page

indicates page number will be displayed on all pages

click to display alignment options

▶ 5. Click the **OK** button. The text box shown in Figure 7-35 appears in the upper-right corner of the Page Header section. The expression =*"Page " & [Page]* in the text box means that the printed report will show the word "Page" followed by a space and the page number.

Page number expression added to the Page Header section | Figure 7-35

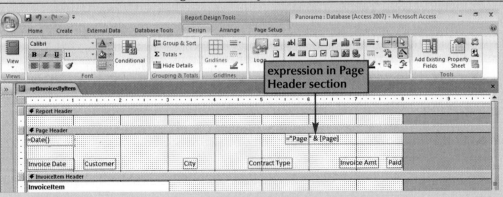

expression in Page Header section

The page number text box is much wider than needed for the page number expression that'll appear in the custom report. You'll decrease its width and right-align it.

▶ 6. Click the **Page Number** text box, decrease its width from the left to one inch total, and then in the Font group on the Design tab, click the **Align Text Right** button 	≡.

▶ 7. Save your report changes, and then switch to Print Preview. See Figure 7-36.

Figure 7-36 | Date and page number in the Page Header section

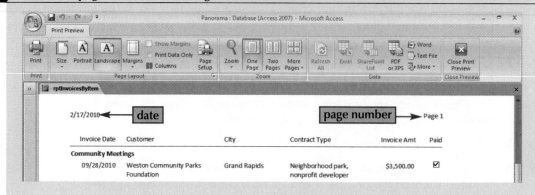

Now you are ready to add the title to the Page Header section.

Adding a Title to a Report

Lucia's report design includes the title "Invoices by Item," which you'll add to the Page Header section centered between the date and the page number.

To add the title to the Page Header section:

▶ **1.** Switch to Design view.

▶ **2.** In the Controls group on the Design tab, click the **Title** button 📄. The title "rptInvoicesByItem," which is name of the report object, appears in the Report Header section in 18-point font.

To match Lucia's design, you need to change the title, set its font size to 14 points, move it to the Page Header section, and then resize the Report Header section to zero height. The title is selected, so typing the new title will replace the current title.

▶ **3.** Type **Invoices by Item**, press the **Enter** key, click the **Font Size** arrow, and then click **14**.

▶ **4.** Right-click an edge of the title, point to **Size**, and then click **To Fit**.

▶ **5.** Right-click an edge of the title, click **Cut**, right-click the **Page Header** section bar, and then click **Paste**. The title is pasted in the upper-left corner of the Page Header section, and the Error Checking Options button ◈ appears to the right of the report title.

▶ **6.** Position the pointer on the **Error Checking Options** button ◈. A ScreenTip is displayed and describes the potential error. See Figure 7-37.

Pasted report title in the Page Header section ◀ **Figure 7-37**

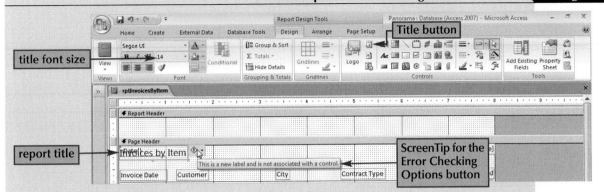

The ScreenTip indicates that the report title, which is a label control, is not associated with any bound or calculated control. Because you don't want a label that contains a report title to be associated with another control, you can ignore this potential error.

▶ **7.** Click the **Error Checking Options** button ⟨⬧⟩, and then click **Ignore Error**.

The report title is still selected, so you can move it so that it's centered between the date and the page number. Because the report title is positioned on top of the date control, there's a chance you might inadvertently also select the date control when you try to drag the report title into position, so you should use the → key to move the report title.

▶ **8.** Move the report title control to the right until it's centered between the date and page number controls.

Finally, you'll align the date, report title, and page number controls on their bottom edges.

▶ **9.** Select the date, report title, and page number controls in the Page Header section, right-click one of the selected controls, point to **Align**, and then click **Bottom**.

▶ **10.** Drag the bottom edge of the Report Header section up all the way to the Report Header section bar to remove the section from the report, and then save your report changes. You completed the design of the custom report. See Figure 7-38.

Figure 7-38 | Completed design of the rptInvoicesByItem report

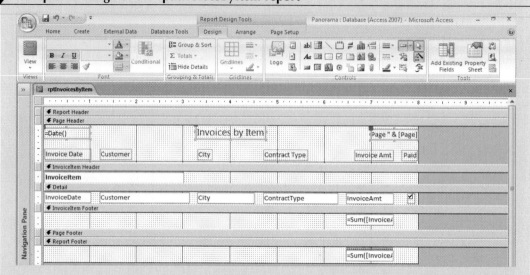

▶ **11.** Switch to Print Preview to review the completed report, and then navigate to the last page of the report. See Figure 7-39.

Figure 7-39 | Completed rptInvoicesByItem report in Print Preview

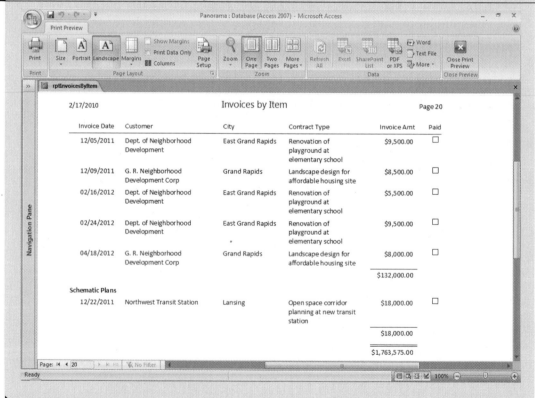

▶ **12.** Close the report.

Next, Sarah wants you to create mailing labels that can be used to address materials to Belmont Landscapes' customers.

Creating Mailing Labels

Sarah needs a set of mailing labels printed for all customers so she can mail a marketing brochure and other materials to them. The tblCustomer table contains the name and address information that will serve as the record source for the labels. Each mailing label will have the same format: first name and last name on the first line; company name (if it exists for the customer) on the second line; address on the third line; and city, state, and zip code on the fourth line.

You could create a custom report to produce the mailing labels, but using the Label Wizard is an easier and faster way to produce them. The **Label Wizard** provides templates for hundreds of standard label formats, each of which is uniquely identified by a label manufacturer's name and number. These templates specify the dimensions and arrangement of labels on each page. Standard label formats can have between one and five labels across a page; the number of labels printed on a single page also varies. Sarah's mailing labels are Avery number C2163; each sheet has 12 1.5-inch by 3.9-inch labels arranged in two columns and six rows on the page.

Creating Mailing Labels and Other Labels | Reference Window

- In the Navigation Pane, click the table or query that'll serve as the record source for the labels.
- In the Reports group on the Create tab, click the Labels button to start the Label Wizard and open its first dialog box.
- Select the label manufacturer and its product number, and then click the Next button.
- Select the label font, color, and style, and then click the Next button.
- Construct the label content by selecting the fields from the record source and specifying their placement and spacing on the label, and then click the Next button.
- Select one or more optional sort fields, click the Next button, specify the report name, and then click the Finish button.

You'll use the Label Wizard to create a report to produce mailing labels for all customers.

To use the Label Wizard to create the mailing label report:

▶ 1. Open the Navigation Pane, click **tblCustomer** to make it the current object that'll serve as the record source for the labels, close the Navigation Pane, and then click the **Create** tab on the Ribbon.

▶ 2. In the Reports group on the Create tab, click the **Labels** button. The first Label Wizard dialog box opens and asks you to select the standard or custom label you'll use.

▶ 3. Make sure that the **English** option button is selected in the Unit of Measure section, that the **Sheet feed** option button is selected in the Label Type section, and that **Avery** is selected in the Filter by manufacturer list box, and then click **C2163** in the Product number list box. See Figure 7-40.

Figure 7-40 | **Selecting a standard label**

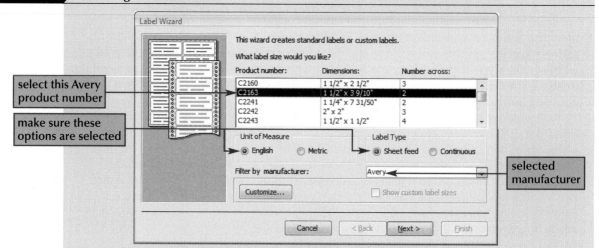

select this Avery product number

make sure these options are selected

selected manufacturer

Because the labels are already filtered for the Avery manufacturer, the top list box shows the Avery product number, dimensions, and number of labels across the page for each of its standard label formats. You can display the dimensions in the list in either inches or millimeters by choosing the appropriate option in the Unit of Measure section. You can also specify in the Label Type section whether the labels are on individual sheets or are continuous forms.

▶ **4.** Click the **Next** button to open the second Label Wizard dialog box, in which you choose font specifications for the labels.

Sarah wants the labels to use 10-point Arial with a medium font weight and without italics or underlines. The font weight determines how light or dark the characters will print; you can choose from nine values ranging from thin to heavy.

▶ **5.** If necessary, select **Arial** for the font name, **10** for the font size, and **Medium** for the font weight; make sure the Italic and the Underline check boxes are not checked and that black is the text color; and then click the **Next** button to open the third Label Wizard dialog box, from which you select the data to appear on the labels.

Sarah wants the mailing labels to print the FirstName and LastName fields on the first line; the Company field on the second line; the Address field on the third line; and the City, State, and Zip fields on the fourth line. One space will separate the FirstName and LastName fields, the City and State fields, and the State and Zip fields.

▶ **6.** Click **FirstName** in the Available fields list box, click the ⟩ button to move the field to the Prototype label box, press the **spacebar**, click **LastName** in the Available fields list box (if necessary), and then click the ⟩ button (see Figure 7-41). The braces around the field names in the Prototype label box indicate that the name represents a field rather than text that you entered.

Trouble? If you select the wrong field or type the wrong text, highlight the incorrect item in the Prototype label box, press the Delete key to remove the item, and then select the correct field or type the correct text.

▶ **7.** Press the **Enter** key to move to the next line in the Prototype label box, and then use Figure 7-41 to complete the entries in the Prototype label box. Make sure you press the **spacebar** after selecting the City field and the State field.

Completed label prototype ◁ **Figure 7-41**

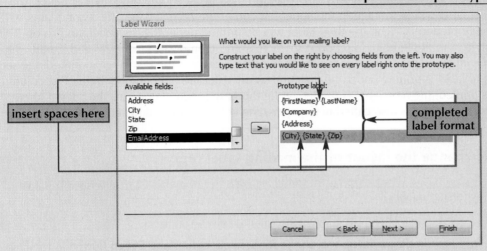

▶ 8. Click the **Next** button to open the fourth Label Wizard dialog box, in which you choose the sort fields for the labels.

Sarah wants Zip to be the primary sort field and LastName to be the secondary sort field.

▶ 9. Select the **Zip** field as the primary sort field, select the **LastName** field as the secondary sort field, and then click the **Next** button to open the last Label Wizard dialog box, in which you enter a name for the report.

▶ 10. Change the report name to **rptCustomerMailingLabels**, and then click the **Finish** button. Access saves the report as rptCustomerMailingLabels and then opens the first page of the report in Print Preview. Note that two columns of labels appear across the page. See Figure 7-42.

Previewing the label content and sequence ◁ **Figure 7-42**

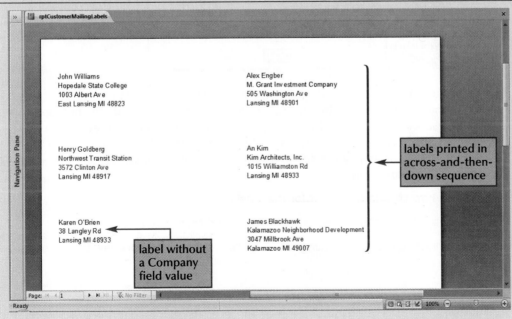

The rptCustomerMailingLabels report is a multiple-column report. The labels will be printed in ascending order by zip code and then in ascending order by last name. The first label will be printed in the upper-left corner on the first page, the second label will be printed to its right, the third label will be printed under the first label, and so on. This style of multiple-column report is the across-and-then-down layout. Instead, Sarah wants the labels to print with the "down, then across" layout—the first label is printed, the second label is printed under the first, and so on. After the bottom label in the first column is printed, the next label is printed at the top of the second column. The "down, then across" layout is also called **newspaper-style columns**, or **snaking columns**.

To change the layout of the mailing label report:

▶ **1.** Switch to Design view. The Detail section, the only section in the report, is sized for a single label.

First, you'll change the layout to snaking columns.

▶ **2.** Click the **Page Setup** tab on the Ribbon, click the **Page Setup** button in the Page Layout group, and then click the **Columns** tab. The Page Setup dialog box displays the Columns options for the report. See Figure 7-43.

| Figure 7-43 | Column options in the Page Setup dialog box |

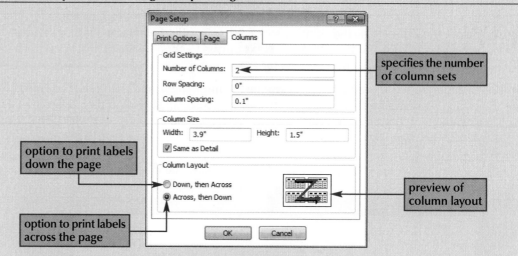

The Columns options in the Page Setup dialog box let you change the properties of a multiple-column report. In the Grid Settings section, you specify the number of column sets and the row and column spacing between the column sets. In the Column Size section, you specify the width and height of each column set. In the Column Layout section, you select between the "down, then across" and the "across, then down" layouts.

You can now change the layout for the labels.

▶ **3.** Click the **Down, then Across** option button, and then click the **OK** button.

You've finished the report changes, so you can now save and preview the report.

Tip

When you select a label using a manufacturer's name and product code, the options in the Grid Settings and Column Size sections are set for you automatically based on your selection.

▶ **4.** Save your report design changes, and then switch to Print Preview. The labels appear in the snaking-columns layout.

You've finished all work on Sarah's reports.

▶ **5.** Close the report, close the Panorama database, make a backup copy of the database, open the **Panorama** database, compact and repair the database, close the database, and then exit Access.

Sarah is very pleased with the modified report and the two new reports, which will provide her with improved information and help expedite her written communications with customers.

Session 7.3 Quick Check | Review

1. What is the function and its format to print the current date in a report?
2. How do you insert a page number in the Page Header section?
3. Clicking the Title button in the Controls group on the Design tab adds a report title to the _____ section.
4. What is a multiple-column report?

Tutorial Summary | Review

In this tutorial, you viewed a report created by the Report tool in Report view, filtered and copied information in the report, and customized the report in Layout view and Design view. You then examined general report design guidelines, learned how to use the guidelines in planning a custom report, and created a query to serve as the record source for the report. In creating the custom report, you sorted and grouped data; added fields and modified report controls; added lines; and added the date, page numbers, and a title. Finally, you created mailing labels.

Key Terms

Can Grow property	Group, Sort, and Total pane	newspaper-style columns
custom report	grouping field	orphaned footer section
Date function	Hide Duplicates property	orphaned header section
detail report	Keep Together property	Report view
Group Footer section	Label Wizard	snaking columns
Group Header section	multiple-column report	summary report

Practice	**Review Assignments**

Practice the skills you learned in the tutorial using the same case scenario.

Data File needed for the Review Assignments: Products.accdb (*cont. from Tutorial 6*)

Sarah wants you to create a custom report for the Products database that prints all companies and the products they offer. She also wants you to customize an existing report. You will perform the tasks for Sarah by completing the following steps:

1. Open the **Products** database located in the Level.02\Review folder provided with your Data Files.
2. Modify the **rptProductsByCompany** report. Figure 7-44 shows a sample of the last page of the completed report. Refer to the figure as you modify the report.

Figure 7-44

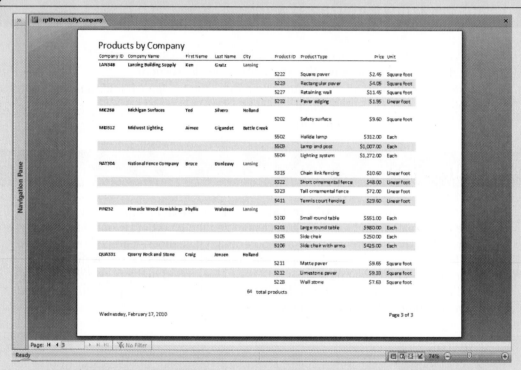

a. Change the Caption property for the report so that it matches the report name.
b. To fit the report on three pages, you might have to change Page Setup properties and reduce the width of the report in Design view after moving the page number to the left.
c. Use the Label tool in the Controls group on the Ribbon to add a label that contains the text **total products** to the right of the count of the total number of products displayed in the Report Footer section.

3. After you've completed and saved your modifications to the rptProductsByCompany report, filter the report in Report view, selecting all records that contain the word "soil" in the ProductType field. Copy the entire filtered report and paste it into a new Word document. Save the document as **rptProductsByCompanyCopy** in the Level.02\Review folder provided with your Data Files. Close Word, and then close the report without saving changes.

4. Create a query that displays the ProductType and CompanyName fields from the tblCompany table, and the ProductType, Price, and Unit fields from the tblProduct table. Sort in ascending order by the first three fields in the query, and then save the query as **qryCompanyProducts**.

5. Create a custom report based on the qryCompanyProducts query. Figure 7-45 shows a sample of the last page of the completed report. Refer to the figure as you create the report.

Figure 7-45

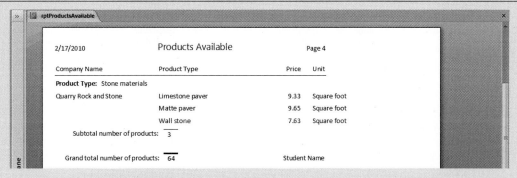

a. Save the report as **rptProductsAvailable**.
b. The ProductType field (from the tblCompany table) is a grouping field.
c. Hide duplicate values for the CompanyName field.
d. Use the Label tool in the Controls group on the Ribbon to add labels for the subtotals, the grand total, and your name.
e. Keep the whole group together on one page.

6. Create a mailing label report according to the following instructions:
a. Use the tblCompany table as the record source.
b. Use Avery C2160 labels, and use the default font and color.
c. For the prototype label, add the ContactFirstName, a space, and ContactLastName on the first line; the CompanyName on the second line; the Address on the third line; and the City, a space, State, a space, and Zip on the fourth line.
d. Sort by Zip and then by CompanyName, and then enter the report name **rptCompanyMailingLabels**.

7. Close the Products database without exiting Access, make a backup copy of the database, open the **Products** database, compact and repair the database, close the database, and then exit Access.

Create	**Case Problem 1**

Use the skills you learned in the tutorial to create reports for a music school.

Data File needed for this Case Problem: Contract.accdb (*cont. from Tutorial 6*)

Pine Hill Music School   Yuka wants you to modify an existing report and to create a custom report and mailing labels for the Contract database. You'll do so by completing the following:

1. Open the **Contract** database located in the Level.02\Case1 folder provided with your Data Files.
2. Modify the **rptStudentContracts** report. Figure 7-46 shows a sample of the last page of the completed report. Refer to the figure as you modify the report.

Figure 7-46

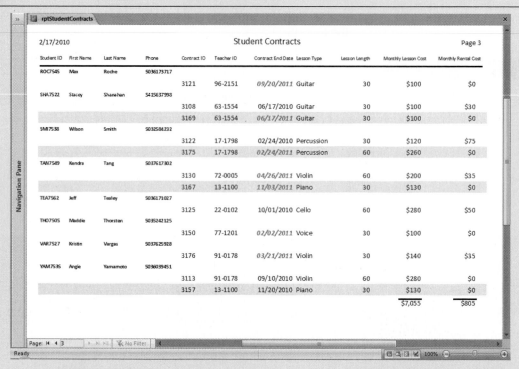

a. Change the conditional formatting rule for the ContractEndDate field to display the date in red, bold, italic font when the date is more recent than 1/1/2011.

b. Add controls to the last page of the report that calculate the total monthly lesson cost and total monthly rental cost below the correct columns.

3. Create a query that displays the LastName and FirstName fields from the tblTeacher table, the LessonType field from the tblContract table, the FirstName and LastName fields from the tblStudent table, and the MonthlyLessonCost and MonthlyRentalCost fields from the tblContract table. Sort in ascending order by the first three fields in the query, and then save the query as **qryTeacherLessons**.

4. Create a custom report based on the qryTeacherLessons query. Figure 7-47 shows a sample of the last page of the completed report. Refer to the figure as you create the report.

Figure 7-47

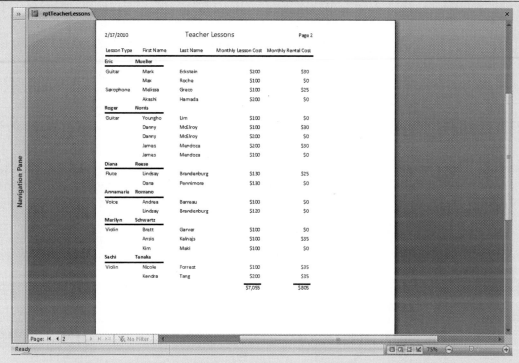

a. Save the report as **rptTeacherLessons**.
b. The LastName field (from the tblTeacher table) is a grouping field.
c. The LessonType field is a sort field, and the LastName field (from the tblStudent table) is a sort field.
d. Hide duplicate values for the LessonType field.
e. Add the FirstName field (from the tblTeacher table) to the Group Header section, and then delete its attached label.

5. Create a mailing label report according to the following instructions:
    a. Use the tblStudent table as the record source.

⊕ EXPLORE

    b. Use Avery C2160 labels, use a larger font size and a heavier font weight, and use the other default font and color options.
    c. For the prototype label, place FirstName, a space, and LastName on the first line; Address on the second line; and City, a space, State, a space, and Zip on the third line.
    d. Sort by Zip and then by LastName, and then enter the report name **rptStudentMailingLabels**.
    e. Change the mailing label layout to snaking columns.

6. Close the Contract database without exiting Access, make a backup copy of the database, open the **Contract** database, compact and repair the database, close the database, and then exit Access.

| Apply | Case Problem 2 |

Apply what you learned in the tutorial to create a report and labels for a health and fitness center.

Data File needed for this Case Problem: Training.accdb (*cont. from Tutorial 6*)

Parkhurst Health & Fitness Center   Martha Parkhurst wants you to create a custom report and mailing labels for the Training database. The custom report will be based on the results of a query you will create. You will create the query, the custom report, and the mailing labels by completing the following steps:

1. Open the **Training** database located in the Level.02\Case2 folder provided with your Data Files.
2. Create a query that displays the ProgramID, ProgramType, and MonthlyFee fields from the tblProgram table, and the MembershipStatus, FirstName, and LastName fields from the tblMember table. Sort in ascending order by the ProgramID, MembershipStatus, and LastName fields, and then save the query as **qryProgramMembership**.
3. Create a custom report based on the qryProgramMembership query. Figure 7-48 shows a sample of the last page of the completed report. Refer to the figure as you create the report.

Figure 7-48

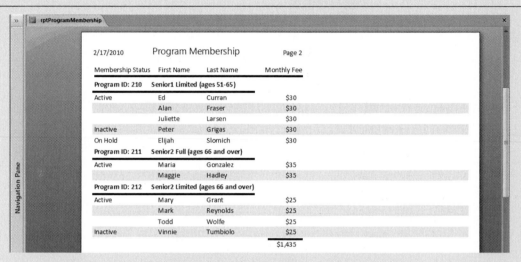

a. Save the report as **rptProgramMembership**.
b. The ProgramID field is a grouping field.
c. The MembershipStatus field is a sort field, and the LastName field is a sort field.
d. Hide duplicate values for the MembershipStatus field.
e. Add the ProgramType field to the Group Header section, and then delete its attached label.

4. Use the following instructions to create the mailing labels:
a. Use the tblMember table as the record source for the mailing labels.
b. Use Avery C2160 labels, and use the default font and color.
c. For the prototype label, place FirstName, a space, and LastName on the first line; Street on the second line; and City, a space, State, a space, and Zip on the third line.
d. Sort by Zip and then by LastName, and then type the report name **rptMemberLabels**.

5. Close the Training database with out exiting Access, make a backup copy of the database, open the **Training** database, compact and repair the database, close the database, and then exit Access.

| Apply | | Case Problem 3 |

Apply what you learned in the tutorial to create a report and labels for a recycling agency.

Data File needed for this Case Problem: Agency.accdb (*cont. from Tutorial 6*)

Rossi Recycling Group Mary Rossi asks you to create a custom report for the Agency database so that she can better track donations made by donors and to create mailing labels. You'll do so by completing the following:

1. Open the **Agency** database located in the Level.02\Case3 folder provided with your Data Files.
2. Create a query that displays the DonationDesc, DonationDate, and DonationValue fields from the tblDonation table, and the FirstName and LastName fields from the tblDonor table. Sort in ascending order by the DonationDesc, DonationDate, and LastName fields, and then save the query as **qryDonorDonations**.
3. Create a custom report based on the qryDonorDonations query. Figure 7-49 shows a sample of the last page of the completed report. Refer to the figure as you create the report.

Figure 7-49

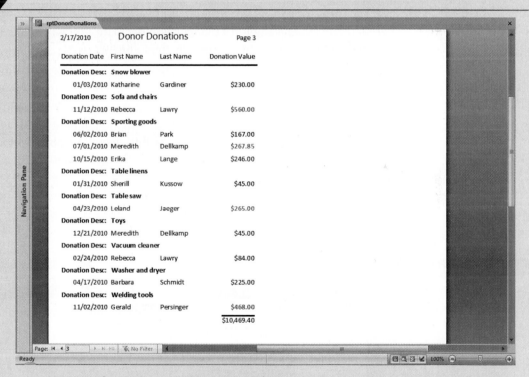

a. Save the report as **rptDonorDonations**.
b. The DonationDesc field is a grouping field.
c. The DonationDate field is a sort field, and the LastName field is a sort field.
d. Hide duplicate values for the DonationDate field.
e. Create a conditional formatting rule for the DonationValue field to display the value in blue, bold font when the amount is more than $250.

⊕ EXPLORE

4. After you've created and saved the rptDonorDonations report, filter the report in Report view, selecting all records whose LastName field value is "Park." Copy the entire filtered report and paste it into a new Word document. Save the document as **rptDonorDonationsCopy**. Close Word, and then close the report without saving it.

5. Use the following instructions to create the mailing labels:

   a. Use the tblAgency table as the record source for the mailing labels.

   b. Use Avery C2160 labels, and use the default font and color.

   c. For the prototype label, place ContactFirstName, a space, and ContactLastName on the first line; AgencyName on the second line; Address on the third line; and City, a space, State, a space, and Zip on the fourth line.

   d. Sort by Zip and then by ContactLastName, and then type the report name **rptAgencyLabels**.

   e. Change the mailing label layout to snaking columns.

6. Close the Agency database without exiting Access, make a backup copy of the database, open the **Agency** database, compact and repair the database, close the database, and then exit Access.

| Create | **Case Problem 4** |

Use the skills you've learned in this tutorial to create a report and labels for a luxury property rental company.

Data File needed for this Case Problem: Vacation.accdb (*cont. from Tutorial 6*)

GEM Ultimate Vacations   Griffin and Emma MacElroy want you to create a custom report and mailing labels for the Vacation database. You will create the custom report and the mailing labels by completing the following steps:

1. Open the **Vacation** database located in the Level.02\Case4 folder provided with your Data Files.

2. Create a query that displays the PropertyName and Country fields from the tblProperty table, the StateProv field from the tblGuest table, and the StartDate, EndDate, and People fields from the tblReservation table. Sort in ascending order by the PropertyName, StateProv, and StartDate fields, and then save the query as **qryPropertyReservations**.

3. Create a custom report based on the qryPropertyReservations query. Figure 7-50 shows a sample of the last page of the completed report. Refer to the figure as you create the report.

Figure 7-50

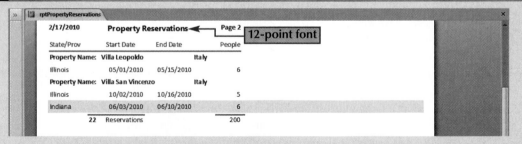

   a. Save the report as **rptPropertyReservations**.

   b. The PropertyName field is a grouping field.

   c. The StateProv field is a sort field, and the StartDate field is a sort field.

   d. Hide duplicate values for the StateProv field.

   ⊕ EXPLORE   e. Add the Country field to the Group Header section.

4. Use the following instructions to create the mailing labels:
    a. Use the tblGuest table as the record source for the mailing labels.
    b. Use Avery C2163 labels, with the default font and color settings. (*Hint*: Be certain the English option button is selected in the Unit of Measure section.)
    c. For the prototype label, place GuestFirstName, a space, and GuestLastName on the first line; Address on the second line; City, a space, StateProv, a space, and PostalCode on the third line; and Country on the fourth line.
    d. Sort by PostalCode, then by GuestLastName, and then enter the report name **rptGuestLabels**.
    e. Change the mailing label layout to snaking columns.

⊕ **EXPLORE**

5. Make a copy of the rptPropertyReservations report. For the copy use the name **rptPropertyReservationsSummary**. Read Access Help to find out how to create a summary report. Modify the rptPropertyReservationsSummary report as follows:
    a. Delete the column heading labels, move up the line in the Page Header section to just below the remaining controls, and then reduce the height of the section.
    b. Add subtotals for the number of reservations and number of people.
    c. Change the report to a summary report.

6. Close the Vacation database without exiting Access, make a backup copy of the database, open the **Vacation** database, compact and repair the database, close the database, and then exit Access.

| Create | **Case Problem 5** |

Work with the skills you've learned in the tutorial to create a report and labels for an Internet service provider.

Data File needed for this Case Problem: ACE.accdb (*cont. from Tutorial 6*)

Always Connected Everyday   Chris and Pat Dixon want you to create a custom report and mailing labels for the ACE database. You'll do so by completing the following:

1. Open the **ACE** database located in the Level.02\Case5 folder provided with your Data Files.

2. Create a query to serve as the record source for the custom report shown in Figure 7-51, and then save the query as **qryAccessPlanCustomers**.

3. Create a custom report based on the qryAccessPlanCustomers query. Figure 7-51 shows a sample of the completed report. Refer to the figure as you create the report. Save the report as **rptAccessPlanCustomers**.

Figure 7-51

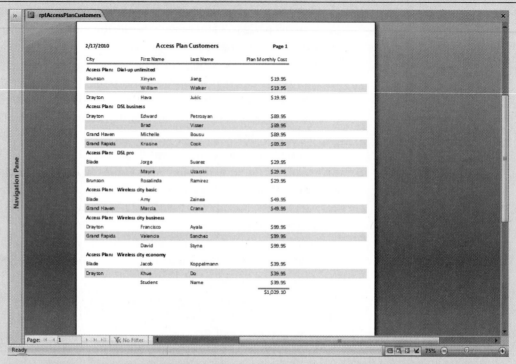

4. After you've created the rptAccessPlanCustomers report, filter the report in Report view, selecting all records that contain a specific value in the city field. Copy the entire filtered report and paste it into a new Word document. Save the document as **rptAccessPlanCustomersCopy**.

5. Use the tblCustomer table as the record source for the mailing labels. Choose appropriate options in the Label Wizard, change the mailing label layout to snaking columns, and save the report as **rptCustomerLabels**.

6. Close the ACE database without exiting Access, make a backup copy of the database, open the **ACE** database, compact and repair the database, close the database, and then exit Access.

Research | Internet Assignments

Use the Internet to find and work with data related to the topics presented in this tutorial.

The purpose of the Internet Assignments is to challenge you to find information on the Internet that you can use to work effectively with this software. The actual assignments are updated and maintained on the Course Technology Web site. Log on to the Internet and use your Web browser to go to the Student Online Companion for New Perspectives Office 2007 at **www.course.com/np/office2007**. Then navigate to the Internet Assignments for this tutorial.

Assess | SAM Assessment and Training

If you have a SAM user profile, you may have access to hands-on instruction, practice, and assessment of the skills covered in this tutorial. Log in to your SAM account (**http://sam2007.course.com**) to launch any assigned training activities or exams that relate to the skills covered in this tutorial.

Review | **Quick Check Answers**

Session 7.1

1. A custom report is a report created by the Report tool or the Report Wizard and that you modify in Layout or Design view, or a report you create from scratch in Layout or Design view.
2. You can apply a filter or you can copy selected portions of the report to the Clipboard.
3. A report sort field that includes a Group Header section before a group of records having the same sort field value and that includes a Group Footer section after the group of records.
4. The Report Header section appears once at the beginning of a report. The Page Header section appears at the top of each page of a report. The Group Header section appears once at the beginning of a new group of records. The Detail section appears once for each record in the underlying table or query. The Group Footer section appears once at the end of a group of records. The Report Footer section appears once at the end of a report. The Page Footer section appears at the bottom of each page of a report.

Session 7.2

1. A detail report is a report that displays fields from the record source in the Detail section. A summary report is a report that displays only summary information, such as grand totals and subtotals.
2. Keep Together
3. orphaned footer
4. Can Grow
5. Hiding duplicate values makes a report easier to read; duplicate values clutter the report.

Session 7.3

1. =Date()
2. Click the Insert Page Number button in the Controls group in Layout or Design view; specify the format, position, and alignment of the page number; and then click the OK button.
3. Report Header
4. A multiple-column report prints the same collection of data in two or more sets across the page.

Ending Data Files

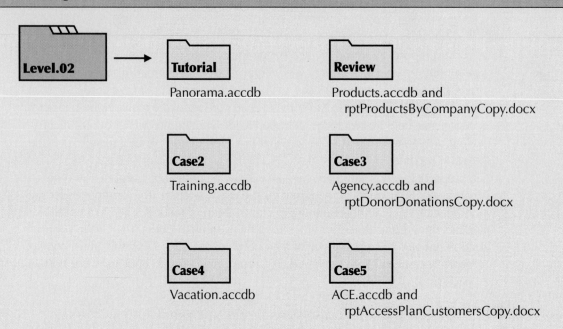

Level.02 → Tutorial
Panorama.accdb

Review
Products.accdb and
rptProductsByCompanyCopy.docx

Case1
Contract.accdb

Case2
Training.accdb

Case3
Agency.accdb and
rptDonorDonationsCopy.docx

Case4
Vacation.accdb

Case5
ACE.accdb and
rptAccessPlanCustomersCopy.docx

Objectives

Session 8.1
- Export an Access table to an HTML document and view the document
- Import a CSV file as an Access table
- Use the Table Analyzer
- Import and export XML files
- Save and run import and export specifications

Session 8.2
- Create a multi-page form using a tab control
- Embed a chart in a form
- Create and modify PivotTables and PivotCharts
- Link data from an Excel worksheet

Sharing, Integrating, and Analyzing Data

Importing, Exporting, Linking, and Analyzing Data in the Panorama Database

Case | Belmont Landscapes

Oren Belmont, Sarah Fisher, and Taylor Sico are pleased with the design and contents of the Panorama database. Oren feels that other employees would benefit from gaining access to the Panorama database and by sharing data among the different programs employees use. Oren and Sarah would also like to be able to analyze the data in the database.

In this tutorial, you will show Oren and Sarah how to import, export, link, and embed data. You will also introduce them to the charting, PivotTable, and PivotChart features of Access.

Starting Data Files

Level.02 →

Tutorial
BelmLogo.gif
BelmTemp.htm
Panorama.accdb *(cont.)*
Products.xlsx
tblCustomerBilling.csv
tblProspect.xml

Review
Ads.xlsx
BelmLogo.gif
BelmTemp.htm
Payables.csv
Products.accdb *(cont.)*
tblPayments.xml

Case1
Contract.accdb *(cont.)*
Instrument.csv
Room.xlsx

Case2
CreditCard.xml
ParkLogo.gif
ParkTemp.htm
Schedule.xlsx
Training.accdb *(cont.)*

Case3
Agency.accdb *(cont.)*
Facility.csv

Case4
Personnel.xlsx
Vacation.accdb *(cont.)*
Works.xml

Case5
ACE.accdb *(cont.)*

Session 8.1

Using the Web

The **Internet** is a worldwide collection of millions of interconnected computers and computer networks that share resources. The **World Wide Web** (or the **Web**) is a vast collection of digital documents available on the Internet. Each digital document on the Web is called a **Web page**, each computer on which an individual or company stores Web pages for access on the Internet is called a **Web server**, and each computer requesting a Web page from a Web server is called a **Web client**. Each Web page is assigned an Internet address, which is also called a **Uniform Resource Locator** (**URL**); the URL identifies where the Web page is stored—the location of the Web server and the name and location of the Web page on the server. For example, http://www.course.com/catalog/default.html is a URL that identifies the Web server (www.course.com), the location path (catalog) on the Web server, and the Web page name (default.html). The beginning of the URL (http) specifies the **Hypertext Transfer Protocol (HTTP)**, which is the data communication method used by Web clients and Web servers to exchange data over the Internet. To view a Web page, you use a computer program called a **Web browser**, such as Microsoft Internet Explorer or Mozilla Firefox. After you start a Web browser, you enter the Web page's URL. The Web browser uses the URL to find and retrieve the Web page, and then displays it on your computer screen.

Each Web page is a text document that contains the necessary codes, called **tags**, that the Web browser interprets to position and format the text in the Web page. A Web page can also contain tags for links to audio files to be played, to graphics and animations to be displayed on the screen, and to other files, which are sent along with the Web page by the Web server. A Web page can also contain tags for **hyperlinks**, which connect Web pages to other Web pages or Web sites or to a location in the same Web page. When you click hyperlink text, the linked page opens. Hyperlinks connect Web pages throughout the Internet.

Web pages are usually created using a programming language called **Hypertext Markup Language (HTML)**. You can create a Web page by typing all the necessary HTML tags into a text document, called an **HTML document**, and saving the document with the .htm or .html file extension. You can also use a program, such as ColdFusion or Adobe Dreamweaver, to create the HTML documents for Web pages without needing to learn HTML. Many programs, including Access, have built-in tools that convert and export objects, such as tables and queries, to HTML documents.

Tip
An intranet is an internal company network that uses software tools and languages, such as HTML, that typically are used on the Internet and the Web. The company that manages or owns the intranet restricts access to it by using passwords.

Exporting an Access Query to an HTML Document

Oren wants to display the customer contact data in the qryCustomersByName query on the company's intranet so that all employees working in the office are able to access it. To store the data on the company's intranet, you'll create a Web page version of the qryCustomersByName query.

Creating the necessary HTML document to provide Oren with the information he wants is not as difficult as it might appear at first. You can use Access to export the query and convert it to an HTML document automatically.

Exporting an Access Query to an HTML Document | Reference Window

- In the Navigation Pane, right-click the object (table, query, form, or report) you want to export, point to Export on the shortcut menu, and then click HTML Document.

or

- In the Navigation Pane, click the object (table, query, form, or report) you want to export, click the External Data tab on the Ribbon, click the More button in the Export group on the External Data tab, and then click HTML Document.
- Enter the filename in the File name text box of the Export - HTML Document dialog box, click the Browse button, select the location where you want to save the file, and then click the Save button.
- Click the Export data with formatting and layout check box to retain most formatting and layout information, check the other two check boxes, as necessary, and then click the OK button.
- If using a template, click the Select a HTML Template check box in the HTML Output Options dialog box, click the Browse button, select the location for the template, click the template filename, and then click the OK button.
- Click the OK button.
- Click the Close button to close the Export - HTML Document dialog box.

To complete the following steps, you need to use Access and a Web browser. The steps in this tutorial are written for Internet Explorer, the Web browser used at Belmont Landscapes. If you use another browser, the steps you need to complete might be slightly different.

You'll export the qryCustomersByName query as an HTML document.

To export the qryCustomersByName query as an HTML document:

▶ **1.** Start Access, and then open the **Panorama** database in the Level.02\Tutorial folder provided with your Data Files.

▶ **2.** Open the Navigation Pane (if necessary), right-click **qryCustomersByName** to display the shortcut menu, point to **Export**, and then click **HTML Document**. The Export - HTML Document dialog box opens.

▶ **3.** Select the text in the File name text box, and then type **Customers by Name**. See Figure 8-1.

| Figure 8-1 | Export - HTML Document dialog box |

The dialog box provides options for exporting the data with formatting and layout, opening the exported file after the export operation is complete, and exporting selected records from the source object (available only when you selected records in an object instead of the object on the Navigation Pane). You need to select the option for exporting the data with formatting and layout and the destination location for the exported file.

▶ 4. Click the **Export data with formatting and layout** check box, click the **Browse** button, navigate to and open the **Level.02\Tutorial** folder, and then click the **Save** button in the File Save dialog box. The File Save dialog box closes, and the File name text box displays the path to your Data Files and the filename Customers by Name.html.

▶ 5. Click the **OK** button. The Export - HTML Document dialog box closes and the HTML Output Options dialog box opens.

This dialog box lets you specify an HTML template or use the default format when saving the object. An **HTML template** is a file that contains HTML instructions for creating a Web page with both text and graphics, together with special instructions that tell Access where to place the Access data in the Web page. Lucia used a text-editing program to create an HTML template named BelmTemp that you'll use to create the Customers by Name HTML document. The template will automatically insert a Belmont Landscapes logo in all Web pages created with it. You need to locate Lucia's template file in your Data Files.

▶ 6. If necessary, click the **Select a HTML Template** check box to select it.

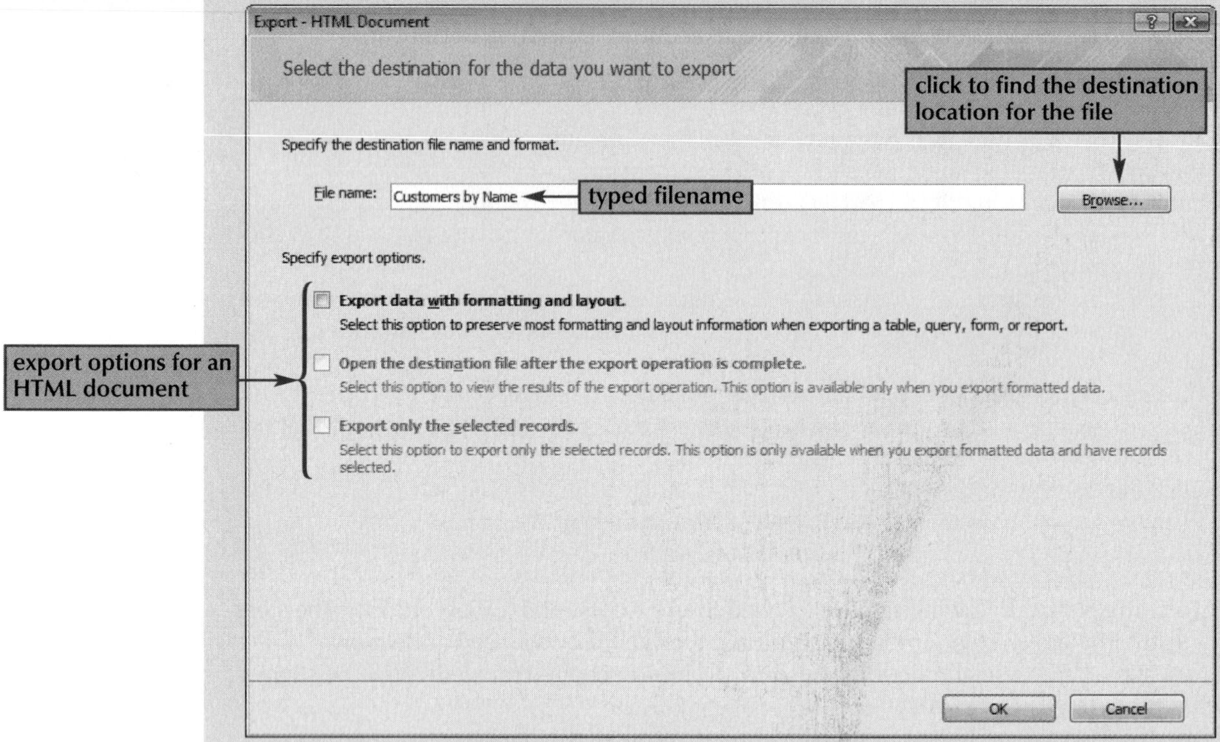

Tip

You should always select the "Export data with formatting and layout" option. Not selecting this option results in an HTML document that's poorly formatted and difficult to read.

7. Click the **Browse** button to open the HTML Template to Use dialog box, navigate to and open the **Level.02\Tutorial** folder, click **BelmTemp**, and then click the **OK** button. Access closes the HTML Template to Use dialog box, returns to the HTML Output Options dialog box, and displays the location and filename for the HTML template. See Figure 8-2.

HTML Output Options dialog box ◀ Figure 8-2

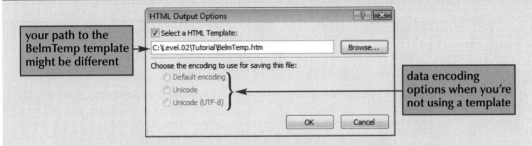

your path to the BelmTemp template might be different

data encoding options when you're not using a template

Trouble? If BelmTemp does not appear in the Level.02\Tutorial folder when you open the HTML Template to Use dialog box, click the Cancel button to return to the HTML Output Options dialog box so you can specify the template filename manually. In the HTML Template text box, type the full path to the BelmTemp.htm file in the Level.02\Tutorial folder—for example, C:\Level.02\Tutorial\BelmTemp.htm.

8. Click the **OK** button. The HTML Output Options dialog box closes, the HTML document named Customers by Name is saved in the Level.02\Tutorial folder, and the Export - HTML Document dialog box asks if you want to save the export steps. You won't save these export steps.

9. Click the **Close** button in the dialog box to close it without saving the steps.

Now you can view the Web page.

Viewing an HTML Document Using Internet Explorer

Oren asks to see the Web page you created. You can view the HTML document that you created using any Web browser. You'll view it using Internet Explorer.

To view the qryCustomersByName query Web page:

1. Open Windows Explorer, and then navigate to and open the **Level.02\Tutorial** folder, which is where you saved the exported HTML document.

2. Right-click **Customers by Name** in the file list to open the shortcut menu, click **Open With**, click **Internet Explorer** in the list of programs in the Open With dialog box, and then click the **OK** button. Internet Explorer starts and opens the Customers by Name Web page. See Figure 8-3.

| Figure 8-3 | qryCustomersByName query in the Internet Explorer window |

query name appears
as the Web page title

graphic supplied
by the template

address for the Web page
(your path might be different)

records from the
qryCustomersByName
query

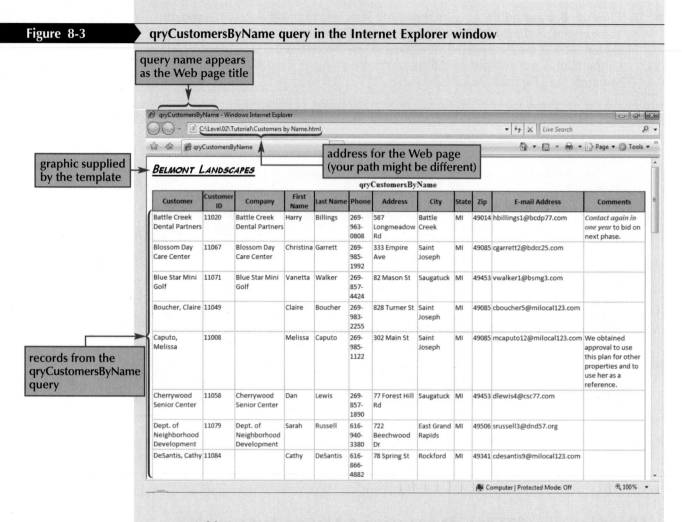

Trouble? If Internet Explorer does not appear in the program list but another Web browser does appear, click the name of that browser. When you use another Web browser, your screens might look slightly different from the screen shown in the figure.

Changes that employees make to the Panorama database will not appear in the Customers by Name Web page that you created because it is a **static Web page**—that is, it reflects the state of the qryCustomersByName query in the Panorama database at the time you created it. If data in the qryCustomersByName query changes, you will need to export the query as an HTML document again.

Because this static Web page is not linked to the qryCustomersByName query on which it is based, you cannot use your browser to make changes to its data. Before closing the Customers by Name Web page, you'll try to change one of its field values.

To attempt to change a field value, and then close the browser:

▸ 1. Double-click **MI** in the State column for the first record (Battle Creek Dental Partners), and then type **NY**. The value of MI remains highlighted and unchanged, because the Customers by Name Web page is a static page.

▸ 2. Click the **Close** button ✕ on the Internet Explorer window title bar to close it and to return to Windows Explorer.

▶ **3.** Click the **Close** button ⊠ on the Windows Explorer window title bar to close it and to return to Access.

Trouble? If the Access window is not active on your screen, click the Microsoft Access program button on the taskbar.

Sarah has a file containing customer billing addresses that she needs to add to the Panorama database. Instead of typing these billing addresses into new records, she asks you to import the data into the Panorama database.

Importing a CSV File as an Access Table

For most customers, the Address, City, State, and Zip fields in the tblCustomer table identify both the customer's location and billing address, which is where Belmont Landscapes sends the customer's invoices. In a few cases, however, the billing address is different from the location address; in addition, the company name used for billing purposes might be different from the company name stored in the tblCustomer table. Sarah has been maintaining an Excel workbook containing customer billing data, and she's exported the data to a CSV file. A **CSV (comma-separated values) file** is a text file in which commas separate values, and each line is a record containing the same number of values in the same positions.

Access can import data from a CSV file directly into a database table. Sarah's CSV file is named tblCustomerBilling, and you'll import it as a table with the same name into the Panorama database.

Importing a CSV File as an Access Table | Reference Window

- Click the External Data tab on the Ribbon.
- In the Import group on the External Data tab, click the Text File button to open the Get External Data - Text File dialog box.
- Click the Browse button in the dialog box, navigate to the location where the file to import is stored, click the filename, and then click the Open button.
- Click the Import the source data into a new table in the current database option button, and then click the OK button.
- In the Import Text Wizard dialog box, click the Delimited option button, and then click the Next button.
- Make sure the Comma option button is selected. If appropriate, click the First Row Contains Field Names check box to select it, and then click the Next button.
- For each field, select the column, type its field name, and select its data type, and then click the Next button.
- Choose the appropriate option button to let Access create a primary key, to choose your own primary key, or to avoid setting a primary key, click the Next button, type the table name, and then click the Finish button.

Now you will import the tblCustomerBilling.csv file as an Access database table.

To import the CSV file as an Access table:

▶ 1. Click the **External Data** tab on the Ribbon, and then in the Import group on the External Data tab, click the **Text File** button (with the ScreenTip "Import text file") to open the Get External Data - Text File dialog box.

▶ 2. Click the **Browse** button, navigate to and open the **Level.02\Tutorial** folder, click **tblCustomerBilling**, click the **Open** button, and then click the **Import the source data into a new table in the current database** option button. The selected path and filename appears in the File name text box. See Figure 8-4.

Figure 8-4	Get External Data - Text File dialog box

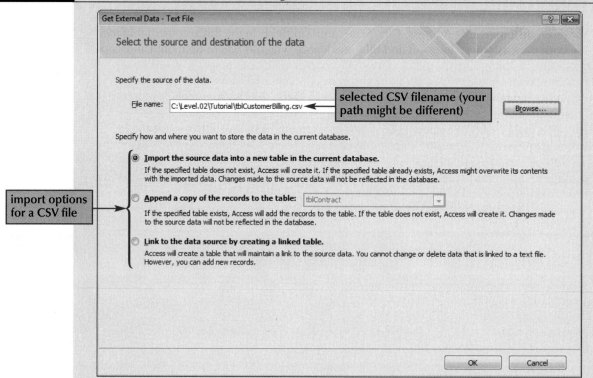

The dialog box provides options for importing the data into a new table in the database, appending a copy of the data to an existing table in the database, and linking to the source data. In the future, Sarah wants to maintain the customer billing data in the Panorama database, instead of using her Excel workbook, so you'll import the data into a new table.

▶ 3. Click the **OK** button to open the first Import Text Wizard dialog box, in which you designate how to identify the separation between field values in each line in the source data. The choices are the use of commas, tabs, or another character to separate, or delimit, the values, or the use of fixed width columns with spaces between each column. The wizard has correctly identified that values are delimited by commas.

▶ 4. Click the **Next** button to open the second Import Text Wizard dialog box, in which you verify the delimiter for values in each line. See Figure 8-5.

Verifying the delimiter for values in the CSV file | Figure 8-5

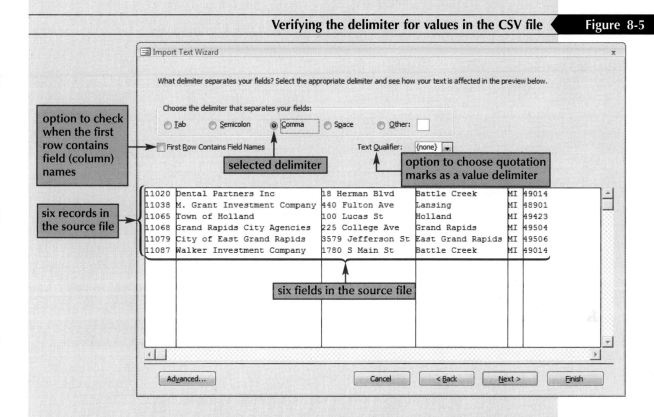

option to check when the first row contains field (column) names

selected delimiter

option to choose quotation marks as a value delimiter

six records in the source file

six fields in the source file

The CSV source file contains six records with six fields in each record. A comma serves as the delimiter for values in each line, so the Comma option button is selected. The first row in the source file contains the first record, not field names, so the First Row Contains Field Names check box is not checked. If the source file uses either single quotation marks or double quotation marks to enclose values, you would click the Text Qualifier arrow to choose the appropriate option.

▶ **5.** Click the **Next** button to open the third Import Text Wizard dialog box, in which you enter the field name and set other properties for the imported fields. You will import all fields from the source file and use the default data type and indexed settings for each field.

▶ **6.** Type **CustomerID** in the Field Name text box, and then click **Field2** in the table list. CustomerID (partially hidden) is the heading for the first column in the table list, and the second column is selected.

▶ **7.** Repeat Step 6 for the rightmost five columns, typing **BillingCompany**, **BillingAddress**, **BillingCity**, **BillingState**, and **BillingZip** in the Field Name text box. See Figure 8-6.

Figure 8-6 ▶ **After setting field names for the six fields in the source file**

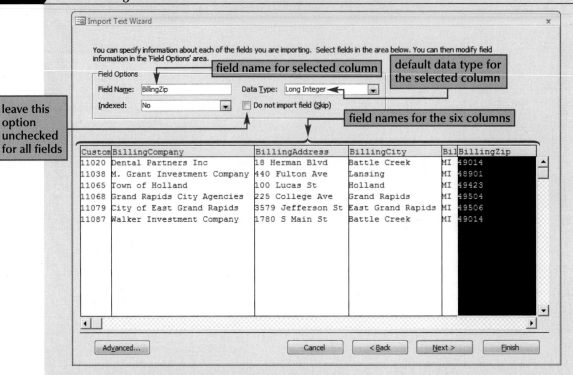

▶ 8. Click the **Next** button to open the fourth Import Text Wizard dialog box, in which you select the primary key for the imported table. CustomerID, the first column, will be the primary key.

▶ 9. Click the **Choose my own primary key** option button, make sure **CustomerID** appears in the list box for the option, click the **Next** button, click the **I would like a wizard to analyze my table after importing the data** check box, and then click the **Finish** button. An Import Text Wizard dialog box opens asking if you want to analyze the table.

After importing data and creating a new table, you can use the Import Text Wizard to analyze the imported table. When you choose this option, you start the Table Analyzer.

Analyzing a Table with the Table Analyzer

Tip

Read the Normalization section in the appendix titled "Relational Databases and Database Design" for more information about normalization and third normal form.

The **Table Analyzer** analyzes a single table and, if necessary, splits it into two or more tables that are in third normal form. The Table Analyzer looks for redundant data in the table. When the Table Analyzer encounters redundant data, it removes redundant fields from the table and then places the redundant fields in new tables.

To use the Table Analyzer to analyze the imported table:

▶ 1. Click the **Yes** button to close the dialog box and to open the first Table Analyzer Wizard dialog box. The diagram and explanation in this dialog box describe the problem when duplicate data is stored in a table.

▶ 2. Click the first **Show me an example** button [»], read the explanation, close the example box, click the second **Show me an example** button [»], read the explanation, close the example box, and then click the **Next** button to open the second Table Analyzer Wizard dialog box. The diagram and explanation in this dialog box describe how the Table Analyzer solves the duplicate data problem.

▶ 3. Click the first **Show me an example** button [»], read the explanation, close the example box, click the second **Show me an example** button [»], read the explanation, close the example box, and then click the **Next** button to open the third Table Analyzer Wizard dialog box. In this dialog box, you choose whether to let the wizard decide which fields go in what tables, if the table is not already normalized. You'll let the wizard decide.

▶ 4. Make sure the **Yes, let the wizard decide** option button is selected, and then click the **Next** button. A message box informs you that the wizard does not recommend splitting the table because the table is normalized and does not contain redundant data.

▶ 5. Click the **Cancel** button to close the message box, exit the wizard, and return to the Get External Data - Text File dialog box, in which you are asked if you want to save the import steps. You don't need to save these steps because you're importing the data only this one time.

▶ 6. Click the **Close** button to close the dialog box.

> **Tip**
>
> You can start the Table Analyzer directly by clicking the Database Tools tab, and then clicking the Analyze Table button in the Analyze group.

The TblCustomerBilling table is now listed in the Tables section in the Navigation Pane. You'll rename the table to change the initial letter to lowercase, and then open the table to verify the import results.

To rename and open the imported TblCustomerBilling table:

▶ 1. Right-click **TblCustomerBilling** in the Navigation Pane, click **Rename**, press the **Home** key, press the **Delete** key, type the letter **t**, and then press the **Enter** key to change the table name to tblCustomerBilling.

▶ 2. Double-click **tblCustomerBilling** in the Navigation Pane to open the table datasheet, resize all columns to their best fit, and then click **11020** in the first row in the CustomerID column to deselect all values. See Figure 8-7.

Imported tblCustomerBilling table datasheet ◀ Figure 8-7

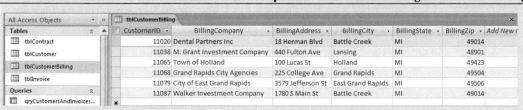

CustomerID	BillingCompany	BillingAddress	BillingCity	BillingState	BillingZip	Add New I
11020	Dental Partners Inc	18 Herman Blvd	Battle Creek	MI	49014	
11038	M. Grant Investment Company	440 Fulton Ave	Lansing	MI	48901	
11065	Town of Holland	100 Lucas St	Holland	MI	49423	
11068	Grand Rapids City Agencies	225 College Ave	Grand Rapids	MI	49504	
11079	City of East Grand Rapids	3579 Jefferson St	East Grand Rapids	MI	49506	
11087	Walker Investment Company	1780 S Main St	Battle Creek	MI	49014	

▶ 3. Save and close the table.

Sarah has some additional data that she wants to import into the Panorama database. The data is stored in XML format.

Using XML

Belmont Landscapes has contacts in the building trade industry and gets customer leads from builders when they sell new homes. One of the builders has several prospective customers available to Sarah in an XML document, which she wants to add to the Panorama database. **XML (Extensible Markup Language)** is a programming language that is similar in format to HTML, but is more customizable and suited to the exchange of data between different programs. Unlike HTML, which uses a fixed set of tags to describe the appearance of a Web page, developers can customize XML to describe the data it contains and how that data should be structured.

Importing an XML File as an Access Table

Access can import data from an XML file directly into a database table. Sarah's XML file is named tblProspect, and you'll import it as a table with the same name into the Panorama database.

Reference Window | **Importing an XML File as an Access Table**

- Click the External Data tab on the Ribbon.
- In the Import group on the External Data tab, click the XML File button to open the Get External Data - XML File dialog box.
- Click the Browse button, navigate to the location for the XML file, click the XML filename, and then click the Open button.
- Click the OK button in the Get External Data - XML File dialog box, click the table name in the Import XML dialog box, click the appropriate option button in the Import Options section, and then click the OK button.
- Click the Close button.
  or
- If you need to save the import steps, click the Save import steps check box, enter a name for the saved steps in the Save as text box, and then click the Save Import button.

Now you will import the tblProspect.xml document as an Access database table.

To import the XML document as an Access table:

▶ 1. Click the **External Data** tab on the Ribbon (if necessary), and then in the Import group on the External Data tab, click the **XML File** button (with the ScreenTip "Import XML file"). The Get External Data - XML File dialog box opens.

▶ 2. Click the **Browse** button, navigate to and open the **Level.02\Tutorial** folder, click **tblProspect**, and then click the **Open** button. The selected path and filename now appear in the File name text box.

▶ 3. Click the **OK** button. The Import XML dialog box opens. See Figure 8-8.

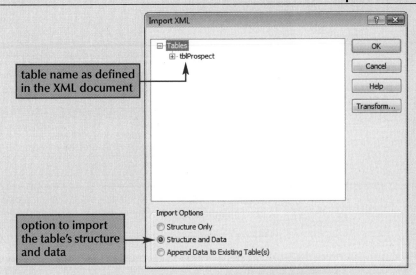

table name as defined in the XML document

option to import the table's structure and data

From the XML file, you can import only the table structure to a new table, import the table structure and data to a new table, or append the data in the XML file to an existing table. You'll import the table structure and data to a new table named tblProspect.

4. Make sure the **Structure and Data** option button is selected, click **tblProspect** in the list box, and then click the **OK** button. The Import XML dialog box closes, and the last Get External Data - XML File dialog box is displayed.

Before reviewing the imported table, you'll save the import steps.

Saving and Running Import Specifications

If you need to repeat the same import procedure many times, you can save the steps for the procedure and expedite future imports by running the saved import steps without using a wizard. Because the builder intends to send Sarah additional lists of prospective customers in the future, you'll save the import steps for Sarah.

To save and run the XML file import steps:

▶ **1.** Click the **Save import steps** check box. The dialog box expands to display additional options for the save operation. See Figure 8-9.

Figure 8-9 Saving the import steps

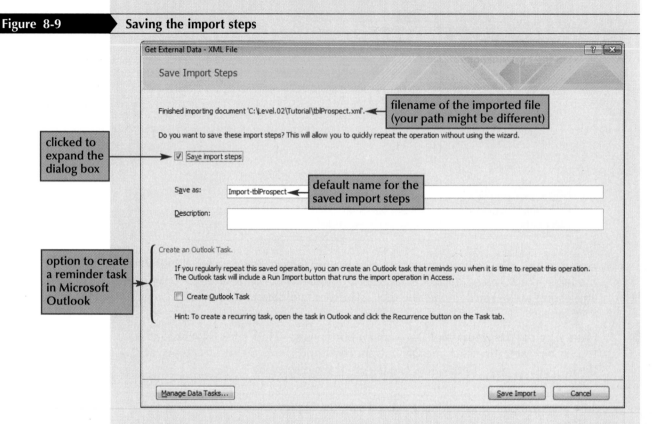

In the expanded dialog box, you can accept the default name for the saved import steps or choose one that you create, and you can enter an optional description. If the import will occur on a set schedule, you can also create a reminder task in Microsoft Outlook. You'll accept the default name for the saved steps, and you won't enter a description or schedule an Outlook task.

▶ **2.** Click the **Save Import** button. The import steps are saved as Import-tblProspect, the Get External Data - XML File dialog box closes, the tblProspect file is imported to the Panorama database, and the table is now listed in the Navigation Pane.

You'll now show Sarah how she can run the saved steps when she receives customer prospects from the builder in the future.

▶ **3.** In the Import group on the External Data tab, click the **Saved Imports** button. The Manage Data Tasks dialog box opens. See Figure 8-10.

Manage Data Tasks dialog box   Figure 8-10

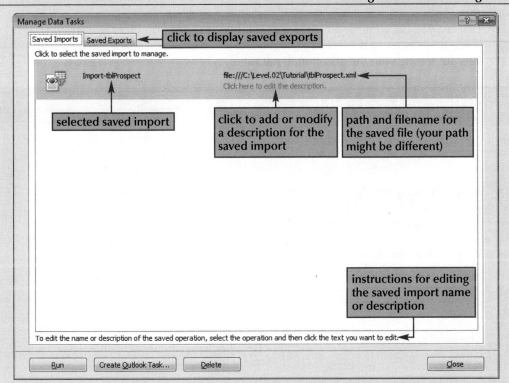

In this dialog box, you can change the saved import name, add or change its description, create an Outlook task for the saved import, run a saved import, or delete a saved import. You can also manage any saved export by clicking the Saved Exports tab. You'll add a description for the saved procedure and review the list of saved exports.

▶ **4.** Click the **Click here to edit the description** link to open an editing box, type **Builder's XML file of customer prospects**, click an unused portion of the orange selection band to close the editing box and accept the typed description, and then click the **Saved Exports** tab. You have not saved any export steps, so no saved exports are displayed.

▶ **5.** Click the **Close** button to close the Manage Data Tasks dialog box.

▶ **6.** Double-click the **tblProspect** table in the Navigation Pane to open the table datasheet, close the Navigation Pane, resize all columns to their best fit, and then click **12001** in the first row in the CustomerID column to deselect all values. See Figure 8-11.

Imported tblProspect table datasheet   Figure 8-11

CustomerID	FirstName	LastName	Phone	Address	City	State	Zip	EmailAddress
12001	Robin & Lee	Freeman	6168669891	3170 Lois Ln	Rockford	MI	49341	freeman@milocal123.com
12002	Marsha & Ted	Strong	6168663946	3184 Lois Ln	Rockford	MI	49341	strongs@milocal123.com
12003	Chris & David	Bowers	6167201093	3142 Kent Cir	Rockford	MI	49341	cdbowers@milocal123.com
12004	Sandy & Frank	Lee	6168663337	3242 Lois Ln	Rockford	MI	49341	sandyfrank@milocal123.com

▶ **7.** Save and close the table.

Sarah next asks you to export the tblInvoice table as an XML file.

Exporting an Access Table as an XML File

Belmont Landscapes uses an accounting package that accepts the data in XML files as input for making accounting entries. Sarah wants to test this capability by exporting the tblInvoice table as an XML file and giving the XML file to the company's accounting manager for testing with the accounting package.

Reference Window | Exporting an Access Table as an XML File

- Right-click the object (table, query, form, or report) in the Navigation Pane, point to Export, and then click XML File.

or

- Click the object (table, query, form, or report) in the Navigation Pane. In the Export group on the External Data tab, click the More button, and then click XML File.
- Click the Browse button in the Export - XML File dialog box, navigate to the location where you will save the XML file, and then click the Save button.
- Click the OK button in the dialog box, select the options in the Export XML dialog box or click the More Options button and select the options in the expanded Export XML dialog box, and then click the OK button.
- Click the Close button.

or

- If you need to save the export steps, click the Save export steps check box, enter a name for the saved steps in the Save as text box, and then click the Save Export button.

InSight | Importing and Exporting Data

You've imported data from an Excel workbook and a text file (TXT extension) in Tutorial 2 and from a text file (CSV extension) and an XML file in this tutorial. Additional Access options include importing an object from another Access database, importing data from other databases (ODBC databases such as SQL Server, dBASE, and Paradox), and importing a Lotus 1-2-3 file, an HTML document, an Outlook folder, or a SharePoint list.

In addition to exporting Access objects as an XML file or an HTML document, Access includes options for exporting data to another Access database, other databases (ODBC database, dBASE, or Paradox), an Excel workbook, a Lotus 1-2-3 file, a text file, a Word document, or a SharePoint list. You can also "export" table or query data to Word's mail merge feature, or export a report to a snapshot file (SNP extension) so you can view it with the Microsoft Snapshot Viewer available from the Microsoft Download Center.

Also available from the Microsoft Download Center is the Microsoft Save as PDF or XPS add-in that you can download and install to export and save objects as PDF or XPS files. Installing this download adds a "PDF or XPS" button in the Export group on the External Data tab. PDF (Portable Document Format) and XPS (XML Paper Specification) are file formats that render reports and other objects in a form viewable on any computer using the free Adobe Reader program for PDF files and an XPS reader program, such as Windows Presentation Foundation, for XPS files.

The steps you follow for all import and export options work similar to the import and export steps you've used in this tutorial and in Tutorial 2. For example, to save an object as an XPS file, right-click the name of the object you want to export in the Navigation Pane, point to Export on the shortcut menu, click PDF or XPS, navigate to the folder where you want to store the file, click the Save as type arrow, click XPS Document, click the Publish button, and then click the Close button.

You can now export the tblInvoice table as an XML file.

To export the tblInvoice table as an XML file:

▶ **1.** Open the Navigation Pane, right-click **tblInvoice** in the Navigation Pane, point to **Export** on the shortcut menu, and then click **XML File**. The Export - XML File dialog box opens.

▶ **2.** Click the **Browse** button, navigate to and open the **Level.02\Tutorial** folder, and then click the **Save** button. The selected path and filename now appears in the File name text box in the Export - XML File dialog box.

▶ **3.** Click the **OK** button. The Export XML dialog box opens.

Clicking the More Options button in the Export XML dialog box expands the dialog box and lets you view and change detailed options for exporting a database object to an XML file.

▶ **4.** Click the **More Options** button to reveal detailed export options in the Export XML dialog box. See Figure 8-12.

Data tab in the Export XML dialog box | **Figure 8-12**

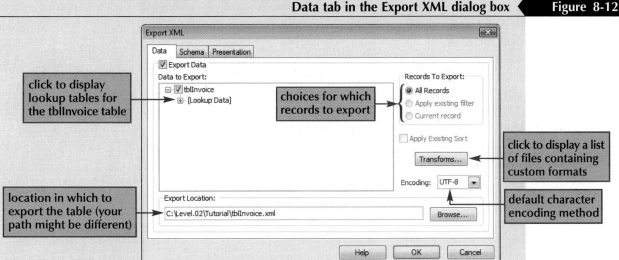

click to display lookup tables for the tblInvoice table

choices for which records to export

click to display a list of files containing custom formats

location in which to export the table (your path might be different)

default character encoding method

The Export Data check box, the Export Location text box, and the Records To Export option group display the selections you made in the previous step. You're exporting all records from the tblInvoice table, including the data in the records and the structure of the table, to the tblInvoice.xml file in the Level.02\Tutorial folder. The encoding option determines how characters will be represented in the exported XML file. The encoding choices are UTF-8, which uses 8 bits to represent each character, and UTF-16, which uses 16 bits to represent each character. You can also click the Transforms button if you have a special file that contains instructions for changing the exported data.

The accounting package doesn't have a transform file and requires the default encoding, but Sarah wants to review the tables that contain lookup data.

▶ **5.** Click the **plus box** to the left of [Lookup Data]. The tblContract table contains lookup data because it's the primary table in the one-to-many relationship with the related tblInvoice table. The accounting package requirements don't include any lookup data from the tblContract table, so make sure the tblContract check box is not checked.

The Data tab settings are correct, so you'll verify the Schema tab settings.

▶ **6.** Click the **Schema** tab. See Figure 8-13.

Figure 8-13 ▶ **Schema tab in the Export XML dialog box**

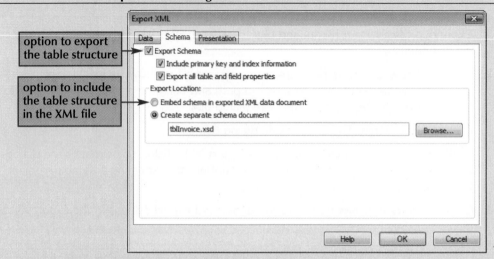

Along with the data from the tblInvoice table, you'll be exporting its table structure, including information about the table's primary key, indexes, and table and field properties. You can include this information in a separate **XSD (XML Structure Definition)** file, or you can embed the information in the XML file. The accounting package expects a single XML file, so you'll embed the structure information in the XML file.

▶ **7.** Click the **Embed schema in exported XML data document** option button to select that option and to dim the "Create separate schema document" text box, and then click the **Presentation** tab.

The Presentation tab options let you export a separate **XSL (Extensible Stylesheet Language)** file containing the format specifications for the tblInvoice table data. Unlike HTML, XML provides no screen formatting information. An XSL file provides formatting instructions so that a browser or another program can display the data in the XML file in a readable way. The accounting package will import the tblInvoice table data directly into its computer program, which contains its own formatting instructions, so you will not export an XSL file.

▶ **8.** Make sure that the **Export Presentation (HTML 4.0 Sample XSL)** check box is not checked, and then click the **OK** button. Access closes the Export XML dialog box, exports the data in the tblInvoice table as an XML file in the Level.02\Tutorial folder, and returns you to the final Export - XML File dialog box.

Sarah plans to make further tests exporting the tblInvoice table as an XML file, so you'll save the export steps.

Saving and Running Export Specifications

Saving the steps to export the tblInvoice table as an XML file will save time and eliminate errors when Sarah repeats the export procedure. You'll save the export steps and then show Sarah how to run the saved export steps.

To save and run the XML file export steps:

▶ **1.** Click the **Save export steps** check box. The dialog box expands to display additional options for the save operation.

The expanded dialog box has the same options you saw earlier when you saved the XML import steps. You'll enter a description, and you won't create an Outlook task because Sarah will be running the saved export steps on an as needed basis.

▶ **2.** In the Description text box, type **XML file accounting entries from the tblInvoice table**. See Figure 8-14.

Saving the export steps ◀ **Figure 8-14**

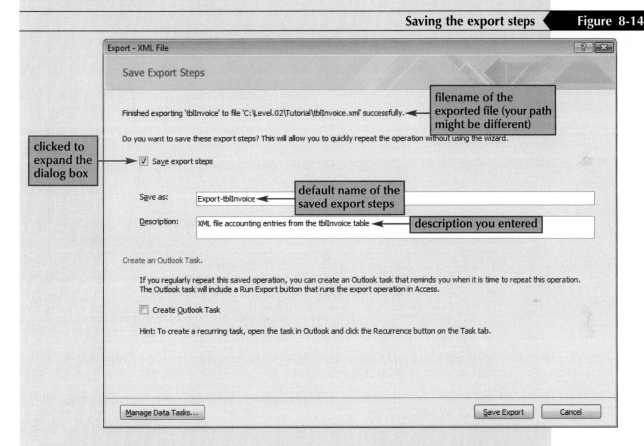

▶ **3.** Click the **Save Export** button. The export steps are saved as Export-tblInvoice, the Export - XML File dialog box closes, and the tblInvoice table is exported as an XML file named tblInvoice.

You'll now show Sarah how she can to run the saved steps.

▶ **4.** Click the **External Data** tab on the Ribbon (if necessary), and in the Export group on the External Data tab, click the **Saved Exports** button. The Manage Data Tasks dialog box opens. See Figure 8-15.

Figure 8-15	Manage Data Tasks dialog box

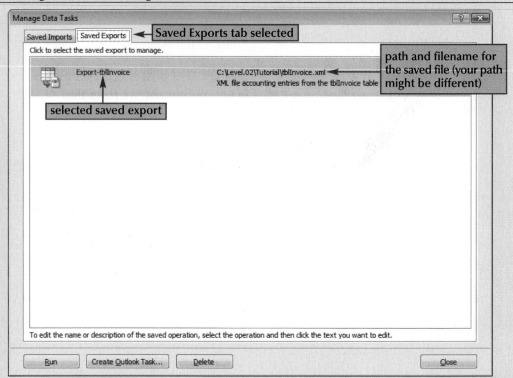

5. Click the **Run** button. The saved procedure runs, and a message box opens, asking if you want to replace the existing XML file you created earlier.

6. Click the **Yes** button to replace the existing XML file. A message box informs you that the export was completed successfully.

7. Click the **OK** button to close the message box, and then click the **Close** button to close the Manage Data Tasks dialog box.

8. If you are not continuing on to the next session, close the Panorama database, and then exit Access.

You've imported and exported data, analyzed a table's design, and saved and run import and export specifications. In the next session, you will analyze data by working with a chart, PivotTable, PivotChart, and linked data, and you will add a tab control to a form.

Review | Session 8.1 Quick Check

1. What is the World Wide Web, and what do you use to view the information it provides?
2. What is a hyperlink?
3. What is HTML?
4. What is an HTML template?
5. What is a static Web page?
6. What is a CSV file?
7. What is the Table Analyzer?
8. _____ is a programming language that describes data and its structure.

Session 8.2

Creating a Multi-page Form Using a Tab Control

You can create a multi-page form in two ways: use the **Page Break tool** to insert a page break control in the form, or use the **Tab Control tool** to insert a control that's called a tab control. If you insert a page break control in a form, users can move between the form pages by pressing the Page Up and Page Down keys. If you use a tab control, the control appears with tabs at the top, with one tab for each page. Users can switch between pages by clicking the tabs.

Sarah wants to include a tab control with two pages in the frmContractsAndInvoices form. The first page of the tab control will contain the frmInvoiceSubform subform that is currently positioned at the bottom of the frmContractsAndInvoices form. The second page of the tab control will contain a chart showing the invoice amounts for the invoices associated with the displayed contract.

To expedite placing the subform in the tab control, you'll cut the subform from the form, add the tab control, and then paste the subform into the left tab on the tab control. You need to perform these steps in Design view.

To add the tab control to the form:

▶ **1.** If you took a break after the previous session, make sure that the Panorama database is open and the Navigation Pane is open.

▶ **2.** Open the **frmContractsAndInvoices** form in Design view, and then close the Navigation Pane.

▶ **3.** Right-click the top edge of the subform control to open the shortcut menu, and then click **Cut** to delete the subform control and place it on the Clipboard.

Trouble? If you do not see Subform in New Window as one of the options on the shortcut menu, you did not click the top edge of the subform control correctly. Right-click the top edge of the subform control until you see this option on the shortcut menu, and then repeat Step 3.

▶ **4.** In the Controls group on the Design tab, click the **Tab Control** button 🗔.

▶ **5.** Position the + portion of the pointer in the Detail section three grid dots from the left edge of the grid and at the 2.5-inch mark on the vertical ruler, and then click the mouse button. Access places a tab control with two pages in the form.

▶ **6.** Right-click the left tab, and then click **Paste** on the shortcut menu. The subform is pasted in the tab control. See Figure 8-16.

Figure 8-16 Subform on the tab control in the Detail section

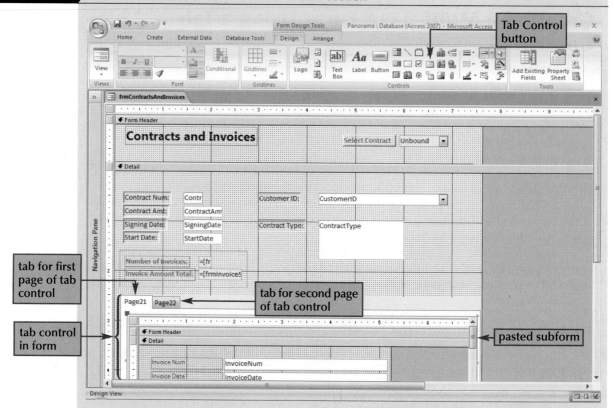

> **7.** Save your form design changes, switch to Form view, and then click **3011** in the ContractNum text box to deselect all controls. The left tab, which represents the first page in the tab control, is the active tab. See Figure 8-17.

Figure 8-17 Subform on the tab control in Form view

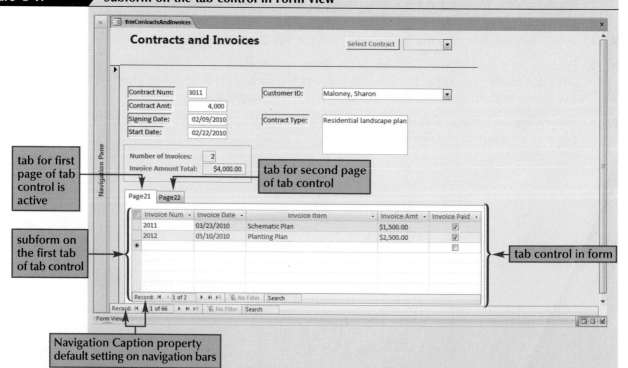

The subform is now displayed on the first page of the tab control and its design is the same as it was before you cut and pasted it to the tab control.

▶ **8.** Click the right tab of the tab control to display the second page, which is empty because you haven't added any controls to it yet.

After viewing the form in Form view, Sarah asks you to edit the labels for the tabs in the tab control, so they indicate the contents of each page. Also, Sarah's staff finds the two sets of navigation buttons confusing—they waste time determining which set of navigation buttons applies to the subform and which to the main form. You'll set the Navigation Caption property for the main form and the subform. The **Navigation Caption property** lets you change the navigation label from the word "Record" to another value. Because the main form displays data about contracts and the subform displays data about invoices, you'll change the Navigation Caption property for the main form to "Contract" and for the subform to "Invoice."

To change the captions for the tabs and the navigation buttons:

▶ **1.** Switch to Design view.

▶ **2.** Click the **form selector** for the main form to select the form control in the main form, open the property sheet to display the properties for the selected form control, click the **Navigation Caption** text box, and then type **Contract**. See Figure 8-18.

| Setting the Navigation Caption property for the main form | Figure 8-18 |

Property Sheet

Selection type: Form

Form ◄──── [form control for the main form is the selected control]

| Format | Data | Event | Other | All |

Record Source	tblContract
Caption	
Pop Up	No
Modal	No
Display on SharePoint Site	Follow Table Setting
Default View	Single Form
Allow Form View	Yes
Allow Datasheet View	No
Allow PivotTable View	No
Allow PivotChart View	No
Allow Layout View	Yes
Picture	(none)
Picture Tiling	No
Picture Alignment	Center
Picture Type	Embedded
Picture Size Mode	Clip
Width	7.625"
Auto Center	No
Auto Resize	Yes
Fit to Screen	Yes
Border Style	Sizable
Record Selectors	Yes
Navigation Buttons	Yes
Navigation Caption	Contract ◄──── [new Navigation Caption property value]
Dividing Lines	No
Scroll Bars	Both

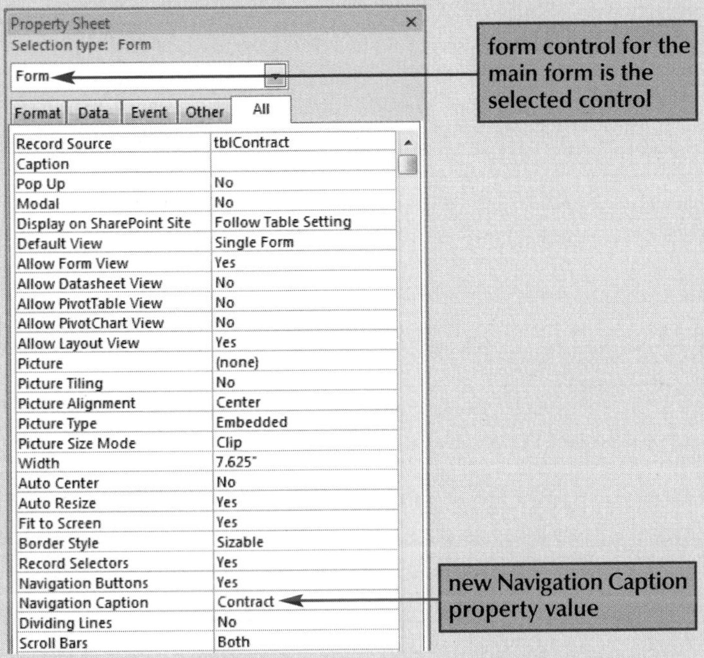

▶ **3.** Click the **form selector** for the subform to select the subform, click the **form selector** for the subform again to select the form control in the subform and display the properties for the selected form control, click the **Navigation Caption** text box, and then type **Invoice**. Navigation buttons don't appear in Design view, so you won't see the effects of the Navigation Caption property settings until you switch to Form view.

4. Click the left tab in the subform to select it, and then type **Invoice Data** in the Caption text box on the property sheet. See Figure 8-19.

| Figure 8-19 | Setting the Caption property for the left tab |

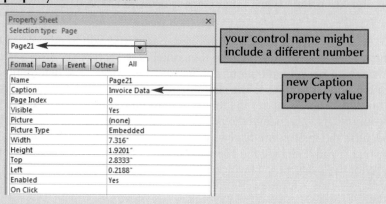

5. Click the right tab in the subform to select it, type **Invoice Chart** in the Caption text box, and then close the property sheet.

6. Save your form design changes, switch to Form view, and then click **3011** in the ContractNum text box to deselect all controls. The tabs and the navigation buttons now display the new caption values. See Figure 8-20.

| Figure 8-20 | Subform on the tab control in Form view |

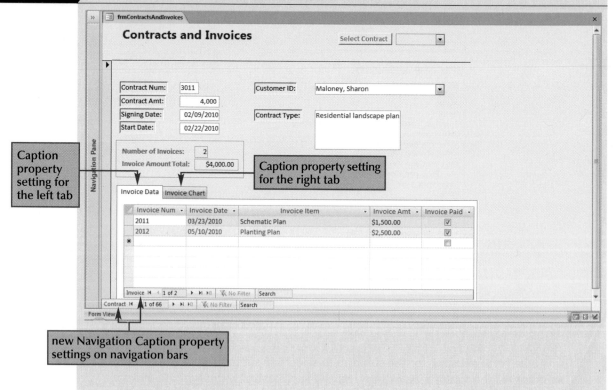

Sarah wants you to add a simple chart to the second page of the tab control.

Integrating Access with Other Programs

When you create a form or report in Access, you include more than just the data from the record source table or query. You've added controls such as lines, rectangles, tab controls, and graphics in your forms and reports to improve their appearance and usability. You can also add charts, drawings, and other objects to your forms and reports, but Access doesn't have the capability to create them. Instead, you create these other objects using other programs and then place them in a form or report using the appropriate integration method.

When you integrate information between programs, the program containing the original information, or object, is called the **source program**, and the program in which you place the information created by the source program is called the **destination program**. Access offers three ways for you to integrate objects created by other programs.

- **Importing**. When you import an object, you include the contents of a file in a new table or append it to an existing table, or you include the contents of the file in a form, report, or field. For example, in Tutorial 2 you added a picture to a form, or imported it into the form, and in this tutorial you imported CSV and XML files as new tables in the Panorama database. The imported picture is a file with a .bmp extension that was created by a graphics program, and the CSV and XML files were created by other programs. Once an object is imported, it has no relation to the program in which it was created. Any changes made to the object using the source program are not reflected in the imported objects.

- **Embedding**. When you embed an object in a form, report, or field, you preserve its connection to the source program, which enables you to edit the object, if necessary, using the features of the source program. Any changes you make to the object are reflected only in the form, report, or field in which it is embedded; the changes do not affect the original object in the file from which it was embedded. Likewise, if you start the source program outside Access and make any changes to the original object, these changes are not reflected in the embedded object.

- **Linking**. When you link an object to a form, report, or field, you include a connection in the destination program to the original file maintained by the source program; you do not store data from the file in the destination program. Any changes you made to the original file using the source program are reflected in the linked file version in the destination program.

InSight | **Importing, Embedding, and Linking Data**

How do you decide which method to use when you need to use data stored in another format in Access? You import a file as a new table or append the records in the file to an existing table when you intend to use Access to maintain the data and no longer need an updated version of the data with the source program. You link to the data when the source program will continue to maintain the data in the file, and you need to use an updated version of the file at all times in the destination program. When linking to the data, you can also maintain the data using the destination program, and the source program will always use the updated version of the file.

For objects in forms or reports, you import an object (such as a picture) when you want a copy of the object in your form or report and you don't intend to make any changes to the object. You embed or link an object when you want a copy of the object in your form or report and you intend to edit the object using the source program in the future. You embed the object when you do not want your edits to the object in the destination program to affect any other copies of the object used by other programs. You link the object when you want your edits to the object in the destination program to affect the object used by other programs.

Sarah wants you to embed a chart on the second page of the tab control.

Embedding a Chart in a Form

The Chart Wizard in Access helps you to embed a chart in a form or report. The chart is actually created by another program, Microsoft Graph, but the Chart Wizard does the work of embedding the chart. After embeddng the chart in a form or report, you can edit it using the Microsoft Graph program.

Reference Window | **Embedding a Chart in a Form**

- In the Controls group on the Design tab in Design view, click the Insert Chart button.
- Position the + portion of the pointer where you want to position the upper-left corner of the chart, and then click the mouse button to start the Chart Wizard.
- Select the record source, fields, and chart type.
- Edit the chart contents, and select the fields that link the object and chart, if necessary.
- Enter a chart title, select whether to include a legend, and then click the Finish button.

The tblInvoice table contains the information needed for the chart Sarah wants you to include in the form's right tab in the tab control.

To add a chart in the tab control and start the Chart Wizard:

1. Switch to Design view, and then click the **Invoice Chart** tab on the tab control, if necessary.

2. In the Controls group on the Design tab, click the **Insert Chart** button, and then move the pointer to the tab control. When the pointer is inside the tab control, the rectangular portion of the tab control you can use to place controls is filled in black.

3. Position the + portion of the pointer in the upper-left corner of the black portion of the tab control, and then click the mouse button. Access places a chart control in the form and opens the first Chart Wizard dialog box, in which you select the record source for the chart.

Sarah wants the chart to provide her staff with a simple visual display of the relative proportions of the invoice amounts for the invoices for the currently displayed contract. You'll use the tblInvoice table as the record source for the chart and select the InvoiceDate and InvoiceAmt fields as the fields to use in the chart.

To create the chart with the Chart Wizard:

1. Click **Table: tblInvoice** in the list box, and then click the **Next** button to display the second Chart Wizard dialog box.

2. Select the **InvoiceDate** and the **InvoiceAmt** fields, and then click the **Next** button to display the third Chart Wizard dialog box, in which you choose the chart type.

3. Click the **Pie Chart** button (row 4, column 1) to select the pie chart as the chart type to use for Sarah's chart. See Figure 8-21.

Selecting the chart type   Figure 8-21

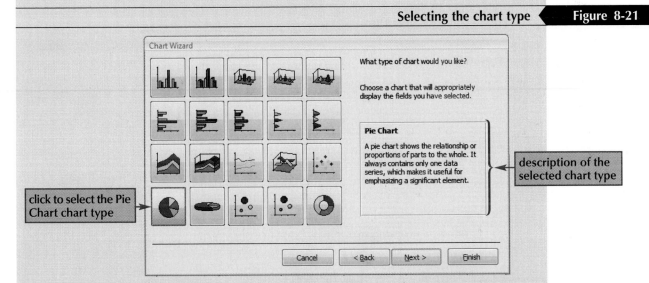

click to select the Pie Chart chart type

description of the selected chart type

4. Click the **Next** button to display the next Chart Wizard dialog box, in which you preview the chart and modify the data and its placement in the chart. Because visualizing the chart from the displayed preview is difficult, you'll use the default layout based on the two selected fields. You can easily modify the chart after you create it.

Tip

The box on the right displays a brief description of the selected chart type.

Tip

The record source for a primary main form must have a one-to-many relationship to the record source for a related subform or chart. The subform or chart object has its Link Master Fields property set to the primary key in the record source to the main form. Its Link Child Fields property is set to the foreign key in the record source to the subform or chart.

▶ 5. Click the **Next** button to display the next Chart Wizard dialog box, in which you choose the fields that link records in the main form, which uses the tblContract table as its record source, to records in the chart, which uses the tblInvoice table as its record source. ContractNum is the common field linking these two tables, and you can use that field as the linking field even though you didn't select it as a field for the chart.

▶ 6. Click the **Next** button to display the final dialog box, in which you enter the title that will appear at the top of the chart and choose whether to include a legend in the chart.

▶ 7. Type **Invoices for this Contract**, make sure the **Yes, display a legend** option button is selected, and then click the **Finish** button. The completed chart appears in the tab control.

You'll view the form in Form view, where it's easier to assess the chart's appearance.

▶ 8. Save your form design changes, switch to Form view, navigate to record 5 in the main form, notice the four contracts displayed in the subform, click the **Invoice Chart** tab to display the chart, and then scroll down the form (if necessary). See Figure 8-22.

Figure 8-22 **Embedded chart in Form view**

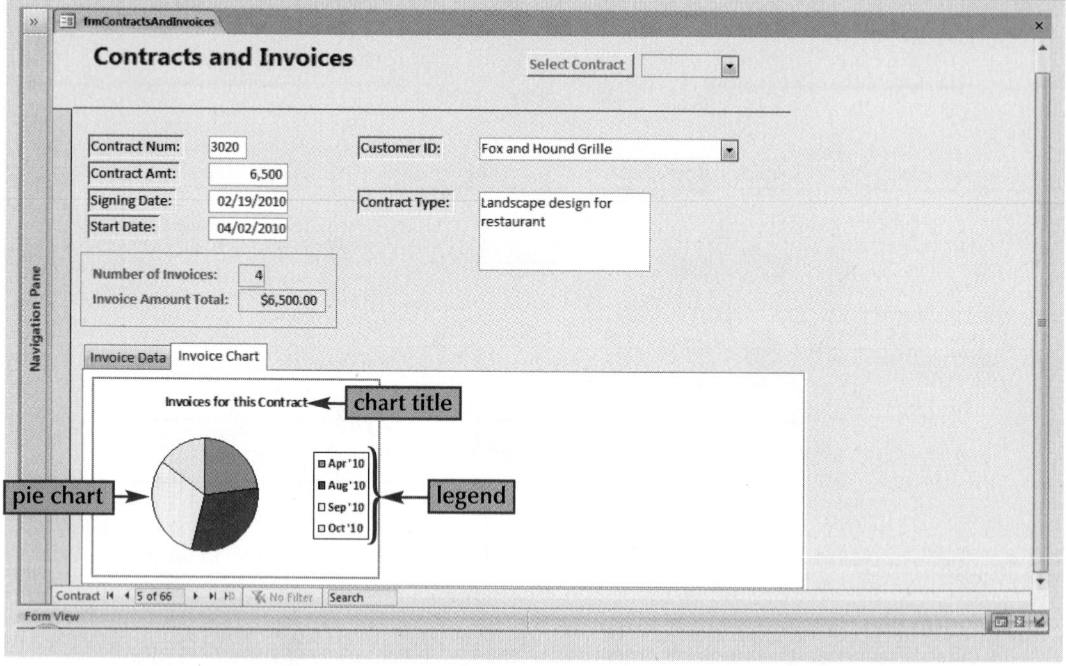

After viewing the chart, Sarah decides it needs some modifications. She wants you to change the chart type from a pie chart to a bar chart, remove the legend, and modify the chart's background color. You'll make these changes by switching to Design view, and then you'll start Microsoft Graph so you can edit the chart.

To edit the chart using Microsoft Graph:

▶ **1.** Switch to Design view, right-click an edge of the chart object to open the shortcut menu, point to **Chart Object**, and then click **Open**. Microsoft Graph starts and displays the chart. See Figure 8-23.

Editing the chart with Microsoft Graph ◄ Figure 8-23

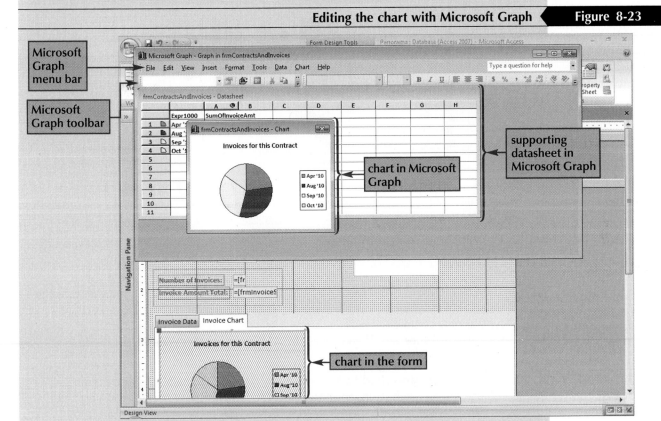

Microsoft Graph is the source program that the Chart Wizard used to create the chart. Because the chart was embedded in the form, editing the chart object starts Graph and allows you to edit the chart using the Graph menu bar and toolbar. In addition to displaying the selected chart, the Graph window displays a datasheet, which contains the data on which the chart is based. You'll now make Sarah's chart changes using Graph.

▶ **2.** Click **Chart** on the Graph menu bar, click **Chart Type** to open the Chart Type dialog box, and then click **Column** in the Chart type list box to display the types of column charts. See Figure 8-24.

Figure 8-24 ▶ **Chart Type dialog box**

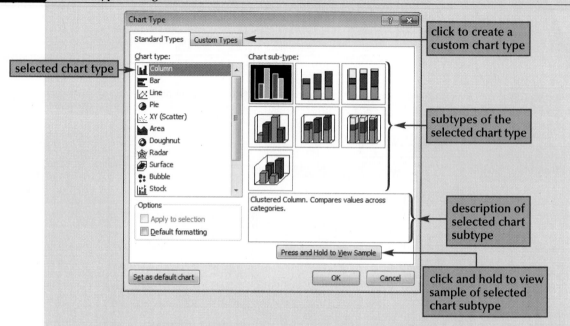

selected chart type ◀

click to create a custom chart type

subtypes of the selected chart type

description of selected chart subtype

click and hold to view sample of selected chart subtype

The Column chart is the selected chart type, and the Clustered Column chart is the default chart subtype (row 1, column 1). A description of the selected chart subtype appears below the chart subtypes. You can create a custom chart by clicking the Custom Types tab. If you click and hold down the Press and Hold to View Sample button, you'll see a sample of the selected subtype.

▶ 3. Click the **Press and Hold to View Sample** button to view a sample of the chart, release the mouse button, and then click the **OK** button to close the dialog box and change the chart to a column chart in the Graph window and in the form.

▶ 4. Click **Chart** on the Graph menu bar, click **Chart Options** to open the Chart Options dialog box, click the **Legend** tab to display the chart's legend options, click the **Show legend** check box to clear it, and then click the **OK** button. The legend is removed from the chart object in the Graph window and in the form.

To change the color or other properties of a chart control—the chart background (or chart area), axes, labels to the left of the y-axis, labels below the x-axis, or data markers (columnar bars for a column chart)—you need to double-click the control.

Tip

A data marker is a bar, dot, segment, or other symbol that represents a single data value.

▶ 5. In the Graph window, double-click one of the blue data markers inside the chart to open the Format Data Series dialog box, and then click the orange box (row 2, column 2) in the color palette in the Area section. See Figure 8-25.

Format Data Series dialog box < **Figure 8-25**

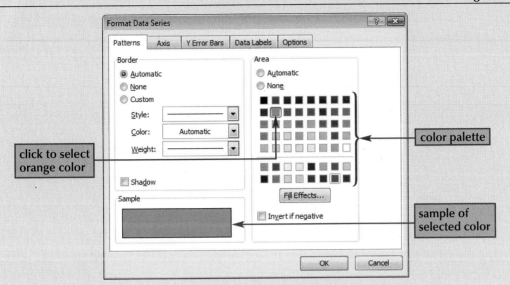

The sample color in the dialog box changes to orange to match the selected color in the color palette.

▶ **6.** Click the **OK** button to close the dialog box and to change the color of the data markers in the chart in the Graph window and in the form to orange.

▶ **7.** In the Graph window, double-click the white chart background to open the Format Chart Area dialog box, click the light orange box (row 5, column 2) in the color palette in the Area section, and then click the **OK** button. The background color changes to light orange in the chart in the Graph window and in the form.

▶ **8.** Click **File** on the Graph menu bar, and then click **Exit & Return to frmContractsAndInvoices** to exit Graph and return to the form.

▶ **9.** Save your form design changes, switch to Form view, navigate to record 5 in the main form, click the **Invoice Chart** tab to display the chart, and then scroll down the form (if necessary). See Figure 8-26.

Figure 8-26 **Completed chart in Form view**

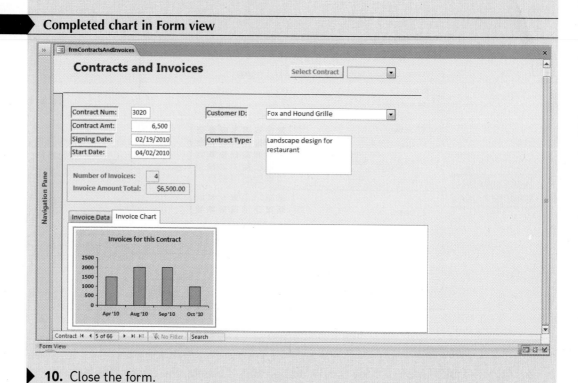

> **10.** Close the form.

Sarah wants to know if Access has other charting and data analysis tools. You'll show her how to create a PivotTable and a PivotChart.

Creating and Using a PivotTable

Sarah wants to be able to analyze Belmont Landscapes' business in a flexible way. You can use PivotTables to provide the flexible analysis that Sarah needs. A **PivotTable** is an interactive table that lets you analyze data dynamically. You can use a PivotTable to view and organize data from a database, look for summary or detail information, and dynamically change the contents and organization of the table. Figure 8-27 shows a PivotTable.

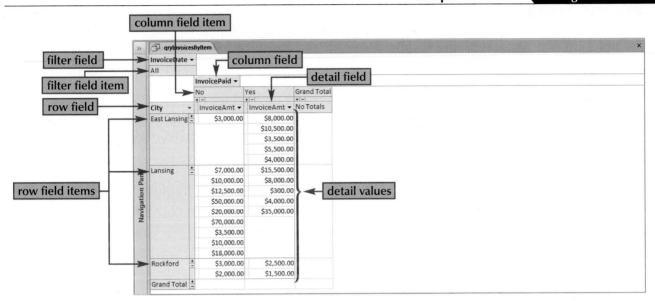

A PivotTable contains the following basic components:

- The **detail area**, consisting of a **detail field** and **detail values**, provides details or totals from a database table or query. In Figure 8-27, the detail field is the InvoiceAmt field from the tblInvoice table, and the detail values are the InvoiceAmt field values.
- The **row area**, consisting of a **row field** and **row field items**, provides row groupings in the PivotTable. In Figure 8-27, the row field is the City field from the tblCustomer table, and the row field items are the City field values.
- The **column area**, consisting of a **column field** and **column field items**, provides column groupings in the PivotTable. In Figure 8-27, the column field is the InvoicePaid field from the tblInvoice table, and the column field items are the InvoicePaid field values.
- The **filter area**, consisting of a **filter field** and **filter field items**, lets you restrict which data appears in the PivotTable. In Figure 8-27, the filter field is the InvoiceDate field from the tblInvoice table, and the filter field item is "All" dates, which means that all InvoiceDate field values are represented in the PivotTable.
- All the PivotTable areas—detail area, row area, column area, and filter area—can have multiple fields with multiple field items.

When you work with PivotTables, you use another program, the **Office PivotTable Component**, which is one of the **Office Web Components** that are part of Office 2007. Therefore, you can use PivotTables with other programs such as Excel. You can create PivotTables with Access tables and queries; the PivotTable view with these Access objects provides this capability.

Creating a PivotTable

Sarah wants to analyze invoice amounts by city and by invoice date in various ways. You'll create a PivotTable using the qryInvoicesByItem query to let her perform this analysis.

To create a PivotTable using a query:

▶ **1.** Open the Navigation Pane, open the **qryInvoicesByItem** query datasheet to display the 172 records in the query, close the Navigation Pane, right-click the **qryInvoicesByItem** tab, and then click **PivotTable View** to switch to PivotTable view. See Figure 8-28.

| Figure 8-28 | PivotTable view for the qryInvoicesByItem query |

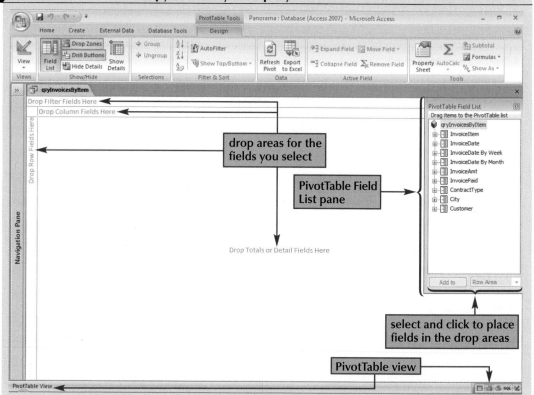

To create a PivotTable, you click a field in the PivotTable Field List pane to select it, and then drag it to one of the four drop areas—row, column, filter, or totals/detail—or click the Add to button at the bottom of the PivotTable Field List pane after selecting one of the four drop areas in the list to the right of the Add to button.

Sarah wants to use the InvoicePaid field as the column field, the City field as the row field, the InvoiceDate field as the filter field, and the InvoiceAmt field as the detail field.

▶ **2.** Click **InvoicePaid** in the PivotTable Field List pane, click the **arrow** on the list box to the right of the Add to button in the PivotTable Field List pane, click **Column Area** in the list, and then click the **Add to** button. Access places the InvoicePaid field and its field values in the column drop area.

▶ **3.** Repeat Step 2 to add the **City** field to the row drop area, the **InvoiceDate** field to the filter drop area, and the **InvoiceAmt** field to the totals or detail drop area. The four selected fields are bold in the PivotTable Field List pane and appear as components in the PivotTable. See Figure 8-29.

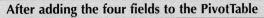

After adding the four fields to the PivotTable | Figure 8-29

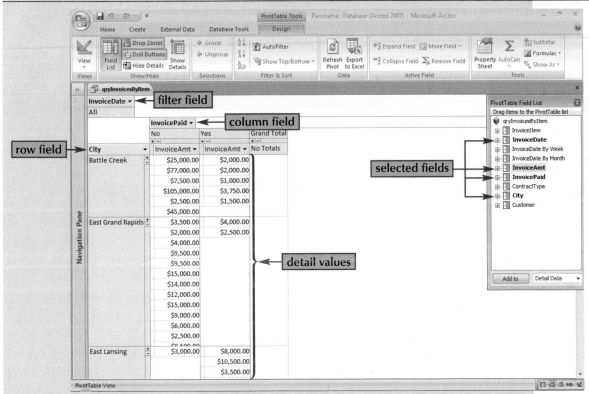

The PivotTable displays all the InvoiceAmt field values from the source query organized by city and invoice status (unpaid or paid).

4. Close the PivotTable Field List pane.

Sarah can filter the PivotTable using one or more of the four selected fields. She can also add total fields and hide the detail values in the PivotTable.

Filtering and Summarizing Data in a PivotTable

A **total field** summarizes values from a source field. For example, Sarah can add subtotals and a grand total of the InvoiceAmt field values to the PivotTable. You'll show Sarah how to filter data in the PivotTable and how to add subtotals by city and a grand total for the InvoiceAmt field values.

To filter data and add a total field in a PivotTable:

▶ **1.** Click the **City** arrow, click the **All** check box to clear all the selections, click the **East Lansing** check box, click the **Lansing** check box, click the **Rockford** check box, and then click the **OK** button. Access applies the City filter and display total invoice amounts for the three selected cities. See Figure 8-30.

Figure 8-30 ▶ **Filtering data by city**

Tip

You've applied a filter to the row field. In a similar way, you can apply filters to the column, filter, and detail fields.

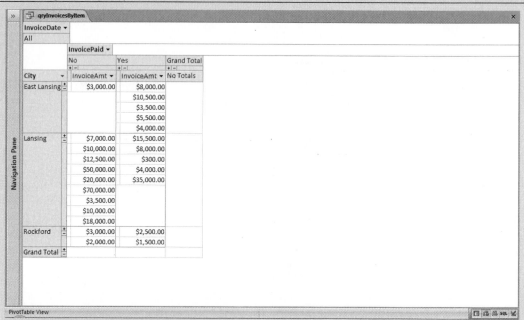

The applied City filter displays all the InvoiceAmt field values from the source query for the cities of East Lansing, Lansing, and Rockford.

▶ **2.** Click one of the **InvoiceAmt** column heading labels; in the Tools group on the Design tab, click the **AutoCalc** button, click **Sum**, and then click to the right of the PivotTable to deselect all values. Access adds a new row for each city in the PivotTable that displays the city's InvoiceAmt total and a new row at the bottom of the PivotTable that displays the grand total for the displayed InvoiceAmt values. See Figure 8-31.

After adding the total field to the PivotTable ◄ Figure 8-31

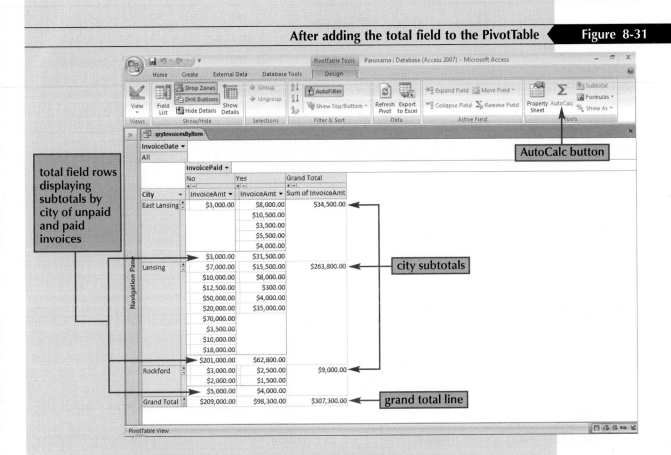

total field rows displaying subtotals by city of unpaid and paid invoices

AutoCalc button

city subtotals

grand total line

3. In the Show/Hide group on the Design tab, click the **Hide Details** button. Access hides the detail lines and displays only the subtotal and grand total lines in the PivotTable. See Figure 8-32.

Subtotals and grand total displayed in the PivotTable ◄ Figure 8-32

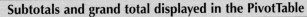
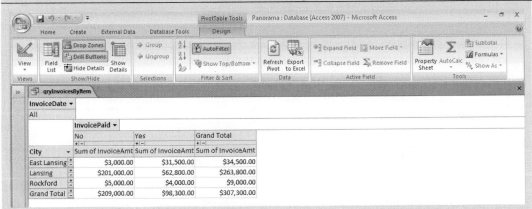

4. In the Show/Hide group on the Design tab, click the **Show Details** button. Access shows the detail lines and the subtotal and grand total lines in the PivotTable for the cities of East Lansing, Lansing, and Rockford.

Sarah asks if you can display the filtered PivotTable data in a chart. You'll switch to PivotChart view to satisfy Sarah's request.

Creating a PivotChart

Office 2007 provides the **Office PivotChart Component** to assist you in adding a chart to a table or query. Using the Office PivotChart Component, you can create a **PivotChart**, an interactive chart that provides capabilities similar to a PivotTable. You can open a table or query, switch to PivotChart view, add fields to the PivotChart's drop areas, just as you did when you created the PivotTable, and then filter the data in the PivotChart. When you create a PivotChart, you can switch to PivotTable view to view and further filter the charted data in a PivotTable. Likewise, after creating a PivotTable, you can switch to PivotChart view to view and further filter the tabular data in a PivotChart.

You'll switch to PivotChart view to show Sarah the PivotChart of the PivotTable data.

To switch to PivotChart view:

▶ 1. Right-click the **qryInvoicesByItem** tab, and then click **PivotChart View** on the shortcut menu to switch to PivotChart view. See Figure 8-33.

| Figure 8-33 | Filtered PivotTable data in a PivotChart |

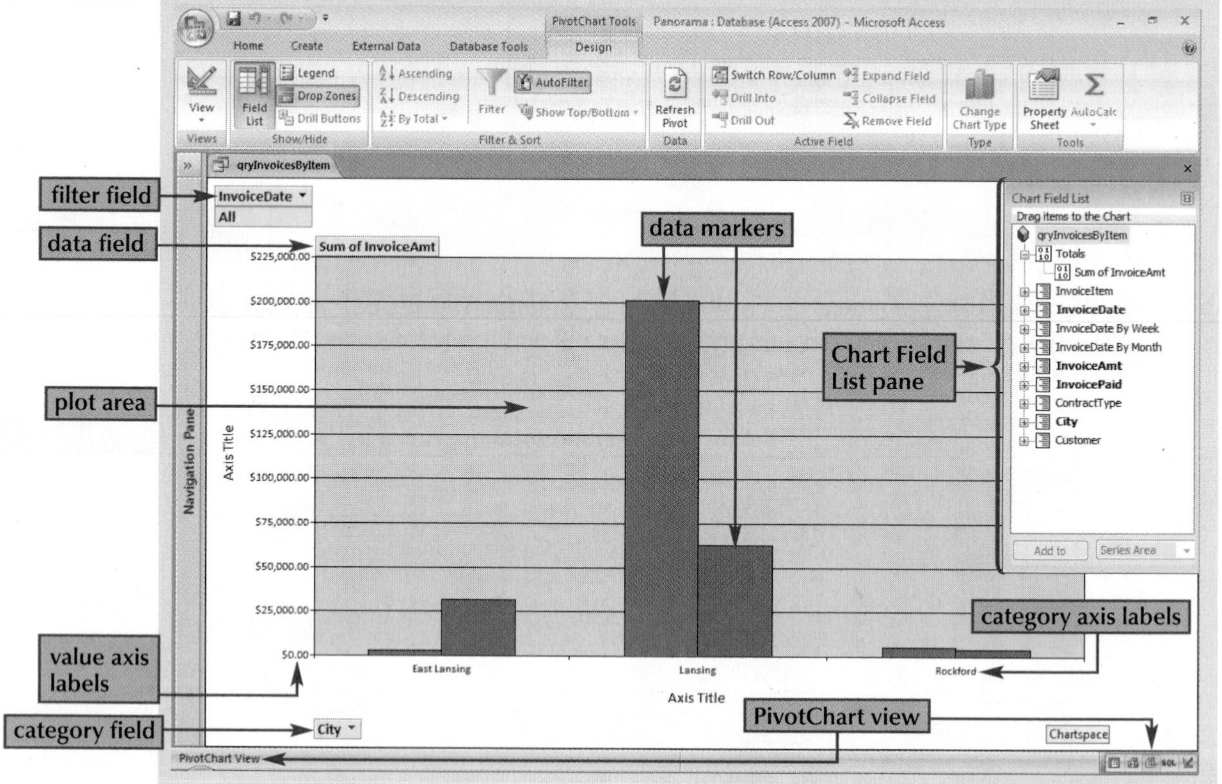

A PivotChart contains the following basic components:

- The **plot area** provides a background for the data markers and gridlines. A **data marker** is a bar, dot, segment, or other symbol that represents a single data value. The **data field**, which is the Sum of InvoiceAmt field in Figure 8-33, identifies which values the data markers represent and identifies each value displayed as a **value axis label**. Each **gridline**, which appears in Figure 8-33 as one of the horizontal lines in the plot area, makes it easier to see the values represented by the data markers.

- The **category field** identifies each value that's displayed as a **category axis label**; each category axis label identifies an individual data marker. In Figure 8-33, the City field is the category field; East Lansing, Lansing, and Rockford are the category axis labels. The data markers show the total unpaid and paid InvoiceAmt field values for each city.
- The **filter field** lets you restrict which data appears in the PivotChart. In Figure 8-33, the filter field is the InvoiceDate field. The "All" value below InvoiceDate indicates that no filter has been applied to the filter field.
- The **series field** identifies the data markers' subdivisions or splits. In Figure 8-33, the InvoicePaid field is the series field, and each pair of data markers represent the two values for the InvoicePaid field. (The series field is not visible in Figure 8-33) The left data marker represents unpaid invoices, and the right data marker represents paid invoices. An optional **legend** provides a list of the series field values and how these values are indicated on the data markers. (Figure 8-33 does not include a legend.)

Next, you'll show Sarah how to modify the PivotChart.

To modify the PivotChart:

▶ **1.** Close the Chart Field List pane. The InvoicePaid field, which is the series field for the PivotChart, is now visible to the right of the PivotChart.

▶ **2.** In the Show/Hide group on the Design tab, click the **Legend** button. A legend is displayed below the InvoicePaid field and indicates that the blue bars represent unpaid invoices (No value) and the red bars represent paid invoices (Yes value).

Sarah wants to change the City filter to display data for Grand Rapids, Holland, Kalamazoo, and Lansing.

▶ **3.** Click the **City** arrow, click the **East Lansing** check box to clear it, click the **Rockford** check box to clear it, click the **Grand Rapids** check box to select it, click the **Holland** check box to select it, click the **Kalamazoo** check box to select it, and then click the **OK** button. Access applies the City filter, displays total invoice amounts for the four selected cities, and changes the scale of the vertical axis and its value axis labels. See Figure 8-34.

Figure 8-34 | After changing the City filter and displaying the legend

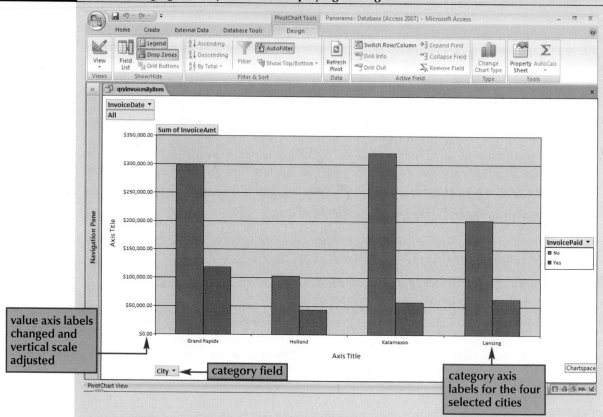

value axis labels changed and vertical scale adjusted

category field

category axis labels for the four selected cities

Sarah wants to change the PivotChart from a column chart to a bar chart to take advantage of the screen width, and she wants to change the colors of the data markers.

4. Click in the white portion of the chart (if necessary) to deselect any chart control, and then in the Type group on the Design tab, click the **Change Chart Type** button, click **Bar** in the left list, and then click the **Clustered Bar** chart (row 1, column 1) in the right list. The chart changes from a clustered column chart to a clustered bar chart.

5. In the chart, click the red data marker for Lansing, hold down the **Shift** key, click the red data marker for Lansing a second time, and then release the **Shift** key. All red data markers are now selected, and any property change you make in the Properties dialog box will apply to all four red data markers.

6. Click the **Border/Fill** tab in the Properties dialog box, click the **Fill Color** arrow, and then click the **DodgerBlue** color (row 3, column 4) in the color palette. The four selected data markers change to the selected DodgerBlue color. See Figure 8-35.

7. Repeat Steps 5-6, selecting the other four data markers (the lower data marker in each set), and clicking the **Tomato** color (row 8, column 13), and then click the **Fill Color** arrow to display the color palette. The four selected data markers change to the Tomato color. See Figure 8-35.

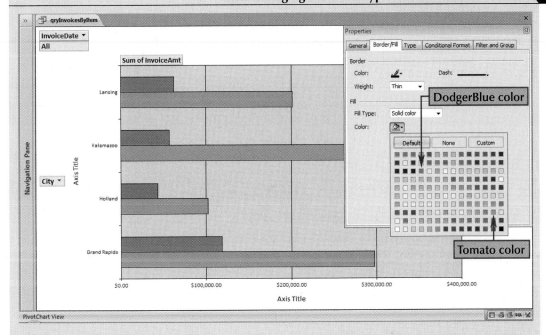

After changing the chart type and data marker colors ◀ **Figure 8-35**

▶ **8.** Close the Properties dialog box, save your PivotTable and PivotChart changes, and then close the query.

▶ **9.** Open the Navigation Pane, open the **qryInvoicesByItem** query datasheet to display the 172 records in the query, switch to PivotChart view to display the saved PivotChart, switch to PivotTable view to display the saved PivotTable, and then close the query.

Sarah's staff maintains an Excel worksheet that tracks the products Belmont Landscapes has used for its landscaping projects. Sarah want to use the product data in the Panorama database.

Linking Data from an Excel Worksheet

Sarah's staff has extensive experience working with Excel and prefers to maintain the data in the Products worksheet using Excel. However, Sarah needs to reference the products data in the Panorama database, and the data she's referencing must always be the current version of the worksheet data. Importing the Excel worksheet data as an Access table would provide Sarah with data that's quickly out of date unless she repeats the import steps each time the data in the Excel worksheet changes. Because Sarah doesn't need to update the products data in the Panorama database, you'll link to the worksheet from the database. When the staff changes the Products worksheet, the changes will be reflected automatically in the linked version of the table in the database. At the same time, Sarah won't be able to update the products data from the Panorama database, which ensures that only the staff members responsible for maintaing the Excel worksheet can update the data.

You'll now link to the data in the Excel worksheet.

To link to the data in the Excel worksheet:

▶ **1.** Click the **External Data** tab on the Ribbon, and then in the Import group on the External Data tab, click the **Excel** button (with the ScreenTip "Import Excel spreadsheet"). The Get External Data - Excel Spreadsheet dialog box opens.

▶ **2.** Click the **Browse** button, navigate to and open the **Level.02\Tutorial** folder, click **Products**, click the **Open** button, and then click the **Link to the data source by creating a linked table** option button. The selected path and filename now appear in the File name text box, and you've set the option to link to the data instead of importing or appending the data. See Figure 8-36.

Figure 8-36	Linking to data in an Excel worksheet

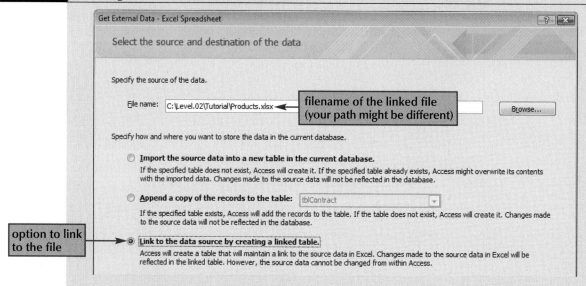

▶ **3.** Click the **OK** button. The Link Spreadsheet Wizard dialog box opens. See Figure 8-37.

Figure 8-37	Linking to data in an Excel worksheet

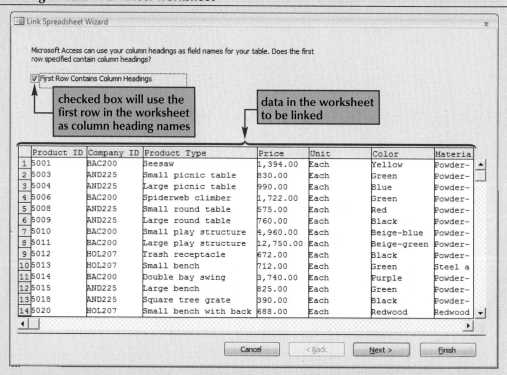

The first row in the worksheet contains column heading names, and each row in the worksheet represents the data about a single product.

▶ **4.** Click the **Next** button to open the next Link Spreadsheet Wizard dialog box, in which you choose a name for the linked table. You'll use the default table name tblProduct.

▶ **5.** Click the **Finish** button. A message box informs you that you've created a linking table to the Excel worksheet file.

▶ **6.** Click the **OK** button to close the message box and complete the linking steps. The tblProduct table now appears in the Navigation Pane. The icon to the left of the table name ⊞ identifies the table as a linked table.

You can open and view the tblProduct table and use fields from the linked table in queries, forms, and reports, but you can't update the products data using the Panorama database. You can update the products data only from the Excel worksheet.

Next, you'll show Sarah how the worksheet and the linked table interact.

To update the Excel worksheet and view the data in the linked table:

▶ **1.** Open Windows Explorer, navigate to and open the **Level.02\Tutorial** folder, right-click **Products**, click **Open With** on the shortcut menu, click **Microsoft Office Excel**, and then click the **OK** button. The Products workbook opens and displays the tblProduct worksheet.

▶ **2.** Click the **Microsoft Office Access** program button on the taskbar to switch to the Panorama database, and then open the **tblProduct** datasheet. The fields and records in the tblProduct table display the same data as the Excel worksheet.

▶ **3.** Select **Yellow** in the first record's Color column, and then type **G**. A warning sound chimes, the message "This Recordset is not updateable" is displayed on the status bar, and the value is not changed.

▶ **4.** Click the **Microsoft Excel** program button on the taskbar to switch to the Products workbook, select **Yellow** in cell F2, type **Green**, and then press the **Enter** key. The value in cell F2 changes from Yellow to Green.

▶ **5.** Click the **Microsoft Office Access** program button on the taskbar to switch to the Panorama database. The first row's Color field value is now Green, because this is the newly changed value in the Excel worksheet.

You've completed your work for Sarah and her staff.

▶ **6.** Close the table.

▶ **7.** Click the **Microsoft Excel** program button on the taskbar to switch to the Products workbook, save your worksheet change, and then exit Excel.

▶ **8.** Close the Panorama database, make a backup copy of the database, open the **Panorama** database, compact and repair the database, close the database, and then exit Access.

Tip

If Excel has the worksheet open at the same time Access is displaying the linked file's data, you must close the table in Access before closing the worksheet in Excel, or Access will display error values in the linked file.

Knowing how to create charts, PivotTables, and PivotCharts and how to link to data maintained by other programs will make it easier for Sarah and her staff to anlayze their operations and to work efficiently in managing data.

Review | **Session 8.2 Quick Check**

1. The _____ property lets you change the navigation label from the word "Record" to another value.
2. When you use the Microsoft Graph program to create and change charts in a form or report, you must _____ the chart.
3. What is a PivotTable?
4. Within a PivotTable you can choose fields form the field list to be a column field, a row field, a detail field, or a(n) _____ field.
5. In a PivotChart, the _____ field identifies which values are shown as value axis labels.
6. You can show/hide a legend for the _____ field in a PivotChart.

Review | **Tutorial Summary**

In this tutorial, you learned how to share and integrate data. You exported an Access query to an HTML document and then used a Web browser to view the document. You imported a CSV file as an Access table, imported and exported XML files, used the Table Analyzer, and saved and executed import and export specifications. Then you created a multi-page form using a tab control, embedded a chart in one of the tab control's pages, and modified the chart. Finally, you created and modified a PivotTable and a PivotChart and linked data from an Excel worksheet.

Key Terms

category axis label	Hypertext Markup	static Web page
category field	Language (HTML)	Tab Control tool
column area	Hypertext Transfer	Table Analyzer
column field	Protocol (HTTP)	tag
column field items	importing	total field
CSV (comma-separated	Internet	Uniform Resource
values) file	legend	Locator (URL)
data field	linking	value axis label
data marker	Navigation Caption property	Web
destination program	Office PivotChart Component	Web browser
detail area	Office PivotTable Component	Web client
detail field	Office Web Component	Web page
detail values	Page Break tool	Web server
embedding	PivotChart	World Wide Web
filter area	PivotTable	XML (Extensible Markup
filter field	plot area	Language)
filter field items	row area	XSD (XML Structure
gridline	row field	Definition)
HTML document	row field items	XSL (Extensible Stylesheet
HTML template	series field	Language)
hyperlink	source program	

| Practice | **Review Assignments** |

Practice the skills you learned in the tutorial using the same case scenario.

Data Files needed for the Review Assignments: Ads.xlsx, BelmLogo.gif, BelmTemp.htm, Payables.csv, Products.accdb (*cont. from Tutorial 7*), and tblPayments.xml

Sarah wants you to integrate the data in the Products database with other programs and she wants to be able to analyze the data in the database. You'll help her achieve these goals by completing the following:

1. Open the **Products** database located in the Level.02\Review folder provided with your Data Files.
2. Export the qryCompanyList query as an HTML document to the Level.02\Review folder, using the HTML template file named BelmTemp, which is located in the Level.02\Review folder, and saving the file as **qryCompanyList**. Do not save the export steps.
3. Import the CSV file named Payables, which is located in the Level.02\Review folder, as a new table in the database. Choose your own primary key, name the table **tblPayables**, run the Table Analyzer, and record the Table Analyzer's recommendation. Do not save the import steps.
4. Import the XML file named tblPayments, which is located in the Level.02\Review folder, as a new table named **tblPayments** in the database. Save the import steps.
5. Export the tblCompany table as an XML file named **tblCompany** to the Level.02\Review folder; do not create a separate XSD file. Save the export steps.
6. Link to the Ads workbook, which is located in the Level.02\Review folder, using **tblAd** as the table name. Change the cost of the flyer for Ad Num 5 to **$300**.
7. Modify the **frmCompaniesWithProducts** form in the following ways:
   a. Add a tab control to the bottom of the Detail section, and place the existing subform on the first page of the tab control.
   b. Change the caption for the left tab to **Product Data** and for the right tab to **Product Chart**.
   c. Change the caption for the main form's navigation buttons to **Company** and for the subform's navigation buttons to **Product**.
   d. Add a chart to the second page of the tab control. Use the tblProduct table as the record source, select the ProductType, Price, and Unit fields, use the 3-D Column Chart type, include a legend, and use **Products Offered** as the chart title.
   e. Change the chart to a Clustered Column chart, and change the blue colored data marker to pink.
8. Open the **tblPayments** table and create a PivotTable with PaymentAmt as the detail field, PaymentDate as the column field, CompanyID as the row field, and PaymentID as the filter field.
9. Switch to PivotChart view. Filter the CompanyID field, selecting BAC200, BEL273, and CHE802, select PaymentAmt as the data field, display the legend, and then save the table.
10. Close the Products database without exiting Access, make a backup copy of the database, open the **Products** database, compact and repair the database, close the database, and then exit Access.

Apply | **Case Problem 1**

Apply the skills you learned in the tutorial to import and export data and create charts for a music school.

Data Files needed for this Case Problem: Contract.accdb (*cont. from Tutorial 7*), **Instrument.csv, and Room.xlsx**

Pine Hill Music School   Yuka wants you to integrate the data in the Contract database with other programs, and she wants to be able to analyze the data in the database. You'll help her achieve these goals by completing the following:

1. Open the **Contract** database located in the Level.02\Case1 folder provided with your Data Files.

⊕ EXPLORE

2. Export the rptTeacherLessons report as an HTML document to the Level.02\Case1 folder; do not use a template or save the export steps. Use your Web browser to open the **rptTeacherLessons** HTML document. Then scroll to the bottom of the page; use the First, Previous, Next, and Last links to navigate through the document.

3. Import the CSV file named Instrument, which is located in the Level.02\Case1 folder, as a new table in the database. Choose your own primary key, name the table **tblInstrument**, run the Table Analyzer, and record the Table Analyzer's recommendation, but do not accept the recommendation. Do not save the import steps.

4. Export the tblTeacher table as an XML file named **tblTeacher** to the Level.02\Case1 folder; do not create a separate XSD file. Save the export steps.

5. Link to the Room workbook, which is located in the Level.02\Case1 folder, using **tblRoom** as the table name. Add a new record to the Room workbook as follows: Room Num **5**, Rental Cost **$25**, and Type **Private**.

6. Open the qryLessonsByTeacher query, and create a PivotTable with MonthlyLessonCost as the detail field, LessonType as the column field, LastName as the row field, and LessonLength as the filter field. Filter the LessonType field, selecting Guitar, Piano, and Saxophone. Add subtotals and a grand total for the MonthlyLessonCost field values.

7. Switch to PivotChart view. Display the legend (if necessary), change the color of the Saxophone data markers to yellow, and then save the query.

8. Close the Contract database without exiting Access, make a backup copy of the database, open the **Contract** database, compact and repair the database, close the database, and then exit Access.

Apply | **Case Problem 2**

Use the skills you learned in the tutorial to analyze the data for a health and fitness center.

Data Files needed for this Case Problem: CreditCard.xml, ParkLogo.gif, ParkTemp.htm, Schedule.xlsx, and Training.accdb (*cont. from Tutorial 7*)

Parkhurst Health & Fitness Center   Martha Parkhurst wants you to integrate the data in the Training database with other programs, and she wants to be able to analyze the data in the database. You'll help her achieve these goals by completing the following:

1. Open the **Training** database located in the Level.02\Case2 folder provided with your Data Files.

2. Export the qryPhysicalsNeeded query as an HTML document to the Level.02\Case2 folder, using the HTML template file named ParkTemp, which is located in the Level.02\Case2 folder, and saving the file as **qryPhysicalsNeeded**. Save the export steps.

⊕ EXPLORE

3. Export the rptProgramMembership report as an HTML document to the Level.02\Case2 folder; do not use a template or save the export steps. Use your Web browser to open the **rptProgramMembership** HTML document. Then scroll to the bottom of the page; use the First, Previous, Next, and Last links to navigate through the document.

4. Import the XML file named CreditCard, which is located in the Level.02\Case2 folder, as a new table named **tblCreditCard**. Save the import steps.

5. Export the tblProgram table as an XML file named **tblProgram** to the Level.02\Case2 folder; do not create a separate XSD file. Save the export steps.

6. Link to the Schedule workbook, which is located in the Level.02\Case2 folder, using **tblSchedule** as the table name. For ClassID 301, change the ClassDay value to **F**.

7. Modify the **frmProgramsAndMembers** form in the following ways:
   a. Add a tab control to the bottom of the Detail section, and place the existing subform on the first page of the tab control.
   b. Change the caption for the left tab to **Member Data** and for the right tab to **Member Chart**.
   c. Change the caption for the main form's navigation buttons to **Program** and for the subform's navigation buttons to **Member**.
   d. Add a chart to the second page of the tab control. Use the tblMember table as the record source, select the ProgramID and MembershipStatus fields, use the Clustered Column chart type, include a legend, and use **Membership Status** as the chart title.
   e. Change the color of the right data marker (or the middle data marker, depending on whether you see two or three data markers) to red.

8. Open the **qryMonthlyFeeStatus** query and create a PivotTable with MonthlyFee as the detail field, MonthlyFeeStatus as the column field, LastName as the row field, and ProgramType as the filter field. Add subtotals and a grand total of the MonthlyFee values, hide the details, and filter the ProgramType field to display only programs for juniors.

9. Switch to PivotChart view for the qryMonthlyFeeStatus query. Change the chart type to Clustered Bar, display the legend, change the data markers to colors of your choice, and then save the query.

10. Close the Training database without exiting Access, make a backup copy of the database, open the **Training** database, compact and repair the database, close the database, and then exit Access.

Challenge | Case Problem 3

Use the skills you learned in the tutorial to integrate and analyze data about an agency that recycles household goods.

Data Files needed for this Case Problem: Agency.accdb (*cont. from Tutorial 7*) and **Facility.csv**

Rossi Recycling Group Mary Rossi wants you to integrate the data in the Agency database with other programs, and she wants to be able to analyze the data in the database. You'll help her achieve these goals by completing the following:

1. Open the **Agency** database located in the Level.02\Case3 folder provided with your Data Files.

2. Export the qryNetDonationsCrosstab query as an HTML document to the Level.02\Case3 folder; do not use a template. Save the file as **qryNetDonationsCrosstab**. Save the export steps.

⊕ EXPLORE

3. Export the frmDonationInfo form as an HTML document to the Level.02\Case3 folder; do not use a template or save the export steps. Use your Web browser to open the **frmDonationInfo** HTML document and review its contents.

⊕ EXPLORE

4. Import the CSV file named Facility, which is located in the Level.02\Case3 folder, as a new table in the database. Choose your own primary key, name the table **tblTemporary**, and run the Table Analyzer. Accept the Table Analyzer's recommendations, rename the tables as **tblStorage** and **tblFacility**, make sure each table has the correct primary key, and let the Table Analzyer create a query. Do not save the import steps. Review the tblTemporary query, review the tblTemporary table (it might be named tblTemporary_OLD), and then review the tblStorage and tblFacility tables.

5. Export the tblDonation table as an XML file named **tblDonation** to the Level.02\Case3 folder; do not create a separate XSD file. Save the export steps.

6. Modify the **frmDonorDonations** form in the following ways:
   a. Add a tab control to the bottom of the Detail section, and place the existing subform on the first page of the tab control.
   b. Change the caption for the left tab to **Donation Data** and for the right tab to **Donation Chart**.
   c. Change the caption for the main form's navigation buttons to **Donor** and for the subform's navigation buttons to **Donation**.
   d. Add a chart to the second page of the tab control. Use the tblDonation table as the record source; select the AgencyID, DonationValue, PickupRequired, and DonationDate fields; use the 3-D Column Chart type; include a legend; and use **Donations by Agency** as the chart title.
   e. Change the chart to a Clustered Bar chart, and change the color of the maroon data marker to red.

7. Open the **qryNetDonations** query and create a PivotTable with NetDonation as the detail field, AgencyName as the column field, DonationDesc as the row field, and PickupRequired as the filter field. Filter the DonationDesc field to display only cash donations.

8. Switch to PivotChart view. Select NetDonation as the data field, filter the AgencyName by removing the first five agencies, leaving the data for five agencies in the chart, display the legend, change the chart type to Clustered Bar, and then save the query.

9. Close the Agency database without exiting Access, make a backup copy of the database, open the **Agency** database, compact and repair the database, close the database, and then exit Access.

Apply | **Case Problem 4**

Use the skills you learned in the tutorial to analyze the data for a luxury property rental company.

Data Files needed for this Case Problem: Personnel.xlsx, Vacation.accdb (*cont. from Tutorial 7*), **and Works.xml**

GEM Ultimate Vacations Griffin and Emma MacElroy want you to integrate the data in the Vacation database with other programs, and they want to be able to analyze the data in the database. You'll help them achieve these goals by completing the following:

1. Open the **Vacation** database located in the Level.02\Case4 folder provided with your Data Files.

2. Export the qryPropertiesByRate query as an HTML document to the Level.02\Case4 folder; do not use a template. Save the file as **qryPropertiesByRate**. Save the export steps.

3. Import the XML file named Works, which is located in the Level.02\Case4 folder, as a new table in the database named **tblWorks**. Save the import steps.

4. Export the qryPropertyReservations query as an XML file named **qryPropertyReservations** to the Level.02\Case4 folder; do not create a separate XSD file. Save the export steps.

5. Link to the Personnel workbook, which is located in the Level.02\Case4 folder, using **tblPersonnel** as the table name. Change the name in the fourth record from Edward Leary to **Marie Leary**.

6. Modify the **frmGuestsWithReservations** form in the following ways:
   a. Add a tab control to the bottom of the Detail section, and place the existing subform on the first page of the tab control.
   b. Change the caption for the left tab to **Reservation Data** and for the right tab to **Reservation Chart**.
   c. Change the caption for the main form's navigation buttons to **Guest** and for the subform's navigation buttons to **Reservation**.
   d. Add a chart to the second page of the tab control. Use the tblReservation table as the record source, select the StartDate, PropertyID, and RentalRate fields, use the Column Chart chart type, include a legend, and use **Reservations** as the chart title.

7. Open the **qryGuestsAndReservations** query, and create a PivotTable with RentalRate as the detail field, StateProv as the column field, the Quarters component of the StartDate By Month entry in the PivotTable Field List as the row field, and PropertyID as the filter field. Add subtotals and a grand total of the RentalRate field, and then hide the details.

8. Switch to PivotChart view. Display the legend, change the green color to yellow, and then save the query.

9. Close the Vacation database without exiting Access, make a backup copy of the database, open the **Vacation** database, compact and repair the database, close the database, and then exit Access.

| Create | **Case Problem 5** |

Use the skills you learned in this tutorial to integrate and analyze the data for an Internet service provider.

Data File needed for this Case Problem: ACE.accdb (*cont. from Tutorial 7*)

Always Connected Everyday   Chris and Pat Aquino want you to integrate the data in the ACE database with other programs, and they want to be able to analyze the data in the database. You'll help them achieve these goals by completing the following:

1. Open the **ACE** database located in the Level.02\Case5 folder provided with your Data Files.

2. Export the tblAccessPlan table as an HTML document to the Level.02\Case5 folder; do not use a template or save the import steps. Save the file as **tblAccessPlan**.

⊕ EXPLORE

3. Export the rptAccessPlanCustomers report as an HTML document to the Level.02\Case5 folder; do not use a template or save the export steps. Use your Web browser to open and review the HTML document.

4. Export the tblCustomer table as an XML file named **tblCustomer** to the Level.02\Case5 folder; do not create a separate XSD file. Save the export steps.

5. Modify one of the existing forms or create a new form so that the form uses a tab control. Change the caption for the navigation buttons, and set the captions for the tab labels.

6. For one of the existing queries (or create a new query), create a PivotTable, add subtotals and a grand total, apply a filter, and hide details. In PivotChart view, display the legend and make any other appropriate changes.

7. Close the ACE database without exiting Access, make a backup copy of the database, open the **ACE** database, compact and repair the database, close the database, and then exit Access.

Research | Internet Assignments

Use the Internet to find and work with data related to the topics presented in this tutorial.

The purpose of the Internet Assignments is to challenge you to find information on the Internet that you can use to work effectively with this software. The actual assignments are updated and maintained on the Course Technology Web site. Log on to the Internet and use your Web browser to go to the Student Online Companion for New Perspectives Office 2007 at **www.course.com/np/office2007**. Then navigate to the Internet Assignments for this tutorial.

Assess | SAM Assessment and Training

If you have a SAM user profile, you may have access to hands-on instruction, practice, and assessment of the skills covered in this tutorial. Log in to your SAM account (**http://sam2007.course.com**) to launch any assigned training activities or exams that relate to the skills covered in this tutorial.

Review | Quick Check Answers

Session 8.1

1. a vast collection of digital documents available on the Internet; Web browser
2. links one Web page to another Web page or Web site, or to another location in the same Web page
3. language used to create most Web pages
4. An HTML template is a file that contains HTML instructions for creating a Web page with both text and graphics, together with special instructions that tell Access where to place the Access data in the page.
5. shows the state of the database at the time the page was created; any subsequent changes made to the database object, such as updates to field values in records, are not reflected in a static Web page
6. a text file in which commas separate values, and each line is a record containing the same number of values in the same positions
7. an Access tool that analyzes a single table and, if necessary, splits it into two or more tables that are in third normal form
8. XML (Extensible Markup Language)

Session 8.2

1. Navigation Caption
2. embed
3. an interactive table that lets you analyze data dynamically
4. filter
5. data
6. series

Ending Data Files

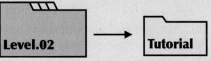

Level.02 →

Tutorial
Customers by Name.html
Panorama.accdb
Products.xlsx
tblInvoice.xml

Review
Ads.xlsx
Products.accdb
qryCompanyList.html
tblCompany.xml

Case1
Contract.accdb
Room.xlsx
rptTeacherLessons.html
rptTeacherLessonsPage2.html
tblTeacher.xml

Case2
qryPhysicalsNeeded.html
rptProgramMembership.html
rptProgramMembershipPage2.html
Schedule.xlsx
tblProgram.xml
Training.accdb

Case3
Agency.accdb
frmDonationInfo.html
qryNetDonationsCrosstab.html
tblDonation.xml

Case4
Personnel.xlsx
qryPropertiesByRate.html
qryPropertyReservations.xml
Vacation.accdb

Case5
ACE.accdb
rptAccessPlanCustomers.html
tblAccessPlan.html
tblCustomer.xml

Reality Check

You interact with databases whenever you place an order on the Internet, check out at a retail store or restaurant, verify your bank account balance, or register for classes. Most businesses use databases, and you can also use databases to track data in your personal life. Examples of personal database use include tracking personal collections, such as DVDs or books; hobby data, such as family histories or antiques; or items related to sports teams, theater clubs, or other organizations to which you might belong. In this exercise, you'll use Access to create a database that will contain information of your choice, using the Access skills and features you've learned in Tutorials 5 through 8.

Note: Please be sure *not* to include any personal information of a sensitive nature in the database you create to be submitted to your instructor for this exercise. Later on, you can update the data in your database with such information for your own personal use.

1. Create a new Access database to contain personal data you want to track. (If you completed Tutorials 1-4 of this book and the Reality Check at the end of Tutorial 4, you can use and enhance the database you've already created, and you can skip this step.) The database must include two or more tables that you can join through one-to-many relationships. Define the properties for each field in each table. Make sure you include a mix of data types for the fields (for example, do not include only Text fields in each table). Specify a primary key for each table, define the table relationships and enforce referential integrity, and enter records in each table.

2. Create queries that include at least the following: pattern query match, list-of-values match, parameter, crosstab, find duplicates, find unmatched, and the use of a conditional value in a calculated field.

3. For one or more fields, apply an input mask and specify field validation rules.

4. Create a split form and modify the form.

5. Create a custom form that uses at least the following: combo box for a lookup, combo box to find records, subform, lines and rectangles, and a tab control. Add one or more calculated controls to the main form based on the subform's calculated control(s), and add a chart, if appropriate. Check the main form's tab order, and improve the form's appearance.

6. Create a custom report that uses at least the following: grouping field, sort field(s), lines, and rectangles. Hide duplicates, and add the date, page numbers, and a report title.

7. Export two or more objects in different formats, and save the step specifications.

8. Create a PivotTable and PivotChart for one of the tables or queries.

9. Designate a trusted folder, backup the database, and compact and repair it.

10. Submit your completed database to your instructor as requested. Include printouts of any database objects, if required.

Objectives

- Learn the characteristics of a table
- Learn about primary, candidate, alternate, composite, and foreign keys
- Study one-to-one, one-to-many, and many-to-many relationships
- Learn to describe tables and relationships with entity-relationship diagrams and with a shorthand method
- Study database integrity constraints for primary keys, referential integrity, and domains
- Learn about determinants, functional dependencies, anomalies, and normalization
- Understand the differences among natural, artificial, and surrogate keys
- Learn about naming conventions

Relational Databases and Database Design

Appendix

This appendix introduces you to the basics of database design. Before trying to master this material, be sure you understand the following concepts: data, information, field, field value, record, table, relational database, common field, database management system (DBMS), and relational database management system (RDBMS).

Tables

A relational database stores its data in tables. A **table** is a two-dimensional structure made up of rows and columns. The terms table, **record** (row), and **field** (column) are the popular names for the more formal terms **relation** (table), **tuple** (row), and **attribute** (column), as shown in Figure A-1.

Figure A-1   ▶   **A table (relation) consisting of records and fields**

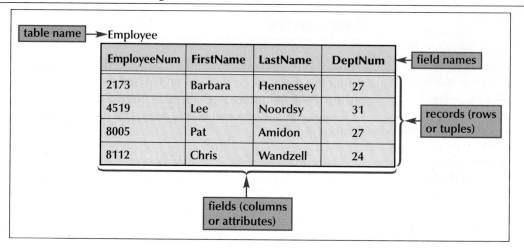

The Employee table shown in Figure A-1 is an example of a relational database table, a two-dimensional structure with the following characteristics:

- Each row is unique. Because no two rows are the same, you can easily locate and update specific data. For example, you can locate the row for EmployeeNum 8005 and change the FirstName value, Pat, the LastName value, Amidon, or the DeptNum value, 27.
- The order of the rows is unimportant. You can add or view rows in any order. For example, you can view the rows in LastName order instead of EmployeeNum order.
- Each table entry contains a single value. At the intersection of each row and column, you cannot have more than one value. For example, each row in Figure A-1 contains one EmployeeNum value, one FirstName value, one LastName value, and one DeptNum value.
- The order of the columns is unimportant. You can add or view columns in any order.
- Each column has a unique name called the **field name**. The field name allows you to access a specific column without needing to know its position within the table.
- The entries in a column are from the same domain. A **domain** is a set of values from which one or more columns (fields) draw their actual values. A domain can be broad, such as "all legitimate last names of people" for the LastName column, or narrow, such as "24, 27, or 31" for the DeptNum column. The domain of "all legitimate dates" could be shared by the BirthDate, StartDate, and TerminationDate columns in a company's employee table.
- Each row in a table describes, or shows the characteristics of, an entity. An **entity** is a person, place, object, event, or idea for which you want to store and process data. For example, EmployeeNum, FirstName, LastName, and DeptNum are characteristics of the employees of a company. The Employee table represents all the employee entities and their characteristics. That is, each row of the Employee table describes a different employee of the company using the characteristics of EmployeeNum, FirstName, LastName, and DeptNum. The Employee table includes only characteristics of employees. Other tables would exist for the company's other entities. For example, a Department table would describe the company's departments and a Position table would describe the company's job positions.

Knowing the characteristics of a table leads directly to a definition of a relational database. A **relational database** is a collection of tables (relations).

Note that this book uses singular table names, such as Employee and Department, but some people use plural table names, such as Employees and Departments. You can use either singular table names or plural table names, as long as you consistently use the style you choose.

Keys

Primary keys ensure that each row in a table is unique. A **primary key** is a column, or a collection of columns, whose values uniquely identify each row in a table. In addition to being *unique*, a primary key must be *minimal* (that is, contain no unnecessary extra columns) and must not change in value. For example, in Figure A-2 the State table contains one record per state and uses the StateAbbrev column as its primary key.

A table and its keys ◀ **Figure A-2**

primary key		alternate keys		
State				
StateAbbrev	**StateName**	**EnteredUnionOrder**	**StateBird**	**StatePopulation**
CT	Connecticut	5	American robin	3,510,297
MI	Michigan	26	robin	10,120,860
SD	South Dakota	40	pheasant	775,933
TN	Tennessee	16	mockingbird	5,962,959
TX	Texas	28	mockingbird	22,859,968

Could any other column, or collection of columns, be the primary key of the State table?

- Could the StateBird column serve as the primary key? No, because the StateBird column does not have unique values (for example, the mockingbird is the state bird of more than one state).
- Could the StatePopulation column serve as the primary key? No, because the StatePopulation column values change periodically and are not guaranteed to be unique.
- Could the StateAbbrev and StateName columns together serve as the primary key? No, because the combination of these two columns is not minimal. Something less, such as the StateAbbrev column by itself, can serve as the primary key.
- Could the StateName column serve as the primary key? Yes, because the StateName column has unique values. In a similar way, you could select the EnteredUnionOrder column as the primary key for the State table. One column, or a collection of columns, that can serve as a primary key is called a **candidate key**. The candidate keys for the State table are the StateAbbrev column, the StateName column, and the EnteredUnionOrder column. You choose one of the candidate keys to be the primary key, and each remaining candidate key is called an **alternate key**. The StateAbbrev column is the State table's primary key in Figure A-2, so the StateName and EnteredUnionOrder columns become alternate keys in the table.

Figure A-3 shows a City table containing the fields StateAbbrev, CityName, and CityPopulation.

| Figure A-3 | A table with a composite key |

What is the primary key for the City table? The values for the CityPopulation column periodically change and are not guaranteed to be unique, so the CityPopulation column cannot be the primary key. Because the values for each of the other two columns are not unique, the StateAbbrev column alone cannot be the primary key and neither can the CityName column (for example, there are two cities named Madison and two cities named Portland). The primary key is the combination of the StateAbbrev and CityName columns. Both columns together are needed to identify—uniquely and minimally—each row in the City table. A multiple-column primary key is called a **composite key** or a **concatenated key**.

The StateAbbrev column in the City table is also a foreign key. A **foreign key** is a column, or a collection of columns, in one table in which each column value must match the value of the primary key of some table or must be null. A **null** is the absence of a value in a particular table entry. A null value is not blank, nor zero, nor any other value. You give a null value to a column value when you do not know its value or when a value does not apply. As shown in Figure A-4, the values in the City table's StateAbbrev column match the values in the State table's StateAbbrev column. Thus, the StateAbbrev column, the primary key of the State table, is a foreign key in the City table. Although the field name StateAbbrev is the same in both tables, the names could be different. However, all experts use the same name for a field stored in two or more tables to broadcast clearly that they store similar values.

Figure A-4 StateAbbrev as a primary key (State table) and a foreign key (City table)

primary key (State table)

State

StateAbbrev	StateName	EnteredUnionOrder	StateBird	StatePopulation
CT	Connecticut	5	American robin	3,510,297
MI	Michigan	26	robin	10,120,860
SD	South Dakota	40	pheasant	775,933
TN	Tennessee	16	mockingbird	5,962,959
TX	Texas	28	mockingbird	22,859,968

composite primary key (City table)

foreign key

City

StateAbbrev	CityName	CityPopulation
CT	Hartford	124,397
CT	Madison	18,812
CT	Portland	9,543
MI	Lansing	115,518
SD	Madison	6,223
SD	Pierre	14,052
TN	Nashville	549,110
TX	Austin	690,252
TX	Portland	16,219

A **nonkey field** is a field that is not part of the primary key. In the two tables shown in Figure A-4, all fields are nonkey fields except the StateAbbrev field in the State and City tables and the CityName field in the City table. *Key* is an ambiguous word because it can refer to a primary, candidate, alternate, or foreign key. When the word key appears alone, however, it means primary key and the definition for a nonkey field consequently makes sense.

Relationships

In a database, a table can be associated with another table in one of three ways: a one-to-many relationship, a many-to-many relationship, or a one-to-one relationship.

One-to-Many Relationship

The Department and Employee tables, shown in Figure A-5, have a one-to-many relationship. A **one-to-many relationship** (abbreviated **1:M** or **1:N**) exists between two tables when each row in the first table (sometimes called the **primary table**) matches many rows in the second table and each row in the second table (sometimes called the **related table**) matches at most one row in the first table. “Many” can mean zero rows, one row, or two or more rows. The DeptNum field, which is a foreign key in the Employee table and the primary key in the Department table, is the common field that ties together the rows of the two tables. Each department has many employees; and each employee works in exactly one department or hasn't been assigned to a department, if the DeptNum field value for that employee is null.

Figure A-5	▶	A one-to-many relationship

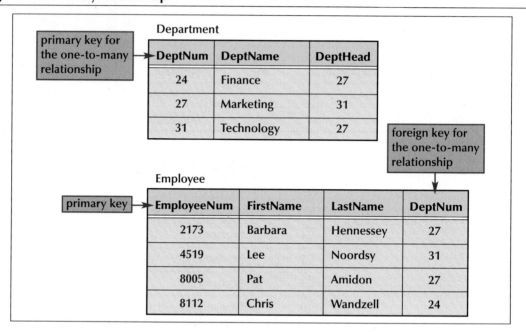

Many-to-Many Relationship

In Figure A-6, the Employee table (with the EmployeeNum field as its primary key) and the Position table (with the PositionID field as its primary key) have a many-to-many relationship. A **many-to-many relationship** (abbreviated as **M:N**) exists between two tables when each row in the first table matches many rows in the second table and each row in the second table matches many rows in the first table. In a relational database, you must use a third table (often called an **intersection table**, **junction table**, or **link table**) to serve as a bridge between the two many-to-many tables; the third table has the primary keys of the two many-to-many tables as its primary key. The original tables now each have a one-to-many relationship with the new table. The EmployeeNum and PositionID fields represent the primary key of the Employment table that is shown in Figure A-6. The EmployeeNum field, which is a foreign key in the Employment table and the primary key in the Employee table, is the common field that ties together the rows of the Employee and Employment tables. Likewise, the PositionID field is the common field for the Position and Employment tables. Each employee has served in many different positions within the company over time, and each position in the company has been filled by many different employees over time.

A many-to-many relationship ◄ **Figure A-6**

primary key
(Position table)

Employee

primary key
(Employee
table)

EmployeeNum	FirstName	LastName	DeptNum
2173	Barbara	Hennessey	27
4519	Lee	Noordsy	31
8005	Pat	Amidon	27
8112	Chris	Wandzell	24

Position

PositionID	PositionDesc	PayGrade
1	Director	45
2	Manager	40
3	Analyst	30
4	Clerk	20

composite key of the
intersection table

Employment

foreign keys related
to the Employee and
Position tables

EmployeeNum	PositionID	StartDate	EndDate
2173	2	12/14/2008	
4519	1	04/23/2010	
4519	3	11/11/2004	04/22/2010
8005	3	06/05/2009	08/25/2010
8005	4	07/02/2007	06/04/2009
8112	1	12/15/2009	
8112	2	10/04/2008	12/14/2009

One-to-One Relationship

In Figure A-5, recall that there's a one-to-many relationship between the Department table (the primary table) and the Employee table (the related table). Each department has many employees, and each employee works in one department. The DeptNum field in the Employee table serves as a foreign key to connect records in that table to records with matching DeptNum field values in the Department table.

Furthermore, each department has a single employee who serves as the head of the department, and each employee either serves as the head of a department or simply works in a department without being the department head. Therefore, the Department and Employee tables not only have a one-to-many relationship, but these two tables also have a second relationship, a one-to-one relationship. A **one-to-one relationship** (abbreviated **1:1**) exists between two tables when each row in each table has at most one matching row in the other table. As shown in Figure A-7, each DeptHead field value in the Department table represents the employee number in the Employee table of the employee who heads the department. In other words, each DeptHead field value in the Department table matches exactly one EmployeeNum field value in the Employee table. At the same time, each EmployeeNum field value in the Employee table matches at most one DeptHead field value in the Department table—matching one DeptHead field value if the employee is a department head, or matching zero DeptHead field values if the employee is not a department head. For this one-to-one relationship, the EmployeeNum field in the Employee table and the DeptHead field in the Department table are the fields that link the two tables, with the DeptHead field serving as a foreign key in the Department table and the EmployeeNum field serving as a primary key in the Employee table.

Some database designers might use EmployeeNum instead of DeptHead as the field name for the foreign key in the Department table, because they both represent the employee number for the employees of the company. However, DeptHead better identifies the purpose of the field and would more commonly be used as the field name.

| Figure A-7 | A one-to-one relationship |

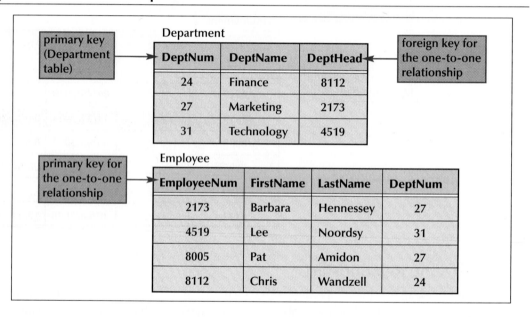

Entity Subtype

Suppose the company awards annual bonuses to a small number of employees who fill director positions in selected departments. As shown in Figure A-8, you could store the Bonus field in the Employee table, because a bonus is an attribute associated with employees. The Bonus field would contain either the amount of the employee's bonus (record 4 in the Employee table) or a null value for employees without bonuses (records 1 through 3 in the Employee table).

Bonus field added to the Employee table ◄ **Figure A-8**

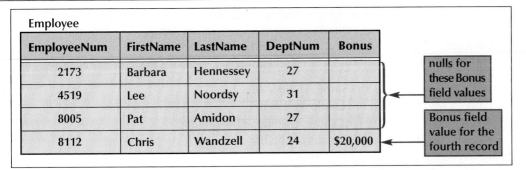

Figure A-9 shows an alternative approach, in which the Bonus field is placed in a separate table, the EmployeeBonus table. The EmployeeBonus table's primary key is the EmployeeNum field, and the table contains one row for each employee earning a bonus. Because some employees do not earn a bonus, the EmployeeBonus table has fewer rows than the Employee table. However, each row in the EmployeeBonus table has a matching row in the Employee table, with the EmployeeNum field serving as the common field; the EmployeeNum field is the primary key in the Employee table and is a foreign key in the EmployeeBonus table.

Storing bonus values in a separate table, an entity subtype ◄ **Figure A-9**

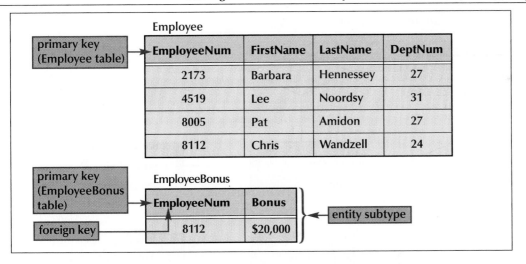

The EmployeeBonus table, in this situation, is called an **entity subtype**, a table whose primary key is a foreign key to a second table and whose fields are additional fields for the second table. Database designers create an entity subtype in two situations. In the first situation, some users might need access to all employee fields, including employee bonuses, while other employees might need access to all employee fields except bonuses. Because most database management systems allow you to control which tables a user can access, you can specify that some users can access both tables and that other users can access the Employee table but not the EmployeeBonus table, keeping the employee bonus information hidden from the latter group. In the second situation, you can create an entity subtype when a table has fields that could have nulls, as was the case for the Bonus field stored in the Employee table in Figure A-8. You should be aware that database experts are currently debating the validity of the use of nulls in relational databases, and many experts insist that you should never use nulls. This warning against nulls is partly based on the inconsistent way different RDBMSs treat nulls and partly due to the lack of a firm theoretical foundation for how to use nulls. In any case, entity subtypes are an alternative to the use of nulls.

Entity-Relationship Diagrams

A common shorthand method for describing tables is to write the table name followed by its fields in parentheses, underlining the fields that represent the primary key and identifying the foreign keys for a table immediately after the table. Using this method, the tables that appear in Figures A-5 through A-7 and Figure A-9 are described in the following way:

Department (<u>DeptNum</u>, DeptName, DeptHead)
    Foreign key: DeptHead to Employee table
Employee (<u>EmployeeNum</u>, FirstName, LastName, DeptNum)
    Foreign key: DeptNum to Department table
Position (<u>PositionID</u>, PositionDesc, PayGrade)
Employment (<u>EmployeeNum</u>, <u>PositionID</u>, StartDate, EndDate)
    Foreign key: EmployeeNum to Employee table
    Foreign key: PositionID to Position table
EmployeeBonus (<u>EmployeeNum</u>, Bonus)
    Foreign key: EmployeeNum to Employee table

    Another popular way to describe tables *and their relationships* is with entity-relationship diagrams. An **entity-relationship diagram (ERD)** shows a database's entities and the relationships among the entities in a symbolic, visual way. In an entity-relationship diagram, an entity and a table are equivalent. Figure A-10 shows an entity-relationship diagram for the tables that appear in Figures A-5 through A-7 and Figure A-9.

Figure A-10	An entity-relationship diagram

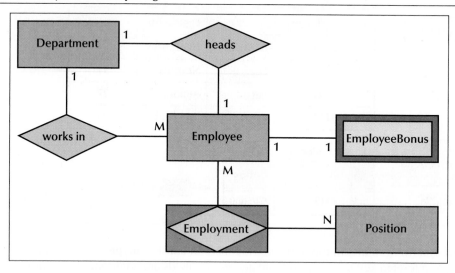

    Entity-relationship diagrams have the following characteristics:

- Entities, or tables, appear in rectangles, and relationships appear in diamonds. The entity name appears inside the rectangle, and a verb describing the relationship appears inside the diamond. For example, the Employee rectangle is connected to the Department rectangle by the "works in" diamond and is read: "an employee works in a department."
- The 1 by the Department entity and the M by the Employee entity identify a one-to-many relationship between these two entities. In a similar manner, a many-to-many relationship exists between the Employee and Position entities and one-to-one relationships exist between the Department and Employee entities and between the Employee and EmployeeBonus entities.

- A diamond inside a rectangle defines a composite entity. A **composite entity** is a relationship that has the characteristics of an entity. For example, Employment connects the Employee and Position entities in a many-to-many relationship and acts as an entity by containing the StartDate and EndDate fields, along with the composite key of the EmployeeNum and PositionID fields.
- An entity subtype, for example, EmployeeBonus, appears in a double rectangle and is connected without an intervening diamond directly to its related entity, Employee.

You can also show fields in an ERD by placing each individual field in a bubble connected to its entity or relationship. However, typical ERDs have large numbers of entities and relationships, so including the fields might confuse rather than clarify the ERD.

Integrity Constraints

A database has **integrity** if its data follows certain rules; each rule is called an **integrity constraint**. The ideal is to have the DBMS enforce all integrity constraints. If a DBMS can enforce some integrity constraints but not others, the other integrity constraints must be enforced by other programs or by the people who use the DBMS. Integrity constraints can be divided into three groups: primary key constraints, foreign key constraints, and domain integrity constraints.

- One primary key constraint is inherent in the definition of a primary key, which says that the primary key must be unique. The **entity integrity constraint** says that the primary key cannot be null. For a composite key, none of the individual fields can be null. The uniqueness and nonnull properties of a primary key ensure that you can reference any data value in a database by supplying its table name, field name, and primary key value.
- Foreign keys provide the mechanism for forming a relationship between two tables, and referential integrity ensures that only valid relationships exist. **Referential integrity** is the constraint specifying that each nonnull foreign key value must match a primary key value in the primary table. Specifically, referential integrity means that you cannot add a row with an unmatched foreign key value. Referential integrity also means that you cannot change or delete the related primary key value and leave the foreign key orphaned. In some RDBMSs, if you try to change or delete a primary key value, you can specify one of these options: restricted, cascades, or nullifies. If you specify **restricted**, the DBMS updates or deletes the value only if there are no matching foreign key values. If you choose **cascades** and then change a primary key value, the DBMS changes the matching foreign key values to the new primary key value, or, if you delete a primary key value, the DBMS also deletes the matching foreign key rows. If you choose **nullifies** and then change or delete a primary key value, the DBMS sets all matching foreign key values to null.
- Recall that a domain is a set of values from which one or more fields draw their actual values. A **domain integrity constraint** is a rule you specify for a field. By choosing a data type for a field, you impose a constraint on the set of values allowed for the field. You can create specific validation rules for a field to limit its domain further. As you make a field's domain definition more precise, you exclude more and more unacceptable values for the field. For example, in the State table, shown in Figures A-2 and A-4, you could define the domain for the EnteredUnionOrder field to be a unique integer between 1 and 50 and the domain for the StateBird field to be any name containing 25 or fewer characters.

Dependencies and Determinants

Tables are related to other tables. Fields are also related to other fields. Consider the modified Employee table shown in Figure A-11. Its description is:

Employee (<u>EmployeeNum</u>, <u>PositionID</u>, LastName, PositionDesc, StartDate, HealthPlan, PlanDesc)

Figure A-11 ➤ **A table combining fields from three tables**

primary key						

Employee

EmployeeNum	PositionID	LastName	PositionDesc	StartDate	HealthPlan	PlanDesc
2173	2	Hennessey	Manager	12/14/2008	B	Managed HMO
4519	1	Noordsy	Director	04/23/2010	A	Managed PPO
4519	3	Noordsy	Analyst	11/11/2004	A	Managed PPO
8005	3	Amidon	Analyst	06/05/2009	C	Health Savings
8005	4	Amidon	Clerk	07/02/2007	C	Health Savings
8112	1	Wandzell	Director	12/15/2009	A	Managed PPO
8112	2	Wandzell	Manager	10/04/2008	A	Managed PPO

The modified Employee table combines several fields from the Employee, Position, and Employment tables that appeared in Figure A-6. The EmployeeNum and LastName fields are from the Employee table. The PositionID and PositionDesc fields are from the Position table. The EmployeeNum, PositionID, and StartDate fields are from the Employment table. The HealthPlan and PlanDesc fields are new fields for the Employee table, whose primary key is now the combination of the EmployeeNum and PositionID fields.

In the Employee table, each field is related to other fields. To determine field relationships, you ask "Does a value for a particular field give me a single value for another field?" If the answer is Yes, then the two fields are related. For example, a value for the EmployeeNum field determines a single value for the LastName field, and a value for the LastName field depends on the value of the EmployeeNum field. In database discussions, the word functionally is used, as in: "EmployeeNum functionally determines LastName" and "LastName is functionally dependent on EmployeeNum." In this case, EmployeeNum is called a determinant. A **determinant** is a field, or a collection of fields, whose values determine the values of another field. A field is functionally dependent on another field (or a collection of fields) if that other field is a determinant for it.

You can graphically show a table's functional dependencies and determinants in a **bubble diagram**; a bubble diagram is also called a **data model diagram** and a **functional dependency diagram**. Figure A-12 shows the bubble diagram for the Employee table shown in Figure A-11.

A bubble diagram for the modified Employee table ◀ **Figure A-12**

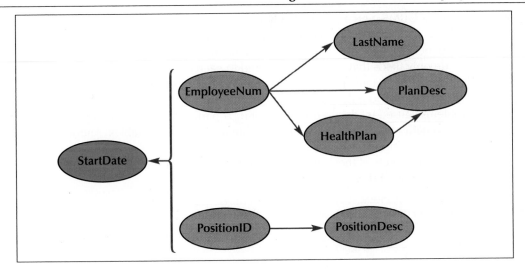

You can read the bubble diagram in Figure A-12 as follows:

- The EmployeeNum field is a determinant for the LastName, HealthPlan, and PlanDesc fields.
- The PositionID field is a determinant for the PositionDesc field.
- The StartDate field is functionally dependent on the EmployeeNum and PositionID fields together.
- The HealthPlan field is a determinant for the PlanDesc field.

Note that EmployeeNum and PositionID together is a determinant for the StartDate field and for all fields that depend on the EmployeeNum field alone and the PositionID field alone. Some experts include these additional fields and some don't. The previous list of determinants does not include these additional fields.

An alternative way to show determinants is to list the determinant, a right arrow, and then the dependent fields, separated by commas. Using this alternative, the determinants shown in Figure A-12 are:

EmployeeNum → LastName, HealthPlan, PlanDesc
PositionID → PositionDesc
EmployeeNum, PositionID → StartDate
HealthPlan → PlanDesc

Only the StartDate field is functionally dependent on the table's full primary key, the EmployeeNum and PositionID fields. The LastName, HealthPlan, and PlanDesc fields have partial dependencies because they are functionally dependent on the EmployeeNum field, which is part of the primary key. A **partial dependency** is a functional dependency on part of the primary key, instead of the entire primary key. Does another partial dependency exist in the Employee table? Yes, the PositionDesc field has a partial dependency on the PositionID field.

Because the EmployeeNum field is a determinant of both the HealthPlan and PlanDesc fields, and the HealthPlan field is a determinant of the PlanDesc field, the HealthPlan and PlanDesc fields have a transitive dependency. A **transitive dependency** is a functional dependency between two nonkey fields, which are both dependent on a third field.

How do you know which functional dependencies exist among a collection of fields, and how do you recognize partial and transitive dependencies? The answers lie with the questions you ask as you gather the requirements for a database application. For each field and entity, you must gain an accurate understanding of its meaning and relationships in the context of the application. **Semantic object modeling** is an entire area of study within the database field devoted to the meanings and relationships of data.

Anomalies

When you use a DBMS, you are more likely to get results you can trust if you create your tables carefully. For example, problems might occur with tables that have partial and transitive dependencies, whereas you won't have as much trouble if you ensure that your tables include only fields that are directly related to each other. Also, when you remove data redundancy from a table, you improve that table. **Data redundancy** occurs when you store the same data in more than one place.

The problems caused by data redundancy and by partial and transitive dependencies are called **anomalies** because they are undesirable irregularities of tables. Anomalies are of three types: insertion, deletion, and update.

To examine the effects of these anomalies, consider the modified Employee table that is shown again in Figure A-13.

| Figure A-13 | A table with insertion, deletion, and update anomalies |

primary key

Employee

EmployeeNum	PositionID	LastName	PositionDesc	StartDate	HealthPlan	PlanDesc
2173	2	Hennessey	Manager	12/14/2008	B	Managed HMO
4519	1	Noordsy	Director	04/23/2010	A	Managed PPO
4519	3	Noordsy	Analyst	11/11/2004	A	Managed PPO
8005	3	Amidon	Analyst	06/05/2009	C	Health Savings
8005	4	Amidon	Clerk	07/02/2007	C	Health Savings
8112	1	Wandzell	Director	12/15/2009	A	Managed PPO
8112	2	Wandzell	Manager	10/04/2008	A	Managed PPO

- An **insertion anomaly** occurs when you cannot add a record to a table because you do not know the entire primary key value. For example, you cannot add the new employee Cathy Corbett with an EmployeeNum of 3322 to the Employee table if you do not know her position in the company. Entity integrity prevents you from leaving any part of a primary key null. Because the PositionID field is part of the primary key, you cannot leave it null. To add the new employee, your only option is to make up a PositionID field value, until you determine the correct position. This solution misrepresents the facts and is unacceptable, if a better approach is available.

- A **deletion anomaly** occurs when you delete data from a table and unintentionally lose other critical data. For example, if you delete EmployeeNum 2173 because Hennessey is no longer an employee, you also lose the only instance of HealthPlan B in the database. Thus, you no longer know that HealthPlan B is the "Managed HMO" plan.

- An **update anomaly** occurs when you change one field value and either the DBMS must make more than one change to the database or else the database ends up containing inconsistent data. For example, if you change a LastName, HealthPlan, or PlanDesc field value for EmployeeNum 8005, the DBMS must change multiple rows of the Employee table. If the DBMS fails to change all the rows, the LastName, HealthPlan, or PlanDesc field now has different values in the database and is inconsistent.

Normalization

Database design is the process of determining the content and structure of data in a database in order to support some activity on behalf of a user or group of users. After you have determined the collection of fields users need to support an activity, you need to determine the precise tables needed for the collection of fields and then place those fields into the correct tables. Crucial to good database design is understanding the functional dependencies of all fields; recognizing the anomalies caused by data redundancy, partial dependencies, and transitive dependencies when they exist; and knowing how to eliminate the anomalies. Failure to eliminate anomalies leads to data redundancy and can cause data integrity and other problems as your database grows in size.

The process of identifying and eliminating anomalies is called **normalization**. Using normalization, you start with a collection of tables, apply sets of rules to eliminate anomalies, and produce a new collection of problem-free tables. The sets of rules are called **normal forms**. Of special interest for our purposes are the first three normal forms: first normal form, second normal form, and third normal form. First normal form improves the design of your tables, second normal form improves the first normal form design, and third normal form applies even more stringent rules to produce an even better design. Note that normal forms beyond third normal form exist; these higher normal forms can improve a database design in some situations but won't be covered in this section.

First Normal Form

Consider the Employee table shown in Figure A-14. For each employee, the table contains EmployeeNum, which is the primary key; the employee's first name, last name, health plan code and description; and the ID, description, pay grade, and start date of each position held by the employee. For example, Barbara Hennessey has held one position, while the other three employees have held two positions. Because each entry in a table must contain a single value, the structure shown in Figure A-14 does not meet the requirements for a table, or relation; therefore, it is called an **unnormalized relation**. The set of fields that includes the PositionID, PositionDesc, PayGrade, and StartDate fields, which can have more than one value, is called a **repeating group**.

Repeating group of data in an unnormalized Employee table ◄ **Figure A-14**

Employee

EmployeeNum	PositionID	FirstName	LastName	PositionDesc	PayGrade	StartDate	HealthPlan	PlanDesc
2173	2	Barbara	Hennessey	Manager	40	12/14/2008	B	Managed HMO
4519	1 3	Lee	Noordsy	Director Analyst	45 30	04/23/2010 11/11/2004	A	Managed PPO
8005	3 4	Pat	Amidon	Analyst Clerk	30 20	06/05/2009 07/02/2007	C	Health Savings
8112	1 2	Chris	Wandzell	Director Manager	45 40	12/15/2009 10/04/2008	A	Managed PPO

First normal form addresses this repeating-group situation. A table is in **first normal form (1NF)** if it does not contain repeating groups. To remove a repeating group and convert to first normal form, you expand the primary key to include the primary key of the repeating group, forming a composite key. Performing the conversion step produces the 1NF table shown in Figure A-15.

Figure A-15	After conversion to 1NF

Employee

primary key →

EmployeeNum	PositionID	FirstName	LastName	PositionDesc	PayGrade	StartDate	HealthPlan	PlanDesc
2173	2	Barbara	Hennessey	Manager	40	12/14/2008	B	Managed HMO
4519	1	Lee	Noordsy	Director	45	04/23/2010	A	Managed PPO
4519	3	Lee	Noordsy	Analyst	30	11/11/2004	A	Managed PPO
8005	3	Pat	Amidon	Analyst	30	06/05/2009	C	Health Savings
8005	4	Pat	Amidon	Clerk	20	07/02/2007	C	Health Savings
8112	1	Chris	Wandzell	Director	45	12/15/2009	A	Managed PPO
8112	2	Chris	Wandzell	Manager	40	10/04/2008	A	Managed PPO

The alternative way to describe the 1NF table is:

Employee (<u>EmployeeNum</u>, <u>PositionID</u>, FirstName, LastName, PositionDesc, PayGrade, StartDate, HealthPlan, PlanDesc)

The Employee table is now a true table and has a composite key. The table, however, suffers from insertion, deletion, and update anomalies. (As an exercise, find examples of the three anomalies in the table.) The EmployeeNum field is a determinant for the FirstName, LastName, HealthPlan, and PlanDesc fields, so partial dependencies exist in the Employee table. It is these partial dependencies that cause the anomalies in the Employee table, and second normal form addresses the partial-dependency problem.

Second Normal Form

A table in 1NF is in **second normal form (2NF)** if it does not contain any partial dependencies. To remove partial dependencies from a table and convert it to second normal form, you perform two steps. First, identify the functional dependencies for every field in the table. Second, if necessary, create new tables and place each field in a table, so that the field is functionally dependent on the entire primary key, not part of the primary key. If you need to create new tables, restrict them to ones with a primary key that is a subset of the original composite key. Note that partial dependencies occur only when you have a composite key; a table in first normal form with a single-field primary key is automatically in second normal form.

First, identifying the functional dependencies leads to the following determinants for the Employee table:

EmployeeNum → FirstName, LastName, HealthPlan, PlanDesc
PositionID → PositionDesc, PayGrade
EmployeeNum, PositionID → StartDate
HealthPlan → PlanDesc

The EmployeeNum field is a determinant for the FirstName, LastName, HealthPlan, and PlanDesc fields. The PositionID field is a determinant for the PositionDesc and PayGrade fields. The HealthPlan field is a determinant for the PlanDesc field. The composite key EmployeeNum and PositionID is a determinant for the StartDate field. Performing the second step in the conversion from first normal form to second form produces the three 2NF tables shown in Figure A-16.

Employee

	EmployeeNum	FirstName	LastName	HealthPlan	PlanDesc
primary key →	**EmployeeNum**	**FirstName**	**LastName**	**HealthPlan**	**PlanDesc**
	2173	Barbara	Hennessey	B	Managed HMO
	4519	Lee	Noordsy	A	Managed PPO
	8005	Pat	Amidon	C	Health Savings
	8112	Chris	Wandzell	A	Managed PPO

Position

	PositionID	PositionDesc	PayGrade
primary key →	**PositionID**	**PositionDesc**	**PayGrade**
	1	Director	45
	2	Manager	40
	3	Analyst	30
	4	Clerk	20

Employment

primary key

EmployeeNum	PositionID	StartDate
2173	2	12/14/2008
4519	1	04/23/2010
4519	3	11/11/2004
8005	3	06/05/2009
8005	4	07/02/2007
8112	1	12/15/2009
8112	2	10/04/2008

The alternative way to describe the 2NF tables is:

Employee (EmployeeNum, FirstName, LastName, HealthPlan, PlanDesc)
Position (PositionID, PositionDesc, PayGrade)
Employment (EmployeeNum, PositionID, StartDate)
   Foreign key: EmployeeNum to Employee table
   Foreign key: PositionID to Position table

All three tables are in second normal form. Do anomalies still exist? The Position and Employment tables show no anomalies, but the Employee table suffers from anomalies caused by the transitive dependency between the HealthPlan and PlanDesc fields. (As an exercise, find examples of the three anomalies caused by the transitive dependency.) That is, the HealthPlan field is a determinant for the PlanDesc field, and the EmployeeNum field is a determinant for the HealthPlan and PlanDesc fields. Third normal form addresses the transitive-dependency problem.

Third Normal Form

A table in 2NF is in **third normal form (3NF)** if every determinant is a candidate key. This definition for 3NF is referred to as **Boyce-Codd normal form (BCNF)** and is an improvement over the original version of 3NF. What are the determinants in the Employee table? The EmployeeNum and HealthPlan fields are the determinants; however, the EmployeeNum field is a candidate key because it's the table's primary key, and the HealthPlan field is not a candidate key. Therefore, the Employee table is in second normal form, but it is not in third normal form.

To convert a table to third normal form, remove the fields that depend on the non-candidate-key determinant and place them into a new table with the determinant as the primary key. For the Employee table, the PlanDesc field depends on the HealthPlan field, which is a non-candidate-key determinant. Thus, you remove the PlanDesc field from the table, create a new HealthBenefits table, place the PlanDesc field in the HealthBenefits table, and then make the HealthPlan field the primary key of the HealthBenefits table. Note that only the PlanDesc field is removed from the Employee table; the HealthPlan field remains as a foreign key in the Employee table. Figure A-17 shows the database design for the four 3NF tables.

| Figure A-17 | After conversion to 3NF |

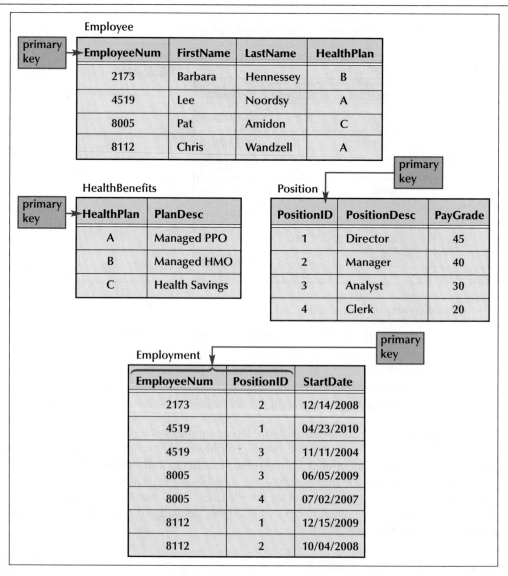

The alternative way to describe the 3NF relations is:

HealthBenefits (<u>HealthPlan</u>, PlanDesc)
Employee (<u>EmployeeNum</u>, FirstName, LastName, HealthPlan)
   Foreign key: HealthPlan to HealthBenefits table
Position (<u>PositionID</u>, PositionDesc, PayGrade)
Employment (<u>EmployeeNum</u>, <u>PositionID</u>, StartDate)
   Foreign key: EmployeeNum to Employee table
   Foreign key: PositionID to Position table

The four tables have no anomalies because you have eliminated all the data redundancy, partial dependencies, and transitive dependencies. Normalization provides the framework for eliminating anomalies and delivering an optimal database design, which you should always strive to achieve. You should be aware, however, that experts sometimes denormalize tables to improve database performance—specifically, to decrease the time it takes the database to respond to a user's commands and requests. Typically, when you denormalize tables, you combine separate tables into one table to reduce the need for the DBMS to join the separate tables to process queries and other informational requests. When you denormalize a table, you reintroduce redundancy to the table. At the same time, you reintroduce anomalies. Thus, improving performance exposes a database to potential integrity problems. Only database experts should denormalize tables, but even experts first complete the normalization of their tables.

Natural, Artificial, and Surrogate Keys

When you complete the design of a database, your tables should be in third normal form, free of anomalies and redundancy. Some tables, such as the State table (see Figure A-2), have obvious third normal form designs with obvious primary keys. The State table's description is:

State (<u>StateAbbrev</u>, StateName, EnteredUnionOrder, StateBird, StatePopulation)

Recall that the candidate keys for the State table are StateAbbrev, StateName, and EnteredUnionOrder. Choosing the StateAbbrev field as the State table's primary key makes the StateName and EnteredUnionOrder fields alternate keys. Primary keys such as the StateAbbrev field are sometimes called natural keys. A **natural key** (also called a **logical key** or an **intelligent key**) is a primary key that consists of a field, or a collection of fields, that is an inherent characteristic of the entity described by the table and that is visible to users. Other examples of natural keys are the ISBN (International Standard Book Number) for a book, the SSN (Social Security number) for a U.S. individual, the UPC (Universal Product Code) for a product, and the VIN (vehicle identification number) for a vehicle.

Is the PositionID field, which is the primary key for the Position table (see Figure A-17), a natural key? No, the PositionID field is not an inherent characteristic of a position. Instead, the PositionID field has been added to the Position table only as a way to identify each position uniquely. The PositionID field is an **artificial key**, which is a field that you add to a table to serve solely as the primary key and that is visible to users.

Another reason for using an artificial key arises in tables that allow duplicate records. Although relational database theory and most experts do not allow duplicate records in a table, consider a database that tracks donors and their donations. Figure A-18 shows a Donor table with an artificial key of DonorID and with the DonorFirstName and DonorLastName fields. Some cash donations are anonymous, which accounts for the fourth record in the Donor table. Figure A-18 also shows the Donation table with the DonorID field, a foreign key to the Donor table, and the DonationDate and DonationAmt fields.

Figure A-18   **Donor and Donation tables**

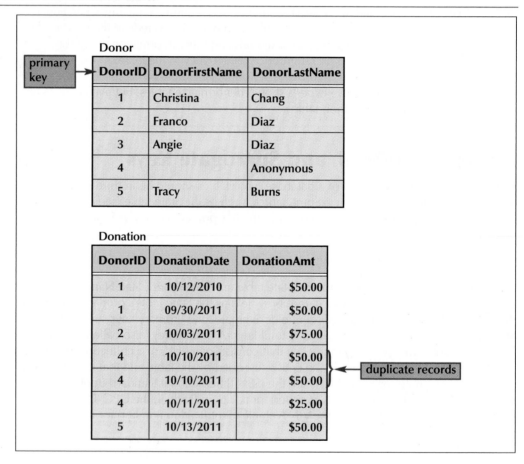

What is the primary key of the Donation table? No single field is unique, and neither is any combination of fields. For example, on 10/10/2011 two anonymous donors (DonorID value of 4) donated $50 each. You need to add an artificial key, DonationID for example, to the Donation table. The addition of the artificial key makes every record in the Donation table unique, as shown in Figure A-19.

| Donation table after adding DonationID, an artificial key | Figure A-19 |

Donation

artificial key →

DonationID	DonorID	DonationDate	DonationAmt
1	1	10/12/2010	$50.00
2	1	09/30/2011	$50.00
3	2	10/03/2011	$75.00
4	4	10/10/2011	$50.00
5	4	10/10/2011	$50.00
6	4	10/11/2011	$25.00
7	5	10/13/2011	$50.00

The descriptions of the Donor and Donation tables now are:

Donor (<u>DonorID</u>, DonorFirstName, DonorLastName)
Donation (<u>DonationID</u>, DonorID, DonationDate, DonationAmt)
   Foreign key: DonorID to Donor table

For another common situation, consider the 3NF tables you reviewed in the previous section (see Figure A-17) that have the following descriptions:

HealthBenefits (<u>HealthPlan</u>, PlanDesc)
Employee (<u>EmployeeNum</u>, FirstName, LastName, HealthPlan)
   Foreign key: HealthPlan to HealthBenefits table
Position (<u>PositionID</u>, PositionDesc, PayGrade)
Employment (<u>EmployeeNum</u>, <u>PositionID</u>, StartDate)
   Foreign key: EmployeeNum to Employee table
   Foreign key: PositionID to Position table

Recall that a primary key must be unique, must be minimal, and must not change in value. In theory, primary keys don't change in value. However, in practice, you might have to change EmployeeNum field values that you incorrectly entered in the Employment table. Further, if you need to change an EmployeeNum field value in the Employee table, the change must cascade to the EmployeeNum field values in the Employment table. Also, changes to a PositionID field value in the Position table must cascade to the Employment table. For these and other reasons, many experts add surrogate keys to their tables. A **surrogate key** (also called a **synthetic key**) is a system-generated primary key that is hidden from users. Usually you can use an automatic numbering data type, such as the Access AutoNumber data type, for a surrogate key. Figure A-20 shows the four tables with surrogate keys added to three of the four tables.

Figure A-20 Using surrogate keys

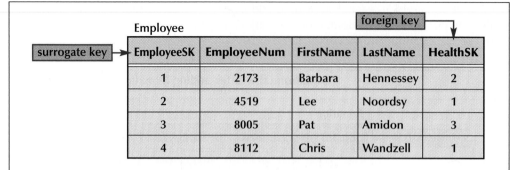

Employee

surrogate key → EmployeeSK	EmployeeNum	FirstName	LastName	HealthSK ← foreign key
1	2173	Barbara	Hennessey	2
2	4519	Lee	Noordsy	1
3	8005	Pat	Amidon	3
4	8112	Chris	Wandzell	1

HealthBenefits

surrogate key → HealthSK	HealthPlan	PlanDesc
1	A	Managed PPO
2	B	Managed HMO
3	C	Health Savings

Position

artificial key → PositionID	PositionDesc	PayGrade
1	Director	45
2	Manager	40
3	Analyst	30
4	Clerk	20

Employment

surrogate key → EmploymentSK	EmployeeSK	PositionID	StartDate
1	1	2	12/14/2008
1	2	1	04/23/2010
1	4	3	11/11/2004
2	2	3	06/05/2009
3	1	4	07/02/2007
3	2	1	12/15/2009
4	3	2	10/04/2008

foreign key

The HealthSK field replaces the HealthPlan field as a foreign key in the Employee table, and the EmployeeSK field replaces the EmployeeNum field in the Employment table. When you change an incorrectly entered EmployeeNum field value in the Employee table, you don't need to cascade the change to the Employment table. When you change an incorrectly entered HealthPlan field value in the HealthBenefits table, you don't have to cascade the change to the Employee table.

As you design a database, you should *not* consider the use of surrogate keys, and you should use an artificial key only for the rare table that has duplicate records. At the point when you implement a database, you might choose to use artificial and surrogate keys, but be aware that database experts debate their use and effectiveness. Some of the trade-offs between natural and surrogate keys that you need to consider are:

- Use surrogate keys to avoid cascading updates to foreign key values. Surrogate keys can also replace lengthier foreign keys when those foreign keys reference composite fields.
- You don't need a surrogate key for a table whose primary key is not used as a foreign key in another table, because cascading updates is not an issue.
- Tables with surrogate keys require more joins than do tables with natural keys. For example, if you need to know all employees with a HealthPlan field value of A, the surrogate key in Figure A-20 requires that you join the Employee and HealthBenefits tables to answer the question. Using natural keys as shown in Figure A-17, the HealthPlan field appears in the Employee table, so no join is necessary.
- Although surrogate keys are meant to be hidden from users, they cannot be hidden from users who create SQL statements and use other ad hoc tools.
- Because you need a unique index for the natural key and a unique index for the surrogate key, your database size is larger and index maintenance takes more time when you use a surrogate key. On the other hand, a foreign key using a surrogate key is usually smaller than a foreign key using a natural key, especially when the natural key is a composite key, so those indexes are smaller and faster to access for lookups and joins.

Microsoft Access Naming Conventions

In the early 1980s, Microsoft's Charles Simonyi introduced an identifier naming convention that became known as Hungarian notation. Microsoft and other companies use this naming convention for variable, control, and other object naming in Basic, Visual Basic, and other programming languages. When Access was introduced in the early 1990s, Stan Leszynski and Greg Reddick adapted Hungarian notation for Microsoft Access databases; their guidelines became known as the Leszynski/Reddick naming conventions. In recent years, the Leszynski naming conventions, the Reddick naming conventions, and other naming conventions have been published. Individuals and companies have created their own Access naming conventions, but many are based on the Leszynski/Reddick naming conventions, as are the naming conventions covered in this section.

An Access database can contain thousands of objects, fields, controls, and other items, and keeping track of their names and what they represent is a difficult task. Consequently, you should use naming conventions that identify the type and purpose of each item in an Access database. You can use naming conventions that identify items generally or very specifically.

For objects, include a prefix tag to identify the type of object, as shown in Figure A-21. In each example in Figure A-21, the final object name consists of a three-character tag prefixed to the base object name. The form name of frmEmployeesAndPositions, for example, consists of the frm tag and the EmployeesAndPositions base form name.

Figure A-21 ▷ **Object naming tags**

Object type	Tag	Example
Form	frm	frmEmployeesAndPositions
Macro	mcr	mcrCalculations
Module	bas	basCalculations
Query	qry	qryEmployee
Report	rpt	rptEmployeesAndPositions
Table	tbl	tblEmployee

The tags in Figure A-21 identify each object type in general. If you want to identify object types more specifically, you could expand Figure A-21 to include tags such as fsub for a subform, qxtb for a crosstab query, tlkp for a lookup table, rsub for a subreport, and so on.

For controls in forms and reports, a general naming convention uses lbl as a prefix tag for labels and ctl as a prefix tag for other types of controls. For more specific naming conventions for controls, you'd use a specific prefix tag for each type of control. Figure A-22 shows the prefix tag for some common controls in forms and reports.

Control naming tags | Figure A-22

Control type	Tag
Check box	chk
Combo box	cbo
Command button	cmd
Image	img
Label	lbl
Line	lin
List box	lst
Option button	opt
PivotTable	pvt
Rectangle	shp
Subform/Subreport	sub
Text box	txt

Some database developers use a prefix tag for each field name to identify the field's data type (for example, dtm for Date/Time, num for Number, and chr for Text or Character), others use a prefix tag for each field name to identify in which table the field is located (for example, emp for the Employee table and pos for the Position table), and still others don't use a prefix tag for field names.

You might use suffix tags for controls that might otherwise have identical names. For example, if you have two text boxes in a form for calculated controls that display the average and the sum of the OrderAmt field, both could legitimately be named txtOrderAmt unless you used suffix tags to name them txtOrderAmtAvg and txtOrderAmtSum.

You should ensure that any name you use does not duplicate a property name or any keyword Access reserves for special purposes. In general, you can avoid property and keyword name conflicts by using two-word field, control, and object names. For example, use StudentName instead of Name, and use OrderDate instead of Date to avoid name conflicts.

All database developers avoid spaces in names, mainly because spaces are not allowed in server database management systems (DBMSs), such as SQL Server, Oracle, and DB2. If you are prototyping a Microsoft Access database that you'll migrate to one of these server DBMSs, or if future requirements might force a migration, you should restrict your Access identifier names so that they conform to the rules common to them all. Figure A-23 shows the identifier naming rules for Access, SQL Server, Oracle, and DB2.

Figure A-23 ▷ **Identifier naming rules for common database management systems**

Identifier naming rule	Access	SQL Server	Oracle	DB2
Maximum character length	64	30	30	30
Allowable characters	Letters, digits, space, and special characters, except for period (.), exclamation point (!), accent grave (`), and square brackets ([ ])	Letters, digits, dollar sign ($), underscore (_), number symbol (#), and at symbol (@)	Letters, digits, dollar sign ($), underscore (_), and number symbol (#)	Letters, digits, at symbol (@), dollar sign ($), underscore (_), and number symbol (#)
Special rules		No spaces; first character must be a letter or at symbol (@)	No spaces; first character must be a letter; stored in the database in uppercase	No spaces; first character must be a letter, at symbol (@), dollar sign ($), or number symbol (#); stored in the database in uppercase

In this appendix, you learned about tables and their characteristics, keys (primary, candidate, alternate, composite, and foreign), relationships (one-to-many, many-to-many, one-to-one, and entity subtypes), entity-relationship diagrams, integrity constraints (entity, referential, and domain), dependencies and determinants, and anomalies. You also learned how to design a database using normalization to place all tables in third normal form. Finally, you learned about natural, artificial, and surrogate keys, and you examined naming conventions.

Key Terms

alternate key

anomalies

artificial key

attribute

Boyce-Codd normal
    form (BCNF)

bubble diagram

candidate key

cascades

composite entity

composite key

concatenated key

data model diagram

data redundancy

database design

deletion anomaly

determinant

domain

domain integrity constraint

entity

entity integrity constraint

entity subtype

entity-relationship
    diagram (ERD)

field

field name

first normal form (1NF)

foreign key

functional dependency
    diagram

insertion anomaly

integrity

integrity constraint

intelligent key

intersection table

junction table

link table

logical key

many-to-many
    relationship (M:N)

natural key

nonkey field

normal forms

normalization

null

nullifies

one-to-many
    relationship (1:M or 1:N)

one-to-one relationship (1:1)

partial dependency

primary key

primary table

record

referential integrity

related table

relation

relational database

repeating group

restricted

second normal form (2NF)

semantic object modeling

surrogate key

synthetic key

table

third normal form (3NF)

transitive dependency

tuple

unnormalized relation

update anomaly

1. What are the formal names for a table, for a row, and for a column? What are the popular names for a row and for a column?
2. What is a domain?
3. What is an entity?
4. What is the relationship between a primary key and a candidate key?
5. What is a composite key?
6. What is a foreign key?
7. Look for an example of a one-to-one relationship, an example of a one-to-many relationship, and an example of a many-to-many relationship in a newspaper, magazine, book, or everyday situation you encounter. For each one, name the entities and select the primary and foreign keys.
8. When do you use an entity subtype?
9. What is a composite entity in an entity-relationship diagram?
10. What is the entity integrity constraint?
11. What is referential integrity?
12. What does the cascades option, which is used with referential integrity, accomplish?
13. What are partial and transitive dependencies?
14. What three types of anomalies can be exhibited by a table, and what problems do they cause?
15. Figure A-24 shows the Employee, Position, and Employment tables with primary keys EmployeeNum, PositionID, and both EmployeeNum and PositionID, respectively. Which two integrity constraints do these tables violate and why?

Figure A-24

Employee

EmployeeNum	ClientName	LastName	HealthPlan
2173	Barbara	Hennessey	B
4519	Lee	Noordsy	A
8005	Pat	Amidon	C
8112	Chris	Wandzell	A

Position

PositionID	PositionDes	PayGrade
1	Director	45
2	Manager	40
3	Analyst	30
4	Clerk	20

Employment

EmployeeNum	PositionID	StartDate
2173	2	12/14/2008
4519	1	04/23/2010
4519		11/11/2004
8005	3	06/05/2009
8005	4	07/02/2007
8112	1	12/15/2009
9876	2	10/04/2008

16. The State and City tables, shown in Figure A-4, are described as follows:
    State (StateAbbrev, StateName, EnteredUnionOrder, StateBird,
        StatePopulation)
    City (StateAbbrev, CityName, CityPopulation)
        Foreign key: StateAbbrev to State table
    Add the field named CountyName for the county or counties in a state containing the
    city to this database, justify where you placed it (that is, in an existing table or in a
    new one), and draw the entity-relationship diagram for all the entities. Counties for
    some of the cities shown in Figure A-4 are Travis and Williamson counties for Austin
    TX; Hartford county for Hartford CT; Clinton, Eaton, and Ingham counties for Lansing
    MI; Davidson county for Nashville TN; Hughes county for Pierre SD; and Nueces and
    San Patricio counties for Portland TX.

17. Suppose you have a table for a dance studio. The fields are dancer's identification number, dancer's name, dancer's address, dancer's telephone number, class identification number, day that the class meets, time that the class meets, instructor name, and instructor identification number. Assume that each dancer takes one class, each class meets only once a week and has one instructor, and each instructor can teach more than one class. In what normal form is the table currently, given the following alternative description?

    Dancer (<u>DancerID</u>, DancerName, DancerAddr, DancerPhone, ClassID, ClassDay, ClassTime, InstrName, InstrID)

    Convert this relation to third normal form and represent the design using the alternative description method.

18. Store the following fields for a library database: AuthorCode, AuthorName, BookTitle, BorrowerAddress, BorrowerName, BorrowerCardNumber, CopiesOfBook, ISBN (International Standard Book Number), LoanDate, PublisherCode, PublisherName, and PublisherAddress. A one-to-many relationship exists between publishers and books. Many-to-many relationships exist between authors and books and between borrowers and books.

    a. Name the entities for the library database.

    b. Create the tables for the library database and describe them using the alternative method. Be sure the tables are in third normal form.

    c. Draw an entity-relationship diagram for the library database.

19. In the following database, which consists of the Department and Employee tables, add one record to the end of the Employee table that violates both the entity integrity constraint and the referential integrity constraint.

Figure A-25

Department

DeptID	DeptName	Location
M	Marketing	New York
R	Research	Houston
S	Sales	Chicago

Employee

EmployeeID	EmployeeName	DeptID
1111	Sue	R
2222	Pam	M
3333	Bob	S
4444	Chris	S
5555	Pat	R
6666	Meg	R

20. Consider the following table:

    Patient (PatientID, PatientName, BalanceOwed, DoctorID, DoctorName, ServiceCode,
          ServiceDesc, ServiceFee, ServiceDate)

    This is a table concerning data about patients of doctors at a clinic and the services the
    doctors perform for their patients. The following dependencies exist in the Patient table:

    PatientID → PatientName, BalanceOwed

    DoctorID → DoctorName

    ServiceCode → ServiceDesc, ServiceFee

    PatientID, DoctorID, ServiceCode → PatientName, BalanceOwed,
          DoctorName, ServiceDesc, ServiceFee, ServiceDate

    a. Based on the dependencies, convert the Patient table to first normal form.

    b. Next, convert the Patient table to third normal form.

21. Suppose you need to track data for mountain climbing expeditions. Each member of
    an expedition is called a climber, and one of the climbers is named to lead an expe-
    dition. Climbers can be members of many expeditions over time. The climbers in
    each expedition attempt to ascend one or more peaks by scaling one of the many
    faces of the peaks. The data you need to track includes the name of the expedition,
    the leader of the expedition, and comments about the expedition; the first name, last
    name, nationality, birth date, death date, and comments about each climber; the
    name, location, height, and comments about each peak; the name and comments
    about each face of a peak; comments about each climber for each expedition; and
    the highest height reached and the date for each ascent attempt by a climber on a
    face with commentary.

    a. Create the tables for the expedition database and describe them using the alterna-
    tive method. Be sure the tables are in third normal form.

    b. Draw an entity-relationship diagram for the expedition database.

22. What is the difference among natural, artificial, and surrogate keys?

23. Why should you use naming conventions for the identifiers in a database?

Ending Data Files

There are no ending Data Files needed for this appendix.

Adding Special Effects to a Presentation

Preparing and Customizing a Sales Presentation

Objectives

Session 3.1
- Insert slides from another presentation
- Create and apply a custom theme
- Add a background picture
- Customize bullets
- Add a textured background

Session 3.2
- Apply sound clips and a movie
- Create and format a chart (graph)
- Create, modify, and format an organization chart
- Apply slide transitions and animations
- Use the pointer pen during a slide show
- Hide slides in a presentation
- Prepare a presentation to run on another computer
- Give a presentation in podium mode

Case | Classic Flowers, Inc.

Sophie De Graff is a horticulturalist who works as the sales manager at Classic Flowers, Inc., in Bainbridge, Georgia. Classic Flowers grows and distributes flowers to retail stores throughout Georgia. One of Sophie's responsibilities is to obtain and manage new accounts. This involves giving sales presentations to large retail stores (Sam's Club, Costco, Wal-Mart, Piggly Wiggly, Kroger, and so forth) that have floral departments. Sophie wants you to help her prepare the Microsoft PowerPoint presentation. She emphasizes the importance of preparing a high-quality presentation that includes a custom theme, graphics, sound effects, animations, charts, graphs, and other elements to maximize the visual effects of the presentation.

In this tutorial, you'll insert slides from one presentation into another presentation; create a custom theme; add a digital image, movie, and sound clip to slides; create a graph and organization chart; apply special visual effects to the slides; learn how to give the slides show in podium mode; and save the presentation to a CD so it can be run on another computer.

Starting Data Files

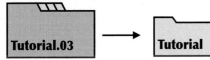

Tutorial.03 → **Tutorial**

Tutorial
Applause.wav
CFISound.wav
CFSales.pptx
Flowers.pptx
PinkFlowerBG.jpg
RightMove.avi

Review
Farm.avi
HotSprings.pptx
HSProposal.pptx
Knock.wav

Case1
CompCase.avi
eBayCase.pptx
JustInCase.pptx
PhoneCase.jpg

Case2
Wedding01.jpg
...
Wedding10.jpg
(10 photos)

Case3
MntMap.jpg
MntPlateau1.jpg
MntPlateau2.jpg

Case4
(none)

Planning the Presentation

Before you begin to create Sophie's slide show, she discusses with you the purpose of, and the audience for, her presentation:

- **Purpose of the presentation**: To present information about products and services of Classic Flowers
- **Type of presentation**: Persuasive (sales)
- **Audience**: Floral department managers and store managers
- **Audience needs**: Details of products and services and information on potential profits
- **Location of the presentation**: Small meeting rooms
- **Format**: On-screen slide show

With this general plan for the presentation, Sophie prepares the text and some of the pictures for the sales presentation.

Inserting Slides from Another Presentation

After Sophie discusses her presentation planning with you, she gives you two presentation files: Flowers, which contains the text and some pictures to include with her sales presentation, and CFSales, a presentation that includes additional information about Classic Flowers's sales. First, you'll open the Flowers presentation and look through it to see what information Sophie has already included. Then, you'll add slides to it from the CFSales presentation.

To insert slides from another presentation, you first need to open the presentation to which you want to add the slides. Then, you use the Reuse Slides command on the New Slide menu to insert specific slides from any other presentation. If the inserted slides have a different design than the current presentation, the design of the current presentation will override the design of the inserted slides.

Inserting Slides from Another Presentation | Reference Window

- Go to the slide in your current presentation after which you want to insert the slides from another presentation.
- In the Slides group on the Home tab, click the New Slide button arrow.
- Click Reuse Slides to display the Reuse Slides task pane.
- In the task pane, click the Browse button, and then click Browse File to open the Browse dialog box.
- Navigate to the location of the presentation that contains the slides you want to insert into the presentation in the PowerPoint window, click the file, and then click the OK button.
- In the task pane, select or deselect the Keep source formatting check box to retain or not retain the formatting of the slides you want to import.
- Click each slide that you want inserted into your presentation.

To open the Flowers presentation and save it with a new name:

▶ **1.** Start PowerPoint, and then open the file **Flowers** located in the **Tutorial.03\Tutorial** folder included with your Data Files.

▶ **2.** Change the subtitle ("Sophie De Graff") to your name.

▶ **3.** Save the presentation file as **Flower Sales** in the Tutorial.03\Tutorial folder. See Figure 3-1.

Slide 1 of Flower Sales ◀ Figure 3-1

▶ **4.** Look through the three slides of the presentation so you have an idea of its current content. Notice that the presentation has a modified blank Office theme (black text on white background), with the Calibri font for the slide titles and body text. The modifications to the Office theme include the long, slender photograph ("panel") of pink flowers on the slides with bulleted lists, resized placeholders for the body text, and inserted and modified footer and slide number.

Your first task is to insert slides from the presentation file CFSales. Sophie tells you that she wants you to insert all five slides from CFSales.

To insert slides from one presentation into another:

▶ **1.** Go to **Slide 3** of Flower Sales. When you insert slides from another presentation, they are inserted after the current slide.

▶ **2.** In the Slides group on the Home tab, click the **New Slide button arrow**. A menu appears with slide layouts for the Office theme and other items.

▶ **3.** Click **Reuse Slides**. The Reuse Slides task pane opens on the right side of the window.

▶ **4.** In the task pane, click the **Browse** button, and then click **Browse File**. The Browse dialog box opens.

▶ **5.** Navigate to the **Tutorial.03\Tutorial** folder, and then double-click **CFSales**. The five slides from the CFSales presentation appear in the Reuse Slides task pane. See Figure 3-2.

Figure 3-2 ▶ **Slide 3 and the Reuse Slides task pane**

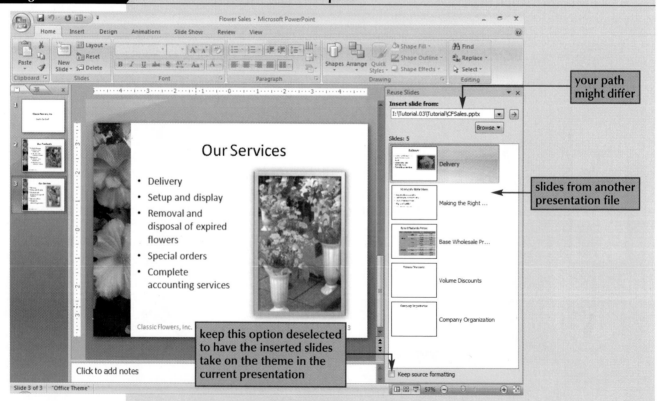

6. At the bottom of the task pane, make sure the **Keep source formatting** check box is unchecked. You don't want to keep the formatting of the inserted slides, but rather you want the new slides to take on the formatting (the theme) of the current Flower Sales presentation.

7. Point to the first slide, "Delivery," in the task pane. The slide increases in size so that you can read its content.

8. Click the **Delivery** slide. It is inserted into the Flower Sales presentation after the current slide (Slide 3).

9. Insert the other four slides, one at a time. See Figure 3-3.

Slide 8 after inserting five slides from another presentation | Figure 3-3

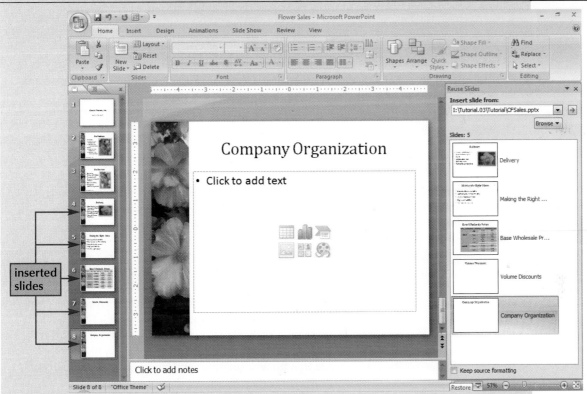

10. In the task pane title bar, click the **Close** button ⊠.

The five slides from CFSales are now Slides 4 through 8 of Flower Sales. Some of the new slides contain bulleted lists or a table of sales information; others contain only a title. Notice that the newly inserted slides take on the modified Office theme of the current presentation.

With most of the slides now created for the presentation, you're ready to create a custom theme.

Creating a Custom Theme

As you recall, a theme is a presentation design that contains the color, attributes, and format for the titles, bulleted lists, other text, and background for the presentation. You have already used several themes that come with PowerPoint. Sometimes, however, you'll want to design your own, custom theme. After you create a custom theme, you can save the presentation as a normal PowerPoint presentation file and then create a new presentation based on the customized presentation, or you can save a presentation as an Office theme, which you can easily apply to other presentations.

Reference Window | **Creating and Saving a Custom Theme**

- Using an existing or new presentation, create the desired theme colors, bullets, fonts, background color, and background graphics.
- Click the Office Button, click Save As to open the Save As dialog box, click the Save as type arrow, and then click Office Theme; *or* click the Design tab on the Ribbon, in the Themes group, click the More button, and then click Save Current Theme to open the Save Current Theme dialog box with Office Theme already selected in the Save as type box.
- Navigate to the desired location, type a filename, and then click the Save button.

Tip

You can press the F12 key to open the Save As dialog box.

For the sales presentation for Classic Flowers, Sophie doesn't want you to use any of the built-in themes; instead, she wants you to create a completely original one designed for her business. She likes the panel of pink flowers in the Slide Master and wants the new theme to match the subject and the colors of the picture. You'll complete the task of creating the custom theme.

Creating Custom Theme Colors

Theme colors are coordinating colors that make up the background, title fonts, body fonts, and other elements of the presentation. Each of the built-in PowerPoint themes, including the default Office theme, has a set of colors associated with it.

InSight | **Selecting Theme Colors**

It's easy to select colors that don't match or make text illegible; for example, red text on a blue background might seem like a good combination, but it's actually difficult to read for an audience at a distance from the screen. It's usually safer, therefore, to select one of the built-in theme colors and stick with it, or make only minor modifications. If you do create a new set of theme colors, select colors that go well together and that maximize legibility of your slides.

The PowerPoint theme colors are a set of 12 colors that have general purposes. These are the 12 colors:

- **Text/Background – Dark 1**, **Text/Background – Light 1**, **Text/Background – Dark 2**, and **Text/Background – Light 2**: These four colors provide you with two possible schemes for light text on a dark background and two possible schemes for dark text on a light background. In practice, you would never select dark text on dark background or light text on light background.
- **Accent 1** through **Accent 6**: These six colors provide colors for lines, shapes, charts, tables, shadows, picture borders, and other objects that might appear on your presentation slides.
- **Hyperlink**: This is the default color for hyperlinked text.
- **Followed hyperlink**: This is the default color for hyperlinks that have been followed. In other words, if you click on a hyperlink and thereby jump to another location, when you return to the original slide, the color of the hyperlink text will be changed to indicate that you have followed that hyperlink.

After you have specified a coordinated set of theme colors, they will appear by default in text and objects, but you can use any of the 12 colors to change the default color of text, fills, shadows, and so forth.

The current presentation uses the color theme called "Office," which is the default set of colors used when the Office theme is applied. The default background color is white and the default text color is black (except for the gray subtitle on the title slide). Sophie feels that this simple theme doesn't fit well with the sales presentation on potted flowers and bouquets. In fact, as you look at the pictures of the flowers in Sophie's presentations, you see mostly warm colors—pinks, reds, violets, oranges, and yellows—so you'll create a set of theme colors using those colors, as well as some greens to match leaf colors and to offer contrast.

You can create the theme colors with any slide in the slide pane, but here you'll want to move to Slide 2 so you can see how the color changes appear on a slide that contains bulleted text and a photograph. You'll create the theme colors now.

To create custom theme colors:

▶ **1.** Go to **Slide 2**, so that a bulleted-list slide appears in the slide pane.

▶ **2.** Click the **Design** tab on the Ribbon. The Ribbon changes to display the available themes, the Colors button, the Fonts button, and others.

▶ **3.** In the Themes group, click the **Colors** button to display the Colors menu. See Figure 3-4. PowerPoint displays the built-in color sets, a set of eight color tiles, for each of the built-in themes. The eight tiles correspond to the second two Text/Background colors and the six accent colors.

Viewing the Colors menu | Figure 3-4

Colors button

built-in theme color sets (you might see additional sets on your screen)

click to create new theme colors

Create New Theme Colors...

▶ **4.** Click **Create New Theme Colors** at the bottom of the Colors menu. The Create New Theme Colors dialog box opens. Here, you can see color tiles representing each of the 12 theme colors of the Office theme. The Sample section of the dialog box shows sample slides with dark and light backgrounds. You'll change most of these colors, beginning with the Text/Background – Dark 1 color, which you'll change to dark green.

▶ **5.** Click the **Text/Background – Dark 1** button to display the Theme Colors palette. Because no dark-green tile appears in the palette, you'll look at more colors.

▶ **6.** At the bottom of the palette, click **More Colors** to display the Colors dialog box, and then, if necessary, click the **Standard** tab. See Figure 3-5.

Figure 3-5	▶ Colors dialog box with theme colors

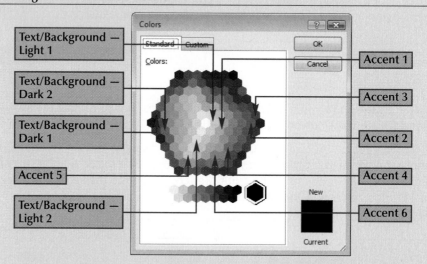

▶ **7.** Click the dark-green tile for Text/Background – Dark 1 as indicated in Figure 3-5, and then click the **OK** button. The Colors dialog box closes. The Text/Background – Dark 1 color changes from black to dark green, and the title text in the right panel in the Sample area of the Create New Theme Colors dialog box changes to dark green also.

You'll now change the color of the light text on the dark background from white to light pink.

▶ **8.** Click the **Text/Background – Light 1** button to display the Theme Colors gallery again. The lightest pink tile in the gallery is not light enough.

▶ **9.** Click **More Colors**, click the light-pink tile shown in Figure 3-5, and then click the **OK** button. The title text on the dark background in the panel on the left in the Sample area changes to light pink.

So far, you have changed the first two theme colors. You'll now change several of the others.

To change more theme colors and save the custom colors:

▶ **1.** With the Create New Theme Colors dialog box still open, click the **Text/Background – Dark 2** button, click **More Colors**, click the **Standard** tab, click the green tile as indicated in Figure 3-5, and then click the **OK** button.

2. Change each of the next seven theme colors to the color indicated in Figure 3-5. (Do not change the Hyperlink or Followed Hyperlink colors.)

3. In the Create New Theme Colors dialog box, select all of the text in the **Name** text box, and then type **Flower**. See Figure 3-6.

Create New Theme Colors dialog box with new colors ◄ **Figure 3-6**

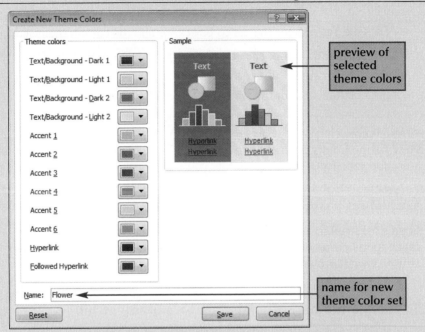

Trouble? If you clicked the Save button before you changed the name, you can edit it. On the Design tab, in the Themes group, click the Colors button, and then locate the custom theme you created. It will appear at the top of the menu and will be named "Custom" followed by a number. Right-click the custom theme, and then, on the shortcut menu, click Edit. Continue with Step 4.

4. Click the **Save** button in the Create New Theme Colors dialog box. The dialog box closes and the theme is applied.

5. In the Themes group, click the **Colors** button. The Flower custom color theme you created appears at the top of the list under "Custom."

6. Press the **Esc** key to close the menu.

7. Save the presentation using the default name.

As you can see in Slide 2, the title and body text are now dark green and the background is light pink. If you look at the slide thumbnails in the pane on the left, you see that those slides also have dark-green text with light-pink background.

Deleting Custom Theme Colors

You can delete a custom theme or theme colors. If you've applied the theme or the theme colors to a presentation, and then saved that presentation, the theme and colors will still be applied to that presentation even if you delete the theme or theme colors from the hard drive. You'll delete the custom theme colors you created. To access the Colors menu, a presentation must be open.

To delete custom theme colors:

▶ **1.** Click the **Design** tab on the Ribbon, and then, in the Themes group, click the **Colors** button. The Colors menu opens.

▶ **2.** Right-click the **Flower** theme color set at the top of the list under Custom.

▶ **3.** On the shortcut menu, click **Delete**. A dialog box opens asking if you want to delete these theme colors.

▶ **4.** Click the **Yes** button. The dialog box closes and the custom theme colors are deleted.

▶ **5.** In the Themes group, click the **Colors** button. Note that the Flower theme colors are deleted.

▶ **6.** Click a blank area of the window to close the menu.

You'll now change the background style of the slides. You've already used the Create New Theme Colors dialog box to change the background to a solid light pink, but if you want special effects, such as shading, you must use the Background Styles gallery.

Creating a Custom Background

Sophie asks you to add shading to the background to add interest and a professional touch to the presentation. You decide to use a **gradient fill**, which is a type of shading in which one color blends into another or varies from one shade to another.

To change the background style to a gradient fill:

▶ **1.** Make sure **Slide 2** appears in the slide pane and the **Design** tab is the active tab on the Ribbon.

▶ **2.** In the Background group, click the **Background Styles** button. The Background Styles gallery appears. See Figure 3-7.

Background Styles gallery ◄ Figure 3-7

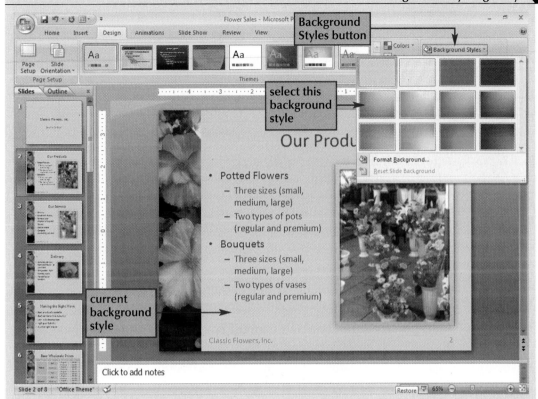

The Background Styles gallery includes 12 styles—four solid colors along the top row corresponding to the four Text/Background theme colors and two gradient styles for each of those colors.

▶ **3.** Click **Style 5**, which is the second background style from the top in the first column. The backgrounds of the slides now vary from dark pink (or violet) in the lower-left corner to light pink in the upper-right corner.

▶ **4.** Save the presentation using the default filename.

As you can see from the slide pane and the slide thumbnails in the pane on the left, all of the slides now have a background with a gradient fill. You'll now add a picture to the background of Slide 1.

Adding a Background Picture

Sophie now wants you to add a photo of a bed of flowers to the background of Slide 1. You'll add it to the Title Slide layout in the Slide Master so it becomes part of the design theme. As you might recall, the Slide Master contains the objects that appear on the slide layouts, and the Title Slide layout contains the objects that appear only on the title slide.

To apply a background picture to a slide:

▶ **1.** Click the **View** tab on the Ribbon, and then, in the Presentation Views group, click the **Slide Master** button. Slide Master view opens and the Ribbon changes to display the Slide Master tab.

2. Click the **Title Slide Layout** thumbnail, the second thumbnail from the top in the pane on the left.

3. In the Background group on the Slide Master tab, click the **Background Styles** button. The Background Styles gallery again appears on the screen.

4. Below the gallery in the menu, click **Format Background**. The Format Background dialog box opens with Fill selected in the list on the left.

5. Click the **Picture or texture fill** option button. The dialog box changes to display commands for customizing a background with a texture or a picture.

6. Click the **File** button. The Insert Picture dialog box opens.

7. Navigate to the **Tutorial.03\Tutorial** folder, click the picture file **PinkFlowerBG**, and then click the **Insert** button. The Insert Picture dialog box closes and the picture is inserted into the background of Slide 1 behind the Format Background dialog box.

   Sophie likes the background picture, but is concerned that it is too bright and has too much contrast, making it hard for the audience to read the text on the slide. You'll adjust the brightness and contrast.

8. Click **Picture** in the left pane of the Format Background dialog box. The dialog box changes to include commands for modifying the picture on the background.

9. Drag the **Brightness** slider to the left until the box indicates **–30%**. Watch the picture change behind the dialog box.

10. Change the **Contrast** to **–40%**. The picture becomes a little darker but with less contrast.

11. Click the **Close** button in the dialog box. See Figure 3-8.

Tip

Type directly in the box or click the up and down arrows to set the percentage to an exact number.

Figure 3-8 | **Picture background in the Title Slide Layout master**

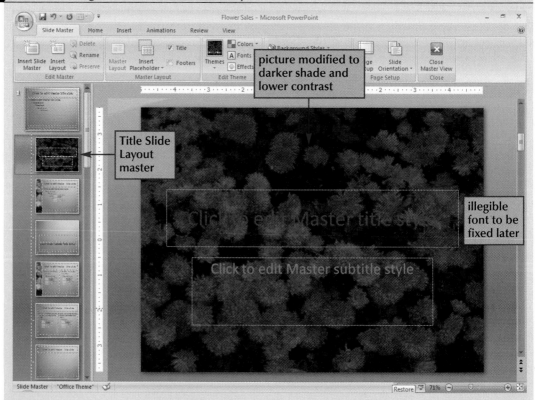

The backgrounds appear as Sophie wants them, but she now wants you to make the title text on the slides stand out more. You'll change the title text font, and then modify its size, style, and color.

Modifying Fonts and Bullets

The font used for all of the text in the presentation is Calibri. This is a good, general-purpose font, but Sophie feels that it doesn't stand out enough as a title font. You'll change the title font, increase its size, and format it as bold. By making the changes in Slide Master view, you'll change the fonts on all the slides in the presentation.

To modify the fonts in Slide Master view:

▶ 1. Click the **Office Theme Slide Master**, the large thumbnail at the top of the left pane.

▶ 2. Click the edge of the title placeholder, which contains the phrase "Click to edit Master title style." Make sure the title box has a solid line around it, not just a dashed line, so the entire text box is selected.

▶ 3. Click the **Home** tab, and then, in the Font group, click the **Font button arrow** to display a menu of fonts.

▶ 4. Click **Arial Rounded MT Bold**.

   Trouble? If Arial Rounded MT Bold doesn't appear in your list of fonts, select Arial Black, AvantGarde Md BT, or some other font that stands out.

▶ 5. In the Font group, click the **Font Size button arrow**, and then click **48** to increase the font size to 48 points.

   The title fonts on all the slides stand out more now, except on the Title Slide Master, where the dark background with dark text makes the text illegible. You'll fix that problem now.

▶ 6. Click the **Title Slide Layout** thumbnail, and then select the title text placeholder, which currently contains dark-green text.

▶ 7. Click the **Font Color button arrow** A ⏷ to display the theme colors palette.

▶ 8. Click the **Light Yellow, Background 2** tile, located third from the left in the top row in the palette under Theme Colors.

▶ 9. Using the same method, change the subtitle to **Yellow, Accent 5** (located second from the right in the top row of tiles).

▶ 10. Deselect the text box. See Figure 3-9.

Figure 3-9 | Title Slide Layout master with modified title text

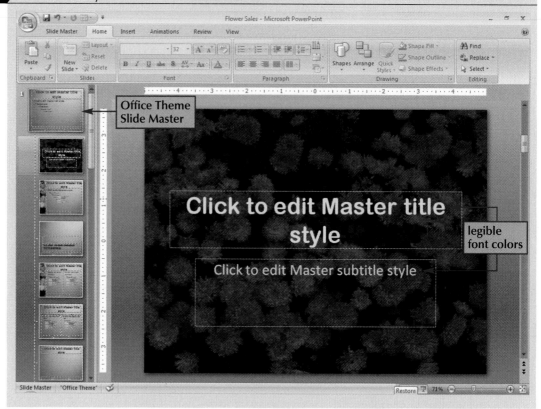

You have changed the font attributes so the title text stands out more. Now you'll change the bullets.

To change the bullets style in Slide Master view:

▶ 1. Click the **Office Theme Slide Master** thumbnail to display the Slide Master in the slide pane.

▶ 2. Click anywhere in the first bulleted item, which says "Click to edit Master text styles."

▶ 3. In the Paragraph group on the Home tab, click the **Bullets button arrow** to display the Bullets gallery. You could select one of the standard bullets shown here in the gallery, but instead, Sophie wants you to select a picture bullet.

▶ 4. Click **Bullets and Numbering** at the bottom of the Bullets gallery to display the Bullets and Numbering dialog box with the Bulleted tab on top.

Picture Bullet dialog box ◄ **Figure 3-10**

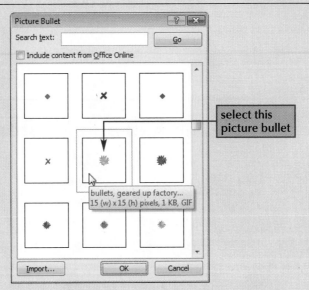

7. Click the bullet indicated in Figure 3-10, and then click the **OK** button. Both dialog boxes close, and the picture bullet you selected becomes the first-level bullet in the body text. Now you'll change the second-level bullet.

8. Click anywhere in the "Second level" line, and then open the Bullets and Numbering dialog box with the Bulleted tab on top.

9. Click the **Filled Square Bullets** style in the top row. Sophie wants you to change the color to the Accent 5 theme color (yellow).

10. Click the **Color** button 🖌️ ▾ in the lower-left corner of the dialog box, and then click the **Yellow, Accent 5** tile, the same color you selected for the subtitle text on the Title Master.

11. Click the **OK** button in the Bullets and Numbering dialog box.

12. Select the footer and slide number placeholders at the bottom of the slide, and then change the color of the text to **Yellow, Accent 5**. Deselect the placeholders. See Figure 3-11.

Figure 3-11 **Slide Master with modified bullets**

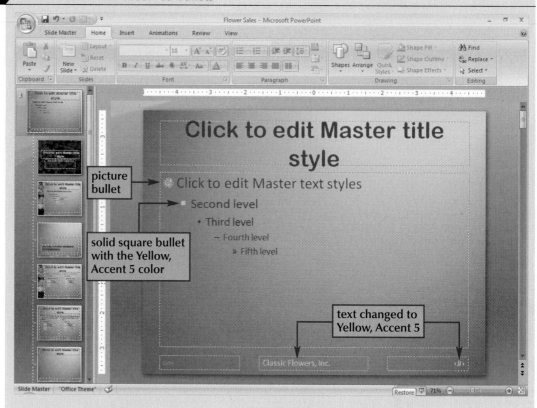

You'll now return to Normal view, see how the slides look, and then save the presentation.

To view the presentation and save it:

▶ **1.** On the status bar, click the **Normal** button ▣. Slide Master view closes and the Slide Master tab disappears from the Ribbon. You see the changes you made in Slide 2.

▶ **2.** Go to **Slide 4**. As you can see, the new font didn't automatically change to match the Slide Masters on the slides that you inserted from the other presentation file, and the footer and slide number don't appear on the slide. You'll fix these problems now.

▶ **3.** Click the **Insert** tab on the Ribbon, and then, in the Text group click the **Header & Footer** button. The Header and Footer dialog box opens with the Slide tab on top.

▶ **4.** Click the **Slide number** and **Footer** check boxes to select them, and then click the **Apply to All** button. The dialog box closes and the slide number and footer appear on all the slides.

▶ **5.** Click the **Home** tab, and then, in the Slides group, click the **Reset** button. The Reset button resets the position, size, and formatting of the slide placeholders in the current slide to the default settings, meaning to the settings found in the Slide Masters. Notice that the border on the picture of the rose disappeared because this setting is not part of the Slide Masters. You'll restore the border now.

▶ **6.** Click the picture to select it, and then click the Picture Tools **Format** contextual tab.

▶ **7.** In the Picture Styles group, click the **Metal Frame** style.

▶ **8.** Drag the picture up so that its top is aligned with the first bullet in the bulleted list.

▶ **9.** Proceed through all the slides, and on each slide, as necessary, reset the title font to the Slide Master font and reposition the table in Slide 6.

▶ **10.** Save the presentation using the default filename.

Your custom theme is now complete, with its customized theme colors, gradient background, new fonts, and pictures of flowers in the background of all the slides. Sophie asks you to save the custom theme so she can apply it to other presentations.

Saving a Custom Theme

In earlier tutorials, you applied built-in themes by clicking the Design tab on the Ribbon to display the Themes group, and then selecting the desired theme. What if you wanted to apply the flower theme in a similar way? That's exactly what Sophie wants to do. To make that possible, she wants you to save the presentation as an Office theme. An **Office theme** is the file type that serves as a design theme. It has the filename extension ".thmx". You can use an Office theme file to apply a custom theme to an existing PowerPoint presentation or you can create a new presentation based on the custom theme.

The default location for saving a PowerPoint presentation as a theme is the Document Themes folder located in the Templates folder, but you can save a theme in any folder. No matter where you save your theme, you can create a new presentation based on that theme by clicking Browse for Themes at the bottom of the Themes gallery.

Understanding the Difference Between a Theme and a Template	InSight

When you save a PowerPoint presentation as a theme, only the design elements (including background graphics) are saved, not the content, that is, not the text or objects applied to the slides. If you want to save a theme with the contents for use in other presentations, you would instead save the presentation as a PowerPoint template.

You've saved your work as a normal PowerPoint presentation. Now you'll save it as a theme, and then test it by creating a new presentation based on this theme.

To save a presentation as a theme:

▶ **1.** Click the **Office Button** , and then click **Save As**. The Save As dialog box opens.

▶ **2.** Click the **Save as type arrow** near the bottom of the dialog box.

▶ **3.** Click **Office Theme** in the list. The current folder changes to Document Themes, but you want to save your theme file in the same location where you saved Flower Sales (in the Tutorial.03\Tutorial folder included with your Data Files).

▶ **4.** Change the current folder to the **Tutorial.03\Tutorial** folder included with your Data Files (or to the location where you saved Flower Sales).

▶ **5.** Edit the text in the File name text box to **Flower**, and then click the **Save** button. PowerPoint saves the file as a theme.

If you had saved the theme to the default Themes folder, it would have appeared as a custom theme in the Themes gallery when you clicked the More button. To delete a custom theme, you right-click it, and then click Delete on the shortcut menu.

You have now created a custom theme that Sophie and others can use with any new presentation.

Using a Custom Theme

You decide to test your new custom theme on a new presentation.

To start a new presentation using a custom theme:

▶ **1.** Click the **Office Button** 🔘, click **New**, and then with the Blank Presentation selected in the Blank and recent section of the New Presentation dialog box, click the **Create** button. PowerPoint creates a new presentation.

▶ **2.** Click the **Design** tab on the Ribbon, and then, in the Themes group, click the **More** button.

▶ **3.** Below the Themes gallery click **Browse for Themes**. The Choose Theme or Themed Document dialog box opens.

▶ **4.** Navigate to the **Tutorial.03\Tutorial** folder included with your Data Files, and then double-click the Office theme file **Flower**. This is the theme you created and saved. The new presentation now has the Flower theme applied. It has only one slide, the title slide, and it has no text.

▶ **5.** Close the presentation without saving it. Keep Flower Sales open in PowerPoint.

You can now report to Sophie that your custom theme works as planned. You can still make changes to customize the background of a slide after a theme is applied. You'll make a change to the background of one of the slides now.

Adding a Textured Background

Sophie wants to highlight Slide 6, which contains a table of the base wholesale prices of Classic Flowers's products. She decides that she wants you to add a textured background to the slide. You'll do that now.

Applying a Textured Background | Reference Window

- Go to the slide to which you want to apply the textured background.
- Click the Design tab on the Ribbon.
- In the Background group, click the Background Styles button, and then click Format Background at the bottom of the backgrounds gallery to open the Format Background dialog box.
- Click the Picture or texture file option button.
- Click the Texture button to display a gallery of textured backgrounds.
- Click the desired texture and then click the Close button if you want to apply the textured background just to the current slide, or click the Apply to All button if you want to apply the textured background to all the slides in the presentation.

You'll now apply a "pink tissue paper" texture to the background of Slide 6.

To add a textured background:

▶ 1. Go to **Slide 6**, and then, if necessary, click the **Design** tab on the Ribbon.

▶ 2. In the Background group, click the **Background Styles** button, and then click **Format Background**. The Format Background dialog box opens with Fill selected on the left.

▶ 3. Click the **Picture or texture fill** option button. The dialog box changes to include commands for inserting a picture or a fill.

▶ 4. Click the **Texture button** 🖼 ▾ . **A gallery of textured backgrounds appears. As you can see, PowerPoint has 25 built-in textures to choose from.**

▶ 5. Click the **Pink tissue paper** texture, located in row 4, column 3. The background of the slide changes to pink tissue paper behind the dialog box.

▶ 6. Click the **Close** button. See Figure 3-12.

Figure 3-12 | Slide 6 with textured background

7. Save the presentation using the default filename.

Sophie is pleased with how Slide 6 stands out from the others, and is happy with the progress you're making on the presentation.

Review | Session 3.1 Quick Check

1. Describe how you insert slides from one presentation into another.
2. What are theme colors?
3. In creating a custom theme, what are four (or more) elements in your presentation that you might want to change?
4. What is a gradient fill, as it pertains to a slide background?
5. Describe how you save a PowerPoint presentation as an Office theme.
6. How do you apply a textured background to a slide?

Session 3.2

Inserting Sounds and Movies into Your Presentation

PowerPoint allows you to add various types of graphics and sounds to your presentation. You're already familiar with adding clip art, drawn images, and digital photos to a slide. In fact, the original Flowers and CFSales presentation files came with images of flowers and bouquets, and you have already inserted the image of a flower bed into the slide background of the title slide. In addition to still photos and other graphics, you can insert sounds and movies into a presentation.

Inserting a Sound into a Presentation | Reference Window

- Go to the slide in which you want to insert the sound.
- Click the Insert tab on the Ribbon.
- In the Media Clips group, click the Sound button arrow, and then on the menu, click the desired source of the sound file.
- Select the sound file from a specified folder and click the OK button.
- When asked how you want the sound to start in the slide show, click the Automatically or When Clicked button.

Sophie feels that you can improve the Flower Sales presentation by adding sound clips, a video clip, and other special effects. You'll use sound and video files that are included with your Data Files. In other presentations, you might have to acquire the sounds and videos in other ways. For example, you can do the following:

- Record sound files with a microphone attached to your computer and appropriate software.
- Use a digital camera with video capture or use a video camera to take digital videos.
- Create images or movies using graphics software.
- Download images or sound clips from the Internet.
- Insert images or sounds from the Clip Organizer, which might include sound or movie files that you have made and that you have downloaded from Office Online.
- Use built-in PowerPoint sound effects.

Inserting Sound Clips

Sophie wants you to add two sound clips, a recording of "Welcome to Classic Flowers" and a sound clip of applause. Sophie's recordings are in .wav files, which is the most common file format for short sound clips.

You can add a sound clip to a slide in several ways. You can use the Insert Media Clip button in a content layout placeholder, or you can use the Insert tab on the Ribbon. You'll add the sound files now using the Insert tab.

To add sound clips to the presentation:

▶ 1. If you took a break after Session 1, start PowerPoint and make sure the Flower Sales presentation is open.

▶ 2. Go to **Slide 1**, and then click the **Insert** tab on the Ribbon.

▶ **3.** In the Media Clips group, click the **Sound** button. The Insert Sound dialog box opens.

▶ **4.** Navigate to the **Tutorial.03\Tutorial** folder included with your Data Files. This folder contains two sound files, Applause and CFISound.

▶ **5.** Click **CFISound**, and then click the **OK** button. A dialog box opens displaying the question "How do you want the sound to start in the slide show?" Sophie wants the sound to start automatically when she displays Slide 1 in Slide Show view.

▶ **6.** Click the **Automatically** button. The dialog box closes and a sound icon ◀ appears in the middle of the slide to indicate that a sound clip is available on that slide. Notice that a special effects icon appears below the slide in the Slides tab. See Figure 3-13.

Figure 3-13 ▶ **Slide 1 with sound icon**

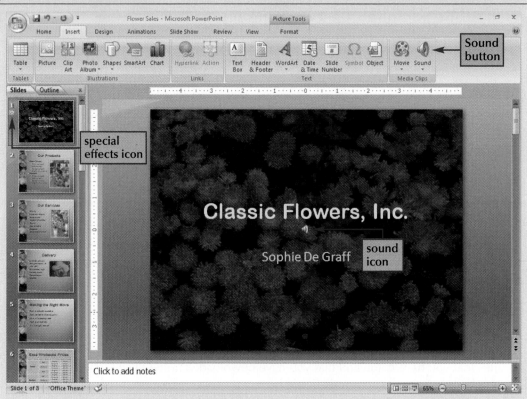

▶ **7.** Double-click the **sound** icon ◀ to play the sound clip. In Slide Show view, the sound will automatically play whenever you display Slide 1. You can also click the sound icon during the slide show to make the sound play again.

Now that you know how to insert a sound clip, Sophie wants you to insert another one in Slide 4.

To add another sound clip:

▶ **1.** Go to **Slide 4** ("Delivery"). Sophie wants you to insert the applause sound clip to celebrate the positive features of the Classic Flowers delivery system.

▶ **2.** Insert the sound clip **Applause**, located in the **Tutorial.03\Tutorial** folder included with your Data Files, into Slide 4, and again select the **Automatically** button in the dialog box asking how you want the sound clip to start.

▶ **3.** Double-click the **sound** icon 🔊 to test the sound clip. Sophie doesn't want this sound icon to be visible on the screen during the slide show, so you'll hide it behind the flower picture.

▶ **4.** Drag the **sound** icon 🔊 so it's located anywhere on top of the framed flower picture on the right of the text.

▶ **5.** With the sound icon still selected, click the **Format** tab below Picture Tools on the Ribbon.

▶ **6.** In the Arrange group, click the **Send to Back** button. The selected sound icon disappears behind the flower picture. You can still see the sizing handles of the sound icon.

▶ **7.** Click a blank area of the slide to deselect the sound icon.

▶ **8.** Save the presentation using the default filename.

Now, when Sophie uses Flower Sales in a sales presentation, the slide show will have sound effects to add interest.

Inserting a Movie

A **video clip**, or **digital movie**, is an animated picture file. PowerPoint supports various file formats, but the most common one for PowerPoint presentations is the Windows video file, which has the extension ".avi".

Sophie wants you to insert a short video of a chess piece being moved as part of Slide 5, "Making the Right Move."

Inserting a Movie into a Presentation | Reference Window

- Go to the slide in which you want to insert the movie.
- Change the layout to include an empty content layout, and then click the Insert Media Clip button in the content layout placeholder to open the Insert Movie dialog box, *or* click the Insert tab on the Ribbon, in the Media Clips group, click the Movie button. The Insert Movie dialog box opens.
- Navigate to the folder containing the movie, click the movie filename from a specified folder, and then click the OK button.
- When asked how you want the movie or sound to start in the slide show, click the Automatically or When Clicked button.

You can insert a video clip in two different ways. You can change the layout to one of the content layouts, click the Insert Media Clip button, and then use the Insert Movie dialog box, or you can use the Movie button in the Media Clips group on the Insert tab. You'll add the movie now using the Insert Media Clip button in a content layout.

To add a movie to a slide:

▶ **1.** Go to **Slide 5** ("Making the Right Move") and then, if necessary, click the **Home** tab on the Ribbon.

▶ **2.** In the Slides group, click the **Layout** button, and then click the **Two Content** layout.

3. Click the **Insert Media Clip** button in the content placeholder. The Insert Movie dialog box opens.

4. Navigate to the **Tutorial.03\Tutorial** folder included with your Data Files, click **RightMove**, and then click the **OK** button. The dialog box asks if you want to play the movie automatically or when you click the icon.

5. Click the **Automatically** button. The first frame of the movie appears in the right side of the slide. Now you'll change the Picture Style of the movie.

6. With the movie frame selected, click the **Format** tab below Picture Tools on the Ribbon.

7. In the Picture Styles group, click the **Metal Frame** style (the third thumbnail from the left). See Figure 3-14. Now the frame around the movie photo matches the frame around the other pictures in the presentation.

| **Figure 3-14** | **Slide 5 with movie** |

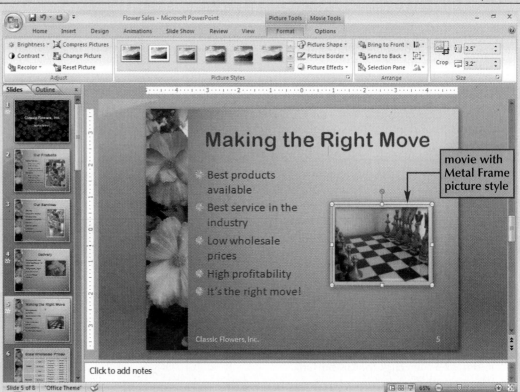

Having inserted the digital movie and changed its picture style, you are now ready to view it.

8. Double-click the picture of the movie. As you can see, the movie shows a chess player making the first move.

Trouble? If the movie was slow to start, don't worry. On some computers, it might take a moment after you double-click the picture for the movie to begin.

Because you clicked the Automatically button when you inserted the movie, it will play when Slide 5 appears during the slide show.

When you insert a movie, you can choose from a few other options to play the movie. You can play the movie full screen, so that it fills the entire screen. You can also set the movie to Loop Until Stopped, which means the movie will play over and over again until you advance to the next slide in Slide Show view. Finally, you can choose the Rewind the Movie After Playing option, which means that, when it's over, the picture on the slide returns to the first frame of the movie rather than stopping on the last frame. Sophie wants the movie to play full screen.

To set the movie to full-screen viewing:

▶ **1.** Make sure the movie is still selected, and then click the **Options** tab below Movie Tools on the Ribbon, if necessary.

▶ **2.** In the Movie Options group, click the **Play Full Screen** check box. Now you'll see what the movie looks like in Slide Show view.

▶ **3.** On the status bar, click the **Slide Show** button 🖵 to start the slide show from the current slide. Slide 5 appears in Slide Show view and the movie plays once in full screen, ending with the final frame, and the slide appears again on the screen.

▶ **4.** Press the **Esc** key. The slide show terminates and you return to Normal view.

   Trouble? You might need to press the Esc key twice to stop the movie and the slide show.

▶ **5.** Save the presentation using the default filename.

Creating a Chart (Graph)

A **chart**, or **graph**, is a visual depiction of data in a spreadsheet. The **spreadsheet** is a grid of cells in a Microsoft Excel worksheet. **Cells** are the boxes that are organized in rows and columns, in which you can add data and labels. The rows are numbered 1, 2, 3, and so on, and the columns are labeled A, B, C, and so forth. You can use a chart to show an audience data trends and patterns or to visually compare data.

Creating a Chart (Graph) | Reference Window

- Change the slide layout to one of the content layouts, and then click the Insert Chart button in the content placeholder; *or* click the Insert tab, and then, in the Illustrations group, click the Chart button. The Insert Chart dialog box opens.
- Click one of the chart icons in the Insert Chart gallery, and then click the OK button. PowerPoint automatically opens a Microsoft Excel worksheet.
- Edit the information in the worksheet for the data that you want to plot.
- Modify the chart layout, style, format, data, or other features, as desired.
- Click outside the chart area to make the chart inactive.

Sophie now wants you to create a chart in Slide 7. The chart will give the volume discount prices from the base wholesale prices given in Slide 6. You'll create the chart now.

To insert a chart:

▶ **1.** Go to **Slide 7** ("Volume Discounts"), and then click the **Insert Chart** button 📊 in the content placeholder. The Insert Chart dialog box opens, displaying a gallery of charts. See Figure 3-15.

Figure 3-15 ▶ **Insert Chart dialog box**

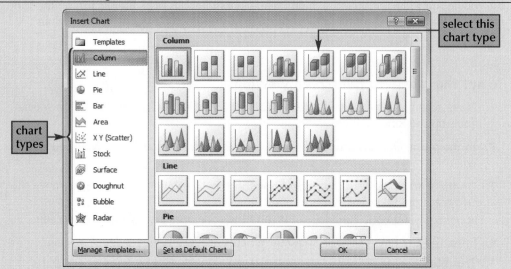

▶ **2.** Click the **Stacked Column in 3D** chart type, which is in the first row, fifth column of the gallery, and then click the **OK** button. PowerPoint inserts a sample chart into Slide 7 and opens a Microsoft Excel worksheet with sample data. See Figure 3-16. You can now use Excel features for inserting and editing data in a worksheet.

Excel spreadsheet with data for chart | Figure 3-16

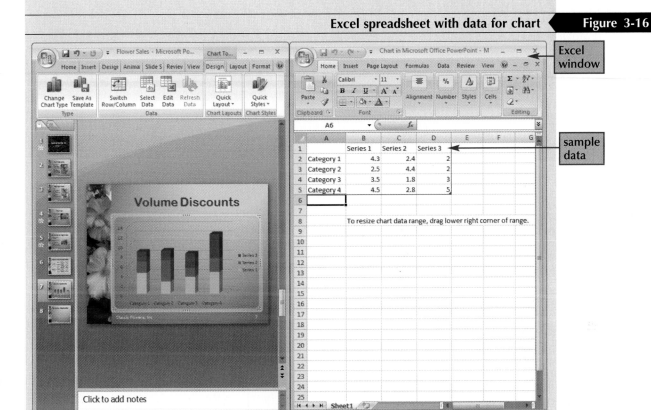

To create the chart for Sophie's presentation, you simply edit the information in the sample spreadsheet on the screen. When you work with a spreadsheet, the cell in which you are entering data is the **active cell**. The active cell has a thick black border around it. In this chart, you want only two columns, one with the number of units ordered (per month) and one with the percent discount. You'll begin by deleting the third and fourth columns of data on the spreadsheet.

To modify the spreadsheet:

▶ **1.** Move the mouse pointer to the top of column C so that the pointer changes to ⬇.

▶ **2.** Click and drag the mouse pointer to select both columns C and D. See Figure 3-17.

Figure 3-17 | **Excel spreadsheet with selected columns**

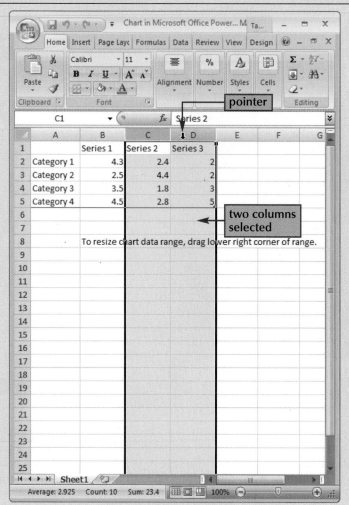

3. Click the **Cells** button on the Home tab in the Excel window, and then click the **Delete** button.

   Trouble? If you see the Cells group instead of the Cells button on the Home tab, just click the Delete button located there.

   A dialog box opens warning you that a formula in the worksheet contains one or more invalid references.

▶ **4.** Click the **OK** button. After you finish editing the data, Excel and PowerPoint will fix the problem of invalid references automatically.

▶ **5.** Click cell **B1**, which currently contains the column label "Series 1."

▶ **6.** Type **Discount %**, and then press the **Enter** key. Again, you'll get the warning of invalid references, which you will get after each data entry until you finish the chart.

▶ **7.** Click the **OK** button in the dialog box.

You need to finish modifying the spreadsheet.

To finish modifying the spreadsheet:

▶ **1.** Click cell **A2** ("Category 1"), type **11-50 Units/Mo**, press the **Enter** key, and then click the **OK** button. The text is entered into cell A2 and cell A3 becomes the active cell. The text in cell A2 is too wide to fit within the cell because the column is too narrow. You'll solve that problem in a moment.

▶ **2.** Type **51-100 Units/Mo** in cell A3, press the **Enter** key, and then click the **OK** button.

▶ **3.** Enter **101-300 Units/Mo** in cell A4 and **>300 Units/Mo** in cell A5. Click the **OK** button in the warning dialog box each time it appears.

▶ **4.** Position the pointer on the divider line between the column A and B headings so that the pointer changes to ╬ , and then double-click. The width of column A is automatically resized so that the widest entry in the column fits in its cell.

▶ **5.** Click the **OK** button in the warning dialog box.

▶ **6.** Click cell **B2**, type **3**, press the **Enter** key, and then click the **OK** button.

▶ **7.** Enter **8** in cell B3, **15** in cell B4, and **20** in cell B5, clicking the OK button each time the warning dialog box appears. The new values appear in cells B2 through B5 in Excel and are reflected in the chart in PowerPoint. See Figure 3-18.

| Figure 3-18 | Complete Excel spreadsheet with data for chart |

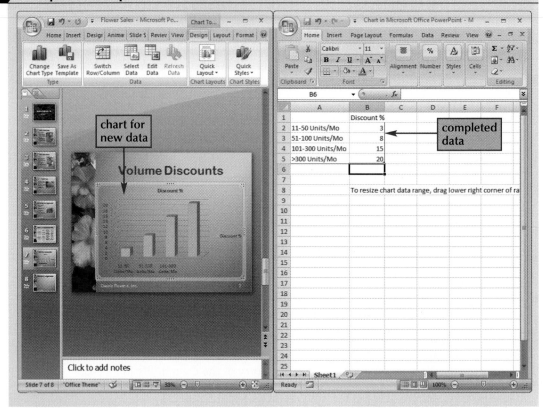

The spreadsheet contains all the necessary data to make the chart. You'll now exit Excel.

To exit Excel and edit the chart:

1. In the title bar in the Excel window, click the **Close** button ☒. The Excel window closes, the Excel data is saved in the PowerPoint presentation, the PowerPoint window expands to fill the full screen, and the new chart appears in Slide 7. See Figure 3-19.

Slide 7 with chart — Figure 3-19

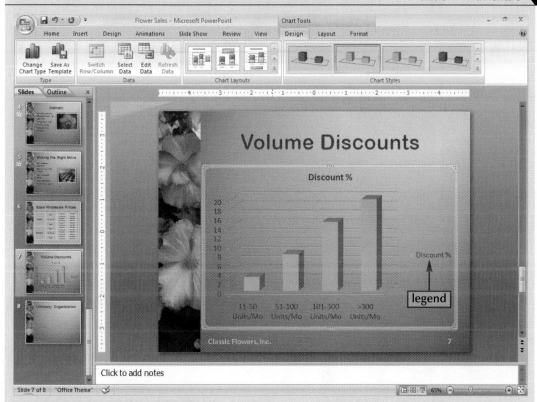

Sophie realizes that the legend on the right side of the chart is unnecessary because all the columns in the chart refer to the discount percentage. You'll now delete the legend.

▶ **2.** Click the **legend** to the right of the chart columns. The legend is selected.

▶ **3.** Press the **Delete** key. The legend disappears from the chart, and the graph expands to fill the space that was occupied by the text box you deleted. You'll now change the chart style.

▶ **4.** If necessary, click the **Design** tab below Chart Tools on the Ribbon.

▶ **5.** In the Chart Styles group, click **Style 4**, the rightmost style in the Chart Styles gallery. The column colors change from pink to purple.

▶ **6.** Click outside the chart region to deselect the chart. See Figure 3-20.

Tip

You can also delete the legend using a command on the Ribbon. With the chart selected, click the Layout tab on the Ribbon, in the Labels group click the Legend button, and then click None.

Figure 3-20 | **Chart after deleting legend**

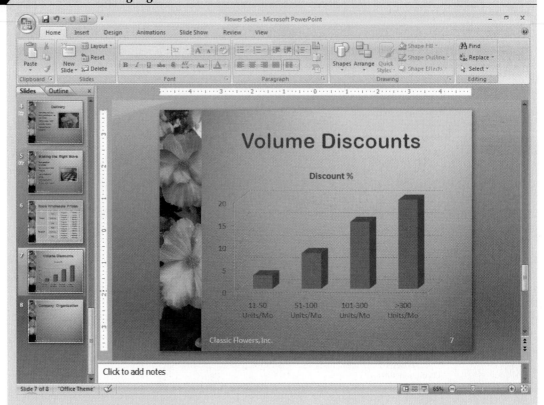

▶ **7.** Save your presentation.

The chart is almost complete, but Sophie wants you to include additional labels on the chart and to make some other minor changes.

To add labels to the chart and make other changes:

▶ **1.** Click anywhere on the chart to make it active, and then click the border around the chart to select the entire chart.

▶ **2.** Click the **Layout** tab below Chart Tools on the Ribbon.

▶ **3.** In the Labels group, click the **Data Labels** button, and then click **Show**. Now the actual values of the discount percent appear on the columns in the chart. Now you'll add vertical gridlines to the chart.

▶ **4.** In the Axes group, click the **Gridlines** button, point to **Primary Vertical Gridlines**, and then click **Major Gridlines**. Now you can see not only horizontal but also vertical gridlines. See Figure 3-21.

Chart after displaying column values and gridlines ◄ Figure 3-21

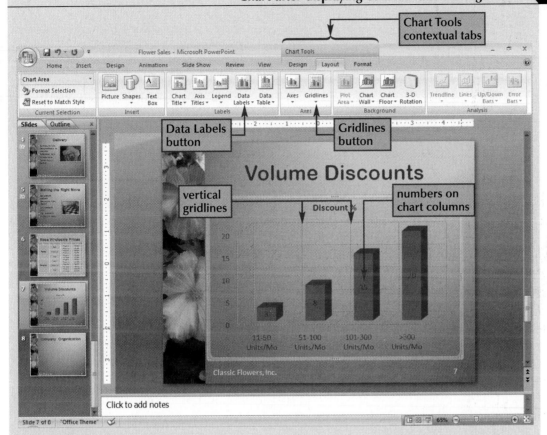

Next, Sophie wants you to add a label to the vertical axis on the left. You'll add rotated text along that axis.

▶ **5.** In the Labels group, click the **Axis Titles** button, point to **Primary Vertical Axis Title**, and then click **Rotated Title**. A text box, rotated so it reads bottom to top parallel to the vertical axis, appears on the chart with the text "Axis Title." The new text box is selected, so you can just start typing to replace it.

▶ **6.** Type **Percent Discount**. The text "Axis Title" is changed to "Percent Discount."

▶ **7.** Click the edge of the chart to select the entire object, and then click the **Format** tab below Chart Tools on the Ribbon.

▶ **8.** In the Shape Styles group, click the **Shape Fill button arrow** to display the theme colors palette.

▶ **9.** Click the **Lavender, Background 1** tile, the first tile in the first row of theme colors. The background of the chart changes to solid light pink.

▶ **10.** Click outside the chart to deselect it. You have now completed the chart. See Figure 3-22.

Figure 3-22 ▶ **Chart with light-pink background**

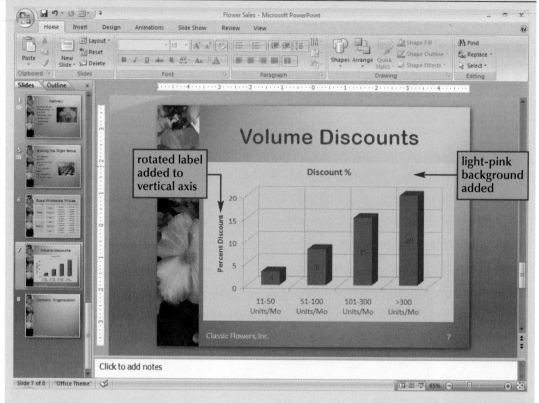

> **11.** Save the presentation.

Sophie is pleased with your chart, which graphically displays the volume discounts offered to customers of Classic Flowers.

Building and Modifying an Organization Chart

Sometimes, potential clients like to know the company organization of Classic Flowers so they know more about the company personnel. Therefore, Sophie wants you to create an organization chart showing key personnel at Classic Flowers. An **organization chart** is a diagram of boxes connected with lines, showing the hierarchy of positions within an organization. Fortunately, PowerPoint provides a feature for easily creating and modifying an organization chart.

Creating an Organization Chart | Reference Window

- Go to the slide in which you want to insert an organization chart.
- Change the slide layout, if necessary, to one of the content layouts, and then click the Insert SmartArt Graphic button, *or* click the Insert tab, and then, in the Illustrations group, click the SmartArt button. The Choose a SmartArt Graphic dialog box opens.
- Click Hierarchy in the pane on the left side of the dialog box to select the type of SmartArt graphic you want.
- In the SmartArt gallery of hierarchy graphics, click Organization Chart, and then click the OK button.
- In the organization chart boxes, type the personnel names, positions, or other information, as desired.
- Add subordinate and coworker boxes as desired.
- Click anywhere outside the organization chart area.

Now you'll insert an organization chart in Slide 8.

To create an organization chart:

▶ **1.** Go to **Slide 8** ("Company Organization"), and then click the **Insert SmartArt Graphic** button ⬚ in the content placeholder. The Choose a SmartArt Graphic dialog box opens.

▶ **2.** Click **Hierarchy** in the pane on the left side of the dialog box to display SmartArt only in that category.

▶ **3.** In the SmartArt gallery of hierarchy graphics, click the **Organization Chart** type (the first chart in the first row), and then click the **OK** button. A sample organization chart, with empty text boxes, appears in the slide.

▶ **4.** Click in the top (Level 1) box. The placeholder text disappears and the insertion point blinks in the box.

▶ **5.** Type **Marjory Cordova**, press the **Enter** key, and then type **President and CEO**. The text is difficult to read because it's light pink on darker pink, but you'll fix the problem later.

▶ **6.** Click the edge of the box just below and to the left of the Level 1 box so that a solid line appears around the box and the entire box is selected. This box represents an assistant to the Level 1, but Sophie doesn't want to show assistants in the organization chart.

▶ **7.** Press the **Delete** key. The assistant box is deleted from the organization chart.

▶ **8.** Click in the leftmost subordinate (Level 2) box, type **Darrell McCarty**, press the **Enter** key, and then type **Director of Operations**.

▶ **9.** Click in the middle Level 2 box, type **Priscilla Rollins**, press the **Enter** key, and then type **Comptroller**.

▶ **10.** Click the rightmost Level 2 box, type **Sophie De Graff**, press the **Enter** key, and then type **Sales Manager**.

▶ **11.** Click outside the Level 2 box but inside the organization chart area to deselect the Level 2 box but keep the entire chart selected. See Figure 3-23.

Figure 3-23 | Slide 8 with organization chart

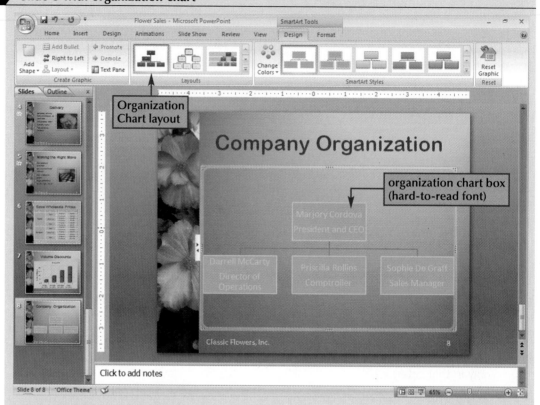

12. Save the presentation.

You have completed part of the organization chart. You'll need to add new boxes, including one more Level 2 box and several subordinate (Level 3) boxes. But first, you'll change the SmartArt style of the organization chart so that the text is more legible.

Changing the Organization Chart Color and Style

To make the text more visible in the organization chart, you could change the text color to, for example, dark green, so it is legible against the pink background, or you could change the background color of the boxes to a darker shade. You'll make the boxes darker.

To change the fill color of the organization chart boxes:

1. With the organization chart still selected, click the **Design** tab, if necessary, below SmartArt Tools on the Ribbon.

2. In the SmartArt Styles group, click the **Change Colors** button. The Change Colors gallery appears.

3. Click the **Dark 2 Fill** icon, the third icon in the first row (under Primary Theme Colors). Now the text is more legible because the boxes have a darker background color. Sophie wants you to add a little interest to the organization chart.

4. In the SmartArt Styles group, click the **Intense Effect** style on the far right of the SmartArt Styles gallery. See Figure 3-24.

Organization chart with new layout and style | Figure 3-24

Now you're ready to add more organization boxes to your organization chart.

Adding Boxes to an Organization Chart

Sophie now wants you to add a box to the organization chart for Kathleen Bahlmann, the chief horticulturalist for the company. She also reports to Marjory Cordova.

To add boxes to the organization chart:

▶ **1.** Click the "Priscilla Rollins" box. You'll add a new box to the right of this box.

▶ **2.** In the Create Graphic group on the Design tab, click the **Add Shape button arrow** to display the Add Shape menu, and then click **Add Shape After**. A new Level 2 box appears between Pricilla Rollins and Sophie De Graff. The new box is selected and ready for you to enter text in it.

▶ **3.** Type **Kathleen Bahlmann**, press the **Enter** key, and then type **Chief Horticulturalist**. You're now ready to add some Level 3 boxes.

▶ **4.** With the "Kathleen Bahlmann" box still selected, in the Create Graphic group click the **Add Shape button arrow**, and then click **Add Shape Below**. A box appears below Kathleen Bahlmann.

▶ **5.** Type **Kyle Wootton**, press the **Enter** key, and then type **Plant Biologist**.

▶ **6.** Click the "Sophie De Graff" box, and then in the Create Graphic group click the **Add Shape** button. A new box is added below the current box. Clicking the button instead of the arrow below the button inserts the type of box inserted the previous time you clicked the Add Shape button.

▶ **7.** Type **Alberto Pendergrass**, press the **Enter** key, and then type **Sales Rep**.

Sophie doesn't like the way the bent lines look between the Level 2 and Level 3 boxes, so she asks you to modify the style of the chart so that the lines go straight down.

▶ **8.** In the Layouts group, point to each of the three styles in the gallery to see how each one looks.

▶ **9.** Click the **Labeled Hierarchy** button. Now you need to increase the font size within the boxes of the organization chart.

▶ **10.** With the organization chart still selected, click the **Home** tab.

▶ **11.** In the Font group, click the **Font Size button arrow**, click **16**, and then deselect the organization chart. See Figure 3-25.

Figure 3-25 ▶ **Slide 8 with completed organization chart**

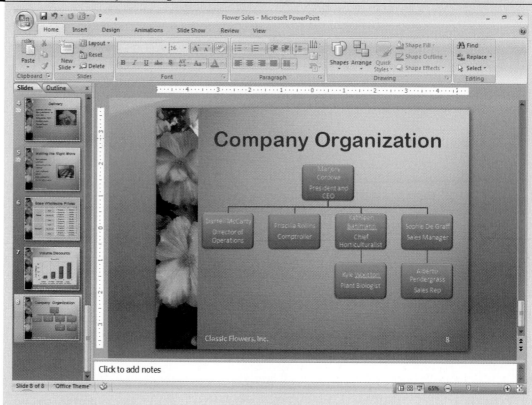

▶ **12.** Save the presentation.

This completes Slide 8 with its organization chart, and completes the text and content of all the slides in the Flower Sales presentation. The only thing left to do is add some special effects and animations.

Applying Special Effects

Special effects—such as fading out of one slide as another appears, animated (moving) text, and sound effects to accompany these actions—can liven up your presentation, help hold your audience's attention, and emphasize key points. On the other hand, special effects can also distract or even annoy your audience. Your goal is to apply special effects conservatively and tastefully so that, rather than making your presentation look gawky and amateurish, they add a professional look and feel to your slide show.

Sophie wants you to add a few special effects to your presentation. The first special effect that you will add is slide transitions.

Adding Slide Transitions

A slide **transition** is a method of moving one slide off the screen and bringing another slide onto the screen during a slide show. Although applying transitions is usually easier in Slide Sorter view because you can easily select several (or all) slides at once, you can also apply a transition in Normal view.

Adding Slide Transitions | Reference Window

- Switch to Slide Sorter view, and then select the slide(s) to which you want to add a transition.
- Click the Animations tab on the Ribbon.
- In the Transition to This Slide group, click the More button to display the gallery of transition effects.
- Click the desired transition effect in the gallery.
- In the Transition to This Slide group, click the Transition Sound button arrow to insert a sound effect that accompanies each transition.
- In the Transition to This Slide group, click the Transition Speed button arrow to modify the speed of the transition.
- In the Transition to This Slide group, click the Apply To All button to apply the transition to all the slides in the presentation.

You'll add a transition to all the slides in the presentation.

To add a transition effect:

▶ 1. On the status bar, click the **Slide Sorter** button 🏁 to switch to Slide Sorter view.

▶ 2. Drag the **Zoom** slider on the status bar to the left to set the zoom to about 95% so you can see all eight slides at once and still have the slides as large as possible.

3. Click the **Animations** tab on the Ribbon. You're going to apply a transition to all the slides in the presentation. You must select at least one slide to make the commands on this tab available.

4. Click **Slide 2**.

5. In the Transition to This Slide group, click the **More** button to display the gallery of slide transitions.

6. Click the **Wipe Right** transition located in the top row, third column under Wipes. PowerPoint previews the transition, and a special effects icon ⭐ appears below the lower-left corner of Slide 2. See Figure 3-26.

Figure 3-26 ▶ **Presentation in Slide Sorter view after applying transition effect**

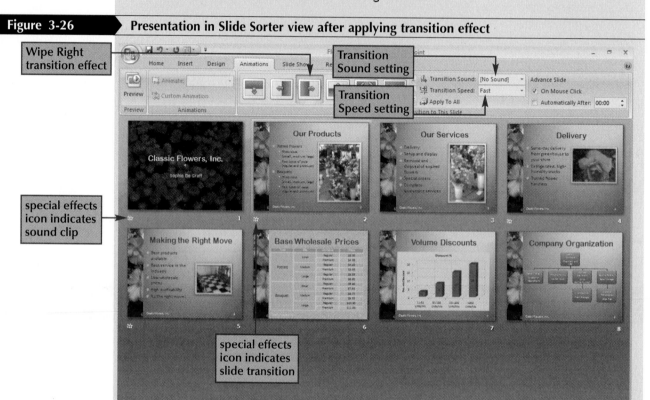

You can change the speed of the transition using the Transition Speed button arrow.

7. In the Transition to This Slide group, click the **Transition Speed button arrow**, and then click **Medium**. This sets the speed at medium, rather than fast or slow. PowerPoint previews the transitions so you can see the type of transition and the speed.

8. In the Transition to This Slide group, click the **Transition Sound button arrow**, and then click **Chime**. This causes a chime to be played during the transition while in Slide Show view.

   Now that you have set the desired transition, speed, and sound to one slide, you can apply it to all the slides in the presentation.

9. In the Transition to This Slide group, click the **Apply To All** button. As indicated in the ScreenTip for this button, clicking this button applies the transition of the current slide to all the other slides.

10. Click a blank area of the slide sorter pane to deselect the slides. Now you'll test the transition.

▶ **11.** Click the **special effects** icon ⭐ below Slide 2. PowerPoint momentarily displays the Slide 1 image at that location, and then performs the Wipe Right transition to Slide 2.

Now, when Sophie advances from one slide to another during a slide show, each slide will wipe onto the screen as a chime sounds.

Now that you've added transitions to the slides, you're ready to add animation.

Animating Bulleted Lists

A PowerPoint **animation** is a special visual or audio effect applied on a slide to an object, such as a graphic or a bulleted list. For example, you can add an animation to display bulleted items on a slide one item at a time. This process is called **progressive disclosure**. When a slide with a bulleted list has a progressive disclosure animation added, only the slide title appears when you first display the slide in your slide show. Then, when you advance the slide show by clicking the left mouse button (or pressing the spacebar or the → key), the first bulleted item appears. When you advance the slide show again, the second bulleted item appears, and so on. The advantage of this type of animation effect is that you can focus your audience's attention on one item at a time, without the distractions of items that you haven't discussed yet.

Applying an Animation | Reference Window

- In Normal view, select the object to which you want to add an animation effect.
- Click the Animations tab on the Ribbon.
- In the Animations group, click the Animate button arrow to display a menu of animations, and then click the desired animation.

or

- In the Animations group, click the Custom Animation button to open the Custom Animation task pane.
- Click the Add Effect button, point to a style, and then click More Effects to open the Add Entrance Effect dialog box.
- Click the desired effect, and then click the OK button.
- Click the Start arrow to choose when the animation starts.
- Click the Speed arrow to choose the speed of the animation.

Because objects on a slide are animated, not the slide itself, the presentation must be in Normal view and an object must be selected for you to choose an animation.

Applying a Custom Animation to Bulleted Lists

PowerPoint Custom Animation supports four general types of animations: Basic (the simplest and most conservative animations), Subtle (less conservative but unobtrusive), Moderate (moderately simple and moderately conservative animations), and Exciting (more complex and less conservative animations). For academic or business presentations, you should generally stick with Basic or Subtle and sometimes Moderate animations. If you're giving a casual or informal presentation, such as one describing a group game or explaining an exciting travel vacation, you might want to use Exciting animations. For this presentation on flowers, you'll apply a Subtle animation.

Now you'll add an animation effect to the bulleted lists in Sophie's presentation. For some presentations, you might include only one or two animations, but Sophie wants to try various animation effects before she completes her final presentation. Because Sophie wants to add the same animation to all the slides that contain a bulleted list and other content, she'll do it all at once by applying the animation to a master layout.

To add an animation to a Slide Master:

▶ **1.** Click the **View** tab on the Ribbon, and then in the Presentation Views group, click the **Slide Master** button.

▶ **2.** Click the **Two Content Layout** thumbnail, which is the fifth thumbnail from the top in the pane to the left of the slide pane. The ScreenTip informs you that this layout is used by Slides 2–5.

▶ **3.** Click the edge of the left content placeholder of the Slide Master in the slide pane. You have to select the object to which you want to apply an animation.

▶ **4.** Click the **Animations** tab on the Ribbon, and then in the Animations group, click the **Animate button arrow**. A menu appears with three general types of animation: Fade, Wipe, and Fly In, and Custom Animation, which you can use to access a wide variety of animation types.

▶ **5.** Click **Custom Animation**. PowerPoint displays the Custom Animation task pane on the right side of the PowerPoint window. See Figure 3-27.

Figure 3-27 ▶ Slide Master with Custom Animation task pane

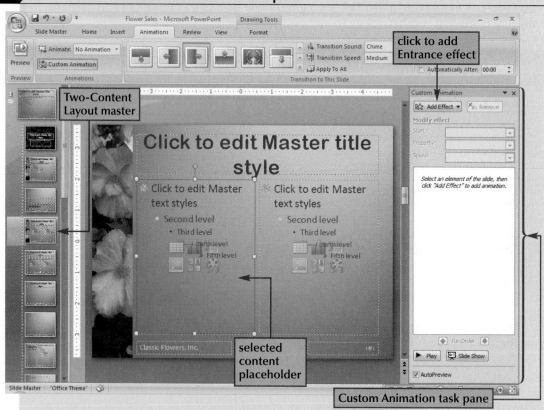

▶ **6.** In the Custom Animation task pane, click the **Add Effect** button, point to **Entrance**, and then click **More Effects** at the bottom of the menu. The Add Entrance Effect dialog box opens. This dialog box shows the various built-in animation effects with which an object can enter the slide during a slide show. You'll test an effect now.

▶ **7.** Click the **Preview Effect** check box, if necessary, at the bottom of the dialog box so that it's selected. This allows you to click an animation effect in the list and watch the animation in the slide pane.

▶ **8.** In the Basic section of the dialog box, click **Fly In**. PowerPoint plays the slide transition you applied earlier, including the sound effect, and then animates the text of the bulleted list in the placeholder. As you can see, Fly In causes the text to scroll up into the slide. Feel free to test other animation entrance effects.

   Trouble? If you can't see the list, drag the dialog box out of the way by its title bar.

▶ **9.** In the Subtle section of the dialog box, click **Expand**. PowerPoint previews the effect for you. You decide to apply this effect to the bulleted lists in the Flower Sales presentation.

▶ **10.** Click the **OK** button. The object is listed in the task pane. See Figure 3-28. The mouse icon next to the object in the task pane indicates that the animation will occur when you advance the slide show.

Custom Animation task pane after adding animation ◀ **Figure 3-28**

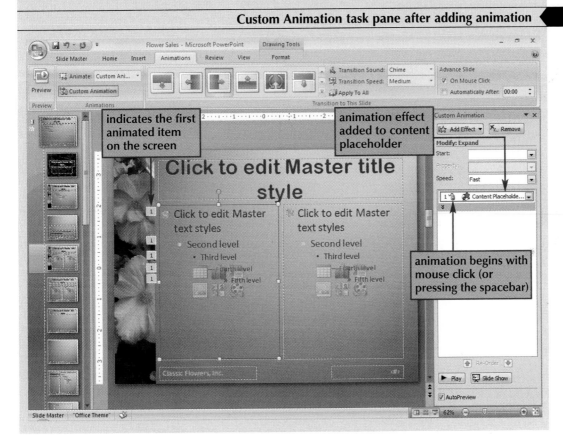

The bulleted items in the left content placeholder are marked with a "1" in little light-blue boxes. This indicates that all five bulleted levels will be animated first among the list of animated objects in this slide. Here, however, you have only one object animated, so you don't see any other numbers besides 1. You'll change that later.

You'll now test the transitions and animation effects you applied to the presentation.

To run a slide show with transitions and animation effects:

▶ **1.** On the status bar, click the **Slide Show** button to start the slide show. PowerPoint displays Slide 1 with the Wipe Right transition effect, makes the chime sound, and then runs the sound clip "Welcome to Classic Flowers, Inc."

▶ **2.** Press the **spacebar** to go to Slide 2, "Our Products." Notice that the title and picture appear in the slide, but not the bulleted list. It will appear, one item at a time in progressive disclosure, as you press the spacebar or the ➔ key or click the left mouse button.

▶ **3.** Press the **spacebar** to display the first-level bulleted item and the two second-level bulleted items below it. Sophie wants you to set up the animation so that the second-level items also appear one at a time in progressive disclosure. You'll do that by modifying the animation effect.

▶ **4.** Continue pressing the **spacebar** to progress through the slide show, and then return to Slide Master view.

▶ **5.** Save the presentation using the default filename.

Modifying the Bulleted-List Animation

Now you'll change the custom animation so that the second-level bulleted items also appear through progressive disclosure.

To set second-level bulleted items to progressive disclosure:

▶ **1.** In the Custom Animation task pane, click the **Click to expand contents arrow** ⬇ located just below the "Content Placeholder" item listed in the task pane. This expands the list of animation items to show the second- through fifth-level bulleted items.

▶ **2.** In the list of animated items, click **Second level**, and then click the **Start** arrow, near the top of the task pane. A three-item menu appears with *On Click* (meaning that the animation begins when you click the left mouse button or press the Spacebar or the ➔ key), *With Previous* (meaning that the animation occurs with the previous animated item, in this case the first-level bulleted item), and *After Previous* (meaning that the animation occurs after the previous animation).

▶ **3.** Click **On Click**. A mouse icon appears next to the second-level item in the task pane. Now the second- through fifth-level bulleted items will animate as a group, but only after you click the mouse button after the first-level bulleted item has animated onto the screen during a slide show. See Figure 3-29.

Slide Master with second-level animation ◄ **Figure 3-29**

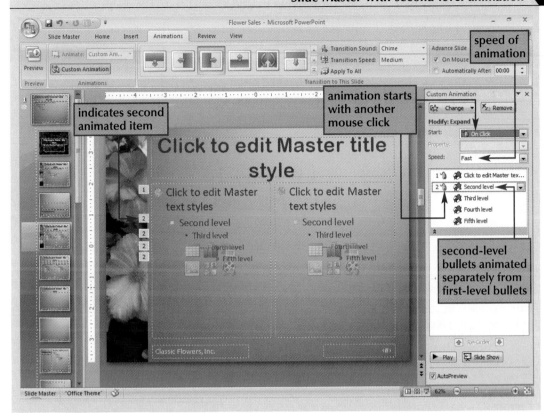

Next, Sophie wants you to add a special feature to the progressive disclosure: dimming after animation. When a bulleted item dims after animation, it changes color, usually to a lighter color, as the next bulleted item animates onto the screen during a slide show.

To set the bulleted items to dim after animation:

▶ **1.** In the Custom Animation task pane, click the **Click to edit Master...** box (the first animated item in the list), and then click the arrow that appears on the right side of that box, which displays a menu of items that allow you to change the animation effect.

▶ **2.** Click **Effect Options** on the menu. The Expand dialog box opens.

▶ **3.** Click the **After animation** arrow, and then click the dark purple color tile, located on the far right in the first row of color tiles.

▶ **4.** Click the **OK** button. PowerPoint plays the animation and demonstrates the dimming after animation.

   Trouble? If you don't see the animation, click the Play button at the bottom of the Custom Animation task pane.

▶ **5.** Repeat this procedure for the second-level bulleted items so that they also dim after animation to the same purple color.

Now you'll view the modified animations.

To view progressive disclosure with dimming after animation:

▶ 1. On the status bar, click the **Slide Show** button to start the slide show.

▶ 2. Press the **spacebar** to advance to Slide 2, and then press the **spacebar** again to display the first bulleted item. This time, the second-level bulleted items don't automatically appear with the first-level item.

▶ 3. Press the **spacebar** again. The first-level bulleted item dims to purple, and the second-level bulleted item appears in the normal color (dark green). See Figure 3-30.

Figure 3-30 ▶ Slide 2 in Slide Show view

▶ 4. Continue advancing through the slide show for two or three more slides so you can see how the animation works.

▶ 5. Press the **Esc** key to terminate the slide show and return to Slide Master view.

▶ 6. On the status bar, click the **Normal** button to return to Normal view.

▶ 7. Save the presentation.

Applying a Custom Animation to a Chart

Sophie now wants you to apply an animation effect to the chart in Slide 7. You'll use PowerPoint's Custom Animation feature, which works for any type of graphic—chart, graph, pictures, and so forth.

To animate a chart:

▶ **1.** Go to **Slide 7** ("Volume Discounts"), click anywhere in the chart, and then click the edge of the chart to select the entire object.

▶ **2.** Make sure the Custom Animation task pane is still open in the PowerPoint window.

▶ **3.** In the Custom Animation task pane, click the **Add Effect** button. For this animation, rather than selecting a method by which the object enters the screen, you'll select an animation effect that emphasizes an object that already appears on the screen in Slide Show view.

▶ **4.** Point to **Emphasis**, and then click **More Effects**. The Add Emphasis Effect dialog box opens.

▶ **5.** In the Moderate section, click **Teeter**. This effect causes the object to teeter back and forth for a second when it appears on the slide.

▶ **6.** Click the **OK** button.

▶ **7.** At the top of the task pane, click the **Speed** arrow, and then click **Slow**. The teetering motion will occur slowly.

▶ **8.** At the top of the task pane, click the **Start** arrow, and then click **With Previous**. The teetering will occur as the slide appears on the screen in Slide Show view, rather than when you click the mouse button after the slide appears.

▶ **9.** Click the **Play** button at the bottom of the Custom Animation task pane to preview the animations in Slide 7.

▶ **10.** In the task pane, click the Close button ✕ , and then save the presentation.

This completes the presentation. You could edit each slide, one at a time, with custom animations to focus on key information or to add interest and excitement to the slide. But Sophie feels that the presentation has enough animation.

Now you'll run through the entire slide show to see how all of the animation effects, transitions, video clip, and so on will appear.

To view the entire slide show:

▶ **1.** Go to **Slide 1**, and then on the status bar click the **Slide Show** button 🖵 . The slide show starts with Slide 1 "wiping right" onto the screen and playing the sound clip. These are the special effects you added to Slide 1.

▶ **2.** While still in Slide 1, click the **sound** icon ◀ . This demonstrates that, even though you've set the sound clip to play automatically when the slide starts, you can also play the sound clip anytime while Slide 1 appears on screen.

▶ **3.** Click the left mouse button or press the **spacebar** to move to Slide 2, and then press the **spacebar** as needed to advance through the animation of the bulleted list, until the last bulleted item dims (changes to purple text).

▶ **4.** Press the **spacebar** to continue through the slide show until the title of **Slide 4** ("Delivery") appears on the screen, and then click the left mouse button or press the **spacebar** three more times to display the three bulleted items. The sound clip of applause automatically plays just after the third item appears.

▶ **5.** Advance to **Slide 5** ("Making the Right Move"), click the left mouse button or press the **spacebar** until all the bulleted items have appeared and dimmed on the screen. The movie then runs automatically in full-screen view.

6. Advance to **Slide 6** ("Base Wholesale Prices"), the slide with the pink tissue paper textured background. This slide has no animation, except for the slide transition.

7. Advance to **Slide 7** ("Volume Discounts"). The column chart slowly and automatically teeters back and forth for three seconds.

8. Press the **spacebar** three more times to finish the slide show and return to Normal view.

9. Save the presentation using the default filename.

Sophie now wants to practice her presentation, including marking slides with the pointer pen.

Marking Slides During a Slide Show

During a slide show, you can mark the slides to emphasize a point using the pointer pen. The **pen** is a mouse pointer that allows you to draw lines on the screen during a slide show. For example, you might use it to underline a word or phrase that you want to emphasize, or to circle a graphic that you want to point out. PowerPoint gives you the option of three pen types: Ballpoint Pen (draws thin, usually blue lines), Felt Tip Pen (draws thicker, usually red lines), and Highlighter (draws thick, usually yellow, transparent lines). You can change the ink color of any of the pens you select. You can also select the Eraser tool to remove pen lines that you've already drawn.

After you go through a presentation and mark it, PowerPoint gives you the choice of keeping the markings or discarding them. Now you'll show Sophie how to use the pointer pen.

To use the pen during a slide show:

1. Go to **Slide 7** and start the slide show. The graph appears and then teeters.

2. Move the mouse until you see the mouse pointer. The pointer appears on the screen, but it will disappear again if you don't move the mouse for a couple seconds.

3. Right-click anywhere on the screen, point to **Pointer Options** on the shortcut menu, and then click **Felt Tip Pen**. You can use the Pointer Options shortcut menu to select the type of pen, the ink color, and other options. After you have selected the Felt Tip Pen, the mouse pointer becomes a small, red dot. By clicking and dragging the pen on the screen, you can draw lines.

4. Click the left mouse button, and then drag to draw a circle around the second column (the one that represents 8% discount) to draw attention to it. See Figure 3-31.

Slide 7 in Slide Show view with felt-tip pen ink mark ◀ Figure 3-31

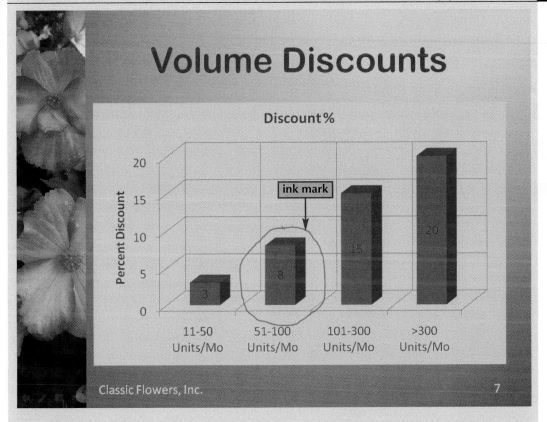

5. Press the **spacebar** to move to **Slide 8**. Note that you can't click the left mouse button to proceed through the slide show while a pointer pen is selected. Also note that the Felt Tip Pen is still active when you change slides, so you can now draw on Slide 8.

6. Click and drag to underline Sophie De Graff's name on the organization chart.

7. Right-click anywhere on the slide, point to **Pointer Options** on the shortcut menu, and then click **Arrow**. The mouse pointer changes back to the ordinary arrow pointer. Now you can click the mouse button to advance the slide show.

8. Click the left mouse button to terminate the slide show and display a blank screen, and then click the left mouse button again to return to Normal view. A dialog box opens asking if you want to keep your ink annotations. You don't want to save the marks with your presentation.

9. Click the **Discard** button.

As you can see, the pointer pen is a powerful tool for highlighting and pointing out information during a slide show.

Hiding Slides

Sophie tells you that some slides aren't appropriate for all prospective clients. For example, if she is giving the presentation to a manager of a small floral shop, she doesn't want to show the manager the volume discounts. In that case, she can temporarily hide that slide so it won't even show up during the presentation. She asks you to show her how to hide a slide.

To hide and unhide a slide:

▶ **1.** Go to **Slide 7**, if necessary. This is the slide you want to hide.

▶ **2.** Click the **Slide Show** tab on the Ribbon.

▶ **3.** In the Set Up group, click the **Hide Slide** button. The button is selected and PowerPoint marks the slide number in the Slides tab so that you know that the slide will be hidden during the slide show. See Figure 3-32. Now you'll see your slides in Slide Show view.

Figure 3-32 **Slide 7 after hiding slide**

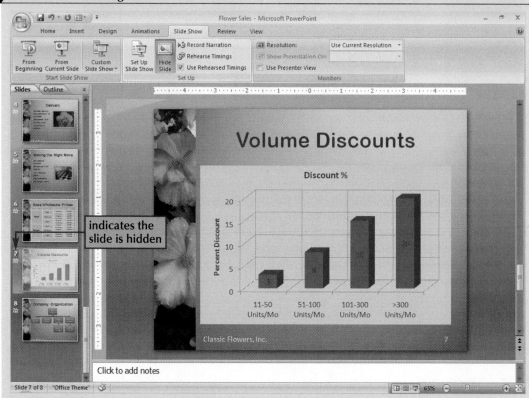

indicates the slide is hidden

▶ **4.** Go to **Slide 6**, and then on the status bar click the **Slide Show** button ⬚. Slide 6 appears in Slide Show view.

▶ **5.** Press the **spacebar** or click the left mouse button. Slide 8 ("Company Organization") appears on screen. The slide show skipped Slide 7 ("Volume Discounts") as you intended.

▶ **6.** Press the **Esc** key to end the slide show.

Now that you've seen how to hide a slide, you should go back and "unhide" it so it will be available for Sophie's presentation to the board of directors.

To unhide a slide:

▶ **1.** In Normal view, go to **Slide 7**.

▶ **2.** In the Set Up group on the Slide Show tab, click the **Hide Slide** button again. This toggles the Hide Slide effect off for Slide 7. The hidden slide icon disappears from the Slides tab.

▶ **3.** Go to **Slide 6**, switch to Slide Show view, and then press the **spacebar** to view Slide 7, verifying that it does indeed show up in the slide show now.

▶ **4.** Return to Normal view, and then save your presentation using the default filename.

▶ **5.** Submit the presentation in electronic or printed form as requested by your instructor.

Sophie is confident that her presentation will go smoothly, providing the needed information to her audiences in an engaging manner. Your final tasks are to help her prepare the materials to run not only on her computer, but also on the computers in the rooms where she'll give her presentations.

Preparing the Presentation to Run on Another Computer

Sophie will present the electronic (on-screen) slide show to store and floral department managers in conference rooms, classrooms, and other locations that might or might not have PowerPoint installed on their computers. She knows that she doesn't need Power-Point installed because she can use **PowerPoint Viewer**, a separate program that you can install and use on any computer that runs Windows to show your PowerPoint presentation. Sophie can't modify any of the slides using the PowerPoint Viewer, and some of the special effects might not work with the Viewer, but she could at least give the complete presentation.

To prepare the presentation to run on any computer, you can use the **Package for CD** feature to create a CD or a folder that you can store on portable media, such as a USB flash drive, that contains a copy of the presentation and PowerPoint Viewer. Sophie can then use this CD or flash drive to install the Viewer and run the presentation file.

Because each computer that runs Windows can have different fonts installed, you can save the presentation with the fonts embedded. With embedded fonts, the presentation will always have the desired fonts, even if they are not installed on the computer where you present the slide show. Be aware, however, that embedding fonts increases the size of the presentation file, so if you plan to embed fonts, make sure the final file size of the packaged presentation will still fit on the CD or flash drive.

Before completing the following steps, consult with your instructor. You'll need a computer with a CD or DVD writer (often called a CD or DVD "burner") and a blank, unused, writable CD or DVD, or you'll need a flash drive with at least 20 MB of free space.

The following steps show you how to complete the process using a flash drive, but the process works almost the same using a CD or DVD. If you create a CD or DVD, insert the blank disc in the computer drive before you start the steps.

To package the presentation to a folder:

▶ **1.** Click the **Office Button** 🔘, point to **Publish**, and then click **Package for CD**. The Package for CD dialog box opens. See Figure 3-33. First, you'll make sure the fonts will be embedded in the packaged presentation.

Trouble? If PowerPoint displays a message warning you about updating to compatible file formats, click the OK button.

Figure 3-33	Package for CD dialog box

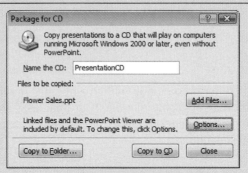

▶ **2.** Click the **Options** button. The Options dialog box opens. See Figure 3-34.

Figure 3-34	Options dialog box for creating a Package for CD

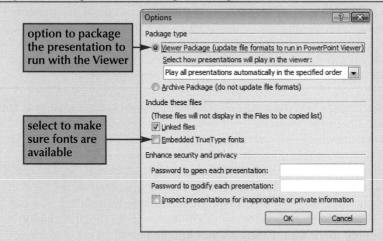

option to package the presentation to run with the Viewer

select to make sure fonts are available

▶ **3.** If necessary, click the **Embedded TrueType fonts** check box to select it. This ensures that the computer on which you run the slide show will have the necessary fonts.

▶ **4.** Click the **OK** button. The Options dialog box closes and the Package for CD dialog box is visible again.

▶ **5.** Click the **Copy to Folder** button. The Copy to Folder dialog box opens.

Trouble? If you are copying your presentation to a CD or DVD, click Cancel to close this dialog box, click the Copy to CD button, and then skip to Step 8.

▶ **6.** Click the **Browse** button and navigate to your flash drive or to the **Tutorial.03\ Tutorial** folder, and then click the **Select** button. You won't change the default name for the folder, PresentationCD.

▶ **7.** Click the **OK** button. A dialog box opens asking if you want to include linked files in your package.

▶ **8.** Click the **Yes** button. Another dialog box opens briefly as PowerPoint copies all the necessary files to the PresentationCD folder or disc, including the file Flower Sales, any needed TrueType fonts, and PowerPoint Viewer.

Trouble? If a dialog box appears warning you that the movie file couldn't be processed, click the OK button. PowerPoint will display only a still photo in place of the movie when you show the presentation with the PowerPoint Viewer.

▶ **9.** Click the **Close** button in the Package for CD dialog box.

You should test the packaged presentation to make sure it works.

To run the PowerPoint presentation from a folder:

▶ **1.** If you packaged the presentation to a USB flash drive, insert the flash drive into an available USB port on your computer. The Removable Disk dialog box opens.

Trouble? If the Removable Disk dialog box doesn't appear, use Explorer to navigate to the flash drive, and then proceed with Step 3.

Trouble? If you packaged the presentation to the Tutorial.03\Tutorial folder, open an Explorer window, and then skip to Step 3.

Trouble? If you packaged the presentation on a CD or DVD, insert the CD or DVD into the drive, and then skip to Step 5.

▶ **2.** Click the **Open folder to view files** button in the dialog box, and then click the **OK** button. An Explorer window opens.

▶ **3.** Navigate in the window to the **PresentationCD** folder on the flash drive or in the Tutorial.03\Tutorial folder, and then double-click the folder to open it.

▶ **4.** Double-click the file **PPTVIEW**. This is the PowerPoint Viewer.

A dialog box opens with only one file visible, Flower Sales.

Trouble? If a dialog box opens asking if you want to run this file, click the Run button.

Trouble? If a dialog box opens containing the PowerPoint Viewer license agreement, read through the agreement, and then click the Accept button.

▶ **5.** Double-click **Flower Sales**. The slide show starts.

▶ **6.** Advance through the presentation by clicking the left mouse button or pressing the **spacebar** or the → key.

Trouble? If, after the movie plays in Slide 5, you cannot proceed to the next slide by pressing the spacebar or the → key, move the mouse until the mouse pointer appears, and then click the left mouse button.

Trouble? If the presentation doesn't work exactly as you prepared it, don't worry. Some features don't translate to the packaged presentation exactly.

▶ **7.** After the blank screen appears at the end of the presentation, click the left mouse button or press the **spacebar** to end the presentation. The PowerPoint Viewer dialog box appears again.

▶ **8.** Close the Microsoft Office PowerPoint Viewer dialog box, and then close the Explorer window.

Now Sophie can show her presentation on any computer, even if that computer does not have PowerPoint installed.

Delivering a Presentation with Two Monitors (Podium Mode)

Sophie knows she will deliver her presentation in lecture halls with large projection screens and wants to take advantage of a special PowerPoint feature: delivering a presentation with two monitors. This is sometimes called **podium mode** because it involves one monitor at the podium that only the presenter can see and another monitor (such as a projection screen) that the audience can see. For example, in properly equipped lecture halls, Sophie will connect her laptop computer to the video projector, set up her laptop for multiple monitors, set up PowerPoint to run on multiple monitors, and then use podium mode to give her presentation.

In podium mode, the presenter and the audience see the normal Slide Show view on the second monitor, and the presenter also sees a special PowerPoint window, called **Presenter View**, on the first (podium) monitor. In the Presenter View window, you can do the following:

- View thumbnails of the presentation slides. The thumbnails help you see the next slides before you display them and see previous slides. You can click any thumbnail to jump to that slide in your presentation. This is especially valuable while answering questions when you might need to jump back to a previous slide.
- See the speaker's notes in large, readable type so you can easily read the notes and use them as a script for your presentation.
- Blank out the screen at any time during a presentation. This allows you to stop and answer questions, take a break in the middle of the presentation, or pause for group discussion in the middle of a presentation without the distraction of the PowerPoint presentation on the projection screen.
- See (in large type) the time of day, time elapsed since starting your presentation, and pen options (so you can switch the mouse pointer to a pen without having to right-click on the screen viewed by the audience).

Sophie asks you to prepare her laptop computer for podium mode.

Note: These steps assume that you have a laptop computer and a separate monitor. If you do not have this equipment, read through the next set of steps without executing them.

To turn on multiple-monitor support:

> 1. With your laptop computer turned off, connect a second monitor to the external monitor port.

> 2. Turn on the second monitor and your laptop computer.

> 3. After Windows is started on your laptop, right-click the Windows desktop, and then click **Personalize** on the shortcut menu.

> 4. In the Personalization window, click the **Display Settings** link. The Display Settings dialog box opens. See Figure 3-35.

Tip

You can also turn on Podium mode and access the Display Settings dialog box by clicking the Slide Show tab, and then, in the Monitors group, clicking the Use Presenter View check box.

Display Settings for setting up for two-monitor presentation ◀ **Figure 3-35**

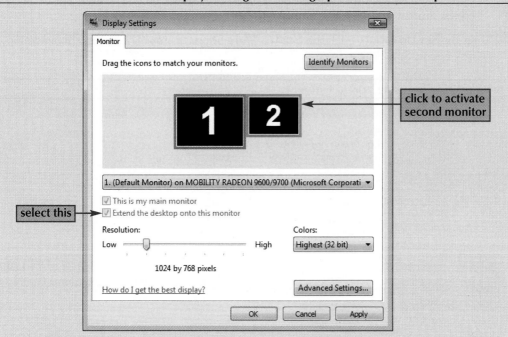

Display Settings for setting up for two-monitor presentation ◀ Figure 3-35

5. Click the arrow of the drop-down menu box below the monitor icons, and then click the option that corresponds to the video card on your computer that supports multiple monitors.

Trouble? If none of the options listed in the Display list include the phrase "(Multiple Monitors)", it probably means that your laptop doesn't support an external monitor, in which case you won't be able to complete these steps. Click the Cancel button, and then read, but do not perform, the rest of these steps.

6. Make a note of the resolution of the laptop monitor, and then click the **monitor 2** thumbnail in the Monitor tab of the dialog box, as indicated in Figure 3-35.

7. Click the **Extend the desktop onto this monitor** check box, if necessary, to make sure it's selected.

8. If necessary, drag the **Resolution** slider, if allowed to do so, until the resolution is the same as on your laptop.

Trouble? If you can't adjust the resolution of the second monitor, just leave it as is and continue these steps. The two-monitor system will probably still work properly.

9. Click the **OK** button.

10. If Windows warns you that your desktop has been reconfigured and tells you that it will revert to the old configuration automatically in a certain number of seconds, click the **Yes** button to accept the changes.

Trouble? If both monitors are not displaying the desktop properly, repeat the preceding steps, as necessary, but try a different resolution for the second monitor in Step 8.

Now that the desktop appears on both monitors, you're ready to set up podium mode in PowerPoint and show your presentation with two monitors.

To set up a slide show for podium mode:

▶ **1.** With the Flower Sales presentation open on the laptop, click the **Slide Show** tab on the Ribbon, if necessary.

▶ **2.** In the Set Up group, click the **Set Up Slide Show** button. The Set Up Show dialog box opens. See Figure 3-36.

Figure 3-36 ▶ Set Up Show for using podium view

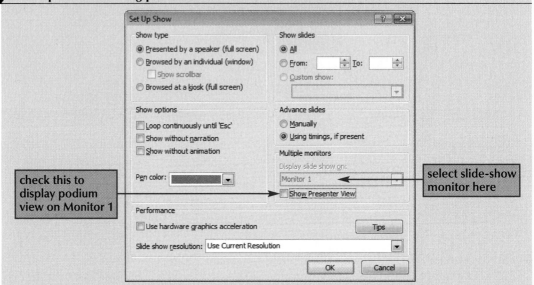

check this to display podium view on Monitor 1

select slide-show monitor here

▶ **3.** In the Multiple monitors section of the dialog box, click the **Display slide show on arrow**, and then, if necessary, click **Monitor 2 Default Monitor** or **Monitor 2 Plug and Play Monitor**, whichever of these two phrases appears in the menu. If you followed the steps in the previous set of steps, Monitor 1 is your laptop; monitor 2 is the external monitor.

▶ **4.** Click the **Show Presenter View** check box. This tells PowerPoint that you want to see the podium-view window.

▶ **5.** Click the **OK** button to close the dialog box.

Now you're ready to use podium mode to deliver the presentation.

To give a slide show in podium mode:

▶ **1.** In the Start Slide Show group, click the **From Beginning** button. Slide 1 of your presentation appears on monitor 2 in normal Slide Show view, and on monitor 1 (the laptop) in the PowerPoint Presenter View window. See Figure 3-37. Look over this figure so you understand the features of Presenter View.

Podium view during a slide show ◀ Figure 3-37

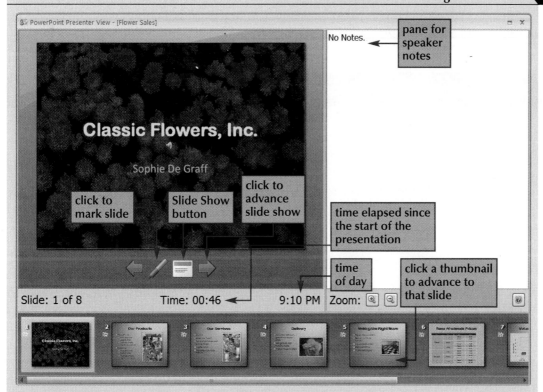

Trouble? If your laptop shows the slide and the other monitor displays the Presenter View window, close the Presenter View window, which automatically terminates the presentation in the other monitor, and then repeat the previous set of steps, but change the monitors in Step 3.

▶ **2.** In the Presenter View window, click the large blue right arrow button to advance to Slide 2. In Presenter View, you can't click the left mouse button to advance the presentation, but you can use the spacebar and the arrow keys on your laptop keyboard, or you can click the thumbnails at the bottom of the Presenter View window. Slide 2 appears in the Presenter View window and on the second monitor.

▶ **3.** Click the **Slide 5** thumbnail at the bottom of the Presenter View window. Slide 5 appears on both monitors.

▶ **4.** Display the animated lists in Slide 5, and then continue on to **Slide 6**.

▶ **5.** Click the **Pointer Options** button 🖊, select one of the pens, and then underline the title on the slide in the Presenter View window.

▶ **6.** Note that you can use your mouse to draw on either the slide in Slide Show view on monitor 2 or on the slide in the slide pane in Presenter View.

▶ **7.** When you have finished, click the **Slide Show** button in the Presenter View window, and then click **End Show**.

▶ **8.** In the dialog box that opens asking if you want to save your annotations, click the **Discard** button.

▶ **9.** Close the presentation.

You have completed Sophie's presentation. Sophie believes that the graphics, sound, and special effects for the on-screen slide show will help her audience stay focused on her presentation. She is pleased to be prepared with a packaged presentation containing the PowerPoint Viewer and with the option of giving the presentation in podium mode. She thanks you for your help.

Review | **Session 3.2 Quick Check**

1. What is a video clip?
2. Describe how you insert a chart into a slide.
3. What is an organization chart?
4. How do you insert an organization chart into a slide?
5. Define the following terms:
   a. transition effect
   b. animation effect
   c. sound effect
   d. pointer pen
   e. podium mode
6. Describe how you add a transition effect to a slide.
7. What is the PowerPoint Viewer?

Review | **Tutorial Summary**

In this tutorial, you learned how to insert slides from another presentation and how to create a theme by creating custom theme colors and backgrounds and by changing the font typeface and font color. You also learned how to add a background image, apply graphics and sound in the form of digital images, video clips, and audio clips, and add a textured background. You also learned how to create a chart (graph) and an organization chart, and how to apply special effects such as slide transitions and animations. You learned how to use the pointer pen to mark slides during a slide show, to hide a slide, and to prepare the presentation to run on another computer. Finally, you learned how to run the slide show with two monitors (podium mode).

Key Terms

active cell	Office theme	progressive disclosure
animation	organization chart	special effect
cell	Package for CD	spreadsheet
chart	pen	theme colors
digital movie	podium mode	transition
gradient fill	PowerPoint Viewer	video clip
graph	Presenter View	

| Practice | **Review Assignments** |

Practice the skills you learned in the tutorial using the same case scenario.

Data Files needed for the Review Assignments: Farm.avi, HotSprings.pptx, HSProposal.pptx, Knock.wav

The chief horticulturalist for Classic Flowers, Inc., Kathleen Bahlmann, recently became aware that a particular farm in southern Georgia is for sale. The farm is special because it has a natural hot spring on its premises. The farm owner has set up a system to use water from the hot spring to heat his barns during the winter. Now that the farm is for sale, Kathleen sees this as an opportunity to improve the profitability of Classic Flowers by purchasing the farm, converting the barns to greenhouses, and using the water from the hot spring to heat the greenhouses. This has the potential of saving millions of dollars on heating expenses over the next several years. Kathleen wants to present her idea to the board of directors of Classic Flowers, and she has asked you to help her create the PowerPoint presentation. She has already created a couple of PowerPoint presentation files; one contains a title slide with some elements that she wants to use for a design theme, and the other contains some of the text that she wants in the final presentation.

1. Open the file **HSProposal**, located in the Tutorial.03\Review folder included with the Data Files, change the subtitle from "Kathleen Bahlmann" to your name, and then save the file as **Hot Springs Proposal** in the same Tutorial.03\Review folder.

2. Modify the current theme colors, which are the Flower theme colors that you created earlier in this tutorial by changing the Text/Background – Dark 1 color from dark green to dark purple and changing the Text/Background – Light 2 from light yellow to white. For the Text/Background – Dark 1 color, pick the dark purple that appears on the Standard tab of the Colors dialog box on the far-right corner of the hexagonal palette of color tiles. For the Text/Background – Light 2 color, use the pure white, large, hexagonal tile near the lower-left corner of the dialog box, to the left of the double row of grayscale tiles. Save the new color set using the name **HotSprings**.

3. In Slide Master view, change the background color of the Office Theme Slide Master to "Dark Purple, Text 1," which is the dark purple color you set for Text/Background Dark 1. (*Hint*: Open the Format Background dialog box, and then, with the Solid fill option button selected, click the Color button.) Apply this dark purple color to all the slides.

4. Change the background style to Style 12, which is a gradient from dark purple in the upper-left corner of the background to lighter purple in the lower-right corner.

5. In the Office Theme Slide Master, do the following:
   a. Change the title text to white.
   b. Change the color of the first-level bulleted-list text to Lavender, Text 1.
   c. Change the second-level bulleted-list text color to the lightest yellow color available in the palette.
   d. Change the third-level bulleted-list text color to white.
   e. Change the first-level bullet to a picture of a yellow-gold square.
   f. Change the second-level bullet to a picture of a smaller green and pale green square.

6. In the Title Slide Layout master, change the subtitle text color to Yellow, Accent 5.

7. Save the presentation using the default filename, and then save it as a new Office theme to the Tutorial.03\Review folder using the filename **Flower2**.

8. Close the PowerPoint presentation file, but leave PowerPoint running.

9. Start a new, blank PowerPoint presentation, and then change its design theme to Flower2.

10. Insert the slide from the file **Hot Springs Proposal**, and then delete the extra (blank) title slide, leaving only one title slide.

11. Insert Slides 2 through 7 (that is, all but the first slide) from the file **HotSprings**, located in the **Tutorial.03\Review** folder.

12. To Slide 1, apply the slide transition Comb Horizontal in the Stripes and Bars section, and then change the slide-transition speed to Medium.

13. Add the sound effect Whoosh to the slide transition, and then apply the transition for Slide 1 to all the slides.

14. In Slide 2, change the animation so that the bulleted list uses progressive disclosure with dimming. Use the Animate button to set the animation to the Fade effect, and then use the Custom Animation task pane to set the dimming color to dark green.

15. In Slide 3, select the two text boxes (but not the slide title) and apply the custom animation Zoom, located in the Moderate section of the Add Entrance Effect dialog box.

16. In Slide 4, insert a chart using the 3-D Clustered Column style.

17. In the Excel spreadsheet for the PowerPoint chart, do the following:
    a. Change cell B1 to **Heating Costs (in millions)**.
    b. Change cell C1 to **Profits (in millions)**.
    c. Delete the column with Series 3.
    d. Change Category 1 through Category 4 (cell A2 through cell A5) to the years **2006** through **2009**, and then add **2010** in cell A6.
    e. In cells B2 through B6 (below Heating Costs), replace the current cell contents with **1.8**, **2.2**, **2.7**, **3.3**, **4.1**. Format these cells as Currency by clicking the Accounting Number Format button in the Number group. Decrease the decimal to one place by clicking the Decrease Decimal button in the Number group.
    f. In cells C2 through C6 (below Profits), replace the current cell contents with **3.2**, **3.1**, **2.9**, **2.7**, **2.5**. On the Home tab in the Excel window, click the Number button, and then click the Accounting Number Format button to format these numbers as currency.

18. In Slide 5, click in the bulleted list text box, click the Home tab, in the Paragraph group, click the Convert to SmartArt Graphic button, and then click the Organization Chart graphic in the gallery.

19. After "Tom Briggs" in the top box, press the Enter key, and then type **Farm Manager**. Similarly, add the title **Greenhouse Manager** to the three second-level boxes. Don't add titles to the three subordinate boxes below Alice Abernathy.

20. Change the layout of the organization chart to Hierarchy, and then change the color of the organization chart to Dark 2 Outline (green).

21. In Slide 6, add the movie **Farm** located in the Tutorial.03\Review folder. Set it to start When Clicked.

22. In Slide 7, insert the sound clip **Knock**, located in the Tutorial.03\Review folder. Set it to start Automatically.

23. Add the Zoom custom animation entrance effect to each of the two text items in Slide 7, and then set the Start option to After Previous so that they play one after another. Drag the Knock sound in the animation pane so it is second in the list.

24. Hide Slide 5.

25. Save the presentation using the filename **Hot Springs Proposal**, so that it replaces the current file of that name in the Tutorial.03\Review folder. Run the slide show, making sure you click the movie in Slide 6 to play it. Use the Felt Tip Pen tool to underline the title in Slide 7. Discard this annotation.

26. Delete the custom color set HotSprings.

27. Package the presentation for a CD, either to a CD or DVD, a USB flash drive, or to the Tutorial.03\Review folder. Name the CD or the folder **Packaged Hot Springs**. If you get an error that PowerPoint can't package the file Farm.avi, continue anyway.

28. Insert the CD or open an Explorer window and navigate to the location of the packaged presentation, start the PowerPoint Viewer, and then run the packaged presentation. Close the PowerPoint Viewer dialog box and the Explorer window when you are finished.

29. Submit the final presentation and the packaged presentation in printed or electronic form, as directed by your instructor.

| Apply | | Case Problem 1 |

Apply the skills you learned to create a presentation for an eBay store.

Data Files needed for this Case Problem: CompCase.avi, eBayCase.pptx, JustInCase.pptx, PhoneCase.jpg

Just in Case, an eBay Store Jergen Oleson is a small-electronics aficionado. He had the latest in electronic gadgets—MP3 player, cell phone, palm computer, laptop, GPS receiver, digital camera, and so forth. But he was always frustrated in trying to find proper cases for these items. He was surprised, in fact, by the dearth of companies that sold cases for electronic gadgets. So he decided to start his own company, which he called Just in Case, and to sell his products through his own eBay store. He now asks you to help him create a theme for his PowerPoint presentations and to start creating a presentation that he will give to potential manufacturers of his cases. Do the following:

1. Open the presentation file **JustInCase**, located in the Tutorial.03\Case1 folder included with the Data Files. This is a file with the Just in Case logo placed on three of the slide masters and with modifications to the size, location, and text justification of some of the placeholders. You'll continue creating the Office theme file from here.

2. Create a new set of theme colors using the colors shown in Figure 3-38. Save the theme colors using the name **JustInCase**.

Figure 3-38

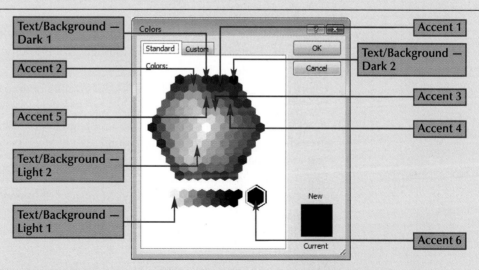

3. Apply the background style Style 4 (solid dark blue, the Text/Background – Dark 1 color).

4. In the Office Theme Slide Master, do the following:
   a. Change the title font to Arial Black.
   b. Change the body text font to Times New Roman.
   c. Change the first-level bullet to a filled square bullet with the Light Yellow, Text 2 theme color.
   d. Change the second-level bullet to a filled round bullet with the Light Blue, Accent 3 theme color.
   e. Change the third-level bullet to a white, hollow, round bullet.
   f. Change the second-level text color to the Light Yellow, Text 2 theme color.
5. Save the presentation as an Office Theme file to the Tutorial.03\Case1 folder using the filename **Just in Case**. Close the file without saving it.
6. Open a new, blank presentation and apply the Just in Case theme. Delete the JustinCase theme color set.
7. On the title page, insert the title **Case Manufacturing and Order Fulfillment Services**. Insert your name as the subtitle.
8. Save the presentation in the Tutorial.03\Case1 folder using the filename **Case Manufacturing**.
9. Insert into this presentation file all seven slides from the file **eBayCase**, located in the Tutorial.03\Case1 folder.
10. In Slide 2, change the layout to Two Content, insert the picture **PhoneCase** from the Tutorial.03\Case1 folder, and then apply the picture style Reflected Rounded Rectangle.
11. In Slide 3, insert the movie **CompCase**, so that it plays when clicked during a slide show, and then apply the picture style Reflected Rounded Rectangle.
12. In Slide 6, insert a chart as follows:
    a. Insert the Line with Markers chart, in the Line section in the Insert Chart dialog box.
    b. Change "Category 1" through "Category 4" to **2010**, **2011**, **2012**, and **2013** to represent the years.
    c. Change "Series 1" to **Sales (in $Thousands)** and "Series 2" to **Profits (in $Thousands)**.
    d. In the Sales column (cells B2 through B5), insert the values **850**, **1000**, **1100**, **1250**.
    e. In the Profits column (cells C2 through C5), insert the values **80**, **180**, **280**, **400**.
    f. Delete column D.
13. Change the Chart Style to Style 45 (located on the bottom row, fifth column of the Design gallery).
14. In Slide 7, insert an organization chart. Change the Layouts style to Hierarchy, and then change the colors to Colorful Range – Accent Colors 3 to 4. Add the following text to the chart, adding and deleting boxes as needed:
    a. First-level box: **Fulfillment Manager**
    b. Second-level boxes: **Inventory Manager**, **Shipping Manager**, and **Accounts Manager**.
    c. Third-level boxes under Shipping Manager: **Processing Manager** and **Mail Manager**.
15. In Slide 8, add the Purple mesh textured background.
16. In Slides 2, 4, and 5, animate the bulleted lists using the Dissolve In entrance animation. Set the dim color to light blue-green.
17. In Slide 2, animate the picture to enter the screen using the Fly In entrance effect.

18. To all the slides, apply the slide transition Fade Smoothly, and then set the transition speed to Slow.

19. Go through the presentation in Slide Show view. Using the red felt-tip pointer pen, draw a rough circle around "Fulfillment Manager" on Slide 7. When you finish the slide show, save the ink marking.

20. Save the presentation using the default name.

21. Submit the presentation in printed or electronic format, as directed by your instructor.

| Challenge | **Case Problem 2** |

Go beyond the skills you've learned to create a self-running presentation for a photographer.

Data Files needed for this Case Problem: Wedding01.jpg through Wedding10.jpg

Ultimate Videos   Sharah-Renae Wabbinton has a home business of taking pictures or scanning photos for special occasions—primarily graduations, weddings, family reunions, and religious events—and preparing "videos" using PowerPoint. Her products aren't true videos, but rather self-running, animated, PowerPoint presentations created using the Photo Album feature. She gives you a copy of 10 photographs from a recent wedding, and has asked you to prepare not only a PowerPoint presentation using those photos but also a custom Office theme that she can use with other "videos." Do the following:

1. Start a new, blank presentation (using the Office theme).

⊕ EXPLORE   2. Change the background style to a gradient fill, with the preset colors design called Nightfall. Apply this background to all slides. (*Hint*: Use the Preset colors button arrow in the Format Background dialog box.)

⊕ EXPLORE   3. In the Office Theme Slide Master, change all the text placeholders to white text, and then draw a rectangle that is the same shape and almost the same size as the entire slide, so that a white border appears between the rectangle and the outer edges of the slide approximately one-quarter of an inch from the edge of the slides. (*Hint*: Use the rectangle Shape tool to draw the rectangle so that it completely covers the slide of the Slide Master, and then, while holding down the Alt key, drag the resize handles to slightly reduce the size of the rectangle on all four sides.)

⊕ EXPLORE   4. Set the Shape Fill of the rectangle to No Fill, and set the Shape Outline to a white, 3-point line.

⊕ EXPLORE   5. With the Slide Master still in the slide pane, set the slide transition to Random Transition. (*Hint*: Random Transition is the last transition in the Transition gallery.)

⊕ EXPLORE   6. Set up the slide show to advance automatically from one slide to the next, with about 5 seconds on each slide. (*Hint*: With the Slide Master still in the slide pane, on the Animations tab in the Transition to This Slide group, deselect the On Mouse Click check box, and then select the Automatically After check box. Change the Automatically After time from 00:00 to **00:05**.)

7. In Normal view, save the presentation as an Office theme titled **Wedding** in the Tutorial.03\Case2 folder included with the Data Files.

8. Close the current presentation without saving it, and then start a new, blank presentation.

⊕ EXPLORE   9. In the Illustrations group on the Insert tab, use the Photo Album button to insert all 10 photographs, **Wedding01** through **Wedding10**, located in the Tutorial.03\Case2 folder. (*Hint*: In the Photo Album dialog box, click the File/Disk button, navigate to the folder containing the pictures, select all the pictures, and then click the Insert button.)

⊕ **EXPLORE**   10. While still viewing the Photo Album dialog box, in the Album Layout section, set the Picture layout to 1 picture (meaning, 1 picture per slide). Set the Frame shape to Simple Frame, White. Apply the theme to the Wedding theme you created and saved in the Tutorial.03\Case2 folder. Click the Create button at the bottom of the Photo Album dialog box to create the photo album. (*Hint*: If you already closed the Photo Album dialog box, click the Photo Album button arrow, and then click Edit Photo Album.)

11. In Slide 1, change the title to **Curtis and Cassandra**, and change the name in the subtitle to your name.

12. In Slides 2 through 11, apply a different Entrance animation effect to each photograph. Use only animations in the Exciting group in the Add Entrance Effect dialog box. Test each animation to make sure it works well.

13. For each picture animation, change the Start setting to With Previous, and then change the Speed to Medium.

⊕ **EXPLORE**   14. Set up the presentation to loop automatically, so that it automatically starts over when it reaches the end. (*Hint*: On the Slide Show tab, in the Set Up group, click the Set Up Slide Show button, and then click the Loop continuously until 'Esc' check box.)

15. Start the slide show and make sure that it runs on its own and continues to run until you press the Esc key.

16. Save the presentation as **Wedding Video** in the Tutorial.03\Case2 folder.

17. If your instructor asks you to do so, print the slide show as a handout with 6 slides per page.

Create	**Case Problem 3**

Use the skills you learned to create a custom theme and presentation for a cartography company.

Data Files needed for this Case Problem: MntMap.jpg, MntPlateau1.jpg, MntPlateau2.jpg

Cartography Research Systems   Barrett Worthington is founder and president of Cartography Research Systems (CRS), a company that maps geological formations and nearby areas. Sample geological areas include glaciers, caves, canyons, river beds, and wilderness sites. CRS clients mostly are energy and mineral exploration companies, but they also include the National Parks Service and land developers.

Barrett has asked you to create and save a design theme that his company can use for their presentations to their clients. He then asks you to help him prepare a portion of a presentation to one of his clients, Eckstein Energy. Do the following:

1. Create a new set of theme colors as shown in Figure 3-39. Your colors don't have to be exactly the same as those shown in the figure. Just try to select each theme color as close as you can. Save the theme colors as **CRScolors**.

Figure 3-39

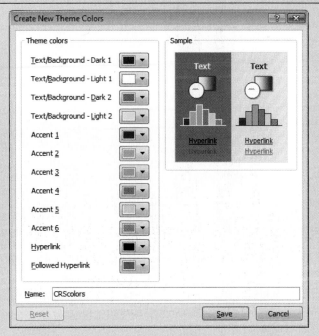

EXPLORE

2. Use the slide masters to apply the background style, font attributes (titles light yellow, bold), bullets, and title border shown in Figure 3-40. (*Hint*: To create the title border, use the Shape Outline button in the Shape Styles group on the Format tab to add the border, and change the color and thickness—called the weight—of the line. If you're not sure of a particular color, just pick any theme color that is close. Similarly, just get the line thickness (weight) as close as you can to the title border in Figure 3-40.)

Figure 3-40

3. Use the slide masters to add progressive disclosure (without dimming) to the bulleted lists and content placeholders. Use the Fly In (from bottom) entrance animation. Modify the animation so that the second- and third-level bulleted items enter the screen separately during a slide show. Refer to Figure 3-40. (*Hint*: To apply the custom animation to all content, not just bulleted lists, apply it to the content placeholder on the Slide Master.)

4. Save the file as an Office theme in your Tutorial.03\Case3 folder using the filename **CRStheme**, and then close the presentation without saving changes.

5. Start a new PowerPoint presentation, and then apply the theme you created, CRStheme. Delete the CRScolors theme color set.

6. Add content to the new presentation, as shown in Figure 3-41. Refer to the following as you add the content:

Figure 3-41

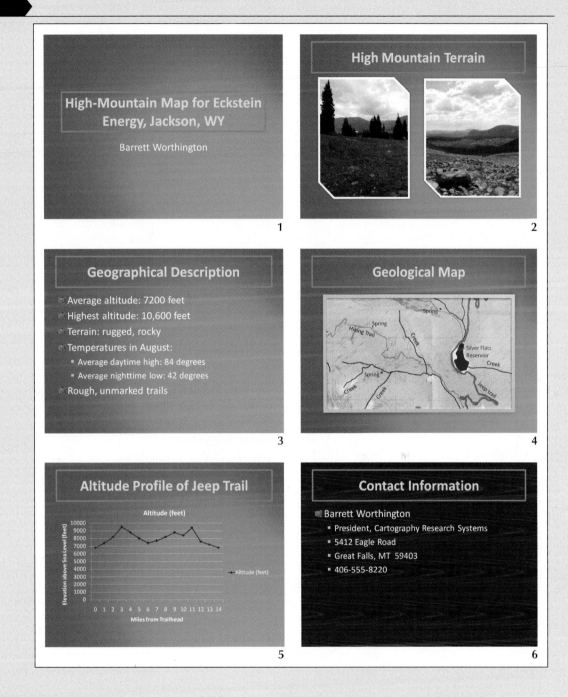

    a. In Slide 1, add the title shown, but use your own name for the subtitle.

    b. In Slide 2, insert the photos **MntPlateau1** and **MntPlateau2**, and then apply the picture style called Snip Diagonal Corner, White.

    c. In Slide 3, type the title and bulleted list, as shown in Figure 3-41.

    d. In Slide 4, insert the picture **MntMap**, and then apply the picture style called Metal Frame.

    e. In Slide 6, after you enter the information, apply the textured background called Walnut.

EXPLORE   7. In Slide 5, create an elevation chart using the Line type chart format called Line with Markers. Delete all the data from the spreadsheet. (*Hint*: Press the Ctrl+A keys to select all, and then press the Delete key.) Enter the data shown in this table, where the upper-left (empty) cell is cell A1, the label "Altitude (feet)" is cell B1, and so forth:

	Altitude (feet)		Altitude (feet)
0	6800	8	8200
1	7400	9	8800
2	8200	10	8400
3	9500	11	9400
4	8800	12	7600
5	8000	13	7200
6	7400	14	6800
7	7700		

EXPLORE   8. Select the data for the chart in Slide 5. (*Hint*: Select the chart placeholder, and then, in the Data group on the Design tab, click the Select Data button. Drag the pointer over all the cells that you entered into the spreadsheet, and then click the OK button in the Select Data Source dialog box.)

    9. Add axis titles to the horizontal and vertical axes, as shown in Figure 3-41. Along the primary horizontal (X) axis, the text is "Miles from Trailhead," and along the primary vertical (Y) axis, the text is "Elevation above Sea Level (feet)."

    10. In Slide 4, insert, rotate, and then color the text boxes that label the reservoir, springs, creeks, and trails, as shown.

    11. Animate all the text boxes using the Appear entrance effect. (*Hint*: First apply the animation to the "Sliver Flats Reservoir" text box, and then select all the "Creek" text boxes and apply the animation to all of them at once. Then select all the "Spring" text boxes and apply the animation effect to all of them at once, and then finally select the two "trail" text boxes and apply the effect to them.)

EXPLORE   12. To each of the four groups of animations, apply the sound effect Click. (*Hint*: For each of the animation groups, click the arrow to the right of the text box number in the Custom Animation task pane, click Effect Options, and then on the Effect tab, set the Sound to Click.)

    13. Test the slide in Slide Show view to make sure that, after the slide appears, you have to click once to have the map "fly in" to the slide, then click four more times to display each of the four groups of text boxes, which appear with a clicking sound. If necessary, edit the text boxes and animation so they work as described.

    14. Save the presentation in the Tutorial.03\Case3 folder using the filename **High-Mnt Map**.

    15. Submit the presentation in electronic or printed form, as requested by your instructor.

| Create | **Case Problem 4** |

Use the skills you learned to create a presentation about a collection for a volunteer group.

There are no Data Files needed for this Case Problem.

Cabot Collectibles Cabot Collectibles is a group of volunteer collectors who create PowerPoint presentations about personal collections. They make these presentations available to anyone who wants to present information on collectibles to schools, churches, civic organizations, clubs, and so forth. They rely on collectors to prepare the PowerPoint presentations. Your task is the following:

1. Select a type of collectible: stamps, coins, foreign currency, baseball cards, jewelry, comic books, artwork, rocks, dolls, figurines, chess sets, or almost anything else.

2. Plan your presentation so your audience learns basic information about your chosen collectible and sees pictures, with descriptions, of sample items from the collection.

3. Acquire pictures of sample items. You can take the pictures yourself with a digital camera, take the pictures with a film camera and scan the photographs, scan flat items directly (stamps, bills, cards, book covers, and so forth), or get pictures from the Web.

4. Gather information about the items depicted in your graphics. You might want to include some of the following: name of item, age of item, origin (purchase location or place of manufacture), date of purchase, dimensions, and special characteristics (handmade, natural dyes, first edition, and so forth).

5. Create a custom theme appropriate for your presentation. In selecting theme fonts and theme colors, take into account the nature of the collection and the common colors found in the graphics that you're going to include. Your theme should include the following:
   a. Custom theme colors
   b. At least one graphic—logo, picture, ready-made shape (rectangle, circle, triangle, and so forth), or textured background
   c. A custom set of bullets; include a picture bullet for the first-level bulleted items
   d. Progressive disclosure, with dimming, of the bulleted lists

6. Create a new presentation based on your custom theme.

7. Include a title slide, at least two slides with bulleted lists, and at least six slides with pictures of collectibles.

8. Apply slide transitions to your slide presentation.

9. Animate at least one graphic.

⊕ EXPLORE 10. If you have access to a microphone on your computer, create at least one sound clip and insert it in your presentation. Keep the recording shorter than 3 seconds. For example, record your voice saying a hard-to-pronounce noun or a foreign word associated with a collectible item, or record a sound effect, like a knock on the door, a bell, or a whistle. (*Hint:* Use the Sound Recorder installed with Windows. Click the Start button, point to All Programs, click Accessories, and then click Sound Recorder. With your microphone ready, click the Record button. When you're finished recording, click the Stop button.)

⊕ EXPLORE 11. If you have access to a digital camera with video capture and have the technical know-how, create a video shorter than 5 seconds of one of your collectibles or of someone admiring your collectibles. Insert the video into one of the slides of your presentation.

12. Save the presentation in the Tutorial.03\Case4 folder using the filename **Collection**.

13. Save the theme in the Tutorial.03\Case4 folder using the filename **Collectible**.

14. Submit your presentation in electronic or printed form, as requested by your instructor.

Research	**Internet Assignments**

Go to the Web to find information you can use to create presentations.

The purpose of the Internet Assignments is to challenge you to find information on the Internet that you can use to work effectively with this software. The actual assignments are updated and maintained on the Course Technology Web site. Log on to the Internet and use your Web browser to go to the Student Online Companion for New Perspectives Office 2007 at **www.course.com/np/office2007**. Then navigate to the Internet Assignments for this tutorial.

Assess	**SAM Assessment and Training**

If you have a SAM user profile, you may have access to hands-on instruction, practice, and assessment of the skills covered in this tutorial. Log in to your SAM account (**http://sam2007.course.com**) to launch any assigned training activities or exams that relate to the skills covered in this tutorial.

Review	**Quick Check Answers**

Session 3.1

1. In the Slides group on the Home tab, click the New Slide button arrow, click Reuse Slides, browse to the location of the presentation with the slide you want to insert, and then click the slide thumbnails of the desired slides.
2. Theme colors are the set of matching colors that makes up the background, fonts, and other elements of the presentation.
3. In creating a custom theme, you might want to change the following elements: background style, fonts, font sizes, font colors, bullets, and background graphics.
4. Gradient fill is a type of shading in which one color blends into another or varies from one shade to another.
5. Click the Office Button, click Save As to open the Save As dialog box, click the Save as type arrow, click Office Theme, navigate to the desired location, type a filename, and then click the Save button.
6. In the Background group on the Design tab, click the Background Styles button arrow, click Format Background, click the picture or texture fill option button, click the Texture button arrow, and then click the desired texture.

Session 3.2

1. A video clip is an animated picture file, usually with the filename extension .avi.

2. Change the slide layout to a different content layout (if necessary), click the Chart button in the content placeholder, select the type of chart, edit the spreadsheet, and then change other chart options as desired.

3. An organization chart is a diagram of boxes, connected with lines, showing the hierarchy of positions within an organization.

4. Change the slide layout to a different content layout (if necessary), click the Insert SmartArt Graphic button in the content placeholder, select a Hierarchy graphic (usually Organization Chart or Hierarchy), click the OK button, type text into the boxes, and then add and remove organization chart boxes as desired.

5. a. **Transition effect**: A method of moving one slide off the screen and bringing another slide onto the screen during a slide show

    b. **Animation effect**: A special visual or audio effect applied to an object (such as graphics or bulleted text)

    c. **Sound effect**: A sound that takes place during a slide show

    d. **Pointer pen**: A PowerPoint mouse pointer that allows you to draw lines on the screen during a slide show

    e. **Podium mode**: A slide show mode involving two monitors, one that's usually at a podium and that only the presenter can see, and another one (such as a projection screen) that the audience can see

6. With the desired slide in the slide pane, click the Animations tab, and then, in the Transition to This Slide group, select the desired transition. If desired, modify the transition to include a sound effect or to execute at a faster or slower rate. If desired, click the Apply To All button to apply the same transition to all slides in the presentation.

7. PowerPoint Viewer is a separate program that you can use to give your slide show on any Windows computer.

Ending Data Files

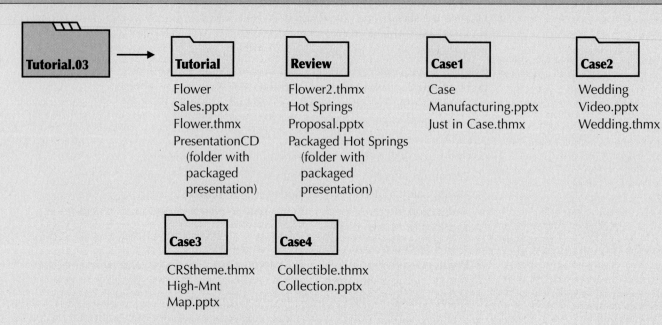

Tutorial.03 →

Tutorial
Flower
Sales.pptx
Flower.thmx
PresentationCD
(folder with
packaged
presentation)

Review
Flower2.thmx
Hot Springs
Proposal.pptx
Packaged Hot Springs
(folder with
packaged
presentation)

Case1
Case
Manufacturing.pptx
Just in Case.thmx

Case2
Wedding
Video.pptx
Wedding.thmx

Case3
CRStheme.thmx
High-Mnt
Map.pptx

Case4
Collectible.thmx
Collection.pptx

Objectives

Session 4.1
- Apply a design theme from another presentation
- Import, modify, and export a Word outline
- Import graphics into a presentation
- Copy an object from another presentation
- Embed and modify a table from Word
- Link and modify an Excel chart

Session 4.2
- Create and edit hyperlinks
- Insert text into shapes
- Add action buttons to a presentation
- View a slide show with embedded or linked objects
- Print a presentation as an outline
- Customize handouts
- Publish a presentation as a Web page
- Learn about Windows Meeting Space
- Identify features not supported by previous versions
- Use the Document Inspector

Integrating PowerPoint with Other Programs and Collaborating with Workgroups

Presenting Information About Clinical Trial Results

Case | Landon Pharmaceuticals Testing, Inc.

Allysa Byington is director of customer service at Landon Pharmaceuticals Testing (LPT), a company that performs clinical trial testing of medicinal drugs developed by other pharmaceutical companies. Allysa works with the pharmaceutical companies to develop effective testing protocols, and then she prepares presentations on the results of the testing. Allysa asks you to help create an effective Microsoft PowerPoint presentation on the results of a pharmaceutical clinical trial for a client, Pamerleau Biotechnologies of Newton, Massachusetts. Pamerleau has developed a drug, with the code name Asperitol and code number PB0182, for the treatment of autoimmune diseases such as rheumatoid arthritis and lupus.

In this tutorial, you apply a design theme from another presentation, you'll import, modify, and export a Microsoft word outline to and from your presentation, and you'll import pictures into your presentation. You'll also embed and modify a Word table in your presentation and link and modify a Microsoft Excel chart. You'll then create and edit hyperlinks, and add action buttons. Finally, you'll learn how to print the presentation outline, to customize handouts, to publish a presentation on the World Wide Web, and to share your presentation with others over the Internet.

Starting Data Files

Tutorial.04

Tutorial
Chart.xlsx
Clinical.pptx
ClinOtl.docx
Demogr.docx
Landon.pptx
Pills.jpg
X-ray.jpg

Review
Hospitals.docx
Landon.pptx
LPTChart.xlsx
LPTInfo.docx
Patient.jpg
Placebos.jpg

Case1
CredUnion.jpg
FLCUChart.xlsx
FLCUDes.pptx
FLCUOtln.docx
FLCUTbl.docx
Money.jpg

Case2
BirdBlt.jpg
FlwBlt.jpg
WMCchart.xlsx
WMCDes.pptx
WMCOtl.docx

Case3
72HrKit.jpg
EPR.pptx
EPRChart.xlsx
EPROtl.docx
EPRTabl.docx
Flood.jpg
Wheat.jpg

Case4
Wetland1.jpg
Wetland2.jpg
Wetland3.jpg
Wetland4.jpg
Weland5.jpg

Session 4.1

Planning the Presentation

Before you begin to create Allysa's slide show, she discusses with you her plans for the presentation.

- **Purpose of the presentation**: To present an overview of the fund-raising clinical-trial report and assign responsibilities
- **Type of presentation**: Report
- **Audience for the presentation**: Management team of Pamerleau Biotechnologies
- **Audience needs**: An overview of efficacy of their drug in treating arthritis
- **Location of the presentation**: Meeting room at the headquarters of Landon Pharmaceuticals Testing, Inc., and online
- **Format**: On-screen slide show and online Web presentation

With the preceding general plan for the presentation, Allysa prepared the outline of the presentation, as well as some of the key information about the presentation to Pamerleau.

Applying a Design Theme from Another Presentation

You already know how to apply a design theme from a theme file. You can use a similar method to apply a design from any other presentation file. For the clinical-trial presentation, Allysa wants you to use the design theme from an existing presentation she recently prepared for another clinical-trial presentation. You'll apply that design theme now.

To apply a design theme from the Landon presentation:

▶ 1. Open the file **Clinical** from the **Tutorial.04\Tutorial** folder included with your Data Files, and then save the file with the new filename **Clinical Report** to the same folder. The title slide appears on the screen with the name of the presenter, Allysa Byington. The presentation has the Technic design theme applied. Notice that this presentation includes only this one slide. See Figure 4-1. You'll create additional slides later.

Title page of new presentation with Technic theme applied ◄ **Figure 4-1**

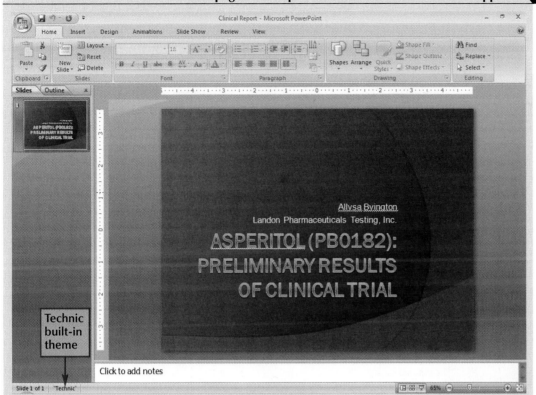

2. Change the subtitle from "Allysa Byington" to your own name, so your instructor can identify you as the author of this presentation.

3. Click the **Design** tab on the Ribbon, and then in the Themes group, click the **More** button. You won't use one of the built-in or custom themes, but rather a slide design already created in another presentation file.

4. Click **Browse for Themes**, and then navigate to the **Tutorial.04\Tutorial** folder included with your Data Files. The dialog box displays all the presentation files within the folder. Now you'll select the presentation Allysa prepared earlier.

5. Click **Landon**, and then click the **Apply** button. The design theme from the presentation Landon is applied to the Clinical Report presentation.

6. Click the **Insert** tab on the Ribbon.

7. In the Text group, click the **Header & Footer** button to display the Header and Footer dialog box, and then click the **Slide number** check box to select it.

8. Click the **Footer** check box to select it, and then type **Landon Pharmaceuticals Testing** in the Footer box.

9. Click the **Apply to All** button. The footer appears on all the slides, including the title slide. See Figure 4-2.

Figure 4-2 ▶ **Presentation with new theme from Landon presentation**

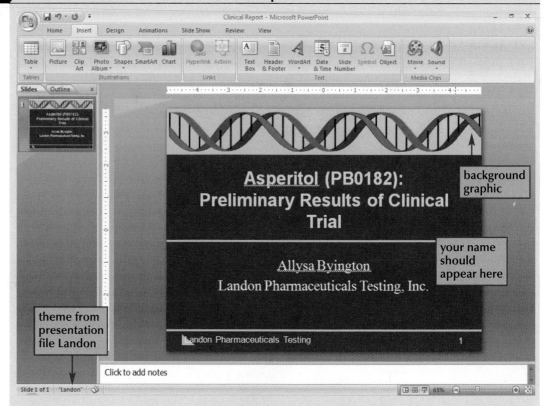

▶ **10.** Save the file with its new design using the default filename.

In Figure 4-2, you can see some of the design elements that Allysa created in her original presentation, including the color scheme with a solid brown background, yellow title text, white body text, and a background graphic of a DNA double helix.

Now you're ready to add more slides to your presentation. All the slides you'll add exist in some format already; your job will be to integrate files created in other programs into the presentation. First, however, you must understand about importing, embedding, and linking objects.

Using Integration Techniques: Importing, Embedding, and Linking

An **object** is anything in a presentation that you can manipulate as a whole. This includes clip art, photos, and text boxes, as well as other graphics, diagrams, and charts that you've already worked with. In addition, you can insert objects, such as a word-processing document or a spreadsheet chart, that were created in other Office programs. The program in which an object is created is the **source program**; the program into which an object is inserted is the **destination program**.

When you insert objects, you import, embed, or link them. Refer to Figure 4-3 as you read the definitions of each of these following terms.

Integration techniques ◄ Figure 4-3

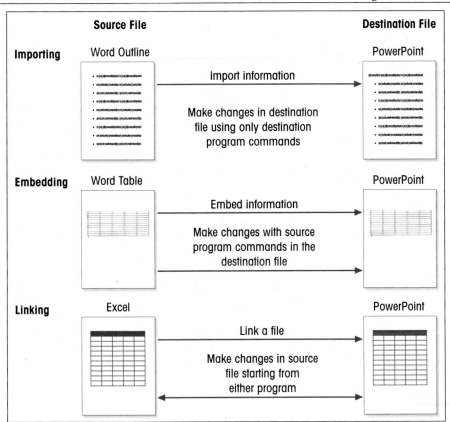

Importing an object means simply copying a file that was created using one program into the file of another program. For example, when you insert graphics and sounds into a presentation, you actually import them. Imported objects become part of the Power-Point presentation. When you import a file, the source program and the destination program don't communicate with each other in any way, as illustrated in Figure 4-3. For example, if you want to modify a graphic (such as change its size or colors) after importing it into PowerPoint, you make these changes in PowerPoint rather than in the graphics program. If you want to access the commands of the source program to modify the object, you need to start the source program and open and modify the file in the source program. The changes will not be reflected in the destination program unless you import the object again.

Embedding is similar to importing but allows a one-way connection to be maintained with the source program, not the source file. For example, if you embed a Word table in a Power-Point presentation and then double-click the table, you will be able to access and use Word commands to edit the table while still in PowerPoint. When you finish editing the embedded table and return to PowerPoint, the changes you made to the table will appear in the object in PowerPoint only; the changes do not appear in the original Word file that you used to create the table. This is because the embedded object is a copy of the original Word file, not the Word file itself. Therefore, if you make subsequent changes to the original Word file using Word, the changes will not be reflected in the embedded Word table in PowerPoint. In other words, an embedded object has no relationship to the original source file, but it does maintain a connection to the source program.

When you **link** an object, you create a connection between the source file and the linked object. You don't place a copy of the source file in the destination file; instead, you place a representation of the actual source file in the destination file. When an object is linked, you can make changes to the source file, and those changes are reflected in the representation of the linked object in the destination file. For the object in the destination file to be updated, the source file must be available to the destination file. For example, when you link an Excel spreadsheet to a PowerPoint slide, the spreadsheet file must be available to the PowerPoint presentation file if you want to edit the file; otherwise, PowerPoint treats the spreadsheet as an embedded file.

You should be aware that not all software allows you to embed or link objects. Only those programs that support **object linking and embedding** (or **OLE**, pronounced oh-LAY) let you embed or link objects from one program to another. Fortunately, sophisticated programs, such as PowerPoint, Word, and Excel, are all OLE-enabled programs and fully support object linking and embedding.

Allysa has created an outline in Word listing the text of many of the slides she wants to include in her presentation. Your next task is to import the Word outline into the presentation.

Importing and Exporting a Word Outline

If your presentation contains quite a bit of text, it might be easier to create the outline of your presentation in Word, so that you can take advantage of the extensive text-editing features available in that program. Fortunately, if you create an outline in a Word document, you don't need to retype it in PowerPoint. You can import it directly into your presentation.

Although you can create handouts in PowerPoint, sometimes you might want to take advantage of Word's formatting commands to make the text easier to read. You might also want to use the presentation of the outline as the outline for a more detailed document. To do this, you can export the outline to a Word document.

First, you'll import an outline into your presentation.

Importing the Word Outline

As you know, when you work in the Outline tab in PowerPoint, each level-one heading (also called Heading 1 or A head) automatically becomes a slide title; each level-two heading (also called Heading 2 or B head) automatically becomes a level-one bulleted paragraph; each level-three heading (also called Heading 3 or C head) automatically becomes a level-two bulleted paragraph, and so forth. Similarly, Word has an Outline view in which you can create outline text that automatically becomes level-one text, level-two text, and so forth, in the Word document. The level-one text becomes a built-in Heading 1 style; level-two text becomes a built-in Heading 2 style, and so forth. So Allysa created a Word document using Outline view (alternatively, she could have simply applied the built-in headings to the outline text). Your next task, then, is to import her outline into PowerPoint.

To import a Word outline:

▶ 1. Click the **Home** tab on the Ribbon, and then, in the Slides group, click the **New Slide button arrow**.

▶ 2. On the menu below the New Slide gallery, click **Slides from Outline**. The Insert Outline dialog box opens.

▶ 3. Navigate to the **Tutorial.04\Tutorial** folder included with your Data Files, click **ClinOtl**, and then click the **Insert** button. The Word outline is inserted as new slides after the current slide in the PowerPoint presentation, with all the level-one text becoming new slide titles. Unfortunately, PowerPoint uses the fonts and text colors of the outline document rather than of the PowerPoint theme. But you can easily fix that.

▶ **4.** On the status bar, to the left of the Zoom slider, click the **Slide Sorter** button ▦ .

▶ **5.** Click **Slide 2** to select it, press and hold the **Shift** key, and then click **Slide 9** (the last slide) to select all the slides from Slide 2 to 9.

▶ **6.** In the Slides group, click the **Layout** button, and then click **Title and Content**. The Title and Content layout is applied to the selected slides. Now you need to reset the slides to the default settings from the Slide Master.

▶ **7.** In the Slides group, click the **Reset** button. The font style and color are "reset" to the design theme. Now, you want to add the footer and page number to the imported slides.

▶ **8.** Click the **Insert** tab on the Ribbon, and then in the Text group, click the **Header & Footer** button to display the Header and Footer dialog box.

▶ **9.** Click the **Slide number** check box, click the **Footer** check box, and then click the **Apply to All** button. Now all the slides have a footer and page number.

▶ **10.** Double-click **Slide 2** to return to Normal view with Slide 2 in the slide pane. See Figure 4-4. The imported Word outline is now in the PowerPoint slides with the proper design theme applied.

Presentation with imported Word outline ◀ **Figure 4-4**

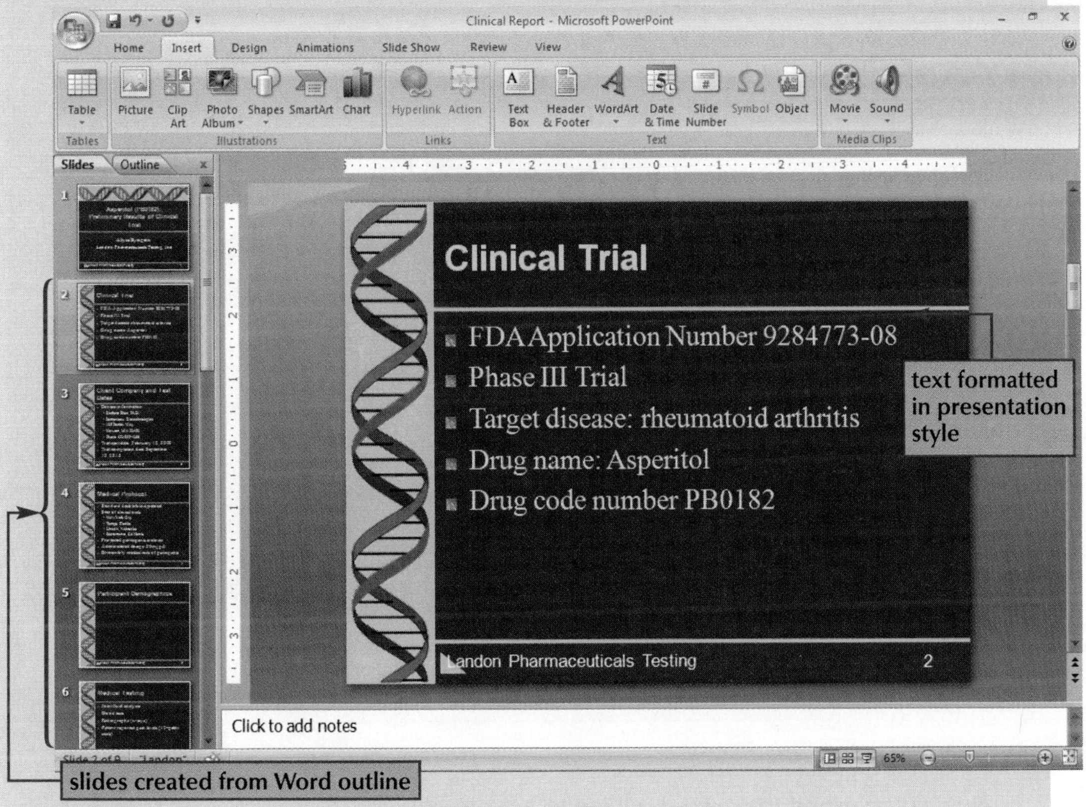

Because you imported the outline, the text is now part of PowerPoint and has no relationship with the Word file ClinOtl. Any changes you make to the PowerPoint text will have no effect on the ClinOtl file.

Exporting the Outline to Word

After looking over the presentation, Allysa wants Slide 9 ("Contents") to become Slide 2, so that her audience gets an overview of the contents of the presentation near the beginning. She then wants you to export the revised text as a Word document so that she can create a written report based on the revised outline. You'll do this now.

To modify the presentation outline in Slide Sorter view:

▶ **1.** Switch to Slide Sorter view.

▶ **2.** Drag the **Slide 9** thumbnail to the right of Slide 1 (and to the left of Slide 2). The Contents slide becomes the new Slide 2. The old Slide 2 ("Clinical Trial") becomes the new Slide 3, the old Slide 3 becomes the new Slide 4, and so forth.

▶ **3.** Double-click **Slide 1** to return to Normal view, and then click the **Outline** tab in the pane on the left so you can see the text of the outline. By changing the order of the slides, you changed the outline. See Figure 4-5.

Figure 4-5 ▶ **Presentation outline after "Contents" slide is moved**

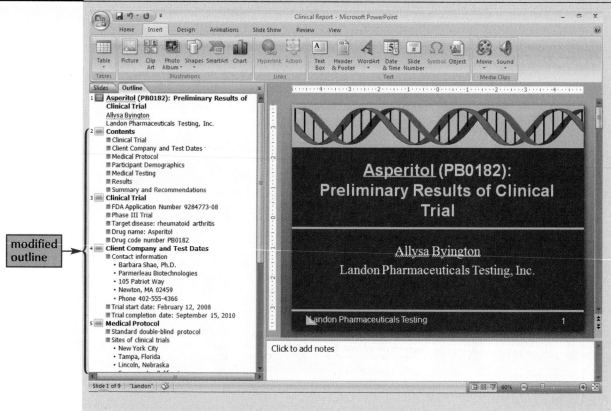

Now you'll export the revised outline to a Word file.

To export the outline to Word:

▶ **1.** Click the **Office Button**, and then click **Save As**. The Save As dialog box opens.

▶ **2.** Click the **Save as type** arrow, and then click **Outline/RTF**. *RTF* means Rich Text Format (RTF), which is a text format that preserves most formatting and can be read by most word processors.

▶ **3.** Click the **Save** button. PowerPoint saves the text of the PowerPoint file as an RTF file with the filename **Clinical Report**. The file is saved in your Tutorial.04\Tutorial folder because it is the default folder.

▶ **4.** Start Microsoft Word 2007, and then open the document **Clinical Report**, located in the **Tutorial.04\Tutorial** folder. As you can see, the text is barely visible because PowerPoint created the RTF file with the same font sizes and colors as in the presentation. You'll now make the text more visible.

▶ **5.** Press the **Ctrl+A** keys; all the text in the document is selected.

▶ **6.** Change the font to **Times New Roman**, change the font size to **12**, and then change the font color to **Automatic** (black).

▶ **7.** Click anywhere to deselect the text. Now you can read the text. See Figure 4-6.

Exported outline in Microsoft Word ◀ **Figure 4-6**

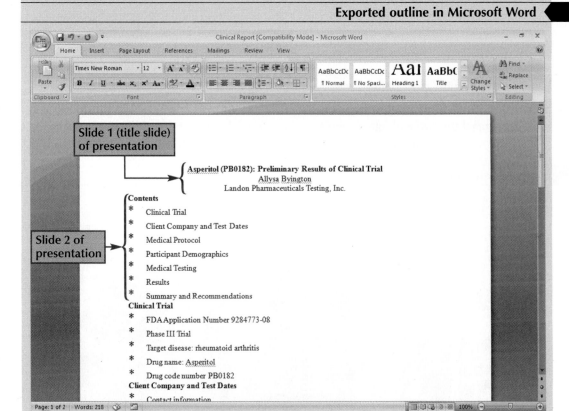

Trouble? If you are unfamiliar with Microsoft Word 2007, skip this and the subsequent steps on modifying and saving the RTF file.

▶ **8.** Click the **Office Button** 🔘, point to **Save As**, and then click **Word Document**. The Save As dialog box opens with Word Document listed in the Save as type box.

▶ **9.** Click the **Save** button. Word saves the Clinical Report outline as a Word document.

Trouble? If you are asked about saving the document to the new Word 2007 format, click the OK button to verify that you do indeed want to save the file in Word 2007 format.

▶ **10.** Exit Word. PowerPoint is the active window again.

Allysa or one of her associates can now reformat the Clinical Report outline using the formatting commands in Word, and then add explanatory text under each heading, as desired.

Now, Allysa wants you to import digital photographs into the presentation. You'll do that now.

Importing Graphics

You already know how to import graphics, as you have inserted digital images and clip art into earlier presentations. Now, to make the Clinical Report presentation more attractive, you'll import digital photographs to illustrate key slides.

To import (insert) graphics into the presentation:

▶ 1. Click the **Slides** tab. The Outline tab is hidden, and the slide thumbnails appear.

▶ 2. Go to **Slide 3** ("Clinical Trial"), and then, if necessary, click the **Home** tab on the Ribbon.

▶ 3. In the Slides group, click the **Layout** button, and then click **Two Content**. Slide 3 changes to the Two Content layout, with the bulleted list on the left and a placeholder on the right, where you will insert a picture.

▶ 4. In the placeholder, click the **Insert Picture from File** button 🖾, navigate to the **Tutorial.04\Tutorial** folder, and then double-click the filename **Pills**. A photo of the asperitol and placebo look-alike pills appears on the slide. See Figure 4-7.

| Figure 4-7 | Slide 3 after importing picture |

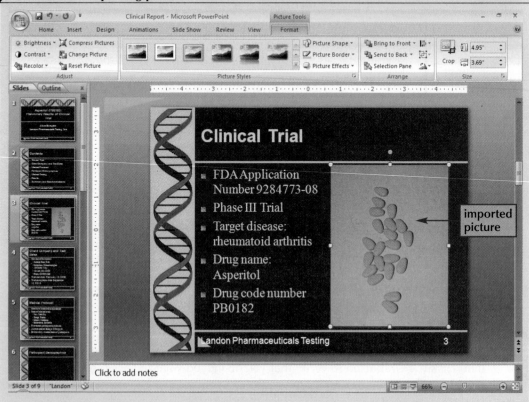

Now Allysa wants you to compress the picture. This will reduce the file size of the presentation, which saves disk space and increases transfer times when she shares the presentation with her colleagues and clients.

To compress pictures in the presentation:

▶ **1.** With the picture still selected, click the **Format** tab below Picture Tools, if necessary.

▶ **2.** In the Adjust group, click the **Compress Pictures** button. The Compress Pictures dialog box opens.

▶ **3.** Click the **Options** button. The Compression Settings dialog box opens.

▶ **4.** Make sure both check boxes in the Compression options group are selected, so that PowerPoint automatically performs a basic compression when you save the file and deletes cropped areas from the picture, if you happen to perform a crop. (Cropping is the process of trimming the pictures on one or more of its sides.)

▶ **5.** Click the **OK** button to close the Compression Settings dialog box, and then click the **OK** button again to close the Compress Pictures dialog box. Now PowerPoint will compress all the pictures you import into this presentation.

▶ **6.** Using the same procedure, apply the Two Content layout to Slide 7, and insert the picture file **X-ray**, located in the **Tutorial.04\Tutorial** folder, into the slide.

▶ **7.** Save the presentation using the default filename.

You can also import graphics (and other objects) by copying (or cutting) from one presentation and pasting into the current presentation. Allysa wants you to do that now.

Copying an Object from Another Presentation

You'll now do a copy-and-paste operation by copying the Landon Pharmaceuticals Testing (LPT) logo from one file into your Clinical Report.

To copy an object from the Landon presentation:

▶ **1.** With the Clinical Report presentation still in the PowerPoint window, open the presentation **Landon**, which is located in your **Tutorial.04\Tutorial** folder.

▶ **2.** In Slide 1 in the Landon presentation, click anywhere in the logo to activate it, and then click the outermost edge to select the entire object. See Figure 4-8.

Figure 4-8 Selected logo in Slide 1 of the Landon presentation

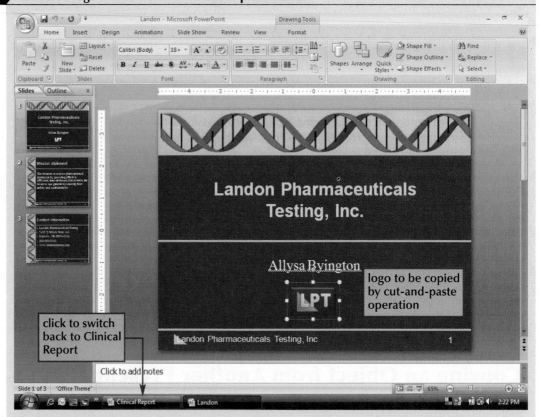

▶ **3.** In the Clipboard group, click the **Copy** button ⧉ . The logo is copied to the Clipboard.

▶ **4.** Click the **Clinical Report** button on the taskbar at the bottom of your screen to switch to the Clinical Report presentation.

Trouble? If you don't see the Clinical Report button on the taskbar, you should see a Microsoft Office PowerPoint button. Click it, and then click Clinical Report to make that presentation active.

▶ **5.** In the Clinical Report presentation, go to **Slide 1**, and then in the Clipboard group, click the **Paste** button. The logo appears below your name on the slide, but overlaps the company name.

▶ **6.** Press the **Down Arrow** key three or four times to center the logo between the company name and the yellow line above the footer.

▶ **7.** Click in a blank area of the slide to deselect the pasted object. See Figure 4-9.

Slide 1 with pasted logo centered below company name | Figure 4-9

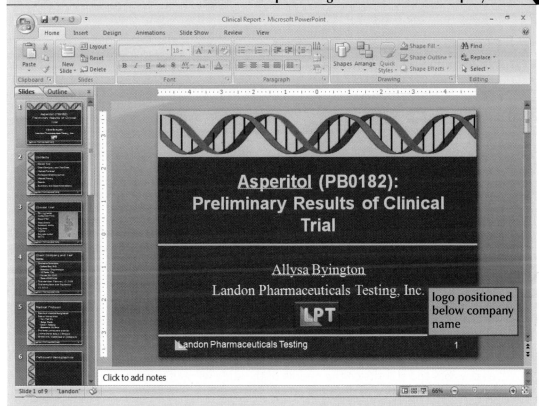

8. Save the presentation using the default filename.

9. Switch back to the Landon presentation, and then close the file.

The Clinical Report presentation now has the desired design theme, text slides, pictures, and logo. Your next task will be to embed a table into one of the slides in the presentation.

Embedding and Modifying a Word Table

You know how to use PowerPoint commands to create a table in a slide, but what if you've already created a table using Word? You don't have to re-create it in PowerPoint; instead, you can copy the table and place it in a slide. If you embed the table instead of importing it, you can then edit it using Word's table commands.

Alyssa created a table in a Word document that lists the demographics of the participants in the trials. You're going to embed that Word table in a slide. Allysa created the table with a black font on a white background, so it is legible in a Word document. But as you'll see, it's not legible in the PowerPoint presentation, with its dark background.

To embed a Word file in a presentation:

1. Go to **Slide 6**, and then click the **Insert** tab on the Ribbon.

2. In the Text group, click the **Object** button. The Insert Object dialog box opens. You can now create a new embedded file or use an existing one. You'll use an existing file.

▶ **3.** Click the **Create from file** option button, and then click the **Browse** button to open the Browse dialog box.

▶ **4.** Navigate to the **Tutorial.04\Tutorial** folder included with your Data Files, click the Word filename **Demogr**, and then click the **OK** button. See Figure 4-10.

Figure 4-10 ▶ **Insert Object dialog box for embedding Word table**

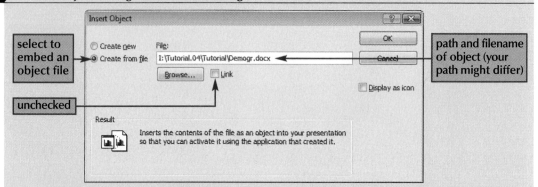

In Figure 4-10, the path and name of the file appear in the File text box. (Note that the path shown on your computer might be different.)

▶ **5.** Make sure the **Link** check box is not selected, as shown in Figure 4-10, and then click the **OK** button. The embedded table appears in Slide 6.

▶ **6.** Resize the table by dragging the corner sizing handles so that the table is as large as possible and still fits on the middle of the slide without overlapping background objects. You will have to drag the object border beyond the edges of the slide to make the table as big as possible. See Figure 4-11.

Figure 4-11 ▶ **Slide 6 with embedded Word table**

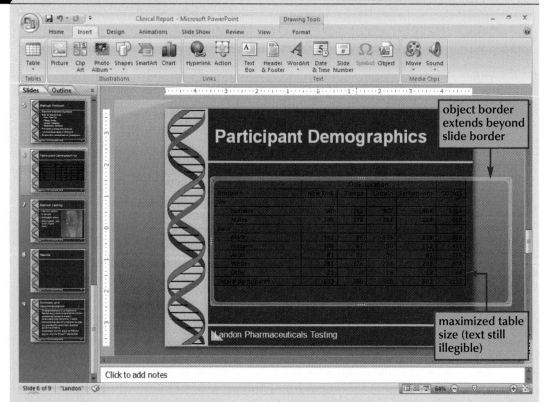

▶ **7.** Click a blank area of the slide to deselect the table.

▶ **8.** Save the presentation using the default filename.

Allysa asks you to modify the embedded table by changing the table color scheme and font size. Because you embedded the table, you will use the program that created the object (in this case, Word) to make the changes.

To modify an embedded table:

▶ **1.** Double-click anywhere in the **table** in Slide 6. The embedded table object becomes active in Word; the Word ruler appears above and to the left of the table, and the Word menu bar and toolbars replace the PowerPoint menu bar and toolbars. See Figure 4-12.

Slide 6 with embedded Word table made active ◀ **Figure 4-12**

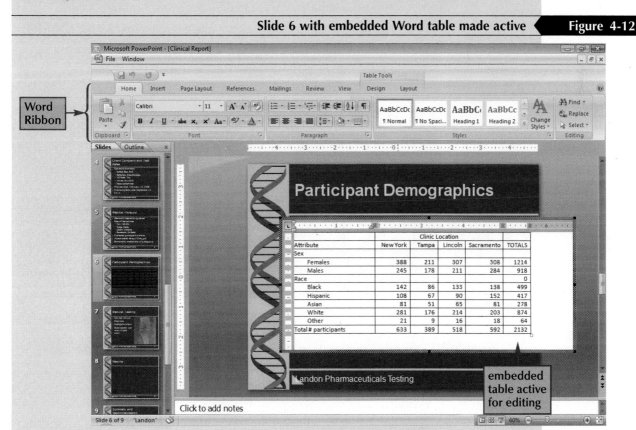

▶ **2.** Drag the mouse pointer from the upper-left cell to the bottom-right cell to select the entire table, and then, if necessary, click the **Home** tab on the Ribbon.

▶ **3.** In the Font section, click the **Font button arrow**, and then click **Times New Roman**.

▶ **4.** Click in the **Font Size** text box, type **13**, and press the **Enter** key. The text of the table is now 13-point Times New Roman.

▶ **5.** Click the **Font Color button arrow** ⬚, and click the white color tile. The font in the Word window seems to disappear, because it is white on a white background.

Trouble? The text will disappear when you change the color to white, because in Word, the background is white. Don't worry about this, because in the PowerPoint presentation, with its dark brown background, the text will show up nicely.

▶ **6.** In the Paragraph group, click the **Borders button arrow** , and then click **Borders and Shading** at the bottom of the gallery. The Borders and Shading dialog box opens.

▶ **7.** Click the **Color** arrow, click the **Yellow tile** at the bottom of the palette under Standard Colors, and then click the **OK** button.

▶ **8.** Click in a blank area of the slide to exit Word and return to PowerPoint, and then click a blank area again to deselect the table. See Figure 4-13.

| Figure 4-13 | Slide 6 with modified table |

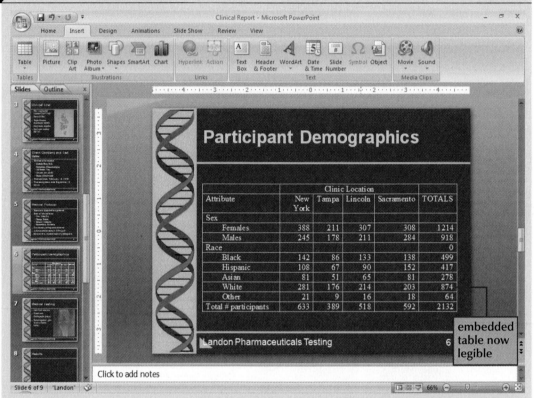

Trouble? If your table doesn't look similar to the one in Figure 4-13, make any adjustments now.

▶ **9.** Save the presentation using the default filename.

You have now completed Slide 6, which contains the embedded object. You have also edited the object using Microsoft Word. Keep in mind that the changes to the object did not change the original table in the Word document because embedding maintains a connection only with the program that was used to create the object, not with the original object itself.

Importing vs. Embedding an Object | InSight

Why would you want to embed rather than import an object into PowerPoint? In the case of a table, you wouldn't, because PowerPoint has all the same table commands as Word, so it's easier to modify the table directly using PowerPoint table commands rather than Word commands. However, sometimes you might want to embed an object because PowerPoint lacks the necessary editing commands. For example, you might want to embed in Power-Point a drawing created using Adobe Illustrator or CorelDRAW. In this case, if you ever wanted to modify the drawing, you'd want Adobe Illustrator or CorelDRAW commands to be available to make the changes.

Next, you'll link an Excel chart to the presentation.

Linking and Modifying an Excel Chart

Now you know how to insert objects into a PowerPoint slide by importing them and by embedding them. What if you needed to include in your presentation data that might change? For example, you might need to include data from an Excel worksheet, but you know that the final numbers won't be available for a while or that the numbers will change over time. In this case, you can link the data. Then, when the source file is updated, you can automatically update the linked object in the destination file so that it reflects the changes made to the source file.

Allysa wants to include a bar graph of the results of the clinical trial of the drug in the Clinical Report presentation. She chooses a bar graph because it emphasizes the effects of the drug-trial participants. The bar graph was created already using Excel, based on data in an Excel workbook, but Allysa anticipates that she will have to modify the work-book after she creates the PowerPoint presentation because some of the trial results were incomplete. Allysa wants any changes made to the workbook to be reflected in the Pow-erPoint file, so rather than retype or import the data into a PowerPoint chart, she asks you to link the Excel workbook to the PowerPoint presentation.

You'll link the Excel graph of income and expenses in Slide 8 in Allysa's presentation now.

To insert a chart linked to an Excel worksheet:

▶ **1.** Go to **Slide 8** ("Results"), and then change the slide layout to **Title Only**.

▶ **2.** Start Microsoft Office Excel 2007, open the file **Chart** located in the **Tutorial.04\ Tutorial** folder, and then save it as **Clinical Chart** in the same folder. Now you can make changes to the chart without modifying the original document.

▶ **3.** Click the edge of the chart to make it active, and then press the **Ctrl+C** keys to copy the chart to the Clipboard.

▶ **4.** Switch back to the Clinical Report presentation, and then press the **Ctrl+V** keys to paste the chart into Slide 8.

▶ **5.** Drag the corners of the object to resize the chart so it fits within the large blank region of the slide. See Figure 4-14.

Tip

When you copy and paste an object from another program into a PowerPoint presentation, the object is normally imported, not embedded or linked. But Microsoft Office 2007 is set up so that when you copy and paste a chart from Excel into PowerPoint, the chart is automatically linked in PowerPoint to Excel.

Figure 4-14 Slide 8 with linked Excel chart

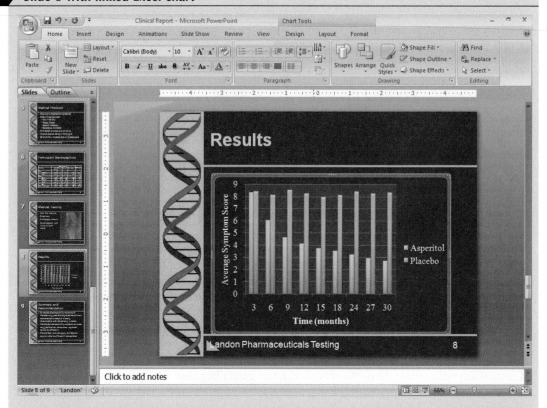

Notice that the linked chart doesn't keep the color theme as it appeared in Excel but rather takes on the color theme of the PowerPoint presentation. Also be aware that, for Excel charts, when you do a copy-and-paste operation, PowerPoint automatically links the file rather than imports or embeds the file.

▶ **6.** Click outside the chart in a blank area of the slide to deselect the object.

▶ **7.** Save the presentation using the default filename.

Another method for linking a file to a PowerPoint presentation is to use the Paste Special command in the Clipboard group on the Home tab. You select the object in the source file that you want to link, and then press the Ctrl+C keys in the source program. Next, you switch to the destination file in PowerPoint, and in the Clipboard group on the Home tab, click the Paste button arrow, and then click Paste Special to open the Paste Special dialog box. Click the Paste link option button, and then click the OK button.

After you linked the chart, Allysa received updated information about one of the results in the clinical-trial report. As it turns out, the scientists at Landon estimated that the average symptom score after 30 months would be 2.7, but after all the data was collected, the value was actually 3.1. Allysa asks you to make changes to the Excel worksheet data, which will then be reflected in the chart, both in the Excel and PowerPoint files.

To modify the linked chart:

▶ **1.** Click anywhere in the **chart** in Slide 8, and then, if necessary, click the **Design** tab on the Ribbon below Chart Tools.

▶ **2.** In the Data group, click the **Edit Data** button. The screen becomes split in two, with the PowerPoint window on the left and the Excel window on the right.

▶ **3.** In the Excel window (on the right), click the **Sheet1** tab at the bottom of the window, and then click in cell **B10** (at the bottom of the Asperitol column).

▶ **4.** Type **3.1**, but don't press the Enter key yet. Look at the chart in the PowerPoint window on the left. Focus on the rightmost yellow bar, which indicates the average symptom score at 30 months.

▶ **5.** Press the **Enter** key. The rightmost yellow bar in the chart in the PowerPoint window changed.

   Trouble? If you didn't see the change, click the Undo button on the Quick Access Toolbar of Excel, and then, while watching the PowerPoint chart, click the Redo button on the Excel Quick Access Toolbar. Make sure you leave the value at 3.1, not 2.7, in cell B10.

▶ **6.** In the Excel window, click the **Close** button ⊠, and then click the **Yes** button when asked if you want to save the changes to the Excel file. PowerPoint now fills the screen again.

▶ **7.** On the status bar at the bottom of the PowerPoint window, click the **Slide Show** button 🖵 to see how the chart looks in Slide Show view. See Figure 4-15.

Linked and modified chart in Slide Show view ◄ **Figure 4-15**

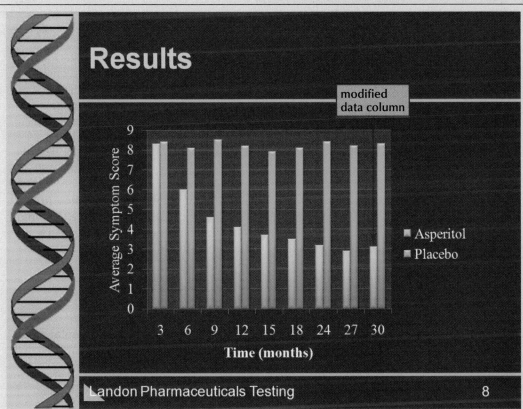

▶ **8.** Press the **Esc** key to exit Slide Show view and return to Normal view.

▶ **9.** Save the presentation using the default filename.

You have now linked and edited an Excel chart from PowerPoint. If you decide later to make further changes to the data in the workbook, you can do so either by directly starting Excel and opening Clinic Chart or using the Edit Chart button in PowerPoint. Either way, any changes made to the workbook will be reflected in the linked object in the PowerPoint slide.

| Review | **Session 4.1 Quick Check** |

1. How does applying a design theme from another presentation differ from applying a design theme from built-in themes?
2. Describe how you use a Word outline to create slides in PowerPoint.
3. Define or describe:
   a. import
   b. embed
   c. link
4. If you modify the source file of a linked object, such as an Excel chart linked to a PowerPoint slide, what happens to the linked object in the PowerPoint slide?
5. If you insert a picture created with scanning software and hardware, is the picture file imported, embedded, or linked?
6. Why would you link an object rather than embed it?

Session 4.2

Creating and Editing Hyperlinks

As you know, a **hyperlink** (or **link**) is a word, phrase, or graphic image that you click to "jump to" (or display) another location, called the **target**. The target of a link can be a location within the same document (presentation), a different document, or a page on the World Wide Web. Graphic hyperlinks are visually indistinguishable from graphics that are not hyperlinks, except when you move the mouse pointer over the link, the pointer changes to 🖑. Text links are usually underlined and are a different color than the rest of the text. After clicking a text link during a slide show, the link changes to another color to reflect the fact that it has been clicked, or **followed**.

Allysa wants to easily move from Slide 2, which lists the presentation contents, to the other slides, because she knows that as her audience asks questions, she'll need to jump around through the slides. Therefore, she asks you to create hyperlinks between each item in Slide 2 and the corresponding slides in the presentation, and then to create hyperlinks from each slide back to Slide 2.

To create a hyperlink to another slide in the presentation:

▶ 1. If you took a break after the last session, open the **Clinical Report** presentation located in the **Tutorial.04\Tutorial** folder included with your Data Files, and then, if necessary, switch to Normal view.

▶ 2. Go to **Slide 2**. First, you'll link the text "Clinical Trial" on Slide 2 to the slide that gives key information about the clinical trial.

▶ 3. In the first bulleted item, select the text **Clinical Trial**.

▶ 4. Click the **Insert** tab on the Ribbon, and then, in the Links group, click the **Hyperlink** button. The Insert Hyperlink dialog box opens. See Figure 4-16.

Insert Hyperlink dialog box   **Figure 4-16**

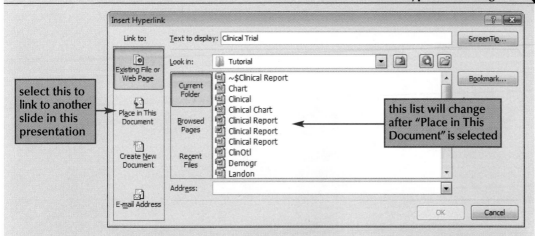

You need to identify the file or location to which you want to link. In this case, you're going to link to a place in the existing document, so you'll want to select that option in the Link to panel on the left side of the dialog box.

▸ **5.** In the Link to panel on the left side of the dialog box, click **Place in This Document**. The dialog box changes to list all of the slides in the presentation.

▸ **6.** In the Select a place in this document list, click **3. Clinical Trial**. The Slide preview area on the right side of the dialog box shows Slide 3. This is the slide the text will be linked to. See Figure 4-17.

Insert Hyperlink dialog box after selecting a slide in current document   **Figure 4-17**

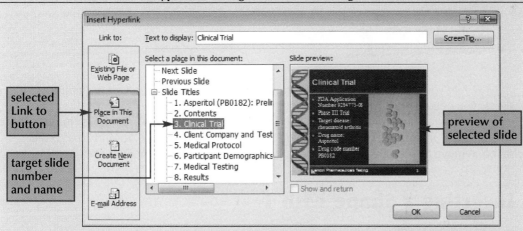

▸ **7.** Click the **OK** button, and then click a blank area of the slide to deselect the text. The text "Clinical Trial" is now a hyperlink, and it is now formatted as green and underlined. (Recall that you can specify the hyperlink color when you set the presentation theme color.)

▸ **8.** Repeat this procedure to add hyperlinks for each of the other bulleted items in Slide 2 so that each item is a hyperlink to its corresponding slide. Slide 2 should then look like Figure 4-18.

Figure 4-18 | Slide 2 with hyperlinks to other slides in presentation

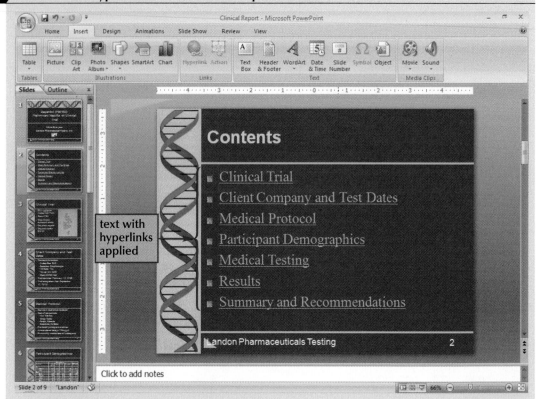

Trouble? If you make a mistake, repeat the procedure. The Edit Hyperlink dialog box will open in place of the Insert Hyperlink dialog box. You can then change the target of the hyperlink.

9. Save the presentation.

Now that you have added hyperlinks from the text in Slide 2 to the corresponding slides, you need hyperlinks from all the other slides back to Slide 2. This way, Allysa can easily jump to any desired slide, jump back to the contents on Slide 2, and then jump to another slide. To create a link back to Slide 2, you will insert a shape, insert text into that shape, remove the borders of the shape, and then convert it to a hyperlink back to Slide 2.

Inserting a Shape with Text

You'll create a hyperlinked shape by first inserting and positioning the shape, and then inserting text into the shape.

Slide 3 with Shapes gallery open   Figure 4-19

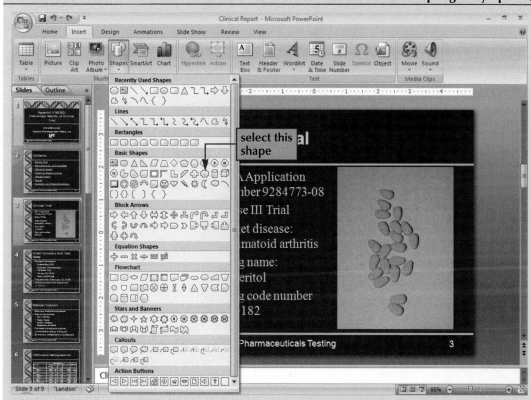

▶ **4.** Move the pointer down between the footer and the slide number near the bottom of the slide.

▶ **5.** Drag the mouse pointer down and to the right to make the shape shown in Figure 4-20. Don't worry about the exact location and size of the shape; you can fix it later.

Figure 4-20 | Slide 3 after plaque shape is inserted

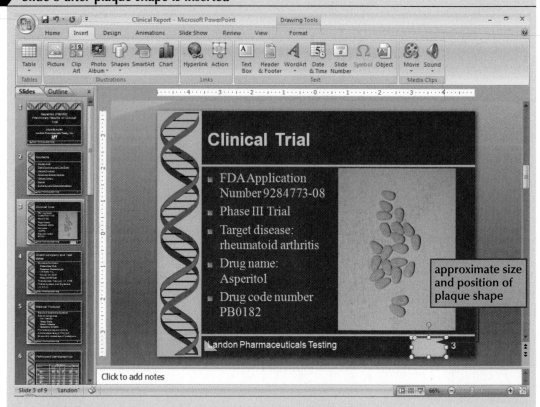

6. With the shape still selected, click the **Format** tab below Drawing Tools on the Ribbon, and then, in the Shape Styles group, click the **More** button.

7. In the Shape Styles gallery, click the **Intense Effect – Dark 1** button located in the first column in the last row in the gallery. The plaque shape changes to a beveled dark brown, similar in color to the background color of the slide but with a subtle gradient fill.

Now that you have the shape to which you'll add a hyperlink, you'll next add text.

To add text to a shape:

1. With the shape still selected on Slide 3, type **Contents**. This will remind Allysa that clicking this shape will jump back to the Contents slide. You might need to adjust the shape size.

2. If necessary, drag the middle sizing handle on the left or right edge of the shape until the shape is big enough to fit the word "Contents" on one line. You might need to make the adjustment two or three times to get the shape just the right size.

3. Deselect the shape. See Figure 4-21.

Slide 3 with completed shape with text and hyperlink | Figure 4-21

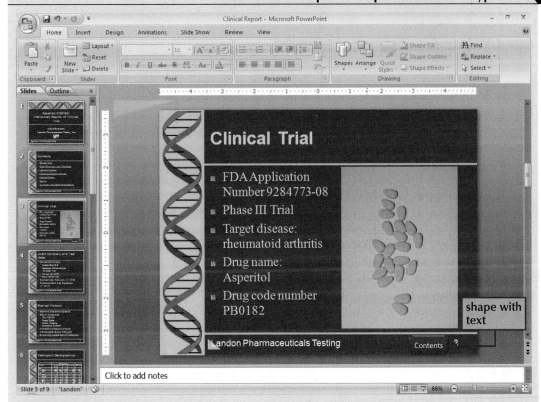

Trouble? If the size and position of the shape in your slide doesn't look like Figure 4-21, make any adjustments now.

You're now ready to make the "Contents" plaque a hyperlink.

To create a hyperlink from the plaque shape to Slide 2:

▶ **1.** Click the edge of the shape to select it.

   Trouble? If you selected the slide number placeholder instead, click in a different location on the shape's edge, for example, on the bottom edge of the Contents plaque.

▶ **2.** Click the **Insert** tab, and then in the Links group, click the **Hyperlink** button. The Insert Hyperlink dialog box opens.

▶ **3.** In the Link to panel on the left side of the dialog box, make sure **Place in This Document** is selected, and then click **2. Contents**. This is the target of the hyperlink.

▶ **4.** Click the **OK** button. The dialog box closes and the shape is formatted as a hyperlink to Slide 2.

   Notice that the entire shape is a hyperlink, not just the text inside the shape, and therefore, the text doesn't change to the green hyperlink color. Shapes and other non-text objects don't change color when they become hyperlinked.

Now you'll copy and paste the hyperlinked Contents shape on the rest of the slides. Because all the links will jump to the same slide, you can copy the shape, its text, and its hyperlink from Slide 3 to the other slides.

To copy the plaque hyperlink to the other slides:

▶ **1.** Make sure the shape is still active, and then press the **Ctrl+C** keys.

▶ **2.** Go to **Slide 4**, and then press the **Ctrl+V** keys. The link text is copied to the same position on Slide 4 as it was on Slide 3. Now you'll verify that the pasted link on Slide 4 has the same target as the original link on Slide 3.

▶ **3.** Right-click the edge of the newly pasted linked shape, and then click **Edit Hyperlink** on the shortcut menu. The Edit Hyperlink dialog box opens.

Trouble? If you don't see Edit Hyperlink on the shortcut menu, you clicked the text box border instead of the link text. Repeat Step 3, but make sure you right-click the link text.

▶ **4.** In the Select a place in this document list, verify that **2. Contents** is selected, and then click the **Cancel** button.

▶ **5.** Repeat Step 2 to paste the link text to Slides 5 through 9 (that is, all the slides that are targets of the hyperlinks on Slide 2).

▶ **6.** Save the presentation.

With all the items on Slide 2 hyperlinked to the other slides and then back again, you're ready to test the results.

To use hyperlinks to jump to specific slides:

▶ **1.** Go to **Slide 2**, and then on the status bar, click the **Slide Show** button 🖵. You'll test the hyperlinks in Slide Show view because they aren't active in Normal view.

▶ **2.** Click the **Clinical Trial** hyperlink. PowerPoint displays Slide 3 ("Clinical Trial").

▶ **3.** Click the **Contents** hyperlink on Slide 3. PowerPoint again displays Slide 2. See Figure 4-22. The Clinical Trial link text is now yellow, indicating that the hyperlink was followed.

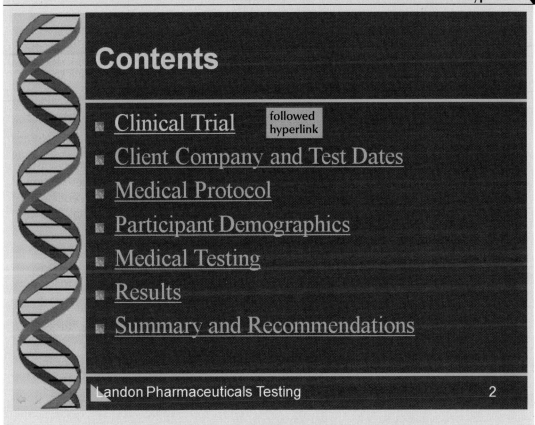

4. Try all the other hyperlinks to make sure they work, and then return to Slide 2 in Normal view.

You have completed the set of hyperlinks within the presentation.

In addition to creating hyperlinks among the slides, you can add action buttons that have essentially the same effect or that can be hyperlinked to another presentation. Allysa wants you to insert an action button that will add a link to another presentation.

Adding Action Buttons

An **action button** is a ready-made shape for which you can easily define a hyperlink to other slides or documents, as well as several other actions. You can use one of the 12 action buttons in PowerPoint, such as Action Button: Home or Action Button: Sound.

Reference Window | **Adding an Action Button as a Link to Another Presentation**

- Click the Insert tab. In the Illustrations group, click the Shapes button.
- Click an action button in the Action Buttons section at the bottom of the menu.
- Click the pointer at the location on the slide where you want the action button to appear.
- In the Action Settings dialog box, click the Hyperlink to option button, click the Hyperlink to list arrow, and then click Other PowerPoint Presentation to open the Hyperlink to Other PowerPoint Presentation dialog box.
- Select the presentation to which you want to jump, and then click the OK button.
- Click the OK button in the Action Settings dialog box.
- Resize and reposition the action button icon as desired.

Allysa wants you to add a link between her presentation and the Landon presentation, which gives the mission statement and contact information of Landon Pharmaceuticals Testing. You'll create a hyperlink to that presentation by adding an action button.

To add an action button to link to another presentation:

▶ 1. Go to **Slide 2**, if you're not there already, and then, if necessary, click the **Insert** tab on the Ribbon.

▶ 2. In the Illustrations group, click the **Shapes** button. The gallery of shapes appears, with the action buttons at the bottom.

▶ 3. Click the **Action Button: Document** button 🗎 located fourth from the right in the bottom row of the gallery. The gallery closes and the pointer changes to $+$.

▶ 4. Click to the left of the slide number near the bottom of Slide 2, at about the same location as you placed the hyperlinked plaque shape on the other slides. A large button with a document icon appears on the slide and the Action Settings dialog box opens.

▶ 5. In the dialog box, click the **Hyperlink to** option button, click the **Hyperlink to** arrow, scroll down, and then click **Other PowerPoint Presentation**. The Hyperlink to Other PowerPoint Presentation dialog box opens. It is similar to the Open dialog box.

▶ 6. Navigate to the **Tutorial.04\Tutorial** folder included with your Data Files, if necessary, click **Landon**, and then click the **OK** button. The Hyperlink to Slide dialog box opens.

▶ 7. With **1. Landon Pharmaceuticals Testing, Inc.** selected, click the **OK** button, and then click **OK** in the Actions Settings dialog box.

▶ 8. Adjust the size and position of the action button, as shown in Figure 4-23.

Slide 2 with Action Button: Document | **Figure 4-23**

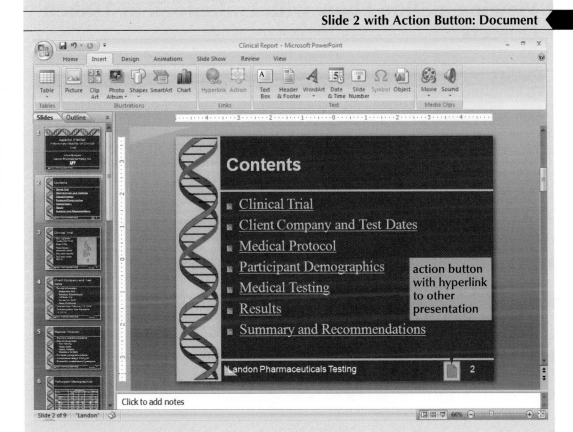

You're now ready to test the action button.

To use the action button to start another presentation:

1. Switch to Slide Show view with Slide 2 ("Contents"), on the screen, and then click the **action button**. Slide 1 of the Landon presentation appears on the screen.

2. Go through the slides of the Landon presentation until you reach the blank slide at the end, and then press the **spacebar** once more. PowerPoint returns to Slide 2 of the Clinical Report presentation.

3. Return to Normal view, and then save the presentation using the default filename.

Tip

To return to the original presentation from a linked presentation, press the Esc key or right-click any slide, and then click End Show on the shortcut menu.

Allysa looks at your work so far and is pleased with your progress. The presentation now includes an imported table from Word, an Excel chart, text links to other slides in the presentation, shapes with hyperlinks back to the Contents slide, and an action button with a link to another presentation.

Viewing a Slide Show with Embedded or Linked Objects

When you present a slide show using a presentation with linked files, those files must be available on a disk so that PowerPoint can access them; and when you embed a file, the source program must be available if you want to edit the embedded object. This is because a copy of the linked file or source program for an embedded file is not included within the PowerPoint file itself; only the path and filename for accessing the linked file are there. Therefore, you should view the presentation on the system that will be used for running the slide show to make sure it has the necessary files and that the hyperlinks are set up properly. If embedded or linked objects don't work when you run the slide show, you'll have to edit the object path so that PowerPoint can find the objects on your disk.

To view the slide show:

1. Go to **Slide 1**, and then on the status bar, click the **Slide Show** button ⊞. Slide 1 appears in Slide Show view.

2. Click the left mouse button (or press the **spacebar**) to go to Slide 2, and then click the **action button** to jump to the other slide show. Slide 1 of the Landon presentation appears on the screen.

3. Press the **Esc** key. The Landon slide show ends and Slide 2 of the Clinical Report presentation appears again.

4. While on Slide 2, test some of the hyperlinks, using the "Contents" hyperlinked shape on each slide to jump back to Slide 2.

5. After viewing all the slides and testing the hyperlinks, return to Slide 1 in Normal view.

InSight | **Editing Hyperlinks**

If you want to copy the presentation file Clinical Report from, for example, your hard drive to your flash drive, you also have to copy the linked files: the presentation file Landon and the Excel file containing the chart. But you'll find that the links to the Landon presentation and to the Excel chart don't work if you try to run the Clinical Report presentation from your jump drive on another computer. This is because the links include the original path and file-name to the files on the hard drive of the computer where you created the links. Therefore, you need to update the links. To update an action button link, you right-click the action but-ton, click Edit Hyperlink on the shortcut menu, and then change the path in the Hyperlink to pathname box. To update the link to an Excel chart, you need to click the Office Button, point to Prepare, and then click Edit Links to Files to open the Links dialog box. Then, you can change the path to the source file.

Allysa is pleased with how well the embedded and linked objects work in her slide show. She now asks you to print the slides in several different formats, to meet the needs of her various audiences.

To prepare the presentation to print in grayscale:

▶ **1.** Click the **Office Button** 🔘 , point to **Print**, and then click **Print Preview**.

▶ **2.** In the Page Setup group on the Print Preview tab, make sure the **Print What** box displays **Slides**.

▶ **3.** In the Print group, click the **Options** button, point to **Color/Grayscale**, and then click **Grayscale**. The presentation now appears in grayscale.

▶ **4.** In the Preview group, click the **Next Page** button five times until you get to Slide 6 ("Participant Demographics"). As you can see, the text of the table isn't visible. This is because you changed the text to white so it would be visible on the dark background, but now with a white background, the text is invisible. The only solution that will allow you to print this slide on a black-and-white printer is to change the text back to black. You'll do that now.

▶ **5.** In the Preview group, click the **Close Print Preview** button, double-click the outer edge of the table on Slide 6, and then drag to select the entire table.

▶ **6.** In the Font group on the Home tab, click the **Font Color button arrow** 🅰️▾ , and then click **Automatic** to change the font to black.

▶ **7.** Click a blank area of the slide twice, once to deselect the Word interface and a second time to deselect the table completely. Now the black text on a brown background is hard to read, but the text will be visible when you print the slides in grayscale.

Now you're ready to print the presentation in grayscale.

To print the presentation as handouts:

▶ **1.** Return to Print Preview, and then go to **Slide 6**. See Figure 4-24. As you can see, the text in the table is now visible.

Figure 4-24 ▶ **Slide 6 in grayscale Print Preview with modified table**

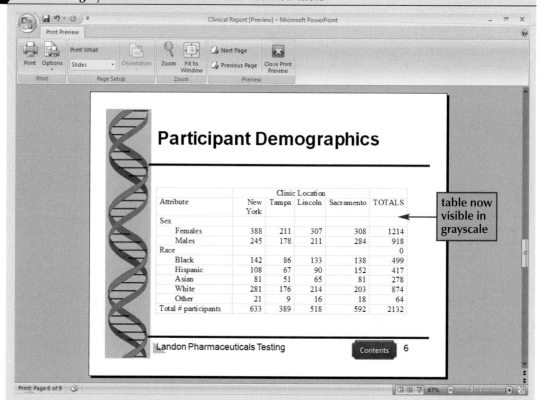

If your instructor asks you to do so, print the presentation as handouts in grayscale.

▶ **2.** In the Page Setup group, click the **Print What arrow**, and then click **Handouts (6 Slides Per Page)**.

▶ **3.** In the Print group, click the **Print** button. The Print dialog box opens.

▶ **4.** Click the **OK** button. The printed presentation should be clear and legible.

▶ **5.** Close the Print Preview window. Now you'll want to undo the change you made to the table text color.

▶ **6.** In the Quick Access Toolbar, click the **Undo** button ⟲. This restores the color of the text on Slide 6.

Printing the Presentation as an Outline

Now Allysa wants you to see what the presentation will look like if she decides to print it in Outline view.

To print the presentation as an outline:

▶ **1.** Click the **Office Button** ⊙, point to **Print**, and then click **Print Preview**.

▶ **2.** In the Page Setup group, click the **Print What arrow**, and then click **Outline View**. The Print Preview window shows your presentation in Outline view.

▶ **3.** In the Zoom group, click the **Zoom** button. The Zoom dialog box opens.

4. Click the **100%** option button, and then click the **OK** button.

5. Scroll down until the text of Slide 1 is at the top of the pane and at least part of the text of Slide 5 is visible near the bottom of the screen. See Figure 4-25.

Print Preview of Outline view   Figure 4-25

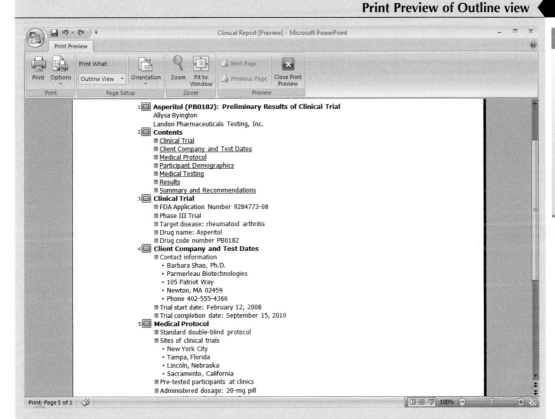

As you can see, only the text of the presentation appears on the page, and the entire presentation fits on one page. Print the outline if your instructor asks you to do so.

6. In the Print group, click the **Print** button to open the Print dialog box, and then click the **OK** button. The outline prints.

7. In the Preview group, click the **Close Print Preview** button.

Allysa decides not to copy the Outline view printout for her audience because the outline lacks the important table in Slide 6 and the chart in Slide 8.

Customizing Handouts

Allysa still wants to give her audience handouts, but she doesn't want them to appear like the usual PowerPoint handouts. Therefore, she asks you to customize the Handout Masters.

To customize the Handout Masters:

1. Click the **View** tab on the Ribbon, and then in the Presentation Views group, click **Handout Master**. The commands on the Handout Master tab appear.

▶ **2.** In the Placeholders group, click the **Header** check box to deselect it, click the **Date** check box to deselect it, and then make sure the **Footer** and **Page Number** check boxes are selected.

▶ **3.** In the lower-left corner of the Handout Master, click the edge of the Footer placeholder to select it, click the **Home** tab on the Ribbon, and then change the font size to **20** points.

▶ **4.** Similarly, change the font size of the text in the page number placeholder located in the lower-right corner of the Handout Master.

▶ **5.** Click in the Footer placeholder, type **Clinical Report of Asperitol**, and then deselect the placeholder.

▶ **6.** Click the **Handout Master** tab.

▶ **7.** In the Background group, click the **Background Styles** button, and then click **Style 2** in the gallery. The gallery closes and the page background changes from white to light tan. You have now modified the Handout Master according to Allysa's specifications. See Figure 4-26.

Figure 4-26 ▶ **Customized Handout Master**

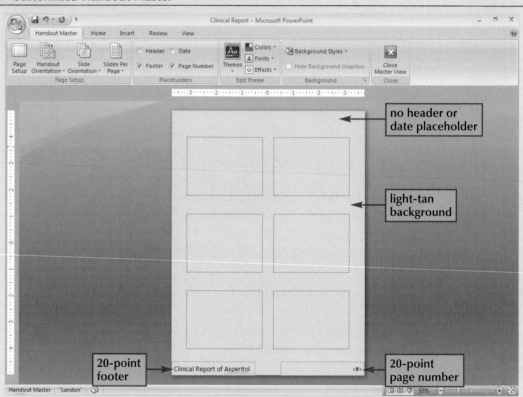

▶ **8.** In the Close group, click the **Close Master View** button, and then save the presentation.

Allysa likes the customized handouts and makes printed color copies of handouts with nine slides per page so that all nine slides of the presentation fit on one page.

Now Allysa wants you to help her prepare the presentation for posting on the Web.

Publishing Presentations on the World Wide Web

As you probably know, the **Internet** is a network of thousands of smaller networks, all joined together electronically as part of a global information-sharing system called the **World Wide Web** (also called simply the **Web**). The Web allows you to find and view electronic documents called **Web pages**. Organizations and individuals make their Web pages available by placing them on a **Web server**, a dedicated network computer with high-capacity hard disks. The Web, then, is a connected network of these Web servers. The location of a particular set of Web pages on a server is called a **Web site**. You can access a particular Web site by specifying its address, also called its **Uniform Resource Locator** (**URL**). To specify URLs and to view Web pages, you use a **Web browser**, a software program that sends requests for Web pages, retrieves them, and then interprets them for display on the computer screen. Two of the most popular browsers are Microsoft Internet Explorer and Mozilla Firefox.

Most Web sites contain a **home page**, a Web page that contains general information about the site. Home pages are like "home base"—they are starting points for online viewers. They usually contain links to the rest of the pages in the Web site.

Publishing a Web page usually means copying files (or saving them) to a Web server so that others can view the Web page. In PowerPoint, you'll use the Save As command to save your presentation as Web pages. When you select the Web pages file type, the Save As dialog box provides options by which you can customize the Web page you are saving.

Normally, you and the organization for which you work would create Web pages using a **Web page editor**, software specifically designed for this purpose, such as Microsoft Expression Web. But sometimes you want to publish a PowerPoint presentation, for example, as a link from the organization's home page. Therefore, Allysa wants you to save the Clinical Report presentation as Web pages so they can be copied onto Landon Pharmaceuticals Testing's Web site. After being placed on the Web site, the presentation will be available to company and client personnel who have access to the Web pages.

To prepare Allysa's PowerPoint presentation (or any presentation) for viewing on the World Wide Web, first you have to convert it to a file format called **HTML**, with the filename extension .htm or .html. HTML stands for **Hypertext Markup Language**, a special software language for describing the format of a Web page so that Web browsers can interpret and display the Web pages. The HTML markings in a file tell the browser how to format the text, graphics, tables, and other objects. Fortunately, you don't have to learn Hypertext Markup Language to create HTML documents; PowerPoint does the work for you. You can easily save any PowerPoint presentation as an HTML document using PowerPoint's Save As command and selecting Web Page or Single File Web Page as the file type. This procedure allows you to create a Web page file (with the filename extension .htm) that includes all the necessary images and controls to produce a professional online presentation.

If you want to edit a resulting HTML document, you'll have to use either a word processor that supports HTML editing (for example, Microsoft Word) or, better still, a dedicated HTML editor (for example, Microsoft Expression Web). PowerPoint doesn't support direct editing of HTML documents. You can, of course, make editing changes in PowerPoint and then save the results again as a Web page.

Publishing the Web Pages

Allysa wants you to save the Clinical Report presentation as a Web page so that she can copy it to the company's Web site. You remember that you added an action button to link to the Landon presentation, so that presentation will need to be saved as a Web page as well. You'll do that first.

To save a presentation as a single file Web page:

▶ **1.** Open the presentation **Landon** from the **Tutorial.04\Tutorial** folder included with your Data Files.

▶ **2.** Click the **Office Button**, and then click **Save As**.

▶ **3.** Click the **Save as type** arrow, and then click **Single File Web Page**. The bottom part of the Save As dialog box now displays options for publishing the Web page. See Figure 4-27.

Figure 4-27 | Save As dialog box for saving presentation as a single file Web page

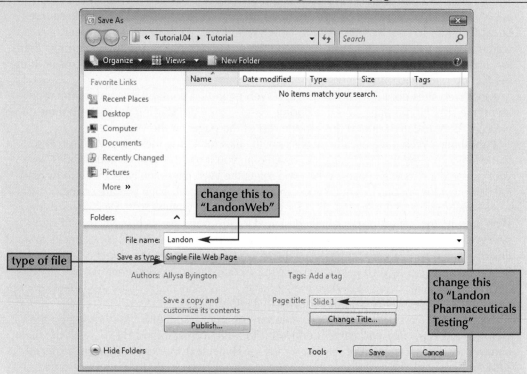

You'll now change the Web page title, which is the title of the page displayed in the title bar of the Web browser.

▶ **4.** Click the **Change Title** button. The Set Page Title dialog box opens.

▶ **5.** If necessary, change the page title to **Landon Pharmaceuticals Testing**, and then click the **OK** button. Now you're ready to publish the Web page.

▶ **6.** In the Save As dialog box, change the File name to **LandonWeb** (no spaces). This ensures that any type of browser can open the file, even browsers that don't accept spaces in the filenames. See Figure 4-28.

Completed Save As dialog box ◀ **Figure 4-28**

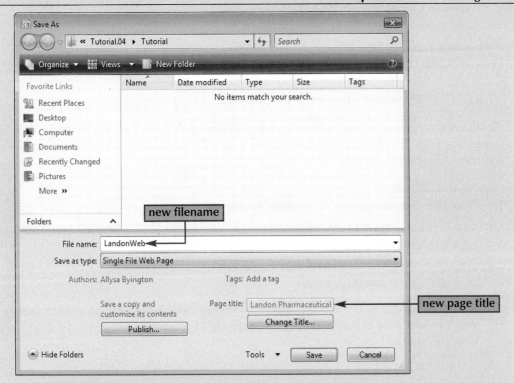

Trouble? If any of the options in your dialog box are different from those in Figure 4-28, make the changes now.

▶ **7.** Click the **Save** button in the Save As dialog box to save the presentation as a single file Web page in the Tutorial.04\Tutorial folder.

▶ **8.** Close the LandonWeb presentation without saving changes.

Having saved the Landon presentation as a Web page file named LandonWeb, you now need to fix the hyperlinked action button in the Clinical Report presentation so that its target is the Web page file LandonWeb rather than the PowerPoint presentation file Landon. You need to do this before you save Clinical Report as a Web page because you cannot edit Web page files within PowerPoint.

To edit the hyperlink target and save the presentation as a Web page:

▶ **1.** With the Clinical Report presentation in the PowerPoint window, go to **Slide 2** in Normal view.

▶ **2.** Right-click the **action button**, and then click **Edit Hyperlink** on the shortcut menu. The Action Settings dialog box opens with the Mouse Click tab on top. Now you want to change the target file from Landon to the Web page LandonWeb.

▶ **3.** Click the **Hyperlink to** arrow, and then click **Other File**, if necessary.

▶ **4.** Navigate to the **Tutorial.04\Tutorial** folder, if necessary, click **LandonWeb**, and then click the **OK** button.

▶ **5.** Click the **OK** button in the Action Settings dialog box. Now you're ready to save Clinical Report as a Web page.

▶ **6.** Using the procedure previously described, save the Clinical Report presentation as a single file Web page with the page title **Clinical Report of Asperitol** and the filename **ClinicalReportWeb** (without spaces).

Now that you saved the presentation as a Web page file, you're ready to see how it looks in a Web browser.

Viewing a Presentation in a Web Browser

It's always a good idea to see exactly what the presentation looks like in a browser before you actually publish it to a Web server. Use your Windows Explorer to navigate to and open ClinicalReportWeb.

To view the presentation in a Web browser:

▶ **1.** Right-click the **Start** button 🔘 in the lower-left corner of your screen, and then click **Explore** on the quick menu.

▶ **2.** Navigate to the **Tutorial.04\Tutorial** folder included with your Data Files, and then double-click **ClinicalReportWeb**.

At this point, you might see the message "This presentation contains content that your browser may not be able to show properly. If you would like to proceed anyway, click here."

▶ **3.** If the message appears, click the **here** link in the preceding phrase.

If you are using Internet Explorer, you might see a partial display of Slide 1 of ClinicalReportWeb, with the Information bar above it that says "To help protect your security, Internet Explorer has restricted this webpage from running scripts or ActiveX controls that could access your computer. Click here for options." You might also see the Information Bar dialog box. Because you created the content, you don't have to worry about viruses and other dangers, so you can allow it to open.

▶ **4.** If the Information Bar dialog box is open, click the **Close** button.

▶ **5.** If the Information bar is at the top of the window, click it, click **Allow Blocked Content** on the menu that opens, and then click **Yes** in the dialog box that opens to verify that you do indeed want to use active content.

▶ **6.** If necessary, maximize the browser window and close the Favorites or other type of pane in the window. Slide 1 of the presentation appears in the large pane on the right, and the slide titles appear in the Outline pane on the left. See Figure 4-29.

Clinical Report presentation Web page in browser ◀ **Figure 4-29**

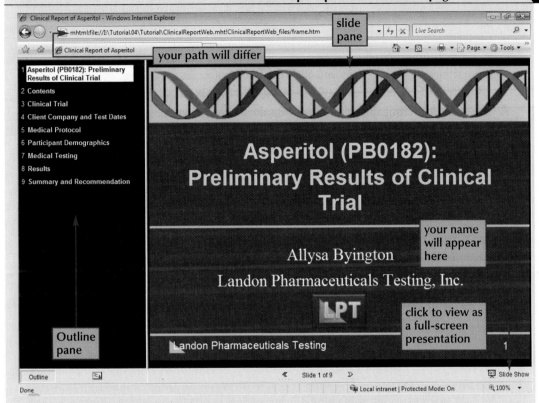

Trouble? If you don't see the outline, click the Outline button at the bottom of the screen.

Now you're ready to browse through the presentation Web page using the navigation controls and the hyperlinks.

To navigate through the presentation in the Web browser:

▶ **1.** On the navigation toolbar at the bottom of the Web page, click the **Next Slide** button ⧐ . The slide pane now displays Slide 2 of the presentation.

▶ **2.** In the Outline pane of the Web page, click **8 Results**. The slide pane now displays Slide 8.

▶ **3.** On the navigation toolbar at the bottom of the Web page, click the **Previous Slide** button ⧏ . Slide 7 ("Medical Testing") appears on the screen. As you can see, the navigation buttons help you easily move one slide forward or backward, whereas the outline hyperlinks allow you to jump from one slide to any other—in any order.

▶ **4.** In the Outline pane, click **2 Contents**, and then click the **action button** on the slide. Slide 1 of the LandonWeb page appears in the browser window, or in a new window of the browser.

Trouble? You'll probably see the same warning messages as before. Repeat the preceding steps until Slide 1 of the LandonWeb page appears.

▶ **5.** Go through the slides of LandonWeb as desired.

▶ **6.** To the left of the Address bar at the top of the browser window, click the **Back** button in the upper-left corner of the browser toolbar as many times as necessary to return to Slide 2 of the ClinicalReportWeb presentation. (In the browser, you can't just press Esc to exit the LandonWeb Web page and return to the ClinicalReportWeb Web page.)

Trouble? If Slide 1 of the LandonWeb presentation stays in your browser window no matter how many times you click the Back button, click the Recent Pages button, and then click the top Clinical Report of Asperitol.

▶ **7.** Look through ClinicalReportWeb as you desire, and then exit your Web browser.

Trouble? If a second instance of Internet Explorer started when you used the action button on Slide 2, close both Internet Explorer windows.

▶ **8.** In the Explorer window, click the **Close** button ![X].

Allysa is pleased with how the presentation looks in the browser and sends the files to the company's technical support person to publish to the Landon Pharmaceuticals Testing Web site. Next, she wants to schedule a specific time to broadcast her presentation over the Internet to get feedback from others.

Sharing and Collaborating with Others

PowerPoint provides various methods for delivering your presentations and collaborating with others, including sending presentations via e-mail, making a presentation available on the World Wide Web, and sharing files through Windows Meeting Space, available with the Windows Vista operating system. You're probably already familiar with e-mail, and you just learned about publishing a presentation as a Web page. This section focuses on holding online meetings and sharing files through Windows Meeting Space.

An **online meeting** is a method of sharing and exchanging information with people at different locations in real time (the actual time during which an event takes place), as if all the participants were together in the same room. To hold an online meeting, you can use **Windows Meeting Space**, a program that manages file sharing and online meetings. It allows participants to write notes or draw sketches on an electronic "whiteboard," send and receive typed messages, share handouts, exchange files, and to log activities that occur during the meeting.

Windows Meeting Space requires that you have the Windows Vista operating system to initiate a meeting and that all attendees likewise have Vista.

Setting Up an Online Meeting with Windows Meeting Space | Reference Window

- To initiate an online meeting, click the Start Button in the lower-left corner of your Vista screen, click All Programs, and then click Windows Meeting Space. The Meeting Space window opens.
- Click Start a new meeting, type a meeting name in the indicated box, type a password in the indicated box, and then click the Create a meeting button (a green circle with a right arrow). The Windows Meeting Space dialog box now has three sections. The large section on the left allows you to share a program or your desktop; the section in the upper right lists the participants and allows you to invite other people to the meeting; and the section in the lower right allows you to add handouts to the meeting.
- To invite participants, click the Invite people icon on the right side of the Meeting Space window. The Invite people dialog box opens. If other people are on your local area network (LAN), their names will appear in the Invite people dialog box. Click the names of those you want to invite. You can also invite anyone else who is running Vista and for whom you have an e-mail address. Click the Invite others button at the bottom of the Invite people dialog box, click Send an invitation in e-mail to open an Outlook e-mail window (you have to be set up to send e-mails in Outlook), type the e-mail address of the invitee, click the Office Button, and then click Send.
- To accept an invitation to the online meeting, open the e-mail invitation, open the attachment to the e-mail, save the attachment to your hard drive, run Windows Meeting Space (as explained previously), open an invitation file, and then select the file you just saved.
- To pass a text note (for typing text messages) or an ink note (for drawing diagrams, equations, and so forth), right-click the attendee to whom you want to send the note, click Note or Ink, type or draw your note, and then click Send.
- To share handouts, which each participant (one at a time) can change and have those changes appear on all participants' handouts, click the Add a handout button in the Handouts section of the Windows Meeting Space dialog box, navigate to the file that you want to share as a handout, and then click the Open button.
- To leave a meeting, click Meeting on the Windows Meeting Space menu bar, and then click Exit.
- To end the online meeting, click Meeting on the menu bar, and then click Exit.

Allysa decides to arrange an online meeting of her presentation for the people in the headquarters of her clients at Parmerleau Biotechnologies. Then, she and her staff give a successful presentation of the clinical-trial report of Asperitol.

Besides holding an online meeting, Allysa wants to prepare the presentation for maximum sharing with others. She asks you to help her identify features of the presentation not supported by previous versions (in case other interested parties haven't upgraded to PowerPoint 2007), to use the Document Inspector to make sure the presentation is in proper order, to use the Information Rights Manager to make sure only those who should view the presentation can view it, and to prepare customized handouts based on the presentation.

Identifying Features Not Supported by Previous Versions

Allysa realizes that some of her clients and colleagues haven't yet upgraded to Power-Point 2007, so she asks you to check the Clinical Report presentation for features not supported by previous versions. For this purpose, you'll use the Microsoft Office Power-Point Compatibility Checker.

To check for features not supported by previous versions:

▶ **1.** Click the **Office Button** 🔘, point to **Prepare**, and then click **Run Compatibility Checker**. PowerPoint searches your presentation for features that aren't supported by earlier versions of PowerPoint, and then opens the Microsoft Office PowerPoint Compatibility Checker dialog box. See Figure 4-30.

| Figure 4-30 | Compatibility Checker dialog box |

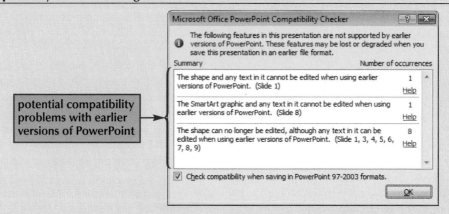

potential compatibility problems with earlier versions of PowerPoint

▶ **2.** Look over the features in the dialog box. As you can see, some of the Office 2007 features are not compatible with PowerPoint 97–2003 formats, but none of the issues is serious. Most of the incompatible features would probably show up properly; you just wouldn't be able to edit them. You inform Allysa of these incompatibilities so she can decide later if she wants to save the presentation in an early format.

▶ **3.** Click the **OK** button. The dialog box closes.

Using the Document Inspector

The **Document Inspector** is a tool you can use to check a presentation for hidden data, such as the author's name and other personal information. Allysa decides that she should check the Clinical Report presentation for hidden data. She asks you to do this now.

To check the document using the Document Inspector:

▶ **1.** Click the **Office Button** 🔘, point to **Prepare**, and then click **Inspect Document**. The Document Inspector dialog box opens.

▶ **2.** If any of the check boxes in this dialog box are not checked, click them. See Figure 4-31.

Document Inspector dialog box ◄ Figure 4-31

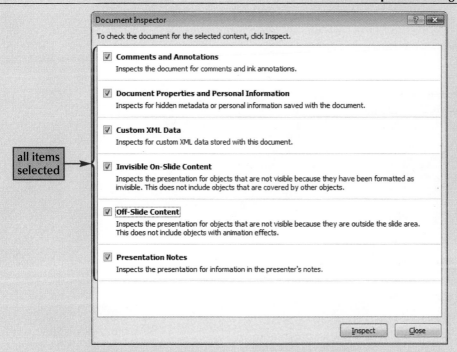

all items selected

3. Click the **Inspect** button at the bottom of the dialog box. After a moment, the Document Inspector displays the results. Your presentation will probably have no problem items except document properties (which include the author's name) and Publish to Web Page information (which includes the Web page title that you used when you saved the presentation as a single file Web page). Allysa doesn't feel that these pieces of information are private, so she sees no reason to remove them.

4. Look over the various types of items that the Document Inspector checks. For example, if you happen to import, embed, or link an object that extends beyond the edges of a slide, the Off-Slide Content feature would have detected the problem.

5. Click the **Close** button on the dialog box.

6. Switch to Slide Sorter view and adjust the zoom to approximately **85%** so that all nine slides appear at once at maximum size in the slide sorter window. See Figure 4-32.

Figure 4-32 | **Completed Clinical Report presentation**

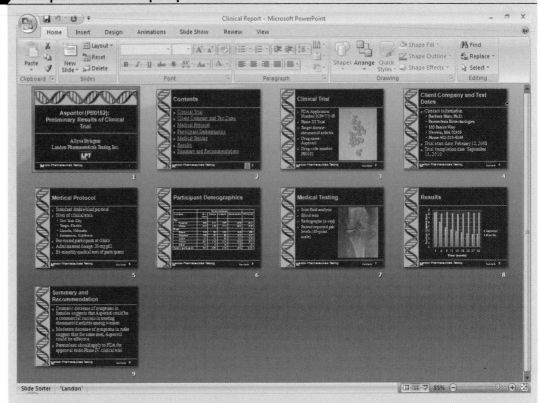

▶ **7.** Submit the file to your instructor in either electronic or printed form as requested, and then close the file.

Marking the Presentation as Final

Before Allysa shares the Clinical Report with others, she wants to make the presentation read-only, which means that others can read but cannot modify the presentation. In PowerPoint, to make a presentation read-only, you use the Mark as Final command, which disables all typing and editing commands. You'll mark Clinical Report as final now.

To mark the presentation as final (read-only):

▶ **1.** Click the **Office Button** , point to **Prepare**, and then click **Mark as Final**. PowerPoint displays a dialog box so you can confirm that you want to mark the presentation as final.

▶ **2.** Click the **OK** button. PowerPoint marks the document, disables typing and editing features, and then saves the document. Another dialog box opens telling you that the document has been marked as final.

▶ **3.** Click the **OK** button.

Trouble? The dialog box telling you that the document has been marked as final might not appear.

The Marked as Final icon appears in the status bar.

Managing Information Rights

Now Allysa wants you to use the **Information Rights Manager** (**IRM**), which allows you to specify access permissions to your presentation. This is extremely important for sensitive information such as the results of a clinical trial, where confidentiality is essential but yet you'll be e-mailing the presentation to many people.

To use the IRM, your computer and the computers of those with whom you are going to share sensitive information must have installed Windows Rights Management Services (RMS). This software is automatically installed on all computers that use Windows Vista. However, the IRM comes only with Microsoft Office 2007 Professional Plus or Office 2007 Ultra, so you might not have IRM available.

Using the Information Rights Manager | Reference Window

- Open the presentation that you want to share.
- Click the Office Button, point to Prepare, point to Restrict Permissions (if this doesn't appear on your computer, you can't use the IRM), and then click Do Not Distribute. The Permissions dialog box opens.
- Select the Restrict permission to this document check box, and then select the desired access level that you want for each user to whom you plan to send the presentation. The permission levels are Read (users can only read the presentation but not edit, print, or copy it), Change (users can read, modify, and save the new version of the presentation), or Full Control (users have full rights to do anything the author can do).

Allysa uses the IRM to distribute secure copies of the Clinical Report to colleagues and customers.

Session 4.2 Quick Check | Review

1. What is a hyperlink?
2. What is an action button?
3. How do you save a presentation as a single file Web page?
4. Describe what a presentation looks like in your browser.
5. What appears on the printed page when you print your presentation as an outline?
6. Describe how to hold an online meeting using Windows Meeting Space.
7. What does the Document Inspector reveal?

Review | **Tutorial Summary**

In this tutorial, you learned how to apply a design theme created in one PowerPoint presentation to another presentation, and how to import, modify, and export a Microsoft Word outline to your presentation and import a digital photograph. You learned how to embed and modify a Word table in your presentation and link and modify an Excel chart. You also learned how to create and edit hyperlinks, add action buttons, publish a presentation as a Web page, and securely share your presentation and collaborate with others over the Internet.

Key Terms

action button
destination program
Document Inspector
embed
follow
home page
HTML (Hypertext Markup
  Language)
hyperlink (link)
import

Information Rights
  Manager (IRM)
Internet
link
object
object linking and embed-
  ding (OLE)
online meeting
publish
source program
target

Uniform Resource
  Locator (URL)
Web browser
Web page
Web page editor
Web server
Web site
Windows Meeting Space
World Wide Web (Web)

| Practice | **Review Assignments** |

Get hands-on practice of the skills you learned in the tutorial using the same case scenario.

Data Files needed for the Review Assignments: Hospitals.docx, Landon.pptx, LPTChart.xlsx, LPTInfo.docx, Patient.jpg, Placebos.jpg

Allysa not only gives reports to clients of Landon Pharmaceuticals Testing clinical trials but also gives presentations to prospective clients. She now asks you to help prepare an information presentation on Landon Pharmaceuticals Testing. Complete the following:

1. Open a new, blank presentation, and then import the Word outline **LPTInfo** located in the Tutorial.04\Review folder included with your Data Files.

2. Type "Getting to Know Landon Pharmaceuticals Testing" as the title in the title slide, and type your name as the subtitle in the title slide, and then save the presentation to the Tutorial.04\Review folder using the filename **Landon Info**.

3. Apply the design theme from the presentation file **Landon**, located in the Tutorial.04\Review folder.

4. Turn on slide numbering in the Header and Footer dialog box, and set the Footer to **Landon Pharmaceuticals Testing** for all slides, including the title slide.

5. In Slide Sorter view, select all the slides except Slide 1 (title slide), apply the Title and Content layout to all the selected slides, and then reset the slides.

6. Still in Slide Sorter view, select Slides 4 and 5, and then apply the Two Content layout to the selected slides.

7. In Slide 4 in Normal view, import the picture **Patient.jpg**, located in the Tutorial.04\Review folder.

8. In Slide 5, import the picture **Placebos.jpg**, located in the Tutorial.04\Review folder. If necessary, resize the picture so it's as large as possible without covering the background objects.

9. In Slide 8, embed the Word table from the Word file **Hospitals**, located in the Tutorial.04\Review folder.

10. Make the Word program active, change the font size for all the text in the table to 20 points, and then adjust the size of the table by increasing the width of the columns so the table appears as large as possible on the slide.

11. Change the font color in the table to white, click the Design Tab under Table Tools, and then, in the Table Styles group, click the Light List – Accent 6 style. Close the Word Ribbon and return to PowerPoint.

12. Start Excel, open the Excel file **LPTChart**, located in the Tutorial.04\Review folder, and then save it as **Landon Cost Chart** in the same folder.

13. Copy the chart, and then return to the Landon Info presentation (but do not close the Landon Cost Chart workbook). Click the edge of the content placeholder, and then paste the chart onto Slide 9.

14. Display the PowerPoint and the Excel windows side by side, go to Sheet1 in the Excel window, edit the cost per patient in 2006 to $3417, and then save the file and exit Excel. (Resize the chart on Slide 9, if necessary.)

15. Open the **Landon** presentation file, located in the Tutorial.04\Review folder, and then copy the main text box containing the mission statement on Slide 2. Switch to the Landon Info presentation, go to Slide 2, change the layout to Title Only, and then paste the mission statement into the slide.

16. Copy the contact information from Slide 3 of the Landon presentation, go to Slide 10 in the Landon Info presentation, change the layout to Title Only, and then paste the contact information into the slide.

17. In Slide 3, use the bulleted items to create hyperlinks to the corresponding slides in the rest of the presentation.

18. In Slide 3, create a Plaque shape in the lower-right corner of the slide. Add text to the shape with the text **Mission Statement**. Resize the shape so it fits to the left of the slide number and below the yellow horizontal line, and so the text fits inside the shape. Make the shape a hyperlink to Slide 2.

19. In Slide 4, insert the Action Button: Home at the bottom of the slide, between the footer and slide number. Click Slide in the Hyperlink to list, and then select 3. "What We Will Cover".

20. Adjust the size of the action button so that it fits between the yellow line at the bottom of the slide just to the left of the slide number.

21. Change the shape style of the action button to Intense Effect – Accent 6, located in the lower-right corner of the Shape Style gallery.

22. Copy the action button to Slides 5 through 10.

23. View the slide show, test all the links, and then save the presentation using the default filename.

24. Customize the Handout Master so that it displays only the date and the page number, view the presentation in grayscale, make any adjustments necessary so that all the elements are legible, and then, if requested by your instructor, print the presentation as handouts with four slides per page and print the outline.

25. Save the presentation as a single Web page named **LandonInfoWeb** (no spaces), with the page title **Landon Pharmaceuticals Testing Information**. View the Web page in your browser, test the links, and then close your browser.

26. Export the outline to a Rich Text file named **Landon Info Final** in the Tutorial.04\Review folder.

27. Start Word, open the file **Landon Info Final**, located in the Tutorial.04\Review folder, and then change all the text to 12-point, black Times New Roman. Save the document as a Word document using the same file name. Exit Word.

28. Check the presentation for features not supported by earlier versions of PowerPoint, and then inspect the document for hidden data.

29. Submit the completed presentation in printed or electronic form, as requested by your instructor, and then close all open files.

Apply | **Case Problem 1**

Apply the skills you learned in this tutorial to create a presentation to recruit new customers for a credit union.

Data Files needed for this Case Problem: CredUnion.jpg, FLCUChart.xlsx, FLCUDes.pptx, FLCUOtln.docx, FLCUTbl.docx, Money.jpg

Flat Lake Credit Union Dwayne Harris is the manager of the Flat Lake Credit Union in Safford, Arizona. One of his responsibilities is to give presentations to potential customers about the services and benefits of membership in the credit union. Complete the following:

1. Open a new, blank presentation, type **Services and Benefits of Credit Union Membership** as the title in the title slide, and then type your name as the subtitle in the title slide.

2. Import the Word outline **FLCUOtln**, located in the Tutorial.04\Case1 folder included with your Data Files.

3. Apply the design theme from the presentation file **FLCUDes**, located in the Tutorial.04\Case1 folder.

4. Apply the Title and Content layout to all the slides with bulleted lists. (*Hint*: Switch to Slide Sorter view, select Slides 2 through 7, and in the Slides group on the Home tab, use the Layout button.)

5. With Slides 2 through 7 still selected in Slide Sorter view, reset the selected slides.

6. Save the presentation to the Tutorial.04\Case1 folder using the filename **FLCUServices**.

7. Add the footer **Flat Lake Credit Union**, and display slide numbers. Do not display the footer or the slide numbers on the title slide.

8. In Slide 3, change the slide layout to Two Content and import the picture file **Money.jpg**, with the bulleted list on the left and the picture on the right.

9. In Slide 7, without changing the slide layout, insert the picture **CredUnion.jpg**, and then resize and position it below the bulleted list and above the footer.

10. Add a new Slide 8 to the presentation, type the slide title **Credit Union Branches**, and embed a Word table from the file **FLCUTbl**, located in the Tutorial.04\Case1 folder. Resize the table so it appears as large as possible.

11. Edit the table so that the text is yellow and the borders are white.

12. Add a new Slide 9 with the title **Credit Union Earnings**, change the layout to Title Only, and then link the chart in the Excel worksheet **FLCUChart** (located in your Tutorial.04\Case1 folder) to that slide using a copy-and-paste operation. Resize the chart as large as possible on the slide.

13. Change the Chart Style (in the Design tab) to Style 6 and set the font size of the two axis labels ("Earnings ($Millions)" and "Year") to 28 points.

EXPLORE 14. Copy Slide 2 from FLCUDes to make it Slide 10 of FLCUServices. (*Hint*: With FLCUDes open, click the miniature of Slide 2 in the Slides tab on the left edge of the PowerPoint window, use the Copy command to copy the slide, and then, in FLCUServices, with Slide 9 as the active slide, paste the new slide.)

15. In Slide 10, insert the Action Button: Home and make it a hyperlink to the first slide in the presentation. (*Hint*: Change the Hyperlink to value to First Slide.) This will allow Dwayne to easily jump from the end to the beginning of the slide show.

EXPLORE 16. Resize the action button to 0.75 by 0.75 inches. (*Hint*: With the action button selected, click the Format tab below Drawing Tools, and in the Size group, set the desired vertical and horizontal dimensions.)

17. Move the action button to the lower-left corner of the slide, so it's near the bottom of the picture panel of Flat Lake, and then change the Shape Style to Intense Effect – Accent 1 (located on the bottom row, second from the left, in the Shape Style gallery).

18. After completing the slide show, save the presentation using the default filename.

19. View the slide show in Slide Show view and test the action button that you inserted.

20. Submit the completed presentation in printed or electronic form, as requested by your instructor. If you print the presentation in grayscale, hide the background graphics on Slide 1. After printing in grayscale, make sure you unhide the background graphics before you proceed to the next step.

21. Save the presentation as a single file Web page with the filename **FLCUWeb** with the Page title "Services and Benefits of Credit Union Membership."

22. View the Web page in your browser, and then close all open windows.

Challenge | **Case Problem 2**

Expand the skills you learned in this tutorial to create a presentation for a wildlife management company.

Data Files needed for this Case Problem: BirdBlt.jpg, FlwBlt.jpg, WMCchart.xlsx, WMCDes.pptx, WMCOtl.docx

Wildlife Management Consultants Hillary Trejo of DeForest, Wisconsin, is president of Wildlife Management Consultants (WMC), a small company that contracts with the Wisconsin Division of Natural Resources and the Bureau of Wildlife Management to manage wildlife (plants and animals) in wildlife refuges and state forests. Hillary asks you to help her prepare and publish a presentation on the services offered by WMC. Complete the following:

1. Open the presentation file **WMCDes** located in the Tutorial.04\Case2 folder included with your Data Files. Hillary wants you to modify this file so you can use it in other presentations as a design theme.

2. Switch to Slide Master view, and then click the Office Theme Slide Master at the top of the pane on the left side of the window.

⊕ **EXPLORE** 3. Click the placeholder text of the level-1 (top) bullet, and change the bullet to the picture **BirdBlt** (head of a bird), located in the Tutorial.04\Case2 folder. (*Hint*: Open the Picture Bullet dialog box, click the Import button, navigate to the Tutorial.04\Case2 folder, and then import **BirdBlt**.)

⊕ **EXPLORE** 4. Repeat the procedure in Step 3 to make the second-level bullet the picture **FlwBlt** (flower bullet), and then reduce its size to 80% of normal. (*Hint*: To adjust the size, use the Size feature in the Bullets and Numbering dialog box.)

5. Return to Normal view, save the presentation to the Tutorial.04\Case2 folder using the filename **WMCDesign**, but leave the presentation open as you complete the remaining steps.

6. Open a new, blank presentation, type **Services of Wildlife Management Consultants** in the title placeholder, and then type your name in the subtitle placeholder.

7. Apply the design theme **WMCDesign**, which you saved to the Tutorial.04\Case2 folder.

8. Import the Word outline in the file **WMCOtl**, located in the Tutorial.04\Case2 folder. Reapply the Title and Content layout to all the slides with bulleted lists, and then reset the slides to follow the default design theme.

⊕ **EXPLORE** 9. Insert the current date, the footer **Wildlife Management**, and the slide number on all the slides including the title slide. (*Hint*: To insert the date, use the same dialog box that you use to insert a footer and the slide number.)

10. Save the presentation as **WMCServices** in the Tutorial.04\Case2 folder.

⊕ **EXPLORE** 11. Change the layout of Slide 3 to Two Content, and then into the left content placeholder on Slide 3, import a photograph of one of the animal species listed on the slide. Use the Microsoft online clip art and media service to find this photo. (*Hint*: Make sure your computer is connected to the Internet, and then click the Clip Art button in the content placeholder to open the Clip Art task pane. In the Results should be list, select only Photographs and deselect all the others.)

12. Make each of the bulleted items in Slide 2 a link to the corresponding slide in the presentation.

⊕ **EXPLORE** 13. Format the background image Wilderness (text with overlaid plants and animals) as a hyperlink to Slide 2. (*Hint*: Switch to Slide Master view, click the WMCDesign Slide Master, make the "Wilderness" object a hyperlink to Slide 2, and then return to Normal view.)

✪ EXPLORE 14. In Slide 3, swap the bulleted list in the left content placeholder with the photograph on the right. (*Hint*: Use the Cut and Paste commands to move the bulleted list.) Adjust the size and position of the photograph as desired.

15. In Slide 8, change the layout to Title Only, and then link the Excel chart **WMCchart**, located in the Tutorial.04\Case2 folder. Resize the chart so it fits on the slide.

✪ EXPLORE 16. Change the color of all the text in the chart to white. (*Hint*: Select the entire chart by clicking the outer edge of the object, and then change the font color.)

✪ EXPLORE 17. Change the chart design to Style 45. (*Hint*: Click the Design tab below the Chart Tools, click the Chart Styles More button, and select Style 45 located on the bottom row, fifth column from the right.)

✪ EXPLORE 18. Copy Slide 2 from WMCDesign, to make it Slide 10 of WMCServices. (*Hint*: With WMCDesign open, click the miniature of Slide 2 in the Slides tab on the left edge of the PowerPoint window, copy the slide, and then, in WMCServices, make sure Slide 9 is the active slide, and paste the new slide.)

✪ EXPLORE 19. Customize the Handout Master in the following ways:
    a. Change the font size of the header, date, footer, and page number to 20 points.
    b. Add the footer text **Wildlife Management Consultants**.
    c. Add the header text **WMC Services**.
    d. Increase the width of the footer so the footer text fits all on one line.
    e. Set the background to a light-yellow color. (*Hint*: Click Format Background located at the bottom of the Background Style gallery, set the Fill to Solid fill, and select a light-yellow color from the Colors palette of color tiles.)

20. In Slide Show view, check all the hyperlinks.

21. Check the presentation for features not supported by earlier versions of PowerPoint. Make a note of these features.

22. Save the presentation using the default filename.

23. Export the outline to an RTF file named **WMCServices Outline**. Start Word, and then open the file you created. Reformat the text so that it is 10-point, black Calibri. Go to the end of the document, and add text describing the features of the presentation that are not supported in earlier versions of PowerPoint. Save your changes.

24. Return to the presentation, save it as a single file Web page with the filename **WMCWeb**, and then view the slide show in your browser.

25. Submit the completed presentation in printed (including the custom handouts) or electronic form, as requested by your instructor, and then close all open files.

| Create | **Case Problem 3** |

Create a presentation for a company that sells emergency preparedness products.

Data Files needed for this Case Problem: 72HrKit.jpg, EPR.pptx, EPRChart.xlsx, EPROtl.docx, EPRTabl.docx, Flood.jpg, Wheat.jpg

Emergency Preparedness Resources   Emergency Preparedness Resources (EPR) is a growing business in West Wendover, Nevada. The owner and president of EPR, Parker Salvatore, gives presentations on his company's products at emergency preparedness seminars, conferences, and trade shows. Parker asks you to set up a PowerPoint presentation on his company's products. Create the finished presentation, as shown in Figure 4-33, and then create a Web page of the presentation.

Figure 4-33

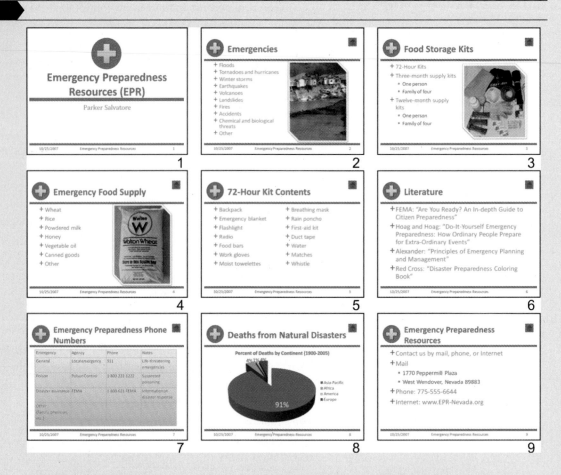

Read all the steps before you start creating your presentation. Not all the necessary steps are included below. You'll have to figure out on your own some necessary steps to complete the assignment.

1. The presentation is created from the **EPR** presentation, located in the Tutorial.04\Case3 folder included with your Data Files. Change the name "Parker Salvatore" on Slide 1 to your name, and save it as **EPRProducts**.

2. The text for the subsequent slides in the presentation comes from the Word outline file **EPROtl**, located in the Tutorial.04\Case3 folder. Adjust the slides with bulleted lists by reapplying the slide layout and then resetting the slides. Make sure the current date, footer, and slide number appear on all the slides.

3. Images that appear in Slides 2 through 4 are **Flood**, **72HrKit**, and **Wheat**, respectively, located in the Tutorial.04\Case3 folder.

4. In Slide 5, because the double-columned bulleted list appears as a single list when you first import the outline, change the slide layout to Two Content and use a cut-and-paste operation to move the last seven bulleted items to a second content placeholder.

5. The table of contact numbers on Slide 7 comes from the file **EPRTabl**, located in the Tutorial.04\Case3 folder. You'll have to modify the table later so that its size, fonts, and borders are legible and attractive, as shown in Figure 4-33. (*Hint*: In EPRTabl, click anywhere in the table, and then click the small button located above the upper-right corner of the table to select the entire table. Use copy and paste to copy the table from the Word document to the PowerPoint presentation.)

6. The pie chart in Slide 8 comes from the Excel file **EPRChart**, located in the Tutorial.04\Case3 folder.

7. The Action Button: Home buttons shown in the upper-right corner of Slide 2 through 9 are hyperlinked to Slide 1.

8. Save your final presentation using the default filename, and then save it as a Web page using the filename **EPRWeb** and the Page title **Emergency Preparedness Resources**.

9. Submit the completed presentation in printed or electronic form, as requested by your instructor, and then close the file.

| Apply | **Case Problem 4** |

Apply the skills you learned in this tutorial to create a presentation about wetlands.

Data Files needed for this Case Problem: Wetland1.jpg, Wetland2.jpg, Wetland3.jpg, Wetland4.jpg, Wetland5.jpg

Campus Conservation Consortium The Campus Conservation Consortium (CCC) is an organization of college students that gives presentations to other students on conserving America's wetlands. Prepare a presentation to your classmates on information about wetlands. You might choose a topic such as grants and scholarships on wetland conservation, analysis and information about wetlands in a particular state, legislation on wetland conservation, description of wetland types (saltwater habitats, freshwater habitats, and upland habitat), use of wetlands by migratory birds or other animals, information about an organization involved in wetland conservation, conservation plans for private owners of wetlands, or other related topics. Do the following:

🌐 EXPLORE

1. Using Microsoft Word, create an outline of your presentation on wetland conservation. Include at least six titles, which will become slide titles. (Remember to switch to Outline view in Word to type your slide titles, which will be formatted with the Heading 1 style.) Under each title, add information (content) items (formatted in the Heading 2 style), which will become the bulleted lists on each slide. Use books and magazines from your college library, encyclopedia, the Internet, or other sources of information to get the necessary information on wetland conservation. If you haven't covered Microsoft Word in your courses and don't know how to create an outline with heading styles, use the Help feature of Word.

2. Save the Word file using the filename **WetlandOtl** to the Tutorial.04\Case4 folder included with your Data Files.

3. In another Word document, create a table. Your table might list various wetland preserves, their total area, examples of major wildlife in the area, or other information. You might be able to find a table on the Internet from which you can extract the data.

4. Save the Word file with the table using the filename **WetlandTbl** to the Tutorial.04\Case4 folder included with your Data Files.

5. Open a new, blank presentation, and include an appropriate title of your choosing and a subtitle with your name as the presenter.

6. Import the Word outline into PowerPoint.

7. Apply the built-in design theme Flow.

8. Reapply the slide layouts to, and reset, the slide, as needed, so they use the proper font and have the proper format.

9. Embed your table into a slide of your presentation. Resize, reposition, and reformat it as needed to maximize its readability.

10. Include a text box either on the first slide or the last slide acknowledging the sources of your information.

11. Insert at least one action button into your presentation with a link to another slide within your presentation.

12. Include at least two text hyperlinks in your presentation, with links to other slides. The text of the hyperlinks can be bulleted items, text in a table cell, or text boxes.

13. Add graphics and slide transitions to the slide show, as desired. If you want, you can use any of the pictures **Wetland1** through **Wetland5** located in the Tutorial.04\Case4 folder.

14. Save your presentation using the filename **Wetlands**.

15. Save your presentation as a single file Web page, with the Page title **Wetland Conservation** and the filename **WetWeb**.

16. Submit the completed presentation in printed or electronic form, as requested by your instructor, and then close the file.

Research	**Internet Assignments**

Go to the Web to find information you can use to create presentations.

The purpose of the Internet Assignments is to challenge you to find information on the Internet that you can use to work effectively with this software. The actual assignments are updated and maintained on the Course Technology Web site. Log on to the Internet and use your Web browser to go to the Student Online Companion for New Perspectives Office 2007 at **www.course.com/np/office2007**. Then navigate to the Internet Assignments for this tutorial.

Assess	**SAM Assessment and Training**

If you have a SAM user profile, you may have access to hands-on instruction, practice, and assessment of the skills covered in this tutorial. Log in to your SAM account (**http://sam2007.course.com**) to launch any assigned training activities or exams that relate to the skills covered in this tutorial.

Review	**Quick Check Answers**

Session 4.1

1. For a built-in theme, you use the Themes gallery on the Design tab. To use a theme from a presentation file, you use the More button on the Themes group, click Browse for Themes, and navigate to the file with the desired theme.

2. On the Home tab, click the New Slide button arrow, click Slides from Outline, select the Word file with the outline, and then click the Open button.

3. a. Import means to insert a file that was created using one program into another program's file.

   b. Embed means to insert a file so that a connection with the source program is maintained.

   c. Link means to insert a file so that a connection between the source file and the destination file is maintained, and changes made to the source file are reflected in the linked object in the destination file.

4. The object is updated to reflect the changes made to the source file.

5. imported

6. so that modifications you make to the source file are reflected in the destination file

Session 4.2

1. A hyperlink is a word, phrase, or graphic that you click to display an object at another location.
2. An action button is a ready-made shape for which you can easily define hyperlinks to other slides or documents.
3. Click the Office Button, click Save As, set Save as type to Single File Web Page, and then click the Save button.
4. A frame on the left contains an outline of the slides, the slide itself appears in a frame on the right, and navigation buttons appear at the bottom of the slide.
5. The slide numbers, slide titles, and bulleted lists on the slides, but no graphics.
6. To initiate an online meeting, click the Start button in the lower-left corner of your Vista screen, click All Programs, and click Windows Meeting Space. The Meeting Space window opens. To invite participants, click the Invite people icon on the right side of the Meeting Space window. Click the names of those you want to invite or invite anyone else who is running Vista and for whom you have an e-mail address. Open the presentation that you want to broadcast, click Slide Show, point to Online Broadcast, and then click Begin Broadcast.
7. Comments and annotations, document properties and personal information, custom XML data, invisible on-slide content, off-slide content, and presentation notes.

Ending Data Files

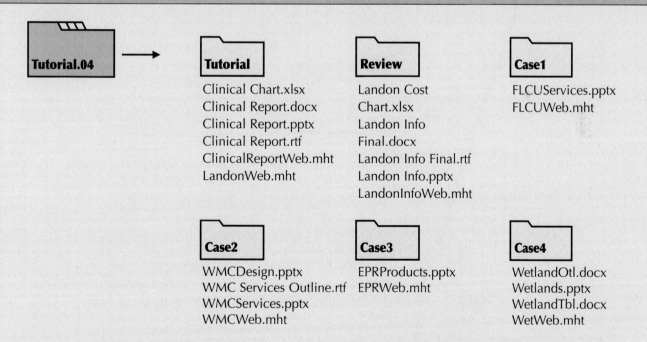

Tutorial.04 →

Tutorial
Clinical Chart.xlsx
Clinical Report.docx
Clinical Report.pptx
Clinical Report.rtf
ClinicalReportWeb.mht
LandonWeb.mht

Review
Landon Cost
Chart.xlsx
Landon Info
Final.docx
Landon Info Final.rtf
Landon Info.pptx
LandonInfoWeb.mht

Case1
FLCUServices.pptx
FLCUWeb.mht

Case2
WMCDesign.pptx
WMC Services Outline.rtf
WMCServices.pptx
WMCWeb.mht

Case3
EPRProducts.pptx
EPRWeb.mht

Case4
WetlandOtl.docx
Wetlands.pptx
WetlandTbl.docx
WetWeb.mht

Reality Check

Have you been on a trip lately? Perhaps you traveled somewhere for Spring Break, went on a camping trip, traveled home during a semester break, spent a semester studying abroad, or went on tour with a college musical group. Whatever your travel experience, others might be interested in your trip. A good vehicle for sharing your trip with family and friends is a PowerPoint presentation or possibly a Web page created from a Power-Point presentation. In this exercise, you'll use PowerPoint to create a presentation about your travels using the skills and features presented in Tutorials 3 and 4.

Note: Please be sure *not* to include any personal information of a sensitive nature in the documents you create to be submitted to your instructor for this exercise. Later on, you can update the documents with such information for your own personal use.

1. Start a new, blank PowerPoint presentation.
2. Create a new set of theme colors, and save it with an appropriate name.
3. Using your theme colors, create an attractive, tasteful design theme using slide masters. Choose design elements that match your travels. For example, if your trip was a serious culture experience (like a visit to European museums), your design should be conservative, but if your trip was festive (like a trip to a football bowl game), your design could be more exciting. In the appropriate slide masters, use picture bullets for the bulleted lists. Save the file as an Office Theme.
4. Start a new presentation using the theme that you created. Save it with an appropriate name.
5. On Slide 1, type an informative title for your presentation. For example, if you traveled to New York City for an internship, your title could be "My New York City Internship," or if you spent a year with the Peace Corps in Bolivia, your title might be "My Year in the Peace Corps in Bolivia." Add your name as a subtitle.
6. Create at least six slides (not counting the title slide) about your trip. Include things such as the purpose of your trip, information about the places you visited, special experiences during your trip, scenic vistas (described in words and shown in pictures), modes of travel you used (airplane, private vehicle, subway, taxi, and so forth), and recommendations for others who might be thinking of a similar trip.
7. Your presentation should include pictures. You can use pictures that you or your friends took, or you could scan printed photos, postcards, ticket stubs, showbills, or other items from your trip. If necessary, go online to find appropriate pictures for your presentation. Apply styles to your pictures.
8. Add movies and recorded sounds to your presentation if you have any.
9. Add slide transitions and custom animations to your presentation. Add sound effects if they will enhance the presentation. Decide whether you want the animations to start automatically (after the previous item) or if you want to let the user control them with the mouse.
10. Use hyperlinks and action buttons to allow the person viewing the presentation to easily jump to different slides.
11. Apply a picture background to one of your slides, and include appropriate footer information.
12. View your presentation in Slide Show view. Make sure the transitions, animations, sound, movies, and links work as you expected. Save your final presentation.
13. If you want to publish the presentation to a Web server, edit links as necessary, and then save the presentation as a single file Web page. Give the Web page a page title that makes sense.
14. Submit the completed presentation in printed or electronic form, as requested by your instructor, and then close the file.

Glossary/Index

Note: Boldface entries include definitions.

Special Characters

<< >> (chevrons), WD 278

= (equal sign), AC 365

A

action button A ready-made shape for which you can easily define a hyperlink to other slides or documents, as well as perform several other actions. PPT 187–189

active cell In a spreadsheet, the cell in which you are entering data; it has a thick black border around it. PPT 115

active sheet The worksheet currently displayed in the workbook window. EX 319

alternate key A candidate key that was not chosen to be the primary key. AC A 3

ampersand (&) operator A concatenation operator that joins text expressions. AC 211, AC 213

Anchor property A form control property that automatically resizes a control and places the control in the same relative position on the screen as the screen size and resolution change. AC 277–278

AND criteria range, EX 375

AND function A logical function that returns a TRUE value if all the logical conditions are true and a FALSE value if any or all of the logical conditions are false. EX 343–344

animation A special visual or audio effect applied on a slide to an object, such as a graphic or a bulleted list. PPT 129–136

    custom, bulleted lists, PPT 129–134

    custom, charts, PPT 134–136

    dimming items after, PPT 133

anomalies Undesirable irregularities of tables caused by data redundancy and by partial and transitive dependencies. Anomalies are of three types: insertion, deletion, and update. AC A 14

Append Only property A field property for a Memo field that lets you edit the field value and, when set to Yes, causes Access to keep a historical record of all versions of the field value. You can view each version of the field value, along with a date and time stamp of when each version change occurred. AC 246

application, Excel. See Excel application

Apply Names dialog box, EX 406

artificial key A field that you add to a table to serve solely as the primary key and that is visible to users. AC A 20–A 21

ascending order Sorts text alphabetically from A to Z, numbers from smallest to largest, and dates from oldest to newest. EX 227

Assign Macro dialog box, EX 437

attribute The formal term for a column in a relation (table). AC A 2

AutoFilter An Access feature that enables you to quickly sort and display field values in various ways.

    filtering data, AC 209–211

AutoFormat A predefined style that you can apply to a form or report. AC 317

AVERAGEIF function A function that calculates the average of values in a range that meet criteria you specify. EX 370–371

AVERAGEIFS function A function that calculates the average of values within a range of cells that meet multiple conditions. EX 372

B

background

    custom themes, PPT 98–99

    pictures, PPT 99–100

    textured, PPT 106–108

background effect, WD 356–357

balloons An oblong box in the margin that displays comments or information about tracked changes. WD 316

BCNF. See Boyce-Codd normal form (BCNF)

Begins with criteria range, EX 376

BETWEEN criteria range, EX 375

bookmark When creating a hyperlink in a document to a location within the same document, an electronic marker used to specify the location you want the hyperlink to jump to. WD 348

    creating, WD 350

    hyperlinks to, WD 348–352

bound control A control that is connected, or bound, to a field in the database based on the record source, or the underlying table or query, and that is used to display and maintain a table field value. AC 283

bound form A form that has a table or query as its record source and is used for maintaining and displaying table data. AC 282

boxes in organization charts, PPT 125–126

Boyce-Codd normal form (BCNF) A second normal form table is in Boyce-Codd normal form if every determinant is a candidate key. BCNF is also called third normal form in this book, although BCNF is an improvement over the original version of third normal form. AC A 18

break (a link) To disrupt the link between a linked object and the source file, thereby making the linked object an embedded object. WD 365

browser A program that displays Web pages. WD 347

    viewing Web pages, WD 365–367

bubble diagram A diagram that graphically shows a table's functional dependencies and determinants. Also known as a data model diagram and a functional dependency diagram. AC A 12

bullet, custom themes, PPT 102–105

Task Reference

TASK	PAGE #	RECOMMENDED METHOD
3-D reference, use	EX 290	*See* Reference Window: Entering a Function That contains a 3-D Reference
Action button, add	PPT 186	*See* Reference Window: Adding an Action Button as a Link to Another Presentation
Animation, apply	PPT 129	*See* Reference Window: Applying an Animation
AutoFilter, use in a table or query datasheet	AC 209	Click arrow on column heading, click filter option
Background, add textured	WD 357	Click Page Layout tab, click Page Color button in Page Background group, click Fill Effects, click Texture tab, click a texture, click OK
Background, set style of	PPT 98	Click Design tab, click Background Styles button, click desired style (or click Format Background and create a custom background)
Background, set to picture	PPT 99	Click Design tab, click Background Styles button, click desired style (or click Format Background and create a custom background)
Background, textured, apply to slide	PPT 107	*See* Reference Window: Applying a Textured Background
Bookmark, create	WD 349–350	Move insertion point to desired location, click Insert tab, click Bookmark button in Links group, type bookmark name, click Add
Bullets, change style	PPT 102	Click next to bullet (or select bulleted text box), click Home tab, click Bullets button arrow, click desired bullet style
Bullets, change to picture	PPT 102	Click next to bullet (or select bulleted text box), click Home tab, click Bullets button arrow, click Bullets and Numbering, click Picture button, click the desired picture, click OK, click OK
Caption, change for a form's navigation bar	AC 411	Click the form selector, open the property sheet, type the value in the Navigation Caption text box, press Enter
Caption, change for a label	AC 292	*See* Reference Window: Changing a Label's Caption
Cell or range, select by name	EX 398	Click Name box arrow, click defined name
Cell or range name, create	EX 397	*See* Reference Window: Creating a Name for a Cell or Range
Cells, lock or unlock	EX 415	Select cell or range, in Font group on the Home tab, click Dialog Box Launcher, click Protection tab, check or uncheck Locked check box, click OK
Cells, reference in other worksheets	EX 288	Enter reference in the following format: =SheetName!CellRange
Character spacing, adjust	WD 219	*See* Reference Window: Adjusting Character Spacing
Chart, create	PPT 113	*See* Reference Window: Creating a Chart (Graph)
Chart, edit with Microsoft Graph	AC 417	In Design view, right-click the chart's edge, point to Chart Object, click Open, make desired changes, click File, click Exit & Return
Chart, embed in a form	AC 414	*See* Reference Window: Embedding a Chart in a Form
Color, change an object's background	AC 318	Click the object, click the arrow for 🎨, click the desired color
Combo box, add to a form	AC 299	*See* Reference Window: Adding a Combo Box to Find Records
Comment, delete (Excel)	EX 420	Click cell with comment, in Comments group on the Review tab, click the Delete button
Comment, insert (Excel)	EX 418	*See* Reference Window: Inserting a Comment
Comment, show or hide (Excel)	EX 419	Click cell with comment, in the Comments group on the Review tab, click the Show/Hide Comment button

TASK	PAGE #	RECOMMENDED METHOD
Comments, delete (Word)	WD 329	*See* Reference Window: Accepting and Rejecting Changes and Deleting Comments
Comments, insert (Word)	WD 317	*See* Reference Window: Inserting Comments
Comments, show or hide all (Excel)	EX 419	In the Comments group on the Review tab, click the Show All Comments button
Conditional Formatting Rules Manager, use	EX 363	In the Styles group on the Home tab, click the Conditional Formatting button, click Manage Rules
Control, anchor in a form	AC 277	In Layout view, select the control(s) to anchor, click Arrange tab, click Anchoring button in Position group, click option in gallery
Control, apply special effect	AC 317	Select the control, click the arrow for 🔲, click the special effect
Control, delete	AC 289	Right-click the control, click Delete
Control, move in a form	AC 285	*See* Reference Window: Selecting and Moving Controls
Control, resize in a form	AC 289	*See* Reference Window: Resizing a Control
Control, select	AC 285	*See* Reference Window: Selecting and Moving Controls
Control layout, remove control from in a form	AC 276	In Layout view, click ✛, select the control, click Arrange tab, click Remove button in Control Layout Group
Control tip property, set for a form control	AC 312	In Layout view, right-click the control, click Properties, click Other tab, type the tip in the ControlTip Text property, press Enter
Controls, align selected	AC 287	Right-click one of the selected controls, point to Align, click desired alignment
Criteria filters, specify complex criteria	EX 239	Click filter arrow, point to Number Filters, Text Filters, or Date Filters, specify filter criteria, click OK as needed
Crosstab query, create	AC 219	*See* Reference Window: Using the Crosstab Query Wizard
CSV file, import as an Access table	AC 395	*See* Reference Window: Importing a CSV File as an Access Table
Custom formats, create	EX A13	In the Number group on the Home tab, click the Dialog Box Launcher, on Number tab, click Custom in the Category box, enter format codes in the Type box, click OK
Data, create error alert message	EX 408	*See* Reference Window: Validating Data
Data, create input message	EX 408	*See* Reference Window: Validating Data
Data, create validation rule	EX 408	*See* Reference Window: Validating Data
Data, group in a report	AC 356	*See* Reference Window: Sorting and Grouping Data in a Report
Data, sort in a report	AC 356	*See* Reference Window: Sorting and Grouping Data in a Report
Data source, create for mail merge	WD 269	*See* Reference Window: Creating A Data Source for a Mail Merge
Data source, edit in Word	WD 285	*See* Reference Window: Editing a Data Source in Word
Data source, sort	WD 288	*See* Reference Window: Sorting a Data Source
Date and time, add to a report	AC 366	*See* Reference Window: Adding the Date and Time to a Report
Date field, insert	WD 276	Click Insert tab, click Date & Time button in Text group, click a date format, select Update automatically checkbox if desired, click OK
Developer tab, display or hide on the Ribbon	EX 420	Click 🔘, click Excel Options button, check or uncheck the Show Developer tab in the Ribbon check box, click OK
Document, inspect	PPT 200	Click 🔘, point to Prepare, click Inspect Document, click Inspect, read inspection report, click Close

TASK	PAGE #	RECOMMENDED METHOD
Documenter, use	AC 267	*See* Reference Window: Using the Documenter
Documents, compare or combine	WD 325	*See* Reference Window: Comparing and Combining Documents
Duplicate records, highlight	EX 361	In the Styles group on the Home tab, click Conditional Formatting button, point to Highlight Cells Rules, click Duplicate Values
Duplicate values, hide	AC 363	*See* Reference Window: Hiding Duplicate Values in a Report
Embedded object, create	EX B5	Copy selection, place insertion point where you want to place the object, in the Clipboard group on the Home tab, click the Paste button arrow, click Paste Special, click Paste option button, select object type, click OK
Embedded object, edit	EX B6	Double-click the embedded object, make edits, deselect object
Embedded object, modify	WD 340	Double-click object, use commands and tools of source program to modify object, click outside embedded object
Excel table, add record	EX 225	*See* Reference Window: Adding a Record to an Excel table
Excel table, create	EX 222	On Insert tab, in Tables group, click Table button, verify range of data, click OK
Excel table, format	EX 224	In Table Style Options group on Table Tools Design tab, click an option
Excel table, rename	EX 224	Click in table, in Properties group on Table Tools Design tab, select name in Table Name box, type name
Excel worksheet, link data from	AC 429	Click External Data tab, click Excel button in Import group, click Browse, select the workbook, click Open, click Link to the data source by creating a linked table, click OK, follow the steps in the Link Spreadsheet Wizard
Export steps, save	AC 407	Click Save export steps check box in Export dialog box, click Save Export
External reference formula, create	EX 299	Click cell in destination file, type=, click cell in source file, complete formula as usual
Field, add to a form or report	AC 283	In Design view, click Add Existing Fields button in Tools group, click the record source, double-click the field
Filter, clear from column	EX 237	Click column filter arrow, click Clear Filter command
Filter, clear from entire table	EX 240	In Sort & Filter group on Data tab, click the Clear button
Filter, select multiple items in a column	EX 238	Click filter arrow, check two or more items, click OK
Filter, use multiple columns	EX 236	Filter for one column, then repeat to filter for additional columns
Filter, use one column	EX 233	Click the column's filter arrow, check item to filter by, click OK
Filter arrows, display or hide	EX 233	In Sort & Filter group on Data tab, click Filter button
Filter by color, apply	EX 364	Click filter arrow, point to Filter by Color, click a color in the palette
Find duplicates query, create	AC 226	*See* Reference Window: Using the Find Duplicates Query Wizard
Find unmatched query, create	AC 227	*See* Reference Window: Using the Find Unmatched Query Wizard
Font, change	PPT 101	Select text or text holder, click Home tab, click Font button arrow, click desired font style, click Font Size button arrow, click desired size, click Font Color button arrow, click desired color
Form, create a custom	AC 282	*See* Reference Window: Creating a Form in Design View
Form, create using the Datasheet tool	AC 270	Select record source in Navigation Pane, click Create tab, click More Forms button in Forms group, click Datasheet
Form, create using the Multiple Items tool	AC 271	Select record source in Navigation Pane, click Create tab, click Multiple Items button in Forms group

TASK	PAGE #	RECOMMENDED METHOD
Form, create using the Split Form tool	AC 273	Select record source in Navigation Pane, click Create tab, click Split Form button in Forms group
Form, select in Design view	AC 299	Click the form selector
Form Footer, add	AC 296	*See* Reference Window: Adding and Removing Form Header and Form Footer Sections
Form Footer, remove	AC 296	*See* Reference Window: Adding and Removing Form Header and Form Footer Sections
Form Header, add	AC 296	*See* Reference Window: Adding and Removing Form Header and Form Footer Sections
Form Header, remove	AC 296	*See* Reference Window: Adding and Removing Form Header and Form Footer Sections
Formula, reference another worksheet	EX 288	*See* Reference Window: Entering a Formula That References Another Worksheet
Formula results, copy and paste as values	EX A8	Copy range with formula results, click first cell in paste location, in the Clipboard group on the Home tab, click the Paste button arrow, click Paste Values
Formulas, add names to existing	EX 406	*See* Reference Window: Adding Defined Names to Existing Formulas
Graph, create	PPT 113	*See* Reference Window: Creating a Chart (Graph)
Handouts, customize	PPT 191–192	Click View tab, click Handout Master, edit handout master slide, click Close Master View button
Horizontal line, insert	WD 360	On Home tab in Paragraph group, click Borders and Shading list arrow, click Borders and Shading, click Horizontal Line, click a line style, click OK
HTML document, export a query as	AC 391	*See* Reference Window: Exporting a Query to an HTML Document
Hyperlink to an existing file or Web page, format text as	WD 353	*See* Reference Window: Creating a Hyperlink to Another Document
Hyperlink, create (Excel)	EX 311	*See* Reference Window: Inserting a Hyperlink
Hyperlink, create (PowerPoint)	PPT 178	Select the object to which you want to apply the hyperlink, click Insert tab, click Hyperlink button in Links group, select the target of the hyperlink, click OK
Hyperlink, edit	EX 312	Right-click cell with hyperlink, click Edit Hyperlink, make edits in Edit Hyperlink dialog box, click OK
Import steps, save	AC 402	Click Save import steps check box in Import dialog box, click Save Import
Information rights, manage	PPT 203	*See* Reference Window: Using the Information Rights Manager
Input Mask Wizard, activate	AC 235	Click the field's Input Mask text box, click [...], specify your choices in the Input Mask Wizard dialog boxes
Input message, create	EX 408	*See* Reference Window: Validating Data
Invalid data, circle	EX 414	In the Data Tools group on the Data tab, click the Data Validation button arrow, click Circle Invalid Data
Legend, add to PivotChart	AC 427	Click Design tab, click Legend button in Show/Hide group
Line, add to a form or report	AC 315	*See* Reference Window: Adding a Line to a Form or Report
Link, break	WD 364	*See* Reference Window: Breaking the Link to a Source File
Link, update	WD 344	In destination file, right-click linked object and then click Update Link

TASK	PAGE #	RECOMMENDED METHOD
Linked object, edit	EX B5	Edit as usual in source file, or double-click the linked object in the destination file, make edits, deselect object
Linked object, paste to another file	EX B4	Copy selection, place insertion point where you want to place the link, in the Clipboard group on the Home tab, click the Paste button arrow, click Paste Special, click Paste link option button, select object type, click OK
Linked workbooks, update	EX 304	Click in source file and edit as usual
Links, manage	EX 306	In the Connections group on the Data tab, click the Edit Links button, select desired option, click OK
Lookup field, change to Text field	AC 265	Display the table in Design view, select the field, click the Lookup tab, set the Display Control property to Text Box
Lookup field, create	AC 231	Click the Data Type arrow, click Lookup Wizard, specify your choices in the Lookup Wizard dialog boxes
Macro, edit	EX 432	*See* Reference Window: Editing a Macro
Macro, record	EX 425	*See* Reference Window: Recording a Macro
Macro, run	EX 427	*See* Reference Window: Running a Macro
Macro, set security level for	EX 423	*See* Reference Window: Setting Macro Security in Excel
Macro, view code	EX 432	*See* Reference Window: Editing a Macro
Macro button, create	EX 436	*See* Reference Window: Creating a Macro Button
Macro button, move	EX 438	Right-click the button, press Esc, drag the button by its selection border to a new location
Macro button, resize	EX 438	Right-click the button, press Esc, drag a selection handle
Mail Merge, perform	WD 264	Click Mailings tab, click Start Mail Merge in Start Mail Merge group, click Step by Step Mail Merge Wizard, follow steps in Mail Merge task pane
Mailing labels, create (Access)	AC 373	*See* Reference Window: Creating Mailing Labels and Other Labels
Mailing labels, create (Word)	WD 291	Click Mailings tab, click Start Mail Merge in Start Mail Merge group, click Step by Step Mail Merge Wizard, click Labels, click Next: Starting document, click Label options, select label type, click OK, click Next: Select Recipients, select or create data source, click Next: Arrange your labels, insert merge fields, click Update all labels, click Next: Preview your labels, click Next: Complete the merge
Memo field, change properties of	AC 245	Display the table in Design view, select the memo field, click the Text Format property or click the Append Only property
Merge fields, insert in main document	WD 277	Click Mailings tab, click Insert Merge Field in Write & Insert Fields group, click a merge field
Movie, insert	PPT 111	*See* Reference Window: Inserting a Movie into a Presentation
Multiple-column report, modify	AC 376	In Design view, click Page Setup tab, click Page Setup button, click the Columns tab, set the column options, click OK
Name, add to existing formulas	EX 406	*See* Reference Window: Adding Defined Names to Existing Formulas
Name, create for cell or range	EX 397	*See* Reference Window: Creating a Name for a Cell or Range
Object, copy from another presentation	PPT 169–170	Open another presentation, select object(s), click the Copy button in the Clipboard group, return to first presentation, click the Paste button in the Clipboard group

TASK	PAGE #	RECOMMENDED METHOD
Object, embed	WD 337	Select and copy object in source program, return to Word, click destination location, on Home tab in Clipboard group click the Paste button arrow, click Paste Special, select Paste option button if necessary, in As list box select option that will paste object as an Object, click OK
Object, link	WD 342	Select and copy object in source program, return to Word, click destination location, on Home tab in Clipboard group click Paste button arrow, click Paste Special, select Paste link option, in As list box select option that will paste object as an Object, click OK
Object dependencies, identify	AC 239	Click Database Tools tab, click Object Dependencies button in Show/Hide group, click the object, click ⊞
Object (file), embed	PPT 171–172	Click Insert tab, click Object button in Text group, click Create from file option button, click Browse button, navigate to folder with file, click filename, click OK, click OK
Object (file), link	PPT 175	Click Insert tab, click Object button in Text group, click Create from file option button, click Browse button, navigate to folder with file, click filename, click OK, click Link check box, click OK
Online meeting, set up	PPT 199	*See* Reference Window: Setting Up an Online Meeting with Windows Meeting Space
Organization chart, create	PPT 123	*See* Reference Window: Creating an Organization Chart
Outline, create and edit	WD 238	*See* Reference Window: Creating and Editing Outlines
Outline, export to RTF	PPT 166–167	Click (🔵), click Save As, click Save as type arrow, click Outline/RTF, click Save button
Outline, import from Word document	PPT 164	Click Home tab, in the Slides group, click New Slide button arrow, click Slides from Outline, navigate to Word file, click Insert
Outline, print	PPT 190	Click (🔵), point to Print, click Print Preview, click Print What arrow, click Outline View, click Print button
Padding, change in a form control	AC 277	In Layout view, click the control, click Arrange tab, click Control Padding button, click the desired setting
Page numbers, add to a report	AC 368	*See* Reference Window: Adding Page Numbers to a Report
Paragraph spacing, adjust	WD 221	*See* Reference Window: Adjusting Spacing Between Paragraphs
Parameter query, create	AC 215	*See* Reference Window: Creating a Parameter Query
Picture, insert (import)	PPT 168	Click Home tab, click Layout button in Slides group, click desired content layout, click Insert Picture from File button in content placeholder, navigate to picture file, click picture file, click Insert
PivotChart, add to a table or query	AC 426	Open the table or query in Datasheet view, right-click the object tab, click PivotChart View, drag the fields from the Field List pane into the PivotChart
PivotChart, create	EX 269	In the Tools group on the PivotTable Tools Options tab, click the PivotChart button, complete the Insert Chart dialog box, click OK
PivotTable, add a total field to	AC 424	Click a detail field's column heading, click Design tab, click AutoCalc button in Tools group, click an aggregate option
PivotTable, add to a table or query	AC 422	Open the table or query in Datasheet view, right-click the object tab, click PivotTable View, drag the fields from the Field List pane into the PivotTable

TASK	PAGE #	RECOMMENDED METHOD
PivotTable, create	EX 248	*See* Reference Window: Creating a PivotTable
PivotTable, rearrange	EX 255	Drag field buttons in the PivotTable Field List
PivotTable, refresh	EX 264	In the Data group on the PivotTable Tools Options tab, click the Refresh button
PivotTable, show or hide details	AC 425	Click Design tab, click Show Details or Hide Details in Show/Hide group
PivotTable field, remove	EX 263	In PivotTable Field List, uncheck items in the field area
PivotTable fields, filter	EX 258	Click the field arrow button in the PivotTable for the data you want to filter, then check and uncheck items
PivotTable items, group	EX 267	In the Group group on the PivotTable Tools Options tab, click the Group Field button, select options in the Grouping dialog box, click OK
PivotTable report layout, change	EX 255	In the Layout group on the PivotTable Tools Design tab, click the Report Layout button, click a layout
PivotTable style, apply	EX 253	In the PivotTable Styles group on the PivotTable Tools Design tab, click More button; click a style
PivotTable value fields, format	EX 254	Click cell in PivotTable, in the Active Field group on the PivotTable Tools Options tab, click Field Settings button, click Number Format button, select format, click OK
Presentation, mark as final	PPT 202	Click (🔘), point to Prepare, click Mark as Final, click OK, click OK
Property sheet, open or close for a report control	AC 214	Select the control, click Design tab, click Property Sheet button in form or Show/Hide group
Record, delete from Excel table	EX 227	Select the record, in Cells group on Home tab, click Delete button arrow, and then click Delete Table Rows
Records, find and replace in Excel table	EX 226	Click in table, in Editing group on Home tab, click the Find & Select button, use Find and Replace dialog box as usual
Rectangle, add to a form or report	AC 316	*See* Reference Window: Adding a Rectangle to a Form or Report
Report, create a custom	AC 353	*See* Reference Window: Creating a Blank Report in Layout View
Report, filter in Report view	AC 335	Right-click the value to filter, point to Text Filters, click filter option
Report, select and copy data in Report view	AC 337	Click the top of the selection, drag to the end of the selection, click Home tab, click 🗐 in Clipboard group
Report filter, add to a PivotTable	EX 257	In the PivotTable Field List, drag a field button to the Report Filter box
Report filter, modify	EX 257	Click the report filter arrow, click filter items
Research task pane, open	WD 249	Click Review tab, in Proofing group click Research button, Thesaurus button, or Translate button
Research task pane, use	WD 248–249	Connect to the Internet if possible, open Research task pane, type term you want to research in Search for text box, click the list arrow and select a reference work, click 🔲
Ribbon, minimize or maximize	EX 440	Double-click any tab
Row(s) and column(s), freeze	EX 221	Click cell below and to right of row(s) and column(s) to freeze. On View tab, in Window group, click Freeze Panes button, click option
Row(s) and column(s), unfreeze	EX 221	On View tab, in Window group, click Freeze Panes button, click Unfreeze Panes
Saved export, run	AC 407	Click External Data tab, click Saved Exports button in Export group, click the saved export, click Run

TASK	PAGE #	RECOMMENDED METHOD
Saved import, run	AC 402	Click External Data tab, click Saved Imports button in Import group, click the saved import, click Run
Shape, create	PPT 180	Click Insert tab, click Shapes button in Illustrations group, click desired shape, drag ╋ in slide
Slide, hide or unhide	PPT 138	Go to slide you want to hide, click Slide Show tab, click Hide Slide button
Slide, insert from another presentation	PPT 91	*See* Reference Window: Inserting Slides from Another Presentation
Slides, mark during slide show	PPT 136	In Slide Show view, move mouse to activate pointer, right-click screen, point to Pointer Options, click desired pen type, drag pen to mark slide
Slide Show, deliver on two monitors (podium mode)	PPT 142	Plug second monitor into computer, set up computer to run both monitors, click Slide Show tab, click Set Up Slide Show button, click Display slide show on arrow, click whichever monitor you want to display slide show, click Show Presenter View check box, click OK, run slide show
Slide transitions, add	PPT 127	*See* Reference Window: Adding Slide Transitions
Sort, create a custom list	EX 231	*See* Reference Window: Creating a Custom List
Sort, multiple columns	EX 229	*See* Reference Window: Sorting Data Using Multiple Sort Fields
Sort, one column	EX 228	Click 🔼 or 🔽
Sound clip, insert	PPT 109	*See* Reference Window: Inserting a Sound into a Presentation
Spacing, change in a form control	AC 277	In Layout view, click the control, click Arrange tab, click Control Margins button in Control Layout group, click the desired setting
Special formats, use	EX A12	In the Number group on the Home tab, click the Dialog Box Launcher, on Number tab, click Special in the Category box, select a format, click OK
Style, apply from Styles window	WD 224–225	Select text you want to format, click style in Styles window
Style, create a new	WD 227	*See* Reference Window: Creating a New Style
Style, modify	WD 223	*See* Reference Window: Modifying Styles
Styles window, open	WD 223	In Styles group on Home tab, click Styles Dialog Box Launcher
Subform, open in a new window	AC 305	Right-click the subform, click Subform in New Window
Subform/Subreport Wizard, activate	AC 302	Make sure 🔲 is selected, click 🔳, click in the grid at the upper-left corner for the subform/subreport
Subtotal Outline view, use	EX 245	Click an outline button to show or hide the selected outline level
Subtotals, insert	EX 243	*See* Reference Window: Calculating Subtotals for a Range of Data
Subtotals, remove	EX 246	In Outline group on the Data tab, click Subtotal button, click Remove All button, click OK
Tab Control, add to a form	AC 409	Click Design tab, click Tab Control button in Controls group, click in the grid at the upper-left corner for the tab control
Tab order, change in a form	AC 313	In Design view, click Arrange tab, click Tab Order button in Control Layout group, drag the rows into the desired order, click OK
Tab Stop property, change for a form control	AC 312	In Layout view, right-click the control, click Properties, click Other tab, set the Tab Stop property
Table of Contents, add text to	WD 233	*See* Reference Window: Working with a Table of Contents
Table of Contents, create	WD 233	*See* Reference Window: Working with a Table of Contents
Table of Contents, update	WD 233	*See* Reference Window: Working with a Table of Contents

TASK	PAGE #	RECOMMENDED METHOD
Table, analyze	AC 399	Select the table, click Database Tools tab, click Analyze Table button in Analyze group
Template, create custom	EX 317	*See* Reference Window: Creating a Custom Template
Template, saving a document as	WD 233	*See* Reference Window: Saving a Document as a Template
Template, use an HTML	AC 392	Click the Export data with formatting and layout check box in the Export - HTML Document dialog box, click the Select a HTML Template check box, click Browse, select template, click OK
Text, insert into a shape	PPT 180–181	Insert a shape (*see* Shape, insert), with shape selected, type text
Theme, create a custom (PowerPoint)	PPT 94	*See* Reference Window: Creating and Saving a Custom Theme
Theme, create a custom (Word)	WD 210	*See* Reference Window: Customizing the Document Theme
Theme colors, create	PPT 95	Click Design tab, click Colors button in Themes group, click Create New Theme Colors, click item button, click More Colors (as desired), select color, click OK, name theme color set, click Save
Theme colors, customize	WD 215	*See* Reference Window: Creating Custom Theme Colors and Theme Fonts
Theme colors, delete	PPT 98	Click Design tab, click Colors button, right-click theme color set, click Delete
Theme fonts, customize	WD 215	*See* Reference Window: Creating Custom Theme Colors and Theme Fonts
Title, add to a form or report	AC 296	In Controls group, click Title button, click and edit the title control, press Enter
Top values query, create	AC 229	*See* Reference Window: Creating a Top Values Query
Total row, add or remove from Excel table	EX 240	In Table Style Options group on the Table Tools Design tab, check or uncheck Total Row check box
Total row, select summary statistics	EX 240	Click arrow button in Total row cell, click summary function
Totals, calculating in a report	AC 343	In Layout view, click any value in the column to calculate, click Format tab, click Totals button in Groupings & Totals group, click Sum
Track Changes, accept and reject	WD 329	*See* Reference Window: Accepting and Rejecting Changes and Deleting Comments
Track Changes, use	WD 316	*See* Reference Window: Tracking Changes in a Document
Transitions, add to slides	PPT 127	*See* Reference Window: Adding Slide Transitions
Trusted folder, create	AC 246	Click (icon), click Access Options, click Trust Center, click Trust Center Settings, click Trusted Locations, click Add new location, click Browse, navigate to the desired folder, click OK four times
Validation circles, clear all	EX 414	In the Data Tools group on the Data tab, click the Data Validation button, click Clear Validation Circles
Validation circles, clear from a cell	EX 414	Enter valid data
Validation circles, create	EX 414	In the Data Tools group on the Data tab, click the Data Validation button, click Circle Invalid Data
Validation rule, create	EX 408	*See* Reference Window: Validating Data
Validation Rule property, set	AC 243	Display the table in Design view, select the field, enter the rule in the Validation Rule text box
Validation Text property, set	AC 241	Display the table in Design view, select the field, enter the text in the Validation Text text box

TASK	PAGE #	RECOMMENDED METHOD
VBA, insert a command	EX 434	Open the Visual Basic Editor, display the macro in the Code window, click at the end of a VBA command, press Enter, type the new command
VBA code, view	EX 432	*See* Reference Window: Editing a Macro
Visual Basic Editor, open or close	EX 432	*See* Reference Window: Editing a Macro
Web page, create from a workbook, worksheet, or range	EX 326	*See* Reference Window: Saving a Workbook, Worksheet, or Range as a Web Page
Web page, publish a presentation to	PPT 194	Click ⬤, click Save As, click Save as type arrow, click Single File Web Page, change options as desired, click Save button
Web page, save document as	WD 359	*See* Reference Window: Saving a Word Document as a Web Page
Web page, view in Web Layout view	WD 355	Click 🔲
Workbook, create from template	EX 314	*See* Reference Window: Creating a Workbook Based on a Template
Workbook, protect	EX 417	*See* Reference Window: Protecting a Workbook
Workbook, save as a Web page	EX 326	*See* Reference Window: Saving a Workbook, Worksheet, or Range as a Web Page
Workbook, save earlier version in Excel 2007 file format	EX A2	In Save As dialog box, select save location, enter filename, click the the Save as type button, click Excel Workbook, click Save
Workbook, save in earlier Excel file format	EX A17	In Save As dialog box, change filename, select save location, click the Save as type button, click Excel 97-2003 Workbook, click Save
Workbook, save with macros	EX 440	In Save As dialog box, select save location, enter filename, click the Save as type button, click Excel Macro-Enabled Workbook, click Save
Workbooks, arrange	EX 298	*See* Reference Window: Arranging Workbooks
Workbooks, link	EX 296	Enter a formula in the following form: =[WorkbookName]WorksheetName!CellRange
Workbooks, switch	EX 297	In the Window group on the View tab, click the Switch Windows button, click the workbook to make active
Worksheet, protect	EX 415	*See* Reference Window: Protecting a Worksheet
Worksheet, unprotect	EX 418	Make worksheet active, in Changes group on the Review tab, click the Unprotect Sheet button
Worksheet group, print	EX 293	Select worksheet group, set up worksheets and print as usual
Worksheets, copy to another workbook	EX 287	*See* Reference Window: Copying Worksheets to Another Workbook
Worksheets, group or ungroup	EX 283	*See* Reference Window: Grouping and Ungrouping Worksheets
Workspace, create	EX 309	Open and arrange workbooks as desired, in the Window group on the View tab, click the Save Workspace button, type a filename, select save location, click Save
XML file, export an Access table to	AC 404	*See* Reference Window: Exporting an Access Table as an XML File
XML file, import as a table	AC 400	*See* Reference Window: Importing an XML File as an Access Table